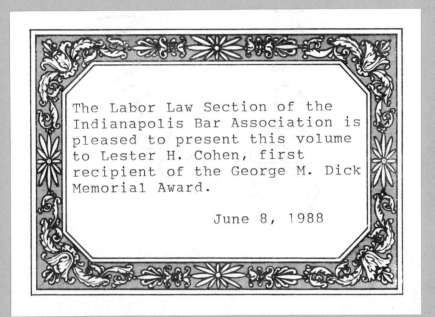

The Labor Law Section of the
Indianapolis Bar Association is
pleased to present this volume
to Lester H. Cohen, first
recipient of the George M. Dick
Memorial Award.

June 8, 1988

How To Take a Case Before the NLRB

FIFTH EDITION

HOW TO TAKE A CASE
BEFORE THE
NLRB

Fifth Edition

Kenneth C. McGuiness
Jeffrey A. Norris
Partners
McGuiness & Williams
Washington, D.C.

The Bureau of National Affairs, Inc., Washington, D.C.

Library of Congress Cataloging-in-Publication Data

McGuiness, Kenneth C.
  How to take a case before the NLRB.

  Includes index.
  1. United States. National Labor Relations
Board.   I. Norris, Jeffrey A.   II. Title.
KF3372.M25   1986   344.73'01'0269   86-14699
ISBN 0-87179-493-4   347.30410269

International Standard Book Number: 0-87179-493-4
Printed in the United States of America

Preface to Fifth Edition

The Fiftieth Anniversary of the National Labor Relations Act is an appropriate milestone at which to review and update what has become a standard text in the field of labor relations. A comparison of the table of contents of this volume with that of the first edition published in 1949 reveals that many of the fundamental principles of NLRB practice and procedure remain the same. That same comparison, however, also indicates that much has changed, and the changes almost invariably have served to make Board practice more complex and specialized.

Much of the evolution of Board practice in recent years has been internally generated. Greater reliance on the establishment of bargaining relationships through remedial bargaining orders, vacillation in the development of standards for preelection conduct, and wide fluctuations in the degree of deference to be accorded grievance-arbitration procedures are just a few of the more significant examples. Other influences on Board practice have been externally generated. The 1974 hospital amendments added a unique and highly complex industry to the Board's jurisdiction; the Freedom of Information Act for the first time opened many of the Board's internal practices to public scrutiny; and the Equal Access to Justice Act now requires that substantial care be exercised by the Board in its deliberative processes. Board practice thus is not static and is not likely to become so in the future. A significant advantage, therefore, is likely to flow to the advocate who is familiar with the intricacies of Board procedure.

This revision retains the objective of previous editions in describing the Board's procedural rules and practices "in orderly fashion and in simple statement." The Board's Rules and Regulations, Statements of Procedure, Casehandling Manual, and 280 volumes of decisions have been distilled into a step-by-step analysis of how the Board processes election petitions and unfair labor practice charges. For those who do not regularly practice before the Board, illustrative charts and forms have been included. For the more experienced lawyers and practitioners, numerous citations to the Board's regulations and Casehandling Manual have been added. The case citations are intended to be illustrative rather than exhaustive, and as with past editions no effort has been made to comment upon the merit of current Board practice.

Every effort has been made to update the legal citations throughout the drafting and revision process. The case citations include Board and court decisions through mid 1986.

The Board's regulations include Equal Access to Justice Act amendments effective May 15, 1986 (51 Fed. Reg. 17,732), revisions to procedures for issuing advisory opinions effective June 1, 1986 (51 Fed. Reg. 15,612), amendments to the Board's rule regarding filing of exceptions and briefs effective June 1, 1986 (51 Fed. Reg. 15,613), and modifications to rules pertaining to time filing periods which will become effective on September 29, 1986 (51 Fed. Reg. 23,744). At the time of publication, the Board had not conformed either the Statements of Procedure or the Casehandling Manual to the modified regulations.

A number of individuals have been particularly helpful in completing this revision. Mark Baker, Margaret Best, James McDonald, Eve Subrin, and Gerri Ratliff all provided valuable research, drafting, and editorial services. As always, personnel at the Board were most cooperative in furnishing research material, forms and charts, and in commenting on portions of the manuscript. In this regard, special thanks go to Executive Secretary John Truesdale, Deputy General Counsel John Higgins, former Assistant General Counsel Standau Weinbrecht, Regional Director Louis D'Amico, and Berton Subrin, Director of the Office of Representation Appeals. Finally, a special word of appreciation for our friends at The Bureau of National Affairs, Inc., Louise Goines, Mary Hughes, and John Kenny for their guidance and assistance in making this volume a reality. Our thanks to you all.

KENNETH C. MCGUINESS
JEFFREY A. NORRIS

Washington, D.C.
August 1986

Foreword

Although this fifth edition of *How To Take a Case Before the NLRB* lists both Jeffrey A. Norris and myself as authors, the manuscript is almost entirely the work of Mr. Norris. While following the format of the previous editions, the content has been completely rewritten. New sources, unavailable before the Freedom of Information Act, have been used, a large amount of new material added, and all citations have been reviewed and updated.

Mr. Norris was able to contribute much of the new material in this edition with the benefit of firsthand experience. He was employed by the NLRB in Washington, D.C., from 1972 to 1977 during a period that the Board was extending its influence in several new areas, including universities and nonprofit hospitals. During his tenure at the Board Mr. Norris worked for several Board members in a variety of capacities, including service as Chief Counsel to Member Peter D. Walther. He deserves great credit for the conversion of a handbook on NLRB procedure that many have found useful into an indispensable resource for all those who practice before the Board.

KENNETH C. MCGUINESS

Washington, D.C.
August 1986

Summary Contents

V. RECORDS AND FILING REQUIREMENTS

Detailed Contents

III. UNFAIR LABOR PRACTICE PROCEEDINGS

IV. SUPPLEMENTAL PROCEEDINGS

V. RECORDS AND FILING REQUIREMENTS

24. Records and Information   535

25. Filing and Service of Papers   544

Exhibits

I
Overview

1

What the Law Provides

The basic labor-management relations policy of the United States and the means adopted by Congress to carry out that policy are found in the National Labor Relations Act as amended. It is this statute that established the National Labor Relations Board and that, in turn, is administered by the Board.

Background

The policy as set forth in the original Act (the Wagner Act) is a simple but sweeping declaration of purpose, stated in terms of eliminating the causes of obstructions to the free flow of commerce arising out of industrial strife and mitigating and eliminating such obstructions when they have occurred. Two methods of accomplishing the desired result were adopted—the encouragement of collective bargaining and the protection of the exercise by workers of full freedom of association, self-organization, and designation of representatives.[1] Both the purpose and the methods remain unchanged. Major amendments—the Labor Management Relations Act of 1947 (Taft-Hartley Act) and the Labor-Management Reporting and Disclosure Act of 1959 (Landrum-Griffin Act)—clarified the right of workers to refrain from union activity, enhanced the protection afforded workers, included safeguards for the public, and improved the Board's organization and procedures.

The law in its present form, with more than 275 volumes of Board cases interpreting and applying its provisions, constitutes an exceedingly complex code of conduct for employers, employees, and unions. The statute consists of five titles. The full text appears in Appendix A. The first, and most extensive, includes the establishment and

---

[1]National Labor Relations Act §1, 29 U.S.C. §151 (1976).

function of the National Labor Relations Board, the procedures for determining the exclusive bargaining agent of employees in a bargaining unit, and the conduct of employers, unions, and their agents which constitute unfair labor practices. Title II establishes the Federal Mediation and Conciliation Service and the procedures for handling national emergency disputes. Title III provides for suits by and against labor organizations. Title IV creates a now-defunct joint committee of Congress to study and report on labor relations problems, and Title V is limited to certain definitions and a saving and separability provision.

This book is concerned solely with those clauses of the statute, all in Title I, that are administered by the National Labor Relations Board. The substance of the principal provisions is set forth in this chapter. The portion of the statute that shapes the structure of the enforcing agency is treated in chapter 2.[2]

Coverage of the Act

§1.1   Businesses

Not everyone is subject to the provisions of the Act. The Board has broad jurisdiction over all businesses where materials, products, or services cross state lines or where the operations of other companies engaged in such activity are affected.[3] However, the Board in its discretion may decline to assert jurisdiction provided that the standards which it uses are not more restrictive than those prevailing on August 1, 1959.[4] Businesses not covered by the Act generally are governed by state and local laws.

The statute empowers the Board to grant states and territories jurisdiction over cases involving industries that are engaged in or affect interstate commerce.[5] However, the Board has never exercised this power and ceded its jurisdiction because of the prerequisite that the state law and its interpretation by the appropriate state tribunal must be consistent with the federal law. Thus far no state has qualified.

---

[2]This book focuses primarily on NLRB procedures and discusses the substance of the National Labor Relations Act only to the extent necessary to afford context and meaning to those procedures. Considerable reliance is placed upon the Board's Rules and Regulations and Statements of Procedure, Series 8, as amended (reprinted as Appendix B) and the Board's Casehandling Manual. For a more extended discussion of the substantive law as it has been developed by the Board and the courts, *see* THE DEVELOPING LABOR LAW: THE BOARD, THE COURTS AND THE NATIONAL LABOR RELATIONS ACT (C. Morris ed., 2d ed., BNA BOOKS, 1983) (hereinafter cited as THE DEVELOPING LABOR LAW).

[3]*NLRB v. Fainblatt*, 306 U.S. 601, 4 LRRM 535 (1939). *See generally* chapter 3 and THE DEVELOPING LABOR LAW at chapter 30.

[4]Sec. 14(c)(1).

[5]Sec. 10(a); *Guss v. Utah Labor Relations Board*, 352 U.S. 817, 39 LRRM 2567 (1957).

§1.2 Employers and Employees

The statute provides that the term "employer" includes any person acting directly or indirectly as an employer except:[6]

- The United States government;
- States or their political subdivisions;
- Federal Reserve banks;
- Wholly owned government corporations;
- Any employer who is subject to the terms of the Railway Labor Act; and
- Labor organizations and their officers and agents except when acting as employers.

Any person who works for an employer is considered to be an "employee" unless specifically exempted from the Act.[7] Individuals not presently working can also be employees if their non-working status is due to a labor dispute or an unfair labor practice and they have not obtained other substantially equivalent employment. Unless the statute otherwise provides, its guarantees apply to employees generally and are not restricted to the employees of any particular employer. The statute specifically exempts the following individuals from its coverage:[8]

- Agricultural laborers;
- Domestic servants;
- Any individual employed by his or her parent or spouse;
- Any individual employed by an employer who is subject to the Railway Labor Act;
- Independent contractors;
- Supervisors; and
- Any individual employed by an employer exempt from the Act (e.g., government employees, employees of wholly owned government corporations, or Federal Reserve banks).

§1.3 Supervisors, Independent Contractors, and Agricultural Laborers

The exemption of supervisors and independent contractors, and to a lesser extent agricultural laborers, has been most troublesome to the Board. The statute specifically states that it is not illegal for

---

[6]Sec. 2(2); *see* THE DEVELOPING LABOR LAW at 1440–1449.

[7]Sec. 2(3); *see* THE DEVELOPING LABOR LAW at 1450–1451. The term "employee" includes undocumented aliens who work for statutory employers. *Sure-Tan, Inc. v. NLRB*, 467 U.S. 883, 116 LRRM 2857 (1984).

[8]Sec. 2(3); *see* THE DEVELOPING LABOR LAW at 1450–1451.

supervisors to organize; they are not, however, accorded the protections of the Act or the use of its election procedures.[9] While a comprehensive definition of the term "supervisor" is found in the Act,[10] the Board and the courts also have developed certain secondary tests of supervisory status.[11]

Neither independent contractors nor agricultural employees are defined by the Act, and the Board has therefore been forced to evolve its own concepts. In determining whether or not an individual is an independent contractor, the Board has consistently applied the common law "right of control" test. If the recipient of the services in question has a right to control not only the result to be achieved but also the manner in which the work is to be performed, an employer-employee relationship exists as a matter of law; otherwise, there exists an independent contractor relationship.[12] The Board has turned to interpretations of Section 3(f) of the Fair Labor Standards Act as its principal guideline in defining agricultural laborers.[13] When dealing with employees in any of the foregoing categories, particular care must be exercised to determine whether the exemptions apply.

§1.4   Labor Organizations and Representatives

The Act defines a labor organization as any organization, agency, employee representation committee, or plan in which employees participate and which exists for the purpose of dealing with employers concerning grievances, wages, labor disputes, rates of pay, hours of employment, or conditions of work.[14] Employee "representatives" include both individuals and labor organizations.[15] An organization need not engage in collective bargaining to be qualified as a labor

---

[9]Sec. 14(a); supervisors are protected under Sec. 8(a)(4) from reprisals for filing unfair labor practice charges. *General Services, Inc.*, 229 NLRB 940, 95 LRRM 1174 (1977). In addition, the discharge of a supervisor is unlawful under Sec. 8(a)(1) when it interferes with the rights of employees to exercise their rights under Sec. 7. *Parker-Robb Chevrolet, Inc.*, 262 NLRB 402, 110 LRRM 1289 (1982).

[10]Sec. 2(11); *see* THE DEVELOPING LABOR LAW at 1451–1457.

[11]*E.g., NLRB v. Bell Aerospace Co.*, 416 U.S. 267, 85 LRRM 2945 (1974) (distinguishing "mangerial employees"); *NLRB v. Berger Transfer & Storage Co.*, 678 F.2d 679, 110 LRRM 2865 (7th Cir. 1982) (incidental and extraordinary exercise of supervisory function not sufficient to make an employee a supervisor); *Kern Council Services to the Developmentally Disabled, Inc.*, 259 NLRB 817, 109 LRRM 1018 (1981) (individual having constant possession of supervisory authority is a supervisor even if authority exercised infrequently).

[12]*See, e.g., Air Transit, Inc.*, 271 NLRB 1108, 117 LRRM 1058 (1984) (taxicab drivers independent contractors because the employer lacked control over the manner and means by which the drivers conduct business after leaving the garage); *see* THE DEVELOPING LABOR LAW at 1464–1466.

[13]*Bayside Enters. Inc. v. NLRB*, 429 U.S. 298, 94 LRRM 2199 (1977); *see* THE DEVELOPING LABOR LAW at 1461–1463.

[14]Sec. 2(5); *see* THE DEVELOPING LABOR LAW at 1488–1493.

[15]Sec. 2(4).

organization.[16] When an employee association or organization is dominated by supervisors, however, it will not be recognized as a qualified representative of employees because of the possibility of a conflict of interest.[17] The labor organization need not be a union; a committee will suffice.[18]

Protected Rights of Employees

The basic rights of employees which the statute seeks to guarantee are stated in Section 7. This provision declares:

"Employees shall have the right to self-organization, to form, join or assist labor organizations, to bargain collectively through representatives of their own choosing, and to engage in other concerted activities for the purpose of collective bargaining or other mutual aid or protection, and [employees] shall also have the right to refrain from any or all such activities."

Employees thus have a statutory right to select and bargain with their employer through representatives of their own choosing, to engage in other concerted activities for their mutual benefit, or to refrain from such conduct. In order to fall within the guarantees of Section 7, an individual's conduct must be both "concerted" and "protected." Activities by a single individual undertaken on his or her own behalf which are determined to be purely personal in nature are not deemed to be concerted; in order to be concerted under the Act an activity must "be engaged in with or on the authority of other employees, and not solely by and on behalf of the employee himself."[19] Examples of conduct found to be personal rather than concerted include the following:

- Filing claims for workers' compensation[20] or similar benefits;[21]

---

[16]*NLRB v. Cabot Carbon Co.*, 360 U.S. 203, 44 LRRM 2204 (1959); (statutory phrase "dealing with" means more than simply collective bargaining); *Armco, Inc.*, 271 NLRB 350, 116 LRRM 1407 (1984) (bargaining history is not dispositive of the issue of whether employees form an organization); *Edward A. Utlaut Mem. Hosp.*, 249 NLRB 1153, 104 LRRM 1434 (1980) (intent of the organization, not its actual performance or development, is critical in determining organization status).

[17]*Exeter Hosp.*, 248 NLRB 377, 103 LRRM 1441 (1980).

[18]*NLRB v. Cabot Carbon Co.*, 360 U.S. 203, 44 LRRM 2204 (1959); *accord South Nassau Community Hosp.*, 247 NLRB 527, 103 LRRM 1175 (1980); *see* THE DEVELOPING LABOR LAW at 1488.

[19]*Meyers Indus., Inc.*, 268 NLRB 493, 115 LRRM 1025 (1984), *enforcement denied sub nom. Prill v. NLRB*, 755 F.2d 941, 118 LRRM 2649 (D.C. Cir. 1985). General Counsel Memorandum No. 84-3 (February 16, 1984), reprinted at 1984 LAB. REL. YRBK. (BNA) 339, provides guidance concerning the *Meyers* standard.

[20]*E.g., Wabco Constr. & Mining Equip. Group*, 270 NLRB 887, 116 LRRM 1171 (1984); *Central Georgia Elec. Membership Corp.*, 269 NLRB 635, 115 LRRM 1311 (1984); *Schreiber Materials & Cartage Co.*, 268 NLRB 1457, 115 LRRM 1162 (1984).

[21]*Briley Marine*, 269 NLRB 697, 115 LRRM 1310 (1984) (filing lawsuit to recover compensation for chemical poisoning injury).

- Filing claims for unemployment benefits;[22]
- Filing a safety complaint with the Occupational Safety and Health Administration;[23]
- Seeking vacation pay assertedly due by filing a claim against the employer with a state agency;[24] and
- Initiating steps to acquire a pay raise by inquiring about union wage scales with another employer.[25]

As these examples illustrate, employee conduct undertaken in furtherance of perfectly legitimate claims generally will not be protected by Section 7 if initiated on a purely personal basis. The one exception is where an individual employee seeks to enforce an existing collective bargaining agreement. In *NLRB v. City Disposal Systems, Inc.*,[26] the Supreme Court approved the Board's *Interboro* doctrine which provides that an individual's assertion of a right grounded in a collective bargaining agreement is recognized as concerted activity, and therefore accorded the protection of Section 7.[27] Accordingly, the filing of an individual grievance predicated upon an honest and reasonable belief that contract rights are being denied constitutes concerted activity.[28]

In addition to being concerted, employee conduct must also be protected in order to fall within Section 7. The Board and the courts, however, have ruled that not all "union" or "concerted" activities are protected by Section 7. Among the activities held to be unprotected by the Act are:

---

[22]*Bearden & Co., Inc.*, 272 NLRB No. 135, 117 LRRM 1417 (1984); *D&D Health Assoc., Inc.*, 270 NLRB 181, 116 LRRM 1056 (1984).

[23]*Certified Serv., Inc.*, 270 NLRB 360, 116 LRRM 1098 (1984). In contrast, the Board in *J.T. Cullen Co.*, 271 NLRB 114, 116 LRRM 1339 (1984), held that an employee's refusal to work for safety reasons constituted concerted activity because it was based upon a mutual employee decision jointly communicated to the employer. *But see Ewing v. NLRB*, 768 F.2d 51, 119 LRRM 3273 (2d Cir. 1985), in which the court rejected the Board's *Meyers* rule and held that "it is clearly within the Board's discretion to find that an individual's reasonable and good faith invocation of an employment-related statutory right is not 'so remotely related to the activities of fellow employees that it cannot reasonably be said that the employee is engaged in concerted activity.'" (citing *NLRB v. City Disposal Sys.*, 465 U.S. 822, 833 n.10).

[24]*Access Control Sys.*, 270 NLRB 823, 116 LRRM 1145 (1984).

[25]*Allied Erecting and Dismantling Co.*, 270 NLRB 277, 116 LRRM 1076 (1984).

[26]465 U.S. 822, 115 LRRM 3193 (1984).

[27]*Interboro Contractors, Inc.*, 157 NLRB 1295, 61 LRRM 1537 (1966). The Board in *Interboro* reasoned that the assertion of a right contained in a collective bargaining agreement is an extension of the concerted action that produced the agreement, and the assertion of such a right affects the rights of all employees covered by the contract.

[28]*Compare Vanport Sand and Gravel, Inc.*, 270 NLRB 1358, 116 LRRM 1372 (1984) (grievance based upon alleged denial of contract seniority rights concerted) *with ABF Freight Sys., Inc.*, 271 NLRB 35, 116 LRRM 1330 (1984) (employee's refusal to operate allegedly unsafe vehicle not concerted because employee not reasonably and honestly invoking a collectively-bargained right, but obstructively raising petty and/or unfounded complaints). *See also Alcan Cable*, 269 NLRB 184, 116 LRRM 1065 (1984), where an employee's filing a complaint under the employer's own *noncontractual* grievance procedure was found not to be in reliance upon a collective bargaining agreement and therefore not concerted.

- Activities which are not in furtherance of a legitimate union interest or which are contrary to an overriding policy of the labor laws;[29]
- Strikes or walkouts unrelated to terms and conditions of employment, or concerted work stoppages which are unlawful, violent, or in breach of contract;[30]
- Activities carried on in an "illegal" manner; for example, destruction of property,[31] sitdown strikes,[32] mass picketing,[33] or slowdown strikes;[34]
- Actions which are indefensible because they evidence a degree of disloyalty to the employer unnecessary to the attainment of union goals;[35]
- Work stoppages which are partial or intermittent, or which unreasonably interfere with the business of the employer without imposing comparable economic hardships on the employees;[36]
- Activities which disparage the employer's product "in a manner reasonably calculated to harm the company's reputation and reduce its income";[37]
- Affirmative interference with the employer's equipment, such as turning off machinery which could have operated for weeks unattended;[38]
- Insubordinate refusal to follow legitimate plant rules.[39]

When employee conduct is determined not to be "concerted" under Section 7—or if concerted then not "protected"—the employer is

---

[29]For a detailed treatment of unprotected concerted activity *see* THE DEVELOPING LABOR LAW at 159–164 and *NLRB v. G.A.I.U. Local 13-B, Graphic Arts Int'l Union*, 682 F.2d 304, 110 LRRM 2984 (2d Cir. 1982).

[30]*Keyway, a Div. of P.H.A.S.E. Inc.*, 263 NLRB 1168, 111 LRRM 1196 (1982); *Virginia Elec. and Power*, 262 NLRB 1119, 111 LRRM 1054 (1982). In *Clear Pine Mouldings, Inc.*, 268 NLRB 1044, 115 LRRM 1113 (1984), the Board for the first time concluded that threatening remarks made by strikers which are unaccompanied by physical acts can be unprotected if, under the circumstances, they reasonably tend to coerce or intimidate employees in the exercise of rights protected under the Act.

[31]*NLRB v. Indiana & Mich. Elec. Co.*, 318 U.S. 9, 11 LRRM 763 (1943); *Teamsters, Local 695 (Wisconsin Supply Corp.)*, 204 NLRB 866, 83 LRRM 1650 (1973).

[32]*NLRB v. Fansteel Metallurgical Corp.*, 306 U.S. 240, 4 LRRM 515 (1939).

[33]*Allen-Bradley Local No. 1111 v. Wisconsin Employment Relations Board*, 315 U.S. 740, 10 LRRM 520 (1942); *Burgreen Contracting Co.*, 195 NLRB 1067, 79 LRRM 1700 (1972).

[34]*NLRB v. AAA Elec., Inc.*, 472 F.2d 444, 82 LRRM 2326 (6th Cir. 1973); *Elk Lumber Co.*, 91 NLRB 333, 26 LRRM 1493 (1950).

[35]*NLRB v. Washington Aluminum Co.*, 370 U.S. 9, 50 LRRM 2235 (1962), and cases cited therein.

[36]*Shelly and Anderson Furniture Mfg. Co. v. NLRB*, 497 F.2d 1200, 86 LRRM 2619 (9th Cir. 1974).

[37]*NLRB v. Electrical Workers Local 1229*, 346 U.S. 464, 33 LRRM 2183 (1953). *But see Interstate Sec. Servs.*, 263 NLRB 6, 110 LRRM 1535 (1982) (publication of newspaper article about labor dispute protected where not malicious, disloyal, or a disparagement of employer).

[38]*Can-Tex Indus. v. NLRB*, 683 F.2d 1183, 110 LRRM 3196 (8th Cir. 1982).

[39]*Bird Engineering*, 270 NLRB 1415, 116 LRRM 1302 (1984).

free to discipline or discharge the employees involved,[40] or may decline to bargain with the union responsible for the conduct.[41]

Unfair Labor Practices

Section 7 is immediately followed by provisions which set forth employer and union unfair labor practices. These are broadly worded descriptions of conduct prohibited under the Act. The employer unfair labor practices set forth in Section 8(a) are diagrammed in Exhibit 1. Certain union unfair labor practices found in Section 8(b) are diagrammed in Exhibits 2 and 3. Unfair labor practice proceedings are described in chapters 12 through 18.

§1.5   Employer Unfair Labor Practices

(a) In general. It is an unfair labor practice for an employer:

- To interfere with, restrain, or coerce employees in the exercise of the rights guaranteed in Section 7 (Section 8(a)(1));
- To dominate or interfere with the formation or administration of any labor organization or contribute financial or other support to it (Section 8(a)(2));
- To encourage or discourage membership in any labor organization by discrimination in regard to hire or tenure or conditions of employment, with the one exception of the valid union shop (Section 8(a)(3));
- To discharge or otherwise discriminate against an employee for filing charges or giving testimony under the Act (Section 8(a)(4));
- To refuse to bargain collectively with the majority representative of the employees (Section 8(a)(5)); and
- To enter into a "hot cargo" agreement with a union, that is, an agreement under which the employer promises not to do business with, or not to handle or otherwise deal in any of the products of, any other person (Section 8(e)).

(b) Discharges Pursuant to a Union-Shop Clause. The statute recognizes only one situation in which it is legal for an employer to discharge an employee upon the request of a union because

---

[40]*NLRB v. Fansteel Metallurgical Corp.*, 306 U.S. 240, 4 LRRM 515 (1939).

[41]*Timken Roller Bearing Co. v. NLRB*, 161 F.2d 949, 20 LRRM 2204 (6th Cir. 1947); *Artcraft Mantel and Fireplace Co.*, 174 NLRB 737, 70 LRRM 1294 (1969). It should be noted that the employer's right to decline to bargain lasts only as long as the illegal strike activity continues. *See United Elastic Corp.*, 84 NLRB 768, 24 LRRM 1294 (1949); *Dorsey Trailers Inc.*, 80 NLRB 478, 23 LRRM 1112 (1948).

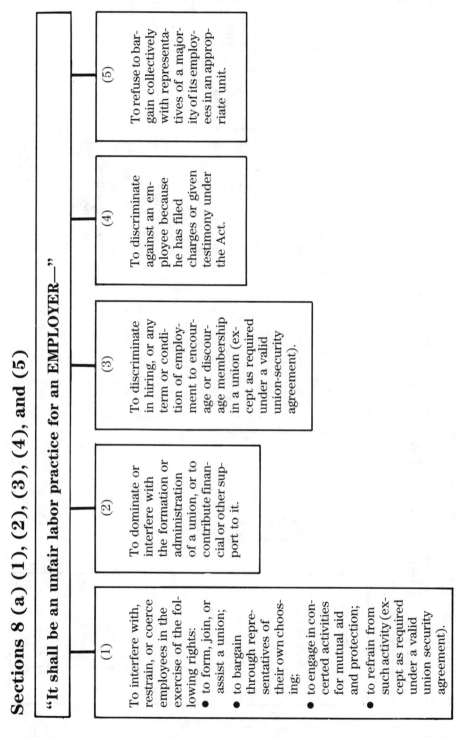

Sections 8 (a) (1), (2), (3), (4), and (5)

"It shall be an unfair labor practice for an EMPLOYER—"

(1)

To interfere with, restrain, or coerce employees in the exercise of the following rights:

● to form, join, or assist a union;

● to bargain through representatives of their own choosing;

● to engage in concerted activities for mutual aid and protection;

● to refrain from such activity (except as required under a valid union security agreement).

(2)

To dominate or interfere with the formation or administration of a union, or to contribute financial or other support to it.

(3)

To discriminate in hiring, or any term or condition of employment to encourage or discourage membership in a union (except as required under a valid union-security agreement).

(4)

To discriminate against an employee because he has filed charges or given testimony under the Act.

(5)

To refuse to bargain collectively with representatives of a majority of its employees in an appropriate unit.

Exhibit 1.   Provisions of Sections 8 (a) (1), (2), (3), (4), and (5)

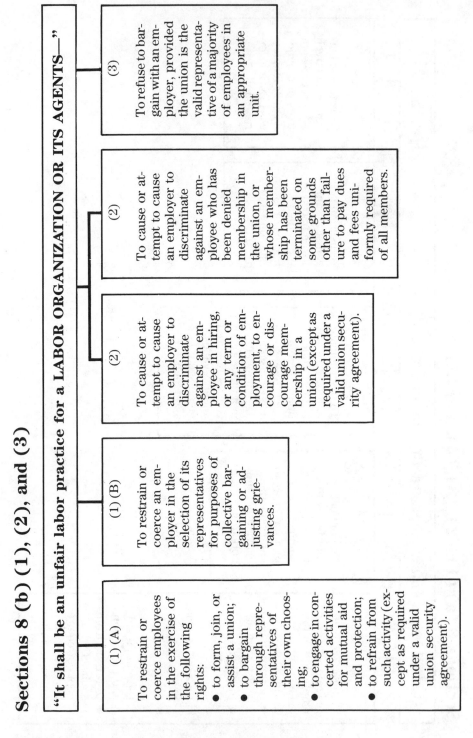

Sections 8 (b) (1), (2), and (3)

"It shall be an unfair labor practice for a LABOR ORGANIZATION OR ITS AGENTS—"

(1) (A)

To restrain or coerce employees in the exercise of the following rights:

- to form, join, or assist a union;
- to bargain through representatives of their own choosing;
- to engage in concerted activities for mutual aid and protection;
- to refrain from such activity (except as required under a valid union security agreement).

(1) (B)

To restrain or coerce an employer in the selection of its representatives for purposes of collective bargaining or adjusting grievances.

(2)

To cause or attempt to cause an employer to discriminate against an employee in hiring, or any term or condition of employment, to encourage or discourage membership in a union (except as required under a valid union security agreement).

(2)

To cause or attempt to cause an employer to discriminate against an employee who has been denied membership in the union, or whose membership has been terminated on some grounds other than failure to pay dues and fees uniformly required of all members.

(3)

To refuse to bargain with an employer, provided the union is the valid representative of a majority of employees in an appropriate unit.

Exhibit 2.   Provisions of Sections 8 (b) (1), (2), and (3)

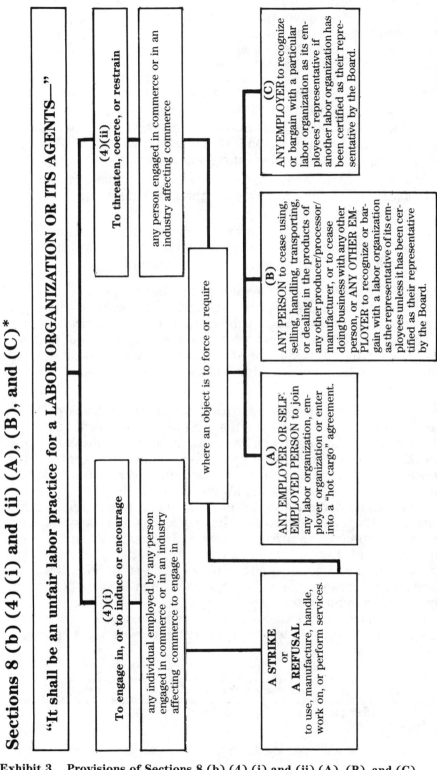

Sections 8 (b) (4) (i) and (ii) (A), (B), and (C)*

"It shall be an unfair labor practice for a LABOR ORGANIZATION OR ITS AGENTS—"

(4)(i)
To engage in, or to induce or encourage

any individual employed by any person engaged in commerce or in an industry affecting commerce to engage in

A STRIKE
or
A REFUSAL
to use, manufacture, handle, work on, or perform services.

(4)(ii)
To threaten, coerce, or restrain

any person engaged in commerce or in an industry affecting commerce

where an object is to force or require

(A)
ANY EMPLOYER OR SELF-EMPLOYED PERSON to join any labor organization, employer organization or enter into a "hot cargo" agreement.

(B)
ANY PERSON to cease using, selling, handling, transporting, or dealing in the products of any other producer/processor/manufacturer, or to cease doing business with any other person, or ANY OTHER EMPLOYER to recognize or bargain with a labor organization as the representative of its employees unless it has been certified as their representative by the Board.

(C)
ANY EMPLOYER to recognize or bargain with a particular labor organization as its employees' representative if another labor organization has been certified as their representative by the Board.

*The statute assigns priority to the handling of such cases and directs that an injunction must be requested if there is reasonable cause to believe that, they have merit.

Exhibit 3.   Provisions of Sections 8 (b) (4) (i) and (ii) (A), (B), and (C)

of nonmembership in the union.[42] Such discharges may be made pursuant to a union-shop agreement which binds all employees to become and remain members of the union 30 or more days after hire as a condition of continued employment. A discharge under such a clause is permitted by the statute only if:

- The union is both free from employer domination or assistance and is the majority-designated representative;
- The union's authority to make such an agreement has not been rescinded in a Board-conducted election within one year preceding the effective date of the agreement;
- The employer has reason to believe that membership was available to the employee on the same terms applicable to other members; and
- The employer has reason to believe that membership was denied or terminated by the union only because of failure of the employee to offer to pay dues or initiation fees.

In 1980 the Act was amended to provide that employees who belong to bona fide religious organizations with conscientious objections to joining or financially supporting a labor organization may not be required to join or support a union as a condition of employment. Such individuals may, however, be required to pay an amount of money equal to union dues and fees to a charitable organization.[43]

(c) Employer Responsibility for Unfair Labor Practices. An employer is responsible for unfair labor practices committed by any person acting as its agent, directly or indirectly,[44] and "[i]n determining whether any person is acting as an 'agent' . . . the question of whether the specific acts performed were actually authorized or subsequently ratified shall not be controlling."[45]

The tests for determining the existence of an agency relationship between an employer and some other person (usually a supervisor) have been expressed in sweeping terms. The Sixth Circuit, for example, has held that "if there is a connection between management and the employee's actions, either by way of instigation, direction, approval, or at the very least acquiescence, then the acts of the employee will be imputed to the company."[46]

Often, courts have found an agency relationship by reference to a "reasonable employee" test, that is, would a reasonable employee

---

[42]Sec. 8(a)(3).

[43]Sec. 19. The employee is not free to contribute to any charity of his or her choice. The employer and union may provide in their contract a list of at least three nonreligious, nonlabor organizations to which contributions in lieu of dues must be made. *Stern v. Teamsters General Local 200,* ——— F. Supp. ———, 121 LRRM 2416 (E.D. Wis. 1986).

[44]Sec. 2(2).

[45]Sec. 2(13).

[46]*NLRB v. Dayton Motels, Inc.,* 474 F.2d 328, 330, 82 LRRM 2651, 2652 (6th Cir. 1973).

conclude that the alleged agent was representing the company's interests?[47] In applying this test, the courts look not to the status or title of the purported agent, but rather to surrounding facts which would reasonably give rise to a belief that the agent was acting for the company.[48] Accordingly, an employer has been held to have committed unfair labor practices because of the acts of a warehouse foreman,[49] a bookkeeper,[50] a secretary,[51] the son of the only two corporate officers in a closely-held family corporation,[52] and a member of the Board of Directors.[53]

Where the purported agent also is a member of a labor union representing company employees, varying standards have been articulated. The Board has urged that under these circumstances, as with other questions of agency, the test should be the reasonable belief of the employees that the individual in question spoke for the company. The Second Circuit rejected this standard, ruling instead that the company would be responsible for such an agent's activity only if it "encouraged, authorized, or ratified—in other words affirmatively participated in—the supervisor's activities."[54] Agency also has been found and an employer held liable for the acts of a community businessmen's committee which included former owners of the business.[55]

Furthermore, a successor employer, one acquiring and continuing a predecessor's business with the knowledge that the former employer had committed an unfair labor practice in the discharge of an employee, may be ordered by the Board to reinstate the employee with backpay.[56] However, an employer may successfully avoid an unfair labor practice finding by immediately and effectively repudiating unlawful statements made by its agents.[57]

§1.6 Union Unfair Labor Practices

(a) In General. It is an unfair labor practice for a labor organization or its agents:

- To restrain or coerce employees in the exercise of their rights under Section 7 or an employer in the selection of represen-

---

[47]*NLRB v. Berger Transfer & Storage Co.*, 678 F.2d 679, 110 LRRM 2865 (7th Cir. 1982) and cases cited therein.

[48]*Id.* at 688.

[49]*Id.*

[50]*Indian Head Lubricants*, 261 NLRB 12, 109 LRRM 1374 (1982).

[51]*Id.* at 13.

[52]*Id.*

[53]*Progressive Medical Group, Inc.*, 260 NLRB 258, 109 LRRM 1231 (1982).

[54]*Connecticut Distrib., Inc. v. NLRB*, 681 F.2d 127, 129, 110 LRRM 2788, 2289 (2d Cir. 1982); *see also Delta Hosiery Inc.*, 259 NLRB 1005, 109 LRRM 1063 (1982); *Community Cash Stores, Inc.*, 238 NLRB 265, 99 LRRM 1256 (1978).

[55]*Colson Corp.*, 148 NLRB 827, 57 LRRM 1078 (1964).

[56]*Golden State Bottling Co. v. NLRB*, 414 U.S. 168, 84 LRRM 2839 (1973).

[57]*Broyhill Co.*, 260 NLRB 1366, 109 LRRM 1314 (1982).

tatives for purposes of collective bargaining or the adjustment of grievances (Section 8(b)(1)(A) and (B));

- To cause or attempt to cause an employer to discriminate against an employee on account of membership or nonmembership in a labor organization with the one exception of the valid union shop (Section 8(b)(2));
- To refuse to bargain collectively with an employer, provided the union has been designated or selected by a majority of the employees as their representative (Section 8(b)(3));
- To engage in, or to induce or encourage an employee to engage in, a strike or refusal to handle goods, or to threaten, coerce, or restrain any person, where an object of such activity is (Section 8(b)(4)):
  - —To require any employer or self-employed person to join a labor or employer organization or to enter into a "hot cargo" agreement (Section 8(b)(4)(A));
  - —To require any person to cease using, selling, handling, or transporting the products of any other employer, or to cease doing business with any other person or to require some other employer to recognize or bargain with a labor organization which has not been certified by the Board as the representative of that other employer's employees (Section 8(b)(4)(B));
  - —To require any employer to bargain with a labor organization where another labor organization has already been certified by the Board as the representative of its employees (Section 8(b)(4)(C)) (these complex provisions are usually referred to as the "secondary boycott" provisions and are diagrammed in Exhibit 3); and
  - —To require an employer to assign work to members of a particular union or craft rather than to members of another union or craft (Section 8(b)(4)(D));
- To charge excessive or discriminatory initiation fees where a union shop is in effect (Section 8(b)(5));
- To cause or attempt to cause an employer to pay for work which is not to be performed (i.e., "feather bedding") (Section 8(b)(6));
- To engage in picketing or threats of picketing where an object is either to organize employees or to force an employer to recognize or bargain with a union (Section 8(b)(7));
- To enter into a "hot cargo" agreement with an employer (Section 8(e)); and
- To require any employee to join or financially support a labor organization against his or her religious beliefs (Section 19).

(b) Union Responsibility for Unfair Labor Practices. The above provisions constitute unfair labor practices only when engaged in by "a labor organization or its agents." Employees or individuals cannot commit unfair labor practices unless they are acting as agents for the labor organization. Rules used to determine responsibility of a labor organization for the acts of an agent are the same as those set forth above for employers.

Application of these rules to specific situations has resulted in rulings that a union was responsible for the acts of a union attorney,[58] district representatives and officers,[59] a union organizing committee,[60] an employee,[61] a business agent,[62] a shop steward,[63] and a foreman with authority to enforce union "working rules."[64] A union also has been found responsible for the acts of the wife of its business representative,[65] a business agent's secretary,[66] a council formed for bargaining purposes by local unions,[67] and an assistant in the union's training program.[68]

§1.7 Injunctions[69]

(a) Mandatory Injunctions. Section 10(l) imposes a mandatory duty on the Board to petition for "appropriate injunctive relief" against a labor organization or its agents charged with a violation of Section 8(b)(4)(A), (B), and (C), or Section 8(b)(7), and against an employer or union charged with a violation of Section 8(e), whenever the General Counsel's investigation reveals "reasonable cause to believe that such charge is true and a complaint should issue." In cases arising under Section 8(b)(7), however, a district court injunction may not be sought if a charge under Section 8(a)(2) of the Act has been filed alleging that the employer has dominated or interfered with the formation or administration of a labor organization and, after investigation, there is "reasonable cause to believe such charge is true and that a complaint should issue." Section 10(l) also provides that its provisions shall be applicable, "where such relief is appropriate," to

---

[58]*NLRB v. Pacific Intermountain Express Co.*, 228 F.2d 170, 37 LRRM 2226 (8th Cir. 1955).

[59]*Local 1814, Int'l Longshoremen's Ass'n v. NLRB*, 735 F.2d 1384, 116 LRRM 2291 (D.C. Cir. 1984) (criminal conduct of union officers attributable to union); *NLRB v. United Mine Workers, Dist. 31*, 198 F.2d 389, 30 LRRM 2445 (4th Cir. 1956).

[60]*PPG Indus., Inc. v. NLRB*, 671 F.2d 817, 109 LRRM 2721 (4th Cir. 1982).

[61]*NLRB v. Urban Tel. Corp.*, 499 F.2d 239, 86 LRRM 2704 (7th Cir. 1974). *See generally Coronado Coal Co. v. Mine Workers*, 268 U.S. 295, 304 (1925) (for union to be accountable, actions of agents must be in accordance with the "fundamental agreement of association"); *Carbon Fuel Co. v. Mine Workers*, 44 U.S. 212, 102 LRRM 3017 (1979).

[62]*NLRB v. United Bhd. of Carpenters & Joiners, Local 517*, 230 F.2d 256, 37 LRRM 2623 (1st Cir. 1956).

[63]*NLRB v. IUE Local 745*, 759 F.2d 533, 118 LRRM 3407 (6th Cir. 1985); *NLRB v. United Hoisting Co.*, 198 F.2d 465, 30 LRRM 2507 (3d Cir. 1952).

[64]*Teamsters, Local 326 (Eazor Express, Inc.)*, 208 NLRB 666, 85 LRRM 1415 (1974); *Teamsters, Local 695 (Wis. Supply Corp.)*, 204 NLRB 866, 83 LRRM 1650 (1973); *NLRB v. Electrical Workers, IBEW, Local 3 (N.Y. Tel. Co.)*, 467 F.2d 1158, 81 LRRM 2483 (2d Cir. 1972); *NLRB v. Cement Masons Local No. 555*, 225 F.2d 168, 36 LRRM 2426 (9th Cir. 1955).

[65]*NLRB v. Local 90, Plasterers*, 606 F.2d 189, 102 LRRM 2482 (7th Cir. 1979).

[66]*Q.V.L. Const., Inc.*, 260 NLRB 1096, 109 LRRM 1277 (1982).

[67]*Berry-Mahurin Const., Inc.*, 258 NLRB 1259, 108 LRRM 1243 (1981).

[68]*Boilermakers, Local Union No. 154*, 253 NLRB 747, 106 LRRM 1030 (1980).

[69]A more extensive discussion of injunctions appears in chapter 21.

violations of Section 8(b)(4)(D) of the Act, which prohibits strikes and other coercive conduct in support of jurisdictional disputes. In practice, injunctions uniformly are sought where the jurisdictional dispute is interfering with the progress of the work. In addition, under Section 10(l) a temporary restraining order pending the hearing on the petition for an injunction may be obtained, without notice to the respondent, upon a showing that "substantial and irreparable injury to the charging party will be unavoidable" unless immediate injunctive relief is granted. Such *ex parte* relief, however, may not extend beyond five days.

(b) Discretionary Injunctions. In addition to Section 10(l) mandatory injunctions, after an unfair labor practice complaint has been issued against an employer or a labor organization, Section 10(j) authorizes the Board to petition a U.S. district court for appropriate temporary relief or restraining order in aid of the pending unfair labor practice proceeding. This is sometimes called the discretionary injunction provision because, unlike Section 10(l), it does not require that injunctive relief be sought, but only makes it possible for the Board to do so in cases where it is considered appropriate. The statute does not define any limits within which the discretion may or may not be used.

The Board looks upon such injunctions as extraordinary remedies which should be used sparingly and acts only in unusual circumstances. Consequently, the cases in which the Board has authorized the General Counsel to request such injunctions generally have been those where the effect of the alleged unfair labor practices was widespread, the public interest was seriously affected, the Board's processes were being interfered with, or the Board's ultimate remedy under the circumstances would have been clearly inadequate and the conduct was clear-cut and flagrant.

A district court is empowered to grant such injunctive relief "as it deems just and proper."[70] Its action in denying or granting the Board's petition is taken in an independent proceeding. The court does not pass upon the ultimate merits of the unfair labor practices charged,[71] and its ruling in no way controls or binds the Board in its subsequent decision on the merits.[72] If the district court issues an injunction, it is dissolved upon issuance of the Board's decision, or upon court enforcement of the Board's order.[73] However, in issuing an injunction, the district court has discretion to limit its duration to a term short of the Board's final decision.[74]

---

[70]Sec. 10(j); *McLeod v. General Elec. Co.*, 385 U.S. 533, 64 LRRM 2129 (1967).

[71]*Kennedy v. Teamsters, Local 542*, 443 F.2d 627, 77 LRRM 2607 (9th Cir. 1971); *Angle v. Sacks*, 382 F.2d 655, 66 LRRM 2111 (10th Cir. 1967).

[72]*Boire v. Teamsters*, 479 F.2d 778, 83 LRRM 2128 (5th Cir. 1973).

[73]*Barbour v. Central Cartage*, 583 F.2d 335, 99 LRRM 2252 (7th Cir. 1978).

[74]*Eisenberg v. Hartz Mountain Corp.*, 519 F.2d 138, 89 LRRM 2705 (3d Cir. 1975).

Neither discretionary nor mandatory injunctions may be obtained directly by the charging party. Only the Board, acting through the General Counsel, has this privilege.

§1.8 Duty to Bargain

One of the principal purposes of the Act is to encourage "the practice and procedure of collective bargaining."[75] In defining what constitutes collective bargaining, the statute prescribes certain rules which are binding upon both employers and labor organizations:[76]

- They have the mutual obligation to meet at reasonable times and to confer in good faith concerning wages, hours, and other terms and conditions of employment;
- They must execute a written contract incorporating any agreement reached if requested by either party; and
- They are not compelled to agree to a proposal or required to make a concession.

The employer is also under an obligation to furnish the union, upon request, with sufficient information to enable it to understand and intelligently discuss the issues raised in bargaining.

The duty to bargain is broad. It extends to all subjects which fall within the general phrase "wages, hours, and other terms and conditions of employment."[77] The outer limits of the duty to bargain cannot be defined with precision, but must be expressed only in the most general of terms. At one extreme, there is no obligation to bargain over minor departures from past practice which affect employees' working conditions, but which cannot be said to be material, substantial, or significant.[78] At the other extreme, managerial decisions relating to the nature and direction of the business, decisions which are said to lie at the "core of entrepreneurial control," may be made unilaterally by an employer without first bargaining with the union, although there may be an obligation to negotiate concerning the *effects* of such decisions on employees.[79]

---

[75]Sec. 1.

[76]Sec. 8(d).

[77]An exhaustive study of this topic is beyond the scope of this book, but is treated in THE DEVELOPING LABOR LAW at 757–869.

[78]*E.g.*, *United Nuclear Corp.*, 268 NLRB 841, 115 LRRM 1111 (1984) (no duty to bargain over employer's decision to administer oral tests to employees because oral test represented a change of form but not of substance, and "there arises no obligation to bargain concerning changes which depart in an insignificant manner from established practice while leaving the practice intact"). *See also Benchmark Indus., Inc.*, 270 NLRB 22, 116 LRRM 1032 (1984) (no duty to bargain over employer's decision to discontinue three-year practice of giving employees Christmas hams and dinners because the hams and dinners were "merely gifts" and not a condition of employment).

[79]*E.g.*, *First Nat'l Maintenance Corp. v. NLRB*, 452 U.S. 666, 107 LRRM 2705 (1981) (decision to close part of a business for economic reasons not a mandatory subject of bargaining, but effects of such decision are mandatory); *Otis Elevator Co.*, 269 NLRB 891, 115 LRRM 1281 (1984) (decision to discontinue research and development activities at one facility and consolidate them with operations at another facility not a mandatory subject of bargaining).

While the Board may compel an employer and the representative of its employees to engage in collective bargaining, and may determine whether they are bargaining in good faith,[80] it may not attempt to dictate the actual terms of an agreement.[81]

§1.9 Limitations on the Board's Discretion in Unfair Labor Practice Cases

The statute limits the Board's discretion in certain aspects of unfair labor practice case handling. For example, the Board must:

- Refuse to issue a complaint upon a charge filed and served more than six months after the unfair labor practice occurred;[82]
- Apply the same rules of decision to company-assisted or company-dominated unions whether or not such unions are independent or affiliates of national labor organizations;[83]
- Seek injunctions in Section 8(b)(4)(A), (B), or (C), 8(e), and 8(b)(7) cases as soon as the investigating officer finds merit in such charges;[84]
- Give top priority to the handling of Section 8(b)(4)(A), (B), or (C), 8(e) or 8(b)(7) cases;[85]
- Give priority to Section 8(a)(3) or 8(b)(2) cases over cases other than those given top priority under Sections 8(b)(4)(A), (B) or (C), 8(e) and 8(b)(7);[86] and
- Refuse to cede jurisdiction to any state whose labor relations requirements are inconsistent with the Act.[87]

Representation Elections

§1.10 Types of Elections

In addition to defining unfair labor practices, the statute also seeks to promote the practice and procedure of collective bargaining by "protecting the exercise by workers of full freedom of association, self-organization, and designation of representatives of their own

---

[80]Secs. 8(a)(5), 8(b)(1)(A).
[81]*H.K. Porter Co. v. NLRB*, 397 U.S. 99, 72 LRRM 2561 (1970).
[82]Sec. 10(b).
[83]Sec. 10(c).
[84]Sec. 10(l).
[85]*Id.*
[86]Sec. 10(m).
[87]Sec. 10(a).

choosing."[88] Representation proceedings are described in chapters 4 through 11.

The statute recognizes four different types of elections:[89]

- The *collective bargaining* election to determine the majority status of a labor organization. A petition for such an election may be filed by a labor organization, a group of employees, an individual, or by an employer;
- The *decertification* election to determine whether a certified or currently recognized labor organization still represents a majority of the employees. A petition for such an election may be filed by a labor organization, a group of employees, or by an individual;[90]
- The *deauthorization* election to determine whether the employees wish to remove the labor organization's authority to have a union-shop agreement. A petition for such an election may be filed by a group of employees representing at least 30 percent of those covered by the agreement;[91] and
- The *national emergency* election to determine whether employees wish to accept the final offer of settlement made by their employer.[92] This election must be conducted between 60–75 days after a federal district court has issued an injunction against a strike or lockout which imperils or threatens to imperil the national safety.

§1.11 Determination of the Unit

The statute provides that "the Board shall decide in each case whether, in order to assure to employees the fullest freedom in exercising the rights guaranteed by this Act, the unit appropriate for the purposes of collective bargaining shall be the employer unit, craft unit, plant unit, or subdivision thereof."[93] Beyond this provision, the statute carries specific proscriptions concerning craft units, guards, and professional employees.[94]

(a) Craft Units. The Board cannot decide that any craft unit is inappropriate for bargaining purposes on the ground that a different unit has been established by a prior Board determination,

---

[88]Sec. 1.

[89]Sec. 9.

[90]Decertification elections are discussed in chapter 11.

[91]Deauthorization elections are discussed in chapter 11.

[92]Sec. 209(b).

[93]Sec. 9(b).

[94]*Id.* See the discussion of appropriate bargaining units in §8.5 and THE DEVELOPING LABOR LAW at chapter 11.

unless a majority of the employees in the proposed craft unit vote against separate representation.[95]

(b) Guards. The Board may not include guards in the same unit with other employees.[96] Furthermore, a union cannot be certified as exclusive bargaining representative for guards if it admits to membership employees other than guards, or if it is affiliated "directly or indirectly" with a labor organization which admits to membership employees other than guards.[97]

The statute defines a guard as "any individual employed as a guard to enforce against employees and other persons rules to protect property of the employer or to protect the safety of persons on the employer's premises."[98] Individuals with both guard and nonguard responsibilities will be deemed guards only if their guard functions constitute an essential part of their duties.[99] In addition, guards are not limited to persons who protect the employer's property, but may include individuals such as armored car company employees who protect the property of others.[100]

The statute prohibits the Board from certifying a union in a unit which includes both guard and nonguard employees but does not prohibit an employer and union from combining them voluntarily.[101] In such situations the Board relaxes its normal restrictions on severance and decertification procedures when the guards desire separate representation.[102] In addition, if the employer withdraws its voluntary recognition at a time when the union still represents a majority of the unit employees, the Board will not find an unfair labor practice and issue a bargaining order thereby giving the union indirectly through the bargaining order what it could not achieve directly through a certification.[103]

---

[95]Sec. 9(b)(2).

[96]Sec. 9(b)(3).

[97]*Id.* Unions disqualified from certification by Sec. 9(b)(3) may not intervene in Board election proceedings to appear on the ballot, *University of Chicago,* 272 NLRB No. 126, 117 LRRM 1377 (1984), and may not file a unit clarification petition, *Brink's, Inc.,* 272 NLRB No. 125, 117 LRRM 1385 (1984). These issues are discussed further in §§7.6(b) and 10.16, respectively.

[98]Sec. 9(b)(3).

[99]*Chance Vought Aircraft, Inc.,* 110 NLRB 1342, 35 LRRM 1338 (1954).

[100]*Purolator Courier Corp.,* 254 NLRB 599, 106 LRRM 1116 (1981); *Brink's, Inc.,* 226 NLRB 1182, 94 LRRM 1022 (1976).

[101]*NLRB v. J.J. Collins' Sons, Inc.,* 332 F.2d 523, 56 LRRM 2375 (7th Cir. 1964).

[102]*Los Angeles Bonadventure Hotel,* 235 NLRB 96, 97 LRRM 1453 (1978); *Fisher-New Center Co.,* 170 NLRB 909, 67 LRRM 1502 (1968).

[103]*Wells Fargo Armored Serv. Corp.,* 270 NLRB 787, 116 LRRM 1129 (1984), *enforced, Truck Drivers Local Union No. 807 v. NLRB,* 755 F.2d 5, 118 LRRM 2613 (2d Cir. 1985). If, however, an employer feels that continued recognition of a union is no longer required because some of the employees in the unit are guards, a unit classification proceeding rather than withdrawal of recognition is the proper method for raising the issue. *ACL Corp.,* 278 NLRB No. 76, 122 LRRM 1012 (1986).

(c) Professional Employees. The Board may not include professional employees in the same unit with other employees unless a majority of the professionals first vote separately in favor of such inclusion.[104] This principle is an acknowledgment that professional employees may have unique interests which can become submerged in a broader unit.[105] As with guards, however, the statutory proscription applies only to the Board, and a union and employer may voluntarily execute a contract on behalf of both professional and nonprofessional employees without first running an election.[106]

The statute affords two definitions of a "professional employee."[107] One definition includes employees engaged in work:

- Predominantly intellectual and varied in character, as opposed to routine mental, manual, mechanical, or physical work;
- Involving consistent exercise of discretion and judgment;
- Requiring advanced knowledge in a field of science or learning usually acquired by a prolonged course of specialized intellectual instruction in an institution of higher learning or in a hospital; and
- Whose output cannot be standardized by time measurement.

The second definition includes employees who have completed the specialized intellectual instruction referred to above, but who in essence are serving an apprenticeship by performing related work under the supervision of a professional person in order to qualify as a professional.[108]

The statutory definition generally is applied on a case-by-case basis by the Board with the nature of the work performed and the qualifications of the employee serving as the major determinants.[109]

§1.12 Limitations on the Board's Discretion in Election Cases

In certain areas involving elections, the statute speaks in mandatory terms and deprives the Board of any discretion. For example, the Board may not:

---

[104]Sec. 9(b)(1); *Leedom v. Kyne*, 358 U.S. 184, 43 LRRM 2222 (1958).

[105]Sec. 2(12); *see* THE DEVELOPING LABOR LAW at 422–424.

[106]*Retail Clerks Local 324*, 144 NLRB 1247, 54 LRRM 1226 (1963).

[107]Sec. 2(12).

[108]*Id.*

[109]*Illinois Valley Community Hosp.*, 261 NLRB 1048, 110 LRRM 1202 (1982) (medical technologists held professionals based upon nature of work); *Utah Power and Light Co.*, 258 NLRB 1059, 108 LRRM 1145 (1981) (engineers held professionals on basis of job and necessary qualifications); *Catholic Bishop of Chicago*, 235 NLRB 776, 98 LRRM 1037 (1978) (teachers and social workers held professionals based upon educational background and experience); *Express-News Corp.*, 223 NLRB 627, 91 LRRM 1489 (1976) (journalists held not professionals because only general college degree required).

- Place professional employees in a unit with nonprofessional employees unless the professionals are first given the opportunity, and do, vote in favor of inclusion;[110]
- Decide that any craft unit is inappropriate on the ground that a different unit has been established by a prior Board decision, unless a majority of the employees in the craft unit vote against separate representation;[111]
- Find a unit of guards appropriate when nonguard employees are included in the same unit;[112]
- Certify a union as exclusive bargaining agent for a unit of guards unless it, as well as its parent body, restricts its membership to guards;[113]
- Conduct a collective bargaining or decertification election in a unit in which a valid election was conducted within the preceding 12-month period;[114]
- Give controlling weight to the extent to which the employees have been organized in determining an appropriate bargaining unit;[115]
- Conduct a deauthorization election where one was conducted within the preceding 12-month period.[116]

The statute also places certain affirmative obligations on the Board with respect to conducting elections. For example, the Board must:

- Apply the same rules in determining whether a question of representation affecting commerce exists irrespective of the identity of the person filing the petition (e.g., employer, labor organization, or individual) and the kind of relief sought;[117]
- Conduct a runoff election between the two choices receiving the largest and second largest number of valid votes cast in situations where none of the choices on the ballot receives a majority;[118]
- Conduct a deauthorization election to determine whether a contractual union-shop provision should be rescinded whenever 30 percent or more of the employees covered by the agreement request such an election.[119]

---

[110]Sec. 9(b)(1).
[111]Sec. 9(b)(2).
[112]Sec. 9(b)(3).
[113]*Id.*
[114]Sec. 9(c)(3).
[115]Sec. 9(c)(5).
[116]Sec. 9(e)(2).
[117]Sec. 9(c)(2).
[118]Sec. 9(c)(3).
[119]Sec. 9(e)(1).

Types of Cases

The National Labor Relations Board identifies 14 different types of cases based on the provisions of the Act involved. (See Exhibit 4.) Following is a brief description of each type and, in parentheses after each, the designation assigned by the Board:

1. An unfair labor practice charge filed by any person, usually an individual or a labor organization, against an employer alleging a violation of Sections 8(a)(1), (2), (3), (4), or (5) of the Act (CA case);

2. An unfair labor practice charge filed by any person, usually an employer or an individual, against a labor organization alleging a violation of Sections 8(b)(1), (2), (3), (5), or (6) of the Act (CB case);

3. An unfair labor practice charge alleging a violation of Sections 8(b)(4)(i)(ii), (A), (B), or (C) filed by any person, usually an employer, against a labor organization (CC case);

4. An unfair labor practice charge involving a jurisdictional dispute within the meaning of Section 8(b)(4)(D) filed by any person, usually an employer or a labor organization (CD case);

5. An unfair labor practice charge involving Section 8(b)(7) filed by any person, usually an employer, against a labor organization (CP case);

6. An unfair labor practice charge involving Section 8(e) filed by any person, usually an employer, against an employer or labor organization or both (CE case);

7. An unfair labor practice charge filed by any person, usually an employer, against a union alleging a failure to provide the notices required by Section 8(g) before striking, picketing, or engaging in a work stoppage at a health care institution (CG case);

8. A petition for a collective bargaining election filed by an individual, a group, or a labor organization (RC case);

9. A petition for a collective bargaining election filed by an employer (RM case);

10. A petition for an election filed by an individual, a group, or a labor organization challenging the current majority status of a labor organization (RD case);

11. A petition filed by an individual, a group, or a labor organization seeking an election to remove the authority of a labor organization to have a union-shop agreement (UD case);

1. Section 8 Unfair Labor

Charge Against Employer		Charge Against
CA Case	**CB Case**	**CP Case**
8(a)(1) Interfere with, restrain, or coerce employees in exercise of their rights under Sec. 7 (to join or assist a labor organization or to refrain). 8(a)(2) Dominate or interfere with the formation or administration of a labor organization or contribute financial or other support to it. 8(a)(3) Encourage or discourage membership in a labor organization (discrimination in regard to hire or tenure). 8(a)(4) Discourage or otherwise discriminate against an employee because he has given testimony under the Act. 8(a)(5) Refuse to bargain collectively with representatives of its employees.	8(b)(1)(A) Restrain or coerce employees in exercise of their rights under Section 7 (to join or assist a labor organization or to refrain). 8(b)(1)(B) Restrain or coerce an employer in the selection of its representatives for collective bargaining or adjustment of grievances. 8(b)(2) Cause or attempt to cause an employer to discriminate against an employee. 8(b)(3) Refuse to bargain collectively. 8(b)(5) Require of employees the payment of excessive or discriminatory fees for membership. 8(b)(6) Cause or attempt to cause an employer to pay or agree to pay money or other thing of value for services which are not performed or not to be performed.	8(b)(7) To picket, cause, or threaten the picketing of any employer where an object is to force or require an employer to recognize or bargain with a labor organization as the representative of his employees, or to force or require the employees of an employer to select such labor organization as their collective bargaining representative, unless such labor organization is currently certified as the representative of such employees: (A) where the employer has lawfully recognized any other labor organization and a question concerning representation may not appropriately be raised under Section 9(c), (B) where within the preceding 12 months a valid election under 9(c) has been conducted, or (C) where picketing has been conducted without a petition under 9(c) being filed within a reasonable period of time not to exceed 30 days from the commencement of such picketing.

2. Section 9 Representation

RC Case	RD Case	RM Case
9(c)(1)(A)(i) Asserting the designation of filing party as bargaining agent.*	9(c)(1)(A)(ii) Asserting that the certified or recognized bargaining agent is no longer the representative.*	9(c)(1)(B) Alleging that one or more claims for recognition as exclusive bargaining agent have been received by employer.*

*This statement is not applicable if an 8(b)(7) charge is
on file involving the same employer; however, the "R" designation applies.

Exhibit 4.   Types of Cases

Practices (C Cases)

Labor Organization			Charge Against Labor Organization and Employer
CC Case	CD Case	CG Case	CE Case

8(b)(4)(i) To engage in, or induce or encourage any individual employed by any person engaged in commerce or in an industry affecting commerce to engage in, a strike or a refusal in the course of his employment to use, manufacture, process, transport, or otherwise handle or work on any goods or to perform any services; or (ii) To threaten, coerce or restrain any person engaged in commerce or in an industry affecting commerce, where in either case an object thereof is:

(A) To force or require any employer or self-employed person to join any labor or employer organization or to enter into any agreement prohibited by Sec. 8(e).

(B) To force or require any person to cease using, selling, handling, transporting, or otherwise dealing in the products of any other producer, processor, or manufacturer, or cease doing business with any other person, or force or require any other employer to recognize or bargain with a labor organization as the representative of his employees unless such labor organization has been so certified.

(C) To force or require any employer to recognize or bargain with a particular labor organization as the representative of its employees if another labor organization has been certified as the representative.

(D) To force or require any employer to assign particular work to employees in a particular labor organization or in a particular trade, craft, or class rather than to employees in another trade, craft, or class, unless such employer is failing to conform to an appropriate Board order or certification.

8(g) To fail to provide any health care institution and the Federal Mediation and Conciliation Service with at least ten days' written notice before engaging in any strike, picketing or other concerted refusal to work at the health care institution. Special notice requirements apply in cases where the parties are negotiating their initial agreement following certification or recognition.

8(e) To enter into any contract or agreement (any labor organization and any employer) whereby such employer ceases or refrains or agrees to cease or refrain from handling or dealing in any product of any other employer, or to cease doing business with any other person.

Petitions (R Cases)

UC Case	UD Case	AC Case
9(b) Clarification of an existing bargaining unit.*	9(e)(1) Employees wish to rescind a union security clause.*	9(b) Amendment of certification.

Exhibit 4—*cont'd*

12. A petition filed by a certified or currently recognized representative of a bargaining unit, or by an employer of employees in such a unit, to clarify the bargaining unit (UC case);

13. A petition filed by a certified representative of a bargaining unit, or by an employer of employees in such a unit, for amendment of the certification to reflect changed circumstances (AC case); and

14. A national emergency election conducted by the Board to determine whether or not employees wish to accept their employer's final offer of settlement (X case).

The foregoing explanation of the provisions of the law covers only its most important points. There are now literally thousands of Board decisions interpreting both the unfair labor practice and representation sections of the statute.

2

The Machinery of the National
Labor Relations Board

Background

The first National Labor Relations Board took office on August 27, 1935, shortly after the Wagner Act was passed. That law authorized establishment of the Board as the agency responsible for administration and enforcement of the Act. Congress gave little guidance as to the structure of the agency, however, and the Board, on its own initiative, established an administrative mechanism which made it prosecutor, judge, and jury.

The system aroused such criticism that, when Congress added major amendments to the original law as part of the Labor Management Relations Act of 1947, a unique system for the administration of the statute was included. In effect, Congress retained the concept of a single enforcement agency but divided authority over it into two independent units—the Board and the Office of the General Counsel.

Both the statute and the legislative history indicate that the Office of the General Counsel was created to perform the all-important preliminary functions of investigation and prosecution of unfair labor practice cases. The Board, on the other hand, was to restrict itself to quasi-judicial functions, operating essentially as an appellate court and making decisions on the basis of a formal record. This organizational structure was left unchanged when Congress passed the Labor-Management Reporting and Disclosure Act of 1959 (Landrum-Griffin Act) except provision was made for the temporary filling of a vacancy in the Office of the General Counsel.

While the congressional intent to separate prosecutorial and adjudicative responsibilities is clear, the failure of the language used to delineate fully the agency's work led to sharp conflicts between the Board and the General Counsel as to which had authority in

29

specific areas. To resolve these differences the Board in 1955 adopted a statement in which it delegated various powers and functions to the General Counsel. There have been fluctuations in the scope of this delegation, but it is now reasonably well defined and complete.[1]

With respect to unfair labor practice cases, the Board more nearly resembles a court than a regulatory agency. Its principal function is judicial in character and it is wholly divorced from the investigation and prosecution of unfair labor practice charges which are the responsibility of the General Counsel. It has no authority over issuance of formal complaints and therefore rules only upon those unfair labor practice cases which the General Counsel decides to prosecute. The General Counsel has absolute authority over whether or not a complaint shall issue in a given proceeding and the scope of the complaint. There is no appeal from the General Counsel's refusal to prosecute and the Board has neither authority to require action on the General Counsel's part nor jurisdiction to hear an action brought by a charging party. The Board does have veto power over requests for Section 10(j) discretionary injunctions prior to the institution of court proceedings but, again, rules only on those requests which first have been approved by the General Counsel.

The Board has complete authority over representation matters. Pursuant to the Labor-Management Reporting and Disclosure Act of 1959, however, the Board delegated its powers over these matters to the regional directors, retaining a right to review any of their decisions.[2] In practice, the General Counsel indirectly exerts some influence on such cases through supervision of the regional offices.

The Board

§2.1   Functions of the Board

The Board has two primary and three secondary functions. The primary functions are: (1) conducting secret-ballot elections among employees in appropriate bargaining units to determine whether they wish to be represented by a labor organization,[3] and (2) preventing and remedying unfair labor practices committed by employers, labor organizations, or their agents.[4] Secondary functions include conducting union deauthorization elections to determine whether em-

---

[1] A memorandum describing the authority and assigned responsibilities of the General Counsel was first issued in 1955 and amended several times thereafter. The full text of the current delegation, as amended, appears in Appendix C.

[2] See Appendix D for the full text of the Board's delegation of authority to regional directors in representation matters.

[3] Secs. 9(b) and (c). This authority has been delegated to the regional directors. See Appendix D.

[4] Sec. 10(a).

ployees wish to rescind an outstanding union-shop clause,[5] resolving
jurisdictional disputes by determining which of the competing groups
of employees is entitled to perform the work in dispute,[6] and polling
employees on their employer's last offer in "national emergency"
situations.[7]

§2.2   Structure of the Board and the Decision-Making Process

The Board consists of five public members who are appointed for
five-year terms by the President with Senate approval.[8] One member
is designated by the President to serve as chairman. Each Board
member has a chief counsel, a deputy chief counsel, and a staff of
approximately 20 attorneys who serve that particular member.

While all five Board members may participate in a decision and
frequently do in cases which establish or change policy, decision-
making authority in most cases is delegated to three-member panels.[9]
Each Board member is the head of one panel and a member of two
others. Typically, a case will be assigned by the Executive Secretary
to a particular Board member, and thus becomes a case of that member's panel. The case is referred to one of that member's staff counsel.
The entire record, including all of the pleadings, briefs, the administrative law judge's or regional director's decision, and the transcript,
is analyzed by the counsel.[10] The case then is considered and discussed
by a "subpanel"—i.e., senior staff members representing the three
Board members who constitute the panel for that case. The subpanel
recommends a disposition and the counsel drafts a legal memorandum for Board consideration or a proposed Board Decision and Order
in accordance with the subpanel recommendations. Draft opinions
are reviewed by the Board members and, if approved, are issued by
the Executive Secretary. Cases which are novel or which establish
or modify policy often are considered at meetings of the full Board.
Draft opinions are then prepared and circulated to all Board members
and are issued over the signatures of either the three panel members
or all five Board members.[11]

---

[5]Sec. 9(e). This authority has been delegated to the regional directors. See Appendix D.

[6]Sec. 10(k).

[7]Sec. 209(b). This authority has been delegated to the General Counsel. See Appendix C, para. I.C.

[8]Sec. 3(a). The Board's statement of its organization, functions, and field office structure is published in its Rules and Regulations at Part 201. The field office structure appears as Appendix E.

[9]Sec. 3(b). A statement prepared for 1983 congressional oversight hearings describes in detail the manner in which cases are processed at the Board level. See Appendix F.

[10]Sec. 4(a).

[11]The Board's case deliberations are closed to the public as are most of the Board's meetings. NLRB Rules and Regulations §§102.137–102.142. The Board's Rules and Regulations and Statements of Procedure, Series 8, as amended, appear in Appendix B.

§2.3   Board Staff

(a) *Executive Secretary.*   The Executive Secretary is the chief administrative and judicial management officer of the Board. The Office of the Executive Secretary is responsible for tracking all cases as they are processed by the Board. This includes assigning cases to the staffs of Board members and monitoring their progress through the various stages leading to issuance of a Board opinion; assigning case-handling priorities; receiving, docketing, and acknowledging all formal documents filed with the Board; certifying documents in the Board's files or records; and issuing and serving on the parties all Board Decisions and Orders. The Executive Secretary also represents the Board in communicating with the parties, with members of Congress, and with the public. Finally, the Executive Secretary supervises the operations of the Information Division.

(b) *Information Division.*   The Information Division is the Board's link with the public. Press releases concerning personnel appointments, major Board decisions, changes in Board operations, and other items of public interest originating both with the Board and the General Counsel are prepared and distributed by the Information Division. As discussed in chapter 24, the Division also publishes weekly summaries of Board decisions.

(c) *Solicitor.*   The Solicitor is the Board's chief legal advisor on questions of law and policy. In addition, the Solicitor provides advice concerning the adoption or modification of agency regulations, pending legislation affecting the Act, and litigation which may influence Board operations. Advisory opinions, declaratory orders, and summary judgment decisions frequently are drafted for the Board by the Solicitor.

(d) *Division of Judges.*   The Division of Judges consists of administrative law judges who conduct the hearings on unfair labor practice complaints. Formerly called trial examiners, these judges are independent of both the Board and the General Counsel. The statute forbids any review of the judges' findings or recommendations before issuance of their formal reports.[12] Furthermore, the administrative law judges are subject to the rules of the Office of Personnel Management which govern appointment and tenure.

Administrative law judges resemble federal district court judges, and act in a purely judicial capacity. They render an initial recommended decision, yet have nothing to do with its eventual disposition or consideration by the Board.[13] They are supervised by the Chief

---

[12]Sec. 4(a).
[13]*Id.*

Administrative Law Judge, who has the final authority to designate which judge will conduct a hearing, to assign dates for such hearings, and to rule upon requests for extensions of time within which to file briefs, proposed findings, and conclusions.[14] For administrative convenience the administrative law judges are based in Washington, D.C., San Francisco, New York City, and Atlanta. To the extent possible, hearings are conducted in the locality where the unfair labor practices occurred.

(e) Office of Representation Appeals. The Office of Representation Appeals is a special unit consisting of a director, three supervisors, and approximately 12 attorneys which is attached to the Chairman's office. Referred to as the "R unit" it is responsible for handling all requests for review of regional director's decisions in representation cases. Review may be requested from Direction of Elections; Decisions and Orders dismissing petitions, clarifying bargaining units, or amending certifications; administrative dismissals; and Supplemental Decisions on election objections and challenged ballots.

Because they often raise crucial election issues, requests for review are processed expeditiously. The R unit prepares a "screen" which (1) summarizes the regional director's findings, (2) describes the specific points raised in the request for review, (3) provides a recommended disposition, and (4) analyzes the facts, arguments and precedents involved in the appeal. The screens along with the director's decision and request for review are circulated to the Board members. As soon as the votes of the Board members are recorded, the parties are notified by mailgram of the disposition of the request for review. In most cases where the request for review is granted, the full record will be reviewed and the Board opinion drafted by attorneys in the R unit.

The General Counsel

§2.4   Functions of the General Counsel

The General Counsel's responsibilities flow both from the provisions of the statute and from the authority delegated by the Board. Section 3(d) provides that the General Counsel shall have final authority to investigate unfair labor practice charges, issue complaints based upon such charges, and prosecute the complaints before the Board. Thus, the General Counsel has statutory authority to accept and investigate charges filed, to enter into and approve informal

---

[14]*See* NLRB Rules and Regulations §201.1.3.

settlements of charges, to dismiss charges, to determine matters concerning consolidation and severance of cases before a complaint issues, to issue complaints and notices of hearing, to appear before administrative law judges in hearings on complaints, and to initiate and prosecute injunction proceedings as provided for in Section 10(l) of the Act. The General Counsel's discretion with regard to the issuance of complaints is broad, and a refusal to issue a complaint is not reviewable by the Board or the courts.[15] In addition, the General Counsel frames the issues to be litigated and the legal theories upon which the complaint will be based.[16]

Section 3(d) also provides that the General Counsel shall supervise all employees in the regional offices and all attorneys with the exception of those serving as administrative law judges or as legal assistants to the Board members. Prior Board approval is required, however, for the appointment, transfer, demotion, or discharge of any regional director or of any officer-in-charge of a subregional office.

In addition to statutory responsibilities, the General Counsel also has been delegated responsibilities by the Board.[17] The delegation of powers touches upon a variety of areas and authorizes the General Counsel to:

- Seek compliance with the Board's orders either by filing petitions for enforcement in the United States courts of appeals pursuant to Section 10(e) of the Act, or through resisting petitions for review filed by aggrieved parties pursuant to Section 10(f) of the Act (para. IB);

- With Board approval, seek temporary restraining orders and injunctive relief pursuant to Section 10(j) of the Act (para. IB);

- Initiate and conduct appeals to the Supreme Court (para. IB);

- Facilitate receipt and processing of election petitions in representation cases, and conduct national emergency elections pursuant to Section 209(b) of the Act (para. IC);

- Attempt to resolve jurisdictional disputes through hearings conducted pursuant to Section 10(k) of the Act (para. ID);

- Serve as agency liaison with other governmental agencies including the Federal Mediation and Conciliation Service (para. IV);

- Perform administrative functions of the agency including the provision of administrative and housekeeping services (paras. VII(1) and (3));

---

[15]*Vaca v. Sipes*, 386 U.S. 171, 64 LRRM 2369 (1967); *see* THE DEVELOPING LABOR LAW at 1601–1602.

[16]*Electrical Workers, Local 1186 (Pac. Elec. Contractors Ass'n)*, 264 NLRB 712, 111 LRRM 1667 (1982); *Penntech Papers, Inc.*, 263 NLRB 264, 111 LRRM 1622 (1982).

[17]See Appendix C.

• In coordination with the Board, submit annual budget requests, apportion and allocate funds, and establish personnel ceilings (para. VII(4)).

The decision of Congress to separate the functions of the Board and the General Counsel sometimes leads to a conclusion that there are, in reality, two wholly independent agencies. An organization chart gives this impression (see Exhibit 5), but the Board's participation in personnel actions involving regional directors and officers-in-charge, its delegation of functions to the General Counsel which, upon occasion, has been withdrawn, and its participation in budget and other administrative matters show that the NLRB is truly a single agency. Its unique feature is its two heads.

§2.5   Structure of the Office of the General Counsel

The statute provides a four-year term for the General Counsel who is appointed by the President with Senate approval. The General Counsel maintains headquarters and staff, except for the personnel in the regional offices, in Washington, D.C. The Deputy General Counsel substitutes for the General Counsel and is accountable for the overall coordination of the General Counsel's organization. The General Counsel's Washington staff consists of four main divisions: Division of Operations-Management, Division of Advice, Division of Enforcement Litigation, and Division of Administration. Each of the first three is supervised by an Associate General Counsel, while the fourth is headed by a Director of Administration.

(a) Division of Operations-Management. The Associate General Counsel for the Division of Operations-Management supervises all field operations and is charged with the management of cases in all of the Washington divisions of the General Counsel. This Division also is responsible for developing systems to achieve effective integration of Washington and field case-processing activities.

(b) Division of Advice. The Associate General Counsel for the Division of Advice oversees the functions of legal advice to regional offices, the injunction work of the district court branch, and the legal research and special projects office. All questions involving mandatory or discretionary injunction proceedings are coordinated with the Assistant General Counsel for Injunction Litigation, who serves as an expert advisor and counsel in the area of injunction cases which have statutory priority and are subject to mandatory proceedings in the federal district courts.

(c) Division of Enforcement Litigation. The Associate General Counsel for Enforcement Litigation is responsible for conduct of litigation seeking the enforcement or defense of Board orders in the

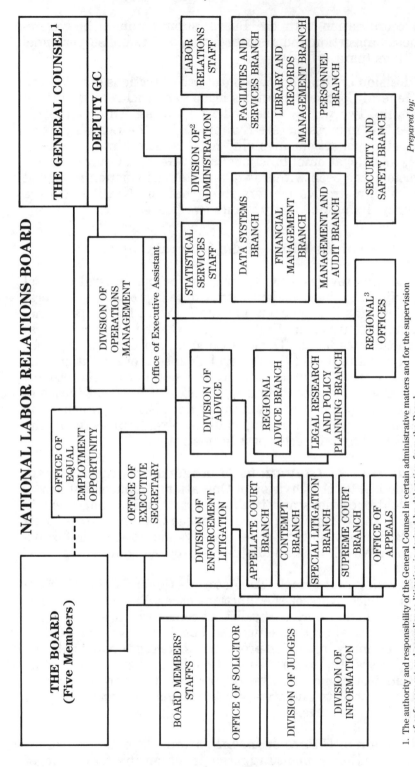

NATIONAL LABOR RELATIONS BOARD

THE BOARD (Five Members)

THE GENERAL COUNSEL[1]

DEPUTY GC

OFFICE OF EQUAL EMPLOYMENT OPPORTUNITY

OFFICE OF EXECUTIVE SECRETARY

DIVISION OF OPERATIONS MANAGEMENT
Office of Executive Assistant

DIVISION OF[2] ADMINISTRATION

LABOR RELATIONS STAFF

FACILITIES AND SERVICES BRANCH

LIBRARY AND RECORDS MANAGEMENT BRANCH

PERSONNEL BRANCH

SECURITY AND SAFETY BRANCH

STATISTICAL SERVICES STAFF

DATA SYSTEMS BRANCH

FINANCIAL MANAGEMENT BRANCH

MANAGEMENT AND AUDIT BRANCH

REGIONAL[3] OFFICES

DIVISION OF ADVICE

REGIONAL ADVICE BRANCH

LEGAL RESEARCH AND POLICY PLANNING BRANCH

DIVISION OF ENFORCEMENT LITIGATION

APPELLATE COURT BRANCH

CONTEMPT BRANCH

SPECIAL LITIGATION BRANCH

SUPREME COURT BRANCH

OFFICE OF APPEALS

BOARD MEMBERS' STAFFS

OFFICE OF SOLICITOR

DIVISION OF JUDGES

DIVISION OF INFORMATION

Prepared by:
National Labor Relations Board

1. The authority and responsibility of the General Counsel in certain administrative matters and for the supervision of enforcement and compliance litigation is derived by delegation from the Board.

2. Division of Administration is also responsible to the Board for administrative support services required in the performance of Board functions.

3. Includes exercise by Regional Director of Board authority under Section 9 of the Act, in representation cases, by delegation from the Board.

Exhibit 5.   National Labor Relations Board Organization Chart

United States courts of appeals and the United States Supreme Court, conduct of contempt litigation, and conduct of miscellaneous litigation in the federal and state courts to protect the Board's processes and functions.[18]

The Division of Enforcement Litigation also has an Office of Appeals which reviews appeals from regional directors' refusals to issue complaints in unfair labor practice cases. The Director of the Office of Appeals may grant requests of representatives of the parties to make informal presentations regarding the merits of the appeals.

(d) Division of Administration.   The Director of Administration is responsible for administrative management and the fiscal and personnel work of the General Counsel. These functions also are performed on behalf of the Board.

(e) Regional Directors.   The United States is divided into 33 regions for purposes of administering the statute. Each region has an office which handles all cases arising in that area.[19] The staff in each office consists of a regional director, regional attorney, field examiners, and field attorneys. The regional director is the chief officer in the region. There are, at the present time, three subregional offices and 16 resident offices. Each is under the direction of a supervisor who reports to the regional director in that region.

---

[18]See Appendix C, note 1, regarding the supervisory role exercised by the Board over the General Counsel's conduct of court litigation.

[19]The locations of these offices and the areas they cover are set forth in Appendix E.

3

Jurisdiction of the Board

Statutory Jurisdiction

The Board's jurisdiction over both representation proceedings and unfair labor practices extends to all enterprises with operations which "affect" interstate or foreign commerce.[1] The courts have construed this to mean that the Board's jurisdiction encompasses "the fullest jurisdictional breadth constitutionally permissible under the commerce clause,"[2] and is precluded only in situations where an employer's activities have a *"de minimis"* effect on interstate commerce.[3]

Before accepting either an election petition or an unfair labor practice charge, it is incumbent upon the Board to establish that it has statutory jurisdiction to proceed.[4] Thus, the Board must determine (1) whether a "labor dispute"[5] exists, (2) whether "employers," "employees," and "labor organizations" are involved,[6] and (3) whether the employer's operations "affect interstate or foreign commerce." Once established, the Board's jurisdiction is exclusive and is not subject to other means of dispute adjustment which may be established

---

[1]Secs. 9(c), 10(a); *see also* definitions of "commerce" and "affecting commerce" set forth in Secs. 2(6), 2(7), respectively.

[2]*NLRB v. Reliance Fuel Oil Corp.*, 371 U.S. 224, 52 LRRM 2046 (1963); *NLRB v. Mars Sales & Equip. Co.*, 626 F.2d 567, 105 LRRM 2138 (7th Cir. 1980).

[3]*NLRB v. Fainblatt*, 306 U.S. 601, 4 LRRM 535 (1939); *Children's Communities, Inc.*, 210 NLRB 6, 86 LRRM 1092 (1974).

[4]*NLRB v. First Termite Control Co.*, 646 F.2d 424, 108 LRRM 2336 (9th Cir. 1981). A challenge to the Board's statutory jurisdiction may be raised at any time. *International Total Serv., Inc.*, 270 NLRB 645, 116 LRRM 1147 (1984) (first raised after issuance of administrative law judge's decision finding existence of unfair labor practice violations).

[5]Sec. 2(9).

[6]The definitions of "employers," "employees," and "labor organizations" appear in Secs. 2(2), (3), and (5) of the Act. The terms also are discussed at §§1.2, 1.4 *supra*.

by law, by private agreement, or otherwise.[7] Neither the courts nor state agencies have concurrent jurisdiction to identify and remedy unfair labor practices.[8]

Discretionary Jurisdiction

Despite its extensive statutory grant of jurisdiction, the Board has never exercised its full authority. Instead, it has considered only those cases which, in its opinion, have a substantial effect on commerce.[9] In approving this practice, the U.S. Supreme Court has noted that Congress left it to the Board to ascertain whether proscribed practices would in particular situations adversely affect commerce,[10] and it has recognized that, even when the effect on interstate commerce is adequate, the Board sometimes properly declines to assert jurisdiction when, in the Board's judgment, the policies of the Act would not be served.[11]

The Board has, over the years, developed a series of jurisdictional standards, expressed in terms of minimum annual dollar volume, to aid in determining whether it will effectuate the policies of the Act to assert jurisdiction. This practice was given statutory recognition by the Labor-Management Reporting and Disclosure Act of 1959. Congress there stated that the Board might continue to decline jurisdiction over any labor dispute within its statutory jurisdiction, provided that it does not decline to assert jurisdiction over any labor dispute over which it would have asserted jurisdiction under the standards prevailing on August 1, 1959.[12] The Board's jurisdictional standards may be established either through a Board decision or through a formal rule-making proceeding pursuant to the Administrative Procedure Act.[13]

The Board thus may expand but not contract its jurisdiction. In the 1959 amendments [14] Congress also resolved the troublesome problem of conflicting federal and state jurisdiction by providing that the

---

[7]*Operating Eng'r, Local 926 v. Jones*, 460 U.S. 669, 112 LRRM 3272 (1983); *United Automobile Workers, Local 1519 v. NLRB*, 619 F.2d 580, 104 LRRM 2050 (6th Cir. 1980).

[8]The preemptive effect of NLRB jurisdiction is discussed in THE DEVELOPING LABOR LAW at 1504–1598; *see also Operating Eng'r, Local 926 v. Jones*, 460 U.S. 669, 112 LRRM 3272 (1983) (state court action by supervisor against union alleging interference with employment contract held preempted by National Labor Relations Act).

[9]*NLRB v. Denver Bldg. Trades Council*, 341 U.S. 675, 28 LRRM 2108 (1951).

[10]*Polish Nat'l Alliance v. NLRB*, 322 U.S. 643, 14 LRRM 700 (1944).

[11]*Guss v. Utah Labor Relations Board*, 352 U.S. 817, 39 LRRM 2567 (1957).

[12]Sec. 14(c)(1).

[13]*Id. K and E Bus Lines, Inc.*, 255 NLRB 1022, 107 LRRM 1239 (1981). The Board exercises plenary jurisdiction in the District of Columbia which means that it may assert jurisdiction over enterprises otherwise in commerce without regard to the monetary standards. *Board of Jewish Educ. of Greater Washington*, 210 NLRB 1037, 86 LRRM 1253 (1974); *Trustees of the Corcoran Gallery of Art*, 186 NLRB 565, 75 LRRM 1380 (1970).

[14]Sec. 14(c)(2).

states may assert jurisdiction over labor disputes which the Board declines to accept.[15]

§3.1   General Jurisdictional Standards

The Board's current jurisdictional standards are:

- *Nonretail Enterprises.* Sales of goods to consumers in other states, directly or indirectly (outflow), or purchases of goods from suppliers in other states, directly or indirectly (inflow), of at least $50,000 per year.[16]

   Direct Outflow is defined as goods shipped or services furnished by the employer outside the state.

   Indirect Outflow is defined as the sale of goods or services within the state to users meeting any of the Board's jurisdictional standards, with the exception of the indirect outflow or indirect inflow standard.[17]

   Direct Inflow is defined as goods or services furnished the employer directly from outside the state.

   Indirect Inflow is defined as goods or services which originated outside the state, but which the employer purchased from a seller or supplier within the state.

   In applying this standard, the Board will add direct and indirect outflow, or direct and indirect inflow; it will not add outflow and inflow.

- *Retail Enterprises.* An annual volume of business of at least $500,000, including sales and excise taxes.[18]

- *Retail and Manufacturing Enterprises Combined.* Either the retail or the nonretail standard, when a single, integrated enterprise manufactures a product as well as sells it directly to the public.[19]

- *Retail and Wholesale Enterprises Combined.* The nonretail standard, when a company is involved in both retail and wholesale operations.[20]

- *Instrumentalities, Links, and Channels of Interstate Commerce.* An annual income of at least $50,000 from furnishing inter-

---

[15]See *infra* text accompanying notes 81–83; *see also* THE DEVELOPING LABOR LAW at 1431.

[16]*American Home Sys.*, 200 NLRB 1151, 82 LRRM 1183 (1972); *Siemons Mailing Serv.*, 122 NLRB 81, 43 LRRM 1056 (1958).

[17]*N&G Coal Co., Inc.*, 274 NLRB No. 45, 118 LRRM 1030 (1985).

[18]*Acme Paper Box Co.*, 201 NLRB 240, 82 LRRM 1333 (1973); *Carolina Supplies and Cement Co.*, 122 NLRB 723, 43 LRRM 1060 (1958). The volume of business is determined by gross sales rather than some other yardstick such as sales commission. *Pit Stop Market*, 279 NLRB No. 161, 122 LRRM 1130 (1986).

[19]*American Home Sys.*, 200 NLRB 1151, 82 LRRM 1183 (1972); *Man Prods. Inc.*, 128 NLRB 546, 46 LRRM 1353 (1960).

[20]*Dominick's Finer Foods Inc.*, 188 NLRB 873, 76 LRRM 1607 (1971); *Pease Oil Co.*, 122 NLRB 344, 43 LRRM 1128 (1958).

state passenger and freight transportation services or performing services valued at $50,000 or more for enterprises that meet any of the standards except indirect outflow or indirect inflow established for nonretail enterprises.[21]

- *National Defense.* The enterprise has a substantial impact on national defense whether or not it satisfies any other jurisdictional standard.[22]

- *Territories and the District of Columbia.* The normal standards as applied in the states are applicable to the territories. Plenary jurisdiction is exercised in the District of Columbia.[23]

- *Multiemployer Bargaining Associations.* Regarded as a single employer in that the annual business of all members is totaled to determine whether any of the standards apply.[24]

- *Multistate Establishments.* The annual business of all establishments is totaled to determine whether any of the standards apply.[25]

- *Nonprofit Organizations.* The same standards as if the organization were operated for profit.[26]

- *Union Employers.* The appropriate nonretail standard.[27]

§3.2 Jurisdictional Standards for Specific Industries

The Board's current jurisdictional standards for specific industries are:

- *Accounting Firms.* The Board has asserted jurisdiction over certified public accounting firms without specifying a precise jurisdictional standard. In the leading case, the firm received gross annual revenues in excess of $10 million.[28]

---

[21]*Panorama Air Tour Inc.*, 204 NLRB 45, 83 LRRM 1276 (1973); *HPO Serv., Inc.*, 122 NLRB 394, 43 LRRM 1127 (1958).

[22]*Trico Disposal Serv., Inc.*, 191 NLRB 104, 77 LRRM 1330 (1971); *Ready Mix Concrete and Materials Inc.*, 122 NLRB 318, 43 LRRM 1115 (1958).

[23]*Van Camp Sea Food Co.*, 212 NLRB 537, 86 LRRM 1573 (1974); *Contract Serv., Inc.*, 202 NLRB 862, 82 LRRM 1757 (1973); *Carribe Lumber and Trading Co.*, 148 NLRB 277, 56 LRRM 1506 (1964); *Westchester Corp.*, 124 NLRB 914, 44 LRRM 1327 (1959).

[24]*Hotel and Restaurant Employees (Assoc. Union St. Restaurants) v. NLRB*, 501 F.2d 794, 86 LRRM 2828 (D.C. Cir. 1974); *Seine & Line Fishermen's Union of San Pedro (Fishermen's Coop. Ass'n)*, 136 NLRB 1, 49 LRRM 1707 (1962); *see also* cases cited in THE DEVELOPING LABOR LAW at 1497 n. 387.

[25]*Quality Courts Motels, Inc.*, 194 NLRB 1035, 79 LRRM 1303 (1972); *Rodgers Lumber Co.*, 117 NLRB 1732, 40 LRRM 1063 (1957).

[26]*Harborcreek School for Boys*, 249 NLRB 1226, 104 LRRM 1271 (1980); *Rhode Island Catholic Orphan Asylum*, 224 NLRB 1344, 92 LRRM 1355 (1976). *But cf. NLRB v. Catholic Bishop of Chicago*, 440 U.S. 490, 100 LRRM 2913 (1979) (Board does not have jurisdiction over church-operated schools).

[27]*Civil Serv. Employees Ass'n*, 181 NLRB 766, 73 LRRM 1475 (1970); *Chain Serv. Restaurant*, 132 NLRB 960, 48 LRRM 1457 (1961).

[28]*Ernst & Ernst Nat'l Warehouse*, 228 NLRB 590, 94 LRRM 1637 (1977).

- *Arbitration Associations.* The Board has asserted jurisdiction over the American Arbitration Association, but has failed to establish a jurisdictional standard.[29]
- *Architects.* The Board has applied its nonretail business standards to architectural firms.[30]
- *Art Museums.* Gross annual revenues in excess of $1 million.[31]
- *Automobile Dealers.* Treated as retail operations, even if the dealer has a franchise from a national manufacturer.[32]
- *Building and Construction.* The appropriate jurisdictional standard in cases involving a single building trades employer, or the multiemployer standard if the employer is part of a multiemployer bargaining association.[33]
- *Colleges, Universities, and Secondary Schools.* At least $1 million total annual income from all sources except those designated by the grantor as not available for operating costs. This applies to both profit and nonprofit institutions.[34]
- *Country Clubs.* Treated as retail concerns.[35]
- *Day Care Centers.* Gross annual revenues of at least $250,000.[36]
- *Entertainment and Amusement.* Treated as retail concerns. The Board will not assert jurisdiction over horse and dog racing tracks.[37]
- *Federal Credit Unions.* At least $500,000 annual gross income from loans, deposits, investments, etc.[38]
- *Gambling Casinos.* At least $500,000 gross annual revenue.[39]
- *Guard Services.* Companies furnishing plant guards to employers involved in interstate commerce are themselves subject to Board jurisdiction if the value of the services meets one of the Board's basic jurisdictional standards. The Board also

---

[29]*American Arbitration Ass'n, Inc.*, 225 NLRB 291, 92 LRRM 1483 (1976); *see also* the discussion of this case in THE DEVELOPING LABOR LAW at 1500 n. 407.

[30]*Wurster, Bernardi & Emmons, Inc.*, 192 NLRB 1049, 78 LRRM 1050 (1971).

[31]*Helen Clay Frick Found.*, 217 NLRB 1100, 89 LRRM 1195 (1975); *Trustees of the Corcoran Gallery of Art*, 186 NLRB 565, 75 LRRM 1380 (1970); *see also Colonial Williamsburg Found.*, 224 NLRB 718, 92 LRRM 1509 (1976).

[32]*Wilson Oldsmobile*, 110 NLRB 534, 35 LRRM 1062 (1954).

[33]*NLRB v. Denver Bldg. Trades Council*, 341 U.S. 675, 28 LRRM 2108 (1951); *Charles E. Forrester*, 189 NLRB 519, 76 LRRM 1622 (1971).

[34]NLRB Rules and Regulations §103.1. *Windsor School Inc.*, 199 NLRB 457, 81 LRRM 1246 (1972); *Cornell Univ.*, 183 NLRB 329, 74 LRRM 1269 (1970).

[35]*Yorba Linda Country Club*, 199 NLRB 730, 81 LRRM 1302 (1972); *Walnut Hills Country Club*, 145 NLRB 81, 54 LRRM 1335 (1963).

[36]*Rhode Island Catholic Orphan Asylum*, 224 NLRB 1344, 92 LRRM 1355 (1976); *Salt & Pepper Nursery School*, 222 NLRB 1295, 91 LRRM 1338 (1976).

[37]*Universal Sec. Consultants*, 203 NLRB 1195, 83 LRRM 1262 (1973); *League of N.Y. Theatres Inc.*, 129 NLRB 1429, 47 LRRM 1210 (1961); NLRB Rules and Regulations §103.3.

[38]*Auto Truck Fed. Credit Union*, 232 NLRB 1024, 97 LRRM 1088 (1977); *Lansing Fed. Credit Union*, 150 NLRB 1122, 58 LRRM 1195 (1965).

[39]*El Dorado, Inc.*, 151 NLRB 579, 58 LRRM 1455 (1965).

has asserted jurisdiction over a company providing escort guard services where the nonretail standard was met.[40]

- *Health Care Institutions.* The Board's jurisdiction extends to "any hospital, convalescent hospital, health maintenance organization, health clinic, nursing home, extended care facility, or other institution devoted to the care of sick, infirm, or aged person."[41] Federal, state, and municipal hospitals are exempt, as are administrative employers in the health field.[42] The Board will assert jurisdiction over nursing homes, visiting nurse associations, and related facilities with gross revenues over $100,000 per year and over proprietary and nonprofit hospitals and other types of health care institutions with gross revenues over $250,000 per year.[43]

- *Hotels, Motels, Apartments, and Condominiums.* At least $500,000 total annual volume of business, whether an establishment is residential or nonresidential.[44]

- *Law Firms and Legal Aid Programs.* Gross annual revenues of at least $250,000.[45]

- *Office Buildings, Shopping Centers, and Parking Lots.* At least $100,000 total annual income, of which $25,000 or more is paid by other organizations which meet any of the standards, except the indirect outflow and indirect inflow nonretail standards.[46]

- *Postal Service.* Full jurisdiction as provided in the Postal Reorganization Act of 1970.[47]

- *Printing, Publishing, and Newspapers.* At least $200,000 total annual volume of business, and the employer must hold membership in or subscribe to interstate news services, publish nationally syndicated features, or advertise nationally sold products.[48]

- *Public Utilities.* At least $250,000 total annual volume of business or $50,000 outflow or inflow, direct or indirect. This stan-

---

[40]*Andover Protective Serv.*, 225 NLRB 485, 92 LRRM 1512 (1976) (escort guards); *Burns Detective Agency*, 110 NLRB 995, 35 LRRM 1179 (1954) (plant guards).

[41]Sec. 2(14).

[42]Sec. 2(2).

[43]*East Oakland Community Health Alliance, Inc.*, 218 NLRB 1270, 89 LRRM 1372 (1975).

[44]*A. J. Clarke Mgt. Corp.*, 249 NLRB 1143, 104 LRRM 1271 (1980) (apartments); *30 Sutton Place Corp.*, 240 NLRB 752, 100 LRRM 1335 (1979) (condominiums) reaffirmed in *Imperial House Condo., Inc.*, 279 NLRB No. 154 (1986); *Penn-Keystone Realty Corp.*, 191 NLRB 800, 77 LRRM 1600 (1971) (hotels and motels).

[45]*Kleinberg, Kaplan, Wolff, Cohen & Burrows, P.C.*, 253 NLRB 450, 105 LRRM 1611 (1980); *Camden Regional Legal Serv., Inc.*, 231 NLRB 224, 95 LRRM 1545 (1977); *Foley, Hoag & Eliot*, 229 NLRB 456, 95 LRRM 1041 (1977).

[46]*BHL Assoc.*, 272 NLRB No. 163, 117 LRRM 1448 (1984); *Air Lines Parking, Inc.*, 196 NLRB 1018, 80 LRRM 1179 (1972); *Carol Mgt. Corp.*, 133 NLRB 1126, 48 LRRM 1782 (1961); *Mistletoe Operating Co.*, 122 NLRB 1534, 43 LRRM 1333 (1958).

[47]*United States Postal Serv.*, 208 NLRB 948, 85 LRRM 1212 (1974).

[48]*Nutley Sun Printing Co.*, 128 NLRB 58, 46 LRRM 1260 (1960); *Belleville Employing Printers*, 122 NLRB 92, 43 LRRM 1125 (1958).

dard applies to retail gas, power, and water companies, as well as to electric cooperatives. Wholesale utilities are subject to the general nonretail standards.[49]

- *Radio, Television, Telegraph, and Telephone Companies.* At least $200,000 total annual volume of business.[50]
- *Restaurants.* Treated as retail operations.[51]
- *Service Establishments.* Treated as retail operations.[52]
- *Sports, Professional.* The Board has refused to apply any specific jurisdictional standard to professional sports, but has regarded the industry as one affecting interstate commerce and has asserted jurisdiction in several cases.[53]
- *Symphony Orchestras.* At least $1 million total annual income, compiled from all sources except those designated by the donor as not available for operating costs.[54]
- *Taxicab Companies.* At least $500,000 total annual volume of business.[55]
- *Transit Companies.* At least $250,000 total annual volume of business.[56]
- *Union Employers.* The Supreme Court has held that the Board may not refuse to assert jurisdiction over unions as a class when they act in the capacity of employers.[57] The Board generally asserts jurisdiction over local unions which are affiliated with national organizations and which remit to them dues or other fees across state lines.[58]

§3.3   Jurisdiction Over Labor Disputes Involving Foreign Countries

The Board will assert jurisdiction over most labor disputes which arise in the territorial United States or its possessions, but not over

---

[49]*Tri-County Elec. Membership Corp.*, 145 NLRB 810, 55 LRRM 1057 (1964); *Sioux Valley Empire Elec. Ass'n*, 122 NLRB 92, 43 LRRM 1061 (1958).

[50]*Mesnikoff*, 238 NLRB 1236, 99 LRRM 1435 (1978); *Raritan Valley Broadcasting Co.*, 122 NLRB 90, 43 LRRM 1062 (1958).

[51]*Furusato Hawaii, Ltd.*, 192 NLRB 105, 77 LRRM 1668 (1972); *Bickford's Inc.*, 110 NLRB 1904, 35 LRRM 1341 (1954).

[52]*OK Barber Shop*, 187 NLRB 190, 76 LRRM 1178 (1971); *Claffery Beauty Shoppes*, 110 NLRB 620, 35 LRRM 1079 (1954).

[53]*See Major League Rodeo, Inc.*, 246 NLRB 743, 103 LRRM 1015 (1979); *North Am. Soccer League*, 236 NLRB 1317, 98 LRRM 1445 (1978); *Volusia Jai Alai, Inc.*, 221 NLRB 1280, 91 LRRM 1065 (1975); *American Basketball Ass'n*, 215 NLRB 280, 88 LRRM 1096 (1974); *National Football League Mgmt. Council*, 203 NLRB 958, 83 LRRM 1203 (1973); *American League of Professional Baseball Clubs*, 180 NLRB 190, 72 LRRM 1545 (1969).

[54]NLRB Rules and Regulations §103.2.

[55]*Red and White Airway Cab Co.*, 123 NLRB 83, 43 LRRM 1392 (1959).

[56]*Air Cal.*, 170 NLRB 18, 67 LRRM 1385 (1968); *Charleston Transit Co.*, 123 NLRB 1296, 44 LRRM 1123 (1959).

[57]*Office Employees Int'l Union, Local 11 (Oregon Teamsters) v. NLRB*, 353 U.S. 313, 40 LRRM 2020 (1957).

[58]*Louisiana Council No. 17, AFSCME*, 250 NLRB 880, 104 LRRM 1485 (1980); *Chain Serv. Restaurant, Luncheonette & Soda Fountain Employees, Local 11*, 132 NLRB 960, 48 LRRM 1457 (1961).

those which arise in a location under the control of another country even if U.S. employees are involved. Jurisdiction has been asserted over labor disputes in American Samoa[59] and Puerto Rico,[60] but denied in a dispute arising in the Danish possession of Greenland even though the employees were hired in the United States, paid from the United States, and returned to the United States following completion of their assignment.[61]

Conversely, the issue of Board jurisdiction over the labor disputes of foreign corporations doing business in the United States depends upon the nature of the foreign business. The Supreme Court has held that the Board does not have jurisdiction over foreign flag vessels operating in the United States even though the vessels belong to a wholly owned American corporation.[62] The Court relied in part on "the well-established rule in international law that the law of the flag state ordinarily governs the internal affairs of a ship."[63] In similar fashion, international organizations such as the World Bank, the Inter-American Development Bank, and the International Monetary Fund enjoy "the privileges and immunities from the laws of the sovereignty" and are exempt from coverage under the Act.[64]

In contrast, the Board will assert jurisdiction when foreign governments or their agents actually act as employers doing business in the territorial United States.[65]

§3.4 Jurisdiction Over Political Subdivisions

The exclusion of "political subdivisions" of state governments from the statutory definition of "employer"[66] has proven to be particularly difficult for the Board to apply in practice.[67] The Board and the courts have held that an organization is an exempt political subdivision if it (1) was created directly by the state and operates as a department or administrative arm of the government, or (2) is administered by individuals who are responsible to public officials or

---

[59]*Van Camp Sea Food Co.*, 212 NLRB 537, 86 LRRM 1573 (1974).

[60]*NLRB v. Security Nat'l Life Ins. Co.*, 494 F.2d 336, 85 LRRM 2737 (lst Cir. 1974).

[61]*RCA Oms, Inc.*, 202 NLRB 228, 82 LRRM 1531 (1973); *cf. GTE Automatic Elec., Inc.*, 226 NLRB 1222, 93 LRRM 1449 (1976).

[62]*McCulloch v. Sociedad Nacional de Marineros de Honduras*, 372 U.S. 10, 52 LRRM 2425 (1963); *Benz v. Compania Naviera Hidalgo*, 353 U.S. 138, 39 LRRM 2636 (1957).

[63]*McCulloch v. Sociedad Nacional de Marineros de Honduras*, 372 U.S. 10, 52 LRRM 2425 (1963).

[64]*National Detective Agencies, Inc.*, 237 NLRB 451, 99 LRRM 1007 (1978) (International Development Bank and International Monetary Fund); *Herbert Harvey, Inc.*, 171 NLRB 238, 68 LRRM 1053 (1968) (World Bank).

[65]*German School of Washington*, 260 NLRB 1250, 109 LRRM 1305 (1982); *Great Lakes Dredge & Dock Co.*, 240 NLRB 197, 100 LRRM 1284 (1978); *S K Prods. Corp.*, 230 NLRB 1211, 95 LRRM 1498 (1977); *State Bank of India*, 229 NLRB 838, 95 LRRM 1141 (1977).

[66]Sec. 2(2).

[67]*See generally* THE DEVELOPING LABOR LAW at 1447–1449 and cases cited therein.

to the general electorate.[68] In addition, the Board for several years refused to assert jurisdiction in situations where there was an "intimate connection" between the purposes of the exempt institution and the services provided by the otherwise nonexempt employer.[69]

The intimate connection standard was abandoned in 1979 and the Board now determines whether the employer itself meets the statutory definition of employer and, if so, determines whether the employer retains sufficient control over the employment conditions of the employees to enable it to bargain with a labor organization as their representative.[70]

§3.5   Application of the Jurisdictional Standards

In applying the dollar volume standards, the Board has developed certain rules of application. Among the more significant of these are:

- There is no need for a separate showing of legal jurisdiction if the employer does enough interstate business to satisfy the indirect inflow or outflow tests. However, when the standards involved are exclusively in terms of gross dollar volume of business, proof of legal jurisdiction is necessary to ensure that not all of the employer's required volume of business has been done within the confines of a single state.[71]

- The Board will assert jurisdiction in any proceeding where the record establishes legal jurisdiction, whether or not the applicable dollar-volume standard is met, if the employer, after being afforded proper opportunity, fails to cooperate in the production of necessary commerce information.[72]

---

[68]*NLRB v. Natural Gas Util. Dist. of Hawkins County*, 402 U.S. 600, 77 LRRM 2348 (1971); *Founders Soc'y Detroit Inst. of Arts*, 271 NLRB 285, 116 LRRM 1376 (1984). With regard to the first standard, *compare Cowden-Clark Mem. Hosp.*, 221 NLRB 945, 91 LRRM 1024 (1975) and *New York Inst. for the Edu. of the Blind*, 254 NLRB 664, 106 LRRM 1113 (1980) (exemption granted) *with Grey Nuns of the Sacred Heart*, 221 NLRB 1225, 91 LRRM 1099 (1975) and *Morristown-Hamblen Hosp. Ass'n*, 226 NLRB 76, 93 LRRM 1166 (1976) (exemption denied). With regard to the second standard, *compare Northern Community Mental Health Center, Inc.*, 241 NLRB 323, 100 LRRM 1492 (1979) and *Community Health and Home Care, Inc.*, 251 NLRB 509, 105 LRRM 1092 (1980) (exemption granted) *with Truman Medical Center, Inc.*, 239 NLRB 1067, 100 LRRM 1102 (1978) (exemption denied). In *Rosenberg Library Ass'n*, 269 NLRB 1173, 116 LRRM 1054 (1984), the Board held that a library was exempt, in part because it was heavily dependent upon public funds for operating expenses and its librarian and board of directors held the same positions for the county library.

[69]*Rural Fire Protection Co.*, 216 NLRB 584, 88 LRRM 1305 (1975); *Herbert Harvey, Inc.*, 171 NLRB 238, 68 LRRM 1053 (1967).

[70]*National Transp. Serv., Inc.*, 240 NLRB 565, 100 LRRM 1263 (1979). In order to be engaged in meaningful bargaining, an employer must retain ultimate authority to establish the entire package of employee compensation. *Compare Res-Care, Inc.*, 280 NLRB No. 78, 122 LRRM 1265 (1986) (jurisdiction declined where government agency had ultimate authority) *with Long Stretch Youth Home, Inc.*, 280 NLRB No. 79, 122 LRRM 1272 (1986) (jurisdiction asserted where employer had ultimate authority).

[71]*Wurster, Bernardi & Emmons, Inc.*, 192 NLRB 1049, 78 LRRM 1050 (1971); *Southern Dolomite*, 129 NLRB 1342, 47 LRRM 1173 (1961).

[72]*Quality Courts Motels, Inc.*, 194 NLRB 1035, 79 LRRM 1303 (1972); *Tropicana Prods., Inc.*, 122 NLRB 121, 43 LRRM 1077 (1958).

- When asserting jurisdiction in secondary boycott cases, the Board views the primary employer as the one with whom the union has a direct dispute and the secondary employer as the one whose employees the union is trying to "induce" to stop handling the primary employer's goods. If necessary for the application of jurisdiction, the Board will consider the operations of the primary and the secondary employer together. When considering the secondary employer's operations, the Board will consider the entire business of the secondary employer with the primary employer at the location affected by the boycott. If the secondary employer meets the jurisdictional standards, the Board will assert authority, regardless of whether or not the primary employer satisfies the standards. Finally, if more than one secondary employer is involved, jurisdiction will be asserted as long as one or more of the secondary employers meets the standards.[73]

- In applying its jurisdictional standards the Board normally determines business volume on the basis of the employer's experience for the most recent calendar or fiscal year preceding the Board's hearing, rather than on the basis of future operations.[74] If annual figures are not available, those for a period of less than one year may be projected to obtain annual volume.[75]

- In order to protect its administrative processes, the Board will assert jurisdiction in a Section 8(a)(4) proceeding whenever there is statutory jurisdiction whether or not the applicable discretionary standard has been met.[76]

§3.6 Advisory Opinions and Declaratory Orders

Even with the published standards it is sometimes difficult to predict whether or not the Board will assert jurisdiction. In recognition of this fact, procedures have been established whereby parties to a dispute before a state court or agency, or the court or agency itself, may petition the Board for an advisory opinion on jurisdiction.[77] The advisory opinion procedures "are designed primarily to determine questions of jurisdiction by the application of the Board's dis-

---

[73]*Plumbers, Local 460 (L.J. Constr.)*, 236 NLRB 1435, 98 LRRM 1589 (1978); *Teamsters Local 866 (Ada Transit Mix)*, 130 NLRB 788, 47 LRRM 1409 (1961); *Commission House Drivers, Teamsters Local 400 (Euclid Foods, Inc.)*, 118 NLRB 130, 40 LRRM 1135 (1957).

[74]*Aroostock Fed. of Farmers, Inc.*, 114 NLRB 538, 36 LRRM 1611 (1955).

[75]*McLeod v. Drug and Hosp. Union, Local 119 (666 Cosmetics, Inc.)*, 80 LRRM 2503 (S.D.N.Y. 1972); *United Mine Workers Dist. 2*, 96 NLRB 1389, 29 LRRM 1043 (1951).

[76]*Midtown Serv. Center, Inc.*, 271 NLRB 1061, 117 LRRM 1103 (1984); *A.A. Electric Co.*, 177 NLRB 504, 71 LRRM 1595 (1969).

[77]NLRB Rules and Regulations §§102.98–102.104.

cretionary standards to the 'commerce' operations of an employer."[78] The Board will dismiss a petition for an advisory opinion when issues other than the application of its discretionary jurisdictional standards are raised.[79]

The General Counsel also may petition the Board and obtain a declaratory order disposing of jurisdictional issues where both an unfair labor practice charge and a representation petition relating to the same employer are pending in a regional office.[80] Unlike the advisory opinions, these orders are final.

Effect of Board Decision to Decline Jurisdiction

As noted earlier, the Board's jurisdiction is exclusive and state courts and agencies do not have concurrent jurisdiction to identify and remedy unfair labor practices. There are two ways, however, that states may be granted authority to process cases which fall within the Board's statutory jurisdiction.

Section 10(a) of the Act authorizes agreements between the Board and state or territorial agencies in which the Board may cede jurisdiction over unfair labor practice cases which arise in certain industries. Such agreements are permissible only in situations where, in the opinion of the Board, the state law is consistent with the Act.

Second, Section 14(c)(2) provides that state and territorial agencies may assume jurisdiction over any labor dispute over which the Board declines or would decline to assert jurisdiction.[81] Most petitions for advisory opinions which are filed with the Board result from the commencement of state proceedings in situations where it is unclear whether the Board would assert jurisdiction. If a Board decision to decline jurisdiction is not based upon an application of its statutory or discretionary standards, but rather upon a determination that it would be contrary to national labor policy to assert jurisdiction, then the states also are precluded from acting.[82] In most cases where state jurisdiction has been asserted under Section 14(c)(2), the states have applied their own substantive laws rather than federal law.[83]

---

[78]*Child, Inc.*, 266 NLRB 578, 112 LRRM 1402 (1983); *Globe Sec. Sys., Inc.*, 209 NLRB 35, 85 LRRM 1327 (1974).

[79]*Western Pa. School for the Deaf*, 262 NLRB 240, 110 LRRM 1301 (1982); *see also* THE DEVELOPING LABOR LAW at 1502 n. 420 and cases cited therein. In addition, petitions for advisory opinions will be dismissed if there are pending unfair labor practice proceedings in which the jurisdictional issue can be addressed, and there are no other reasons why an immediate determination of the jurisdictional issue should be made. *Chieppo Bus Co.*, 278 NLRB No. 71, 121 LRRM 1210 (1986).

[80]NLRB Rules and Regulations §§102.105–102.110.

[81]*Radio and Television Broadcast Techns. Local 1264 v. Broadcast Serv. of Mobile, Inc.*, 380 U.S. 255, 58 LRRM 2545 (1965).

[82]*Beasley v. Food Fair of N.C., Inc.*, 416 U.S. 653, 86 LRRM 2196 (1974); *NLRB v. Committee of Interns and Residents*, 566 F.2d 810, 96 LRRM 2342 (2d Cir. 1977).

[83]*See* THE DEVELOPING LABOR LAW at 1431 n. 46 and cases cited therein.

II

Representation Proceedings

4

Designation of a Bargaining Agent Without an Election

The statute provides that a labor organization designated or selected by a majority of employees in an appropriate bargaining unit shall be the exclusive bargaining agent for those employees.[1] The "preferred" and most widely used method of determining a union's status as bargaining representative is the Board's secret ballot election procedures set forth in Section 9 of the Act. These procedures are described in chapters 5 through 12. There are two additional methods by which bargaining status may be established which are described in this chapter. The first is voluntary recognition by an employer in response to a union's claim of majority support in an appropriate unit. The second is Board-ordered recognition without an election in situations where pervasive unlawful conduct by the employer has made a meaningful election impossible.

Voluntary Recognition

Before resorting to the Board's formal election procedures, labor organizations often seek voluntary recognition from the employer. The request for recognition need not be in any particular form and can range from a simple verbal request to a formal written demand. In responding to requests for recognition employers must be satisfied that the requesting union does in fact represent a majority of the

---

[1]Sec. 9(a).

employees in the unit. Extending voluntary recognition to a minority union constitutes a violation of Section 8(a)(2) of the Act.[2]

Labor organizations most often seek to demonstrate their support by proffering union authorization cards signed by a majority of the employees in the unit. Such cards may evidence actual union membership or application for membership on the part of the employee,[3] dues checkoff authorization,[4] or may simply indicate that the employee desires to designate the union as exclusive bargaining representative.[5] The Board has established an elaborate set of principles concerning both the form of the authorization cards and the manner in which they may be solicited. Many of these principles are discussed in chapter 5 in connection with the "showing of interest" that is required to be submitted in support of election petitions.[6]

An employer faced with a demand for recognition purportedly supported by a majority of the unit employees need not extend recognition to and bargain with the requesting union. The employer may simply decline the request for recognition and insist that the union petition for a Board election to determine the true sentiments of the employees.[7] There are two exceptions to this rule. First, if the employer independently has verified the majority support of the union through procedures such as employee polls,[8] surveys,[9] or third-party examination of authorization cards,[10] recognition and bargaining may be required. Second, in situations where the employer denies recognition and then commits serious unfair labor practices which make it unlikely that a fair election can be held, the Board may in certain circumstances direct that the employer bargain with the union.[11] These cases are discussed further in the next section.

Occasionally two or more unions may compete for the right to represent currently unrepresented employees. For approximately 35 years the Board required employers to maintain strict neutrality and held that voluntary recognition of one of the competing unions con-

---

[2]*Garment Workers (Bernhard-Altmann Textile Corp.) v. NLRB*, 366 U.S. 731, 48 LRRM 2251 (1961). In determining whether recognition lawfully has been extended, the Board applies a twofold test. At the time of recognition (1) the employer must employ a substantial and representative complement of its projected workforce (i.e., the jobs or job classifications designated for the operation must be substantially filled), and (2) the employer must be engaged in its normal business operations. *Hilton Inn Albany*, 270 NLRB 1364, 116 LRRM 1366 (1984).

[3]*Raley's Inc.*, 227 NLRB 670, 94 LRRM 1443 (1976).

[4]*Lebanon Steel Foundry v. NLRB*, 130 F.2d 404, 10 LRRM 760 (D.C. Cir. 1942).

[5]*NLRB v. Stow Mfg. Co.*, 217 F.2d 900, 35 LRRM 2210 (2d Cir. 1954).

[6]*See generally* THE DEVELOPING LABOR LAW at 503–505 and NLRB REPRESENTATION ELECTIONS—LAW, PRACTICE AND PROCEDURE (J. Feerick, H. Baer, and J. Arfa 1979/80) at 71–83 (hereafter NLRB REPRESENTATION ELECTIONS).

[7]*Linden Lumber Div., Sumner & Co. v. NLRB*, 419 U.S. 301, 87 LRRM 3236 (1974).

[8]*Struksnes Constr. Co.*, 165 NLRB 1062, 65 LRRM 1385 (1967).

[9]*Sullivan Elec. Co.*, 199 NLRB 809, 81 LRRM 1313 (1972).

[10]*Amay's Bakery and Noodle Co.*, 227 NLRB 214, 94 LRRM 1165 (1976).

[11]*NLRB v. Gissel Packing Co.*, 395 U.S. 575, 71 LRRM 2481 (1969); *Drug Package Co.*, 228 NLRB 108, 94 LRRM 1570 (1977), *enforced as modified*, 570 F.2d 1340, 97 LRRM 2851 (8th Cir. 1978).

stituted unlawful assistance under Section 8(a)(2).[12] Neutrality was required even in situations where the union seeking voluntary recognition had valid authorization cards from an overwhelming majority of the employees and the rival union or unions had minimal support.[13] In 1982 the Board abandoned the *Midwest Piping* doctrine and concluded that in initial organizing cases an employer voluntarily could recognize a union which produced evidence of majority support up to the point that a rival union filed a valid petition for a Board election. Once a valid petition was filed the neutrality obligations attached pending the results of the election.[14]

Although Section 9(b)(3) precludes the Board from certifying as bargaining representative in a unit of guards a union which directly or indirectly admits nonguards to membership, there is nothing unlawful about an employer voluntarily extending recognition to such a union. In such cases, however, the employer is free to withdraw that recognition at any time, even at a time when the union retains the overwhelming support of the unit employees.[15]

Board-Imposed Bargaining Orders

In addition to voluntary recognition, a union may acquire bargaining privileges by virtue of a bargaining order issued by the Board as a remedy for serious unfair labor practices committed by the employer. Bargaining orders are viewed as extraordinary remedies to be imposed only in situations where fair elections cannot be held.

§4.1 When Warranted

Recent Board decisions pertaining to the issuance of remedial bargaining orders rely upon the principles established by the Su-

---

[12]*Midwest Piping and Supply Co.*, 63 NLRB 1060, 17 LRRM 40 (1945).

[13]*See, e.g., American Bread Co.*, 170 NLRB 85, 67 LRRM 1430, *enforcement denied*, 411 F.2d 147, 71 LRRM 2243 (6th Cir. 1969).

[14]*Bruckner Nursing Home*, 262 NLRB 955, 110 LRRM 1374 (1982). The prohibition against voluntarily recognizing one union in the face of a valid petition filed by another union applies even in cases where the employees clearly support the union seeking recognition, and the petition has become stale because its processing has been "blocked" by a prolonged unfair labor practice proceeding. As stated in *Haddon House Food Prods., Inc.*, 269 NLRB 338, 115 LRRM 1209 (1984):

"[S]o long as a valid representation petition seeking to represent an employer's employees remains outstanding and has not been withdrawn or dismissed, the prolonged litigation of concurrent unfair labor practice proceedings involving the same employer cannot serve to invalidate the strict requirement of employer neutrality set forth in Bruckner Nursing Home." 269 NLRB at 341, 115 LRRM at 1211.

For an analysis of the employer's right to continue bargaining with an incumbent union in the face of a valid election petition filed by a challenging union, *see RCA Del Caribe, Inc.*, 262 NLRB 963, 110 LRRM 1369 (1982).

[15]*Wells Fargo Armored Serv. Corp.*, 270 NLRB 787, 116 LRRM 1129 (1984), *enf'd*, 755 F.2d 5 (2d Cir. 1985).

preme Court in its 1969 *Gissel* decision.[16] The Supreme Court there
determined that bargaining orders are appropriate remedies for employer refusals to bargain in situations where the "employer has
committed unfair labor practices which have made the holding of a
fair election unlikely or which have in fact undermined the union's
majority and caused an election to be set aside."[17] The Court enumerated three categories of cases in which it would consider authorizing
remedial bargaining orders:[18]

- Where the employer has committed "outrageous" and "pervasive" unfair labor practices which have made the holding of
  a free and fair election impossible;
- Where the employer has committed less pervasive unfair labor
  practices which "nonetheless still have the tendency to undermine majority strength and impede the election processes;"
  and
- Where the employer's unlawful practices are so minor that,
  "because of their minimal impact on the election machinery,
  [they] will not sustain a bargaining order."[19]

For cases falling in the first category the Court observed that a
bargaining order would be appropriate "without need of inquiry into
majority status on the basis of cards or otherwise."[20] The Board has
been reluctant to issue bargaining orders in situations where the
union has not at some point demonstrated majority strength.[21] It was
not until 12 years after *Gissel* was decided that the Board first cau-
tiously issued a bargaining order in a case where the union argued
that the employer's unfair labor practices prevented it from acquiring
majority support which it otherwise would have received.[22] Within
a matter of a few years a reconstituted Board determined that it
lacked authority under Section 10(c) to order an employer to bargain
with a union as a remedy for unfair labor practices if the union never
enjoyed majority support among the unit employees.[23] According to
the Board:

---

[16]*NLRB v. Gissel Packing Co.*, 395 U.S. 575, 71 LRRM 2481 (1969). The issue of remedial
bargaining orders is discussed extensively in THE DEVELOPING LABOR LAW at chapter 12, and
NLRB REPRESENTATION ELECTIONS at chapter 14.

[17]*NLRB v. Gissel Packing Co.*, 395 U.S. 575, 610, 71 LRRM 2481, 2494 (1969).

[18]*Id.* 395 U.S. at 613–614, 71 LRRM at 2495–2496.

[19]*Id.*

[20]*Id.* 395 U.S. at 613, 71 LRRM at 2495.

[21]The Board has not always insisted that majority support be demonstrated through authorization cards signed by a majority of the unit employees. In *Pinter Bros.*, 227 NLRB 921,
94 LRRM 1284 (1977), the Board combined 14 votes cast for the union in an election which
the union lost 14–18 with authorization cards signed by six nonvoting employees to conclude
that the union actually represented 20 of 39 unit employees on the date of the election.

[22]*United Dairy Farmers Coop. Ass'n*, 242 NLRB 1026, 101 LRRM 1278 (1979), *aff'd and
remanded*, 633 F.2d 1054, 105 LRRM 3034 (3d Cir. 1980), *on remand*, 257 NLRB 772, 107
LRRM 1577 (1981); *see also Conair Corp.*, 261 NLRB 1189, 110 LRRM 1161 (1982), *enforcement
denied*, 721 F.2d 1355, 114 LRRM 3169 (D.C. Cir. 1983).

[23]*Gourmet Foods Inc.*, 270 NLRB 578, 116 LRRM 1105 (1984).

"Our own review of the statute, its legislative history, Board and court precedent and legal commentary has convinced us that the majority rule principle is such an integral part of the Act's current substance and procedure that it must be adhered to in fashioning a remedy, even in the most 'exceptional' cases. We view the principle as a direct limitation on the Board's existing statutory remedial authority as well as a policy that would render improper exercise of any remedial authority to grant non-majority bargaining orders which the Board might possess."[24]

The great majority of bargaining orders are issued in cases falling within the second *Gissel* category—i.e., cases in which the union at one point had attained majority status which was dissipated through the employer's unlawful conduct.[25] In such instances it is incumbent upon the Board to evaluate the extensiveness of the employer's unfair labor practices in terms of their past effect on election conditions and the likelihood of their recurrence in the future. If the Board concludes that the possibility of conducting a free election is slight and the employees' previous demonstration of support for the union is a more reliable indicator of their true sentiments, a bargaining order generally is issued.[26]

Although the Board has considerable discretion in determining when to award bargaining orders, the courts require that it "clearly explicate its reasons for issuing a bargaining order and include [specific] findings as to why a fair election cannot be held."[27] In reaching its conclusions, the Board applies an objective standard rather than inquiring into the employer's subjective motivations,[28] and also considers the union's conduct in evaluating the totality of the circumstances.[29] Only when a direct causal relationship has been established between the employer's conduct and the inability to conduct a fair election is a bargaining order appropriate.[30]

---

[24]*Id.* 270 NLRB at 583, 116 LRRM at 1111.

[25]*NLRB v. Gissel Packing Co.*, 395 U.S. 575, 71 LRRM 2481 (1969). As noted, the Court determined that bargaining orders are not appropriate in cases falling within the third category where the employer's unlawful practices are relatively minor.

[26]*Id.* 394 U.S. at 614–615, 71 LRRM at 2496. Employers often defend against the issuance of bargaining orders by arguing that the union's demonstration of support is not a reliable indicator of employee sentiment, offering such reasons as the authorization cards were revoked prior to the recognition demand; the authorization cards were signed only because of misrepresentations made by the individuals soliciting them; or the authorization cards were forged. If the employer successfully challenges the validity of the union's claim of majority support, a bargaining order will not be issued. *See* THE DEVELOPING LABOR LAW at 528–537 and cases cited therein.

[27]*NLRB v. Armcor Indus., Inc.*, 535 F.2d 239, 244, 92 LRRM 2374, 2378 (3d Cir. 1976); *see also The Exchange Bank v. NLRB*, 732 F.2d 60, 64, 115 LRRM 3692, 3695 (6th Cir. 1984) (Board's articulation of reasons why bargaining order necessary sufficient under "the heightened level of scrutiny to which we have held bargaining orders must be subjected").

[28]*Elling v. Halvorson*, 222 NLRB 534, 91 LRRM 1179 (1976).

[29]*See, e.g., NLRB v. Triumph Curing Center*, 571 F.2d 462, 98 LRRM 2047 (9th Cir. 1978); *Donovan v. NLRB*, 520 F.2d 1316, 89 LRRM 3127 (2d Cir. 1975).

[30]*Clark Equipment Co.*, 278 NLRB No. 85, 121 LRRM 1258 (1986) (no bargaining order issued notwithstanding numerous 8(a)(1) violations because "considering the nature of the violations [i.e., interrogations], especially in the context of the large size of the unit, and the lack of evidence of any dissemination of the misconduct which involved only nine employees, we do not believe that the effects of Respondent's misconduct will linger to prevent a fair election").

The Board has determined that the proper time period to evaluate the effect of the employer's conduct is when the case is first presented to the Board rather than when the Board's order issues. While the passage of time between the violations and the order, substantial turnover of unit employees, a switch in management, or other changed circumstances may be considered by the Board in determining the appropriateness of a bargaining order, they are not dispositive and the Board is not precluded from issuing such an order because of these factors.[31]

§4.2   Elements of Proof

In situations where a union has made a request for recognition in an appropriate bargaining unit and the employer has responded with serious unfair labor practices, a bargaining order can be issued on the basis that the employer has unlawfully refused to bargain under Section 8(a)(5) of the Act. In such cases the burden is on the General Counsel to establish that a demand for recognition was made, that it was made at a time when the union had majority support, that the requested unit is appropriate, and that the employer's unlawful conduct has undermined the union's majority status and has precluded the holding of a free election.[32]

Bargaining orders also may be issued in situations where an employer's refusal to recognize the union does not constitute an independent violation of Section 8(a)(5) because the union has not made a request for recognition.[33] Such orders are predicated upon flagrant Section 8(a)(1) and (3) violations which tend to undermine the union's majority status and prevent the holding of a fair election.[34] The elements required for Section 8(a)(1) and (3) bargaining orders are the same as those for Section 8(a)(5) orders except that a demand for recognition by the union and a refusal by the employer need not be established.[35]

The Board has relied upon many different types of unlawful conduct to support bargaining orders.[36] Conduct which adversely af-

---

[31]*NLRB v. Pacific Southwest Airlines*, 550 F.2d 1148, 94 LRRM 2772 (9th Cir. 1977); *Granite City Journal, Inc.*, 262 NLRB 1153, 111 LRRM 1045 (1982); *Bandag, Inc.*, 228 NLRB 1045 n.1, 96 LRRM 1094 n.1 (1977); *but see NLRB v. J. Coty Messenger Serv.*, 763 F.2d 92, 119 LRRM 2779 (2d Cir. 1985); *United Serv. for the Handicapped v. NLRB*, 678 F.2d 661, 110 LRRM 3231 (6th Cir. 1982); *NLRB v. Jamacia Towing, Inc.*, 632 F.2d 208, 105 LRRM 2959 (2d Cir. 1980); *Hedstrom Co. v. NLRB*, 558 F.2d 1137, 95 LRRM 3069 (3d Cir. 1977) (suggesting that Board should consider effect of changed circumstances).

[32]*Trading Port, Inc.*, 219 NLRB 298, 89 LRRM 1565 (1975); *see also* NLRB General Counsel's Memorandum on *Trading Port, reprinted in* 4 LAB. L. REP. ¶9078 (CCH 1978) and THE DEVELOPING LABOR LAW at 503–516.

[33]*Hambre Hombre Enters., Inc.*, 228 NLRB 136, 94 LRRM 1590 (1977); *Beasley Energy, Inc.*, 228 NLRB 93, 94 LRRM 1563 (1977).

[34]*Steel-Fab, Inc.*, 212 NLRB 363, 86 LRRM 1474 (1974).

[35]*See* NLRB General Counsel's Memorandum on *Trading Port, supra* note 32.

[36]Thorough analyses of conduct cited by the Board in support of bargaining orders appear in THE DEVELOPING LABOR LAW at 508–516 and NLRB REPRESENTATION ELECTIONS at 586–591; *see also Regency Manor Nursing Home*, 275 NLRB No. 171, 119 LRRM 1273 (1985) (Dennis concurring opinion).

fects the employment status of unit employees such as discrimina-torily motivated plant closings, transfers of unit work, layoffs, and discharges frequently are used as the basis of bargaining orders be-cause of their long-lasting effects.[37] Threats of discharge, plant clos-ings, and other forms of reprisal also have been found sufficient to support bargaining orders,[38] as have promises of benefits if the em-ployees reject the union.[39] Pervasive Section 8(a)(1) violations such as coercive employee interrogations, surveillance of union activities, preventing employees from talking about the union until after the election, and so forth, also can support orders to bargain.[40] The Board has refused to apply the *Gissel* standards mechanically and instead has examined the totality of the circumstances to determine whether the employer's conduct has made it unlikely that a free and fair election can be held.[41]

§4.3 Effective Date

The effective date of the Board's bargaining order depends upon the sequence of events. In the typical case involving a Section 8(a)(5) violation, the union secures a card majority, requests recognition, and the employer immediately responds with unfair labor practices. In such cases the bargaining order is made retroactive to the union's request for recognition.[42] The bargaining order also is dated from the request for recognition when the unfair labor practices predate the request.[43] When there is a lapse of time between the union's attain-ment of majority support/demand for recognition and the commence-ment of the employer's unlawful conduct, the bargaining order is retroactive to the point at which the employer "embarked on a clear course of unlawful conduct or has engaged in sufficient unfair labor practices to undermine the union's majority status."[44]

In cases involving only Section 8(a)(1) and (3) violations where there is no union demand for recognition, the bargaining order dates from the day the employer embarked on a course of unlawful conduct or the union's attainment of majority status, whichever occurs later.[45] If all of the operative events (i.e., union attainment of majority status,

---

[37]*Ja-Wex Sportswear, Ltd.*, 260 NLRB 1229, 109 LRRM 1341 (1982); *Checker Cab Co.*, 260 NLRB 955, 109 LRRM 1253 (1982); *Spiegel Trucking Co.*, 257 NLRB 230, 107 LRRM 1492 (1981).

[38]*Air Prods. & Chemicals, Inc.*, 263 NLRB 341, 111 LRRM 1024 (1982); *Scott Glass Prod., Inc.*, 261 NLRB 906, 110 LRRM 1131 (1982).

[39]*Glengarry Contracting Indus., Inc.*, 258 NLRB 1167, 108 LRRM 1315 (1981); *J. J. New-berry Co.*, 249 NLRB 991, 104 LRRM 1244 (1980).

[40]*Gentile Pontiac*, 260 NLRB 429, 109 LRRM 1228 (1982).

[41]*Faith Garment Co.*, 246 NLRB 299, 102 LRRM 1515 (1979).

[42]*Parker-Robb Chevrolet, Inc.*, 262 NLRB 402, 110 LRRM 1289 (1982).

[43]*Trading Port, Inc.*, 219 NLRB 298, 89 LRRM 1565 (1975).

[44]*Id.* 219 NLRB at 301, 89 LRRM at 1569; *Jasta Mfg. Co.*, 246 NLRB 48, 102 LRRM 1610 (1979); *Kroger Co.*, 228 NLRB 149, 94 LRRM 1586 (1977).

[45]*Beasley Energy, Inc.*, 228 NLRB 93, 94 LRRM 1563 (1977).

demand for recognition, and commencement of unlawful conduct) occur more than six months prior to the filing of the unfair labor practice charge, the bargaining order is retroactive to the first day of the Section 10(b) six-month limitations period.[46]

Benefits of an NLRB Certification

While a union whose representative status has been established voluntarily or by virtue of a bargaining order is legally entitled to serve as the exclusive bargaining agent of unit employees, additional benefits are accorded to unions that have been granted an NLRB certification following a Board-conducted election:

- The employer is obligated to bargain with a certified union for at least one year (the "certification year"), absent unusual circumstances.[47] Unusual circumstances include such things as a schism within the certified union, its dissolution, or a substantial change in the size of the bargaining unit within a short period of time.[48] The certification year has been interpreted by the Board to mean one year of good faith bargaining rather than a calendar year. Accordingly, if an employer initially refuses to bargain in good faith with a certified union, the certification year begins not with the Board's issuance of the certification, but with the commencement of the employer's good faith bargaining.[49]

- The employer's obligation to bargain continues throughout the certification year notwithstanding the fact that the original bargaining unit may no longer be appropriate,[50] the union's majority support has been dissipated,[51] or the employer entertains a good faith doubt about the union's continued majority support.[52] During the certification year there is an irrebuttable presumption of majority status; following expiration of the certification year the presumption continues, but may be rebutted by evidence establishing a basis for raising a good faith doubt.[53]

---

[46]*Chromalloy Mining and Minerals*, 238 NLRB 688, 99 LRRM 1642 (1978).

[47]*Ray Brooks v. NLRB*, 348 U.S. 96, 35 LRRM 2158 (1954); *U.S. Eagle Inc.*, 202 NLRB 530, 82 LRRM 1561 (1973).

[48]*Ray Brooks v. NLRB*, 348 U.S. 96, 35 LRRM 2158 (1954).

[49]*Mar-Jac Poultry, Inc.*, 136 NLRB 785, 49 LRRM 1854 (1962); *see also Lamar Hotel*, 137 NLRB 1271, 50 LRRM 1366 (1962).

[50]*McLeod v. National Maritime Union*, 334 F. Supp. 34 (S.D.N.Y. 1971).

[51]*Ray Brooks v. NLRB*, 348 U.S. 96, 35 LRRM 2158 (1954).

[52]*United Supermarkets, Inc.*, 214 NLRB 958, 87 LRRM 1434 (1974).

[53]*Id.*

- Where the parties have not yet signed an agreement, any petition for an election filed within a year of certification will be dismissed, absent unusual circumstances.[54]
- The parties are virtually assured that their contractual relationship will not be disturbed by a Board election if the contract is signed within a year of the issuance of the certification and the contract contains no unlawful provisions.[55] However, where the contract is due to expire within the certification year, the Board has entertained a timely petition for an election filed within that year.[56]
- A certification is added "insurance" against a strike by an outside union. It is illegal under Section 8(b)(4)(C) of the Act for one union to exert pressure for recognition on behalf of employees for whom a rival union has received a Board certification. Such pressure is not unlawful when the current representative lacks a certification.[57]
- If an employer refuses to honor a certification and to bargain, the certified union may request employees of other employers such as suppliers to strike their employer in order to bring pressure on the offending employer.[58]
- If a union is certified as bargaining agent for employees doing a certain type of work and the employer gives this work to employees belonging to another union, the certified union may strike to compel the employer to honor the certification.[59] Without a certification, a strike to force the employer to assign work to members of one union rather than another may be illegal.

Voluntary recognition and bargaining orders may accord legally enforceable bargaining rights to labor organizations, but as outlined above substantial additional protections are available to unions that are certified following a Board-conducted election.

---

[54]*Aleo Mfg. Co.*, 109 NLRB 1297, 34 LRRM 1554 (1954); *see also Firestone Tire and Rubber Co.*, 185 NLRB 63, 74 LRRM 1761 (1970).

[55]*Pine Transp. Inc.*, 197 NLRB 256, 80 LRRM 1334 (1972); *F. J. Kress Box Co.*, 97 NLRB 1109, 29 LRRM 1212 (1952).

[56]*Ludlow Typograph Co.*, 108 NLRB 1463, 34 LRRM 1249 (1954).

[57]*Perry Norvell Co.*, 80 NLRB 225, 23 LRRM 1061 (1948).

[58]Sec. 8(b)(4)(B).

[59]Sec. 8(b)(4)(D).

5

The Petition for an Election

Representation proceedings—which concern employees' right to select or reject a bargaining agent—are the heart of the National Labor Relations Act. Section 7 guarantees to employees the right to form, join, or assist labor organizations, to bargain collectively through representatives of their own choosing, and to engage in other concerted activities for the purpose of collective bargaining or other mutual aid or protection. Section 9 sets forth the procedures which employees may use to exercise the right to select, or reject, a union representative by means of secret ballot elections.

For nearly 25 years a large proportion of the Board's workload was devoted to resolving issues raised in representation proceedings. As the Board's caseload grew, the representation matters became increasingly burdensome. Recognizing the routine nature of many of these cases and the relative stability of the Act's interpretation in this area, Congress, as a part of the 1959 amendments, authorized the Board to delegate the bulk of its authority over election cases to the regional directors.[1]

The Board exercised this authority in 1961, and today the regional directors play a leading role in representation case processing. (See Exhibit 6.) This was accomplished by a formal delegation (reprinted as Appendix D) in which the Board gave authority to the regional directors to:

- Decide whether a question concerning representation exists;
- Determine the appropriate collective bargaining unit;
- Direct an election;
- Certify the results of the election; and
- Make findings and issue rulings on objections and challenged ballots.

---

[1]Sec. 3(b).

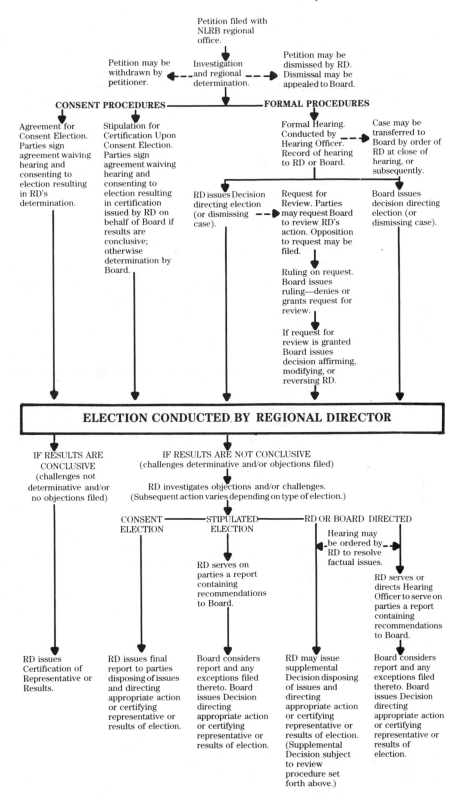

Petition filed with
NLRB regional
office.

Petition may be
withdrawn by
petitioner.

Investigation
and regional
determination.

Petition may be
dismissed by RD.
Dismissal may be
appealed to Board.

CONSENT PROCEDURES

FORMAL PROCEDURES

Agreement for
Consent Election.
Parties sign
agreement waiving
hearing and
consenting to
election resulting
in RD's
determination.

Stipulation for
Certification Upon
Consent Election.
Parties sign
agreement waiving
hearing and
consenting to
election resulting
in certification
issued by RD on
behalf of Board if
results are
conclusive;
otherwise
determination by
Board.

Formal Hearing.
Conducted by
Hearing Officer.
Record of hearing
to RD or Board.

Case may be
transferred to
Board by order of
RD at close of
hearing, or
subsequently.

RD issues Decision
directing election
(or dismissing
case).

Request for
Review. Parties
may request Board
to review RD's
action. Opposition
to request may be
filed.

Board issues
decision directing
election (or
dismissing case).

Ruling on request.
Board issues
ruling—denies or
grants request for
review.

If request for
review is granted
Board issues
decision affirming,
modifying, or
reversing RD.

ELECTION CONDUCTED BY REGIONAL DIRECTOR

IF RESULTS ARE
CONCLUSIVE
(challenges not
determinative and/or
no objections filed)

IF RESULTS ARE NOT CONCLUSIVE
(challenges determinative and/or objections filed)

RD investigates objections and/or challenges.
(Subsequent action varies depending on type of election.)

CONSENT
ELECTION

STIPULATED
ELECTION

RD OR BOARD DIRECTED

Hearing may
be ordered by
RD to resolve
factual issues.

RD serves on
parties a report
containing
recommendations
to Board.

RD serves or
directs Hearing
Officer to serve on
parties a report
containing
recommendations
to Board.

RD issues
Certification of
Representative or
Results.

RD issues final
report to parties
disposing of issues
and directing
appropriate action
or certifying
representative or
results of election.

Board considers
report and any
exceptions filed
thereto. Board
issues Decision
directing
appropriate action
or certifying
representative or
results of election.

RD may issue
supplemental
Decision disposing
of issues and
directing
appropriate action
or certifying
representative or
results of election.
(Supplemental
Decision subject
to review
procedure set
forth above.)

Board considers
report and any
exceptions filed
thereto. Board
issues Decision
directing
appropriate action
or certifying
representative or
results of
election.

Exhibit 6.   Outline of Representation Procedures Under Section 9(c)

As described in chapter 8, the Board retained a limited form of review to assure uniform and consistent application of its interpretation of law and policy. The propriety of the Board's delegation of authority over representation cases under the amendment to Section 3(b) is now well established. The authority is exercised as a part of the Board's function to interpret the Act, subject to review by the courts.[2]

Types of Petitions

The authority for Board election proceedings is contained in Section 9 of the Act.[3] Before the Board may proceed, however, a petition must be filed. Neither the Board nor the General Counsel is empowered to determine the bargaining representative or to investigate a claim of majority status on its own initiative.[4] The petition is a formal request addressed to the Board to determine whether or not a majority of employees in a bargaining unit wish to be represented by a particular labor organization for the purposes of collective bargaining. The statute provides that a petition for an investigation and certification of representative may be filed by:

- Any individual, an employee, or group of employees acting on behalf of employees;[5]
- An employer, but only when one or more individuals or labor organizations present a claim to be recognized as the exclusive bargaining representative;[6]
- A labor organization acting on behalf of employees.[7]

§5.1   Individual Petitions

An individual who files a timely petition need only show that it is supported by at least 30 percent of the employees in the proposed bargaining unit and that representative status is being sought for the purpose of collective bargaining.[8] Since a supervisor cannot represent employees for bargaining purposes, the Board will dismiss petitions filed by supervisors.[9]

---

[2]*NLRB v. Magnesium Casting Co.*, 427 F.2d 114, 74 LRRM 2234 (lst Cir. 1970); *Wallace Shops Inc.*, 133 NLRB 36, 48 LRRM 1564 (1961).

[3]Secs. 9(c), 3(b).

[4]Sec. 9(c)(1).

[5]Sec. 9(c)(1)(A).

[6]Sec. 9(c)(1)(B).

[7]*Id.*

[8]*Hofmann Packing Co.*, 87 NLRB 601 n.2, 25 LRRM 1182 n.2 (1949), *overruled on other grounds, Grand Union Co.*, 123 NLRB 1665, 44 LRRM 1201 (1959).

[9]*Kennecott Copper Corp.*, 98 NLRB 75, 29 LRRM 1300 (1952); *see also Buckeye Village Mkt. Inc.*, 175 NLRB 271, 70 LRRM 1529 (1969).

§5.2   Employer Petitions

An employer may file a petition (referred to as an RM petition) when there is no currently certified or recognized incumbent union and one or more individuals or labor organizations present a claim to be recognized.[10] The claim for recognition need not be in any particular form and may be inferred from conduct alone such as the submission of contract proposals[11] or picketing for recognition or organization.[12] The union or unions, however, must claim to represent a majority of the unit employees.[13] If the employer's petition does not indicate that a claim for recognition has been made, it will be dismissed.[14]

Employers also may file RM petitions in situations where there is an incumbent certified or recognized union and the employer can "demonstrate by objective considerations that it has some reasonable grounds for believing that the union has lost its majority status since its certification [or recognition]."[15] The RM petition must be supported by a letter, statement, affidavit, or other signed document setting forth the "objective considerations" on which the employer relies in requesting an election.

The validity of an employer's objective considerations is determined administratively by the regional director and is not an issue to be litigated at the representation hearing. In the absence of unusual circumstances no independent investigation is made of the objective considerations, and the crucial question is not whether the union has in fact lost its majority status, but whether the employer has a reasonable basis for believing that such a loss has occurred.

The Board examines the totality of the circumstances in determining whether objective considerations exist. Factors frequently relied upon include union inactivity in negotiations or in the processing of grievances; statements by employees that they no longer desire representation; substantial employee turnover in the unit; a

---

[10]Sec. 9(c)(1)(B); NLRB Statements of Procedure ¶101.17. *See generally United States Postal Serv.*, 256 NLRB 502, 107 LRRM 1249 (1981).

[11]*Johnson Bros. Furniture Co.*, 97 NLRB 246, 29 LRRM 1089 (1951); *Kimel Shoe Co.*, 97 NLRB 127, 29 LRRM 1069 (1951).

[12]*Coca-Cola Bottling Co.*, 80 NLRB 1063, 23 LRRM 1160 (1948).

[13]*Albuquerque Insulation Contractor, Inc.*, 256 NLRB 61, 107 LRRM 1254 (1981).

[14]*Horseshoe Club Operating Co.*, 172 NLRB 1703, 69 LRRM 1048 (1968); *Herman Loewenstein, Inc.*, 75 NLRB 377, 21 LRRM 1032 (1947).

[15]*United States Gypsum Co.*, 157 NLRB 652, 656, 61 LRRM 1384, 1386 (1966). *See generally* NLRB Casehandling Manual ¶11042. The right to file RM petitions in these situations is subject to the timeliness requirements of both the certification year (§5.5 *infra*) and contract bar (§5.8 *infra*) doctrines. Moreover, a finding of objective considerations sufficient to support an RM petition does not mean that the presumption of the union's on-going majority status has been rebutted and the employer is therefore justified in withdrawing recognition from the union and refusing to bargain. *Hydro Conduit Corp.*, 278 NLRB No. 164, 121 LRRM 1349 (1986).

decrease in checkoff authorizations; and admissions on the part of union officials that they no longer have majority support.[16] While many of these factors standing alone may not give rise to a finding of objective considerations, in combination or in light of other surrounding circumstances they may be found sufficient to support an RM petition.

After the employer files an RM petition, if the union issues a clear and unequivocal disclaimer of interest in representing the employees, and does not thereafter act in a manner inconsistent with such disclaimer, the petition will be dismissed.[17]

§5.3 Union Petitions

A labor organization may petition for an election in one of three circumstances:

- Where the employer has not recognized it as exclusive bargaining representative, and the union seeks such recognition. In such cases, a formal demand for recognition need not precede the filing of the petition.[18]

- Where the union, despite its recognition by the employer and the negotiation of a collective bargaining agreement, files a petition for an election in order to obtain the benefits of a certification.[19]

- Where two or more labor organizations file a joint petition for an election in which they seek certification as the joint representative for a single group of employees. Authorization cards submitted in support of the petition do not have to stipulate whether the employees desire joint or individual representation.[20] If a joint representative is certified, the employer may insist that they bargain jointly.[21]

(a) Disqualification of Union. In some cases the Board is urged to dismiss a union's election petition on the basis that the union should be disqualified from representing the unit employees. As a

---

[16]*See, e.g., NLRB v. Gallaro Bros.*, 419 F.2d 97, 73 LRRM 2043 (2d Cir. 1969); *Lodge 1746 and 743 Machinists v. NLRB (United Aircraft Corp.)*, 416 F.2d 809, 71 LRRM 2336 (D.C. Cir. 1969); *Riverside Produce Co.*, 242 NLRB 615, 101 LRRM 1371 (1979); *Viking Lithographers, Inc.*, 184 NLRB 139, 74 LRRM 1407 (1970).

[17]*Josephine Furniture Co.*, 172 NLRB 404, 68 LRRM 1311 (1968); *Ny-Lint Tool & Mfg. Co.*, 77 NLRB 642, 22 LRRM 1061 (1948).

[18]*Gray Drug Stores, Inc.*, 197 NLRB 924, 80 LRRM 1449 (1972); *"M" Sys., Inc.*, 115 NLRB 1316, 38 LRRM 1055 (1956); *Advance Pattern Co.*, 80 NLRB 29, 23 LRRM 1022 (1948).

[19]*McGraw-Edison Co.*, 199 NLRB 1017, 81 LRRM 1439 (1972); *Montgomery Ward and Co.*, 137 NLRB 346, 50 LRRM 1137 (1962); *General Box Co.*, 82 NLRB 678, 23 LRRM 1589 (1949). See the discussion concerning the benefits of certification in chapter 4 notes 47–59.

[20]*Pharmaseal Labs.*, 199 NLRB 324, 81 LRRM 1215 (1972); *Hamburg Indus., Fidelity Serv., and Indus. Technical Serv.*, 193 NLRB 67, 78 LRRM 1130 (1971); *Mid-South Packers, Inc.*, 120 NLRB 495, 41 LRRM 1526 (1958); *Stickless Corp.*, 115 NLRB 979, 37 LRRM 1466 (1956).

[21]*Swift and Co.*, 115 NLRB 752, 37 LRRM 1392 (1956).

general rule such contentions are rejected when based upon the qualifications, character, or internal affairs of the union. In the Board's view, "absent certain statutory limitations, the choice of a bargaining representative rests upon the desires of the employees."[22]

There are situations, however, where a union has been disqualified from representing certain employees. One common source of disqualification is a conflict of interest. A union may not represent employees where such union also competes with the employer for business.[23] Likewise, a union will be disqualified if any of its officers or agents have interests which may conflict with "the single-minded purpose of protecting and advancing the interests of the employees who have selected [the union] as their bargaining agent."[24] A union also will be disqualified from representing a unit of guards if it already represents nonguard employees.[25]

(b) No-Raiding Procedures. The AFL-CIO has established programs for handling representation disputes between affiliates. No-raiding agreements also exist between the Teamsters and other international unions. To the extent possible, the Board modifies its representation procedures to accommodate these private programs.[26]

The Board takes the following action whenever a petition is filed in a case involving at least two affiliates of the AFL-CIO, one of which has either been recognized by the employer for at least one year or has been certified by the Board or by a state agency as collective bargaining agent for the employees involved:

- The regional director sends immediate notification of the fact of filing to the presidents of the AFL-CIO and the parent international unions involved, to all parties, and to the Board's Executive Secretary.
- The regional director undertakes the customary informal investigation of the merits of the petition.
- If the petitioner is an affiliate of the AFL-CIO, the regional director delays any necessary formal notice (i.e., issuance of notice of a hearing) for a period of 30 days from the date of the above notification in order to permit use of the settlement provisions of the no-raiding agreement.
- If the petitioner is not an affiliate of the AFL-CIO, the regional director has the discretion to delay formal action as above, including but not limited to those situations where the peti-

---

[22]*Auto Transports, Inc.*, 100 NLRB 272, 30 LRRM 1272 (1952).

[23]*Visiting Nurses Ass'n, Inc.*, 254 NLRB 49, 106 LRRM 1100 (1981).

[24]*Bausch & Lomb Optical Co.*, 108 NLRB 1555, 1559, 34 LRRM 1222, 1224 (1954). *See, e.g., St. Louis Labor Health Inst.*, 230 NLRB 180, 95 LRRM 1347 (1977) (union's president also employer's principal labor negotiator); *Harlem Rivers Consumers Coop.*, 191 NLRB 314, 77 LRRM 1883 (1971) (union agent a principal of employer's supplier).

[25]*Wackenhut Corp.*, 196 NLRB 278, 79 LRRM 1673 (1972).

[26]*See generally* NLRB Casehandling Manual ¶¶11050–11056.

tioner voluntarily requests a delay to permit operation of a no-raiding agreement.

- At the expiration of the 30-day period, the case will be processed in accordance with normal procedures unless an active proceeding under the AFL-CIO no-raiding agreement has been initiated.

When a request to suspend processing of a representation petition is based upon other no-raiding agreements, the regional director files a copy or a description of the agreement with the Board. The director also submits all information available concerning the status of any relevant proceedings which may have been brought under the agreement. When it appears that the parties may be able to resolve their differences through their private agreement, the Board will suspend its proceedings for 30 days or take other appropriate action to encourage a voluntary resolution.

Timeliness of Petition

The periods of time during which an election petition may be filed are limited both by statute and by Board decision. Accordingly, when a party decides to file a petition the question of timeliness must first be addressed.

§5.4   Statutory Bar

The Board will not conduct an election in a unit or subdivision of a unit in which a valid election has been held in the preceding 12 months.[27] The election may have been conducted by the Board or by a state agency which comports with NLRB election policies.[28] In situations where no union is certified, the year begins to run from the date of the election even if postelection objections or challenges are filed and take several months to resolve.[29]

The statutory bar applies only to valid elections in which the results are conclusive. If an election is set aside on the basis of meritorious postelection objections, a second election may be conducted within the year.[30] Similarly, runoff or rerun elections may be held

[27]Sec. 9(a)(3).

[28]*We Transport, Inc.*, 198 NLRB 949, 81 LRRM 1010 (1972); *Modern Litho Plate Corp.*, 134 NLRB 66, 49 LRRM 1110 (1961); *Olin Mathieson Chem. Corp.*, 115 NLRB 1501, 38 LRRM 1099 (1956).

[29]*Tri-Ex Tower Corp.*, 230 NLRB 1006, 96 LRRM 1490 (1977); *Bendix Corp.*, 179 NLRB 140, 72 LRRM 1264 (1969); *Palmer Mfg. Co.*, 103 NLRB 336, 31 LRRM 1520 (1953). For situations in which the election does result in the issuance of a certification, see discussion of the certification bar at §5.5 *infra*.

[30]*NAPA N.Y. Warehouse, Inc.*, 76 NLRB 840, 21 LRRM 1251 (1948).

in situations where the results of the first election are inconclusive.[31] Deauthorization elections to rescind a union shop provision are always timely except within 12 months of a previous deauthorization election.[32]

The statutory bar precludes elections only in any "bargaining unit or any subdivision" of a unit within which a previous election has been held. Thus, while a second election could not be conducted within a year in a segment of a larger unit, the statute does not preclude elections in broader units which encompass the original unit in which the election was held.[33] In addition, the statutory bar applies to elections rather than petitions. Accordingly, petitions filed within 60 days of the anniversary date of the election will be accepted and processed so long as the election itself is not conducted until after the anniversary date.[34] A petition filed more than 60 days before the election anniversary date will be dismissed as being untimely.[35]

§5.5 Certification Bar

Where a union is certified as bargaining representative after winning a Board election, the parties are given a full year (the "certification year") within which to negotiate an initial agreement. During this period the union's continuing majority status generally is presumed. The effect of the presumption is that during the certification year petitions for elections are barred[36] and the employer must, in the absence of unusual circumstances, continue to bargain in good faith even in the face of objective evidence that the union has, in fact, lost its majority status.[37] Unlike the statutory bar which runs for a year following the election and has a 60-day open period for the filing of election petitions, the certification bar begins with the issuance of the certification and runs for a full year.[38] In addition, the statutory bar merges into the certification bar once a certification is issued. Thus, a petition filed after the anniversary date of an election and therefore timely under the statutory bar doctrine in the absence of a certification will be dismissed as being untimely if a certification was issued and the certification year has not yet expired.

In unusual circumstances the Board may abbreviate or extend the certification year. For example, a certified union may lose its

---

[31]*See* NLRB Casehandling Manual ¶11350.3.

[32]Sec. 9(e)(2); *Monsanto Chem. Co.*, 147 NLRB 49, 56 LRRM 1136 (1964).

[33]*Vickers, Inc.*, 124 NLRB 1051, 44 LRRM 1585 (1959); *Robertson Bros. Dept. Store, Inc.*, 95 NLRB 271, 28 LRRM 1335 (1951).

[34]*Vickers, Inc.*, 124 NLRB 1051, 44 LRRM 1585 (1959).

[35]*Id. See also Randolph Metal Works, Inc.*, 147 NLRB 973, 56 LRRM 1348 (1964).

[36]*Midstate Tele. Co.*, 179 NLRB 85, 72 LRRM 1279 (1969).

[37]*Ray Brooks v. NLRB*, 348 U.S. 96, 35 LRRM 2158 (1954); *see also Rockwell Valves, Inc.*, 115 NLRB 236, 37 LRRM 1271 (1956).

[38]*Ray Brooks v. NLRB*, 348 U.S. 96, 35 LRRM 2158 (1954).

preferred status if within the certification year it is dissolved, becomes defunct, or an internal schism develops.[39] In addition, a drastic fluctuation in the size of the workforce within a relatively short period of time may result in a reduction of the certification year.[40] If the parties negotiate a contract which expires prior to the expiration of the certification year, the expiration of the contract rather than the expiration of the certification year determines when an election petition can be filed.[41]

On the other hand, when an employer refuses to bargain in good faith with a newly certified union the certification year may be extended by the Board so as to ensure a minimum of one year of lawful bargaining.[42] Petitions filed during the extension period will be dismissed as being untimely. In addition, if the parties successfully negotiate a contract during the certification year the contract bar principles discussed in §5.8 below become effective and may preclude the filing of rival election petitions even after the expiration of the certification year.[43]

§5.6   Voluntary Recognition Bar

Voluntary recognition agreements entered into by an employer and a union may bar an election petition for "a reasonable time."[44] As with the certification bar, the voluntary recognition bar is intended to afford the parties to a new bargaining relationship ample time to negotiate an initial agreement.

In order to constitute a bar the recognition agreement must be valid. It may be oral or written,[45] but the union must have the support of a majority of the employees in the unit.[46] In addition, voluntary recognition may not be extended to a preferred union in order to inhibit the organizing efforts of a rival union which already has substantial support in the unit.[47] Voluntary recognition agreements

---

[39]*Id.*

[40]*Renaissance Center Partnership*, 239 NLRB 1247, 100 LRRM 1121 (1979).

[41]*Ludlow Typograph Co.*, 108 NLRB 1463, 34 LRRM 1249 (1954).

[42]*Mar-Jac Poultry Co.*, 136 NLRB 785, 49 LRRM 1854 (1962); *see also Nansemond Convalescent Center, Inc.*, 255 NLRB 563, 107 LRRM 1092 (1981).

[43]*Ludlow Typograph Co.*, 108 NLRB 1463, 34 LRRM 1249 (1954). The contract bar doctrine is discussed at §5.8 *infra.*

[44]*Keller Plastics Eastern, Inc.*, 157 NLRB 583, 61 LRRM 1396 (1966); *see also Josephine Furniture Co.*, 172 NLRB 404, 68 LRRM 1311 (1972); *Dale's Super Valu, Inc.*, 181 NLRB 698, 73 LRRM 1427 (1970).

[45]*Mojave Elec. Coop., Inc.*, 210 NLRB 88, 86 LRRM 1085 (1974).

[46]*Jack L. Williams, D.D.S.*, 231 NLRB 845, 97 LRRM 1532 (1977); *Keller Plastics Eastern, Inc.*, 157 NLRB 583, 61 LRRM 1396 (1966). Where a successor employer voluntarily recognizes a union which has been certified for a year or more, the union enjoys a rebuttable presumption of majority status only. A successor may lawfully withdraw recognition if it can show that the union in fact lost its majority status at the time of the refusal to bargain or that the refusal to bargain was grounded on a good faith doubt based on objective factors that the union continued to command majority support. *Harley Davidson Transp. Co.*, 273 NLRB No. 192, 118 LRRM 3040 (1985).

[47]*Whitemarsh Nursing Center*, 209 NLRB 873, 85 LRRM 1492 (1974).

may not constitute election bars in cases where recognition has been extended in an inappropriate bargaining unit.[48]

A voluntary recognition agreement will bar an election petition only for a "reasonable time." The determination of what constitutes a reasonable period of time within which to negotiate a contract is made on a case-by-case basis.[49]

§5.7 Bargaining Order Bar

In situations where a bargaining order is issued against an employer as a remedy for serious unfair labor practices, the parties are required to bargain in good faith for a reasonable period of time.[50] During the period of compliance bargaining a petition for an election will be dismissed as being untimely.[51] As with the voluntary recognition bar, what constitutes a reasonable period of time must be determined in light of the surrounding circumstances.[52]

§5.8 Contract Bar

The Board generally will not direct an election where there is a valid collective bargaining agreement in existence. Known as the "contract bar doctrine," this rule is intended to strike a balance between the twin objectives of stable labor relations and affording employees freedom of choice in selecting bargaining representatives.[53] The contract bar principles are not statutorily mandated but have been developed through the exercise of Board discretion. They may therefore be applied or waived by the Board as circumstances require.[54]

(a) Duration of Contract Bar. In order to bar an election petition a contract must have a reasonable and definite duration. Contracts of less than 90 days as well as those with no fixed term, of unreasonable or indefinite duration, or those which are terminable at will do not constitute bars for any period of time.[55]

---

[48]*Cf. Central Gen. Hosp.*, 223 NLRB 110, 91 LRRM 1433 (1976).

[49]*Tajon, Inc.*, 269 NLRB 327, 115 LRRM 1233 (1984) (three months and two bargaining sessions); *Brennan's Cadillac, Inc.*, 231 NLRB 225, 96 LRRM 1004 (1977) (three months); *Down River Forest Prods., Inc.*, 205 NLRB 14, 83 LRRM 1504 (1973) (five months).

[50]Remedial bargaining orders are discussed in chapter 4.

[51]*See Hermet, Inc.*, 207 NLRB 671, 84 LRRM 1536 (1973).

[52]See note 49 *supra.*

[53]*See generally* THE DEVELOPING LABOR LAW at 361–376.

[54]*NLRB v. Circle A & W Prods. Co.*, 647 F.2d 924, 107 LRRM 2923 (9th Cir. 1981).

[55]*Crompton Co.*, 260 NLRB 417, 109 LRRM 1161 (1982); *Pacific Coast Ass'n of Pulp and Paper Mfgrs.*, 121 NLRB 990, 42 LRRM 1477 (1958).

Assuming a reasonable duration, a contract will bar an election petition filed by the contracting parties for its entire term.[56] If the contracting union does not have a Board certification however, the contract will not preclude it from filing a petition seeking such certification.[57] Election petitions filed by nonincumbent unions are barred for the duration of the contract or for three years, whichever is less.[58] If during the term of the contract the parties agree on an amendment or a new contract with a termination date after the termination date of the existing contract, the amendment or new contract will be deemed to be a "premature extension" and will not bar an otherwise timely petition based on the original expiration date.[59]

Notwithstanding the existence of an unexpired contract, an election petition is timely if filed within the contract's 30-day "open period."[60] For contracts of three years or less, the period between 90 and 60 days prior to contract expiration is the open period; for contracts in excess of three years, it is the 90–60 day period prior to the third anniversary of the contract's execution.[61] Thus, the 60-day period immediately prior to a contract's termination is "insulated" against the filing of petitions. In the health care industry the open period is between 120 and 90 days prior to contract termination.[62] Exhibits 7 and 8 indicate the open periods for health care and non-health care institution contracts expiring on any given day of the year. Petitions filed before the open period or during the insulated period will be dismissed as untimely. Petitions filed on the sixtieth day before and including the termination date are untimely.[63] In situations where a contract is in effect "to" or "until" a certain date, the date indicated should not be included in the 60-day calculation.[64]

If the employer and the incumbent union successfully execute a new contract during the "insulated" 60-day period prior to expiration of the old contract, the new contract will serve as an election bar. If, on the other hand, the old contract expires without a new one being executed, a petition will be timely up to the point that a successor agreement is reached.[65]

---

[56]*Absorbent Cotton Co.*, 137 NLRB 908, 50 LRRM 1258 (1962).

[57]*General Box Co.*, 82 NLRB 678, 23 LRRM 1589 (1948).

[58]*General Cable Corp.*, 139 NLRB 1123, 51 LRRM 1444 (1962); *see also Penn-Keystone Realty Corp.*, 191 NLRB 800, 77 LRRM 1600 (1971). Ambiguities concerning the effective date of a contract for purposes of applying the contract bar rules will be resolved against finding a bar. *Marriott Corp.*, 259 NLRB 157, 108 LRRM 1317 (1981).

[59]*Southwestern Portland Cement Co.*, 126 NLRB 931, 45 LRRM 1412 (1960); *but see Shen-Valley Meat Packers, Inc.*, 261 NLRB 958, 110 LRRM 1121 (1982).

[60]*Deluxe Metal Furniture Co.*, 121 NLRB 995, 42 LRRM 1470 (1958); *see also Leonard Wholesale Meats, Inc.*, 136 NLRB 1000, 49 LRRM 1901 (1962). To be timely, the petition must be received by the Board during the open period, not simply placed in the mail. NLRB Rules and Regulations §102.111(b)(5).

[61]*Abbey Medical/Abbey Rents, Inc.*, 264 NLRB 969, 111 LRRM 1683 (1982); *Vanity Fair Mills, Inc.*, 256 NLRB 1104, 107 LRRM 1331 (1981).

[62]*Trinity Lutheran Hosp.*, 218 NLRB 199, 89 LRRM 1238 (1975).

[63]*Vanity Fair Mills, Inc.*, 256 NLRB 1104, 107 LRRM 1331 (1981).

[64]*Hemisphere Steel Prods. Inc.*, 131 NLRB 56, 47 LRRM 1595 (1961).

[65]*Deluxe Metal Furniture Co.*, 121 NLRB 995, 42 LRRM 1470; *see* The Developing Labor Law at 375–376 for special rules pertaining to the application of the contract bar principles following expiration of the old contract.

FORM NLRB-5254
(9-82)

TIMELY FILING OF PETITIONS - HEALTH CARE INDUSTRY ONLY

CONTRACT EXPIRATION DATE *	PETITION TIMELY IF FILED ON OR BETWEEN DATES	CONTRACT EXPIRATION DATE *	PETITION TIMELY IF FILED ON OR BETWEEN DATES	CONTRACT EXPIRATION DATE *	PETITION TIMELY IF FILED ON OR BETWEEN DATES	CONTRACT EXPIRATION DATE *	PETITION TIMELY IF FILED ON OR BETWEEN DATES
Jan 1	Sep 4 – Oct 3	Feb 1	Oct 5 – Nov 3	Mar 1	Nov 2 – Dec 1	Apr 1	Dec 3 – Jan 1
2	5 – 4	2	6 – 4	2	3 – 2	2	4 – 2
3	6 – 5	3	7 – 5	3	4 – 3	3	5 – 3
4	7 – 6	4	8 – 6	4	5 – 4	4	6 – 4
5	8 – 7	5	9 – 7	5	6 – 5	5	7 – 5
6	9 – 8	6	10 – 8	6	7 – 6	6	8 – 6
7	10 – 9	7	11 – 9	7	8 – 7	7	9 – 7
8	11 – 10	8	12 – 10	8	9 – 8	8	10 – 8
9	12 – 11	9	13 – 11	9	10 – 9	9	11 – 9
10	13 – 12	10	14 – 12	10	11 – 10	10	12 – 10
11	14 – 13	11	15 – 13	11	12 – 11	11	13 – 11
12	15 – 14	12	16 – 14	12	13 – 12	12	14 – 12
13	16 – 15	13	17 – 15	13	14 – 13	13	15 – 13
14	17 – 16	14	18 – 16	14	15 – 14	14	16 – 14
15	18 – 17	15	19 – 17	15	16 – 15	15	17 – 15
16	19 – 18	16	20 – 18	16	17 – 16	16	18 – 16
17	20 – 19	17	21 – 19	17	18 – 17	17	19 – 17
18	21 – 20	18	22 – 20	18	19 – 18	18	20 – 18
19	22 – 21	19	23 – 21	19	20 – 19	19	21 – 19
20	23 – 22	20	24 – 22	20	21 – 20	20	22 – 20
21	24 – 23	21	25 – 23	21	22 – 21	21	23 – 21
22	25 – 24	22	26 – 24	22	23 – 22	22	24 – 22
23	26 – 25	23	27 – 25	23	24 – 23	23	25 – 23
24	27 – 26	24	28 – 26	24	25 – 24	24	26 – 24
25	28 – 27	25	29 – 27	25	26 – 25	25	27 – 25
26	29 – 28	26	30 – 28	26	27 – 26	26	28 – 26
27	30 – 29	27	31 – 29	27	28 – 27	27	29 – 27
28	Oct 1 – 30	28	Nov 1 – 30	28	29 – 28	28	30 – 28
29	2 – 31	**29	2 – Dec 1	29	30 – 29	29	31 – 29
30	3 – Nov 1			30	Dec 1 – 30	30	Jan 1 – 30
31	4 – 2			31	2 – 31		

* "Contract Expiration Date" is the last effective date of contract. A contract "to" or "until" a date does not include that date and the last effective date is the preceding day, unless there is evidence to show that the parties intended the contract to be effective on the "to or until date". A contract for a period in excess of three years is not effective beyond the end of the third year, and the expiration date is the last day of the third year.

** Leap Year Adjustment - Add one day to each of the petition timely dates when contract expires March 1 - May 29 inclusive.
Add one day to the first of the petition timely dates when contract expires May 30 - June 27 inclusive.

Exhibit 7. Timely Filing of Petitions—Health Care Industry Only (Form NLRB-5254)

TIMELY FILING OF PETITIONS - HEALTH CARE INDUSTRY ONLY

FORM NLRB-5254 (9-92)

CONTRACT EXPIRATION DATE *	PETITION TIMELY IF FILED ON OR BETWEEN DATES		CONTRACT EXPIRATION DATE *	PETITION TIMELY IF FILED ON OR BETWEEN DATES		CONTRACT EXPIRATION DATE *	PETITION TIMELY IF FILED ON OR BETWEEN DATES		CONTRACT EXPIRATION DATE *	PETITION TIMELY IF FILED ON OR BETWEEN DATES	
May 1	Jan 2	Jan 31	Jun 1	Feb 2	Mar 3	Jul 1	Mar 4	Apr 2	Aug 1	Apr 4	May 3
2	3	Feb 1	2	3	4	2	5	3	2	5	4
3	4	2	3	4	5	3	6	4	3	6	5
4	5	3	4	5	6	4	7	5	4	7	6
5	6	4	5	6	7	5	8	6	5	8	7
6	7	5	6	7	8	6	9	7	6	9	8
7	8	6	7	8	9	7	10	8	7	10	9
8	9	7	8	9	10	8	11	9	8	11	10
9	10	8	9	10	11	9	12	10	9	12	11
10	11	9	10	11	12	10	13	11	10	13	12
11	12	10	11	12	13	11	14	12	11	14	13
12	13	11	12	13	14	12	15	13	12	15	14
13	14	12	13	14	15	13	16	14	13	16	15
14	15	13	14	15	16	14	17	15	14	17	16
15	16	14	15	16	17	15	18	16	15	18	17
16	17	15	16	17	18	16	19	17	16	19	18
17	18	16	17	18	19	17	20	18	17	20	19
18	19	17	18	19	20	18	21	19	18	21	20
19	20	18	19	20	21	19	22	20	19	22	21
20	21	19	20	21	22	20	23	21	20	23	22
21	22	20	21	22	23	21	24	22	21	24	23
22	23	21	22	23	24	22	25	23	22	25	24
23	24	22	23	24	25	23	26	24	23	26	25
24	25	23	24	25	26	24	27	25	24	27	26
25	26	24	25	26	27	25	28	26	25	28	27
26	27	25	26	27	28	26	29	27	26	29	28
27	28	26	27	28	29	27	30	28	27	30	29
28	29	27	28	Mar 1	30	28	31	29	28	May 1	30
29	30	28	29	2	31	29	Apr 1	30	29	2	31
30	31	Mar 1	30	3	Apr 1	30	2	May 1	30	3	Jun 1
31	Feb 1	2				31	3	2	31	4	2

* "Contract Expiration Date" is the last effective date of contract. A contract "to" or "until" a date does not include that date and the last effective date is the preceding day, unless there is evidence to show that the parties intended the contract to be effective on the "to or until date". A contract for a period in excess of three years is not effective beyond the end of the third year, and the expiration date is the last day of the third year.

** Leap Year Adjustment - Add one day to each of the petition timely dates when contract expires March 1 - May 29 inclusive.
Add one day to the first of the petition timely dates when contract expires May 30 - June 27 inclusive.

Exhibit 7—*page 2*

FORM NLRB-5254 (9-92)

TIMELY FILING OF PETITIONS - HEALTH CARE INDUSTRY ONLY

CONTRACT EXPIRATION DATE *	PETITION TIMELY IF FILED ON OR BETWEEN DATES	CONTRACT EXPIRATION DATE *	PETITION TIMELY IF FILED ON OR BETWEEN DATES	CONTRACT EXPIRATION DATE *	PETITION TIMELY IF FILED ON OR BETWEEN DATES	CONTRACT EXPIRATION DATE *	PETITION TIMELY IF FILED ON OR BETWEEN DATES
Sep 1	May 5 – Jun 3	Oct 1	Jun 4 – Jul 3	Nov 1	Jul 5 – Aug 3	Dec 1	Aug 4 – Sep 2
2	6 – 4	2	5 – 4	2	6 – 4	2	5 – 3
3	7 – 5	3	6 – 5	3	7 – 5	3	6 – 4
4	8 – 6	4	7 – 6	4	8 – 6	4	7 – 5
5	9 – 7	5	8 – 7	5	9 – 7	5	8 – 6
6	10 – 8	6	9 – 8	6	10 – 8	6	9 – 7
7	11 – 9	7	10 – 9	7	11 – 9	7	10 – 8
8	12 – 10	8	11 – 10	8	12 – 10	8	11 – 9
9	13 – 11	9	12 – 11	9	13 – 11	9	12 – 10
10	14 – 12	10	13 – 12	10	14 – 12	10	13 – 11
11	15 – 13	11	14 – 13	11	15 – 13	11	14 – 12
12	16 – 14	12	15 – 14	12	16 – 14	12	15 – 13
13	17 – 15	13	16 – 15	13	17 – 15	13	16 – 14
14	18 – 16	14	17 – 16	14	18 – 16	14	17 – 15
15	19 – 17	15	18 – 17	15	19 – 17	15	18 – 16
16	20 – 18	16	19 – 18	16	20 – 18	16	19 – 17
17	21 – 19	17	20 – 19	17	21 – 19	17	20 – 18
18	22 – 20	18	21 – 20	18	22 – 20	18	21 – 19
19	23 – 21	19	22 – 21	19	23 – 21	19	22 – 20
20	24 – 22	20	23 – 22	20	24 – 22	20	23 – 21
21	25 – 23	21	24 – 23	21	25 – 23	21	24 – 22
22	26 – 24	22	25 – 24	22	26 – 24	22	25 – 23
23	27 – 25	23	26 – 25	23	27 – 25	23	26 – 24
24	28 – 26	24	27 – 26	24	28 – 26	24	27 – 25
25	29 – 27	25	28 – 27	25	29 – 27	25	28 – 26
26	30 – 28	26	29 – 28	26	30 – 28	26	29 – 27
27	31 – 29	27	30 – 29	27	31 – 29	27	30 – 28
28	Jun 1 – 30	28	Jul 1 – 30	28	Aug 1 – 30	28	31 – 29
29	2 – Jul 1	29	2 – 31	29	2 – 31	29	Sep 1 – 30
30	3 – 2	30	3 – Aug 1	30	3 – Sep 1	30	2 – Oct 1
		31	4 – 2			31	3 – 2

* "Contract Expiration Date" is the last effective date of contract. A contract "to" or "until" a date does not include that date and the last effective date is the preceding day, unless there is evidence to show that the parties intended the contract to be effective on the "to or until date". A contract for a period in excess of three years is not effective beyond the end of the third year, and the expiration date is the last day of the third year.

** Leap Year Adjustment - Add one day to each of the petition timely dates when contract expires March 1 - May 29 inclusive.
Add one day to the first of the petition timely dates when contract expires May 30 - June 27 inclusive.

Exhibit 7—*page 3*

FORM NLRB-4645 (9-82)

TIMELY FILING OF PETITIONS - (NOT FOR USE IN HEALTH CARE CASES)

CONTRACT EXPIRATION DATE*	PETITION TIMELY IF FILED ON OR BETWEEN DATES	CONTRACT EXPIRATION DATE*	PETITION TIMELY IF FILED ON OR BETWEEN DATES	CONTRACT EXPIRATION DATE*	PETITION TIMELY IF FILED ON OR BETWEEN DATES	CONTRACT EXPIRATION DATE*	PETITION TIMELY IF FILED ON OR BETWEEN DATES
Jan 1	Oct 4 Nov 2	Feb 1	Nov 4 Dec 3	**Mar 1	Dec 2 Dec 31	Apr 1	Jan 2 Jan 31
2	5 3	2	5 4	2	3 Jan 1	2	3 Feb 1
3	6 4	3	6 5	3	4 2	3	4 2
4	7 5	4	7 6	4	5 3	4	5 3
5	8 6	5	8 7	5	6 4	5	6 4
6	9 7	6	9 8	6	7 5	6	7 5
7	10 8	7	10 9	7	8 6	7	8 6
8	11 9	8	11 10	8	9 7	8	9 7
9	12 10	9	12 11	9	10 8	9	10 8
10	13 11	10	13 12	10	11 9	10	11 9
11	14 12	11	14 13	11	12 10	11	12 10
12	15 13	12	15 14	12	13 11	12	13 11
13	16 14	13	16 15	13	14 12	13	14 12
14	17 15	14	17 16	14	15 13	14	15 13
15	18 16	15	18 17	15	16 14	15	16 14
16	19 17	16	19 18	16	17 15	16	17 15
17	20 18	17	20 19	17	18 16	17	18 16
18	21 19	18	21 20	18	19 17	18	19 17
19	22 20	19	22 21	19	20 18	19	20 18
20	23 21	20	23 22	20	21 19	20	21 19
21	24 22	21	24 23	21	22 20	21	22 20
22	25 23	22	25 24	22	23 21	22	23 21
23	26 24	23	26 25	23	24 22	23	24 22
24	27 25	24	27 26	24	25 23	24	25 23
25	28 26	25	28 27	25	26 24	25	26 24
26	29 27	26	29 28	26	27 25	26	27 25
27	30 28	27	30 29	27	28 26	27	28 26
28	31 29	28	Dec 1 30	28	29 27	28	29 27
29	Nov 1 30	**29	2 31	29	30 28	29	30 28
30	2 Dec 1			30	31 29	30	31 Mar 1
31	3 2			31	Jan 1 30		

* "Contract Expiration Date" is the last effective date of contract. A contract "to" or "until" a date does not include that date and the last effective date is the preceding day, unless there is evidence to show that the parties intended the contract to be effective on the "to or until date". A contract for a period in excess of three years is not effective beyond the end of the third year, and the expiration date is the last day of the third year.

** Leap Year Adjustment - Add one day to each of the petition timely dates when contract expires March 1 - April 29 inclusive. Add one day to first of the petition timely dates when contract expires April 30 - May 28 inclusive.

Exhibit 8.   Timely Filing of Petitions (Except Health Care) (Form NLRB-4645)

FORM NLRB-4645 (9-92)

TIMELY FILING OF PETITIONS - (NOT FOR USE IN HEALTH CARE CASES)

CONTRACT EXPIRATION DATE *	PETITION TIMELY IF FILED ON OR BETWEEN DATES	CONTRACT EXPIRATION DATE *	PETITION TIMELY IF FILED ON OR BETWEEN DATES	CONTRACT EXPIRATION DATE *	PETITION TIMELY IF FILED ON OR BETWEEN DATES	CONTRACT EXPIRATION DATE *	PETITION TIMELY IF FILED ON OR BETWEEN DATES
**May 1	Feb 1 – Mar 2	Jun 1	Mar 4 – Apr 2	Jul 1	Apr 3 – May 2	Aug 1	May 4 – Jun 2
2	2 – 3	2	5 – 3	2	4 – 3	2	5 – 3
3	3 – 4	3	6 – 4	3	5 – 4	3	6 – 4
4	4 – 5	4	7 – 5	4	6 – 5	4	7 – 5
5	5 – 6	5	8 – 6	5	7 – 6	5	8 – 6
6	6 – 7	6	9 – 7	6	8 – 7	6	9 – 7
7	7 – 8	7	10 – 8	7	9 – 8	7	10 – 8
8	8 – 9	8	11 – 9	8	10 – 9	8	11 – 9
9	9 – 10	9	12 – 10	9	11 – 10	9	12 – 10
10	10 – 11	10	13 – 11	10	12 – 11	10	13 – 11
11	11 – 12	11	14 – 12	11	13 – 12	11	14 – 12
12	12 – 13	12	15 – 13	12	14 – 13	12	15 – 13
13	13 – 14	13	16 – 14	13	15 – 14	13	16 – 14
14	14 – 15	14	17 – 15	14	16 – 15	14	17 – 15
15	15 – 16	15	18 – 16	15	17 – 16	15	18 – 16
16	16 – 17	16	19 – 17	16	18 – 17	16	19 – 17
17	17 – 18	17	20 – 18	17	19 – 18	17	20 – 18
18	18 – 19	18	21 – 19	18	20 – 19	18	21 – 19
19	19 – 20	19	22 – 20	19	21 – 20	19	22 – 20
20	20 – 21	20	23 – 21	20	22 – 21	20	23 – 21
21	21 – 22	21	24 – 22	21	23 – 22	21	24 – 22
22	22 – 23	22	25 – 23	22	24 – 23	22	25 – 23
23	23 – 24	23	26 – 24	23	25 – 24	23	26 – 24
24	24 – 25	24	27 – 25	24	26 – 25	24	27 – 25
25	25 – 26	25	28 – 26	25	27 – 26	25	28 – 26
26	26 – 27	26	29 – 27	26	28 – 27	26	29 – 27
27	27 – 28	27	30 – 28	27	29 – 28	27	30 – 28
28	28 – 29	28	31 – 29	28	30 – 29	28	31 – 29
29	Mar 1 – 30	29	Apr 1 – 30	29	May 1 – 30	29	Jun 1 – 30
30	2 – 31	30	2 – May 1	30	2 – 31	30	2 – Jul 1
31	3 – Apr 1			31	3 – Jun 1	31	3 – 2

*"Contract Expiration Date" is the last effective date of contract. A contract "to" or "until" a date does not include that date and the last effective date is the preceding day, unless there is evidence to show that the parties intended the contract to be effective on the "to or until date". A contract for a period in excess of three years is not effective beyond the end of the third year, and the expiration date is the last day of the third year.

** Leap Year Adjustment - Add one day to each of the petition timely dates when contract expires March 1 - April 29 inclusive.
Add one day to first of the petition timely dates when contract expires April 30 - May 28 inclusive.

Exhibit 8—*page 2*

FORM NLRB-4645 (9-82)

TIMELY FILING OF PETITIONS - (NOT FOR USE IN HEALTH CARE CASES)

CONTRACT EXPIRATION DATE *	PETITION TIMELY IF FILED ON OR BETWEEN DATES	CONTRACT EXPIRATION DATE *	PETITION TIMELY IF FILED ON OR BETWEEN DATES	CONTRACT EXPIRATION DATE *	PETITION TIMELY IF FILED ON OR BETWEEN DATES	CONTRACT EXPIRATION DATE *	PETITION TIMELY IF FILED ON OR BETWEEN DATES
Sep 1	Jun 4 - Jul 3	Oct 1	Jul 4 - Aug 2	Nov 1	Aug 4 - Sep 2	Dec 1	Sep 3 - Oct 2
2	5 - 4	2	5 - 3	2	5 - 3	2	4 - 3
3	6 - 5	3	6 - 4	3	6 - 4	3	5 - 4
4	7 - 6	4	7 - 5	4	7 - 5	4	6 - 5
5	8 - 7	5	8 - 6	5	8 - 6	5	7 - 6
6	9 - 8	6	9 - 7	6	9 - 7	6	8 - 7
7	10 - 9	7	10 - 8	7	10 - 8	7	9 - 8
8	11 - 10	8	11 - 9	8	11 - 9	8	10 - 9
9	12 - 11	9	12 - 10	9	12 - 10	9	11 - 10
10	13 - 12	10	13 - 11	10	13 - 11	10	12 - 11
11	14 - 13	11	14 - 12	11	14 - 12	11	13 - 12
12	15 - 14	12	15 - 13	12	15 - 13	12	14 - 13
13	16 - 15	13	16 - 14	13	16 - 14	13	15 - 14
14	17 - 16	14	17 - 15	14	17 - 15	14	16 - 15
15	18 - 17	15	18 - 16	15	18 - 16	15	17 - 16
16	19 - 18	16	19 - 17	16	19 - 17	16	18 - 17
17	20 - 19	17	20 - 18	17	20 - 18	17	19 - 18
18	21 - 20	18	21 - 19	18	21 - 19	18	20 - 19
19	22 - 21	19	22 - 20	19	22 - 20	19	21 - 20
20	23 - 22	20	23 - 21	20	23 - 21	20	22 - 21
21	24 - 23	21	24 - 22	21	24 - 22	21	23 - 22
22	25 - 24	22	25 - 23	22	25 - 23	22	24 - 23
23	26 - 25	23	26 - 24	23	26 - 24	23	25 - 24
24	27 - 26	24	27 - 25	24	27 - 25	24	26 - 25
25	28 - 27	25	28 - 26	25	28 - 26	25	27 - 26
26	29 - 28	26	29 - 27	26	29 - 27	26	28 - 27
27	30 - 29	27	30 - 28	27	30 - 28	27	29 - 28
28	Jul 1 - 30	28	31 - 29	28	31 - 29	28	30 - 29
29	2 - 31	29	Aug 1 - 30	29	Sep 1 - 30	29	Oct 1 - 30
30	3 - Aug 1	30	2 - 31	30	2 - Oct 1	30	2 - 31
		31	3 - Sep 1			31	3 - Nov 1

* "Contract Expiration Date" is the last effective date of contract. A contract "to" or "until" a date does not include that date and the last effective date is the preceding day, unless there is evidence to show that the parties intended the contract to be effective on the "to or until date". A contract for a period in excess of three years is not effective beyond the end of the third year, and the expiration date is the last day of the third year.

** Leap Year Adjustment - Add one day to each of the petition timely dates when contract expires March 1 - April 29 inclusive. Add one day to first of the petition timely dates when contract expires April 30 - May 28 inclusive.

Exhibit 8—*page 3*

(b) Circumstances of Execution. In order to constitute a bar a contract must be bona fide; that is, it must be the product of good-faith arms-length bargaining between an employer and the majority representative of its employees. The Board presumes that an agreement has been legitimately executed,[66] but if there is evidence that the contract is not legitimate it will not bar an election petition. The Board has found no bar, for example, in situations where the employer forced employees to sign the contract's signatory page without affording them an opportunity to review the contract terms;[67] where a union agent made false representations concerning the circumstances of the contract's execution;[68] where employees agreed to the terms of a contract before they were even hired by the contracting employer;[69] and where a contract which provided for employee ratification was not so ratified.[70]

A contract will not serve as an election bar if it is executed (1) at a time when the contracting parties are aware that a rival union claims representation rights or (2) at a time when an election petition already is pending before the Board.[71]

(c) Status of Contracting Union as Representative. In order to constitute a bar, a contract must be executed with a bona fide labor organization with an ability and an interest in representing the unit employees. The status of the contracting union initially is reviewed at the time the contract is executed. A contract executed with a minority union will not constitute a bar,[72] but once majority status has been established the subsequent loss of majority support during the term of the contract will not remove the contract as a bar. There are instances, however, when the status of the contracting labor organization during the life of the contract may be reviewed. For example, the union may become defunct, may develop an internal schism, or may disclaim further interest in representing the employees. In such instances the contract ceases to constitute a bar to an election petition filed by a rival labor organization.

● *Defunctness.* A union is considered defunct only if it is unwilling or unable to represent the employees. Neither a temporary inability to function nor the loss of all employees in the unit constitute defunctness if the union otherwise continues in existence and is will-

---

[66]*Pepsi Cola Bottling Co.*, 187 NLRB 15, 76 LRRM 1558 (1970).

[67]*Frank Hager, Inc.*, 230 NLRB 476, 96 LRRM 1117 (1977).

[68]*Air Lacarte, Fla. Inc.*, 212 NLRB 764, 86 LRRM 1663 (1975).

[69]*Mego Corp.*, 223 NLRB 279, 92 LRRM 1080 (1976).

[70]*Merico, Inc.*, 207 NLRB 101, 84 LRRM 1395 (1973); *American Broadcasting Co.*, 114 NLRB 7, 36 LRRM 1494 (1955).

[71]*Bridgeport Jai Alai, Inc.*, 227 NLRB 1519, 94 LRRM 1435 (1977); *United Serv. Co.*, 227 NLRB 1469, 94 LRRM 1250 (1977). *But see RCA Del Caribe, Inc.*, 262 NLRB 963, 110 LRRM 1369 (1982).

[72]*Pepsi Cola Bottling Co.*, 187 NLRB 15, 76 LRRM 1558 (1970).

ing and able to represent the employees.[73] The absence of affirmative steps toward dissolution; the presence of members, officers, and stewards; the administration of health and welfare and pension funds; and the processing of grievances all are evidence that a union is not defunct.

● *Schism*. Disagreements may exist among unit employees regarding the nature of their representation. In most instances these disagreements do not fragment the unit to such a degree that the stability of the bargaining relationship is jeopardized and the employees' interest is best served by a new election.[74] When, however, there is a fundamental split over basic policy issues which reaches from the local to the highest levels of the international, and where the employees have taken affirmative steps to change the incumbent representative because of these differences, then a schism has developed and an existing contract will not serve as an election bar.[75]

● *Relinquishment or Abandonment of Jurisdiction*. The Board has held that a contract will not serve as a bar when the contracting union affirmatively abandons or relinquishes jurisdiction over the employees and thereafter takes no action inconsistent with its disclaimer.[76] In some instances the union's conduct may be prompted by employees' dissatisfaction with the quality of the representation which they have been receiving.[77] In other instances it may be the result of collusion between two unions in which an incumbent seeks to disavow an unfavorable existing contract in order to allow the other union an opportunity to negotiate a more advantageous one. In such a case the Board may not honor the disclaimer.[78]

(d) Adequacy of Contract Form and Substance. In striking a balance between stabilizing labor relations through deference to labor contracts and affording employees freedom of choice in the selection of bargaining representatives, the Board has established certain principles regarding the form and substance of contracts which serve as election bars:

---

[73]*Hershey Chocolate Corp.*, 121 NLRB 901, 42 LRRM 1460 (1958); *see also Kent Corp.*, 272 NLRB No. 115, 117 LRRM 1333 (1984); *Automated Business Sys.*, 189 NLRB 124, 76 LRRM 1549 (1971); *Bennett Stone Co.*, 139 NLRB 1422, 51 LRRM 1518 (1962).

[74]*Yates Indus., Inc.*, 264 NLRB 1237, 112 LRRM 1231 (1982); *Standard Brands, Inc.*, 214 NLRB 72, 87 LRRM 1261 (1974); *Allied Chem. Corp.*, 196 NLRB 483, 80 LRRM 1026 (1972).

[75]*Hershey Chocolate Corp.*, 121 NLRB 901, 42 LRRM 1460 (1958); *Great Atl. & Pac. Tea Co.*, 120 NLRB 656, 42 LRRM 1022 (1958). Only Communism and corruption have been considered schismatic in the past. *Aelo Mfg. Co.*, 109 NLRB 1297, 34 LRRM 1554 (1954); *Hershey Chocolate Corp., supra.*

[76]*American Sunroof Corp.*, 243 NLRB 1128, 102 LRRM 1086 (1979).

[77]In *East Mfg. Corp.*, 242 NLRB 5, 101 LRRM 1079 (1979), the Board refused to honor a union's disclaimer predicated upon employee dissatisfaction because to allow a union to disavow its contractual commitments would impugn the integrity of the collective bargaining process and encourage circumvention of that process.

[78]*See American Sunroof Corp.*, 243 NLRB 1128, 102 LRRM 1086 (1979).

- An oral agreement will not constitute a bar even if the parties consider themselves bound by its terms;[79]
- The agreement must be signed by all parties and dated prior to the filing of the petition in order to constitute a bar;[80]
- While an "informal" agreement may constitute a bar, the contract must contain substantial terms and conditions of employment sufficient to stabilize the bargaining relationship; an agreement limited to wages, for example, would be inadequate;[81]
- To constitute a bar, the agreement clearly must encompass the employees in an appropriate bargaining unit sought to be represented;[82]
- A contract which is not applied equally to both union member and nonmember employees (i.e., a "members only" contract) will not constitute a bar;[83]
- A contract containing a union security provision which is clearly unlawful on its face, or which has been found to be unlawful by the Board in an unfair labor practice proceeding, may not bar a representation petition.[84] If the unlawful clause is eliminated by a proper revision or amendment, or if the contract contains a provision "clearly defining the effectiveness" of the offending clause, the contract will be considered cured;[85]
- As with an unlawful union security provision, a contract containing a checkoff provision which is unlawful on its face or which has been held unlawful in an unfair labor practice proceeding or in a court proceeding brought by the Attorney General will not bar an election petition;[86]

---

[79]*Appalachian Shale Prods. Co.*, 121 NLRB 1160, 42 LRRM 1506 (1958); *see also Empire Screen Printing Inc.*, 249 NLRB 718, 104 LRRM 1198 (1980); *Diversified Servs., Inc.*, 225 NLRB 1092, 93 LRRM 1068 (1976).

[80]*Crothall Hosp. Serv. Inc.*, 270 NLRB 1420, 117 LRRM 1072 (1984); *Roosevelt Mem. Park, Inc.*, 187 NLRB 517, 76 LRRM 1047 (1976). The parties' initials on an agreement may be sufficient. *Gaylord Broadcasting Co.*, 250 NLRB 198, 104 LRRM 1360 (1980). If two unions are jointly certified as bargaining representative, a contract serves as a bar even if signed by only one of the unions. *Pharmaseal Labs.*, 199 NLRB 324, 81 LRRM 1215 (1972).

[81]*Radio Free Europe/Radio Liberty, Inc.*, 262 NLRB 549, 110 LRRM 1330 (1982); *Farrel Rochester Div. of USM Corp.*, 256 NLRB 996, 107 LRRM 1358 (1981); *Hotel Employers Ass'n of San Francisco*, 159 NLRB 143, 62 LRRM 1215 (1966); *Appalachian Shale Prods. Co.*, 121 NLRB 1160, 42 LRRM 1506 (1958).

[82]*Levi Strauss and Co.*, 218 NLRB 625, 89 LRRM 1402 (1975); *Moore-McCormack Lines*, 181 NLRB 510, 73 LRRM 1457 (1970); *Mathieson Alkali Works, Inc.*, 51 NLRB 113, 12 LRRM 251 (1943).

[83]*Bob's Big Boy Family Restaurants v. NLRB*, 625 F.2d 850, 104 LRRM 3169 (9th Cir. 1980); *Appalachian Shale Prods. Co.*, 121 NLRB 1160, 42 LRRM 1506 (1958).

[84]*Paragon Prods. Corp.*, 134 NLRB 662, 49 LRRM 1156 (1961). Examples of unlawful clauses would include those which fail to honor the 30-day grace period set forth in Sec. 8(a)(3) or those which afford preferential treatment to union members in terms of hiring, layoff, or other terms and conditions of employment. *Peabody Coal Co.*, 197 NLRB 1231, 81 LRRM 1156 (1972).

[85]*NLRB v. News Syndicate Co.*, 365 U.S. 695, 47 LRRM 2916 (1961); *International Typographical Union (Haverhill Gazette) v. NLRB*, 365 U.S. 705, 47 LRRM 2920 (1961).

[86]*NLRB v. Martin Bldg. Material Co.*, 431 F.2d 1246, 75 LRRM 2161 (5th Cir. 1970); *Gary Steel Supply Co.*, 144 NLRB 470, 54 LRRM 1082 (1963); *Paragon Prods. Corp.*, 134 NLRB 662, 49 LRRM 1156 (1961).

- A contract which discriminates against classes of persons on the basis of race will not serve as a bar;[87]

- A contract containing clauses unlawful under Section 8(e) of the Act may still operate as an election bar. Unlike a union security provision, a hot cargo clause is not deemed to restrain the selection of a bargaining representative;[88]

- The Board will honor an automatic renewal provision so that a contract of reasonable duration can continue to serve as a bar beyond its initial term if it is allowed to renew.[89] Timely notices to reopen, modify, or terminate the contract, however, will forestall operation of the automatic renewal provision; and[90]

- Contract extensions which are negotiated prior to the 90–60 day "open period" of the initial contract are considered by the Board to be "premature" and will not operate as an election bar.[91] Extension agreements negotiated during the insulated 60-day period prior to expiration of the contract, however, are not premature and will constitute a bar so long as the other contract bar requirements are satisfied.[92]

(e) *Changed Circumstances Within Contract Term.*

- *Change in Nature of Operations.* The Board has determined that a contract will not bar an election petition if between the time the contract is executed and the petition is filed there is a substantial change in the "*nature* as distinguished from the *size* of the operations."[93] Such situations include those in which there has been (1) a merger of two or more operations into a completely new operation,[94] or (2) a renewal of operations at the same or a new location with new employees after a substantial lapse of time.[95] In contrast, when there is simply the relocation of an existing enterprise rather than the establishment of a new one, a pre-existing contract will serve as an election bar.[96]

---

[87]*Jno. H. Swisher & Son, Inc.*, 209 NLRB 68, 85 LRRM 1280 (1974); *Pioneer Bus Co.*, 140 NLRB 54, 51 LRRM 1546 (1962).

[88]*Food Haulers, Inc.*, 136 NLRB 394, 49 LRRM 1774 (1962).

[89]*Providence Television, Inc.*, 194 NLRB 759, 79 LRRM 1079 (1971).

[90]*Ideal Can Co.*, 219 NLRB 59, 89 LRRM 1618 (1975).

[91]See note 59 *supra*.

[92]*Crompton Co.*, 260 NLRB 417, 109 LRRM 1161 (1982).

[93]*General Extrusion Co.*, 121 NLRB 1165, 42 LRRM 1508 (1958).

[94]*Martin Marietta Refractories Co.*, 270 NLRB 821, 116 LRRM 1150 (1984); *Denver Publishing Co.*, 238 NLRB 207, 99 LRRM 1222 (1978); *Mego Corp.*, 223 NLRB 279, 92 LRRM 1080 (1976); *Boston Gas Co.*, 221 NLRB 628, 91 LRRM 1034 (1975); *Kroger Co.*, 155 NLRB 546, 60 LRRM 1351 (1965).

[95]*Rheem Mfg. Co.*, 188 NLRB 436, 76 LRRM 1311 (1971); *Slater Sys. Md., Inc.*, 134 NLRB 865, 49 LRRM 1294 (1961); *General Extrusion Co.*, 121 NLRB 1165, 42 LRRM 1508 (1958).

[96]*Westwood Import Co. v. NLRB*, 681 F.2d 664, 110 LRRM 3248 (9th Cir. 1982); *see also NLRB v. Marine Optical Co.*, 671 F.2d 11, 109 LRRM 2593 (1st Cir. 1982).

● *Purchases and Accretions.* When a good faith purchaser buys a business and does not agree in writing to assume an existing contract, the contract will not serve as a bar.[97] When, however, an employer acquires or establishes a new facility or operation after a contract has been executed, the effect of the contract as a bar will depend upon whether the new facility or operation is deemed to be an "accretion" to the existing bargaining unit. Under the Board's accretion doctrine, when the newly-acquired employees share a common interest in working conditions with the employees covered by the contract, the new employees will be considered as an addition or accretion to the existing unit and the contract will serve as a bar to an election in the expanded unit.[98]

The key element in determining whether certain employees constitute an accretion is the "community of interest" of the two groups; i.e., do the new employees share a mutual interest in working conditions with the represented employees, or do they have separate interests which are likely to be ignored if they are absorbed into the existing bargaining unit.[99] In applying the community of interest standard, the Board examines such factors as: (1) similarity of working conditions, (2) job classification, (3) skills and functions, (4) similarity of products, (5) interchangeability of employees, (6) geographical proximity, (7) functional integration of the business, (8) centralization of managerial control, (9) collective bargaining history, and (10) the size and number of employees at the facility to be acquired as compared with the existing operation.[100] The Board does not give determinative weight to any single factor, but considers the totality of the circumstances in ascertaining whether the new employees share common interests with those in the existing bargaining unit.

● *Expanding Units and Prehire Agreements.* In some instances a contract will be executed and the unit covered by the agreement will increase substantially in size. In *General Extrusion Co.*, 121 NLRB 1165, 42 LRRM 1508 (1958), the Board set forth a series of principles to govern when an election should be directed in the expanded unit notwithstanding the existence of a valid, unexpired contract.

Contracts which have been executed before any employees have been hired,[101] or before a "substantial increase" in personnel, will

---

[97]*Illinois Bell Tel. Co.*, 222 NLRB 485, 91 LRRM 1274 (1976); *Southern Moldings, Inc.*, 219 NLRB 119, 89 LRRM 1623 (1975). If however, the purchaser does agree in writing to assume the labor agreement and the union acquiesces, the contract may be asserted as a bar. *American Concrete Pipe of Hawaii, Inc.*, 128 NLRB 720, 46 LRRM 1373 (1960).

[98]*Cf. Boston Gas Co.*, 235 NLRB 1354, 98 LRRM 1146 (1978). *See generally* THE DEVELOPING LABOR LAW at 369–371 and cases cited therein.

[99]*Lammert Indus. v. NLRB*, 578 F.2d 1223, 98 LRRM 2992 (7th Cir. 1978).

[100]*Universal Sec. Instruments, Inc. v. NLRB*, 649 F.2d 247, 107 LRRM 2518 (4th Cir. 1981).

[101]Section 8(f) of the Act authorizes "prehire" agreements in the construction industry— i.e., agreements executed with a minority union before any or most employees have been hired. Until the union is able to demonstrate majority support such agreements will not bar an election petition. *Sunray Ltd.*, 258 NLRB 517, 108 LRRM 1129 (1981); *Mishara Constr. Co.*, 171 NLRB 471, 68 LRRM 1120 (1968).

not bar an election petition. A substantial increase exists if over 70 percent of the employees are hired after the contract is executed, or if there is a change in over 50 percent of the job classifications.[102]

(f) As Bar to Representation of Excluded Groups.   In *Briggs Indiana Corp.*, 63 NLRB 1270, 17 LRRM 46 (1945), the Board held that where a union promises not to represent certain employees during the term of its collective bargaining agreement, the Board will not during the term of that agreement entertain a petition by the union seeking to represent such employees.[103] The *Briggs Indiana* rule

> "will be applied only where the contract itself contains an *express* promise on the part of the union to refrain from seeking representation of the employees in question or to refrain from accepting them into membership; such a promise will not be implied from a mere unit exclusion, nor will the rule be applied on the basis of an alleged understanding of the parties during contract negotiations."[104]

§5.9   Pendency of Other Proceedings

Pursuant to its "blocking charge" doctrine, the Board generally will hold a representation case in abeyance where unfair labor practice charges have been filed by a party to the representation case that are based upon conduct serious enough to have a tendency to interfere with employee free choice in an election.[105] Charges alleging (1) company domination of a labor organization (Section 8(a)(2)), (2) bad faith bargaining by either the company or the union (Sections 8(a)(5) and (b)(3)), or (3) recognitional or organizational picketing by a union (Section 8(b)(7)) will block the processing of a petition even when filed by a person not a party to the representation proceeding. In the Board's view the nature of these violations and the remedies which could be imposed might condition or preclude the existence of the question concerning representation sought to be raised by the petition.[106]

If upon investigation of the charges the regional director concludes that they lack merit, processing of the representation case generally will be resumed. This is true notwithstanding the fact that

---

[102]*California Labor Indus., Inc.*, 249 NLRB 600, 104 LRRM 1179 (1980); *West Penn Hat and Cap Corp.*, 165 NLRB 543, 65 LRRM 1417 (1967); *General Extrusion Co.*, 121 NLRB 1165, 42 LRRM 1508 (1958).

[103]*United Broadcasting Co.*, 223 NLRB 908, 92 LRRM 1141 (1976). *See also Allis-Chalmers Mfg. Co.*, 179 NLRB 1, 72 LRRM 1241 (1967).

[104]*Cessna Aircraft Co.*, 123 NLRB 855, 857, 44 LRRM 1001, 1002 (1959); *United Broadcasting Co.*, 223 NLRB 908, 92 LRRM 1141 (1976).

[105]*Carson Pirie Scott & Co.*, 69 NLRB 935, 17 LRRM 44 (1946); *United States Coal and Coke Co.*, 3 NLRB 398, 1A LRRM 551 (1937). The blocking charge doctrine does not apply to Sec. 8(e) unfair labor practice charges filed by the employer. *Holt Bros.*, 146 NLRB 383, 55 LRRM 1310 (1964).

[106]*Big Three Indus., Inc.*, 201 NLRB 197, 82 LRRM 1411 (1973).

the regional director's dismissal of the charges has been appealed to the General Counsel.[107] If, on the other hand, the regional director finds that the charges are meritorious and decides to issue a complaint, the representation petition will be held in abeyance pending final disposition of the complaint. If the allegations found meritorious involve refusals to bargain (Sections 8(a)(5) or (b)(3)) or employer domination of the petitioning union (Section 8(a)(2)), the petition will be dismissed rather than held in abeyance; it may, however, be reinstated by the petitioner upon final disposition of the unfair labor practice case.[108]

There are four exceptions to the blocking charge rule in which the Board will continue to process the election petition notwithstanding the pendency of the unfair labor practice charges:

- When the charging party requests that the representation case continue by filing a request to proceed. (See Exhibit 9.) By filing a request to proceed the charging party specifically waives any right to rely upon the alleged unfair labor practice as a basis for objections to the election.[109] In Section 8(a)(2), (a)(5), or (b)(3) situations where the nature of the allegations, if established, would condition or preclude the existence of a question concerning representation, requests to proceed normally will not be honored absent specific authorization by the Board.[110]

- When the regional director feels that under the circumstances employees could exercise their free choice in an election notwithstanding the pendency of the charge.[111] Advice from the Board often is sought by the director. Among the factors to be considered are the character and scope of the charge and its tendency to impair the employees' free choice; the size of the unit and the number of employees involved in the events upon which the charge is based; the interest of the employees in an

---

[107]NLRB Casehandling Manual ¶11730.2; *Stewart-Warner Corp.*, 112 NLRB 1222, 36 LRRM 1176 (1955). If the charges on appeal involve allegations of Sec. 8(a)(2), (a)(5), (b)(3), or (b)(7), Board approval must be secured before an election can be conducted.

[108]NLRB Casehandling Manual ¶11730.3. A regional director's decision to dismiss a petition or hold it in abeyance pending disposition of meritorious unfair labor practice charges may be appealed to the Board. *See* NLRB Casehandling Manual ¶11730.11; NLRB Rules and Regulations §102.71(b). There is little practical difference between the Board's holding a petition in abeyance or dismissing it subject to reinstatement upon application of the petitioner after disposition of the unfair labor practice proceeding. NLRB Casehandling Manual ¶11730.11 assures notification to the petitioner of the disposition of the charge by requiring that the petitioner "be considered a party in interest in the ULP proceeding with an interest limited solely to receipt of a copy of the order or other document which operates to finally dispose of the proceeding."

[109]Regional directors also are authorized, upon Board approval, to honor the waiver of a petitioner who indicates a willingness to withdraw a Sec. 8(a)(2) assistance charge in the event the allegedly assisted union is certified. NLRB Casehandling Manual ¶11730.4; *Carlson Furniture Indus., Inc.*, 157 NLRB 851, 61 LRRM 1457 (1966). Charging parties who withdraw refusal to bargain or unlawful domination or assistance charges, however, may not be able to reinstate them after the election. *Fernandes Supermarkets, Inc.*, 203 NLRB 568, 83 LRRM 1138 (1973).

[110]*E. & R. Webb, Inc.*, 194 NLRB 1135, 79 LRRM 1163 (1972).

[111]NLRB Casehandling Manual ¶11730.5.

FORM NLRB-4551
(10-62)

UNITED STATES OF AMERICA
NATIONAL LABOR RELATIONS BOARD

REQUEST TO PROCEED

In the matter of _____

(Name of Case)

_____

(Number of Case)

The undersigned hereby requests the Regional Director to proceed with the above-captioned representation case, notwithstanding the charges of unfair labor practices filed in Case No. _____.

It is understood that the Board will not entertain objections to any election in this matter based upon conduct occurring prior to the filing of the petition.

Date _____

By _____

_____

(Title)

GPO 883-931

Exhibit 9.   Request to Proceed (Form NLRB-4551)

expeditious election; the relationship of the charging parties to the unions involved in the representation case; the showing of interest, if any, demonstrated by the charging party in the representation case; and the timing of the charge.[112]

● When the conditions of the immediately preceding exception are met, the unfair labor practice and representation cases raise common issues, and the regional director feels that processing the representation case will also resolve issues in the unfair labor practice case.[113]

● When an election has been scheduled and unfair labor practice charges are filed too close to the election to permit a thorough investigation, the regional director may (1) postpone the election pending disposition of the charges, (2) hold the election and impound the ballots until the charges are resolved, or (3) conduct the election, issue a certification if the union wins, and then proceed with the investigation of the charges.[114]

Once the blocking charges have been resolved the representation proceeding may be resumed. Where the respondent in the unfair labor practice case has taken all appropriate remedial measures but the time for posting the required notice has not yet expired, the regional director may conduct a hearing, negotiate a consent election agreement, or issue a decision either directing an election or dismissing the petition. Absent a waiver from the charging party, however, the actual election will not be conducted until after the expiration of the posting period.[115]

§5.10 Fluctuating Workforce

The regional director will dismiss a petition which requests an election in an inappropriate bargaining unit, a one-person unit,[116] or in a unit with a fluctuating workforce. An election will be directed only if it appears that there is a substantial and representative employee complement in the bargaining unit.[117] In situations where a substantial and representative complement does not exist, the general practice is to dismiss the petition as untimely rather

---

[112]*Id.*

[113]NLRB Casehandling Manual ¶11730.6; *Panda Terminals*, 161 NLRB 1215, 63 LRRM 1419 (1966); *Krist Gradis, et al.*, 121 NLRB 601, 42 LRRM 1395 (1958).

[114]NLRB Casehandling Manual ¶11730.7.

[115]*Id.* at ¶11730.8. Where the remedy in the unfair labor practice case includes an order directing the employer to withdraw and withhold recognition of a union until it has been certified, neither an RC petition filed by that union nor an RM petition filed by the employer will be accepted until after the expiration of the posting period. Any showing of interest in support of the RC petition also must be dated after the expiration of the posting period. *Id.*

[116]*Roman Catholic Orphan Asylum*, 229 NLRB 251, 95 LRRM 1118 (1977).

[117]*K-P Hydraulics Co.*, 219 NLRB 138, 89 LRRM 1601 (1975).

than direct an election at a future date.[118] The dismissal, however, will be without prejudice to its being refiled at a more appropriate time.

The Board examines both the percentage of the employee complement and the percentage of the job classifications filled in determining whether a substantial and reasonable complement exists. The *General Extrusion* standards for use in contract bar situations[119] do not necessarily apply to the determination of whether an election should be conducted in an expanding unit.[120] Instead, the Board considers one or more of the following factors:

- The size of the employee complement at the time the election is directed which may be more substantial and representative than at the time of the hearing.[121]

- Whether the jobs which remain to be filled entail responsibilities and require skills which are similar to those already occupied; if so, a substantial and representative complement finding is more likely.[122]

- The timing of the unit expansion. A two-year expansion period has been found to be too long to deny current employees an election, while a one-year date has been deemed "a more realistic date for measuring the substantiality of the present force."[123]

- The definiteness of the employer's expansion plans. An election petition will not be dismissed on the basis of plans which are speculative.[124]

The guidelines which the Board has established for the dismissal of petitions in expanding units apply equally to situations in which the unit is contracting.[125] In cases where the expanding and contracting work force results from the seasonal nature of the employer's business, the Board will direct that the election be held at or about the seasonal peak.[126]

---

[118]*Id.*

[119]See note 102 *supra.*

[120]*Bell Aerospace Co.,* 190 NLRB 509, 77 LRRM 1278 (1971); *Endicott Johnson de Puerto Rico, Inc.,* 172 NLRB 1676, 69 LRRM 1002 (1968).

[121]*Bell Aerospace Co.,* 190 NLRB 509, 77 LRRM 1278 (1971); *Celotex Corp.,* 180 NLRB 62, 72 LRRM 1583 (1969).

[122]*Frolic Footwear, Inc.,* 180 NLRB 188, 72 LRRM 1611 (1969); *Redman Indus., Inc.,* 174 NLRB 1065, 70 LRRM 1404 (1969).

[123]*Gerlach Meat Co.,* 192 NLRB 559, 77 LRRM 1832 (1971); *Bekaert Steel Wire Corp.,* 189 NLRB 561, 76 LRRM 1698 (1971).

[124]*Canterbury of Puerto Rico, Inc.,* 225 NLRB 309, 92 LRRM 1486 (1976); *Meramec Mining Co.,* 134 NLRB 1675, 49 LRRM 1386 (1961).

[125]*Plum Creek Lumber Co.,* 214 NLRB 619, 87 LRRM 1587 (1974).

[126]*Dick Kelchner Excavating Co.,* 236 NLRB 1414, 98 LRRM 1442 (1978); *Cleveland Cliffs Iron Co.,* 117 NLRB 668, 39 LRRM 1319 (1957).

Filing of Petition

§5.11 Where to File and Contents of Petition

The petition is filed in person or by mail with the NLRB regional office in the region in which the bargaining unit is located. The location of these offices and the areas they cover are set forth in Appendix E. If the proposed unit is located in two or more regions, the petition may be filed in any one of the regions.[127] The General Counsel also may permit a petition to be filed in Washington, D.C., when necessary to effectuate the purposes of the Act or avoid unnecessary expense or delay.[128] Assistance in the preparation of the petition will be furnished by personnel in the regional office upon request. If a petition is filed through the mails, it is suggested, though not required, that it be sent by registered or certified mail. The petition form, in brief, contains the name and address of the filing party, the name and address of the employer's establishment, a description of the unit claimed to be appropriate, the approximate number of employees involved, and the names of all labor organizations which claim to represent the employees.[129] (See Exhibit 10.)

While attention to filing requirements is encouraged, the Board has held that a petition can be valid where blanks are left unanswered,[130] or where there are technical defects such as failure to indicate the number of employees supporting the petition or the fact that a request for recognition has been made to the employer.[131] While the validity of the petition is usually upheld where the defects are cured at the subsequent hearing,[132] it is better practice to fill out the form completely and special care should be taken to show the employer's name accurately. If the petitioner is aware of claims by other unions to represent the same employees, those claims must be disclosed to the Board.[133] Where the petitioner has withheld such information, the Board has set aside the election.[134]

In filling out the petition, particular care should be taken in describing the desired unit of employees; inaccurate or ambiguous language may: (1) invite argument as to the employees covered and thus block the possibility of complete agreement on a consent election; (2) lead to intervention from other labor organizations; (3) render the

---

[127]NLRB Rules and Regulations §102.60; *National Van Lines*, 117 NLRB 1213, 39 LRRM 1408 (1957).

[128]NLRB Rules and Regulations §102.72(a).

[129]*Id.* at §102.61.

[130]*Petco Corp.*, 98 NLRB 150, 29 LRRM 1311 (1952).

[131]*Padgett Printing and Lithographing Co.*, 101 NLRB 144, 31 LRRM 1024 (1952).

[132]*NLRB v. National Truck Rental Co.*, 239 F.2d 422, 38 LRRM 2781 (D.C. Cir. 1956).

[133]*Somerville Iron Works, Inc.*, 117 NLRB 1702, 40 LRRM 1073 (1957).

[134]*Id.*

FORM NLRB-502
(11-64)

UNITED STATES OF AMERICA
NATIONAL LABOR RELATIONS BOARD

FORM EXEMPT UNDER
44 U.S.C. 3512

PETITION

DO NOT WRITE IN THIS SPACE
CASE NO.
DATE FILED

INSTRUCTIONS.—Submit an original and four (4) copies of this Petition to the NLRB Regional Office in the Region in which the employer concerned is located.
If more space is required for any one item, attach additional sheets, numbering item accordingly.

The Petitioner alleges that the following circumstances exist and requests that the National Labor Relations Board proceed under its proper authority pursuant to Section 9 of the National Labor Relations Act.

1. Purpose of this Petition *(If box RC, RM, or RD is checked and a charge under Section 8(b) (7) of the Act has been filed involving the Employer named herein, the statement following the description of the type of petition shall not be deemed made.)*
(Check one)

☐ RC—CERTIFICATION OF REPRESENTATIVE —A substantial number of employees wish to be represented for purposes of collective bargaining by Petitioner and Petitioner desires to be certified as representative of the employees.

☐ RM—REPRESENTATION (EMPLOYER PETITION)—One or more individuals or labor organizations have presented a claim to Petitioner to be recognized as the representative of employees of Petitioner.

☐ RD—DECERTIFICATION—A substantial number of employees assert that the certified or currently recognized bargaining representative is no longer their representative.

☐ UD—WITHDRAWAL OF UNION SHOP AUTHORITY—Thirty percent (30%) or more of employees in a bargaining unit covered by an agreement between their employer and a labor organization desire that such authority be rescinded.

☐ UC—UNIT CLARIFICATION—A labor organization is currently recognized by employer, but petitioner seeks clarification of placement of certain employees: *(Check one)* ☐ In unit not previously certified
☐ In unit previously certified in Case No. _____.

☐ AC—AMENDMENT OF CERTIFICATION—Petitioner seeks amendment of certification issued in Case No._____.

Attach statement describing the specific amendment sought.

2. NAME OF EMPLOYER	EMPLOYER REPRESENTATIVE TO CONTACT	PHONE NO.

3. ADDRESS(ES) OF ESTABLISHMENT(S) INVOLVED *(Street and number, city, State, and ZIP Code)*

4a. TYPE OF ESTABLISHMENT *(Factory, mine, wholesaler, etc.)*	4b. IDENTIFY PRINCIPAL PRODUCT OR SERVICE

5. Unit Involved *(In UC petition, describe PRESENT bargaining unit and attach description of proposed clarification.)*

Included

Excluded

6a. NUMBER OF EMPLOYEES IN UNIT:

PRESENT _____

PROPOSED (BY UC/AC)
_____

6b. IS THIS PETITION SUPPORTED BY 30% OR MORE OF THE EMPLOYEES IN THE UNIT?*

☐ YES ☐ NO

*Not applicable in RM, UC, and AC.

(If you have checked box RC in 1 above, check and complete EITHER item 7a or 7b, whichever is applicable)

7a. ☐ Request for recognition as Bargaining Representative was made on .... and Employer
(Month, day, year)
declined recognition on or about .... *(If no reply received, so state)*
(Month, day, year)

7b. ☐ Petitioner is currently recognized as Bargaining Representative and desires certification under the act.

8. Recognized or Certified Bargaining Agent *(If there is none, so state)*

NAME	AFFILIATION
ADDRESS	DATE OF RECOGNITION OR CERTIFICATION

9. DATE OF EXPIRATION OF CURRENT CONTRACT, IF ANY *(Show month, day, and year)*	10. IF YOU HAVE CHECKED BOX UD IN 1 ABOVE, SHOW HERE THE DATE OF EXECUTION OF AGREEMENT GRANTING UNION SHOP *(Month, day, and year)*

11a. IS THERE NOW A STRIKE OR PICKETING AT THE EMPLOYER'S ESTABLISHMENT(S) INVOLVED? YES .... NO	11b. IF SO, APPROXIMATELY HOW MANY EMPLOYEES ARE PARTICIPATING?

11c. THE EMPLOYER HAS BEEN PICKETED BY OR ON BEHALF OF .... A LABOR
ORGANIZATION, OF .... *(Insert name)* SINCE ....
(Insert address) *(Month, day, year)*

12. ORGANIZATIONS OR INDIVIDUALS OTHER THAN PETITIONER (AND OTHER THAN THOSE NAMED IN ITEMS 8 AND 11c), WHICH HAVE CLAIMED RECOGNITION AS REPRESENTATIVES AND OTHER ORGANIZATIONS AND INDIVIDUALS KNOWN TO HAVE A REPRESENTATIVE INTEREST IN ANY EMPLOYEES IN THE UNIT DESCRIBED IN ITEM 5 ABOVE. (IF NONE, SO STATE.)

NAME	AFFILIATION	ADDRESS	DATE OF CLAIM *(Required only if Petition is filed by Employer)*

I declare that I have read the above petition and that the statements therein are true to the best of my knowledge and belief.

....
(Petitioner and affiliation, if any)

By...   ....
(Signature of representative or person filing petition)   *(Title, if any)*

Address ....
(Street and number, city, State, and ZIP Code)   *(Telephone number)*

WILLFULLY FALSE STATEMENT ON THIS PETITION CAN BE PUNISHED BY FINE AND IMPRISONMENT (U.S. CODE, TITLE 18, SECTION 1001)

GPO 883-928

Exhibit 10.   Petition Used in Election, Decertification, Union Shop Deauthorization, Unit Clarification, and Amendment of Certification Cases   (Form NLRB-502)

unit inappropriate under the provisions of the statute or the Board's rulings; or (4) provide a basis for challenging ballots.

The petitioner's description of the bargaining unit should include sufficient detail to make identification of the included employees as simple as possible. Also, the classifications of employees to be excluded from the unit should be specified. For example, where a unit of "production and maintenance employees" is sought, the petitioner also should indicate such exclusions as "all guards, professional employees, and supervisors as defined in the Act." A petition will not be dismissed, however, because it fails to list such exclusions.[135]

§5.12 Showing of Interest

(a) In General. The Act itself does not require that election petitions be accompanied by evidence of employee interest in acquiring or retaining union representation. The Board, however, administratively has imposed a "showing of interest" requirement to limit elections to those situations where there is sufficient employee interest in an election to justify expenditure of the Board's resources.[136] Of course, it is the result of the election and not the showing of interest which determines the union's majority status.[137]

The showing of interest is a nonlitigable administrative matter to be determined by the Board. (See Exhibit 11.) While information offered by any party bearing on the validity of the showing of interest generally is received by the Board, weighed, and if appropriate acted upon, there is no right in any party to litigate the subject either directly in the representation case or collaterally in a related case.[138] Thus, the showing submitted by the petitioner is always held in confidence by the Board,[139] and no party has the right to litigate such issues as the adequacy of the showing of interest,[140] timeliness of its submission,[141] currency of dates,[142] authenticity,[143] or subsequent revocation of authorizations.[144]

---

[135]*See Sealed Power Corp.*, NLRB Case No. 7-RC-2109, 32 LRRM 1186 (1953).

[136]*NLRB v. Metro-Truck Body, Inc.*, 613 F.2d 746, 104 LRRM 2498 (9th Cir. 1980); *Big Y Foods Inc.*, 238 NLRB 855, 99 LRRM 1299 (1978). *See generally* NLRB Casehandling Manual ¶¶11020–11039; *S.H. Kress & Co.*, 137 NLRB 1244, 50 LRRM 1361 (1962).

[137]*Northeastern Univ.*, 218 NLRB 247, 89 LRRM 1862 (1975).

[138]NLRB Casehandling Manual ¶¶11020, 11028.4; *NLRB v. J. I. Case Co.*, 201 F.2d 597, 31 LRRM 2330 (9th Cir. 1953).

[139]*The Midvale Co.*, 114 NLRB 372, 36 LRRM 1575 (1955).

[140]*Modern Plastics Corp.*, 169 NLRB 716, 67 LRRM 1261 (1968); *Morganton Full Fashioned Hosiery Co.*, 102 NLRB 134, 31 LRRM 1288 (1953).

[141]*Rappahannock Sportswear Co.*, 163 NLRB 703, 64 LRRM 1417 (1967); *Wyman-Gordon Co.*, 117 NLRB 75, 39 LRRM 1176 (1957).

[142]*Cleveland Cliffs Iron Co.*, 117 NLRB 668, 39 LRRM 1319 (1957).

[143]*Riviera Manor Nursing Home*, 200 NLRB 333, 81 LRRM 1411 (1972); *Barber-Colman Co.*, 130 NLRB 478, 47 LRRM 1373 (1961).

[144]*Reliable Mailing Serv. Co.*, 113 NLRB 1263, 36 LRRM 1459 (1955).

FORM NLRB-4069
(9-83)

UNITED STATES OF AMERICA
NATIONAL LABOR RELATIONS BOARD

Case

REPORT ON INVESTIGATION OF INTEREST

The undersigned agent of the National Labor Relations Board has investigated the evidence of representation submitted by the labor organization(s) claiming an interest in the above-entitled case. The statistical results of this investigation are set forth below.

1. The following organizations were requested in writing on the indicated dates to submit evidence of representation, if any, but have failed to do so.

Name and Affiliation of Labor Organization	Date of Request

2. a. Designation and payroll information pertaining to the unit claimed appropriate by the labor organization listed in the first column according to a *(Complete) (Spot)* check of the employer's payroll for the period ending _____ , 19____.
   b. Although requested, no payroll list submitted. ☐ *(Check here)*

NAME OF UNION *(Abbreviate)*	NUMBER OF EMPLOYEES IN UNIT	Percent of names in claimed unit found on payroll among the timely designations submitted by each union *(if interest is based on contract, so indicate)*			
		Indicate Category 1, 2, or 3			
		1. LESS THAN 10% **2. 10% TO LESS THAN 30%**		**3. 30% OR ABOVE**	
A		UNION **A** CATEGORY _____ DESIGNATIONS ARE CURRENT: ☐ CHECK HERE	UNION **B**	UNION **C**	UNION **D**
B		UNION **B** CATEGORY _____ DESIGNATIONS ARE CURRENT: ☐ CHECK HERE	UNION **A**	UNION **C**	UNION **D**
C		UNION **C** CATEGORY _____ DESIGNATIONS ARE CURRENT: ☐ CHECK HERE	UNION **A**	UNION **B**	UNION **D**
D		UNION **D** CATEGORY _____ DESIGNATIONS ARE CURRENT: ☐ CHECK HERE	UNION **A**	UNION **B**	UNION **C**

3. Unit(s) different from those claimed by the unions listed above, contended as appropriate by the employer.

TYPE OF UNIT CLAIMED APPROPRIATE	NUMBER OF EMPLOYEES IN UNIT	UNION **A**	UNION **B**	UNION **C**	UNION **D**

GPO 902-572

_____   _____
(Date of Report)   *(Board Agent)*

Exhibit 11.   Report on Investigation of Interest   (Form NLRB-4069)

(b) Extent of Interest Required by Petitioners. The extent
of the showing of interest which is required depends upon both the
type of election sought and whether the party submitting the showing
is a petitioner or intervenor. The rules for petitioners are as follows:

- *"RC" Petition.* If the petition is filed by an employee, a group
of employees, or a labor organization and the petitioner is not a party
to a current or recently expired contract, it must be accompanied by
a showing that at least 30 percent of the employees in the appropriate
unit desire the union to be their bargaining agent or wish to have
an NLRB election to make such a determination.[145] If the petitioning
union is the certified or currently recognized bargaining agent of the
employees involved, or if it is a party to a current or recently expired
contract covering the employees, no additional showing of interest is
necessary.[146]

During a strike, the petition must be accompanied by a showing
of interest of 30 percent of the number employed at the time the
strike began. This 30 percent may come from the strikers, the non-
strikers, the replacements, or any combination thereof.[147] In seasonal
industries, it is sufficient to submit a showing of 30 percent of those
currently employed in the unit at the time the petition is filed; it is
not necessary to submit a 30-percent showing of those employed at
the peak of the season.[148]

Where a joint petition is filed by more than one union seeking
joint representation of the unit employees, it is immaterial whether
the authorization cards indicate a desire for individual or joint representation; all the cards are accepted and counted in support of the
joint petition.[149]

- *"RM" Petition.* When an employer files a petition in response
to a claim for recognition by one or more unions, no showing of
interest is required.[150] When, however, the employer's petition is filed
in order to test the continuing majority status of an incumbent union,
a statement of the objective considerations demonstrating reasonable
grounds for believing that the union has lost its majority support
must be submitted.[151]

- *"RD" Petition.* The petitioner must establish that at least 30
percent of the employees in the bargaining unit support the petition
before a decertification election will be conducted.[152]

---

[145]NLRB Statements of Procedure §101.18. No showing of interest is required when an
expedited election is requested under Sec. 8(b)(7)(C). Expedited elections are discussed at
§§20.9–20.11.

[146]NLRB Casehandling Manual ¶11022.1.

[147]*Id.* at ¶11022.3.

[148]*Bordo Prods. Co.,* 117 NLRB 313, 39 LRRM 1220 (1957).

[149]*St. Louis Indep. Packing Co.,* 169 NLRB 1106, 67 LRRM 1338 (1968); *Vanadium Corp.,*
117 NLRB 1390, 40 LRRM 1010 (1957); *Stickless Corp.,* 115 NLRB 979, 37 LRRM 1466 (1956).

[150]Sec. 9(c)(1)(b); NLRB Casehandling Manual ¶11022.2.

[151]*United States Gypsum Co.,* 157 NLRB 652, 61 LRRM 1384 (1966). This requirement is
discussed further at §5.2 *supra.*

[152]NLRB Statements of Procedure §101.18.

• *"UD" Petition.* Section 9(e)(1) of the Act requires that an election to rescind a union security provision in a labor contract can be conducted only upon the request of 30 percent or more of the employees in the unit.

• *"UC" and "AC" Petitions.* Petitions to clarify or amend an existing certification need not be supported by a showing of interest.[153]

(c) Extent of Interest Required of Intervenors.   A "full intervenor" is a union which seeks intervention for the purpose of blocking a consent election agreement or participating fully in the hearing. A 10-percent showing of interest by the intervenor in the unit claimed by the petitioner is required.[154]

A "participating intervenor" is a union which does not seek to block the consent election, but which does want its name placed on the ballot. So long as one employee in the unit supports the intervening union, it may be accorded a place on the ballot under the terms agreed upon by the other parties and, if a hearing is held, may participate fully.[155]

An intervenor which seeks a unit different from the one sought by the petitioner must make a 30-percent showing of interest in the unit which it seeks.[156] All authorization cards submitted by intervenors must be dated prior to the close of the hearing or execution of a consent election agreement.[157]

(d) Time for Submission of Showing of Interest.   Where an individual, a group of employees, or a labor organization files the petition for an election, the showing of interest must be submitted along with the petition or within 48 hours thereafter, "but in no event later than the last day on which the petition might timely be filed."[158] Upon the failure to produce the data within the 48 hours, the petition is subject to dismissal. However, upon a showing of good cause, the regional director may, prior to dismissal, grant an extension of time within which the data may be submitted.[159] For example, the designations may not be readily available because the employees are scattered over a large area.

Where the employer files the petition for an election, no showing of interest is required but proof must be submitted to the regional

---

[153]*Id.* at §101.17.

[154]NLRB Casehandling Manual ¶11022.3d.

[155]*See Union Carbide & Carbon Corp.,* 89 NLRB 460, 25 LRRM 1585 (1950).

[156]NLRB Casehandling Manual ¶11022.3b; *Great Atl. & Pac. Tea Co.,* 130 NLRB 226, 47 LRRM 1303 (1961).

[157]*Caesar's Palace,* 194 NLRB 818, 79 LRRM 1069 (1972).

[158]NLRB Statements of Procedure §101.17; *Mallinckrodt Chem. Works,* 200 NLRB 1, 81 LRRM 1375 (1972).

[159]NLRB Casehandling Manual ¶11026.1; *Rappahannock Sportswear Co.,* 163 NLRB 703, 64 LRRM 1417 (1967); *Channel Master Corp.,* 114 NLRB 1486, 37 LRRM 1196 (1955).

office of a demand by the labor organization for recognition. If there is an incumbent union, evidence of the objective considerations which justify the employer's doubt concerning the union's continued majority status must be submitted along with the petition or within 48 hours. Such proof may consist of a letter from the union containing the demand, an affidavit of an oral demand, or other evidence which establishes the raising of a question concerning representation. Otherwise, the petition is subject to dismissal.

An intervening union also must submit its evidence of interest at the time intervention is requested or within 48 hours thereafter.[160] An intervenor's showing of interest may be accepted by the regional director notwithstanding expiration of the 48-hour period under the following circumstances:

- If submitted *before* a consent election agreement has been approved or a hearing concluded, full intervention may be granted;
- If submitted *after* the approval of an agreement or the close of a hearing, the union may not participate in the proceedings but may, with the consent of the parties, appear on the ballot; and
- If no preconsent or prehearing notice was given to the intervening union, intervention may be permitted only where the showing of interest predates the approval of the agreement or close of the hearing.[161]

(e) Validity of Showing of Interest. Authorization cards on which employees apply for membership in the labor organization and/or authorize the union to represent them are most frequently submitted as evidence of interest.[162] In passing upon the sufficiency of a petitioner's submitted showing of interest, the Board has established the following principles:

- Authorization cards must be signed and dated;[163]
- Authorization cards are presumed to be valid in the absence of objective considerations questioning their authenticity;[164]
- Authorization cards solicited by supervisors are generally invalid for establishing interest;[165]
- An employee's subjective state of mind in signing an authorization card cannot negate a clear statement on the card that the signer is designating the union as bargaining agent;[166]

---

[160]NLRB Casehandling Manual ¶11024.2.

[161]*Id.* at ¶11026.2.

[162]*Potomac Elec. Power Co.*, 111 NLRB 553, 35 LRRM 1527 (1955).

[163]Casehandling Manual ¶11028.5.

[164]*Id.* at ¶11028.

[165]*Southeastern Newspapers, Inc.*, 129 NLRB 311, 46 LRRM 1541 (1960). *But cf. El Rancho Mkt.*, 235 NLRB 468, 98 LRRM 1153 (1978).

[166]*Gary Steel Prods. Corp.*, 144 NLRB 1160, 54 LRRM 1211 (1963).

- Authorization cards signed by a single employee for more than one union may be counted by both unions;[167]
- Authorization cards should specifically name the petitioning party;[168]
- Authorization cards which name an organizing committee acting on behalf of a petitioning district or local are accepted as evidence of interest;[169]
- Authorization cards which name the petitioner's parent organization are accepted as evidence of petitioner's interest[170] and are added to those cards which designate the petitioning affiliate;[171]
- Authorization cards signed before the petitioner transferred affiliation to another international are not accepted as evidence of the employees' interest in the new affiliation;[172] the Board requires the petitioner to make a new showing;
- Authorization cards signed before the name of the petitioning local was changed to that of another local of the same international are accepted as evidence of a showing of interest;[173]
- Authorizations to revoke checkoff are rejected as evidence of a showing of interest in support of an individual's petition to rescind union shop authority;[174]
- Where a union's petition is dismissed because of an inadequate showing of interest, it may file a new petition supported by the required number of authorization cards.[175] The petitioner in this situation may use the same authorization cards provided the petition is timely and the authorization cards are still current; and
- A valid current or recently expired contract with an employer covering all or part of the employees in the bargaining unit sought may be used as the showing of interest by the union signatory to the agreement.[176]

The petitioner should always remember that where the Board finds appropriate a unit other than the one sought in the petition, the showing of interest originally submitted may be inadequate in

---

[167]*Brooklyn Borough Gas Co.*, 110 NLRB 18, 34 LRRM 1589 (1954).

[168]*Olin Mathieson Chem. Corp.*, 114 NLRB 948, 37 LRRM 1073 (1955).

[169]*Cab Serv. and Parts Corp.*, 114 NLRB 1294, 37 LRRM 1181 (1955).

[170]*United States Gypsum Co.*, 118 NLRB 20, 40 LRRM 1120 (1957).

[171]*NLRB v. Bradford Dyeing Ass'n*, 310 U.S. 318, 6 LRRM 684 (1940).

[172]*Mohawk Business Machs. Corp.*, 118 NLRB 168, 40 LRRM 1145 (1957); NLRB Case-handling Manual ¶11028.

[173]*Atlantic Mills Serv. Corp.*, 118 NLRB 1023, 40 LRRM 1305 (1957).

[174]*Valencia Baxt Express, Inc.*, NLRB Case No. 24-UD-21, 49 LRRM 1446 (1962).

[175]*U.S. Rubber Co.*, 91 NLRB 293, 26 LRRM 1477 (1950).

[176]*Bush Terminal Co.*, 121 NLRB 1170, 42 LRRM 1530 (1958).

the new unit. This may result in either a dismissal of the petition[177] or a later request for submission of an additional showing of interest.[178]

To avoid either result, the petitioner should submit its fullest showing of interest in any possible alternative unit which the petitioner, the employer, or another union may be seeking. Where the alternative unit is smaller than the one set forth in the petition, the showing of interest should be broken down so as to indicate the support in the smaller (e.g., craft) unit or units.

(f) Attack on Showing of Interest. As indicated above, parties cannot, as a matter of right, attack a petitioner's showing of interest.[179] Furthermore, NLRB hearing officers are under instructions not to permit litigation of the showing of interest in a representation hearing,[180] and the Board's Rules and Regulations provide no administrative procedure whereby interest may be contested by a party. However, the Board has conducted special investigations into the nature of the showing of interest (e.g., whether the authorization cards were tainted by supervisory solicitation or were otherwise fraudulent).[181] To obtain such an investigation a party must submit data (e.g., affidavits) which are of sufficient weight to cast doubt on the reliability of the petitioner's showing of interest.[182] This data will not be accepted as evidence at the representation hearing, but should be submitted to the regional director.[183] If the investigation discloses that the remaining valid showing of interest falls below the required 30 percent, the petition will be dismissed.[184] However, if the remaining valid showing of interest satisfies the 30-percent interest requirement, the petition ordinarily will be processed but the invalid portion of the showing may be turned over to a U.S. Attorney for possible prosecution.[185]

---

[177]*E.I. du Pont de Nemours & Co.*, 116 NLRB 286, 38 LRRM 1242 (1956).

[178]*E.I. du Pont de Nemours & Co.*, 117 NLRB 1048, 39 LRRM 1381 (1957); NLRB Casehandling Manual ¶11030.5.

[179]*NLRB v. J. I. Case Co.*, 201 F.2d 597, 31 LRRM 2330 (9th Cir. 1953); see §5.12(a) *supra.*

[180]NLRB Casehandling Manual ¶11028.4; *Plains Coop. Oil Mill*, 123 NLRB 1709, 44 LRRM 1217 (1959).

[181]*Globe Iron Foundry*, 112 NLRB 1200, 36 LRRM 1170 (1955).

[182]*Id. See also Georgia Kraft Co.*, 120 NLRB 806, 42 LRRM 1066 (1958).

[183]*Royal Jet, Inc.*, 113 NLRB 1064, 36 LRRM 1477 (1955).

[184]NLRB Casehandling Manual ¶11028.2; *Columbia Records*, 125 NLRB 1161, 45 LRRM 1244 (1959).

[185]18 U.S.C. §1001; NLRB Casehandling Manual ¶11028.2.

6

Prehearing Handling of the Election Petition

Preliminary Investigation

§6.1 Notification to the Parties

Immediately upon the docketing of a petition for a representation election, a written notification of its filing is sent by the regional director to the employer and to all interested parties.[1] Interested parties include all labor organizations and individuals who claim or who are believed to claim to represent any employee within the unit or whose contractual interests would be affected by the disposition of the petition. Examples include (1) the petitioner; (2) the employer, if other than the petitioner; (3) any individual or labor organization which is a party to a currently existing or recently expired labor contract covering any of the employees in the unit; (4) any labor organization which has notified the regional office within the past six months that it represents or is seeking to represent unit employees; and (5) any labor organization which recently participated in another case involving the same employees.[2]

The notification to the parties contains a copy of the petition and the name of the Board agent to whom the case has been assigned. The parties may be asked to submit certain information including copies of any existing or recently expired contracts, documentary material such as letters which bear upon the question concerning representation, and the names of any other interested persons who should be informed of the proceedings.[3] (See Exhibits 12–14.)

---

[1]NLRB Casehandling Manual ¶11008.
[2]*Id.* at ¶11008.1.
[3]*Id.* at ¶11008.4.

NATIONAL LABOR RELATIONS BOARD

REGION 5

Candler Building - 4th Floor

109 Market Place

Baltimore, MD   21202

January 2, 1986

Mr. Jack Smith, President
Janco Computer Services, Inc.
8181 Greensboro Drive
McLean, VA   22102

Re: Janco Computer Services, Inc.
Case No. 5-RC (RD)-1234

Dear Mr. Smith:

Enclosed is a copy of a petition filed in the above case. Also enclosed is a copy of Form NLRB-4812 pertaining to our procedures.

Investigation of this matter has been assigned to the staff member named below who will communicate with you promptly. However, in order to expedite the processing of this case

> YOU ARE HEREBY NOTIFIED that if, after preliminary investigation, the undersigned has reasonable cause to believe that a question concerning representation exists within the meaning of Section 9(c) and 3(b) of the Act, a Notice of Hearing will issue scheduling a formal hearing in this matter for [date] unless a firm commitment is received from each party within five days that it will waive hearing and enter into an election agreement or good cause is shown within five days why the proposed hearing date cannot be met.

The issuance of the notice of formal hearing in this case does not mean that the matter cannot be disposed of by agreement of the parties. On the contrary, it is the policy of this office to encourage voluntary adjustments. The examiner or attorney assigned to the case will be pleased to receive and to act promptly upon your suggestions or comments to this end. An agreement between the parties, approved by the Regional Director, would serve to cancel the hearing. If a hearing is scheduled, the parties will be contacted by a staff member approximately five (5) days before the hearing date, at which time the parties should be prepared to discuss the matters to be raised at the hearing as well as possible stipulations.

In the interim, please submit as soon as possible to this office the following information

> (a) The attached commerce questionnaire filled out in the appropriate sections;

Exhibit 12.   Letter to Employer When Representation Petition (RC) Filed by Union or Employees, or Decertification Petition Filed (RD)

-2-

(b)   Copies of correspondence and existing or recently-expired collective-bargaining contracts, if any, covering any of the the employees in the unit alleged in the petition;

(c)   An alphabetized list of employees described in the petition, together with their job classifications for the payroll period immediately preceding the date of this letter;

(d)   Your position as to the appropriateness of the unit sought.

In the event an election is agreed to or directed in this case, a list of names and addresses of all the eligible voters must be filed by the Employer with the undersigned, who will in turn make it available to all parties to the case. The list must be furnished to the undersigned within seven (7) days of the direction or approval of agreement for election. We are advising you now of this procedure so that you will have ample time to prepare for the eventuality that such a list may become necessary.

The list referred to in the preceding paragraph is in addition to the list of employees requested in the proposed unit by job classification in Item (c).

Please advise this office if you have information concerning other interested parties who should be apprised of this petition.

It has been our experience that by the time a petition such as this one has been filed, employees also have questions about what is going on and what may happen. At this point in the handling of this case, we, of course, do not know what disposition will be made of the petition, but experience tells us that an explanation of rights, responsibilities, and Board procedures can be helpful to your employees.

The Board believes that employees should have readily-available information about their rights and the proper conduct of employee-representation elections. At the same time, employers and unions should be apprised of their responsibilities to refrain from conduct which could impede employees' freedom of choice. Accordingly, you are requested to post the enclosed Notice to Employees in conspicuous places in areas where employees such as those described in the enclosed petition work and to advise me whether they have been posted. Copies of this notice are being made available to the labor organization(s) involved. In the event an election is not conducted pursuant to this petition, you are requested to remove the posted Notice.

I will appreciate your cooperation in this matter.

Very truly yours,

Louis J. D'Amico
Regional Director

Attachments

CERTIFIED MAIL - RETURN RECEIPT REQUESTED

CASE ASSIGNED TO:
TELEPHONE NUMBER:

Exhibit 12—*page 2*

NATIONAL LABOR RELATIONS BOARD

REGION 5

Candler Building - 4th Floor

109 Market Place

Baltimore, MD 21202

January 2, 1986

Ms. Jean Jones, Business Agent
Local 007
United Computer Operators International Union
P. O. Box 10
Arlington, VA 22207

Re: Janco Computer Services, Inc.
Case No. 5-RM-1234

Dear Ms. Jones:

Attached is a copy of the petition filed in the above case. This case has been assigned to the staff member named below. Also enclosed is a copy of Form NLRB-4812 pertaining to our procedures.

Will you please advise us within 48 hours whether or not you claim an interest among any of the employees involved in this petition. If you have a current or recently-expired collective-bargaining agreement covering any of these employees, please send us a copy of the contract.

It has been our experience that by the time a petition such as this one has been filed, employees may have questions about what is going on and what may happen. At this point in the handling of this case, we of course do not know what disposition will be made of the petition, but experience tells us that an explanation of rights, responsibilities, and Board procedures can be helpful to the employees involved.

The Board believes that employees should have readily available information about their rights and the proper conduct of employee representation elections. At the same time, employers and unions should be apprised of their responsibilities to refrain from conduct which could impede employees' freedom of choice.

Accordingly, the employer has been requested to post the enclosed Notice to Employees in conspicuous places in areas where employees such as those described in the enclosed petition work.

Very truly yours,

Louis J. D'Amico
Regional Director

CERTIFIED MAIL - RETURN RECEIPT REQUESTED

CASE ASSIGNED TO:
TELEPHONE NUMBER:

Exhibit 13. Letter to Union When Representation Petition Filed by Employer (RM)

NATIONAL LABOR RELATIONS BOARD

REGION 5

Candler Building - 4th Floor

109 Market Place

Baltimore, MD   21202

January 2, 1986

Mr. Jack Smith, President
Janco Computer Services, Inc.
8181 Greensboro Drive
McLean, VA 22102

                        Re: Janco Computer Services, Inc.
                             Case No. 5-RM-1234

Dear Mr. Smith:

This is to advise you that the petition which you recently filed in the
above case has been assigned to the staff member named below who will
communicate with you promptly. Enclosed is a copy of Form NLRB-4812
pertaining to our procedures.

Please submit as soon as possible to this office the following information:

    (a) The attached commerce questionnaire filled out in the
        appropriate sections, if you have not submitted such
        information in prior cases;

    (b) Proof of demand for recognition of the labor organization;

    (c) An alphabetized list of employees described in the petition,
        together with their job classifications for the payroll
        period immediately preceding the date of this letter.

In the event an election is agreed to or directed in this case, a list of
names and addresses of all the eligible voters must be filed by the
Employer with the undersigned, who will in turn make it available to all
parties to the case. The list must be furnished to the undersigned within
seven (7) days of the direction or approval of agreement for election. We
are advising you now of this procedure so that you will have ample time to
prepare for the eventuality that such a list may become necessary.

The list referred to in the preceding paragraph is in addition to the list
of employees requested in the proposed unit by job classification in Item
(c).

Please advise this office if you have information concerning other
interested parties who should be apprised of this petition.

**Exhibit 14.   Letter to Employer When Representation Petition Filed by
Employer (RM)**

-2-

It has been our experience that by the time a petition such as this one has been filed, employees also have questions about what is going on and what may happen. At this point in the handling of this case, we of course do not know what disposition will be made of the petition, but experience tells us that an explanation of rights, responsibilities, and Board procedures can be helpful to your employees.

The Board believes that employees should have readily-available information about their rights and the proper conduct of employee-representation elections. At the same time, employers and unions should be apprised of their responsibilities to refrain from conduct which could impede employees' freedom of choice. Accordingly, you are requested to post the enclosed Notice to Employees in conspicuous places in areas where employees such as those described in the enclosed petition work and to advise me whether they have been posted. Copies of this notice are being made available to the labor organization(s) involved. In the event an election is not conducted pursuant to this petition, you are requested to remove the posted Notice.

I will appreciate your cooperation in this matter.

Very truly yours,

Louis J. D'Amico
Regional Director

Enclosures

CERTIFIED MAIL - RETURN RECEIPT REQUESTED

CASE ASSIGNED TO:
TELEPHONE NUMBER:

Exhibit 14—*page 2*

Included with the initial letter to the parties are three other forms. Form 4812 (Exhibit 15) notifies the parties of their right to be represented by counsel and contains a brief statement of representation case procedures. Form 4701, Notice of Appearance, (Exhibit 16) is used by a party to notify the Board of the name and address of counsel or other representative and may be filed at any stage of the proceeding. Form 4813, Notice of Designation of Representative as Agent for Service of Documents, (Exhibit 17) is filed whenever a party wishes to designate its representative as agent for the exclusive service of documents. With the exception of charges, amended charges, subpoenas, directions of elections, or notices of elections which always are served on the parties, all other documents and written communications relating to the proceedings are served on the designated agent.[4]

In addition to the information mentioned above, the employer ordinarily is asked to submit the following:

- Information showing the nature of the company's business and its volume of operations for jurisdictional purposes if such information has not been provided in prior cases.[5] (See Exhibit 18.)
- A payroll list identifying the employees in the alleged bargaining unit alphabetically and by job classification. This list should include those employees employed during the payroll period ending on or immediately preceding the date of the filing of the petition. It will be used to verify the showing of interest submitted in support of the petition.[6] If the employer refuses to supply the list, the petitioner's estimate of the number of employees involved will be viewed as accurate, and those who designate the union as their bargaining agent will be considered to be within the unit. If a strike is in progress the payroll list as of the date of the start of the strike will be requested, as will lists for all other dates on which additional employees joined the strike.
- A position statement on the appropriateness of the bargaining unit requested in the petition and whether or not the employer is willing to consent to an election.[7]

Included in the initial notification to the parties is a request that they post a notice to employees containing information about employee rights and the proper conduct of employee representation elections. (See Exhibit 19.) This is a request only and failure to post the notice is not considered sufficient cause to set aside an election.

---

[4]*Id.* at ¶11008.7.
[5]*Id.* at ¶11009a.
[6]*Id.* at ¶11009c.
[7]*Id.* at ¶11009d.

FORM NLRB-4812
(2 81)

NATIONAL LABOR RELATIONS BOARD

NOTICE: PARTIES INVOLVED IN A REPRESENTATION PETITION SHOULD BE AWARE OF THE FOLLOWING PROCEDURES:

Right to be represented by counsel

Any party has the right to be represented by counsel or other representative in any proceeding before the National Labor Relations Board and the courts. In the event you wish to have a representative appear on your behalf, please have your representative complete Form NLRB-4701, Notice of Appearance, and forward it to the respective regional office as soon as counsel is chosen.

Designation of representative as agent for service of documents

In the event you choose to have a representative appear on your behalf, you may also, if you so desire, use Form NLRB-4813 to designate that representative as your agent to receive exclusive service on your behalf of all formal documents and written communications in the proceeding, excepting decisions directing an election and notices of an election, and further excepting subpoenas, which are served on the person to whom they are addressed. If this form is not filed, both you and your representative will receive copies of all formal documents. If it is filed, copies will be served only upon your representative, and that service will be service upon you under the statute. The designation once filed shall remain valid unless a written revocation is filed with the Regional Director.

Investigation of petition

Immediately upon receipt of the petition, the regional office conducts an impartial investigation to determine if the Board has jurisdiction, whether the petition is timely and properly filed, whether the showing of interest is adequate, and if there are any other interested parties to the proceeding or other circumstances bearing on the question concerning representation.

Withdrawal or dismissal

If it is determined that the Board does not have jurisdiction or that other criteria for proceeding to an election are not met, the petitioner is offered an opportunity to withdraw the petition. Should the petitioner refuse to withdraw, the Regional Director dismisses the petition and advises the petitioner of the reason for the dismissal and of the right to appeal to the Board.

Agreement and conduct of election

Upon the determination that the criteria are met for the Board to conduct a secret ballot election to resolve the question concerning representation, the parties are afforded the opportunity to enter into a consent election agreement. There are two forms: (1) Form NLRB-651, Agreement for Consent Election, provides that the parties accept the final determination of the Regional Director. (2) Form NLRB-652, Stipulation for Certification Upon Agreement for Consent Election, provides for the right of appeal to the Board on postelection matters. The secret ballot election will be conducted by an agent of the NLRB under the terms of the agreement and the parties shall have the right to observe and certify to the conduct of the election.

Hearing

If there are material issues which the parties cannot resolve by agreement, the Regional Director may issue a notice of hearing on the petition. At the hearing, all parties will be afforded the opportunity to state their positions and present evidence on the issues.

Scheduling of a hearing does not preclude the possibility of a consent election agreement. Approval of an agreement will serve as withdrawal of the notice of hearing.

Names and addresses of eligible voters

Upon approval of an election agreement, or upon issuance of a direction of election, the employer will be required to prepare a list of the names and addresses of eligible voters. The employer must file the eligibility list with the Regional Director within seven days after approval of the election agreement, or after the Regional Director or the Board has directed an election. The Regional Director then makes the list available to all other parties. The employer is advised early of this requirement so that there will be ample time to prepare for the eventuality that such a list becomes necessary. *(This list is in addition to list of employees in the proposed unit and their job classifications to be used to verify the showing of interest by a union).*

GPO 879 433

Exhibit 15.   Statement of Procedures in Representation Proceedings (Form NLRB-4812)

FORM NLRB-4701
(3-83)

NATIONAL LABOR RELATIONS BOARD
NOTICE OF APPEARANCE

CASE NO.

TO: *(Check one Box Only)* 1/
☐   REGIONAL DIRECTOR

☐   EXECUTIVE SECRETARY
NATIONAL LABOR RELATIONS BOARD
WASHINGTON, D. C. 20570

☐   GENERAL COUNSEL
NATIONAL LABOR RELATIONS BOARD
WASHINGTON, D. C. 20570

THE UNDERSIGNED HEREBY ENTERS APPEARANCE AS REPRESENTATIVE OF _____

IN THE ABOVE-CAPTIONED MATTER.

SIGNATURE OF REPRESENTATIVE *(PLEASE SIGN IN INK)*	REPRESENTATIVE'S NAME, ADDRESS, ZIP CODE *(PRINT OR TYPE)*
DATE	AREA CODE TELEPHONE NUMBER

1/   IF CASE IS PENDING IN WASHINGTON AND NOTICE OF APPEARANCE IS SENT TO THE GENERAL COUNSEL OR THE EXECUTIVE
SECRETARY A COPY SHOULD BE SENT TO THE REGIONAL DIRECTOR OF THE REGION IN WHICH THE CASE WAS FILED SO THAT
THOSE RECORDS WILL REFLECT THE APPEARANCE.

Exhibit 16.   Notice of Appearance   (Form NLRB-4701)

FORM NLRB-4813
(11-81)

National Labor Relations Board

**NOTICE OF DESIGNATION OF REPRESENTATIVE
AS AGENT FOR SERVICE OF DOCUMENTS**

CASE NO.

TO: Regional Director,

I, the undersigned party, hereby designate my representative, whose name and address appear below and who has entered an appearance on my behalf in this proceeding, as my agent to receive exclusive service of all documents and written communications relating to this proceeding, including complaints and decisions and orders, but not including charges, amended charges, subpoenas, directions of elections or notices of elections, and I authorize the National Labor Relations Board to serve all such documents only on said representative. This designation shall remain valid until a written revocation of it, signed by me, is filed with the Board.

Full name of party	Representative's name, address, zip code *(print or type)*
Signature of party *(please sign in ink)*	
Title	
Date	Area Code / Telephone Number

GPO 906-298

**Exhibit 17.   Notice of Designation of Representative as Agent for
Service of Documents   (Form NLRB-4813)**

FORM NLRB-5081 (8-83)	NATIONAL LABOR RELATIONS BOARD **QUESTIONNAIRE ON COMMERCE INFORMATION**	FORM EXEMPT UNDER 44 U.S.C. 3512

Please read carefully. Answer all applicable items and return to the Regional Office. If additional space is required, use plain bond paper and identify item number.

CASE NAME	CASE NUMBER

1. TYPE OF BUSINESS
   [ ] CORPORATION   [ ] PARTNERSHIP   [ ] SOLE PROPRIETORSHIP

2. CLASSIFICATION WHICH DESCRIBES YOUR BUSINESS

[ ] WHOLESALING	[ ] NEWSPAPER	[ ] OFFICE OF INDUSTRIAL BUILDING	[ ] RETAIL
[ ] HOSPITAL	[ ] HOTEL - MOTEL	[ ] MANUFACTURING/PROCESSING	[ ] SERVICE ORGANIZATION
[ ] TRUCKING	[ ] PUBLIC UTILITY	[ ] BROADCASTING STATION	[ ] NURSING HOME
[ ] TRANSIT SYSTEM	[ ] BUILDING AND CONSTRUCTION	[ ] OTHER *(Describe)*	

3. EXACT LEGAL TITLE OF FIRM

4. IF A CORPORATION

A. INCORPORATED IN STATE OF:	B. NAME(s) AND ADDRESS(es) OF PARENT, SUBSIDIARY, OR RELATED CORPORATION, IF ANY, AND DESCRIBE RELATIONSHIP

5. IF A PARTNERSHIP
   FULL NAME AND COMPLETE ADDRESS OF ALL PARTNERS:

6. IF A PROPRIETORSHIP
   FULL NAME AND COMPLETE ADDRESS OF PROPRIETOR:

7. BRIEFLY DESCRIBE THE NATURE OF YOUR BUSINESS *(General products handled or manufactured, or nature of services performed)*

8. PRINCIPAL PLACE OF BUSINESS LOCATED AT:	BRANCH(es) LOCATED AT:

9. NUMBER OF PERSONNEL PRESENTLY EMPLOYED BY YOUR FIRM

A. TOTAL	B. AT THE ADDRESS INVOLVED IN THIS PROCEEDING:

10. DURING THE PAST [ ] CALENDAR, [ ] FISCAL YEAR *(If Fiscal Year indicate dates)* OR [ ] LAST 12 MONTHS *(Check appropriate box)*:

A. DID GROSS REVENUE FROM SALES OR PERFORMANCE OF SERVICES DIRECTLY TO CUSTOMERS OUTSIDE THE STATE EXCEED $50,000 [ ] YES [ ] NO IF LESS THAN $50,000 INDICATE AMOUNT	$
B. DID GROSS AMOUNT OF PURCHASES OF MATERIALS OR SERVICES DIRECTLY FROM OUTSIDE THE STATE EXCEED $50,000 [ ] YES [ ] NO IF LESS THAN $50,000 INDICATE AMOUNT	$
C. DID GROSS REVENUE FROM YOUR SALES OR PERFORMANCE OF SERVICES EQUAL OR EXCEED $50,000 TO FIRMS WHICH DIRECTLY MADE SALES TO CUSTOMERS OUTSIDE THE STATE AND/OR TO CUSTOMERS WHICH MADE PURCHASES FROM DIRECTLY OUTSIDE THE STATE [ ] YES [ ] NO IF LESS THAN $50,000 INDICATE AMOUNT	$
D. IF THE ANSWER TO 10(c) IS NO, DID GROSS REVENUE FROM SALES OR PERFORMANCE OF SERVICES EQUAL OR EXCEED $50,000 TO PUBLIC UTILITIES, TRANSIT SYSTEMS, NEWSPAPERS, HEALTH CARE INSTITUTIONS, BROADCASTING STATIONS, COMMERCIAL BUILDINGS, EDUCATIONAL INSTITUTIONS AND/OR RETAIL CONCERNS [ ] YES [ ] NO IF LESS THAN $50,000 INDICATE AMOUNT	$
E. DID GROSS AMOUNT OF YOUR PURCHASES EQUAL OR EXCEED $50,000 FROM FIRMS WHICH IN TURN, PURCHASED THOSE GOODS DIRECTLY FROM OUTSIDE THE STATE [ ] YES [ ] NO IF LESS THAN $50,000 INDICATE AMOUNT	$
F. GROSS REVENUE FROM ALL SALES OR PERFORMANCE OF SERVICES *(Check largest amount which firm equaled or exceeded)*: [ ] $100,000 [ ] $200,000 [ ] $250,000 [ ] $500,000 [ ] $1,000,000 IF LESS THAN $100,000 INDICATE AMOUNT	$

11. ARE YOU A MEMBER OF, OR PARTICIPATE IN, AN ASSOCIATION OR OTHER EMPLOYER GROUP THAT ENGAGES IN COLLECTIVE BARGAINING?
    [ ] YES   [ ] NO   *(If Yes, give Name and Address of association or group)*.

12. DID FIRM PERFORM NATIONAL DEFENSE WORK DURING THE PERIOD INDICATED IN 10 ABOVE? [ ] YES [ ] NO *(If Yes, amount of dollar volume and name(s) and address(es) for whom work was performed)*.	$

13. PROVIDE NAME & TITLE OF YOUR REPRESENTATIVE BEST QUALIFIED TO GIVE FURTHER INFORMATION CONCERNING THE OPERATIONS OF YOUR BUSINESS

NAME	TITLE	TELEPHONE NUMBER

SIGNATURE OR AUTHORIZED REPRESENTATIVE COMPLETING THIS QUESTIONNAIRE

NAME AND TITLE *(Type or Print)*	SIGNATURE	DATE

GPO : 1983 O - 413-948

Exhibit 18.   Questionnaire on Commerce Information   (Form NLRB-5081)

NOTICE TO EMPLOYEES

FROM THE

National Labor Relations Board

A PETITION has been filed with this Federal agency seeking an election to determine whether certain employees want to be represented by a union.

The case is being investigated and NO DETERMINATION HAS BEEN MADE AT THIS TIME by the National Labor Relations Board. IF an election is held Notices of Election will be posted giving complete details for voting.

It was suggested that your employer post this notice so the National Labor Relations Board could inform you of your basic rights under the National Labor Relations Act.

YOU HAVE THE RIGHT under Federal Law

- To self-organization
- To form, join, or assist labor organizations
- To bargain collectively through representatives of your own choosing
- To act together for the purposes of collective bargaining or other mutual aid or protection
- To refuse to do any or all of these things unless the union and employer, in a state where such agreements are permitted, enter into a lawful union security clause requiring employees to join the union.

It is possible that some of you will be voting in an employee representation election as a result of the request for an election having been filed. While NO DETERMINATION HAS BEEN MADE AT THIS TIME, in the event an election is held, the NATIONAL LABOR RELATIONS BOARD wants all eligible voters to be familiar with their rights under the law IF it holds an election.

The Board applies rules which are intended to keep its elections fair and honest and which result in a free choice. If agents of either Unions or Employers act in such a way as to interfere with your right to a free election, the election can be set aside by the Board. Where appropriate the Board provides other remedies, such as reinstatement for employees fired for exercising their rights, including backpay from the party responsible for their discharge.

NOTE:

The following are examples of conduct which interfere with the rights of employees and may result in the setting aside of the election.

- Threatening loss of jobs or benefits by an Employer or a Union
- Promising or granting promotions, pay raises, or other benefits, to influence an employee's vote by a party capable of carrying out such promises
- An Employer firing employees to discourage or encourage union activity or a Union causing them to be fired to encourage union activity
- Making campaign speeches to assembled groups of employees on company time within the 24-hour period before the election
- Incitement by either an Employer or a Union of racial or religious prejudice by inflammatory appeals
- Threatening physical force or violence to employees by a Union or an Employer to influence their votes

Please be assured that IF AN ELECTION IS HELD every effort will be made to protect your right to a free choice under the law. Improper conduct will not be permitted. All parties are expected to cooperate fully with this agency in maintaining basic principles of a fair election as required by law. The National Labor Relations Board as an agency of the United States Government does not endorse any choice in the election.

NATIONAL LABOR RELATIONS BOARD

an agency of the

UNITED STATES GOVERNMENT

THIS IS AN OFFICIAL GOVERNMENT NOTICE AND MUST NOT BE DEFACED BY ANYONE

Exhibit 19.   Notice to Employees   (Form NLRB-666)

Finally, the initial letter advises the employer that at some point in the future it will be required to furnish to the regional director a list of the names and addresses of all eligible voters in the event that an election is directed or a consent election agreement is approved. This list, generally referred to as the *Excelsior* list, must be filed with the regional director within seven days of the direction of, or agreement to, an election.[8] The names and addresses should be listed in a systematic manner (e.g., alphabetically, or by time clock or card numbers, either as a whole unit or by departments). This list will be used as the voting list and should be kept up to date.

§6.2　The Board Agent's Investigation

Approximately three days after the petition and notification are sent to the parties the Board agent will begin a preliminary investigation.[9] In general, this investigation is designed to determine whether the Board has jurisdiction, whether the petition has been properly filed, and whether there is any possibility that the parties will be able to consent to an election.[10] Thus, the Board agent's inquiries will focus on the following types of issues:

- Whether the employer's operations affect commerce within the meaning of the statute.
- Whether the union qualifies as a labor organization.
- Whether the petition has been timely filed.
- Where a labor organization is petitioning for the election, whether there is a valid showing of interest from at least 30 percent of the employees in the requested unit.
- Where an employer is the petitioner, whether a demand for collective bargaining rights has been made or whether objective evidence has been submitted to support a claim that the incumbent union's continued majority status is in doubt.
- If a strike is currently taking place, all pertinent data, including date of commencement of the strike, nature of the strike, number of employees, and whether strikers have been replaced.[11]
- The extent to which intervenors may participate in the proceedings.
- The appropriateness of the requested bargaining unit.

---

[8]The list derives its name from *Excelsior Underwear, Inc.*, 156 NLRB 1236, 61 LRRM 1217 (1966). The *Excelsior* list is discussed in NLRB Casehandling Manual ¶11312 and at §9.1.

[9]NLRB Casehandling Manual ¶11010.

[10]See discussion of consent election procedures at §§6.8–6.10 *infra; see also* NLRB Statements of Procedure §101.18(a).

[11]Sec. 9(c)(3).

Frequently the Board agent will rely on telephone consultations, information submitted in response to the regional director's initial letter, or personal contact with individual parties in making these determinations, but joint conferences of the parties also may be arranged. The informal conferences are intended to determine the respective positions of the parties and to secure pertinent information. If it appears that the petition should be dismissed, the Board agent will recommend to the petitioner that the petition be amended to eliminate the perceived defect, or if it cannot be cured by amendment, that it be withdrawn voluntarily. If, on the other hand, it appears that the petition is valid, the Board agent will encourage the parties to consent to an election in order to avoid the time and expense of a formal hearing.

§6.3 Amendment of Petition

The petition may be amended at any time prior to a hearing and may be amended during the hearing at the discretion of the hearing officer.[12] If the petition is amended after the issuance of a notice of hearing but before the hearing opens, the regional director will amend the notice of hearing.[13]

In some instances an amendment may be required as a result of events which occur during the proceedings. For example, if the bargaining unit described in a consent election agreement or the unit requested during a hearing departs substantially from that set forth in the petition, the petition description should be amended.[14]

A petition is amended by typing "Amended" (or "Second Amended," "Third Amended," etc.) before the word "Petition" on the petition form and by rewriting the contents of the petition to reflect the desired changes. A document supplementing the original petition which merely describes additions or deletions to be made should not be used.[15] As with the original petition, it is perfectly proper for the petitioner to ask the assistance of the Board agent in preparing the amendment. In the event the petitioner seeks a unit larger than the one originally requested, a 30-percent showing of support in the larger unit is required.[16]

Informal Disposition of Petitions

A petition may be disposed of before a formal hearing in four ways: (1) withdrawal of the petition by the petitioning party; (2)

---

[12]NLRB Statements of Procedure §101.18(a); NLRB Casehandling Manual ¶11014; *Atlantic Richfield Co.*, 208 NLRB 142, 85 LRRM 1222 (1974); *Peabody Coal Co.*, 197 NLRB 1231, 81 LRRM 1156 (1972); *Cohn Goldwater Mfg. Co.*, 103 NLRB 399, 31 LRRM 1531 (1953).

[13]NLRB Casehandling Manual ¶11140.1.

[14]*Id.* at ¶11014.

[15]*Id.*

[16]See discussion at §5.12.

dismissal of the petition by the regional director; (3) disclaimer of interest by the union; or (4) adjustment by consent of the parties to an election.

§6.4   Withdrawal of Petition

At any time prior to the close of a hearing the petitioner may on its own motion ask to withdraw the petition or the Board agent may request that the withdrawal be made because, among other possible reasons, the desired unit is not appropriate; the petition is untimely under the contract bar or related doctrines;[17] the petition is not supported by an adequate showing of interest;[18] or further processing of the petition is blocked by unresolved unfair labor practice charges.[19]

Where the petitioner seeks to withdraw the petition, a form for that purpose will be supplied. (See Exhibit 20.) Prior to the close of the formal hearing a petition may be withdrawn only with the consent of the regional director. The case is closed as soon as the withdrawal is approved by the director.[20]

Approval of a withdrawal request, while generally favored by the Board,[21] is not automatic.[22] Special rules pertaining to requirements for withdrawal requests made after the close of a hearing or after an election agreement has been reached are discussed in chapter 8.[23]

§6.5   Dismissal of Petition

If a petition is not withdrawn as requested by the Board agent, it generally will be dismissed by the regional director, who will send a letter to the parties informing them of this action.[24] (See Exhibit 21.) The letter will state the grounds for the regional director's dismissal. In the absence of a timely appeal, the case is closed at this point.

Any party has 14 days from service of the regional director's letter in which to appeal the dismissal.[25] This is done by filing a

---

[17]See discussion at §§5.4–5.8.

[18]See discussion at §5.12; NLRB Statements of Procedure §101.18(b).

[19]See discussion at §5.9.

[20]NLRB Rules and Regulations §102.60.

[21]*Westinghouse Elec. Corp.*, 144 NLRB 455, 54 LRRM 1079 (1963).

[22]*Private Medical Group of New Rochelle*, 218 NLRB 1315, 89 LRRM 1501 (1975).

[23]See discussion at §8.12(b).

[24]NLRB Statements of Procedure §101.18(c); NLRB Casehandling Manual ¶¶11100–11104.3.

[25]NLRB Rules and Regulations §102.71(c). See discussion of how time is computed under the Board's rules at §25.3. The request for review procedures for appeals from regional director decisions dismissing election petitions during representation hearings are set forth in the Board's Rules and Regulations §102.71(a). They are similar but not identical to request for review procedures applicable to appeals of regional director determinations made after completion of the administrative investigation (*see* NLRB Rules and Regulations §102.67(b) and discussion at §8.9) and those applicable to director decisions to dismiss a petition or hold it in abeyance pending resolution of blocking charges (*see* NLRB Rules and Regulations §102.71(b) and discussion at §5.9, note 108).

FORM NLRB-601
(7-57)

UNITED STATES OF AMERICA
NATIONAL LABOR RELATIONS BOARD

WITHDRAWAL REQUEST

In the matter of _____ _____
                      (Name of case)   *(Number of case)*

This is to request withdrawal of the *(petition)* *(charge)* in the above case.

_____
(Name of Party Filing)

By _____
      (Name of Representative)

_____
(Title)

Date _____

Withdrawal request approved

_____
(Date)

Regional Director,
National Labor Relations Board.

☆ U.S. Government Printing Office: 1965—469-330/28388

Exhibit 20.   Withdrawal Request (Petition or Charge) (Form NLRB-601)

NATIONAL LABOR RELATIONS BOARD

REGION 5

Candler Building - 4th Floor

109 Market Place

Baltimore, MD   21202

January 2, 1986

Ms. Jean Jones, Business Agent
Local 007
United Computer Operators International Union
P.O. Box 10
Arlington, VA   22207

> Re: Janco Computer Services, Inc.
>   Case No. 5-RC-1234

Dear Ms. Jones:

The above-captioned case, petitioning for an investigation and determination of representatives under Section 9(c) of the National Labor Relations Act, as amended, has been carefully investigated and considered.

As a result of the investigation, it appears that, because it would not effectuate the purposes of the Act to assert jurisdiction herein [the petitioner has failed to submit evidence of designation as bargaining agent of substantial number of employees involved] [the unit of employees for which petitioner seeks to act as bargaining agent (seeks decertification) is inappropriate for collective bargaining purpose] [other], further proceedings are not warranted at this time. I am, therefore, dismissing the petition in this matter.

Pursuant to the National Labor Relations Board Rules and Regulations Section 102.19 you may obtain a review of this action by filing a request therefor with the Executive Secretary, National Labor Relations Board, Washington, D.C. 20570. This request must contain a complete statement setting forth the facts and reasons upon which it is based. The request for review (eight copies) must be received by the Executive Secretary by the close of business on [date]. Upon good cause shown, however, the Executive Secretary may grant special permission for a longer period within which to file. Any any such request for extension of time should be submitted to the Executive Secretary and a copy submitted to me and to each of the other parties to this proceeding.

The request for review and any request for extension of time must include a statement that a copy has been served on me and on each of the other parties to this proceeding, and the copy must be served in the same or faster manner as that used in filing the request with the Board. When filing with the Board is accomplished by personal service, however, the other parties shall be promptly notified of such action by telephone, followed by service of a copy by mail or telegraph.

                         Very truly yours,

                         Louis J. D'Amico
                         Regional Director

Exhibit 21.   Letter Informing Petitioner of the Petition Dismissal

request for review with the Board in Washington, D.C. (See Exhibit 22.) Eight copies must be filed and a copy sent to the regional director and to each of the other parties within the same 14 days. The request for review should contain a complete statement setting forth the facts and reasons upon which the appeal is based. It may be granted by the Board upon one or more of the following grounds only: (1) a substantial question of law or policy is raised due to the absence of, or departure from, Board precedent; (2) there are compelling reasons for reconsideration of an important Board rule or policy; (3) the request for review is accompanied by documentary evidence previously submitted to the regional director raising serious doubts as to the regional director's factual findings; (4) the regional director's action is, on its face, arbitrary or capricious; or (5) the petition raises issues which can best be resolved upon the basis of a record developed at a hearing.[26]

Where a party desires an extension of time in which to file an appeal, a request should be addressed to the Board in Washington with copies to the other parties. The request addressed to the Board must be accompanied by proof of service upon the other parties.[27]

During the period before a request for review is filed, the regional director retains authority over the case and may revoke the dismissal. Once the appeal has been filed with the Board, however, the director must obtain the Board's approval before reconsidering the initial determination.[28]

When the request for review is received by the Board, notice of its receipt will be sent to the other parties by the Board's Executive Secretary. (See Exhibit 23.) Likewise, when the appeal has been decided by the Board, all parties will be notified of the action taken.

The Board may deny the request for review, which closes the case, or may grant review and (1) reverse the regional director and order further processing of the case; or (2) uphold the regional director's dismissal of the case, stating the grounds for its action and citing appropriate Board precedents. (See Exhibit 24.)

§6.6   Disclaimer of Interest

In some instances an election petition may be resolved informally on the basis of a claim by the union that it does not wish to represent the employees.[29] Such a disclaimer may be made by a union with an outstanding certification or an unexpired contract covering some or all of the employees sought to be represented by a rival union ("RC" petition). Disclaimers frequently are used, however, in situations

---

[26]NLRB Rules and Regulations §102.71(a).
[27]*Id.*
[28]NLRB Casehandling Manual ¶11100.3.
[29]*Id.* at ¶¶11120–11124.4.

FORM NLRB-4916
(9-82)

UNITED STATES OF AMERICA
NATIONAL LABOR RELATIONS BOARD

INSTRUCTIONS FOR FILING REQUEST FOR REVIEW OF
ADMINISTRATIVE DISMISSAL OF REPRESENTATION PETITION

Pursuant to the National Labor Relations Board Rules and Regulations, Series 8, as amended, you may obtain a review of this action by filing a request therefor with the National Labor Relations Board, addressed to the Executive Secretary, National Labor Relations Board, Washington, D.C., 20570. A copy of such request for review must be served on the Regional Director and each of the other parties to the proceeding. This request for review must contain a complete statement setting forth the facts and reasons upon which it is based. The request for review (*eight copies*) must be received by the Executive Secretary of the Board in Washington, D.C., by the close of business on _____ .

Upon good cause shown, however, the Board may grant special permission for a longer period within which to file. The request for extension of time should be submitted to the Executive Secretary of the Board in Washington, D.C., and a copy of any such request for extension of time should be submitted to the Regional Director, and to each of the other parties to this proceeding.

The request for review and any request for extension of time for filing must include a statement that a copy has been served on the Regional Director and on each of the other parties to this proceeding, and the copy must be served in the same or faster manner as that utilized in filing the request with the Board. When filing with the Board is accomplished by personal service, however, the other parties shall be promptly notified of such action by telephone, followed by service of a copy by mail or telegraph.

**Exhibit 22.   Instructions for Filing Request for Review of Administrative
Dismissal of Representation Petition   (Form NLRB-4916)**

FORM NLRB-1419
(10-82)

NATIONAL LABOR RELATIONS BOARD

WASHINGTON, DC   20570

Date:

In re:

This is to acknowledge receipt of your

filed with the Board in the above-entitled matter, which has been transferred to the Board for consideration

Very truly yours,

Exhibit 23.   Notice Acknowledging Receipt of Appeal (Form NLRB-1419)

TELEGRAPHIC MESSAGE

NAME OF AGENCY	PRECEDENCE	SECURITY CLASSIFICATION
NLRB – ORDER SECTION	ACTION: INFO:	

ACCOUNTING CLASSIFICATION	DATE PREPARED 4/3/85 10:00 am	FILE

FOR INFORMATION CALL

NAME XYZ/MRT	PHONE NUMBER 254-9001	TYPE OF MESSAGE ☐ SINGLE ☐ BOOK ☐ MULTIPLE-ADDRESS

THIS SPACE FOR USE OF COMMUNICATION UNIT

MESSAGE TO BE TRANSMITTED (Use double spacing and all capital letters)

TO:

(LIST NAMES AND ADDRESSES OF
PARTIES ABOVE TELEGRAPHIC MESSAGE)

RE: (CASE NAME AND NUMBER) HAVING DULY CONSIDERED THE PETITIONER'S

APPEAL OF THE REGIONAL DIRECTOR'S ADMINISTRATIVE DISMISSAL OF THE

INSTANT PETITION, THE BOARD CONCLUDES THAT THE APPEAL RAISES NO

SUBSTANTIAL ISSUES WARRANTING REVIEW. ACCORDINGLY, REGIONAL DIRECTOR'S

DISMISSAL OF PETITION IS AFFIRMED. BY DIRECTION OF THE BOARD: DATED,

WASHINGTON, D. C.   1985.

_____
                                              Deputy Executive Secretary

	SECURITY CLASSIFICATION
PAGE NO.	NO. OF PGS.	

STANDARD FORM 14
 REVISED 11-80
 GSA FPMR (41 CFR) 101-35.306
 Previous editions usable NSN 7540-00-634-3968
 ☆ GPO : 1981 O – 341-576 (7041)
 14-103

Exhibit 24.   Board Order Affirming Regional Director's Dismissal of Petition

where the employer has sought an election ("RM" petition) or an individual or group of employees seek to decertify an incumbent union ("RD" petition).

A disclaimer should be in writing and should be clear and unequivocal. In addition, the union must not take any action inconsistent with the disclaimer such as petitioning for recognition or pressing a grievance. If the disclaimer is accepted the union will be dropped as a party in the RC case and the RM and RD petitions, if not withdrawn by the parties, will be dismissed.[30] If the disclaimer of interest is by a certified union, the dismissal will be accompanied by a revocation of the outstanding certification.[31] When the disclaimer is made prior to the execution of an election agreement or the opening of a hearing, it generally is approved without prejudice to the union's ability to reassert an active interest in representing the employees at any time.[32]

§6.7 Voluntary Consents

The fourth way to resolve an election petition informally without need of a hearing is for the parties to consent voluntarily to the conduct of the election. The advantages and requirements for election agreements are discussed below.

Election Agreements and Stipulations

If the investigation discloses that the requirements for an election have been met, the Board agent will attempt to persuade the parties to adjust the representation dispute by agreeing to use the Board's informal election machinery. There are two types of informal adjustment: (1) the consent election agreement, and (2) the stipulated election agreement.[33]

Both consent agreements and stipulated agreements may be entered into by the parties at any stage of an election proceeding before issuance of the regional director's decision. Either type of adjustment becomes effective only upon approval by the regional director. Prior to such approval, any party may insist upon changes in the terms of the adjustment or withdraw entirely.[34]

The date of the representation election often is the most significant factor in the success or failure of a union organizing campaign.

---

[30]*Id.* at ¶¶11122, 11124.1, 11124.2.

[31]*Id.*

[32]*Id.* Disclaimers of interest filed after an election agreement has been signed or after the opening of a hearing are discussed at §8.13.

[33]NLRB Rules and Regulations §102.62. *See generally* NLRB Statements of Procedure §101.19; NLRB Casehandling Manual ¶¶11084–11098.1.

[34]Requirements for withdrawal after approval by the regional director are discussed at §8.12(b).

A vote at the peak of the drive is most desirable from the union's point of view and the filing of the petition is usually timed with this in mind. The employer, on the other hand, frequently tries to delay the election, both to gain time to persuade the employees they are better off without the union and to let the inherent difficulty of sustaining interest in any such program take its toll. Since the election date is set in the agreement or stipulation these are the types of tactical considerations which weigh heavily on the decision of whether or not to consent to an election.

Other factors to be considered are:

- Avoiding employee resentment sometimes caused by what appears to be a party's effort to delay or avoid the bargaining process.
- Saving the time and expense of a formal and public hearing.
- Psychological advantages flowing from the practice of resolving disputes (including representation issues) by direct negotiation and agreement.
- Advantage to the employer of resolving the representation issue quickly where rival unions are organizing and there is disruption in the plant.
- Possibility of compromising differences over the scope of the bargaining unit, unit status of particular employees, and voter eligibility.

Under both types of informal adjustment the parties agree that:

- The employer is engaged in commerce, as illustrated by a brief statement of the commerce facts.
- An appropriate unit exists and precisely which employees that unit includes.
- An election shall be conducted at a certain date, time, and place.[35]
- A specific payroll shall be used to determine eligibility.[36]
- As soon after the election as possible, the votes shall be counted and tabulated. Upon the conclusion of the counting, each party will be served with a tally of ballots.

§6.8   Agreement for Consent Election

The terms of the agreement for a consent election are set forth in printed forms available at the Board's regional offices. (See Exhibit

---

[35]In cases where the parties consent to an election but cannot agree on details such as time, place, and location, they may leave such matters "to be designated by the regional director" in which case the regional director may unilaterally schedule the election. Resolution of major disagreements such as the appropriate bargaining unit, however, should not be left to the regional director. NLRB Casehandling Manual ¶11084.3.

[36]The regional director will not approve an election agreement when it is known in advance that the eligibility of a substantial number of employees will be relegated to the challenged ballot procedure. *Id.*

25.) Under the terms of the consent agreement, in addition to those specified above, the parties agree that:

- They waive their right to a hearing at any stage of the proceeding.
- The rulings of the regional director on all questions relating to the election (for example, eligibility to vote, validity of challenged ballots and objections) shall be final and binding. The Board cannot entertain any objections to the regional director's rulings unless they are arbitrary and capricious. The Board itself has said: "In the absence of fraud, misconduct, or *such gross mistakes as imply bad faith on the part of the Regional Director*, we deem his determination to be final in consent elections, even though we might have reached a different conclusion." (Emphasis in original.)[37]
- If challenged ballots are sufficient in number to affect the results of the count, the regional director shall conduct an investigation and rule upon the challenged ballots.
- If objections to the conduct of the election or to conduct affecting the results of the election are filed with the regional director within seven days after the tally of ballots has been prepared, the regional director shall conduct an investigation and rule upon the objections.
- If the regional director finds that the objections have merit, the director may: (a) set aside the results of the election; and (b) conduct a new election at a date, time, and place to be determined.
- The regional director shall issue to the parties a certificate of results (where a majority of the employees have voted against representation), or a certification of representative (where a labor organization has received a majority of the valid ballots cast). (See Exhibits 26 and 27, respectively.) In either event, the regional director's certification has the same force and effect as if issued by the Board.[38]
- Any rulings by the regional director with respect to any amendment of the certification shall be final.[39]

From the foregoing it is apparent that the effect of the consent agreement is, for the most part, like that of the directed election after a hearing. Thus, in both instances the regional director rules on all questions relating to the election, investigates and rules upon challenged ballots and objections, and certifies the results. The principal difference is found in the scope of review of the director's action. In

---

[37]*McMullen Leavens Co.*, 83 NLRB 948, 955, 24 LRRM 1175, 1178 (1949).
[38]NLRB Rules and Regulations §102.62(a).
[39]*Id.* at §§102.62(a) and 102.63(b).

FORM NLRB-651
(3-84)

UNITED STATES OF AMERICA
NATIONAL LABOR RELATIONS BOARD

AGREEMENT FOR CONSENT ELECTION

Pursuant to a petition duly filed under Section 9 of the National Labor Relations Act, as amended, and subject to the approval of the Regional Director for the National Labor Relations Board (herein called the Regional Director), the undersigned parties hereby waive a hearing, agree that the petition is hereby amended to conform to this Agreement and that approval of this Agreement constitutes a withdrawal of any Notice of Representation Hearing previously issued in this matter, and further **AGREE AS FOLLOWS:**

1. **SECRET BALLOT.** — An election by secret ballot shall be held under the supervision of the said Regional Director, among the employees of the undersigned Employer in the unit defined below, at the indicated time and place, to determine whether or not such employees desire to be represented for the purpose of collective bargaining by (one of) the undersigned labor organization(s). Said election shall be held in accordance with the National Labor Relations Act, the Board's Rules and Regulations, and the applicable procedures and policies of the Board, provided that the determination of the Regional Director shall be final and binding upon any question, including questions as to the eligibility of voters, raised by any party hereto relating in any manner to the election, and provided further that rulings or determination by the Regional Director in respect of any amendment of any certification resulting therefrom shall also be final.

2. **ELIGIBLE VOTERS.** — The eligible voters shall be those employees included within the unit described below, who were employed during the payroll period indicated below, and also employees who did not work during said payroll period because they were ill or on vacation or temporarily laid off, employees in the military service of the United States who appear in person at the polls, employees engaged in an economic strike which commenced less than 12 months before the election date and who retained their status as such during the eligibility period and their replacements, but *excluding* any employees who have since quit or been discharged for cause and employees engaged in a strike who have been discharged for cause since the commencement thereof, and who have not been rehired or reinstated prior to the date of the election and employees engaged in an economic strike which commenced more than 12 months prior to the date of the election and who have been permanently replaced. At a date fixed by the Regional Director, the parties, as requested, will furnish to the Regional Director an accurate list of all the eligible voters, together with a list of the employees, if any, specifically excluded from eligibility.

3. **NOTICES OF ELECTION.** — The Regional Director shall prepare a Notice of Election and supply copies to the parties describing the manner and conduct of the election to be held and incorporating therein a sample ballot. The parties, upon the request of and at a time designated by the Regional Director, will post such Notice of Election at conspicuous and usual posting places easily accessible to the eligible voters.

4. **OBSERVERS.** — Each party hereto will be allowed to station an equal number of authorized observers, selected from among the nonsupervisory employees of the Employer, at the polling places during the election to assist in its conduct, to challenge the eligibility of voters, and to verify the tally.

5. **TALLY OF BALLOTS.** — As soon after the election as feasible, the votes shall be counted and tabulated by the Regional Director, or Board agent or agents. Upon the conclusion of the counting, the Regional Director shall furnish a Tally of Ballots to each of the parties. When appropriate, the Regional Director shall issue to the parties a certification of representative or of results of election, as may be indicated.

6. **OBJECTIONS, CHALLENGES, REPORTS THEREON.** — Objections to the conduct of the election or conduct affecting the results of the election, or to a determination of representatives based on the results thereof, may be filed with the Regional Director within 5 days after issuance of the Tally of Ballots. Copies of such objections must be served on the other parties at the time of filing with the Regional Director. The Regional Director shall investigate the matters contained in the objections and issue a report thereon. If objections are sustained, the Regional Director may in the report include an order voiding the results of the election and, in that event, shall be empowered to conduct a new election under the terms and provisions of this Agreement at a date, time, and place to be determined by the Regional Director. If the challenges are determinative of the results of the election, the Regional Director shall investigate the challenges and issue a report thereon. The method of investigation of objections and challenges, including the question whether a hearing should be held in connection therewith, shall be determined by the Regional Director, whose decision shall be final and binding.

7. **RUNOFF PROCEDURE.** — In the event that more than one labor organization is signatory to this Agreement and in the event that no choice on the ballot in the election receives a majority of the valid ballots cast, the Regional Director shall proceed in accordance with the Board's Rules and Regulations.

8. **COMMERCE.** — The Employer is engaged in commerce within the meaning of Section 2 (6) and (7) of the National Labor Relations Act.

(Over)

Exhibit 25.   Agreement for Consent Election   (Form NLRB-651)

9. WORDING ON THE BALLOT. — Where only one labor organization is signatory to this Agreement, the name of the organization shall appear on the ballot and the choice shall be "Yes" or "No." In the event that more than one labor organization is signatory to this Agreement, the choices on the ballot will appear in the wording indicated below and in the order enumerated below, reading from left to right on the ballot, or, if the occasion demands, from top to bottom. *(If more than one union is to appear on the ballot, any union may have its name removed from the ballot by the approval of the Regional Director of a timely request, in writing, to that effect.)*

First.

Second.

Third.

10. PAYROLL PERIOD FOR ELIGIBILITY - THE PERIOD ENDING _____ .

11. DATE, HOURS, AND PLACE OF ELECTION. —

12. THE APPROPRIATE COLLECTIVE-BARGAINING UNIT. —

--	--
(Employer)	*(Name of organization)*
By ------------------------------------	**By** ------------------------------------
(Name) *(Date)*	*(Name)* *(Date)*
--	--
(Title)	*(Title)*
Recommended:	
--	--
(Board Agent) *(Date)*	*(Name of other Organization)*
Date approved -------------------------	**By** ------------------------------------
	(Name) *(Date)*
--	--
Regional Director *National Labor Relations Board*	*(Title)*

Case _____

GPO : 1984 O – 437–082

Exhibit 25—*page 2*

FORM NLRB-4280
(5-84)

RC-RM-RD

UNITED STATES OF AMERICA
NATIONAL LABOR RELATIONS BOARD

TYPE OF ELECTION

(Check One) | *(Also check box*
☐ **Consent Agreement** | *below where*
☐ **Stipulation** | *appropriate)*
☐ **Board Direction**
☐ **RD Direction** | ☐ **8(b)(7)**

Case

CERTIFICATION OF RESULTS OF ELECTION

An election having been conducted in the above matter under the supervision of the Regional Director of the National Labor Relations Board in accordance with the Rules and Regulations of the Board; and it appearing from the Tally of Ballots that no collective bargaining representative has been selected; and no objections having been filed to the Tally of Ballots furnished to the parties, or to the conduct of the election, within the time provided therefor;

Pursuant to authority vested in the undersigned by the National Labor Relations Board,

IT IS HEREBY CERTIFIED that a majority of the valid ballots has not been cast for any labor organization appearing on the ballot, and that no such organization is the exclusive representative of all the employees, in the unit herein involved, within the meaning of Section 9(a) of the National Labor Relations Act, as amended.

Signed at

On the   day of   19

Regional Director, Region
National Labor Relations Board

Exhibit 26.   Certification of Results of Election   (Form NLRB-4280)

FORM NLRB-4279
(12-63)

UNITED STATES OF AMERICA

NATIONAL LABOR RELATIONS BOARD

RC—RM—RD

TYPE OF ELECTION

(Check one)
☐ Consent Agreement
☐ Stipulation
☐ Board Direction
☐ RD Direction

(Also check box below
where appropriate)
☐ 8(b)(7)

Case

CERTIFICATION OF REPRESENTATIVE

An election having been conducted in the above matter under the supervision of the Regional Director of the National Labor.Relations Board in accordance with the Rules and Regulations of the Board; and it appearing from the Tally of Ballots that a collective bargaining representative has been selected; and no objections having been filed to the Tally of Ballots furnished to the parties, or to the conduct of the election, within the time provided therefor;

Pursuant to authority vested in the undersigned by the National Labor Relations Board, **IT IS HEREBY CERTIFIED** that a majority of the valid ballots have been cast for

and that, pursuant to Section 9(a) of the National Labor Relations Act, as amended, the said labor organization is the exclusive representative of all the employees in the unit set forth below, found to be appropriate for the purposes of collective bargaining in respect to rates of pay, wages, hours of employment, or other conditions of employment.

UNIT:

Signed at
On the

day of

19

On behalf of

NATIONAL LABOR RELATIONS BOARD

Regional Director, Region
National Labor Relations Board

Exhibit 27.   Certification of Representative   (Form NLRB-4279)

the case of the consent election, the Board or a court will consider only those actions of the director which are arbitrary and capricious. In the case of directed elections, as more fully explained in the discussion of requests for review (see §8.9), rulings will be set aside if erroneous.

§6.9   Agreement for Stipulated Election

The terms of the stipulated election agreement differ from those of the consent election agreement in two significant respects. First, in the stipulated agreement the parties agree to waive their rights to any hearing *before the election*; in the consent election agreement the parties' waiver applies to both pre- and post-election hearings. Second, in the stipulated agreement the parties agree that the Board shall finally determine all questions relating to the election (for example, validity of challenged ballots and objections to the conduct of the election);[40] in the consent election agreement the parties agree that the regional director shall make the final and binding decisions on such matters.

As with consent elections, the terms of stipulated elections also are set forth in printed forms which are available at the Board's regional offices. (See Exhibit 28.) Postelection procedures under stipulations are similar but not identical to those followed in contested cases where the regional director or the Board orders that the election be conducted, but final determination is made by the Board rather than the regional director.[41] These procedures are discussed in chapter 10.

§6.10   Withdrawal From Election Agreements

Once a consent or a stipulated election agreement has been executed, the regional director will permit a party to withdraw only upon a showing of unusual circumstances or by agreement of all parties.[42] If the withdrawal is desired in order to conduct a hearing or enter into a new agreement on different terms, the request will be considered in light of the cause shown, the timeliness of the request, and the positions of the other parties. As a general rule the regional director will strive to honor the terms of the agreement.[43]

---

[40]NLRB Rules and Regulations §102.62(b).
[41]*Compare* NLRB Rules and Regulations §102.69(c)(2) (stipulated elections) *with* §102.69(c)(3) (directed elections).
[42]NLRB Casehandling Manual ¶11098.
[43]*Id.*

FORM NLRB-652
(5-80)

UNITED STATES OF AMERICA
NATIONAL LABOR RELATIONS BOARD

STIPULATION FOR CERTIFICATION UPON CONSENT ELECTION

Pursuant to a petition duly filed under Section 9 of the National Labor Relations Act, as amended, and subject to the approval of the Regional Director for the National Labor Relations Board (herein called the Regional Director), the undersigned parties hereby agree that the petition is hereby amended to conform to this Stipulation and that the approval of this Stipulation constitutes a withdrawal of any Notice of Representation Hearing previously issued in this matter, and further AGREE AS FOLLOWS:

1. SECRET BALLOT.—An election by secret ballot shall be held under the supervision of the said Regional Director, among the employees of the undersigned Employer in the unit defined below, at the indicated time and place, to determine whether or not such employees desire to be represented for the purpose of collective bargaining by (one of) the undersigned labor organization(s). Said election shall be held in accordance with the National Labor Relations Act, the Board's Rules and Regulations, and the applicable procedures and policies of the Board.

2. ELIGIBLE VOTERS.—The eligible voters shall be those employees included within the unit described below, who were employed during the payroll period indicated below, and also employees who did not work during said payroll period because they were ill or on vacation or temporarily laid off, employees in the military services of the United States who appear in person at the polls, employees engaged in an economic strike which commenced less than 12 months before the election date and who retained their status as such during the eligibility period and their replacements, but *excluding* any employees who have since quit or been discharged for cause and employees engaged in a strike who have been discharged for cause since the commencement thereof, and who have not been rehired or reinstated prior to the date of the election, and employees engaged in an economic strike which commenced more than 12 months prior to the date of the election and who have been permanently replaced. At a date fixed by the Regional Director, the parties, as requested, will furnish to the Regional Director an accurate list of all the eligible voters, together with a list of the employees, if any, specifically excluded from eligibility.

3. NOTICES OF ELECTION.—The Regional Director shall prepare a Notice of Election and supply copies to the parties describing the manner and conduct of the election to be held and incorporating therein a sample ballot. The parties, upon the request of and at a time designated by the Regional Director, will post such Notice of Election at conspicuous and usual posting places easily accessible to the eligible voters.

4. OBSERVERS.—Each party hereto will be allowed to station an equal number of authorized observers, selected from among the nonsupervisory employees of the Employer, at the polling places during the election to assist in its conduct, to challenge the eligibility of voters, and to verify the tally.

5. TALLY OF BALLOTS.—As soon after the election as feasible, the votes shall be counted and tabulated by the Regional Director, or Board agent or agents. Upon the conclusion of the counting, the Regional Director shall furnish a Tally of Ballots to each of the parties.

6. POSTELECTION AND RUNOFF PROCEDURE.—All procedures subsequent to the conclusion of counting ballots shall be in conformity with the Board's Rules and Regulations.

7. RECORD.—The record in this case shall be governed by the appropriate provisions of the Board's Rules and Regulations and shall include this Stipulation. Hearing and notice thereof, Direction of Election, and the making of Findings of Fact and Conclusions of Law by the Board prior to the election are hereby expressly waived.

**Exhibit 28.   Stipulation for Certification Upon Consent Election
(Form NLRB-652)**

8. COMMERCE.—The Employer is engaged in commerce within the meaning of Section 2 (6) and (7) of the National Labor Relations Act, and a question affecting commerce has arisen concerning the representation of employees within the meaning of Section 9 (c). *(Insert commerce facts.)*

9. WORDING ON THE BALLOT.—Where only one labor organization is signatory to this agreement, the name of the organization shall appear on the ballot and the choice shall be "Yes" or "No." In the event that more than one labor organization is signatory to this Stipulation, the choices on the ballot will appear in the wording indicated below and in the order enumerated below, reading from left to right on the ballot, or, if the occasion demands, from top to bottom. *(If more than one union is to appear on the ballot, any union may have its name removed from the ballot by the approval of the Regional Director of a timely request, in writing, to that effect.)*

First.

Second.

Third.

10. PAYROLL PERIOD FOR ELIGIBILITY - THE PERIOD ENDING_____.

11. DATE, HOURS, AND PLACE OF ELECTION.—

12. THE APPROPRIATE COLLECTIVE-BARGAINING UNIT.—

(Employer)	*(Name of Organization)*
By _____ *(Name)* _____ *(Date)*	By _____ *(Name)* _____ *(Date)*
_____ *(Title)*	_____ *(Title)*
Recommended:	_____ *(Name of other Organization)*
_____ *(Board Agent)* _____ *(Date)*	By _____ *(Name)* _____ *(Date)*
Date approved _____	_____ *(Title)*
_____ Regional Director, National Labor Relations Board.	Case No._____

GPO : 1981 O - 351-733

Exhibit 28—*page 2*

7

The Representation Hearing

Prehearing Procedures

§7.1 Notice of Hearing

If the parties cannot agree on one of the informal methods of determining the union's majority status, the regional director takes formal action by serving a notice of hearing on all interested parties.[1] (See Exhibit 29.) The notice of hearing fixes the time and place of the hearing. There is no formal requirement as to the minimum number of days' notice the regional director must give to the parties, but generally at least five days are given.

Accompanying the notice of hearing will be a copy of the representation petition, a copy of National Labor Relations Board Form 4669 (Exhibit 30) which outlines the procedures for conducting the hearing and filing briefs, and a supplemental notice (Exhibit 31) which informs the parties that they may still dispose of the petition through an informal adjustment of the case and outlines the requirements for obtaining a postponement of the hearing.

In seeking a postponement of the hearing, a party must demonstrate good and sufficient grounds therefor and must:[2]

- Submit an original and two copies of the request in writing to the regional director;
- Set forth reasons, in detail, for the request;
- Suggest alternative dates for any rescheduled hearing;
- Obtain and set forth the positions of all other parties; and
- Serve copies of the request simultaneously on all other parties.

---

[1]NLRB Rules and Regulations §102.63.
[2]NLRB Casehandling Manual ¶11142.1.

FORM NLRB-852
(7-82)

UNITED STATES OF AMERICA

BEFORE THE NATIONAL LABOR RELATIONS BOARD

CASE NO.

NOTICE OF REPRESENTATION HEARING

The Petitioner, above named, having heretofore filed a Petition pursuant to Section 9(c) of the National Labor Relations Act, as amended, 29 U.S.C. Sec. 151 et seq., copy of which Petition is hereto attached, and it appearing that a question affecting commerce has arisen concerning the representation of employees described by such Petition.

YOU ARE HEREBY NOTIFIED that, pursuant to Sections 3(b) and 9(c) of the Act, on the day of _____ , 19 _____ , at

a hearing will be conducted before a hearing officer of the National Labor Relations Board upon the question of representation affecting commerce which has arisen, at which time and place the parties will have the right to appear in person or otherwise, and give testimony. *(Form NLRB-4669, Statement of Standard Procedures in Formal Hearings Held Before The National Labor Relations Board Pursuant to Petitions Filed Under Section 9 of The National Labor Relations Act, as Amended, is attached.)*

Signed at _____ on the _____ day of _____ ,19 _____

Regional Director, Region
National Labor Relations Board

Exhibit 29.　Notice of Representation Hearing　(Form NLRB-852)

FORM NLRB-4669
(3-83)

(R Cases)

SUMMARY OF STANDARD PROCEDURES IN FORMAL HEARINGS HELD BEFORE THE NATIONAL LABOR RELATIONS BOARD PURSUANT TO PETITIONS FILED UNDER SECTION 9 OF THE NATIONAL LABOR RELATIONS ACT, AS AMENDED

The hearing will be conducted before a Hearing Officer of the National Labor Relations Board.

Parties may be represented by an attorney or other representative and present evidence relevant to the issues. *(Copies of exhibits should be supplied to the Hearing Officer and other parties at the time the exhibit is offered in evidence.)*

An official reporter will make the only official transcript of the proceedings and all citations in briefs or arguments must refer to the official record. After the close of the hearing, one or more of the parties may wish to have corrections made in the record. All such proposed corrections, either by way of stipulation or motion, should be forwarded to the Regional Director or to the Board in Washington *(if the case is transferred to the Board)* instead of to the Hearing Officer, inasmuch as the Hearing Officer has no power to make any rulings in connection with the case after the hearing is closed. All matter that is spoken in the hearing room will be recorded by the official reporter while the hearing is in session. In the event that any party wishes to make off-the-record remarks, requests to make such remarks should be directed to the Hearing Officer and not to the official reporter.

Statements of reasons in support of motions or objections should be as concise as possible. Objections and exceptions may upon appropriate request be permitted to stand to an entire line of questioning. Automatic exceptions will be allowed to all adverse rulings.

All motions shall be in writing or, if made at the hearing, may be stated orally on the record and shall briefly state the order or relief sought and the grounds for such motion. An original and two copies of written motions shall be filed with the Hearing Officer and a copy thereof immediately shall be served on the other parties to the proceeding.

The sole objective of the Hearing Officer is to ascertain the respective positions of the parties and to obtain a full and complete factual record upon which the duties under Section 9 of the National Labor Relations Act may be discharged by the Regional Director of the Board. It may become necessary for the Hearing Officer to ask questions, to call witnesses, and to explore avenues with respect to matters not raised by the parties. The services of the Hearing Officer are equally at the disposal of all parties to the proceedings in developing the material evidence.

After the close of hearing, any party who desires to file a brief may do so in the appropriate manner described below.

1. Briefs filed with the Regional Director

Unless transfer of the case to the Board is announced prior to close of hearing, the brief should be filed in duplicate with the Regional Director. A typed brief with a carbon copy is acceptable. A copy must also be served on each of the other parties and proof of such service must be filed with the Regional Director at the time the briefs are filed. *Briefs submitted are to be double-spaced on 8½ by 11 inch paper.*

The briefs shall be filed within 7 days after the close of the hearing unless an extension of time, not to exceed an additional 14 days, is granted by the Hearing Officer. A request for extension must be made before the hearing closes and for good cause.

Any request for an extension of time made after the close of the hearing must be received by the Regional Director, in writing, not later than 3 days before the date the briefs are due and copies thereof must be served immediately on the other parties.

(OVER)

Exhibit 30. Summary of Procedures in Representation Case Hearings (Form NLRB-4669)

FORM NLRB-4669 (3-83) Continued

2. Briefs filed with the Board in Washington, D.C.

a. If transfer of case to The Board is announced at the hearing:

Should any party desire to file a brief with the Board, eight copies thereof shall be filed with the Board in Washington, D.C. Immediately upon such filing, a copy shall be served on each of the other parties. Proof of such service must be filed with the Board simultaneously with the briefs. Such brief shall be printed or otherwise legibly duplicated: Provided, however, that carbon copies of typewritten matter shall not be filed and if submitted will not be accepted. No reply brief may be filed except upon special leave of the Board. *Any brief filed after transfer of the case to the Board shall be double-spaced on 8½ by 11 inch paper.*

The briefs shall be filed within 7 days after the close of hearing unless an extension of time, not to exceed an additional 14 days upon request made for good cause, before the hearing closes, is granted by the Hearing Officer.

b. Transfer of cases to The Board effected after close of hearing:

Pursuant to Section 102.67 of the Board's Rules and Regulations, the Regional Director may, at any time after the close of hearing and before decision, transfer a case to the Board for decision. The order transferring the case will fix a date for filing briefs in Washington.

If brief has already been filed with the Regional Director, the parties may file eight copies of the same brief with the Board in the same manner as set forth in "a," above, except that service on other parties is not required. No further briefs shall be submitted except by special permission of the Board.

If the case is transferred to the Board before the time expires for filing of briefs with the Regional Director and before the parties have filed briefs, such briefs shall be filed as set forth in "a," above.

c. Request for extension of time to file briefs with the Board:

Any request for extension of time to file briefs with the Board in Washington, made after the close of hearing, must be received by the Washington Office not later than 3 days before the date the briefs are due. Such request must be in writing and a copy shall be served immediately on each of the other parties and the Regional Director and shall contain a statement that such service has been made.

As provided in Section 102.112 of the Board's Rules and Regulations, service on all parties of a request for an extension of time shall be made in the same manner as that utilized in filing the paper with the Board; however, when filing with the Board is accomplished by personal service, the other parties shall be promptly notified of such action by telephone, followed by service of a copy by mail or telegraph.

GPO 906-789

Exhibit 30—*page 2*

FORM NLRB-4338
(7-82)

NATIONAL LABOR RELATIONS BOARD

NOTICE

Case No. _____

The issuance of the notice of formal hearing in this case does not mean that the matter cannot be disposed of by agreement of the parties. On the contrary, it is the policy of this office to encourage voluntary adjustments. The examiner or attorney assigned to the case will be pleased to receive and to act promptly upon your suggestions or comments to this end. An agreement between the parties, approved by the Regional Director, would serve to cancel the hearing.

However, unless otherwise specifically ordered, the hearing will be held at the date, hour, and place indicated. Postponements *will not be granted* unless good and sufficient grounds are shown *and* the following requirements are met:

(1)   The request must be in writing. An original and two copies must be served on the Regional Director;

(2)   Grounds thereafter must be set forth in *detail;*

(3)   Alternative dates for any rescheduled hearing must be given;

(4)   The positions of all other parties must be ascertained in advance by the requesting party and set forth in the request; *and*

(5)   Copies must be simultaneously served on all other parties *(listed below)*, and that fact must be noted on the request.

Except under the most extreme conditions, no request for postponement will be granted during the three days immediately preceding the date of hearing.

Exhibit 31.   Supplemental Notice Regarding Settlements and Postponements of Representation Case Hearings   (Form NLRB-4338)

Before ruling upon a request for postponement of hearing, the regional director usually waits until all parties have had an opportunity to submit their positions. The director's ruling is served on all parties. (See Exhibit 32.)[3]

§7.2 Amendment of Notice of Hearing

In addition to ruling on requests for postponements, the regional director also may amend the notice of hearing in other respects prior to the opening of the hearing.[4] The place or hour of the hearing may be changed; an amendment to the underlying petition may necessitate an amendment to the notice of hearing; or the representation proceeding may be consolidated with or severed from related pending cases. In addition, the regional director retains the authority to withdraw the notice of hearing entirely and, when appropriate, dismiss the petition at any time until the case is transferred to the Board. These actions may be taken on the director's own motion or at the request of one or more of the parties.[5]

§7.3 Prehearing Motions

All motions made by the parties before the opening of the hearing must be filed with the regional director.[6] An original and two copies of motions should be filed. They should state briefly the action requested and the grounds for the request. For example, if the moving party desires to intervene, a statement should be made of the grounds upon which the party claims an interest in the proceeding. Copies of motions must be served immediately upon each of the parties.

The regional director may rule upon all prehearing motions and serve a copy of the ruling upon each of the parties. The regional director has the option of referring some or all of the motions to the hearing officer assigned to the case. Motions to amend the notice of hearing or to dismiss the petition usually are ruled upon by the regional director while most other motions are referred to the hearing officer.[7]

The regional director's rulings on motions to revoke subpoenas become part of the hearing record only upon request of the aggrieved party. Otherwise, all prehearing motions and rulings automatically become part of the record.[8] Unless expressly authorized by the Board's regulations, prehearing rulings by the regional director (other than

---

[3]*Id.* at ¶11142.2.

[4]NLRB Rules and Regulations §102.63; NLRB Casehandling Manual ¶¶11140, 11146.

[5]*Id.*

[6]NLRB Rules and Regulations §102.65(a); NLRB Casehandling Manual ¶11140.2.

[7]NLRB Casehandling Manual ¶11114.

[8]NLRB Rules and Regulations §102.65(c).

FORM NLRB-859
(9-75)

UNITED STATES OF AMERICA

BEFORE THE NATIONAL LABOR RELATIONS BOARD

Case No.

ORDER RESCHEDULING HEARING

IT IS HEREBY ORDERED that the hearing in the above-entitled matter be and the same hereby is rescheduled

from

DATED at   this   day of   , 19

Regional Director, Region
National Labor Relations Board

Exhibit 32.   Order Rescheduling Hearing   (Form NLRB-859)

dismissals of petitions) may not be appealed directly to the Board but may be considered by the Board in connection with a request for review of the regional director's decision or whenever the case is transferred to it for decision.[9]

Conduct of the Hearing

§7.4   Nature of the Representation Hearing

The purpose of the representation hearing is to gather factual information necessary for the regional director or the Board to rule upon a question concerning representation. Theoretically the hearing is investigative rather than adversarial in nature.[10] Hearings generally are conducted in the region where the election petition originates and, with rare exception, are open to the public. A verbatim transcript is made by an official reporter retained by the Board's regional office. This constitutes the official record of the hearing. Copies may be purchased by the parties but must be ordered from the official reporter. A copy also is placed in the regional office formal file. Although the regional office's copy is available to parties and to the public, the regional director will not permit removal of the transcript from the office. All citations and references made in briefs and motions must refer to the official record.

   (a) Role of the Hearing Officer.   The officer presiding over the hearing normally is a Board attorney or field examiner from the region in which the hearing is held. The hearing officer is an agent of the regional director.[11] As the hearing is considered to be part of the investigation, it is the hearing officer's function to assure that the record includes a full presentation of factual material upon which the regional director or the Board can decide the issues involved.[12]

   The hearing officer has authority to call, examine, and cross-examine witnesses and to request that documentary evidence be introduced into the record. Indeed, the Board has ruled that it is not improper for a hearing officer to develop "most of the evidence" on a critical issue by examination of witnesses where the parties have failed to call their own witnesses.[13]

---

   [9]*Id.* Prehearing orders dismissing petitions may be appealed in accordance with the procedures set forth in §102.71 of the Board's Rules and Regulations. *See* NLRB Rules and Regulations §102.65(a).

   [10]NLRB Casehandling Manual ¶11180; NLRB Statements of Procedure §101.20.

   [11]*Rochester Metal Prods.*, 94 NLRB 1779, 28 LRRM 1289 (1951).

   [12]NLRB Casehandling Manual ¶11184.1; *Altamont Knitting Mills, Inc.*, 101 NLRB 525, 31 LRRM 1103 (1952).

   [13]*United States Smelting, Refining & Mining Corp.*, 116 NLRB 661, 662, 38 LRRM 1314 (1956).

The hearing officer has the power to limit the testimony to relevant issues. Thus, the hearing officer can stop examination of witnesses[14] or refuse to permit a line of testimony which produces no evidence.[15] Although leading questions may be asked of witnesses, the hearing officer may stop such questioning where the practice is being abused.[16] The hearing officer is empowered[17] and required[18] to rule on all motions (except motions to dismiss the petition) referred by the regional director or made at the hearing. Any motion to dismiss the petition must be referred by the hearing officer to the regional director or to the Board, as the case may be.[19] The hearing officer also has the discretion to postpone the hearing or to adjourn it to a later date or to a different place. This may be done either by oral announcement at the hearing or in writing.[20]

(b) Role of the Parties. Any party has the right to appear at a hearing in person, by counsel, or by other representative. The Board does not prescribe rules of admission to practice before it or its hearing officers, and parties are not required to be represented by attorneys.[21] Misconduct of an aggravated character on the part of any attorney or other representative may cause the Board to refuse the offender permission to practice further before it.[22]

The parties are given full opportunity to present their respective positions and to present evidence in support of their contentions. Each party has the power to call, examine, and cross-examine witnesses.[23] Any party may file objections to the conduct of the hearing including objections relating to the introduction of evidence. Such objections must be stated orally or in writing and will be included in the hearing record. Further participation in the hearing will not be viewed as a waiver of the objection.[24]

(c) Rules of Evidence. Theoretically, representation hearings are nonadversarial, investigatory proceedings. The issues, however, often are vigorously contested. The Act does not set forth rules of evidence to be used in representation proceedings but the Board, through its Rules and Regulations, states that the rules of evidence

---

[14]*Ravenna Arsenal, Inc.*, 98 NLRB 1 n.1, 29 LRRM 1283 (1952).

[15]*Sears, Roebuck & Co.*, 112 NLRB 559 n.1, 36 LRRM 1060 n.1 (1955).

[16]*Altamont Knitting Mills, Inc.*, 101 NLRB 525, 31 LRRM 1103 (1952).

[17]NLRB Rules and Regulations §102.65(a).

[18]*Father & Son Shoe Stores, Inc.*, 117 NLRB 1479, 40 LRRM 1032 (1957).

[19]NLRB Rules and Regulations §102.65(a).

[20]*Id.* at §102.64(b).

[21]*Id.* at §102.38. The Board has, however, established certain restrictions on the ability of former agency employees to participate in cases which were pending during the period of their employment. *See id.* at §§102.119–120.

[22]*Id.* at §§102.44, 102.66(d); NLRB Casehandling Manual ¶11182.1.

[23]NLRB Rules and Regulations §102.66(a).

[24]*Id.* at §102.66(b).

prevailing in the courts shall not be controlling.[25] Thus, hearing officers may overrule objections which raise technicalities concerning the presentation of evidence.[26] Furthermore, it has been held that the provisions of the Administrative Procedure Act do not apply to the conduct of representation hearings.[27]

§7.5   Sequence of the Hearing

Most hearings proceed in the following sequence:

- The hearing officer notes for the record the appearances on behalf of the parties.
- The hearing officer places in the record the so-called "formal papers." These consist of the petition, the notice of hearing, any prehearing motions and the rulings thereon, and affidavits of service.[28]
- Factual agreements on such matters as the status of the labor organization or the operations of the company are then placed in the record by stipulation.
- If the size or composition of the unit is a contested issue, the petitioner will be asked to proceed with relevant testimony. Other parties then produce direct testimony. Witnesses called by any party are subject to cross-examination.
- The same procedure is followed on other contested issues.
- At the conclusion of the hearing, the parties are entitled, upon request, to engage in oral argument.[29]

§7.6   Motions Before the Hearing Officer

All motions made at the hearing must be made in writing or stated on the record.[30] If in writing, an original and two copies must be filed, and a copy served immediately upon each of the other parties.[31] The motion should state briefly the relief sought and the grounds for such motion.

The hearing officer must rule on every motion filed at the hearing or referred by the regional director except a motion to dismiss the

---

[25]*Id.* at §102.66(a).

[26]*See Jerome E. Mundy Co.*, 116 NLRB 1487, 39 LRRM 1019 (1956).

[27]*Operating Eng'rs, Local No. 148 v. Operating Eng'rs, Local No. 2*, 173 F.2d 557, 23 LRRM 2517 (8th Cir. 1949). Once the hearing opens, however, *ex parte* communications by interested persons with the regional director, the Board, or members of their staffs are prohibited. NLRB Rules and Regulations §102.128(a).

[28]NLRB Casehandling Manual ¶11192.

[29]NLRB Rules and Regulations §102.66(e).

[30]*Id.* at §102.65(a); NLRB Casehandling Manual ¶11202.

[31]NLRB Rules and Regulations §102.65(a); NLRB Casehandling Manual ¶11202.

petition.[32] A motion to dismiss, which may be made in writing or orally,[33] must be referred to the regional director or to the Board. Rulings of the hearing officer may be made orally on the record or in writing.[34] If in writing, a copy will be served on each party. All motions, rulings, and orders become part of the record, except rulings on motions to revoke subpoenas.[35] The petition to revoke a subpoena, any answer filed, and a ruling thereon become part of the record only upon specific request of the aggrieved party.[36]

All rulings by the hearing officer ultimately are considered when the entire record is reviewed by the regional director or the Board. In limited instances rulings by the hearing officer may be appealed during the hearing by special permission of the regional director.[37] A written request for special permission to appeal from the hearing officer's ruling, along with a copy of the appeal itself, should be filed with the regional director stating the reasons why special permission should be granted and the grounds relied upon for the appeal. Copies of the request for special permission and the appeal are served on all other parties who shall have an opportunity to respond in writing. If the regional director grants the request for special permission, the appeal is reviewed on its merits.[38]

(a) Amendment or Withdrawal of Petition. The petitioner may move during the hearing to withdraw or amend the petition.[39] The rules for withdrawing petitions before the hearing apply also to requests filed at the hearing. (See discussion at §6.4.) It is the Board's settled policy to allow the parties to litigate all issues raised by an amendment to the petition which have not been fully litigated previously.[40]

A petition amended during the hearing does not constitute a new petition where the amendment merely particularizes the composition of the unit,[41] the categories of employees involved in the amended petition are covered in the original petition,[42] or the petition is amended

---

[32]NLRB Rules and Regulations §102.65(a). The Board's Casehandling Manual provides that motions to transfer the case to the Board or for oral argument before the regional director or the Board also should be referred by the hearing officer to the regional director or to the Board. NLRB Casehandling Manual ¶11202.

[33]*Valley Concrete Co.*, 88 NLRB 519, 25 LRRM 1354 (1950).

[34]NLRB Rules and Regulations §102.65(a).

[35]*Id.* at §102.65(c).

[36]*Id.* at §§102.65(c), 102.66(c).

[37]NLRB Casehandling Manual ¶11234. The same limited appeal right exists with respect to the Board in cases where the regional director already has transferred the case to the Board. *Id.*

[38]*Id.*

[39]NLRB Casehandling Manual ¶¶11204 (amendment), 11208 (withdrawal).

[40]*De Laval Separator Co.*, 97 NLRB 544, 29 LRRM 1124 (1951).

[41]*Blatz Brewing Co.*, 94 NLRB 1277, 28 LRRM 1182 (1951); *see also Atlantic Richfield Co.*, 208 NLRB 142, 85 LRRM 1222 (1974) (amendment adding several hundred employees to unit and deleting a like amount of other employees held within discretion of hearing officer).

[42]*Rauland Corp.*, 97 NLRB 1333, 29 LRRM 1258 (1952).

so as to seek, in the alternative, separate units rather than the single unit originally requested.[43] Where the petition is amended during the hearing to embrace a substantially larger unit, however, the Board has held that the petitioner must submit the required showing of interest in the larger unit.[44] If no party is prejudiced and no valid collective bargaining agreement is executed by the company and another union between the time of filing the original petition and the amendment, the amended petition will not be dismissed.[45]

(b) Motions to Intervene. Hearing officers also may be required to rule upon motions to intervene filed by labor organizations which seek to participate in a representation proceeding started by another labor organization, by an employer, by an individual, or by a group of employees. While the statute does not provide any standards or procedures regarding intervention, the Board's Rules and Regulations state that intervention may be granted to any person having an interest in the proceeding "to such extent and upon such terms as [the regional director or hearing officer] may deem proper."[46] If intervention is granted the intervenor becomes a party to the proceeding.[47]

Prehearing motions to intervene often are referred to the hearing officer by the regional director. Motions made at the hearing may be written or stated orally on the record; in each instance the normal requirements for filing motions apply, including a statement of the reason why the motion should be granted.[48] If the motion for intervention is filed after the transfer of the case to the Board, it must be filed in writing with the Board in Washington, D.C.[49]

Requests for intervention will be granted only to persons able to demonstrate an interest in the representation proceeding. The required interest may be demonstrated in a variety of ways. First, a union which is party to an existing or recently expired contract covering the employees in the requested unit may intervene.[50] Second, a union which has been certified or is the currently recognized representative of the employees involved has a sufficient interest in the

---

[43]*Crossett Paper Mills*, 98 NLRB 542, 29 LRRM 1396 (1952).

[44]*Carbide & Carbon Chems. Corp.*, 88 NLRB 437, 25 LRRM 1341 (1950).

[45]*Cohn Goldwater Mfg. Co.*, 103 NLRB 399, 31 LRRM 1531 (1953); *see also Hyster Co.*, 72 NLRB 937, 19 LRRM 1238 (1947).

[46]NLRB Rules and Regulations §102.65(b). Labor organizations which cannot be certified as the representative of unit employees may not intervene in the representation proceeding. *University of Chicago*, 272 NLRB No. 126, 117 LRRM 1377 (1984) (union precluded by Sec. 9(b)(3) from representing guard unit not permitted to intervene).

[47]NLRB Rules and Regulations §102.65(b).

[48]*Id.* at §102.65(a); NLRB Casehandling Manual ¶11194.

[49]NLRB Rules and Regulations §102.65(a). *Northeastern Univ.*, 218 NLRB 247, 89 LRRM 1862 (1975).

[50]NLRB Casehandling Manual ¶11194.1. *Peabody Coal Co.*, 197 NLRB 1231, 81 LRRM 1156 (1972); *Penn-Keystone Realty Corp.*, 191 NLRB 800, 77 LRRM 1600 (1971).

proceeding to justify intervention.[51] Third, a union which submits some timely showing of interest among the employees in the unit, such as a signed petition or authorization cards, may be permitted to intervene.[52]

When the motion to intervene is based upon signed authorization cards or other expressions of employee interest, the degree to which the intervenor will be permitted to participate in the proceedings will depend upon the extent of the demonstrated employee support. A "participating intervenor" is one which submits a showing of interest from less than 10 percent of employees in the requested unit. A single authorization card is a sufficient basis upon which to grant participating intervention.[53] Participating intervenors may appear on the ballot and may participate fully in the hearing, but may not "block" a consent election.[54] If a 10 percent or greater showing of interest is submitted, "full" intervention status is granted and the intervening union may "block" a consent election in addition to appearing on the ballot and participating in the hearing.[55]

In the absence of a 30-percent showing of interest, a participating or full intervenor may appear on the ballot for an election in the unit specified in the petition, but may not request its own unit. An intervening union can both oppose the unit sought by the petitioner and seek its own unit if its showing of interest includes at least 30 percent of the employees in the latter unit.[56] For example, an intervenor must submit at least a 30-percent showing in the craft unit if it seeks to sever a craft unit from the petitioner's industrial unit,[57] or a 30-percent showing in a unit which is substantially larger than that sought by the petitioner.[58] Accordingly, if the issue of an appreciably different unit is raised by an intervenor which has at least a 30-percent showing in its desired unit, it need not file a separate petition for that unit.[59]

Where an intervening union is party to a consent election agreement and the petitioning union withdraws from that agreement, the intervenor must submit a showing of at least 30 percent before the election will be conducted.[60] Similarly, the intervenor must have a showing of at least 30 percent to oppose withdrawal of a petition,

---

[51]*FWD Corp.*, 138 NLRB 386, 51 LRRM 1042 (1962).

[52]NLRB Casehandling Manual ¶¶11022.3, 11194.2.

[53]*See Manhattan College*, 195 NLRB 65, 79 LRRM 1253 (1972).

[54]NLRB Casehandling Manual ¶11022.3(d). Consent election agreements are discussed at §§6.8 and 6.9.

[55]*Id.* at ¶11022.3(c).

[56]*Salvation Army, Inc.*, 225 NLRB 406, 93 LRRM 1085 (1976).

[57]*Boeing Airplane Co.*, 86 NLRB 368, 24 LRRM 1624 (1949).

[58]*Electric Auto-Lite Co.*, 87 NLRB 129, 25 LRRM 1079 (1949).

[59]*Tennessee Coach Co.*, 88 NLRB 253, 25 LRRM 1321 (1950); *Tin Processing Corp.*, 80 NLRB 1369, 23 LRRM 1253 (1948).

[60]*Dierks Paper Co.*, 120 NLRB 290, 41 LRRM 1490 (1958).

unless the petition was filed by an employer.[61] Where the petition was filed by an employer and the employer seeks withdrawal, the intervenor may obtain the election originally sought without submitting any showing of interest.[62]

As a general rule the showing of interest must be submitted along with the motion to intervene or within 48 hours of its filing.[63] In the absence of any such evidence of employee support, the labor organization has no standing in the case. The Board has, however, avoided application of an inflexible rule and has developed a series of exceptions. If the intervenor's showing of interest is submitted after the 48-hour period but before a consent election agreement is approved or before the hearing has ended, intervention may be permitted.[64] If the intervenor has been notified of the 48-hour rule but nevertheless fails to submit its showing until after a consent election agreement has been approved or until after the hearing has ended, it will not be permitted to participate in the case.[65] Its name may be added to the ballot in a consent election, however, if the parties to the consent election agreement agree to the addition.[66] In situations where the interest of a labor organization does not become apparent until after a consent election agreement is approved or until after the close of the hearing, a delayed motion to intervene will be granted to the extent that the showing of interest submitted in support of the motion predates the approval of the agreement or close of hearing.[67] If the showing of interest postdates approval of a consent election agreement, the intervenor nevertheless may appear on the ballot if the parties to the agreement consent.[68]

The discussion thus far has focused upon unions which seek to intervene for purposes of appearing on the ballot. In some instances, however, unions may wish to intervene solely for purposes of commenting upon the appropriateness of the requested bargaining unit. This may occur when the intervening union represents other employees in the plant, represents employees at other plants of the employer, or has a substantial number of collective bargaining agreements in the industry involved. Intervention in such cases may be sought simply to ensure that the parties do not agree to a bargaining unit which includes employees already represented by the intervenor, or may be sought to disavow any interest in the unit requested by the petitioner. Such motions generally are granted.[69] Intervention will not be granted, however, to employee or employer committees

---

[61]*International Aluminum Corp.*, 117 NLRB 1221, 39 LRRM 1407 (1957).

[62]*Id.*

[63]NLRB Casehandling Manual ¶11024.2.

[64]NLRB Casehandling Manual ¶11026.2(a).

[65]*Union College*, 247 NLRB 531, 103 LRRM 1196 (1980); *Consolidated Fibres, Inc.*, 205 NLRB 557, 84 LRRM 1020 (1973).

[66]NLRB Casehandling Manual ¶11026.2(b).

[67]*Id.* at ¶11026.2(c).

[68]*Id.*

[69]*Id.* at ¶11194.3.

not purporting to be labor organizations, or to organizations which have been determined by the Board to be company-dominated and therefore ordered disestablished.[70]

(c) Applications for Subpoenas. Subpoenas are available to any party. There are two basic types of subpoenas: (1) *subpoena ad testificandum* which requires the party served to appear for the sole purpose of giving testimony (see Exhibit 33), and (2) *subpoena duces tecum* which requires the party served to appear both to give testimony and to present documents named in the subpoena (see Exhibit 34). Both are obtained by filing a written application with the regional director if made before the opening of the hearing, or with the hearing officer at the hearing.[71] The application need not name either the witness or the documents sought. Questions pertaining to the adequacy of the subpoena or to the relevancy of the information requested are reviewed not upon issuance of the subpoena, but upon a motion to revoke. Also, notice of such application need not be communicated to the other parties.[72] The regional director or the hearing officer must furnish the subpoenas requested.[73] If the person against whom the subpoena is issued does not intend to comply, a petition to revoke may be filed with the regional director within five working days from the date of service. Upon receipt of such petition, the regional director or hearing officer will give immediate notice to the party upon whose request the subpoena was issued.[74]

The regional director or hearing officer may revoke the subpoena for a number of reasons. Most often it is revoked because it seeks evidence which does not relate to any matter under investigation or it does not describe with sufficient particularity the evidence sought. The regional director or hearing officer must provide reasons for their rulings.[75] Failure to file a timely petition to revoke a subpoena may bar the party from making a subsequent attack on that subpoena, thereby compelling production of the desired data.

The petition to revoke a subpoena, any answer filed thereto, and the regional director's or hearing officer's ruling on the petition become part of the record only upon request of the aggrieved party.[76]

(d) Postponements. There are a variety of reasons why it may be desirable or necessary to have a postponement during the course

---

[70]*Id.*

[71]NLRB Rules and Regulations §102.66(c); NLRB Casehandling Manual ¶¶11210–11214. Procedures for acquiring subpoenas in preparation for or during unfair labor practice hearings are similar. See discussion §15.13 and §16.20.

[72]NLRB Rules and Regulations §102.66(c).

[73]*Id.* NLRB Casehandling Manual ¶11140.3.

[74]NLRB Rules and Regulations §102.66(c). Petitions to revoke must be received by the regional director within the five-day period, not simply placed in the mails. NLRB Rules and Regulations §102.111(b)(4).

[75]*Id.*

[76]NLRB Rules and Regulations §§102.65(c), 102.66(c).

☆U. S. GOVERNMENT PRINTING OFFICE: 1984—435-443

FORM NLRB-32
(1-83)

SUBPOENA

UNITED STATES OF AMERICA
NATIONAL LABOR RELATIONS BOARD

To _____

_____

Request therefor having been duly made by _____

_____

whose address is _____
        (Street)   (City)   (State)

YOU ARE HEREBY REQUIRED AND DIRECTED TO APPEAR Before _____

_____ of the National Labor Relations Board,

at _____

in the City of _____

on the   day of   , 19   , at   o'clock   m.   of that day, to testify in the

Matter of

_____

_____

_____

_____

A- 843050

In testimony whereof, the seal of the National Labor Relations Board is affixed hereto, and the undersigned, a member of said National Labor Relations Board, has hereunto authorized the issuance hereof.

Issued at

this   day of   19

Robert P. Hunter

NOTICE TO WITNESS.—Witness fees for attendance, subsistence, and mileage, under this subpoena are payable by the party at whose request the witness is subpoenaed. A witness appearing at the request of the General Counsel of the National Labor Relations Board shall submit this subpoena with the voucher when claiming reimbursement.

Exhibit 33. Subpoena Ad Testificandum (Form NLRB-32)

☆U.S. GOVERNMENT PRINTING OFFICE 1983-398-502

FORM NLRB-31
(1-83)

SUBPOENA DUCES TECUM

UNITED STATES OF AMERICA
NATIONAL LABOR RELATIONS BOARD

To

Request therefor having been duly made by

whose address is

YOU ARE HEREBY REQUIRED AND DIRECTED TO APPEAR BEFORE

of the National Labor Relations Board,

at

in the City of

on the   day of   , 19   , at   o'clock   m. of that day, to testify in the

Matter of

And you are hereby required to bring with you and produce at said time and place the following books, records, correspondence, and documents:

B- 413003

In testimony whereof, the seal of the National Labor Relations Board is affixed hereto, and the undersigned, a member of said National Labor Relations Board, has hereunto authorized the issuance hereof.

Issued at

this   day of   , 19

Robert P. Hunter

NOTICE TO WITNESS.—Witness fees for attendance, subsistence, and mileage, under this subpoena are payable by the party at whose request the witness is subpoenaed. A witness appearing at the request of the General Counsel of the National Labor Relations Board shall submit this subpoena with the voucher when claiming reimbursement.

Exhibit 34.   Subpoena Duces Tecum (Form NLRB-31)

of a hearing. For example, the hearing may be recessed in order to allow the parties to negotiate a consent agreement,[77] to allow the petitioner to withdraw the petition,[78] or to permit one of the parties to issue and enforce a subpoena.[79] If a consent agreement is reached or a withdrawal request filed, the hearing will be adjourned indefinitely pending approval by the regional director. With regard to subpoenas, if the hearing officer feels that the testimony or the documentary evidence sought to be acquired through the subpoena is relevant and there are no more expeditious ways of acquiring the information, a reasonable adjournment will be granted.[80]

The parties also may seek postponements in order to allow new counsel to become familiar with the case, or in order to acquire additional relevant evidence not immediately available. When considering such requests the hearing officer will balance the desirability of prompt hearings against the need for a complete record. Brief continuances of a few days generally are granted upon good cause shown, but longer delays are discouraged and the hearing officer may seek to accommodate the parties' interests in other ways. If the postponement is requested in order to acquire additional evidence, for example, the hearing officer may adjourn the proceedings to a more convenient location, or may seek a stipulation from the parties.[81] The hearing officer also may suggest that the closing of the hearing be made subject to the introduction of a later acquired exhibit.[82]

Postponements may be to a day certain or may be indefinite. In the latter instance the hearing will be resumed upon issuance of an order from the hearing officer to the parties which will be made a part of the record. If the reason for resuming the hearing no longer exists, it will be closed by an order of the hearing officer.[83]

§7.7   Presentation of Evidence

(a) *Issues Excluded From Representation Hearing.* The Board through its decisions has developed rules with respect to the types of evidence which will not be permitted to be introduced at representation hearings. Following are some basic areas in which testimony will not be received in the representation hearing:

- The adequacy of the showing of interest submitted by a union.[84]

---

[77]NLRB Casehandling Manual ¶11188.

[78]*Id.* at ¶11208.

[79]*Id.* at ¶11214.

[80]*Id.*

[81]*Id.* at ¶11238.2.

[82]*Id.* at ¶11224.7.

[83]*Id.* at ¶11238.3.

[84]*Neighborhood Legal Servs., Inc.,* 236 NLRB 1269, 98 LRRM 1414 (1978); NLRB Casehandling Manual ¶11196.

- Allegations that authorization cards were procured by misrepresentation or coercion,[85] or that they have been revoked,[86] or that they are stale,[87] or that supervisors influenced or participated in the union's acquisition of a showing of interest.[88]

- The manner, method, or procedure employed by the Board in evaluating the showing of interest or determining whether an employer petition is supported by "objective considerations."[89]

- Alleged commission of unfair labor practices by one of the parties, unless such matters are material to the issue of whether a question concerning representation exists.[90]

- The meaning of a contract's provisions, where the contract's language is clear and unambiguous.[91]

- The practices of the contracting parties under union-security or checkoff clauses regardless of the contract's ambiguity.[92]

- The eligibility of employees for union membership.[93]

- The extent to which economic strikers have been replaced.[94]

- Whether the union maintains discriminatory membership policies.[95]

- Alleged union violation of federal statutes.[96]

- While evidence pertaining to the scope and composition of the requested bargaining unit is appropriate, evidence with respect to a substantially different bargaining unit sought by a union will not be received absent an adequate showing of interest in the alternate unit.

(b) Stipulations at Hearing. From time to time in the course of the hearing—either on or off the record—the hearing officer may try to obtain all-party stipulations. These are factual agreements

---

[85]*American Beauty Baking Co.*, 198 NLRB 327, 81 LRRM 1228 (1972); *Standard Cigar Co.*, 117 NLRB 852, 39 LRRM 1332 (1957). If evidence of *fraud* is sought to be introduced at the hearing, the party seeking its introduction should bring it to the attention of the regional director within five working days for administrative investigation. The hearing should not be interrupted. NLRB Casehandling Manual ¶11196.1.

[86]*General Dynamics Corp.*, 175 NLRB 1035, 71 LRRM 1116 (1969).

[87]*Cleveland Cliffs Iron Co.*, 117 NLRB 668, 39 LRRM 1319 (1957).

[88]*Adelphi Univ.*, 195 NLRB 639, 79 LRRM 1545 (1972); *Southeastern Rubber Mfg. Co.*, 173 NLRB 797, 69 LRRM 1434 (1968). NLRB Casehandling Manual ¶11228.

[89]*Milwaukee Indep. Meat Packers Ass'n*, 223 NLRB 922, 92 LRRM 1138 (1976).

[90]*Foothill Elec. Corp.*, 120 NLRB 1350, 42 LRRM 1184 (1958); NLRB Casehandling Manual ¶11228.

[91]*Reading Hardware Corp.*, 85 NLRB 610, 24 LRRM 1446 (1949); *see also Knife River Coal Mining Co.*, 96 NLRB 1, 28 LRRM 1474 (1951).

[92]*Paragon Prods. Corp.*, 134 NLRB 662, 49 LRRM 1160 (1961).

[93]*Northern Redwood Lumber Co.*, 88 NLRB 272, 25 LRRM 1307 (1950).

[94]*Eastern Camera & Photo Corp.*, 140 NLRB 569, 52 LRRM 1068 (1963).

[95]*United Constr. Contractors Ass'n*, 212 NLRB 767, 86 LRRM 1734 (1974); *S. H. Kress & Co.*, 212 NLRB 132, 86 LRRM 1508 (1974); *Petrie Stores Corp.*, 212 NLRB 130, 86 LRRM 1509 (1974).

[96]*S. H. Kress & Co.*, 212 NLRB 132, 86 LRRM 1508 (1974).

issues pertinent to the hearing, undertaken to narrow the contested issues and to shorten the hearing.[97] The regional director or the Board will not be bound by any stipulation that is inconsistent with the statute or Board policy. Thus, contrary to all-party stipulations, the Board has excluded guards[98] and supervisors[99] from agreed-upon units. Likewise, the parties' stipulation that an employer is engaged in commerce within the meaning of the Act and that the Board should exercise jurisdiction is not binding. The Board may still determine whether assertion of jurisdiction would be contrary to its policy.[100]

Although the language of a stipulated unit may not in all respects be that usually employed by the Board, the regional director or the Board will decline to disturb the agreed-upon unit as long as it does not violate Board policy.[101] The Board has ruled, however, that stipulated units, even though not contrary to law or policy, do not establish Board policy with respect to unit composition.[102]

When entering into stipulations covering the composition of a unit, parties should make certain that they are acquainted with the duties of the employees who are to be included in or excluded from the unit. Referring to its well-established "policy of honoring concessions made in the interest of expeditious handling of representation cases,"[103] the regional director or Board will refuse to reopen a record on the posthearing plea of a party's oversight or lack of knowledge at the time it entered into the stipulation.[104]

(c) Witnesses. When stipulations cannot be reached, the record is developed through testimonial and documentary evidence. As noted earlier, the rules of evidence used in the federal courts are not controlling,[105] but they frequently are used as guidance. Relevance and completeness are the principal considerations in determining the admissibility of evidence.[106]

All witnesses are sworn by the hearing officer prior to testifying and are subject to cross-examination.[107] The refusal of a witness to answer a proper question is grounds for striking all testimony previously given by the witness on related matters.[108] All objections to

---

[97]*See generally* NLRB Casehandling Manual ¶11222.

[98]*Colonial Shirt Corp.*, 114 NLRB 1214, 37 LRRM 1136 (1959).

[99]*Central Cigar & Tobacco Co.*, 112 NLRB 1094, 36 LRRM 1151 (1955).

[100]*East Newark Realty Corp.*, 115 NLRB 483, 37 LRRM 1328 (1956). Jurisdictional requirements are discussed in chapter 3.

[101]*Buckley Southland Oil*, 210 NLRB 1060, 86 LRRM 1340 (1974).

[102]*Eavey Co.*, 115 NLRB 1779, 38 LRRM 1177 (1956).

[103]*New York Shipping Ass'n*, 109 NLRB 1075, 1077–1078, 34 LRRM 1492, 1493 (1954).

[104]*Sport Coach Corp.*, 203 NLRB 145, 83 LRRM 1152 (1973); *Cruis Along Boats, Inc.*, 128 NLRB 1019, 46 LRRM 1419 (1960); *Stanley Aviation Corp.*, 112 NLRB 461, 36 LRRM 1028 (1955).

[105]NLRB Rules and Regulations §102.66(a).

[106]NLRB Casehandling Manual ¶11216.

[107]NLRB Casehandling Manual ¶11220.

[108]*Id.* NLRB Rules and Regulations §102.66(d)(3).

questions asked and all motions to strike testimony must be ruled on by the hearing officer. Upon rejection of proffered testimony, a party may make an offer of proof or be requested by the hearing officer to do so.[109]

Witness fees and mileage are paid by the party at whose request the witness appears.[110] The fees paid are the same as those paid in the federal courts.

(d) Exhibits. Documents and records which are material and relevant to the issues under consideration may be introduced into evidence once their authenticity has been established. Unlike unfair labor practice hearings, exhibits need not be submitted in duplicate.[111] In an effort to maintain a clear and concise record, the hearing officer may ask the parties to read or otherwise identify portions of lengthy documents which they feel are pertinent.

Close of the Hearing

§7.8   Oral Argument and Briefs

Any party is entitled, upon request, to a reasonable period for oral argument before the hearing officer at the close of the hearing.[112] Such oral argument will be included in the stenographic report of the hearing.

Parties also have the right to file briefs with the regional director or the Board, as the case may be, within seven days after the close of the hearing.[113] However, the hearing officer is empowered to grant an additional 14 days for the submission of briefs, provided that the request for an extension of time is made before the close of the hearing.[114] Such request and supporting reasons must be stated on the record.

The granting of extension requests is discretionary with the hearing officer. Factors considered include (1) the reasons offered by the requesting party, (2) the length of the transcript, (3) the complexity of the issues, (4) the time anticipated to receive the transcript, (5) the length of time the parties have had to prepare the case, and (6)

---

[109]NLRB Casehandling Manual ¶11226.

[110]NLRB Rules and Regulations §102.66(g). See §16.9 regarding fees paid to witnesses in unfair labor practice proceedings.

[111]NLRB Casehandling Manual ¶11224.

[112]NLRB Rules and Regulations §102.66(e); NLRB Casehandling Manual ¶11240.

[113]NLRB Rules and Regulations §102.67(a), (i). In Sec. 8(b)(7) cases the parties may not file briefs unless special permission is granted by the regional director or by the Board. See §20.10 and NLRB Casehandling Manual ¶11244.2.

[114]NLRB Rules and Regulations §102.67(a).

previous delays or postponements granted to the requesting party.[115] If the parties object to the hearing officer's ruling, extensions may be requested of the regional director or the Board following the close of the hearing.[116]

§7.9   The Hearing Officer's Report

Shortly after the close of the hearing, the hearing officer submits a report to the regional director or to the Board, as the case may be.[117] It consists of an analysis of the issues presented at the hearing and a summary of the evidence. The statute prohibits the hearing officer from including any recommendations in the report.[118] The Board repeatedly has ruled that the report is an administrative document and therefore is not available for inspection by any of the parties.[119]

---

[115]NLRB Casehandling Manual ¶11244.3.
[116]*Id.*
[117]NLRB Rules and Regulations §102.66(f).
[118]Sec. 9(c)(1).
[119]*Radio Corp.*, 89 NLRB 699, 26 LRRM 1022 (1950).

8

Posthearing Procedures, Withdrawals, and Disclaimers

Procedures Before the Regional Director

§8.1 Transmittal of Record and Filing of Briefs

After the close of the hearing, the entire record in the case is forwarded to the regional director or, upon issuance by the regional director of an order transferring the case,[1] to the Board in Washington. The record includes: the petition, notice of hearing with affidavit of service, motions, rulings, orders, the stenographic report of the hearing, stipulations, and exhibits.[2]

There are certain established requirements for all formal documents—motions and briefs for example—which are submitted for consideration:

- If a brief or motion is filed with the regional director, an original and one copy must be presented; if the case is before the Board, eight copies must be filed.[3]
- Typed carbon copies of original documents will be accepted by regional directors, but not by the Board. In addition, the Board requires that all documents be double spaced and filed on 8-1/2 by 11-inch paper.[4]

---

[1]NLRB Rules and Regulations §102.67(h).

[2]*Id.* at §102.68. The record subsequently may be supplemented with the stenographic transcript of any oral argument before the regional director, affidavits of service, any briefs or other legal memoranda submitted by the parties to the regional director or to the Board, and the regional director's decision.

[3]*Id.* at §§102.67(a), 102.67(k)(1).

[4]*Id.*

- Copies must be served upon all other parties and proof of such service must be filed with the documents.[5]

Parties who wish to file briefs with the regional director generally must do so within seven days of the close of the hearing. For good cause, the hearing officer at the hearing may grant an extension not to exceed an additional 14 days.[6] Requests for further extensions should be addressed to the regional director, or if the case has been transferred to the Board, to the Board's Executive Secretary. The need for the extension must be explained. Extension requests should be served immediately upon the other parties, including the regional director if the request is filed with the Board, and should be made no later than three working days before the date the briefs are due.[7]

Parties do not have an absolute right to file reply briefs, but may do so upon receipt of special permission.[8] Special leave must also be obtained by an organization desiring to present its views as an *amicus curiae*, and such leave usually is granted.[9]

§8.2   Posthearing Motions

All motions filed after the close of the hearing must be filed directly with the regional director or, if the case has been transferred to the Board, with the Board. Such motions should state briefly the order or relief sought and the grounds therefor.[10] Any party, including the regional director, may file an answer to a motion. The answer should be filed promptly in the same form and manner as other documents.[11]

In general, posthearing motions for reconsideration of the regional director's decision or report, for reopening of the record, or for rehearing are not favored. They may be granted by the regional director or by the Board, however, in "extraordinary circumstances."[12] Such motions will not be granted with regard to any matter which could have been but was not raised at the hearing.

Motions for reconsideration must specifically state the error relied upon and refer to appropriate portions of the record. Motions for reopening the record or for rehearing also must specify:

- The error alleged to require a rehearing or hearing *de novo*;

---

[5]*Id.* at §§102.67(a), 102.67(k)(2).

[6]*Id.* at §§102.67(a), 102.67(i).

[7]*Id.* at §102.67(k)(3).

[8]*Id.* at §§102.67(a), 102.67(i).

[9]*United States Gypsum Co.*, 118 NLRB 20, 40 LRRM 1120 (1957).

[10]NLRB Rules and Regulations §102.65(a); NLRB Casehandling Manual ¶11262.

[11]NLRB Casehandling Manual ¶11264; *Westinghouse Elec. Corp.*, 108 NLRB 556, 34 LRRM 1039 (1954).

[12]NLRB Rules and Regulations §102.65(e)(1).

- The prejudice to the requesting party resulting from such error;
- The additional evidence sought to be introduced and why it was not previously presented; and
- The result which would be required if the evidence were introduced and credited.[13]

If the record is reopened, only evidence discovered since the hearing or evidence which the regional director or the Board believes should have been taken will be admitted.

Motions for reconsideration or for rehearing must be filed within 14 days after service of the regional director's decision or report.[14] Motions to reopen the record must be filed promptly upon discovery of the information sought to be introduced. Requests for extensions of time to file a motion must be received three days prior to the due date and must be served upon the other parties. The fact that a posthearing motion is pending will not delay implementation of an order that certain action be undertaken.[15] If, however, the motion indicates that the eligibility of certain individuals to vote in the election may be affected if the motion is granted, the ballots of those individuals will be challenged and impounded pending a ruling on the motion.[16]

§8.3 Oral Argument

Any party desiring to supplement the briefs with oral argument may file a request with the regional director or the Board after the close of the hearing and before issuance of the decision.[17] Regional directors occasionally permit oral argument in novel situations. Due to the large volume of cases, however, permission is rarely granted by the Board. Neither the right of the regional director nor that of the Board to order oral argument is dependent upon a request from the parties. Either may set a date for hearing oral argument at their discretion in cases before them for decision.

Whenever a request for oral argument is granted by the Board, all parties are served with a notice of hearing. (See Exhibit 35.) The regional director's notice of hearing for oral argument is similar in style. The oral argument is conducted in the regional office if before the regional director or in Washington if before the Board. Each party to the proceeding normally is entitled to a 30-minute argument. Requests for additional time may not be granted unless timely appli-

---

[13]*Id.*

[14]*Id.* at §102.65(e)(2).

[15]*Id.* at §102.65(e)(3).

[16]The Board's "vote and impound" policies are discussed further at §§8.9, 8.11, and 9.9.

[17]NLRB Rules and Regulations §102.67(a); NLRB Statements of Procedure §101.21(b).

UNITED STATES OF AMERICA

BEFORE THE NATIONAL LABOR RELATIONS BOARD

JANCO COMPUTER SERVICES, INC.

      and   Case No. 5-RC-1234

LOCAL 007, UNITED COMPUTER OPERATORS
  INTERNATIONAL UNION

NOTICE OF HEARING

PLEASE TAKE NOTICE that, pursuant to the authority invested in the National Labor Relations Board under the National Labor Relations Act, as amended, a hearing will be held before the National Labor Relations Board on February 2, 1986, in Room 640, 1717 Pennsylvania Avenue, N.W., Washington, D.C., for the purpose of oral argument in the above-entitled proceeding.

Dated, Washington, D.C., 2 January 1986.

By direction of the Board:

_____
      Associate Executive Secretary

Exhibit 35. Notice of Oral Argument

cation is made in advance of oral argument. It is not unusual for persons who have filed *amicus curiae* briefs to be permitted to argue orally.

§8.4 Decision of the Regional Director or the Board

The decision by the regional director, or by the Board if the case has been transferred to it, is made on the basis of the entire record. The decision sets forth the facts of the case, the issues in dispute, the contentions of the parties, and a determination of the issues with supporting reasons. Issues most frequently resolved in these decisions include the timeliness of the petition, the appropriateness of the bargaining unit, and the eligibility of disputed employees to vote. In most instances the regional director or the Board will either dismiss the petition or direct an election.

(a) Decision and Order. Regional directors, or the Board in transferred cases, dismiss election petitions through issuance of a Decision and Order. (See Exhibit 36.) The director will review any objections to the rulings made by the hearing officer at the hearing, determine whether the employer satisfies the Board's statutory and discretionary jurisdictional standards,[18] and evaluate whether the labor organizations involved wish to represent employees of the employer. Even in cases where these prerequisites are satisfied, however, the regional director or the Board may nevertheless dismiss the petition on the basis that a question concerning representation does not exist. In addition to jurisdictional defects, petitions often are dismissed on the basis that they are untimely,[19] are not supported by an adequate showing of interest,[20] or seek representation rights in an inappropriate bargaining unit.[21]

(b) Decision and Direction of Election. Regional directors, or the Board in transferred cases, direct elections through issuance of a Decision and Direction of Election. (See Exhibit 37.) As with Decisions and Orders, the hearing officer's rulings are reviewed, the application of the Board's jurisdictional standards to the employer are evaluated, and the interest of the labor organizations involved in representing the employer's employees is determined. After concluding that a question affecting commerce exists, the director or the Board then defines the appropriate bargaining unit and describes the eligible voters.

---

[18] See discussion at chapter 3.
[19] See discussion at §§5.4–5.10 *supra*.
[20] See discussion at §5.12 *supra*.
[21] See discussion at §8.5 *infra*.

FORM NLRB-4479
(3-84)

UNITED STATES OF AMERICA
BEFORE THE NATIONAL LABOR RELATIONS BOARD

DECISION AND ORDER

Upon a petition duly filed under Section 9(c) of the National Labor Relations Act, as amended, a hearing was held before a hearing officer of the National Labor Relations Board.

Pursuant to the provisions of Section 3(b) of the Act, the Board has delegated its authority in this proceeding to the undersigned.

Upon the entire record in this proceeding, the undersigned finds:

1. The hearing officer's rulings made at the hearing are free from prejudicial error and are hereby affirmed.

2. The Employer is engaged in commerce within the meaning of the Act and it will effectuate the purposes of the Act to assert jurisdiction herein.

3. The labor organization(s) involved claim(s) to represent certain employees of the Employer.

4. No question affecting commerce exists concerning the representation of certain employees of the Employer within the meaning of Section 9(c) (1) and Section 2(6) (7) of the Act, for the following reasons:

ORDER

IT IS HEREBY ORDERED that the petition(s) filed herein be, and it (they) hereby is (are), dismissed.

RIGHT TO REQUEST REVIEW

Under the provisions of Section 102.67 of the Board's Rules and Regulations, a request for review of this Decision may be filed with the National Labor Relations Board, addressed to the Executive Secretary, 1717 Pennsylvania Avenue, NW., Washington, D.C. 20570. This request must be received by the Board in Washington by

Dated _____

at _____

_____
Regional Director, Region

Exhibit 36. Decision and Order Dismissing Petition (Form NLRB-4479)

FORM NLRB-4477
(8-63)

UNITED STATES OF AMERICA
BEFORE THE NATIONAL LABOR RELATIONS BOARD

DECISION AND DIRECTION OF ELECTION

Upon a petition duly filed under Section 9(c) of the National Labor Relations Act, as amended, a hearing was held before a hearing officer of the National Labor Relations Board; hereinafter referred to as the Board.

Pursuant to the provisions of Section 3(b) of the Act, the Board has delegated its authority in this proceeding to the undersigned.

Upon the entire record in this proceeding, the undersigned finds:

1. The hearing officer's rulings made at the hearing are free from prejudicial error and are hereby affirmed.

2. The Employer is engaged in commerce within the meaning of the Act and it will effectuate the purposes of the Act to assert jurisdiction herein.

3. The labor organization(s) involved claim(s) to represent certain employees of the Employer.

4. A question affecting commerce exists concerning the representation of certain employees of the Employer within the meaning of Section 9(c)(1) and Section 2(6) and (7) of the Act.

5. The following employees of the Employer constitute a unit appropriate for the purpose of collective bargaining within the meaning of Section 9(b) of the Act:

DIRECTION OF ELECTION

An election by secret ballot shall be conducted by the undersigned among the employees in the unit(s) found appropriate at the time and place set forth in the notice of election to be issued subsequently, subject to the Board's Rules and Regulations. Eligible to vote are those in the unit(s) who were employed during the payroll period ending immediately preceding the date of this Decision, including employees who did not work during that period because they were ill, on vacation, or temporarily laid off. Also eligible are employees engaged in an economic strike which commenced less than 12 months before the election date and who retained their status as such during the eligibility period and their replacements. Those in the military services of the United States may vote if they appear in person at the polls. Ineligible to vote are employees who have quit or been discharged for cause since the designated payroll

OVER

Exhibit 37.　Decision and Direction of Election　(Form NLRB-4477)

period, employees engaged in a strike who have been discharge for cause since the commencement thereof and who have not been rehired or reinstated before the election date, and employees engaged in an economic strike which commenced more than 12 months before the election date and who have been permanently replaced. Those eligible shall vote whether or not they desire to be represented for collective bargaining purposes by

LIST OF VOTERS

In order to insure that all eligible voters may have the opportunity to be informed of the issues in the exercise of their statutory right to vote, all parties to the election should have access to a list of voters and their addresses which may be used to communicate with them. **Excelsior Underwear, Inc.,** 156 NLRB 1236 *(1966)*; **N.L.R.B.** v. **Wyman-Gordon Company,** 394 U.S. 759 *(1969)*. Accordingly, it is hereby directed that within 7 days of the date of this Decision _____ copies of an election eligibility list, containing the names and addresses of all the eligible voters, shall be filed by the Employer with the undersigned/Officer-in-Charge of the Subregion who shall make the list available to all parties to the election. In order to be timely filed, such list must be received in the

on or before   No extension of time to file this list shall be granted except in extraordinary circumstances, nor shall the filing of a request for review operate to stay the requirement here imposed.

RIGHT TO REQUEST REVIEW

Under the provisions of Section 102.67 of the Board's Rules and Regulations, a request for review of this Decision may be filed with the National Labor Relations Board, addressed to the Executive Secretary, 1717 Pennsylvania Avenue, NW., Washington D.C. 20570. This request must be received by the Board in Washington by

Dated _____

at _____   _____

                                    Regional Director, Region

Exhibit 37—*page 2*

§8.5 Appropriate Bargaining Unit

The description of the appropriate bargaining unit is the most common issue in a representation case. The Board, however, has not developed strict rules for defining bargaining units in all cases. Its guiding principle is that employees in a bargaining unit should share a "community of interest." Such a community of interest typically is found in similarity of wages and hours, common supervision, frequent interchange or functional integration with other employees, and area practice and bargaining history.[22] It should be noted that the Board is required only to designate *an* appropriate unit; it need not define the *most* appropriate bargaining unit.[23]

(a) Statutory Limitations. While the Board generally exercises wide discretion in determining bargaining units, it is limited by some basic rules provided in the Act:

- A unit may not include both professional and nonprofessional employees unless a majority of the professional employees vote to be included in such a unit.[24]

- The Board may not find a proposed craft unit inappropriate on the ground that a different unit has been established by a prior Board determination unless a majority of employees in the proposed craft unit vote against separate representation.[25]

- Guards may not be included in a unit with nonguard employees and the Board may not certify a guard union if it admits nonguards to membership or is affiliated directly or indirectly with a union containing nonguard members.[26]

---

[22]*St. Francis Hosp.*, 271 NLRB 948 n.35, 116 LRRM 1465 n.35 (1984) and cases cited therein.

[23]*Roman Catholic Diocese of Brooklyn*, 236 NLRB 1 n.1, 98 LRRM 1359 (1978); *Morand Bros. Beverage Co.*, 91 NLRB 409, 26 LRRM 1501 (1950).

[24]Sec. 9(b)(1). Sec. 2(12) of the Act defines a "professional" employee as

"(a) any employee engaged in work (i) predominantly intellectual and varied in character as opposed to routine mental, manual, mechanical, or physical work; (ii) involving the consistent exercise of discretion and judgment in its performance; (iii) of such a character that the output produced or the result accomplished cannot be standardized in relation to a given period of time; (iv) requiring knowledge of an advanced type in a field of science or learning customarily acquired by a prolonged course of specialized intellectual instruction and study in an institution of higher learning or a hospital, as distinguished from a general academic education or from an apprenticeship or from training in the performance of routine mental, manual, or physical processes; or (b) any employee, who (i) has completed the courses of specialized intellectual instruction and study described in clause (iv) of paragraph (a), and (ii) is performing related work under the supervision of a professional person to qualify himself to become a professional employee as defined in paragraph (a)."
See also §1.11(c) regarding the definition of a "professional employee," §§8.6(b) and 9.12(b) regarding self-determination elections for professional employees, and THE DEVELOPING LABOR LAW at 422–424.

[25]Sec. 9(b)(2). Craft severance election procedures also are discussed at §§8.6 and 9.12.

[26]Sec. 9(b)(3). Special rules pertaining to the representation of guards are discussed at §1.11(b).

- The appropriateness of a unit may not turn on the extent to which it already is organized by the union.[27]

The Board also has established special rules concerning the exclusion of specific types of employees from bargaining units.

(b) Confidential Employees.   An employee may be excluded from a rank-and-file bargaining unit as a confidential employee only if the employee assists "persons who formulate, determine *and* effectuate management policies in the field of labor relations,"[28] or regularly has access to confidential information concerning collective bargaining negotiations.[29]

(c) Managerial Employees.   Managerial employees are those who

> "formulate and effectuate management policies by expressing and making operative the decisions of their employer, and those who have discretion in the performance of their jobs independent of their employer's established policy."[30]

These employees are excluded from the coverage of the Act[31] as well as from rank-and-file bargaining units in order to avoid any division of loyalty between management and the union.[32]

(d) Supervisory Employees.   Supervisory employees are defined as

> "individuals . . . having authority in the interest of the employer, to hire, transfer, suspend, lay off, recall, promote, discharge, assign, reward, or discipline other employees, or responsibility to direct them, or to adjust their grievances, or effectively to recommend such action, if in connection with the foregoing the exercise of such authority is not of a merely routine or clerical nature, but requires the use of independent judgment."[33]

Supervisory employees are excluded from coverage of the Act,[34] and cannot be included in a rank-and-file bargaining unit. They may,

---

[27]Sec. 9(c)(5).

[28]*B.F. Goodrich Co.*, 115 NLRB 722, 724, 37 LRRM 1383, 1384 (1956), *quoted with approval in NLRB v. Hendricks County Rural Elec. Membership Corp.*, 454 U.S. 170, 108 LRRM 3105 (1981). *See also Trailways, Inc.*, 271 NLRB 612, 117 LRRM 1023 (1984) (secretary to individual who formulates and effectuates labor relations policies excluded from unit as confidential employee even though individual's labor relations authority did not encompass unit employees).

[29]*Pullman Standard Div. of Pullman, Inc.*, 214 NLRB 762, 87 LRRM 1370 (1974).

[30]*General Dynamics Corp.*, 213 NLRB 851, 75 LRRM 1705 (1974), *cited with approval in NLRB v. Bell Aerospace Co.*, 416 U.S. 267, 85 LRRM 2945 (1974); *See also NLRB v. Yeshiva Univ.*, 444 U.S. 672, 103 LRRM 2576 (1980) (managerial status of university faculty) and *FHP, Inc.*, 274 NLRB No. 168, 118 LRRM 1525 (1985) (managerial status of physicians and dentists).

[31]*NLRB v. Bell Aerospace Co.*, 416 U.S. 267, 85 LRRM 2945 (1974).

[32]*See* THE DEVELOPING LABOR LAW at 1457–1459.

[33]Sec. 2(11).

[34]*Id.*

however, without Board sanction join units composed only of supervisors, and employers may bargain voluntarily with such groups.[35]

(e) Clerical Employees. Clerical employees are categorized as either office clerical, considered to be "white collar" office workers, or plant clerical, considered to have interests similar to those involved in production. Office clericals typically are excluded from a rank-and-file bargaining unit while plant clericals usually are included.[36]

In addition to special rules regarding certain types of employees, the Board also has developed criteria for determining the appropriateness of bargaining units in certain situations.

(f) Health Care Institutions. In 1974 Congress amended the Act to cover all hospitals, nursing homes, extended-care facilities, and health maintenance organizations,[37] but in doing so warned the Board that "due consideration should be given . . . to preventing proliferation of bargaining units in the health care industry."[38] Congress intended to limit the number of bargaining units in health care facilities in order to minimize labor disruptions which might interfere with patient care.

The Board in late 1982 announced a two-step procedure for determining the appropriateness of health care bargaining units.[39] In the first step, the unit sought by the petitioning union generally had to conform to one of the seven classifications of employees commonly found in health care institutions: physicians, registered nurses, other professional employees (e.g., pharmacists, physical therapists, lab technologists, social workers), technical employees (which usually includes licensed practical nurses), business office clerical employees, service and maintenance employees, and skilled maintenance employees.[40] Requested units which were defined more narrowly than those classifications (a unit consisting of only pharmacists, for example) were not granted unless "extraordinary and compelling facts" existed which justified the smaller unit.[41] Only after the first step test was satisfied would the regional director apply the Board's traditional "community of interest" test as the second step. Not only was a sufficient community of interest among employees within the

---

[35]Sec. 14(a).

[36]*Rish Equip. Co.*, 257 NLRB 808, 107 LRRM 1607 (1981); *Jensen's Motorcycle, Inc.*, 254 NLRB 1248, 107 LRRM 1095 (1981).

[37]Section 2(2) was amended to delete the exclusion of nonprofit hospitals from the definition of an "employer" covered by the Act.

[38]S. REP. No. 93-766, 93d Cong., 2d Sess. 5 (1974); H.R. REP. No. 93-1051, 93d Cong., 2d Sess. 7 (1974).

[39]*St. Francis Hosp.*, 265 NLRB 1025, 112 LRRM 1153 (1982) (*St. Francis I*).

[40]*Id.* For a more extensive treatment of these categories, *see* THE DEVELOPING LABOR LAW at 436–451.

[41]*St. Francis Hosp.*, 265 NLRB 1025, 112 LRRM 1153 (1982) (*St. Francis I*).

unit required, but this interest also had to have been sufficiently *distinct* from the interests of all other employees of the institution for the requested unit to be granted.[42]

In 1984, the Board abandoned its two-step approach to health care unit determinations and replaced it with a "disparity-of-interests" test in order to more fully effectuate Congress' admonition against unit proliferation.[43] The disparity-of-interests test starts with the premise that all health care employees should be included in a separate professional or nonprofessional unit unless their interests are so disparate as to justify a separate unit. The Board in *St. Francis II* summarized its new approach as judging the appropriateness of the petitioned-for unit "in terms of normal criteria, but sharper than usual differences (or 'disparities') between the wages, hours, and working conditions, etc., of the requested employees and those in an overall professional or nonprofessional unit must be established to grant the unit."[44] The Board felt that by focusing on disparities of interests, fewer units would result thus fulfilling Congress' intent.

The Board cautioned that the disparity-of-interests test should not be so narrowly construed as to provide for only a professional and nonprofessional unit. Rejecting such a *per se* approach, the Board held that separate representation must be justified on each factual record in light of the disparity-of-interests test.[45]

(g) Multiplant Units. The Board considers the single-plant unit to be presumptively appropriate in most cases.[46] A multiplant unit may be found appropriate, however, where a high degree of functional

---

[42]*Id.* Several courts of appeals took somewhat different approaches to this issue. The Ninth and Tenth Circuits established tests under which broad units (e.g., one unit of professional and one unit of nonprofessional employees) were presumed to be appropriate, with more narrow units justified only if their interests were sufficiently *dissimilar* to those of the broader unit. *Presbyterian/St. Luke's Medical Center v. NLRB*, 653 F.2d 450, 107 LRRM 2953 (10th Cir. 1981); *NLRB v. St. Francis Hosp.*, 601 F.2d 404, 101 LRRM 2943 (9th Cir. 1979). On the other hand, the Second, Eighth, and Eleventh Circuits rejected any rigid "disparity of interests" test, maintaining that the Board must strictly observe the congressional admonition against undue proliferation in making unit determinations. *NLRB v. Walker County Medical Center*, 722 F.2d 1535, 115 LRRM 2553 (11th Cir. 1984); *Watonwan Mem. Hosp. v. NLRB*, 711 F.2d 848, 113 LRRM 3481 (8th Cir. 1983); *Trustees of Masonic Hall and Asylum Fund v. NLRB*, 699 F.2d 626, 112 LRRM 2908 (2d Cir. 1982).

[43]*St. Francis Hosp.*, 271 NLRB 948, 116 LRRM 1465 (1984) (*St. Francis II*).

[44]*Id.*, 271 NLRB at 953, 116 LRRM at 1470 (footnote omitted).

[45]No clear pattern has emerged from the Board's post-*St. Francis II* decisions. In *Southern Maryland Hosp. Center*, 274 NLRB No. 212, 118 LRRM 1599 (1985), the Board found a unit limited to technical employees to be appropriate thereby indicating that units smaller than all professionals or all nonprofessionals will be approved in some cases. On the other hand, in *St. Luke's Mem. Hosp.*, 274 NLRB No. 202, 118 LRRM 1545 (1985), the Board vacated a previous certification in a unit limited to licensed and graduate practical nurses, finding that no "sharper than usual" differences existed between the nurses and other technical employees in the hospital. Finally, in *Kirksville College of Osteopathic Medicine, Inc.*, 274 NLRB No. 121, 118 LRRM 1443 (1985), the Board reversed its 1978 decision in *Albany Medical College*, 239 NLRB 853, 100 LRRM 1279 (1978), and held that medical schools which are affiliated with a hospital will be considered health care institutions under the Act when the functions, administration, and work force of the medical school are so highly integrated with those of the hospital that separating them for representation purposes would be impractical.

[46]*Wyandotte Sav. Bank*, 245 NLRB 943, 102 LRRM 1349 (1979).

integration exists among several separate facilities of the same employer. Factors which the Board considers include (1) prior bargaining history, (2) centralization of management, particularly with regard to labor relations, (3) extent of employee interchange, (4) degree of interdependence or autonomy among facilities, (5) difference or similarity in skills and functions of employees, and (6) relative geographical location of the facilities.[47]

(h) Multiemployer Units. A bargaining unit containing the employees of more than one employer will be found appropriate only if all affected employers and the union clearly consent to the arrangement.[48] The Board requires that employers manifest this consent either by participating in bargaining as a group[49] or by designating a joint agent to bargain for them.[50] While a bargaining history of multiemployer units is an important consideration, it will not itself justify a multiemployer unit absent the express consent of all parties.[51] Finally, an employer's participation in multiemployer bargaining with respect to some of its employees does not require that units of its remaining employees also bargain on a multiemployer basis.[52] A single-employer unit (of, for example, clerical employees[53]) will be found appropriate if the employees constitute a "homogeneous, separately identifiable group with internal cohesiveness."[54]

§8.6 Self-Determination Elections

In designating an appropriate unit, the Board sometimes will defer to the desires of affected employees as expressed in an election.

(a) "Globe" Elections. Frequently a group of employees may constitute two equally appropriate units—a smaller, craft or departmental unit, or one component of a comprehensive plantwide unit. In such cases the Board may allow the employees involved to choose one of the two units. This is known as a *Globe* election.[55]

---

[47]*Trustees of Columbia Univ.*, 222 NLRB 309, 91 LRRM 1276 (1976); *see also* THE DEVELOPING LABOR LAW at 432–436.

[48]*Tampa Bay Area Glazing Contractors Ass'n, Inc.*, 228 NLRB 360, 94 LRRM 1744 (1977).

[49]Employers may bargain together but execute separate contracts with the union that represents their employees. *Kroger Co.*, 148 NLRB 569, 57 LRRM 1021 (1964).

[50]*Greenhoot, Inc.*, 205 NLRB 250, 83 LRRM 1656 (1973).

[51]*Tampa Bay Area Glazing Contractors Ass'n, Inc.*, 228 NLRB 360, 94 LRRM 1744 (1977).

[52]*Joseph E. Seagram & Sons*, 101 NLRB 101, 31 LRRM 1022 (1952).

[53]*San Jose Motel*, 174 NLRB 1009, 70 LRRM 1378 (1969).

[54]*St. Luke's Hosp.*, 234 NLRB 130, 131, 97 LRRM 1099, 1100 (1978); *Los Angeles Statler Hilton Hotel*, 129 NLRB 1349, 47 LRRM 1194 (1961).

[55]*Globe Mach. & Stamping Co.*, 3 NLRB 294, 1A LRRM 122 (1937). This policy was approved by the Supreme Court in *Pittsburgh Plate Glass Co. v. NLRB*, 313 U.S. 146, 8 LRRM 425 (1941).

A necessary precondition to a *Globe* election is that a proposed separate craft or departmental unit be an appropriate one.[56] The Board considers the following factors in determining the appropriateness of a separate craft unit:

- Whether or not the proposed unit consists of a distinct and homogeneous group of skilled journeymen craftsmen performing the functions of their craft on a nonrepetitive basis, or of employees constituting a functionally distinct department, working in trades or occupations for which a tradition of separate representation exists.
- The history of collective bargaining of the employees sought and at the plant involved, and at other plants of the employer, with emphasis on whether the existing patterns of bargaining are productive of stability in labor relations, and whether such stability will be unduly disrupted by the destruction of the existing patterns of representation.
- The extent to which the employees in the proposed unit have established and maintained their separate identity during the period of inclusion in a broader unit, and the extent of their participation or lack of participation in the establishment and maintenance of the existing pattern of representation and the prior opportunities, if any, afforded them to obtain separate representation.
- The history and pattern of collective bargaining in the industry involved.
- The degree of integration of the employer's production processes, including the extent to which their continued normal operation is dependent upon the performance of the assigned functions of the employees in the proposed unit.
- The qualifications of the union seeking to "carve out" a separate unit, including that union's experience in representing employees like those involved in the severance action.[57]

Where a separate departmental (i.e., noncraft) unit is sought, the Board's standards of inquiry are less well-defined. While most determinations are made on a case-by-case basis, factors commonly considered include (1) differences in skills, (2) differences in training, (3) degree of common supervision, (4) interchange with other employees, and (5) differences in methods of performance evaluation.[58]

Globe elections may be held in a variety of situations. Where a plant is unorganized, employees in the proposed craft or departmental

---

[56]*Memphis Furniture Mfg. Co.*, 259 NLRB 401, 108 LRRM 1361 (1981).

[57]*Mallinckrodt Chem. Works*, 162 NLRB 387, 397, 64 LRRM 1011, 1016 (1966). Since *Mallinckrodt*, the Board has given the greatest weight to whether there has been a history of bargaining on a basis broader than the craft unit. *See Memphis Furniture Mfg. Co.*, 259 NLRB 401, 108 LRRM 1361 (1981).

[58]THE DEVELOPING LABOR LAW at 431.

unit will be given three choices: (1) representation by the petitioning craft or departmental union, (2) representation by the petitioning plantwide union, or (3) no union.[59] If only one union is seeking to represent unorganized employees on a plantwide basis, but a smaller unit is found appropriate along with the plantwide unit, separate elections may be ordered. If the union receives a majority vote of employees in both the smaller unit and the plantwide unit, the smaller unit will be included in the plantwide unit. If the union does not receive a majority in the smaller unit, the smaller unit will be found to be a separate, appropriate unit and will not be represented by the plantwide union.[60]

Where a plant is already organized and a union seeks to sever a craft or department from the plantwide unit to be represented separately, an election will be held within the smaller group. Employees will choose between (1) representation by the present plantwide union and (2) representation by a craft or departmental union. Employees in this situation may not vote "no union."[61]

(b) "Professional" Elections. The Act provides that the Board shall not find appropriate a unit which includes both professional and nonprofessional employees, unless a majority of the professional employees vote for inclusion in such a unit.[62] This election must be held even though professionals may greatly outnumber nonprofessionals in the proposed unit.[63] In addition, even though a majority of professionals may have voted for inclusion with nonprofessionals in the past, if a rival union petitions to represent the entire unit the professionals must again be given the opportunity to choose separate representation.[64]

In this type of election, professionals are given ballots containing two questions. The first asks whether the professional employee desires to be included in a unit with nonprofessionals. The second asks which union, if any, the employee wishes to have as the bargaining representative.[65]

(c) "Residual" Elections. In a partially organized plant, those employees who are not represented are generally known as "residual" or "fringe" employees. Where these employees were initially excluded

---

[59]*See Massachusetts Elec. Co.*, 248 NLRB 155, 103 LRRM 1404 (1980).

[60]*Underwood Mach. Co.*, 59 NLRB 42, 15 LRRM 109 (1944). *See also* THE DEVELOPING LABOR LAW at 420.

[61]NLRB Casehandling Manual ¶11090.1.

[62]Sec. 9(b)(1). Note that professionals may be represented together with nonprofessionals without an election in situations where the union is recognized voluntarily by the employer. The election is required only when the Board establishes such a unit. *Retail Clerks Local 324*, 144 NLRB 1247, 54 LRRM 1226 (1963).

[63]*See Leedom v. Kyne*, 358 U.S. 184, 43 LRRM 2222 (1958).

[64]*Westinghouse Elec. Corp.*, 115 NLRB 530, 37 LRRM 1341 (1956).

[65]NLRB Casehandling Manual ¶11090.1(b).

from the plantwide unit but their inclusion would have been appropriate, they may be granted the opportunity to vote for inclusion in the plantwide unit and representation by the union representing that unit.[66] If a second union seeks to represent only residual employees, these employees will choose between inclusion in the plantwide unit or representation by a separate union, constituting a separate bargaining unit.[67] Where a question concerning representation arises in the plantwide unit and at that time the incumbent union seeks to include residual employees in the larger unit, the Board will not allow residual employees to choose a separate unit; they must vote in the same way as their nonresidual counterparts.[68]

§8.7   Voter Eligibility

The eligibility of an employee to vote in a representation election generally turns upon two factors: (1) status as an "employee" during the eligibility period and on the election date[69] and (2) whether the employee is "sufficiently identified with the bargaining unit to have a community of interest with its other members."[70] The eligibility period typically is the payroll period which immediately precedes the direction of election.[71]

The Board has developed eligibility rules for the following classes of employees:

(a) Part-Time Employees.   Regular part-time employees are eligible.[72] Those part-time employees who work only irregularly are not eligible.[73] "Dual-function" employees, who spend only part time on bargaining unit work, are eligible if they have a substantial interest in conditions of employment in the bargaining unit.[74]

(b) Temporary and Seasonal Employees.   Temporary employees are eligible to vote only if they are employed during the

---

[66]*Armour & Co.*, 40 NLRB 1333, 10 LRRM 100 (1942); NLRB Casehandling Manual ¶11090.1(c)(1).

[67]NLRB Casehandling Manual ¶11090.1(c)(2).

[68]*D.V. Displays Corp.*, 134 NLRB 568, 49 LRRM 1199 (1961).

[69]*Famous Indus., Inc.*, 220 NLRB 484, 90 LRRM 1581 (1975).

[70]*NLRB v. Certified Testing Labs., Inc.*, 387 F.2d 275, 67 LRRM 2111 (3d Cir. 1967). *See generally* L. Modjeska, NLRB PRACTICE 228–229 (1983).

[71]*Heavenly Valley Ski Area v. NLRB*, 552 F.2d 269, 94 LRRM 3157 (9th Cir. 1977); *Gator Prods., Inc.*, 250 NLRB 282, 104 LRRM 1359 (1980) (an employee need not work during the entire eligibility period; he or she need only work at some time during that period).

[72]*Motz Poultry Co.*, 244 NLRB 573, 102 LRRM 1198 (1979); *Mount Sinai Hosp.*, 233 NLRB 507, 97 LRRM 1017 (1977).

[73]*NLRB v. Wehrenberg Theatres, Inc.*, 690 F.2d 159, 111 LRRM 2684 (8th Cir. 1982); *NLRB v. Boston Beef Co., Inc.*, 652 F.2d 223, 107 LRRM 3090 (1st Cir. 1981).

[74]*R.B.P., Inc.*, 176 NLRB 163, 71 LRRM 1195 (1969); *Berea Pub. Co.*, 140 NLRB 516, 52 LRRM 1051 (1963).

eligibility period and their tenure of employment is uncertain.[75] An employee's tenure is considered uncertain so long as no definite termination date is known, even though the employee may be aware that the employment will be shortlived.[76] An employee temporarily assigned to work outside of the bargaining unit, or to supervisory duties, is eligible to vote.[77] Seasonal employees may vote only if they have a reasonable expectation of reemployment.[78]

(c) Probationary Employees. Probationary employees may vote if their duties and working conditions are similar to those of regular employees and they have a reasonable expectation of permanent employment.[79]

(d) Employees on Leave of Absence or Temporary Layoff. Employees on sick leave or other leave of absence are eligible to vote if they will be restored to their jobs when they are ready to resume work.[80] Laid-off employees may vote if they have a reasonable expectation of recall.[81] A determination of this expectation depends upon objective factors, including the past experience of the employer regarding layoffs, the employer's future plans, the circumstances of the layoff, and representations made to employees by the employer.[82] This determination must be made upon information available at the time of the election, not upon any subsequent developments.[83]

(e) Employees Whose Employment Has Been Terminated. Employees who have voluntarily quit or have been discharged for cause are ineligible to vote.[84] Employees who have been discharged[85] or laid off discriminatorily[86] are eligible. Employees allegedly discharged in violation of the Act are permitted to vote subject to challenge. If the number of challenged ballots could affect

---

[75]*Personal Prods. Corp.*, 114 NLRB 959, 37 LRRM 1079 (1955).

[76]*NLRB v. New England Lithographic Co., Inc.*, 589 F.2d 29, 100 LRRM 2001 (1st Cir. 1978); *Pen Mar Packaging Corp.*, 261 NLRB 874, 110 LRRM 1148 (1982); *see also* THE DEVELOPING LABOR LAW at 387.

[77]*E.I. du Pont de Nemours & Co.*, 210 NLRB 395, 86 LRRM 1155 (1974).

[78]*NLRB v. Broyhill Co.*, 528 F.2d 719, 91 LRRM 2109 (8th Cir. 1976); *Case-Swayne Co.*, 209 NLRB 1069, 85 LRRM 1598 (1974).

[79]*Vogue Art Ware & China Co.*, 129 NLRB 1253, 47 LRRM 1169 (1961).

[80]*Keeshin Charter Serv.*, 250 NLRB 780, 105 LRRM 1030 (1980).

[81]*Queen City Paving Co.*, 243 NLRB 71, 101 LRRM 1472 (1979).

[82]*High Energy Corp.*, 259 NLRB 747, 109 LRRM 1015 (1981); *Precision Tumbling Co.*, 252 NLRB 1014, 105 LRRM 1365 (1980). A reasonable expectation of recall must be based upon the totality of the evidence. In *S&G Concrete Co.*, 274 NLRB No. 116, 118 LRRM 1420 (1985), the Board found that two employees had no reasonable expectation of recall notwithstanding statements made by the plant manager at the time of their layoffs that the layoffs would be temporary in view of other evidence indicating that they were permanent.

[83]*Thomas Engine Corp.*, 196 NLRB 706, 80 LRRM 1755 (1972).

[84]*Spray Sales and Sierra Rollers*, 225 NLRB 1089, 93 LRRM 1025 (1976).

[85]*P.R.S. Ltd.*, 237 NLRB 628, 99 LRRM 1027 (1978).

[86]*Simley Corp.*, 233 NLRB 391, 97 LRRM 1218 (1977).

the result of the election, the Board will resolve them after completion of the unfair labor practice proceeding.[87]

(f) Strikers. Economic strikers who have been permanently replaced are eligible to vote in any election held within 12 months of the commencement of the strike.[88] While an employee does not necessarily lose the right to vote by taking a job elsewhere,[89] voting eligibility will be lost if the employee abandons any interest in the former job.[90] Unfair labor practice strikers, by contrast, are eligible to vote regardless of how much time has elapsed from the beginning of the strike.[91] Strikers will be presumed to be economic strikers, however, until they are found by the Board to be on strike because of their employer's unfair labor practices.[92]

(g) Replacements of Strikers. Replacements of economic strikers employed on a permanent basis are eligible to vote if they are employed during the eligibility period and on the election date.[93] If a strike occurs after the eligibility period has passed, permanent replacements working on election day may vote.[94] Replacements for unfair labor practice strikers are not permitted to vote.[95]

(h) Relatives of Management. Individuals employed by a parent or spouse are statutorily excluded from the definition of "employee,"[96] and thus may not vote in representation elections. Other relatives may be excluded from the bargaining unit and therefore ineligible to vote if they are found to have a greater affinity with the interests of management than with the interests of the bargaining unit.[97]

---

[87]*Gary Aircraft Corp.*, 193 NLRB 108, 78 LRRM 1535 (1971).

[88]Sec. 9(c)(3); *Bio-Science Labs. v. NLRB*, 542 F.2d 505, 93 LRRM 2154 (9th Cir. 1976).

[89]*Pacific Tile & Porcelain Co.*, 137 NLRB 1358, 50 LRRM 1394 (1962).

[90]*Lake Development Mgmt. Co.*, 259 NLRB 791, 109 LRRM 1027 (1981) (employee expressly told employer he intended to terminate his employment); *P.B.R. Co.*, 216 NLRB 602, 89 LRRM 1259 (1975) (employee's failure to accept offer of reinstatement constituted abandonment). *But see Q-T Tool Co.*, 199 NLRB 500, 81 LRRM 1520 (1972) (employee's telling *new* employer that he had no intention of returning to old job held not to prove that employee intended to abandon former employment).

[91]*Kellburn Mfg. Co.*, 45 NLRB 322, 11 LRRM 142 (1942).

[92]*Bright Foods, Inc.*, 126 NLRB 553, 45 LRRM 1343 (1960).

[93]*Famous Indus.*, 220 NLRB 484, 90 LRRM 1581 (1975); *Pacific Tile & Porcelain Co.*, 137 NLRB 1358, 50 LRRM 1394 (1962); *see also* L. Modjeska, NLRB PRACTICE 231.

[94]*Tampa Sand & Material Co.*, 129 NLRB 1273, 47 LRRM 1166 (1961).

[95]*Larand Leisurelies, Inc.*, 222 NLRB 838, 91 LRRM 1305 (1976).

[96]Sec. 2(3). In the context of corporations, the Board has limited the Sec. 2(3) exclusion to the children or spouse of an individual with at least a 50 percent ownership interest. *See Cerni Motor Sales, Inc.*, 201 NLRB 918, 82 LRRM 1404 (1973).

[97]*International Metal Prods. Co.*, 107 NLRB 65, 33 LRRM 1055 (1953). Close relatives of owners may be excluded from the bargaining unit without showing that they enjoy special job-related privileges by virtue of the family relationship. *NLRB v. Action Automotive, Inc.*, 469 U.S. _____, 118 LRRM 2577 (1985). Employees related to nonowner supervisors, however, will be included in the unit in the absence of a showing that they enjoy a special status on the job. *Burlington Food Store, Inc.*, 272 NLRB No. 51, 117 LRRM 1279 (1984); *Pargas of Crescent City, Inc.*, 194 NLRB 616, 78 LRRM 1712 (1971).

The Board will defer to an express written agreement between the parties (a "consent" election agreement or "stipulated" election agreement[98]) which addresses specific issues of voter eligibility, provided such agreement does not conflict with the Act or Board policy.[99] The Board will also honor an explicit oral agreement of the parties to specific issues of eligibility.[100]

Procedures Before the Board

§8.8 Cases Transferred From the Regional Director

As noted earlier in this chapter, the regional director may at any time issue an order to be effective at the close of the hearing transferring the case to the Board. (See Exhibit 38.)[101] Such transfers generally are restricted to novel or extremely complex cases in which prompt Board guidance is desirable. In such instances the director does not issue a decision and the Board itself proceeds to decide the case. The parties' requests for oral argument and all posthearing briefs are filed with the Board rather than with the regional director.[102]

§8.9 Request for Review of the Regional Director's Decision

In instances where the regional director does not transfer the case to the Board but rather issues a decision on the merits, the parties may appeal from the director's decision by filing a request for review with the Board.[103] Since the Board will grant requests for review only where "compelling reasons" exist, such requests must be based on one of four grounds:

- That a substantial question of law or policy is raised because of the absence of or the departure from officially reported Board precedent;
- That the regional director's decision on a substantial factual issue is clearly erroneous on the record and such error prejudicially affects the rights of a party;

---

[98]See §§6.8 and 6.9.

[99]*Norris-Thermador Corp.*, 119 NLRB 1301, 41 LRRM 1283 (1958). *See also* THE DEVELOPING LABOR LAW at 390.

[100]*Banner Bedding, Inc.*, 214 NLRB 1013, 87 LRRM 1417 (1974).

[101]NLRB Rules and Regulations §102.67(h).

[102]*Id.* at §§102.67(i), (j).

[103]*Id.* at §102.67(b). Separate request for review procedures apply for appeals from regional director's decisions dismissing an election petition during the hearing (see NLRB Rules and Regulations §102.71(a) and discussion §6.5) and decisions dismissing petitions or holding them in abeyance pending resolution of "blocking" charges (see NLRB Rules and Regulations §102.71(b) and discussion §5.9 n.108).

FORM NLRB-4481
(1-67)

UNITED STATES OF AMERICA
BEFORE THE NATIONAL LABOR RELATIONS BOARD

Case No.

ORDER TRANSFERRING REPRESENTATION CASE
TO THE NATIONAL LABOR RELATIONS BOARD

IT IS HEREBY ORDERED, pursuant to Section 102.67 of the National Labor Relations Board Rules and Regulations, that the above-entitled matter be and it hereby is transferred to and continued before the Board in Washington, D. C.

Subject to the provisions of Section 102.67 (i)* of the aforementioned rules and regulations, briefs may be filed with the Executive Secretary, National Labor Relations Board, Washington, D. C., 20570, on or before

By direction of the Regional Director for Region

Dated _____   _____
                                                            (Signature)

                                               _____
                                                            (Title)

*(i) If any case is transferred to the Board for decision after the parties have filed briefs with the regional director, the parties may, within such time after service of the order transferring the case as is fixed by the regional director, file with the Board eight copies of the brief previously filed with the regional director. Such copies shall be printed or otherwise legibly duplicated: Provided, however, That carbon copies of typewritten matter shall not be filed and if submitted will not be accepted. No further briefs shall be permitted except by special permission of the Board. If the case is transferred to the Board before the time expires for the filing of briefs with the regional director and before the parties have filed briefs, such briefs shall be filed as set forth above and served in accordance with subsection (b) of this section, within the time set by the regional director. If the order transferring the case is served on the parties during the hearing, the hearing officer may, prior to the close of the hearing and for good cause, grant an extension of time within which to file a brief with the Board for a period not to exceed an additional 14 days. Requests for extension of time in which to file a brief with the Board under authority of this section not addressed to the hearing officer during the hearing shall be filed in writing with the Board and copies thereof shall immediately be served on the other parties and the regional director. Requests for extension of time shall be received by the Board not later than 3 days before the date such briefs are due in Washington, D. C. A copy of any such request shall be served immediately on the other parties and the regional director and shall contain a statement that such service has been made. No reply brief may be filed except upon special leave of the Board.

**Exhibit 38.   Order Transferring Representation Case to NLRB
(Form NLRB-4881)**

- That the conduct of the hearing or any ruling made in connection with the proceeding has resulted in prejudicial error; or
- That there are compelling reasons for reconsideration of an important Board rule or policy.[104]

Requests for review (eight copies) must be filed with the Board in Washington, D.C., within 14 days after service of the regional director's decision or order.[105] Copies must be served on all parties including the regional director.[106] The request must be a self-contained document and should set forth reasons for seeking review in sufficient detail for the Board to rule without having to research the case record.[107] Any party may file a statement opposing the request within seven days after the last day on which the request for review must be filed.[108] While the facts which the Board considers generally are restricted to those included in the request and the statement in opposition, the Board may examine other portions of the record in evaluating the request.[109]

All requests for review, statements in opposition, and supporting briefs must be double spaced on 8-½ by 11-inch paper and, in the absence of special permission, shall not exceed 50 pages in length exclusive of subject index and table of authorities. All briefs which exceed 20 pages shall contain a subject index with page references and a table of cases and other authorities cited.[110] Requests for extensions of time to file these documents shall be filed with the Board or the regional director, as appropriate, not less than three days before the document is due.[111]

The parties may at any time waive their right to request review (see Exhibit 39)[112] or may, with the permission of the Board, withdraw a request previously filed.[113] The effect of any such waiver or withdrawal will be to preclude the parties from relitigating in any related unfair labor practice proceeding any issue which was, or could have been, raised in the representation proceeding.[114]

(a) Effect of Denying Review. Denial of a request for review amounts to Board approval of the regional director's action. (See Exhibit 40.) It also precludes relitigating any such issues in a related

---

[104]*Id.* at §102.67(c).

[105]*Id.* at §102.67(b).

[106]*Id.* at §102.67(k)(2). A statement of service must be filed simultaneously with the Board. *Id.* and §102.67(e).

[107]*Id.* at §102.67(d).

[108]*Id.* at §102.67(e).

[109]*Id.* at §102.67(d); *see Bon Secours Hosp., Inc.,* 248 NLRB 115, 103 LRRM 1375 (1980).

[110]NLRB Rules and Regulations at §102.67(k)(1).

[111]*Id.* at §102.67(k)(3).

[112]*Id.* at §102.67(f).

[113]*Id.* at §102.67(g).

[114]*Id.* at §102.67(f); *A. S. Horner, Inc.,* 246 NLRB 393, 102 LRRM 1535 (1979).

FORM NLRB-4480
(5-84)

UNITED STATES OF AMERICA
NATIONAL LABOR RELATIONS BOARD

WAIVER

IN THE MATTER OF _____

(Name of Case)

_____
(Number of Case)

PURSUANT TO SECTION 102.67 AND 102.69 OF THE RULES AND REGULATIONS OF THE NATIONAL LABOR RELATIONS BOARD. THE UNDERSIGNED PARTY WAIVES ITS RIGHT TO REQUEST REVIEW OF OR FILE EXCEPTIONS TO THE REGIONAL DIRECTOR'S AND/OR HEARING OFFICER'S

_____
(Name of document or applicable documents)

_____   IN THE ABOVE-
(Date of document)

OR ☐ CHECK IF DOCUMENT NOT YET ISSUED.

CAPTIONED MATTER.

_____
(Name of Party)

BY _____
(Name of Representative)

_____
(Title)

DATE _____

**Exhibit 39.   Waiver of Right to Request Review of Regional Director's
Determination   (Form NLRB-4480)**

TELEGRAPHIC MESSAGE

NAME OF AGENCY	PRECEDENCE	SECURITY CLASSIFICATION
NLRB–ORDER SECTION	ACTION: INFO:	

ACCOUNTING CLASSIFICATION	DATE PREPARED 4/3/85 10:00 am	FILE

FOR INFORMATION CALL		

NAME XYZ/MRT	PHONE NUMBER 254-9119	TYPE OF MESSAGE ☐ SINGLE ☐ BOOK ☐ MULTIPLE-ADDRESS

THIS SPACE FOR USE OF COMMUNICATION UNIT

MESSAGE TO BE TRANSMITTED *(Use double spacing and all capital letters)*

TO:

(LIST NAMES AND ADDRESSES OF
PARTIES ABOVE TELEGRAPHIC MESSAGE)

RE: (CASE NAME AND NUMBER) EMPLOYER'S REQUEST FOR REVIEW OF THE

REGIONAL DIRECTOR'S DECISION AND ORDER IS HEREBY DENIED AS IT

RAISES NO SUBSTANTIAL ISSUES WARRANTING REVIEW. BY DIRECTION OF THE

BOARD: DATED   1985.

————————————————
Deputy Executive Secretary

SECURITY CLASSIFICATION

PAGE NO.	NO. OF PGS.

STANDARD FORM 14
REVISED 11-80
GSA FPMR (41 CFR) 101-35.306

Previous editions usable   NSN 7540-00-634-3968

14-103

✿ GPO : 1981 O - 341-526 (7046)

**Exhibit 40.   Order Denying Employer's Request for Review of
Regional Director's Decision**

subsequent unfair labor practice proceeding.[115] Unpublished Board decisions affirming a regional director's determinations, however, have no binding precedential value.[116]

(b) Effect of Granting Review. If the request for review is granted, the parties are afforded 14 days within which to file additional briefs with the Board unless the Board already has ruled upon the issues on review in the order granting review.[117] Such briefs shall be limited to the issues on which review was granted. The Board will consider the entire record in the light of the grounds relied upon for review. The Board proceeds upon the record or after oral argument or the submission of briefs or upon further hearing to decide the issues referred to it or to review the decision of the regional director. It will then direct a secret ballot election of the employees, dismiss the petition, affirm or reverse the regional director's order in whole or in part, or make such other disposition of the matter as it deems appropriate.[118]

The granting of the request for review shall not stay the regional director's decision unless otherwise ordered by the Board.[119] Accordingly, the regional director will schedule and conduct an election directed by the decision even though a request for review has been filed with or granted by the Board. If the request for review is still pending on the day of the election, the ballots whose validity is in dispute shall be segregated and all ballots shall be impounded and remain unopened pending Board disposition of the request for review.[120]

---

[115]NLRB Rules and Regulations §102.67(f); *Wickes Furniture*, 261 NLRB 1062, 110 LRRM 1184 (1982).

[116]*Educational and Recreational Servs., Inc.*, 261 NLRB 448, 110 LRRM 1102 (1982).

[117]NLRB Rules and Regulations §102.67(g).

[118]*Id.* at §102.67(j).

[119]Sec. 3(b); NLRB Rules and Regulations §102.67(g).

[120]*Id.* at §102.67(b). Section 3(b) has been interpreted to mean that when the regional director orders the parties to act (e.g., directing an election) they must do so regardless of the pendency of an appeal. It was not intended, however, to preclude enforcement of a Board order reversing a regional director's decision when no stay has been granted. Thus, in *NLRB v. Sav-On Drugs, Inc.*, 728 F.2d 1254, 115 LRRM 3421 (9th Cir. 1984), the Board found that the employer unlawfully discharged two pharmacist managers for engaging in union activities even though the employer's decision to terminate the managers was based upon a regional director's determination—subsequently reversed by the Board—that the managers were supervisors, unprotected by the Act.

Questions regarding the legitimacy of the election may arise when the Board grants review and eventually determines that the appropriate unit is considerably smaller than the one in which the election was held. In *Hamilton Test Sys. v. NLRB*, 743 F.2d 136, 117 LRRM 2248 (2d Cir. 1984), an election was conducted in a unit which encompassed the entire workforce. The unit subsequently found appropriate by the Board constituted approximately 45 percent of the workforce, and a union certification was issued based upon the ballots cast by those employees. The court refused to enforce the certification on the basis that the employees were misled regarding the scope of the unit, and might have voted against union representation had they known that the unit would be reduced by more than 50 percent. *Accord NLRB v. Lorimar Productions, Inc.*, 771 F.2d 1294, 120 LRRM 2425 (9th Cir. 1985). The Board has interpreted the *Hamilton Test* decision narrowly and has attempted to limit it to its unique facts. *See Parsons School of Design*, 275 NLRB No. 18, 119 NLRB 1021 (1985).

Motions for Reconsideration, Rehearing, and Reopening the Record

§8.10 When Appropriate

After the close of a hearing a party may, because of "extraordinary circumstances," move to reopen the record. In addition, following issuance of the regional director's decision or report a party may request reconsideration, a rehearing, or the reopening of the record.[121] Such motions should be filed with the regional director or with the Board, as appropriate.

A regional director may treat a request for review as if it were a motion for reconsideration. If the director feels that a change in the original decision is warranted, the Board will be notified and will suspend action on the pending request until such time as the regional director advises the Board that further proceedings are being handled in the region or that the Board should resume consideration of the request for review.

No motion for reconsideration will be entertained regarding any matter which could have been but was not raised earlier in the representation proceeding. The motion should describe in detail the error relied upon and should refer to specific pages in the record concerning alleged errors of fact. Similarly, motions for rehearing or to reopen the record should specify (1) the error relied upon, (2) the prejudice resulting from the error, (3) the additional evidence sought to be introduced, (4) why such evidence was not introduced earlier, and (5) the result which would obtain if the evidence was introduced and credited. Only newly discovered evidence or evidence which should have been accepted earlier will be taken at a reopened hearing.[122]

§8.11 Effect of Filing

Motions for reconsideration must be filed within 14 days after service of the decision or report; motions to reopen must be filed "promptly" upon discovery of the evidence sought to be introduced.[123] As with requests for review, the filing of motions for reconsideration, for rehearing, or to reopen the record will not operate as a stay of any action directed to be taken in the decision or report, including the running of an election. If the granting of any such motion will affect the eligibility of certain individuals to vote, their ballots will be challenged and impounded pending disposition of the motion.[124]

---

[121]*Id.* at §102.65(e)(1).
[122]*Id.*
[123]*Id.* at §102.65(e)(2).
[124]*Id.* at §102.65(e)(3).

A motion for reconsideration, for rehearing, or to reopen the record is not a prerequisite to the exhaustion of administrative remedies.[125]

Withdrawals and Disclaimers

In addition to directions of election, consent election procedures, and dismissals, representation petitions may be disposed of in two other ways: by withdrawal or disclaimer. Thus, a party who has filed a representation petition or who has intervened in a pending case may decide that it does not wish to proceed. In that event the petitioner, whether an employer or a union, or the intervening union, files a request for withdrawal with the regional director. When an employer has filed a petition or a group of individual employees seeks to decertify a union, the union may submit a disclaimer of interest which has the same effect as a request for withdrawal.

A request for withdrawal of petition may be granted, with or without prejudice to the filing of a new petition, or it may be denied. A disclaimer of interest may be accepted or rejected.

§8.12 Withdrawal of Petition

(a) *Withdrawal Before Close of Hearing or Approval of Election Agreement.*   Prior to the close of the hearing or approval of an election agreement the petitioner may, for legitimate reasons, seek to withdraw the petition voluntarily. In addition, the Board agent investigating the petition may recommend that the petition be withdrawn because absent withdrawal it will be dismissed. This might occur, for example, if the requested unit is inappropriate, the petition is not supported by an adequate showing of interest, or the petition is untimely or "blocked" by a pending unfair labor practice charge.[126]

In such instances the petition may be withdrawn with the consent of the regional director with whom the petition was filed.[127] A petitioner's genuine desire to withdraw usually is honored, and the request may be granted without prejudice to the later filing of a new petition at any time.[128] As soon as the withdrawal is approved by the regional director the case is closed.[129] If, however, the withdrawal request is accompanied by conduct indicative of an ongoing interest in representing the employees such as a strike or recognitional pick-

---

[125]*Id.*

[126]See discussion at chapter 6.

[127]NLRB Rules and Regulations §102.60(a); NLRB Casehandling Manual ¶11110.

[128]*Wyman-Gordon Co.*, 117 NLRB 75, 39 LRRM 1176 (1957).

[129]NLRB Rules and Regulations §102.60(a).

eting, then the withdrawal request will be denied and an election conducted.[130]

(b) **Withdrawal After Close of Hearing or Approval of Election Agreement but Before Election.**   After the hearing has been closed or an election agreement has been reached, withdrawal requests must be filed with the regional director or with the Board in cases transferred to it.[131] The disposition of such requests will depend upon what type of election petition has been filed and whether intervening unions are involved.

If a petitioning union seeks to withdraw an RC petition and there are no intervening unions, the request generally will be granted with six months' prejudice to the filing of a new petition. The election will be cancelled even if the employer involved wishes to proceed with the vote.[132] If, however, there is an intervening union and if that union is able to acquire the requisite 30-percent showing of interest in the unit on its own behalf, then the election may be held with only the intervening union's name on the ballot.[133] The intervenor's showing of interest need not antedate the election agreement or the close of the hearing, and a reasonable period of time for acquiring and submitting the required showing of interest will be provided. Should the intervening union subsequently seek to withdraw, the six-month prejudice period applicable to petitioners also would apply.[134]

If an employer which has filed an RM petition seeks to withdraw the petition and there is no opposition from any union, the request generally will be granted without prejudice to the filing of another petition at any time. If, however, opposition is expressed by a union other than a certified incumbent and the protesting union can demonstrate a 30-percent showing of interest in the unit, the election will be held as scheduled.[135]

Similarly, requests to withdraw filed by RD petitioners generally will be granted without prejudice. If, however, an intervenor other than a certified incumbent union can establish the requisite showing of interest within a reasonable period of time, the election will proceed as scheduled.[136]

As noted, withdrawal requests granted after the close of the hearing or the execution of an election agreement generally are with prejudice for a period of six months. They will be granted without prejudice, however, in instances in which the election has been di-

---

[130]NLRB Casehandling Manual ¶11110.1.
[131]NLRB Rules and Regulations §102.60(a); NLRB Casehandling Manual ¶11114.
[132]NLRB Casehandling Manual ¶11114.1(a).
[133]*Cf. Anheuser-Busch, Inc.*, 246 NLRB 29, 102 LRRM 1422 (1979).
[134]NLRB Casehandling Manual ¶11114.1(b).
[135]*Id.* at ¶11114.2.
[136]*Id.* at ¶11114.3.

rected in a unit substantially different from the one sought by the petitioner.[137]

(c) Withdrawal of Petition After an Election.   Withdrawal requests filed after a valid election should be submitted to the regional director. Such requests generally are not granted if it appears that the request is prompted by a desire to circumvent the effect of a Board certification. If the regional director feels that the request should be granted, prior approval must be secured from the Board through its Executive Secretary.[138]

While a request to withdraw a *petition* submitted while objections to an election are pending generally will not be granted, withdrawal of the *objections* may be approved if the petitioner seeks to make the results of the election final. Such requests may be granted without prejudice to the petitioner's right to file a new petition at an appropriate time based upon a new showing of interest.[139] A withdrawal request submitted after the election has been set aside on the basis of petitioner's objections may be approved by the regional director without prejudice.[140]

§8.13   Disclaimers of Interest

Whenever two or more labor organizations are competing in an election either participant may have its name removed from the ballot by filing a request with the regional director.[141] In addition, in an RM proceeding where a petition has been filed by an employer or in an RD proceeding where a petition for decertification has been filed, the currently certified or recognized union, or the union found to be seeking recognition, may have its name removed from the ballot by providing timely notice to all parties and to the regional director disclaiming any interest in representing the employees.[142] The Board neither provides nor requires any special form for the making of a disclaimer of interest. Usually the disclaimer merely states that the union waives or disclaims any right to represent the affected employees.

In order to be effective a disclaimer must be "clear and unequivocal" and must not be accompanied by any inconsistent conduct such as striking or picketing for recognition, urging the execution of a

---

[137]*Id.* at ¶11114.4.
[138]*Id.* at ¶11116.
[139]*Id.* at ¶11116.1.
[140]*Id.* at ¶11116.2.
[141]NLRB Rules and Regulations §102.69(a); NLRB Casehandling Manual ¶11120.
[142]NLRB Rules and Regulations §102.69(a); NLRB Casehandling Manual ¶11124.

collective bargaining agreement, or seeking to press grievances.[143] If a disclaimer is invalid, the representation proceeding will continue with all participants. If it is valid, the disclaiming union will be disregarded as a party and any certification previously issued to such union will be revoked.[144] In some circumstances, if the disclaiming union is a party to a current collective bargaining contract and no other labor organization demonstrates an interest in or an ability to represent the employees and administer the contract, the agreement will not serve as a bar to the filing of an election petition.[145]

(a) Timing of Disclaimers. Disclaimers may be filed at any time during a representation proceeding. A disclaimer filed prior to the execution and approval of an election agreement or the opening of a hearing may result in the dismissal of the petition without prejudice to any party to refile at any time.[146] A union which has filed a disclaimer may not block the making of a subsequent election agreement.[147]

If a disclaimer of interest is filed during the hearing, the hearing officer will refer it to the regional director. If the regional director accepts the disclaimer as valid and unequivocal, the hearing will be adjourned indefinitely, the notice of hearing will be withdrawn, and the petition will be dismissed without prejudice.[148] The Board has held that the failure of a union to appear at the hearing does not constitute a disclaimer.[149]

Where a union's disclaimer is filed after the regional director's approval of an election agreement, consent or stipulated, or after the close of the hearing, the election will be cancelled, whether or not the petitioner—i.e., the employer, or the individual or group of employees seeking decertification–objects. The petition will be dismissed with prejudice, but may be reinstated upon request of the petitioner if the union should make a claim for recognition upon the employer within six months from the date of the regional director's dismissal.[150] In addition, any petition filed by the disclaiming union within those six months will not be entertained, unless good cause is shown to the contrary.[151]

---

[143]NLRB Casehandling Manual ¶¶11122, 11124.1; *McClintock Market, Inc.*, 244 NLRB 555, 102 LRRM 1141 (1979); *Roberts Tires*, 212 NLRB 405, 86 LRRM 1507 (1974); *Plough, Inc.*, 203 NLRB 121, 83 LRRM 1086 (1973).

[144]NLRB Casehandling Manual ¶¶11122, 11124.1.

[145]Compare *American Sunroof Corp.-West Coast, Inc.*, 243 NLRB 1128, 102 LRRM 1086 (1979) (contract not a bar) *with East Mfg. Corp.*, 242 NLRB 5, 101 LRRM 1079 (1979) (contract is a bar).

[146]NLRB Casehandling Manual ¶¶11124.1 and 11124.2.

[147]*Id.* at ¶11122.

[148]*Id.* at ¶¶11124.1, 11124.2.

[149]*Central Optical Co.*, 88 NLRB 246, 25 LRRM 1318 (1950).

[150]NLRB Casehandling Manual ¶11124.2; *Campos Dairy Prods., Ltd.*, 107 NLRB 715, 33 LRRM 1233 (1954).

[151]*Id.*

If a disclaimer is filed at any time after the execution of an election agreement or the close of the hearing and an intervening union with a 30-percent showing of interest in the unit wishes to proceed with the election, the disclaiming union's name will be dropped from the ballot and the vote will be taken.[152] The showing of interest need not antedate the approval of the agreement or the close of the hearing and a reasonable period of time to procure the necessary showing will be afforded. Should the intervening union subsequently withdraw from the election, the six-month prejudice period to the filing of a new petition shall apply both to the disclaiming union and to the intervenor unless good cause is shown.[153]

(b) Petitions Filed Within the Six-Month Prejudice Period.

As noted above, in certain withdrawal or disclaimer cases the regional director or the Board provides that "any petition filed within six months will not be entertained unless good cause is shown to the contrary." When a union files a new petition within that six-month period, the regional director must determine whether "good cause" in fact exists.

If the regional director decides that good cause does exist, a notice of hearing will be issued and the question of good cause will be considered at the hearing. If the regional director's conclusion is sustained and an appeal is taken, the Board may ultimately decide whether or not the director's determination was correct.[154] If the regional director determines that good cause does not exist, the petition will be dismissed and the petitioning union may thereupon seek review of the dismissal by appealing to the Board.[155]

What constitutes sufficient good cause to entertain a petition within the prohibited six-month period is not stated comprehensively by the Board; instead, it judges each case individually. Examples of what the Board may consider good cause include: the disclaimer or withdrawal of the original petition was made because of the expansion or contraction of the unit; the union did not wish to proceed to an election on the original petition in the presence of an outstanding unfair labor practice complaint; and the employer has agreed to a consent election at the request of the petitioning union.[156]

The Board has ruled that withdrawal of a petition with prejudice to the filing of another petition for six months applies only to a

---

[152]*Id.* at ¶11124.4.

[153]*Id.*

[154]NLRB Rules and Regulations §102.67(c); NLRB Casehandling Manual ¶11118; *Agawam Food Mart, Inc.*, 162 NLRB 1420, 64 LRRM 1197 (1967).

[155]NLRB Rules and Regulations §102.71(a); NLRB Casehandling Manual ¶11118. See discussion at §6.5 regarding appeals from the regional director's dismissal of election petitions.

[156]*See generally* NLRB Casehandling Manual ¶11118.1.

petitioner; it does not apply to an intervening union. Accordingly, an interested union is permitted to intervene in an election proceeding even though less than six months have elapsed since withdrawal with prejudice of its petition for the same bargaining unit.[157]

---

[157]NLRB Casehandling Manual ¶11118.2; *California Furniture Shops, Ltd.*, 115 NLRB 1399, 38 LRRM 1080 (1956).

9

The Election

Background

The heart of the representation case is the election itself, and it is here that the Board exercises considerable power. Pursuant to the broad grant of authority in Section 9(c), the Board alone controls the procedural conduct of the election,[1] and its control over the substantive content of the campaign is substantial. Courts often have repeated the Supreme Court's early holding that the Board enjoys a "wide degree of discretion in establishing the procedure and safeguards necessary to insure the fair and free choice of bargaining representatives by employees."[2] In exercising this discretion, the Board has delegated much of its authority to the regional directors. The directors and their agents therefore bear the primary responsibility for the proper conduct of the election.[3]

Preelection Matters

§9.1 The *Excelsior* List

Within seven days after a consent election agreement has been approved, or after an election has been directed (except expedited elections—see chapter 20), the employer must file with the regional director an "*Excelsior* list." This list, named for the Board decision

---

[1]*NLRB v. Waterman Steamship Corp.*, 309 U.S. 206, 5 LRRM 682 (1940).

[2]*NLRB v. A.J. Tower Co.*, 329 U.S. 324, 19 LRRM 2128 (1946); *see, e.g., NLRB v. New Columbus Nursing Home, Inc.*, 720 F.2d 726, 114 LRRM 3304 (lst Cir. 1983) (quoting *Tower*); *TRW-United Greenfield Div. v. NLRB*, 716 F.2d 1391, 114 LRRM 2921 (11th Cir. 1983) (Board has broad power in conducting and supervising elections).

[3]NLRB Rules and Regulations §102.69(a); NLRB Casehandling Manual ¶11300. The Board's delegation of election responsibilities to the regional directors appears as Appendix D.

first requiring its submission, must contain the names and addresses of all potentially eligible voters. Upon receiving the list the regional director is required to forward a copy to all parties involved in the case. Failure to furnish the list is grounds for setting aside the election.[4]

Although the *Excelsior* requirement may not be waived,[5] whether an employer has satisfied the rule is measured by a "substantial compliance" standard.[6] Errors and omissions in the list, or tardiness in filing it, may be grounds for finding that the employer has not substantially complied. The Board requires that an employer make at least a "good faith" effort to minimize errors and to make a timely submission.[7] Generally, omissions of names or addresses from the list are considered a more serious breach than are inaccuracies,[8] while a failure to submit the list by the prescribed deadline will usually be excused if the effect of the delay is *de minimis*.[9] To assure compliance, the employer should make every effort to compile a complete, accurate list, and to file it with the regional director within the prescribed seven-day period.

§9.2 Preelection Conference and Voter Eligibility

After the direction of an election, the regional director or the director's agent may arrange an informal conference of all the parties. The purpose of this meeting is to settle the details of the election by obtaining the parties' agreement on such matters as voting time and location, voter eligibility, and election observers.[10] The preelection conference is a useful tool for assuring a smooth election, but the decision to make use of this tool lies within the discretion of the regional director. The Board's Rules and Regulations do not require the conference.[11] Accordingly, any objection to an election based upon the failure to hold a preelection conference will be overruled.[12]

---

[4]*Excelsior Underwear, Inc.*, 156 NLRB 1236, 61 LRRM 1217 (1966); *NLRB v. Wyman-Gordon Co.*, 394 U.S. 759, 70 LRRM 3345 (1969). *See generally* NLRB Casehandling Manual ¶¶11312–11313.1(2).

[5]NLRB Casehandling Manual ¶11312.1.

[6]*Texas Christian Univ.*, 220 NLRB 396, 90 LRRM 1274 (1975) (*Excelsior* rule not to be applied mechanically); *Program Aids Co.*, 163 NLRB 145, 65 LRRM 1244 (1967) (establishing the substantial compliance standard).

[7]*Texas Christian Univ.*, 220 NLRB 396, 90 LRRM 1274 (1975) (election not set aside where employer acts in good faith); *Telonic Instruments*, 173 NLRB 588, 69 LRRM 1398 (1968) (insubstantial defects in list permitted where employer not grossly negligent or unwilling to afford union full access to employees).

[8]*EDM of Texas*, 245 NLRB 934 n.1, 102 LRRM 1405 (1979); *Lobster House*, 186 NLRB 148, 75 LRRM 1309 (1970).

[9]*Excelsior Underwear, Inc.*, 156 NLRB 1236, 61 LRRM 1217 (1966).

[10]In a consent election, most of the details of the election are settled in the consent election agreement, although eligibility questions may be addressed in a preelection conference. *See* NLRB Statements of Procedure §101.19(a)(1).

[11]*See* NLRB Rules and Regulations §102.69.

[12]*Eisner Grocery Co.*, 116 NLRB 976, 38 LRRM 1376 (1956).

If a conference is scheduled, the parties should be prepared to articulate their positions on when and where the voting should take place, who is eligible to vote, and who will serve as official observers, as well as other matters. The regional director has final authority to decide these questions in a directed election, and absent unusual circumstances the Board will not interfere with the director's election arrangements.[13] At the preelection conference, however, the parties have an opportunity to influence the regional director's exercise of this broad discretion. By working with each other and with the regional director, the parties often can reach agreement on important details of the election, thus assuring its smooth operation.

The primary focus of the conference usually is on developing a definitive voter eligibility list. Using the *Excelsior* list as a starting point, the parties will seek to resolve their differences over which employees should be permitted to vote. The mere checking and preparation of an eligibility list, however, does not constitute a final and binding agreement on all eligibility questions.[14] As long as the parties do not enter into a written stipulation of the eligible voters, they remain free during the actual voting to make ballot challenges at variance with the eligibility list.[15] If it becomes clear that a significant number of challenges will be made, the regional director may withdraw approval of the election agreement or reconvene the parties for clarification.[16]

The freedom to make challenges at variance with the list is lost when the parties enter into "a *written and signed agreement* which *expressly* provides that issues of eligibility resolved therein shall be final and binding."[17] The Board considers "such an agreement, and only such an agreement, a final determination of the eligibility issues treated therein unless it is, in part or in whole, contrary to the Act or established Board policy."[18] The stipulation procedure provides the great advantage of reducing the possibility of postelection hearings on voter challenges. In turn, a more expeditious resolution of the representation question can be achieved. Because stipulated voter lists are the sole basis upon which later questions of eligibility will

---

[13]*Independent Rice Mill, Inc.*, 111 NLRB 536, 35 LRRM 1509 (1955).

[14]*Norris-Thermador Corp.*, 119 NLRB 1301, 41 LRRM 1283 (1958).

[15]*Id.*

[16]NLRB Casehandling Manual ¶¶11094, 11312.4.

[17]*Norris-Thermador Corp.*, 119 NLRB 1301, 41 LRRM 1283 (1958) (emphasis in original).

[18]*Id. See Illinois Valley Community Hosp.*, 249 NLRB 410, 104 LRRM 1154 (1980) (parties may not agree that certain employees, admittedly in the bargaining unit, may not vote). In general, a deviation from the stipulated list will be permitted only where the question of eligibility turns on a "statutory exclusion," rather than on the employees' "community of interests" with other employees in the unit. *Pilgrim Foods, Inc.*, 234 NLRB 136, 137 n.5, 97 LRRM 1187, 1189 n.5 (1978); *see also Rosehill Cemetery Ass'n*, 262 NLRB 1289, 110 LRRM 1430 (1982) (stipulation not binding on statutory question of employee's status as "supervisor," regardless of whether the stipulation has included or excluded the employee).

be resolved, however, the parties should exercise utmost care before entering into a written agreement.[19]

§9.3   Date, Hours, and Location of Election

The date, hours, and location of the election are important matters that are determined with the aim of maximizing the opportunity for voter participation. In a consent election the time and location of the voting usually are prescribed in the election agreement, but the parties may leave these matters to be decided by the regional director.[20] In a directed election the preelection conference usually will produce agreement on these matters. Where this agreement is not forthcoming, or where the parties to a consent election have so designated, the regional director will make the decision.[21] Regardless of whether the parties' agreement or the regional director's decision sets the time and location, the Board's wide discretion and ultimate power in scheduling elections guarantees that the same general policies and guidelines will be followed.[22]

(a) Date.   The date selected should reflect a consideration of the parties' desires and operational needs, as well as the goals of conducting a prompt and timely election and maximizing voter participation.[23] The balance of these considerations usually requires that the selected date *not* be one on which all or part of the plant will be closed, on which absenteeism is likely to be high, or on which many employees will be away on company business or on vacation.[24] These general guidelines place the primary constraints upon the date chosen.

The time frame within which the chosen date must fall varies according to the type of election being held. Usually, no election may be held sooner than ten days after the regional director receives the *Excelsior* list. If the parties desire a very prompt election, the employer may submit the list before the required seven-day deadline, and the ten-day period will be calculated provisionally from the date the list is expected to arrive at the regional office. If the tenth day falls on a holiday, a weekend, or a shutdown date, and all parties

---

[19]In *Banner Bedding, Inc.*, 214 NLRB 1013, 87 LRRM 1417 (1974), the Board permitted a *narrow* exception to the requirement of an express writing. Where both parties admitted that an oral agreement on a voter's eligibility was concluded in the presence of a Board agent, the Board recognized that agreement as a binding stipulation.

[20]NLRB Casehandling Manual ¶11084.3.

[21]*Id.* at ¶11302.

[22]*Daylight Grocery Co. v. NLRB*, 678 F.2d 905, 110 LRRM 2915 (11th Cir. 1982) ("Board has wide discretion in scheduling elections" and may be reversed only for "abuse of discretion which denies an employee the opportunity to vote"); *Beck Corp. v. NLRB*, 590 F.2d 290, 100 LRRM 2719 (9th Cir. 1978) (Board has wide discretion in scheduling elections).

[23]NLRB Casehandling Manual ¶11302.1.

[24]*Id.*

agree, the election may be held on the ninth day following receipt of the list. Limited exceptions to the ten-day requirement may also be granted where there is an impending strike or picketing, the employer has submitted the list promptly, and all parties agree to the waiver.[25]

At the opposite end of the time frame, the date of a Board-directed election must generally fall within thirty days of the date of the direction. A directed election ordered by the regional director usually will be held between twenty-five and thirty days after the order. If the twenty-fifth day falls on a weekend, the election will be ordered for a later rather than an earlier date.[26]

The particular day within this time period selected for the election will be one on which substantially all eligible employees will have an opportunity to vote.[27] Paydays frequently are selected because absenteeism usually is at a minimum.[28] As noted above, the aim of maximizing the opportunity for voter participation is fundamental in setting the election date.

The importance of this goal is reflected in the Board's handling of several "special situations." In industries with seasonal or cyclical employment patterns, the Board or regional director may order an election but require that it be held at a later date when employment is at "peak," with voter eligibility to be determined immediately preceeding issuance of the election notice.[29] A similar postponement may be ordered where there is an "expanding unit." If an election is directed for a unit that soon will be augmented, the vote may be scheduled for a later date when a fuller complement of employees is present.[30] For postponement to be avoided, the existing complement of employees must be "substantial and representative" of the skills and types of employees who eventually will comprise the total complement.[31] Reflecting its concern that the election date be one on which a truly representative vote can be taken, the Board often has

---

[25]*Id.*

[26]*Id.*

[27]*Glenn McClendon Trucking Co.*, 255 NLRB 1304, 107 LRRM 1081 (1981) (important part of Board procedures in conducting elections is that all employees have opportunity to vote). *See also Daylight Grocery Co. v. NLRB*, 678 F.2d 905, 110 LRRM 2915 (11th Cir. 1982) (Board's exercise of its wide discretion in scheduling elections will be reversed only for an abuse that denies an employee the opportunity to vote).

[28]*But see Beck Corp. v. NLRB*, 590 F.2d 290, 100 LRRM 2719 (9th Cir. 1978) (Board did not abuse discretion in refusing employer's request to hold election on payday).

[29]*Dick Kelchner Excavating Co.*, 236 NLRB 1414, 98 LRRM 1442 (1978); *Industrial Forestry Ass'n*, 222 NLRB 295, 91 LRRM 1234 (1976). *But see NLRB v. Broyhill Co.*, 528 F.2d 719, 91 LRRM 2109 (8th Cir. 1976) (regional director did not abuse discretion in refusing employer's request to delay election until peak period, where 70 percent of average peak-period employee complement currently was working).

[30]*See, e.g., St. John of God Hosp., Inc.*, 260 NLRB 905, 109 LRRM 1209 (1982); *Bryant Elec. Co.*, 216 NLRB 933, 88 LRRM 1595 (1975).

[31]*St. John of God Hosp., Inc.* 260 NLRB 905, 109 LRRM 1209 (1982); *Premium Foods, Inc. v. NLRB*, 709 F.2d 623, 113 LRRM 3261 (9th Cir. 1983) ("substantial and representative" standard embodies balance between early representation and maximum participation).

reversed regional directors' decisions refusing postponement until a "peak" employment period or until a unit has fully expanded.[32]

(b) Hours. As with the determination of the election date, the central concern in setting the hours for voting is that all eligible employees have an adequate opportunity to cast their ballots. The hours ultimately depend upon the circumstances of each case, but the time of day and length of the voting period should allow for all employees to vote on company time or on their own time without making a special trip from home especially to vote.[33] The Board's guidelines suggest that the polls be open at and around the beginning and ending of each work shift.[34] "Split-session" voting is common where the employer operates more than one shift. Under this scheme, polls are open only long enough for employees on a shift to vote, and are reopened for voting by employees on other shifts.[35] A final variation in the voting hours is the "traveling election," where, in a multiemployer or multiplant bargaining unit, voting is conducted at one location and the polls are then closed and moved to another location.[36]

(c) Location. The election usually will be held on the employer's premises, where accessibility to the voters can best be achieved.[37] Although the voting location is within the regional director's discretion,[38] a site off the premises is permitted only upon a showing of good cause by the party preferring the off-premises location. If such a site is selected, it must be a public building "reasonably close" (within one to four blocks) to the employer's premises such as would normally be used for municipal voting.[39] The employer's premises presumptively are the most suitable election site and a party who desires that the voting take place off company property must suggest available alternatives.[40]

Wherever the election is held, the Board agent usually endeavors to have the actual polling place spatially and visually separated from other activity, and away from any area where supervisors can observe the voting. Typically, an office or shipping room large enough to contain all election equipment and personnel will be selected.[41] Vot-

---

[32]*See, e.g., Industrial Forestry Ass'n,* 222 NLRB 295, 91 LRRM 1234 (1976) (seasonal operation); *St. John of God Hosp., Inc.,* 260 NLRB 905, 109 LRRM 1209 (1982) (expanding unit); *Bryant Elec. Co.,* 216 NLRB 933, 88 LRRM 1595 (1975) (expanding unit).

[33]NLRB Casehandling Manual ¶11302.3.

[34]*Id.*

[35]*Id.* at ¶11332 (opening and closing of each voting session treated like opening and closing of elections).

[36]*Id.* at ¶11334.1.

[37]*Id.* at ¶11302.2.

[38]*Halliburton Servs.,* 265 NLRB 1154, 112 LRRM 1330 (1982).

[39]NLRB Casehandling Manual ¶11302.2.

[40]*Id.*

[41]*Id.*

ing may be held at more than one location, usually when the unit is very large or when a "traveling election" is held for a multiple-location unit.[42]

§9.4   The Ballot

Ballots for the election are provided by the Board and may be handled only by Board agents and by the individual voter.[43] The ballot itself as well as its contents must meet guidelines specified by the Board. A blank sheet of paper—the same size, color, and type used for the ballots in the election—cannot serve as an official ballot, even if a voter has clearly designated his choice on it.[44] The color of the ballot will not be disclosed to the parties prior to the opening of the polls, and different colors will be used for different groups or units voting at the same time. In an election with both manual and mail balloting, both types of ballots will be the same color.[45]

The question on the ballot varies according to the type of election and the number of labor organizations involved. The consent election agreement or the direction of election will dictate what form the question is to take and what choices the voters are to have.[46] In an election involving a single labor organization, the ballot will provide the employees the opportunity to vote on the question: "Do you wish to be represented for purposes of collective bargaining by (name of union)?" Spaces are provided for voting "yes" or "no." (See Exhibit 41.) Where a bilingual election is being conducted, the ballot will have the same format with all headings, instructions, and questions printed in both languages.[47] (See Exhibit 42.)

If two or more labor organizations are participating in an election, the voter is given a wider range of choices. The ballot provides the employee with an opportunity to choose representation by either one of the unions or to select no representative at all. (See Exhibit 43.) The positioning of the choices on the ballot ideally will be agreed upon by the various parties to the election. Where agreement is not reached, the order in which the choices appear will be determined

---

[42]For a case involving a very large unit requiring numerous polling locations, *see Newport News Shipbuilding and Dry Dock Co.*, 239 NLRB 82, 99 LRRM 1518 (1978). On the handling of elections involving multiple polling places generally, *see* NLRB Casehandling Manual ¶11334.

[43]NLRB Casehandling Manual ¶11306.

[44]*McCormick Lumber Co.*, 206 NLRB 314, 84 LRRM 1267 (1973); *Knapp-Sherrill Co.*, 171 NLRB 1547, 68 LRRM 1286 (1968).

[45]NLRB Casehandling Manual ¶11306.4.

[46]*Id.* at ¶11306.1.

[47]Bilingual ballots will be furnished where a substantial number of employees do not speak English and where the parties so request. *King's River Pine*, 227 NLRB 299 n.2, 94 LRRM 1029 (1976). Stipulations by the parties as to the use of bilingual ballots will be upheld unless it is shown that failure to use such ballots adversely affected the employees' ability to cast an informed vote. *Norwestern Prods., Inc.*, 226 NLRB 653, 93 LRRM 1322 (1976). Where a multi-language ballot had a tendency to confuse and was defective on its face, the Board set aside the election even though there was no evidence of any actual voter confusion. *Kraft, Inc.*, 273 NLRB No. 184, 118 LRRM 1242 (1985).

UNITED STATES OF AMERICA
National Labor Relations Board
FORM NLRB-707N2 (RC, RM, RD CASES) (4-84)

OFFICIAL SECRET BALLOT

For certain employees of

Janco Computer Services, Inc.

Do you wish to be represented for purposes of collective bargaining by -

Local 007, United Computer Operators
International Union

MARK AN "X" IN THE SQUARE OF YOUR CHOICE

YES	NO
☐	☐

DO NOT SIGN THIS BALLOT Fold and drop in ballot box.
If you spoil this ballot return it to the Board Agent for a new one.

**Exhibit 41.   Sample Ballot Used in Collective Bargaining Election
Involving One Union**

UNITED STATES OF AMERICA
ESTADOS UNIDOS DE AMERICA

National Labor Relations Board
Junta Nacional De Relaciones Del Trabajo

OFFICIAL SECRET BALLOT
PAPELETA SECRETA OFICIAL
For Certain Employees of
Para Ciertos Empleados De

Janco Computer Services, Inc.

Do you wish to be represented for purposes of collective bargaining by—

¿Desea usted estar representado para los fines de negociar colectivamente por

Local 007, United Computer Operators
International Union

MARK AN "X" IN THE SQUARE OF YOUR CHOICE
MARQUESE CON UNA "X" DENTRO DEL CUADRO DE SU SELECCION

| YES | NO |
| SI | NO |

DO NOT SIGN THIS BALLOT. Fold and drop in ballot box. FORM NLRB-707N2A and 707N2ASP (5-80)
NO FIRME ESTA PAPELETA. Dóblela y depósitela en la urna electoral.

If you spoil this ballot return it to the Board Agent for a new one.
Si usted daña esta papeleta devuélvala al Agente da la Junta y pídale una nueva.

**Exhibit 42. Sample Bilingual Ballot Used in Collective Bargaining Election
Involving One Union (Form NLRB-707N2ASP)**

UNITED STATES OF AMERICA
National Labor Relations Board

OFFICIAL SECRET BALLOT

For certain employees of
Janco Computer Services, Inc.

This ballot is to determine the collective bargaining representative, if any, for the unit in which you are employed.

MARK AN "X" IN THE SQUARE OF YOUR CHOICE

Local 007, United Computer Operators International Union	NEITHER	Local 1212 International Alliance of High-Tech Workers
☐	☐	☐

FORM NLRB-707N3 (RC, RM, RD CASES) (5-80)

DO NOT SIGN THIS BALLOT. Fold and drop in ballot box.
If you spoil this ballot return it to the Board Agent for a new one.

GPO 869 465

Exhibit 43.   Sample Ballot Used in Collective Bargaining Election Involving More Than One Union (Form NLRB-707N3)

by chance (for example, by the toss of a coin).[48] To avoid confusion in an election involving numerous units, the same relative places on the ballots for each unit will be maintained.[49] If the Board inadvertently reverses the determined ballot positions, the election will not be set aside unless there is clear evidence that the reversal affected the outcome of the election.[50] As with a single-union election, special bilingual ballots will be furnished if necessary.

Other variations of the ballot appear in "self-determination" elections.[51] In severance elections, where a group of employees vote on whether they wish to be severed from a larger unit, the voters will be afforded a choice between the incumbent union and the new union or unions seeking to sever part of the existing unit.[52] The ballot will list the names of the contending unions. (See Exhibit 44.) Unlike the normal representation election involving more than one union, a choice of no representation is not available in a severance election.[53] If the election is conducted in a unit which includes professional employees, the ballot carries two questions: one asking for a "yes" or "no" choice of whether the professionals wish to be included in a single unit with nonprofessionals, the other asking by which union, if any, the professionals desire to be represented.[54] In a residual election, unrepresented employees in a partially organized plant vote on which union, if any, will represent them. Here the ballot offers a choice between representation by any one of the petitioning unions or no representation at all.[55]

Any labor organization seeking representation rights must be clearly designated on the ballot. Where the name "AFL-CIO and/or its Appropriate Affiliate" appeared on a petition, the Board held that such a designation on the ballot would not sufficiently identify the labor organization to accord employees their Section 7 right to select bargaining representatives *of their own choosing.*"[56] A union may, however, request the use of a shortened name on the ballot. Regardless of whether the matter was raised initially at a hearing, the regional director may grant such a request.[57] But the shortened name may be used only *in addition to* the full name and the director must find that the voters will not be misled by use of the additional name.[58]

---

[48]NLRB Casehandling Manual ¶11306.3.

[49]*Id.*

[50]*NLRB v. Bayliss Trucking Corp.*, 432 F.2d 1025, 75 LRRM 2501 (2d Cir. 1970) (the reversal of positions was immaterial since a sample ballot had been posted for one week, the Board agent explained the ballot to the voters, and all the voters could read the clearly distinct union names on the ballot).

[51]See §8.6 for a discussion of "self-determination" elections.

[52]NLRB Casehandling Manual ¶11090.1(a).

[53]*Id.*

[54]*Id.* at ¶11090.1(b).

[55]*Id.* at ¶11090.1(c).

[56]*O & T Warehousing Co.*, 240 NLRB 386, 100 LRRM 1212, 1213 (1979) (emphasis added).

[57]NLRB Casehandling Manual ¶11306.2.

[58]*Id.*

UNITED STATES OF AMERICA

National Labor Relations Board

OFFICIAL SECRET BALLOT

FOR CERTAIN EMPLOYEES OF

Janco Computer Services, Inc.

This ballot is to determine the collective bargaining representative, if any, for the unit in which you are employed.

MARK AN "X" IN THE SQUARE OF YOUR CHOICE

Local 007, United Computer Operators International Union	Local 1212, International Alliance of High-Tech Workers
☐	☐

DO NOT SIGN THIS BALLOT. Fold and drop in ballot box.
If you spoil this ballot return it to the Board Agent for a new one.

Exhibit 44.   Sample Ballot Used in Severance Election

If used, the shortened name will appear in parentheses below the union's official title.[59]

§9.5 The Election Notice

Standard notice of election forms will be furnished by the Board agent so that eligible voters can be informed of the election details.[60] The notice contains a sample ballot like the one to be used in the election, a description of the bargaining unit, the eligibility cutoff date, and the date, hours, and location of the voting.[61] The mechanics of the voting procedure and the rights of employees also are described, and other pertinent instructions (concerning the voting eligibility of strikers, for example) are given.[62] (See Exhibit 45.) Supplements prepared or approved by the regional office, such as voting schedules or lists of eligible voters, may also be provided along with the election notice.[63]

At least one copy of the notice and any approved supplements are provided for each location at the workplace where employee notices customarily are posted. In addition, a copy will be provided for each party to the election and each legal representative. The parties may obtain a reasonable number of additional copies upon request.[64]

When a substantial number of the eligible voters do not read or write English, notices printed in the appropriate foreign language will be furnished. (See Exhibit 46.) If a foreign language notice is used, that language must also appear on a bilingual ballot.[65] The foreign language notices posted must contain *all* of the same information found in the English ballot.[66] Unless it is shown that failure to provide multilingual notices and ballots adversely affected the employees' ability to cast an informed vote, the Board will uphold the parties' stipulation to conduct an election solely in English.[67]

While the Board alone bears responsibility for the content of the election notice and for furnishing it to the appropriate parties,[68] the

---

[59]*Id.*

[60]NLRB Casehandling Manual ¶11314.

[61]*Id.* For split session, multiple site, and mail ballot elections, the time and place for mingling and counting the ballots will also be included. *Id.*

[62]*Id.* For "self-determination" elections, the notice also contains an appropriate explanation of how the vote of the various groups will be considered in determining the election results. *Id.* at ¶¶11314.1, 11090.1. See also §8.6.

[63]NLRB Casehandling Manual ¶11314.2.

[64]*Id.* at ¶11314.

[65]*Id.*

[66]*Rattan Art Gallery, Ltd.*, 260 NLRB 255, 109 LRRM 1149 (1982) (election set aside where Sec. 7 right to refrain from engaging in union activity was omitted from foreign language ballot); *Flo-Tronic Metal Mfg., Inc.*, 251 NLRB 1546, 105 LRRM 1144 (1980) (failure to include full statement of rights in both English and Spanish was grounds for invalidating election).

[67]*Norwestern Prods., Inc.*, 226 NLRB 653, 93 LRRM 1322 (1976).

[68]Where the Board neglects this responsibility by failing to supply an adequate number of copies of the notice, an election may still be set aside on grounds of inadequate notice to the employees. *Thermalloy Corp.*, 233 NLRB 428, 96 LRRM 1505 (1977) (there was "no question

UNITED STATES OF AMERICA ★ NATIONAL LABOR RELATIONS BOARD

NOTICE OF ELECTION

RIGHTS OF EMPLOYEES

Under the National Labor Relations Act, employees have the right:

- To self-organization
- To form, join, or assist labor organizations
- To bargain collectively through representatives of their own choosing
- To act together for the purposes of collective bargaining or other mutual aid or protection
- To refuse to do any or all of these things unless the Union and Employer, in a State where such agreements are permitted, enter into a lawful union security clause requiring employees to join the Union.

It is the responsibility of the National Labor Relations Board to protect employees in the exercise of these rights.

The Board wants all eligible voters to be fully informed about their rights under Federal law and wants both Employers and Unions to know what is expected of them when it holds an election.

If agents of either Unions or Employers interfere with your right to a free, fair, and honest election, the election can be set aside by the Board. Where appropriate the Board provides other remedies, such as reinstatement for employees fired for exercising their rights, including backpay from the party responsible for their discharge.

The following are examples of conduct which interferes with the rights of employees and may result in the setting aside of the election:

- Threatening loss of jobs or benefits by an Employer or a Union
- Promising or granting promotions, pay raises, or other benefits to influence an employee's vote by a party capable of carrying out such promises
- An Employer firing employees to discourage or encourage union activity or a Union causing them to be fired to encourage union activity
- Making campaign speeches to assembled groups of employees on company time within the 24 hour period before the election
- Incitement by either an Employer or a Union of racial or religious prejudice by inflammatory appeals
- Threatening physical force or violence to employees by a Union or an Employer to influence their votes.

The National Labor Relations Board protects your right to a free choice

Improper conduct will not be permitted. All parties are expected to cooperate fully with this agency in maintaining basic principles of a fair election as required by law. The National Labor Relations Board as an agency of the United States Government does not endorse any choice in the election.

NATIONAL LABOR RELATIONS BOARD
an agency of the
UNITED STATES GOVERNMENT

UNITED STATES OF AMERICA
National Labor Relations Board
OFFICIAL SECRET BALLOT

For certain employees of

Janco Computer Services, Inc.

Do you wish to be represented for purposes of collective bargaining by -

Local 007, United Computer Operators
International Union

MARK AN "X" IN THE SQUARE OF YOUR CHOICE

YES	NO
☐	☐

PURPOSE OF THIS ELECTION — This election is to determine the representative, if any, desired by the eligible employees for purposes of collective bargaining with their Employer. (See VOTING UNIT in this Notice of Election, for description of eligible employees.) A majority of the valid ballots cast will determine the results of the election.

SECRET BALLOT — The election will be by SECRET ballot under the supervision of the Regional Director of the National Labor Relations Board. Voters will be allowed to vote without interference, restraint, or coercion. Electioneering will not be permitted at or near the polling place. Violations of these rules should be reported immediately to the Regional Director or the agent in charge of the election. Your attention is called to Section 12 of the National Labor Relations Act:

ANY PERSON WHO SHALL WILLFULLY RESIST, PREVENT, IMPEDE, OR INTERFERE WITH ANY MEMBER OF THE BOARD OR ANY OF ITS AGENTS OR AGENCIES IN THE PERFORMANCE OF DUTIES PURSUANT TO THIS ACT SHALL BE PUNISHED BY A FINE OF NOT MORE THAN $5,000 OR BY IMPRISONMENT FOR NOT MORE THAN ONE YEAR, OR BOTH.

An agent of the Board will hand a ballot to each eligible voter at the voting place. Mark your ballot in secret in the voting booth provided. DO NOT SIGN YOUR BALLOT. Fold the ballot before leaving the voting booth, then personally deposit it in a ballot box under the supervision of an agent of the Board.

A sample of the official ballot is shown at the center of this Notice.

ELIGIBILITY RULES — Employees eligible to vote are those described under VOTING UNIT in this Notice of Election, including employees who did not work during the designated payroll period because they were ill or on vacation or temporarily laid off, and also including employees in the military service of the United States who appear in person at the polls. Employees who have quit or been discharged for cause since the designated payroll period and who have not been rehired or reinstated prior to the date of this election are not eligible to vote.

CHALLENGE OF VOTERS — An agent of the Board or an authorized observer may question the eligibility of a voter. Such challenge MUST be made before the voter's ballot has been placed in the ballot box.

AUTHORIZED OBSERVERS — Each of the interested parties may designate an equal number of observers, this number to be determined by the Regional Director or agent in charge of the election. These observers (a) act as checkers at the voting place and at the counting of ballots, (b) assist in the identification of voters, (c) challenge voters and ballots, and (d) otherwise assist the Regional Director or agent.

INFORMATION CONCERNING ELECTION — The Act provides that only one valid representation election may be held in a 12 month period. Any employee who desires to obtain any further information concerning the terms and conditions under which this election is to be held or who desires to raise any question concerning the holding of an election, may do so by communicating with the Regional Director or agent in charge of the election.

WARNING: THIS IS THE ONLY OFFICIAL NOTICE OF THIS ELECTION AND MUST NOT BE DEFACED BY ANYONE

Exhibit 45. Notice of Election (Form NLRB-707)

ESTADOS UNIDOS DE AMERICA ★ JUNTA NACIONAL DE RELACIONES DEL TRABAJO

AVISO DE ELECCION

INSTRUCCIONES A EMPLEADOS ELEGIBLES QUE VOTEN POR CORREO DE LOS ESTADOS UNIDOS

DERECHOS DE LOS EMPLEADOS

Conforme a lo dispuesto en la Ley Nacional de Relaciones del Trabajo, los empleados tienen el derecho a:

- Organizarse
- Constituir, ingresar en, o ayudar a organizaciones obreras
- Negociar colectivamente por conducto de representantes seleccionados por ellos mismos
- Actuar concertadamente con el fin de negociar colectivamente u otro fin de ayuda o protección mutua
- Negarse a hacer cualesquiera o todas estas cosas a menos que, en un Estado en donde tales convenios sean permitidos, la unión y el patrono concierten una cláusula legal de seguridad de la unión que requiera que los empleados ingresen en la unión.

La Junta Nacional de Relaciones del Trabajo tiene la responsabilidad de proteger a los empleados en el ejercicio de estos derechos.

PROPOSITO DE ESTA ELECCION

VOTO SECRETO

REGLAS DE ELEGIBILIDAD

RECUSACION DE VOTANTES

OBSERVADORES AUTORIZADOS

INFORMACION CONCERNIENTE A LA ELECCION

LA JUNTA NACIONAL DE RELACIONES DEL TRABAJO PROTEGE SU DERECHO A UNA LIBRE SELECCION

No se permitirá conducta impropia. Se espera de todas las partes que cooperen cabalmente con esta agencia en el mantenimiento de los principios básicos de una elección imparcial según requiere la ley. La Junta Nacional de Relaciones del Trabajo como una agencia del Gobierno de los Estados Unidos no endosa ninguna de las selecciones en la elección.

JUNTA NACIONAL DE RELACIONES DEL TRABAJO
una agencia del
GOBIERNO DE LOS ESTADOS UNIDOS

ADVERTENCIA: ESTE ES EL UNICO AVISO OFICIAL DE ESTA ELECCION Y NO DEBE SER MUTILADO POR NINGUNA PERSONA

Exhibit 46.   Election Notice in Spanish (Form NLRB-4910SP)

employer's cooperation is necessary for the actual posting of the notice. An employer is not *required* to submit to the use of his property for this purpose.[69] A Board agent, however, will investigate employer intransigence or complaints of insufficient posting, and although lacking authority to compel posting of the notices, can usually gain the employer's cooperation. Arguments based on a desire to avoid objections by other parties to the election, or to avoid the employer being estopped from making objections, are usually successful in convincing the employer to post the notices.[70] Where the Board agent thinks it necessary, notices may be distributed by mail or in person to employees not working during the posting period. Even newspaper or radio publicity is permissible in extraordinary circumstances.[71]

When the employer agrees to post the notices, they should be displayed in conspicuous places such as on bulletin boards and near timecard racks.[72] Because of the exigencies of each case, the Board has never established a specified time prior to an election for the posting of the election notice.[73] Instead, this detail is left to the discretion of the regional director who is in a better position to assess the circumstances of each case.[74] Where an employer offers no valid explanation for a late posting of notices, the Board often has ordered a new election regardless of whether employees were otherwise notified of the election and despite the fact that nearly all of the eligible voters participated in the election.[75] Ultimately, the facts of each case will be evaluated to determine if an employer has posted the election notice in adequate time to inform the employees of their rights and of the pending election.[76]

Election Procedures

§9.6   Role of Board Personnel

The Board's Rules and Regulations require that, unless otherwise directed, "all elections shall be conducted under the supervision

---

of fault on the part of the employer"). *But see Cerlo Mfg. Corp. v. NLRB*, 585 F.2d 847, 99 LRRM 3054 (7th Cir. 1978) (reversing the Board, the court refused to set aside an election where the official notices never arrived and the employer posted a notice prepared by his attorney and a copy of the official stipulation for certification upon consent election).

[69]NLRB Casehandling Manual ¶11314.3.

[70]*Id.*

[71]*Id.*

[72]*Id.*

[73]*Kilgore Corp.*, 203 NLRB 118, 83 LRRM 1010 (1973).

[74]*Id. See also Congoleum Indus.*, 227 NLRB 108, 93 LRRM 1503 (1976) (on the basis of *Kilgore*, posting two days before election was unsatisfactory).

[75]*Associated Air Freight, Inc.*, 247 NLRB 990, 103 LRRM 1270 (1980).

[76]*See, e.g., Printhouse Co.*, 246 NLRB 741, 102 LRRM 1663 (1979) (election not set aside "in view of all the circumstances" where notices were posted one day before the balloting).

of the regional director in whose region the proceeding is pending."[77] In practice, one or more agents of the regional office will conduct the election. The number and type of Board agents present will depend upon such factors as the size, complexity, and duration of the election.[78] Generally, one Board agent will be stationed at the "checking table" for each polling place, and others may be present for "challenge tables," relief, and supervision.[79] The agent in charge of the election is responsible for properly "manning" the polls and for insuring that proper voting procedures are followed.[80]

The Board personnel conducting the election are required to follow the Board's established procedures and to maintain a neutral stance at all times. In some cases, postelection objections are made on the basis of the conduct of Board agents. Most frequently these objections arise from Board personnel failing to observe the designated voting hours, leaving the polls or ballots unattended, making statements that violate Board neutrality, or acting improperly in challenging voters. In each of these areas, there are relatively well-defined standards regulating the conduct of Board personnel.

Objections alleging a deviation from the designated voting hours usually are concerned with either late opening of the polls or failure to keep the polls open beyond the closing time to accommodate late voters. The Board will not set aside an election solely because Board agents arrive late and cause the election to be delayed.[81] Rather, an election will be invalidated because of the agents' tardiness when it is shown that "the votes of those possibly excluded could have been determinative" of the election outcome.[82] Where the possibly excluded votes could not have been determinative, but there are circumstances indicating that the late opening may have affected the vote, the Board may also set aside the election.[83]

For objections arising from the handling of voters who arrive after the designated closing time of the polls, the Board will defer to the "reasonable discretion" of the agent conducting the election.[84] In determining whether a late voter should be permitted to cast a ballot, the following factors usually are considered: (1) why the employee was late; (2) how late the employee was; (3) the length of the voting

---

[77]NLRB Rules and Regulations §102.69(a).

[78]NLRB Casehandling Manual ¶11308.

[79]*Id.*

[80]*Id.*

[81]*Jim Kraut Chevrolet, Inc.*, 240 NLRB 460, 100 LRRM 1227 (1979) (election upheld where polls opened one and one-half hours late).

[82]*Jobbers Meat Packing Co.*, 252 NLRB 41, 105 LRRM 1184 (1980) (polls opened two hours late; election upheld); *see also Celotex Corp.*, 266 NLRB 802, 113 LRRM 1052 (1983) (reaffirming the *Jobbers Meat* standards).

[83]*Jobbers Meat Packing Co.*, 252 NLRB 41, 105 LRRM 1184 (1980). In *V.I.P. Limousine, Inc.*, 274 NLRB No. 90, 118 LRRM 1399 (1985), the polls opened on time, but the Board nevertheless set the election aside because a snowstorm prevented a substantial number of employees from reaching the polls, thereby destroying the integrity of the election process.

[84]*Kerrville Bus Co.*, 257 NLRB 176, 107 LRRM 1466 (1981).

period; and (4) whether the ballot box had been opened or the tally commenced when the employee arrived.[85] Board agents are encouraged to afford employees the broadest possible opportunity to participate in the election so long as the election procedures are not hampered.[86] In practice, however, late voters usually are not permitted to cast ballots more than a few minutes after the scheduled close of the election.[87] Thus, in a case where a voter arrived after the slot in the ballot box had been taped to signal the close of the election, the Board upheld its agent's decision to deny the voter a ballot.[88]

Beyond minor deviations from the designated voting hours, the conduct of Board agents may give rise to objections if the agents leave the polls or ballots unattended. The standard by which such objections are judged is whether "a reasonable possibility of irregularity inhered in the conduct of [the] election."[89] Where a Board agent left unmarked ballots out of her sight for approximately five minutes, but there was no evidence that anyone approached the area where the ballots were resting, an objection to the election was dismissed.[90] An objection also was dismissed in a case where it was alleged that the Board agent's lax supervision permitted a small number of unused ballots to remain in a voting booth during the balloting. The Board ruled that such an isolated incident, which could not be found determinative of the election results, did not interfere with a free and fair election.[91]

Because Board personnel conducting an election must remain neutral, objections frequently are based on allegedly biased statements or conduct of these persons. Acts of Board agents which tend to destroy confidence in the Board's election processes may be grounds for upholding an objection.[92] The Board and reviewing courts usually focus on whether voting employees were exposed to the allegedly biased comments or action. In most cases, the Board agent's conduct is not grounds for setting aside the election if there was no such employee exposure.[93] Even where employees do witness the agent's allegedly biased conduct, an election will not be invalidated unless the bias is clear and has a marked effect upon the voters. For example,

---

[85]*Id.*

[86]*Id.*

[87]*Southland Corp.*, 232 NLRB 631, 96 LRRM 1279 (1977).

[88]*Atlantic Int'l Corp.*, 228 NLRB 1308, 94 LRRM 1740 (1977).

[89]*Trico Prods. Corp.*, 238 NLRB 380, 381, 99 LRRM 1265, 1266 (1978), *quoting Peoples Drug Stores, Inc.*, 202 NLRB 1145, 82 LRRM 1763 (1973).

[90]*Trico Prods. Corp.*, 238 NLRB 380, 99 LRRM 1265 (1978).

[91]*Newport News Shipbuilding and Dry Dock Co.*, 239 NLRB 82, 99 LRRM 1518 (1978).

[92]*Athbro Precision Eng'g Corp.*, 166 NLRB 966, 65 LRRM 1699 (1967); *see also Sioux Prods., Inc. v. NLRB*, 703 F.2d 1010, 112 LRRM 3219 (7th Cir. 1983).

[93]*See, e.g., NLRB v. Sonoma Vineyards, Inc.*, 727 F.2d 860, 115 LRRM 3151 (9th Cir. 1984) (election upheld where Board agent stated, outside the earshot of employees, he thought union could easily prove its ballot challenges); *NLRB v. Allen's I.G.A. Foodliner*, 652 F.2d 594, 108 LRRM 2341 (6th Cir. 1980) (Board agent's statement that "if the employees had been treated right she would not be there holding the election," although improper, was not prejudicial because no voters heard the comment).

an election was upheld against a challenge that a Board agent acted improperly by holding up a ballot and, using his finger, making an imaginary "X" over the petitioning union's box as part of the instructions to voters. This demonstration was not prejudicial, the Board ruled, because the agent orally stated that voters should "make an X in the box of their choice."[94] In contrast, the Board invalidated an election in which a Board agent, who could not speak Spanish, delegated to a union observer the responsibility to explain voting procedures to Spanish-speaking employees.[95]

The final area in which Board agents must carefully remain neutral and follow established procedures is the process for challenging voters. The challenge procedure permits a voter's eligibility to be called into question before that voter casts a ballot (see §9.9 *infra*). The Board agent is required to challenge any voter whose name is not on the eligibility list and any voter the agent reasonably believes is ineligible to vote. In the latter case, the agent will make the challenge only after the parties have failed to do so.[96] The Board agent will not *make* challenges on behalf of the parties, regardless of whether the parties have their own observers present.[97] If, however, a party genuinely cannot obtain an observer, the Board agent may *state* that party's challenges that are based upon good cause. In this case the challenge is not made on behalf of the Board, and the Board assumes no responsibility for assuring that certain voters will be challenged.[98]

The distinction between "making" a challenge on behalf of a party and "stating" the challenge of a party who genuinely cannot obtain an observer is a fine one. It is the responsibility of the parties to *initiate* their own challenges. The Board agent, in addition to initiating the Board's challenges based on eligibility, may *state* those initiated by a party who is unable to have an observer present.[99] The burden presumptively rests with the parties to state their own challenges unless there is an "unexpected occurrence" that makes it impossible for a party to be represented by an observer. An observer's mistake or inadvertence is not an occurrence requiring the Board agent to act.[100]

In addition to the standards controlling voting hours, supervision of the polls and ballots, violations of Board neutrality, and the chal-

---

[94]*Newport News Shipbuilding and Dry Dock Co.*, 239 NLRB 82, 87 n.18, 99 LRRM 1518, 1524 n.18 (1978).

[95]*Alco Iron & Metal Co.*, 269 NLRB 590, 115 LRRM 1322 (1984).

[96]NLRB Casehandling Manual ¶11338.

[97]*Id.*

[98]*Id.*

[99]*NLRB v. Schwartz Bros., Inc.*, 475 F.2d 926, 82 LRRM 2376 (D.C. Cir. 1973).

[100]*Fern Labs., Inc.*, 232 NLRB 379, 97 LRRM 1315 (1977). *Cf. Laubenstein & Portz, Inc.*, 226 NLRB 804, 93 LRRM 1367 (1976) (Board agent acted improperly in not stating a challenge where the agent was fully aware of a settlement agreement calling for the challenge and the challenging party had no observer present).

lenge process, Board agents are bound by detailed election procedures. Those procedures are discussed below in §§9.7 through 9.15.

§9.7 Election Observers

Each party to the election usually will be represented at the polls
by an equal number of predesignated observers chosen to assist in
the conduct of the election.[101] Non-participating unions and "no-union"
employee groups may not be represented by observers.[102] The Board
agent will determine the number of observers per party based on the
size of the election, the number of polling places, the length of voting
hours, etc. This determination usually will be made after consultation
with the parties. Although a party may, either expressly or by default,
waive the opportunity to have observers, the agent conducting the
election will provide each party every opportunity for representation.[103]

There are some restrictions on who may serve as an observer.
Unless the parties agree otherwise, all observers must be nonsupervisory employees of the employer, and cannot be representatives of
"no-union" groups.[104] In addition, "persons clearly identified with
management," even though they are nonsupervisory employees, cannot act as observers.[105] The Board has found that an employer's attorney,[106] a company president's wife,[107] and an office manager[108] all
were ineligible to act as observers. However, a nun who was a co-
owner of an employer-hospital by virtue of being a member of the
order of sisters who maintained the institution was found *not* to be
"closely identified" with the employer.[109] It is permissible for a union
official,[110] or an employee allegedly discriminated against because of
his or her pro-union activity,[111] to serve as an observer.

The Board requires that the names of proposed observers be
submitted to the Board agent early enough to permit a check of

---

[101]NLRB Rules and Regulations §102.69(a); NLRB Casehandling Manual ¶11310.

[102]NLRB Casehandling Manual ¶11310.

[103]*Id.; See Summa Corp. v. NLRB*, 625 F.2d 293, 105 LRRM 2364 (9th Cir. 1980) (election
invalidated where, contrary to the parties' stipulation, union had more observers present than
the employer). In *Sonicraft, Inc.*, 276 NLRB No. 44, 120 LRRM 1208 (1985), the Board set
aside an election because the presence of three union observers in contrast with the employer's
single observer might have created an impression among voters that the Board was partial to
the union and the union was running the election.

[104]NLRB Casehandling Manual ¶11310.

[105]*Masoneilan Int'l*, 223 NLRB 965, 92 LRRM 1025 (1976); *see also Peabody Eng. Co.*, 95
NLRB 952, 28 LRRM 1391 (1951).

[106]*Peabody Eng. Co.*, 95 NLRB 952, 28 LRRM 1391 (1951).

[107]*Wiley Mfg., Inc.*, 93 NLRB 1600, 27 LRRM 1623 (1951).

[108]*Watkins Brick Co.*, 107 NLRB 500, 33 LRRM 1176 (1953).

[109]*St. Joseph Riverside Hosp.*, 224 NLRB 721, 92 LRRM 1340 (1976).

[110]*New England Lumber v. NLRB*, 646 F.2d 1, 107 LRRM 2165 (1st Cir. 1981).

[111]NLRB Casehandling Manual ¶11310.

nonsupervisory status,[112] and the parties usually will agree upon a slate of eligible observers at the preelection conference. An election may be set aside for use of an ineligible observer, so it is important that the parties make their selections carefully.

All observers are given detailed, written instructions by the Board agent either at a preelection meeting or immediately before the election itself. (See Exhibit 47.) Observers are asked to assist in identifying voters, record those employees who have voted, challenge voters on behalf of the parties, and serve as checkers in the counting of ballots. An observer for each party will be stationed at the checking table where voters enter the polls and at the ballot box. In large elections, more observers may be used for ushering and other assistance.[113] While carrying out their duties, election observers, as a matter of right, may keep lists of the names of voters they intend to challenge.[114] However, the official eligibility list is the only list that observers may use to record those who have or have not voted.[115]

Official observers are identified by a badge provided by the Board, and are strongly urged to refrain from wearing other insignia related to the election.[116] Observers are prohibited from electioneering during their hours of duty, whether at or away from the polling place, and they may not engage in conversation with incoming voters.[117] To insure this ban on electioneering, observers away from the polling area will usually be accompanied by a representative of the opposing party.[118] In short, election observers are expected to carry out their assigned duties without partisan displays.

§9.8 Mechanics of the Election

The actual voting is always conducted and supervised by NLRB agents.[119] The agents will arrange the physical layout of the polling place—i.e., the checking tables, the voting booths, and the ballot box—in a manner which minimizes confusion and avoids backups of waiting voters.[120] The Board will furnish all the necessary election

---

[112]*Id.*

[113]*Id.*

[114]*Tom Brown Drilling Co.*, 172 NLRB 1267, 68 LRRM 1473 (1968); *Bear Creek Orchards*, 90 NLRB 286, 26 LRRM 1204 (1950).

[115]NLRB Casehandling Manual ¶11322.1; *Piggly-Wiggly #011 and #228 Eagle Food Centers, Inc.*, 168 NLRB 792, 66 LRRM 1360 (1967).

[116]NLRB Casehandling Manual ¶¶11310, 11326.1; *see also Glacier Packing Co.*, 210 NLRB 571, 86 LRRM 1178 (1974) (quoting Item 7 of "Things Not to Do" in Instructions to Observers); *cf. Nestle Co.*, 248 NLRB 732, 103 LRRM 1567 (1980) (objection to observer wearing pro-union button overruled).

[117]NLRB Casehandling Manual ¶11326.2; *cf. Amalgamated Indus. Union, Local 76B*, 246 NLRB 727 n.2, 102 LRRM 1666 n.2 (1979) (not impermissible for union observer to urge employees to come in and vote or to answer questions concerning whether certain employees had already voted).

[118]NLRB Casehandling Manual ¶11326.2.

[119]NLRB Statements of Procedure §101.19(a)(2).

[120]NLRB Casehandling Manual ¶11316.

UNITED STATES OF AMERICA

NATIONAL LABOR RELATIONS BOARD

INSTRUCTIONS TO ELECTION OBSERVERS

DUTIES *(General):*

1. Act as checkers and watchers.

2. Assist in identification of voters.

3. Challenge voters and ballots.

4. Otherwise assist agents of the Board.

THINGS TO DO *(Specific):*

1. Identify voter.

2. Check off the name of the person applying to vote. One check before the name by one organization. One check after the name by the other organization or the Company.

3. See that only one voter occupies a booth at any one time.

4. See that each voter deposits a ballot in the ballot box.

5. See that each voter leaves the voting room immediately after depositing ballot.

6. Report any conflict as to the right to vote to the agent of the Board at your table.

7. Remain in the voting place until all ballots are counted in order to check on the fairness of the count, if ballots are counted at that time. If they are not counted immediately, you will be informed as to when and where ballots will be counted.

8. Report any irregularities to the Board agent as soon as noticed.

9. Challenge of Voters - An agent of the Board or an authorized observer may question eligibility of a voter. Such challenge MUST be made before the voter's ballot has been placed in the ballot box.

10. Wear your observer badge at all times during the conduct of the election.

11. BE ON TIME. *(One-half hour before the time for the opening of the polls.)*

THINGS NOT TO DO *(Specific):*

1. Give any help to any voter. Only an agent of the Board can assist the voter.

2. Electioneer any place during the hours of the election.

3. Argue regarding the election.

4. Leave the polling place without the agent's consent.

5. Use intoxicating liquors.

6. Keep any list of those who have or have not voted.

As an official representative of your organization, you should enter upon this task with a fair and open mind. Conduct yourself so that no one can find fault with your actions during the election. You are here to see that the election is conducted in a fair and impartial manner, so that each eligible voter has a fair and equal chance to express themselves freely and in secret.

NATIONAL LABOR RELATIONS BOARD

GPO 883-664

Exhibit 47.   Instructions to Election Observers   (Form NLRB-722)

equipment, such as portable voting booths and ballot boxes.[121] In a smoothly run election, one checking table can accommodate 250–400 voters per hour.

Prior to opening the polls, the Board agents conducting the election will assemble the observers and possibly "outside" (non-observer) representatives of the parties. At this meeting, observers will receive their badges and final instructions, and the parties' outside representatives will be allowed to inspect the polling area and voice any objections. These objections usually will be disposed of at this time by the supervising Board agent. Finally, the ballot box will be inspected by all observers and then sealed by the agent. The parties' outside representatives are required to leave the polling area before the polls open. Voters who arrive before the polls open cannot vote early and will be asked to wait outside the polling area.[122]

At the scheduled time, the polls will be opened and voting will begin.[123] Voters will enter the polling place at a designated entrance and proceed to the appropriate checking table where a Board agent and an observer for each party will be stationed. The voter will be asked to identify him or herself by name or number (such as a pay or badge number) and the observers then will check off the voter's name on the eligibility list.[124] After the voter has been identified and checked off, the Board agent will give him or her an unmarked ballot.[125]

The voter will then proceed to an unoccupied voting booth to mark the ballot by placing an "X" in the desired box. Only one occupant per voting booth is permitted and there may not be conversation between occupants at different booths.[126] If a voter spoils a ballot, a fresh one will be provided by the Board agent. After registering his on her choice, the voter will leave the voting booth and deposit the folded ballot into the ballot box. Observers will be stationed near the ballot box but they may not handle any voter's ballot. Having completed this process, the voter will leave the polling area.[127]

At the scheduled time, the polls will be closed, even if the election started late. Employees waiting in line to vote at the scheduled closing time will be permitted to cast ballots. The slot in the ballot box will be sealed upon the conclusion of the voting and the Board agent will, unless the parties agree otherwise, maintain personal custody of the box until the count.[128] If a voter arrives after the polls have

---

[121]*Id.* at ¶¶11304–11304.5.

[122]*Id.* at ¶¶11318–11318.5.

[123]*Id.* at ¶11320.

[124]See discussion at §9.9 *infra* on the procedure for challenging voters.

[125]NLRB Casehandling Manual at ¶11322.1. In *Newport News Shipbuilding and Dry Dock Co.*, 239 NLRB 82, 99 LRRM 1518 (1978), the Board refused to set aside an election where more employee names were checked off on the eligibility list than there were actual ballots counted. The discrepancy was too small to affect the outcome in the 17,000-vote election, and the Board assigned the discrepancy to human error and inadvertence.

[126]NLRB Casehandling Manual ¶11322.2.

[127]*Id.* at ¶11322.4.

[128]*Id.* at ¶11324.

closed, but before the ballot box is opened for counting, the Board agent will attempt to obtain the parties' agreement on whether the voter should be permitted to cast a ballot. Failing such agreement, the employee may be permitted to cast a ballot that the Board agent will then challenge. The Board generally defers to its agents' discretion in the handling of late voters.[129]

The final stage of the election itself is the signing of the certification on the conduct of the election. (See Exhibit 48.) Each observer will be asked to sign this document, which declares that the balloting was fairly conducted, that all eligible voters were given an opportunity to cast secret ballots, and that the ballot box was protected to insure a fair and secret vote. If an observer refuses to sign the certification, he or she will be asked for a signed, written explanation for the refusal. If a party was not represented by an observer, the Board agent will note this on the certification form.[130]

The reference in the certification on conduct of election to the opportunity for employees to vote "in secret" reflects an interest that the Board carefully safeguards. The opportunity for voting in secrecy is insured by the precise procedures Board agents are required to follow, such as the use of isolated voting booths [131] and the requirement that only the voter may handle his or her marked ballot.[132]

Election objections frequently are grounded on alleged breaches of the secrecy requirement. Where, for example, the voting booths were arranged so that employees could be observed while marking their ballots, the Board set aside an election.[133] Any arrangement at the polling place that could give voters the impression they are being observed as they vote may be grounds for invalidating an election.[134] Secrecy also may not be impaired by the presence of two persons in a voting booth at one time, even where one person is attempting to explain the voting procedure to a non-English speaking co-employee.[135] Because the Board views ballot secrecy as "a matter of public concern rather than a personal privilege subject to waiver," the Board will void the vote of an employee who places identifying markings on his or her ballot or openly marks it for others to see.[136]

---

[129]*Id.* See also text accompanying notes 84-88 *supra*.

[130]NLRB Casehandling Manual ¶11324. Signing the certificate does not deny a party the right to make objections that may serve as a basis for invalidating the election. *F.J. Stokes Corp.*, 117 NLRB 951, 39 LRRM 1338 (1957). The same procedures for opening and closing elections discussed in the preceding paragraphs are followed for each session of a split-session election. NLRB Casehandling Manual ¶11332.

[131]NLRB Casehandling Manual ¶11322.2.

[132]*Id.* at ¶11322.4.

[133]*Royal Lumber Co.*, 118 NLRB 1015, 40 LRRM 1304 (1957).

[134]*Sewell Plastics, Inc.*, 241 NLRB 887 n.4, 100 LRRM 1589 (1979); *see Crown Cork & Seal Co. v. NLRB*, 659 F.2d 127, 108 LRRM 2224 (10th Cir. 1981).

[135]NLRB Casehandling Manual ¶11322.2; *Magic Pan, Inc. v. NLRB*, 627 F.2d 105, 105 LRRM 2559 (7th Cir. 1980).

[136]*General Photo Prods.*, 242 NLRB 1371, 101 LRRM 1352 (1979).

FORM NLRB-75:
(9-8?)

UNITED STATES OF AMERICA
NATIONAL LABOR RELATIONS BOARD

CERTIFICATION ON CONDUCT OF ELECTION

Name of employer _____   Case No. _____

Date of election _____ Place _____

The undersigned acted as agents of the Regional Director and as authorized obervers, respectively, in the conduct of the balloting at the above time and place.

WE HEREBY CERTIFY that such balloting was fairly conducted, that all eligible voters were given an opportunity to vote their ballots in secret, and that the ballot box was protected in the interest of a fair and secret vote.

For   For the Regional Director, Region

_____   _____

_____   _____

_____   _____

_____   _____

_____   _____

For   For

_____   _____

_____   _____

_____   _____

_____   _____

_____   _____

Exhibit 48.   Certification on Conduct of Election   (Form NLRB-750)

Where there is no evidence a possible impairment of secrecy could have affected the election outcome or intimidated voters, the Board usually will not set aside the election.[137] Where the presence of more than one employee in the voting booth was an isolated incident, the election was upheld.[138] In another case, where observers were able to see the markings on certain ballots as voters approached the ballot box, the election was upheld because the voters were unaware of the breach and could not have been intimidated in making their choice.[139] Thus, an impairment of ballot secrecy, while serious, will not be cause for a new election in every case.

§9.9 Challenging a Voter

Some voters will not be merely "checked off" at the checking table and permitted to vote in the usual manner. Any Board agent or authorized election observer has the right to challenge a voter's eligibility to participate in the election.[140] The challenge procedure permits the questioning of a voter's eligibility and the impoundment of the challenged voter's marked ballot pending a determination of the eligibility question. As noted in §9.6 *supra*, the Board agent must challenge (1) any voter whose name is not on the eligibility list; and (2) any voter, not challenged by one of the parties' observers, who the agent has reason to believe is ineligible. The agent will not *initiate* challenges on behalf of a party, regardless of whether or not that party has observers present. In some cases, however, a Board agent may *state* well-founded challenges previously initiated by a party who is genuinely unable to have an observer present.[141] The parties' observers are entitled to challenge any voter for cause, and the ground for a challenge must be stated when it is made.[142] Most challenges are based on the ground that a voter is ineligible because he or she is not included in the specified unit or is a "supervisor" within the meaning of the Act.

Challenges should be made when the voter comes to the checking table, *before* he or she receives a ballot. A challenge voiced any time before the voter's ballot is deposited in the ballot box will, however, usually be honored.[143] A party cannot remedy failure to make timely challenges by filing objections to the election on the basis of the unchallenged votes.[144] Nor does a party's statement at the opening

---

[137]*Sewell Plastics, Inc.*, 241 NLRB 887, 100 LRRM 1589 (1979); *see Crown Cork & Seal Co. v. NLRB*, 659 F.2d 127, 108 LRRM 2224 (10th Cir. 1981).

[138]*Machinery Overhaul Co.*, 115 NLRB 1787, 38 LRRM 1168 (1956).

[139]*Crown Cork & Seal Co. v. NLRB*, 659 F.2d 127, 108 LRRM 2224 (10th Cir. 1981).

[140]NLRB Rules and Regulations §102.69(a).

[141]NLRB Casehandling Manual ¶11338. See *supra* notes 96-100 and accompanying text.

[142]NLRB Casehandling Manual ¶11338.

[143]*Id.* at ¶11338.3.

[144]*NLRB v. A.J. Tower Co.*, 329 U.S. 324, 19 LRRM 2128 (1946).

of the polls that it challenges each and every voter constitute a proper challenge. Each voter must be challenged individually.[145]

When a voter is challenged, the observers will place a small "c" beside his or her name, or the voter's name will be placed on a supplemental list if the name does not appear on the eligibility list. The Board agent will fill out the stub of a "challenge envelope" identifying the voter, the challenging party, and the reason for the challenge. (See Exhibit 49.) The voter is then given the envelope and a ballot. The agent directs the voter to mark the ballot at the voting booth, place the ballot in the envelope, seal the envelope and drop it in the ballot box.[146] Arguments on the merits of a challenge are not permitted during the voting process,[147] but the Board agent may refuse the casting of even a challenged ballot by persons in job classifications specifically excluded by the decision and direction of election.[148]

The challenged ballot envelopes are segregated from the other ballots at the time of the count, but a party may withdraw any challenge before the count.[149] Only if the number of challenged ballots is sufficient to affect the outcome of the election will the eligibility of challenged voters be determined. The procedure for resolution of challenges is set forth in chapter 10.

§9.10   Mail Balloting

Where long distances are involved, or where voters are dispersed over a large geographical area, voting may be conducted by mail. It is within the regional director's discretion to determine whether to employ mail balloting, either in whole or in part.[150] If one of the parties is not agreeable to the use of mail balloting, however, Board guidelines recommend that the procedure be used only when a manual election is clearly not feasible.[151] Specific provision in the direction of election for mail balloting is not required, and the omission of such a provision is not a sufficient basis for setting aside an election.[152]

If an election includes both mail and manual voting, only employees who cannot vote in person because of "employer action" (e.g., assignment to duties at a location far away from the polling place) are permitted the use of mail ballots. Pipeline employees, seamen,

---

[145]*William R. Whittaker Co.*, 94 NLRB 1151, 28 LRRM 1150 (1951).

[146]NLRB Casehandling Manual ¶11338.1.

[147]*Id.* at ¶11338.4.

[148]*Id.* at ¶11338.5.

[149]*Sears, Roebuck & Co.*, 117 NLRB 522, 39 LRRM 1278 (1957).

[150]NLRB Casehandling Manual ¶11336; *see J. Ray McDermott & Co. v. NLRB*, 571 F.2d 850, 98 LRRM 2191 (5th Cir. 1978) (regional director acted properly in holding mail ballot election where a prior mail vote had secured high degree of participation and employees worked a variety of shifts in scattered locations).

[151]NLRB Casehandling Manual ¶11336.

[152]*J.R. Simplot Co.*, 107 NLRB 1211, 33 LRRM 1357 (1954).

CHALLENGED BALLOT

Secret ENVELOPE

FORM NLRB-4646
(2-65)

IDENTIFICATION STUB

NAME

CLOCK NO. UNIT

JOB CLASS

COMPANY

POLLING PLACE DATE

REASON FOR CHALLENGE

CHALLENGED BY

BOARD AGENT

PUT ADDITIONAL INFORMATION ON
THE BACK OF THIS STUB

Exhibit 49. Challenged Ballot Envelope (Form NLRB-4646)

and traveling public utility crewmembers are typical mail voters. Employees who are in the armed forces, are ill, on vacation, or on voluntary leaves of absence are not permitted to use mail balloting. Mail ballots may be sent to employees on layoff status only if all parties to the election agree.[153]

The procedure for mail elections is straightforward. A notice of election will be posted at the employer's place of business and, if possible, at any scattered bases of operation. This notice will instruct employees on the nature of the election, the date for mailing and returning ballots, and the procedure for notifying the regional office if the employee fails to receive a ballot by the prescribed date.[154] At least 24 hours before the Board mails ballots to the voters, the parties will receive written notice of the time and date on which the ballots will be dispatched, along with the deadline by which they must be returned to the regional office. In mixed manual-mail elections, the return deadline will precede the date of the manual voting. After the parties have received their written notice, the Board will mail each voter a balloting kit. This kit contains: (1) a notice of election and instructions for voting (see Exhibit 50); (2) a ballot; and (3) a postage-paid return envelope with an attached stub for the voter to sign and fill in with identifying information. (See Exhibit 51.)[155]

As in any election, a list of eligible voters will be prepared and will include the last known address of each person who is to vote by mail. A balloting kit will be forwarded to each mail voter the parties agree is eligible and to each voter that any party alleges is eligible. A "key number" is assigned to each name on the eligibility list and is written on the return envelope stub that each voter receives. This numbering system permits monitoring of the returned ballots to insure that voters who receive duplicates do not vote twice.[156]

The Board generally is flexible in applying its guidelines for the handling of mail ballots.[157] Ballots received after the designated return deadline, but before the count is made, usually will be accepted as valid. Where, for example, the postmark showed that voters mailed their ballots at a time when they could reasonably anticipate timely receipt by the Board, the ballots were counted.[158] In another case, where the regional director insisted on voiding late ballots despite the parties' waiver of the return deadline, the Board overruled the

---

[153]NLRB Casehandling Manual ¶11336.1.

[154]*Id.* at ¶11336.3. *See id.* at ¶11336.4 on the procedures for mailing "duplicate kits" to employees who do not receive their ballots in time, or who have spoiled their original ballots.

[155]NLRB Casehandling Manual ¶11336.2.

[156]*Id.*

[157]*Id.* at ¶11336.4. The Casehandling Manual provides that late ballots should be voided unless the parties agree to waive the deadline, and that ballots returned in unsigned envelopes should always be voided. *Id.*

[158]*Kerrville Bus*, 257 NLRB 176, 107 LRRM 1466 (1981) (ballots mailed three days before deadline from within city of receipt); *Queen City Paving Co.*, 243 NLRB 71, 101 LRRM 1472 (1979) (postmarked three days prior to return deadline).

UNITED STATES OF AMERICA
NATIONAL LABOR RELATIONS BOARD

NOTICE OF ELECTION OF REPRESENTATIVE
and
INSTRUCTIONS TO ELIGIBLE EMPLOYEES VOTING BY
UNITED STATES MAIL

NOTICE OF ELECTION

An election by secret ballot is being conducted under the supervision of the Regional Director of the National Labor Relations Board among the eligible voters to determine the representative, if any, desired by them for the purpose of collective bargaining with the employer named on the enclosed ballot. Your name appears on the list of those who are eligible to vote in this election.

PLEASE SEE THE OTHER SIDE OF THIS PAGE FOR AN IMPORTANT STATEMENT CONCERNING YOUR RIGHTS UNDER FEDERAL LAW AND HOW THE NLRB PROTECTS YOUR RIGHT TO A FREE CHOICE AND A FAIR ELECTION.

An OFFICIAL BALLOT and a RETURN-ADDRESSED SECRET ENVELOPE are enclosed. To vote by mail, carry out the following instructions:

INSTRUCTIONS TO ELIGIBLE EMPLOYEES VOTING BY UNITED STATES MAIL
(Read Carefully)

FROM THE TIME YOU OPEN THE ENVELOPE CONTAINING THE BALLOT, YOU SHOULD CONSIDER YOURSELF IN THE SAME POSITION AS THOUGH IN A VOTING BOOTH IN A MANUALLY CONDUCTED ELECTION. YOU SHOULD THEREFORE FOLLOW THE INSTRUCTIONS BELOW AND DROP YOUR BALLOT IN THE UNITED STATES MAIL BEFORE DISCUSSING IT WITH ANYONE. Read the official ballot carefully. *Ignore the instruction on the ballot to* "Fold and drop in ballot box," as this does not apply to persons who vote by mail. Mark an "X" in the square of your choice. Fold the ballot and put it in the envelope addressed to the National Labor Relations Board. Seal this envelope. *Sign (do not print) your name, preferably as it appears on the employer's payroll, on the outside of the envelope in the space provided after the word "Signature."* Deposit the envelope, which requires no postage, in the United States mail *so that your ballot will be RECEIVED at the place shown on the return envelope not later than*

_____
(Date)

To insure that your ballot is counted, it must be received by the date shown. Mail your ballot immediately, or sufficiently before this date to insure timely receipt.

This is a secret ballot election. YOUR BALLOT WILL BE VOID AND WILL NOT BE COUNTED *UNLESS* you:

1. Mark on the ballot only in the place provided for marking; *do not* identify yourself on the ballot.
2. Return the ballot in the same envelope which you received for that purpose.
3. Sign your name in your *own* handwriting on the outside of that envelope after the word "Signature," so that your name can be checked against the eligibility list.

After your name is checked against the eligibility list the detachable part of the envelope, the stub upon which your name appears, will be removed and destroyed. The remaining section of the envelope containing the ballot will be mixed with all other ballot sections before it is opened by agents of the Board and your ballot removed, thus insuring secrecy.

If you have any question about this election you can contact the Regional Director or designated agent at the address below.

NATIONAL LABOR RELATIONS BOARD

FORM NLRB-4175
(5-78)

Exhibit 50. **Notice of Election and Instructions for Voting by Mail (Form NLRB-4175)**

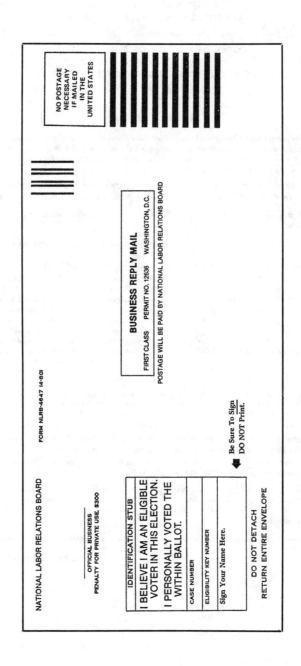

Exhibit 51.   Mail Ballot Envelope   (Form NLRB-4647)

director and ordered the ballots counted.[159] As a matter of policy, the Board attempts to accord mail voters the same "broad participation" in elections that manual voters receive, as long as election procedures are not unduly hampered.[160] But the Board has refused to count unsigned ballots,[161] and has refused to set aside an election in which, through no fault of the parties, a sufficient number of ballots to affect the outcome were not received at all.[162]

At the time scheduled for the count, the closed and returned envelopes are treated in the same way as ballots cast by voters in a manual election. Observers representing the parties will be present to check off the envelopes against the eligibility list, and challenges may be made at this time. The stubs containing identification information are detached from those envelopes that are unchallenged and the unmarked envelopes are shuffled before being opened. The marked ballots are then counted or, in a mixed manual-mail election, mixed with the ballot box votes and counted. As in a manual election, all observers are requested to sign a certification on conduct of election.[163]

§9.11 Counting the Ballots

The counting of ballots usually will take place soon after the close of voting. If the election has been lengthy and the count is expected to be drawn out, the Board agent may allow a rest period or meal break before the count. If multiple polling places have been used, the count will not take place until all the boxes have been collected. Typically, the count is made at the polling place or at some other central location.[164] Board agents and the parties' observers will participate in the count, and persons excluded during the voting (such as supervisors and attorneys) may be present.[165]

Prior to the actual counting, the parties may "clear" some challenged ballots by consent. A party may unilaterally withdraw a challenge or one may be sustained by joint agreement. Where a challenge

---

[159]*Sadler Bros. Trucking & Leasing Co.*, 225 NLRB 194, 92 LRRM 1477 (1976); *see also* NLRB Casehandling Manual ¶11336.4.

[160]*Kerrville Bus*, 257 NLRB 176, 107 LRRM 1466 (1981).

[161]*Northwest Packing Co.*, 65 NLRB 890, 17 LRRM 249 (1946); *see also* NLRB Casehandling Manual ¶11336.4.

[32]*J. Ray McDermott & Co. v. NLRB*, 571 F.2d 850, 98 LRRM 2191 (5th Cir. 1978) (reviewing court found the Board's decision supported by the parties' interest in the finality of the representation proceedings and the lapse of over one year since the union first petitioned for an election); *cf. NLRB v. Pinkerton's, Inc.*, 621 F.2d 1322, 104 LRRM 2743 (6th Cir. 1980) (evidentiary hearing required on whether four employees, from whom ballots were never received, were actually sent ballots). *See also Security '76/Div. of Int'l Total Serv., Inc.*, 272 NLRB No. 23, 117 LRRM 1238 (1984), where a mail ballot election was set aside on the basis that since seven of the 31 mailed ballots were returned as undeliverable, 23 percent of the eligible voters were not afforded notice and an opportunity to vote.

[163]NLRB Casehandling Manual ¶11336.5.

[164]*Id.* at ¶11340.1.

[165]*Id.* at ¶11340.2.

is withdrawn, any other party will be given the opportunity to challenge the same voter. The Board's guidelines emphasize, however, that this opportunity for "clearing" challenges is not intended to produce extended argument on the merits that will unduly delay the count. If a challenge is cleared, the parties will be asked to sign a written notation of their agreement on the stub of the challenge envelope. The ballot then will be removed from the envelope and dropped, still folded, into the ballot box. Unresolved challenge envelopes will be segregated and those ballots not counted.[166]

The clearing of challenges completed, the Board agent will announce to the parties the "rules" of the count: that a majority of the valid votes cast will decide the election; that a ballot containing any means of identifying the voter will be declared void; and that any ballot clearly reflecting the voter's intention will be counted, regardless of unorthodox markings. The agent then will instruct the participating representatives as to the procedures for tallying the vote. At this point the box(es) are opened and the contents thoroughly intermixed.[167]

While the observers may assist with the tally, only Board agents are permitted to handle marked ballots. It is the agent's responsibility to interpret the ballots and try to determine the voter's intention when there are unorthodox markings. If one of the observers questions the agent's interpretation and the parties cannot reach agreement, the ballot will be segregated and treated as a challenge.[168] The agent will either place the ballots in separate stacks and then count them aloud, or call out the preference expressed on each ballot and then place it in the appropriate stack. The observers record the voters' preferences, with one party's representative checking the tally of the other party's. When the number of votes for a party reaches 50, the tally is recounted, with subsequent recounts at each 50-vote interval.[169]

§9.12   Counting the Ballots in Self-Determination Elections

As noted above, a majority of the valid votes cast in an election determines the result.[170] Self-determination elections, however, require that special procedures be followed in the segregation, pooling, and counting of ballots.[171] There are three types of self-determination elections: (a) "severance" elections, in which a union seeks to sever

---

[166]*Id.* at ¶11340.3. *See id.* at ¶11344 concerning how the Board handles and stores challenged ballots and ballots from which the voters' intent is unclear.

[167]*Id.* at ¶11340.4.

[168]*Id.* at ¶11304.7.

[169]*Id.* at ¶11340.5 ("Informal Method" of Counting) and ¶11340.6 ("Formal Method" of Counting).

[170]*Id.* at ¶11340.4.

[171]See §8.6 for a discussion of self-determination elections in general.

and represent part of an established unit; (b) "professional elections," in which "professional" employees vote on whether to be included in a single unit with nonprofessional employees; and (c) "residual" elections, in which unrepresented employees in a partially organized plant vote on whether to become part of a larger unit. In each type of election, the smaller group's ballots are usually segregated and counted before those of any larger group that may be voting.

(a) Severance Elections. A typical severance election is one in which one union seeks to sever and represent a unit of craftsmen only, while another union seeks a larger unit of production workers as well as craftsmen. The counting procedures in such an election depend upon whether the existing, larger group (production workers) is voting simultaneously with the group considering severance.

Where Both Groups Are Voting Simultaneously: If a majority of the employees in the craft group select representation by the union seeking severance, then that group will be severed and considered a separate bargaining unit. If a majority of these employees do not select the union seeking severance, they remain a part of the existing unit and their ballots are pooled and counted with those of the production employees in the existing unit.[172] In this comprehensive count, votes for the union seeking severance will be counted as valid votes cast, but will not be counted for or against the union seeking the larger unit, while all other ballots will be accorded their face value.[173]

Where Only the Severance Group Is Voting: If a majority of the employees in the voting group (the craft group) select a union seeking severance, these employees will be certified as a separate bargaining unit. If there is no such majority, the craft employees will remain a part of the existing unit and the election results will be certified to that effect.[174]

(b) Professional Elections. Section 9(b)(1) of the Act requires that professional employees not be included in a unit with nonprofessional employees unless the professionals vote for such inclusion. As a result, professional employees involved in an election vote on whether they wish to be included with nonprofessionals, and on whether they desire representation by either union or by no union. The ballots of the professionals are counted first.[175]

If a majority of the ballots favor inclusion, the votes of the professionals will be pooled and counted with those of the nonprofessionals to determine the entire unit's representative. If a majority of the

---

[172]NLRB Casehandling Manual ¶11090.1(a).

[173]*American Potash & Chemical Corp.*, 107 NLRB 1418 at n.12, 33 LRRM 1380 at n.12 (1954).

[174]NLRB Casehandling Manual ¶11090.1(a). *See Memphis Furniture Mfg. Co.*, 259 NLRB 401, 108 LRRM 1361 (1981), for an example of a case involving a severance election.

[175]NLRB Casehandling Manual ¶11090.1(b).

professional employees vote against inclusion, they will be considered as a separate unit and their votes will be counted separately to determine their representative, if any.[176] Where there is only one petitioning union, that union may, within 10 days of a Direction of Election, notify the regional director that it does not wish to represent the professional employees as a separate unit, even if those employees vote for such representation. In such a case the professionals would remain unrepresented.[177] Finally, where there is only a single professional employee voting, a ballot favoring inclusion in a larger unit is pooled and counted with the ballots of the nonprofessionals to determine the unit's representative, if any. A vote against inclusion, however, leaves the single professional unrepresented because a one-person unit is impermissible.[178]

    (c) Residual Elections. There are various types of elections involving "fringe" or "residual" groups of unrepresented employees. The procedures for handling the ballots vary depending upon the number of unions and voting groups involved. Only some of the numerous possible configurations are discussed here.

    Where an incumbent union in a partially organized plant seeks to add a group of unrepresented employees to its existing unit, a self-determination election in the residual group is not held. Instead, there will be a single vote of all the employees.[179] If a majority of the ballots are cast for the incumbent union, that union will be certified as the representative of the entire unit, now including the residual employees. If such a majority is not attained, the entire unit will be unrepresented.[180]

    In some elections an incumbent union seeks to add the unrepresented residual group to its existing unit, while a second union wishes to represent the residual group as a separate unit.[181] Here, the single voting group will be the unrepresented employees. If the incumbent union receives a majority, the residual group will be incorporated into the existing unit. If the union seeking separate representation receives a majority, the residual group will be certified as a separate unit to be represented by that union. The residual group will remain unrepresented if neither of the competing unions receives a majority of the valid ballots cast.[182]

---

[176]*Montgomery County Opportunity Board, Inc.*, 249 NLRB 880, 104 LRRM 1238 (1980).

[177]*See, e.g., Evergreen Legal Services*, 246 NLRB 964, 103 LRRM 1028 (1979).

[178]*Lutheran Ass'n for Retarded Children*, 218 NLRB 1278, 89 LRRM 1467 (1975). For the handling of professional employees' votes in decertification elections, *see Utah Power & Light Co.*, 258 NLRB 1059, 108 LRRM 1145 (1981).

[179]*D.V. Displays Corp.*, 134 NLRB 568, 49 LRRM 1199 (1961).

[180]NLRB Casehandling Manual ¶11090.1(c)(1).

[181]*Cf. Folger Coffee Co.*, 250 NLRB 1, 104 LRRM 1293 (1980), where the incumbent sought a single unit of all residual employees and an outside union sought a narrower unit.

[182]NLRB Casehandling Manual ¶11090.1(c)(2).

Finally, there may be cases in which an incumbent union seeks an election only in the existing unit, while a second union seeks to represent both the existing unit and the residual group as a single unit. Two voting groups—the existing unit and the unrepresented fringe employees—will be established and the ballots counted separately. If the incumbent union receives a majority of votes from the employees in the existing unit, then that union retains its status as the unit's representative, and the outside union's representation is limited to the residual group. If a majority of the employees in the existing unit do not select the incumbent, all the ballots are pooled and the outside union's bargaining status is determined by the combined count.[183]

In this count, votes for the incumbent are considered valid, but count neither for nor against the outside union seeking the more comprehensive unit. All other votes, whether for the outside union, or for no representation, are accorded their face value. If a majority of the valid ballots have not been cast either for the outside union or for no representation, the election is deemed inconclusive. A second election will then be held among the employees in the more comprehensive unit to determine whether the outside union shall be certified.[184]

§9.13 Determining the Validity of Disputed Ballots

As noted above, the Board agent will rule on the validity of each ballot during the count and will, if possible, determine the voter's intention if the ballot bears unorthodox markings. When one of the parties seriously questions the agent's interpretation of a ballot, it will be segregated and treated as a challenged ballot.[185] If the number of such disputed ballots is sufficient to affect the outcome of the election, it becomes necessary to determine the validity of those ballots. The Board has developed relatively clear principles for making this determination. These principles also guide the Board agent in passing on the validity of disputed ballots during the count.

The Board will make every effort to ascertain the voter's choice, so long as that choice is clearly manifested. A uniform marking of the ballot is not required.[186] Any ballot whose markings identify the voter, however, will be declared void and that voter will not be given an opportunity to vote again.[187] Reviewing courts generally enforce this rule, but the Seventh Circuit has reversed a Board decision that

---

[183]*Id.* at ¶11090.1(c)(3).

[184]*Id.*

[185]*Id.* at ¶11340.7.

[186]*Id.*; *Hydro Conduit Corp.*, 260 NLRB 1352, 109 LRRM 1320 (1982); *J.L.P. Vending Co.*, 218 NLRB 794, 89 LRRM 1385 (1975).

[187]*A.G. Parrot Co.*, 255 NLRB 259 n.3, 106 LRRM 1324 n.3 (1981) (signed ballot invalidated); *General Photo Prods.*, 242 NLRB 1371, 101 LRRM 1352 (1979).

a "smiling face" drawn on a ballot sufficiently identified the voter to justify invalidating the ballot.[188]

Although the determination of whether a ballot "clearly manifests" the voter's choice ultimately depends upon an examination of each disputed ballot, several rules have been established. In a decision that cured a longstanding split between the Board and several appellate courts, the Board ruled that it will observe any unambiguous expression of the voter's choice expressed on the the ballot.[189] Previously the Board would not observe expressions of intent written on the back of the ballot, but now a mere "Yes" or "No" written there will be taken as the voter's choice.[190] The Board also has clearly established that any markings in only one box on an otherwise unmarked ballot will presumptively establish that box as the voter's choice. A variation from the normal "X" will not be cause for voiding the ballot.[191] If a voter writes "No" in both boxes, the ballot will be taken to indicate a vote against union representation, as will a ballot with an "X" in the No box and a phrase uncomplimentary to the union written in the Yes box.[192] Finally, where a ballot bears markings in more than one box, but it is clear that the employee attempted to erase or scratch out the markings in one of the boxes, the ballot will not be voided. The Board will accept the erasure or scratch-out as designating a denial of that choice.[193]

Ballots invalidated for failure to indicate the voter's choice or because they identify the voter will be counted as void. Postelection objections may be made to the Board agent's ruling on the validity of a ballot.

§9.14   Tally of Ballots

After all the ballots have been counted, with void and challenged ballots appropriately segregated, the Board agent will prepare an official tally of ballots. (See Exhibits 52 and 53.) This tally will list the "approximate number of eligible voters" (the number originally appearing on the eligibility list plus those not on the list who nevertheless cast a ballot), the number of void ballots and the number of votes cast for the various choices available to the voters.[194] The tally

---

[188]*Sioux Prods., Inc.*, 703 F.2d 1010, 112 LRRM 3219 (7th Cir. 1983).

[189]*Hydro Conduit Corp.*, 260 NLRB 1352, 109 LRRM 1320 (1982).

[190]*Id.; see also NLRB v. Connecticut Foundry Co.*, 688 F.2d 871, 110 LRRM 3307 (2d Cir. 1982).

[191]*Kaufman's Bakery, Inc.*, 264 NLRB 225, 111 LRRM 1261 (1982).

[192]*Harry Lunstead Designs, Inc.*, 265 NLRB 799, 112 LRRM 1007 (1983); *see also NLRB v. Connecticut Foundry Co.*, 688 F.2d 871, 110 LRRM 3307 (2d Cir. 1982) ("no" in both boxes).

[193]*J.L.P. Vending Co.*, 218 NLRB 794, 89 LRRM 1385 (1975) (erasure); *see Daylight Grocery Co. v. NLRB*, 678 F.2d 905, 110 LRRM 2915 (11th Cir. 1982) (erasure); *Abtex Beverage Corp.*, 237 NLRB 1271, 99 LRRM 1107 (1978) (scratch-out markings).

[194]NLRB Casehandling Manual ¶11340.8.

FORM NLRB-760
(12-82)

UNITED-STATES OF AMERICA
NATIONAL LABOR RELATIONS BOARD

Date Filed

Case No. _____

Date Issued _____

Type of Election
(Check one:)
☐ Stipulation
☐ Board Direction
☐ Consent Agreement
☐ RD Direction
Incumbent Union *(Code)*

(If applicable check
either or both:)
☐ 8(b) (7)
☐ Mail Ballot

TALLY OF BALLOTS

The undersigned agent of the Regional Director certifies that the results of the tabulation of ballots cast in the election held in the above case, and concluded on the date indicated above, were as follows:

1. Approximate number of eligible voters .... _____

2. Number of Void ballots .... _____

3. Number of Votes cast for _____ .... _____

4. Number of Votes cast for _____ .... _____

5. Number of Votes cast for _____ .... _____

6. Number of Votes cast against participating labor organization(s) .... _____

7. Number of Valid votes counted (sum of 3, 4, 5, and 6) .... _____

8. Number of Challenged ballots .... _____

9. Number of Valid votes counted plus challenged ballots (sum of 7 and 8) .... _____

10. Challenges are (not) sufficient in number to affect the results of the election.

11. A majority of the valid votes counted plus challenged ballots (Item 9) has (not) been cast for _____

For the Regional Director _____

The undersigned acted as authorized observers in the counting and tabulating of ballots indicated above. We hereby certify that the counting and tabulating were fairly and accurately done, that the secrecy of the ballots was maintained, and that the results were as indicated above. We also acknowledge service of this tally.

For _____   For _____

For _____   For _____

Exhibit 52.   Tally of Ballots   (Form NLRB-760)

FORM NLRB-4168
(12-82)

UNITED STATES OF AMERICA
NATIONAL LABOR RELATIONS BOARD

Case No. _____

Date Issued _____

Type of Election *(Check one:)*   *(Also check box below*
                                       where appropriate)

□ Consent Agreement   □ 8 (b)(7)
□ Stipulation
□ Board Direction
□ RD Direction

REVISED TALLY OF BALLOTS
(Counting of Challenged Ballots)

The undersigned agent of the Regional Director certifies that the results of counting the challenged ballots directed to be counted by the

on _____ and the addition of these ballots to the original Tally of Ballots,

executed on _____ , were as follows:

	Original Tally	Challenged Ballots Counted	Final Tally
Approximate number of eligible voters	_____		
Number of Void ballots	_____	_____	_____
Number of Votes cast for _____	_____	_____	_____
Number of Votes cast for _____	_____	_____	_____
Number of Votes cast for _____	_____	_____	_____
Number of Votes cast against participating labor organization(s) ...	_____	_____	_____
Number of Valid votes counted	_____		_____
Number of Undeterminated challenged ballots	_____		_____
Number of Valid votes counted plus challenged ballots	_____		_____
Number of Sustained challenges *(voters ineligible)*			_____

The remaining undetermined challenged ballots, if any, shown in the Final Tally column are (not) sufficient to affect the results of the election. A majority of the valid votes plus challenged ballots as shown in the Final Tally column has (not) been cast for _____

_____

For the Regional Director _____

The undersigned acted as authorized observers in the counting and tabulating of ballots indicated above. We hereby certify that this counting and tabulating, and the compilation of the Final Tally, were fairly and accurately done, and that the results were as indicated above. We also acknowledge service of this Tally.

For _____   For _____

_____   _____

_____   _____

For _____   For _____

_____   _____

_____   _____

Exhibit 53. Revised Tally of Ballots   (Form NLRB-4168)

also will show the number of challenged ballots and, if that number is insufficient to affect the results, the outcome of the election.

In determining whether the challenges might affect the results, the requirement that a union must receive more than 50 percent of the valid votes cast in order to win is important. If the number of challenged ballots, added to the trailing choice, would shift the majority, the challenges might affect the results. The challenges will not affect the results if such a shift would not occur. Thus, for the election results to be determined at the time of the tally, the number of challenged ballots must be too small to affect the election outcome. Stated differently, for the tally to be determinative a single choice must receive a majority of the combined total of the valid votes counted plus the challenged ballots.[195]

With the official tally filled out according to the preceding rules, the Board agent and observers for each party will sign the document, certifying that the count was fair and accurate and that the secrecy of the ballots was maintained.[196] A copy of the tally then will be served upon a responsible representative of each party, either in person or by certified mail.[197] This completes the election procedures, but the Board will retain possession of all marked ballots and all challenged or impounded ballots.[198] In addition, a file on the election containing the voter list, copies of the tally, and memos respecting abnormal occurrences will be retained.[199]

§9.15 Majority Rule and the Representative Character of the Vote

Section 9(a) of the Act provides that "the majority of the employees in a unit" shall select or designate their representative for collective bargaining purposes. The simple phrase "majority of the employees" could be interpreted in a number of ways, but it is now well-settled that a majority of the valid votes cast in an election will determine the outcome. The Board adopted this rule shortly after passage of the Act and it has remained unquestioned ever since.[200] Thus, a majority of the unit employees need not participate in an election for it to be determinative. In following this rule, the Board has adopted the generally accepted principle that voters who do not participate in a democratic election assent to the will of the majority of those voting.[201] If the count of valid votes cast reveals a tie vote,

---

[195]*Id. See id.* at ¶11340.8(b) for the tally of ballots in self-determination elections.

[196]*Id.* at ¶11340.9.

[197]*Id.* at ¶11340.10.

[198]*See id.* at ¶11344 for Board procedures in storing and maintaining uncounted determinative challenged and impounded ballots.

[199]Id. at ¶11342.

[200]*R.C.A. Mfg. Co.*, 2 NLRB 159, 1 LRRM 95 (1936).

[201]*Id.*

the union has not received a majority and the employees will remain unrepresented.[202]

This reliance on a majority of the votes cast does not remove all questions concerning whether a vote is "representative." In those rare cases in which only a minority of the eligible employees vote, these questions may still arise. In ruling on the representative character of such minority votes, the Board has not established a definitive standard. Rather, the Board examines each case to consider whether each eligible employee had an opportunity to cast a secret ballot and whether any compulsion was placed upon employees to force them not to vote. The circumstances of each case, in light of these considerations, determine whether a vote is representative.[203] "In the absence of any showing that any employee eligible to vote was denied the right to vote or prevented from exercising his free choice in voting, or other unusual circumstances, the reasons for neglect to vote are not material to the issue."[204]

In practice, the Board's treatment of questions concerning the representative character of the vote has not always been predictable. A union was certified in one case in which only 31 percent of the eligible electorate voted and only 19 percent of the eligible employees voted for the union.[205] Where there were only two eligible voters and one of them did not vote, the Board set aside the election and ordered a rerun.[206] But where there were two eligible voters who both cast ballots and one of those ballots was unmarked, the Board certified the election.[207] It appears that the Board's willingness to uphold a vote as "representative" increases as the size of the electorate and the number actually voting increase.

In a related line of cases, the Board has held that if a voter is kept from voting by his employer's actions or job-related emergencies and that voter's ballot could affect the election results, an election will be set aside. Thus, where an employee whose vote could have been determinative could not vote because he was making emergency repairs on a propane tank, a new election was ordered.[208] In another case, where an employer told an employee on sick leave that he was ineligible to vote, the Board also set aside the election.[209] The Board's

---

[202]*John W. Thomas Co.*, 111 NLRB 226, 35 LRRM 1444 (1955).

[203]*Stiefel Const. Corp.*, 65 NLRB 925, 17 LRRM 251 (1946).

[204]*Id.* 65 NLRB at 927, 17 LRRM at 252.

[205]*Valencia Serv. Co.*, 99 NLRB 343, 30 LRRM 1074 (1952); *cf. Mechling Barge Lines*, 69 NLRB 838, 18 LRRM 1270 (1946) (election set aside in which 21 percent of eligible voters participated); *V.I.P. Limousine, Inc.*, 274 NLRB No. 90, 118 LRRM 1399 (1985) (decertification election set aside where a 20 inch snow storm occurred on election day and 67 of 89 eligible voters cast ballots).

[206]*Kit Mfg. Co.*, 198 NLRB 1, 81 LRRM 1136 (1971).

[207]*Global Automotive Enters.*, 198 NLRB 950, 81 LRRM 1020 (1972).

[208]*Cal Gas Redding, Inc.*, 241 NLRB 290, 100 LRRM 1486 (1979); *see also Glenn McClendon Trucking Co.*, 255 NLRB 1304, 107 LRRM 1081 (1981) (truckdrivers assigned to unusually long routes).

[209]*Kansas City Bifocal Co.*, 236 NLRB 1663, 98 LRRM 1592 (1978).

willingness to set aside elections in which a possibly determinative voter is denied the opportunity to vote does have limitations. Either the Board or one of the parties must cause the inability to vote. Sickness or some unplanned occurrence that results in a voter's disenfranchisement will not be cause for a new election, even where the disenfranchised voter's ballot might effect the election results.[210]

Campaign Standards

§9.16 Overview of Campaign Regulation

The preceding discussion has detailed the election procedures by which employees express their choice on representation questions. Before the election itself, however, the contending parties engage in a vigorous campaign to sway the voters and affect that choice. Pursuant to its broad powers under Section 9(c) of the Act, the Board exercises considerable control over the content of the campaign.[211]

Although Section 8(c) of the Act protects the right of employers and unions to express any views, argument, or opinion, this protection is available only in unfair labor practice cases. Section 8(c) does not prevent otherwise protected statements from being used as a basis for setting aside representation elections. Moreover, statements containing threats of reprisal or force, or promises of benefit, are explicitly excluded from the Section 8(c) protection. The Board's power to regulate campaign conduct is therefore not hampered by statutory protections of the parties. This power is further broadened by the Board's own doctrine that conduct constituting an unfair labor practice is sufficient grounds for setting aside an election.

The topics that most frequently receive the Board's attention are false or misleading propaganda, threats of reprisal or promises of benefit, and propaganda objectionable for its form or timing. The highlights of these and other areas are discussed below.

§9.17 False or Misleading Propaganda

The Board's handling of postelection objections alleging misrepresentations in election propaganda has fluctuated considerably over the years. The Board has shifted from a policy of carefully scrutinizing alleged misrepresentations,[212] to a policy of refusing to examine the

---

[210]*Berryfast, Inc.*, 265 NLRB 82, 111 LRRM 1450 (1982); *Versail Mfg., Inc.*, 212 NLRB 592, 86 LRRM 1603 (1974).

[211]*See generally* R. Williams, NLRB REGULATION OF ELECTION CONDUCT (1985). In addition to the Board's election rules, Sec. 12 of the Taft-Hartley Act provides for the imposition of a fine and imprisonment for up to one year for persons who interfere with the Board's election processes.

[212]*Hollywood Ceramics Co.*, 140 NLRB 221, 51 LRRM 1600 (1962).

substance of campaign propaganda,[213] back to a policy of close scrutiny,[214] and back again to the policy of not scrutinizing the substance of campaign statements.[215] Presently, the Board will not

> "probe into the truth or falsity of the parties' campaign statements, and . . . will not set elections aside on the basis of misleading campaign statements. [The Board] will, however, intervene in cases where a party has used forged documents which render the voters unable to recognize propaganda for what it is."[216]

This refusal to examine the substance of campaign statements is limited to cases alleging misrepresentations, for the Board will still enforce rules against threats, promises of benefit, and other impermissible conduct.

The current position on this issue is not the one that has prevailed for most of the Board's history. But ongoing friction with reviewing courts, and especially changes in the Board's membership, have produced stark fluctuations in Board policy since the late 1970's. The primary justifications for the current rule are: (1) it is clear and easy to apply while rendering predictable results; (2) it views employees as mature individuals capable of recognizing campaign propaganda for what it is; and (3) it reduces the Board's caseload and the opportunity for parties to delay the resolution of representation questions.[217] Although the current Board membership solidly accepts these justifications, the continuing validity of the current rule is likely to be questioned as new members are appointed.

§9.18   Threats of Reprisal or Promises of Benefit

As noted above, the protections in Section 8(c) of the Act do not extend to the context of a representation election. Even where those protections do apply—in unfair labor practice cases—statements containing threats of reprisal or force or promises of benefit are expressly excepted from the protection. In practice, the Board's regulation of threats of reprisal or promises of benefit has been primarily directed against employers. Union promises or predictions of the adverse impact of not unionizing traditionally have been subject to much less pervasive regulation.

The Supreme Court has summarized the narrow permissible scope of an employer's campaign statements regarding the possible consequences of unionization: "The prediction must be *carefully phrased* on the basis of *objective fact* to convey an employer's belief as to

---

[213]*Shopping Kart Food Market, Inc.*, 228 NLRB 1311, 94 LRRM 1705 (1977).

[214]*General Knit*, 239 NLRB 619, 99 LRRM 1687 (1978).

[215]*Midland Nat'l Life Ins. Co.*, 263 NLRB 127, 110 LRRM 1489 (1982).

[216]*Id.* 263 NLRB at 133, 110 LRRM at 1494.

[217]*Id.* 263 NLRB at 131–132, 110 LRRM at 1493–1494.

demonstrably probable consequences beyond his control."[218] If there is any implication that action is to be taken for anti-union reasons rather than reasons of economic necessity, the statement will be considered a threat of reprisal.[219] Such a statement may be grounds for setting aside an election.

Applying these standards, the Board has invalidated elections where the following types of employer statements were found to constitute threats against employees: (1) predictions that unionization would cause loss of business and plant closure;[220] (2) statements that unionization inevitably would cause a loss of jobs;[221] (3) warnings that a loss of wages or benefits would result from unionization;[222] (4) suggestions that strikes or shutdowns would inevitably result;[223] (5) statements indicating that the employer would "bargain from scratch;"[224] and (6) references to the fact that the employer would no longer directly communicate with the employees.[225] These are the most common types of statements that the Board finds to be objectionable threats of reprisal.

In a number of recent cases, the Board's scrutiny of allegedly threatening statements has become more lenient. For example, where an employer's president referred to a blank piece of paper "as an example of how you could lose with the union, as there are no guarantees that you would keep all your present pay and benefits," the Board reversed an administrative law judge's decision finding the comments objectionable. These references, the Board found, merely reflected the realities of the bargaining process.[226]

In another case, a union objected to such statements as "can wages or benefits be negotiated downward[?] You are damn right

---

[218]*NLRB v. Gissel Packing Co.*, 395 U.S. 575, 618, 71 LRRM 2481, 2497 (1969) (emphasis added).

[219]*Id.*

[220]*Rosewood Mfg. Co.*, 263 NLRB 420, 111 LRRM 1023 (1982) (statements linking selection of union with unprofitability, low productivity, subsequent plant closure, and loss of jobs); *General Dynamics Corp.*, 250 NLRB 719, 104 LRRM 1438 (1980) (intensive campaign creating impression that strikes, plant closure, job loss, and other adverse consequences would result).

[221]*Patsy Bee, Inc.*, 266 NLRB 635, 113 LRRM 1016 (1983) (threatened loss of employment and withholding of benefits); *Alpha Cellulose Corp.*, 265 NLRB 177, 111 LRRM 1458 (1982) (threats that economic strikers would lose their jobs); *A.J. Schmidt Co.*, 265 NLRB 1646, 112 LRRM 1126 (1982) (implied threat of loss of jobs).

[222]*Patsy Bee, Inc.*, 266 NLRB 635, 113 LRRM 1016 (1983); *BRK Electronics*, 248 NLRB 1275, 104 LRRM 1039 (1980) (statement that benefits listed in existing employee handbook would become "null and void").

[223]*Turner Shoe Co.*, 249 NLRB 144, 104 LRRM 1336 (1980) (statements associating union with strikes objectionable in light of repeated threats of plant closure); *General Dynamics Corp.*, 250 NLRB 719, 104 LRRM 1438 (1980). *But see Clark Equipment Co.*, 278 NLRB No. 85, 121 LRRM 1258 (1986) (no violation found where repeated references to possibility of strikes accompanied by references to bargain in good faith).

[224]*General Merchandise Distribs., Inc.*, 263 NLRB 931, 111 LRRM 1138 (1982) (senior company official stated company would "start bargaining . . . from nothing"); *BRK Electronics*, 248 NLRB 1275, 104 LRRM 1039 (1980).

[225]*Mead Nursing Home, Inc.*, 265 NLRB 1115, 112 LRRM 1019 (1982) (statement that employees might have to deal with employer solely "through union representatives").

[226]*Riley-Beaird, Inc.*, 271 NLRB 155, 117 LRRM 1070 (1984); *accord Clark Equipment Co.*, 278 NLRB No. 85, 121 LRRM 1258 (1986) (employer's statements "accurately reflected the obligations and possibilities of the bargaining process"). *See also National Micronetics, Inc.*, 277 NLRB No. 95, 121 LRRM 1035 (1985), where the Board determined that the employer

they can and I have done some," made by the employer's corporate
industrial relations manager. The Board reversed its regional director's decision and found that the employer's "communications with
respect to reductions in wages were attempts to balance the [union's]
rosy predictions as to the effect of unionization." Apparently looking
for more than an *implied* threat, the Board found that the employer's
statements did not "in any way threaten employees that it would
retaliate by reducing wages or benefits" if the employees unionized.[227]
Although the Board has by no means ceased regulation of alleged
employer threats, these cases represent the current Board's trend
toward less exacting scrutiny of such statements.[228]

In addition to threats of reprisal by an employer, promises of
benefit also may be grounds for invalidating an election. The Board
has set aside elections in several cases in which employers stated
that nonunionized employees already received benefits equal to those
of unionized employees, and that employees would continue to receive
such benefits whether represented by a union or not. Such statements,
the Board has found, constitute "the promise of a benefit to encourage
employees to reject the union."[229] But in a more recent case, the Board
did not find objectionable an employer's campaign leaflet that stated
in part: "Your company has promised a first rate benefits program
from the first . . . we have kept our promises. You can also depend
on us to do so in the future." This statement, the Board ruled, merely
explained the employer's track record and did not promise to continue
existing benefits "only in the absence of a union."[230] The current
Board's position in these cases is that an unlawful promise of benefits
will be found only where an employer states that it is company policy
to treat unionized and nonunionized employees alike, and that employees are currently receiving all they could expect a union to get
for them.[231]

Finally, there is a small body of law regulating threats and promises by unions. The Board has ruled that "a union agent's threats of
bodily harm, damage to personal property, or the like" tend to have
a substantial destructive effect on campaign discussion. Such threats

---

did not interfere with an election when it responded to union misrepresentations by distributing
highlighted portions of an NLRB decision articulating the ongoing rights of an employer
following a union election victory.

[227]*Caradco Corp.*, 267 NLRB 1356, 114 LRRM 1217 (1983).

[228]*See also Metz Metallurgical Corp.*, 270 NLRB 889, 116 LRRM 1170 (1984) (employee
who failed to follow directions was told, "You don't need any union, your job is on the line.");
Bardcor Corp., 270 NLRB 1083, 116 LRRM 1231 (1984) (supervisor's statement regarding the
firing of union activists during an organizing campaign not objectionable because it was made
in jest and not attributable to management); *Fiber Indus., Inc.*, 267 NLRB 840, 114 LRRM
1210 (1983) (statements suggesting that employees could not speak to management themselves
found unobjectionable).

[229]*Pacific Tel. Corp.*, 256 NLRB 449, 107 LRRM 1269 (1981); *see also American Telecom-
munications Corp.*, 249 NLRB 1135, 104 LRRM 1282 (1980).

[230]*John W. Galbreath & Co.*, 266 NLRB 96, 112 LRRM 1279 (1983). *See also Clark Equipment Co.*, 278 NLRB No. 85, 121 LRRM 1258 (1986) (employer's statements not a promise of
benefits, but merely a reminder of how good conditions were at the plant, including ongoing
improvements initiated prior to the union campaign).

[231]*Cafe Tartuffo, Inc.*, 261 NLRB 281, 110 LRRM 1032 (1982).

are therefore sufficient grounds for invalidating an election, even when they are "couched in terms of possible future conduct."[232] An election also may be set aside if a union agent threatens to "black-list" nonunion employees and keep them from gaining future employment,[233] or to report illegal alien employees to the Immigration Service.[234] The proper test for whether union conduct interfered with the election is "whether the conduct reasonably tends to interfere with the employees' free and uncoerced choice."[235] Acts of employees who are not under the actual or apparent authority of the union are given "less weight" in determining whether the employees' freedom of choice was affected.[236] As for objections based on union promises, they are not often made and rarely succeed.[237]

§9.19 Propaganda Objectionable for Its Form or Timing

Some campaign propaganda may be objectionable, not for its content, but for the time, place, or manner of its presentation. The types of conduct most commonly found objectionable on these grounds are discussed below.

(a) Employer Questioning, Polling, or Surveillance. Section 8(a)(1) of the Act makes it an unfair labor practice for an employer "to interfere with, restrain, or coerce employees" in the exercise of their protected rights. Such a practice may also be grounds for setting aside an election. The Board's view of when questioning of employees about their union preferences violates this prohibition has, like its regulation of misrepresentations, undergone considerable change over the years.[238] These changes have reflected the Board members' differing views of whether questioning or "interrogation" is "inherently coercive."

The Board's current position is that an employer's questioning of open and active union supporters about their union sentiments, in the absence of threats or promises, is not necessarily unlawful. The basic test for deciding objections alleging unlawful questioning is "whether under all of the circumstances the interrogation reasonably tends to restrain, coerce, or interfere with rights guaranteed by the Act." The Board will consider such factors as the background of the charges, the nature of the information sought, the identity of the

---

[232]*Home & Industrial Disposal Serv.*, 266 NLRB 100, 112 LRRM 1257 (1983).

[233]*United Broadcasting Co.*, 248 NLRB 403, 103 LRRM 1421 (1980).

[234]*Local 300, Cosmetic and Novelties Workers' Union*, 257 NLRB 1335, 108 LRRM 1085 (1981).

[235]*Baja's Place, Inc.*, 268 NLRB 868, 115 LRRM 1122 (1984).

[236]*See, e.g., ATR Wire and Cable Co.*, 267 NLRB 204, 114 LRRM 1006 (1983).

[237]*See, e.g., National Duct Corp.*, 265 NLRB 413, 111 LRRM 1628 (1982).

[238]*See Syracuse Color Press, Inc.*, 103 NLRB 377, 31 LRRM 1473 (1953) (interrogation of employees *per se* unlawful); *Blue Flash Express, Inc.*, 109 NLRB 591, 34 LRRM 1384 (1954) (rejection of *per se* rule in favor of a broad, three-prong test); *PPG Indus.*, 251 NLRB 1146, 105 LRRM 1434 (1980) (clear restatement of *per se* rule).

questioner, and the place and method of interrogation. Usually, either the words of the question or the context in which they are used must suggest coercion of the employee.[239] This "totality of the circumstances" test obviously makes line-drawing difficult and means that each case will be judged individually.

There also are restrictions on more systematic forms of questioning such as polling of employees. If an employer polls or systematically questions employees about their union sentiments, five safeguards must generally be present to avoid a Section 8(a)(1) violation or election interference: (1) the poll must be intended only to determine the truth of a union's claim of majority support; (2) this purpose must be communicated to the employees; (3) assurances against reprisal must be given; (4) the polling must be by secret ballot; and (5) the employer must not have committed other unfair labor practices or created a coercive atmosphere.[240] The Board applies these criteria rigidly against employers,[241] but generally will permit union polling without such restrictions.[242]

Surveillance of employees is another form of conduct that both violates Section 8(a)(1) and constitutes election interference.[243] Conduct calculated to create the impression that management has had union activities under surveillance is treated similarly.[244] The mere presence of a company official or agent at a place where a union meeting is being conducted, however, is not objectionable in the absence of evidence showing an improper purpose.[245]

(b) Visiting Voters' Homes.   Systematic preelection visits to employees' homes by employer representatives are grounds for automatically invalidating an election, even if only a small portion of the electorate is actually visited. This rule applies regardless of whether the employer's remarks during the visit are coercive in character.[246] Home visits by union representatives, on the other hand, are permissible as long as they are not accompanied by threats or coercion. This disparate treatment is premised on the notion that unions have

---

[239]*Rossmore House*, 269 NLRB 1176, 116 LRRM 1025 (1984), *enf'd*, 760 F.2d 1006, 119 LRRM 2624 (9th Cir. 1985); *see also Clark Equipment Co.*, 278 NLRB No. 85, 121 LRRM 1258 (1986); *Meadow Crest, Inc.*, 272 NLRB No. 181, 117 LRRM 1484 (1984).

[240]*Struksnes Const. Co.*, 165 NLRB 1062, 65 LRRM 1385 (1967).

[241]*See, e.g., Judson School*, 209 NLRB 677, 86 LRRM 1248 (1974).

[242]*Springfield Discount, Inc.*, 195 NLRB 921, 79 LRRM 1542 (1972); *see also Kusan Mfg. Co. v. NLRB*, 749 F.2d 362, 117 LRRM 3394 (6th Cir. 1984).

[243]*Crown Cork & Seal Co.*, 254 NLRB 1340, 106 LRRM 1270 (1981) (note-taking and observation of handbilling); *Richman-Gordman Stores, Inc.*, 220 NLRB 453, 90 LRRM 1349 (1975) (store manager parked car at motel where union meeting being held and observed entrance to meeting room).

[244]*Phelps Dodge Corp.*, 177 NLRB 531, 71 LRRM 1385 (1969).

[245]*Osco Drug, Inc.*, 237 NLRB 231, 99 LRRM 1150 (1978); *Atlanta Gas Light Co.*, 162 NLRB 436, 64 LRRM 1051 (1966).

[246]*Peoria Plastic Co.*, 117 NLRB 545, 39 LRRM 1281 (1957).

limited access to employees and are less likely than employers to intimidate employees by visiting them at home.[247]

(c) "Captive Audience" Speeches on the Eve of the Election. Neither the employer nor any union may make an election speech "on company time to massed assemblies of employees within 24 hours before the scheduled time for conducting an election."[248] A violation of this rule is grounds for setting aside an election, for the Board views such last-minute captive audience speeches as interference with the employees' "sober and thoughtful" choice. Speeches during the 24-hour period, on or off company premises, are not prohibited so long as attendance is *voluntary and* on the employees *own time.* Distribution of campaign literature and the use of other campaign media are not covered by the rule.[249]

Numerous Board decisions have addressed the question of what exactly is a "speech on company time to massed assemblies of employees." There is no question that an employer's remarks to individual employees at their work stations are beyond the scope of the rule, even where the employer systematically addresses each employee during the 24-hour period.[250] The Board has found violations, however, where employer representatives addressed small groups of employees (six employees out of 266 eligible voters), and where a supervisor asked a small group of employees if they had any questions about a company "fact sheet" and answered their questions.[251] Finally, only speeches that concern the election and urge employees to vote in a particular manner are covered by the rule.[252]

(d) Electioneering and Other Conduct Near the Polls. The Board has made it clear that the campaign is not to extend into or near the polling place. The Board agents conducting the election will make every effort to keep the polls and surrounding areas free of electioneering. In some cases the agents may determine an area surrounding the polling place in which all electioneering is prohibited.[253] Although waiting voters need not remove campaign insignia and may talk so long as they do not cause a disturbance,[254] the parties and their agents are held to stricter standards of conduct.

---

[247]*Plant City Welding & Tank Co.*, 119 NLRB 131, 41 LRRM 1014 (1957).

[248]*Peerless Plywood Co.*, 107 NLRB 427, 429, 33 LRRM 1151, 1152 (1953).

[249]*Id.* 107 NLRB at 427–430, 33 LRRM at 1151–1152. *See also Livingston Shirt Corp.*, 107 NLRB 400, 33 LRRM 1156 (1953) (all other lawful means of persuasion permitted during the 24-hour period); *Belcor, Inc.*, 263 NLRB 1078, 111 LRRM 1533 (1982) (rule inapplicable where union party within 24-hour period not held on company time or premises, no speech given, and attendance not mandatory).

[250]*Land O'Frost*, 252 NLRB 1, 105 LRRM 1250 (1980); *Electro-Wire Prods., Inc.*, 242 NLRB 960, 101 LRRM 1271 (1979).

[251]*Honeywell, Inc.*, 162 NLRB 323, 64 LRRM 1002 (1966).

[252]*See, e.g., Malone & Hyde, Inc.*, 115 NLRB 498, 37 LRRM 1327 (1956).

[253]NLRB Casehandling Manual ¶11326.4.

[254]*Id.* at ¶11326.3.

In an effort to establish a clear rule for dealing with conversations between employer or union agents and voters near the polls, the Board has held that prolonged conversations are conduct that, in itself, will invalidate an election. The actual content and effect of the conversations are immaterial. An election will not necessarily be set aside, however, because of an isolated, innocuous comment or question by an employer or union official to a voter.[255] The rule applies only when the voters are in the polling area or in line waiting to vote, and only when the polls are actually open.[256]

Other forms of conduct also have been found to invalidate an election: (1) distribution of literature in the "no electioneering" area during voting hours and in full view of employees waiting to vote;[257] (2) use of a sound truck to broadcast electioneering propaganda that could be heard in the voting area;[258] (3) the unexplained presence of a supervisor near the polling area, even though the supervisor's work area was nearby;[259] and (4) a union business agent buying drinks for the voters before and during the polling hours.[260] Where, however, a supervisor had a legitimate purpose for being near the polling area, and the employees had been informed beforehand of the reasons for the supervisor's presence, an election objection was overruled.[261]

§9.20   Other Objectionable Campaign Conduct

Other preelection conduct will support objections to the election if it occurs under circumstances from which the Board can infer probable interference with the voters' choice.

(a) Benefits and Inducements.   In the heat of the campaign, the parties sometimes will be prompted to confer benefits as rewards to employees for their support. Such rewards may be found objectionable. In the employer's case, these rewards may take the form of increased wages or other changes in the conditions of employment. For the union, the most commonly used inducement is the waiver of initiation fees for employees who support the union. The Board will

---

[255]*Milchem, Inc.*, 170 NLRB 362, 67 LRRM 1395 (1968); *see also Modern Hard Chrome Serv. Co.*, 187 NLRB 82, 75 LRRM 1498 (1970) (a "chance hello" will not suffice to set aside an election).

[256]*Alson Mfg. Aerospace*, 230 NLRB 735, 96 LRRM 1340 (1977); *Lincoln Land Moving & Storage*, 197 NLRB 1238, 80 LRRM 1489 (1972) (polls must be open).

[257]*Pastoor Bros. Co.*, 223 NLRB 451, 91 LRRM 1577 (1976); *Continental Can Co.*, 80 NLRB 785, 23 LRRM 1126 (1948); *cf. Boston Insulated Wire & Cable Co.*, 259 NLRB 1118, 109 LRRM 1081 (1982) (no interference where union agents distributing literature were separated from voting line by glass door).

[258]*Alliance Ware, Inc.*, 92 NLRB 55, 27 LRRM 1040 (1950).

[259]*Electric Hose & Rubber Co.*, 262 NLRB 186, 110 LRRM 1282 (1982); *Volt Technical Corp.*, 176 NLRB 832, 71 LRRM 1608 (1969) (supervisor also spoke with employees waiting to vote).

[260]*Labor Servs., Inc.*, 274 NLRB No. 68, 118 LRRM 1407 (1985).

[261]*American Induction Heating Corp.*, 221 NLRB 180, 90 LRRM 1466 (1975).

examine the circumstances of each case to see if the grant of benefits was motivated by the pending election.

When an employer raises wages or confers other benefits on employees while an election is pending, the Board usually will find election interference unless the change was based upon (1) the culmination of events that began prior to the commencement of union activity;[262] (2) justifiable economic considerations;[263] or (3) independent industry or corporate policy.[264] The employer bears the burden of showing that the challenged action had a legitimate justification. "The crucial determinate is whether the wage increase or other benefits were granted for the purpose of influencing the employees' vote in the election and were of a type reasonably calculated to have that effect."[265]

Changes in a variety of benefits may give rise to a finding of election interference. Where an employer granted the employees a dental plan, and there was collateral evidence of union-related animus, the Board upheld an objection.[266] In another case, the Board sustained an objection based on the employer suddenly providing bus service for employees for a short period of time preceding the election.[267] However, minor "fringes" such as distribution of caps and tee-shirts are generally not considered the types of benefits that unduly influence voters, for these gifts have "no intrinsic value."[268]

Unions frequently offer employees a waiver of union dues, in one form or another, as an encouragement to support the union. The Supreme Court has held that a union unlawfully interferes with an election if it offers to waive initiation fees for employees who sign union "recognition slips" before the election.[269] Applying this rule, the Board will invalidate any election in which a waiver of dues is made contingent upon joining the union *before* the election.[270] If the waiver is extended to employees who join the union after the election, as well as those who join before, it does not constitute an impermissible inducement.[271]

---

[262]*Red's Express*, 268 NLRB 1154, 115 LRRM 1213 (1984) (planned wage increase acceptable); *Coronet Instr. Media*, 250 NLRB 940, 104 LRRM 1470 (1980) (implementation of previously developed retirement plan).

[263]*Red's Express*, 268 NLRB 1154, 115 LRRM 1213 (1984) (increased profit justified wage increase).

[264]*Royal Coach Sprinklers, Inc.*, 268 NLRB 1019, 116 LRRM 1167 (1984) (increased vacation benefits granted, in part, to keep up with other firms in area).

[265]*Red's Express*, 268 NLRB 1154, 1155, 115 LRRM 1213, 1214–1215 (1984).

[266]*Brooks Bros.*, 261 NLRB 876, 110 LRRM 1126 (1982).

[267]*F.W.I.L. Lundry Bros. Restaurant*, 248 NLRB 415, 103 LRRM 1520 (1980).

[268]*R.L. White Co.*, 262 NLRB 575, 111 LRRM 1078 (1982). The Board, however, did set aside an election in *Owens-Illinois, Inc.*, 271 NLRB 1235, 117 NLRB 1104 (1984), where jackets with union insignias were given away. *White* was distinguished on the basis of the price of the items given away.

[269]*NLRB v. Savair Mfg. Co.*, 414 U.S. 270, 84 LRRM 2929 (1973).

[270]*Equitable Constr. Co.*, 266 NLRB 668, 113 LRRM 1020 (1983).

[271]*Movielab Video, Inc.*, 272 NLRB No. 11, 117 LRRM 1195 (1984); *King Wholesale, Inc.*, 266 NLRB 1163, 113 LRRM 1106 (1983); *Circleville Metal Workers, Inc.*, 266 NLRB 719, 113 LRRM 1012 (1983).

(b) Appeals to Racial Prejudice. The Board long has recognized that appeals to racial prejudice in a representation campaign must be circumscribed. The Board's traditional approach, as set forth in its *Sewell Manufacturing* decision,[272] has been that if a party deliberately sought to overstress and exacerbate racial sentiments by irrelevant, inflammatory appeals, an election would be set aside. Only discussions of race limited to *truthfully* setting forth another party's position on racial matters would be permitted. Moreover, the party using a racial message would bear the burden of establishing that it was truthful and germane to the campaign.

These basic rules remain in force, but their scope has been modified by subsequent Board decisions. Essentially, only racial appeals or arguments that "have no purpose except to inflame the racial feelings of voters in the election" are fully covered by the *Sewell Manufacturing* rules. Racial propaganda aimed at increasing racial pride and concerted action to overcome inequality is permitted.[273] Thus, "consciousness raising" racial appeals—such as a supervisor's expression of his opinion that a potential union steward would disfavor Blacks—have been permitted when temperately presented.[274] Some courts of appeals have held that the *Sewell* test for truth and relevancy is applicable only to inflammatory racial appeals, and that false but noninflammatory statements are reviewed according to the usual test for misrepresentation.[275] Even with the somewhat narrowed scope of the rules stated above, however, racially prejudicial remarks made in an atmosphere of intimidation and coercion will be grounds for invalidating an election.[276]

---

[272]138 NLRB 66, 50 LRRM 1532 (1962).

[273]*Bancroft Mfg. Co.*, 210 NLRB 1007, 86 LRRM 1376 (1974).

[274]*Coca-Cola Bottling Co.*, 232 NLRB 717, 96 LRRM 1289 (1977); *see also Bancroft Mfg. Co.*, 210 NLRB 1007, 86 LRRM 1376 (1974) (not unlawful for union to claim Blacks would lose their jobs if union lost the election where mostly Black employees were laid off during the campaign and the claim was temperately presented); *NLRB v. Sumter Plywood Corp.*, 535 F.2d 917, 92 LRRM 3508 (5th Cir. 1976).

[275]*NLRB v. Utell Int'l, Inc.*, 750 F.2d 177, 36 FEP Cases 897 (2d Cir. 1984); *Peerless of America, Inc. v. NLRB*, 576 F.2d 119, 17 FEP Cases 838 (7th Cir. 1978); *NLRB v. Bancroft Mfg. Co.*, 516 F.2d 436, 10 FEP Cases 1429 (5th Cir. 1975).

[276]*YKK (U.S.A.) Inc.*, 269 NLRB 82, 115 LRRM 1186 (1984) (racist anti-Japanese comments); *see also NLRB v. Silverman's Men's Wear, Inc.*, 656 F.2d 53, 107 LRRM 3273 (3d Cir. 1981) (regional director improperly denied a hearing on employer's objections to anti-Jewish remarks made by union agent).

10

Postelection Procedures

The Board has three parallel procedures for resolving issues raised by challenged ballots and postelection objections. The procedure which is used in any given case will depend primarily upon whether the election was conducted pursuant to a consent election agreement (see Exhibit 54), a stipulated election agreement (see Exhibit 55), or was directed either by the regional director or the Board (see Exhibit 56).[1] The procedure will vary also depending upon whether postelection issues are investigated administratively or through a hearing, and whether the regional director issues a determination or a recommendation to the Board. It is crucial, therefore, that all parties be aware of which procedure is being used and the time, service, and other regulatory requirements applicable to that particular procedure.

Filing of Challenges and Objections

§10.1   Timeliness and Service

In order to be valid, challenges to voters must be made before the challenged ballot is placed into the ballot box.[2] Objections to the election which amount to postelection challenges to certain voters will not be investigated.[3]

There are two types of postelection objections—those which relate to the manner in which the election itself was conducted, and

---

[1]Consent agreements and stipulated elections are discussed at §§6.8 and 6.9; directed elections are discussed in chapter 8.

[2]NLRB Rules and Regulations §102.69(a); NLRB Casehandling Manual ¶¶11338, 11360; see discussion at §9.9.

[3]*NLRB v. A.J. Tower Co.*, 329 U.S. 324, 19 LRRM 2128 (1946); NLRB Casehandling Manual ¶11360.

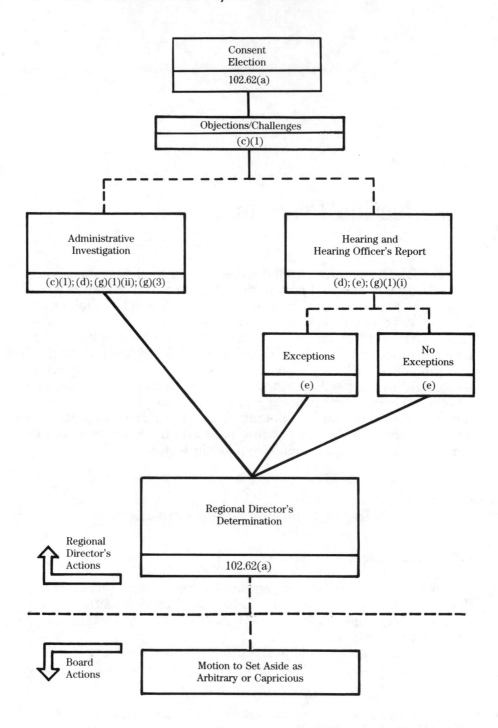

**Exhibit 54. Postelection Procedures in Consent Election Cases
(Citations are to NLRB Rules and Regulations § 102.69
unless otherwise noted.)**

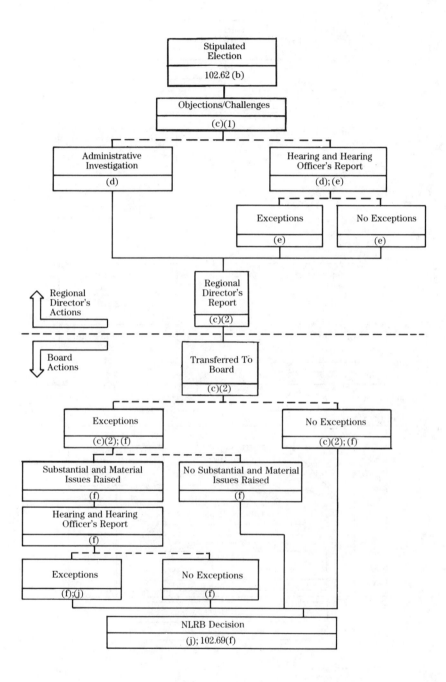

**Exhibit 55.   Postelection Procedures in Stipulated Election Cases
(Citations are to NLRB Rules and Regulations § 102.67
unless otherwise noted.)**

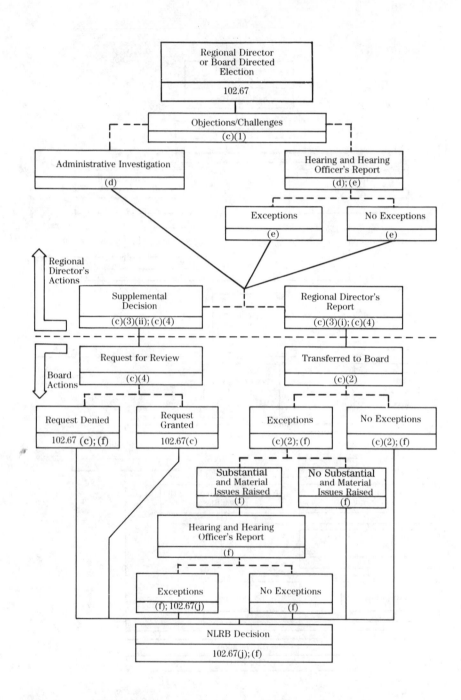

**Exhibit 56. Postelection Procedures in Directed Election Cases
(Citations are to NLRB Rules and Regulations § 102.69
unless otherwise noted.)**

those which relate to conduct which affected the results of the election.[4] The applicable procedures for investigating the allegations are the same for both types of objections. They may be filed only by the employer involved, the petitioner (who may be an individual), or any labor organization or individual whose name appeared on the ballot.[5]

Objections must be filed by the close of business on the seventh day after the tally of ballots has been prepared.[6] In most instances the tally is served on the day of the election immediately after the ballots have been counted.[7] The date of filing with the regional director is the date of receipt of the objections at the regional office, rather than the date they are deposited in the mail.[8] Objections must be timely filed in order to be considered, even in situations where the challenged ballots are sufficient in number to affect the results of the election[9] or where the other party has not been prejudiced by the late filing.[10] In 1986 the Board overruled its prior practice of accepting late filings received by mail in situations where the objecting party could demonstrate that it took every precaution necessary to assure compliance with the filing requirement. Objections must be *received* on or before the close of business of the last day for filing.[11]

An original and five copies of the objections must be filed with the regional director. The director shall serve a copy of the objections on the other parties to the proceeding.[12] Notwithstanding the director's acceptance of this responsibility, however, the Board expects that, "as a matter of courtesy, objecting parties will continue to serve objections [on other parties] as well."[13]

When a regional director rules that objections are not timely, they will be rejected and returned to the filing party.[14] A request for leave to appeal the rejection may be filed in the same manner as appeals from other rulings of the regional director.[15]

---

[4]NLRB Rules and Regulations §102.69(a). For a comprehensive study of postelection objections, see R. Williams, NLRB REGULATION OF ELECTION CONDUCT (1985).

[5]NLRB Rules and Regulations §102.69(a); NLRB Casehandling Manual ¶11392.3. Employees are not "parties" under NLRB Rules and Regulations §102.8 and therefore may not file objections. *Clarence E. Clapp*, 279 NLRB No. 51, 122 LRRM 1067 (1986).

[6]NLRB Rules and Regulations §102.69(a). As revised in 1986, §102.69(a) of the Rules and Regulations provides that the seven-day period begins to run from the time the tally of ballots is prepared and "made available" to the parties.

[7]NLRB Rules and Regulations §102.69(a).

[8]*General Elec. Co.*, 103 NLRB 108, 31 LRRM 1506 (1953).

[9]NLRB Rules and Regulations §102.69(a).

[10]*Alfred Nickles Bakery, Inc.*, 209 NLRB 1058, 85 LRRM 1571 (1974).

[11]NLRB Rules and Regulations §102.111(b)(3). See §25.3 *infra*.

[12]NLRB Rules and Regulations §102.69(a).

[13]47 Fed. Reg. 54,432 (December 3, 1982).

[14]NLRB Casehandling Manual ¶11392.2.

[15]See discussion at §8.9.

§10.2   Obligation to Furnish Supporting Documentation

Parties must submit with their objections a short but specific statement of the underlying reasons therefor.[16] Objections which fail to include such a statement will be rejected.[17] Unless the regional director affords a longer period of time, the objecting party has seven days to furnish evidence in support of the objections.[18] Such evidence should include a list of witnesses, a brief description of their testimony, and any other information identifying the nature of the conduct upon which the objections are based. If the objecting party is unable to submit sufficient evidence to establish a *prima facie* case in support of the objections, or if the objections, even if true, are insufficient to set aside the election, the regional director is not required to pursue the investigation[19] and the objections may be overruled.[20]

Investigation of Challenges and Objections

§10.3   Administrative Investigation by Regional Director

If the challenged ballots are sufficient in number to affect the results of the election, or if timely objections have been filed, the regional director will initiate an administrative investigation.[21] The investigative procedure is identical for consent, stipulated, and directed elections.[22] All challenges and objections are investigated. Written position statements are secured from the parties; witnesses are identified, interviewed, and, where possible, their testimony recorded in affidavits; and relevant documents are reviewed.[23]

The scope of the investigation initially is determined by the regional director. The director has the discretion to limit the investigation to the specific challenges filed and objections raised by the parties. On the other hand, if evidence is uncovered during the investigation which indicates that the election may in some manner have been tainted, the regional director is not precluded from considering such conduct simply because it was not specifically alleged

[16]NLRB Rules and Regulations §102.69(a); NLRB Casehandling Manual ¶11392.4; *Midland Nat'l Life Ins. Co.*, 244 NLRB 3, 102 LRRM 1156 (1979).

[17]*Warner Elec. Brake & Clutch*, 194 NLRB 499, 78 LRRM 1688 (1971).

[18]NLRB Rules and Regulations §102.69(a); NLRB Casehandling Manual ¶11392.5.

[19]NLRB Casehandling Manual ¶11392.5; *Cumberland Nursing & Convalescent Center*, 248 NLRB 322, 103 LRRM 1417 (1980); *Newport News Shipbuilding and Dry Dock Co.*, 239 NLRB 82, 99 LRRM 1518 (1978).

[20]*Flinkote Co.*, 260 NLRB 1247, 109 LRRM 1339 (1982).

[21]NLRB Rules and Regulations §102.69(c)(1).

[22]NLRB Casehandling Manual ¶11364 (challenges) and ¶11396 (objections).

[23]*Id.*

in the objections.[24] In order to serve as a basis for invalidating an election, however, the conduct must have occurred after the filing of the petition, or after the date of the prior election if the objections relate to a rerun or runoff election.[25]

At the conclusion of the administrative investigation the regional director issues a report or supplemental decision.[26] The director either resolves the challenges or objections on the basis of the administrative record or directs that additional evidence on some or all of the issues be taken at a hearing.

§10.4 Hearing on Challenges and Objections

At any point during the administrative investigation of the challenges and objections the regional director has the discretion to direct a hearing on some or all of the outstanding issues.[27] The Board's Rules and Regulations, however, require that a hearing be held for challenges and objections which the director concludes "raise substantial and material factual issues."[28] Substantial credibility issues over material facts must be resolved at a hearing and not simply upon the basis of an evaluation of the results of an administrative investigation.[29]

The party seeking a hearing must furnish specific evidence of objectionable conduct; vague, general allegations are insufficient.[30] This evidence should include exact dates of the conduct complained of, as well as names of those persons involved and names of any witnesses.[31] In the case of a consent election, exceptions to the regional director's determinations must state the specific findings that are controverted and must offer factual evidence to support a contrary conclusion. A party's mere disagreement with the regional director's

---

[24]NLRB Casehandling Manual ¶11394; *Red Carpet Bldg. Maintenance Corp.*, 263 NLRB 1285, 111 LRRM 1232 (1982); *American Safety Equip. Corp.*, 234 NLRB 501, 97 LRRM 1305 (1978); *Pure Chem Corp.*, 192 NLRB 681, 77 LRRM 1923 (1971).

[25]NLRB Casehandling Manual ¶11394; *Ideal Elec. & Mfg. Co.*, 134 NLRB 1275, 49 LRRM 1316 (1961).

[26]Regional director reports and supplemental decisions are discussed further at §10.5 *infra*. Once a director's decision has been issued, the parties are precluded from engaging in *ex parte* communications with Board members and their staffs. NLRB Rules and Regulations §102.128(c).

[27]NLRB Rules and Regulations §102.69(d); NLRB Casehandling Manual ¶11364.1 (challenges) and ¶11396.1 (objections). *NLRB v. ARA Servs., Inc.*, 717 F.2d 527, 114 LRRM 2377 (3d Cir. 1983).

[28]NLRB Rules and Regulations §102.69(d).

[29]NLRB Casehandling Manual ¶11396.2; *River Walk Manor, Inc.*, 269 NLRB 831, 115 LRRM 1318 (1984) (conflicting affidavits submitted during administrative investigation made hearing necessary). Other evidence, not contained in a petitioner's objections but discovered in the course of the regional director's investigation, may also raise substantial and material factual issues which warrant a hearing. *American Safety Equip. Corp.*, 234 NLRB 501, 97 LRRM 1305 (1978); *Dayton Tire & Rubber Co.*, 234 NLRB 504, 97 LRRM 1308 (1978).

[30]*Magnolia Screw Prods., Inc. v. NLRB*, 548 F.2d 130, 94 LRRM 3255 (6th Cir. 1976).

[31]*Id.*; *McCrometer, Div. of Ametek, Inc.*, 261 NLRB 947, 110 LRRM 1187 (1982).

reasoning or conclusions does not raise a substantial and material factual issue.[32]

In consent and directed election cases the regional director retains jurisdiction over issues which have been set down for a hearing. In stipulated cases, however, a director's notice of hearing on challenges or objections has the effect of automatically transferring the case to the Board for a final decision.[33] In such cases the parties may object to the notice of hearing by requesting special permission to appeal to the Board.[34]

The postelection hearing procedures are the same for all three kinds of elections (i.e., consent, directed, and stipulated) and for all types of issues (i.e., challenges alone, objections alone, or both considered together).[35] In situations where related unfair labor practice charges have been filed, the challenges, objections, and unfair labor practice charges may be consolidated for a hearing before an administrative law judge.[36] In cases involving directed and stipulated elections, both the representation issues and the unfair labor practice issues may be transferred to the Board for decision; in consent election cases the representation issues must be severed at the conclusion of the hearing and returned to the regional director for a final determination.[37]

As with preelection hearings discussed in chapter 7, postelection hearings are investigatory rather than adversarial,[38] and are conducted by a hearing officer or an administrative law judge.[39] The hearing officer generally is assigned from the region in which the hearing is held. If the hearing raises an issue concerning the conduct of a Board agent from that same region, or if the hearing has been directed by the Board to examine credibility findings made by the regional director, a hearing officer from another region may be designated.[40]

The conduct of the hearing is similar to that described in chapter 7 regarding preelection proceedings. The hearing officer or administrative law judge opens the hearing,[41] the formal papers are introduced,[42] the party filing the challenges or objections introduces its

---

[32]*NLRB v. Tennessee Packers, Inc.*, 379 F.2d 172, 65 LRRM 2619 (6th Cir. 1967).

[33]NLRB Rules and Regulations §102.69(i)(1); NLRB Casehandling Manual ¶11396.1(b).

[34]NLRB Rules and Regulations §§102.65(c), 102.69(i)(1); NLRB Casehandling Manual ¶11396.1(b).

[35]NLRB Rules and Regulations §102.69(e); NLRB Casehandling Manual ¶¶11370.4, 11420.

[36]NLRB Rules and Regulations §102.33(a)(2); NLRB Casehandling Manual ¶¶11420.1–11420.2.

[37]NLRB Casehandling Manual ¶11420.2.

[38]*Id.* at ¶11422.

[39]*Id.* at ¶¶11424, 11424.2. Even though the hearing is investigatory rather than adversarial, once the hearing begins the parties are precluded from making *ex parte* communications to the hearing officer, the regional director, the Board, and members of their staffs. NLRB Rules and Regulations §102.128(b).

[40]NLRB Casehandling Manual ¶11424.2.

[41]*Id.* at ¶11428.2.

[42]*Id.* at ¶11428.3.

evidence followed by the presentations of opposing parties.[43] The regional director may assign a representative from the regional office to attend the hearing to ensure that all of the evidence contained in the investigative file is introduced into the record.[44] While regional representatives may examine and cross-examine witnesses, raise objections, and so on, they are instructed to refrain from introducing evidence until such time as it is apparent that the desired information will not be offered by one of the other parties.[45] Posthearing briefs may be filed in cases where the order directing the hearing provides for the filing of briefs.[46]

In most cases the hearing officer or administrative law judge will prepare and serve on the parties a report containing credibility resolutions, findings of fact, and—in contrast with preelection proceedings—recommendations concerning the disposition of each issue.[47] The report will be filed with the regional director or with the Board, as appropriate.[48] Within 14 days of the issuance of the report any party may file exceptions.[49] If filed with the regional director, an original and one copy must be submitted; if filed with the Board, eight copies are required.[50] Opposing parties must be served with copies of exceptions and supporting briefs, and have seven days from the last date on which exceptions may be filed within which to file an answering brief.[51]

§10.5 Regional Director's Report or Supplemental Decision on Challenges and Objections

After reviewing the hearing officer's report and exceptions, the regional director will proceed to resolve the issues raised by the chal-

---

[43]*Id.* at ¶11428.4. Rules pertaining to the use of witness statements in unfair labor practice hearings also apply in postelection hearings on objections and challenged ballots. See NLRB Rules and Regulations §102.118(c) and discussion at §16.9(c) *infra*.

[44]*Id.* at ¶11424.4.

[45]*Id.* at ¶¶11424.4, 11428.4.

[46]*Id.* at ¶11430.

[47]*Id.* at ¶¶11376, 11432; NLRB Rules and Regulations §102.69(e). The hearing officer's recommendations must not extend beyond the issues considered at the hearing. In *Iowa Lamb Corp.*, 275 NLRB No. 35, 119 LRRM 1041 (1985), the Board refused to adopt a hearing officer's recommendation that the election be set aside on the basis of the employer's statement made the day before the election promising improved insurance benefits. The Board found that the statement was not alleged by the union to be objectionable, the regional director did not identify it as an issue in ordering the hearing, and the hearing officer did not notify the parties that he would consider it in his report. The statement, therefore, was not fully litigated and was unrelated to the issues set for hearing.

[48]*Id.* at ¶11432. As discussed at §10.9 *infra*, hearings sometimes are ordered by the Board in the course of reviewing a regional director's determination made on the basis of an administrative investigation. In such cases, the hearing officer's report is filed with the Board rather than with the regional director.

[49]NLRB Rules and Regulations §102.69(e) (if filed with the regional director) and §102.69(f) (if filed with the Board).

[50]NLRB Casehandling Manual ¶11434.

[51]NLRB Rules and Regulations §102.69(e).

lenges and objections.[52] Where the election was held pursuant to a consent agreement or a stipulation, the regional director will issue a report. If the election was directed by either the Board or the regional director, the director has the option of issuing a report (in which case the proceeding is transferred to the Board) or a supplemental decision (in which case the proceeding will be reviewed by the Board only if a request for review is granted).[53]

In consent election cases the parties have agreed that the regional director's rulings shall be final. Accordingly, in such proceedings the director's report contains a final determination of each issue.[54] At the opposite extreme, the parties in stipulated cases have negotiated for final rulings by the Board so that the regional director's report contains recommendations rather than determinations.[55] In directed cases, the regional director's report contains recommendations and the supplemental decision contains determinations.[56] Regional director reports and supplemental decisions generally describe the background of the case, the issues in dispute along with a description of each party's position, and a final resolution of each issue.[57] Reports and supplemental decisions are served on the parties by certified mail.[58]

Board Consideration of Regional Director's Report or Supplemental Decision

The availability of Board review depends primarily upon the type of election that was conducted. As noted earlier, in consent election cases the regional director's determination is final absent arbitrary and capricious conduct. As stated by the Board:

> "In the absence of fraud, misconduct, or *such gross mistakes as imply bad faith on the part of the Regional Director*, we deem his determination to be final in consent elections of this character, even though we might have reached a different conclusion."[59]

---

[52]As noted at §10.4 *supra*, directing a hearing in a stipulated case automatically transfers the case to the Board so that any posthearing determinations would be made by the Board rather than by the regional director.

[53]NLRB Rules and Regulations §102.69(c)(3); NLRB Casehandling Manual ¶¶11368 (challenges), 11400 (objections).

[54]NLRB Casehandling Manual ¶¶11368.3 (challenges), 11400.3 (objections).

[55]*Id.*

[56]*Id.*

[57]*See generally* NLRB Casehandling Manual ¶¶11368.4 (challenges), 11400.4 (objections).

[58]*Id.* at ¶¶11368.7, 11400.6.

[59]*McMullen Leavens Co.*, 83 NLRB 948, 955, 24 LRRM 1175, 1178 (1949) (emphasis in original; footnote omitted); *accord Lowell Corrugated Container Corp.*, 177 NLRB 169, 72 LRRM 1419 (1969).

In stipulated and directed elections in which a report has been issued, Board review is secured through the filing of exceptions; in directed cases where the regional director has issued a supplemental decision, a request for review must be filed.[60]

§10.6 Filing of Exceptions

Exceptions to a regional director's report must be filed with the Board within 14 days of its issuance.[61] Requests for extensions of time to file exceptions must be received by the Board no later than three days before they are due. The granting of extension requests is discretionary with the Board.

Eight copies of the exceptions and supporting brief, if any, must be filed.[62] In addition, if no hearing was held during the regional director's investigation, a party may supplement the exceptions and briefs with copies of documentary evidence, including affidavits, which were timely submitted to the director during the investigation, but which were not included in the report.[63] Thereafter such evidence will become a part of the record. Failure to submit such evidence on a timely basis to the regional director, or to append it to the exceptions filed with the Board, will preclude that party from using such evidence in a subsequent related unfair labor practice proceeding.[64] Copies of exceptions, briefs, and supporting documentation must be served upon opposing parties and the regional director "immediately," and a statement of service must accompany the exceptions filed with the Board.[65]

Within seven days from the last date on which exceptions may be filed, an opposing party may file an answering brief, and if no hearing was held, supplementary documentation also may be submitted on the same conditions as are applicable to parties filing exceptions.[66] The service requirements for answering briefs are the same as those for exceptions.[67]

---

[60]NLRB Rules and Regulations §102.69(c)(2) and (4); NLRB Casehandling Manual ¶11370.1 and .2 and ¶11402.1 and .2.

[61]*See generally* NLRB Rules and Regulations §102.69(c)(2).

[62]*Id.* Carbon copies of typewritten material will not be accepted by the Board.

[63]*Id.* at §102.69(g)(3).

[64]*Id.*

[65]*Id.* at §102.69(c)(2).

[66]*Id.* at §§102.69(c)(2), (g)(3). *Seth Thomas Div., General Time Corp.*, 262 NLRB 715, 110 LRRM 1382 (1982).

[67]NLRB Rules and Regulations §§102.69(c)(2), (g)(3). *See also* revised and renumbered §102.111 of the Board's Rules and Regulations and Table 1, Part VIII.

§10.7   Filing of Requests for Review

In situations where the regional director following a directed election has issued a supplemental decision determining the issues in dispute rather than a report to the Board containing recommendations, Board review is secured not through exceptions but through the filing of a request for review.[68] The grounds upon which review will be granted and the procedures applicable in requesting review are the same as those used in seeking Board review of the regional director's preelection determinations.[69] As with exceptions, in situations where the regional director has failed to conduct a hearing, the request for review may be supplemented with documentary evidence, including affidavits, which were timely submitted to the director but not included in the supplemental decision.[70]

§10.8   Administrative Record Before the Board

Whenever the regional director issues an order transferring the case to the Board, or issues a report on challenges and/or objections, or whenever the Board grants a request for review of a supplemental decision, the "record" of the proceeding is transferred to the Board.[71] The precise contents of the record depend upon whether a hearing was held during the regional director's investigation.

If a hearing was held the record consists of:

- The notice of hearing; motions, rulings, and orders made during the hearing; stipulations and exhibits introduced at the hearing along with the stenographic report of the proceedings;
- The objections which were filed; the report on objections or challenged ballots issued by the hearing officer or administrative law judge; and the briefs or other legal memoranda supported by the parties;
- The decision of the regional director, if any; and
- The record of any preelection hearing which may have been conducted.[72]

If no hearing was held, the record includes:

- The objections which were filed; briefs and other legal memoranda submitted by the parties; any report on objections or challenged ballots along with any exceptions to such report;

---

[68]*Id.* at §102.69(c)(4).
[69]See discussion at §8.9.
[70]NLRB Rules and Regulations §§102.69(c)(4), (g)(3).
[71]*Id.* at §102.69(g)(2).
[72]*Id.* at §102.69(g)(1)(i).

- The regional director's decision on objections and challenged ballots and any request for review of such decision; and

- Documentary evidence—excluding witness statements—relied upon by the regional director in issuing the report or supplemental decision; and any other motions, rulings, or orders made by the director.[73]

As noted earlier in the discussion of filing exceptions and requests for review, the parties may submit to the Board documentary evidence including witness statements which were timely presented to the regional director, but which were not included in the director's report or supplemental decision. Once submitted, such evidence also becomes part of the official record of the proceedings.[74]

§10.9   Board Decision on Exceptions or Review

If a request for review has been granted or exceptions filed, the Board proceeds to resolve the outstanding issues.[75] If the Board concludes that substantial and material factual issues do not exist, it may decide the case on the basis of the administrative record alone. If it concludes that substantial and material factual issues do exist, the Board may direct that a hearing be held before a hearing officer.[76]

The hearing is conducted in the same manner as those held prior to the election and those directed by the regional director to investigate challenges and objections.[77] At the conclusion of the hearing, the hearing officer will, if requested by the Board, issue a written report resolving questions of credibility and containing recommendations regarding the disposition of all outstanding issues. The rules regarding the timely filing of exceptions, supporting briefs, and answering briefs are the same as those applicable to hearings ordered by the regional director.[78] If, however, the representation proceeding has been consolidated with an unfair labor practice case for purposes

---

[73]*Id.* at §102.69(g)(1)(ii).

[74]*Id.* at §102.69(g)(3). It is important that any party desiring to supplement the record with affidavits and other evidence submitted to the regional director do so promptly while the director's decision is being considered by the Board. In *Riveredge Hosp.*, 274 NLRB No. 124, 118 LRRM 1423 (1985), an employer sought to defend against a refusal to bargain charge by alleging that the record before the Board in the earlier representation case had been incomplete. The Board held that the employer's failure to timely raise the issue of the inadequacy of the record transmitted to the Board in either the representation proceeding or at the appropriate point in the unfair labor practice proceeding (see §102.69(g)(3) of the Board's Rules and Regulations) constituted a waiver precluding it from raising the issue as a defense to its alleged refusal to bargain.

[75]*Id.* at §§102.67(j) (request for review), 102.69(f) (exceptions).

[76]*Id.* and NLRB Casehandling Manual ¶¶11370.3 (challenges), 11404 (objections).

[77]See discussion at §§7.4–7.7 regarding preelection hearings and §10.4 *supra* regarding hearings on challenges and objections directed by the regional director.

[78]NLRB Rules and Regulations §102.69(f); see discussion at §10.4 *supra*.

of a hearing, the rules for filing exceptions and briefs to an administrative law judge's decision apply.[79]

Decisions as to both objections and challenges are made on the basis of the entire written record. Challenged ballots need not be ruled upon where the outcome of the election would not be affected either way.[80] Where a conclusive election may result from opening and counting a group of challenged ballots, the Board or the regional director may refuse to rule upon an additional group of challenged ballots.[81]

If it is determined that the challenged ballots were cast by ineligible voters, the ballots remain unopened and are not counted. If, on the other hand, the challenges are overruled, the regional director opens and counts the ballots and issues a revised tally. (See Exhibit 53.) Where only one challenged ballot is involved and it is ruled to be the vote of an eligible voter, it is opened and counted even though the secrecy of the vote is destroyed.[82]

The counting procedures are the same as those at the original count. Any party may file objections with the regional director to the revised tally within seven days after receiving it.[83] If timely objections are filed, the procedures that follow are the same as those which apply to objections filed after the election. If timely objections are not filed, and the results of the election are decisive, the regional director will issue a certification.[84]

If the Board or the regional director overrules the objections, and the results of the election are otherwise conclusive, an appropriate certification will be issued—a certification of representative if the union won the election; a certification of results if it lost.[85] If the objections are sustained in whole or in part, the first election will be set aside and a rerun election directed unless the case has been consolidated with an unfair labor practice case and the objectionable conduct is serious enough to warrant issuance of a bargaining order.[86]

Rerun and Runoff Elections

§10.10   Rerun Elections

If the original election is set aside on the basis of meritorious objections, a rerun election will be conducted by the regional direc-

---

[79]NLRB Rules and Regulations §§102.69(f), 102.46. See discussion at §§17.4–17.8.

[80]*Carlisle Paper Box Co. v. NLRB*, 398 F.2d 1, 68 LRRM 2831 (3d Cir. 1968).

[81]*S & S Corrugated Paper Mach. Co.*, 89 NLRB 1363, 26 LRRM 1112 (1950).

[82]*Davison Chem. Co.*, 115 NLRB 786, 37 LRRM 1417 (1956).

[83]NLRB Rules and Regulations §102.69(h).

[84]*Id.*

[85]See discussion at §10.12 *infra.*

[86]See discussion at §§4.1–4.3.

tor.[87] Rerun elections are held as soon as possible after the original election is set aside. In many instances where elections have been set aside on the basis of objectionable conduct, unfair labor practice charges based upon the same or related conduct are pending. In these situations the rerun election may be delayed pursuant to the Board's "blocking charge" doctrine.[88]

For the most part, the rules and procedures for running initial elections apply to rerun elections as well. These include the preparation and preelection checking of voter eligibility lists;[89] the date, hours, and places of conducting the election;[90] voting procedures;[91] the counting of ballots and preparation and service of a tally; [92] and the procedures for filing and considering challenged ballots and post-election objections.[93] The Board does not require the petitioner to produce a new showing of interest, however, even if there has been a considerable lapse of time since the first election.[94]

There are two major areas where the rules for rerun elections differ from those which apply to initial elections: the Notice of Election and the voter eligibility date. Notices informing employees of the details of rerun elections may include a paragraph explaining why the original election was set aside.[95] Consequently, if requested by a party or if deemed warranted by the regional director, the notice will include language reading substantially as follows:

> "NOTICE TO ALL VOTERS. The election conducted on (date), was set aside because the National Labor Relations Board found that certain conduct of the (employer, union, third party, Board agent) interfered with the employees' exercise of a free and reasoned choice. Therefore, a new election will be held in accordance with the terms of this Notice of Election. All eligible voters should understand that the National Labor Relations Act, as amended, gives them the right to cast their ballots as they see fit, and protects them in the exercise of this right, free from interference by any of the parties."

The Board generally grants requests to include this language, but such consent is not mandatory. The regional director, for example, might conclude that its use would be inappropriate in cases where the original election has been set aside on the basis of a stipulation

---

[87]*See generally* NLRB Casehandling Manual ¶¶11450–11452.1. Board orders directing rerun elections are not "final orders" which may be appealed to the courts. *U.S. Elec. Motors v. NLRB*, 722 F.2d 315, 115 LRRM 2036 (6th Cir. 1983).

[88]The "blocking charge" doctrine is discussed at §5.9.

[89]NLRB Casehandling Manual ¶11452.

[90]*Id.*

[91]*Id.* at ¶11454.

[92]*Id.* at ¶11456.

[93]*Id.*

[94]*Provincial House, Inc.*, 236 NLRB 926, 98 LRRM 1307 (1978); *Interlake S.S. Co.*, 178 NLRB 128, 72 LRRM 1008 (1969).

[95]NLRB Casehandling Manual ¶11452.1; *Lufkin Rule Co.*, 147 NLRB 341, 56 LRRM 1212 (1964).

by the parties and there never has been a final determination of the merits of the objections or challenged ballots.[96]

While the voting group in a rerun election will be the same as in the original election, a more recent payroll period may be used for determining voter eligibility.[97] In most instances the voting eligibility date will be either (1) the last full payroll period preceding the date of the decision ordering the rerun,[98] or (2) if the decision is made by the regional director and no review is granted, the last full payroll period preceding the date of issuance of the notice of election.

If objections are filed and the regional director or Board sets aside the rerun election, another rerun election can be held. However, if the results of the rerun are not decisive—that is, no single choice receives a majority of the valid votes cast—no runoff will be conducted if the original election was either a runoff election or a "severance" election.[99]

§10.11   Runoff Elections

(a) When Appropriate.   Section 9(c)(3) of the Act provides in part:

> "In any election where none of the choices on the ballot receives a majority, a run-off shall be conducted, the ballot providing for a selection between the two choices receiving the largest and second largest number of valid votes cast in the election."

Thus, whenever there are three or more choices on the ballot (i.e., at least two representatives and "neither") and no single choice receives a majority of the valid votes cast, the regional director must, with the exception noted below, conduct a runoff election.[100] Runoff elections are automatic and are not dependent upon either a request from the parties or an order of the Board. The Board's Casehandling Manual[101] provides the following examples of situations in which runoff elections would be appropriate:

(1) *Eligible*	17		(2) *Eligible*	77	
Union A	8	(x)	Union A	36	(x)
Union B	8	(x)	Union B	0	
Neither	1		Neither	36	(x)

---

[96]NLRB Casehandling Manual ¶11452.1.

[97]*Id.* at 11452; *Socony-Vacuum Oil Co.,* 84 NLRB 969, 24 LRRM 1331 (1949); *cf. Central Distributors, Inc.,* 266 NLRB 1021, 113 LRRM 1073 (1983).

[98]*Pennington Bros.,* 98 NLRB 965, 29 LRRM 1455 (1952).

[99]NLRB Casehandling Manual ¶11456. Runoff elections are discussed in the next section. Severance elections are discussed at §9.12(a).

[100]*See generally* NLRB Rules and Regulations §102.70 and NLRB Casehandling Manual ¶¶11350–11350.5.

[101]¶11350.2.

(3) *Eligible*	*10*		(4) *Eligible*	*19*	
Union A	4	(x)	Void	1	
Union B	4	(x)	Union A	9	(x)
Neither	0		Union B	9	(x)
			Neither	0	

The two choices designated "(x)" would appear on the runoff ballot.

(b) Timing and Eligibility. Runoff elections are held as soon as possible after the original election but not before the time for filing objections has expired, unless all parties waive their right to file objections.[102] If timely objections are filed, the runoff will not be conducted until they have been resolved. Eligible to vote in the runoff election are those employees who were eligible to vote in the original election and who remain in an eligible category.[103] Thus, the eligibility list may not be adjusted upward by the addition of new names, but may be adjusted downward by the deletion of individuals who have quit or have been discharged for cause since the original eligibility date and who have not been rehired or reinstated.

The general rule that the initial eligibility date shall be used in runoff elections is subject to modification in proper circumstances.[104] In some cases, the long period of time between the original and runoff election, and the high turnover of unit employees, may lead the regional director to conclude that a more current eligibility period would provide a more representative vote.[105] Such cases, however, are rare.[106]

A labor organization which is eliminated from the runoff ballot by the results of the first election may participate in a proceeding involving objections to the runoff election.[107] Any objection to the runoff election will be rejected as untimely if it is based on conduct that occurred before the original election and to which no objections had been filed.[108]

(c) Exceptions. Since there must be at least three choices on the original ballot, runoff elections are not possible in the following situations:

- In a one-union election where the choice is "yes" or "no";[109]

---

[102]*Id.* at ¶¶11350.3, 11350.5.

[103]*Id.* at ¶11350.5; NLRB Rules and Regulations §102.70(b).

[104]*Piper Indus., Inc.*, 212 NLRB 474, 87 LRRM 1277 (1974).

[105]*Interlake S.S. Co.*, 178 NLRB 128, 72 LRRM 1008 (1969) (26 months between elections).

[106]*Lane Aviation Corp.*, 221 NLRB 898, 91 LRRM 1012 (1975); *Piper Indus., Inc.*, 212 NLRB 474, 87 LRRM 1277 (1974).

[107]*American Tobacco Co.*, 93 NLRB 1323, 27 LRRM 1568 (1951).

[108]NLRB Casehandling Manual ¶11350.3.

[109]*Id.* at ¶11350.1. If "yes" receives a majority of the votes cast a certification of representative will be issued to the union; if "no" receives at least 50 percent of the votes cast a certification of results will be issued. See discussion at §10.12 *infra*.

- In a severance election where there are only two choices on the ballot;[110]

- When the disputed election is itself a runoff between the two highest choices of a prior election.[111]

In addition, there are three situations in which an inconclusive election with three or more choices on the ballot will not result in a runoff:

- All choices receive exactly the same number of votes;

- Two choices receive an equal number of votes but a third choice receives a higher but less-than-majority vote; and

- Two or more choices receive an equal number of votes, another receives no votes, there are no challenged ballots, and all eligible voters have voted.[112]

In the first two situations the elections are considered to be nullities. Illustrative examples in the Board's Casehandling Manual[113] are the following:

(1) *Eligible*	*17*	(2) *Eligible*	*16*
Union A	5	Union A	4
Union B	5	Union B	4
Neither	5	Union C	4
		None	4
(3) *Eligible*	*16 or 17*	(4) *Eligible*	*16*
Union A	5	Union A	4
Union B	5	Union B	4
Neither	6	Neither	8
(5) *Eligible*	*40*		
Union A	10		
Union B	10		
Union C	5		
None	15		

Elections which have been nullified are rerun with precisely the same multiple choices on the ballot. If the results of the second election are determinative, an appropriate certification will be issued. If the results are inconclusive, a runoff election will be conducted. However, if the runoff election results in another nullity, the petition will be dismissed.[114]

In the third situation enumerated above, all of the eligible votes have been cast without challenge, two or more choices have received

---

[110]*Id.*

[111]*Id.* at ¶11350.5.

[112]*Id.* at ¶11350.1 and NLRB Rules and Regulations §102.70(d).

[113]¶11350.2.

[114]*Id.*

an equal number of votes and the remaining choice has received no votes at all. Examples offered by the Board[115] are the following:

(1) *Eligible*	18		*(2)* *Eligible*	16
Union A	9		Union A	0
Union B	9		Union B	8
Neither	0		Neither	8

In these cases neither a runoff nor a rerun election will be held. Since no union has received a majority and all possible votes have been cast, a certification of results of the election will be issued. When, however, not all eligible voters cast ballots in the first election, a runoff is appropriate.[116]

Board Certifications

§10.12   Types of Certification

The end product of a representation proceeding is a certification, which can be issued only after an election.[117] There are two main types of certifications:

- CERTIFICATION OF REPRESENTATIVE, issued after an election in which a majority of employees voted for representation by a labor organization. (See Exhibit 27.)
- CERTIFICATION OF RESULTS OF ELECTION, issued after a tie election or an election in which a majority of employees voted against representation. (See Exhibit 26.)

The Board will issue variations on the above certifications patterned to meet specialized situations. For example, a Certificate of Results of Election may be issued after a deauthorization election in which the unit employees determine whether to withdraw their union's authority to negotiate union security clauses in their collective bargaining agreements. (See Exhibit 64.)

The Board will issue a certification of representative only where, in the words of the statute, "the majority of the employees"[118] have cast their ballots in favor of a labor organization. The Board and the courts repeatedly have held that the phrase "the majority of the employees" means majority of the valid votes cast, not a majority of those eligible to vote.[119] Thus, a labor organization may be certified which received less than a majority of those eligible to vote, but more than one-half of the valid votes actually cast.

---

[115]*Id.*

[116]*Community Medical Properties, Ltd.*, 218 NLRB 516, 89 LRRM 1404 (1975).

[117]*Ray Brooks v. NLRB*, 348 U.S. 96, 35 LRRM 2158 (1954).

[118]Sec. 9(a).

[119]See discussion at §9.15.

In all elections involving only one labor organization—the ballot affording choices of "yes" or "no"—a certification of results of election will be issued where the labor organization fails to receive a majority of the valid ballots cast. Thus, where such election results in a tie vote, an equal number of valid votes having been cast for and against the labor organization, the Board will issue a certification of results of election.[120]

The Board need not automatically issue a certification in every instance where a labor organization is designated by a majority of the valid votes cast. The Board may refuse to certify a successful union where, upon its own motion or other proper procedures, the legality of any stage in the representation proceeding is called into question.[121] Certification has been withheld, for example, where the number of employees in the unit was reduced to one after the election.[122] The Board held that it would be contrary to policy to certify a representative for a one-man unit. The Board also has declined to issue a certification where the labor organization was precluded from representing the employees because of supervisory domination or because of some other conflict of interest.[123]

At one time the Board held that allegations of unlawful racial discrimination on the part of a union which had won a Board election could be entertained prior to issuance of a certification of representative.[124] This practice was abandoned in the Board's *Handy Andy* decision, except when Board review is necessary "to preserve the integrity of the Board's own processes."[125] In *Handy Andy* the Board concluded that it was neither statutorily nor constitutionally required to entertain allegations of race discrimination prior to issuance of a certification, and that better practice would be to consider such claims in the context of an unfair labor practice proceeding where "the accused union is accorded the full spectrum of due process, including particularly the right of judicial review."[126] Current Board practice is to consider allegations of invidious race and sex discrimination in unfair labor practice proceedings.[127]

§10.13 Significance of Certification

The certification of representative is merely a determination that a majority of employees in an appropriate unit have selected a par-

---

[120]*John W. Thomas Co.*, 111 NLRB 226, 35 LRRM 1444 (1955); *see also Tullahoma Concrete Pipe Co.*, 168 NLRB 555, 66 LRRM 1325 (1967).

[121]*Worthington Pump and Mach. Corp.*, 99 NLRB 189, 30 LRRM 1052 (1952).

[122]*Cutter Labs.*, 116 NLRB 260, 38 LRRM 1241 (1956).

[123]*See Sierra Vista Hosp., Inc.*, 241 NLRB 631, 100 LRRM 1590 (1979).

[124]*Bekins Moving and Storage Co.*, 211 NLRB 138, 86 LRRM 1323 (1974); *see also NLRB v. Mansion House Center Mgmt. Corp.*, 473 F.2d 471, 82 LRRM 2608 (8th Cir. 1973).

[125]*Handy Andy, Inc.*, 228 NLRB 447, 94 LRRM 1354 (1977).

[126]*Id.* 228 NLRB at 454, 94 LRRM at 1361.

[127]*Bell and Howell Co.*, 230 NLRB 420, 95 LRRM 1333 (1977); *see also Natter Mfg. Corp. v. NLRB*, 580 F.2d 948, 99 LRRM 2963 (9th Cir. 1978).

ticular labor organization as their exclusive bargaining representative.[128] The significance of a certification in terms of stabilizing the bargaining relationship between the employer and union already has been discussed in chapter 4. Certifications are not affected by a change in ownership of the employing entity.[129]

The Board also has ruled that the certification is not a jurisdictional award in the sense that unit employees are forever entitled to perform the work set forth in the unit description. It is true that a certification presupposes a determination that the group of employees involved constitute an appropriate unit for purposes of collective bargaining, and that in making such determination the Board considers the general nature of the duties and work tasks of such employees. However, unlike an award in a jurisdictional dispute,[130] this determination by the Board does not freeze the duties or work tasks of the employees in the unit found appropriate. Thus, the Board's unit finding does not preclude the employer from adding to, or subtracting from, the employees' work assignments. While the unit finding may be determined by, it does not determine, job content; nor does it signify approval, in any respect, of any work task claims which the certified union may have made before the Board or elsewhere.[131]

§10.14 Duration of Certification

The certification identifies the union's status as exclusive bargaining representative with certainty and finality for a reasonable period of time—customarily for one year after date of certification— and indefinitely thereafter until such status is shown to have ceased.[132] Thus, an employer, absent unusual circumstances, must bargain with a certified union during the year following the date of certification even though (1) the union loses a majority of employees from membership[133] or (2) opposing petitions for elections are pending or may be filed with the Board.[134] The Board has ruled that the same effect is to be given to certifications issued by state agencies after secret ballot elections as is given to its own certifications.[135]

The vitality of a certification is not extended or affected in any way where the Board issues a certificate that a currently recognized representative may continue to bargain for a group of employees who,

---

[128]*Dawes Labs. Inc.*, 164 NLRB 935, 65 LRRM 1178 (1967); *Miron Bldg. Prods. Co.*, 116 NLRB 1406, 39 LRRM 1002 (1956).

[129]*See NLRB v. Burns Int'l Sec. Servs.*, 406 U.S. 272, 80 LRRM 2225 (1972).

[130]Jurisdictional disputes are discussed in chapter 19.

[131]*Plumbing Contractors Ass'n*, 93 NLRB 1081, 27 LRRM 1514 (1951).

[132]*Ray Brooks v. NLRB*, 348 U.S. 96, 35 LRRM 2158 (1954); *see also Abrams v. Carrier Corp.*, 434 F.2d 1234, 75 LRRM 2736 (2d Cir. 1970).

[133]*Ray Brooks v. NLRB*, 348 U.S. 96, 35 LRRM 2158 (1954). See also text at notes 51–53, chapter 4.

[134]*NLRB v. Henry Heide, Inc.*, 219 F.2d 46, 35 LRRM 2378 (2d Cir. 1955).

[135]*Doctors Osteopathic Hosp.*, 242 NLRB 447, 101 LRRM 1192 (1979).

in a "severance" or self-determination election, have voted against severance from the existing unit.[136]

§10.15   Who Issues Certification

The same force and effect attach to a certification regardless of whether it is issued by a regional director or by the Board in Washington.[137] The regional director will issue certifications in all cases where the election was held pursuant to an agreement for consent election.[138] In stipulated elections (1) the certification will be issued by the regional director where no objections are filed and challenges are not determinative of the results; or (2) the certification will be issued by the Board where objections are filed or challenges are determinative of results, except that the regional director will issue a certification after the opening and counting of challenged ballots pursuant to a direction of the Board.[139]

In directed elections, certification will be issued (1) by the regional director where no objections are filed and challenges are not determinative; (2) by the regional director in a supplemental decision based on an administrative investigation or hearing where there are objections and/or challenges; (3) by the Board where the regional director's report transferred the case to the Board; or (4) by the regional director after opening and counting challenged ballots pursuant to the director's own direction or that of the Board.[140]

Clarification of Bargaining Units; Amendment or Revocation of Certifications

Issuance of a Board certification does not forever establish the precise parameters of the parties' bargaining relationship. The Board subsequently may clarify the description of the bargaining unit whether the union is certified or has been recognized voluntarily by the employer.[141] In addition, the Board repeatedly has held that its certifications are subject to reconsideration,[142] that it may police its certifications by amendment, clarification, and even by revocation.[143]

---

[136]*B.F. Goodrich Chem. Co.*, 84 NLRB 429, 24 LRRM 1275 (1949).

[137]NLRB Rules and Regulations §102.69(b); NLRB Casehandling Manual ¶11470.

[138]NLRB Casehandling Manual ¶11472.1.

[139]*Id.* at ¶11472.2.

[140]*Id.* at ¶11472.3.

[141]NLRB Rules and Regulations §§102.60(b), 102.61(d), 102.63(b); NLRB Casehandling Manual ¶¶11480–11498.

[142]*Worthington Pump and Machinery Corp.*, 99 NLRB 189, 30 LRRM 1052 (1952).

[143]NLRB Casehandling Manual ¶11478.3; *Independent Metal Workers Local No. 1 (Hughes Tool Co.)*, 147 NLRB 1573, 56 LRRM 1289 (1964).

§10.16 Clarification of Bargaining Units

(a) When Appropriate. Clarification of a bargaining unit is usually sought to resolve the unit placement of disputed classifications of employees. Clarification petitions ("UC" petitions) are appropriate in three kinds of situations:

• *Disputes Concerning Job Classifications.* A petition to clarify a unit is appropriate where the placement of employees who cast challenged ballots in the election remains unresolved,[144] or where the functions of two or more employers are so interrelated that their employees should constitute one unit.[145] Clarification also is appropriate where the employer creates new job classifications subsequent to unit certification or recognition,[146] and where a question arises, due to the assignment of new job duties, whether employees should be added[147] or excluded[148] from the unit.

• *Accretion.* When an employer expands or relocates its operations, questions that arise concerning the inclusion of new or relocated employees in an existing bargaining unit may be determined by a petition for clarification.[149]

• *Consolidation of Existing Units.* Where the same union represents employees in several discrete units of the same employer, it may petition to consolidate those units into one.[150] In ruling upon such a petition, the Board looks to factors such as integration of operations among the units concerned[151] and whether the units are related by bargaining history.[152]

Unit clarification petitions may not be used to settle jurisdictional disputes between competing unions.[153] If the dispute is one concerning which union should represent employees doing particular work, a UC petition is appropriate.[154] If, on the other hand, the controversy is whether work should be performed by one bargaining unit

---

[144]*D'Youville College*, 225 NLRB 792, 92 LRRM 1578 (1976).

[145]*General Envelope Co.*, 222 NLRB 10, 91 LRRM 1081 (1976).

[146]*Lakeshore Manor, Inc.*, 225 NLRB 908, 93 LRRM 1038 (1976); *Southwestern Bell Tel. Co.*, 222 NLRB 407, 91 LRRM 1282 (1976).

[147]*Metromedia, Inc.*, 247 NLRB 392, 103 LRRM 1155 (1980).

[148]*Robintech, Inc.*, 222 NLRB 571, 91 LRRM 1258 (1976).

[149]*Pilot Freight Carriers, Inc.*, 208 NLRB 853, 85 LRRM 1179 (1974). Accretions also are discussed at §5.8(e).

[150]*Libbey-Owens-Ford Glass Co.*, 169 NLRB 126, 67 LRRM 1096 (1968).

[151]*Marion Power Shovel Co.*, 230 NLRB 576, 95 LRRM 1339 (1977).

[152]*Stafford-Lowdon Co.*, 253 NLRB 270, 105 LRRM 1538 (1980). Conversely, changed circumstances may make it appropriate to subdivide an existing unit. In *Rock-Tenn Co.*, 274 NLRB No. 114, 118 LRRM 1377 (1985), the Board held that while it normally places considerable weight on bargaining history, it is not determinative where significant changes in the organizational structure and operations of the business have occurred which negate any community of interest that may have existed previously.

[153]*United Food and Commercial Workers Int'l Union*, 262 NLRB 817, 110 LRRM 1383 (1982); *see also Harley-Davidson Motor Co.*, 234 NLRB 1121, 97 LRRM 1401 (1978).

[154]*Carey v. Westinghouse Elec. Corp.*, 375 U.S. 261, 55 LRRM 2042 (1964).

or another, or where a union "merely seeks additional work for employees already within its unit," the dispute is over jurisdiction and a UC petition is not appropriate.[155]

(b) Processing Petition for Unit Clarification.

Clarification of an existing bargaining unit is requested by filing a petition on the same form used in representation election cases.[156] (See Exhibit 10.) It may be filed by a labor organization currently recognized or certified as bargaining agent of the employees in the bargaining unit or by the employer involved.[157] Neither a rival union nor individual employees are authorized to file such a petition. Petitions for clarification may not be filed when a question concerning representation exists,[158] nor may they be used for purposes of resolving work assignment disputes.[159]

The petition form calls for substantially the same information as required in petitioning for an election except that a description of the proposed clarification, the number of employees in the unit before and after the clarification, the job classifications affected and the number of employees in each, and a statement of reasons for clarification must be included.[160]

Immediately upon docketing the petition will be assigned to a Board agent who will notify all interested parties of the filing.[161] (See Exhibit 57.) The Board agent will review the outstanding certification and labor agreements, if any, as well as any other pertinent information contained in the Board's files or furnished by the parties.[162] If it appears that a question concerning representation is raised or the petition is for some other reason inappropriate, voluntary withdrawal of the petition by the petitioner will be solicited.[163] In the absence of withdrawal, the petition will be dismissed.[164]

---

[155]*Id.* 375 U.S. at 269, 55 LRRM at 2045. Jurisdictional disputes are resolved under Sec. 10(k) of the Act and are discussed in chapter 19.

[156]NLRB Rules and Regulations §102.60(b).

[157]NLRB Rules and Regulations §102.60(b). Because of the Sec. 9(b)(3) prohibition against certifying nonguard unions in guard units, the Board will not entertain a unit clarification petition filed by a mixed guard-nonguard union seeking to clarify a unit of guards in which it has been voluntarily recognized. *Brink's Inc. and Security Leasing Co.*, 272 NLRB No. 125, 117 LRRM 1385 (1984).

[158]*Id*; NLRB Statements of Procedure §101.17.

[159]*Ingersoll Prods. Div. of the Borg-Warner Corp.*, 150 NLRB 912, 58 LRRM 1168 (1965); see chapter 19.

[160]NLRB Rules and Regulations §102.61(d).

[161]NLRB Casehandling Manual ¶11490. Interested parties include: (1) the employer involved, (2) the recognized or certified bargaining agent, (3) labor organizations or individuals who claim or who are believed to claim to represent unit employees or who would be affected by the proposed clarification, (4) any labor organization actively campaigning among the employees of the employer, and (5) any labor organization which has participated as an interested party in a recently-closed case involving the same employees. *Id.* at ¶11490.1.

[162]*Id.* at ¶¶11490.2, 11492.

[163]*Id.* at ¶11492.1.

[164]*Id.* at ¶11494.3.

NATIONAL LABOR RELATIONS BOARD

REGION 5

Candler Building - 4th Floor

109 Market Place

Baltimore, MD   21202

January 2, 1986

Mr. Jack Smith, President
Janco Computer Services, Inc.
8181 Greensboro Drive
McLean, VA 22102

Re: Janco Computer Services, Inc.
     Case No. 5-UC-823

Dear Mr. Smith:

A Petition for Clarification of Bargaining Unit pursuant to provisions of
Section 102.61 of the Rules and Regulations of the National Labor Relations
Board has been filed with this office. A copy is attached. Also enclosed
is a copy of Form NLRB-4812 pertaining to our procedures.

Investigation of this matter has been assigned to the staff member named
below who will communicate with you promptly.

In the meantime please submit as soon as possible to this office the
following information:

> Copies of correspondence pertaining to the matter and of any
> pertinent collective-bargaining agreements;

> A list of employees as to whom the issue is raised by the
> petition, together with their job classifications for the
> payroll period immediately preceding the date of this letter;

> The attached commerce questionnaire filled out in the appropriate
> sections, if you have not submitted such information in prior
> cases;

> A copy of the current collective bargaining agreement and, if
> the bargaining unit is certified, the case name and number;

> Copy of any certification that may be involved;

**Exhibit 57.   Letter Informing Employer of Filing of Petition for Clarification
of Bargaining Unit**

-2-

A description of the proposed clarifications;

Reason why petitioner desires clarification of unit.

Please notify this office of any other interested parties who should be apprised of this petition.

Very truly yours,

Louis J. D'Amico
Regional Director

Enclosures

CERTIFIED MAIL - RETURN RECEIPT REQUESTED

CASE ASSIGNED TO:
TELEPHONE NUMBER:

Exhibit 57—*page 2*

The ultimate responsibility for disposing of the petition rests with the regional director.[165] The director may issue a decision without a hearing, may direct that a hearing be held, or may take any other appropriate action.[166] If a notice of hearing is issued, both the notice and the petition for clarification may be amended or withdrawn at any time prior to the close of the hearing.[167]

All hearing and posthearing procedures in unit clarification cases are the same as those applicable to preelection representation proceedings.[168] The only exception is that where the unit or certification involved arises out of a consent election agreement, the regional director's action is final and not subject to Board review.[169] In all other instances requests for review may be filed with the Board.[170]

§10.17 Amendment of Certifications

Closely aligned with unit clarification procedures are those pertaining to the amendment of an outstanding certification. Both procedures are commenced by the filing of a petition with the regional director, and both are designed to in some way modify an existing bargaining relationship. In contrast with unit clarification cases in which the bargaining relationship may be the product of voluntary recognition, an amendment of certification petition is appropriate only in instances where there has been a prior Board certification.

(a) *When Appropriate.* While regional directors may on their own initiative correct inadvertent errors in a certification which has been issued by the director or the Board, matters of substance must be disposed of through a petition for an amendment (an "AC" petition).[171] AC petitions are appropriate in the following circumstances:

• *Change in Identity of Employer.* Where a new employer becomes the successor to all or part of the old employer's business, an AC petition is appropriate to amend the union's certification to in-

---

[165]*Id.* at ¶11494.

[166]NLRB Rules and Regulations §102.63(b). If the regional director dismisses the petition without a hearing, requests for review of the dismissal must be filed in accordance with the requirements of §102.67 of the Board's Rules and Regulations rather than the requirements of §102.71. *See* NLRB Rules and Regulations §102.63(b) and NLRB Casehandling Manual ¶11494.3. If a hearing is held, the parties are precluded from making any *ex parte* communications with the regional director, Board members, and members of their staffs any time after the hearing opens. NLRB Rules and Regulations §102.128(a).

[167]NLRB Rules and Regulations §102.63(b) (notice); NLRB Casehandling Manual ¶11492.4 (petition).

[168]NLRB Rules and Regulations §102.63(b); NLRB Casehandling Manual ¶11494.4; see generally §§7.4–7.9.

[169]*Id.* Consent election agreements are discussed at §6.8.

[170]NLRB Rules and Regulations §102.63(b). Request for review procedures are discussed at §8.9.

[171]NLRB Casehandling Manual ¶11478.1.

clude the employees of the successor employer.[172] Whether an employer is a successor depends upon continuity in both the workforce and identity of the business enterprise. Continuity of workforce typically will be found where a majority of the new employer's workforce consists of holdovers from the former employer.[173] Continuity in the identity of the business depends upon whether the same business operations, jobs, physical plant, supervision staff, products or services, and methods of production exist under the new employer as under the old.[174]

● *Change in Identity of the Union.* AC petitions may be filed to reflect changes in a local union's identity when it assumes the representation duties of its previously certified international affiliate,[175] affiliates with an international union,[176] merges with another union,[177] or when two international unions merge into a single organization.[178] Certain requirements must be met, however, before the Board will grant an AC petition for any of these reasons. First, there must be a guarantee of continuity of representation.[179] This generally is found where both union leaders and a majority of the membership favor a change in affiliation.[180] Second, the original union must not remain a presently "functioning viable entity" after the affiliation.[181] Third, unit employees must have a reasonable opportunity to approve the affiliation.[182] While the strict standards of a Board representation election do not apply to an affiliation vote, unit employees must have adequate notice of the affiliation election,[183] and the election must be held in an orderly fashion.[184]

● *Change in Identity of the Bargaining Unit.* An AC petition is appropriate where a multiemployer bargaining arrangement is disbanded and the union previously representing the multiemployer unit represents the same employees in single employer units.[185]

---

[172]*Miami Indus. Trucks, Inc.*, 221 NLRB 1223, 91 LRRM 1040 (1975).

[173]*NLRB v. Burns Int'l Sec. Servs.*, 406 U.S. 272, 80 LRRM 2225 (1972).

[174]*Border Steel Rolling Mills, Inc.*, 204 NLRB 814, 83 LRRM 1606 (1973).

[175]*Duquesne Light Co.*, 248 NLRB 1271, 104 LRRM 1043 (1980).

[176]*Seattle-First Nat'l Bank*, 241 NLRB 751, 100 LRRM 1564 (1979).

[177]*McKesson Wine & Spirits Co.*, 232 NLRB 210, 97 LRRM 1495 (1977).

[178]*American Enka Co.*, 231 NLRB 1335, 97 LRRM 1528 (1977).

[179]*Missouri Beef Packers, Inc.*, 175 NLRB 1100, 71 LRRM 1177 (1969).

[180]*Hamilton Tool Co.*, 190 NLRB 571, 77 LRRM 1257 (1971).

[181]*Missouri Beef Packers, Inc.*, 175 NLRB 1100, 1101, 71 LRRM 1177, 1179 (1969).

[182]*Peco, Inc.*, 204 NLRB 1036, 83 LRRM 1428 (1973). Note that while the Board has repeatedly reversed itself on this issue, the present rule is that *all* unit employees, not just union members, must be permitted to vote both on a change in affiliation, *Amoco Production Co.*, 262 NLRB 1240, 110 LRRM 1419 (1982), and on mergers, *F.W. Woolworth Co.*, 268 NLRB 805, 115 LRRM 1120 (1984). *But see Financial Inst. Employees of America, Local 1182 v. NLRB*, 750 F.2d 757, 118 LRRM 2208 (9th Cir. 1984), *cert. granted*, 53 U.S.L.W. 3799 (U.S. May 13, 1985), No. 84-1493 (refusing to apply Board's current rule).

[183]*Noesting Pin Ticket Co.*, 270 NLRB 937, 116 LRRM 1192 (1984); *Ocean Sys., Inc.*, 223 NLRB 857, 92 LRRM 1019 (1976).

[184]*Bear Archery Corp.*, 223 NLRB 1169, 92 LRRM 1097 (1976).

[185]*McKesson Wine & Spirits Co.*, 232 NLRB 210, 96 LRRM 1465 (1977).

An AC petition is not appropriate where a question concerning representation exists,[186] as, for example, where the original representation election was so plagued by procedural flaws as to be invalid.[187] Where a question concerning representation exists, the Board is required by the Act to conduct a representation election.[188]

(b) Processing Petition for Amendment of Certification. Petitions to amend an existing certification may be filed by either the certified bargaining representative or by the employer involved.[189] Such a petition cannot be filed by a bargaining agent which has been recognized voluntarily by the employer, but not certified by the Board. Like petitions to clarify a bargaining unit, petitions to amend a certification may not be filed when a question concerning representation exists.[190]

The petition to amend a certification includes information similar to that found in the representation petition and the same form is used. (See Exhibit 10.) The details of the desired amendment and the reasons for its adoption must be shown.[191] Once the petition is docketed, the procedures for Board agent investigation (see Exhibit 58), ruling by the regional director, and review by the Board are precisely the same as those which apply to petitions for unit clarification.[192] An amendment of a certification does not amount to a new certification, recertification, or extension of the old certification.[193]

§10.18 Revocation of Certification

A regional director has the authority to revoke a certification on a motion by one of the parties, or on his or her own initiative, if it is determined that revocation is appropriate in a given situation.[194] Where the certification arose out of an agreement for consent election, the regional director's action on revocation will be final. However, if the certification arose from a directed or a stipulated election, the regional director's action will be final, subject to the right of the parties to request review by the Board.[195]

---

[186]*Illinois Grain Corp.*, 222 NLRB 495, 91 LRRM 1237 (1976).

[187]*J.H. Day Co.*, 204 NLRB 863, 83 LRRM 1418 (1973).

[188]Sec. 9(c)(1).

[189]NLRB Rules and Regulations §102.60(b).

[190]*Id.*

[191]*Id.* at §102.61(e).

[192]*See generally* NLRB Rules and Regulations §102.63(b); NLRB Casehandling Manual ¶¶11490–11498, and discussion §10.16 *supra*.

[193]*McKesson Wine & Spirits Co.*, 232 NLRB 210, 97 LRRM 1495 (1977); *National Carbon Co.*, 116 NLRB 488, 38 LRRM 1284 (1956).

[194]NLRB Casehandling Manual ¶11478.3.

[195]*Id.*

NATIONAL LABOR RELATIONS BOARD

REGION 5

Candler Building - 4th Floor

109 Market Place

Baltimore, MD   21202

January 2, 1986

Mr. Jack Smith, President
Janco Computer Services, Inc.
8181 Greensboro Drive
McLean, VA 22102

Re: Janco Computer Services, Inc.
     Case No. 5-AC-812

Dear Mr. Smith:

A Petition for Amendment of Certification pursuant to provisions of Section 102.61 of the Rules and Regulations of the National Labor Relations Board has been filed with this office. A copy is attached. Also enclosed is a copy of Form NLRB-4812 pertaining to our procedures.

Investigation of this matter has been assigned to the staff member named below who will communicate with you promptly.

In the meantime, please submit as soon as possible to this office the following information:

> Copies of correspondence pertaining to the matter and of any pertinent collective-bargaining agreements;
>
> The attached commerce questionnaire filled out in the appropriate sections, if you have not submitted such information in prior cases;
>
> Description of the present bargaining unit, and, if the bargaining unit is certified, an identification of the existing certification;
>
> Copy of any certification that may be involved;

Exhibit 58.   Letter Informing Employer of Filing of Petition for Amendment of Certification

-2-

A statement by petitioner setting forth the details of the
desired amendment and reasons therefor;

Reason for desired amendment.

Please notify this office of any other interested parties who should be
apprised of this petition.

Very truly yours,

Louis J. D'Amico
Regional Director

Enclosures

CERTIFIED MAIL - RETURN RECEIPT REQUESTED

CASE ASSIGNED TO:
TELEPHONE NUMBER:

Exhibit 58—*page 2*

Among the reasons more frequently relied upon as a basis for suspension or revocation of a certification are union misconduct,[196] failure to adequately represent all unit employees,[197] conflict of interest,[198] the affiliation of a guard union with a nonguard union following issuance of a certification,[199] and the subsequent issuance of Board or court decisions which make continued certification inappropriate.[200]

Judicial Review of Board Certifications

§10.19   General Rule

The statute limits judicial review to "final orders" of the Board.[201] It is now well established that Board decisions in representation proceedings are not final orders and therefore may not be appealed directly to the federal courts.[202] Congress deliberately insulated such proceedings from direct judicial review so as to avoid the attrition of union support caused by delay in the commencement of collective bargaining.[203]

It is possible, however, to secure review of representation issues indirectly through unfair labor practice proceedings. Section 9(d) of the Act provides that where a Board order in an unfair labor practice case is based in part upon facts determined in a representation proceeding, the records developed in both the representation and unfair labor practice cases shall be transmitted to the court for review.

In the usual case, the Board overrides employer objections to an election and issues a certification of representative to the union. When the union seeks to commence bargaining the employer refuses to negotiate. The union then files an unfair labor practice charge

---

[196]*Union Nacional de Trabajadores (Carborundum Co. of Puerto Rico)*, 219 NLRB 862, 90 LRRM 1023 (1975) (ongoing pattern of union violence and coercion).

[197]*American Mailing Corp.*, 197 NLRB 246, 80 LRRM 1294 (1972) (sex discrimination); *Independent Metal Workers Local No. 1 (Hughes Tool Co.)*, 147 NLRB 1573, 56 LRRM 1289 (1964) (negotiation of contract provisions which tend to perpetuate employment discrimination on basis of race).

[198]*North Shore Univ. Hosp.*, 272 NLRB No. 188, 118 LRRM 1585 (1985); *Sierra Vista Hosp., Inc.*, 241 NLRB 631, 100 LRRM 1590 (1979) (supervisory participation in operation of union creates clear and present danger of conflict of interest in representing nonsupervisory employees); *Catalytic Indus. Maintenance Co.*, 209 NLRB 641, 86 LRRM 1142 (1974) (union representation of employees of both employer and subcontractor created conflict of interest).

[199]*Rock-Hil-Uris, Inc.*, 193 NLRB 313, 78 LRRM 1193 (1971).

[200]*College of Osteopathic Medicine & Surgery*, 265 NLRB 295, 111 LRRM 1523 (1982) (union's certification as representative of faculty members revoked following Board decision to reclassify all faculty members as managerial employees thereby eliminating all statutory employees from the unit); *Cooper-Hewitt Elec. Co.*, 215 NLRB 277, 88 LRRM 1475 (1974) (Supreme Court decision reversing Board precedent concerning the lawfulness of preelection union promises justified revocation of union's certification).

[201]Secs. 10(e), 10(f).

[202]*American Fed'n of Labor v. NLRB*, 308 U.S. 401, 5 LRRM 670 (1940).

[203]*Boire v. Greyhound Corp.*, 376 U.S. 473, 55 LRRM 2694 (1964).

alleging a failure on the part of the employer to bargain in good faith as required by Section 8(a)(5).

During investigation of the charge in these "certification test" or "technical 8(a)(5)" cases, the employer in most instances acknowledges that it is refusing to bargain in order to challenge the Board certification or the proceeding on which it is based. A refusal-to-bargain complaint will be issued and the employer afforded an opportunity to file an answer. If factual issues are involved a hearing will be scheduled before an administrative law judge. If, however, there are no factual issues in dispute and the only question raised is the validity of the certification, the hearing may be bypassed and a motion for summary judgment filed directly with the Board.[204] Either at the hearing or in response to the motion for summary judgment, the employer has an opportunity to challenge the Board's findings and determinations in the representation proceeding and argue that it has no obligation under Section 8(a)(5) to bargain with a union which has been certified improperly.

In nearly all certification test cases the Board affirms the results of the representation proceeding and directs the employer to bargain with the union.[205] Such a direction constitutes a "final order" which may be appealed by the employer to an appropriate federal court of appeals.[206] Alternatively, if the employer refuses to bargain and fails to file an appeal, the General Counsel may seek court enforcement of the Board's order.[207] In either case, the court of appeals may consider the employer's contentions regarding the representation case in ruling upon the validity of the bargaining order.[208]

Since labor organizations which have lost an election may not demand that an employer bargain, the refusal-to-bargain route is not available to unions that seek to challenge a representation proceeding. They may, however, engage in organizational or recognitional picketing[209] with the expectation that the employer will file an unfair labor practice charge under Section 8(b)(7)(B) which prohibits such picketing within 12 months of a valid election. The union's defense to the charge would be that there had been no valid election. As in the technical 8(a)(5) cases, this defense can be raised both before the Board and the court of appeals. Although available to labor organizations, this procedure rarely is used because the time necessary to acquire a court decision invalidating the election results takes far longer than the 12-month period during which the union is statutorily barred from filing a petition for a new election.

---

[204]NLRB Casehandling Manual ¶¶10025 and 10282.

[205]*But see Sub-Zero Freezer Co.*, 271 NLRB 47, 116 LRRM 1281 (1984), where the Board refused to grant summary judgment on the basis of employer complaints of preelection threats by the union which had been rejected during the earlier representation proceeding.

[206]Sec. 10(f).

[207]Sec. 10(e).

[208]Sec. 9(d).

[209]See chapter 20.

§10.20 Exceptions to General Rule

The courts have developed three exceptions to the general rule that Board rulings in representation cases may not be appealed directly to the federal courts:

- Where the Board has acted in excess of its delegated powers and contrary to a specific prohibition in the Act;[210]
- Where a substantial constitutional question is raised;[211] and
- Where the Board's conduct interferes with the federal government's exercise of foreign policy.[212]

All three exceptions generally are construed narrowly by the courts. The first exception was created in *Leedom v. Kyne*,[213] a case in which the Board determined that a bargaining unit containing both professional and nonprofessional employees was appropriate without first affording the professionals an opportunity to decide whether they wished to be included in such a unit as required by Section 9(b)(1) of the Act. Since the Board circumvented a statutory proscription and acted in excess of the authority delegated to it by Congress, the Supreme Court concluded that a direct appeal to a federal district court was appropriate. Subsequent cases have indicated that this exception is available only in extraordinary situations in which the Board clearly has neglected its statutory responsibilities[214] or acted in excess of its statutory authority.[215]

The second exception relating to substantial constitutional issues was created in *Fay v. Douds*.[216] In that case a union objected to the running of a Board election on the basis that it was party to an existing collective bargaining agreement which covered the unit employees. When the election was held the federal district court concluded that it had jurisdiction to review the Board's action on the basis that a constitutional due process of law issue was raised by the Board's denial of a property right to the incumbent union. The *Fay v. Douds* exception also has been construed very narrowly[217] and has

---

[210]*Leedom v. Kyne*, 358 U.S. 184, 43 LRRM 2222 (1958); *see also Inland Empire Dist. Council, Lumber and Sawmill Workers' Union v. Millis*, 325 U.S. 697, 16 LRRM 743 (1945).

[211]*Fay v. Douds*, 172 F.2d 720, 23 LRRM 2356 (2d Cir. 1949).

[212]*McCulloch v. Sociedad Nacional de Marineros*, 372 U.S. 10, 52 LRRM 2425 (1963).

[213]358 U.S. 184, 43 LRRM 2222 (1958).

[214]*Compare Templeton v. Dixie Color Printing Co.*, 444 F.2d 1064, 77 LRRM 2392 (5th Cir. 1971) (judicial review granted) *with Newport News Shipbuilding and Dry Dock Co. v. NLRB*, 633 F.2d 1079, 105 LRRM 2738 (4th Cir. 1980) (judicial review denied).

[215]*E.g., Physicians Nat'l House Staff Ass'n v. Fanning*, 642 F.2d 492, 104 LRRM 2940 (D.C. Cir. 1980).

[216]172 F.2d 720, 23 LRRM 2356 (2d Cir. 1949).

[217]*E.g., Bova v. Pipefitters and Plumbers Local 60*, 554 F.2d 226, 95 LRRM 2793 (5th Cir. 1977); *NLRB v. P.A.F. Equip. Co.*, 528 F.2d 286, 91 LRRM 2204 (10th Cir. 1976).

been applied only in situations presenting clear constitutional conflicts.[218]

The third exception is limited to situations in which the Board's action may conflict with foreign law and therefore interfere with the government's exercise of foreign policy. In the context of representation proceedings, the direction of an election involving foreign employees or at a facility owned or controlled by a foreign government could give rise to such a conflict. For this reason direct judicial review of the Board's determination in such cases is made available.[219]

§10.21 Standard of Court Review

Under the *Universal Camera*[220] doctrine, Board findings regarding questions of fact will be deemed by the courts to be conclusive if supported by substantial evidence in the record considered as a whole. Accordingly, the Board's determinations in representation cases when reviewed by a court of appeals are entitled to considerable weight and generally are not reversed in the absence of evidence that the Board has abused its discretion.[221]

---

[218]*Florida Board of Business Regulation v. NLRB*, 497 F. Supp. 599, 105 LRRM 2858 (M.D. Fla. 1980) (Tenth Amendment); *Grutka v. Barbour*, 549 F.2d 5, 94 LRRM 2584 (7th Cir. 1977); *McCormick v. Hirsch*, 460 F. Supp. 1337, 99 LRRM 3342 (M.D. Pa. 1978); *Caulfield v. Hirsch*, 95 LRRM 3164 (E.D. Pa. 1977) (all raising First Amendment issues involving Board's assertion of jurisdiction over lay teachers employed by parochial schools).

[219]*McCulloch v. Sociedad Nacional de Marineros*, 372 U.S. 10, 52 LRRM 2425 (1963).

[220]*Universal Camera Corp. v. NLRB*, 340 U.S. 474, 27 LRRM 2373 (1951).

[221]See discussion at §§17.16–17.21.

11

Decertification and Union Security Deauthorization Procedures

The Act establishes two types of proceedings intended to give employees the right to rescind or limit authority previously extended to their bargaining representative. Decertification elections are used to determine whether a certified or currently recognized labor organization continues to represent a majority of the employees in the unit.[1] Deauthorization elections are used to determine whether employees desire to rescind the authority of their union to maintain or negotiate union shop or other forms of union security clauses.[2]

Decertification Procedures

§11.1 Filing of Petition

A decertification proceeding is commenced by the filing of a decertification ("RD") petition. The discussion of the processing of other types of election petitions in prior chapters also applies to the processing of decertification petitions except to the extent indicated in this chapter.

Decertification petitions may be filed by any employee, group of employees, or any individual or organization acting on their behalf.[3]

---

[1]Sec. 9(c)(1)(A)(ii).

[2]Sec. 9(e)(1). Union shop clauses are authorized by Sec. 8(a)(3) of the Act and generally require that employees join the union within 30 days as a condition of their continued employment.

[3]NLRB Rules and Regulations §102.60(a).

The employer or its agents may not file a decertification petition.[4] In addition to setting forth information pertaining to the identity of all interested parties and a description of the bargaining unit in which the decertification election is sought, the petition also must contain an allegation that the individuals or labor organizations who have been certified or recognized by the employer no longer have majority support among the unit employees.[5] It is not necessary that employees who wish to file a decertification petition first resign from the union.[6]

§11.2 Appropriate Bargaining Unit

An issue which frequently arises in decertification cases is the appropriate bargaining unit. The Board's general rule is that the bargaining unit in a decertification election must be coextensive with either the certified or recognized bargaining unit.[7] Thus, petitions by special groups of individuals such as craft, technical, or professional employees seeking to carve themselves out of a broader unit and decertify the union as their bargaining representative generally are dismissed as being inappropriate.[8]

Even when there is an outstanding Board certification, however, there are circumstances in which it may be appropriate to conduct the decertification election in a different unit. If following issuance of the certification, for example, the interests of the employees change so that the original unit no longer is appropriate under traditional

---

[4]*Sperry Gyroscope Co.*, 136 NLRB 294, 49 LRRM 1766 (1962). If an employer doubts a union's majority status an RM petition should be filed. See §§5.2 and 5.12. An employer's continuing obligation to bargain with an incumbent union following the filing of a valid decertification petition has varied over the years. In *Telautograph Corp.*, 199 NLRB 892, 81 LRRM 1337 (1972), the Board held that while an incumbent union may continue to administer its contract and process grievances following the filing of a valid decertification petition, the employer may not bargain with the union for a new contract until such time as the question concerning representation raised by the petition has been resolved. *Telautograph* was overruled in *Dresser Indus., Inc.*, 264 NLRB 1088, 111 LRRM 1436 (1982), by a Board which concluded that a rule permitting an employer to withdraw from bargaining solely because a decertification petition has been filed does not accord due weight to the incumbent union's continuing majority status. The continuing viability of the *Dresser* rule, however, has been questioned in more recent cases. *See, e.g., City Markets, Inc.*, 273 NLRB No. 71, 118 LRRM 1279 (1984); *Santa Rosa Mem. Hosp.*, 272 NLRB No. 155, 117 LRRM 1422 (1984); *Auto Fast Freight, Inc.*, 272 NLRB No. 88, 117 LRRM 1336 (1984). In addition, an employer and incumbent union may privately agree to continue negotiating following the filing of a decertification petition and delay the effective date of any agreement reached until after the petition has been resolved. *Kelly Broadcasting Co.*, 273 NLRB No. 206, 118 LRRM 1241 (1985).

[5]NLRB Rules and Regulations §102.61(c); *Kraft Foods Co.*, 76 NLRB 492, 21 LRRM 1214 (1948).

[6]*Kraft Foods Co.*, 76 NLRB 492, 21 LRRM 1214 (1948).

[7]*Fast Food Merchandisers, Inc.*, 242 NLRB 8, 101 LRRM 1087 (1979); *Westinghouse Elec. Corp.*, 227 NLRB 1932, 94 LRRM 1373 (1977); *Brom Mach. and Foundry Co.*, 227 NLRB 690, 94 LRRM 1677 (1977).

[8]*Menasco Mfg. Co.*, 111 NLRB 604, 35 LRRM 1526 (1955) (technical employees); *Campbell Soup Co.*, 111 NLRB 234, 35 LRRM 1453 (1955) (craft employees). *But see Utah Power & Light Co.*, 258 NLRB 1059, 108 LRRM 1145 (1981), where professional employees in a broader mixed unit were allowed to file a decertification petition because they never had been given an opportunity to vote on whether they wished to be included in the broader mixed unit in the first place. Such a vote is required by Sec. 9(b)(1) of the Act.

Board principles, a different unit may be established for the decertification election.[9] Similarly, the fact that the parties may have agreed to the inclusion of statutory supervisors in the original unit does not preclude their exclusion in the decertification proceeding.[10]

The conduct of the parties themselves subsequent to the issuance of the original certification also may render the certified unit inappropriate. In some cases the parties may mutually agree that certain job classifications shall be added to or deleted from the originally certified unit.[11] In other cases collective bargaining may be conducted on a multifacility, multiemployer or some other basis which extends beyond the originally certified bargaining unit. It may be possible that the certified unit becomes "merged" into a broader negotiating unit, in which case a decertification petition limited to the original unit will be dismissed. In *American Consolidating Co.*, [12] for example, a petition was dismissed because employees in the certified unit were considered to have been merged into a multiemployer unit where their employer executed the master agreement negotiated in the larger unit, implemented its wage and benefit provisions, and adhered to its grievance procedure.[13] In contrast, where bargaining on behalf of the certified unit is conducted on a broader basis but the unit retains its individual identity and is not merged into the other units, a decertification petition limited to the original unit will be appropriate.[14]

§11.3   Hearing and Certification

Hearings in decertification cases are conducted in the same manner as in other representation proceedings. This includes the general rule that evidence concerning alleged unfair labor practices will not be received in a decertification hearing. Thus, evidence will not be admitted if it concerns employer participation in the institution of the proceeding, whether such evidence pertains to the showing of interest or to employer responsibility for filing of the petition.[15] Al-

---

[9]*Illinois Canning Co.*, 125 NLRB 699, 45 LRRM 1162 (1959).

[10]*Newhouse Broadcasting Corp.*, 198 NLRB 342, 81 LRRM 1013 (1972).

[11]*Kardon Chevrolet, Inc.*, 249 NLRB 598, 104 LRRM 1129 (1980) (parties mutually agreed to modify certified unit to exclude part-time sales representatives); *Tom Kelly Ford, Inc.*, 264 NLRB 1080, 111 LRRM 1404 (1982) (pattern of bargaining indicated that parties did not consider certain job classifications to be included in unit).

[12]226 NLRB 923, 93 LRRM 1446 (1976).

[13]*Accord Armstrong Rubber Co.*, 208 NLRB 513, 85 LRRM 1147 (1974). *But see Albertsons, Inc.*, 273 NLRB No. 42, 118 LRRM 1090 (1984), where decertification petitions filed at two separate stores following the employer's withdrawal from a multiemployer bargaining association were considered appropriate, notwithstanding the fact that the union had never been recognized as bargaining representative at either location and all prior bargaining had taken place on a multiemployer, multifacility basis.

[14]*Etna Equip. and Supply Co.*, 236 NLRB 1578, 98 LRRM 1591 (1978); *Duval Corp.*, 234 NLRB 160, 97 LRRM 1165 (1978); *Jos. Schlitz Brewing Co.*, 206 NLRB 928, 84 LRRM 1373 (1973); *Food Fair Stores, Inc.*, 204 NLRB 75, 83 LRRM 1257 (1973).

[15]*Typographical Union v. McCulloch*, 222 F. Supp. 154, 54 LRRM 2276 (D.D.C. 1963); *Union Mfg. Co.*, 123 NLRB 1633, 44 LRRM 1188 (1959).

legations that the employer has interfered with employees' rights and tainted the decertification petition by signalling to its employees that it approves and supports the decertification drive must be entertained in an unfair labor practice proceeding.[16]

The certifications issued after decertification elections are the same as those issued in other representation proceedings. (See Exhibts 26 and 27.) A certificate of results of election—certifying that the union is no longer the bargaining representative—will always be issued where the union fails to receive a majority of the valid ballots cast. Thus, where a decertification results in a tie vote, the union will receive a certificate of results just as if a majority had voted to decertify it.[17]

Union Security Deauthorization Procedures

The purpose of a deauthorization proceeding is to determine whether the authority of the bargaining representative to enter into a union security agreement should be rescinded, not whether a majority of the unit employees desire continued representation by the union.[18] While the purpose of deauthorization and decertification elections differ, the procedures involved are similar.[19] The most stringent form of union security clause permissible under the Act—and the one which most often generates deauthorization petitions—is one which binds all employees in the appropriate bargaining unit to become and remain members of the union 30 days (or some longer period) after the date of hire or the date the contract becomes effective, whichever is later.[20] The closed shop, requiring union membership as a condition of obtaining and retaining employment, which was proper under the Wagner Act, is banned completely. Moreover, an employer may not discriminate against an employee for nonmembership in the union if the employee has religious convictions against joining or financially supporting a labor organization or if the employee tenders the periodic dues and initiation fees uniformly required by the union.[21]

According to the statute,[22] a union enters into a valid union shop agreement if the following conditions are satisfied:

---

[16]*E.g., Lomasney Combustion, Inc.*, 273 NLRB No. 157, 118 LRRM 1501 (1984).

[17]*Best Motor Lines*, 82 NLRB 269, 23 LRRM 1557 (1949).

[18]*Dalewood Rehabilitation Hosp., Inc.*, 224 NLRB 1618, 92 LRRM 1372 (1976); *cf.* NLRB Casehandling Manual ¶11500.

[19]*See generally* NLRB Rules and Regulations §§102.83–102.88; NLRB Statements of Procedure §101.26; NLRB Casehandling Manual ¶¶11500–11516.

[20]Sec. 8(a)(3).

[21]*Id.*; Sec. 19.

[22]Sec. 8(a)(3).

- The union is the exclusive bargaining representative of the employees in an appropriate bargaining unit;
- During the year preceding the effective date of the agreement the union's authority to make a union shop agreement was not rescinded in a Board-conducted election;
- The contracting union must be free from employer domination or assistance within the meaning of Section 8(a)(2); and
- The agreement must contain an appropriate 30-day grace period for all employees who are not union members when it takes effect. The required grace period in the building and construction industry is seven days.

While the statute permits the union shop, it also specifically provides that employees covered by such a provision may vote to rescind their bargaining agent's authority to make such an agreement.[23]

A deauthorization ("UD") petition will be entertained where there is any form of union security agreement, including agency shop,[24] regardless of its legality under the Act.[25]

§11.4   Filing of Petition

A deauthorization petition may be filed by an employee or group of employees acting on behalf of 30 percent or more of the employees in the appropriate bargaining unit.[26] The petition must be in writing, signed, and filed with the regional director with jurisdiction over the bargaining unit.[27] If evidence of employee support is not filed with the petition, such evidence must be furnished within 48 hours. In the absence of a timely submission of interest the petition may be dismissed.[28]

In seasonal industries Board elections generally are delayed until such time as a representative number of employees are employed. A deauthorization petition will be accepted prior to the opening of the season, however, based upon the interest of the permanent employees working at the time the petition is filed, or based on some other reasonable formula which satisfies the spirit of the showing of interest requirement.[29]

A deauthorization petition can be filed only if there is in existence a union security agreement between the employer and the union, or

---

[23]Sec. 9(e)(1).

[24]*Monsanto Chem. Co.*, 147 NLRB 49, 56 LRRM 1136 (1964).

[25]*Andor Co.*, 119 NLRB 925, 41 LRRM 1184 (1957); NLRB Casehandling Manual ¶11506.4.

[26]Sec. 9(e)(1); NLRB Rules and Regulations §102.83. Deauthorization petitions may not be filed by an employer or its agents. *Cf. Community Tele-Communications, Inc.*, 249 NLRB 542, 104 LRRM 1155 (1980).

[27]NLRB Rules and Regulations §102.83.

[28]NLRB Casehandling Manual ¶11506.3.

[29]*Id.*

an extension of such an agreement.[30] The normal contract bar principles, pursuant to which the Board dismisses representation petitions filed in the face of valid contracts, are not applied by the Board to deauthorization cases.[31] In the absence of a union security agreement, the Board will dismiss a deauthorization petition.[32]

Where a representation or an unfair labor practice case is pending and it involves some or all of the same employees, a deauthorization petition will not be processed. Instead, it will be suspended until disposition is made of the other case. Also, if investigation of the pending representation case should reveal a question concerning representation and an election is to be held, the deauthorization petition will be dismissed.[33]

The statute prohibits the holding of a deauthorization election in any unit or part of a unit in which a valid deauthorization election was conducted in the preceding 12 months.[34] However, conduct of a representation election within the preceding 12 months does not preclude a deauthorization election.[35]

§11.5 Appropriate Bargaining Unit

The rules regarding appropriate bargaining units in deauthorization elections parallel those which apply in decertification elections.[36] In general, the unit for a deauthorization election must be coextensive with the contractual unit. Deauthorization petitions in which the described unit is not coextensive with the unit covered by the union security agreement will be dismissed.[37] As with decertification proceedings, however, the Board will examine the pattern of bargaining to determine whether the contract unit has been "merged" with other units so that the deauthorization election should be conducted on a broader basis.[38]

§11.6 Hearing and Election

If the required showing of interest and other prerequisites to a deauthorization election have been met, the regional director will

---

[30]*Id.* at ¶11506.4.

[31]*Id.* at ¶11506.5. The Board's contract bar principles are discussed at §5.8.

[32]*Wakefield's Deep Sea Trawlers, Inc.*, 115 NLRB 1024, 37 LRRM 1480 (1956).

[33]NLRB Casehandling Manual ¶¶11506.1 (representation proceeding), 11730 (unfair labor practice proceeding).

[34]Sec. 9(e)(2).

[35]*Monsanto Chem. Co.*, 147 NLRB 49, 56 LRRM 1136 (1964).

[36]See §11.2 *supra*.

[37]*Romac Containers, Inc.*, 190 NLRB 238, 77 LRRM 1105 (1971); NLRB Casehandling Manual ¶11506.6.

[38]*Compare Heck's Inc.*, 234 NLRB 756, 97 LRRM 1359 (1978) (merger found) *with Day and Zimmerman, Inc.*, 246 NLRB 1181, 103 LRRM 1076 (1979) (no merger found). *See also Illinois School Bus Co.*, 231 NLRB 1, 95 LRRM 1502 (1977) (deauthorization election run in unit coextensive with unit established voluntarily by parties even though some included employees spent a majority of their time performing exempt work).

attempt to secure a consent (see Exhibit 59) or stipulated (see Exhibit 60) election agreement from the parties setting forth the time and location of the election, eligible voters, and so forth.[39] If agreement of the parties cannot be reached, the director will direct an election or issue a notice of hearing if substantial issues remain unresolved.[40] The method of conducting the hearing as well as posthearing procedures are the same as those for representation cases.[41] Should the regional director conclude before the close of the hearing that no election should be held, the petition may be dismissed administratively. In such cases the petitioner may obtain Board review of the dismissal by filing with the Board within 14 days a statement setting forth the facts and reasons upon which the request is based.[42]

With one exception, the procedures for running a deauthorization election are the same as those for representation elections. (See Exhibit 61.) In representation elections the union will be certified if it receives a majority of the *votes cast,* irrespective of whether that number also constitutes a majority of the *eligible voters* in the unit. In a deauthorization election, however, a majority of those eligible to vote must vote for rescission of authority before a certification rescinding such authority will be issued.[43] Persons who are ill, on vacation, or temporarily laid off—but not employees in the armed services who fail to appear to vote—will be included as eligible employees.[44]

The question on a deauthorization ballot is "Do you wish to withdraw the authority of your bargaining representative to require under its agreement with the employer that membership in the union be a condition of employment?"[45] (See Exhibit 62.) Postelection procedures including the investigation and disposition of challenged ballots and objections are the same as in representation election cases.[46] Unions may not, however, continue to enforce the terms of their union security clause during the period between an affirmative vote to deauthorize and final Board certification of the results of the election.[47]

As noted above, the decisive majority in a deauthorization election is a majority of the employees eligible to vote, not a majority of the valid votes cast. (See Exhibit 63.) The Board will not conduct a runoff of a deauthorization election.[48] The regional director or the

---

[39]NLRB Rules and Regulations §102.85; NLRB Casehandling Manual ¶11508.1.
[40]NLRB Rules and Regulations §102.85; NLRB Casehandling Manual ¶11508.1.
[41]NLRB Rules and Regulations §102.86; NLRB Casehandling Manual ¶11510.
[42]NLRB Rules and Regulations §102.88.
[43]Sec. 8(a)(3); NLRB Casehandling Manual ¶11512.
[44]*Id.*
[45]*Id.*
[46]*Id.* at ¶11514. See chapter 10.
[47]*Lyons Apparel, Inc.,* 218 NLRB 1172, 89 LRRM 1507 (1975).
[48]NLRB Statements of Procedure §101.29.

Board, as the case may be, will issue a certificate of results. (See Exhibit 64.) Where an affirmative vote is cast for deauthorization, the union cannot enter into a valid union security agreement for a period of one year from the date of the certificate of results.[49]

---

[49]Sec. 8(a)(3).

FORM NLRB-4931
(6-62)

UNITED STATES OF AMERICA
NATIONAL LABOR RELATIONS BOARD

AGREEMENT FOR CONSENT UD ELECTION

Pursuant to a Petition duly filed under Section 9 of the National Labor Relations Act, as amended, and subject to the approval of the Regional Director for the National Labor Relations Board *(herein called the Regional Director)*, the undersigned parties hereby waive a hearing and agree that the petition is hereby amended to conform to this Agreement and that approval of this Agreement constitutes a withdrawal of any Notice of Representation Hearing previously issued in this matter, and further AGREE AS FOLLOWS:

1. SECRET BALLOT. — An election by secret ballot shall be held under the supervision of the said Regional Director, among the employees of the undersigned Employer in the unit defined below, at the indicated time and place, to determine whether or not such employees wish to withdraw the authority of the undersigned union to require under its agreement with the undersigned employer that membership in such union be a condition of employment. Said election shall be held in accordance with the National Labor Relations Act, the Board's Rules and Regulations and the applicable procedures and policies of the Board, provided that the determination of the Regional Director shall be final and binding upon any question, including questions as to the eligibility of voters, raised by any party hereto relating in any manner to the election, and provided further that rulings or determinations by the Regional Director in respect of any amendment of any certification resulting therefrom shall also be final.

2. ELIGIBLE VOTERS. — The eligible voters shall be those employees included within the Unit described below, who were employed during the payroll period indicated below, and also employees who did not work during said payroll period because they were ill or on vacation or temporarily laid off, employees in the military services of the United States who appear in person at the polls, employees engaged in an economic strike which commenced less than twelve *(12)* months before the election date and who retained their status as such during the eligibility period and their replacements, but *excluding* any employees who have since quit or been discharged for cause and employees engaged in a strike who have been discharged for cause since the commencement thereof, and who have not been rehired or reinstated prior to the date of the election, and employees engaged in an economic strike which commenced more that 12 months prior to the date of the election and who have been permanently replaced. At a date fixed by the Regional Director, the parties, as requested, will furnish to the Regional Director, an accurate list of all the eligible voters, together with a list of the employees, if any, specifically excluded from eligibility.

3. NOTICE OF ELECTION. — The Regional Director shall prepare a Notice of Election and supply copies to the parties describing the manner and conduct of the election to be held and incorporating therein a sample ballot. The parties, upon the request of and at a time designated by the Regional Director, will post such Notice of Election at conspicuous and usual posting places easily accessible to the eligible voters.

4. OBSERVERS. — Each party hereto will be allowed to station an equal number of authorized observers, selected from among the nonsupervisory employees of the Employer, at the polling places during the election to assist in its conduct, to challenge the eligibility of voters, and to verify the tally.

5. TALLY OF BALLOTS. — As soon after the election as feasible, the votes shall be counted and tabulated by the Regional Director, or Board agent or agents. Upon the conclusion of the counting, the Regional Director shall furnish a Tally of Ballots to each of the parties. When appropriate, the Regional Director shall issue to the parties a certification of results of election.

6. OBJECTIONS, CHALLENGES, REPORTS THEREON. — Objections to the conduct of the election or conduct affecting the results of the election, may be filed with the Regional Director within 5 days after issuance of the Tally of Ballots. Copies of such objections must be served upon the other parties at the time of filing with the Regional Director. The Regional Director shall investigate the matters contained in the objections and issue a report thereon. If objections are sustained, the Regional Director may in the report include an order voiding the results of the election and, in that event, shall be empowered to conduct a new election under the terms and provisions of this agreement at a date, time and place to be determined by the Regional Director. If the challenges are determinative of the results of the election, the Regional Director shall investigate the challenges and issue a report thereon. The method of investigation of objections and challenges, including the question whether a hearing should be held in connection therewith, shall be determined by the Regional Director, whose decision shall be final and binding.

7. COMMERCE. — The Employer is engaged in commerce within the meaning of Section 2 (6) and (7) of the National Labor Relations Act.

Exhibit 59.   Agreement for Consent Union Security Deauthorization Election (Form NLRB-4931)

8. WORDING ON THE BALLOT. — The name of the labor organization, signatory to this agreement, shall appear on the ballot and the choice shall be "Yes" or "No." The wording on the ballot shall be: "Do you wish to withdraw the authority of your bargaining representative to require, under its agreement with the employer, that membership in the union be a condition of employment?"

9. PAYROLL PERIOD FOR ELIGIBILITY. —

10. DATE, HOURS, AND PLACE OF ELECTION. —

11. THE APPROPRIATE COLLECTIVE BARGAINING UNIT. —

....	....
(Employer)	*(Name of Petitioner)*
....	....
(Address)	*(Address)*
By	By ....
(Name and Title) *(Date)*	*(Name and Title)* *(Date)*
Recommended:	
....	....
(Board Agent) *(Date)*	*(Name of Organization)*
Date approved	
....	....
Regional Director, National Labor Relations Board.	*(Address)*
Case No.	By ....
	(Name and Title) *(Date)*

Exhibit 59—*page 2*

FORM NLRB-4932
(2-83)

UNITED STATES OF AMERICA
NATIONAL LABOR RELATIONS BOARD

STIPULATION FOR CERTIFICATION UPON CONSENT UD ELECTION

Pursuant to a petition duly filed under Section 9 of the National Labor Relations Act, as amended, and subject to the approval of the Regional Director for the National Labor Relations Board *(herein called the Regional Director)*, the undersigned parties hereby agree that the petition is hereby amended to conform to this Stipulation and that approval of this Stipulation constitutes a withdrawal of any Notice of Representation Hearing previously issued in this matter and further AGREE AS FOLLOWS:

1. SECRET BALLOT. — An election by secret ballot shall be held under the supervision of the said Regional Director, among the employees of the undersigned employer in the unit defined below, at the indicated time and place, to determine whether or not such employees wish to withdraw the authority of the undersigned union to require under its agreement with the undersigned employer that membership in such union be a condition of employment. Said election shall be held in accordance with the National Labor Relations Act, the Board's Rules and Regulations, and the applicable procedures and policies of the Board.

2. ELIGIBLE VOTERS. — The eligible voters shall be those employees included within the unit described below, who were employed during the payroll period indicated below, and also employees who did not work during said payroll period because they were ill or on vacation or temporarily laid off, employees in the military services of the United States who appear in person at the polls, employees engaged in an economic strike which commenced less than twelve *(12)* months before the election date and who retained their status as such during the eligibility period and their replacements, but *excluding* any employees who have since quit or been discharged for cause and employees engaged in a strike who have been discharged for cause since the commencement thereof, and who have not been rehired or reinstated prior to the date of the election, and employees engaged in an economic strike which commenced more than twelve *(12)* months prior to the date of the election and who have been permanently replaced. At a date fixed by the Regional Director, the parties, as requested, will furnish to the Regional Director, an accurate list of all the eligible voters, together with a list of the employees, if any, specifically excluded from eligibility.

3. NOTICE OF ELECTION. — The Regional Director shall prepare a Notice of Election and supply copies to the parties describing the manner and conduct of the election to be held and incorporating therein a sample ballot. The parties upon the request of and at a time designated by the Regional Director, will post such Notice of Election at conspicuous and usual posting places easily accessible to the eligible voters.

4. OBSERVERS. — Each party hereto will be allowed to station an equal number of authorized observers, selected from among the nonsupervisory employees of the employer, at the polling places during the election to assist in its conduct, to challenge the eligibility of voters, and to verify the tally.

5. TALLY OF BALLOTS. — As soon after the election as feasible, the votes shall be counted and tabulated by the Regional Director, or Board agent or agents. Upon the conclusion of the counting, the Regional Director shall furnish a Tally of Ballots to each of the parties.

6. POST-ELECTION PROCEDURE. — All procedures subsequent to the conclusion of counting ballots shall be in conformity with the Board's Rules and Regulations.

7. RECORD. — The record in this case shall be governed by the appropriate provisions of the Board's Rules and Regulations and shall include this stipulation. Hearing and notice thereof, Direction of Election, and the making of Findings of Fact and Conclusions of Law by the Board prior to the election are hereby expressly waived.

8. COMMERCE. — The employer is engaged in commerce within the meaning of Section 2 (6) and (7) of the National Labor Relations Act. *(Insert commerce facts.)*

Exhibit 60.   Stipulation for Certification Upon Consent Union Security Deauthorization Election (Form NLRB-4932)

9. WORDING ON THE BALLOT. — The wording on the ballot shall be: "Do you wish to withdraw the authority of your bargaining representative to require, under its agreement with the employer, that membership in the union be a condition of employment?" The choice shall be "Yes" or "No."

10. PAYROLL PERIOD FOR ELIGIBILITY. —

11. DATE, HOURS, AND PLACE OF ELECTION. —

12. THE APPROPRIATE COLLECTIVE BARGAINING UNIT. —

(Employer)	*(Name of Petitioner)*
(Address)	*(Address)*

By _____   By _____

(Name and Title)   *(Date)*   *(Name and Title)*   *(Date)*

Recommended:

_____
(Board Agent)   *(Date)*

                                      (Name of Organization)

Date approved _____

                  Regional Director
       · **National Labor Relations Board**   _____
                                        (Address)

Case _____   By _____

                                   (Name and Title)   *(Date)*

Exhibit 60—*page 2*

Exhibit 61. Notice of Deauthorization Election (Form NLRB-4135)

UNITED STATES OF AMERICA
National Labor Relations Board
FORM NLRB-4135B *(UD CASES)* (4-84)

OFFICIAL SECRET BALLOT
For certain employees of
Janco Computer Services, Inc.

Do you wish to withdraw the authority of your bargaining representative to require, under its agreement with the Employer, that membership in the Union be a condition of employment?

MARK AN "X" IN THE SQUARE OF YOUR CHOICE

YES	NO
☐	☐

DO NOT SIGN THIS BALLOT. Fold and drop in ballot box.
If you spoil this ballot return it to the Board Agent for a new one.

**Exhibit 62. Sample Ballot Used in Deauthorization Election
(Form NLRB-4135B)**

FORM NLRB-4880
(10-81)

UNITED STATES OF AMERICA
NATIONAL LABOR RELATIONS BOARD

CASE NO. _____

DATE FILED

DATE ISSUED _____

TYPE OF ELECTION:
(Check)

☐ Stipulation
☐ Board Direction
☐ Consent Agreement
☐ RD Direction

TALLY OF BALLOTS — UD ELECTION

The undersigned agent of the Regional Director certifies that the results of the tabulation of ballots cast in the election held in the above case, and concluded on the date indicated above, were as follows:

1. Approximate number of eligible voters .... _____

2. Void ballots .... _____

3. Votes cast in favor of withdrawing the authority of the bargaining representative to require, under its agreement with the Employer, that membership in such Union be a condition of employment _____

4. Votes cast against the above proposition .... _____

5. Valid votes counted (sum of 3 and 4) .... _____

6. Challenged ballots .... _____

7. Challenges are (not) sufficient in number to affect the results of the election.

8. The required majority of the eligible voters have (not) cast valid ballots in favor of the proposition.

For the Regional Director

_____

The undersigned acted as authorized observers in the counting and tabulating of ballots indicated above. We hereby certify that the counting and tabulating were fairly and accurately done, that the secrecy of the ballots was maintained, and that the results were as indicated above. We also acknowledge service of this tally.

For _____   For _____
_____   _____
_____   _____
For _____   For _____
_____   _____
_____   _____

**Exhibit 63.   Tally of Ballots—Union Security Deauthorization Election
(Form NLRB-4880)**

FORM NLRB-4889
(10-81)

UNITED STATES OF AMERICA

NATIONAL LABOR RELATIONS BOARD

UD ELECTION

TYPE OF ELECTION
(Check one)

☐ Consent Agreement

☐ Stipulation

☐ Board Direction

☐ RD Direction

Case No.

CERTIFICATION OF RESULTS OF ELECTION

Following the filing of a petition, pursuant to Section 9(e) of the National Labor Relations Act, as amended, an election was conducted herein under the supervision of the Regional Director of the National Labor Relations Board. No objections were filed to the conduct of the election, or to the Tally of Ballots.

Pursuant to the authority vested in the undersigned by the National Labor Relations Board, IT IS HEREBY CERTIFIED that a majority of employees eligible to vote have *(not)* voted to withdraw the authority of

to require, under its agreement with the Employer, that membership in such labor organization be a condition of employment, in conformity with Section 8(a)(3)of the Act, as amended:

Signed at
On the   day of   198

On behalf of

NATIONAL LABOR RELATIONS BOARD

_____

Regional Director, Region
National Labor Relations Board

**Exhibit 64. Certification of Results of Election—Union Security
Deauthorization Proceeding (Form NLRB-4889)**

III

Unfair Labor Practice Proceedings

12

The Unfair Labor Practice Charge and Investigation

The National Labor Relations Board has the exclusive power to prevent employers and labor organizations from engaging in unfair labor practices. It has no authority to investigate the conduct of individuals acting in their private capacities, but only as agents of statutory employers or labor organizations.[1] It is significant, however, that the Board's test of agency focuses upon the perceptions of employees. Thus, individuals may be found to be agents of an employer if that employer "has taken steps that lead its employees reasonably to conclude that those persons were acting on behalf of management."[2]

Neither the Board nor the General Counsel has the authority to investigate alleged unfair labor practices on its own initiative.[3] The filing of an unfair labor practice charge is a condition precedent to, and initiates the investigation of, an unfair labor practice.[4] Only the filing of a charge can provide the spark which starts the machinery of the Act running.[5]

The type of unfair labor practice charge filed depends upon whether it is filed against an employer or a labor organization, and upon which section of the Act is alleged to have been violated:

If the charge is against an employer or its agents, the result is—

---

[1]*International Longshoremen's Union, CIO (Sunset Line & Twine Co.)*, 79 NLRB 1487, 23 LRRM 1001 (1948).

[2]*NLRB v. Proler Int'l Corp.*, 635 F.2d 351, 106 LRRM 2530 (5th Cir. 1981). *Compare Dean Indus.*, 162 NLRB 1078, 64 LRRM 1193 (1967) (agency relationship found) *with Tylertown Wood Prods.*, 251 NLRB 515, 105 LRRM 1120 (1980) (no agency relationship found).

[3]*Nash v. Florida Indus. Comm'n*, 389 U.S. 235, 66 LRRM 2625 (1967); *NLRB v. Houston Distribution Servs., Inc.*, 573 F.2d 260, 98 LRRM 2538 (5th Cir. 1978).

[4]NLRB Casehandling Manual ¶10010.

[5]*See, e.g., Kern's Bakeries, Inc.*, 227 NLRB 1329, 95 LRRM 1165 (1977).

- A "CA" case, alleging violations of one or more subsections of Section 8(a) of the Act.

If the charge is against a labor organization or its agents, the result is—

- A "CB" case, alleging violations of one or more of subsections 8(b)(1), (2), (3), (5), or (6) of the Act; or
- A "CC" case, alleging violations of one or more of subsections 8(b)(4)(i) and/or (ii)(A), (B), or (C) of the Act; or
- A "CD" case, alleging violations of Section 8(b)(4)(i) and/or (ii)(D) of the Act; or
- A "CP" case, alleging violations of one or more subsections of Section 8(b)(7) of the Act; or
- A "CG" case, alleging violations of Section 8(g) of the Act.[6]

If the charge is against a labor organization or its agents and/or an employer or its agents, the result is—

- A "CE" case, alleging violations of Section 8(e) of the Act.

Filing of Unfair Labor Practice Charges

§12.1   Who May File

Any person—an individual, an employer, or a labor organization—may file an unfair labor practice charge.[7] In some instances the validity of Board proceedings have been challenged because of the identity or character of the charging party. The type of person or organization making the charge, or the relationship between such person or organization and the individuals involved in the acts complained of, however, are not limited by the Act. Thus, for example, it has been held that unfair labor practice proceedings may be maintained where the charges are filed by:

- An attorney, on behalf of individual employees;[8]
- An individual, in effect a "stranger," who is not an employee;[9]

---

[6]Health care cases arising under all sections of the Act other than Section 8(g) should be filed in the same manner as non-health care cases.

[7]NLRB Rules and Regulations §102.9; NLRB Casehandling Manual ¶10016.

[8]*NLRB v. Bishop*, 228 F.2d 68, 37 LRRM 2185 (6th Cir. 1955).

[9]*NLRB v. Indiana & Mich. Elec. Co.*, 318 U.S. 9, 11 LRRM 763 (1943); *Carpenters Local 1846 v. Pratt-Farnsworth, Inc.*, 690 F.2d 489, 515 n.11, 111 LRRM 2787, 2804 n.11 (5th Cir. 1982).

- A discriminatorily discharged employee, on behalf of himself and other employees similarly discharged;[10]
- An individual, on behalf of a labor organization, even though he is not authorized to file the charge;[11]
- An employer who is not a member of an employer association in a case where rights of members of that association are involved;[12]
- A labor organization which is not the majority representative;[13]
- A labor organization which has no members in the employ of the charged company;[14]
- A labor organization, against another labor organization, where both parties are affiliated with the same parent federation;[15]
- A civil rights group, on behalf of individual employees;[16]
- A party to a primary dispute, where the charge alleges an illegal secondary boycott.[17]

With regard to the motivation or character of the charging party, the Supreme Court has said that "[d]ubious character, evil or unlawful motives, or bad faith of the informer cannot deprive the Board of its jurisdiction to conduct the inquiry."[18] Thus, the Board's power to process an unfair labor practice case is not affected where it is claimed that the charging party itself has engaged in misconduct,[19] or had filed the charge in bad faith and for unlawful motives.[20] Nor does the fact that a union has engaged in discrimination based on race, sex, or national origin bar it from filing a charge.[21] Similarly, a party to an illegal "hot cargo" contract may attack the validity of the contract by charging the other party to the agreement.[22]

The Board may consider, however, the motivation and character of the charging party in exercising its prosecutorial discretion. The Supreme Court has held that

> "[w]hile . . . misconduct of the union would not deprive the Board of jurisdiction, this does not mean that the Board may not properly con-

---

[10]*Vee Cee Provisions, Inc.*, 256 NLRB 758, 107 LRRM 1416 (1981).

[11]*Terminal Taxi*, 229 NLRB 643, 95 LRRM 1124 (1977).

[12]*Heating, Piping & Air Conditioning Contractors New York City Ass'n*, 102 NLRB 1646, 31 LRRM 1482 (1953).

[13]*Pennsylvania Greyhound Lines*, 303 U.S. 261, 2 LRRM 599 (1938).

[14]*NLRB v. General Shoe Corp.*, 192 F.2d 504, 29 LRRM 2112 (6th Cir. 1951).

[15]*Teamsters Local 404*, 100 NLRB 801, 30 LRRM 1360 (1952).

[16]*Bagley Produce, Inc.*, 208 NLRB 20, 85 LRRM 1349 (1973).

[17]*Wine, Liquor & Distillery Workers Union, Local 1*, 78 NLRB 504, 22 LRRM 1222 (1948).

[18]*NLRB v. Indiana & Mich. Elec. Co.*, 318 U.S. 9, 18, 11 LRRM 763, 767 (1943).

[19]*Union Independiente de Empleados de Servicios Legales de Puerto Rico, Inc.*, 249 NLRB 1044, 104 LRRM 1433 (1980).

[20]*NLRB v. Fred P. Weissman Co.*, 170 F.2d 952, 23 LRRM 2131 (6th Cir. 1948).

[21]*NLRB v. Mangurian's, Inc.*, 566 F.2d 463, 97 LRRM 2477 (5th Cir. 1978).

[22]*Milk Drivers & Dairy Employees, Local 546*, 133 NLRB 1314, 49 LRRM 1001 (1961).

sider such misconduct as material to its own decision to entertain and proceed upon the charge. The Board has wide discretion in the issue of complaints. . . . It is not required by the statute to move on every charge; it is merely enabled to do so. It may decline to be imposed upon or to submit its process to abuse."[23]

§12.2   Prefiling Assistance

Any person considering filing an unfair labor practice charge may seek assistance from a Board agent in a regional office.[24] While Board agents may furnish information concerning statutory requirements and Board procedures, they may not render legal advice or opinions, and may not commit the General Counsel or the Board.[25] Assistance in the preparation of a charge generally includes the furnishing of forms, reasonable clerical and stenographic services, the correction of obvious errors (e.g., citing the wrong section of the Act), and suggestions concerning wording of the charge.[26]

§12.3   Contents

Appropriate forms on which to file charges may be obtained at any NLRB regional office. Three types of forms are available:

- *NLRB 501*. Charge Against Employer (CA) (See Exhibit 65.)
- *NLRB 508*. Charge Against Labor Organization or Its Agent (CB, CC, CD, CG, CP) (See Exhibit 66.)
- *NLRB 509*. Charge Alleging Unfair Labor Practices Under Section 8(e) of the Act (CE) (See Exhibit 67.)

While reasonable facsimiles of the Board forms are acceptable, their use is discouraged.[27] Charges must be sworn to before a notary public, Board agent, or other person authorized to administer oaths, or must contain a declaration by the person signing it that its contents are true and correct to the best of his or her knowledge.[28] In addition, the names and addresses of both the charging and charged parties must be given, along with "a clear and concise statement of the facts constituting the alleged unfair labor practice."[29] The wording of the charge should be specific enough to inform the charged party of the

---

[23]*NLRB v. Indiana & Mich. Elec. Co.*, 318 U.S. 9, 18–19, 11 LRRM 763, 767 (1943); *see also NLRB v. Sears, Roebuck & Co.*, 421 U.S. 132, 143 n.10, 89 LRRM 2001, 2004 n.10 (1975).

[24]*See generally* NLRB Casehandling Manual ¶¶10012.1–10012.7.

[25]*Id.* at ¶10012.5.

[26]*Id.* at ¶10012.6–10012.7.

[27]*Id.* at ¶10020.

[28]NLRB Rules and Regulations §102.11.

[29]*Id.* at §102.12. If the charge is filed by a labor organization, the full name and address of any national or international labor organization of which it is an affiliate or constituent unit also must be furnished.

GPO : 1984 O - 435-440

FORM EXEMPT UNDER 44 U.S.C. 3512

FORM NLRB-501 (8-83)	UNITED STATES OF AMERICA NATIONAL LABOR RELATIONS BOARD **CHARGE AGAINST EMPLOYER**	**DO NOT WRITE IN THIS SPACE**	
		Case	Date Filed

INSTRUCTIONS: File an original and 4 copies of this charge with NLRB Regional Director for the region in which the alleged unfair labor practice occurred or is occurring.

1. EMPLOYER AGAINST WHOM CHARGE IS BROUGHT

a. Name of Employer	b. Number of workers employed

c. Address *(street, city, state, ZIP code)*	d. Employer Representative	e. Telephone No.

f. Type of Establishment *(factory, mine, wholesaler, etc.)*	g. Identify principal product or service

h. The above-named employer has engaged in and is engaging in unfair labor practices within the meaning of section 8(a), subsections (1) and *(list subsections)* _____ of the National Labor Relations Act, and these unfair labor practices are unfair practices affecting commerce within the meaning of the Act.

2. Basis of the Charge *(be specific as to facts, names, addresses, plants involved, dates, places, etc.)*

By the above and other acts, the above-named employer has interfered with, restrained, and coerced employees in the exercise of the rights guaranteed in Section 7 of the Act

3. Full name of party filing charge *(if labor organization, give full name, including local name and number)*

4a. Address *(street and number, city, state, and ZIP code)*	4b. Telephone No.

5. Full name of national or international labor organization of which it is an affiliate or constituent unit *(to be filled in when charge is filed by a labor organization)*

6. DECLARATION

I declare that I have read the above charge and that the statements are true to the best of my knowledge and belief.

By _____   _____
   (signature of representative or person making charge)   *(title if any)*

Address _____
                                        (Telephone No.)   *(date)*

WILLFUL FALSE STATEMENTS ON THIS CHARGE CAN BE PUNISHED BY FINE AND IMPRISONMENT (U. S. CODE, TITLE 18, SECTION 1001)

Exhibit 65.   Charge Against Employer   (Form NLRB-501)

FORM EXEMPT UNDER 44 U.S.C. 3512

FORM NLRB-508 (8-83)	UNITED STATES OF AMERICA NATIONAL LABOR RELATIONS BOARD **CHARGE AGAINST LABOR ORGANIZATION OR ITS AGENTS**	DO NOT WRITE IN THIS SPACE	
		Case	Date Filed

INSTRUCTIONS: File an original and 3 copies of this charge and an additional copy for each organization, each local, and each individual named in item 1 with the NLRB Regional Director of the region in which the alleged unfair labor practice occurred or is occurring.

1. LABOR ORGANIZATION OR ITS AGENTS AGAINST WHICH CHARGE IS BROUGHT

a. Name

b. Union Representative to contact

c. Telephone No.

d. Address *(street, city, state and ZIP code)*

e. The above-named organization(s) or its agents has *(have)* engaged in and is *(are)* engaging in unfair labor practices within the meaning of section 8(b), subsection(s) *(list subsections)* _____ of the National Labor Relations Act, and these unfair labor practices are unfair practices affecting commerce within the meaning of the Act.

2. Basis of the Charge *(be specific as to facts, names, addresses, plants involved, dates, places, etc.)*

3. Name of Employer

4. Telephone No.

5. Location of plant involved *(street, city, state and ZIP code)*

6. Employer representative to contact

7. Type of establishment *(factory, mine, wholesaler, etc.)*

8. Identify principal product or service

9. Number of workers employed

10. Full name of party filing charge

11. Address of party filing charge *(street, city, state and ZIP code)*

12. Telephone No.

13. DECLARATION

I declare that I have read the above charge and that the statements therein are true to the best of my knowledge and belief.

By _____

(signature of representative or person making charge)

_____

(title or office, if any)

Address _____

(Telephone No.)   *(date)*

WILLFUL FALSE STATEMENTS ON THIS CHARGE CAN BE PUNISHED BY FINE AND IMPRISONMENT (U. S. CODE, TITLE 18, SECTION 1001)

Exhibit 66.   Charge Against Labor Organization   (Form NLRB-508)

FORM NLRB-509
(9-82)

UNITED STATES OF AMERICA
NATIONAL LABOR RELATIONS BOARD
CHARGE ALLEGING UNFAIR LABOR PRACTICE UNDER SECTION 8(e) OF THE ACT

FORM EXEMPT UNDER
44 U.S.C. 3512

INSTRUCTIONS: File an original and 3 copies of this charge, and an additional copy for each organization, each local and each individual named in item 1 with the NLRB regional director for the region in which the alleged unfair labor practice occurred or is occurring.

CASE NUMBER	DATE FILED	1. CHARGE FILED AGAINST:		
		Employer and Labor Organization ☐	Employer ☐	Labor Organization ☐

a. Name of Labor Organization (Give full name, including local name and number)	b. Union Representative to Contact	c. Phone Number
d. Address (Street and number, city, State and ZIP Code)		
e. Name of Employer	f. Employer Representative to Contact	g. Phone Number
h. Location of Plant Involved (Street, city, State and ZIP Code)		

i. Type of Establishment (Factory, mine, wholesaler, etc.)	j. Identify Principal Product or Service	k. No. of Workers Employed

The above-named labor organization or its agents, and/or employer has (have) engaged in and is (are) engaging in unfair labor practices within the meaning of section 8(e) of the National Labor Relations Act, and these unfair labor practices are unfair labor practices affecting commerce within the meaning of the Act.

2. Basis of the Charge (Be specific as to facts, names, plants involved, dates, places, etc.)

3. Full Name of Party Filing Charge (If labor organization, give full name, including local name and number)

a. Address (Street and number, city, State and ZIP Code)	b. Telephone Number

4. Full Name of National or International Labor Organization of Which It Is an Affiliate or Constituent Unit (To be filled in when charge is filed by a labor organization)

5. DECLARATION
I declare that I have read the above charge and that the statements therein are true to the best of my knowledge and belief.

By (Type/Print name of representative or person filing charge)	Title, if any	Telephone Number
Address	Signature	Date

WILLFULLY FALSE STATEMENTS ON THIS CHARGE CAN BE PUNISHED BY FINE AND IMPRISONMENT (U.S. CODE, TITLE 18, SECTION 1001)

Exhibit 67.   Charge Alleging Unfair Labor Practice Under Section 8(e) of the Act (Form NLRB-509)

alleged violations and yet broad enough to cover any related unfair labor practices.[30]

It is important to understand the limited function of an unfair labor practice charge. The charge is not a formal pleading and it is not necessary to apprise the charged party of the exact nature of each and every allegation against him. That is the function of the complaint. The purpose of a charge is merely to set in motion the Board's investigative machinery, and put the charged party on notice as to the general nature of the allegations.[31] Often the notice requirement can be satisfied simply by quoting the statutory language alleged to have been violated.[32] The only limitation is that a complaint may not issue on matters so completely unrelated to the charge that the Board may be said to be initiating proceedings on its own.[33]

The charge should not include statements in the nature of evidence.[34] Required factual information, whether in affidavit form or a fact statement, that is furnished in support of the charge may be supplied separately. If such statements are quoted or incorporated by reference into the charge, they must be served on the charged party along with the charge form.

Where more than one party has participated in the commission of an alleged unfair labor practice, it is not mandatory that charges be filed against all parties.[35] The charging party may elect to bring charges against only one or more of them. For example, in a case where an employee is discharged by the employer at the request of a union pursuant to an allegedly illegal contract, the employee may choose to file a charge against the employer, or against the union, or against both. The Board, however, has no authority to issue an order against a participant in an unfair labor practice who has not been named in the charge.

§12.4　Filing and Service

The charge is filed with the regional office in whose area the unfair labor practices are alleged to have occurred. A charge which alleges such practices in two or more regions may be filed with the regional director for any of such regions.[36] (The areas covered by the regional offices are set forth in Appendix E.) On rare occasions it

---

[30]NLRB Casehandling Manual ¶10020.

[31]*Flex Plastics, Inc.*, 262 NLRB 651, 110 LRRM 1365 (1982); *Turner Tool and Joint Rebuilders Corp.*, 256 NLRB 595, 107 LRRM 1303 (1981).

[32]*Supreme Bumpers, Inc.*, 243 NLRB 230, 101 LRRM 1599 (1979).

[33]*Flex Plastics, Inc.*, 262 NLRB 651, 110 LRRM 1365 (1982). NLRB Casehandling Manual ¶¶10020.2–10020.4 set forth additional requirements for CC, CD, CE, and CP unfair labor practice charges.

[34]NLRB Casehandling Manual ¶10020.1.

[35]*Radio Officers Union v. NLRB*, 347 U.S. 17, 33 LRRM 2417 (1954).

[36]NLRB Rules and Regulations §102.10; NLRB Casehandling Manual ¶10018.

may be be possible to file a complaint directly with the General Counsel in order to avoid unnecessary costs or delay.[37]

In filing the charge with the regional office, one original and four copies must be submitted, together with one additional copy for each charged party.[38] The charge may be filed in person at the regional office, by mail, or by handing it to a Board agent away from the regional office.[39] If filed through the mails, it is advisable to send the charge by registered or certified mail.

The regional director, as a matter of course, will serve copies of the charge upon the charged parties. The director, however, assumes no responsibility for compliance with the requirement imposed on charging parties that such service be made.[40] If a regional director has served the charge in a timely fashion, the proceeding is not invalidated because the charging party has failed to do so.[41] Where the six-month statute of limitations is about to expire, the charging party should serve the party against whom the charge is made as soon as it files its charge with the Board's regional office.[42] The date of service is the date of mailing so that service is timely if mailed within the six-month period even though it is not actually received by the charged party until after expiration of that period.[43]

In situations where there are multiple organizations involved, the normal rules of agency apply for purposes of receipt of service. Thus, service on one business or labor organization may be deemed service on another in instances where the enterprises constitute a single employer,[44] alter egos,[45] joint employers,[46] or joint representatives.[47]

§12.5 Supporting Documentation

At the time the charge is filed with the Board's regional office, the charging party should submit an affidavit or statement in writing

---

[37]NLRB Rules and Regulations §102.33(a).

[38]NLRB Rules and Regulations §102.11; NLRB Casehandling Manual ¶10020.

[39]NLRB Casehandling Manual ¶10018.

[40]NLRB Rules and Regulations §102.14; NLRB Casehandling Manual ¶10052.

[41]*T.L.B. Plastics Corp.*, 266 NLRB 331, 112 LRRM 1383 (1983).

[42]"Filing" means that the charge has been received by the regional director or other Board agent; "service" upon the charged party occurs when a copy of the charge is placed in the mails or is hand delivered. Both must occur within six months in order for the charge to be timely. Sec. 10(b); NLRB Casehandling Manual ¶10052; see discussion at §12.6 *infra. But see Westbrook Bowl*, 274 NLRB No. 145, 118 LRRM 1489 (1985) (complaint dismissed where General Counsel failed to introduce evidence that respondent actually received copy of charge within the 10(b) period).

[43]*See, e.g., NLRB v. Preston H. Haskell Co.*, 616 F.2d 136, 104 LRRM 2235 (5th Cir. 1980); *St. John Medical Center*, 252 NLRB 514, 105 LRRM 1380 (1980); *General Marine Transp. Corp.*, 238 NLRB 1372, 99 LRRM 1637 (1978).

[44]*G.W. Wilson*, 240 NLRB 333, 100 LRRM 1276 (1979).

[45]*Sturdevant Sheet Metal & Roofing Co.*, 238 NLRB 186, 99 LRRM 1240 (1978).

[46]*Wright, Schuchart, Harbor/Boecon/Bovee, Crail/Geri, A Joint Venture*, 236 NLRB 780, 98 LRRM 1364 (1978).

[47]*Oregon, Southern Idaho and Wyo. Dist. Council of Laborers*, 243 NLRB 405, 101 LRRM 1559 (1979).

setting forth in detail all relevant facts, including names, dates, and places. In addition, the names and addresses of possible witnesses and other persons who may have knowledge of facts supporting the charge should be submitted along with any documents or other evidence available to the charging party. If a novel theory of law is involved, it is advisable to include an explanation and analysis of appropriate authorities as an aid to the regional office in its investigation and consideration of the case.

§12.6   Timeliness

Section 10(b) of the Act provides that no complaint may be issued on matters which occurred more than six months prior to the filing of a charge and the service of a copy on the respondent unless the charging party is in the armed forces. If the individual is in the armed forces, the six-month period commences upon discharge from the service.[48] Filing with the regional director and service on the respondent both must occur within the six-month period in order for the charge to be timely. Filing occurs when the charge is actually received by the regional director or other Board agent. In contrast, service on the respondent occurs when the charge is placed in the mails or is hand delivered.[49] As noted above, responsibility for timely service rests with the charging party and not with the regional director. A charge which is not timely filed will not be processed.[50]

The six-month limitations period begins to run when the unfair labor practice is committed rather than on the date when its consequences become effective.[51] If the charging party does not have actual or constructive knowledge of the unfair labor practice, however, the period begins to run when such knowledge is received.[52] Similarly, the limitations period may be tolled (i.e., suspended) during the time that respondent fraudulently conceals the unlawful conduct from the charging party.[53] If the unfair labor practice is continuing in nature,

---

[48]Sec. 10(b).

[49]*See* NLRB Rules and Regulations §102.111(b)(1) (charges must be received on or before the close of business of the last day for filing) and §102.112 (service is accomplished when matter is deposited in the mail or delivered in person).

[50]NLRB Casehandling Manual ¶10052. The Board, however, views the Sec. 10(b) period as a statute of limitations which can be waived by the parties, rather than as a jurisdictional requirement. If a Sec. 10(b) defense is not timely raised, it will be considered waived. *Federal Mgmt. Co.*, 264 NLRB 107, 111 LRRM 1296 (1982).

[51]In *United States Postal Serv. Marina Mail Processing Center*, 271 NLRB 397, 116 LRRM 1417 (1984), an employee was notified on February 27 that he would be terminated and was placed on nonduty status on March 3. The Board held that the Sec. 10(b) period commenced on February 27 rather than on March 3.

[52]NLRB Casehandling Manual ¶10052; *see Don Burgess Constr. Corp.*, 227 NLRB 765, 95 LRRM 1135 (1977) (limitations period does not begin to run until person adversely affected is put on notice).

[53]*Danzansky-Goldberg Mem. Chapels, Inc.*, 264 NLRB 840, 112 LRRM 1108 (1982); *Pacific Intercom Co.*, 255 NLRB 184, 106 LRRM 1289 (1981).

the charge is timely filed so long as at least one unlawful act is committed within the preceding six months.[54]

Evidence pertaining to unlawful conduct which occurred prior to the 10(b) period may be introduced and considered by the Board when it is offered not for the purpose of establishing a pre-10(b) violation, but rather for purposes of serving as background for, or explanation of, subsequent conduct which did occur within the 10(b) period.[55] For example, evidence concerning an employer's extreme hostility to union organizers during an organizing campaign one year earlier is admissible as background information in evaluating allegations of unlawful conduct during a current campaign.[56] Similarly, pre-10(b) evidence that a predecessor employer required new employees to join the union and execute checkoff authorization cards on the first day of employment and negotiated a union contract without the consent of any of the unit employees was found to be relevant background in considering whether a subsequent employer's decision to withdraw recognition from the union on the basis of a good-faith doubt of its continuing majority status violated Section 8(a)(5).[57]

In some instances a timely filed charge is either withdrawn voluntarily by the charging party or is dismissed by the regional director. The director may subsequently seek to reinstate the charge more than six months after the alleged unlawful conduct has occurred. Several Board and court decisions have authorized reinstatement of the charge in such circumstances on equitable grounds.[58] In *Winer Motors*[59] the Board reversed itself with regard to charges which had been withdrawn and concluded that such charges may not be reinstated on the basis of equitable considerations in the absence of evidence that the respondent fraudulently concealed the operative facts underlying the charge.[60] Subsequently the Board has applied the same rule to charges which have been dismissed by the regional director.[61] In the Board's view, charges which have been dismissed

---

[54]*See, e.g., Campo Slacks, Inc.*, 266 NLRB 492, 112 LRRM 1432 (1983), where the employer's failure to make insurance fund payments for three years continued into the Sec. 10(b) period because each indebtedness and refusal to pay was considered to be a separate violation. Contracts containing unlawful union security or hot cargo clauses which are executed prior to the six-month period may still be found unlawful if the challenged clauses are enforced or otherwise reaffirmed within the six-month period. *Los Angeles Mailers Union (Hillbro Newspaper Printing Co.)*, 135 NLRB 1132, 49 LRRM 1659 (1962); *Paul W. Speer, Inc.*, 98 NLRB 212, 29 LRRM 1319 (1952).

[55]*Machinists Lodge 1424 v. NLRB (Bryan Mfg. Co.)*, 362 U.S. 411, 45 LRRM 3212 (1960); *Henry J. Kaiser Co.*, 259 NLRB 1, 108 LRRM 1230 (1981).

[56]*Air Prods. & Chemicals, Inc.*, 263 NLRB 341, 111 LRRM 1024 (1982); *cf. City Serv. Insulation Co.*, 266 NLRB 654, 113 LRRM 1018 (1983).

[57]*Pick-Mt. Laurel Corp.*, 259 NLRB 302, 108 LRRM 1342 (1981).

[58]*California Pacific Signs, Inc.*, 233 NLRB 450, 97 LRRM 1085 (1977) (Board allowed reinstatement of dismissed charge on basis of newly discovered evidence); *Silver Bakery*, 150 NLRB 421, 58 LRRM 1070 (1964) (Board authorized reinstatement where withdrawal solicited by Board agent who erroneously told charging party that Board lacked jurisdiction).

[59]*Winer Motors, Inc.*, 265 NLRB 1457, 112 LRRM 1175 (1982).

[60]*See Koppers Co.*, 163 NLRB 517, 64 LRRM 1375 (1967).

[61]*Ducane Heating Corp.*, 273 NLRB No. 175, 118 LRRM 1145 (1985). In *Duff-Norton Co.*, 275 NLRB No. 93, 119 LRRM 1189 (1985), a Board panel majority refused to reinstate a

or withdrawn voluntarily have been disposed of and, in effect, cease to exist.

§12.7 Amendments

Although the Act makes no provision for the amendment of a charge, the Board and the courts have recognized the power of the charging party to do so.[62] A charge may be amended by typing "Amended" (or "Second Amended," "Third Amended," etc.) before the word "Charge" on the regular charge form and either (1) rewriting the entire contents of the charge to include the desired changes, or (2) referring to the existing charge and simply stating what is to be added, deleted, or modified. While both methods of amendment are proper, the former is preferred.[63] Assistance to the extent permitted in connection with the original charge may be rendered by Board agents in connection with the filing of amendments,[64] and once filed the amendments should be served by registered mail on the charged and other interested parties.[65] The amendment of a charge does not constitute a withdrawal of either the original charge or an earlier amendment.[66]

Unfair labor practice charges may be amended for a variety of reasons.[67] During the course of the investigation technical errors in the original charge concerning such items as names and dates may be discovered. The investigation also may uncover evidence of additional violations not encompassed by the original charge which must be cited in a new or amended charge before they can be included in a complaint. Conversely, Board agents may suggest that allegations for which there is no supporting evidence be dropped. Finally, amendments may be appropriate to cover related violations occurring subsequent to the last amendment.

An amended charge also may allege entirely new unfair labor practices which occurred after the original charge but within the six-month period before the filing and service of the amendment.[68] Amendments based upon conduct occurring after the original charge but more than six months before the filing and service of the amended

---

previously dismissed charge in light of subsequent evidence that a supervisor "set up" an employee for termination. The supervisory conduct was not viewed as a fraudulent concealment of operative facts which might justify an untimely reinstatement of the charge; *see also Northwest Towboat Ass'n*, 275 NLRB No. 24, 118 LRRM 1647 (1985) (*Ducane Heating* applied to deny reinstatement of dismissed charge).

[62]*See, e.g., NLRB v. Operating Eng'rs, Local 925*, 460 F.2d 589, 80 LRRM 2398 (5th Cir. 1972). *See generally* NLRB Casehandling Manual ¶10064.

[63]NLRB Casehandling Manual ¶10064.1.

[64]*Id.* at ¶10064.3.

[65]*Id.* at ¶10064.2.

[66]*NLRB v. Kobritz (Star Beef Co.)*, 193 F.2d 8, 29 LRRM 2190 (1st Cir. 1951).

[67]*See generally* NLRB Casehandling Manual ¶¶10064.5–10064.7.

[68]*Philip Carey Mfg. Co.*, 140 NLRB 1103, 52 LRRM 1184 (1963).

charge generally will be untimely.[69] The principal exception to this rule is when the subsequent conduct cited in the amended charge "relates back" to the conduct alleged in the original charge.[70] This may occur, for example, when the amended charge particularizes general allegations in the original charge or is based upon the same or a similar fact pattern.[71] In such cases the amendment will be timely even though some of the conduct may have occurred more than six months earlier. Where the amended charge raises a new and separate cause of action, however, it must independently satisfy the six-month limitation as to filing and service.[72]

Investigation of Unfair Labor Practice Charges

§12.8 Notice to Parties

Upon receipt of a charge by the Board's regional office, it is docketed, given a number, and assigned to a Board agent for investigation.[73] An acknowledgment of the filing naming the field examiner or attorney to whom the charge has been assigned is sent to the charging party along with a request that a written account of the facts and circumstances surrounding the matters complained of in the charge be furnished promptly. (See Exhibit 68.)[74] A similar letter is sent to the party charged along with a copy of the actual charge. (See Exhibit 69.) The charged party also is asked to submit a position statement concerning the allegations in the charge and, if the charged party is an employer, it is asked to submit "commerce" data for purposes of determining whether the Board has jurisdiction.[75] (See Exhibit 18.)

In addition to the charging and charged parties, circumstances may require that notice of the filing of the charge be offered to other parties as well. By way of example, such parties might include (1) a labor organization alleged to be dominated or assisted in a Section 8(a)(2) charge; (2) an employer involved in a secondary boycott or jurisdictional dispute case; (3) in a Section 8(b)(2) case, an employer allegedly being pressured to violate Section 8(a)(3) by the charged union; and (4) any party to a collective bargaining agreement which

---

[69]*Hunter Saw Div. of Asko, Inc.*, 202 NLRB 330, 82 LRRM 1498 (1973); *Bastian-Blessing, Div. of Golconda Corp.*, 194 NLRB 609, 79 LRRM 1010 (1971); *Sunnen Prods.*, 189 NLRB 826, 77 LRRM 1184 (1971).

[70]*Daniel Constr. Co.*, 244 NLRB 704, 102 LRRM 1399 (1979).

[71]*See, e.g., Air Express Int'l Corp.*, 245 NLRB 478, 102 LRRM 1574 (1979); *Schraffts Candy Co.*, 244 NLRB 581, 102 LRRM 1274 (1979); *Staco, Inc.*, 244 NLRB 461, 102 LRRM 1223 (1979).

[72]*NLRB v. Central Power & Light Co.*, 425 F.2d 1318, 74 LRRM 2269 (5th Cir. 1970); *Speed Queen*, 192 NLRB 995, 78 LRRM 1148 (1971).

[73]NLRB Statements of Procedure §101.4; NLRB Casehandling Manual ¶10022.

[74]NLRB Casehandling Manual ¶¶10040.1–10040.2.

[75]NLRB Statements of Procedure §101.4; NLRB Casehandling Manual ¶10040.3.

NATIONAL LABOR RELATIONS BOARD

REGION 5

Candler Building - 4th Floor

109 Market Place

Baltimore, MD   21202

January 2, 1986

Ms. Jean Jones, Business Agent
Local 007
United Computer Operators International Union
P.O. Box 10
Arlington, VA   22207

                         Re: Janco Computer Services, Inc.
                              Case No. 5-CA-1234

Dear Ms. Jones:

This will acknowledge receipt of the unfair labor practice charge filed by
you. Enclosed is a copy of Form NLRB-4541 pertaining to our investigative
and voluntary adjustment procedures.

Investigation of this matter has been assigned to the staff member named
below who will communicate with you promptly.

If you have not already done so please send immediately to this office a
statement outlining the basis for your charge, including therein the dates
of events involved in the case and the names and addresses of persons who
can testify in support of the allegations, together with any documents or
materials available to you which have a bearing on the case, such as
correspondence, contracts, records, et cetera.

Failure to submit evidence promptly may subject the charge to dismissal
without further investigation.

                         Very truly yours,

                         Louis J. D'Amico
                         Regional Director

Enclosures

CERTIFIED MAIL - RETURN RECEIPT REQUESTED

CASE ASSIGNED TO:
TELEPHONE NUMBER:

Exhibit 68.   Letter Acknowledging Receipt of Unfair Labor Practice Charge

NATIONAL LABOR RELATIONS BOARD

REGION 5

Candler Building - 4th Floor

109 Market Place

Baltimore, MD   21202

January 2, 1986

Mr. Jack Smith, President
Janco Computer Services, Inc.
8181 Greensboro Drive
McLean, VA 22102

                          Re: Janco Computer Services, Inc.
                               Case No. 5-CA-1234

Dear Mr. Smith:

Enclosed is a copy of a charge filed in the above case alleging that your
organization has engaged in unfair labor practices under the National Labor
Relations Act. Also enclosed is a copy of Form NLRB-4541 pertaining to our
investigative and voluntary adjustment procedures.

Investigation of this case has been assigned to the staff member named
below who will communicate with you promptly.

In the meantime, we would appreciate having from you a description of the
facts and circumstances and a written statement of your position with
respect to the allegations contained in the charge.

In addition, it is requested that you complete the attached questionnaire
relative to your business and return it to this office as soon as possible.

                          Very truly yours,

                          Louis J. D'Amico
                          Regional Director

Attachments

CERTIFIED MAIL - RETURN RECEIPT REQUESTED

CASE ASSIGNED TO:
TELEPHONE NUMBER:

**Exhibit 69.   Letter Notifying Employer of Filing of Unfair Labor Practice
Charge**

is under challenge.[76] Such interested parties also are asked to submit their version of the facts surrounding the charge.

Along with the initial letters to the parties are enclosed three Board forms. Form NLRB–4541 (see Exhibit 70) advises the parties of their right to be represented by counsel and explains the procedures which will be followed in processing the charge. Form NLRB–4701, Notice of Appearance, (see Exhibit 16) is used by the parties to notify the Board of the name and address of their counsel or other representative. Once counsel or other representative has filed an appearance, copies of all subsequent documents in the case, with the exception of subpoenas, will be served on both the party and the designated representative.[77]

There may be circumstances in which a party wishes to designate its counsel or representative of record as *exclusive* agent for the service of most documents. Form NLRB–4813 is used for this purpose. (See Exhibit 17.) This form must be signed by the party (not by the designated representative) and remains in effect until revoked in writing. If an exclusive agent is designated, all documents and written communications, with the exception of charges, amended charges, and subpoenas, will be served only on the agent and not on the party.[78]

§12.9   Charges Receiving Priority

The statute assigns priorities to the processing of certain types of cases.[79] Thus, in each regional office priority over all other cases will be given to the investigation of charges in the following order:

- Sections 8(b)(4)(A), (B), and (C) cases;
- Section 8(b)(4)(D) cases involving Section 10(l) injunctive relief;[80]
- Section 8(b)(7) cases, including petitions under Section 8(b)(7)(C) and Section 9(c), and charges affecting the disposition of Section 8(b)(7) cases or petitions;
- Section 8(e) cases;
- Section 8(a)(3) cases; and
- Section 8(b)(2) cases.

In determining processing priorities within the six categories, the particular facts of the case including the filing date, nature of

---

[76]NLRB Casehandling Manual ¶10040.4.

[77]*Id.* at ¶10026.

[78]*Id.* at ¶10040.6.

[79]Secs. 10(l), (m).

[80]Whether or not to pursue Sec. 10(l) injunctive relief in Sec. 8(b)(4)(D) cases is discretionary with the General Counsel. When such relief is sought (usually when there is a work stoppage) it is treated as a statutory priority case. When injunctive relief is not pursued, the Sec. 8(b)(4)(D) charge is not given statutory priority and it is investigated in accordance with the Board's normal investigative priorities. NLRB Casehandling Manual ¶11740.2.

FORM NLRB-4541
(5-80)

NATIONAL LABOR RELATIONS BOARD

NOTICE: PARTIES INVOLVED IN AN INVESTIGATION OF AN UNFAIR LABOR PRACTICE CHARGE SHOULD BE AWARE OF THE FOLLOWING PROCEDURES:

Right to be represented by counsel · Any party has the right to be represented by counsel or other representative in any proceeding before the National Labor Relations Board and the courts. In the event you wish to have a representative appear on your behalf, please have your representative complete Form NLRB-4701, Notice of Appearance, and forward it to the respective regional office as soon as counsel is chosen.

Designation of representative as agent for service of documents · In the event you choose to have a representative appear on your behalf, you may also, if you so desire, use Form NLRB-4813 to designate that representative as your agent to receive exclusive service on your behalf of all formal documents and written communications in the proceeding, excepting charges and amended charges, and further excepting subpoenas which are served on the person to whom they are addressed. If this form is not filed, both you and your representative will receive copies of all formal documents, including complaints, orders, and decisions. If it is filed, copies will be served only on your representative, and that service will be considered service on you under the statute. The designation, once filed, shall remain valid unless a written revocation is filed with the Regional Director.

Impartial investigation to determine whether charge has merit · Immediately upon receipt of a charge, the regional office conducts an impartial investigation to obtain all the facts which are material and relevant to the charge. In order to determine whether the charge has merit, the Region interviews the available witnesses. Your active cooperation in making witnesses available and stating your position will be most helpful to the Region.

The Region seeks evidence from all parties. Naturally, if only the charging party cooperates in the investigation, a situation results whereby the evidence presented by the charging party may warrant the issuance of a complaint, in the absence of any explanation from the party charged with having violated the law. Where evidence of meritorious defenses is made available a number of cases are withdrawn or dismissed. Your active cooperation will result in disposing of the case at the earliest possible time, whether the case has merit or not.

If the charge lacks merit, charging party has opportunity to withdraw · If it is determined that the charge lacks merit, the charging party is offered the opportunity to withdraw it. Should the charging party refuse to withdraw the charge, the Regional Director dismisses the charge, advising the charging party of its right to appeal the dismissal to the General Counsel.

If the charge has merit, the matter may be voluntarily adjusted · If the Regional Director determines that the charge has merit, all parties are afforded an opportunity to settle the matter by voluntary adjustment. It is the policy of this office to explore and encourage voluntary adjustment before proceeding with litigation before the Board and courts, which is both costly and time consuming. The Regional Director and members of the staff are always available to discuss adjustment of the case at any stage and will be pleased to receive and act promptly upon any suggestions or comments concerning settlements.

Voluntary adjustments after issuance of complaint · If settlement is not obtained, the Regional Director will issue a complaint which is the basis for litigating the matter before the Board and courts. However, issuance of a complaint does not mean that the matter cannot still be disposed of through voluntary adjustment by the parties. On the contrary, at any stage of the proceeding the Regional Director and staff will be pleased to render any assistance in arriving at an appropriate settlement, thereby eliminating the necessity of costly and time-consuming litigation.

GPO 672 956

Exhibit 70.   Statement of Procedures in Unfair Labor Practice Proceedings (Form NLRB-4541)

the allegations, impact upon the parties and the public, as well as relief sought all are taken into consideration. Cases in which Section 10(l) or 10(j) injunctive relief will be sought receive top priority.[81]

As a matter of policy, the General Counsel processes charges not accorded statutory priority in the following order:

- Other unfair labor practice charges in which Section 10(j) injunctive relief is sought;
- Other Section 8(b)(4)(D) charges;
- Unfair labor practice charges which are "blocking" an election;
- Cases in which a work stoppage or lockout related to the charge or petition is in effect or is imminent;
- Representation cases involving a schism;
- Other representation cases including deauthorization proceedings seeking revocation of union security provisions; and
- All other unfair labor practice cases.[82]

§12.10   Investigation

The Board agent commences the investigation of the charge as quickly as possible after it is assigned, generally within seven days. Under current time targets regional directors attempt to complete the investigation and reach a determination regarding disposition of the charge within 30 days of filing.[83] Most regional directors adhere closely to the time targets and grant extensions to the parties for the submission of evidence to the Board agent only in exceptional circumstances.

The scope of the investigation is determined by the allegations in the charge as modified by any subsequent amendments. In the event that the investigation discloses evidence of violations not encompassed by the charge allegations, they may not be investigated further absent a new or amended charge.[84] Evidence of probable violations of statutes other than the National Labor Relations Act will not be investigated but may be referred to appropriate enforcement agencies.[85]

The investigation consists of interviews with parties and witnesses by one or more Board agents.[86] The investigation is not limited

---

[81]NLRB Casehandling Manual ¶11740.1.

[82]*Id.* at ¶11740.2.

[83]The current time goals for processing priority and non-priority unfair labor practice cases and summary judgment Sec. 8(a)(5) cases are set forth in ¶10051 of the Casehandling Manual and are reproduced in Appendix G.

[84]NLRB Casehandling Manual ¶10054.2.

[85]*Id.* at ¶10054.3. Incidents of obstruction of justice or perjury on the part of persons involved in Board proceedings may be referred to the Department of Justice for consideration. *Id.* at ¶10054.5.

[86]*See generally* NLRB Casehandling Manual ¶10056. If necessary to conduct a thorough investigation, the Board agent may request that the regional director issue an investigative subpoena. NLRB Casehandling Manual ¶¶11770–11770.3.

to witnesses suggested by the parties but may include anyone the agent feels may shed light on the charges. If a party is represented by counsel, the Board generally permits counsel to be present during the interview of the party or any supervisor or agent whose testimony would be binding on the party.[87] In the case of a charging party, the right to have counsel present must be requested.[88] Where a charged party is cooperating with the investigation, counsel may be notified of the interview by the Board agent and afforded an opportunity to be present.[89] In all situations, however, the privilege is contingent upon counsel refraining from interfering with, delaying, or otherwise impeding the Board agent's investigation.

The right of a party to have counsel attend witness interviews does not extend to former supervisors or to other individuals whose statements and actions are not binding on the party.[90] Moreover, a Board agent may receive information from a supervisor or agent without notifying counsel if the individual comes forward voluntarily and specifically requests that counsel not be present.[91]

Requests by nonagent witnesses to have their own counsel or other representative present during an interview generally are granted so long as the interview is not delayed or otherwise hampered.[92] Such requests normally will not be granted, however, when the witnesses' counsel or representative also represents one of the parties. In such instances the regional director has the option of either proceeding with the interview with counsel present, or cancelling the interview and informing the witness that documentary evidence or a written statement may be submitted for consideration.[93]

Board agents generally will attempt to incorporate the statements of all witnesses into sworn affidavits.[94] The charging party ordinarily assists the agent in every way possible in the investigation. In part this is an attempt to persuade the regional director the case has merit but, also, lack of cooperation is sufficient reason for the director to dismiss the charge summarily.[95]

The case of the party charged is somewhat different. Those attorneys who practice before the Board have widely varying views as to the extent they will cooperate in the investigation when they

---

[87]*Id.* at ¶10056.1 (charging party) and ¶10056.5 (charged party).

[88]*Id.* at ¶10056.1.

[89]*Id.* at ¶10056.5. In *Aeroglastics, Inc.*, 228 NLRB 1157, 95 LRRM 1095 (1977), the employer filed a motion to strike the testimony of one of its supervisors on the basis that the Board agent interviewed the supervisor without affording an opportunity for the employer's counsel to be present as required by the Casehandling Manual. The motion was denied on the basis that the Manual confers no substantive legal rights and the employer was not prejudiced by the noncompliance. *See also Montgomery Ward & Co.*, 187 NLRB 956, 76 LRRM 1195 (1971).

[90]NLRB Casehandling Manual ¶10056.5; *cf. Central Freight Lines, Inc. v. NLRB*, 653 F.2d 1023, 108 LRRM 2457 (5th Cir. 1981).

[91]NLRB Casehandling Manual ¶10056.5.

[92]*Id.* at ¶10056.2.

[93]*Id.*

[94]*Id.* at ¶10058.2.

[95]*Id.* at ¶10056.1.

represent the party charged. No single rule applies in every case. The principle to be kept in mind is that the Board agent is acting as an impartial investigator at this stage of the case. If the investigation discloses no merit to the charges, the case will be withdrawn or dismissed. A refusal to cooperate means that this decision will be based on facts developed primarily from the charging party. When it is recognized that a substantial majority of charges filed are found to be without merit as a result of the investigation, it obviously is to the advantage of the party charged that the regional director have an accurate understanding of facts favorable to that party. On the other hand, if a complaint issues, the impartial investigator becomes the prosecutor. Any information turned over during the investigation may be used against the respondent.

If the legal issues involved in the case are either novel or complex, parties should submit their views of the law to the regional office, orally or in writing or both. Frequently, it is advisable to ask for a meeting with the regional director and the director's principal advisors. In the pressure of other work or of meeting case-handling deadlines, facts and legal principles which a party feels are significant may be overlooked by the agent responsible for the investigation. Personal contact with the supervisory staff avoids such omissions.

In particularly difficult cases where the file has been referred to Washington for "advice," such contacts should be made with the General Counsel in Washington, D.C.[96] Parties often are not informed of the referral but, where the regional director does not make final disposition of a charge within 30 days after it is filed, it usually has been sent to Washington for advice.

Disposition of Charges

Upon completion of the investigation, the charge may be disposed of informally, or the regional office may institute formal proceedings. Informal dispositions include withdrawal by the charging party, dismissal or deferral by the regional director, and adjustment by the parties. Withdrawals and dismissals are discussed in this chapter; deferrals and voluntary adjustments are discussed in chapters 13 and 14, respectively.

§12.11 Withdrawal

Withdrawals may be solicited or unsolicited.[97] Where the investigation reveals no violation of the statute or a lack of jurisdiction by the

---

[96]The Division of Advice is discussed at §2.5(b).

[97]*See generally* NLRB Statements of Procedure §101.5 and NLRB Casehandling Manual ¶10120.

Board, the agent will ask the charging party to withdraw the charge. The charging party also is notified that absent withdrawal the charge will be dismissed. If the charge is withdrawn, the party charged is immediately notified by the regional office and the case is closed.

A charging party may, on his or her own initiative, ask to withdraw the charge. However, pursuant to the Board's rules, a "charge may be withdrawn, prior to the hearing, only with the consent of the regional director with whom such charge was filed."[98] The reason for the requirement is that once a charge is filed the General Counsel proceeds not in the vindication of private rights, but as representative of an agency entrusted with the authority and responsibility of enforcing a statute in which the public has an interest.[99] An adjustment by the parties which does not remedy the indicated unfair labor practices, or which is contrary to the public interest, may not be accepted as a basis for withdrawal of a charge. For example, the Board will not recognize a private settlement in which an employer attempts to buy release from unfair labor practice charges by payment of money, nor will withdrawal be permitted where the investigation has disclosed violent conduct by the party charged.[100]

Once the charge is withdrawn with the consent of the regional director, it cannot be revived; it is as if that charge had never been filed. Accordingly, where a charge is refiled, the six-month limitation applies with respect to the date of the refiling and not the filing date of the charge which was withdrawn.[101]

§12.12 Dismissal

If a charge is not withdrawn upon request the regional director may refuse to issue a formal complaint, thereby, in effect, dismissing the charge.[102] The charging party is notified of the dismissal by letter and copies are sent to all interested parties and their counsel. The reasons for the dismissal are stated with sufficient particularity that the charging party may, if desired, direct an appeal to the dispositive aspects of the dismissal.[103] (See Exhibit 71.)

There are numerous reasons why a charge might be dismissed. Among the more common reasons are: (1) legal insufficiency of details

---

[98]NLRB Rules and Regulations §102.9.

[99]*Community Medical Servs.*, 236 NLRB 853, 98 LRRM 1314 (1978).

[100]NLRB Casehandling Manual ¶10120.4. On the other hand, regional directors should not reject the terms of a private settlement and proceed with a complaint in instances where the dispute does not involve broad policy issues, the proposed settlement is acceptable to all parties, and the public interest is better served by encouraging voluntary settlement of disputes than in proceeding with litigation. *Texaco, Inc.*, 273 NLRB No. 164, 118 LRRM 1160 (1985).

[101]NLRB Casehandling Manual ¶10120.5; *see also Winer Motors, Inc.*, 265 NLRB 1457, 112 LRRM 1175 (1982), and discussion at §12.6 *supra*.

[102]*See generally* NLRB Statements of Procedure §101.6 and NLRB Casehandling Manual ¶10122.

[103]NLRB Casehandling Manual ¶10122.3.

NATIONAL LABOR RELATIONS BOARD

REGION 5

Candler Building - 4th Floor

109 Market Place

Baltimore, MD   21202

February 2, 1986

Ms. Jean Jones, Business Agent
Local 007
United Computer Operators International Union
P.O. Box 10
Arlington, VA 22207

> Re: Janco Computer Services, Inc.
>   Case No. 5-CA-1234

Dear Ms. Jones:

The above-captioned case charging a violation under Section 8 of the
National Labor Relations Act, as amended, has been carefully investigated
and considered.

As a result of the investigation, it appears that, because there is
insufficient evidence of violation [a summary report setting forth the
reasons for dismissal will be included here in the dismissal letter if the
charging party desires it], further proceedings are not warranted at this
time. I am, therefore, refusing to issue a complaint in this matter.

Pursuant to the National Labor Relations Board Rules and Regulations
Section 102.19 you may obtain a review of this action by filing a request
for such review with the General Counsel of the National Labor Relations
Board, Washington, D.C. 20570, and a copy with me. This request must
contain a complete statement setting forth the facts and reasons upon which
it is based. The request must be received by the General Counsel in
Washington, D.C., by the close of business on [date]. Upon good cause
shown, however, the General Counsel may grant special permission for a
longer period within which to file. A copy of any such request should be
submitted to me.

Very truly yours,

Louis J. D'Amico
Regional Director

cc: General Counsel
     National Labor Relations Board
     Washington, D.C. 20570

     Janco Computer Services, Inc.
     8181 Greensboro Drive
     McLean, VA 22102

**Exhibit 71.   Letter Informing Parties of Regional Director's Refusal to Issue
Complaint**

on the face of the charge, (2) lack of cooperation by the charging party, (3) apparent lack of Board jurisdiction under current standards, (4) charge not timely filed, (5) insufficient evidence to support the charge allegations, (6) unilateral settlement with the charged party which would effectuate the policies of the Act, and (7) the alleged unlawful conduct is isolated in nature and formal proceedings thus are unnecessary.[104] In the absence of a timely appeal by the charging party, the case is closed upon issuance of a dismissal letter by the regional director.

The charging party has 14 days from service of the dismissal letter within which to appeal a regional director's refusal to issue a complaint.[105] In cases where an election has been directed or where charges relating to a Section 8(b)(7) proceeding are dismissed, an appeal must be filed within seven days.[106] The appeal is filed with the General Counsel in Washington, D.C., and a copy is served on the regional director. (See Exhibit 72.) In addition, Notice of Appeal forms (see Exhibit 73) are used by the charging party to notify the other parties that an appeal has been filed.[107] A request for an extension of time to file an appeal must be in writing and received by the General Counsel, with a copy served on the regional director, prior to the expiration of the filing period. Consideration of an appeal which is untimely filed is within the discretion of the General Counsel upon good cause shown.[108]

The General Counsel will provide all parties with an acknowledgment of the filing of the appeal along with any ruling on a request for an extension of time to appeal.[109] The General Counsel does not as a matter of routine practice disclose the contents of appeals to the charged party. Upon specific request, however, the General Counsel may furnish the charged party with a copy of the appeal after deleting the names of certain witnesses and other information considered to be confidential.[110]

The appeal should contain a complete statement setting forth the facts and reasons upon which it is based. The appeal is processed by the General Counsel's staff in Washington and is decided on the record forwarded by the regional director,[111] the information in the

---

[104]*Id.* at 10122.2.

[105]NLRB Rules and Regulations §102.19(a); NLRB Statements of Procedure §101.6; NLRB Casehandling Manual ¶10122.4.

[106]NLRB Rules and Regulations §102.81(a) (directed elections) and §102.81(c) (Section 8(b)(7) proceedings).

[107]NLRB Rules and Regulations §102.19(a); NLRB Casehandling Manual ¶10122.4 (failure of charging party to notify other parties of appeal shall not affect validity of appeal).

[108]NLRB Rules and Regulations §102.19(a); *North Elec. Co.*, 233 NLRB 1017, 93 LRRM 1203 (1977).

[109]NLRB Rules and Regulations §102.19(a); NLRB Casehandling Manual ¶¶10122.4, 10122.10.

[110]Letter from NLRB General Counsel John S. Irving to Arthur Heitzer, Esq. (November 16, 1977).

[111]In some instances the case may be remanded to the regional director for additional investigation. NLRB Casehandling Manual ¶10122.13.

FORM NLRB-4938
(11-80)

UNITED STATES OF AMERICA

NATIONAL LABOR RELATIONS BOARD

PROCEDURES FOR FILING AN APPEAL

Pursuant to the National Labor Relations Board Rules and Regulations you may obtain a review of this action by FILING AN APPEAL WITH THE GENERAL COUNSEL of the National Labor Relations Board, Washington, D.C. 20570, AND A COPY WITH ME. This appeal must contain a complete statement setting forth the facts and reasons upon which it is based. The appeal must be received by the General Counsel in Washington, D.C. by the close of business on _____. Upon good cause shown, however, the General Counsel may grant special permission for a longer period within which to file. A copy of any such request for extension of time should be submitted to me.

If you file an appeal, please complete the notice forms enclosed with the attached letter and send one copy of the form to each of the other parties whose names and addresses are listed. The notice forms should be mailed at the same time you file the appeal, but mailing the notice forms does not relieve you of the necessity for filing the appeal itself with the General Counsel and a copy of the appeal to me within the time stated above.

GPO 883-927

Exhibit 72. Procedures for Filing an Appeal From Regional Director's Dismissal of Charge (Form NLRB-4938)

FORM NLRB-4767
(1-83)

UNITED STATES OF AMERICA
NATIONAL LABOR RELATIONS BOARD

NOTICE OF APPEAL

Date:

To:

Please be advised that an appeal is being taken to the General Counsel of the National Labor Relations Board from the action of the Regional Director in refusing to issued a complaint on the charge in Case Name(s)

Case No. _____ . *(If more than one case number, include all case numbers in which appeal is taken.)*

_____
(Signature)

**Exhibit 73.   Notice of Appeal From Regional Director's Dismissal of Charge
(Form NLRB-4767)**

appeal itself, and any facts or argument submitted by the party charged. While parties are not encouraged to present their positions to the General Counsel personally, a party wishing to do so may request an appointment.[112] Where this is done, the party will, at a minimum, have an opportunity to present its views of the facts and the law to high-ranking members of the General Counsel's staff. Though referred to as "oral arguments" these are, in fact, informal discussions. Other parties are not present but, where one party is granted such argument, other parties are then given a similar opportunity.[113] In complex cases, a personal interview with the General Counsel or staff is frequently well worth the time and expense involved. The General Counsel has final authority over issuance of the complaint and is not limited in any way by the action of the regional director.

After a review of the case, the General Counsel may reverse the regional director and direct that an unfair labor practice complaint be issued or may uphold the regional director's refusal to proceed— thereby dismissing the case.[114] The General Counsel's refusal to issue a complaint is final; it is not subject to court review.[115] However, the charging party may file a motion for reconsideration of the decision if it states with particularity the error requiring reconsideration and it is filed within 14 days of the service of the decision.[116] The General Counsel may accept motions for reconsideration which are filed beyond the 14-day period so long as they are filed within the Section 10(b) six-month limitations period.[117]

Dismissed charges remain alive during the pendency of an appeal.[118] Thus, when only some of the allegations in a charge are dismissed and a complaint is issued on the meritorious allegations, if an appeal is filed concerning the dismissed allegations a hearing cannot be held on the complaint until after the disposition of the appeal.[119] Similarly, when there are closely related charges filed such as 8(a)(5)/8(b)(3) or 8(b)(7)/8(a)(5) violations, and merit is found in one charge but not in the other, issuance of a complaint generally will be withheld until after the time for filing an appeal has expired or until after the appeal has been decided.[120]

An appeal to the General Counsel from the regional director's refusal to issue a complaint generally will not suspend processing of

---

[112]NLRB Rules and Regulations §102.19(b).

[113]*Id.*

[114]*Id.* at §102.19(c).

[115]*Machinists v. Lubbers,* 681 F.2d 598, 110 LRRM 2977 (9th Cir. 1982); *Pacific Southwest Airlines, Inc. v. NLRB,* 587 F.2d 1032, 103 LRRM 2431 (9th Cir. 1980); *see also Rockford Ready-Mix Co. v. Zipp,* 482 F. Supp. 489, 103 LRRM 2363 (N.D. Ill. 1979) (mandamus action will not lie against regional director to force issuance of complaint).

[116]NLRB Rules and Regulations §102.19(c).

[117]*Ducane Heating Corp.,* 273 NLRB No. 175, 118 LRRM 1145 (1985). See discussion at §12.6 *supra.*

[118]*St. Luke's Mem. Hosp., Inc. v. NLRB,* 623 F.2d 1173, 104 LRRM 2788 (7th Cir. 1980); *Fluid Packaging Co.,* 247 NLRB 1469, 103 LRRM 1415 (1980).

[119]NLRB Casehandling Manual ¶10122.5.

[120]*Id.*

a representation or a decertification petition while the appeal is pending.[121] Thus, the regional director will conduct an election while an unfair labor practice appeal is pending before the General Counsel even though the party appealing is a union appearing on the election ballot. If the charges on appeal involve allegations of 8(a)(2), (a)(5), (b)(3) or (b)(7) violations, Board approval must be secured before an election can be conducted.[122]

---

[121]NLRB Casehandling Manual ¶11730.2.
[122]*Id.*

13

Deferral of Charges to Arbitration

Where an unfair labor practice charge is filed by a party to a collective bargaining agreement which contains a binding grievance arbitration procedure, the General Counsel may "defer" the charge for resolution through the contractual procedure. Similarly, where an unfair labor practice charge is brought after an arbitrator has issued an award in the same matter, the Board may defer to that award.

Deferral to arbitration is not automatic, however. It is purely a matter of Board discretion. Section 10(a) of the Act provides that the Board's power to adjudicate unfair labor practices "shall not be affected by any other means of adjustment or prevention that has been or may be established by agreement." The fact that the same conduct which constitutes an unfair labor practice may also constitute a breach of a collective bargaining agreement does not deprive the Board of jurisdiction or require it to defer.[1]

The Supreme Court has endorsed the Board's deferral policies.[2] While the Court has rejected deferral to arbitration with respect to claims brought under Title VII of the Civil Rights Act of 1964,[3] the Fair Labor Standards Act,[4] and the Civil Rights Act of 1871 (Section 1983),[5] it recently reaffirmed its support for deferral under the National Labor Relations Act.[6]

---

[1]*NLRB v. Strong Roofing & Insulating Co.*, 393 U.S. 357, 70 LRRM 2100 (1969); *see also NLRB v. C & C Plywood Corp.*, 385 U.S. 421, 64 LRRM 2065 (1967).

[2]*NLRB v. City Disposal Sys., Inc.*, 465 U.S. 822, 115 LRRM 3193 (1984); *William E. Arnold Co. v. Carpenters Dist. Council*, 417 U.S. 12, 86 LRRM 2212 (1974).

[3]*Alexander v. Gardner-Denver Co.*, 415 U.S. 36, 7 FEP Cases 81 (1974).

[4]*Barrentine v. Arkansas-Best Freight Sys., Inc.*, 450 U.S. 728, 24 WH Cases 1284 (1981).

[5]*McDonald v. City of West Branch*, 466 U.S. 284, 115 LRRM 3646 (1984).

[6]*NLRB v. City Disposal Sys., Inc.*, 465 U.S. 822, 115 LRRM 3193 (1984). Justice Brennan wrote both the *City Disposal* and *McDonald* opinions, which were issued within a month of one another.

The Board has established policies for deferral of charges to the contractual procedure before actual arbitration proceedings have commenced, after arbitration proceedings have begun but before a resolution is reached, and subsequent to the arbitrator's rendering a final decision. The criteria for deferral differ with respect to each of these stages, and will be examined separately here.

Pre-Arbitral Deferral

In deferring a charge before arbitration commences, the regional director holds the case in abeyance while the parties use their grievance arbitration machinery to resolve the dispute. In *Collyer Insulated Wire*,[7] the Board established that so long as certain requirements were met it would defer to grievance arbitration procedures in Section 8(a)(5) cases even though those procedures had yet to begin. The deferral requirements are that the parties have a long-standing collective bargaining relationship, there is no "enmity" on the part of the employer toward employees' exercise of protected rights, the employer indicates its willingness to arbitrate, the contract's arbitration clause covers the dispute before the Board, and the contract and its meaning lie at the center of the dispute.[8]

The Board subsequently extended its policy of pre-arbitral deferral to cover charges brought under Sections 8(a)(1) and 8(a)(3) of the Act.[9] The Board further extended its deferral policy to cases involving allegations of Section 8(b)(1)(A),[10] 8(b)(1)(B),[11] 8(b)(2),[12] and 8(b)(3)[13] violations. In 1977 the Board cut back its deferral policy to cover only Section 8(a)(5) and 8(b)(3) cases.[14] The Board removed this restriction in 1984 in *United Technologies Corp.*, restoring its policy of deferral in the full range of cases noted above.[15]

Before a charge will be deferred, both the criteria outlined by the Board in its *Collyer* and *United Technologies* decisions and certain procedural requirements must be met. A discussion of these prerequisites follows.

---

[7]192 NLRB 837, 77 LRRM 1931 (1971).

[8]*Id.*

[9]*National Radio Co.*, 198 NLRB 527, 80 LRRM 1718 (1972).

[10]*Teamsters Local 70 (National Biscuit Co.)*, 198 NLRB 552, 80 LRRM 1727 (1972).

[11]*Columbia Typographical Union 101 (Washington Post Co.)*, 207 NLRB 831, 85 LRRM 1018 (1973).

[12]*Newspaper Guild (Enterprise Pub. Co.)*, 201 NLRB 793, 82 LRRM 1337 (1973).

[13]*Teamsters Local 70 (National Biscuit Co.)*, 198 NLRB 552, 80 LRRM 1727 (1972).

[14]*General American Transp. Corp.*, 228 NLRB 808, 94 LRRM 1483 (1977).

[15]*United Technologies Corp.*, 268 NLRB 557, 115 LRRM 1049 (1984). The Board has refused to defer Section 8(a)(4) cases contending that "the duty to preserve the Board's process from abuse is a function of this Board and may not be delegated to the parties or to an arbitrator." *Filmation Assoc.*, 227 NLRB 1721, 94 LRRM 1470, 1471 (1977); *see also International Harvester Co.*, 271 NLRB 647, 117 LRRM 1075 (1984).

§13.1 Timeliness

A request for pre-arbitral deferral must be raised before or during the unfair labor practice hearing.[16] Requests for deferral that are first raised in the posthearing brief to the administrative law judge[17] or in a party's exceptions to the administrative law judge's decision[18] will be denied.

§13.2 The Parties' Bargaining Relationship

The Board in *Collyer* indicated that deferral is appropriate where the parties enjoy "a long and productive collective bargaining relationship."[19] A bargaining relationship short in duration, however, will not in itself preclude deferral. The Board has deferred disputes arising soon after the first collective bargaining agreement between the parties has gone into effect.[20]

The Board has refused to defer, however, where it finds an employer's conduct constitutes a rejection of the principles of collective bargaining and the self-organizational rights of employees.[21] Thus, where an employer has repudiated its bargaining agreements,[22] or dealt directly with employees over such changes,[23] or conditioned employment upon nonmembership in a union,[24] deferral has been denied. Nonetheless, if past and present alleged employer misconduct "does not appear to be of such character as to render the use of [arbitration] machinery unpromising or futile," the Board will not reject deferral on the ground of such misconduct alone.[25]

The Board's prior policy has been to refuse deferral where an unfair labor practice charge alleged an employer's interference with the grievance procedure or retaliation against employees for pursuing a grievance through the contractual mechanism.[26] Thus, the Board refused to defer where an employer discharged an employee for attending an arbitration hearing,[27] and where an employer discharged an employee for refusing to abandon a grievance.[28] The Board appears

---

[16]*E.g., Duchess Furniture,* 220 NLRB 13, 90 LRRM 1160 (1975); *Erie Strayer Co.,* 213 NLRB 344, 87 LRRM 1162 (1974).

[17]*James W. Whitfield,* 220 NLRB 507, 90 LRRM 1250 (1975).

[18]*Asbestos Workers, Local 22 (Rosendahl, Inc.),* 212 NLRB 913, 87 LRRM 1604 (1974).

[19]192 NLRB 837, 77 LRRM 1931 (1971).

[20]*L.E.M., Inc. (Southwest Engraving Co.),* 198 NLRB 694, 81 LRRM 1069 (1972); *Coppus Eng'r Corp.,* 195 NLRB 595, 79 LRRM 1449 (1972).

[21]*Mountain State Constr. Co.,* 203 NLRB 1085, 83 LRRM 1208 (1973).

[22]*Id.*

[23]*Texaco, Inc.,* 233 NLRB 375, 96 LRRM 1534 (1977).

[24]*F.S. Willey Co.,* 224 NLRB 1170, 92 LRRM 1589 (1976).

[25]*United Aircraft Corp.,* 204 NLRB 879, 83 LRRM 1411 (1972).

[26]*Joseph T. Ryerson & Sons, Inc.,* 199 NLRB 461, 81 LRRM 1261 (1972).

[27]*Anthony Co.,* 220 NLRB 886, 90 LRRM 1373 (1975).

[28]*North Shore Pub. Co.,* 206 NLRB 42, 84 LRRM 1165 (1973).

to have relaxed this policy somewhat in its decision in *United Technologies Corp.* In that case the Board ruled that deferral was proper where the unfair labor practice complaint concerned an employer's harassment and intimidation of an employee in an attempt to induce her to withdraw her grievance. It is therefore presently unclear whether the Board will adopt a new policy of deferring Section 8(a)(3) charges involving employer interference with employees' use of contractual grievance procedures or hold fast to its prior policy of declining to defer such cases.[29]

The Board additionally will refuse to defer if the union will not protect or actively advocate the charging party's interest, or is hostile to the charging party or his or her cause. Thus, the Board has refused to defer unfair labor practice charges alleging union discrimination in job referrals,[30] or that a union caused an employee's discharge.[31]

§13.3   The Parties' Willingness to Arbitrate

All parties to a dispute must be willing to submit it to arbitration before the regional director will defer. A party's willingness to arbitrate will not be presumed.[32] Should a party refuse, in response to the regional director's inquiry, to promise unconditionally to proceed to arbitration, the matter will not be deferred.[33] The Board also will refuse deferral where the employer is not willing to waive the procedural defense that a grievance was not timely filed.[34] Furthermore, deferral will be denied in cases where the union declines to take an employee's grievance to arbitration, since in such a case the employee would be deprived of the right to seek redress of a statutory wrong.[35]

---

[29]*See United States Postal Serv.*, 271 NLRB 1297, 117 LRRM 1184 (1984) (employer did not render grievance/arbitration machinery "unpromising or futile" by unilaterally altering location, size, and physical arrangement of stewards' work area; refusing to permit stewards access to typing facilities; denying stewards forms necessary to leave work stations to perform union duties; and permitting only one steward at a time in the stewards' work area); *United States Postal Serv.*, 270 NLRB 1022, 116 LRRM 1206 (1984) (employer refusal to accord precedential value to prior grievance resolution does not constitute renunciation of entire bargaining process where decision based on employer's view of merits of current grievance, not rejection of applicability of arbitration process). *But see* NLRB General Counsel Memorandum No. 84-5, *Guideline Memorandum Concerning United Technologies Corporation* 2–3 (March 6, 1984), reprinted at 1984 LAB. REL. YRBK. (BNA) 344, suggesting that the Board in *United Technologies* reaffirmed earlier principles that deferral is appropriate only where there exists "a workable and freely resorted to grievance procedure." (Copies of the General Counsel memorandum may be obtained from the Board's Information Division.)

[30]*Electrical Workers (IBEW) Local 367*, 230 NLRB 86, 96 LRRM 1182 (1977).

[31]*Machinists Lodge 1129*, 219 NLRB 1019, 90 LRRM 1040 (1975); *Machinists Lodge 68*, 205 NLRB 132, 84 LRRM 1030 (1973).

[32]NLRB General Counsel Memorandum No. 73-17, *Arbitration Deferral Policy Under Collyer—Revised Guidelines* 17 (May 10, 1973). Copies may be acquired from the Board's Information Division.

[33]*Id.* at 15-18.

[34]*Southern Fla. Hotel & Motor Ass'n*, 245 NLRB 561, 102 LRRM 1578 (1979); *Pilot Freight Carriers, Inc.*, 224 NLRB 341, 92 LRRM 1338 (1976).

[35]NLRB General Counsel Memorandum No. 84-5, *supra* n. 29 at 5.

The arbitration procedure must be final and binding upon the parties.[36] The arbitrator must be a neutral figure, not involved in the incident leading to the grievance.[37] The fact that the final step in the grievance procedure is a hearing before a bipartite panel, rather than before an arbitrator, however, will not necessarily cause the Board to refuse deferral.[38]

§13.4 Contractual Coverage of the Dispute

The collective bargaining agreement and its arbitration provision must "clearly encompass" the dispute in order to be deferrable.[39] If no interpretation of a contract clause is involved in the unfair labor practice claim, the Board will not defer to arbitration.[40] Similarly, if the dispute concerns a contractual issue but does not fall within the contract's arbitration clause, the Board will refuse to defer.[41]

In cases where *all* unfair labor practice allegations cannot be disposed of by an arbitrator, the Board may decline to defer. This is because one of the chief rationales behind deferral is the desire to avoid litigation of the same issues in multiple forums.[42] Where, however, the Board must decide a part of the dispute, deferral would create and not eliminate litigation in multiple forums.[43]

Similarly, all parties to the unfair labor practice case must be able to participate in arbitration proceedings for deferral to occur. In cases where third parties, not bound by the contract that provides for arbitration of disputes, are involved in an unfair labor practice claim, the Board will not defer to contractual arbitration procedures. This frequently occurs in cases involving secondary boycotts, "hot cargo" agreements prohibited by Section 8(e) of the Act,[44] and cases where an employer repudiates a contract with one union in favor of other unions.[45]

---

[36]*Wheeler Constr. Co.*, 219 NLRB 541, 90 LRRM 1173 (1975).

[37]*Westinghouse Elec. Corp.*, 206 NLRB 812, 84 LRRM 1580 (1973).

[38]*Teamsters, Local 70 (National Biscuit Co.)*, 198 NLRB 552, 80 LRRM 1727 (1972).

[39]*United Technologies Corp.*, 268 NLRB 557, 115 LRRM 1049 (1984); *Collyer Insulated Wire*, 192 NLRB 837, 77 LRRM 1931 (1971); *see also Atlas Tack Corp.*, 226 NLRB 222, 93 LRRM 1236 (1976); *Operating Engineers Local 400 (Hilde Constr. Co.)*, 225 NLRB 596, 92 LRRM 1494 (1976).

[40]*Struthers Wells Corp.*, 245 NLRB 1170, 102 LRRM 1484 (1979); *Meilman Food Indus., Inc.*, 234 NLRB 698, 97 LRRM 1372 (1978). For this reason, the Board's deferral policy does not apply to intra-union disputes between unions and their members. *Teamsters Local 519 (Rust Engineering Co.)*, 275 NLRB No. 68, 119 LRRM 1143 (1985); *see also Electrical Workers (IBEW) Local 702 (Central Illinois Public Serv. Co.)*, 274 NLRB No. 189, 118 LRRM 1528 (1985) (Member Hunter concurring).

[41]*Machinists, Dist. 10 (Ladish Co.)*, 200 NLRB 1159, 82 LRRM 1081 (1972).

[42]*Sheet Metal Workers' Local 17 (George Koch Sons, Inc.)*, 199 NLRB 166, 81 LRRM 1195 (1972).

[43]*Id.*

[44]*Masters, Mates & Pilots (Seatrain Lines, Inc.)*, 220 NLRB 164, 90 LRRM 1691 (1975).

[45]*Fenix & Scisson, Inc.*, 207 NLRB 752, 85 LRRM 1380 (1973).

§13.5   Matters Within the Board's Special Expertise

Even though a dispute may involve contractual relations between the parties and fall within the contract's arbitration clause, the Board may still decline to defer if the matter is one traditionally within the Board's expertise, or outside the competence of an arbitrator. Such matters include the following:

(a) Accretions.   The Board will not defer where the dispute involves whether a collective bargaining agreement covers certain additional employees at the employer's facility.[46]

(b) Unit Clarifications.   Controversies over the appropriateness of a bargaining unit, brought as contractual grievances, will not be deferred.[47] The Board has declared that

> "[t]he determination of questions of representation, accretion and appropriate unit do not depend upon contract interpretation but involve the application of the statutory policy standards and criteria."[48]

Since many unit clarification cases involve more than one union claiming representational rights under different contracts, resolution of such cases might lead to multiple conflicting arbitration awards. Thus, the Board has determined that unit clarification proceedings, not arbitrations, are the proper means of resolving such disputes.[49]

(c) Contract Conflicts With the Act.   Where terms of the collective bargaining agreement conflict with provisions of the Act, or where it is unclear whether employees' statutory rights are also covered by the contract, the Board will not defer. For example, in *U.S. Steel Corp.*,[50] the Board refused to defer a dispute over the employer's rule banning all distribution of literature, an activity protected in some cases by Section 7 of the Act, because it was unclear whether employees' Section 7 rights were covered by the contract. The Board additionally will refuse to defer where contract language upon which the arbitrator would rely is illegal.[51]

(d) Compliance With Board Orders.   When a dispute concerns a party's compliance with prior Board orders, the Board will not defer to arbitration, even though the grievance might otherwise

---

[46]*Retail Clerks Local 588 (Raley's, Inc.)*, 224 NLRB 1638, 92 LRRM 1381 (1976). Accretions are discussed at §5.8(e).

[47]*Marion Power Shovel Co.*, 230 NLRB 576, 95 LRRM 1339 (1977).

[48]*Id.*

[49]*Crown Cork & Seal Co.*, 203 NLRB 171, 83 LRRM 1088 (1973). Unit clarification procedures are discussed at §10.16.

[50]223 NLRB 1246, 92 LRRM 1158 (1976).

[51]*Electrical Workers (IBEW) Local 901 (Ernest P. Breaux Elec. Co.)*, 220 NLRB 1236, 90 LRRM 1439 (1975).

be arbitrable. In a case where an employee previously reinstated by Board order was laid off, the Board refused to submit the issue of the employer's compliance with its order to an arbitrator, noting that the matter was one "clearly inappropriate for determination by an arbitrator."[52]

(e) Statutory Issues.   The Board has established that "legal questions concerning the . . . Act . . . are within the special competence of the Board rather than of an arbitrator."[53] Thus, the Board has refused to defer where the issue was whether a contract clause concerned a mandatory subject of bargaining under the Act.[54] Similarly, the Board will not defer disputes over an employer's failure to provide information in the course of bargaining,[55] unless the contract contains a clear and effective waiver of the union's right to the information at issue.[56] This is because the duty to provide information is imposed by Section 8(a)(5) of the Act, and is independent of any contractual obligation.[57]

(f) Arbitrator's Inability to Adequately Remedy Misconduct.   Where it appears that a party would disregard an arbitration award and take unilateral action in violation of Section 8(a)(5) of the Act, the Board will not defer.[58] The Board has likewise refused to defer in cases involving unilateral conduct on the part of a union.[59]

§13.6   Compliance With *Spielberg* Criteria

Should the Board defer an unfair labor practice claim to arbitration, it will retain jurisdiction over the matter to ensure that the dispute is promptly settled or arbitrated, and that the procedural requirements established in *Spielberg Manufacturing Co.*[60] are met. These requirements are discussed thoroughly at §§13.10–13.15 *infra*. If a charge is deferred and these criteria are not met, a party may file a motion with the Board requesting that it exercise its jurisdiction and adjudicate the matter.[61]

---

[52]*Ernst Constr. Div.*, 217 NLRB 1069, 89 LRRM 1233 (1975).

[53]*Columbus Printing Pressmen No. 252 (R.W. Page Co.)*, 219 NLRB 268, 270, 89 LRRM 1553, 1556 (1975).

[54]*Id.*

[55]*St. Joseph's Hosp.*, 233 NLRB 1116, 97 LRRM 1212 (1977); *Worcester Polytechnic Institute*, 213 NLRB 306, 87 LRRM 1616 (1974).

[56]*American Standard, Inc.*, 203 NLRB 1132, 83 LRRM 1245 (1973).

[57]*See NLRB v. Acme Indus. Co.*, 385 U.S. 432, 64 LRRM 2069 (1967).

[58]*Texaco, Inc.*, 233 NLRB 375, 96 LRRM 1534 (1977).

[59]*E.g., Communications Workers (Western Elec. Co.)*, 204 NLRB 782, 83 LRRM 1583 (1973).

[60]112 NLRB 1080, 36 LRRM 1152 (1955).

[61]*Arbitration Deferral Policy Under Collyer—Revised Guidelines, supra* n.32 at 47.

§13.7 Procedures for *Collyer* Deferral

When a region receives a charge alleging a violation of Section 8(a)(1), 8(a)(3), 8(a)(5), 8(b)(1)(A), 8(b)(1)(B), 8(b)(2), or 8(b)(3) of the Act, it will first determine whether the allegations of the charge and evidence submitted by the charging party in support of the charge establish an arguable violation of the Act.[62] If this preliminary investigation does not establish a violation of the Act, the charge will be dismissed.[63]

If an arguable violation is found, the region will then examine the case to determine whether the various criteria for deferral, as described above, are met. The parties will be given notice of this aspect of the investigation and given an opportunity to present evidence and views on the issue.[64] If deferral is found not warranted, the region will conduct a full investigation of the merits of the charge and proceed toward a resolution of the case through dismissal, settlement, or issuance of a complaint.[65]

If the region finds deferral of the charge to be warranted, it will inquire informally whether the respondent is willing to proceed to arbitration and waive any contractual time limits for filing grievances, if applicable.[66] If the respondent expresses a willingness to arbitrate, the region will issue a letter (see Exhibit 74) deferring the charge to arbitration.[67] If the respondent does not indicate a willingness to arbitrate, the Board will proceed with a full investigation of the merits of the charge.[68] If the charge is found to warrant issuance of a complaint, the region will inform the respondent that absent settlement a complaint will issue unless the respondent notifies the region, in writing, within seven calendar days, that it is willing to arbitrate.[69] If the respondent indicates its willingness to arbitrate, the region will defer the charge to arbitration.[70] If the respondent does not indicate its willingness to arbitrate within the seven-day period, the region will proceed with its processing of the charge. Should the respondent later attempt to raise a *Collyer* defense or urge deferral, the region will oppose such a move on the grounds of its untimeliness.[71]

If at any time subsequent to issuance of a complaint the region finds for the first time that grounds for deferral exist, the region will give the respondent an opportunity to express its willingness to ar-

---

[62]*Id.* at 36.
[63]*Id.*
[64]*Id.* at 37.
[65]*Id.* at 41.
[66]*Id.*
[67]*Id.* at 42, 44–45.
[68]*Id.* at 42.
[69]*Id.* at 42–43.
[70]*Id.* at 43.
[71]*Id.*

NATIONAL LABOR RELATIONS BOARD

REGION 5

Candler Building - 4th Floor

109 Market Place

Baltimore, MD   21202

January 2, 1986

Mr. Jack Smith, President   Ms. Jean Jones, Business Agent
Janco Computer Services, Inc.   Local 007, United Computer
8181 Greensboro Drive   Operators International Union
McLean, VA 22102   P.O. Box 10
                                      Arlington, VA 22207

                          Re: Janco Computer Services, Inc.
                               Case No. 5-CA-1235

Dear Mr. Smith and Ms. Jones:

In accordance with the National Labor Relations Board's decisions in
<u>Collyer Insulated Wire, A Gulf and Western System Co.</u>, 192 NLRB 837,
and <u>United Technologies Corporation</u>, 268 NLRB 557, I am declining to
issue a complaint on the instant charge based on my determination that
further proceedings on the charge should be administratively deferred for
arbitration.

My reasons for deferring the charge are as follows:

   1. The charge alleges the Employer violated Section 8(a)(1)
       and (3) of the Act by harassing, threatening and repri-
       manding Mary Hughes and by terminating her on August 28, 1985,
       because of her membership in and activities on behalf of
       Local 007, United Computer Operators International Union.

   2. There is a contract between the parties which provides for
       binding arbitration.

   3. There is substantial likelihood that utilization of the
       contractual arbitration procedure would lay this
       dispute to rest.

   4. On December 23, 1985, this office was notified by the Employer
       in this matter that it is now and for a reasonable period
       will be willing to arbitrate the dispute underlying
       the charge in the above-captioned case, notwithstanding
       any contractual limitation on the processing of the
       grievance to arbitration.

Under Section 102.19 of the National Labor Relations Board's Rules and
Regulations, the Charging Party may obtain a review of my administrative
determination to defer further proceedings on this charge by filing an
appeal with the General Counsel addressed to the Office of Appeals,
National Labor Relations Board, Washington, D. C. 20570, addressing a copy

**Exhibit 74. Letter to Parties Deferring Unfair Labor Practice Charge
to Arbitration**

-2-

of the appeal to this Office. This appeal must contain a complete
statement of the facts and reasons on which it is based. The appeal must
be received by the General Counsel in Washington, D.C., by 5:00 p.m. on
[date]. For good cause shown, however, the General Counsel may grant
special permission to extend the time for filing. A request for an
extension of time to file an appeal must be in writing and received by the
Office of Appeals prior to [date]; a copy of such request should be filed
with this Office. If the General Counsel determines that deferral of this
charge to arbitration is unwarranted, the case will be remanded to me for
appropriate action. But if the General Counsel sustains my decision, the
case will be remanded to me for deferral as set forth herein.

It is also my intention to inquire as to the status of this dispute
periodically, and no later than 90 days hence; and to accept and consider
at any time a request and supporting evidence submitted by any party to
this matter for dismissal of the charge, for continued deferral of
administrative action on the charge, or for issuance of a complaint.

It is my intention to revoke my decision to defer and resume processing of
the charge if the dispute underlying the charge is not promptly settled
or submitted for arbitration, or if the interests of the Charging Party
are otherwise now in conflict with those of both parties to the contract.
See, however, the Board's decision in General Dynamics Corporation,
Quincy Shipbuilding Division, 271 NLRB No. 27, concerning the application
of United Technologies Corporation, 268 NLRB 557, to a situation
where the grievant withdrew his grievance after pursuing almost all of
the steps of the grievance-arbitration procedure.

It is my intention to revoke my decision to defer and to resume processing
of this charge in the event the Employer, by conduct inconsistent with its
expression of a willingness to arbitrate, prevents or impedes the prompt
resolution of the underlying dispute through the contract grievance-
arbitration procedures.

If the dispute underlying the charge is not resolved amicably under the
grievance procedure, and resort to arbitration proves necessary, the
Charging Party may obtain a review of the arbitrator's final award by
addressing a request for review to this Office. The request should be in
writing and contain a statement of the facts and circumstances bearing on
whether the arbitral proceedings were fair and regular; whether the unfair
labor practice issues which gave rise to this charge were considered and
decided by the arbitrator; and whether the award is consonant with the
purposes and policies of the Labor Management Relations Act. Spielberg Manufacturing Company, 112 NLRB 1080, Olin Corporation, 268
NLRB 573.

Very truly yours,

Louis J. D'Amico
Regional Director

CERTIFIED MAIL - RETURN RECEIPT REQUESTED

Exhibit 74—*page 2*

bitrate—first informally, then formally in writing with the seven-day limitation described above. If the respondent expresses its willingness to arbitrate, the region will withdraw the complaint and defer the matter to arbitration.[72]

The charging party may obtain a review of the region's deferral of the charge and refusal to issue a complaint by filing an appeal with the Board's Office of Appeals in Washington, D.C. Such an appeal must be filed within 13 days of the region's issuance of its deferral letter, and must set forth the facts and reasons upon which the appeal is based.[73]

Deferral to Pending Arbitration

In *Dubo Manufacturing Corp.*[74] the Board established a policy under which it will defer the further processing of an unfair labor practice case where the matter in dispute has already been submitted to the parties' contractual grievance arbitration machinery, and there is a "reasonable chance" that such machinery will resolve the dispute.[75] Deferral under *Dubo* may be available even though the prerequisites to *Collyer* deferral (described at §§13.1–13.5 *supra*) are not met. For example, *Dubo* deferral would be appropriate where the collective bargaining agreement's arbitration clause does not cover the instant dispute, but where the parties have entered an *ad hoc* agreement to arbitrate the particular dispute.[76] Similarly, a case could be deferred under *Dubo* in spite of a history of employer enmity toward the exercise of protected rights (which might preclude *Collyer* deferral), if the charging party so chose.[77]

§13.8 Requirements for *Dubo* Deferral

One key difference between deferral under *Dubo* and deferral under *Collyer* is that *Dubo* deferral requires voluntary submission to arbitration by all parties involved (the charging party may be compelled to arbitrate in the *Collyer* setting if all of *Collyer's* prerequisites are met). The charging party cannot be forced to arbitrate and forgo his or her claim before the Board under *Dubo*.[78] Deferral under *Dubo* can occur only after both the employee and the charging

---

[72]*Id.* at 43–44.

[73]*Id.* at 45.

[74]142 NLRB 431, 53 LRRM 1070 (1963).

[75]*Id.*; NLRB General Counsel Memorandum No. 79-36, *Procedures for Application of the Dubo Policy to Pending Charges* 1 (May 14, 1979). Copies may be acquired from the Board's Information Division.

[76]*Arbitration Deferral Policy Under Collyer—Revised Guidelines, supra* n.32 at 39 n.64.

[77]*Id.*

[78]*National Rejectors Indus.*, 234 NLRB 251, 97 LRRM 1142 (1978).

union have been given the opportunity to choose between the contractual grievance arbitration machinery and the Board's processes, and they have voluntarily chosen the former.[79]

Dubo requires that a grievance be pending within the contractual grievance arbitration machinery before deferral may occur.[80] Such a grievance may be at any stage in the contractual machinery, but such machinery must contain a final step consisting of binding arbitration.[81] Where the employee involved chooses not to pursue the grievance but the union continues to process it (if, for example, the dispute involves several employees), the region will still defer to arbitration.[82] Where, however, both the employee and union choose to drop the grievance, or the union wishes to drop the grievance but the employee wants to pursue it, (and cannot do so without the union) there will be no deferral because there would no longer be a pending grievance.[83]

§13.9 Procedures for *Dubo* Deferral

When an unfair labor practice charge is filed, the region will inquire of the parties involved whether the matter in dispute has been submitted to grievance arbitration. If it has not, and does not become subject to grievance arbitration subsequently, the region will process the case in its normal manner. If the matter has been submitted to grievance arbitration, but any investigation conducted by the region discloses that the charge has no merit, the case will be dismissed.[84]

If the charge is determined to have merit, the region will advise both the charging party and the union that they must choose between pursuing the unfair labor practice claim before the Board or pursuing the grievance in arbitration. They will be advised that if they choose to pursue grievance arbitration, processing of the case pending before the Board will abate. They will further be advised that if they choose to pursue their unfair labor practice claim (thus abandoning their grievance) and that claim ultimately is found to be without merit, they may be left without any remedy since they would ordinarily be time-barred from reinvoking the grievance machinery.[85]

---

[79]*Procedures for Application of the Dubo Policy to Pending Charges, supra* n.75 at 2–3; *see Youngstown Sheet & Tube Co.,* 235 NLRB 572, 98 LRRM 1347 (1978) (no deferral where charging party not informed of his right to a Board determination).

[80]*Dubo Mfg. Corp.,* 142 NLRB 431, 53 LRRM 1070 (1963).

[81]*United States Postal Serv.,* 225 NLRB 220, 93 LRRM 1089 (1976); *cf. Youngstown Sheet & Tube Co.,* 235 NLRB 572, 98 LRRM 1347 (1978) (no deferral where matter had not been submitted to arbitration and there was "no particular reason to believe it would be").

[82]NLRB General Counsel Memorandum No. 81-39, *Deferral of Charges Under Dubo Manufacturing* (July 17, 1981). Copies may be acquired from the Board's Information Division.

[83]*Procedures for Application of the Dubo Policy to Pending Charges, supra* n.75 at 3.

[84]*Id.*

[85]*Id.* at 3–4.

If the region defers the case to arbitration, it will nonetheless retain jurisdiction pending completion of the arbitration process, just as in a deferral under *Collyer*. (See Exhibit 75.) The arbitral award will be scrutinized by the region in light of the criteria set out in *Spielberg* (see §§13.10–13.15 *infra*).[86] If the *Spielberg* standards are not met, and the region finds merit in the unfair labor practice charge, a complaint will be issued.[87] Finally, since the consent of the charging party is a prerequisite to *Dubo* deferral, the charging party may not later appeal the region's deferral of the case to arbitration.[88]

Post-Arbitral Deferral

The Board established in *Spielberg Manufacturing Co.* that it will defer to an arbitration award where the issues involved in the unfair labor practice claim are decided by the arbitrator.[89] *Spielberg* established three prerequisites to post-arbitral deferral: (1) the arbitration proceedings must have been "fair and regular," (2) all parties must have agreed to be bound, and (3) the decision of the arbitrator is not "clearly repugnant to the purposes and policies of the Act."[90] In *Raytheon Co.*[91] the Board added a fourth requirement for *Spielberg* deferral: the unfair labor practice issue must have been presented to and considered by the arbitrator. These four requirements are examined in more detail below.

§13.10   Fair and Regular Proceeding

The Board requires that the arbitration proceeding comport with the basic standards of due process, that the arbitrator or panel of arbitrators be neutral, and that in cases of individual employee grievances, the union representative vigorously represent the grievant.

(a) **Due Process.** The grievant must be given notice of the arbitration hearing and sufficient time to prepare his or her case.[92] At the hearing the grievant must be allowed to introduce evidence

---

[86]*Spielberg Mfg. Co.*, 112 NLRB 1080, 36 LRRM 1152 (1955).

[87]*Procedures for Application of the Dubo Policy to Pending Charges, supra* n.75 at 3–4.

[88]*Arbitration Deferral Policy Under Collyer—Revised Guidelines, supra* n.32 at 40–41 n.66.

[89]*Spielberg Mfg. Co.*, 112 NLRB 1080, 36 LRRM 1152 (1955). The Board also will defer to grievance settlements where the deferral standards are met. *Alpha Beta Co.*, 273 NLRB No. 194, 118 LRRM 1202 (1985). In *Spann Building Maintenance Co.*, 275 NLRB No. 135, 119 LRRM 1209 (1985), a Board panel majority deferred to a grievance settlement which was reached with the grievant outside of the grievance process.

[90]*Id.*

[91]140 NLRB 883, 52 LRRM 1129 (1963).

[92]*Gateway Transp. Co.*, 137 NLRB 1763, 50 LRRM 1495 (1962) (two days notice afforded grievant insufficient time to prepare).

NATIONAL LABOR RELATIONS BOARD

REGION 5

Candler Building - 4th Floor

109 Market Place

Baltimore, MD   21202

January 2, 1986

Mr. Jack Smith, President   Ms. Jean Jones, Business Agent
Janco Computer Services, Inc.   Local 007, United Computer Operators
8181 Greensboro Drive   International Union
McLean, VA 22102   P.O. Box 10
                                        Arlington, VA 22207

                     Re: Janco Computer Services, Inc.
                          Case No. 5-CA-1236

Dear Mr. Smith and Ms. Jones:

This office has preliminarily considered the charge in the above-captioned
matter alleging the Employer violated Section 8(a)(1) and (3) of the
National Labor Relations Act, as amended, by denying employee Mary Hughes
overtime because of her membership in and activities on behalf of Local
007, United Computer Operators International Union.

Pursuant to the decision of the National Labor Relations Board in Dubo
Manufacturing Co., 142 NLRB 431, I have determined that further proceedings in this charge should be administratively deferred at this time
for the following reasons:

    1. The grievance covering this matter is being processed
        through the grievance and arbitration procedure.

    2. There is substantial likelihood that utilization of the
        contractual arbitration procedure would lay this
        dispute to rest.

It is my intention to inquire as to the status of this dispute periodically, and no later than 90 days hence; and to accept and consider at any
time a request and supporting evidence submitted by any party to this
matter for consideration of the deferral of action in the charge, or for
issuance of a complaint.

The Charging Party may obtain a review of the arbitrator's award by
addressing a request for review to this Office. The request should be in
writing and contain a statement of the facts and circumstances bearing on
whether the arbitral proceedings were fair and regular, and whether the
award is consonant with the purposes and policies of the Labor Management
Relations Act. Spielberg Manufacturing Company, 112 NLRB 1080;
Olin Corporation, 268 NLRB 573.

                     Very truly yours,

                     Louis J. D'Amico
                     Regional Director

**Exhibit 75.   Letter to Parties Administratively Deferring Unfair Labor
Practice Charge to Pending Arbitration Proceedings**

of the alleged statutory violation,[93] and confront and cross-examine opposing witnesses.[94]

(b) Neutral Arbitrator.   Where the tribunal is unfairly biased against the grievant the Board will not defer. Thus, the Board has not deferred where the number of employer representatives on the tribunal was greater than the number of employee representatives.[95] The Board similarly has refused to defer to bipartite tribunals where both the union and employer have committed unfair labor practices against the grievant,[96] and where the grievant was a dissident union member known for his attacks on both the employer and union.[97] Mere verbal abrasiveness on the part of the arbitrator or tribunal toward the grievant during the proceeding, however, typically will not cause the Board to decline deferral.[98]

(c) Vigorous Representation.   Where the grievant is represented by a union at the proceeding, such representation must be vigorous.[99] If the union representative is hostile toward the grievant[100] or has a conflict of interest,[101] the Board will not defer.

§13.11   Agreement of Parties to Be Bound

This requirement is typically met where the union and employer have agreed explicitly in the collective bargaining agreement to be bound by the arbitration procedure established therein. Even where the contract does not contain explicit language binding the parties the Board has inferred that the parties intended to be bound by the contractual arbitration procedure.[102]

§13.12   Award Not Repugnant to the Act

In examining the arbitrator's award, the Board does not engage in a *de novo* review of the case. Rather, it reviews the record of the proceeding for procedural irregularities and obvious errors in the arbitrator's findings of fact, and then examines the arbitrator's legal

---

[93]*Electronic Reproduction Serv. Corp.*, 213 NLRB 758, 87 LRRM 1211 (1974); *Electrical Workers Local 1522 (Western Elec. Co.)*, 180 NLRB 131, 73 LRRM 1091 (1969).

[94]*Versi Craft Corp.*, 227 NLRB 877, 94 LRRM 1207 (1977).

[95]*Harrah's Club*, 150 NLRB 1702, 58 LRRM 1333 (1965).

[96]*T.I.M.E.-D.C., Inc.*, 203 NLRB 1141, 83 LRRM 1509 (1973).

[97]*Roadway Express, Inc.*, 145 NLRB 513, 54 LRRM 1419 (1963).

[98]*Denver-Chicago Trucking Co.*, 132 NLRB 1416, 48 LRRM 1524 (1961); *see also United States Postal Serv.*, 241 NLRB 1253, 101 LRRM 1074 (1979) (Board refused to retract deferral because of arbitrator's alleged verbal abuse of grievant).

[99]*Gateway Transp. Co.*, 137 NLRB 1763, 50 LRRM 1495 (1962).

[100]*Longshoremen's & Warehousemen's Local 27 (Morris R. Bond)*, 205 NLRB 1141, 84 LRRM 1546 (1973).

[101]*Artim Transp. Sys., Inc.*, 166 NLRB 795, 65 LRRM 1594 (1967).

[102]*Champlin Petroleum Co.*, 201 NLRB 83, 82 LRRM 1388 (1973).

conclusion to determine whether it is consistent with Board law.[103]

The test of "repugnancy" is not whether the Board would have reached the same results as the arbitrator, but whether the arbitrator's award is "palpably wrong as a matter of law."[104] So long as the arbitrator's decision is susceptible to an interpretation consistent with the Act, it will not be considered clearly repugnant.[105] The Third Circuit has held that it is an abuse of discretion for the Board to refuse to defer to an arbitration award where "the findings of the arbitrator may arguably be characterized as not inconsistent with Board policy."[106] As the court put it:

> "If the reasoning behind an award is susceptible of two interpretations, one permissible and one impermissible, it is simply not true that the award was 'clearly repugnant' to the Act."[107]

Examples of arbitration awards to which the Board has refused to defer include those upholding an employee's discharge for engaging in union activity,[108] invoking the grievance procedure,[109] seeking relief from the Board,[110] or making anti-employer statements in the exercise of Section 7 rights.[111] The Board has refused deferral where arbitrators have not enforced a party's obligation to bargain, such as in cases involving unilateral changes in terms and conditions of employment,[112] and the failure to provide requested information.[113] The Board has likewise not deferred to awards barring employees from holding union office[114] or penalizing them for not paying union fines.[115]

---

[103]*Kansas City Star Co.*, 236 NLRB 866, 98 LRRM 1320 (1978) (Member Truesdale, concurring).

[104]*Olin Corp.*, 268 NLRB 573, 115 LRRM 1056 (1984); *Inland Steel Co.*, 263 NLRB 1091, 111 LRRM 1193 (1982). *But see Taylor v. NLRB*, 786 F.2d 1516, 122 LRRM 2084 (11th Cir. 1986) (rejecting *Olin* standard).

[105]*Olin Corp.*, 268 NLRB 573, 115 LRRM 1056 (1984); *see also, United States Postal Serv.*, 275 NLRB No. 65, 119 LRRM 1153 (1985); *Cone Mills Corp.*, 273 NLRB No. 188, 118 LRRM 1197 (1985); *Altoona Hosp.*, 270 NLRB 1179, 116 LRRM 1276 (1984). In *John Morrell & Co.*, 270 NLRB 1, 116 LRRM 1177 (1984), the Board refused to defer to an arbitrator's award sustaining the discharge of a union officer because the award was not susceptible to any interpretation consistent with the Supreme Court's opinion in *Metropolitan Edison v. NLRB*, 460 U.S. 693, 112 LRRM 3265 (1983).

[106]*NLRB v. Pincus Bros., Inc.-Maxwell*, 620 F.2d 367, 104 LRRM 2001 (3d Cir. 1980).

[107]*Id.* 620 F.2d at 374, 104 LRRM 2005, *quoting Douglas Aircraft Co. v. NLRB*, 609 F.2d 352, 102 LRRM 2811 (9th Cir. 1979).

[108]*Wagoner Transp. Co.*, 177 NLRB 452, 73 LRRM 1179 (1969).

[109]*Sea-Land Serv.*, 240 NLRB 1146, 100 LRRM 1406 (1979); *Shippers Dispatch, Inc.*, 223 NLRB 439, 92 LRRM 1252 (1976).

[110]*Douglas Aircraft Co.*, 234 NLRB 578, 97 LRRM 1242 (1978); *Super Valu Xenia*, 228 NLRB 1254, 95 LRRM 1444 (1977).

[111]*Union Fork & Hoe Co.*, 241 NLRB 907, 101 LRRM 1014 (1979); *Clara Barton Terrace Convalescent Center*, 225 NLRB 1028, 92 LRRM 1621 (1976); *Hawaiian Hauling Serv.*, 219 NLRB 765, 90 LRRM 1011 (1975).

[112]*NLRB v. Alfred M. Lewis, Inc.*, 587 F.2d 403, 99 LRRM 2841 (9th Cir. 1978). Conversely, the Board will not defer to an arbitrator's award granting representation rights to a union with tainted authorization cards. *Local 1115, Nursing Home and Hosp. Employees*, 275 NLRB No. 45, 119 LRRM 1093 (1985). In *Earl C. Smith, Inc.*, 278 NLRB No. 100, 121 LRRM 1278 (1986), the Board refused to defer to an award that remedied employer refusal to bargain violations by ordering compliance with the terms of a successor contract which was not at issue or in effect at the time of the employer's violations.

[113]*Kroger Co.*, 226 NLRB 512, 93 LRRM 1315 (1976).

[114]*Cessna Aircraft Co.*, 220 NLRB 873, 90 LRRM 1312 (1975).

[115]*Heat & Frost Insulators, Local No. 31 (J&D Carlson, Inc.)*, 222 NLRB 1046, 91 LRRM 1455 (1976).

Finally, the Board has refused to defer to awards upholding illegal "hot cargo" agreements.[116]

§13.13 Statutory Issue Considered by Arbitrator

Since the Board first decreed that any post-arbitral deferral be conditioned upon the arbitrator's having considered the unfair labor practice issue,[117] the Board has changed its policy on several occasions with respect to the degree of consideration of the statutory issue required of the arbitrator.[118]

In early 1984 the Board settled upon a new, more liberal standard for deferral.[119] It announced that it would find that an arbitrator has adequately considered the unfair labor practice issue if:

> "(1) the contractual issue is factually parallel to the unfair labor practice issue, and (2) the arbitrator was presented generally with the facts relevant to resolving the unfair labor practice."[120]

The Board thus rejected the notion, raised in earlier cases,[121] that it should defer only where, upon a *de novo* consideration of the arbitrator's award, it would have disposed of the issues just as the arbitrator had done.[122]

Under the Board's new standard, the arbitrator need not actually discuss or pass upon the unfair labor practice issue in his or her award. It is enough that he or she merely consider evidence relevant to the statutory issue.[123] If the contractual and statutory issues carry different standards of review, the Board will consider whether such a difference renders the award "clearly repugnant" to the Act[124] (see discussion §13.12 *supra*).

---

[116]*Retail Clerks, Local 324 (Federated Dep't Stores, Inc.)*, 235 NLRB 711, 97 LRRM 1556 (1978).

[117]*Raytheon, Inc.*, 140 NLRB 883, 52 LRRM 1129 (1963).

[118]*See, e.g., Suburban Motor Freight, Inc.*, 247 NLRB 146, 103 LRRM 1113 (1980); *Electronic Reproduction Serv. Corp.*, 213 NLRB 758, 87 LRRM 1211 (1974).

[119]*Olin Corp.*, 268 NLRB 573, 115 LRRM 1056 (1984).

[120]*Id.*

[121]*American Freight Sys., Inc.*, 264 NLRB 126, 111 LRRM 1385 (1982); *Professional Porter & Window Cleaning Co.*, 263 NLRB 136, 110 LRRM 1496 (1982).

[122]*Olin Corp.*, 268 NLRB 573, 115 LRRM 1056 (1984).

[123]*Atlantic Steel Co.*, 245 NLRB 814, 102 LRRM 1247 (1979), *cited with approval in Olin Corp.*, 268 NLRB 573, n.6, 115 LRRM 1056, n.6 (1984). In *United Parcel Serv.*, 270 NLRB 290, 116 LRRM 1064 (1984), the Board's conclusion that the arbitration panel considered the statutory issue was based not upon the panel's five-line decision which made no mention of the alleged unfair labor practice, but rather upon the testimony of the panel's chairman who indicated that the unfair labor practice issues were considered by the panel and rejected. In *Wheeling-Pittsburgh Steel Corp.*, 277 NLRB No. 160, 121 LRRM 1101 (1985), the Board refused to defer on the basis that the arbitrator did not have before him the relevant facts pertaining to the alleged unfair labor practice. The arbitrator did not hear three of four crucial witnesses who testified at the unfair labor practice hearing, mischaracterized the testimony of a fourth witness, and made an erroneous finding of fact.

[124]*Olin Corp.*, 268 NLRB 573, 115 LRRM 1056 (1984).

Some U.S. courts of appeals have imposed additional prerequisites for their approval of Board deferrals under *Spielberg*. The District of Columbia Circuit announced two additional requirements for *Spielberg* deferrals: (1) that the arbitrator "clearly decided the issue on which it is later urged that the Board should give deference," and (2) that the arbitrator decided an issue "within its competence."[125] With respect to the first requirement, the court stated that it would approve of deferral only where the arbitrator resolved "*congruent* statutory and contractual issues."[126]

The Ninth Circuit has adopted the District of Columbia Circuit's additional prerequisites, and has further defined them.[127] It has established that for an arbitrator to have "clearly decided" the statutory issue, he must "specifically deal with" it.[128] The Third Circuit, in approving this rule, declared that

> "in order for the Board's deferral policy not to be one of abdication, the Board must be presented with some evidence that the statutory issue has actually been decided."[129]

The court noted that if the arbitrator's decision is "ambiguous as to the resolution of the statutory issue," deferral will not be approved.[130]

With respect to the issue of the arbitrator's "competence," the Ninth Circuit has indicated that the arbitrator's competence is as good as that of the Board's regarding issues of fact and superior to that of the Board's regarding issues of contract interpretation, but that the arbitrator possesses no special competence regarding issues of law. Thus, only where the statutory and contractual issues are congruent is deferral appropriate.[131]

The Board's liberal deferral policy appears to conflict with these additional requirements imposed by the courts. The requirement of some circuits that contractual and statutory issues be "congruent"[132] imposes a higher standard than the Board's rule that the issues merely be "factually parallel."[133] Similarly, the courts' requirement that the arbitrator specifically address the statutory issue[134] is a stricter standard than the Board's rule, which does not require the arbitrator to discuss the unfair labor practice claim.[135] The Board's new liberal

---

[125]*Banyard v. NLRB*, 505 F.2d 342, 347, 87 LRRM 2001, 2005 (D.C. Cir. 1974).

[126]505 F.2d at 348, 87 LRRM at 2005 (emphasis in original).

[127]*Stephenson v. NLRB*, 550 F.2d 535, 94 LRRM 3224 (9th Cir. 1977).

[128]*Id.* 550 F.2d at 538 n.4, 94 LRRM at 3226 n.4.

[129]*NLRB v. General Warehouse Corp.*, 643 F.2d 965, 969, 106 LRRM 2729, 2732 (3d Cir. 1981).

[130]*Id.* at n.16, *quoting Stephenson v. NLRB*, 550 F.2d 535, 94 LRRM 3224 (9th Cir. 1977).

[131]*Stephenson v. NLRB*, 550 F.2d 535, 94 LRRM 3224 (9th Cir. 1977).

[132]*Id.*; *Banyard v. NLRB*, 505 F.2d 342, 87 LRRM 2001 (D.C. Cir. 1974).

[133]*Olin Corp.*, 268 NLRB 573, 115 LRRM 1056 (1984).

[134]*NLRB v. General Warehouse Corp.*, 643 F.2d 965, 106 LRRM 2729 (3d Cir. 1981); *Stephenson v. NLRB*, 550 F.2d 535, 94 LRRM 3224 (9th Cir. 1977); *Banyard v. NLRB*, 505 F.2d 342, 87 LRRM 2001 (D.C. Cir. 1974).

[135]*Olin Corp.*, 268 NLRB 573, 115 LRRM 1056 (1984).

deferral standards, therefore, may meet with disapproval in some federal courts of appeals.

§13.14   Burden of Proof

The Board has, in effect, established a presumption of post-arbitral deferrability. In *Olin Corp.*[136] it established that the party seeking to have the Board *reject* deferral has the burden of showing that the standards enumerated above have *not* been met. Thus, if a respondent establishes that arbitration in the matter brought as an unfair labor practice charge has taken place, the General Counsel bears the burden of persuasion to show that deficiencies in the arbitral process warrant the Board's disregard of the arbitral award and conduct of a *de novo* review.[137]

§13.15   Cases Where Deferral Is Inappropriate

Regardless of whether the *Spielberg* criteria are met, the Board will not defer to arbitration awards in certain types of cases. Such cases include representation cases,[138] cases involving unlawful assistance to a union under Section 8(a)(2) of the Act,[139] and Section 8(a)(4) cases involving employer discrimination against an employee for filing charges or giving testimony under the Act.[140]

---

[136]*Id.*

[137]*Id; see also Ryder Trucklines, Inc.*, 273 NLRB No. 98, 118 LRRM 1092 (1984). This is a reversal of the Board's previous position that the party seeking deferral had the burden of showing that the *Spielberg* criteria were met. *Suburban Motor Freight, Inc.*, 247 NLRB 146, 103 LRRM 1113 (1980); *Yourga Trucking, Inc.*, 197 NLRB 928, 80 LRRM 1498 (1972).

[138]*Commonwealth Gas Co.*, 218 NLRB 857, 89 LRRM 1613 (1975); *cf. Pinkerton's, Inc.*, 270 NLRB 27, 116 LRRM 1135 (1984).

[139]*Servair, Inc.*, 236 NLRB 1278, 99 LRRM 1259 (1978).

[140]*Filmation Assoc.*, 227 NLRB 1721, 94 LRRM 1470 (1977).

14

Settlement of Unfair Labor Practice Charges

If the Board's investigation reveals merit in an unfair labor practice charge, the agent normally will attempt to secure a settlement or voluntary adjustment that will provide a remedy for the alleged unfair labor practice without the necessity of further proceedings.[1] Board agents are encouraged to afford the parties every opportunity to reach a mutually satisfactory resolution at all stages of the Board proceeding since settlement is viewed as the most effective means to improve the parties' relationship and focus Board resources on other cases.[2]

Settlement agreements vary greatly depending upon the circumstances of each case. There are two basic types of Board settlement agreements—informal and formal. An informal agreement consists simply of a commitment on the part of the charged party to remedy the alleged unfair labor practices in exchange for withdrawal or dismissal of the charge. Informal agreements are used far more frequently than formal agreements,[3] and only require approval of the regional director. A formal agreement generally consists of a signed stipulation which, in addition to providing remedies for the alleged unfair labor practices, also provides for the issuance of a cease and desist order by the Board, and in some cases for the entry of a court decree enforcing the Board's order.

The filing of an unfair labor practice charge may result in the charged party undertaking certain conduct which, while not technically coinciding with Board remedies, nevertheless satisfies the

---

[1]NLRB Statements of Procedure ¶101.7. In fiscal year 1981, 82.2 percent of the meritorious unfair labor practice charges were closed through formal or informal settlement agreements. 46 NLRB ANN. REP. Chart 3A (1981).

[2]NLRB Casehandling Manual ¶¶10124–10128.

[3]In fiscal year 1981, 97.2 percent of the settlement agreements were informal and only 2.8 percent were formal. 46 NLRB ANN. REP. Table 7 (1981).

desires of the charging party. In other instances, the charged party may be willing to remedy the unfair labor practices but be unwilling to execute a written agreement. While these actions may be sufficient to warrant withdrawal or dismissal of the unfair labor practice charge, they technically are not settlement agreements.[4] As used by the Board, a settlement agreement is a written document on which the Board has placed its imprimatur, with which the Board will police compliance, and on the basis of which, when complied with, the parties are notified that the matter has been closed.[5]

The parties to a settlement agreement vary with the type of unfair labor practice alleged.[6] The charged party is a necessary signatory to all formal and informal settlements. The charging party is a desirable signatory, but not a necessary one. While the Board makes every effort to negotiate bilateral settlement agreements, unilateral agreements (i.e., without the charging party) are acceptable where the respondent agrees to take all actions necessary to remedy the alleged unfair labor practices.[7] In situations where the remedy provided for in the settlement agreement includes disestablishing or withholding recognition from a labor organization, the union should be a party to the agreement.[8] Similarly, if the proposed remedy involves ceasing to give effect to all or part of an existing collective bargaining contract, both parties to the contract should be signatories to the settlement agreement.[9]

Where a necessary party to an agreement—the illegally assisted or dominated union or the other party to the affected contract, for example—refuses either to join in the settlement agreement or to waive its rights, the regional director will issue a formal complaint and proceed to a hearing. A copy of the complaint and notice of hearing will be served on the objecting party, and if that party thereafter fails to appear at the hearing, a settlement agreement may be executed by the remaining parties.[10]

Informal Settlement Agreements

§14.1 Nature of Informal Settlement Agreements

As noted, informal settlement agreements are the most frequent type of adjustment. They are used in situations where the charged

---

[4]Non-Board settlement agreements are discussed *infra* at notes 75–77.

[5]NLRB Casehandling Manual ¶10140.1.

[6]*See generally* NLRB Casehandling Manual ¶¶10134.1–10134.6.

[7]In some instances a charging party may be unwilling to enter into a settlement agreement, but may be willing to sign a separate document acknowledging the terms of the agreement and stating that no appeal will be taken from the dismissal of the charge. NLRB Casehandling Manual ¶10134.2.

[8]The union may waive its right to be a party to the proceedings or to contest the settlement. *Id.* at ¶10134.3; *see also* ¶10130.5.

[9]*Id.* at ¶¶10130.5, 10134.3, and 10134.4. A similar rule applies to parties to a hot cargo agreement. *See* NLRB Casehandling Manual ¶10134.6.

[10]NLRB Casehandling Manual ¶10134.5

party does not have a history of illegal conduct and there appears to be little likelihood of a repetition of the violation.[11] An informal agreement provides that the charged party will take certain action to remedy the alleged unfair labor practices. It requires approval by the regional director but does not provide for a Board order or the entry of a court decree.[12]

Informal settlement agreements most frequently are executed prior to issuance of a complaint, but may also be entered after a complaint has been issued, or after the hearing has opened.[13] Regional directors have the authority on their own to approve informal settlements executed prior to the hearing.[14] Once the hearing has opened, however, the agreement must be submitted to the administrative law judge for approval.[15]

If the charging party consents to the settlement so that the agreement is bilateral, the charged party is instructed to undertake the remedial action called for in the agreement.[16] If after issuance of the complaint but before opening of the hearing the charging party refuses to consent so that the agreement is unilateral, the regional director informs the charging party by letter of the reasons for the recommended approval and affords the charging party five days from service of the letter to file objections.[17] If the settlement is approved notwithstanding the charging party's objections, the regional director must furnish a brief statement of the reasons for doing so.[18]

§14.2 Terms of Informal Settlement Agreements

The terms of informal settlement agreements vary considerably depending upon the facts of each case. In most instances NLRB Form 4775, or a modification thereof, is used. (See Exhibit 76.) In the standard agreement the charged party agrees (1) to post a notice for 60 consecutive days, (2) to comply with the conditions set forth in the notice, (3) to pay any backpay which may be due, and (4) to notify the regional director of steps undertaken to comply with the terms of the agreement.

In addition to the standard provisions, other terms may be negotiated by the parties. Nonadmission clauses which stipulate that by executing the settlement agreement the charged party does not

---

[11]NLRB Statements of Procedure ¶101.7; NLRB Casehandling Manual ¶¶10140.2, 10146.1.

[12]NLRB Casehandling Manual ¶10146.1.

[13]NLRB Statements of Procedure §§101.9(b)(2) (after complaint issues but before opening of hearing), 101.9(d)(1) (after hearing opens); NLRB Casehandling Manual ¶¶10146.2, 10148.1–10148.4.

[14]NLRB Statements of Procedure §101.9(b)(2); NLRB Casehandling Manual ¶10148.2. In certain limited circumstances the regional director may have to get prior approval from the General Counsel in Washington, D.C. *See* NLRB Casehandling Manual ¶¶10148.1, 11751.2.

[15]NLRB Statements of Procedure §101.9(d)(1); NLRB Casehandling Manual ¶10148.3.

[16]NLRB Casehandling Manual ¶10150.1.

[17]NLRB Statements of Procedure §101.9(c)(1) (this time period was unaffected by the Board's September 1986 rules change); NLRB Casehandling Manual ¶10152.1.

[18]*Id.*

FORM NLRB-4775
(11-85)

UNITED STATES GOVERNMENT
NATIONAL LABOR RELATIONS BOARD
SETTLEMENT AGREEMENT

In the Matter of

The undersigned Charged Party and the undersigned Charging Party, in settlement of the above matter, and subject to the approval of the Regional Director for the National Labor Relations Board, HEREBY AGREE AS FOLLOWS:

POSTING OF NOTICE—Upon approval of this Agreement, the Charged Party will post immediately in conspicuous places in and about its plant/office, including all places where notices to employees/members are customarily posted, and maintain for 60 consecutive days from the date of posting, copies of the attached Notice made a part hereof, said Notices to be signed by a responsible official of the Charged Party and the date of actual posting to be shown thereon. In the event this Agreement is in settlement of a charge against a union, the union will submit forthwith signed copies of said Notice to the Regional Director who will forward them to the employer whose employees are involved herein, for posting, the employer willing, in conspicuous places in and about the employer's plant where they shall be maintained for 60 consecutive days from the date of posting.

COMPLIANCE WITH NOTICE—The Charged Party will comply with all the terms and provisions of said Notice.

BACKPAY—The Charged Party will make whole the employees named below by payment to each of them of the amount opposite each name.

REFUSAL TO ISSUE COMPLAINT—In the event the Charging Party fails or refuses to become a party to this Agreement, and if in the Regional Director's discretion it will effectuate the policies of the National Labor Relations Act, the Regional Director shall decline to issue a Complaint herein *(or a new Complaint if one has been withdrawn pursuant to the terms of this Agreement)*, and this Agreement shall be between the Charged Party and the undersigned Regional Director. A review of such action may be obtained pursuant to Section 102.19 of the Rules and Regulations of the Board if a request for same is filed within 10 days thereof. This Agreement is contingent upon the General Counsel sustaining the Regional Director's action in the event of a review. Approval of this Agreement by the Regional Director shall constitute withdrawal of any Complaint(s) and Notice of Hearing heretofore issued in this case, as well as any answer(s) filed in response.

PERFORMANCE—Performance by the Charged Party with the terms and provisions of this Agreement shall commence immediately after the Agreement is approved by the Regional Director, or if the Charging Party does not enter into this Agreement, performance shall commence immediately upon receipt by the Charged Party of advice that no review has been requested or that the General Counsel has sustained the Regional Director.

NOTIFICATION OF COMPLIANCE—The undersigned parties to this Agreement will each notify the Regional Director in writing what steps the Charged Party has taken to comply herewith. Such notification shall be given within 5 days, and again after 60 days, from the date of the approval of this Agreement. In the event the Charging Party does not enter into this Agreement, initial notice shall be given within 5 days after notification from the Regional Director that no review has been requested or that the General Counsel has sustained the Regional Director. Contingent upon compliance with the terms and provisions hereof, no further action shall be taken in this case.

Charged Party			Charging Party		
By:	Name and Title	Date	By:	Name and Title	Date
Recommended By:		Date	Approved By:		Date
	Board Agent			Regional Director	

Exhibit 76.   Informal Settlement Agreement (Form NLRB-4775)

admit to violating the National Labor Relations Act often are inserted.[19] Special clauses also might be included for situations in which reinstatement is refused or not desired;[20] there is joint and several liability among two or more respondents;[21] or retroactive seniority will require adjustments in existing seniority rosters.[22]

In some cases the regional director may wish to settle some, but not all, of the alleged unfair labor practices set forth in the charge. In such instances the agreement will specify which unfair labor practice allegations are being excluded.[23] If the regional director intends to issue a complaint concerning the excluded allegations, the settlement agreement will provide that the evidence bearing upon the settled allegations may be introduced at the hearing on the unsettled allegations.[24]

If, on the other hand, the unsettled allegations are to be dismissed, the settlement agreement cannot be approved until the appeal period has expired or the appeal has been denied. If the appeal is sustained, however, the regional director must (1) include the additional allegations in the settlement, (2) proceed to complaint only on the appealed allegations, or (3) refuse to approve the partial settlement and proceed to complaint on all of the allegations.[25]

§14.3 Posting of Notices

All informal settlement agreements provide for notice to the employees of the action taken by the charged party to remedy the alleged unfair labor practices.[26] While regional offices have some latitude in tailoring the notice language to the particular case, most notices follow the language of notices in Board orders in comparable cases. It is proper for the Board to require the posting of a notice which declares publicly that a party will conform in the future to the requirements of the Act, but it is not proper to require a party to confess past guilt.[27]

The Board uses various types of prepared notices which are completed by inserting language describing the specific unfair labor practices involved. (See Exhibits 77 and 78.) In the absence of special

---

[19]NLRB Casehandling Manual ¶10130.6. Nonadmission clauses are not included in the posted notices. *Independent Shoe Workers of Cincinnati (United States Shoe Corp.)*, 203 NLRB 783, 83 LRRM 1307 (1973).

[20]NLRB Casehandling Manual ¶¶10130.2, 10130.7.

[21]*Id.* at ¶10130.4.

[22]*Id.* at ¶10130.8.

[23]*Id.* at ¶¶10146.4 (bilateral settlements), 10152.2 (unilateral settlements).

[24]*Id.*

[25]*Id.*

[26]*Id.* at ¶¶10132.1–10132.5, 10136.1–10136.2.

[27]*Id.* at ¶10132.1; *NLRB v. Express Pub. Co.*, 312 U.S. 426, 8 LRRM 415 (1941). According to the Board's Casehandling Manual, statements such as "We violated the law when we fired John Smith" or "We will not fire anyone for union activity again" are not proper.

Form NLRB-4722
(10-70)

NOTICE TO EMPLOYEES

POSTED PURSUANT TO A SETTLEMENT AGREEMENT APPROVED BY A REGIONAL DIRECTOR OF THE NATIONAL LABOR RELATIONS BOARD
AN AGENCY OF THE UNITED STATES GOVERNMENT

The National Labor Relations Act gives all employees these rights:

    To engage in self-organization;
    To form, join, or help labor organizations;
    To bargain collectively through representatives of their own choosing;
    To act together for collective bargaining or other mutual aid or protection;
    To refrain from any or all of these things.

  WE WILL NOT do anything to interfere with, restrain, or coerce our employees in their exercise of these rights.

  WE WILL NOT discriminatorily encourage membership in Local 007, United Computer Operators International Union, by requesting and/or accepting for hire and employment, employees referred to us by Local 007, pursuant to any exclusive hiring hall and/or referral arrangement, when such referrals are made without a structured, systematic, rational or objective referral system.

_____
Janco Computer Services, Inc.

DATED:_____By:_____
                           Jack Smith, President

THIS IS AN OFFICIAL NOTICE AND MUST NOT BE DEFACED BY ANYONE

This notice must remain posted for 60 consecutive days from the date of posting and must not be altered, defaced, or covered by any other material. Any questions concerning this notice or compliance with its provisions may be directed to the Board's Office. Region 5, Candler Building - 4th Floor, 109 Market Place, Baltimore, MD 21202

Exhibit 77.   Notice Used in Informal Settlement of Employer Unfair Labor Practice (Form NLRB-4722)

FORM NLRB-4723
(10-70)

NOTICE TO MEMBERS

POSTED PURSUANT TO A SETTLEMENT AGREEMENT
APPROVED BY A REGIONAL DIRECTOR OF THE
NATIONAL LABOR RELATIONS BOARD
AN AGENCY OF THE UNITED STATES GOVERNMENT

We are posting this Notice to inform you of your rights
guaranteed in the National Labor Relations Act.

The Act gives all employees these rights:

    To organize themselves;
    To form, join or assist labor organizations;
    To bargain as a group through a representative they
        choose;
    To act together for collective bargaining or
        other mutual aid or protection;
    To refuse to do any or all of these things.

We assure our members/participants that:

WE WILL NOT disallow insurance claims or in any other manner deny
our membership/participants benefits, if guaranteed by the
collective bargaining agreement, because they have not paid union
membership dues or for other membership considerations.

WE WILL NOT in any other manner restrain or coerce our members/
participants in the exercise of their rights guaranteed under
Section 7 of the National Labor Relations Act.

WE HAVE offered Mary Hughes full and immediate reinstatement to
insurance coverage by our insurance benefit fund.

_____
Local 007, United Computer Operators
International Union

Dated:_____ By:_____
                         Jean Jones, Business Agent

THIS IS AN OFFICIAL NOTICE AND MUST NOT BE DEFACED BY ANYONE

This notice must remain posted for 60 consecutive days from the date of posting and must not be altered, defaced,
or covered by any other material. Any questions concerning this notice or compliance with its provisions may be directed
to the Board's Office,   Region 5, Candler Building - 4th Floor, 109 Market Place,
             Baltimore, MD   21202

Exhibit 78.   **Notice Used in Informal Settlement of Union Labor Practice**
              (Form NLRB-4723)

permission from Washington, notices are posted for 60 consecutive days.[28] Employer notices are posted at the work location of the affected employees. Union notices are posted at the union hall, at the union meeting place, or if the employer permits, at the work location of the employees. Where the affected employees are widely scattered, the Board may direct that notices be mailed to the employees individually or published in a daily newspaper of general circulation.[29]

§14.4   Appeal of Informal Settlement Agreements

As noted earlier, the regional director (before the hearing has opened) or the administrative law judge (after the hearing has opened but before issuing a decision) may accept the terms of an informal settlement agreement over the objection of the charging party.[30] An appeal from the regional director's acceptance may be taken by the charging party whether the settlement is reached before or after issuance of a complaint.[31] The appeal procedure applicable to dismissal of unfair labor practice charges is used for an appeal from a regional director's acceptance of a unilateral settlement agreement.[32]

Appeals from an administrative law judge's acceptance or rejection of an informal settlement may be taken by any aggrieved party, including the General Counsel.[33] If the administrative law judge dismisses the complaint, a request for review may be filed within 28 days.[34] In all other cases a party wishing to challenge an administrative law judge's ruling must first seek special permission to appeal from the Board.[35]

§14.5   Compliance With Informal Settlement Agreements

If no appeal is taken, the regional director instructs the charged party to take the action called for in the settlement agreement. If an appeal is taken, such instructions are not given unless and until the regional director or administrative law judge's acceptance of the agreement has been sustained by the General Counsel.[36] Informal settlement agreements are policed in the same manner as adminis-

---

[28]*Id.*

[29]*Id.* at ¶10132.4. See NLRB Casehandling Manual ¶10136 for notices used in secondary boycott and hot cargo cases.

[30]See notes 13–15 *supra.*

[31]NLRB Statements of Procedure §§101.7 (before complaint issues), 101.9(c)(2) (after complaint issues).

[32]*Id; see also* NLRB Rules and Regulations §102.19; NLRB Statements of Procedure §101.6; discussion at §12.12.

[33]NLRB Statements of Procedure §§101.9(d)(1), 101.9(d)(2); NLRB Casehandling Manual ¶¶10148.3, 10148.5.

[34]NLRB Rules and Regulations §102.27; NLRB Casehandling Manual ¶10148.5.

[35]NLRB Rules and Regulations §102.26; NLRB Statements of Procedure §101.9(d)(2).

[36]NLRB Casehandling Manual ¶10152.4.

trative law judges' decisions, Board orders, and court judgments.[37] When the regional director is satisfied that all of the terms have been performed—usually after the expiration of the notice-posting period—the parties will be notified that the case has been closed. The notification will provide that continued observance of the terms of the informal settlement is a condition of the case remaining closed.[38]

If a charged party has commenced complying with the terms of the settlement agreement before being instructed to do so by the regional director, the performance eventually required normally will be only that remaining to be performed.[39] Where it appears to the regional director, however, that the terms of the settlement agreement have not or will not be carried out, the parties are notified that the director will undertake whatever action appears appropriate to effectuate the purposes of the Act. In most instances the settlement agreement will be withdrawn, the complaint will be issued or reissued, and the case will proceed as if a settlement agreement never had been reached—i.e., the complaint will be processed on its merits and not on the basis of noncompliance with the agreement.[40]

§14.6   Effect of Informal Board Settlement

A pending representation case will be processed partially while the terms of the settlement agreement are being performed. For example, a hearing may be held, or the regional director or the Board may issue a direction of election. An election will not be held, however, until the terms of the agreement have been performed and the notice-posting period has expired.

Where an informal agreement provides for bargaining in settlement of charges of refusal to bargain or bad faith bargaining, such settlement is not automatically equal to a certification that allows the parties one year in which to negotiate a contract free from rival claims and petitions.[41] The Board has held, however, that under a settlement agreement containing a bargaining provision, the parties must meet and bargain collectively for a "reasonable" period of time following settlement.[42] The length of this period depends upon the particular circumstances of each case.[43] Thus, an employer violates Section 8(a)(5) of the Act by challenging the union's majority status

---

[37]*Id.* at ¶10150.2.

[38]*Id.* at ¶10150.3.

[39]*Id.* at ¶10152.4.

[40]*Id.* at ¶10154; *see also* NLRB Statements of Procedure §101.9(e)(2).

[41]*Ruffalo's Trucking Serv., Inc.*, 114 NLRB 1549, 37 LRRM 1201 (1955).

[42]*All Brand Printing Corp.*, 236 NLRB 140, 98 LRRM 1579 (1978); *Fred Tuch Buick*, 199 NLRB 876, 82 LRRM 1012 (1972).

[43]*WDIV Post-Newsweek Stations, Inc.*, 254 NLRB 550, 107 LRRM 1037 (1981); *All Brand Printing Corp.*, 236 NLRB 140, 98 LRRM 1579 (1978); *Fred Tuch Buick*, 199 NLRB 876, 82 LRRM 1012 (1972).

or withdrawing recognition from the union before this time period has elapsed.[44] Similarly, the Board has held that a settlement agreement and a contract entered into pursuant to that settlement bar a rival union's petition for an election[45] or a petition for decertification prior to the expiration of this period.[46]

It is the Board's policy to honor the settlement agreements to which its agents are parties. Moreover, the Board has held that a settlement agreement disposes of all presettlement conduct of a charged party unless prior violations of the Act were either unknown to the General Counsel and not readily discoverable by investigation, or specifically reserved from the settlement agreement by the mutual understanding of the parties.[47] The Board will go behind a settlement agreement, however, where unfair labor practices continue after its execution,[48] or where that agreement is breached.[49] In such circumstances, the Board litigates the presettlement as well as the post-settlement violation.[50]

Formal Settlement Agreements

§14.7   Nature of Formal Settlement Agreements

A formal settlement agreement is used in situations where (1) there is a likelihood of recurrence or extension of the unfair labor practices charged; (2) there is a history of prior unfair labor practices on the part of the charged party; or (3) there is either continuing violence or the likelihood of continuing violence.[51] Unlike an informal settlement which often is a simple agreement, a formal settlement is a written stipulation containing a Board order specifying that certain remedial action will be undertaken. Formal settlements also often provide for entry of a court judgment enforcing the Board order.[52]

As with informal agreements, formal settlements may be bilateral or unilateral.[53] They may be executed before or after a complaint

---

[44]*Ray's Liquor Store*, 234 NLRB 1136, 98 LRRM 1308 (1978).

[45]*Dick Bros. Inc.*, 110 NLRB 451, 35 LRRM 1016 (1954). See discussion at §5.7.

[46]*Los Angeles Tile Jobbers, Inc.*, 210 NLRB 789, 86 LRRM 1269 (1974).

[47]*E.S.I. Meats, Inc.*, 270 NLRB 1430, 117 LRRM 1065 (1984); *Cambridge Taxi Co.*, 260 NLRB 931, 109 LRRM 1241 (1982).

[48]*East Tex. Motor Freight*, 262 NLRB 868, 110 LRRM 1547 (1982); *Robert Bosch Corp.*, 256 NLRB 1036, 107 LRRM 1418 (1981).

[49]*Interstate Paper Supply Co.*, 251 NLRB 1423, 105 LRRM 1480 (1980).

[50]*Id.*; *International Photographers (IATSE) Local 659*, 197 NLRB 1187, 81 LRRM 1223 (1972).

[51]NLRB Casehandling Manual ¶10164.2.

[52]*Id.* at ¶10164.1.

[53]*Id.* at ¶10164.7.

has issued,[54] as well as before or after the hearing has opened.[55] If reached prior to issuance of a complaint, a complaint is issued simultaneously with execution of the stipulation.[56] If reached after issuance of a complaint and after an answer has been filed, respondents are encouraged but not required to withdraw their answer.[57]

§14.8 Contents of Formal Settlement Agreements

Formal settlement stipulations generally contain several discrete segments.[58] (See Exhibits 79 and 80.)

(a) Jurisdictional Facts.[59] It is not sufficient that the parties consent to Board jurisdiction. The stipulation must specify jurisdictional facts sufficient to indicate to the Board and to the courts that jurisdiction exists under one of the Board's current jurisdictional standards.

(b) Waiver of Hearing.[60] The stipulation must include a waiver of a formal hearing and other additional proceedings.

(c) Enumeration of Record.[61] The stipulation must contain a description of the documents constituting the record in the case. While the exact content of the record may vary from one case to another, typical documents include the stipulation; the charge and any amendments thereto; the complaint and notice of hearing; the answer (if any, or if not previously withdrawn); and any other letter, document, affidavit, or order disposing of the rights of interested parties.

(d) Facts.[62] Except where the respondent has consented to the entry of a court judgment, the Board's order must be predicated upon an unfair labor practice finding. Accordingly, either the pleadings (i.e., complaint allegations which are undenied or admitted) or the facts set forth in the stipulation must be sufficient to support an unfair labor practice determination. If the agreement provides for a bargaining order, the appropriateness of the bargaining unit and the majority status of the union involved must be acknowledged.[63]

---

[54]*Id.* at ¶¶10164.2, 10172.1.

[55]*Id.* at ¶10164.6.

[56]*Id.* at ¶¶10164.2, 10172.1.

[57]*Id.* at ¶10164.3.

[58]*Id.* at ¶10166.2.

[59]*Id.* at ¶10166.3.

[60]*Id.* at ¶10166.4; *see also* NLRB Statements of Procedure §101.9(b)(1).

[61]NLRB Casehandling Manual ¶10166.5.

[62]*Id.* at ¶10166.6.

[63]*Id.*

UNITED STATES OF AMERICA
BEFORE THE NATIONAL LABOR RELATIONS BOARD

Janco Computer Services, Inc.

and   Case No. 5-CA-1237

Local 007, United Computer Operators
  International Union

DECISION AND ORDER

Statement of the Case

On January 2, 1986, Janco Computer Services, Inc., herein called the
Respondent, Local 007, United Computer Operators International Union,
herein called the Union, and the General Counsel of the National Labor
Relations Board entered into a "Stipulation for Board Order and Court
Judgment" subject to approval of the Board, providing for the entry of a
consent order by the Board and a consent judgment by any appropriate United
States Court of Appeals. The parties waived all further and other
procedures before the Board to which they may be entitled under the
National Labor Relations Act, as amended, and the Rules and Regulations of
the Board, and Respondent waived its right to contest the entry of a
consent judgment or to receive further notice of the application therefor.

Pursuant to the provisions of Section 3(b) of the National Labor
Relations Act, as amended, the National Labor Relations Board has delegated
its authority in this proceeding to a three-member panel.

The aforesaid Stipulation is hereby aproved and made a part of the
record herein, and the proceeding is hereby transferred to and continued
before the Board in Washington, D.C., for the entry of a Decision and Order
pursuant to the provisions of the said Stipulation.

Upon the basis of the aforesaid Stipulation and the entire record in
this proceeding, the Board makes the following:

Findings of Fact

1. The business of the Respondent

Respondent is a Commonwealth of Virginia corporation with offices and
place of business at McLean, Virginia. It is engaged in the manufacture,
sale, and distribution of computer hardware, software, and related
services. During the past 12 months, which period is representative of all
times material herein, Respondent, in the course and conduct of its
business operations sold and shipped goods or provided services from its
facilities within the Commonwealth of Virginia, to customers within said
Commonwealth, which customers were themselves engaged in interstate
commerce by other than indirect means, of a total value in excess of
$50,000.

The Respondent admits, and we find, that it is an employer engaged in
commerce within the meaning of Section 2(6) and (7) of the Act.

2. The labor organization involved

The Union is a labor organization within the meaning of Section 2(5)
of the Act. The Union has been at all times material herein the recognized
statutory representative of all employees in the appropriate unit for the
purpose of collective bargaining within the meaning of Section 9(a) of the
Act.

3. The appropriate unit

All customer service and sales representatives employed by Respondent,
excluding all other employees, guards and supervisors as defined in the
Act, constitute a unit appropriate for the purposes of collective
bargaining within the meaning of Section 9(b) of the Act.

Exhibit 79.   Formal Settlement Stipulation of Employer Unfair Labor Practice

-2-

ORDER

Upon the basis of the above findings of fact, the Stipulation, and the entire record in this proceeding, and pursuant to Section 10(c) of the National Labor Relations Act, as amended, the National Labor Relations Board hereby orders that:

The Respondent, Janco Computer Services, Inc., its officers, agents, successors, and assigns, shall:

1. Cease and desist from:

(a) Refusing to bargain collectively with the Union, as the exclusive representative of all its customer service and sales representatives, excluding all other employees, guards and supervisors as defined in the Act.

(b) Refusing, upon request, at reasonable times and locations, to bargain collectively with the Union as the exclusive representative of all of its employees in the unit described above.

(c) In any like or related manner failing or refusing to bargain collectively with the Union, or interfere with, restrain, or coerce employees in the exercise of their rights as guaranteed in Section 7 of the Act.

2. Take the following affirmative action which the National Labor Relations Board finds will effectuate the policies of the National Labor Relations Act, as amended:

(a) Upon request, at reasonable times and locations, bargain collectively with the Union as the exclusive representative of all employees in the aforesaid appropriate unit with respect to rates of pay, wages, hours and other terms and conditions of employment.

(b) Post at its McLean, Virginia, place of business, copies of the attached Notice to Employees. Copies of the Notice, on forms provided by the Regional Director for Region 5, after being duly signed by an authorized representative of the Respondent, shall be posted by the Respondent immediately upon receipt thereof, and be maintained for 60 consecutive days thereafter, in conspicuous places, including all places where notices to employees are customarily posted. Reasonable steps shall be taken by the Respondent to insure that the Notices are not altered, defaced, or covered by any other material.

(c) Notify the Regional Director for Region 5, in writing, within 20 days from the date of this Order, what steps the Respondent has taken to comply herewith.

Dated, Washington, D.C.,

_____
Chairman

_____
Member

_____
Member

NATIONAL LABOR RELATIONS BOARD

(SEAL)

Exhibit 79—*page 2*

UNITED STATES OF AMERICA
BEFORE THE NATIONAL LABOR RELATIONS BOARD

Local 007, United Computer Operators
International Union

and   Case No. 5-CB-1234

Janco Computer Services, Inc.

DECISION AND ORDER

Statement of the Case

On January 2, 1986, Local 007, United Computer Operators International
Union, herein called Respondent, Janco Computer Services, Inc., herein
called Employer, and the General Counsel of the National Labor Relations
Board entered into a Stipulation for the entry of a consent order by the
Board and a consent judgment by any appropriate United States Court of
Appeals. The parties waived all further and other procedures before the
Board to which they may be entitled under the National Labor Relations Act,
as amended, and the Rules and Regulations of the Board, and Respondent
waived its right to contest the entry of a consent judgment or to receive
further notice of the application therefor.

Pursuant to the provisions of Section 3(b) of the National Labor
Relations Act, as amended, the National Labor Relations Board has delegated
its authority in this proceeding to a three-member panel.

The aforesaid Stipulation is hereby approved and made a part of the
record herein, and the proceeding is hereby transferred to and continued
before the Board in Washington, D.C., for the entry of a Decision and Order
pursuant to the provisions of the said Stipulation.

Upon the basis of the aforesaid Stipulation and the entire record in
this proceeding, the Board makes the following:

Findings of Fact

1. The business of the Employer

Employer is now, and has been at all times material herein, a
corporation doing business in the Commonwealth of Virginia with an office
and place of business located in McLean, Virginia, where it is engaged in
the manufacture, sale, and distribution of computer hardware, software, and
related services.

During the past 12 months, the Employer, in the course and conduct of
its business operations, purchased and received at its McLean, Virginia,
location products valued in excess of $50,000 directly from points located
outside the Commonwealth of Virginia, and during the same period of time
the Employer sold and shipped from its McLean, Virginia, location, products
valued in excess of $50,000 directly to points located outside the
Commonwealth of Virginia.

The Respondent and the Employer admit, and we find, that the Employer
is an employer engaged in commerce within the meaning of Section 2(6) and
(7) of the Act.

2. The labor organization involved

Local 007, United Computer Operators International Union, is a labor
organization within the meaning of Section 2(5) of the Act.

Exhibit 80.   Formal Settlement Stipulation of Union Unfair Labor Practice

-2-

ORDER

Upon the basis of the above findings of fact, the Stipulation, and the entire record in this proceeding, and pursuant to Section 10(c) of the National Labor Relations Act, as amended, the National Labor Relations Board hereby orders that:

The Respondent, its officers, agents, and representatives, shall:

1. Cease and desist from:

(a) Attempting to block the ingress and egress of vehicles seeking to leave or enter the premises of the Employer by engaging in mass picketing, scattering tacks and nails, or any other object in the road leading to the entrances to the Employer's premises, or in any other manner, or by any other means obstructing, hindering, preventing or stopping or attempting to obstruct, hinder, prevent or stop any employee or other person from going to or from the Employer's premises.

(b) In any other manner restraining or coercing employees of the Employer in the exercise of rights guaranteed by Section 7 of the National Labor Relations Act, as amended.

2. Take the following affirmative action which the National Labor Relations Board finds will effectuate the policies of the National Labor Relations Act, as amended:

(a) Post at its meeting hall and its business office, copies of the attached Notice to Employees and Members. Copies of said Notice, on forms provided by the Regional Director for Region 5, after being duly signed by the Respondent's representative, shall be posted by the Respondent immediately upon receipt thereof and maintained by it for 60 consecutive days thereafter, in conspicuous places, including all places where notices to members are customarily posted. Reasonable steps shall be taken by the Respondent to insure that such Notices are not altered, defaced, or covered by any other material.

(b) Mail to the Regional Director for Region 5 signed copies of said Notice for posting if Janco Computer Services, Inc., is willing, in the plant of Janco in McLean, Virginia, in the places where notices to employees are customarily posted. Copies of said Notice, on forms provided by the Regional Director for Region 5, after having been signed by Respondent's representative, shall be forthwith returned to the Regional Director for such posting by Janco.

(c) Notify the Regional Director for Region 5, in writing, within 20 days from the date of this Order, what steps the Respondent has taken to comply herewith.

Dated, Washington, D.C.,

                           _____
                               Chairman

                           _____
                               Member

                           _____
                               Member

NATIONAL LABOR RELATIONS BOARD

(SEAL)

Exhibit 80—*page 2*

(e) Backpay.[64]   In most cases the Board will request that the specific amount of backpay due under the agreement not be left to future determination, but be computed and set forth in the stipulation and in the notice. In order to encourage prompt compliance on the part of the respondent, the stipulation may provide for the additional accumulation of backpay and interest if reinstatement of the affected individuals is not accomplished within 10 days of entry of the Board's order.

(f) Consent to Board Order.[65]   The parties must consent in the stipulation to the entry of a Board order without further notice. The terms of the Board order must be set forth with the same precision as in an administrative law judge or Board decision. It is permissible, however, for the parties to substitute the words "shall not" for the traditional phrase "shall cease and desist from."

(g) Consent to Court Judgment.   Ordinarily, formal settlement agreements contain respondent's consent to the Board's application for entry of a decree by the appropriate court of appeals enforcing the Board's order.[66] In situations where a court judgment is entered, it is unnecessary for the respondent to admit in the stipulation that it has engaged in any unlawful conduct. The Board will proceed to issue its order and seek a court judgment even in cases where the respondent immediately has complied with its order.[67]

§14.9   Approval of Formal Settlement Agreements

All formal settlement agreements must be approved by the General Counsel and by the Board.[68] In addition, if the settlement is reached after the opening of the hearing but before a decision has been issued by the administrative law judge, the judge's approval must be acquired as well.[69] Any party, including the General Counsel, aggrieved by a judge's disapproval or acceptance of a formal settlement may request permission of the Board to appeal.[70]

Once a formal settlement agreement is approved by the regional director, the agreement, along with the charging party's objections and the regional director's written analysis, if any, is transmitted to the General Counsel in Washington, D.C., for review. If the General Counsel approves the settlement, the charging party is notified and

---

[64]*Id.* at ¶10164.5.

[65]*Id.* at ¶10166.7; *see also* NLRB Statements of Procedure §101.9(b)(1).

[66]*Id.* at ¶10164.4.

[67]*Id.*

[68]NLRB Statements of Procedure §101.9(c)(2); NLRB Casehandling Manual ¶10164.6A.

[69]NLRB Statements of Procedure §101.9(d)(1); NLRB Casehandling Manual ¶10164.6B.

[70]NLRB Rules and Regulations §102.26; NLRB Statements of Procedure §101.9(d)(2); NLRB Casehandling Manual ¶10164.6B.

the record is forwarded to the Board. Within seven days after service of the notice of submission to the Board, the charging party may file with the Board an additional position statement.[71] The Board must accept or reject the agreement as submitted; it may not modify the agreement and then enforce it as modified.

If the Board accepts the stipulation, the respondent is required to undertake the remedial actions set forth in the order.[72] If on the other hand the stipulation is rejected, the case is returned to the regional office for processing as if no agreement had been reached.[73] If the stipulation is approved but the respondent refuses to comply, the Board may petition an appropriate court for enforcement of its order or, if the stipulation already provides for entry of a court judgment, the Board may simply seek a contempt of court citation.[74]

Non-Board Settlement Agreements

In some cases the charged and the charging parties may reach a mutually acceptable private resolution of their differences without the assistance or approval of the Board. The Board may, but is not required to, honor such agreements.[75] If the charging party seeks permission to withdraw its unfair labor practice charge on the basis of a private agreement, the regional director normally will grant the request so long as the settlement is not repugnant to the purposes of the Act. Since the Board exists to vindicate public rather than private rights, agreement by the immediate parties to the proceeding does not guarantee that permission to withdraw the charge will be granted.[76] In some cases approval of the withdrawal request may be withheld pending full performance of the requirements set forth in the private settlement; in other instances withdrawal may be granted earlier but made conditional upon total performance of the commitments set forth in the private agreement.[77]

---

[71]NLRB Statements of Procedure §101.9(c)(2).

[72]NLRB Casehandling Manual ¶10172.6.

[73]NLRB Casehandling Manual ¶10174. Over the years the Board has accepted the principle that "[s]ettlement agreements are highly favored in the law and will be upheld whenever possible because they are a means of amicably resolving doubts and preventing lawsuits." *Hotel Holiday Inn De Isla Verde v. NLRB*, 723 F.2d 169, 173 n.1, 115 LRRM 2188, 2191 n.1 (1st Cir. 1983). When settlement agreements are rejected by the Board, it generally is because they do not afford employees adequate relief, *Clear Haven Nursing Home*, 236 NLRB 853, 98 LRRM 1314 (1978), or for some other reason do not appear to effectuate the policies of the Act. *E.g.*, *Carpenters 46 Northern Calif. Counties Conf. Bd. (Arntz Contracting Co.)*, 274 NLRB No. 181, 118 LRRM 1588 (1985) (proposed settlement rejected in view of recidivist history of certain union respondents and alleged continuation of similar misconduct).

[74]NLRB Statements of Procedure §101.9(e)(1).

[75]NLRB Casehandling Manual ¶10142, as modified by General Counsel Memorandum 83-16, *Revisions to Sections 101.22, 101.42, 101.44* (August 5, 1983). Such agreements may be oral as well as written. NLRB Casehandling Manual ¶10144, as modified by *Revisions to Sections 101.22, 101.42, 101.44*, *supra*. Copies of the General Counsel Memorandum may be acquired from the Board's Information Division.

[76]*Id.* at ¶10142; *U.S. Contractors, Inc. v. NLRB*, 697 F.2d 692, 112 LRRM 2742 (5th Cir. 1983); *Community Medical Servs.*, 236 NLRB 853, 98 LRRM 1314 (1978).

[77]NLRB Casehandling Manual ¶10142.

15

Unfair Labor Practice Prehearing Procedures

If the investigation reveals that a charge has merit, and if the attempts to settle the case have been unsuccessful, the regional director, on behalf of the General Counsel, commences a formal action by serving a complaint and notice of hearing on all "parties." The "parties" upon whom the complaint is served include:

- The person filing the charge;
- The person against whom the charge is filed;
- Any party to a contract alleged to be unlawful;
- Any labor organization alleged to be company assisted or dominated;
- Any recognized labor organization whose bargaining status is in question; and
- Each labor organization involved in a jurisdictional dispute.[1]

The regional director has the discretion to serve copies of the complaint on interested persons other than those mentioned above,[2] and may limit the participation rights of any party to the extent of that party's interest in the proceeding.[3] Employees affected by the proceeding who are not charging parties generally are not served with a copy of the complaint. There is no fixed period of time after the charge has been filed in which a complaint must issue. The six-month limitation in Section 10(b) of the Act applies only to the filing and service of a charge and not to the issuance of a complaint. Re-

---

[1]NLRB Rules and Regulations §102.8; NLRB Casehandling Manual ¶¶10264, 10270.
[2]NLRB Casehandling Manual ¶10270.
[3]NLRB Rules and Regulations §102.8.

gional directors, however, historically have issued complaints approximately 44 days after the filing of the charge.[4]

Complaint and Notice of Hearing

§15.1 Contents of Complaint

The complaint contains a clear and concise statement of the facts upon which the Board's jurisdiction is predicated and a description of the acts claimed to constitute unfair labor practices. (See Exhibit 81.) If known, the approximate dates and places of such acts and the names of respondent's agents or other representatives who committed the acts are set forth.[5] The typical complaint contains separate numbered paragraphs setting forth: (1) specifics concerning the filing and service of the original and amended charges; (2) recital of jurisdictional facts; (3) identity and nature of the parties; (4) chronology of events; (5) enumeration of the sections of the Act alleged to have been violated; and, in most cases, (6) a prayer for relief.[6]

The allegations of the complaint should be sufficiently detailed to enable the parties to understand the offenses charged and the issues to be litigated.[7] Such things as dates and locations of incidents, names of involved persons, including alleged discriminatees, and descriptions of bargaining units generally are set forth if they are known. It is not necessary, however, that the complaint constitute a mirror image of the underlying unfair labor practice charge. If the investigation of the charge uncovers evidence of additional unlawful conduct, the General Counsel may include such conduct in the complaint so long as it occurred within the appropriate six-month limitations period and is similar in nature or related to the incidents described in the charge.[8] The only limitation is that a complaint may not issue on matters so completely outside the scope of the charge that the Board may be said to be initiating the proceeding on its own motion.[9]

---

[4] 46 NLRB ANN. REP. Table 23 (1981).

[5] NLRB Rules and Regulations §102.15. *See generally* NLRB Casehandling Manual ¶¶10260–10276. Shareholders and corporate officers may be named as individual respondents and may be held personally liable to remedy unfair labor practices in instances where they disregard the corporate form, *Campo Slacks, Inc.*, 266 NLRB 492, 112 LRRM 1432 (1983); *Ski Craft Sales Corp.*, 237 NLRB 122, 98 LRRM 1518 (1978), or where their individual conduct is otherwise so egregious that imposition of personal liability would effectuate the purposes of the Act. *Workroom for Designers, Inc.*, 274 NLRB No. 115, 119 LRRM 1067 (1985).

[6] NLRB Casehandling Manual ¶10262. If the relief requested is routine, it may be omitted from the complaint and requested by counsel for the General Counsel in the opening or closing statements or in the posthearing brief.

[7] *Id.* at ¶10266; *Drukker Communications, Inc.*, 700 F.2d 727, 116 LRRM 2077 (D.C. Cir. 1983); *Sherwood Ford, Inc.*, 264 NLRB 863, 111 LRRM 1464 (1982).

[8] NLRB Casehandling Manual ¶10256.

[9] *NLRB v. Kohler Co.*, 220 F.2d 3, 35 LRRM 2606 (7th Cir. 1955). In *Clark Equipment Co.*, 278 NLRB No. 85, 121 LRRM 1258 (1986), the complaint cited numerous independent 8(a)(1) violations although no specific 8(a)(1) allegations appeared in either the original or amended charge. The Board nevertheless sustained the complaint on the basis of standard language in the Board's charge form.

UNITED STATES OF AMERICA
BEFORE THE NATIONAL LABOR RELATIONS BOARD
FIFTH REGION

Janco Computer Services, Inc.

and   Case No. 5-CA-1238

Local 007, United Computer Operators
International Union

COMPLAINT AND NOTICE OF HEARING

It having been charged by United Computer Operators International
Union, herein called the Union, that Janco Computer Services, Inc., herein
called Respondent, has enaged in, and is engaging in, unfair labor
practices affecting commerce as set forth and defined in the National Labor
Relations Act, as amended, 29 U.S.C. Sec. 151, et seq., herein
called the Act, the General Counsel of the National Labor Relations Board,
on behalf of the National Labor Relations Board, herein called the Board,
by the undersigned, pursuant to Section 10(b) of the Act, and Section
102.15 of the Board's Rules and Regulations, Series 8, as amended, hereby
issues this Complaint and Notice of Hearing and alleges as follows.

1.

The charge in this proceeding was filed by the Union on January 2,
1986, and a copy thereof was served by certified mail on Respondent on
January 2, 1986.

2.

At all times material herein, Respondent, a corporation with an office
and place of business in McLean, Virginia, herein called Respondent's
facility, has been engaged in the manufacture, sale, and distribution of
computer hardware, software, and related services.

3.

(a) Annually, Respondent, in the course and conduct of its business
operations described above in paragraph 2, sold and shipped from its
McLean, Virginia, facility, products, goods and materials valued in excess
of $50,000 directly to points outside the Commonwealth of Virginia.

(b) Annually, Respondent, in the course and conduct of its busness
operations described above in paragraph 2, purchased and received at its
McLean, Virginia, facility, products, goods, and materials valued in excess
of $50,000 directly from points outside the Commonwealth of Virginia.

4.

Respondent is now, and has been at all times material herein, an
employer engaged in commerce within the meaning of Section 2(2), (6) and
(7) of the Act.

Exhibit 81.   Complaint and Notice of Hearing

-2-

5.

The Union is now, and has been at all times material herein, a labor organization within the meaning of Section 2(5) of the Act.

6.

At all times material herein, James Snow occupied the position of General Manager, and is now, and has been at all times material herein, a supervisor of Respondent within the meaning of Section 2(11) of the Act and an agent of Respondent within the meaning of Section 2(13) of the Act.

7.

On or about November 6, 1985, Respondent, acting through James Snow, at its McLean, Virginia, location created an impression among its employees that their union activities were under surveillance by Respondent.

8.

On or about November 8, 1985, Respondent, acting through James Snow:

(a) Interrogated pro-union employee Mary Hughes regarding her union membership, activities and sympathies and the union membership, activities and sympathies of fellow employees.

(b) By soliciting employee complaints and grievances, promised its employees increased benefits and improved terms and conditions of employment.

(c) Threatened its employees with plant closure and loss of jobs if they selected the Union as their bargaining representative.

9.

On or about November 9, 1985, Respondent discharged its employee Mary Hughes.

10.

Respondent engaged in the conduct described above in paragraph 9 and has failed and refused and continues to fail and refuse to reinstate said employee because the employee named therein joined, supported, or assisted the Union, and engaged in other mutual aid or protection, and in order to discourage employees from engaging in such activities or other concerted activities for the purpose of collective bargaining or other mutual aid or protection.

11.

By the acts and conduct described above in paragraphs 7 and 8, and by each of said acts, Respondent has interfered with, restrained and coerced, and is interfering with, restraining and coercing employees in the exercise of their rights protected in Section 7 of the Act, and Respondent thereby has been engaging in unfair labor practices within the meaning of Section 8(a)(1) of the Act.

Exhibit 81—*page 2*

-3-

12.

By the acts and conduct described above in paragraphs 9 and 10, and by each of said acts, Respondent has discriminated, and is discriminating, in regard to the hire or tenure or terms or conditions of employment of its employees, thereby discouraging membership in a labor organization, and Respondent thereby has been engaging in unfair labor practices within the meaning of Section 8(a)(1) and (3) of the Act.

13.

The unfair labor practices of Respondent described above affect commerce within the meaning of Section 2(6) and (7) of the Act.

PLEASE TAKE NOTICE that commencing at 9:30 o'clock in the forenoon (EST) on the [Date], and on consecutive days thereafter, a hearing will be conducted in a conference room of the National Labor Relations Board, Fifth Region, 109 Market Place, Suite 4200, Baltimore, Maryland, before a duly designated administrative law judge of the National Labor Relations Board on the allegations set forth in the above complaint, at which time and place you will have the right to appear in person, or otherwise, and give testimony.

You are further notified that, pursuant to Sections 102.20 and 102.21 of the Board's Rules and Regulations, Series 8, as amended, Respondent shall file with the undersigned, acting in this matter as an agent of the National Labor Relations Board, an original and four (4) copies of an answer to said complaint within 14 days from the service thereof, and that, unless it does so, all of the allegations in the complaint shall be deemed to be admitted to be true and shall be so found by the Board. You are also notified that pursuant to said Rules and Regulations, Respondent shall serve a copy of the answer on each of the other parties.

Form NLRB-4668, Statement of Standard Procedure in Formal Hearings Held Before the National Labor Relations Board in Unfair Labor Practice Cases, is attached.

Dated at Baltimore, Maryland, this 2nd day of January, 1986.

Region 5
National Labor Relations Board
Candler Building, Fourth Floor
109 Market Place
Baltimore, Maryland 21201

Attachment

Exhibit 81—*page 3*

§15.2 Amendments to Complaint

A complaint may be amended at any time prior to issuance of a Board order.[10] Complaints may be amended: (1) before the commencement of the hearing by the regional director who issued the complaint; (2) during the hearing and before transfer to the Board by the administrative law judge; and (3) after transfer to the Board by the Board itself.[11] In some situations the General Counsel's request to amend the complaint at the hearing may generate a request by the respondent for a hearing postponement. In order to avoid such a request, the General Counsel may notify the respondent in advance that a motion to amend will be made at the hearing and may provide details of the contemplated amendment.[12]

Amendments made at the hearing must be approved by the administrative law judge upon motion made either in writing, orally on the record, or through interlineations made on the original or amended complaint.[13] If the administrative law judge denies a request to amend, the General Counsel normally will take an immediate appeal rather than renew the request at the end of the trial through an exception to the administrative law judge's decision.[14] Requests for amendments made after the transfer of the case to the Board must be filed with the Board in Washington, D.C.[15]

Due process considerations weigh heavily in ruling upon requests for amendments to the complaint. If the new conduct sought to be included in the amended complaint is similar or related to the conduct set forth in the original complaint, the request is more likely to be granted than if the new conduct is unrelated and the respondent has never before been put on notice that its actions will be challenged.[16] Similarly, an amendment request is likely to be granted when the issue sought to be added to the complaint has been discussed at the hearing and the General Counsel is simply seeking to conform the

---

[10]NLRB Rules and Regulations §102.17; NLRB Casehandling Manual ¶10274.

[11]NLRB Rules and Regulations §102.17; NLRB Casehandling Manual ¶¶10274.1 (prehearing amendment), 10274.2 (amendment at the hearing), 10274.3 (posthearing amendment). Amendments made during the hearing also are discussed at §16.15.

[12]NLRB Casehandling Manual ¶10274.1.

[13]*Id.* at ¶10274.2.

[14]*Id.*

[15]*Id.* at ¶10274.3.

[16]*Compare Cobb Theatres, Inc.*, 260 NLRB 856, 109 LRRM 1267 (1982) (complaint properly amended because additional allegations "related back" to matters in original complaint) *with Taurus Waste Disposal, Inc.*, 263 NLRB 309, 111 LRRM 1031 (1982) (complaint could not be amended because new allegation was unrelated to the allegations contained in original complaint). Proposed amendments to complaints also may raise issues of timeliness. If the conduct alleged as unlawful in the amended complaint occurred more than six months prior to the amendment but within six months of the original charge, the proposed amendment will be untimely if the two events are considered to be distinct and separate violations, *Allied Indus. Workers Local 594 (Warren Molded Plastics)*, 227 NLRB 1541, 94 LRRM 1699 (1977), but timely if viewed as two component incidents of a single integrated event, *Kelly-Goodwin Hardwood Co.*, 269 NLRB 33, 115 LRRM 1240 (1984); *see also Carpenters Local 720 (Stone & Webster Eng'g)*, 274 NLRB No. 219, 118 LRRM 1594 (1985).

complaint to the proof or to add an unfair labor practice which already has been fully litigated.[17] In cases where the amendment request catches the respondent by surprise, the administrative law judge may postpone the hearing in order to afford the respondent an opportunity to prepare a defense to the new allegations.[18]

§15.3   Withdrawal of Complaint

A complaint may be withdrawn before the hearing by the regional director upon his or her own motion, or upon the request of any party.[19] Prehearing withdrawal requests generally are based upon informal settlement agreements reached by the parties[20] that provide for withdrawal of the complaint, or upon the discovery of evidence that the underlying charge lacks merit.

Once the hearing has opened, the administrative law judge must approve any withdrawal of the complaint.[21] A motion is filed by the General Counsel and the administrative law judge may either approve the withdrawal request or simply dismiss the complaint. A motion for withdrawal of the complaint may be filed upon full compliance with the terms of an informal settlement agreement reached after the opening of the hearing.[22] If a charging party requests that the charge be withdrawn after the case has been transferred by the administrative law judge to the Board, the General Counsel in those circumstances files a motion directly with the Board requesting that the complaint be dismissed rather than withdrawn.[23]

§15.4   Notice of Hearing and Hearing Postponements

A notice of hearing usually is part of the formal complaint when it is served upon the parties.[24] The notice of hearing fixes the time

---

[17]*NLRB v. Iron Workers, Local 433*, 600 F.2d 770, 101 LRRM 3119 (9th Cir. 1979) (NLRB warranted in finding that union violated Section 8(b)(1)(A) by threats and violence. Although Board's complaint did not specifically allege threats and violence, the issues were fully and fairly litigated at the hearing); *Nebraska Bulk Transp., Inc.*, 240 NLRB 135, 100 LRRM 1340 (1979) (General Counsel permitted to amend complaint against employer to include additional allegations where the motion to amend was predicated on testimony from the employer's witnesses and from one of the employer's exhibits, and additional allegations were similar to those in original complaint). *But see Charles Batchelder Co.*, 250 NLRB 89, 104 LRRM 1342 (1980) (General Counsel's request for an additional Section 8(a)(1) finding was not deemed timely nor was it considered properly raised and was therefore denied). Motions to conform the pleadings to the proof are discussed further at §16.21.

[18]NLRB Casehandling Manual ¶10406.2.

[19]NLRB Rules and Regulations §102.18; NLRB Casehandling Manual ¶10275.1. *Olympia Fields Osteopathic Med. Center*, 278 NLRB No. 119, 121 LRRM 1246 (1986).

[20]Prehearing *formal* settlement agreements do not provide for either the withdrawl or dismissal of a complaint. NLRB Casehandling Manual ¶¶10164–10174.

[21]NLRB Casehandling Manual ¶10275.3. See also discussion at §§16.15 and 16.21.

[22]NLRB Casehandling Manual ¶10275.3.

[23]*Id.* at ¶10275.4.

[24]*Id.* at ¶10267. In *Van Heusen Co.*, 221 NLRB 732, 90 LRRM 1687 (1975), the Board held that the respondent was not denied due process when the notice of hearing was issued six months after the complaint when the proceeding was consolidated with another complaint.

and place of the hearing before an administrative law judge. The hearing date is set at least 14 days after the time of the receipt of the complaint and, in most cases, much later.

The Board's general rule is that unfair labor practice hearings will be conducted on the dates scheduled and that postponements will be granted only when good cause can be shown.[25] The rules and regulations, however, do provide that the regional director issuing the complaint may extend the hearing date or change the location of the hearing upon his or her own motion, or when good cause can be shown by any other party.[26]

Motions for postponement must be in writing. An original and two copies are submitted to the regional director and copies served simultaneously on all other parties.[27] The motion must contain a detailed statement of the reasons for the postponement request and should contain suggestions for alternative hearing dates. The positions of the other parties regarding postponement should be ascertained in advance and set forth in the motion.[28] Except in emergency situations, requests for postponement should be filed at least three days before the scheduled hearing date.[29]

Answer

§15.5 Contents of Answer

The respondent has 14 days from the service of the complaint to file an answer.[30] (See Exhibit 82.) The answer must specifically admit, deny, or explain each and every fact alleged in the complaint. A general statement in a letter or otherwise that the respondent denies having engaged in unlawful conduct will not satisfy the Board's specificity requirements.[31] If the respondent has no knowledge concerning an allegation, the answer should clearly state that the respondent is without knowledge to admit or deny the truth of the allegation and such answer will be treated by the Board as a denial.[32]

---

[25]NLRB Casehandling Manual ¶¶10258, 10294.1. Postponements requested during the hearing are discussed at §16.16.

[26]NLRB Rules and Regulations §102.16.

[27]NLRB Casehandling Manual ¶10294.2.

[28]*Id.*

[29]*Id.*

[30]NLRB Rules and Regulations §102.20. *See generally* NLRB Casehandling Manual ¶¶10280–10280.4.

[31]*Contractors Excavating, Inc.*, 270 NLRB 1189, 116 LRRM 1248 (1984) (unsigned and undated document purporting to be an answer but failing to conform to Board's rules rejected); *American Steel Line Co.*, 249 NLRB 380, 104 LRRM 1188 (1980) (employer's answer not acceptable under Board's rules and regulations because it did not address the alleged violations).

[32]NLRB Rules and Regulations §102.20; NLRB Casehandling Manual ¶10280. A respondent, however, may not seek to raise a material issue of fact by denying knowledge of its own actions. *DPM of Kansas, Inc.*, 261 NLRB 220, 110 LRRM 1022 (1982).

UNITED STATES OF AMERICA
BEFORE THE NATIONAL LABOR RELATIONS BOARD

Janco Computer Services, Inc.

    and   Case No. 5-CA-1238

Local 007, United Computer Operators
  International Union

ANSWER

Comes now Janco Computer Services, Inc. and within the time set forth by the Board's Rules and Regulations, files this Answer to the Complaint filed by the Regional Director in the above-styled case.

1. Admitted.

2. Admitted.

3. (a) Admitted.

   (b) Admitted.

4. Admitted.

5. Admitted.

6. Admitted, with the exception that James Snow is General Operations Manager.

7. Denied.

8. (a) Respondent is without knowledge as to whether Mary Hughes is a pro-union employee. This paragraph otherwise is denied.

   (b) Denied.

   (c) Denied.

9. Admitted.

10. Denied.

11. Denied.

12. Denied.

13. Denied.

Wherefore, having fully answered all counts of this Complaint, Respondent Janco Computer Services, Inc. respectfully moves that it be dismissed on all counts.

                   Respectfully submitted,

                   _____

                   Jonathan R. Lewis, Senior Attorney
                   Janco Computer Services, Inc.
                   8181 Greensboro Drive
                   McLean, Virginia 22102

Exhibit 82.   Answer

If a timely answer is not filed, the allegations in the complaint will be deemed by the Board to be admitted as true. Similarly, any complaint allegation which is not specifically denied or explained will be considered to be admitted as true unless the respondent states that it is without knowledge or unless good cause to the contrary can be shown.[33] The same rules apply to amended complaints. If the respondent files an answer to the original complaint but fails to file an answer to an amended complaint, the Board may consider the allegations in the amended complaint to be admitted as true.[34]

An original and four copies of the answer must be filed with the regional director who issued the complaint and copies served immediately upon the other parties.[35] A party represented by counsel must have one attorney of record sign the answer and furnish an address; parties not represented by counsel must sign the answer in their own names and provide their own addresses.[36] As a general rule, answers need not be verified or accompanied by an affidavit. However, answers which are not properly signed, which are filed strictly for purposes of delay, or which contain scandalous or indecent material may be stricken in whole or in part,[37] and any attorney filing such an answer may be subject to disciplinary action.[38]

§15.6 Timeliness of Answer

The answer must be filed within 14 days of service of the complaint.[39] This time may be extended by the regional director, however, either upon his or her own motion or upon the request of any other party if good cause can be shown.[40] In most cases the Board is not anxious to determine the substantive rights of the parties on the basis of failure to comply with the 14-day filing requirement. While regional directors are inclined to accept late filings if good cause can be shown,[41] the Board has made it clear that reasons such as the

---

[33]NLRB Rules and Regulations §102.20; NLRB Casehandling Manual ¶10280.1.

[34]*Oldwick Materials, Inc.*, 264 NLRB 1152, 111 LRRM 1451 (1982). Similarly, where a complaint is withdrawn as part of a settlement agreement and subsequently refiled because of noncompliance with the settlement terms, a second answer is required. *Orange Data, Inc.*, 274 NLRB No. 156, 118 LRRM 1441 (1985).

[35]NLRB Rules and Regulations §102.21.

[36]*Id.*

[37]NLRB Casehandling Manual ¶10280.2. Motions to strike filed by the General Counsel are carefully considered by the Board. Requests to strike statements in an answer which do not constitute a defense to the complaint allegations will be denied when it appears that the respondent is attempting to preserve its position. *Coca-Cola Bottling Co.*, 264 NLRB 94, 111 LRRM 1254 (1982); *Westin Hotel*, 261 NLRB 1005, 110 LRRM 1145 (1982); *G.F. Business Equip., Inc.*, 256 NLRB 262, 107 LRRM 1244 (1981).

[38]NLRB Rules and Regulations §102.21.

[39]*Id.* at §102.20.

[40]*Id.* at §102.22.

[41]*See NLRB v. Zeno Table Co.*, 610 F.2d 567, 102 LRRM 2540 (9th Cir. 1979), where the court made it clear that the Board should apply a "good cause" standard rather than a more onerous "extraordinary circumstances" standard in evaluating an employer's reasons for filing a late answer.

failure to have an attorney,[42] the attorney's delinquency in reviewing the complaint,[43] or simply the attorney's failure to file a timely answer[44] do not constitute good cause.

If an answer has not been filed within the allotted period, the Board attorney assigned to the case generally will attempt to contact the respondent or its counsel in writing and notify it that the answer has not been received. An additional one week for filing an answer may be offered, and only if an answer is not received within the extended time period will a motion for summary judgment be filed.[45]

§15.7 Amendments to Answer

A respondent may amend the answer at any time prior to the opening of the hearing.[46] Once the hearing has opened, the answer may be amended in response to an amendment of the complaint and, at the discretion of the administrative law judge or the Board, may be amended even in the absence of a complaint modification.[47] Such factors as the nature of the new allegations, the extent to which the respondent should reasonably have been able to anticipate them, and the amount of notice afforded are considered by the administrative law judge in deciding whether and during what period of time the respondent should be permitted to amend the answer.[48]

If an answer is withdrawn rather than amended, the legal effect is the same as if no answer had ever been filed, and all of the allegations in the complaint are considered to be admitted as true.[49]

Prehearing Motions

§15.8 Filing and Appeal of Prehearing Motions

There are a wide variety of possible prehearing motions. The nature of the motion determines where and with whom it is filed.[50] The following motions are filed with the regional director: (1) post-

---

[42]*Urban Labs., Inc.*, 249 NLRB 867, 104 LRRM 1233 (1980).

[43]*Sherwood Coal Co.*, 252 NLRB 497, 105 LRRM 1354 (1980).

[44]*Hillcrest Packing Co.*, 247 NLRB 1389, 103 LRRM 1330 (1980). The Board noted that the respondent had notice that the answer had not been filed, had indicated an intention to file an answer on its own, and failed to do so. *Id.*

[45]NLRB Casehandling Manual ¶10280.3.

[46]NLRB Rules and Regulations §102.23; NLRB Casehandling Manual ¶10280.4.

[47]*Id.*

[48]*Cf.* NLRB Casehandling Manual ¶10406.

[49]*D & L Contracting, Inc.*, 266 NLRB No. 20, 112 LRRM 1271 (1983).

[50]*See generally* NLRB Rules and Regulations §§102.24–102.33; NLRB Casehandling Manual ¶¶10290–10292. Procedures applicable to motions filed during the hearing are discussed at §16.14.

ponement of the hearing date,[51] (2) extension of time to file an answer, (3) intervention in the hearing, and (4) taking of a deposition.[52] Motions for summary judgment are filed with the Board[53] and all other motions are filed with the chief, deputy chief, or associate chief administrative law judge, as appropriate.[54]

All prehearing motions should be filed with an original and four copies[55] and additional copies served immediately upon the other parties. The motion should state briefly the order or relief requested and the reasons why the request is appropriate. All motions and responses should be filed promptly to expedite the proceeding.[56] Motions submitted to the administrative law judges will be assigned to a judge who may or may not eventually be assigned to hear the case. If the judge's ruling is issued prior to the opening of the hearing, it will be in writing and a copy served on each of the parties.[57]

In most cases a party aggrieved by a ruling on a prehearing motion will not seek an immediate appeal, but rather will wait until the administrative law judge has issued a decision and then file an exception to the adverse ruling with the Board. If an immediate appeal is desired, however, a request for special permission to appeal—accompanied by the actual appeal itself—must be filed promptly with the Board.[58] The request must be in writing and should describe briefly the reasons why special permission should be granted and the appeal sustained. After the other parties have been given an opportunity to respond, the Board will rule upon the request for special permission to appeal and, if granted, upon the appeal itself.[59]

§15.9 Motions to Consolidate or Sever Cases

In some situations it may be advisable for two or more related cases to be consolidated for purposes of a hearing and Board review. In other situations changed circumstances may dictate that cases which previously were consolidated now should be severed and processed separately. Prior to the hearing the regional director has the authority to consolidate or sever cases pending in his or her region.[60]

---

[51]See discussion at §15.4 *supra.*

[52]NLRB Rules and Regulations §§102.24, 102.30(a), 102.33(d).

[53]NLRB Rules and Regulations §102.24; NLRB Casehandling Manual ¶¶10290, 10290.2, 10290.3.

[54]NLRB Rules and Regulations §102.24; NLRB Casehandling Manual ¶¶10290, 10290.2, 10290.3.

[55]A motion for summary judgment is filed with the Board and therefore requires eight copies. See §15.18 *infra.*

[56]NLRB Rules and Regulations §102.24; NLRB Casehandling Manual ¶¶10290, 10290.1.

[57]NLRB Rules and Regulations §102.25; NLRB Casehandling Manual ¶10290.3.

[58]NLRB Rules and Regulations §102.26; NLRB Casehandling Manual ¶10290.4. Copies must be served on the other parties and, if the appeal is from an administrative law judge's ruling, a copy must be served on the administrative law judge as well.

[59]NLRB Rules and Regulations §102.26.

[60]*Id.* at §§102.33(c), (d).

If one of the parties rather than the regional director seeks consolidation or severance, however, a motion must be filed.[61] Motions prior to the hearing are filed with the chief, deputy chief, or associate chief administrative law judge, as appropriate, while those filed during the hearing are submitted to the administrative law judge.[62]

The Board has determined that consolidation may be appropriate in the following circumstances:[63]

- Representation cases involving the same employer or the same employer association;
- Unfair labor practice cases involving the same employer;
- Unfair labor practice cases involving the same union where the fact situations are related, e.g., an illegal contract or an association-wide strike;
- Unfair labor practice cases against an employer and a union which arise from the same set of facts, e.g., a discharge, a strike, or negotiations where both sides are alleged to have engaged in bad faith bargaining; and
- Where a hearing has been directed in a representation case concerning conduct which also has been alleged to constitute an unfair labor practice.

Cases which previously have been consolidated may be severed if consolidation no longer appears to be appropriate.[64]

Decisions on consolidation and severance are discretionary with the regional director or the administrative law judge. Administrative efficiency, however, is the principal consideration. To the extent that two or more cases arise out of the same set of operative facts, involve the same respondent, raise the same or similar legal issues, and require the testimony of the same witnesses, administrative efficiency is enhanced through consolidation.[65] In contrast, no interest is served by consolidating cases presenting unrelated issues even if they do share a common respondent.[66] Rulings by the administrative law judge on motions to consolidate or sever may be appealed to the Board on the same basis as other motions filed before or during the hearing.[67]

---

[61]*Id.* at §102.33(d); NLRB Casehandling Manual ¶11720.4.

[62]NLRB Rules and Regulations §102.33(d); NLRB Casehandling Manual ¶11720.4; *see also* NLRB Rules and Regulations §102.24.

[63]NLRB Casehandling Manual ¶11720.2.

[64]*Id.* at ¶11720.3.

[65]*Free-Flow Packaging Corp.*, 219 NLRB 925, 90 LRRM 1230 (1975) (representation case and unfair labor practice case consolidated where it was determined that "the unfair labor practices charged, the designated objections, and various challenged ballots, constituted a single overall controversy").

[66]*See, e.g., United States Postal Serv.*, 263 NLRB 357, 111 LRRM 1534 (1982) (not appropriate to consolidate cases involving different units of employees, different factual backgrounds, and different allegations); *Albert Einstein Med. Center*, 245 NLRB 140, 102 LRRM 1508 (1979).

[67]NLRB Rules and Regulations §102.33(d); see also discussion at §15.8 *supra*.

§15.10 Motions to Intervene

Persons having an interest in an unfair labor practice proceeding may seek to intervene either before or after the hearing starts. If intervention is sought prior to the hearing, a written motion must be filed with the regional director.[68] The regional director may rule upon the motion or refer it to the administrative law judge.[69]

Motions to intervene may be granted to the extent and upon such terms as the regional director or the administrative law judge deems appropriate. A request to intervene may be denied if intervention is sought in an unfair labor practice case for purposes of relitigating issues considered in an earlier representation proceeding.[70] On the other hand, intervention requests by persons who appear to be "interested parties" generally are granted.[71]

§15.11 Motions for Bill of Particulars

One of the most common prehearing motions is for a bill of particulars addressed to the complaint.[72] Bills of particulars also may be addressed to affirmative defenses raised in an answer.[73] A bill of particulars is appropriate in situations where the pleading to which it is addressed lacks specificity in describing the acts which are claimed to constitute the unlawful conduct. Board attorneys are instructed to furnish the particulars requested in all situations where a complaint is, or may arguably be, insufficient.[74]

§15.12 Applications for Depositions

The Federal Rules of Civil Procedure which provide for compulsory pretrial discovery are not applicable to Board proceedings.[75] Prehearing depositions for purposes of discovery are not allowed. Depositions may, however, be used for purposes of preserving the

---

[68]NLRB Rules and Regulations §102.29. The normal rules regarding service and the number of copies which must be filed apply to such motions. See discussion §15.8 *supra*. Motions to intervene made at the hearing are discussed at §16.17.

[69]*Id.*

[70]*Dow Chemical, U.S.A.*, 229 NLRB 1162, 95 LRRM 1287 (1977); *United States Steel Corp.*, 189 NLRB 119, 76 LRRM 1570 (1971).

[71]*See, e.g., Camay Drilling Co.*, 239 NLRB 997, 100 LRRM 1136 (1978) (pension fund trustees permitted to intervene where employer was alleged to have unlawfully terminated pension fund contributions); *Taylor Bros., Inc.*, 230 NLRB 861, 96 LRRM 1040 (1977) (employees permitted to intervene to be given an opportunity to vote on bargaining representative); *Electrical Workers Local 3 (N.Y. Tel. Co.)*, 197 NLRB 866, 80 LRRM 1630 (1972) (international union permitted to intervene on basis of contract administered by affiliated local).

[72]NLRB Casehandling Manual ¶10292.1.

[73]*Id.* at ¶10292.2.

[74]*Id.* at ¶10292.1. NLRB Casehandling Manual ¶10266 requires that the complaint be "sufficiently detailed to enable the parties to understand the offenses charged and the issues to be met."

[75]*Id.* at ¶10292.4.

testimony of witnesses who, because of illness or distance, will be unable to attend the hearing.[76]

Application for a deposition, if made before the opening of the hearing, must be filed in writing with the regional director.[77] The application must set forth the reasons why, when, and where such deposition should be taken and the matters about which it is expected the witness will testify. The application should be served upon the regional director at least seven days before the desired date for the deposition. The regional director may grant the application only if "good cause" has been shown. As noted, "good cause" may be found in the unavailability of a witness, either due to illness or great distance from the place of hearing.[78] If the application is granted and an order and notice of deposition is issued, the procedure followed is identical to that used when an administrative law judge grants a similar application.[79]

§15.13　Applications for Subpoenas

The Act provides that the Board shall, upon the application of any party, issue a subpoena requiring the attendance and testimony of witnesses or the production of evidence at the hearing.[80] Applications filed prior to the hearing are submitted to the regional director while those filed at the hearing are submitted to the administrative law judge.[81] There are two basic trial subpoenas: (1) *subpoena ad testificandum* which requires the party served to appear for the sole purpose of giving testimony (see Exhibit 33), and (2) *subpoena duces tecum* which requires the party served to appear both to give testimony and to present documents named in the subpoena (see Exhibit 34). The application for a subpoena may be made *ex parte* and it is not necessary to furnish the name of the witness to be served or a description of the documents sought to be produced.[82] The application is granted by the regional director in the name of the Board.

---

[76]*NLRB v. Interboro Contractors, Inc.*, 432 F.2d 854, 75 LRRM 2459 (2d Cir. 1970); *Flite Chief, Inc.*, 258 NLRB 1124, 108 LRRM 1303 (1981).

[77]NLRB Rules and Regulations §102.30(a); NLRB Casehandling Manual ¶10352.2; *Ford Paint & Varnish Co.*, 264 NLRB 1189, 112 LRRM 1033 (1982).

[78]NLRB Casehandling Manual ¶10352.3; *Valley Mold Co.*, 215 NLRB 211, 88 LRRM 1514 (1974) (expense and inconvenience of having employer's employees appear as witnesses at hearing does not constitute good cause for taking their depositions).

[79]See discussion at §16.19.

[80]Sec. 11(1); *see also* NLRB Rules and Regulations §102.31 and NLRB Casehandling Manual ¶¶11770–11828. The discussion in this section relates to trial subpoenas. Special rules apply for investigative subpoenas (*see* NLRB Casehandling Manual ¶¶11770–11770.3) and for subpoenas issued in situations where the witness has refused or is likely to refuse to testify or provide other information on the basis of the privilege against self-incrimination (*see* NLRB Rules and Regulations §102.31(c) and NLRB Casehandling Manual ¶11770).

[81]NLRB Rules and Regulations §102.31(a); NLRB Casehandling Manual ¶11772.1. Requests for subpoenas filed during the hearing are discussed in the next chapter at §16.20. Subpoena enforcement proceedings are discussed at §§21.15–21.20.

[82]NLRB Casehandling Manual ¶11772.1.

Subpoenas may be served personally, by registered mail, by telegraph, or by delivery at the principal office or business address of the person required to be served.[83] If a person served is represented by counsel, a copy of the subpoena also must be served upon the attorney. Whenever possible, the subpoena should be served at least five days before the testimony is scheduled to be given or the requested documents produced.[84]

If the person served does not intend to comply, a petition to revoke the subpoena must be filed within five days after the subpoena has been served.[85] Petitions to revoke filed before the hearing are submitted to the regional director and referred to the administrative law judge or to the Board for a ruling.[86] Copies of the petition to revoke are furnished to the person who requested the subpoena. The subpoena generally will be revoked if it is determined that (1) the evidence sought to be produced does not relate to any matter under investigation, (2) the subpoena does not describe with sufficient particularity the evidence sought to be produced, or (3) if for any other reason sufficient in law the subpoena is otherwise invalid.[87] Unless specifically requested by the party aggrieved by the ruling, a petition to revoke a subpoena and related documents are not made a part of the official record.[88]

§15.14 Preliminary Section 10(j) Injunctive Relief

In the great majority of cases the charging party must wait until the unfair labor practice case has been settled or completed through issuance of a Board or court order before receiving remedial relief. Section 10(j) of the Act provides, however, that upon issuance of a complaint the Board may petition an appropriate United States district court for temporary relief or a restraining order.[89] Section 10(j) was enacted because of the realization that several months or even years may elapse between the filing of a complaint and issuance of a final order. Accordingly, the "injunctive relief provided for in Section 10(j) is interlocutory in nature; it is designed to fill the considerable time gap between the filing of a complaint by the Board and

---

[83]Sec. 11(4); NLRB Casehandling Manual ¶11778. A *subpoena duces tecum* should be served on the individual having custody of the documents desired, not merely on any company or union representative. NLRB Casehandling Manual ¶11776.

[84]NLRB Casehandling Manual ¶11778.

[85]NLRB Rules and Regulations §102.31(b); NLRB Casehandling Manual ¶¶11782–11782.5. Petitions to revoke must actually be received within the designated five-day period, not simply placed in the mails. NLRB Rules and Regulations §102.111(b)(4).

[86]NLRB Rules and Regulations §102.31(b); NLRB Casehandling Manual ¶11782.1.

[87]NLRB Rules and Regulations §102.31(b); NLRB Casehandling Manual ¶11782.

[88]NLRB Rules and Regulations §102.31(b); NLRB Casehandling Manual ¶11782.5.

[89]The nature of Section 10(j) relief is discussed in NLRB Rules and Regulations §102.94 and the specific procedures for acquiring Section 10(j) relief in the federal courts are discussed at §21.11 *infra*.

issuance of its final decision, in those cases in which considerable harm may occur in the interim."[90]

Unlike Section 10(l) injunctions which are mandatory and which are authorized by the regional director, Section 10(j) injunctive relief is discretionary and must be authorized by the Board. The statute does not provide any criteria for the exercise of Section 10(j) authority, but the Board has considered certain factors in determining whether proceedings under that section are appropriate:[91]

- The clarity of the alleged violations;
- Whether the case involves the shutdown of important business operations which, because of their special nature, would have an extraordinary impact on the public interest;
- Whether the alleged unfair labor practices involve an unusually wide geographic area, thus creating special problems of public concern;
- Whether the unfair labor practices create special remedy problems that would make it impossible either to restore the status quo or to dissipate effectively the consequences of the unfair labor practices through use of the regular procedures provided in the Act for Board orders and subsequent enforcement proceedings;
- Whether the unfair labor practices involve interference with the conduct of an election or constitute a clear and flagrant disregard of Board certification of a bargaining representative or other Board procedures;
- Whether the continuation of the alleged unfair labor practices will result in exceptional hardship to the charging party;
- Whether the current unfair labor practice is of a continuing or repetitious pattern;
- Whether, if violence is involved, it is out of control of local authorities or otherwise widespread and susceptible to control by Section 10(j) relief.

In cases where the regional director has decided to issue a complaint and has concluded that Section 10(j) relief would be appropriate, a memorandum is prepared setting forth the fact findings to be relied upon, the legal analysis which establishes a violation, the reason why Section 10(j) relief is considered necessary, and the specific interim relief to be requested. This memorandum is submitted to the General Counsel in Washington, D.C., who reviews the request,

---

[90]*Fuchs v. Hood Indus., Inc.*, 590 F.2d 395, 397, 100 LRRM 2547, 2548 (1st Cir. 1979).

[91]NLRB Casehandling Manual ¶10310.2. NLRB General Counsel Memorandum No. 79-77 (October 15, 1979) delineates 14 categories of cases which may be appropriate for Section 10(j) relief. These categories are discussed at §21.9(a)–(o) *infra*.

and, if he or she concurs in the recommendation, passes it through to the Board for approval.[92]

Stipulations

§15.15 When Appropriate

In some instances the parties may agree on the material facts but disagree as to the appropriate law. This may occur, for example, in Section 8(a)(5) refusal to bargain cases in which representation issues in a prior related proceeding are sought to be tested, in cases raising new legal or policy questions, and in cases where the facts already have been litigated in an earlier ancillary proceeding.[93] In these situations, a hearing before an administrative law judge may not be necessary and it would be faster and less expensive for the parties to stipulate to the agreed-upon facts and submit the case directly to the administrative law judge or to the Board for a decision.

In order to stipulate a case, the facts being stipulated must be sufficiently detailed to form the basis for findings, and they must be agreed upon. The parties cannot stipulate a case which requires the resolution of credibility conflicts. If there is disagreement not over the existence of certain facts but over the relevance of those facts to the disposition of the case, the case may nevertheless still be stipulated. In such instances all of the facts are included in the stipulation along with a statement that not all parties concede their relevance. Any party questioning relevance may thereafter set forth its position in its brief.[94]

§15.16 Stipulations to the Administrative Law Judge

Stipulations may be submitted either to an administrative law judge or to the Board. Those submitted to an administrative law judge waive the right to a hearing, stipulate the facts, and agree that an administrative law judge may issue a decision upon the basis of the submission. Where this is done, the parties may specifically reserve the right to submit briefs to the administrative law judge. Such a stipulation does not in any way affect the parties' right to take to the Board any exceptions they may wish to file to the administrative law judge's decision. The stipulation is submitted in duplicate to the chief administrative law judge in Washington, D.C.[95]

---

[92]NLRB Casehandling Manual ¶10310.1.
[93]*Id.* at ¶10284.
[94]*Id.*
[95]*Id.* at ¶10286.

§15.17   Stipulations to the Board

A stipulation to the Board is accomplished by an agreement in which the parties stipulate the facts, waive their right to a hearing and to an administrative law judge's decision,[96] and agree that the Board may rule upon the basis of the submission. In addition, the parties may ask the Board to set a time for the filing of briefs. This stipulation does not bind the parties to accept the Board's decision; the right to appeal to the appropriate court of appeals remains unaffected. Such a submission is made by filing eight copies with the Board's Executive Secretary in Washington, D.C.[97]

Summary Procedures

There are instances in which the General Counsel may wish to dispense with a hearing before an administrative law judge and request an order against the respondent through summary proceedings.

§15.18   Summary Judgment

The most frequently used form of summary proceeding is a motion for summary judgment. Such motions may be filed when an answer is inadequate, untimely, or not filed at all.[98] They also are used in "technical 8(a)(5)" or "certification test" proceedings in which the employer is refusing to bargain in order to acquire court review of the underlying Board certification.[99] Similarly, summary judgment motions may be filed when an employer is attempting to relitigate in an unfair labor practice proceeding issues which were or could have been litigated in the prior representation proceeding (e.g., jurisdiction, appropriate unit, objections, challenged ballots, amendment of certification).[100] Respondents also may file motions for summary judgment when the General Counsel's complaint, on its face, fails to allege a violation of the Act.[101]

---

[96]Both parties must agree to waive the hearing before the administrative law judge. The administrative law judge has no authority to grant a request to dispense with the preparation and issuance of a decision over the objection of any party. *Lodge No. 1129, Machinists (Victoria Horwath)*, 216 NLRB 630, 89 LRRM 1265 (1975).

[97]NLRB Casehandling Manual ¶10288.

[98]*Id.* at ¶10280.3; *Contractors Excavating, Inc.*, 270 NLRB 1189, 116 LRRM 1248 (1984); *Parisian Manicure Mfg. Co.*, 258 NLRB 203, 108 LRRM 1128 (1981) (answer inadequate); *Clean and Shine*, 255 NLRB 1144, 107 LRRM 1056 (1981) (answer not filed).

[99]NLRB Casehandling Manual ¶¶10025, 10282; see also discussion of certification test proceedings at §10.19.

[100]*E.g., Divine Providence Hosp.*, 248 NLRB 521, 103 LRRM 1439 (1980).

[101]In *Manville Forest Prods. Corp.*, 269 NLRB 390, 115 LRRM 1266 (1984), the employer's motion for summary judgment was granted upon a showing that the only conduct alleged in the complaint to be a violation was unprotected activity.

Motions for summary judgment may be filed only in situations where there are no factual issues warranting a hearing.[102] Prior to granting the motion, the Board will issue to the respondent a Notice to Show Cause affording an opportunity to show cause why the motion should not be granted.[103]

§15.19 Judgment on the Pleadings and Default Judgment

In situations where the respondent fails to file an answer or where the answer admits the allegations in the complaint, the General Counsel may seek to secure a Board order without a hearing by filing a motion for judgment on the pleadings[104] or for default judgment.[105] Default judgments lack any precedential value.[106]

---

[102]NLRB Casehandling Manual ¶10282.1.

[103]NLRB Casehandling Manual ¶10282.2.

[104]*I.S.G. Extrusion Toolings, Inc.*, 262 NLRB 114, 110 LRRM 1248 (1982); *Dullinger Excavating, Inc.*, 261 NLRB 371, 110 LRRM 1096 (1982); *V. Pangori & Sons, Inc.*, 248 NLRB 405, 103 LRRM 1427 (1980).

[105]*E.g., Handy Dan's Convenience Store*, 275 NLRB No. 61, 119 LRRM 1142 (1985); *Standard Steel Treating Co.*, 266 NLRB No. 139, 113 LRRM 1072 (1983); *D & J Gravel Co.*, 261 NLRB 391, 110 LRRM 1096 (1982).

[106]*Brown Fox Mining Co.*, 270 NLRB No. 107, 116 LRRM 1360 (1984).

16

The Unfair Labor Practice Hearing

Nature of Unfair Labor Practice Hearing

§16.1 In General

Hearings for the purpose of taking evidence upon a complaint are conducted by an administrative law judge.[1] The judges are assigned by the chief administrative law judge in Washington, D.C., the deputy chief judge in San Francisco, or one of the associate chief judges in New York or Atlanta, and the parties are not entitled to know in advance the identity of the judge assigned to their case.[2] The hearing usually is open to the public[3] and is conducted in the region where the charge originated. An explanation of the mechanics of the hearing is enclosed with the complaint. (See Exhibit 83.)

All parties have the right to appear at the hearing either in person, by counsel, or by another representative; may call, examine, and cross-examine witnesses; and may introduce documentary and other evidence into the record.[4] The General Counsel is represented by an attorney, generally one assigned to the regional office issuing the complaint. Charging parties and respondents usually are represented by counsel. The Board, however, does not have rules requiring that parties be represented by an attorney so parties sometimes rely upon their own employees or professional consultants.

---

[1]*See generally* NLRB Rules and Regulations §§102.34–102.44; NLRB Statements of Procedure §101.10; NLRB Casehandling Manual ¶¶10380–10412; THE DEVELOPING LABOR LAW at 1621–1623. While the Board and individual Board members also may conduct unfair labor practice hearings, this authority rarely is exercised. NLRB Rules and Regulations §102.34.

[2]NLRB Rules and Regulations §102.34. Unauthorized *ex parte* communications may not be made with the administrative law judge, Board members, or staff once a complaint or notice of hearing has issued, or once the communicator learns that a complaint or notice of hearing will issue. NLRB Rules and Regulations §102.128(e).

[3]The Board and the administrative law judge have the authority to close the hearing to the public. NLRB Rules and Regulations §102.34.

[4]NLRB Rules and Regulations §102.38.

FORM NLRB-4668
(3-83)

(C Cases)

SUMMARY OF STANDARD PROCEDURES IN FORMAL HEARINGS HELD BEFORE THE NATIONAL LABOR RELATIONS BOARD IN UNFAIR LABOR PRACTICE PROCEEDINGS PURSUANT TO SECTION 10 OF THE NATIONAL LABOR RELATIONS ACT, AS AMENDED

The hearing will be conducted by an Administrative Law Judge of the National Labor Relations Board who will preside at the hearing as an independent, impartial trier of the facts and the law whose decision in due time will be served on the parties. The offices of the Administrative Law Judges are located in Washington, D.C.; San Francisco, California; New York, New York; and Atlanta, Georgia.

At the date, hour, and place for which the hearing is set, the Administrative Law Judge, upon the joint request of the parties, will conduct a "prehearing" conference, prior to or shortly after the opening of the hearing, to assure that the issues are sharp and clearcut; or the Administrative Law Judge may independently conduct such a conference. The Administrative Law Judge will preside at such conference, but may, if the occasion arises, permit the parties to engage in private discussions. The conference will not necessarily be recorded, but it may well be that the labors of the conference will be evinced in the ultimate record, for example, in the form of statements of position, stipulations, and concessions. Except under unusual circumstances, the Administrative Law Judge conducting the prehearing conference will be the one who will conduct the hearing; and it is expected that the formal hearing will commence or be resumed immediately upon completion of the prehearing conference. No prejudice will result to any party unwilling to participate in or make stipulations or concessions during any prehearing conference.

(This is not to be construed as preventing the parties from meeting earlier for similar purposes. To the contrary, the parties are encouraged to meet prior to the time set for hearing in an effort to narrow the issues.)

Parties may be represented by an attorney or other representative and present evidence relevant to the issues.

An official reporter will make the only official transcript of the proceedings, and all citations in briefs and arguments must refer to the official record. The Board will not certify any transcript other than the official transcript for use in any court litigation. Proposed corrections of the transcript should be submitted, either by way of stipulation or motion, to the Administrative Law Judge for approval.

All matter that is spoken in the hearing room while the hearing is in session will be recorded by the official reporter unless the Administrative Law Judge specifically directs off-the-record discussion. In the event that any party wishes to make off-the-record statements, a request to go off the record should be directed to the Administrative Law Judge and not to the official reporter.

Statements of reasons in support of motions and objections should be specific and concise. The Administrative Law Judge will allow an automatic exception to all adverse rulings and, upon appropriate order, an objection and exception will be permitted to stand to an entire line of questioning.

All exhibits offered in evidence shall be in duplicate. Copies of exhibits should be supplied to the Administrative Law Judge and other parties at the time the exhibits are offered in evidence. If a copy of any exhibit is not available at the time the original is received, it will be the responsibility of the party offering such exhibit to submit the copy to the Administrative Law Judge before the close of hearing. In the event such copy is not submitted, and the filing thereof has not for good reason shown been waived by the Administrative Law Judge, any ruling receiving the exhibit may be rescinded and the exhibit rejected.

Any party shall be entitled, upon request, to a reasonable period at the close of the hearing for oral argument, which shall be included in the stenographic report of the hearing. In the absence of a request, the Administrative Law Judge may ask for oral argument if, at the close of the hearing, it is believed that such argument would be beneficial to the understanding of the contentions of the parties and the factual issues involved.

(OVER)

Exhibit 83. Summary of Standard Procedures in Unfair Labor Practice Hearings (Form NLRB-4668)

FORM NLRB-4668 (3-83) Continued

Any party shall be entitled, upon request made before the close of the hearing, to file a brief or proposed findings and conclusions, or both, with the Administrative Law Judge who will fix the time for such filing. *Any such filing submitted shall be double-spaced on 8½ by 11 inch paper.*

Attention of the parties is called to the following requirements laid down in Section 102.42 of the Board's Rules and Regulations, Series 8, as amended, with respect to the procedure to be followed before the proceeding is transferred to the Board:

No request for an extension of time within which to submit briefs or proposed findings to the Administrative Law Judge will be considered unless received by the Chief Administrative Law Judge in Washington, D.C. *(or, in cases under the San Francisco, California branch office, the Deputy Chief Administrative Law Judge; or in cases under the branch offices in New York, New York, and Atlanta, Georgia, the Associate Chief Administrative Law Judge)* at least 3 days prior to the expiration of time fixed for the submission of such documents. Notice of request for such extension of time must be served simultaneously on all other parties, and proof of such service furnished to the Chief Administrative Law Judge, Deputy Chief Administrative Law Judge or the Associate Chief Administrative Law Judge, as the case may be. All briefs or proposed findings filed with the Administrative Law Judge must be submitted in triplicate, and may be printed or otherwise legibly duplicated with service on the other parties.

In due course the Administrative Law Judge will prepare and file with the Board a decision in this proceeding, and will cause a copy thereof to be served on each of the parties. Upon filing of this decision, the Board will enter an order transferring this case to itself, and will serve copies of that order, setting forth the date of such transfer, on all parties. At that point, the Administrative Law Judge's official connection with the case will cease.

The procedure to be followed before the Board from that point forward, with respect to the filing of exceptions to the Administrative Law Judge's decision, the submission of supporting briefs, requests for oral argument before the Board, and related matters, is set forth in the Board's Rules and Regulations, particularly in Section 102.46 and following sections. A summary of the more pertinent of these provisions will be served on the parties together with the order transferring the case to the Board.

Adjustments or settlements consistent with the policies of the Act reduce government expenditures and promote amity in labor relations. If adjustment appears possible, the Administrative Law Judge may suggest discussions between the parties or, upon request, will afford reasonable opportunity during the hearing for such discussions.

GPO 899-558

Exhibit 83—*page 2*

A verbatim transcript is made by an official court reporter retained by the Board.[5] The transcript constitutes the official record of the hearing and all citations and references made in briefs, arguments and motions must refer to the official record. If any party desires to purchase copies of the transcript, special arrangements must be made with the court reporter. The regional office obtains one copy of the transcript. The region's copy of the transcript technically is available to all parties, but its use by non-Board personnel is discouraged.

As discussed in greater detail below, at the conclusion of the hearing the parties may argue orally before the administrative law judge and submit briefs and proposed findings.[6] The administrative law judge thereafter issues a written decision containing proposed findings of fact, conclusions of law, and a recommended order. Upon the filing of exceptions by one or more of the parties, the judge's decision will be reviewed by the Board in Washington, D.C.

§16.2 Role of the Administrative Law Judge

Administrative law judges are selected by the Board from a civil service roster furnished by the Office of Personnel Management. Although the judges are selected by the Board and are required to adhere to Board precedent in deciding cases, the statute affords them an independent status. Section 4(a) of the Act precludes review of judges' opinions either before or after publication by anyone other than the Board members or attorneys on their staffs. In addition, administrative law judges are prohibited from advising or consulting with Board members regarding a decision to which exceptions have been filed.[7]

Administrative law judges function in much the same manner as trial court judges. As presiding officers, they are responsible for the orderly conduct of the hearing and the preservation of the parties' rights. The Board's Rules and Regulations[8] provide that administrative law judges shall have authority to:

- Administer oaths and affirmations;
- Grant applications for subpoenas;
- Rule upon petitions to revoke subpoenas;
- Rule upon offers of proof and receive relevant evidence;

---

[5]The parties voluntarily may waive their right to a written transcript. NLRB Rules and Regulations §102.35(i); *George Williams Sheet Metal Co.*, 201 NLRB 1050, 82 LRRM 1617 (1973).

[6]NLRB Rules and Regulations §102.42.

[7]Sec. 4(a). Prior to the Taft-Hartley amendments in 1947, decisions of administrative law judges (then called trial examiners) were reviewed by supervisors prior to issuance and, upon appeal to the Board, were evaluated by a Review Section rather than by attorneys reporting directly to Board members. THE DEVELOPING LABOR LAW at 1616.

[8]NLRB Rules and Regulations §102.35.

- Take or cause depositions to be taken;
- Regulate the course of the hearing including, if necessary, excluding persons or counsel from the hearing for contemptuous conduct, and striking all related testimony of witnesses who refuse to answer any proper question;
- Hold conferences for the settlement or simplification of the issues by consent of the parties, but not to adjust cases;[9]
- Dispose of procedural requests, including motions referred by the regional director and motions to amend pleadings; also to dismiss complaints or portions of complaints; and to order hearings reopened or consolidated prior to issuance of a decision;
- Approve stipulations voluntarily entered into by all parties which dispense with a verbatim transcript of the oral testimony adduced at the hearing, and which waive the parties' right to file with the Board exceptions to the findings of fact (but not to the conclusions of law or recommended order) which the administrative law judge shall make in the decision;
- Make and file decisions in conformity with Section 8 of the Administrative Procedure Act, Public Law 89-54, U.S.C., Sec. 557;
- Call, examine, and cross-examine witnesses, and introduce into the record documentary or other evidence;
- Request the parties at any time during the hearing to state their respective positions concerning any issue in the case or theory in support thereof; and
- Take any other action authorized by the published Rules and Regulations of the Board.

The administrative law judge also is charged with the duty of seeing that a complete record is made and that all pertinent facts are elicited. "The [judge] is not required to sit idly by and permit a confused or meaningless record to be made."[10] It is for this reason that the Board has delegated to the administrative law judges the authority to examine and cross-examine witnesses and, on their own motion, to call witnesses to the stand.[11]

On the other hand, administrative law judges must direct hearings so that they are focused on material issues and are conducted as expeditiously as possible. There is considerable variation in the approach of the individual administrative law judges, and a litigant sometimes faces the uncomfortable necessity of insisting on the right to full presentation of his or her case despite the obvious interest of the administrative law judge in expediting the hearing.

---

[9]Sec. 4(a) of the Act prohibits the Board from appointing individuals to conciliate or mediate disputes.

[10]*NLRB v. Bryan Mfg. Co.*, 196 F.2d 477, 30 LRRM 2008 (7th Cir. 1952).

[11]NLRB Rules and Regulations §102.35(k).

At any time during a proceeding the administrative law judge may withdraw voluntarily and another judge will be designated.[12] In addition, up until the time the decision is issued any party may request that the judge withdraw on the basis of personal bias or disqualification.[13] Such a request is made by filing with the judge an affidavit setting forth in detail the matters alleged to constitute grounds for disqualification. If the judge feels that the affidavit has been filed with due diligence and is sufficient on its face, he or she will withdraw from the case. Otherwise, the judge will deny the request on the record and will proceed with the hearing.[14]

The standards applied by the Board and the courts in determining whether an administrative law judge's display of hostility and bias requires disqualification are stringent ones. The use of intemperate language,[15] the resolution of all issues in favor of one party,[16] or the crediting of all witnesses for one party[17] generally will be insufficient, standing alone, to justify disqualification. In addition, the alleged bias must appear on the face of the record and cannot be based upon off-the-record discussions or conduct unrelated to the hearing.[18] In general, only conduct which deprives the hearing of that degree of fundamental fairness required by due process will justify disqualification.[19]

In the event an administrative law judge designated to hear a case for any reason becomes unavailable after the hearing has opened,

---

[12]NLRB Rules and Regulations §102.37 (withdrawal), §102.36 (designation of replacement).

[13]NLRB Rules and Regulations §102.37. Requests for disqualification which are filed after the issuance of the administrative law judge's decision will be rejected as untimely. *Sanford Home for Adults*, 253 NLRB 1132, 106 LRRM 1219 (1981); *Overnite Transp. Co.*, 245 NLRB 423, 102 LRRM 1453 (1979).

[14]A ruling denying a request for disqualification can be appealed to the Board on the terms specified in §102.26 of the Board's Rules and Regulations. Parties to Board proceedings are given considerable latitude to present their respective positions and supporting arguments to the Board, and administrative law judges are precluded by §102.26 of the Board's Rules and Regulations from regulating the content of such submission. *District No. 1, Pacific Coast Dist. Engineers Beneficial Ass'n (Crest Tankers, Inc.)*, 274 NLRB No. 215, 118 LRRM 1547 (1985) (Hunter concurring).

[15]*Ohio Power Co.*, 215 NLRB 165, 88 LRRM 1007 (1974) (judge characterized himself as one of a "new breed"); *NLRB v. Jack August Enters., Inc.*, 583 F.2d 575, 99 LRRM 2582 (1st Cir. 1978) (judge used words and phrases incisively descriptive and damning to employer).

[16]*Penn Color, Inc.*, 261 NLRB 395, 110 LRRM 1115 (1982); *Dimensions in Metal, Inc.*, 258 NLRB 563, 108 LRRM 1308 (1981); *Tom's Ford, Inc.*, 253 NLRB 888, 106 LRRM 1063 (1980).

[17]*Twin County Trucking, Inc.*, 259 NLRB 576, 108 LRRM 1390 (1981); *K.W. Norris Printing Co.*, 232 NLRB 985, 97 LRRM 1080 (1977).

[18]*Heads & Threads Co.*, 261 NLRB 800, 110 LRRM 1137 (1982) (contention that judge's former service as counsel for General Counsel interfered with his fairness and impartiality rejected in absence of statements or other evidence on record indicating bias or prejudice); *Centeno Super Markets, Inc.*, 220 NLRB 1151, 90 LRRM 1732 (1975) (judge not disqualified simply because while in private practice he represented charging party eight or nine years earlier).

[19]*NLRB v. Webb Ford, Inc.*, 689 F.2d 733, 111 LRRM 2555 (7th Cir. 1982) (although some findings of administrative law judge were not supported by substantial evidence, and although he exceeded his statutory authority in certain respects, his findings did not reveal such extreme bias as to be set aside). *District No. 1, Pacific Coast Dist. Engineers Beneficial Ass'n (Crest Tankers, Inc.)*, 274 NLRB No. 215, 118 LRRM 1547 (1985) (Hunter concurring) (judge disqualified from presiding at trial in light of exclusion of counsel from hearing because of appeal taken to one of judge's evidentiary rulings, injudicious statements made to the parties, and an apparent overriding concern for the protection of his own personal reputation).

another judge may be designated to continue the hearing or take other appropriate action.[20] If the original judge dies or otherwise becomes unavailable after the hearing has closed, the necessity for additional testimony will depend principally upon whether a new judge can render a decision on the basis of the record already developed. If credibility resolutions involving evaluations of demeanor are required, a trial *de novo* generally must be held.[21]

§16.3   Role of Counsel for the General Counsel

Prior to issuance of a complaint the General Counsel's role is that of an impartial investigator weighing the facts which rebut, as well as those which support, charges which have been filed.[22] At this stage the General Counsel has complete control over the case. Once a complaint has been issued, however, the General Counsel's role begins to shift from that of investigator to prosecutor. Until the opening of the hearing before an administrative law judge, the General Counsel continues to rule—through the regional directors—on minor matters, such as changes in the hearing dates, requests for subpoenas, motions to intervene, and settlements. Once the hearing starts, control over the case passes to the Board, acting through the administrative law judge, and the General Counsel becomes merely one of the parties.

At the hearing, the General Counsel is represented by an attorney, usually assigned to the regional office issuing the complaint. Counsel for the General Counsel is responsible for introducing evidence in support of the complaint allegations.[23] The burden of proof for establishing the violation rests with the General Counsel.[24]

§16.4   Role of Counsel for the Respondent and Charging Party

Both the respondent and the charging party are entitled to appear at the hearing in person, by counsel or through another representative.[25] Parties who elect to represent themselves will not be

---

[20]NLRB Rules and Regulations §102.36.

[21]*Illinois Bell Tel. Co.*, 259 NLRB 1240, 109 LRRM 1111 (1982) (Board sustained credibility findings of judge who wrote decision after first judge died where credibility findings were based upon factors other than demeanor); *Wellington Hall Nursing Home, Inc.*, 240 NLRB 639, 100 LRRM 1480 (1979) (*de novo* hearing not required upon death of first judge where there was no conflict in testimony and no credibility resolutions were required); *Roger's I.G.A., Inc.*, 232 NLRB 1053, 96 LRRM 1420 (1977) (hearing *de novo* ordered after death of first judge where disposition of issues rested on credibility resolutions based upon demeanor evaluations).

[22]The General Counsel's role as investigator is described in chapter 12.

[23]NLRB Casehandling Manual ¶10380.

[24]*NLRB v. Transportation Mgmt. Corp.*, 462 U.S. 393, 113 LRRM 2857 (1983); *Behring Int'l, Inc. v. NLRB*, 675 F.2d 83, 109 LRRM 3265 (3d Cir. 1982).

[25]NLRB Rules and Regulations §102.38.

allowed to rely upon their unfamiliarity with the Board's procedures as an excuse for unreasonably delaying the proceedings,[26] nor may they cite the absence of counsel as justification for a new hearing.[27]

Counsel representing the respondent may call, examine and cross-examine witnesses, and may present documentary evidence.[28] Counsel for the charging party also is entitled to participate in the hearing,[29] and is entitled to examine witnesses and to introduce evidence as long as it does not jeopardize the prosecution of the complaint by the General Counsel. It is to the charging party's advantage to work closely with, and in support of, the counsel for the General Counsel. Charging party's counsel can be helpful in assisting the General Counsel's office in getting the facts. The manner and degree of participation in the hearing by the representative for the charging party should be carefully worked out with the counsel for the General Counsel. The prime responsibility for proving the case rests with the latter and the charging party who tries to "take over" from counsel for the General Counsel usually meets resistance from both that individual and the administrative law judge.[30]

One role of counsel is to ensure proper conduct of the parties and their witnesses. Persons who engage in misconduct at the hearing may be summarily excluded by the administrative law judge.[31] If an attorney or other representative, after due notice and hearing, is found to have engaged in aggravated misconduct, he or she may be suspended or disbarred from further practice before the Board.[32]

Certain restrictions apply to the ability of former Board personnel to represent parties in cases which were pending at the time they were employed by the Board. Persons who worked in a regional office may not file an appearance in any case which was pending in that office at the time of their employment.[33] Persons employed in Washington, D.C., are precluded from filing an appearance in all cases pending at the time of their employment, whether pending in Washington or in any of the regional offices.[34] Any person who violates the Board's rules will be disqualified from further participation in the case.[35] In addition, if a material advantage accrues to a party improperly represented by a former Board attorney, the attorney's

---

[26]*Serendippity-Un-Ltd and Tigerrr, Inc.*, 263 NLRB 768, 111 LRRM 1263 (1982).

[27]*California Pacific Signs, Inc.*, 233 NLRB 450, 97 LRRM 1085 (1977).

[28]NLRB Rules and Regulations §102.38.

[29]*Spector Freight Sys., Inc.*, 141 NLRB 1110, 52 LRRM 1456 (1963).

[30]*Cf.* NLRB Casehandling Manual ¶10380.3.

[31]NLRB Rules and Regulations §102.44(a).

[32]*Id.* at §102.44(b); *Herbert J. Nichol*, 111 NLRB 447, 35 LRRM 1489 (1955) (union representative who made threatening statements to charging party suspended for six months); *Robert S. Cahoon*, 106 NLRB 831, 32 LRRM 1568 (1953) (attorney who assaulted opposing counsel during hearing suspended for 90 days).

[33]NLRB Rules and Regulations §102.119.

[34]*Id.* at §102.120.

[35]*Beverly Enters.*, 266 NLRB 758, 113 LRRM 1034 (1983).

entire law firm may be disqualified from further participation.[36] The
Board, however, has not been sympathetic to suggestions that the
complaints of improperly represented charging parties be dismissed.[37]

§16.5   Rules of Evidence

Section 10(b) of the Act provides that unfair labor practice proceedings shall "so far as practicable, be conducted in accordance with
the rules of evidence applicable in the district courts of the United
States. . . ."[38] Rule 43(b) of the Federal Rules of Civil Procedure provides that whenever a statute or rule of the state in which the hearing
is held favors the reception of evidence, the statute or rule shall
govern rather than the federal rule of evidence if the latter is narrower. Attorneys and other representatives participating in Board
proceedings thus should be familiar both with the Federal Rules of
Civil Procedure and with the rules of evidence in the state where the
hearing is held.

As might be expected, there is considerable variation in the latitude with which different administrative law judges apply these
rules. The Board rarely reverses an administrative law judge because
of rulings on the admissibility of evidence. Similarly, the courts of
appeals generally defer to the Board's evidentiary rulings.[39]

Sequence of Unfair Labor Practice Hearing

§16.6   Pretrial Conference

The administrative law judge, upon the request of the parties or
upon his or her own motion, may conduct a pretrial conference. Historically, the pretrial conference has been conducted immediately
prior to or shortly after the opening of the hearing. In recent years

---

[36]*Id.* In *Paul E. Iacono Structural Eng'r, Inc. v. Humphrey*, 722 F.2d 435, 113 LRRM 3516
(9th Cir. 1983), the court held that where a former Board attorney had substantial responsibility
for investigating an unfair labor practice charge, the law firm which subsequently hired the
attorney was disqualified by Canon 9 of the American Bar Association's Model Code of Ethics
from thereafter representing one of the parties in a §303 damage action arising out of the same
set of facts as the earlier unfair labor practice charge.

[37]*Alumbaugh Coal Corp.*, 247 NLRB 895, 103 LRRM 1210 (1980) (complaint not dismissed
where former Board attorney's participation in case was minimal and respondent failed to
show prejudice).

[38]*See also* NLRB Rules and Regulations §102.39; NLRB Casehandling Manual ¶10390.

[39]*Carpenter Sprinkler Corp. v. NLRB*, 605 F.2d 60, 102 LRRM 2199 (2d Cir. 1979) (Board
exclusion of secret tape recording affirmed even though tape might have been admissible in
federal district court because "the Board is not required to observe automatically all the rules
of evidence governing the trial of cases in court"); *J.C. Penney Co. v. NLRB*, 384 F.2d 479, 66
LRRM 2069 (10th Cir. 1967) (affidavit of witness admissible as past recollection recorded where
witness had no current recollection of statements in affidavit).

some administrative law judges have conducted pretrial conferences through joint telephone calls with the parties a few days before the scheduled hearing. The objectives of the pretrial conference are to: (1) avoid surprise and confusion by clarifying the issues and theories of the complaint and answer; (2) simplify the issues and eliminate the taking of evidence on matters about which there is no dispute; and (3) provide the parties another opportunity to negotiate a settlement under the guidance of the administrative law judge.[40]

§16.7 Stipulations

In advance of the hearing or shortly after the hearing has opened, the parties may explore the possibility of stipulating to facts which are not in dispute and to the validity of documents or other exhibits whose authenticity is acknowledged.[41] Stipulations may range from an oral agreement on a single fact stated orally on the record to a formal written agreement dispensing with a verbatim written transcript of the hearing and waiving the right of the parties to challenge the administrative law judge's findings of fact.[42]

Time devoted to the preparation of stipulations generally is time well spent. The issues which must be litigated and for which witnesses must be procured are minimized, hearings are shorter and less complex, the record is smaller, and it may be possible to include as part of an agreement to a series of facts a fact which may otherwise be particularly difficult to prove. The General Counsel may enter into a stipulation with the respondent over the objections of the charging party. The charging party, however, is entitled to introduce evidence either to contradict or to explain parts of the stipulation.[43]

Stipulations must pertain to facts rather than to legal conclusions. For example, a stipulation that the Board has jurisdiction in a proceeding would not be binding, while a stipulation as to facts which establish jurisdiction under one of the Board's discretionary jurisdictional standards would be binding.[44] In addition, it is possible to stipulate to the existence of a fact without acknowledging that the fact is relevant to the outcome of the proceeding.[45]

§16.8 Opening of the Hearing

The hearing generally opens at the place, date, and hour scheduled. It is not uncommon for several cases to be set for hearing, on

---

[40]NLRB Casehandling Manual ¶¶10350, 10381, 10381.1.

[41]*See generally* NLRB Rules and Regulations §102.40; NLRB Casehandling Manual ¶10392.

[42]NLRB Rules and Regulations §102.35(i); NLRB Statements of Procedure §101.10(b)(4).

[43]*UAW v. NLRB (Borg-Warner)*, 231 F.2d 237, 37 LRRM 2744 (7th Cir. 1956).

[44]NLRB Casehandling Manual ¶10392.

[45]*Id.*

a "calendar call" basis, at the same place, date, and hour. This generally occurs when multiple cases are ready for trial at approximately the same time, where they are to be tried in the same general geographical area (i.e., within 30 or 40 miles of each other) and where each case is not likely to take more than four days to be tried.[46] The administrative law judge officially will open the hearing for each case on the calendar at or about the time mentioned in the notice of hearing. The parties will discuss the order in which the cases will be tried (generally the shortest case first), the estimated trial time, and then establish a schedule for when each case will begin.[47] The cases are then adjourned until the time established in the schedule for trial.

The hearing, in general, follows the usual sequence of a trial in court. A brief opening statement may be made by the counsel for the General Counsel,[48] the prosecutor, followed by a similar statement made by the respondent, the defendant. The latter's statement often is reserved until after the General Counsel's case has been presented. Counsel for the General Counsel then introduces into evidence the formal documents. These include the original charge, any amended charges, the complaint and notice of hearing, Form NLRB-4668 (see Exhibit 83), written postponement requests, and other pretrial motions along with the rulings thereon, and all affidavits of service.[49] Evidence then is presented in support of the complaint allegations, followed by that in defense and, in turn, by rebuttal.

§16.9   Testimony of Witnesses

The administrative law judge, the counsel for the General Counsel, and representatives of all parties to the proceeding have the right to call, examine, and cross-examine witnesses.[50] Witnesses who are subpoenaed to testify are entitled to fees and expenses for mileage equal to those paid witnesses in the federal courts. At the present time witnesses are paid $30 for each day they are required to appear, 20.5 cents per mile to and from the hearing, and, where required by travel distance to be away from home overnight, an additional $50–$75 per day.[51] Since the overnight expenses vary from one location

---

[46]*Id.* at ¶10258.

[47]*Id.* at ¶10382.

[48]Opening statements generally are made in cases which involve novel legal theories; where certain issues, without prior explanation, would appear to be irrelevant; or where the context of the case needs to be described. The primary purpose of the opening statement is to provide sufficient advance explanation of the case to permit appropriate evidentiary rulings. NLRB Casehandling Manual ¶10386.

[49]NLRB Casehandling Manual ¶10384. Petitions to revoke subpoenas and rulings thereon are not included in the formal papers unless specifically requested by the aggrieved party. NLRB Casehandling Manual ¶11782.5.

[50]NLRB Rules and Regulations §102.38.

[51]*See* NLRB Casehandling Manual ¶11780.

to another and the terms of the other reimbursements are adjusted periodically, it is advisable to acquire from the counsel for the General Counsel current terms and rates. Witness fees and mileage are paid by the party at whose request the witnesses appear[52] and a claim for reimbursement should be filed at the time the witness is discharged.[53]

(a) *Sequestration.* Any party at the hearing may ask the administrative law judge to exclude prospective witnesses from the hearing room.[54] Such a request might be made in order to avoid a witness being influenced by the testimony of others, or out of concern that the mere presence of certain individuals (e.g., supervisors) might have an intimidating effect. Parties are, however, entitled to have at least one "main representative" in addition to counsel present in the hearing room at all times whether or not that person intends to testify.[55]

Charging parties and discriminatees generally are permitted to remain in the hearing room. In the absence of extraordinary circumstances mandating either their constant presence or total exclusion, discriminatees may be excluded from the hearing room only during periods of time when other witnesses are testifying about events which the discriminatees already have testified about, or which they will or may testify about before the hearing concludes.[56]

(b) *Examination.* Witnesses in Board proceedings are examined in much the same manner as witnesses in the federal courts. Leading questions of a party's own witnesses are to be avoided except with respect to preliminary or immaterial matters.[57] Rule 611(c) of the Federal Rules of Evidence and Rule 43(b) of the Federal Rules of Civil Procedure apply to Board proceedings so that a party may call hostile witnesses and conduct their examination through leading questions.[58] The refusal of a witness to answer any question that has been ruled to be proper shall, in the discretion of the administrative law judge, be grounds for striking all of the testimony previously given by the witness on related matters.[59]

---

[52]NLRB Casehandling Manual ¶11780. Failure of a respondent to pay the required witness fees and expenses constitutes an unfair labor practice. *Howard Mfg. Co.*, 231 NLRB 731, 96 LRRM 1633 (1977).

[53]NLRB Casehandling Manual ¶11780.

[54]*Id.* at ¶10394.1.

[55]*Id.*

[56]*Unga Painting Corp.*, 237 NLRB 1306, 99 LRRM 1141 (1978). The *Unga Painting* rule does not apply in representation proceedings. *See Fall River Sav. Bank*, 246 NLRB 831, 102 LRRM 1667 (1979).

[57]NLRB Casehandling Manual ¶10394.2; *Boatel Alaska, Inc.*, 236 NLRB 1458, 99 LRRM 1005 (1978) (administrative law judge permitted leading questions regarding preliminary matters and instances in which witness appeared to have exhausted his recollection).

[58]NLRB Casehandling Manual ¶10394.3.

[59]NLRB Rules and Regulations §102.44(c); *Feld & Sons, Inc.*, 263 NLRB 332, 111 LRRM 1038 (1982).

(c) Use of Witness Statements or Affidavits. During the investigation of an unfair labor practice charge, a Board agent may acquire unsworn statements or sworn affidavits from individuals who subsequently are called as witnesses. Such statements are useful as a basis for developing questions to be asked of the witness, for purposes of refreshing the witness' failed recollection, for purposes of impeachment, and under certain conditions, may be introduced as substantive evidence.[60] The Board has held, with Supreme Court approval, that such statements and affidavits need not be disclosed to the respondent prior to the time that the witness has testified.[61] Even then, however, there are limits on the Board's obligation to produce the statements.

First, not all statements are disclosable. Only those that are signed or otherwise adopted by the witness, and those that amount to contemporaneously recorded verbatim recitals of statements made by the witness to the Board agent need be turned over.[62] In addition, since only statements that are in existence at the time the witness testifies need be disclosed, parties are not entitled to statements submitted to the Board by witnesses after the conclusion of their testimony at the hearing.[63]

Second, statements are required to be made available only for purposes of conducting cross-examination. If the statement contains material concerning issues not addressed in the witness' direct examination, counsel for the General Counsel may seek permission from the administrative law judge to excise the unrelated portions of the statement.[64] After examining the document the administrative law judge may direct that certain portions be excised, or may direct that the entire document be furnished if the portions of the statement unrelated to the witness' direct testimony nevertheless relate to other matters raised by the pleadings.[65]

---

[60]NLRB Casehandling Manual ¶10394.6 citing *Alvin J. Bart & Co.*, 236 NLRB 242, 98 LRRM 1257 (1978), and Rules 612, 613, 801 and 803(5) of the Federal Rules of Evidence.

[61]NLRB Rules and Regulations §102.118(b); *NLRB v. Robbins Tire & Rubber Co.*, 437 U.S. 214, 98 LRRM 2617 (1978). The rules regarding the availability of witness statements to respondents apply equally to charging parties who seek such statements. *Senftner Volkswagen Corp.*, 257 NLRB 178, 107 LRRM 1488 (1981).

[62]Specifically, §102.118(d) of the Board's Rules and Regulations provides:
"The term statement . . . means: (1) a written statement made by said witness and signed or otherwise adopted or approved by him; or (2) a stenographic, mechanical, electrical, or other recording, or a transcription thereof, which is a substantially verbatim recital of an oral statement made by said witness to an agent of the party obligated to produce the statement and recorded contemporaneously with the making of such oral statement."
See Coca-Cola Bottling Co., 250 NLRB 1341, 105 LRRM 1204 (1980) (writing made by Board agent while witness spoke does not qualify as a disclosable statement under Board's rules).

[63]*Kawasaki Motors Corp.*, 257 NLRB 502, 107 LRRM 1541 (1981).

[64]NLRB Casehandling Manual ¶10394.10. Statements which do not relate in any respect to the subject matter of the witness' direct testimony need not be furnished. *Allou Distribs.*, 201 NLRB 47, 82 LRRM 1102 (1973).

[65]NLRB Rules and Regulations §102.118(b)(2); NLRB Casehandling Manual ¶10394.10; see *Carpenters Local 1437 (Associated Gen. Contractors of Cal., Inc.)*, 210 NLRB 359, 86 LRRM 1080 (1974) (not an abuse of discretion for an administrative law judge to bar disclosure of statement relating to emotional stress of witness when this issue not raised during direct examination).

As a general rule, counsel for the General Counsel will furnish copies of witness statements to all respondents immediately upon completion of the witness' testimony. Respondents are allowed to retain the statements until the hearing is closed, including during periods of recess, but must then return them along with any copies which may have been made.[66] There is no obligation to return a witness statement that has been introduced into the record as substantive evidence.[67]

(d) Offers of Proof. In situations where the administrative law judge refuses to permit a witness to testify about a certain issue or issues, counsel may consider making an offer of proof. An offer of proof is simply a statement of counsel as to what the witness would say if permitted to testify. The offer may be in writing or stated verbally on the record, and may be in narrative or question and answer form.[68] Offers of proof should be specific and set forth with precision the facts which would be revealed in the testimony. Once the administrative law judge is made aware of the exact nature of the excluded testimony, the initial ruling may be reversed or limited. In any event, with the offer of proof in the record the Board will be made aware of the excluded evidence.

§16.10 Documentary Evidence

(a) In General. In addition to calling witnesses and presenting oral testimony, all parties have the right to introduce into the record documentary or other evidence to the extent permitted by the administrative law judge.[69] All exhibits must be introduced in the form of an original and one copy unless it can be established that the original is unobtainable. In most cases, once an exhibit has been authorized and introduced, the administrative law judge will authorize the substitution of a copy for the original.[70] The party offering an exhibit must make copies available to other parties upon request.

Exhibits which are admitted into evidence become part of the official record. If a proffered exhibit is not allowed by the administrative law judge to be admitted into evidence, it may upon request of the offering party be placed into the "Rejected Exhibits" file.[71] The rejected exhibits file is made available to the administrative law judge, to the Board and to the courts during their review of the case, so that it may be advantageous to request that a significant document

---

[66]NLRB Casehandling Manual ¶10394.11.
[67]*Id.*
[68]*Id.* at ¶10396.
[69]NLRB Rules and Regulations §102.38.
[70]NLRB Casehandling Manual ¶10398.2.
[71]*Id.* at ¶10398.3.

rejected by the administrative law judge be placed in the rejected exhibits file.

Upon occasion a party may ask permission to submit a particular document after the hearing officially has closed. In such instances, the parties generally stipulate on the record that the additional exhibit or exhibits may be received, provide a brief description of the documents expected to be introduced, and reserve appropriate exhibit numbers. Entering into such an agreement does not preclude a party from thereafter inspecting and objecting to the admissibility of the proffered evidence.[72]

(b) Documents in the Possession of the Board. A party also may wish to procure files, reports, memoranda or other documents in the possession of the Board, or may seek to have a regional director, field examiner, attorney, or other Board official testify. As a general rule the Board rejects all such requests and will seek to revoke or quash any subpoena soliciting such information, whether issued in connection with a lawsuit, Board proceeding, or administrative proceeding of another agency.[73] If such information or testimony is desired, however, a special written request may be filed identifying the documents to be produced or the person whose testimony is sought, the nature of the pending proceeding, and the purpose to be served by the production of the document or the testimony.[74] The request is filed with the Board or its chairman for documents or officials under the control of the Board, and with the General Counsel for documents or officials in the regional offices or under the General Counsel's control in Washington, D.C.[75]

§16.11   Consideration of Representation Issues

The Board and the courts have held that a representation proceeding and a subsequent unfair labor practice case based on that proceeding "are really one."[76] Accordingly, issues relating to the va-

---

[72]*Id.* at ¶10398.5.

[73]NLRB Rules and Regulations §102.118(a)(1); NLRB Casehandling Manual ¶¶10400.1, 11820–11828. Under certain circumstances parties may be entitled to prehearing statements made by individuals who testify at a Board unfair labor practice or representation case hearing. See discussion at §16.9(c), *supra.* In addition, certain information in the possession of the Board may be acquired under the Freedom of Information Act. *See* NLRB Rules and Regulations §107.117(a)–(d) and discussion at §§24.3 and 24.4. Special rules apply to the production of Board documents during backpay proceedings. See discussion at §§18.8 and 18.11.

[74]Board officials should not be called for purposes of eliciting testimony concerning settlement discussions. The fact that settlement offers were made or discussed generally are not admissible. Admissions of fact, however, whether made during settlement discussions or at some other time usually are admissible. NLRB Casehandling Manual ¶10402.

[75]NLRB Rules and Regulations §102.118(a)(1); NLRB Casehandling Manual ¶¶11820–11828.

[76]*Pittsburgh Plate Glass Co. v. NLRB*, 313 U.S. 146, 158, 8 LRRM 425, 430 (1941); *see also Adrian Belt Co.*, 224 NLRB 1231, 92 LRRM 1431 (1976); *Smith Co.*, 200 NLRB 772, 82 LRRM 1269 (1972).

lidity of a Board certification resulting from a representation proceeding and decided in that proceeding may not be tried again in a later unfair labor practice hearing.[77] Thus, an administrative law judge will reject evidence on any issue which was litigated in a prior representation case where the evidence sought to be introduced was available at the time of the earlier proceeding.[78] Furthermore, the Board has held that the administrative law judge lacks the authority to make a unit finding contrary to the earlier determination made by the Board in the representation proceeding.[79]

§16.12   Oral Argument

Any party is entitled, upon request, to a reasonable period at the close of the hearing to argue orally before the administrative law judge. Such arguments are included in the stenographic record of the hearing.[80] Oral argument may not be necessary in every case or on every issue, but the parties should be prepared to argue orally in response to a request from the administrative law judge. If it appears that additional explanation of novel legal questions or complex factual issues would be helpful to the administrative law judge, oral argument may be desirable. Conversely, if the case is relatively straightforward, oral argument may be presented in lieu of a post-hearing brief. If made, the argument should be confined to the points on which clarification or emphasis appears to be necessary. The essential facts should be emphasized, arguments as to credibility of witnesses made, and the legal principles involved pointed out.

§16.13   Briefs and Proposed Findings

In most cases, a more effective argument can be made by means of a written brief. Such briefs, as well as proposed findings, may be filed as a matter of right upon request made prior to the close of the hearing.[81] The importance of an effective brief cannot be over-emphasized. At the close of the hearing, all facts upon which the case will be decided are a part of the record, but they have not yet been organized into a coherent story. The party who carefully and accurately marshals the facts in a brief to the administrative law judge will often find the case being considered, in substantial part, in light of that statement of the facts.

---

[77]*Id.*

[78]*Dewey Portland Cement Co.*, 142 NLRB 951, 53 LRRM 1196 (1963); *see also Fall River Sav. Bank v. NLRB*, 649 F.2d 50, 107 LRRM 2653 (1st Cir. 1981).

[79]*Kearney & Trecker Corp.*, 101 NLRB 1577, 31 LRRM 1255 (1952).

[80]NLRB Rules and Regulations §102.42; NLRB Casehandling Manual ¶10408.

[81]NLRB Rules and Regulations §102.42; NLRB Casehandling Manual ¶10410.

A party's treatment of the law is equally important. Most administrative law judges are thoroughly versed in the application of the Act, but it is a complex law, subject to many interpretations, and a well-reasoned legal argument will carry great weight.

The brief should be concise. Long briefs containing repetitious factual statements, implausible legal arguments, or personal attacks on the Board, the administrative law judge, or opposing counsel are apt to receive little consideration. Briefs to the administrative law judge must be filed on 8-½ by 11-inch paper, but the 50-page limit applicable to briefs filed with the Board[82] does not apply.[83] A copy of the brief must be served on each party. An original and two copies of the brief and a statement of service upon the other parties should be filed with the administrative law judge.[84]

The administrative law judge fixes the time, not to exceed 35 days from the close of the hearing, for the filing of briefs. Requests for extensions of time in which to file must be addressed to the chief administrative law judge in Washington, D.C., the deputy chief administrative law judge in San Francisco, or the associate chief administrative law judges in New York or Atlanta, as appropriate, and must be received at least three days prior to the due date. Such requests, if reasonable, usually are given favorable consideration. If one extension is granted, requests for additional time will be denied except in unusual circumstances. Notice of a request for extension of time must be served upon all other parties, and proof of such service should accompany the request.[85]

Motions Filed With the Administrative Law Judge During the Hearing

§16.14   Filing and Appeal of Motions

The procedure for filing motions during the hearing and for appealing adverse rulings from the administrative law judge parallel those which apply to prehearing motions discussed in the previous chapter.[86] All motions made at the hearing should be submitted in writing to the administrative law judge or stated orally on the record.[87] Motions filed after the hearing has closed but prior to the

---

[82]NLRB Rules and Regulations §102.46(j).
[83]NLRB Supplementary Information printed at 47 Fed. Reg. 40,770 (September 15, 1982).
[84]NLRB Rules and Regulations §102.42.
[85]*Id.*
[86]See discussion at §15.8.
[87]NLRB Rules and Regulations §102.24.

transfer of the case to the Board should be filed with the chief, deputy chief, or associate chief administrative law judge, as appropriate.[88]

All motions should state briefly the order or relief requested, along with reasons why the request is appropriate. An original and four copies of the motion should be filed and copies immediately served on the other parties. Motions and responses to motions should be filed promptly and within such time as not to delay the proceeding.[89] The administrative law judge's rulings, if made during the hearing, are stated orally on the record. In all other instances such rulings are made in writing and served on the parties, or are contained in the judge's written decision disposing of the case.[90]

The Board discourages interlocutory appeals from the rulings of an administrative law judge.[91] The preferred procedure is for the parties to proceed with the hearing and then challenge the validity of the judge's ruling or order through exceptions to his or her decision.[92] The Board will, however, entertain requests for special permission to take interlocutory appeals.[93] Such requests for special permission to appeal, together with a copy of the appeal itself, should be filed promptly, in writing, with the Board.[94] The request should set forth reasons why special permission should be granted and the grounds relied upon for the appeal. Copies must be served on the other parties and on the administrative law judge. Any opposition to the request must be filed promptly, in writing, and also served on the other parties and the administrative law judge. After all parties have had an opportunity to be heard, the Board will proceed to rule upon the request for special permission to appeal and, if granted, upon the appeal itself.[95]

As with prehearing motions, there are a wide variety of possible motions which may be filed with the administrative law judge during the hearing. Some of the more common motions are discussed in the following sections.

---

[88]*Id.* After the case has been transferred to the Board all motions should be filed with the Board's Executive Secretary as provided in §102.47 of the Rules and Regulations.

[89]*Id.* at §102.24.

[90]*Id.* at §102.25. If the administrative law judge has reserved ruling on a motion and the Board requests that the case be transferred and continued before it or one of its members (see NLRB Rules and Regulations §102.50), the Board itself will rule on the pending motion.

[91]*See* NLRB Casehandling Manual ¶10404.

[92]NLRB Rules and Regulations §102.26.

[93]*Id.* and NLRB Casehandling Manual ¶10404. The Board's attorneys have been instructed that unless the administrative law judge's ruling undermines a substantial portion of the General Counsel's case, requests for special permission to appeal should not be filed if they are likely to delay the hearing for more than half a day. Similarly, Board attorneys have been told to resist requests filed by opposing counsel which are likely to result in a hearing delay in excess of half a day. NLRB Casehandling Manual ¶10404.

[94]As discussed at §16.15 *infra*, the parties do not need to seek special permission to appeal a ruling by the administrative law judge dismissing the complaint. Such appeals are a matter of right. NLRB Rules and Regulations §102.27.

[95]NLRB Rules and Regulations §102.26.

§16.15   Amendment or Dismissal of the Complaint

As noted in the previous chapter,[96] the General Counsel may file a motion during the hearing to amend the complaint.[97] No other party, including the charging party, may seek to amend the complaint.[98] If a motion to amend the complaint is denied, counsel for the General Counsel normally will seek special permission to file an interlocutory appeal with the Board rather than raising the matter by exception to the administrative law judge's decision.[99]

If a motion to dismiss the complaint in its entirety is granted by the administrative law judge prior to issuance of a decision in the case, the parties need not seek special permission to file an interlocutory appeal but may acquire Board review simply by filing a written request.[100] The request must set forth the grounds for review and copies must be served on all parties and on the regional director who issued the complaint. If no appeal is taken within 28 days of the date of the order of dismissal, the case is closed.[101]

§16.16   Postponements of the Hearing

Administrative law judges have the authority to continue the hearing from day to day or to adjourn the hearing to a later date or another location either on their own motion or at the request of one of the parties.[102] There are many reasons which may warrant a request for postponement. One of the most frequently cited reasons is that of "surprise" originating from an amendment of the complaint at the hearing or from some other unanticipated event.[103] The absence

---

[96]See discussion at §15.2.

[97]NLRB Rules and Regulations §102.17; NLRB Casehandling Manual ¶10274.2. Once the hearing opens, the General Counsel's prosecutional discretion to amend the complaint ends and permission to amend must be sought from the administrative law judge. *See Sheet Metal Workers, Local 263,* 272 NLRB No. 13, 117 LRRM 1176 (1984), *citing Woodlawn Hosp.,* 233 NLRB 782, 97 LRRM 1386 (1977), and *Watkins Furniture Co.,* 160 NLRB 188, 62 LRRM 1599 (1966).

[98]*Sunbeam Plastics Corp.,* 144 NLRB 1010, 54 LRRM 1174 (1963).

[99]NLRB Casehandling Manual ¶10274.2.

[100]NLRB Rules and Regulations §102.27. In *Consumers Distribution Co.,* 274 NLRB No. 50, 119 LRRM 1015 (1985), the Board distinguished posthearing motions to *withdraw* and *dismiss* complaints. Motions to dismiss, the Board ruled, contemplate a decision on the merits and are governed by §102.27 of the Board's regulations. Motions to withdraw complaints, on the other hand, do not extinguish the underlying charge, and appeals must be taken in accordance with the requirements of §102.26.

[101]NLRB Rules and Regulations §102.27.

[102]*Id.* at §102.43. Prehearing postponements are discussed at §15.4.

[103]NLRB Casehandling Manual ¶10406.2; *J.M. Tanaka Constr., Inc.,* 249 NLRB 238, 104 LRRM 1219 (1980) (request denied where factual basis for amendment to complaint arose from material submitted by respondent and respondent could not claim surprise as to legal implications of furnished documents); *Woodville Plant,* 244 NLRB 119, 102 LRRM 1127 (1979) (surprise over amendment to complaint not established); *Meat Workers Local 248 (Milwaukee Indep. Meat Packers Ass'n),* 222 NLRB 1023, 91 LRRM 1307 (1976) (request denied where amendments to complaint made at hearing nearly identical to those alleged in original complaint).

of necessary witnesses[104] or documentation,[105] the engagement of new counsel,[106] scheduling conflicts of counsel in other proceedings,[107] and the unavailability of respondents' officials[108] also are examples of reasons often given for postponement requests.

As a general rule administrative law judges do not look with favor upon postponement requests, particularly those that are made during or immediately prior to the hearing. Counsel for the General Counsel also can be expected to resist the granting of such requests.[109] In instances where it can be established that through no fault of the moving party the failure to grant a postponement will jeopardize the party's due process rights, postponements of reasonable duration may be granted.[110] It is advisable, therefore, for the parties to prepare their cases sufficiently in advance of the hearing date to allow adequate time to collect all required documents and ensure that arrangements are made for the attendance of all witnesses.

§16.17 Intervention

Prehearing motions to intervene were discussed in the previous chapter.[111] Such motions also may be filed with the administrative law judge during the hearing.[112] Such motions may be made either in writing or orally upon the record, and must set forth the grounds upon which the movant claims an interest in the proceeding.[113] The motion to intervene may be granted to the extent and upon such terms as the administrative law judge considers to be proper.[114] Intervention may be granted in person or by counsel or other representative.[115]

---

[104]*Flite Chief, Inc.*, 258 NLRB 1124, 108 LRRM 1303 (1981) (request denied where counsel knew two months before hearing that witness would be difficult to serve with subpoena); *Quebecor Group, Inc.*, 258 NLRB 961, 108 LRRM 1301 (1981) (request denied where witness named in complaint and respondent did not show why it could not have secured witness' appearance at the hearing).

[105]*Ampco-Pittsburgh Corp.*, 247 NLRB 660, 103 LRRM 1217 (1980) (request denied where party had notice that document would be necessary and had ample time to procure it).

[106]NLRB Casehandling Manual ¶10406.1.

[107]*SEIU Local 32E (Cadillac Fairview Shopping Centers)*, 259 NLRB 771, 109 LRRM 1036 (1981) (request denied where counsel scheduled court appearance after Board proceeding already had been postponed once); *Louisiana Cement Co.*, 241 NLRB 536, 101 LRRM 1053 (1979) (request denied where one continuance granted earlier and pretrial statements of witnesses already had been furnished to employer).

[108]*Holyoke Motel, Inc.*, 219 NLRB 61, 90 LRRM 1132 (1975) (not abuse of discretion for administrative law judge to deny request for continuance based in part upon illness of owner).

[109]*See generally* NLRB Casehandling Manual ¶¶10406–10406.4.

[110]*Id.* at 10406.2.

[111]See §15.10.

[112]NLRB Rules and Regulations §102.29; NLRB Casehandling Manual ¶10388.1.

[113]If in writing, an original and four copies must be filed with the administrative law judge and copies must be served on all of the parties. NLRB Rules and Regulations §102.29; see also discussion at §16.14 *supra*.

[114]See cases cited at §15.10 notes 70–71.

[115]NLRB Rules and Regulations §102.29.

§16.18   Objection to Conduct of Hearing

Any objection with respect to the conduct of the hearing, including any objection to the introduction of evidence, may be stated orally or in writing. The objection should be accompanied by a statement of the grounds on which it is based. Both are included in the record of the hearing. Objections are not considered waived by further participation in the hearing.[116] Exception need not be taken to each adverse ruling upon objection since automatic exceptions are allowed.

If the administrative law judge rules any question to be improper, the witness need not answer it. If the administrative law judge rules the question to be proper and the witness still refuses to answer, the administrative law judge has the discretion to strike from the record all testimony previously given by the witness on related matters.[117]

§16.19   Depositions

As noted in the previous chapter,[118] depositions are not permitted under the Board's rules for purposes of discovery, but may be used after a complaint has issued in order to preserve the testimony of individuals who will be unable to attend the hearing.[119] The procedures for seeking a deposition during the hearing, or after the hearing but before transfer of the case to the Board, are similar to those for prehearing depositions.

Applications for depositions must be filed in writing with the administrative law judge and with all other parties at least seven days prior to the time when it is desired that the deposition be taken.[120] The application must set forth the reasons why, when, and where the deposition is to be taken, and the matters concerning which it is expected the witness will testify. In addition, the name and address of both the person to be deposed and the officer before whom the deposition is to be taken should be given.[121]

---

[116]*Id.* at §102.41.

[117]*Id.* at §102.44(c).

[118]See discussion at §15.12.

[119]*See* NLRB Casehandling Manual ¶¶10352.1, 10352.3.

[120]NLRB Rules and Regulations §102.30(a). If the deposition is to be taken outside of the continental United States, 15 days notice must be given. *Id.*

[121]*Id.* Any agent of the Board authorized to administer oaths, or any person authorized to administer oaths by the laws of the United States or of the place where the examination is to be taken, may preside at the deposition. Depositions held in foreign countries may be taken before any secretary of embassy or legation, consul general, consul, vice consul, or consular agent of the United States. NLRB Rules and Regulations §102.30(b). The parties may, however, by written stipulation, agree that the deposition may be taken before any person, at any time or place, and in any manner without affecting the validity of the deposition. NLRB Rules and Regulations §102.30(f).

If the administrative law judge concludes that "good cause" for taking the deposition has been established,[122] an Order and Notice of Deposition will be issued and served on all parties. The Order and Notice sets forth the name of the witness whose deposition is to be taken, the date, hour, and place of the deposition, and the officer before whom the deposition is to be taken.[123] The designated officer need not necessarily be the one requested in the application.[124] The officer or a court reporter under the officer's direction will record the testimony at the expense of the party requesting the deposition.[125]

All parties are given an opportunity to examine and cross-examine the witness under oath.[126] All objections to questions or evidence must be made at the time of the examination or else they will be deemed waived. The officer before whom the examination is taken does not have the power to rule upon the objections, but simply notes them upon the deposition.[127] The testimony must be subscribed by the witness, and if for any reason the witness is unable or refuses to sign the deposition, that fact is noted in the officer's certificate.[128]

An original and two copies of the deposition are transmitted to the administrative law judge who then rules upon the admissibility of the deposition in whole or in part.[129] Parties who had objections to questions or to the evidence when the deposition was being taken should renew them before the administrative law judge. However, errors or irregularities regarding compliance with the Board's rules for taking depositions will be deemed waived in the absence of a prompt motion to supress part or all of the deposition.[130]

§16.20 Subpoenas

Applications for prehearing subpoenas were discussed in the previous chapter.[131] The requirements and procedures for requesting prehearing subpoenas apply equally to applications for subpoenas made during the hearing except that the application is filed with the administrative law judge rather than with the regional director.[132]

---

[122]As noted, "good cause" generally requires a showing that the witness will not be available to testify at the hearing either because of illness, distance from the hearing location, or other circumstance. NLRB Casehandling Manual ¶10352.3.

[123]NLRB Rules and Regulations §102.30(a).

[124]*Id.* NLRB Casehandling Manual ¶10352.4.

[125]NLRB Casehandling Manual ¶10352.6.

[126]NLRB Rules and Regulations §102.30(c).

[127]*Id.*

[128]*Id.* The officer's certificate states that the deposition is a true record of the testimony and exhibits given by the witness, and that the officer is not of counsel or attorney to any of the parties, and has no personal interest in the proceeding. *Id.*

[129]*Id.* at §102.30(d).

[130]*Id.* at §102.30(e); NLRB Casehandling Manual ¶10352.7.

[131]See discussion at §15.13.

[132]*See generally* NLRB Rules and Regulations §102.31(a); NLRB Casehandling Manual ¶¶11772–11780.

Similarly, the requirements for petitions to revoke a subpoena are the same with the exception that those filed during the hearing are filed directly with the administrative law judge.[133]

In situations where a party seeks primary evidence such as a particular document but has secondary evidence available, a notice to produce may be preferable to issuance of a subpoena if it is anticipated that the person in possession of the document will resist the subpoena. A subpoena enforcement proceeding may be time consuming.[134] On the other hand, a failure to produce following service of a notice to produce would provide the necessary foundation for immediate introduction of secondary evidence.[135]

§16.21 Conforming the Pleadings

There are several different types of motions designed to conform the pleadings to the proof. If at the end of the General Counsel's case there has been an unquestioned failure of proof with regard to one or more allegations in the complaint, counsel for the General Counsel may seek to drop the allegation through a motion to strike or a motion to amend the complaint.[136] If there has been a total failure of proof with regard to the entire complaint, a motion to dismiss may be filed.[137]

At the conclusion of the case, counsel for the General Counsel may file a motion to conform the pleadings to the proof. The purpose of such motion is to eliminate minor and immaterial variances in the record regarding names, dates, and other nonsubstantive details.[138] If portions of the transcript already have been received and there are material inaccuracies, one or more of the parties may seek to have the transcript corrected through either a stipulation or a motion to correct.[139]

---

[133]NLRB Rules and Regulations §102.31(b); NLRB Casehandling Manual ¶¶11782–11782.5.

[134]Subpoena enforcement proceedings are discussed at §§21.15–21.20.

[135]NLRB Casehandling Manual ¶10400.2.

[136]*Id.* at ¶10388.4.

[137]*Id.* Related to these motions is a motion to dismiss filed by respondent's counsel either at the end of the General Counsel's presentation of evidence or at the end of the entire case. *See* NLRB Casehandling Manual ¶10388.2 and discussion at §16.15 *supra.*

[138]NLRB Casehandling Manual ¶10388.3.

[139]*Id.* at ¶10412.

17

Unfair Labor Practice Posthearing Procedures

Administrative Law Judge's Decision

§17.1 Nature and Effect of Decision

After the close of the hearing and the submission of briefs, if any, the administrative law judge prepares a written decision.[1]

(a) Nature of Decision. The administrative law judge's decision is based upon the judge's consideration of all of the evidence, the briefs, and his or her view of the applicable law. The decision contains findings of fact and conclusions of law regarding all material issues raised in the complaint.[2] Judges occasionally will include rulings on conduct not specifically cited in the complaint. If the conduct is closely related to actions alleged to be unlawful in the complaint, and was fully litigated at the hearing, the variance between the complaint and the findings generally will be ignored by the Board.[3]

The administrative law judge may recommend that the complaint be dismissed in its entirety or sustained in whole or in part. If any part of the complaint is sustained, the administrative law judge will recommend that the accused party cease and desist from the

---

[1]*See* NLRB Rules and Regulations §102.45(a), NLRB Statements of Procedure §101.11, and NLRB Casehandling Manual ¶10430.

[2]*Cardio Data Sys. Corp.*, 264 NLRB 37, 111 LRRM 1266 (1982) (administrative law judges have an obligation to make findings of fact and reach conclusions of law with respect to all allegations of misconduct set forth in the complaint).

[3]*Compare Inland Steel Co.*, 259 NLRB 191, 108 LRRM 1334 (1981) (supervisor's statement to employee properly held unlawful threat even though not alleged in complaint because it was closely related to subject matter of complaint and was fully litigated) *with Camay Drilling Co.*, 254 NLRB 239, 106 LRRM 1096 (1981) (no violation when complaint did not challenge employer's unilateral implementation of final wage offer because issue not sufficiently litigated and employer did not have opportunity to present a defense).

unlawful conduct and take affirmative action to remedy its effects.[4] The administrative law judge must follow prior Board precedent notwithstanding his or her personal view of that precedent unless and until reversed or modified by the Board or by the United States Supreme Court.[5]

The administrative law judge files the decision with the Board, and copies are served on all parties.[6] The decision thus performs two important functions for the parties: (1) it affords the respondent an opportunity for immediate and voluntary compliance without the necessity of a Board order or a possible court decree, and (2) it serves to define the issues to be argued before the Board in cases where exceptions are filed by a party who disagrees with the administrative law judge's appraisal of the case.

(b) Effect of Decision.   Upon receipt of the administrative law judge's decision the Executive Secretary immediately enters an order transferring the case to the Board. (See Exhibit 84.) The record of the case transferred to the Board consists of the charge, the complaint and notice of hearing, the answer, any amendments to the foregoing documents, motions, rulings, orders, the stenographic report of the hearing, stipulations, exhibits, documentary evidence, depositions, and the administrative law judge's decision.[7] Even rejected exhibits are included in a rejected exhibits file. Thus, everything considered by the administrative law judge in ruling on the case is forwarded to the Board except the parties' briefs to the administrative law judge and motions and rulings on revocation of subpoenas which the moving party has not asked to be made a part of the record.[8] If exceptions, cross-exceptions, or answering briefs subsequently are filed, these too become a part of the record before the Board.[9]

Although entitled to great weight, the administrative law judge's findings and recommendations are by no means binding on the Board.[10] The Board may adopt, reject, or modify a judge's decision in whole or in part. The Board, however, generally is reluctant to reject the findings of an administrative law judge that are predicated upon the resolution of conflicting testimony. Because of the judge's opportunity to observe the demeanor of the witnesses, the Board usually accepts credibility determinations and will not overturn them unless a clear

---

[4]For a discussion of Board orders and remedies, *see* THE DEVELOPING LABOR LAW at chapter 33.

[5]*E.g.*, *Consolidated Casinos Corp.*, 266 NLRB 988, 113 LRRM 1081 (1983).

[6]NLRB Rules and Regulations §102.45(a).

[7]*Id.* at §102.45(b).

[8]Unless specifically requested by the party aggrieved by the ruling, a petition to revoke a subpoena and related documents are not made a part of the official record. NRLB Rules and Regulations §102.31(b).

[9]*Id.* at §102.45(b).

[10]*See Universal Camera Corp. v. NLRB*, 340 U.S. 474, 27 LRRM 2373 (1951).

FORM NLRB-1406
(10-82)

UNITED STATES OF AMERICA
BEFORE THE NATIONAL LABOR RELATIONS BOARD

Janco Computer Services, Inc.

and

Local 007, United Computer
Operators International Union

Case   5-CA-1238

ORDER TRANSFERRING PROCEEDING TO THE
NATIONAL LABOR RELATIONS BOARD

A hearing in the above-entitled proceeding having been held before a duly designated Administrative Law Judge and the Decision of the said Administrative Law Judge, a copy of which is annexed hereto, having been filed with the Board in Washington, D.C.,

IT IS HEREBY ORDERED, pursuant to Section 102.45 of National Labor Relations Board Rules and Regulations, that the above-entitled matter be, and it hereby is, transferred to and continued before the Board.

Dated, Washington, D.C.,

By direction of the Board:

_____
Executive Secretary

NOTE: Communications concerning compliance with the Decision of the Administrative Law Judge should be with the Director of the Regional Office issuing the complaint.

Attention is specifically directed to the excerpts from the Rules and Regulations appearing on the pages attached hereto. Note particularly the limitations on length of briefs and on size of paper.

Exceptions to the Decision of the Administrative Law Judge in this proceeding must be received by the Board in Washington, D.C., on or before

Exhibit 84.   Order Transferring Case to Board (Form NLRB-1406)

preponderance of all the relevant evidence convinces the Board that the resolutions are incorrect.[11]

In cases where a district court has issued a Section 10(j) injunction[12] but the administrative law judge recommends dismissal of the complaint, the General Counsel will advise the district court of the judge's recommendation.[13] Discretion then lies with the district court to modify or terminate the injunction.

§17.2   Voluntary Compliance and Failure to File Exceptions

The party against whom the complaint was issued may comply with the recommendations made in the administrative law judge's decision. All communications concerning such compliance should be addressed to the regional director who issued the complaint. Immediately upon receipt of the administrative law judge's decision, the regional director mails a letter in which assistance is offered to achieve early compliance. (See Exhibit 85.) Such a letter will not be sent in any case where the General Counsel disagrees with the decision and intends to file exceptions with the Board. If, however, the parties accept and comply with the recommendations of the administrative law judge, the proceedings normally conclude at this point.[14]

As discussed later in this chapter,[15] the parties may file exceptions to the administrative law judge's decision with the Board. In the absence of timely or proper exceptions, however, the findings, conclusions, and recommendations of the judge automatically become the decision and order of the Board.[16] The administrative law judge's decision thus acquires the force and effect of a Board order.[17] In such cases the Board rarely seeks enforcement in the court of appeals, but where it does, it assumes that the parties have waived all objections and exceptions for all purposes.[18]

Where the Board in the absence of exceptions seeks automatic enforcement of its decision, the court may concern itself only with two questions: (1) whether the party against whom the order was

---

[11]*Standard Dry Wall Prods., Inc.*, 91 NLRB 544, 26 LRRM 1531 (1950). The Board, however, is not absolutely bound by the judge's credibility determinations and may independently evaluate them in light of the record evidence. *Humes Elec., Inc.*, 263 NLRB 1238, 111 LRRM 1268 (1982).

[12]See §15.14 and chapter 21.

[13]NLRB Rules and Regulations §102.94(b).

[14]NLRB Statements of Procedure §101.11(b).

[15]See §17.4 *infra.*

[16]Sec. 10(c) of the Act; NLRB Rules and Regulations §102.48(a). *See also* NLRB Rules and Regulations §102.46(h) ("[n]o matter not included in exceptions or cross-exceptions may thereafter be urged before the Board, or in any further proceeding").

[17]The Board, however, is not bound by the administrative law judge's reasoning simply because no exceptions have been filed, and may reevaluate the decision in light of the record evidence. *Yellow Taxi Co.*, 262 NLRB 702, 110 LRRM 1346 (1982). *See Hedstrom Co. v. NLRB*, 629 F.2d 305, 105 LRRM 2183 (3d Cir. 1980) (even if exception not filed to finding of administrative law judge, finding not final and may be revised by Board).

[18]NLRB Rules and Regulations §102.48(a).

NATIONAL LABOR RELATIONS BOARD

REGION 5

Candler Building - 4th Floor

109 Market Place

Baltimore, MD   21202

January 2, 1986

Mr. Jack Smith, President
Janco Computer Services, Inc.
8181 Greensboro Drive
McLean, VA 22102

Re: Janco Computer Services, Inc.
     Case No. 5-CA-1238

Dear Mr. Smith:

You have recently received the Administrative Law Judge's Decision in the above case. The matter has been assigned to me for the purpose of assisting you to effect compliance with its terms. I trust that you will immediately initiate compliance so as to avoid any further litigation and notify me to this effect within 20 days.

I am enclosing herewith a number of notices with the request that they be immediately posted as ordered. If further notices are required, they will be forwarded to you upon request. A certification of posting is also enclosed. This form, with information as to when and where such posting was made, should be returned to this office with three signed and dated copies of the notice.

With respect to the backpay portion of the Decision, please assemble the necessary records and I shall call you in the near future to arrange a time for us to meet and discuss the computation.

Copies of the letter offering Ms. Hughes reinstatement should be furnished to this office.

If there are any questions or problems, please feel free to call upon me. Your cooperation will be appreciated.

                    Very truly yours,

                    Shelley L Korch
                    Shelley L. Korch
                    Compliance Officer

Enclosures

cc: All Other Parties
     Respondent or Designated Representative of Record

Exhibit 85.   Letter Regarding Compliance With Decision of Administrative Law Judge

issued is subject to the Act; and (2) whether the Board has jurisdiction to issue the order.[19] Beyond that, failure to file exceptions to the administrative law judge's decision is conclusive as to all issues, and the court automatically will enforce the Board's order.[20] Thus, for example, the court will not consider objections that:

- There is no substantial evidence to support the Board's findings;[21]
- The Board's remedial order is invalid;[22]
- Exceptions were made orally during a telephone conversation with a Board employee.[23]

These cases are the exception. In most instances, the parties either comply with the administrative law judge's decision voluntarily or file exceptions.

§17.3 Postdecision Motions

All motions filed after issuance of the administrative law judge's decision must be filed with the Board in Washington, D.C.[24]

(a) Intervention. The Board's rules do not provide specifically for intervention after issuance of the administrative law judge's decision.[25] On rare occasions, however, the Board has entertained motions and granted permission for such intervention. Thus, for example, the Board granted permission to intervene where: (1) an employer sought to file exceptions to an administrative law judge's findings which related to its agreement with the union involved in the proceeding,[26] and (2) an international union sought to intervene in a proceeding involving one of its locals in order to file exceptions so as to protect "interests of the international and all of its other subordinate locals."[27]

The Board also allows intervention for the purpose of filing *amicus curiae* briefs in important cases, particularly by trade associations or parent labor organizations. When the Board is considering adoption of a new policy, it may solicit such briefs.

---

[19]*NLRB v. Hansen*, 220 F.2d 733, 35 LRRM 2675 (1st Cir. 1955).

[20]*See NLRB v. Pugh & Barr, Inc.*, 194 F.2d 217, 29 LRRM 2382 (4th Cir. 1952) (failure to file exceptions precludes right to have sufficiency of evidence reviewed by court); *see also Alexander Dawson, Inc. v. NLRB*, 586 F.2d 1300, 99 LRRM 3105 (9th Cir. 1978) (court may not consider issues not raised in exception).

[21]*NLRB v. Noroian*, 193 F.2d 172, 29 LRRM 2201 (9th Cir. 1951).

[22]*NLRB v. Puerto Rico S.S. Ass'n*, 211 F.2d 274, 33 LRRM 2755 (1st Cir. 1954).

[23]*NLRB v. Mooney Aircraft*, 310 F.2d 565, 51 LRRM 2615 (5th Cir. 1962).

[24]NLRB Rules and Regulations §102.47.

[25]§102.29 of the Board's Rules and Regulations provides only for intervention in proceedings before the administrative law judge.

[26]*Newspaper & Mail Deliverers' Union*, 101 NLRB 589, 31 LRRM 1105 (1952).

[27]*Honolulu Star-Bulletin, Ltd.*, 123 NLRB 395, 43 LRRM 1449 (1959).

(b) Withdrawal of Charge. After issuance of the administrative law judge's recommended order, an unfair labor practice charge may be withdrawn only with the consent of the Board.[28] Upon withdrawal of the charge the complaint is dismissed. As with withdrawal requests made prior to or during the hearing, they are most likely to be granted when the alleged unfair labor practices have been remedied and no party objects to the request.[29]

(c) Severance. In a consolidated proceeding against more than one party, the Board may sever the proceeding when one of the parties complies fully with the recommendations of the administrative law judge.[30] The case against the complying party usually will be closed; the case against the remaining party will continue. This sometimes occurs where an employer and a union are charged by an individual with maintaining an illegal hiring arrangement. If the remedy includes backpay, the complying party will have paid half the amount due. The case is not closed, however, and, if the noncomplying party prevails over the complying party on appeal, the Board will look to the complying party for the balance of the backpay.

Exceptions to Administrative Law Judge's Decision

§17.4 Exceptions

Any party to the proceeding, including the General Counsel, may file exceptions to the administrative law judge's decision.[31] Parties also may file exceptions to any other portion of the record or proceedings, including rulings on motions made by the regional director or the administrative law judge prior to or during the hearing.[32]

The purpose of exceptions is to identify specifically the issues of substance or procedure which the Board is being asked to resolve. Accordingly, the Board's Rules and Regulations provide that each exception shall:

- Set forth specifically the questions of procedure, fact, law, or policy to which exception is taken;

---

[28]NLRB Rules and Regulations §102.9.

[29]See §12.11 *infra.*

[30]*Atlantic Freight Lines, Inc.*, 117 NLRB 464, 39 LRRM 1256 (1957).

[31]NLRB Rules and Regulations §102.46(a). *See generally* NLRB Rules and Regulations §102.46(b), NLRB Statements of Procedure §101.11(b), and NLRB Casehandling Manual ¶10438. Only parties are entitled to file exceptions. Accordingly, discriminatees who are not charging parties because a union or other representative has filed the charge on their behalf may not file exceptions to an administrative law judge's decision. *Giacalone v. NLRB*, 682 F.2d 427, 110 LRRM 2981 (3d Cir. 1982); *Lincoln Technical Inst., Inc.*, 256 NLRB 176, 107 LRRM 1185 (1981).

[32]NLRB Rules and Regulations §102.46(a).

- Identify the part of the administrative law judge's decision to which objection is made;
- Designate by page the portions of the record upon which the exception is based; and
- Concisely state the basis for the exception including a citation of authorities whenever a supporting brief is not filed.[33]

Exceptions should be as specific and precise as possible. The Board will disregard broad general exceptions which fail to identify clearly the issues, and will review the administrative law judge's decision as if the parties had waived the right to file exceptions.[34] The Board also will disregard documents attached to the exceptions which were not introduced into evidence,[35] and new testimony introduced through the exceptions.[36]

Parties must file exceptions within 28 days from the date of service of the order transferring the case to the Board, or within such further period as the Board may allow.[37] Requests for extensions of time must be in writing and must be received by the Board at least three days prior to the due date.[38] Eight copies of the exceptions, which should be double spaced and on 8-½ by 11-inch paper, are required. In addition, all parties, including the regional director, must be served with a copy of the exceptions.[39]

Parties should comply strictly with these filing requirements. While the Board on occasion will show some leniency in situations where a noncomplying party is inexperienced or where no prejudice has been shown,[40] there is no reason to jeopardize one's case by being careless in following the filing rules.

In addition to paying close attention to the filing requirements, parties should exercise great care in analyzing the administrative

---

[33]*Id.* at §102.46(b)(1). If a supporting brief is *not* filed, the exceptions including citations and argument may not exceed 50 pages in length. If a supporting brief *is* filed, the 50-page limit does not apply, but the exceptions may not contain any argument or citation of authority. *Id.*

[34]*Id.*; *McDonnell Douglas Corp.*, 271 NLRB 1528, 117 LRRM 1332 (1984); *Izzi (Pat Izzi Trucking Co.)*, 149 NLRB 1097, 57 LRRM 1474 (1964); *see also Wismer & Becker, Contracting Engrs.*, 251 NLRB 687, 105 LRRM 1214 (1980) (exceptions lacked specificity required by Board's Rules and Regulations) and *Fiesta Pub. Co.*, 268 NLRB 660, 115 LRRM 1081 (1984) (motion to strike exceptions granted where exceptions did not allege with particularity what error, mistake, or oversight administrative law judge committed, or on what grounds findings should be overturned).

[35]*Consolidated Casinos Corp.*, 266 NLRB 988, 113 LRRM 1081 (1983); *Feld & Sons, Inc.*, 263 NLRB 332, 111 LRRM 1038 (1982).

[36]*Fiesta Pub. Co.*, 268 NLRB 660, 115 LRRM 1081 (1984) (Board granted motion to strike exceptions which renounced testimony given by two principal witnesses at the hearing and asked Board to accept new testimony).

[37]NLRB Rules and Regulations §102.46(a); see also discussion at §25.3.

[38]NLRB Rules and Regulations §102.46(a). Copies of the request must promptly be served on the other parties. *Id.*

[39]*Id.* at §102.46(j).

[40]*See, e.g., St. Bernadette's Nursing Home*, 234 NLRB 835, 97 LRRM 1553 (1978) (motion to dismiss exceptions as untimely denied where exceptions mailed with sufficient time to permit timely delivery in the normal course, and where prejudice not established because respondent had adequate time, and did, file response to exceptions).

law judge's decision and making certain that all disputed findings are the subject of an exception. Under the Board's Rules and Regulations, "[n]o matter not included in exceptions or cross-exceptions may thereafter be urged before the Board, or in any further proceeding."[41] In addition, Section 10(e) of the Act provides that, "[n]o objection that has not been urged before the Board . . . shall be considered by the court, unless the failure or neglect to urge such objection shall be excused because of extraordinary circumstances." Failure to draft the exceptions properly, therefore, may preclude a party from challenging a crucial finding of the administrative law judge either before the Board or subsequently in court.[42]

§17.5   Briefs in Support of Exceptions

Parties are entitled to submit a brief supporting their exceptions.[43] These briefs are intended to supplement rather than duplicate the exceptions. If a brief is filed, the exceptions may not contain any argument or citations to authority; if a brief is not filed, the exceptions may contain both citations and argument, but the document may not exceed 50 pages in length.[44] The best practice is to identify in the exceptions by section, page, or paragraph the portion of the administrative law judge's decision to which exception is taken, and use the brief to set forth the basis for the exceptions (e.g., improper credibility resolution, misapplication of case precedent, etc.), citations to the transcript which afford evidentiary support for the exceptions, and any relevant legal authorities. Discussion in the briefs may not extend beyond the exceptions, and to the extent that the briefs are overinclusive they will be ignored.[45]

The Board's Rules and Regulations provide that briefs in support of exceptions shall contain, in the order indicated, the following:

- A concise statement of the case containing all information material to the questions presented;
- A specification of the questions involved and to be argued together with a reference to the specific exceptions to which they relate; and
- The argument, presenting clearly the points of fact and law supporting the brief's position on each question, with specific page references to the record and the legal or other supporting material.[46]

---

[41]NLRB Rules and Regulations §102.46(h).

[42]*NLRB v. Laborers, Local 282 (Alberici-Fruin-Colnon)*, 567 F.2d 833, 97 LRRM 2275 (8th Cir. 1977) (assertion of a mistaken ruling by administrative law judge could not be raised before Board because no exceptions to ruling had been filed); *Barton Brands, Ltd. v. NLRB*, 529 F.2d 793, 91 LRRM 2241 (7th Cir. 1976) (statute of limitations defense could not be raised before court when not raised in exceptions or cross-exceptions before Board).

[43]NLRB Rules and Regulations §102.46(a).

[44]NLRB Rules and Regulations §102.46(b)(1).

[45]*Jones Dairy Farm*, 245 NLRB 1109, 102 LRRM 1475 (1979).

[46]NLRB Rules and Regulations §102.46(c).

In addition, briefs are to be double spaced on 8-½ by 11-inch paper and are not to exceed 50 pages in length, excluding subject index and table of authorities. To request permission to exceed the maximum page length, parties must file a motion at least 10 days prior to the date the brief is due.[47] If the brief exceeds 20 pages in length, a subject index with page references and an alphabetical table of cases and other authorities cited also are required.[48]

The brief to the Board, like that to the administrative law judge, should be concise. Care should be taken to correct factual errors or misplaced emphasis in the administrative law judge's decision. Discussion of applicable law should both present the party's view of the case and specifically address any conflicting legal theories found in the decision.

Incorporation by reference of the brief to the administrative law judge is not recommended. The brief to the administrative law judge was directed to a single individual who heard the case and observed the witnesses. Moreover, since it was prepared prior to issuance of the administrative law judge's decision, it can provide little direct support for exceptions taken to that decision.[49] A brief to the Board must interest and persuade the Board members and their legal counsel, none of whom will have previously participated in the case and all of whom will be working from the formal written record. Moreover, the Board members themselves rarely read the record but must rely for both the facts and the law on briefs of the parties and memoranda prepared by their legal assistants. Their time is limited. Short, accurate briefs which avoid repetition and irrelevancies are more likely to be read and digested.

The brief in support of exceptions should be filed and served at the same time and in the same manner as the exceptions, but as a separate document.[50]

§17.6 Answering Briefs and Briefs in Support of Administrative Law Judge's Decision

Any party who is completely satisfied with the administrative law judge's decision may, within the time period prescribed for filing exceptions, file a brief in support of the decision.[51] A more common practice, however, is for a satisfied party to wait and see whether or not any of the other parties file exceptions, and if they do then prepare an answering brief directed specifically at the issues raised in the exceptions. Answering briefs must be filed within 14 days, or such

---

[47]*Id.* at §102.46(j).

[48]*Id.*

[49]*Cf. Ditch Witch*, 248 NLRB 452, 103 LRRM 1446 (1980) (brief previously submitted to administrative law judge failed to fulfill requirements for exceptions).

[50]See discussion at §17.4 *supra*, notes 37–39.

[51]NLRB Rules and Regulations §102.46(a); NLRB Casehandling Manual ¶10438.6.

further period as the Board may allow, from the last date on which exceptions and any supporting brief may be filed.[52] Therefore, a party has a longer period of time after issuance of the administrative law judge's decision to prepare an answering brief than a brief in support.[53]

Many of the Board's rules regarding briefs in support of exceptions apply equally to answering briefs. For example, answering briefs may not extend beyond issues raised in the exceptions and supporting brief;[54] pages of the record which support challenged portions of the administrative law judge's decision should be cited;[55] requests for extensions of time for filing must be received by the Board three days prior to the due date;[56] and requirements pertaining to page size, length of briefs, subject index, table of authorities, and the number of copies which must be filed[57] also apply to answering briefs.

§17.7 Reply Briefs

As a general rule the parties are entitled to file one brief in support of, and one brief in opposition to, each set of exceptions.[58] Accordingly, the Board's Rules and Regulations do not authorize an excepting party to respond to an answering brief with a reply brief, and most efforts to file such briefs are unsuccessful. If such a brief is desired, special leave of the Board must be acquired.[59]

§17.8 Cross-Exceptions and Answering Briefs

Within 14 days after the last date on which exceptions may be filed, any party who has not already done so may file its own set of exceptions (referred to as "cross-exceptions") to the administrative law judge's decision along with a supporting brief.[60] Requirements pertaining to the format, length and timeliness of exceptions and supporting briefs also apply to cross-exceptions and supporting briefs.[61] Within 14 days after the last day on which cross-exceptions may be

---

[52]NLRB at §102.46(d)(1).

[53]Nevertheless, the Board has accepted briefs in support even after the filing deadline. In *Otis Elevator Co.*, 255 NLRB 235, 106 LRRM 1343 (1981), the Board denied a request to strike as untimely certain portions of the General Counsel's brief in support of the administrative law judge's decision. The Board simply treated the brief in support as a timely answering brief noting that the Board's filing requirements are to be liberally construed and no prejudice had been shown as a result of the Board's acceptance of the brief.

[54]NLRB Rules and Regulations §102.46(d)(2).

[55]*Id.*

[56]*Id.* at §102.46(d)(3).

[57]*Id.* at §102.46(j).

[58]*Save-It Discount Foods, Inc.*, 263 NLRB 689, 111 LRRM 1110 (1982).

[59]NLRB Rules and Regulations §102.46(g).

[60]*Id.* at §102.46(e).

[61]*Id.* at §102.46(b), (e), (f)(2), (j), and §102.111.

filed, any other party may file an answering brief.[62] Rules with respect to filing answering briefs to exceptions apply equally to answering briefs to cross-exceptions,[63] including the requirement that
the scope of the answering brief may not exceed the issues raised in
the cross-exceptions.[64]

Frequently the administrative law judge will dismiss certain
allegations in a complaint and sustain others. When this occurs a
party may consider that, for all practical purposes, the case has been
won, even though there may be disagreement with the administrative
law judge's findings on minor issues. As a result, if the opposing party
does not file exceptions, the party who won may not be interested in
taking the case to the Board by filing exceptions with respect to the
minor issues. At the same time, the winning party may be uncertain
as to whether the loser will file exceptions, in which event the winner
would want to file a brief in support of the administrative law judge's
decision and exceptions to the minor issues lost.

When faced with this set of circumstances, the winning party
may do nothing until the time for filing exceptions has expired. If
the loser files exceptions, the winner may then file cross-exceptions
to the portion of the decision considered to be adverse and file a brief
in support of these cross-exceptions. In other words, the filing of
exceptions by either party serves to keep the entire matter alive and
thus enables the other party to protect his or her position by filing
cross-exceptions to any portion of the decision. Moreover, although
a brief in support of the decision must be filed within the 28-day time
limit for filing exceptions,[65] if such a brief is not filed by the winner
and exceptions are filed by the loser, the winner can file an answering
brief which, from a practical standpoint, would serve the same purpose as the brief in support.

§17.9   Oral Argument Before the Board

Any party desiring to argue orally before the Board should address a written request to the Executive Secretary simultaneously
with the filing of its statement of exceptions or cross-exceptions.[66]
Although there have been many comments, including some from
Board members themselves, about the desirability of more oral arguments, pressure of the Board's workload has kept the number to

---

[62]*Id.* at §102.46(f)(1).

[63]*Id.* at §102.46(c), (f)(1), (f)(2), (j), and §102.111.

[64]*Thermo King Corp.*, 247 NLRB 296, 103 LRRM 1204 (1980). In *Save-It Discount Foods,
Inc.*, 263 NLRB 689, 111 LRRM 1110 (1982), the Board rejected respondent's answering brief
to the General Counsel's cross-exceptions because the brief was responsive not to the cross-
exceptions, but to the brief which the General Counsel had filed in answer to respondent's
exceptions.

[65]NLRB Rules and Regulations §102.46(a).

[66]*Id.* at §102.46(i).

a small fraction of the Board's caseload. As a rule, the Board has granted such requests only where the case involves:

- A basic policy question;
- A question whose resolution may establish new precedent;
- Matters on which the Board may wish to hear arguments more fully developed than those set forth in written briefs.

Whenever the Board grants a party's request for oral argument, all parties are served with a notice of hearing. (See Exhibit 35.) The oral argument is usually conducted before the Board in Washington, D.C. Each party to the proceeding is entitled to 30 minutes' argument. Requests for additional time may not be granted unless timely application is made in advance of the argument.[67]

Decision and Order of the Board

§17.10   Review of Administrative Law Judge's Decision

In the absence of timely exceptions, the administrative law judge's decision automatically becomes the decision and order of the Board.[68] If exceptions are filed to the administrative law judge's decision, the Board makes its decision on the basis of the entire written record.[69] Where exception is taken to a factual finding of the administrative law judge, however, the Board, in determining whether the finding is contrary to a preponderance of the evidence, may limit its consideration to such portions of the record as are specified in the exceptions, the supporting brief, and the answering brief.[70] In reviewing the administrative law judge's decision, the Board is precluded from consulting with the administrative law judge or with any agent of the General Counsel.[71]

While all five Board members may participate in the review of an administrative law judge's decision, and frequently do in cases which establish or change policy, decision-making authority in most cases is delegated to three-member panels.[72] Typically, a case will be assigned by the Executive Secretary to a particular Board member, and referred to one of that member's staff counsel. The entire record,

---

[67]*Id.*

[68]*Id.* at §102.48(a). See discussion at §17.2 *supra.*

[69]*Id.* at §102.48(b). See §17.1(b) *supra* for what constitues the record before the Board.

[70]*Id.* at §102.48(c). Although neither the Act nor the Board's rules provide that *parties* may request reopening of the record after issuance of the administrative law judge's decision and before issuance of the Board's decision, the *Board* has authority to order the record reopened (NLRB Rules and Regulations §102.48(b)), and it has entertained motions filed for this purpose. It has then ruled on the basis of whether or not material evidence sought to be introduced was known and available at the time of the hearing.

[71]Sec. 4(a) of the Act; NLRB Statements of Procedure §101.12(a).

[72]Sec. 3(b).

including all of the pleadings, briefs, administrative law judge's decision and the transcript will be analyzed by the counsel.[73] The case then will be considered and discussed by a "subpanel"—i.e., senior staff members representing the three Board members who constitute the panel for that case. The subpanel will recommend a disposition, and the counsel will draft a proposed Board Decision and Order in accordance with the subpanel recommendations. The draft opinion will be reviewed by the Board members and, if approved, will be issued by the Executive Secretary. Cases which are novel or which establish or modify policy often are considered at full-Board agendas and are issued over the signatures of all five Board members.

§17.11 Form of Board Decision and Order

The Board may adopt, reject, or modify the findings, conclusions, and recommendations of the administrative law judge. The Board will issue either a "short form" or "long form" decision. A "short form" decision is used when the Board affirms the administrative law judge and simply incorporates the administrative law judge's decision and recommended order into its own opinion without substantial elaboration. A "long form" opinion is used when the Board departs from the administrative law judge's analysis in some manner and, therefore, issues its own findings of fact, conclusions of law, and order.

There is a tendency on the part of some to believe that cases in which a long form decision is issued have been more carefully considered than those in which the Board has issued a short form adoption. This is inaccurate. All cases follow the decisional process outlined in the previous section, and it is improper to assume that a case was reviewed superficially simply because the Board adopted the administrative law judge's decision without further comment. Both short form and long form decisions, however, must be based upon explicit findings. An agency's "action[s] cannot be upheld [by a court] merely because findings might have been made and considerations disclosed which would justify its order. . . . There must be . . . a responsible finding."[74]

The Board's decision may uphold or dismiss the entire complaint, or it may uphold and dismiss various allegations of the complaint. Where unfair labor practices are found, the Board is authorized to frame an order in two parts:[75] (1) a negative part, ordering the party found guilty of the unfair labor practices to cease and desist from such practices, and (2) an affirmative part, directing that certain action be taken to remedy the violations.

---

[73]Sec. 4(a).

[74]*S.E.C. v. Chenery Corp.*, 318 U.S. 80, 94 (1943).

[75]Sec. 10(c) provides that the Board may issue "an order requiring such person to cease and desist from such unfair labor practice, and to take such affirmative action, including reinstatement of employees with or without backpay, as will effectuate the policies of the Act."

§17.12   Cease and Desist Orders

Cease and desist orders are a form of injunctive relief enjoining the respondent from continuing its unlawful conduct in the future. Cease and desist orders may be narrow or broad. A narrow order is one which prohibits continuation of the specific conduct found to be unlawful. Narrow orders also contain a provision requiring the respondent to cease and desist from engaging in "like or related" conduct.[76] Broad orders prohibit a wide range of unlawful conduct by stipulating that the respondent shall cease and desist from violating the Act "in any other manner."[77]

Broad orders are appropriate only in situations where the record demonstrates a proclivity on the part of the respondent to violate the Act, or where there has been widespread or egregious misconduct.[78] In addition, while cease and desist orders generally apply only to the geographic location involved in the particular case, they may cover all of an employer's facilities or the entire area where a union has jurisdiction if there has been a pattern or practice of unlawful conduct.[79]

Cease and desist orders are enforceable through judicial contempt proceedings and penalties.[80] Accordingly, it often is of considerable interest to the parties whether a narrow or broad order is issued. If the Board seeks to challenge the conduct of a party against whom a broad cease and desist order has been entered, the initiation of contempt proceedings may be all that is required. In contrast, if a narrow order has been issued and the challenged conduct is not covered, an entirely new unfair labor practice proceeding may be necessary.

---

[76]For example, "The ABC Corp. shall cease and desist from interrogating employees about their union sympathies *or in any like or related manner* interfering with their right to join or refrain from joining a labor organization"; or "The XYZ Union shall cease and desist from restraining or coercing *the employees of ABC Corp.* from delivering goods to the municipal building jobsite."

[77]For example, "The ABC Corp. shall cease and desist from interrogating employees about their union sympathies *or in any other manner* interfering with their right to join or refrain from joining a labor organization"; or "The XYZ Union shall cease and desist from restraining or coercing *the employees of any employer* from delivering goods to the municipal building jobsite." *See* NLRB Casehandling Manual ¶10522.3.

[78]*Hickmott Foods, Inc.*, 242 NLRB 1357, 101 LRRM 1342 (1979); *see Coil-ACC, Inc.*, 262 NLRB 76, 110 LRRM 1262 (1982) (broad order appropriate where employer's egregious and widespread misconduct demonstrated general disregard for employees' fundamental statutory rights); *Clark Manor Nursing Home Corp.*, 254 NLRB 455, 106 LRRM 1231 (1981) (broad order warranted where employer's unfair labor practices may not have been widespread, but they were numerous, varied, egregious and demonstrated a deliberate disregard for employees' Sec. 7 rights); *Teamsters, Local 945 (Newark Disposal Serv.)*, 232 NLRB 1, 97 LRRM 1103 (1977) (broad order justified against union where there were four instances of unlawful conduct over relatively short time, prior Board orders did not restrain unlawful conduct, and union's course of conduct demonstrated a proclivity to repeat secondary boycotts). In *Operating Eng'r Local 12*, 270 NLRB 1172, 116 LRRM 1268 (1984), the Board reversed earlier precedent and concluded that prior administrative law judges' decisions to which no exceptions were filed could be relied upon to demonstrate a proclivity to violate the Act.

[79]*J. P. Stevens & Co.*, 240 NLRB 33, 100 LRRM 1342 (1979).

[80]*Sure-Tan, Inc. v. NLRB*, 467 U.S. 883, 116 LRRM 2857 (1984); NLRB Casehandling Manual ¶10510.

§17.13 Affirmative Remedial Orders

Unlike cease and desist orders which are mandatory whenever an unfair labor practice has been found,[81] the Board's authority to order that affirmative action be undertaken by a respondent is discretionary. The Board's remedial authority is broad and is subject to only limited judicial review.[82] It is not, however, without limit. For example, the Board may not:

- Compel a party to make a bargaining concession or agree to a proposal;[83]
- Issue an order which is punitive in nature;[84]
- Remedy unfair labor practices which occurred outside of the six-month statute of limitations period specified in Section 10(b) of the Act;[85]
- Issue a remedial order which is unclear and fails to inform the respondent of what conduct is prohibited.[86]

Within these limitations, however, the Board exercises broad authority to develop, to the extent possible, remedies calculated to return the parties to the situation as it existed prior to the commencement of the unlawful conduct.[87]

(a) Section 8(a)(1) Violations.   The Board generally issues an appropriate cease and desist order against employers who have interferred with, restrained, or coerced employees in the exercise of their Section 7 rights. The posting of a Board notice for 60 consecutive days also is required.[88]

(b) Section 8(a)(2) Violations.   Where an employer has dominated a union, the Board generally directs that the union be dises-

---

[81]*See NLRB v. Express Pub. Co.*, 312 U.S. 426, 8 LRRM 415 (1941). The Board, however, may refuse to issue any remedial order where the unfair labor practices found are of such an isolated or *de minimus* nature that they do not warrant remedial action. *E.g., American Federation of Musicians, Local 76 (Jimmy Wakely Show)*, 202 NLRB 620, 82 LRRM 1591 (1973); *Kohl Motors, Inc.*, 185 NLRB 324, 76 LRRM 1747 (1970).

[82]*Sure-Tan, Inc. v. NLRB*, 467 U.S. 883, 116 LRRM 2857 (1984) (the Board has the primary responsibility and broad discretion to devise remedies that effectuate the policies of the Act, subject only to limited judicial review); *NLRB v. Food Store Employees Local 347 (Heck's Inc.)*, 417 U.S. 1, 86 LRRM 2209 (1974) (Congress invested Board, not courts, with broad discretion to fashion remedial orders).

[83]*H.K. Porter Co. v. NLRB*, 397 U.S. 99, 73 LRRM 2561 (1970).

[84]*Republic Steel Corp. v. NLRB*, 311 U.S. 7, 7 LRRM 287 (1940) ("The Act is essentially remedial. It does not carry a penal program declaring the described unfair labor practices to be crimes.").

[85]*But cf. Pacific Intercom Co.*, 255 NLRB 184, 106 LRRM 1289 (1981) (Sec. 10(b) period of limitation tolled when party frauduently conceals its unlawful conduct).

[86]*Cf. NLRB v. National Garment Co.*, 166 F.2d 233, 21 LRRM 2215 (8th Cir. 1948).

[87]*See generally* NLRB Casehandling Manual ¶¶10524–10524.7 and THE DEVELOPING LABOR LAW at chapter 33.

[88]Cease and desist orders are discussed at §17.12 *supra* and Board notices are discussed at §17.14 *infra*.

tablished.[89] Where there has been assistance and support of the union which falls short of actual domination, the normal remedy is to order the employer to withdraw and withhold recognition until such time as the union is certified by the Board.[90]

(c) Section 8(a)(3) and (4) Violations. In a typical 8(a)(3) or (4) case, an employee is discriminated against or terminated for having engaged in union activities, or for having filed a charge or testified under the Act. In addition to a cease and desist order and a 60-day notice tailored to the specific unlawful conduct found, the Board generally will require reinstatement and backpay for the affected employee.[91] Reinstatement to the employee's former job or a substantially equivalent job usually is ordered unless the employer can show that the employee engaged in serious misconduct making reinstatement inappropriate,[92] or would have been terminated in any event for lawful reasons.[93] Reinstatement and backpay are discussed in detail in the next chapter.

(d) Section 8(a)(5) Violations. In most instances an employer's unlawful refusal to bargain will be remedied through a cease and desist order and instructions to bargain collectively in good faith with the appropriate union, upon request, over rates of pay, wages, hours of work, and other terms and conditions of employment.[94]

These are examples of the traditional remedies utilized in routine cases brought against employers. In situations where an employer's unlawful conduct is particularly flagrant or egregious, extraordinary remedies such as the mailing of individual Board notices to employees, granting the union access to the employer's premises for purposes of posting notices on bulletin boards or talking with employees during nonworking time, ordering employers to pay for litigation costs, attorneys' fees, and union expenses also may be imposed.[95]

---

[89]*Carpenter Steel Co.*, 76 NLRB 670, 21 LRRM 1232 (1948); *see also South Nassau Communities Hosp.*, 247 NLRB 527, 103 LRRM 1175 (1980) (disestablishment of nursing advisory committee not ordered since there was no allegation of employer domination of the committee), and NLRB Casehandling Manual ¶10524.1.

[90]*Carpenter Steel Co.*, 76 NLRB 670, 21 LRRM 1232 (1948).

[91]Sec. 10(c). *See generally* NLRB Casehandling Manual ¶10528 (reinstatement) and ¶¶10530–10546 (backpay).

[92]*PBA Inc.*, 270 NLRB 998, 116 LRRM 1162 (1984) and *Clear Pine Mouldings*, 268 NLRB 1044, 115 LRRM 1113 (1984) (picket line misconduct of striking employees disqualified them from reinstatement).

[93]*Keeshin Charter Serv., Inc.*, 250 NLRB 780, 105 LRRM 1030 (1980) (discriminatee not ordered reinstated because he lawfully would have been laid off since he was a driver and insurance carriers refused to insure him). *See generally* NLRB Casehandling Manual ¶10528.

[94]NLRB Casehandling Manual ¶¶10524.4–10524.6; *NLRB v. Gissel Packing Co.*, 395 U.S. 575, 71 LRRM 2481 (1969). Minor or limited unfair labor practices, however, will not sustain a bargaining order. Bargaining orders are discussed in chapter 4.

[95]*See generally* THE DEVELOPING LABOR LAW at 1678–1682.

(e) Section 8(b)(1)(A) and (B) Violations. Labor organizations, like employers, are subject to cease and desist orders and notice posting requirements. Similarly, affirmative relief ordered to be taken by a union is tailored to afford a remedy for the specific violation found.[96] For example, the remedy for unlawfully imposed fines generally is rescission of the fine and reimbursement of monies paid;[97] dues illegally checked off are returned;[98] employees or supervisors who lost their jobs as a result of improper union pressure exerted against employers are awarded backpay;[99] and the union memberships of supervisors unlawfully expelled are restored.[100] In cases where actual or threatened physical violence has occurred, the normal remedy is a cease and desist order. If employees are unable to work as a result of such conduct, backpay generally is not assessed against the union,[101] although in extreme cases the union's certification as exclusive bargaining agent may be revoked.[102]

(f) Section 8(b)(2) Violations. When the unlawful conduct consists of a union's attempt to cause an employer to commit a Section 8(a)(3) violation, the usual remedy is a cease and desist order and the posting of a notice.[103] When the union's efforts are successful and actual discrimination occurs, however, affirmative relief also is ordered the nature of which depends upon the circumstances. Generally, the union must send a notice to both the employer and to the discriminatee indicating that it no longer objects to the individual's employment on nondiscriminatory terms or to the restoration of full employment benefits.[104]

If the discriminatee has lost income as a result of the unlawful conduct, backpay may be awarded. In most cases the employer and the union will be jointly and severally liable.[105] In situations where the employer initially resists the union's demands but finally acquiesces under extraordinary pressure, the union's liability for lost wages may be primary and the employer's liability secondary.[106] If

---

[96]*Id.* at 1682–1694.

[97]*Stationary Eng'rs, Local 39 (Kaiser Foundation Hosps.)*, 268 NLRB 115, 114 LRRM 1244 (1983). Union members also may be reimbursed for lost wages and travel and other expenses incurred in resisting retaliatory disciplinary proceedings brought against them by their union. *Laborers Local 294 (Hayward Baker Co.)*, 275 NLRB No. 48, 119 LRRM 1033 (1985).

[98]*Teamsters Local 886 (United Parts Co.)*, 119 NLRB 222, 41 LRRM 1056 (1957).

[99]*See, e.g., Western Pub. Co.*, 263 NLRB 1110, 111 LRRM 1537 (1982) (employee); *Silver Bay Local 962 (Alaska Lumber & Pulp Co.)*, 215 NLRB 414, 88 LRRM 1370 (1974) (supervisor). Board policy concerning backpay awards in situations involving union-procured employer discrimination has been inconsistent. *See Iron Workers, Local 111 v. NLRB*, _____ F.2d _____, 122 LRRM 2611 (D.C. Cir. 1986).

[100]*United Marine Div., Local 333*, 233 NLRB 387, 96 LRRM 1609 (1977).

[101]*Teamsters, Local 901 (Lock Joint Pipe & Co.)*, 202 NLRB 399, 82 LRRM 1525 (1973).

[102]*Union Nacional de Trabajadores (Carborundum Co.)*, 219 NLRB 862, 90 LRRM 1023 (1975).

[103]*See National Maritime Union*, 78 NLRB 971, 22 LRRM 1289 (1948).

[104]*Operating Eng'rs, Local 450 (Houston Chapter, Associated Gen. Contractors)*, 267 NLRB 775, 114 LRRM 1201 (1983).

[105]*Acme Mattress Co.*, 91 NLRB 1010, 26 LRRM 1611 (1950).

[106]*See Union Boiler Co.*, 245 NLRB 719, 102 LRRM 1473 (1979) (since union suggested conduct which violated Sec. 8(a)(3), union held primarily liable, employer secondarily liable).

only the union is charged with unlawful conduct, its responsibility for backpay is exclusive.[107] In all cases, a union may limit its backpay liability by notifying the employer that it no longer objects to employment of the employee or employees involved on a nondiscriminatory basis. If the employer continues the discriminatory conduct following such notice, it alone becomes responsible for backpay which accrues beginning five days after the notice is given.[108] Similar make-whole remedies are utilized in cases where the unlawful conduct consists of a labor organization's discriminatory operation of a hiring hall, pension funds, or health and welfare funds.[109]

(g) Section 8(b)(3) Violations. As with employer remedies under Section 8(a)(5), unions which refuse to bargain collectively with an employer will be ordered to cease and desist from such conduct and directed to bargain in good faith.[110] In addition, unions may be ordered to furnish information relevant to the collective bargaining process,[111] execute an agreed-upon contract,[112] or reimburse the employer for additional expenditures incurred pursuant to inappropriate contract clauses.[113] The Board, however, generally does not require a union to reimburse employees for wages lost as a result of its refusal to execute an agreed-upon contract.[114]

(h) Section 8(b)(4) Violations.[115] In addition to the usual cease and desist and notice posting requirements, there are a variety of affirmative remedies which may be imposed on unions that engage in unlawful secondary activity. Employees who have been fired, expelled from union membership, or otherwise disciplined for refusing to participate in unlawful activity are entitled to monetary reimbursement and restoration of their union status;[116] contracts which

---

[107]*Radio Officers' Union v. NLRB*, 347 U.S. 17, 33 LRRM 2417 (1954).

[108]*Harsh Inv. Corp.*, 260 NLRB 1088, 109 LRRM 1280 (1982); *see Sheet Metal Workers' Local 355 (Zinsco Elec. Prods.)*, 254 NLRB 773, 106 LRRM 1137 (1981).

[109]*See* THE DEVELOPING LABOR LAW at 1685–1686.

[110]*American Radio Ass'n*, 82 NLRB 1344, 24 LRRM 1006 (1949).

[111]*National Union of Hosp. & Health Care Employees (Sinai Hosp.)*, 248 NLRB 631, 103 LRRM 1459 (1980) (union ordered to ask trustees to furnish information relating to health and welfare plan); *Asbestos Workers, Local 80 (W. Va. Master Insulators Ass'n)*, 248 NLRB 143, 103 LRRM 1370 (1980) (union ordered to furnish information relating to referral system).

[112]*District 1199C, Nat'l Union of Hosp. & Health Care Employees*, 241 NLRB 270, 101 LRRM 1030 (1979); *Truck Drivers Local 807 (Relay Transp.)*, 195 NLRB 603, 79 LRRM 1462 (1972).

[113]*See NLRB v. Warehousemen's Local 17*, 451 F.2d 1240, 78 LRRM 3056 (9th Cir. 1971) (union required to reimburse employer for expenditures under contract which was illegally obtained); *Laborers Local 264 (J.J. Dalton)*, 216 NLRB 40, 88 LRRM 1192 (1975) (industry advancement funds); *Carpenters Local 964, (Contractors & Suppliers Ass'n)*, 184 NLRB 625, 74 LRRM 1081 (1970) (same).

[114]*Graphic Arts Local 280 (James H. Barry Co.)*, 235 NLRB 1084, 98 LRRM 1188 (1978); *Teamsters, Local 427 (Edward D. Sultan Co.)*, 223 NLRB 1342, 92 LRRM 1144 (1976).

[115]Sec. 8(b)(4)(A), (B), and (C) violations may be remedied temporarily through Sec. 10(l) injunction proceedings. See chapter 21. Sec. 8(b)(4)(D) violations cannot be remedied prior to the culmination of Section 10(k) proceedings. See chapter 19.

[116]*Carpenters Local 112 (Summit Valley Indus., Inc.)*, 217 NLRB 902, 89 LRRM 1799 (1975).

have been executed through unlawful secondary pressures may be rescinded; fines levied against employers must be repaid;[117] and the union may be required to notify employees in writing that it will no longer support or sponsor secondary picketing.[118] In cases where a union has demonstrated a proclivity to engage in unlawful secondary activity, the Board may direct that its compliance notice be published in a newspaper of general circulation in the geographical area where the union is located.[119]

(i) Section 8(b)(5) Violations.   When a union exacts a discriminatory or excessive initiation fee from an employee, the Board directs that the employee be refunded the difference between the fee paid and the regular fee paid by other individuals.[120]

(j) Section 8(b)(6) Violations.   When the Board finds that a union has exacted funds from an employer for work not performed, the usual remedy is an order directing that the employer be refunded the difference between the wages paid and the amount normally paid for the work which actually was performed;[121] if no work was performed at all, the entire amount of the wages paid is refunded.[122]

(k) Section 8(b)(7) Violations.   Most instances of unlawful picketing under Section 8(b)(7) are considered under the mandatory injunction provisions of Section 10(l).[123] If an unfair labor practice is found by the Board, however, the normal remedy is a cease and desist order and the posting of a notice.[124]

(l) Section 8(e) Violations.   When both the employer and union are found to have entered into an unlawful "hot cargo" contract, the Board directs that they cease and desist from giving effect to the challenged provisions, and refrain from entering into such agreements in the future.[125] When only the union has been charged and

---

[117]*See United Marine Div., Local 333*, 226 NLRB 1214, 94 LRRM 1100 (1976) (union ordered to return monies unlawfully exacted from secondary employer who continued doing business with primary employer).

[118]*See, e.g., Teamsters, Local 554 (Clark Bros. Transfer Co. & Coffey's Transfer Co.) v. NLRB*, 262 F.2d 456, 43 LRRM 2197 (D.C. Cir. 1958); *Electrical Workers, Local 481 (J.A. Constr.)*, 234 NLRB 297, 97 LRRM 1221 (1978).

[119]*Service Employees, Local 73 (Andy Frain, Inc.)*, 239 NLRB 295, 99 LRRM 1667 (1978).

[120]*Boilermakers, Local 749*, 192 NLRB 502, 77 LRRM 1839 (1971); *General Longshore Workers, Local 1419 (New Orleans S.S. Ass'n)*, 186 NLRB 674, 75 LRRM 1411 (1970); *Automobile Workers, Local 153 (Richard Stacker)*, 99 NLRB 1419, 30 LRRM 1169 (1952).

[121]*Metallic Lathers Local 46 (Expanded Metal Eng'g Co.)*, 207 NLRB 631, 84 LRRM 1570 (1973).

[122]*Local 456, Teamsters (J.R. Stevenson Corp.)*, 212 NLRB 968, 87 LRRM 1101 (1974).

[123]See chapter 21 and the discussion of expedited elections in chapter 20.

[124]*See Drug and Hosp. Employees, Local 1199 (Janel Sales Corp.)*, 136 NLRB 1564, 50 LRRM 1033 (1962); *Local 182, Teamsters (Woodward Motors, Inc.)*, 135 NLRB 851, 49 LRRM 1576 (1962).

[125]*See Feifer (American Feed Co.)*, 133 NLRB 214, 48 LRRM 1622 (1961).

found guilty of a violation, the Board's order will be directed only against the union, and the scope of the prohibition will vary depending upon whether the union sought to enforce the hot cargo provision against a single employer, a few employers, or an entire class of employers.[126] The Board has held that monetary make-whole remedies such as reimbursement to employees of initiation fees, dues, benefit contributions, and repayment of lost income are not appropriate for Section 8(e) violations.[127]

(m) Section 8(g) Violations. When a labor organization fails to provide timely notice before engaging in a strike, picketing, or concerted refusal to work at a health care institution, the usual remedy is a cease and desist order until such time as the appropriate notice is given.[128]

§17.14 Board Notices

Every Board order carries a requirement for the posting of notices "expressed in simple and readily understandable language"[129] setting forth the action which will be taken to remedy the specific unfair labor practices found.[130] In the absence of special permission, the notices are to remain posted for 60 consecutive days.[131]

In the case of unfair labor practices committed by employers, the notices are to be posted in conspicuous places at the employer's premises.[132] Notices pertaining to unfair labor practices committed by unions may be posted at the union hall, at the union's meeting place, on the employer's premises, or may be mailed individually to the employees against whom the unfair labor practices were committed.[133] In situations where the affected employees cannot be located or where the unlawful conduct is widespread, the Board also may direct that the notice be published in a daily newspaper of general circulation.[134] Various types of prepared notices are available at the

---

[126]*Milk Drivers & Dairy Employees, Local 537 (Sealtest Foods)*, 147 NLRB 230, 56 LRRM 1193 (1964); *Retail Clerks, Local 770 (Frito Co.)*, 138 NLRB 244, 51 LRRM 1010 (1962).

[127]In *Building Material & Dump Truck Drivers, Teamsters Local 36 (Cal. Dump Truck Owners Ass'n)*, 249 NLRB 386, 104 LRRM 1279 (1980), 669 F.2d 759, 108 LRRM 3153 (D.C. Cir. 1981), *aff'd sub nom. Shepard v. NLRB*, 459 U.S. 344, 112 LRRM 2369 (1983), the Supreme Court confirmed that the NLRB is not required to reflexively order complete relief.

[128]*See, e.g., Electrical Workers, Local 388 (Hoffman Co.)*, 220 NLRB 665, 90 LRRM 1390 (1975).

[129]*Bilyeu Motor Corp.*, 161 NLRB 982, 983, 63 LRRM 1471 (1966).

[130]The notice requirements for Board orders and settlement agreements are similar. See NLRB Casehandling Manual ¶10132.1c and discussion at §14.3.

[131]*See* NLRB Casehandling Manual ¶¶10132.1a (settlements), 10526.1 (Board orders).

[132]*Id.* at ¶10132.4.

[133]*Id.*

[134]*Id. See* NLRB Casehandling Manual ¶10136.2 for notices used in secondary boycott and hot cargo cases.

regional offices, each notice tailored to fit the particular unfair labor practices found. (See Exhibits 86-92.)

§17.15   Motions for Reconsideration, Rehearing, and Reopening the Record

Any party to a Board proceeding may file a motion for reconsideration, rehearing, or reopening of the record because of extraordinary circumstances.[135] The motion must be filed within 28 days of service of the Board's decision and order, or within such further period as the Board may allow.[136] Motions to introduce additional evidence must be filed promptly upon discovery of such evidence.[137] Requests for extensions of time to file such motions must be received by the Board at least three days prior to the due date, and copies of all motions must promptly be served on the other parties to the proceeding.[138] Unless specifically so ordered by the Board, the filing of postdecision motions shall not operate to delay implementation of the Board's order.[139]

(a) Motions for Reconsideration.   Motions for reconsideration must specify the material error alleged to have occurred, and with respect to findings of fact, must specify the pages of the record relied upon.[140] Until such time as the transcript is filed in court, the Board may modify or set aside all or a portion of its findings of fact, conclusions of law, or order.[141] Motions for reconsideration generally are referred to the same Board panel that issued the initial decision. The panel may, however, refer the motion to the full Board for its consideration.[142] Motions for reconsideration have been granted to consider whether the Board's decision and order are unsupportable on the record[143] or when an intervening court decision renders the Board's original order inappropriate.[144] Such motions will be denied,

---

[135]NLRB Rules and Regulations §102.48(d)(1); NLRB Casehandling Manual ¶10452.

[136]NLRB Rules and Regulations §102.48(d)(2).

[137]*Id.*

[138]*Id.*

[139]*Id.* at §102.48(d)(3). Motions for reconsideration or rehearing are not necessary to exhaust administrative remedies. *Id.*

[140]*Id.* at §102.48(d)(1).

[141]*Id.* at §102.49; *See Hadden House Food Prods., Inc.*, 260 NLRB 1060, 109 LRRM 1233 (1982) (motion for reconsideration rejected when filed with Board after court enforcement of Board's order).

[142]*Columbia Typographical Union 101 (Byron S. Adams Printing, Inc.)*, 214 NLRB 27, 87 LRRM 1275 (1974); *Enterprise Indus. Piping Co.*, 118 NLRB 1, 40 LRRM 1114 (1957).

[143]*John S. Barnes Corp.*, 197 NLRB 32, 80 LRRM 1607 (1972).

[144]*See, e.g., R & H Masonry Supply, Inc.*, 258 NLRB 1220, 108 LRRM 1199 (1981) (order modified to delete language no longer necessary in view of court's refusal to enforce Board's instructions that the employer reestablish its trucking operation).

FORM NLRB–4726
(4–71)

NOTICE TO MEMBERS

POSTED BY ORDER OF THE
NATIONAL LABOR RELATIONS BOARD
AN AGENCY OF THE UNITED STATES GOVERNMENT

WE WILL NOT engage in, or induce or encourage any individual employed by Lincor Software Company to engage in a strike or refusal in the course of such individual's employment to use, manufacture, process, transport, or otherwise handle or work on any goods, articles, materials or commodities, or to perform any services, where an object thereof is to force or require Lincor Software Company to cease doing business with persons engaged in commerce, or in an industry affecting commerce, or to force or require persons engaged in commerce or an industry affecting commerce to cease doing business with Janco Computer Services, Inc.

WE WILL NOT threaten, coerce or restrain Lincor Software Company, or any other person engaged in commerce or in an industry affecting commerce, where an object thereof is to force or require Lincor Software Company to cease doing business with persons engaged in commerce or in an industry affecting commerce to cease doing business with Janco Computer Services, Inc.

Local 007, United Computer Operators
International Union

Dated_____ By_____
                         Jean Jones, Business Agent

THIS IS AN OFFICIAL NOTICE AND MUST NOT BE DEFACED BY ANYONE

This notice must remain posted for 60 consecutive days from the date of posting and must not be altered, defaced, or covered by any other material. Any questions concerning this notice or compliance with its provisions may be directed to the Board's Office, Region 5, Candler Building – 4th Floor, 109 Market Place, Baltimore, MD 21202

Exhibit 86. Notice Used in Secondary Boycott Case (Form NLRB-4726)

FORM NLRB—4820
(5-72)

NOTICE

TO ALL PRESENT AND FORMER EMPLOYEES
OF JANCO COMPUTER SERVICES, INC.

PURSUANT TO

A DECISION AND ORDER

of the National Labor Relations Board, and in order to effectuate
the policies of the National Labor Relations Act, as amended, we
hereby give notice that:

WE, LOCAL 007, UNITED COMPUTER OPERATORS INTERNATIONAL
UNION, WILL NOT threaten employees of Janco Computer
Services, Inc. with loss of employment or other
reprisals if they do not join said labor organization.

WE WILL NOT assault, attempt to assault, or threaten
the Company's employees with reprisals if they refuse
to support a strike at the Company's said plant; or
engage in picketing in such a manner as to bar
employees from entering or leaving the plant; or in any
other manner restrain or coerce the Company's employees
in the exercise of their right to self-organization, to
form, join, or assist labor organizations, to bargain
collectively through representatives of their own
choosing, and to engage in other concerted activities
for the purpose of collective or other mutual aid or
protection, and to refrain from any or all of such
activities as guaranteed to them by Section 7 of the
Act.

_____
Local 007, United Computer Operators
International Union

Dated_____ By_____
Jean Jones, Business Agent

_____

THIS IS AN OFFICIAL NOTICE AND MUST NOT BE DEFACED BY ANYONE

This notice must remain posted for 60 consecutive days from the date of posting and must not be altered, defaced,
or covered by any other material. Any questions concerning this notice or compliance with its provisions may be directed
to the Board's Office, Region 5, Candler Building – 4th Floor, 109 Market Place,
Baltimore, MD 21202

Exhibit 87.   Notice Used in Case of Union Coercion (Form NLRB-4820)

FORM NLRB—4820
(5—72)

NOTICE

TO ALL OFFICERS, REPRESENTATIVES, AGENTS AND MEMBERS
OF THE UNITED COMPUTER OPERATORS INTERNATIONAL UNION

PURSUANT TO

A DECISION AND ORDER

of the National Labor Relations Board, and in order to effectuate
the policies of the National Labor Relations Act, as amended, we
hereby notify you that:

WE WILL NOT refuse to bargain collectively as the
exclusive representative of the employees in the unit
found appropriate in the Recommended Decision of the
Administrative Law Judge in Case No. 5-CB-1234 with
Janco Computer Services, Inc. with respect to rates of
pay, wages, hours of employment, and other conditions
of employment;

WE WILL NOT require, instruct, or induce our
representatives or agents to require that the
above-named company execute contracts which expressly,
or in their performance, make membership in United
Computer Operators International Union a condition of
employment, except in accordance with the provisos in
Section 8(a)(3) of the aforesaid Act.

WE WILL NOT direct, instigate, encourage, approve, or
ratify strike action for the purpose of requiring that
the above-named Company execute contracts which
expressly, or in their performance, make membership in
United Computer Operators International Union a
condition of employment, except in accordance with the
provisos in Section 8(a)(3) of the aforesaid Act.

WE WILL NOT cause, or attempt to cause, the above-named
company to discriminate in any manner against their
employees, in violation of Section 8(a)(3) of the
aforesaid Act.

```
                              _____
                              Local 007, United Computer
                              Operators International Union


Dated_____  By_____
                              Jean Jones, Business Agent
```

THIS IS AN OFFICIAL NOTICE AND MUST NOT BE DEFACED BY ANYONE

This notice must remain posted for 60 consecutive days from the date of posting and must not be altered, defaced,
or covered by any other material. Any questions concerning this notice or compliance with its provisions may be directed
to the Board's Office, Region 5, Candler Building - 4th Floor, 109 Market Place,
Baltimore, MD 21202

**Exhibit 88. Notice Used in Case of Union's Refusal to Bargain and Insistence
Upon Illegal Hiring Clause (Form NLRB-4820)**

FORM NLRB–4727
(9–69)

NOTICE TO EMPLOYEES

POSTED BY ORDER OF THE
NATIONAL LABOR RELATIONS BOARD
AN AGENCY OF THE UNITED STATES GOVERNMENT

WE are posting this Notice to inform you of your rights
guaranteed by the National Labor Relations Act and we give you
these assurances:

The Act gives all our employees these rights:

To organize themselves;
To form, join or assist labor organizations;
To act together for collective bargaining or other
mutual aid or protection; and
To refuse to do any or all of these things.

WE WILL NOT do anything that interferes with these rights.

_____
Janco Computer Services, Inc.

Dated:_____   By_____
Jack Smith, President

_____

THIS IS AN OFFICIAL NOTICE AND MUST NOT BE DEFACED BY ANYONE

This notice must remain posted for 60 consecutive days from the date of posting and must not be altered, defaced,
or covered by any other material. Any questions concerning this notice or compliance with its provisions may be directed
to the Board's Office, Region 5, Candler Building – 4th Floor, 109 Market
Place, Baltimore, MD 21202

**Exhibit 89. Notice Used in Case of Employer Interference or Coercion
(Form NLRB-4727)**

FORM NLRB–4727
(9–69)

NOTICE TO EMPLOYEES

POSTED BY ORDER OF THE
NATIONAL LABOR RELATIONS BOARD
AN AGENCY OF THE UNITED STATES GOVERNMENT

WE WILL NOT in any manner interfere with, restrain or coerce our employees in the exercise of their right to self-organization, to form labor organizations, to join or to assist Local 007, United Computer Operators International Union or any other labor organization, to bargain collectively through representatives of their own choosing, or to engage in concerted activities for the purpose of collective bargaining or other mutual aid or protection, or to refrain from any or all of such activities except to the extent that such right may be affected by an agreement requiring membership in a labor organization as a condition of employment as authorized in Section 8(a)(3) of the Act, as modified by the Labor-Management Reporting and Disclosure Act of 1959.

WE WILL OFFER to the employees named below immediate and full reinstatement to their former or substantially equivalent positions without prejudice to any seniority or other rights and privileges previously enjoyed, and make them whole for any loss of pay suffered as a result of the discrimination against them, with interest.

      Mary Hughes
      Christopher Wren

All our employees are free to become or remain members of the above-named union or any other labor organization. We will not discriminate in regard to hire or tenure of employment or any term or condition of employment against any employee because of membership in or activity on behalf of any such labor organization.

                     _____
                     Janco Computer Services, Inc.

Dated_____ By_____
                     Jack Smith, President

THIS IS AN OFFICIAL NOTICE AND MUST NOT BE DEFACED BY ANYONE

This notice must remain posted for 60 consecutive days from the date of posting and must not be altered, defaced, or covered by any other material. Any questions concerning this notice or compliance with its provisions may be directed to the Board's Office,   Region 5, Candler Building – 4th Floor, 109 Market Place, Baltimore, MD 21202

Exhibit 90.   Notice Used in Case of Discriminatorily Discharged Employees (Form NLRB-4727)

FORM NLRB–4727
(9–69)

NOTICE TO EMPLOYEES

POSTED BY ORDER OF THE
NATIONAL LABOR RELATIONS BOARD
AN AGENCY OF THE UNITED STATES GOVERNMENT

Section 7 of the National Labor Relations Act guarantees employees the following rights:

> To self-organization or to form, join, or assist a labor organization;
> To bargain collectively with their employer through representatives of their own choosing;
> To engage in other activities together for the purpose of collective bargaining or other mutual aid or protection;
> To refrain from any or all of the above activities except to the extent that such activities may be affected by an agreement requiring membership in a labor organization as a condition of employment as authorized in Section 8(a)(3) of the Act.

In recognition of these rights, we hereby notify our employees that:

> WE WILL NOT fail or refuse to bargain collectively in good faith with Local 007, United Computer Operators International Union, herein called Local 007, as the exclusive bargaining representative of our employees in the appropriate bargaining unit described below regarding wages, hours and other terms and conditions of employment:
>
> > All customer service and sales representatives employed by Respondent, excluding all other employees, guards and supervisors as defined in the Act.
>
> WE WILL, upon request, at reasonable times and locations, bargain collectively with Local 007, in the above appropriate unit.
>
> WE WILL NOT in any like or related manner, fail or refuse to bargain collectively with Local 007, or interfere with, restrain, or coerce our employees in the exercise of their rights as guaranteed in Section 7 of the Act.

_____
Janco Computer Services, Inc.

Dated_____   By_____
                                Jack Smith, President

THIS IS AN OFFICIAL NOTICE AND MUST NOT BE DEFACED BY ANYONE

This notice must remain posted for 60 consecutive days from the date of posting and must not be altered, defaced, or covered by any other material. Any questions concerning this notice or compliance with its provisions may be directed to the Board's Office, Region 5, Candler Building – 4th Floor, 109 Market Place, Baltimore, MD 21202

Exhibit 91.   Notice Used in Case of Employer's Refusal to Bargain (Form NLRB-4727)

FORM NLRB–4727
(9–69)

NOTICE TO EMPLOYEES

POSTED BY ORDER OF THE
NATIONAL LABOR RELATIONS BOARD
AN AGENCY OF THE UNITED STATES GOVERNMENT

We post this notice to inform you of the rights guaranteed to you in the National Labor Relations Act.

The Act gives all employees these rights:

 To organize themselves;
 To form, join, or assist a union;
 To bargain as a group through a representative
  they choose;
 To act together for collective bargaining or
  mutual aid or protection; and
 To refuse to do any or all of these things.

We assure our employees that:

 WE WILL NOT do anything to interfere with these rights.

 WE WILL NOT sponsor, render aid to, dominate, assist or support Local 007, United Computer Operators International Union or any other labor organization.

 WE WILL NOT recognize or bargain with Local 007, United Computer Operators International Union as representative of our employees.

 WE WILL withdraw and withhold all recognition from Local 007, United Computer Operators International Union and disestablish it as a representative of our employees for the purpose of dealing with us concerning grievances, labor disputes, rates of pay, hours of employment or other conditions of work.

—————————————————————
Janco Computer Services, Inc.

Dated_____ By_____
        Jack Smith, President

THIS IS AN OFFICIAL NOTICE AND MUST NOT BE DEFACED BY ANYONE

This notice must remain posted for 60 consecutive days from the date of posting and must not be altered, defaced or covered by any other material. Any questions concerning this notice or compliance with its provisions may be directed to the Board's Office, Region 5, Candler Building - 4th Floor, 109 Market Place, Baltimore, MD 21202

Exhibit 92. Notice Used in Case of Employer Domination or Interference With Formation or Administration of Labor Organization (Form NLRB-4727)

however, when all matters raised in the motion have been previously considered by the Board.[145]

(b) Motions for Reopening the Record and for Rehearing. A motion to reopen the record must describe the additional evidence sought to be introduced, indicate why it was not presented earlier, and explain why the new evidence would require a different result.[146] Similarly, motions for rehearing must specify the error requiring a new hearing and an explanation of the prejudice to the moving party resulting from such error.[147] Only newly discovered evidence, evidence which has become available since the close of the hearing, or evidence which the Board feels should have been taken at the original hearing but was not taken shall be admitted at any further hearing.[148]

In addition to receiving supplemental evidence, cases may be remanded to the administrative law judge for purposes of making vital credibility resolutions,[149] making additional findings of fact,[150] or explaining in greater detail the basis for the decision. Remands also may be appropriate upon direction of an appellate court[151] in cases where there has been perjured testimony[152] or where the administrative law judge did not properly conduct the hearing.[153]

Judicial Review and Enforcement of the Board's Order

Following issuance of the Board decision, all communications and conferences pertaining to compliance with the Board's order should be directed to the regional director who issued the complaint.[154] Immediately upon receipt of the Board's decision, the regional director sends a letter offering assistance in achieving early compliance. (See Exhibit 93.) If compliance cannot be secured, the regional director will notify the Board.

---

[145]*See, e.g., Kahn's & Co.*, 256 NLRB 930, 107 LRRM 1316 (1981) (motion for reconsideration denied where it raised no substantial issue not previously considered by Board in issuing its original decision and order).

[146]NLRB Rules and Regulations §102.48(d)(1); *See Exchange Bank*, 264 NLRB 822, 111 LRRM 1602 (1982) (motion to reopen record denied where evidence sought to be introduced, even if considered, would not alter Board's decision).

[147]NLRB Rules and Regulations §102.48(d)(1).

[148]*Id. Washington Street Brass & Iron Foundry, Inc.*, 268 NLRB 338, 114 LRRM 1276 (1983) (motion to remand and reopen record denied where allegedly suppressed evidence would not affect the result and was not shown to be newly discovered or previously unavailable).

[149]*See, e.g., Crown Cork de Puerto Rico, Inc.*, 243 NLRB 569, 101 LRRM 1499 (1979).

[150]*See, e.g., Warehouse Groceries Mgmt., Inc.*, 254 NLRB 252, 106 LRRM 1171 (1981).

[151]*See, e.g., Charles H. McCauley Assocs.*, 266 NLRB 649, 113 LRRM 1017 (1983).

[152]*See, e.g., Electrical Workers, Local 745 (Nat'l Elec. Coil)*, 268 NLRB 308, 114 LRRM 1269 (1983).

[153]*See, e.g., Dayton Power & Light Co.*, 267 NLRB 202, 114 LRRM 1009 (1983).

[154]See generally chapter 18.

NATIONAL LABOR RELATIONS BOARD

REGION 5

Candler Building - 4th Floor

109 Market Place

Baltimore, MD   21202

January 2, 1986

Mr. Jack Smith, President
Janco Computer Services, Inc.
8181 Greensboro Drive
McLean, VA 21202

                            Re: Janco Computer Services, Inc.
                                  Case No. 5-CA-1239

Dear Mr. Smith:

You have recently received the Decision and Order of the Board [Judgment of
the Court of Appeals] in the above case. Pursuant thereto, you are
required to notify me within 20 days of the receipt of that document what
steps you have taken or will take to comply.

Further formal action in this matter can be avoided by complying promptly
and completely with the Decision and Order of the Board [Judgment of the
Court of Appeals]. Compliance Officer Shelley L. Korch will assist you in
effecting compliance. If you have any questions, please write or telephone
Ms. Korch.

I am enclosing 12 copies of the notice you will need in order to comply
with the terms of the Order [Judgment]. Please sign and date these; post
an appropriate number; and return three signed and dated copies with a
covering letter stating exactly where and when you posted other copies.

As soon as you offer reinstatement to Ms. Hughes, please advise us and we
shall assist you in computing back pay.

If and when the charging union requests bargaining meetings, it would be
appreciated if you would keep a complete file of all correspondence and
memoranda so that the character of the bargaining may be evaluated if it
becomes necessary to do so.

At the end of the posting period please advise me that the notices were
continuously and conspicuously posted. If and when you have fully complied
with the affirmative terms of the Order [Judgment] and there are no
reported violations of its negative provision, we shall notify you that the
case has been "closed" on compliance.

                            Very truly yours,

                            Louis J. D'Amico
                            Regional Director

**Exhibit 93.   Letter Regarding Compliance With Decision and Order of Board or
Court Judgment**

A Board decision and order is not self-enforcing. The mere failure to comply with a Board order does not itself constitute an independent violation of the Act, and there are no fines, jail sentences, or other sanctions for noncompliance. To secure enforcement, the Board must file a petition in an appropriate United States court of appeals.[155] (See Exhibit 94.) While such petitions are permissive rather than mandatory, it is the Board's routine practice to seek enforcement unless satisfactory compliance can be achieved within a reasonable time after its order issues. Similarly, Section 10(f) of the Act confers upon any person aggrieved by a Board order the right to petition an appropriate court of appeals for review.

§17.16   Final Orders

Only "final orders" of the Board may be reviewed by the courts under Sections 10(e) and (f). Final orders are those which are entered pursuant to Section 10(c) at the conclusion of an unfair labor practice proceeding either dismissing the complaint in whole or in part, or finding a violation and providing a remedy. Preliminary matters such as a determination that the Board has jurisdiction over a respondent, a regional director's refusal to issue a complaint,[156] the denial of a request for a subpoena,[157] or the Board's assignment of work in a Section 10(k) jurisdictional dispute case[158] are not reviewable final orders. Similarly, Board decisions in representation proceedings are not final orders and therefore may not be appealed directly to the federal courts. Review of representation issues must be secured indirectly through refusal to bargain unfair labor practice proceedings.[159]

§17.17   Parties Entitled to Seek Court Enforcement or Review

The Board alone has the right and the responsibility to seek court enforcement of its orders under Section 10(e). A successful charging party has no standing to enforce unfair labor practice violations found by the Board, and conversely a respondent may not

---

[155]Sec. 10(e); NLRB Statements of Procedure §101.14.

[156]*George Banta Co. v. NLRB*, 626 F.2d 354, 104 LRRM 3103 (4th Cir. 1980); *see, e.g., Saez v. Goslee*, 463 F.2d 214, 80 LRRM 2808 (1st Cir. 1972).

[157]Subpoena enforcement proceedings are discussed at §§21.15–21.20.

[158]*International Tel. & Tel. Corp. v. IBEW, Local 134*, 419 U.S. 428, 88 LRRM 2227 (1975); *Henderson v. Int'l Longshoremen's & Warehousemen's Union, Local 50*, 457 F.2d 572, 79 LRRM 2903 (9th Cir. 1972). Jurisdictional dispute awards may be reviewable, however, in the context of a subsequent Sec. 8(b)(4)(D) unfair labor practice proceeding. See §19.7(c).

[159]The general principles concerning nonreviewability of representation issues are discussed at §10.19 and the limited exceptions to those principles are discussed at §10.20.

NLRB ORDER ENFORCEMENT CHART

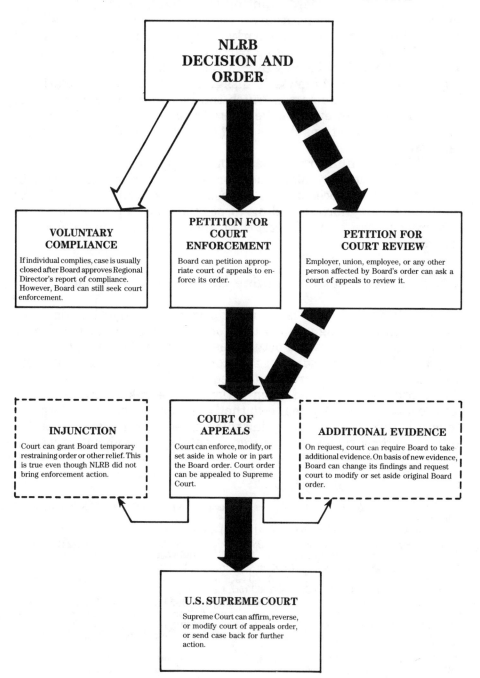

NLRB DECISION AND ORDER

VOLUNTARY COMPLIANCE

If individual complies, case is usually closed after Board approves Regional Director's report of compliance. However, Board can still seek court enforcement.

PETITION FOR COURT ENFORCEMENT

Board can petition appropriate court of appeals to enforce its order.

PETITION FOR COURT REVIEW

Employer, union, employee, or any other person affected by Board's order can ask a court of appeals to review it.

INJUNCTION

Court can grant Board temporary restraining order or other relief. This is true even though NLRB did not bring enforcement action.

COURT OF APPEALS

Court can enforce, modify, or set aside in whole or in part the Board order. Court order can be appealed to Supreme Court.

ADDITIONAL EVIDENCE

On request, court can require Board to take additional evidence. On basis of new evidence, Board can change its findings and request court to modify or set aside original Board order.

U.S. SUPREME COURT

Supreme Court can affirm, reverse, or modify court of appeals order, or send case back for further action.

Exhibit 94. NLRB Order Enforcement Chart

request enforcement of a Board order dismissing all or portions of a complaint.[160]

Section 10(f), however, provides that "any person aggrieved by a final order of the Board granting or denying in whole or in part the relief sought" may petition an appropriate court of appeals[161] for review of the Board's order. A party against whom an order is issued is "aggrieved," as is a charging party with respect to any portion of a complaint which is dismissed.[162] A victorious party does not become "aggrieved" simply because it disagrees with adverse underlying findings or conclusions upon which the Board's order is based.[163] A charging party, however, can be treated as aggrieved when the Board finds all of the violations charged, but fails to grant all of the remedies requested.

While prevailing respondents or charging parties may not on their own petition for enforcement or review, they may intervene in an enforcement proceeding in support of the Board's order.[164] As intervenors they have standing to petition the Supreme Court for certiorari in the event the court of appeals refuses to enforce the order.[165]

§17.18　Procedures for Seeking Enforcement or Review

(a) Jurisdiction. The court of appeals acquires jurisdiction over a case upon the filing of a petition for enforcement or review. Prior to the time that the record actually is filed with the court, however, the Board retains jurisdiction to reconsider, set aside, or modify its order either *sua sponte* or upon the request of one of the parties. After the record has been filed, such action can be taken only with the court's approval.[166] A remand to the Board for further consideration generally divests the court of jurisdiction, so that a new petition for enforcement or review is required if subsequent judicial review is desired.[167]

---

[160]*See, e.g., Amalgamated Util. Workers v. Consolidated Edison Co.*, 309 U.S. 261, 6 LRRM 669 (1940).

[161]Appropriate venue is discussed at §17.18(b) *infra.*

[162]*United Automobile Workers, Local 283 v. Scofield*, 382 U.S. 205, 60 LRRM 2479 (1965). *See also Albrecht v. NLRB*, 181 F.2d 652, 26 LRRM 2158 (7th Cir. 1950) (individual discriminatees may seek review of Board's order dismissing complaint).

[163]*Boeing Co. v. NLRB*, 526 F.2d 587, 89 LRRM 2672, (4th Cir. 1975); *Deaton Truck Line, Inc. v. NLRB*, 337 F.2d 697, 57 LRRM 2209 (5th Cir. 1964).

[164]*United Automobile Workers, Local 283 v. Scofield*, 382 U.S. 205, 60 LRRM 2479 (1965). Respondents also may intervene in the Board's application for enforcement of a settlement agreement in situations where the respondent is supporting the Board's order. *NLRB v. Oil, Chemical & Atomic Workers Int'l Union (Catalytic Indus.)*, 476 F.2d 1031, 82 LRRM 3159 (1st Cir. 1973).

[165]*See Newspaper Drivers & Handlers, Local 372 v. Detroit Newspaper Publishers' Ass'n*, 382 U.S. 366, 61 LRRM 2147 (1966) (union which intervened at court of appeals level permitted to file petition for certiorari).

[166]*NLRB v. Marland One-Way Clutch Co.*, 520 F.2d 856, 89 LRRM 2721 (7th Cir. 1975).

[167]*NLRB v. Wilder Mfg. Co.*, 454 F.2d 995, 78 LRRM 2760 (D.C. Cir. 1972).

(b) Filing of Petitions. Petitions for enforcement or review may be filed in any court of appeals having jurisdiction over the area "wherein the unfair labor practice in question occurred or wherein such person resides or transacts business."[168] Persons aggrieved by a Board order also may file a petition for review in the Court of Appeals for the District of Columbia.[169] Only the federal circuit courts of appeals have jurisdiction over such petitions. State courts and federal district courts are without authority to review Board orders or to enjoin Board proceedings except in very rare circumstances.[170]

As a matter of practice, the Board uniformly files its petitions for enforcement in the court of appeals within whose geographical jurisdiction the alleged unfair labor practices occurred. Since persons aggrieved by a Board order may have several different circuits to choose from in filing their petition for review, considerable time often is devoted to identifying the court with the most favorable precedent. If petitions are filed in more than one circuit the Board files the record in the circuit in which "a proceeding with respect to such order was first instituted."[171]

The appellate court having exclusive jurisdiction may, on its own motion or at the request of the parties, transfer the proceeding to any other court of appeals "for the convenience of the parties in the interest of justice."[172] Factors considered by the courts include the location of counsel and the parties, the pendency of related proceedings in other circuits, whether the impact of the litigation is local to one circuit, whether one court is more familiar with the parties and issues involved, and the respective caseloads of the courts.[173]

(c) Timeliness and Effect of Appeal. There is no time limit specified in the Act within which the Board must file a petition for enforcement, and the 60-day limit specified in Rule 73 of the Federal Rules of Civil Procedure is not applicable. Board orders do not become stale and are enforceable even if the respondent already has complied.[174] Similarly, petitions for review are not required to be filed

---

[168]Secs. 10(e), 10(f).

[169]Sec. 10(f).

[170]See §10.20 and THE DEVELOPING LABOR LAW at 1713–1725.

[171]28 U.S.C. §2112(a) (1976). It is this provision which has given rise to the often criticized "race to the courthouse." *Insurance Workers Union v. NLRB,* 360 F.2d 823, 61 LRRM 2415 (D.C. Cir. 1966); *see also Liquor Salesmen's Union Local 2 v. NLRB,* 664 F.2d 1200, 106 LRRM 2953 (D.C. Cir. 1981).

[172]28 U.S.C. §2112(a) (1982).

[173]*Liquor Salesmen's Union Local 2 v. NLRB,* 664 F.2d 1200, 106 LRRM 2953 (D.C. Cir. 1981); *International Union, United Automobile Workers (Preston Prods. Co.) v. NLRB,* 373 F.2d 671, 64 LRRM 2225 (D.C. Cir. 1967).

[174]*NLRB v. Mexia Textile Mills,* 339 U.S. 563, 26 LRRM 2123 (1950); *see NLRB v. Pool Mfg. Co.,* 339 U.S. 577, 26 LRRM 2127 (1950) (two and one-half year delay does not preclude enforcement). At the opposite extreme, the Board also may seek enforcement before the respondent has had an opportunity to comply with its order, *NLRB v. Teamsters Local 85 (Victory Transp. Serv., Inc.),* 454 F.2d 875, 79 LRRM 2437 (9th Cir. 1972), or after the respondent already has complied in full, *NLRB v. Pennsylvania Greyhound Lines, Inc.,* 303 U.S. 261, 2 LRRM 599 (1938).

within a specified period of time although some courts have held that the doctrine of laches is applicable.[175] Once a petition has been filed, however, the party named as respondent must file an answer within the time limits set by the applicable appellate court rules (usually 20 days or less), or else a default judgment enforcing the Board's order may be issued.[176]

Section 10(g) of the Act provides that the filing of petitions for enforcement or review shall not operate as a stay of the Board's order unless specifically directed by the court.

§17.19 Scope of Judicial Review[177]

Section 10(e) provides that upon appeal the courts may consider only those issues which were disputed before the Board unless the failure to raise the issue before the Board was the result of extraordinary circumstances. This requirement has been interpreted to mean that findings of an administrative law judge to which no exceptions have been taken may not be contested on appeal.[178]

The Board's findings of fact are to be treated by the courts as being conclusive so long as they are "supported by substantial evidence on the record considered as a whole."[179] The Supreme Court has interpreted this statutory standard to mean that a reviewing court is entitled to set aside the Board's findings of fact only "when it cannot conscientiously find that the evidence supporting that decision is substantial, when viewed in the light that the record in its entirety furnishes, including the body of evidence opposed to the Board's view."[180]

While the latitude of the courts in reviewing the Board's conclusions of law may be somewhat broader than their latitude in reviewing findings of fact, the Supreme Court nevertheless has admonished the courts that "[i]t is the Board on which Congress conferred the authority to develop and apply fundamental national labor policy . . . 'subject to limited judicial review.'"[181]

§17.20 Court Judgments

The courts of appeals may grant or deny enforcement to the Board's order either in whole or in part. They also have the authority

---

[175]*Schaefer v. NLRB*, 697 F.2d 558, 112 LRRM 2609 (3d Cir. 1983); *see, e.g., Griffith Co. v. NLRB*, 545 F.2d 1194, 93 LRRM 2834 (9th Cir. 1976).

[176]Federal Rules of Civil Procedure, Rule 15(b).

[177]For an expanded discussion of this significant topic, *see* THE DEVELOPING LABOR LAW at 1704–1712.

[178]*Cf. Woelke & Romero Framing, Inc. v. NLRB*, 456 U.S. 645, 110 LRRM 2377 (1982).

[179]Sec. 10(e).

[180]*Universal Camera Corp. v. NLRB*, 340 U.S. 474, 488, 27 LRRM 2373 (1951).

[181]*Beth Israel Hosp. v. NLRB*, 437 U.S. 483, 500–501, 98 LRRM 2727, 2733-2734 (1978); *see also Ford Motor Co. v. NLRB*, 441 U.S. 488, 101 LRRM 2222 (1979) (so long as Board's interpretation of statute is reasonably defensible, it should not be rejected merely because court prefers another view).

to modify the order and enforce it as so modified. If the Board's order is enforced, the court enters a decree which is in the nature of a continuing injunction enforceable through contempt proceedings.[182] Only the Board can institute a contempt proceeding.[183]

The courts of appeals also are authorized to deny enforcement and remand cases to the Board for further proceedings. This may occur, for example, when the Board's dismissal of a complaint is reversed and the case is remanded for purposes of fashioning an appropriate remedy. Since the Board is primarily responsible for developing remedies to effectuate national labor policy,[184] remands to the Board are preferred to court-imposed remedies.

Cases also may be remanded to the Board for purposes of making additional findings, clarifying the original decision and order, considering offers of proof, or for purposes of reconsidering the governing legal principles in light of intervening Board or court decisions. A remand does not have the effect of terminating the proceeding, but of simply returning it to the Board for further action. If the Board accepts the remand,[185] it generally will regard the court's view of the applicable legal principles as being "the law of the case"—i.e., determinative in that particular proceeding, but of no binding effect in subsequent cases raising the same issues.

In cases where a court challenge to the Board's order is found to be frivolous or diliatory, the Board's costs and fees, including attorneys' fees, may be recovered from the offending party.[186] Costs also may be assessed against the Board under the Equal Access to Justice Act when a case is dismissed and it is determined that the General Counsel was not substantially justified in issuing and prosecuting the unfair labor practice complaint.[187]

§17.21 Supreme Court Review

Final review rests with the United States Supreme Court.[188] Board cases are reviewed by the Court either upon certification or upon the granting of a writ of certiorari.[189] Cases which involve important questions of law or policy affecting the administration of

---

[182]*See* NLRB Casehandling Manual ¶¶10510.1–10510.3 for the rules governing contempt proceedings.

[183]*Amalgamated Util. Workers v. Consolidated Edison Co.*, 309 U.S. 261, 6 LRRM 669 (1940).

[184]*NLRB v. Food Store Employees Local 347 (Heck's, Inc.)*, 417 U.S. 1, 86 LRRM 2209 (1974).

[185]As opposed to seeking Supreme Court review by filing a petition for certiorari. See §17.21 *infra*.

[186]*Hedison Mfg. Co. v. NLRB*, 643 F.2d 32, 106 LRRM 2897 (1st Cir. 1981); *see also* NLRB Casehandling Manual ¶¶10521, 11830.

[187]Proceedings under the Equal Access to Justice Act are discussed in chapter 23.

[188]Sec. 10(e).

[189]*Id.*; 28 U.S.C. §1254 (1982).

the Act, or cases presenting issues on which the courts of appeals are split are most likely to be heard by the Court. In instances where the Board's order is not enforced, the Court generally remands the case to the court of appeals for reconsideration in light of the Court's opinion, or instructs the court of appeals to remand the case to the Board for further proceedings.

18

Compliance Proceedings

Absent dismissal of the underlying charge or complaint, most Board unfair labor practice proceedings culminate with an obligation on the part of the respondent to undertake and/or refrain from undertaking certain actions. Whether incorporated into a formal or informal settlement agreement, recommended decision of an administrative law judge, Board order, or court judgment enforcing a Board order, respondents generally are required to cease and desist from engaging in certain practices and undertake affirmative action to remedy the unlawful conduct found.[1] The term "compliance proceedings" refers to those formal and informal steps taken by the Board to ensure that respondents in fact comply with such commitments.

Primary responsibility for monitoring compliance rests with the regional director who issued the underlying complaint. All regions designate one or more individuals as "compliance officers" who are responsible for initiating compliance efforts, determining what actions are necessary to effectuate compliance, monitoring compliance activity, and issuing periodic reports on compliance progress.[2]

Informal Compliance Proceedings

§18.1 Initiation of Compliance Efforts

Every effort is made to encourage the respondent to comply voluntarily. With bilateral informal settlement agreements signed by the charging party, the compliance officer immediately contacts the charged party to solicit voluntary compliance. If, on the other hand, the settlement is unilateral and not signed by the charging party,

---

[1]Typical remedies are discussed at §17.13 and THE DEVELOPING LABOR LAW at chapter 33.
[2]NLRB Casehandling Manual ¶¶10500.2–10500.3.

the charged party is not contacted until after the time for taking an appeal has expired or, if an appeal has been taken, not until the settlement has been sustained by the Board.[3] Similarly, compliance efforts with regard to administrative law judges' recommended orders or Board orders are not undertaken until such time as it is evident that appeals will not be taken.[4] In contrast, immediate compliance with court judgments is sought notwithstanding the filing of a petition for certiorari with the United States Supreme Court unless there has been a stay of the mandate by the court of appeals.[5]

The compliance officer will seek written confirmation of the respondent's compliance intentions. If the respondent intends to comply voluntarily, the compliance officer will offer the region's assistance in such areas as locating discriminatees, furnishing documentation necessary to calculate monetary obligations, and clarifying the nature of respondent's affirmative obligations. Throughout the compliance period the compliance officer will monitor all compliance activity.[6]

§18.2 Noncompliance

If a respondent states that it does not intend to comply, or by its conduct demonstrates an unwillingness to comply, the regional director will recommend that enforcement proceedings be commenced by the Division of Enforcement Litigation.[7]

In some instances, conduct of the respondent during the compliance period will be challenged, but it will be unclear whether the conduct constitutes noncompliance with an outstanding order or simply grounds for an entirely new unfair labor practice charge. A new charge and complaint generally will be appropriate in situations where the new allegations involve circumstances unrelated to the original order. Accordingly, the region is likely to suggest that a new charge be filed in cases where (1) there has been no court enforcement of the Board order to date, (2) the remedial provision allegedly violated is one of the negative (i.e., cease and desist) provisions of the order, or (3) the conduct challenged is not expressly encompassed by the

---

[3]*Id.* at ¶10502.2. Compliance with informal settlement agreements also is discussed at §§14.4 and 14.5.

[4]NLRB Casehandling Manual ¶¶10502.3, 10502.4, and 10502.6.

[5]*Id.* at ¶¶10502.5–10502.6.

[6]*See generally* NLRB Casehandling Manual ¶¶10504.1–10504.8. Cease and desist requirements and affirmative action obligations associated with the various types of statutory violations are discussed at §§17.12 and 17.13. *See also* NLRB Casehandling Manual ¶¶10521–10528.

[7]*See* NLRB Casehandling Manual ¶¶10506–10506.4. See also §§17.16–17.21 relating to enforcement proceedings. In order to assist the Board in monitoring compliance, the General Counsel routinely seeks inclusion of a visitorial clause in the Board's remedial orders and formal settlement agreements. Such clauses constitute advance authorization for the Board to obtain discovery regarding compliance efforts in accordance with the Federal Rules of Civil Procedure from the respondent or from any other person with knowledge of compliance activity. General Counsel Memorandum 85-5 (September 23, 1985) available from the Board's Information Division.

terms of the Board's order.[8] The distinction between noncompliance or a new proceeding can be significant in situations where the conduct occurred more than six months earlier. If deemed to be an independent unfair labor practice, a new charge generally will be untimely.[9]

If noncompliance with a court judgment is alleged, the Board may, following prior written notification to the parties, petition the court for a contempt citation.[10] Contempt is presumed to be appropriate in cases where another Board order or court judgment based upon a new unfair labor practice would add nothing either affirmatively or negatively to an outstanding court judgment.[11]

§18.3   Reinstatement

Individuals who have lost or been denied employment as a result of unlawful conduct generally are entitled to reinstatement as part of their make-whole remedy.[12] The normal order provides for "immediate and full reinstatement to [the discriminatee's] former position or, if that position no longer exists, to a substantially equivalent one without prejudice to seniority or other rights or privileges."[13] If a substantially equivalent position is unavailable, the respondent may be required to offer employment in another area of its operations, or place the discriminatee on a preferential hiring list.[14] Persons on preferential hiring lists are entitled to employment vacancies for which they qualify prior to such positions being offered to other individuals.[15] When a person entitled to reinstatement under a Board order is serving in the armed forces, the respondent must notify the individual of his or her right to reinstatement upon completion of military service.[16]

(a) Reinstatement to Former Position. An obligation to reinstate an employee to his or her "former position" may, but does not necessarily, mean reinstatement to the actual job which the employee had at the time of the termination; rather, it means reinstatement to the position which the individual would have had at the time of reinstatement in the absence of discrimination. Thus, if the discriminatee absent the unlawful conduct would have received wage

---

[8]NLRB Casehandling Manual ¶10508.4.

[9]Sec. 10(b). Timeliness of unfair labor practice charges is discussed at §12.6.

[10]*See* NLRB Casehandling Manual ¶¶10510.1–10510.3.

[11]*Id.* at ¶10510.3b. Contempt may be appropriate also in situations where the outstanding judgment literally covers the new violation even though the new conduct is not identical with, nor does it arise out of, the same dispute as the underlying case. *Id.* at ¶10510.3a.

[12]See §17.13(c).

[13]NLRB Casehandling Manual ¶10528.1; *see, e.g., Lykes Bros., Inc.,* 128 NLRB 606, 46 LRRM 1347 (1960).

[14]*Id.* at ¶¶10528.1, 10528.4.

[15]*See, e.g., Accetta (Venezia Bread Co.),* 147 NLRB 1048, 56 LRRM 1364 (1964).

[16]NLRB Rules and Regulations §103.100; NLRB Casehandling Manual ¶¶10528.1, 10528.11.

or salary increases, promotions, or transfers, the respondent's obligation is to reinstate the individual to the new position at the current rate of compensation.[17]

Individuals who replace unlawfully terminated employees may be discharged in order to accomplish the reinstatement order.[18] If, however, a person occupying a position which is deemed to be the former employee's job would have held that position in the absence of discrimination, that person need not be displaced.[19] Similarly, if there are more discriminatees seeking reinstatement than there are reinstatement positions available, the respondent must, based upon what would have happened absent discrimination, reinstate some discriminatees and make alternative arrangements for the rest.[20]

(b) Reinstatement to Substantially Equivalent Position. If reinstatement to a discriminatee's former position is not possible either because the position no longer exists or because the discriminatee would not be the current incumbent, reinstatement to a substantially equivalent position must be offered.[21] The determination of substantial equivalency is one which must be made based upon all of the surrounding circumstances. Among the factors considered by the Board are the following:

- Whether the new position is temporary or seasonal in nature;[22]

- Whether the new position involves harder, more disagreeable, or less desirable work;[23]

- Whether the new position is in a different job classification, different location, or under different management;[24]

---

[17]NLRB Casehandling Manual ¶10528.2; *Gulf States United Tel. Co.*, 253 NLRB 603, 105 LRRM 1680 (1980) (discharged probationary employee reinstated to permanent position where job performance satisfactory and employee would have acquired permanent status); *George Webel*, 236 NLRB 1192, 99 LRRM 1434 (1978) (reinstatement must be to position employee would have reached through seniority, not position held at time of discriminatory layoff). *But see NLRB v. Ford Motor Co.*, 683 F.2d 156, 110 LRRM 3202 (6th Cir. 1982) (Board could not order supervisory promotions to discharged employees since promotion to supervisory position a management responsibility).

[18]*See, e.g., Pace Oldsmobile, Inc.*, 256 NLRB 1001, 107 LRRM 1414 (1981); *National Car Rental Sys., Inc.*, 252 NLRB 159, 105 LRRM 1263 (1980).

[19]This might occur, for example, when one of two identical jobs is eliminated and the discriminatee rather than the incumbent would legitimately have been laid off. NLRB Casehandling Manual ¶10528.2.

[20]NLRB Casehandling Manual ¶10528.5.

[21]*Id.* at ¶10528.3.

[22]*See, e.g., Lion Uniform*, 247 NLRB 992, 103 LRRM 1264 (1980) (seasonal work); *John L. Lutz Welding & Fabricating, Inc.*, 239 NLRB 582, 99 LRRM 1723 (1978) (temporary position).

[23]*See, e.g., Carruthers Ready Mix, Inc.*, 262 NLRB 739, 110 LRRM 1392 (1982) (more strenuous job); *Flite Chief, Inc.*, 258 NLRB 1124, 108 LRRM 1303 (1981) (shorter hours and night shift). *American Medical Ins. Co.*, 235 NLRB 1417, 98 LRRM 1538 (1978) (file work rather than subscriber relations).

[24]*See, e.g., Carruthers Ready Mix, Inc.*, 262 NLRB 739, 110 LRRM 1392 (1982) (different locations).

- Whether the new position offers lower or less certain compensation, or fewer opportunities for overtime and leave payments;[25]
- Whether the new position is significantly different in terms of job content.[26]

Offers of reinstatement to positions not deemed to be substantially equivalent will not satisfy a respondent's reinstatement obligation, nor will it toll the continued accrual of backpay.

(c) Without Prejudice to Seniority Rights or Other Privileges. Valid reinstatement offers not only must be to the same or substantially equivalent positions, but also must be on terms which do not jeopardize the individual's seniority rights or other privileges of employment. Accordingly, reinstatement offers which require an employee to relinquish or waive seniority,[27] accept payment on an hourly rather than a shift basis,[28] or change from a part-time to a full-time position[29] have been deemed invalid because they entail the relinquishment of valuable employment benefits.

(d) Reinstatement Rights of Strikers. Unfair labor practice strikers (i.e., persons striking in protest over alleged unfair labor practices) are entitled to full reinstatement upon their unconditional offer to return to work.[30] Persons who have been hired to replace the strikers must be displaced if necessary to create vacancies for the returning strikers.[31] Economic strikers (i.e., persons striking for economic or other reasons unrelated to alleged unfair labor practices) are entitled, upon unconditional application, to be reinstated to their former positions. If their former positions no longer are available, economic strikers may remain employees and be reinstated upon the departure of their replacements unless they have in the meantime acquired regular and substantially equivalent employment elsewhere, or unless the employer can prove that reinstatement was not offered for legitimate and substantial business reasons.[32] If at the time of the offer to return to work the economic strikers' jobs are occupied by permanent replacements, the replacements need not be

---

[25]*See, e.g., Midwest Hanger Co.*, 221 NLRB 911, 91 LRRM 1218 (1975) (lower wages or salary for employee David Covey).

[26]*See, e.g., Laredo Packing Co.*, 264 NLRB 245, 112 LRRM 1071 (1982) (discharged truck-drivers not required to accept nondriving positions). In *Interplastic Corp.*, 270 NLRB 1223, 116 LRRM 1225 (1984), the Board concluded that an employee discharge from a part-time job was not entitled to reinstatement to a full-time position in view of the respondent's elimination of all part-time work.

[27]*See Mutual Maintenance Serv. Co.*, 244 NLRB 211, 102 LRRM 1243 (1979).

[28]*East Belden Corp.*, 239 NLRB 776, 100 LRRM 1077 (1978).

[29]*Id.*

[30]*See Mastro Plastics Corp. v. NLRB*, 350 U.S. 270, 37 LRRM 2587 (1956); NLRB Case-handling Manual ¶10528.12.

[31]*See Mastro Plastics Corp. v. NLRB*, 350 U.S. 270, 37 LRRM 2587 (1956).

[32]*Laidlaw Corp.*, 171 NLRB 1366, 68 LRRM 1252 (1968).

displaced and the strikers instead are placed on a preferential hiring list.[33] As a general rule, the respondent must reinstate strikers within five days of their unconditional offer to return to work.[34] Failure to do so could result in the imposition of a backpay obligation for the duration of the delay.[35]

It is not necessary for strikers individually to make unconditional applications to return to work, nor for employers to extend individual reinstatement offers to each striker. Strikers' unions may act as their agents both for the conveyance of the application to, and the receipt of reinstatement offers from, the employers.[36]

§18.4   Backpay

In addition to reinstatement, backpay orders also are used to restore the situation "as nearly as possible, to that which would have obtained but for the illegal discrimination."[37] The Supreme Court has cautioned, however, that "a backpay remedy must be sufficiently tailored to expunge only the *actual*, and not merely *speculative*, consequences of the unfair labor practices."[38] Accordingly, backpay orders, whether imposed upon an employer, a labor organization, or both, are designed only to correct the situation caused by the specific unfair labor practices found. Individuals who have been discriminated against may be made "whole" by paying to them net backpay which is equal to gross backpay (i.e., what the discriminatee would have earned absent the discrimination) less net interim earnings (i.e., what was actually earned from other employment—or what reasonably could have been earned through the exercise of due diligence—during the backpay period, less expenses incurred in seeking and holding interim employment).[39]

(a) Definitions of Backpay Terms. The Board has established certain procedures for cases which involve the payment of backpay. It is important to understand the definitions of the various terms which the Board uses before describing those procedures:[40]

- *Backpay period.* The period of time during which backpay accrues, usually beginning with the date of the discrimination

---

[33]*See NLRB v. Mackay Radio & Telegraph Co.*, 304 U.S. 333, 2 LRRM 610 (1938).

[34]NLRB Casehandling Manual ¶10528.13; *see Trinity Valley Iron & Steel Co.*, 158 NLRB 890, 62 LRRM 1109 (1966).

[35]*Trinity Valley Iron & Steel Co.*, 158 NLRB 890, 62 LRRM 1109 (1966).

[36]*See Shop Rite Foods, Inc.*, 171 NLRB 1498, 70 LRRM 1075 (1968) (application to return to work); *Art Metalcraft Plating Co.*, 133 NLRB 706, 48 LRRM 1701 (1961) (receipt of reinstatement offer); NLRB Casehandling Manual ¶10528.12.

[37]*Phelps Dodge Corp. v. NLRB*, 313 U.S. 177, 194, 8 LRRM 439, 446 (1941).

[38]*Sure-Tan, Inc. v. NLRB*, 467 U.S. 883, 900, 116 LRRM 2857, 2864 (1984) (emphasis in original).

[39]NLRB Casehandling Manual ¶10530.

[40]*See id.* at ¶10530.1.

and ending with the date a bona fide offer of reinstatement is
made.

- *Gross backpay.* The amount of money a discriminatee would
  have earned from the employer absent the discrimination. Included in this term are not only wages but other forms of
  reimbursement as well, such as bonuses, vacation pay, and
  tips.

- *Interim earnings.* The money a discriminatee actually earned
  at other work during the backpay period. Included are net
  earnings from self-employment and the value of perquisites of
  interim employment such as room and board. It does not include money received from a second job held prior to the discrimination, union benefits,[41] or unemployment compensation.[42]
  Amounts of money that a discriminatee might have earned
  had he or she not quit, been discharged, or refused interim
  employment may be deducted from gross backpay in certain
  circumstances.

- *Expenses.* Expenses the discriminatee incurred in seeking and
  holding other employment during the backpay period which
  would not have been incurred absent the discrimination, such
  as transportation, room and board, and family moving expenses.

- *Net interim earnings.* Interim earnings less expenses.

- *Net backpay.* Gross backpay less net interim earnings. This is
  the amount which should be paid to the discriminatee plus
  "fringe" benefits which would have been received less those
  received in interim employment.

- *Excepted period.* A period of time in which the discriminatee
  was not available for work for reasons such as military service,
  strike, pregnancy, or illness. If, however, the discriminatee's
  inability to work was due to events which would not have
  occurred or to environmental factors which would not have
  existed absent the unlawful discrimination, the disability will
  be attributed to the discrimination, and backpay will be
  awarded.[43] During excepted periods gross backpay is not credited to the discriminatee, nor are net interim earnings deducted from gross backpay.

- *Quarterly computations.* Normally net backpay figures are
  computed on a quarterly basis corresponding to the four quarters in the calendar year. The amounts due are calculated
  independently each quarter so that figures reached in one
  quarter neither affect, nor are affected by, experiences in

---

[41]*See, e.g., Madison Courier, Inc.,* 202 NLRB 808, 82 LRRM 1667 (1973) (strike benefits).
[42]*NLRB v. Gullett Gin Co.,* 340 U.S. 361, 27 LRRM 2230 (1951).
[43]*M.F.A. Milling Co.,* 170 NLRB 1079, 68 LRRM 1077 (1968); *American Mfg. Co.,* 167
NLRB 520, 66 LRRM 1122 (1967).

another quarter.[44] Thus, the amount of net backpay due in one quarter will not be reduced because interim earnings exceeded gross backpay in another quarter.

(b) Backpay Recordkeeping Requirements. Upon issuance of a complaint alleging discrimination, the Board's regional office will give each employee involved:

- A pamphlet explaining backpay computations, records the employee should keep, and instructions that he or she is under an obligation to make reasonable efforts to secure other employment during the backpay period. (See Exhibit 95.)
- A Social Security form to be signed and returned by the employee to the Board. This form authorizes the Social Security Administration to supply the Board with a record of the worker's employment and earnings during the backpay period. (See Exhibit 96.)
- A form to keep the regional office informed of where the employee can be reached. (See Exhibit 97.)

As for recordkeeping by the party who committed the unfair labor practice, the Board's backpay order contains the following language:

"Preserve and make available to the Board or its agents upon request, for examination and copying, all payroll records, social security payment records, time cards, personnel records and reports, and all other records necessary to analyze the amounts of backpay due and the rights of employment under the terms of this Order."

At the appropriate time (for example, after issuance of the Board's backpay order), when compliance is being effectuated, the party against whom the order issued will be supplied with a form for computation of gross backpay. (See Exhibit 98.) This form is to be completed and returned to the Board agent.

§18.5 Computing Gross Backpay

There is no single formula for computing gross backpay to cover every situation. The objective in selecting a backpay formula is to restore the discriminatees, as accurately as possible, to the economic positions which they would have enjoyed during the backpay period absent discrimination. Accordingly, gross backpay computations should take into account such variables as the rise and fall of working time, changing rates of pay, job transfers, promotions, and fringe benefits.[45] Exact precision, however, is not required and the Board's backpay

---

[44]*NLRB v. Seven-Up Bottling Co.*, 344 U.S. 344, 31 LRRM 2237 (1953); *F. W. Woolworth Co.*, 90 NLRB 289, 26 LRRM 1185 (1950).

[45]NLRB Casehandling Manual ¶10534.2.

FORM NLRB-4288
(3-82)

NATIONAL LABOR RELATIONS BOARD

INFORMATION ON BACKPAY FOR EMPLOYEES

NOTICE

YOU MAY BE ENTITLED TO BACKPAY

Form NLRB-916, Backpay Claimant Identification, must be filled out **IMMEDIATELY** and mailed in the enclosed envelope which requires no postage. Type or print **ALL** the information asked for on the form.

NOW, read the information in this leaflet carefully and follow each instruction to ensure that you will receive all the money which you may have coming.

1. PURPOSE OF THIS LEAFLET

Your name has been included in a complaint issued by the General Counsel of the National Labor Relations Board. This may result in a decision that you have been illegally discharged, laid off, demoted, or refused employment. The National Labor Relations Board may decide that you are entitled to backpay because of this. We will need your help to find out how much the backpay will be. The purpose of this leaflet is to tell you what backpay is and how you can help us. It is important to remember, however, that the charges concerning your discharge may be dismissed. If this happens, you will not receive backpay.

2. WHAT IS BACKPAY?

Backpay has two parts. The first is what you would have earned if the employer or union had not violated the law and caused you to be discharged, laid off, demoted, or refused employment. This is called gross backpay. The second part is

Exhibit 95.   Information on Backpay for Employees   (Form NLRB-4288)

what you earn while you are kept from your rightful job. This is called interim earnings. The backpay due you is the difference between gross backpay and interim earnings. To use a simple example, suppose you were making $200 a week before you were discharged. The NLRB finds that you were illegally discharged and orders that you be paid for loss of earnings. Immediately after being discharged you take another job for $150 a week. Then, 10 weeks after your discharge the employer who illegally discharged you offers you your old job. The gross backpay is $2,000 *($200 per week for 10 weeks)* and your interim earnings are $1,500 *($150 per week for 10 weeks).* Thus, your backpay would be $500 *($2,000 minus $1,500).*

This calculation for backpay is normally computed for every calendar quarter during which you were entitled to backpay and the backpay due you for a particular quarter will normally not be offset by additional interim earnings from a different calendar quarter.

3. ARE YOU EMPLOYED NOW OR LOOKING FOR WORK?

Read what follows very carefully, it is important

YOU WILL NOT GET BACKPAY FOR TIMES WHEN YOU ARE UNEMPLOYED AND DO NOT LOOK FOR WORK OR ARE UNABLE TO WORK.

You must make a real and sincere effort to obtain work even though you may have been illegally discharged. If you decide to take a fishing trip for a month rather that look for a job, you may not get backpay for that month. If you decide to be a full-time homemaker or go back to school or college full-time, you may not qualify for backpay until you again start looking for a full-time job. Therefore, we must know whether you were looking for work by going to employers, by registering with your state employment service *(or unemployment insurance office)* and in various other ways. You may not remember names of places where you apply for work and are turned down unless you keep a written record of your search for work on a daily or weekly basis. We have provided Form NLRB-5224, Claimant Expense and Search For Work Report, for the purpose of keeping a record of the expenses you have while searching for employment *(such as mileage, phone calls, motels, parking fees, etc.)* and this form will also provide a convenient record of your search for work.

Exhibit 95—*page 2*

YOU WILL BE ABLE TO SHOW THAT YOU LOOKED FOR WORK BY DOING THE FOLLOWING THINGS:

(1) Register at your local employment service *(or unemployment insurance office)*. Keep a record on the Claimant Expense and Search For Work Report *(Part I. A)*, and keep whatever registration card or record that office gives you. Note the date of your registration and the location of the office. When you receive unemployment insurance benefits, keep all records which show the dates of payment of the benefits, etc. If you register with any other state, private, or union employment agency, this information must also be recorded.

(2) Whenever you apply or ask for a job, keep a record on the Claimant Expense and Search For Work Report *(Part I,B)* on the date you asked for work, the name of the employer, its location, whom you talked to and what was said *(e.g., "Sorry, we have no work for you," or "We will let you know if a job opens." etc.)*.

(3) You must also list in the space provided *(Part I, C)* the dates and reasons why you were unavailable for work for any period of time during the calendar quarter.

(4) If you become employed by another employer but for any reason lose the job before the company from which you were illegally discharged asks you to return to work, you must again make a real and sincere effort to obtain work in the manner discussed above.

4. YOUR INTERIM EARNINGS

When you do find another job, you must keep a record of the name and address of the employer, the job classification, when you start, how much you earn, how long you continue working at the job and why your employment ended. Keep this information on Part II, B, of Form NLRB—5224. In addition, keep all records that show what you earn at these other jobs, including pay stubs, W-2 forms or any other record of your earnings.

5. YOUR EXPENSES

You may have to spend money looking for other work or holding another job and you may be entitled to deduct these expenses from your interim earnings. It is important to keep a record of these expenses on the enclosed Form NLRB-5224 *(Part II, A)*.

Exhibit 95—*page 3*

FOR EXAMPLE:

On your new job you may have to pay more money to get to and from work than you had to pay with your old job. You may be entitled to the increased cost as an expense. You may have spent bus fare or used a car looking for work. You may have paid employment agency fees to get a job. You may have had to pay union initiation or work permit fees or dues to keep a job. You may be entitled to a credit for those expenses when your backpay is calculated. Therefore, **it is very important to keep a record of all your expenses on Form NLRB-5224.**

In your search for work you should record your mileage, parking fees, public transportation expenses, etc., on Part II, A, of the form. **SEND THE COMPLETED FORM NLRB-5224 TO THE NLRB REGIONAL OFFICE AT THE END OF EACH CALENDAR QUARTER.**

6. KEEPING RECORDS

In addition to recording the necessary information on the form we have provided, you should keep all the records you have on applications made for work, interim earnings, and expenses as described under items 3, 4, and 5 above until you turn them over to the NLRB agent who requests them.

7. WHEN DO YOU GET YOUR BACKPAY?

If you help by doing the things listed above, we will be able to figure out your backpay without delay. This assumes, of course, that the National Labor Relations Board decides that you are entitled to backpay. Not all cases take the same time. Sometimes an employer or union will settle quickly; others may go to court after the National Labor Relations Board has made its decision. Therefore, we cannot tell you now, when, or if you will get backpay.

REMEMBER TO TELL THE NATIONAL LABOR RELATIONS BOARD REGIONAL OFFICE ABOUT ANY CHANGE IN YOUR ADDRESS. USE THE ENCLOSED POSTAL CARD. ALSO NOTIFY THE EMPLOYER IN THIS CASE.

If the employer is ordered to take you back to your old job and you have moved away from the old address the employer has for you, the offer to take you back may never reach you in time for you to accept it.

KEEP THIS PAMPHLET FOR YOUR INFORMATION

Exhibit 95—*page 4*

FORM NLRB-4180
(12-73)

NATIONAL LABOR RELATIONS BOARD

AUTHORIZATION TO SOCIAL SECURITY ADMINISTRATION
TO FURNISH EMPLOYMENT AND EARNINGS INFORMATION

SOCIAL SECURITY NUMBER	DATE OF BIRTH	FOR OFFICE USE ONLY - DO NOT WRITE IN THIS SPACE
		PLEASE SUPPLY THIS INFORMATION FOR THE PERIOD
NAME *(Please type or print)*		FROM _____ TO _____
NLRB CASE NAME AND NUMBER		

I hereby authorize the Social Security Administration to forward to the Regional Office of the National Labor Relations Board the record (by quarters) of my places of employment, employers' addresses, and corresponding earnings.

Signature _____

(Form must be signed in ink. Please do not type or print signature.)

N.L.R.B. REGIONAL OFFICE ADDRESS:

GPO 933 733

**Exhibit 96. Authorization to Social Security Administration to Furnish
Employment and Earnings Information (Form NLRB-4180)**

FORM NLRB-916
(6-80)

FORM EXEMPT UNDER
44 U.S.C. 3512

NATIONAL LABOR RELATIONS BOARD
BACKPAY CLAIMANT IDENTIFICATION

1. NAME OF CLAIMANT (*Mr., Mrs., Miss., Ms.*)	2. DATE OF BIRTH	3. SOCIAL SECURITY NUMBER
A. MAIDEN NAME, IF MARRIED	B. OTHER NAMES USED, IF ANY	C. SPOUSE'S FIRST AND LAST NAME, MIDDLE INITIAL	D. SPOUSE'S SOCIAL SECURITY NUMBER

4. ADDRESS (*Street and Number, City, State and ZIP Code, NOTIFY REGIONAL OFFICE OF NLRB OF NEW ADDRESS IF YOU MOVE*)

5. TELEPHONE NUMBER.

6. LIST BELOW FRIENDS OR RELATIVES WHO WILL KNOW WHERE YOU ARE IN CASE YOU MOVE:

NAME	ADDRESS	TELEPHONE NUMBER

7. SUPPLY THE FOLLOWING INFORMATION REGARDING YOUR EMPLOYMENT AT:

_____
(Name of Company)

CASE NUMBER

A. NAME OF DEPARTMENT YOU WERE IN AT TIME OF UNFAIR LABOR PRACTICE	B. KIND OF JOB YOU HAD AT TIME OF UNFAIR LABOR PRACTICE	C. DATE YOU STARTED WORKING FOR THIS COMPANY
D. RATE OF PAY AT TIME OF DISCHARGE	E. NUMBER OF HOURS WORKED EACH WEEK	

GPO 893-279

Exhibit 97. Backpay Claimant Identification (Form NLRB-916)

FORM NLRB-4312 (8-83)	COMPUTATION OF BACKPAY		YEAR	QUARTER
CASE NO.			EXCEPTED PERIOD(S)	
NAME		SOCIAL SECURITY NO.		
JOB TITLE AND DEPARTMENT				

BACKPAY COMPUTATION FOR CALENDAR QUARTER

1. NUMBER OF HOURS, DAYS OR WEEKS					
2. HOURLY, DAILY OR WEEKLY RATE OF PAY	$	$	$		
3. PRODUCT: ITEM 1 X ITEM 2	$	$	$		
4. BONUS AND OTHER					
5. QUARTERLY TOTAL GROSS BACKPAY				$	

6. QUARTERLY INTERIM EARNINGS AND EXPENSES	EARNINGS	EXPENSES	
TOTALS	$	$	

7. QUARTERLY NET INTERM EARNINGS		$	
8. NET BACKPAY FOR QUARTER *(Item 5 minus Item 7)*		$	
9. INTEREST *(See Note below)*	FROM: _____ THROUGH _____	No. days _____	$ _____ *Interest*
10. TOTAL NET BACKPAY PLUS INTEREST *(Item 8 plus Item 9)*		$	

NOTE: *Interest will not be computed, usually, until a tender of the backpay due has been made or a date for payment has been agreed upon, since interest accrues until that date.*

Exhibit 98. Computation of Backpay (Form NLRB-4312)

computations may therefore be predicated upon any range of facts, circumstances, or reasonable inferences which afford a rational basis for a conclusion.[46]

Over the years, four basic backpay formulas have been developed by the Board and approved by the courts. The selection of which formula to use will be made by the compliance officer, and will depend upon the circumstances of each case, including the availability of data necessary to apply the formula.

(a) Average Earnings Formula. The discriminatee's average earnings for a representative pay period prior to the commission of the unfair labor practice are computed. Gross backpay is calculated by multiplying the average earnings figure by the number of pay periods in the backpay period. This formula is appropriate in situations where the nature of the discriminatee's job, the discriminatee's level of earnings, and the company's business all remained relatively constant during the pre-unfair labor practice and backpay periods.[47]

(b) Average Hours of Work Formula. In situations where the employer's wage rates changed during the backpay period, a formula based upon the average hours worked by the discriminatee may be more appropriate than one based upon average earnings. Using a representative period prior to the commission of the unfair labor practice, the average number of hours worked by the discriminatee per pay period is computed. This average figure is then multiplied by the applicable hourly rate of pay for each pay period in the backpay period, and the sums totaled in order to compute gross backpay.[48] This formula is most useful in instances where the discriminatee was employed long enough prior to the unfair labor practice to establish a typical working pattern, and the employer's business is not seasonal in nature.[49]

(c) Representative Employee Formula. Under this method an employee is selected who worked both prior to the unfair labor practice and during the backpay period and whose work in terms of content and working conditions was similar to that of the discriminatee. If the employee and the discriminatee historically had comparable earnings, the representative employee's earnings during the backpay period could be viewed as a measure of the discriminatee's backpay. If their earnings differed but hours of work were approximately the same, the number of hours worked by the representative

---

[46]*Id.* citing *Palmer v. Connecticut Ry. & Lighting Co.*, 311 U.S. 544, 561 (1941); *NLRB v. Kartarik, Inc.*, 227 F.2d 190, 37 LRRM 2104 (8th Cir. 1955).

[47]*See* NLRB Casehandling Manual ¶¶10538–10538.4 for a more extensive discussion of the average earnings formula.

[48]*See* NLRB Casehandling Manual ¶¶10540–10540.4 for a more extensive discussion of the average hours of work formula.

[49]NLRB Casehandling Manual ¶10540.2.

employee multiplied by the discriminatee's hourly rate could be used to compute backpay. When there are several representative employees, their average earnings or average hours worked may be used as an appropriate standard. The representative employee formula is particularly useful in cases where there are long backpay periods involving several job and pay changes.[50]

(d) Replacement Employee Formula. In situations where there are no comparable employees who worked during both the pre-unfair labor practice and backpay periods, the individual or group of individuals who replaced the discriminatee may be used for purposes of estimating backpay due. Where the replacement was hired at the same wage rate as the discriminatee, the replacement's earnings may be viewed as a reasonable measure of what the discriminatee might have earned.[51] If, as is often the case, the replacement was hired at a lower rate of pay, then the replacement's hours of work may be used to determine the approximate number of hours which the discriminatee would have worked during the backpay period. These hours then can be multiplied by the discriminatee's hourly rate to calculate gross backpay.[52]

(e) Items Included in Gross Backpay. The formulas described above may be used for computing the discriminatee's earnings during the backpay period. Gross backpay includes all payments which would have been made absent the discrimination including bonuses, commissions, profit-sharing payments, vacation pay, tips, and employer contributions to pension funds.[53]

Fringe benefits which the discriminatee would have received during the backpay period also must be paid. Examples would include health, hospitalization, and life insurance payments;[54] housing subsidies;[55] and pension benefits.[56] While the employer's obligation to

---

[50]*See* NLRB Casehandling Manual ¶¶10542–10542.4 for a more extensive discussion of the representative employee formula.

[51]*See* NLRB Casehandling Manual ¶¶10544–10544.4 for a more extensive discussion of the replacement employee formula.

[52]In cases where the discriminatee was compensated on a commission or other incentive basis, the Board may compute the ratio between the discriminatee's pre-unfair labor practice earnings and those of a similarly situated individual or group of individuals, and apply that ratio to the earnings of the test group during the backpay period to estimate what the discriminatee would have earned. *Boyer Ford Trucks, Inc.*, 270 NLRB 1133, 116 LRRM 1485 (1984); *Story Oldsmobile, Inc.*, 145 NLRB 1647, 55 LRRM 1217 (1964). NLRB Casehandling Manual ¶10545.

[53]NLRB Casehandling Manual ¶10550; *see, e.g., Artim Transp. Sys.*, 193 NLRB 179, 78 LRRM 1607 (1971) (contributions to pension fund); *Finishline Indus.*, 181 NLRB 756, 74 LRRM 1654 (1970) (contributions to pension funds).

[54]NLRB Casehandling Manual ¶10552.1; *see, e.g., East Texas Steel Castings*, 116 NLRB 1336, 38 LRRM 1470 (1956); *Deena Artware*, 112 NLRB 371, 36 LRRM 1028 (1955).

[55]NLRB Casehandling Manual ¶10552.2; *e.g., Climax Spinning Co.*, 101 NLRB 1193, 31 LRRM 1206 (1952).

[56]NLRB Casehandling Manual ¶10552.3; *e.g., Fibreboard Prods. Corp.*, 180 NLRB 142, 72 LRRM 1617 (1969).

reimburse the discriminatee for lost fringe benefits may be offset by the amount of such benefits received from interim employment, interim earnings may not be deducted.[57]

§18.6   Interim Earnings

Gross backpay due a discriminatee will be reduced by the discriminatee's "interim earnings"—i.e., earnings actually received during the backpay period, or earnings which could have been received through the exercise of reasonable efforts. Since the Board requires discriminatees to mitigate backpay liability by securing interim employment,[58] any willful refusal to seek or retain such employment could result in a tolling (i.e., suspension) of the respondent's backpay liability.[59]

(a) Computing Interim Earnings.   All money received by a discriminatee in payment for work or services performed may be regarded as interim earnings. (See Exhibit 99.)[60] Earnings from self-employment, tips, and the value of perquisites of interim employment such as room, board, and use of an automobile are all deductible from gross backpay as interim earnings.[61] In contrast, unearned income such as unemployment insurance payments, the portion of workers' compensation benefits not attributable to lost wages, gifts, earnings on investments, union benefits, and gambling winnings are not interim earnings.[62] Also, since the Board does not require discriminatees to invest extra effort to mitigate a respondent's backpay liability, income derived from a second job held prior to the discrimination, and income derived from hours worked in excess of those which would have been available from respondent, need not be included in interim earnings. Income from a second job must be included only to the extent that not working for respondent allowed the employee to work additional hours at the second job.[63]

---

[57]*See* NLRB Casehandling Manual ¶¶10552, 10552.1; *e.g., Glen Raven Silk Mills, Inc.,* 101 NLRB 239, 31 LRRM 1045 (1952).

[58]*See, e.g., NLRB v. Arduini Mfg. Co.,* 394 F.2d 420, 68 LRRM 2129 (1st Cir. 1968).

[59]*E.g., American Bottling Co.,* 116 NLRB 1303, 38 LRRM 1465 (1956); *see also Shell Oil Co.,* 218 NLRB 87, 89 LRRM 1534 (1975) (backpay to employee who voluntarily quit interim employment reduced by projected amount of lost interim earnings). Discriminatees who willfully conceal interim earnings from the Board will be denied backpay for all quarters in which they engaged in concealed employment. *American Navigation Co.,* 268 NLRB 426, 115 LRRM 1017 (1983). Backpay will be denied entirely if the intentionally concealed employment cannot be attributed to specific quarters. *Ad Art, Inc.,* 280 NLRB No. 114 (1986).

[60]NLRB Casehandling Manual ¶10604.1.

[61]*Id.* at ¶¶10602, 10602.1. To the extent that automobile, gasoline, housing and similar allowances represent reimbursements for job-related expenses rather than perquisites of employment, they are not included as part of interim earnings. *Cf. Boyer Ford Trucks, Inc.,* 270 NLRB 1133, 116 LRRM 1485 (1984).

[62]NLRB Casehandling Manual ¶10604.1.

[63]*Id.* at ¶¶10604.3, 10604.4, and 10606. *See George A. Angle,* 252 NLRB 1156, 105 LRRM 1651 (1980) (income from supplemental job).

FORM NLRB-5230 (2-82)	NATIONAL LABOR RELATIONS BOARD **INTERIM EARNINGS REPORT**	

NAME AND ADDRESS OF INTERIM EMPLOYER

CASE NAME

CASE NUMBER

PLEASE PROVIDE THE FOLLOWING EMPLOYMENT AND EARNINGS INFORMATION FOR:
NAME: SOCIAL SECURITY NUMBER:

1. DATE EMPLOYMENT BEGAN:

2. DATE EMPLOYMENT ENDED:

3. LAST HOURLY RATE:

4. CHECK ONE: FULL TIME ☐ | PART TIME ☐ If part time, indicate average weekly hours:

5. GROSS EARNINGS BY MONTH *(BEFORE ANY WITHHOLDINGS)*

MONTH YEAR	GROSS AMOUNT	MONTH YEAR	GROSS AMOUNT	MONTH YEAR	GROSS AMOUNT	MONTH YEAR	GROSS AMOUNT

6. REASON EMPLOYMENT ENDED:

7. LIST ANY REASONS AND DATES FOR ANY PERIOD OF TIME THIS INDIVIDUAL DID NOT WORK DUE TO ILLNESS, VACATION, LEAVE OF ABSENCE, LAYOFF OR OTHER.

DATES		REASON
FROM	TO	

PREPARED BY: _____   _____
                    (Name of Employer Representative)   *(Title)*

_____   _____
(Date)   *(Signature)*

Exhibit 99.   Interim Earnings Report   (Form NLRB-5230)

Discriminatees are entitled to deduct from their interim earnings all expenses incurred in seeking or retaining interim employment that they would not have incurred had they not been discriminated against. Examples include extra transportation costs, employment agency and other fees associated with the employment search, room and board if the interim employment is away from home, and moving costs.[64] Generally, capital losses sustained in the sale of a home or other personal items are not considered allowable expenses.[65]

(b) Unavailability for Work.   Backpay does not accrue during periods of time that a discriminatee is unavailable for work.[66] Temporary unavailability, for example, may be caused by injury, illness, full-time attendance at school, military service, or institutional confinement.[67] Discriminatees who have retired following their loss of employment may nevertheless be considered "available" and eligible for backpay if they continue actively to seek employment following retirement.[68] Persons who have been deported from the United States as illegal aliens, however, are considered to be "unavailable" for work (thereby tolling further accrual of backpay) during any period that they are not lawfully entitled to be present and employed in this country.[69]

(c) Willful Idleness.   As noted earlier,[70] discriminatees are required to mitigate backpay by making reasonable efforts to secure and retain interim employment. While as a technical matter backpay is not tolled against an individual who fails to make such efforts, in the absence of evidence as to what the discriminatee might have earned "the Board assumes that any other employment would have yielded earnings equal to that of the work from which the discriminatee had been discharged."[71] Since under these circumstances lost interim earnings equal gross backpay, there is no net backpay due.

Discriminatees are not required to go beyond "reasonable exertions" in seeking interim employment.[72] The efforts expected are

---

[64]NLRB Casehandling Manual ¶10610.

[65]*Id.*

[66]NLRB Casehandling Manual ¶10612. *See generally* NLRB Casehandling Manual ¶¶10612–10626.

[67]NLRB Casehandling Manual ¶¶10618.1–10618.3. If an injury or illness arose out of interim employment or was caused by the respondent's unfair labor practices, backpay may not be tolled. *Id.* at ¶10612.1. Similarly, attendance at school may not toll backpay if it can be demonstrated that the discriminatee was looking for work and would have dropped out of school if suitable employment could be found. *Id.* at ¶10618.3. *See Three States Trucking, Inc.*, 252 NLRB 1088, 105 LRRM 1457 (1980); *J.L. Holtzendorff Detective Agency*, 206 NLRB 483, 84 LRRM 1479 (1973).

[68]NLRB Casehandling Manual ¶10620.

[69]*Sure-Tan, Inc. v. NLRB*, 467 U.S. 883, 116 LRRM 2857 (1984).

[70]See *supra* notes 58 and 59.

[71]*Painters, Local 419 (Spoon Tile Co.)*, 117 NLRB 1596, 1598 n.7, 40 LRRM 1051, 1052 n.7 (1957), *quoted in* NLRB Casehandling Manual ¶10612.

[72]*NLRB v. Arduini Mfg. Co.*, 394 F.2d 420, 68 LRRM 2129 (1st Cir. 1968).

those of reasonable persons in similar circumstances taking into account such factors as the discriminatee's skills, qualifications, age, health, and the conditions of the labor market.[73] Registration at public and private employment agencies, written and telephone responses to employment advertisements, job interviews, inquiries of friends and neighbors regarding job vacancies, and so on are factors which the Board examines in determining whether a reasonable search for interim employment has been made.[74] Rejection of a reasonable offer of interim employment, or the loss of such employment through misconduct or a voluntary quit, may be viewed by the Board as a willfull loss of earnings suspending the discriminatee's entitlement to backpay.[75] The burden of establishing that a discriminatee was unavailable for work or engaged in a willful loss of earnings rests with the respondent.[76]

§18.7 Computing and Distributing Net Backpay

Net backpay is computed by deducting net interim earnings (i.e., interim earnings less expenses) from gross backpay. Computations are made on a quarterly basis using NLRB Form 4312. (See Exhibit 98.) In addition, interest is assessed in accordance with the adjusted prime interest rate then in effect.[77] Interest begins to accrue on the last day of each calendar quarter of the backpay period on the amount due and owing for that quarter, and continues until compliance with the order is achieved.[78]

While the Board is anxious to avoid the time and expense of litigation whenever possible, it also is reluctant to compromise the backpay claims of discriminatees. Accordingly, when a respondent disputes the amount of backpay which is due, the Board will attempt to avoid formal proceedings by negotiating a settlement agreement, but will strive in any such agreement to acquire all of the backpay assertedly due.[79] The Board's regional directors, however, are authorized to accept settlements containing at least 80 percent of the claimed backpay without clearance from Washington headquarters.

---

[73]*Pipeline, Local 38 (Hancock-Northwest, J.V.)*, 268 NLRB 167, 114 LRRM 1247 (1983); *see* NLRB Casehandling Manual ¶10616.

[74]*See, e.g., Cumberland Farms Dairy*, 266 NLRB 855, 113 LRRM 1048 (1983); *see* NLRB Casehandling Manual ¶¶10616.1–10616.5. Discharged employees are not confined to the geographical area of their former employer in searching for interim employment. They remain in the labor market by seeking work in any area with comparable work opportunities. *M Restaurants v. NLRB*, 621 F.2d 336, 104 LRRM 2818 (9th Cir. 1980).

[75]*See, e.g., Medline Indus., Inc.*, 261 NLRB 1329, 110 LRRM 1286 (1982) (willful loss of earnings evidenced by discriminatee's propensity to quit jobs for myriad of reasons); *see* NLRB Casehandling Manual ¶10614.

[76]*See* NLRB Casehandling Manual ¶10622. The burden of proof in backpay proceedings is discussed further at §18.11 *infra*.

[77]*Florida Steel Corp.*, 231 NLRB 651, 96 LRRM 1070 (1977).

[78]*Id.; Reserve Supply Corp.*, 140 NLRB 330, 52 LRRM 1012 (1962); *Isis Plumbing & Heating Co.*, 138 NLRB 716, 51 LRRM 1122 (1962); *see* NLRB Casehandling Manual ¶¶10623.1–10624.3.

[79]NLRB Casehandling Manual ¶10628.1.

Any agreement which calls for less than 80 percent of the backpay calculated to be due must be cleared in advance by the Board's Division of Operations Management.[80] Private settlements between the respondent and the discriminatee may not defeat or diminish the discriminatee's backpay claim.[81]

Once net backpay has been computed, the normal procedure is for checks made payable to each discriminatee to be delivered by respondent to the regional office. Appropriate tax and withholding deductions should be made from the gross amount due.[82] The checks then are delivered to the discriminatees either in person or by certified mail. In certain circumstances the Board may permit the respondent to make payments directly to discriminatees on condition that appropriate evidence of payment be submitted to the Board.[83]

Formal Compliance Proceedings

In many cases, agreement cannot be reached regarding either the existence or the amount of a respondent's backpay liability. In such instances a formal hearing before an administrative law judge may be required. As with unfair labor practice proceedings, backpay hearings are conducted by the General Counsel. The General Counsel's authority in compliance matters, however, is limited. Rather than acting on his or her own initiative as in the issuance and prosecution of unfair labor practice complaints, the General Counsel in compliance proceedings serves as an agent of the Board in the effectuation of its order.[84]

Formal compliance proceedings generally are not commenced until after court enforcement of the Board's order, particularly where issues other than backpay remain in dispute or where the backpay period has not ended.[85] In cases where the backpay period ends prior to the commencement of the unfair labor practice proceeding and the

---

[80]*Id.*

[81]*Id.* at ¶10640.3; *e.g., NLRB v. Armstrong Tire & Rubber Co.,* 263 F.2d 680, 43 LRRM 2577 (5th Cir. 1959).

[82]Tax and withholding requirements on backpay payments are discussed in NLRB Casehandling Manual ¶¶10648–10649.6. Respondents are not required to reimburse discriminatees for income tax losses incurred as a result of receiving backpay awards in a lump sum. *Orleans Int'l Inc.,* 274 NLRB No. 169, 119 LRRM 1048 (1985). Board agents, however, generally inform discriminatees who receive lump sum payments that they may be entitled to income average. *Laborers, Local 282 (Austin Co.),* 271 NLRB 878, 117 LRRM 1083 (1984).

[83]NLRB Casehandling Manual at ¶10640.3. Discriminatees have one year within which to collect their backpay awards. Failure to do so is considered to be a forfeiture and the money is returned to the respondent. *Starlite Cutting, Inc.,* 280 NLRB No. 120 (1986).

[84]*Ace Beverage Co.,* 250 NLRB 646, 105 LRRM 1042 (1980).

[85]NLRB Casehandling Manual ¶10650. Special authorization to commence backpay proceedings prior to court enforcement may be granted in situations where the backpay period has ended, and either the respondent will not contest the backpay determination or for some other reason (e.g., bankruptcy) a prompt resolution of backpay is desirable. *Id.* at ¶10652.

backpay issues are relatively straightforward, the formal backpay and unfair labor practice proceedings may be merged.[86]

§18.8   Backpay Specification and Notice of Hearing

Most backpay proceedings are commenced by the regional director issuing a backpay specification accompanied by a notice of hearing.[87] The backpay specification sets out in detail the methodology and the mathematical computations used by the Board in ascertaining net backpay.[88] The purpose of the specification is to inform the respondent of the Board's rationale, and to limit and define the issues in controversy at the backpay hearing.[89] All respondents who may be jointly or severally liable are named in the specification, including those who already may have paid their proportionate share of the backpay assertedly due.[90]

Regional directors also are authorized to issue a notice of hearing without a backpay specification.[91] This procedure is most likely to be used when there is no dispute as to the amount of backpay involved, but there is a disagreement as to the respondent's liability for the backpay (e.g., successorship, joint employer, or alter ego issues).[92]

Copies of the backpay specification and/or notice of hearing are served on all respondents and charging parties at least 21 days prior to the hearing.[93] Discriminatees also are notified of the hearing and informed that their testimony may be required.[94]

Following issuance of the backpay specification or notice of hearing, it is Board policy to make available to respondents for inspection and copying all factual information in documents in the possession of the regional office "relevant to the computation of the net backpay or to other items of reimbursement or restitution."[95] Such information

---

[86]*Id.* at ¶10650.1.

[87]NLRB Rules and Regulations §102.52.

[88]§102.53(a) of the Board's Rules and Regulations provides that the specification "shall specifically and in detail show, for each employee, the backpay periods broken down by calendar quarters, the specific figures and basis of computation as to gross backpay and interim earnings, the expenses for each quarter, the net backpay due, and any other pertinent information." *See also* NLRB Casehandling Manual ¶10656.5.

[89]NLRB Casehandling Manual ¶10656.1. *See* NLRB Casehandling Manual ¶¶10656.1–10656.15 for a detailed discussion of the preparation of backpay specifications.

[90]*Id.* at ¶10656.3.

[91]NLRB Rules and Regulations §102.52. NLRB Rules and Regulations §102.53(b) provides that the notice of hearing shall contain the time and place of the hearing, and a brief statement of the matters in controversy.

[92]NLRB Casehandling Manual ¶10654.2.

[93]*Id.* at ¶10660; NLRB Rules and Regulations §102.52.

[94]NLRB Casehandling Manual ¶10662.

[95]*Id.* at ¶¶10663, 10663.1. Although not standard policy, such information also may be disclosed prior to issuance of a backpay specification or notice of hearing when, in the judgment of the regional director, advance disclosure "will significantly enhance possibilities of settlement." *Id.* at ¶10663.2.

might include, for example, affidavits or documentation relating to discriminatees' employment searches, interim earnings and expenses, periods of unavailability for work, and other forms of reimbursement. Information unrelated or only marginally related to the computation of backpay need not be disclosed.[96]

The Board attempts to prepare the backpay specification as promptly as possible. If there is a delay, however, the courts repeatedly have indicated that the agency's inaction cannot be used as a basis to deny relief to individuals who otherwise would be entitled to recovery.[97]

§18.9   Answer to Backpay Specification

In many respects the requirements for filing an answer to a backpay specification parallel those applicable to an answer filed in response to an unfair labor practice complaint.[98] They must be in writing, signed by the respondent or its designated agent, and must specifically admit, deny or explain each and every allegation in the backpay specification.[99] A statement that the respondent is without knowledge will, as with a regular answer, operate as a denial. Denials must be sufficiently specific to fairly meet the substance of the allegations in the specification which is denied.[100]

Answers to backpay specifications, however, are unique in one significant respect. As to all matters which are within the knowledge of the respondent, a general denial will not be adequate. Thus, for example, if a respondent disputes either the accuracy of the figures contained in the backpay specification or the premises upon which they are based, a general denial will not suffice, and the respondent in such circumstances must specifically state the reasons for the disagreement, setting forth in detail the appropriate premises and furnishing appropriate supporting figures.[101]

Failure to file a timely answer, or an unexplained failure to plead with sufficient particularity is considered by the Board to be an admission. Accordingly, the allegations in the specification will be taken

---

[96]Examples cited in ¶10663.3 of the Board's Casehandling Manual include information (1) pertaining to the agency's deliberative or policy-making processes, (2) reflecting the mental opinions, impressions, conclusions, and legal theories of attorneys and other party representatives, (3) identifying confidential sources of information to the agency, and (4) of an intimate personal nature having only slight relevance to the backpay inquiry.

[97]*NLRB v. Ironworkers, Local 480*, 466 U.S. 720, 116 LRRM 2289 (1984); *NLRB v. J.H. Rutter-Rex Mfg. Co.*, 396 U.S. 258, 72 LRRM 2881 (1969).

[98]See discussion at §§15.5–15.7.

[99]NLRB Rules and Regulations §102.54(b).

[100]*Id.*

[101]*Id.; see, e.g., Tiffany Handbags, Inc.*, 271 NLRB 621, 117 LRRM 1131 (1984); *Normike Contractors, Inc.*, 267 NLRB 836, 114 LRRM 1116 (1983); *see also Kuhns*, 264 NLRB 412, 111 LRRM 1485 (1982) (partial summary judgment granted where respondent filed general denial without specifically denying gross backpay allegations, providing alternative formula, or explaining failure to do so).

as true without the necessity for introduction of supporting evidence, and the respondent thereafter will be precluded from disputing the allegations or raising any issues not properly raised in its answer.[102] The one exception to this rule is interim earnings—since a discriminatee's interim earnings usually are not known to the respondent general denials concerning interim earnings are permitted.[103]

The answer to a backpay specification must be filed within 21 days from the service of the specification.[104] An original and four copies must be served on the regional director issuing the specification, and a copy thereof must be served immediately upon any other respondent who may be jointly liable.[105] If no answer is filed within the designated time period the respondent will be contacted by a Board attorney and an immediate response requested. In the absence of an answer, the General Counsel will file a motion for summary judgment,[106] urge that the Board accept the allegations in the backpay specification as true, and request that an appropriate order be entered without the necessity for additional evidence.[107] No answer, however, is required in response to a notice of hearing which is issued without a backpay specification.[108]

§18.10 Prehearing Procedures

The procedures applicable to formal proceedings in unfair labor practice cases generally are followed in formal backpay proceedings as well.[109] Any time before the hearing opens, the regional director on his or her own motion or for good cause shown may extend the date of the hearing.[110] The regional director on his or her own motion may also withdraw[111] or amend the specification.[112] Similarly, the respondent will be permitted to amend its answer prior to the hearing

---

[102]NLRB Rules and Regulations §102.54(c); *see also* NLRB Casehandling Manual ¶¶10664.2–10664.3, and 10737.3; *Fugazy Continental Corp.*, 260 NLRB 1225, 109 LRRM 1367 (1982); *Nelson Elec.*, 260 NLRB 1, 109 LRRM 1138 (1982).

[103]*See, e.g., Tiffany Handbags, Inc.*, 271 NLRB No. 97, 117 LRRM 1131 (1984); *East Belden Corp.*, 267 NLRB 262, 114 LRRM 1014 (1983).

[104]NLRB Rules and Regulations §102.54(a). The regional director may grant an extension of time to file an answer either upon his or her own motion, or at the request of any respondent for good cause shown. *Id.* at §102.55.

[105]*Id.* at §102.54(a).

[106]Motions for summary judgment are discussed at §15.18.

[107]NLRB Casehandling Manual ¶10664.1.

[108]*Id.*; NLRB Rules and Regulations §102.54(d).

[109]The Board's Casehandling Manual ¶10670 provides that unfair labor practice procedures and trial techniques should be followed "except where they are inconsistent with this manual, the Rules and Regulations, or are otherwise inappropriate or inapplicable." *See also* NLRB Rules and Regulations §102.59.

[110]NLRB Rules and Regulations §102.56.

[111]*Id.* at §102.58; NLRB Casehandling Manual ¶10674.

[112]*Id.* at §102.57; NLRB Casehandling Manual ¶10672.

even in the absence of a modification to the specification.[113] Once the hearing has commenced, the pleadings may be amended and the specification may be withdrawn only with the permission of the administrative law judge or the Board for good cause shown.[114]

Formal backpay hearings often can become very complex in situations where there are many discriminatees, the gross backpay formula used is in dispute, or where the discriminatees' patterns of interim employment are irregular. Parties are well advised, therefore, to prepare thoroughly for the hearing and to consider entering into factual stipulations if possible. Documentation necessary to support or challenge the backpay specification, along with supplementary explanatory tabulations in complex cases, may be acquired in advance. In addition, witnesses qualified to testify about the labor market conditions during the backpay period, particularly with regard to jobs for which the discriminatees are qualified, should be considered for use on the issue of interim employment.

§18.11   Conduct of Backpay Hearing

As noted in the last section, procedures for conducting hearings in unfair labor practice cases generally are applicable to formal backpay proceedings.[115] The one unique aspect to backpay hearings, however, concerns the burden of proof. The General Counsel has the burden of proving gross backpay and expenses incurred by the discriminatees in seeking or maintaining interim employment[116] and the burden of going forward with the evidence if the accuracy of the backpay specification is challenged.[117] The respondent, on the other hand, has the burden of proving legitimate deductions from gross backpay such as interim earnings, willful idleness, misconduct justifying discharge from interim employment, or unavailability for interim employment.[118]

The General Counsel seeks to establish gross backpay principally through the backpay specification. If the respondent does not dispute the computations, or if the respondent has not contested the com-

---

[113]NLRB Rules and Regulations §102.57 (specification modified); *High Performance Tube, Inc.*, JD-(ATL)-45-82 (amendment to answer proper in absence of amendment to specification).

[114]NLRB Rules and Regulations §102.57 (amendment); NLRB Casehandling Manual ¶10672 (amendment); NLRB Casehandling Manual ¶¶10674.2–10674.3.

[115]See generally chapter 16.

[116]NLRB Casehandling Manual ¶10737.2; *Neely's Car Clinic*, 255 NLRB 1420, 107 LRRM 1157 (1981).

[117]*See Big Three Indus. Gas & Equip. Co.*, 263 NLRB 1189, 111 LRRM 1616 (1982) (upon respondent's showing discriminatee quit interim employment, burden shifted to General Counsel to show decision to quit reasonable and thus no willful loss of earnings).

[118]NLRB Casehandling Manual ¶10737.2; *see, e.g., Big Three Indus. Gas & Equip. Co.*, 263 NLRB 1189, 111 LRRM 1616 (1982) (willful misconduct); *Inland Empire Meat Co.*, 255 NLRB 1306, 107 LRRM 1114 (1981) (willful idleness); *Wayne Trophy Corp.*, 254 NLRB 881, 106 LRRM 1460 (1981) (willful idleness). *See also Berry-Mahurin Const., Inc.*, 273 NLRB No. 133, 118 LRRM 1398 (1984) (backpay awarded in light of respondent's failure to sustain burden of establishing that discriminatee would not have been hired absent discrimination).

putations with sufficient particularity and offered alternative methods for computing gross backpay, the allegations are deemed to be admitted and respondent is precluded from controverting the allegations of the specification.[119] In complex cases or cases where the backpay specification properly has been challenged, the compliance officer may be called as a witness by the General Counsel to explain the computations in the backpay specification and identify the defects in the alternative methodologies suggested by the respondent.[120] The General Counsel usually will introduce as part of the case in chief evidence pertaining to expenses incurred by the discriminatees in seeking or retaining interim employment.[121]

In attempting to mitigate gross backpay, respondents often place considerable reliance upon records pertaining to interim earnings and upon the testimony of discriminatees. The Board's policy long has been to cooperate with respondents by furnishing in advance of the hearing such records as Social Security and Railroad Retirement Board reports and letters from interim employers.[122] In addition, even though the General Counsel may not need the testimony of discriminatees for the case in chief, the Board generally will assist respondents in locating discriminatees so that they can be called to testify at the hearing.[123]

Following receipt of all the evidence, the administrative law judge will prepare a written Supplemental Decision and Order resolving the issues in dispute and ordering that the amount of backpay found appropriate be distributed to identified discriminatees. The Supplemental Decision and Order may be appealed to the Board on the same basis as administrative law judges' decisions in unfair labor practice cases.[124]

---

[119]See §18.9 *supra* at notes 101 and 102.

[120]*See* NLRB Casehandling Manual ¶¶10716.1, 10738.

[121]*See Id.* at ¶10740.3.

[122]*Id.* at ¶10732. While making such documentation available to respondents, the Board has cautioned its attorneys not to assume such an active role that they place themselves in the position of having assumed the burden of proof in areas that are properly respondents' responsibility. *Id.* at ¶¶10737.2, 10737.4.

[123]*Id.* at ¶10733. The General Counsel's role in producing discriminatees for examination by the respondent is not mandatory, but merely "advisory and cooperative." *Cornwell Co.*, 171 NLRB 342, n.2, 68 LRRM 1200 (1968).

[124]*See* NLRB Casehandling Manual ¶10670 and discussion at chapter 17.

IV

Supplemental Proceedings

19

Jurisdictional Dispute Proceedings

Jurisdictional disputes—frequently referred to as "work assignment" disputes—are disagreements over which group of employees is entitled to perform certain jobs. In many situations the employer involved is relatively neutral and is more interested in seeing to it that the competing factions reach an accommodation than in which employees actually perform the work. Every disagreement over work assignments has the potential for interfering with or stopping entirely the flow of work. Accordingly, Section 8(b)(4)(D) of the Act provides that it shall be an unfair labor practice for a labor organization to engage in strikes, picketing, boycotts, threats, or coercion for the purpose of

> "forcing or requiring any employer to assign particular work to employees in a particular labor organization or in a particular trade, craft, or class rather than to employees in another labor organization or in another trade, craft, or class unless such employer is failing to conform to an order or certification of the Board determining the bargaining representative for employees performing such work."

Congress realized, however, that a Board determination that a union has engaged in unlawful threats or coercion, and an order that the union cease and desist from such conduct, does not address the underlying dispute—the union might under Section 8(b)(4)(D) be precluded from applying certain forms of pressure in support of its claim to the work, but the merits of that claim would remain unresolved. Accordingly, Congress enacted Section 10(k) of the Act which establishes a procedure for the Board itself to resolve the underlying work assignment dispute in situations where the parties are unable to do so voluntarily.

As discussed in the balance of this chapter, because of the unique characteristics of jurisdictional disputes, the Act contemplates special procedures for processing Section 8(b)(4)(D) charges. Upon receipt of such a charge the Board's regional office will conduct a preliminary

investigation to determine whether there is reasonable cause to believe that the charged union has engaged in proscribed activity. If
reasonable cause is found, the regional office will determine whether
the contesting parties voluntarily have resolved the work assignment
dispute or have agreed upon a method for doing so. In the absence
of such a resolution or agreement, the Board will suspend further
processing of the charge and proceed to resolve the dispute itself in
a Section 10(k) proceeding. Upon completion of the Section 10(k)
proceeding, processing of the Section 8(b)(4)(D) charge is resumed
with disposition of the charge dependent upon the charged union's
willingness to comply with the Board's assignment of the disputed
work.

Nature of Jurisdictional Disputes

§19.1   Conflicting Claims for Work Assignments

As with other Section 8(b)(4) unfair labor practices, there must
be a proscribed *object* (i.e., assignment or reassignment of disputed
work) pursued through proscribed *means* (i.e., inducement or encouragement usually in the form of picketing, threats, coercion, or
other forms of restraint). The mere existence of a disagreement over
which group of employees should perform disputed work is not sufficient in and of itself to activate Section 8(b)(4)(D)—one of the parties
must support its claim to the work through an overt act of encouragement or inducement. This statutory prerequisite, however, is not
difficult to satisfy and often consists of nothing more than a verbal
threat from a union official to an employer that unless the assignment
is made to the union's members there will be a strike or other interruption of the work.[1] When two or more of the parties are anxious
to have the Board resolve the dispute (usually the employer and the
union representing the employees to whom the work initially was
assigned), the opportunity for staged threats is obvious.

Where a union has a good-faith claim to the disputed work based
upon the jurisdictional clause in a collective bargaining agreement,
the initiation of arbitration or Section 301 judicial proceedings to
enforce the clause, or threats to initiate such proceedings, generally
will not be considered prohibited inducement or encouragement under Section 8(b)(4)(D).[2]

---

[1] *See, e.g., International Printing and Graphic Communications Union, Local 51 (Format
Printing Co.),* 266 NLRB 7, 112 LRRM 1193 (1983) (union official said that if union members
lost work union "would pull the whole damn shop").

[2] *Brockton Newspaper Guild (Enterprise Pub. Co.),* 275 NLRB No. 22, 119 LRRM 1008
(1985); *National Ass'n of Broadcast Employees & Technicians (Metromedia, Inc.),* 255 NLRB
372, 106 LRRM 1367 (1981); *Sheet Metal Workers, Local 49 (Los Alamos Constructors, Inc.),*
206 NLRB 473, 84 LRRM 1333 (1973).

In jurisdictional dispute cases the focus generally is not on the proscribed means, but on the proscribed object—i.e., was the challenged union's conduct undertaken in pursuit of a work assignment or some other objective? The Board has held that Sections 8(b)(4)(D) and 10(k) are designed "to resolve competing claims between rival groups of employees, and not to arbitrate disputes between a union and an employer where no such competing claims are involved."[3] Applying this principle, the Supreme Court has determined that "the applicability of Section 8(b)(4)(D) is premised on conflicting claims of unions or groups of employees for the same job."[4] Given this broad definition, jurisdictional disputes have been found in a variety of factual settings. For example, such disputes have been found to exist:

- Where two unions have collective bargaining agreements with one employer and each claims the work for its members;[5]

- Where employees in two separate craft groups belonging to the same local union present competing claims to the disputed work;[6]

- Where employees in two separate local unions belonging to the same international union present competing claims to the disputed work;[7]

- Where the competing claims to the disputed work are made by a union and by unrepresented employees;[8]

- Where the competing claims to the disputed work are made by groups of employees working for different employers;[9]

- Where the employer against whom the threats are made does not employ any of the competing employees, but nevertheless has the authority to determine who will perform the work.[10]

---

[3]*Highway Truckdrivers, Local 107 (Safeway Stores, Inc.)*, 134 NLRB 1320, 1322, 49 LRRM 1343 (1961).

[4]*NLRB v. Plasterers' Local 79 (Tex. State Tile & Terrazzo Co.)*, 404 U.S. 116, 135, 78 LRRM 2897, 2904 (1971).

[5]*E.g., New Orleans Typographical Union, Local 17 v. NLRB*, 368 F.2d 755, 63 LRRM 2467 (5th Cir. 1966); *St. Louis Stereotypers' Union No. 8 (Pulitzer Pub. Co.)*, 152 NLRB 1232, 59 LRRM 1292 (1965). A legitimate jurisdictional dispute exists even when the union making the threat is the one already performing the work. *Cleveland Mailers' Union No. 12 (Art Gravure Corp.)*, 223 NLRB 1402, 92 LRRM 1152 (1962).

[6]*E.g., Bricklayers, Local 1 (Shelby Marble & Tile Co.)*, 188 NLRB 148, 76 LRRM 1280 (1971).

[7]*E.g., Electrical Workers, Local 211 (Sammons Communications)*, 271 NLRB 330, 116 LRRM 1361 (1984); *Bricklayers Union, Local 2 (Decora, Inc.)*, 152 NLRB 278, 59 LRRM 1065 (1965).

[8]*E.g., Millwrights Local 1026 (Intercounty Constr. Corp.)*, 266 NLRB 1049, 113 LRRM 1090 (1983); *Communications Workers (Mountain States Tel. & Tel. Co.)*, 118 NLRB 1104, 40 LRRM 1320 (1957).

[9]*E.g., Electrical Workers, Local 3 (Western Elec. Co.)*, 141 NLRB 888, 52 LRRM 1419 (1963).

[10]*E.g., Teamsters, Local 282 (Active Fire Sprinkler Corp.)*, 233 NLRB 1230, 97 LRRM 1118 (1977) (strike against general contractor to reassign work from a union with whom it has a collective bargaining agreement to a subcontractor employing individuals represented by striking union).

Not all union demands that disputed work be assigned to its members, however, are encompassed by Sections 8(b)(4)(D) and 10(k). For example, jurisdictional disputes do not exist:

- Where the union attempts to force an employer to make assignments which conform to an order or certification previously issued by the Board;[11]
- Where the disputed work is performed by supervisors, managers, or other persons who are not statutory employees;[12]
- Where the union's object is representational or recognitional;[13]
- Where the union's object is to restore lost jobs by demanding reinstatement of discharged employees, or by protesting the employer's change in working conditions which resulted in the termination of union members;[14]
- Where the union's object is to retain bargaining unit work by preventing it from being transferred to another employer;[15]
- Where the two competing groups of employees agree on the appropriate assignment of the work, but the employer does not comply with that agreement.[16]

The Board thus will exercise its authority under Sections 8(b)(4)(D) and 10(k) in situations where two or more groups of employees are competing for the same work, but will refrain from interfering when the union's object is recognitional or representational in nature, or where it is attempting to apply traditional primary economic pressure.

§19.2   Disclaimers of Interest

As noted above, Section 8(b)(4)(D) applies only when there are competing claims for the work.[17] Accordingly, the Board has held that there is no work assignment dispute when a union either has

---

[11]This object is expressly excepted from the Sec. 8(b)(4)(D) prohibitions.

[12]*E.g., Teamsters Local 236 (Maxon Constr. Co.)*, 194 NLRB 594, 79 LRRM 1019 (1971). *But see Bricklayers, Local 44 (Raymond Int'l)*, 207 NLRB 354, 85 LRRM 1088 (1973) (competing claims found where work assigned to nonsupervisory foremen).

[13]*E.g., Communications Workers (Mountain States Tel. & Tel. Co.)*, 118 NLRB 1104, 40 LRRM 1320 (1957) (union not seeking to have work assigned to particular employees, but only to be recognized as representative of employees to whom work is assigned).

[14]*E.g., Chauffeurs Local 331 (Bulletin Co.)*, 139 NLRB 1391, 51 LRRM 1490 (1962) (picketing to protest jobs lost when subcontract terminated); *Highway Truckdrivers, Local 107 (Safeway Stores, Inc.)*, 134 NLRB 1320, 49 LRRM 1343 (1961) (union attempt to retrieve jobs reassigned to other plants); *Electrical Workers, Local 292 (Franklin Broadcasting Co.)*, 126 NLRB 1212, 45 LRRM 1455 (1960) (protest to obtain reinstatement of employees and to persuade employer to sign new contract not a work assignment claim).

[15]*National Maritime Union (Puerto Rico Marine Mgt., Inc.)*, 227 NLRB 1081, 95 LRRM 1291 (1977); *Chicago Web Printing Pressmen, Local 7 (Metropolitan Printing Co.)*, 209 NLRB 320, 85 LRRM 1586 (1974).

[16]*Teamsters, Local 70 (Hills Transp. Co.)*, 136 NLRB 1086, 49 LRRM 1930 (1962).

[17]*NLRB v. Plasterers' Local 79 (Tex. State Tile & Terrazzo Co.)*, 404 U.S. 116, 78 LRRM 2897 (1971).

made no claim to the disputed work or has renounced a prior claim.[18] In determining whether the disclaimer or renunciation is valid, the Board will examine all the surrounding circumstances including its timing[19] and whether the union thereafter engages in conduct inconsistent with its expressed lack of interest in the work. If the disclaimer is found to be "hollow," it will be ignored and the Board will proceed to determine the dispute.[20]

In some cases employees will continue to claim the disputed work notwithstanding disclaimers by their union. The Board has determined, however, that the mere fact that individual employees continue to press their claims for the work in dispute is not inconsistent with an effective disclaimer by their union so long as the disclaimer is clear and unequivocal.[21] If, however, the disclaimer is a sham and the union does nothing to discourage the employees from continuing to press their claims, the Board may discount the disclaimer and proceed to determine the dispute.[22]

An agreement by the union merely to refrain from further Section 8(b)(4)(D) conduct is not an effective disclaimer,[23] nor is a disclaimer limited to a particular construction jobsite effective in situations where there is an ongoing work assignment dispute as evidenced by similar union conduct against the same employer regarding the same type of work at other jobsites.[24]

Processing Jurisdictional Dispute Claims

§19.3 Notice of Charge Filed

Whenever a charge alleging a Section 8(b)(4)(D) violation is filed, the regional office promptly will serve a copy of the charge and a

---

[18]*Sheet Metal Workers, Local 465 (Thorpe Insulation Co.)*, 198 NLRB 1245, 81 LRRM 1131 (1972); *Carpet Layers Local 1905 (Southwestern Floor Co.)*, 143 NLRB 251, 53 LRRM 1324 (1963); *Lathers Int'l Union, Local 328 (Acoustics & Specialities, Inc.)*, 139 NLRB 598, 51 LRRM 1345 (1962); *see* NLRB Casehandling Manual ¶10208.

[19]The Board's prior rule that a disclaimer would be ineffective if made after a Sec. 10(k) notice of hearing had issued, or if made at the 10(k) hearing itself (*cf. Laborers' Int'l Union, Local 935 (Campbell Constr. Co.)*, 194 NLRB 367, 78 LRRM 1619 (1971) (disclaimer does not alter nature of jurisdictional dispute)) was abandoned in *Painters' Local 1396 (C.L. Wolff & Sons Printing Co.)*, 246 NLRB 442, 102 LRRM 1591 (1979).

[20]*Carpenters, Local 102 (Meiswinkel Interiors)*, 260 NLRB 972, 109 LRRM 1245 (1982).

[21]*Teamsters Local 85 (United Cal. Express & Storage Co.)*, 236 NLRB 157, 98 LRRM 1186 (1978), cited in NLRB Casehandling Manual ¶10208.

[22]In *Teamsters Local 85 (United Cal. Express & Storage Co.)*, 236 NLRB 157, 98 LRRM 1186 (1978), the Board held the union's disclaimer valid because while the disclaiming union routinely transmitted grievances of the employees to the employer even after disclaimer, it did not support the grievances and indicated that its official position was to support the rival union's claim.

[23]General Counsel Memorandum No. 73-82 (December 3, 1973) at 7. Copies may be obtained from the Board's Information Division.

[24]*Cf. Journeymen Local 189 (Kahoe Air Balance Co.)*, 197 NLRB 159, 80 LRRM 1374 (1972).

"Notice of Charge Filed" upon all parties.[25] (See Exhibit 100.) The "parties" include the charged union or unions, the charging party, the employer making the work assignment (if not the charging party), and any other union or group of employees claiming the disputed work.[26] If in light of the surrounding circumstances the regional director concludes that Section 10(l) injunctive relief is appropriate, a petition for submission to the appropriate federal district court will be prepared on a priority basis.[27]

The Notice of Charge Filed not only apprises the charged union that the charge has been filed, but further indicates that the Board itself will proceed under Section 10(k) to determine the underlying jurisdictional dispute unless, within 10 days of receipt of the Notice, satisfactory evidence is submitted that the parties either have actually adjusted their dispute or have agreed upon a method for doing so voluntarily.

§19.4 Voluntary Adjustments

If the Board has satisfactory evidence that the parties have adjusted their dispute through voluntary procedures, or have agreed upon a method for doing so, it will either refrain from issuing a notice of a Section 10(k) hearing or will quash the notice if already issued.[28] The Board thus encourages the parties to resolve the dispute privately before exercising its own authority.

An "agreed-upon method" is one to which all parties to the dispute are bound—it must bind the employer who has assigned the disputed work as well as all disputing unions or employee groups.[29] Thus, a contractual obligation between an employer and one of the disputing unions to submit work assignment disputes to arbitration does not constitute an agreed-upon method if the other disputing union is not bound by the same contract.[30] Even if the employer has

---

[25]NLRB Rules and Regulations §102.89; NLRB Statements of Procedure §101.31; NLRB Casehandling Manual ¶10209.

[26]NLRB Casehandling Manual ¶10209. The charging party need not be the employer making the work assignment. *Plumbers Local 195 (Gulf Oil Corp.)*, 275 NLRB No. 69, 119 LRRM 115 (1985).

[27]NLRB Rules and Regulations §102.89; NLRB Statements of Procedure §101.32. Injunctions in the context of Sec. 8(b)(4)(D) proceedings are discussed further at §§21.1–21.7.

[28]*See NLRB v. Plasterers' Local Union No. 79 (Tex. State Tile & Terrazzo Co.)*, 404 U.S. 116, 78 LRRM 2897 (1971); NLRB Rules and Regulations §§102.90, 102.93; NLRB Statements of Procedure §101.33; NLRB Casehandling Manual ¶10210.

[29]*NLRB v. Plasterers' Local 79 (Tex. State Tile & Terrazzo Co.)*, 404 U.S. 116, 78 LRRM 2897 (1971); NLRB Casehandling Manual ¶10212.3.

[30]*E.g., Machinists, Dist. Lodge 27 (Joseph E. Seagram & Sons, Inc.)*, 198 NLRB 407, 80 LRRM 1642 (1972). Similarly, grievance-arbitration procedures which do not bind the employer, *e.g., Teamsters Local 294 (John V. Warren, Inc.)*, 203 NLRB 1255, 83 LRRM 1268 (1973), or which do not bind groups of unrepresented employees claiming the work, *e.g., Laborers Local 231 (C. Iber & Sons, Inc.)*, 204 NLRB 37, 83 LRRM 1278 (1973), will not qualify as agreed-upon methods. It is possible, however, that parties to a dispute may establish an agreed-upon method on an *ad hoc* basis by simply agreeing to be bound by the grievance procedures contained in a contract which the employer has with one of the disputing unions. General Counsel Memorandum 73-82 at 10.

UNITED STATES OF AMERICA
BEFORE THE NATIONAL LABOR RELATIONS BOARD
REGION 5

Local 007, United Computer Operators
  International Union

                          Union
        and

Janco Computer Services, Inc.   Case No. 5-CD-100

                      Charging Party

        and

International Alliance of
  High-Tech Workers, Local 1212

                    Party In Interest

                 NOTICE OF CHARGE FILED

        PLEASE TAKE NOTICE, that pursuant to Section 10(b) of the National
Labor Relations Act, as amended, a charge has been filed alleging the
above-named labor organization, United Computer Operators International
Union, Local 007, has engaged in an unfair labor practice within the
meaning of paragraph (4)(D) of Section 8(b) of the Act. A copy of the
charge is attached hereto.

        YOU ARE FURTHER NOTIFIED, pursuant to Section 10(k) of the Act, that,
unless within 10 days after receipt of this notice of charge filed the
parties to the dispute alleged in said charge submit to the undersigned
satisfactory evidence that they have adjusted said dispute or have agreed
upon methods for the voluntary adjustment thereof, the Board is empowered
and directed to hear and determine the dispute out of which the said unfair
labor practice charge arose if it is determined that the said charge has
merit.

        IN WITNESS WHEREOF, the undersigned Regional Director has caused this
notice of charge filed to be signed at Baltimore, Maryland, on this 2nd day
of January, 1986.

                        LOUIS J. D'AMICO, REGIONAL DIRECTOR
                        NATIONAL LABOR RELATIONS BOARD, REGION 5
                        CANDLER BUILDING - SUITE 4200
                        109 MARKET PLACE
                        BALTIMORE, MARYLAND 21202

CASE ASSIGNED TO: Mr. David R. Levinson
TELEPHONE NUMBER: (202) 254-3238

Exhibit 100.   Notice of Charge Filed in Jurisdictional Dispute Proceeding

separately committed to arbitrate work assignment disputes with each one of the competing unions, such commitments do not constitute agreed-upon methods under Section 10(k) in the absence of one agreement which binds all parties.[31] Similarly, a method of resolution which is binding on the competing unions and a general contractor will not be sufficient absent consent of the subcontractor with control over the disputed work.[32]

If an agreed-upon method of resolution is found to exist, the 8(b)(4)(D) charge will be held in abeyance pending culmination of the private proceedings.[33] If the regional director subsequently is informed that the dispute has been resolved and that the charged union is abiding by the decision, the charge will be dismissed absent withdrawal by the charging party.[34] If, on the other hand, the agreed-upon method is not successful either because the parties have failed to use it or because the charged union refuses to be bound by the determination, the normal procedure is not for the Board to attempt to resolve the dispute in a Section 10(k) proceeding, but rather to issue a Section 8(b)(4)(D) complaint and process the case as a normal unfair labor practice.[35]

§19.5 Notice of Section 10(k) Hearing

In cases where the Section 8(b)(4)(D) charge appears to have merit and the parties do not submit satisfactory evidence that they have voluntarily resolved the dispute or have agreed upon a method for doing so, the Board will proceed to determine the dispute itself

---

[31]*Cf., General Teamsters Local 470 (Philco-Ford Corp.)*, 203 NLRB 592, 83 LRRM 1180 (1973) (separate agreements which conflict are not "agreed-upon" methods).

[32]*Plasterers' Local 502 (Advanced Terrazzo & Tile Co.)*, 272 NLRB No. 121, 117 LRRM 1339 (1984) (agreement by four competing labor organizations to use "composite" crew not an agreed-upon method in absence of employer's willingness to be bound); *Carpenters, Local 1622 (O.R. Karst)*, 139 NLRB 591, 51 LRRM 1379 (1962). Jurisdictional disputes arise most frequently in the construction industry. The AFL-CIO Building and Construction Trades Department has attempted over the years to develop with construction contractors procedures for the private resolution of such disputes. The National Joint Board for the Settlement of Jurisdictional Disputes in the Construction Industry (NJB) was replaced in June 1973 by the Impartial Jurisdictional Disputes Board (IJDB). Dissatisfaction on the part of both union and management officials with IJDB decisions led to a suspension of IJDB proceedings in June 1981. After a moratorium of more than three years, the Building and Construction Trades Department and several construction contractor associations late in 1984 reached tentative agreement on a Plan for the Settlement of Jurisdictional Disputes which provides for expedited arbitration of work assignment disputes.

[33]NLRB Rules and Regulations §102.93; NLRB Statements of Procedure §101.33; NLRB Casehandling Manual ¶10212.4.

[34]NLRB Rules and Regulations §102.93; NLRB Statements of Procedure §101.33; NLRB Casehandling Manual ¶10212.5. If the dispute is resolved by assigning the work to employees represented by the charged union, the complaint will be dismissed irrespective of whether the employer has complied with the determination. NLRB Rules and Regulations §102.93; NLRB Statements of Procedure §101.33; NLRB Casehandling Manual ¶10214.1.

[35]NLRB Rules and Regulations §102.93; NLRB Casehandling Manual ¶10214.1. *See Electrical Workers Local 26 (McCloskey & Co.)*, 147 NLRB 1498, 56 LRRM 1402 (1964).

by issuing to the parties[36] a notice of hearing.[37] (See Exhibit 101.)
The notice contains a simple statement of the issues involved in the
dispute along with a statement of the time and place of the hearing
to be held before a hearing officer not less than 10 days after service
of the notice.[38] Cases involving work performed on missile or space
sites, or otherwise affecting the national defense, may be handled on
an expedited basis.[39]

In cases where Section 10(l) injunctive relief is pursued, the notice of hearing generally is issued within five days of the date upon
which such relief first is sought.[40] If after the notice of hearing is
issued the parties agree upon a method for resolving their dispute,
the notice of hearing will be withdrawn by the regional director even
though the underlying Section 8(b)(4)(D) charge remains pending.[41]
If, on the other hand, the parties submit evidence that there has been
an actual adjustment of the dispute, the notice will be withdrawn
and the charge generally will be dismissed.[42]

§19.6 Section 10(k) Hearing

(a) *Nature of Proceedings.* Section 10(k) hearings closely resemble representation hearings.[43] They are nonadversarial in nature,[44] are held before a hearing officer,[45] and to the extent applicable
conform to representation hearing procedures.[46] (See Exhibit 102.)
The primary role of the hearing officer is to incorporate into the record
all pertinent facts necessary to enable the Board to determine whether
there is reasonable cause to believe that the charged union has

---

[36]*See* NLRB Casehandling Manual ¶10210.1 for the definition of parties who should be
afforded notice.

[37]NLRB Rules and Regulations §102.90; NLRB Statements of Procedure §101.33; NLRB
Casehandling Manual ¶10210.

[38]Sec. 10(k) and NLRB Rules and Regulations §102.90 indicate that the hearing shall be
scheduled for a date not less than 10 days following service of the notice of the filing of the
charge. NLRB Casehandling Manual ¶10210.2a notes, however, that Board practice is to schedule hearings not less than 10 days after the service of the notice of *hearing.*

[39]*See* NLRB Rules and Regulations §102.90 and NLRB Statements of Procedure §101.35
(elimination of briefs; procedure for expedited briefing); NLRB Statements of Procedure §101.33
and NLRB Casehandling Manual ¶10210.2b (hearings held less than 11 days after notice);
NLRB Casehandling Manual ¶10210.3 (expedited hearing transcript).

[40]NLRB Rules and Regulations §102.90; NLRB Casehandling Manual ¶10210.1.

[41]*See* NLRB Casehandling Manual ¶¶10210.4, 10212.4.

[42]*Id.* at ¶10212.5b.

[43]Representation hearings are discussed in chapter 7. The Supreme Court has held that
Sec. 10(k) hearings are not "adjudications" within the meaning of the Administrative Procedure
Act, and therefore need not conform with the procedural requirements of Sec. 5 of that Act.
International Tel. & Tel. Corp. v. Electrical Workers, Local 134, 419 U.S. 428, 88 LRRM 2227
(1975).

[44]NLRB Statements of Procedure §101.34.

[45]*Id.*; NLRB Rules and Regulations §102.90. NLRB Casehandling Manual ¶10210.5 indicates that the designated hearing officer "should not be the same person who investigated
the charge, who acted as attorney for the General Counsel in a companion [secondary boycott]
case based on the same facts, or who may prosecute the [Section 8(b)(4)(D)] unfair labor practice
case which may arise thereafter."

[46]NLRB Rules and Regulations §102.90.

UNITED STATES OF AMERICA
BEFORE THE NATIONAL LABOR RELATIONS BOARD
FIFTH REGION

Local 007, United Computer Operators
International Union

        Union

    and   Case No. 5–CD–100

Janco Computer Services, Inc.

       Charging Party

    and

International Alliance of High-Tech
Workers, Local 1212

       Party In Interest

NOTICE OF HEARING

PLEASE TAKE NOTICE that on the 2nd day of May, 1986, at 11:00 o'clock in the forenoon, Eastern Standard Time, in a hearing room of the National Labor Relations Board, Fifth Region, 109 Market Place, Suite 4200, Baltimore, Maryland 21202, pursuant to Section 10(k) of the National Labor Relations Act, a hearing will be conducted before a Hearing Officer of the National Labor Relations Board upon the dispute alleged in the Charge attached to the Notice of Charge Filed issued in this matter on January 2, 1986. At the hearing, the parties will have the right to appear in person or otherwise and give testimony.

The dispute in this case concerns the assignment of the following tasks:

The installation, maintenance, and repair of all computers and related equipment at the Janco Computer Services, Inc., facility, 8181 Greensboro Drive, McLean, Virginia 22102.

IN WITNESS WHEREOF, the undersigned Regional Director, on behalf of the Board, has caused this Notice of Hearing to be signed at Baltimore, Maryland, on this 2d day of April, 1986.

LOUIS J. D'AMICO, REGIONAL DIRECTOR
NATIONAL LABOR RELATIONS BOARD, REGION 5
CANDLER BUILDING – SUITE 4200
109 MARKET PLACE
BALTIMORE, MARYLAND 21202

Exhibit 101.   Notice of Hearing in Jurisdictional Dispute Proceeding

FORM NLRB-4899
(8-63)

10(k) Cases

STATEMENT OF STANDARD PROCEDURES IN FORMAL HEARINGS HELD BEFORE THE NATIONAL LABOR RELATIONS BOARD PURSUANT TO CHARGES FILED UNDER SECTION 10(k) OF THE NATIONAL LABOR RELATIONS ACT, AS AMENDED

The hearing will be conducted before a Hearing Officer of the National Labor Relations Board.

Parties may be represented by an attorney or other representatives and present evidence relevant to the issues. *(Copies of exhibits should be supplied to the Hearing Officer and other parties at the time the exhibit is offered in evidence.)*

The 10(k) hearing is a nonadversary factfinding hearing and the technical rules of evidence are not controlling. The 10(k) hearing procedure shall conform, insofar as applicable, to the procedures set forth in Sections 102.64 to 102.68, inclusive, of the Rules and Regulations of the National Labor Relations Board and the parties' attention is also called to Sections 102.89 through 102.93, inclusive, of those Regulations.

An official reporter will make the only official transcript of the proceedings and all citations in briefs or arguments must refer to the official record. After the close of the hearing, one or more of the parties may wish to have corrections made in the record. All such proposed corrections, either by way of stipulation or motion, should be forwarded to the Board in Washington instead of to the Hearing Officer, inasmuch as the Hearing Officer has no power to make any rulings in connection with the case after the hearing is closed. All matter that is spoken in the hearing will be recorded by the official reporter while the hearing is in session. In the event that any party wishes to make off-the-record remarks, requests to make such remarks should be directed to the Hearing Officer and not to the official reporter.

Statements of reasons in support of motions or objections should be as concise as possible. Objections and exceptions may upon appropriate request be permitted to stand to an entire line of questioning. Automatic exceptions will be allowed to all adverse rulings.

An original and two copies of all motions submitted during the hearing shall be served on the other parties.

The sole objective of the Hearing Officer is to ascertain the respective positions of the parties and to obtain a full and complete factual record upon which the duties under Section 10(k) of the National Labor Relations Act may be discharged by the Board. It may become necessary for the Hearing Officer to ask questions, to call witnesses, and to explore avenues with respect to matters not raised by the parties. The services of the Hearing Officer are equally at the disposal of all parties to the proceedings in developing the material evidence.

Upon the close of the hearing, the proceeding will be transferred to the Board and the Board will proceed either forthwith upon the record, or after oral argument, or the submission of briefs, or further hearing, to determine the dispute or make other disposition of the matter. Should any party desire to file a brief with the Board, eight copies thereof shall be filed with the Board at Washington, D.C., within 7 days after the close of the hearing: **Provided, however,** that in cases involving the national defense and so designated in the notice of hearing no briefs shall be filed, and the parties, after the close of the evidence, may argue orally upon the record their respective contentions and positions: **Provided further,** that in cases involving the national defense, upon application for leave to file briefs expeditiously made to the Board in Washington, D.C., after the close of the hearing, the Board may for good cause shown grant such leave and thereupon specify the time for filing. Immediately upon such filing, a copy shall be served on the other parties. Proof of such service must be filed with the Board simultaneously with the briefs. Such brief shall be printed or otherwise legibly duplicated: **Provided, however,** that carbon copies of typewritten matter shall not be filed and if submitted will not be accepted. Request for extension of time in which to file a brief shall be in writing and must be received by the Board in Washington, D.C., 3 days prior to the due date with copies thereof served on the other parties. No reply brief may be filed except upon special leave of the Board.

As provided in Section 102.112 of the Board's Rules, service on all parties of a request for an extension of time shall be made in the same manner as that utilized in filing the paper with the Board; however, when filing with the Board is accomplished by personal service, the other parties shall be promptly notified of such action by telephone, followed by service of a copy by mail or telegraph.

An exhibit number may be reserved for posthearing submission of exhibits by stipulation of the parties.

Any party shall be entitled, upon request, to a reasonable period at the close of the hearing for oral argument, which shall be included in the stenographic report of the hearing. In the absence of a request, the Hearing Officer may ask for oral argument if at the close of the hearing it is believed that such arguments would be beneficial to the Board's understanding of the contentions of the parties and the issues involved.

Voluntary adjustments consistent with the policies of the Act reduce Government expenditures and promote amity in labor relations. Upon request, the Hearing Officer will afford reasonable opportunity during the hearing for discussions between the parties if adjustment of the jurisdictional dispute appears possible.

Exhibit 102.   Statement of Procedures in Formal Jurisdictional Dispute Proceedings   (Form NLRB-4899)

violated Section 8(b)(4)(D), and if so, to determine the dispute itself.[47] The parties are permitted to present their positions, introduce evidence in support of their contentions, and argue orally on the record before the hearing officer.[48]

At the close of the hearing, the hearing officer prepares a written report. Unless the case is unusual or complicated, the report should be prepared within 48 hours of the close of the hearing.[49] As with the hearing officer's report in a representation proceeding,[50] the Section 10(k) hearing report analyzes the issues and the evidence, but makes no recommendations or findings.[51] Also consistent with treatment afforded hearing officers' reports in representation proceedings, the Section 10(k) report is considered by the Board to be an administrative document and therefore not served on the parties or their representatives.[52]

Unlike most representation proceedings, however, the final determination is made by the Board rather than by the regional director. Accordingly, upon the close of the hearing the case is transferred to the Board.[53] Briefs may be filed by the parties as a matter of right within seven days after the close of the hearing.[54] In cases involving national defense, the normal procedure is for the parties to dispense with the filing of briefs and instead to argue their positions orally on the record. For good cause shown, however, the Board may authorize the filing of posthearing briefs in national defense cases on an expedited basis.[55] Special permission also must be acquired in all cases for the filing of reply briefs.[56] The Board's determination of the dispute thus is based upon the evidence taken at the hearing, the hearing officer's report, and the posthearing oral arguments and briefs, if any, offered by the parties.[57]

(b) Board Determination of Dispute.   Prior to 1961, the NLRB initially confined itself to determining whether the employer's assignment of the work violated any Board order or certification or any contract between the employer and the striking union. If not, the Board, by a negative determination, would hold that the union was

---

[47]*See* NLRB Statements of Procedure §101.34; NLRB Casehandling Manual ¶10210.5.

[48]NLRB Statements of Procedure §101.34. Once the hearing opens, however, the parties are precluded from making any unauthorized *ex parte* communications with members of the Board or their staffs. NLRB Rules and Regulations §102.128(d).

[49]NLRB Casehandling Manual ¶10210.6.

[50]See discussion at §7.9.

[51]NLRB Statements of Procedure §101.34; NLRB Casehandling Manual ¶10210.6.

[52]NLRB Casehandling Manual ¶10210.6.

[53]NLRB Rules and Regulations §102.90; NLRB Statements of Procedure §101.34.

[54]NLRB Rules and Regulations §102.90; NLRB Statements of Procedure §101.35; *see* NLRB Casehandling Manual ¶10210.7.

[55]NLRB Rules and Regulations §102.90; NLRB Statements of Procedure §101.35; see also note 39 *supra*.

[56]NLRB Rules and Regulations §102.90.

[57]NLRB Statements of Procedure §101.35.

not lawfully entitled to strike or picket to force the assignment of the disputed work to its members. In 1961, however, the United States Supreme Court held that the Board's approach to Section 10(k) proceedings was wrong and henceforth the Board must decide the underlying dispute and make affirmative awards of the disputed work.[58] The Court stated: "It is the Board's responsibility and duty to decide which of two or more employee groups claiming the right to perform certain work tasks is right and then specifically to award such tasks in accordance with its decision." The award is to be made on the basis of such criteria as custom, tradition, and the like "generally used by arbitrators, unions, employers, joint boards or others in wrestling with (the) problem" of jurisdictional disputes.

Following the Supreme Court's decision, the Board now makes an "affirmative" work assignment determination in accordance with the Court's ruling. The Board has held that, in making jurisdictional awards as required by the Court, it could not and would not formulate general rules and that each case would have to be decided on its own facts.[59] The Board said it would consider all relevant factors in determining who is entitled to the work in dispute, such as, the skills and work involved,[60] certifications by the Board, company and industry practice,[61] agreements between unions and between employers and unions,[62] awards of arbitrators,[63] joint boards, and the AFL-CIO in the same or related cases, the assignment made by the employer, and the efficient operation of the employer's business.[64]

While these are the factors most commonly relied upon by the Board, they are not exclusive. The Board also has made work assignments on the basis that the work in dispute replaces work previously performed by one of the competing groups,[65] on the basis of safety considerations,[66] and on the availability of training programs offered by one of the unions.[67] The Board will not, however, entertain

---

[58]*NLRB v. Radio and Television Broadcast Eng'rs, Local 1212 (Columbia Broadcasting Sys.)*, 364 U.S. 573, 47 LRRM 2332 (1961).

[59]*Machinists Lodge 1743 (J.A. Jones Constr. Co.)*, 135 NLRB 1402, 49 LRRM 1684 (1962).

[60]*E.g., Plumbers, Local 201 (Shaker, Travis & Quinn, Inc.)*, 271 NLRB 650, 117 LRRM 1017 (1984); *Mine Workers Dist. 30 (Samoyed Energy Co.)*, 271 NLRB 191, 116 LRRM 1396 (1984).

[61]*E.g., Electrical Workers, Local 3 (Telecom Plus)*, 271 NLRB 739, 117 LRRM 1009 (1984); *Asbestos Workers, Local 4 (Cowper, Inc.)*, 202 NLRB 832, 83 LRRM 1029 (1973).

[62]*E.g., Carpenters, Local 626 (Cassidy Plastering Co.)*, 198 NLRB 446, 80 LRRM 1672 (1972).

[63]*E.g., New York Mailers Union No. 6 (New York News, Inc.)*, 270 NLRB 303,116 LRRM 1200 (1984).

[64]*E.g., Newspaper & Mail Deliverers' Union (New York News, Inc.)*, 270 NLRB 307, 116 LRRM 1271 (1984); *Brewers Local 6 (Anheuser-Busch, Inc.)*, 270 NLRB 219, 116 LRRM 1249 (1984).

[65]*Philadelphia Typographical Union, Local 2 (Phila. Inquirer)*, 142 NLRB 36, 52 LRRM 1504 (1963). *But see New Orleans Typographical Union, Local 17 (E.P. Rivas, Inc.)*, 147 NLRB 191, 56 LRRM 1169 (1964) (although work in dispute replaced work performed by one group, another group received the assignment).

[66]*E.g., Electrical Workers, Local 103 (Siemens Corp.)*, 227 NLRB 685, 94 LRRM 1388 (1976).

[67]*Cleveland Typographical Union 53 (Sherwin-Williams Co.)*, 224 NLRB 583, 92 LRRM 1319 (1976).

in a jurisdictional dispute proceeding claims that certain employees should be disqualified from receiving the disputed work because their union engages in racial discrimination.[68]

In the vast majority of cases, the Board awards the work to the group of employees preferred by the employer. In its opinions the Board has emphasized that "an employer's assignment of disputed work cannot be made the touchstone in determining a jurisdictional dispute."[69] Nevertheless, the agency has acknowledged that it consistently has placed great weight on the factors of contract coverage and employer preference in making work assignment awards.[70]

The Board's work assignment award is made directly to the employees rather than to their union or other representative. The scope of the award generally is limited to the specific work and jobsite mentioned in the notice of hearing. In situations where there is evidence that the dispute is likely to recur elsewhere, the award may be broadened to encompass any jobsite where the territorial jurisdictions of the competing organizations coincide.[71] Similarly, completion of the work which prompted the filing of the charge will not render the dispute moot in situations where the dispute has occurred in the past and there is nothing to indicate that such disputes will not occur again in the future.[72]

§19.7   Posthearing Procedures

(a) Compliance With Determination.   If the parties following issuance of the award submit to the regional director satisfactory evidence of compliance with the determination, the underlying Section 8(b)(4)(D) charge will be dismissed.[73] The charging party thereafter may appeal the dismissal to the Board.[74]

(b) Noncompliance With Determination.   If the parties fail to submit satisfactory evidence of compliance with the determination, the regional director issues a Section 8(b)(4)(D) complaint and notice of hearing.[75] The case thereafter is processed in the same manner as

---

[68]*Plumbers Local 393 (Hall-Way Contracting Co.)*, 232 NLRB 644, 97 LRRM 1153 (1977).

[69]*Millwrights Local 1102 (Don Cartage)*, 160 NLRB 1061, 1078, 63 LRRM 1085, 1091 (1966).

[70]*Id.*, reconsidered *sua sponte* at 244 NLRB 275, 102 LRRM 1134 (1979).

[71]*E.g., Drywall Tapers, Local 2006 (Painting & Drywall Contractors)*, 248 NLRB 626, 103 LRRM 1427 (1980). *But see Laborers' Dist. Council (Paschen Contractors)*, 270 NLRB 327, 116 LRRM 1373 (1984) (broad award denied where no evidence respondent likely to resort to unlawful conduct elsewhere to claim work).

[72]*E.g., Iron Workers Local 350 (Cornell & Co.)*, 271 NLRB 1182, 117 LRRM 1115 (1984).

[73]*See* NLRB Rules and Regulations §102.91; NLRB Statements of Procedure §101.36; NLRB Casehandling Manual ¶10214.

[74]NLRB Casehandling Manual ¶10214. Appeal procedures are discussed in §12.12.

[75]NLRB Rules and Regulations §102.91; NLRB Statements of Procedure §101.36; NLRB Casehandling Manual ¶10214.1. As discussed at §19.4 *supra*, a complaint also is issued when one of the parties refuses to honor an agreed-upon method for resolving the dispute.

any other unfair labor practice proceeding.[76] If the Board, however, determines that employees who are represented by the charged union are entitled to the work, the charge is dismissed by the regional director whether or not the employer complies with the determination.[77]

(c) Judicial Review of Determination. The Board's decision, just as in any other unfair labor practice case, is subject to court review.[78] In cases where a Section 10(k) proceeding has been held and an unfair labor practice proceeding follows, the record in the Section 10(k) proceeding and the resulting determination of the Board become part of the unfair labor practice record and thus subject to examination by the court upon review.[79]

---

[76]NLRB Rules and Regulation §102.91. *See, e.g., Carpenters Local 1102 (Int'l Indus. Contracting Corp.)*, 271 NLRB 414, 117 LRRM 1141 (1984).

[77]NLRB Rules and Regulations §102.91; NLRB Statements of Procedure §101.36; NLRB Casehandling Manual ¶10214.1.

[78]Procedures for enforcement or review of Board unfair labor practice decisions are discussed at §§17.18–17.21.

[79]NLRB Rules and Regulations §102.92.

20

Picketing for Recognition or Organization

Section 8(b)(7) of the Act prohibits a labor organization which is not currently certified as the employees' bargaining representative from picketing or threatening to picket for the purpose of obtaining either recognition by the employer (recognitional picketing) or acceptance by the employees as their bargaining representative (organizational picketing)[1] whenever:

- The employer lawfully has recognized another union and the picketing occurs at a time when a representation election is not appropriate;[2]
- A valid representation election has been conducted by the Board within the preceding 12 months;[3] or
- The picketing has been conducted without a representation petition having been filed "within a reasonable period of time not to exceed thirty days from the commencement of such picketing."[4]

Enacted as part of the 1959 amendments to the Act, Section 8(b)(7) has been described by the Supreme Court as "a comprehensive code governing organizational strikes and picketing."[5] In comment-

---

[1]*See generally* THE DEVELOPING LABOR LAW at 23.

[2]Sec. 8(b)(7)(A).

[3]Sec. 8(b)(7)(B).

[4]Sec. 8(b)(7)(C). As discussed further *infra*, there are two provisos to subsection (C). Under the first proviso, if a timely representation petition has been filed, the Board is required to conduct an expedited election. (Neither a hearing by the regional director nor a showing of interest among the employees by the petitioner is required.) Under the second proviso, picketing or other publicity which truthfully advises the public (including consumers) that an employer does not employ members of, or have a contract with, a union shall not be regarded as unlawful unless an effect of such picketing is to cause an employee of another person not to perform services.

[5]*NLRB v. Drivers Local 639*, 362 U.S. 274, 291, 45 LRRM 2975, 2982 (1960).

ing upon the intended purpose of Section 8(b)(7), the Supreme Court has noted that

> "[t]he use of picketing was of particular concern as a method of coercion in three specific contexts: where employees had already selected another union representative, where employees had recently voted against a labor union, and where employees had not been given a chance to vote on the question of representation. Picketing in these circumstances was thought impermissibly to interfere with the employees' freedom of choice."[6]

Section 8(b)(7), therefore, reflects a strong congressional desire that disputes concerning representation rights be resolved through the Board's election procedures rather than through picketing.

Nature of Proscribed Conduct

§20.1 Picketing and Threats of Picketing

Not all conduct undertaken by a labor organization in support of recognitional or organizational goals is proscribed by Section 8(b)(7). The focus of that section is upon picketing and threats of picketing.

Union representatives patrolling the entrance to an employer's premises with picket signs conveying a recognitional or organizational message clearly are engaging in prohibited Section 8(b)(7) picketing. Neither the patrolling nor the picket signs, however, are essential. The placing of signs at the employer's entrance with union representatives stationed in cars or other shelter nearby has been held to constitute picketing.[7] In addition, signals to employees, customers, or other persons entering the employer's premises to take collective action against the employer can constitute picketing in the absence of written picket signs.[8] Handbilling also may constitute picketing in cases where other union conduct suggests that the purpose of the handbilling is not simply to convey information, but rather to induce collective action against the employer.[9]

---

[6]*NLRB v. Iron Workers Local 103 (Higdon Contracting Co.)*, 434 U.S. 335, 347, 97 LRRM 2333, 2338 (1978).

[7]*Teamsters Local 182 (Woodward Motors, Inc.)*, 135 NLRB 851, 49 LRRM 1576 (1962). *But see NLRB v. Furniture Workers (Jamestown Sterling Corp.)*, 337 F.2d 936, 57 LRRM 2347 (2d Cir. 1964) (court of appeals remanded case to Board to determine whether union representatives were so far out of sight that their conduct could not reasonably be characterized as picketing).

[8]*Teamsters Local 282 (Gen. Contractors Ass'n)*, 262 NLRB 528, 110 LRRM 1342 (1982); *District 30, United Mine Workers (Terry Elkhorn Mining Co.)*, 163 NLRB 562, 64 LRRM 1394 (1967).

[9]*Lawrence Typographical Union No. 570 (Kansas Color Press, Inc.)*, 169 NLRB 279, 67 LRRM 1166 (1968); *Lumber & Sawmill Workers, Local 2797 (Stolze Land & Lumber Co.)*, 156 NLRB 388, 61 LRRM 1046 (1965). *But see Teamsters Local 688 (Levitz Furniture Co.)*, 205 NLRB 1131, 84 LRRM 1103 (1973) (handbilling not designed to and which did not signal collective action does not constitute picketing).

Section 8(b)(7) prohibits threats to picket for recognitional or organizational purposes as well as actual picketing.[10] Threat cases have arisen most frequently in the context of attempts to organize guards by unions that are precluded by Section 9(b)(3) of the Act from being certified in a guard unit because they admit nonguards to membership.[11]

§20.2   Recognitional or Organizational Object

Section 8(b)(7) does not proscribe all picketing, but only picketing with an object of forcing or requiring an employer "to recognize or bargain with a labor organization," or forcing or requiring employees to select the labor organization as their bargaining representative. Accordingly, it is not unlawful under Section 8(b)(7) for a union to picket in order to obtain the reinstatement of a discharged employee;[12] to force the employer to conform to "area standards" wage rates and fringe benefits;[13] or to protest the employer's commission of unfair labor practices—frequently Section 8(a)(5) refusals to bargain or refusals to honor negotiated labor contracts.[14] Picketing to enforce a Section 8(f) prehire agreement by a union which has not yet acquired majority support, however, is considered to be picketing for recognitional purposes under Section 8(b)(7).[15]

Union picketing often is conducted for multiple purposes. So long as "an" object of the picketing is recognitional or organizational, the picketing is unlawful notwithstanding the existence of other lawful reasons.[16] Labor organizations sometimes will attempt to disguise recognitional and organizational picketing with assertions that the object of picketing is for other, lawful reasons. The determination of whether an object of the picketing is recognition or organization is

---

[10]*Service Employees, Local 73 (A-1 Sec. Serv. Co.)*, 224 NLRB 434, 92 LRRM 1393 (1976); *see also Teamsters Local 710 (Univ. of Chicago)*, 274 NLRB No. 142, 118 LRRM 1514 (1985).

[11]*Service Employees, Local 73 (A-1 Sec. Serv. Co.)*, 224 NLRB 434, 92 LRRM 1393 (1976). *See also General Serv. Employees Union Local 73 (William Witsman)*, 240 NLRB 462, 100 LRRM 1477 (1979); *Teamsters Local 344 (Purolator Sec., Inc.)*, 228 NLRB 1379, 95 LRRM 1568 (1977). Section 9(b)(3) restrictions on the representation of guards are discussed at §1.11(b).

[12]*United Auto Workers Local 259 (Fanelli Ford Sales, Inc.)*, 133 NLRB 1468, 49 LRRM 1021 (1961).

[13]*Houston Bldg. & Constr. Trades Council (Claude Everett Constr. Co.)*, 136 NLRB 321, 49 LRRM 1757 (1962).

[14]*E.g., Building & Constr. Trades Council (Sullivan Elec. Co.)*, 146 NLRB 1086, 56 LRRM 1010 (1964).

[15]*NLRB v. Iron Workers Local 103 (Higdon Contracting Co.)*, 434 U.S. 335, 97 LRRM 2333 (1978). Sec. 8(f) authorizes an employer engaged primarily in the building and construction industry to enter into a contract with a union prior to the time that the union has acquired majority support. Until the union does acquire majority status, however, the agreement is voidable by the employer. Picketing by a minority union, therefore, is not deemed to be for the purpose of enforcing an existing contract, but rather for the purpose of acquiring bargaining rights. *Id. But see Jim McNeff, Inc. v. Todd*, 461 U.S. 260, 113 LRRM 2113 (1983) (union may recover in §301 action monetary obligations incurred by employer under a prehire contract prior to its repudiation).

[16]*Retail Store Employees Union Local 345 (Gem of Syracuse, Inc.)*, 145 NLRB 1168, 55 LRRM 1122 (1964).

a mixed question of fact and law for the Board which "normally survives judicial review."[17]

The General Counsel cannot establish a Section 8(b)(7) violation simply by showing that a union is engaging in, or is threatening to engage in, picketing for recognitional or organizational purposes— it is also necessary to establish that such conduct is occurring in one of the three factual contexts described in the statute.

§20.3   Another Union Currently Recognized

Under subparagraph (A) of Section 8(b)(7), recognitional or organizational picketing by an uncertified union is unlawful in instances where the employer has lawfully recognized another union and no question concerning representation can be raised. This provision reflects a congressional desire that where an employer lawfully extends voluntary recognition to a union "both the employer and the employees are entitled to immunity from recognition or organization picketing for prescribed periods."[18]

Subparagraph (A) applies only during periods when a question concerning representation cannot be raised. This means, as a practical matter, that picketing under this subparagraph is prohibited only when the Board's contract bar or other bar doctrines preclude the filing of an election petition.[19] Both the contract bar doctrine and Section 8(b)(7)(A) are intended, in part, to promote stability in established bargaining relationships.[20]

Subparagraph (A) applies only when an employer has "lawfully recognized" a union. The lawfulness of the voluntary recognition, however, can be raised by a picketing union as a defense in a Section 8(b)(7)(A) proceeding only in situations where the recognition can be attacked directly under Sections 8 and 9 of the Act.[21] Unfair labor practices such as unlawful recognition may not be litigated in the context of Section 9 representation proceedings.[22] Accordingly, as a practical matter, a picketing union can challenge the legality of the employer's voluntary recognition only in the context of a timely filed Section 8(a)(2) charge.[23]

---

[17]*NLRB v. Iron Workers Local 103 (Higdon Contracting Co.)*, 434 U.S. 335, 341–343 n.7, 97 LRRM 2333, 2336, n.7 (1978). *See also NLRB v. Teamsters Local 182 (Woodward Motors, Inc.)*, 135 NLRB 851, 49 LRRM 1576 (1962).

[18]*International Hod Carriers, Local 840 (C.A. Blinne Const. Co.)*, 135 NLRB 1153, 1156–1157, 49 LRRM 1638, 1639 (1962).

[19]These doctrines are discussed at §§5.4–5.8.

[20]*International Hod Carriers, Local 1298 (Roman Stone Constr. Co.)*, 153 NLRB 659, 59 LRRM 1430 (1965).

[21]*Id.* In the interest of industrial stability, the Board did not want to permit a rival union to challenge indirectly as a defense in Sec. 8(b)(7)(A) proceedings bargaining relationships immune from direct challenge under Secs. 8 or 9.

[22]*Union Mfg. Co.*, 123 NLRB 1633, 44 LRRM 1188 (1959).

[23]*See International Hod Carriers, Local 1298 (Roman Stone Constr. Co.)*, 153 NLRB 659, 59 LRRM 1430 (1965).

§20.4   Valid Election Held Within 12 Months

Subparagraph (B) of Section 8(b)(7) prohibits recognitional or organizational picketing during the 12-month period following a valid election. This provision is intended to insulate the employer and employees from picketing during the period of time that Section 9(b)(3) of the Act bars a second election in the same unit.[24] The 12-month period runs from the date of the Board's certification of representative (or certification of results) rather from the date of the balloting.[25] The prohibition against picketing applies to unions that did not participate in the earlier election as well as to unions that did, including former incumbent unions that were decertified.[26]

Since a Section 8(b)(7)(B) violation is predicated upon a valid election having been held, the validity of the earlier election often is raised by the picketing union as a defense. When the earlier election was conducted pursuant to the expedited procedures in Section 8(b)(7)(C),[27] the validity of the direction of election itself may be challenged.[28] If the picketing union participated in the earlier election, the Board may not permit the union to relitigate in a Section 8(b)(7)(B) proceeding issues which were or could have been litigated in the earlier representation proceeding.[29]

§20.5   Picketing of Unreasonable Duration Absent a Petition

Recognitional or organizational picketing permissible under subparagraphs (A) and (B) may nevertheless be unlawful under subparagraph (C) if it continues for more than a reasonable period of time without an election petition being filed. A reasonable period of time can never exceed 30 days, and in some circumstances may be less than 30 days. Picketing beyond a reasonable period of time without a petition being filed is an unfair labor practice which can be enjoined under Section 10(l);[30] if a petition is filed the picketing may continue, but the first proviso to Section 8(b)(7)(C) provides for an expedited election procedure. Accordingly, subparagraph (C) was "designed to shield employers and employees from the adverse effects of prolonged recognitional or organizational picketing and to provide a

---

[24]*Operating Engr's, Local 12 (Lamont Pipe Co.)*, 239 NLRB 500, 99 LRRM 1657 (1978).

[25]*Retail Store Employees' Union Local 692 (Irvins, Inc.)*, 134 NLRB 686, 49 LRRM 1188 (1961).

[26]*Lawrence Typographical Union, Local 570 (Kansas Color Press, Inc.)*, 158 NLRB 1332, 62 LRRM 1243 (1966).

[27]The expedited election procedures are discussed at §§20.9–20.11 *infra*.

[28]E.g., *Department & Specialty Store Employees' Union, Local 1265 (Oakland G.R. Kinney Co.)*, 136 NLRB 335, 49 LRRM 1771 (1962).

[29]See *Dallas Gen. Drivers Local 745 (Macatee, Inc.)*, 127 NLRB 683, 46 LRRM 1069 (1960).

[30]Sec. 10(l) injunctions are discussed in chapter 21.

procedure whereby the representation issue that gave rise to the picketing could be resolved as quickly as possible."[31]

The Act does not define what constitutes a "reasonable" period of time, and the Board has viewed the specified 30-day period as an outer limit.[32] The Board may conclude that picketing is unreasonable if continued without a petition being filed for a period of less than 30 days in cases where the picketing is accompanied by violence or intimidation,[33] or where the picketing threatens to cause severe economic harm to the employer.[34] It also is possible that the 30-day standard may be violated notwithstanding the absence of sustained picketing for 30 consecutive days in cases where the picketing is intermittent but prolonged; where separate periods of picketing are combined; where the picketing is conducted on a coordinated basis by two or more unions; or where the picketing is carried out at multiple jobsites.[35] Finally, recognitional or organizational picketing of any duration may be unreasonable if carried out by a labor organization which is statutorily precluded from being certified in the requested unit.[36]

If within a reasonable period of time a petition is filed, the picketing may continue beyond 30 days, but the election will be conducted on an expedited basis.[37] If the picketing union wins the election and is certified as representative of the employees, Section 8(b)(7) no longer is applicable. If on the other hand the picketing union loses the election, further picketing becomes unlawful under Section 8(b)(7)(B) and may be enjoined under Section 10(l).

§20.6 Informational Picketing

In addition to the expedited election proviso, Section 8(b)(7)(C) has a second proviso which states that

"nothing in this subparagraph (C) shall be construed to prohibit any picketing or other publicity for the purpose of truthfully advising the public (including consumers) that an employer does not employ members of, or have a contract with, a labor organization, unless an effect of such picketing is to induce any individual employed by any other

---

[31]*Teamsters, Local 115 (Vila-Barr Co.)*, 157 NLRB 588, 589, 61 LRRM 1386, 1387 (1966).

[32]*Retail, Wholesale & Dep't Store Union Dist. 65 (E. Camera & Photo Corp.)*, 141 NLRB 991, 52 LRRM 1426 (1963).

[33]*E.g., Samoff v. Teamsters Local 115*, 338 F. Supp. 856, 79 LRRM 2562 (E.D. Pa. 1972) (26 days); *Cuneo v. United Shoe Workers*, 181 F. Supp. 324, 45 LRRM 2822 (D.N.J. 1960) (10 days); *Mine Workers Dist. 12 (Traux Traer Coal Co.)*, 177 NLRB 213, 72 LRRM 1634 (1969) (two weeks).

[34]*E.g., Elliott v. Sapulpa Typographical Union, Local 619*, 45 LRRM 2400 (N.D. Okla. 1959) (fifteen days).

[35]*See* THE DEVELOPING LABOR LAW at 1096–1097 and cased cited therein.

[36]*General Serv. Employees Union Local 73 (Andy Frain, Inc.)*, 230 NLRB 351, 95 LRRM 1566 (1977); *Teamsters Local 344 (Purolator Sec., Inc.)*, 228 NLRB 1379, 95 LRRM 1568 (1977); *Service Employees, Local 73 (A-1 Sec. Serv. Co.)*, 224 NLRB 434, 92 LRRM 1393 (1976) (unions with nonguard members precluded by Sec. 9(b)(3) from being certified in guard units).

[37]The expedited election procedures are discussed at §§20.9–20.11 *infra*.

person in the course of his employment, not to pick up, deliver or transport any goods or not to perform any services."

The proviso thus authorizes recognitional or organizational picketing for more than 30 days in the absence of an election petition where (1) the picketing truthfully advises the public that the employer does not employ union members or have a union contract, and (2) such conduct does not induce employees of other employers to cease dealing with the picketed employer. The proviso is not applicable to picketing encompassed by Sections 8(b)(4)(A) and (B),[38] and has the effect of nullifying the expedited hearing procedures in the first proviso to Section 8(b)(7)(C).[39]

The purpose of the proviso is to authorize appeals to the general public for spontaneous pressure against an employer while simultaneously prohibiting such appeals to organized labor groups or members of unions, as such.[40] The legality of picketing under the proviso, therefore, often depends upon the identity of the union's intended audience. This question is determined by the Board on the basis of such factors as the wording on the picket signs, evidence of prior union demands for recognition, failure of the union to disclaim earlier recognitional picketing, and picketing at employee rather than consumer entrances to the employer's premises.[41]

Even if the picketing qualifies as informational rather than recognitional, it still must not have an effect of causing employees of other employers "not to pick up, deliver or transport any goods or not to perform any services." The standard applied by the Board is not qualitative in terms of the number of interruptions over a prescribed period of time, but rather evaluates the actual impact on the picketed employer's business.[42] The test is "whether the picketing has disrupted, interfered with, or curtailed the employer's business"; a test which is not satisfied by isolated delays, but which requires stopping deliveries to a substantial degree.[43]

Processing Section 8(b)(7) Charges

§20.7   Initiation of Proceedings

The Board has adopted a number of special procedures for cases arising under Section 8(b)(7).[44] (See Exhibit 103.) A charge alleging

---

[38]*Drug & Hosp. Employees Union Local 1199 (Janel Sales Corp.)*, 136 NLRB 1564, 50 LRRM 1033 (1962).

[39]*Department & Specialty Store Employees' Union, Local 1265 (Oakland G.R. Kinney Co.)*, 136 NLRB 335, 49 LRRM 1771 (1962); *International Hod Carriers, Local 840 (C.A. Blinne Const. Co.)*, 135 NLRB 1153, 49 LRRM 1638 (1962).

[40]*NLRB v. Electrical Workers Local 3 (Jack Picoult)*, 317 F.2d 193, 53 LRRM 2116 (2d Cir. 1963).

[41]*See* THE DEVELOPING LABOR LAW at 1104–1105.

[42]*Retail Clerks Union Local 324 (Barker Bros. Corp.)*, 138 NLRB 478, 51 LRRM 1053 (1962).

[43]*Id.* at 138 NLRB 491, 51 LRRM 1057.

[44]*See generally* NLRB Rules and Regulations §§102.73–102.82; NLRB Statements of Procedure §§101.22–101.25; NLRB Casehandling Manual ¶¶10240–10248.

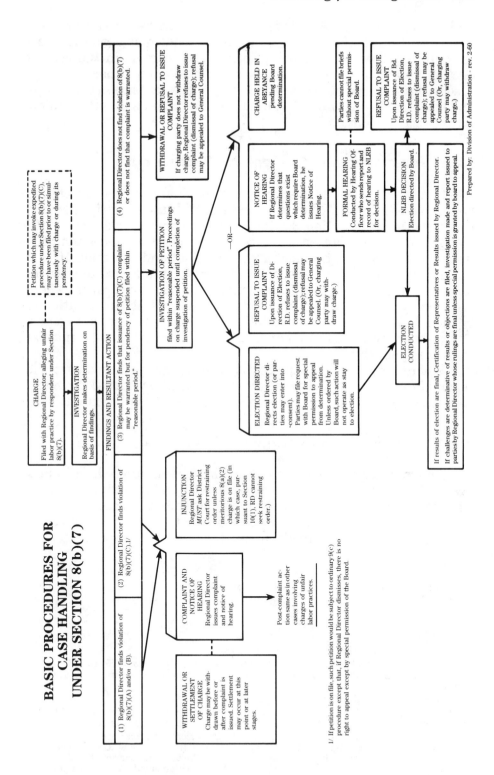

Exhibit 103. Basic Procedures for Case Handling Under Section 8(b)(7)

a violation of Section 8(b)(7) is docketed by the regional office as a "CP" case. The statute requires that it be handled as a priority matter.[45] It is processed as other priority cases except, in the case of Section 8(b)(7)(C), where a representation petition is pending or is filed within a reasonable time thereafter.[46] The contents of the charge and the manner in which it is filed are the same as for other unfair labor practice charges.[47]

§20.8   Investigation of Charge—No Petition Filed

Investigation of the charge by the regional office is expected to be completed within 72 hours of its filing.[48] If the investigation discloses merit in a Section 8(b)(7)(A) or (B) charge, or an 8(b)(7)(C) charge where no representation petition is pending, a complaint is issued and an application for injunctive relief under Section 10(l) is made.[49] Section 10(l) makes it mandatory for the Board to seek injunctive relief with respect to Section 8(b)(7) violations, except where the employer has assisted another union unlawfully in violation of Section 8(a)(2).[50] The Section 8(b)(7) complaint is processed in accordance with regular unfair labor practice procedures to the extent that they are applicable.[51]

Where it appears that the Section 8(b)(7) charge lacks merit, the regional director will not issue a complaint. The regional director's decision may be appealed to the General Counsel.[52] (See Exhibit 104.)

§20.9   Investigation of Charge—Petition Filed

An outstanding election petition changes the procedure in Section 8(b)(7) cases. Whether the election petition is pending when the CP charge is filed, or is timely filed thereafter, processing of the charge is suspended and the petition is investigated on an expedited basis.[53] In order to be timely under the expedited procedures, the

---

[45]Sec. 10(l); *see also* NLRB Rules and Regulations §102.73.

[46]See §20.9 *infra* for a discussion of processing 8(b)(7)(C) charges where a petition has been filed.

[47]NLRB Statements of Procedure §101.22(a). See chapter 12.

[48]NLRB Casehandling Manual ¶10242.

[49]*Id.*; NLRB Statements of Procedure §101.22(b).

[50]*See* NLRB Casehandling Manual ¶10242 regarding the effect of dismissal of the Sec. 8(a)(2) charge in the processing of the Sec. 10(l) petition. Injunctions generally are discussed in chapter 21.

[51]NLRB Rules and Regulations §102.74.

[52]NLRB Rules and Regulations §§102.74, 102.19; NLRB Statements of Procedure §101.22(b). Appeals from the regional director's refusal to issue a complaint are discussed at §12.12.

[53]NLRB Rules and Regulations §102.75; NLRB Statements of Procedure §101.22(b). *But see* NLRB Casehandling Manual ¶10242 which instructs the Board's staff that where the petition is filed at or about the time the CP charge is filed, "[t]he charge should be fully investigated first, and the complete investigation of the petition should await a judgment as to the merits of the charge. . . ."

NATIONAL LABOR RELATIONS BOARD

REGION 5

Candler Building - 4th Floor

109 Market Place

Baltimore, MD   21202

January 2, 1986

Mr. Jack Smith, President
Janco Computer Services, Inc.
8181 Greensboro Drive
McLean, VA 22102

Re: Local 007, United Computer
     Operators International Union
     Case No. 5-CP-181

Dear Mr. Smith:

The above-captioned case, charging a violation under Section 8(b)(7) of the National Labor Relations Act, as amended, has been carefully investigated and considered.

It does not appear that further proceedings on the charge are warranted inasmuch as [statement of reasons for dismissal].

I am, therefore, refusing to issue a complaint in this matter.

Pursuant to the National Labor Relations Board Rules and Regulations, Series 8, as amended, you may obtain a review of this action by filing an appeal with the General Counsel addressed to the Office of Appeals, National Labor Relations Board, Washington, D.C. 20570, and a copy with me. This appeal must contain a complete statement setting forth the facts and reasons upon which it is based. The appeal must be received by the General Counsel in Washington, D.C., by the close of business on [month-day-year]. Upon good cause shown, however, the General Counsel may grant special permission for a longer period within which to file. Any request for extension of time must be submitted to the Office of Appeals in Washington, and a copy of any such request should be submitted to me.

If you file an appeal, please complete the Form NLRB-4767, Notice of Appeal, I have enclosed with this letter and send one copy of the form to each of the other parties whose names and addresses are listed below. The notice forms should be mailed at the same time you file the appeal, but mailing the notice forms does not relieve you of the necessity for filing the appeal itself with the General Counsel and a copy of the appeal with the Regional Director within the time stated above.

Very truly yours,

Louis J. D'Amico
Regional Director

Exhibit 104. Regional Director's Dismissal of CP Charge—No Direction of Election

petition must be filed within 30 days of the commencement of the recognitional or organizational picketing.

If the regional director dismisses the petition and refuses to direct an election, processing of the Section 8(b)(7)(C) charge is resumed.[54] If, on the other hand, an election is directed, the charge is dismissed.[55] (See Exhibit 105.)

A request for the General Counsel to review the dismissal of the charge must be filed within seven days (unlike 14 days in other cases) and must contain a complete statement setting forth the facts and reasons upon which the request is based.[56] The request for review does not operate as a stay of any dismissal action by the regional director.[57] A pending election petition has no effect on Section 8(b)(7)(A) or (B) charges as both subsections speak to circumstances when no petition could properly be filed.[58]

§20.10   Investigation of Petition

The expedited election procedure is used only when the regional office's investigation of a representation petition involving the employees of the employer named in the pending CP charge discloses that

- The employer's operations come within the Board's jurisdictional dollar volume standards;
- Picketing of the employer is being conducted for an object prohibited by Section 8(b)(7);
- Section 8(b)(7)(C) is applicable to the picketing; and
- The petition has been filed within a reasonable period of time not to exceed 30 days from the commencement of the picketing.[59]

If these four requirements are satisfied, the petition may omit certain items normally required under Section 9(c)(1). It is not necessary for the petitioner to allege in the petition that a demand for recognition was made on the employer, nor is it necessary to submit the usual 30-percent showing of interest by the employees.[60]

---

[54]NLRB Rules and Regulations §102.81(b); NLRB Statements of Procedure §101.24(b).

[55]NLRB Rules and Regulations §102.81(a); NLRB Statements of Procedure §101.24(a).

[56]NLRB Rules and Regulations §102.81(a).

[57]*Id.*

[58]*International Hod Carriers, Local 840 (C.A. Blinne Const. Co.),* 135 NLRB 1153, 49 LRRM 1638 (1962). If an 8(b)(7)(C) charge is accompanied by charges that other sections of the statute also have been violated and the regional director dismisses the allegations, an appeal to the General Counsel must be filed on an expedited basis within three days from service of the dismissal. NLRB Rules and Regulations §102.81(c).

[59]NLRB Statements of Procedure §101.23(a).

[60]*See* Sec. 8(b)(7)(C); NLRB Statements of Procedure §101.23(a) n.1.

NATIONAL LABOR RELATIONS BOARD

REGION 5

Candler Building - 4th Floor

109 Market Place

Baltimore, MD   21202

January 2, 1986

Mr. Jack Smith, President
Janco Computer Services, Inc.
8181 Greensboro Drive
McLean, VA 22102

Re: Local 007, United Computer Operators
International Union
Case No. 5-CP-182

Dear Mr. Smith:

The above-captioned case, charging a violation under Section 8(b)(7) of the
National Labor Relations Act, as amended, has been carefully investigated
and considered.

It does not appear that further proceedings on the charge are warranted
inasmuch as a timely valid representation petition involving the employees
of the employer named in the charge has been filed within a reasonable time
from the commencement of the picketing described in said charge, and a
determination has been made that an expedited election should be conducted
upon such petition in accordance with the provisions of Sections 8(b)(7)(C)
and 9(c) of said Act, and the National Labor Relations Board Rules and
Regulations, Series 8, as amended. A notice of such election is being
issued in Case No. 5-RC-1234.

I am, therefore, refusing to issue a complaint in this matter.

Pursuant to the National Labor Relations Board Rules and Regulations,
Series 8, as amended, you may obtain a review of this action by filing an
appeal with the General Counsel addressed to the Office of Appeals,
National Labor Relations Board, Washington, D.C. 20570, and a copy with
me. This appeal must contain a complete statement setting forth the facts
and reasons upon which it is based. The appeal must be received by the
General Counsel in Washington, D.C., by the close of business on
[month-day-year]. Upon good cause shown, however, the General Counsel may
grant special permission for a longer period within which to file. Any
request for extension of time must be submitted to the Office of Appeals in
Washington, and a copy of any such request should be submitted to me.

**Exhibit 105. Regional Director's Dismissal of CP Charge—Direction
of Election**

-2-

If you file an appeal, please complete the Form NLRB-4767, Notice of Appeal, I have enclosed with this letter and send one copy of the form to each of the other parties whose names and addresses are listed below. The notice forms should be mailed at the same time you file the appeal, but mailing the notice forms does not relieve you of the necessity for filing the appeal itself with the General Counsel and a copy of the appeal with the Regional Director within the time stated above.

Very truly yours,

Louis J. D'Amico
Regional Director

Enclosures

CERTIFIED MAIL - RETURN RECEIPT REQUESTED

cc: Local 007, United Computer Operators International Union
     General Counsel, NLRB, Washington, D.C.   20570

bc: Data Processing Section
     Division of Advice, Legal Research and Policy Planning Branch

Exhibit 105—*page 2*

During the course of the regional director's investigation, documentary and other evidence may be submitted by (1) the parties, (2) any individual or labor organization purporting to represent the employees involved, and (3) any labor organization on whose behalf the picketing has been conducted.[61] The regional director, without a hearing, may direct that an election be held in an appropriate unit of the employees.[62] (See Exhibit 106.) When an election is directed without a hearing, any party aggrieved may promptly file a request with the Board for special permission to appeal that action to the Board; the request for review, however, does not stay any action by the regional director unless specifically ordered by the Board.[63]

On the other hand, if the proceedings raise substantial issues which require determination before an election may be held, the regional director is not required to proceed without a hearing but may order that such a hearing be held. (See Exhibit 107.) A hearing is directed only when the regional director determines that certain issues—e.g., proper unit—must be resolved before the election.[64] If held, the procedures followed in connection with such a hearing are similar to those used for regular representation election petitions pursuant to Section 9(c) except that the hearing ordinarily is directed on a shorter notice to the parties and the parties are not permitted to file briefs unless special permission is granted. The parties, however, may state their respective positions fully on the record at the hearing. Any request for review of a decision of the regional director must be filed promptly after issuance of such a decision rather than within the 14 days normally permitted.[65]

If following the investigation the regional director determines that the expedited election procedures are not warranted, the petition will be dismissed absent withdrawal.[66] In some situations the director will notify the parties that while an expedited election may not be warranted, a regular election under Section 9(c)(1) would be appropriate.[67]

If a petition seeking an expedited election is filed and there is no "CP" charge on file with the regional office but the petitioner claims an exemption from the requirements of Section 9(c)(1) of the Act because of the picketing, the claim will not be honored. The regional director, however, will afford the petitioner an opportunity to furnish the necessary evidence to sustain the usual petition processed under Section 9(c)(1) of the Act. (See Exhibit 108.) If within a reasonable time, usually 48 hours after receipt of the letter, the

---

[61]NLRB Rules and Regulations §102.77(a).
[62]*Id.* at §102.77(b); NLRB Statements of Procedure §101.23(b).
[63]NLRB Rules and Regulations §102.80(c); NLRB Statements of Procedure §101.23(b).
[64]NLRB Casehandling Manual ¶10246.
[65]NLRB Rules and Regulations §102.77(b); NLRB Statements of Procedure §101.23(c).
[66]NLRB Rules and Regulations §102.80(a); NLRB Statements of Procedure §101.25.
[67]NLRB Rules and Regulations §102.80(b); NLRB Statements of Procedure §101.25.

NATIONAL LABOR RELATIONS BOARD

REGION 5

Candler Building - 4th Floor

109 Market Place

Baltimore, MD   21202

January 2, 1986

Mr. Jack Smith, President
Janco Computer Services, Inc.
8181 Greensboro Drive
McLean, VA 22102

                    Re: Janco Computer Services, Inc.
                        Case No. 5-RC-1235

Dear Mr. Smith:

On the basis of the investigation made to date in the above matter, it
appears appropriate now to conduct a secret ballot to determine whether or
not the employees of Janco Computer Services, Inc. in the unit of employees
described below wish to be represented for purposes of collective
bargaining by Local 007, United Computer Operators International Union, or
Local 1212, International Alliance of High-Tech Workers pursuant to Section
9(a) of the National Labor Relations Act, or by neither union.

Accordingly, pursuant to Sections 8(b)(7)(C) and 9(c) of said Act, and
Section 102.77 of the National Labor Relations Board Rules and Regulations,
an election by secret ballot will be conducted as provided in the enclosed
Notice of Election among the employees of the above-named employer in a
unit described as follows, which is hereby found to be appropriate:

     All customer service and sales representatives employed by
     Respondent, excluding all other employees, guards and supervisors
     as defined in the Act.

Additional copies of the Notice of Election are being herewith furnished
the employer for posting in conspicuous places.

Your cooperation will be appreciated.

                    Very truly yours,

                    Louis J. D'Amico
                    Regional Director

Enclosures

CERTIFIED MAIL - RETURN RECEIPT REQUESTED

Exhibit 106.   Regional Director's Direction of Election Without Hearing

UNITED STATES OF AMERICA
BEFORE THE NATIONAL LABOR RELATIONS BOARD
FIFTH REGION

Local 007, United Computer
  Operators International Union

                    Petitioner

       and   Case No 5-RC-1236

Janco Computer Services, Inc.

                    Employer

                NOTICE OF REPRESENTATION HEARING

    The above-named Petitioner, having heretofor filed a petition pursuant
to Section 9(c) of the National Labor Relations Act, as amended, a copy of
which petition is attached hereto, and it appearing that, pursuant to said
Section and to Section 8(b)(7)(C) of the said Act, a question affecting
commerce has arisen concerning whether the employees described by such
petition desire a collective-bargaining representative as defined in
Section 9(a) of the Act, and concerning the unit to which an election may
appropriately be conducted to resolve such question.

    YOU ARE HEREBY NOTIFIED that, pursuant to Section 9(c) of the Act, and
the National Labor Relations Board Rules and Regulations, Series 8, as
amended, on the 3rd day of May, 1986, at the National Labor Relations
Board, Fifth Region, 109 Market Place, Suite 4200, Baltimore, MD 21202, a
hearing will be conducted before the hearing officer of the National Labor
Relations Board upon the aforesaid question, at which time and place the
parties will have the right to appear in person, or otherwise, and give
testimony. Form NLRB-4669 is attached.

Signed at Baltimore, Maryland, this 2d day of January, 1986.

                          _____
                          LOUIS J. D'AMICO, REGIONAL DIRECTOR
                          NATIONAL LABOR RELATIONS BOARD, REGION 5
                          CANDLER BUILDING - SUITE 4200
                          BALTIMORE, MARYLAND 21202

Exhibit 107.   Notice of Hearing on Petition Filed Under Section 8(b)(7)(C)

NATIONAL LABOR RELATIONS BOARD

REGION 5

Candler Building - 4th Floor

109 Market Place

Baltimore, MD   21202

January 2, 1986

Ms. Jean Jones, Business Agent
Local 007, United Computer Operators
    International Union
P.O. Box 10
Arlington, VA 22207

                          Re: Janco Computer Services, Inc.
                               5-RC-1236

Dear Ms. Jones:

The above-captioned case, arising from a petition filed pursuant to Section
9(c) of the National Labor Relations Act, as amended, has been carefully
investigated and considered.

It does not appear that expedited procedures pursuant to said Section of
the Act are warranted inasmuch as

> [the petition has not been filed within a reasonable time after the
> commencement of picketing of the employer named in the petition, a
> reasonable time having been determined in the current circumstances to
> be ___ days.]

> [other reason]

I am therefore declining to process the petition under said expedited
procedures, and am proceeding to process the petition in accordance with
the provisions of Section 9(c)(1) of the National Labor Relations Act and
of Subpart C of the National Labor Relations Board Rules and Regulations.

If you have not already done so, furnish evidence that

> [a substantial number of employees wish to be represented by the
> petitioner for the purpose of collective bargaining.]

**Exhibit 108.   Regional Director's Refusal to Process Under Expedited
Procedures**

-2-

[or]

[a substantial number of employees do not desire to be represented for collective-bargaining purposes by the labor organization (individual) currently certified (recognized).]

[or]

[a labor organization or individual has presented a claim to the petitioner to be recognized as the representative of the petitioner's employees as defined in Section 9(c) of the Act.]

Unless such evidence is submited promptly, the petition will be dismissed.

Very truly yours,

Louis J. D'Amico
Regional Director

CERTIFIED MAIL - RETURN RECEIPT REQUESTED

cc: Other Parties
      Excutive Secretary
      National Labor Relations Board
      Washington, D.C.   20570

Exhibit 108—*page 2*

petitioner does not furnish such evidence in compliance with the requirements of Section 9(c)(1), the petition will be dismissed, absent withdrawal.[68] (See Exhibit 109.) There is no right to appeal from the dismissal of a petition filed to invoke the expedited election procedure except by special permission of the Board.[69]

§20.11   Election and Postelection Procedures

When a petition has been filed for an expedited election, the parties may, subject to the approval of the regional director, enter into a consent election agreement. They may not enter into a stipulated election agreement.[70] In the absence of a consent election agreement, the regional director fixes the basis of eligibility of voters and the place, date, and hours of balloting. The mechanics of arranging the balloting and other procedures for the conduct of the election are the same as in the usual election conducted by the Board.[71]

The regional director's rulings on any objections to the conduct of the election or challenged ballots are final and binding, unless the Board, on an application by one of the parties, grants special permission to appeal from the regional director's rulings. The party requesting such review by the Board must do so promptly, in writing, and state briefly the grounds relied upon. A copy must be served on each of the other parties including the regional director. The request for review does not stay the regional director's rulings unless so ordered by the Board.[72]

---

[68]NLRB Casehandling Manual ¶10244.2b.

[69]NLRB Rules and Regulations §102.80(a); NLRB Statements of Procedure §102.25.

[70]NLRB Rules and Regulations §102.79; NLRB Statements of Procedure §101.23(d); NLRB Casehandling Manual ¶10244.4. Consent and stipulated elections are discussed at §§6.8 and 6.9, respectively.

[71]NLRB Rules and Regulations §102.78; NLRB Statements of Procedure §101.23(b). See discussion at §§9.1–9.15.

[72]NLRB Rules and Regulations §102.78; NLRB Statements of Procedure §101.23(b).

NATIONAL LABOR RELATIONS BOARD

REGION 5

Candler Building - 4th Floor

109 Market Place

Baltimore, MD   21202

January 2, 1986

Ms. Jean Jones, Business Agent
Local 007, United Computer Operators
  International Union
P.O. Box 10
Arlington, VA 22207

Re: Janco Computer Services, Inc.
     5-RC-1236

Dear Ms. Jones:

The above-captioned case, arising from a petition filed pursuant to Section 9(c) and a charge filed pursuant to Section 8(b)(7) of the National Labor Relations Act, as amended, has been carefully investigated and considered.

It does not appear that further proceedings are warranted inasmuch as

[the picketing described in the charge is violative of Section 8(b)(7)(A)(B).]

[other reason]

I am, therefore, dismissing the petition in this matter.

Very truly yours,

Louis J. D'Amico
Regional Director

CERTIFIED MAIL - RETURN RECEIPT REQUESTED

cc: Other Parties
     Executive Secretary
     National Labor Relations Board
     Washington, D.C. 20570

Exhibit 109.   Regional Director's Dismissal of Petition

21

Ancillary Judicial Proceedings— Injunctions and Subpoena Enforcement

The Act provides for injunctive relief as a provisional remedy pending Board adjudication of a complaint. Section 10(l) requires the Board to seek a temporary injunction after it files charges in the following unfair labor practice cases: (1) secondary boycotts and other secondary activities,[1] (2) hot cargo agreements,[2] and (3) picketing for organizational or recognitional purposes.[3] In all other unfair labor practice cases, the Board may seek an injunction under Section 10(j) after a complaint has been issued, but it is not required to do so.

The regional director, not the charging party, has standing to seek both mandatory and discretionary injunctions.[4] There is some authority for the proposition that a charging party may be granted permission to intervene in a Section 10(j) case, but the weight of authority is that there is no right to intervene.[5] A charging party

---

[1]Secs. 8(b)(4)(A), (B), (C). In cases involving Sec. 8(b)(4)(D), the Board must seek injunctive relief under 10(l) only "where such relief is appropriate." *See* General Counsel Memorandum No. 73-82 (December 3, 1973) at 18–21 for a discussion of the guidelines used in seeking injunctions and the scope of injunctions in Sec. 8(b)(4)(D) cases. Copies may be obtained from the Board's Information Division.

[2]Sec. 8(e).

[3]Sec. 8(b)(7). See chapter 20.

[4]*Solien v. Miscellaneous Drivers, Local 610*, 440 F.2d 124, 76 LRRM 2780 (8th Cir. 1971) (power to initiate 10(l) injunction suit restricted to Board alone); *Squillacote v. International Union, UAW*, 383 F. Supp. 491, 87 LRRM 2811 (E.D. Wis. 1974) (power to initiate 10(j) injunction suit restricted to Board alone).

[5]*Youngblood v. Scottex Corp.*, 80 LRRM 2619 (N.D. Tex. 1972), permits intervention. Intervention was not permitted in *Squillacote v. International Union, UAW*, 383 F. Supp. 491, 87 LRRM 2811 (E.D. Wis. 1974); *Reynolds v. Marlene Ind. Corp.*, 250 F. Supp. 722, 61 LRRM 2342 (S.D.N.Y. 1966); *Penello v. Burlington Ind.*, 54 LRRM 2165 (W.D. Va. 1963). In Sec. 10(l) proceedings, however, it is clear that parties may not intervene. *Solien v. Miscellaneous Drivers, Local 610*, 440 F.2d 124, 76 LRRM 2780 (8th Cir. 1971). The *Scottex* court reasoned that since 10(l) provides that any person involved in the charge shall be given "an opportunity to appear by counsel and present any relevant testimony," the charging party's participation was limited to that extent. In contrast, 10(j) has no language on participation, and so the court concluded that parties could intervene under FED. R. CIV. P. 24(a)(2).

can file an *amicus curiae* brief[6] and may appeal decisions regarding injunctions.[7] This chapter examines the procedures followed and the standards applied in injunction and subpoena enforcement proceedings.

Mandatory Injunctions Under Section 10(l)

§21.1 Charges Requiring Injunctive Relief Under Section 10(l)

Section 10(l) requires the regional director to seek an injunction in an appropriate federal district court[8] whenever there is reasonable cause to believe that a party has violated Sections 8(b)(4)(A), (B), (C) (secondary activities); Section 8(e) (hot cargo agreements); or Section 8(b)(7) (picketing for recognitional or organizational purposes). When there is reasonable cause to believe that a violation of Section 8(b)(4)(D) has occurred, a Section 10(l) injunction may be sought "where such relief is appropriate." Injunctive relief is considered appropriate in nearly every case where the alleged unlawful conduct is continuing or likely to resume.[9] Regional directors may not, however, seek restraining orders in Section 8(b)(7) cases where a Section 8(a)(2) domination of labor union charge has been filed against the employer and the preliminary investigation indicates that the charge is meritorious.[10]

§21.2 Responsibility of Regional Director to Seek Injunctive Relief

The Act requires the regional director to make the preliminary investigation in Section 10(l) cases "forthwith" and to give these cases "priority over all other cases except cases of a like character."[11] In an effort to ensure that Section 10(l) cases are handled promptly,

---

[6]*San Francisco-Oakland Newspaper Guild v. Kennedy*, 404 F.2d 37, 69 LRRM 2535 (9th Cir. 1968) (10(l)); *NLRB v. Committee of Interns & Residents*, 94 LRRM 2605 (S.D.N.Y. 1976) (10(j)).

[7]*See McLeod v. Teamsters Local 239*, 330 F.2d 108, 55 LRRM 2838 (2d Cir. 1964).

[8]Sec. 10(l) provides that an injunction can be sought in any district court of the United States within any district where the unfair labor practice has occurred, or is alleged to have occurred, or wherein the accused resides or transacts business. Sec. 10(l) further provides that a district court has jurisdiction of a labor organization in the district where the organization maintains its principal office, or in any district where its authorized officers or agents are promoting or protecting the interests of employee members. In addition, service of process on agents constitutes service upon the organization.

[9]General Counsel Memorandum No. 73-82 at 18–19. In general, whenever there is reasonable cause to believe that respondent union is violating Section 8(b)(4)(D), Section 10(k) proceedings are warranted unless all parties have agreed to be bound by a voluntary method for resolution of the dispute or have actually resolved the dispute. See chapter 19. Sec. 10(l) injunctions are warranted in either case. General Counsel Memorandum No. 73-82 at 19.

[10]Sec. 10(l); NLRB Statements of Procedure §101.37; NLRB Casehandling Manual ¶10242.

[11]Sec. 10(l); NLRB Rules and Regulations §102.95(a).

the General Counsel has advised that charging parties should be required to submit their evidence immediately, normally within 24 hours from the time of filing of the charge. Furthermore, the regions are required to complete their investigations within 72 hours with their determinations following immediately.[12]

If the regional director determines that there is "reasonable cause" to believe that the unfair labor practice has been committed, he or she must seek an injunction in an appropriate federal district court.[13] Section 10(l) is mandatory, not discretionary, in nature and *requires* the regional director to seek an injunction when "reasonable cause" is found.[14]

If a petition for injunctive relief is filed, the regional director is required to handle the remainder of the case expeditiously and to give the case priority in successive stages.[15] The complaint generally is issued promptly, normally within five days of the filing of the petition, and the regional director often requests that the chief administrative law judge set a hearing date within three weeks.[16] In addition, at each stage, the region attempts to process the case expeditiously.[17]

Only the regional director in whose office the unfair labor practice charge is filed may seek a Section 10(l) injunction.[18] The charging party may not seek an injunction,[19] but may request that the Board do so.[20]

(a) *Settlement Before Filing Injunction Petition.* Before filing for a Section 10(l) injunction, the regional director may initiate settlement negotiations or encourage the union to cease its unlawful activities.[21] If negotiations become protracted or if the union refuses to cease its activities, the regional director must petition for injunctive relief and file a complaint.[22]

(b) *Settlement of Underlying Case.* Settlement of the underlying unfair labor practice case terminates the Section 10(l) proceed-

---

[12]General Counsel Memorandum No. 77-9 (January 28, 1977) at 1–2; General Counsel Memorandum No. 77-77 (July 27, 1977) at 1. Copies may be obtained from the Board's Information Division.

[13]See *supra* note 8.

[14]*Squillacote v. Meat & Allied Food Workers Local 248*, 534 F.2d 735, 92 LRRM 2089 (7th Cir. 1976); *Retail Clerks Union v. Food Employers Council*, 351 F.2d 525, 60 LRRM 2322 (9th Cir. 1965).

[15]NLRB Rules and Regulations §§102.96–102.97.

[16]General Counsel Memorandum 77-77 at 1; General Counsel Memorandum 77-9 at 2.

[17]General Counsel Memorandum 77-77 at 2; General Counsel Memorandum 77-9 at 3.

[18]*Evans v. International Typographical Union*, 76 F. Supp. 881, 21 LRRM 2375 (D. Ind. 1948).

[19]*Solien v. Miscellaneous Drivers, Local 610*, 440 F.2d 124, 76 LRRM 2780 (8th Cir. 1971).

[20]*Table Talk Pies v. Strauss*, 237 F. Supp. 514, 57 LRRM 2250 (S.D.N.Y. 1964).

[21]NLRB Casehandling Manual ¶10230.

[22]*Id.*

ing, and the charging party does not have the right to a hearing on its objections to the settlement if a complaint has not been filed.[23] If, however, a complaint has been filed, the charging party is entitled to be heard with respect to its objections to a proposed settlement.[24] Even if a settlement is reached, the regional director must institute injunction proceedings if resumption of the allegedly illegal conduct is imminent or likely.[25]

§21.3 Appeal of Regional Director's Decision Not to Seek Injunctive Relief

As mentioned above, the regional director must seek an injunction whenever there is "reasonable cause" to believe that the specified unfair labor practice violations were committed. The charging party may appeal to the General Counsel the regional director's determination that "reasonable cause" did not exist and, if the appeal is sustained, the General Counsel may order the regional director to seek injunctive relief.[26]

§21.4 Section 10(l) Injunction Proceedings in Federal District Court

(a) Parties Participating in Proceedings. The regional director, not the charging party, is the plaintiff in Section 10(l) injunction proceedings.[27] Section 10(l) provides, however, that any person involved in the charge, including the charging party, can appear by counsel and present relevant testimony. Courts have held that the existence of this provision indicates that participation should be thus limited and that parties, therefore, cannot intervene in Section 10(l) proceedings.[28] Similarly, intervention has not been allowed at the appellate level in a 10(l) case.[29] The parties in the underlying case, however, may be granted permission to file *amicus curiae* briefs.[30]

(b) Evidentiary Hearing. In a Section 10(l) case, the district court usually holds an evidentiary hearing to allow the parties to present their evidence. There is no denial of due process if the district

---

[23]*Terminal Freight Coop. Ass'n v. NLRB*, 447 F.2d 1099, 78 LRRM 2097 (3d Cir. 1971).

[24]*See Leeds & Northrup Co. v. NLRB*, 357 F.2d 527, 61 LRRM 2283 (3d Cir. 1966).

[25]NLRB Casehandling Manual ¶10230.

[26]*McLeod v. Teamsters Local 239*, 330 F.2d 108, 55 LRRM 2838 (2d Cir. 1964). Appeal procedures are discussed at §12.12.

[27]*Solien v. Miscellaneous Drivers, Local 610*, 440 F.2d 124, 76 LRRM 2780 (8th Cir. 1971).

[28]*Id.*

[29]*Hirsch v. Building & Constr. Trades Council*, 530 F.2d 298, 91 LRRM 2438 (3d Cir. 1976).

[30]*San Francisco-Oakland Newspaper Guild v. Kennedy*, 404 F.2d 37, 69 LRRM 2535 (9th Cir. 1968).

court decides not to allow oral testimony at the hearing.[31] Furthermore, in some cases, an evidentiary hearing is not required.[32]

(c) Standards Applied by District Court.   In order to acquire an injunction, the regional director must show that there is "reasonable cause" to believe that the alleged unfair labor practice violations were committed.[33] The regional director need not prove that the violations, in fact, were committed.[34] Likewise, district courts are not to usurp the power of the Board by deciding the case on the merits.[35]

The courts of appeals, however, disagree on the definition of "reasonable cause." Some circuits will follow the regional director's recommendation so long as the director's "factual allegations and legal issues are substantial and non-frivolous."[36] Other circuits seem to require a demonstration of "some significant possibility that the Board will enter an enforceable order."[37] Nevertheless, all circuits appear to agree that deference should be accorded to the regional director's resolution of issues of law and fact.[38] In addition, at least one court has indicated that the regional director's burden of proof in a Section 10(l) case is less than that in a Section 10(j) case.[39]

Once the "reasonable cause" test is satisfied, Section 10(l) empowers the district court to grant injunctive relief which it deems "just and proper."[40] Courts have broad discretion in applying this

---

[31]*Kennedy v. Teamsters, Local 542,* 443 F.2d 627, 77 LRRM 2607 (9th Cir. 1971).

[32]*See, e.g., Squillacote v. Graphic Arts Int'l Union,* 540 F.2d 853, 93 LRRM 2257 (7th Cir. 1976) (no denial of due process when no evidentiary hearing held because facts were established in prior proceedings and in affidavits).

[33]*Squillacote v. Teamsters Local 344,* 561 F.2d 31, 95 LRRM 2977 (7th Cir. 1977); *Humphrey v. International Longshoremen's Ass'n,* 548 F.2d 494, 94 LRRM 2374 (4th Cir. 1977).

[34]*Douds v. Teamsters Local 707,* 156 F. Supp. 240, 41 LRRM 2765 (S.D.N.Y. 1957); *see also Squillacote v. Graphic Arts Int'l Union,* 540 F.2d 853, 93 LRRM 2257 (7th Cir. 1976) (regional director need not establish by "clear and convincing evidence" that reasonable cause exists to believe that charge is true).

[35]*See, e.g., Hendrix v. Amalgamated Meat Cutters,* 555 F.2d 175, 95 LRRM 2095 (8th Cir. 1977) (determination of whether violation occurred reserved exclusively for Board with review by court of appeals); *Humphrey v. International Longshoremen's Ass'n,* 548 F.2d 494, 94 LRRM 2374 (4th Cir. 1977) (district court not to decide merits of 10(l) injunction case); *Squillacote v. Teamsters Local 344,* 561 F.2d 31, 95 LRRM 2977 (7th Cir. 1977) (district court not to decide merits of 10(l) injunction case).

[36]*See, e.g., Hendrix v. Operating Eng'rs Local 571,* 592 F.2d 437, 445, 100 LRRM 2704, 2709-2710 (8th Cir. 1979).

[37]*Danielson v. Joint Bd. of Coat Workers' Union,* 494 F.2d 1230, 1244, 85 LRRM 2902, 2912 (2d Cir. 1974). See THE DEVELOPING LABOR LAW at 1648–1649 for a more complete discussion of the standards applied by different circuits.

[38]*See, e.g., Kaynard v. Teamsters Local 282,* 576 F.2d 471, 98 LRRM 2569 (2d Cir. 1978) (district court should defer to statutory interpretation and rational factual inferences of the Board); *Humphrey v. International Longshoremen's Ass'n,* 548 F.2d 494, 94 LRRM 2374 (4th Cir. 1977) (General Counsel's resolution of disputed issues of law and fact should be accorded considerable deference); *Danielson v. International Org. of Masters,* 521 F.2d 747, 89 LRRM 2564 (2d Cir. 1975) (regional director entitled to assume facts and draw inferences regarding disputed issues of fact, and court must sustain those findings where director's choice is rationally based and court not convinced Board's legal position is wrong).

[39]*See, e.g., Eisenberg v. Hartz Mountain Corp.,* 519 F.2d 138, 89 LRRM 2705 (3d Cir. 1975).

[40]*Cf. Danielson v. Electrical Workers, Local 501,* 509 F.2d 1371, 88 LRRM 2625 (2d Cir. 1975) (Sec. 10(l) does not mandate injunction upon finding that reasonable cause exists to believe unfair labor practice occurred, but gives district court discretion in determining whether injunctive relief would be "just and proper").

standard. Injunctions have been found "just and proper" where deemed necessary to preserve the status quo so that the Board's ultimate decision will not be rendered moot by intervening events.[41] They also have been deemed "just and proper" where necessary to prevent disruptions in commerce or future unfair labor practices.[42] Some courts have balanced the effects of grant or denial of an injunction on the union, the employer, and the public;[43] others give primary weight to the public interest.[44] In addition, any delay by the Board in seeking an injunction may be considered.[45] District courts, however, may not use their grant of discretion to challenge the Board's interpretation and application of the Act.[46] Although equitable concerns are considered, the equitable doctrine of "unclean hands" has been held to be unavailable to prevent injunctive relief.[47]

§21.5 Effect and Duration of Section 10(l) Injunctions

A district court's findings in injunction proceedings are not binding on the Board when it adjudicates the underlying unfair labor practice or on the court of appeals reviewing the Board's decision.[48] Until the Board's decision, the parties must abide by the district court's order, and contempt proceedings may be instituted to compel compliance.

Section 10(l) injunctions usually expire when the Board issues its decision in the underlying case.[49] They may not remain in effect pending an appeal of the Board decision to a federal court of appeals.[50]

A district court, however, is not required to grant an injunction remaining in effect through the Board's final adjudication.[51] Some courts have rejected the imposition of a time limit on a Section 10(l)

---

[41]*Union de Tronquistas de Puerto Rico, Local 901 v. Arlook*, 586 F.2d 872, 99 LRRM 3250 (1st Cir. 1978).

[42]*Id.*

[43]*See Squillacote v. Graphic Art Int'l Union*, 540 F.2d 853, 93 LRRM 2257 (7th Cir. 1976) (possibility of delay in proper exercise of economic pressure to gain union's ends balanced against possible economic loss and injury to public resulting from unlawful secondary boycott justified injunction).

[44]*Vincent v. Teamsters Local 445*, 76 LRRM 2409 (S.D.N.Y. 1970) (injunctive relief just and proper given strong public interest in commencement and continuance of college construction against which union was picketing).

[45]*See, e.g., Johansen v. Orange County Dist. Council*, 95 LRRM 3275 (C.D. Cal. 1977) (delay of over six months between filing of charge and court action is factor to be considered in determining whether injunction would be proper); *Danielson v. Electrical Workers, Local 501*, 509 F.2d 1371, 88 LRRM 2625 (2d Cir. 1975) (injunctive relief found unwarranted where Board failed to seek expedited review of district court's denial of injunction which was recognition that there was no real danger of irreparable harm to public interest until Board adjudicated underlying unfair labor practice).

[46]*Squillacote v. Teamsters Local 344*, 561 F.2d 31, 95 LRRM 2977 (7th Cir. 1977).

[47]*Samoff v. Teamsters Local 115*, 338 F. Supp. 856, 79 LRRM 2562 (E.D. Pa. 1972).

[48]*Solien v. Miscellaneous Drivers, Local 610*, 440 F.2d 124, 76 LRRM 2780 (8th Cir. 1971).

[49]*Hirsch v. Building & Constr. Trades Council*, 530 F.2d 298, 91 LRRM 2438 (3d Cir. 1976).

[50]*Sears, Roebuck & Co. v. Carpet Layers, Local 419*, 397 U.S. 655, 74 LRRM 2001 (1970).

[51]*Carpenters v. Sperry*, 170 F.2d 863, 23 LRRM 2040 (10th Cir. 1948).

injection.[52] The Third Circuit has held that Section 10(j) injunctions, and by implication Section 10(l) injunctions, should be limited to a period of six months to encourage expeditious handling of the underlying case.[53] The Eighth Circuit limited a Section 10(l) injunction to the minimum time required for Board adjudication of the case.[54] The court did so because it recognized that the union's purpose for picketing might be destroyed if the proceedings were delayed thereby making the court's decision dispositive.[55]

§21.6　Temporary Restraining Orders Under Section 10(l)

Section 10(l) also provides for the issuance of temporary restraining orders using the same criteria as injunctive relief. In order to obtain a temporary restraining order without notice, the petition must allege that "substantial and irreparable injury to the charging party will be unavoidable."[56] In addition, the temporary restraining order is effective for only five days.[57]

§21.7　Appeal of District Court's Decision in Section 10(l) Injunction Proceedings

The standard for appellate review of a decision to grant a Section 10(l) injunction depends upon the issues being appealed. In general, findings of fact and the finding of "reasonable cause" will be reversed only if clearly erroneous.[58] Any equitable relief granted will be upheld unless the district court committed an abuse of discretion, while legal conclusions are fully reviewable.[59]

The clearly erroneous test for findings of fact does not apply when the denial of an injunction is being appealed. In such cases, the court of appeals may examine all evidence to determine whether the district court erred.[60]

---

[52]*See, e.g., Hendrix v. Operating Eng'rs Local 571*, 592 F.2d 437, 100 LRRM 2704 (8th Cir. 1979) (union's request for definite time limit on Section 10(l) injunction rejected because Congress knew of lengthy Board hearing procedure and did not impose a time limit).

[53]*Eisenberg v. Hartz Mountain Corp.*, 519 F.2d 138, 89 LRRM 2705 (3d Cir. 1975).

[54]*Dawidoff v. Minneapolis Bldg. & Constr. Trades Council*, 550 F.2d 407, 94 LRRM 2801 (8th Cir. 1977) (case remanded to determine minimum time necessary).

[55]*Id.*

[56]Sec. 10(l).

[57]*Id.*

[58]*Local Joint Bd., Hotel & Restaurant Employees v. Sperry*, 323 F.2d 75, 54 LRRM 2298 (8th Cir. 1963).

[59]*Boire v. Teamsters*, 479 F.2d 778, 83 LRRM 2128 (5th Cir. 1973).

[60]*See National Maritime Union v. Commerce Tankers Corp.*, 457 F.2d 1127, 79 LRRM 2954 (2d Cir. 1972).

Discretionary Injunctions Under Section 10(j)

§21.8 Scope of Section 10(j)

Section 10(j) provides that upon issuance of a complaint in an unfair labor practice proceeding, the Board may seek injunctive relief in an appropriate federal district court.[61] The purpose of the injunction is to prevent delays in the Board's administrative process from frustrating the Act's remedial objectives.[62] While Section 10(l) mandates injunctive relief for certain violations, Section 10(j) is discretionary with the regional director. Sections 10(l) and 10(j) also differ in the sense that a complaint must be filed before the regional director can seek a 10(j) injunction while a 10(l) injunction may be sought before a complaint is filed.[63]

Neither statutory nor case law has developed any definite guidelines to determine whether injunctive relief is appropriate in a given case. The Board's Casehandling Manual, however, lists several factors which are considered by the Board in deciding whether injunctive relief should be sought under Section 10(j):[64]

- The clarity of the alleged violations;
- Whether the case involves the shutdown of important business operations which, because of their special nature, would have an extraordinary impact on the public interest;
- Whether the alleged unfair labor practices involve an unusually wide geographic area, thus creating special problems of public concern;
- Whether the unfair labor practices create special remedy problems so that it would probably be impossible either to restore the status quo or effectively dissipate the consequences of the unfair labor practices through resort solely to the regular procedures provided in the Act for Board order and subsequent enforcement proceedings;
- Whether the unfair labor practices involve interference with the conduct of an election or constitute a clear and flagrant disregard of Board certification of a bargaining representative or other Board procedures;

---

[61]The Board may seek a 10(j) injunction in any United States district court within any district where the unfair labor practice in question is alleged to have occurred or where such person resides or transacts business. In contrast to Sec. 10(l), Sec. 10(j) does not provide specifically for jurisdiction over labor unions. See note 8 *supra.* Most injunctions against unions are handled under Sec. 10(l). THE DEVELOPING LABOR LAW at 1643.

[62]*See, e.g., Solien v. Merchants Home Delivery Serv., Inc.*, 557 F.2d 622, 95 LRRM 2596 (8th Cir. 1977) (Senate report evidences concern that delays inherent in administrative process may frustrate Act's remedial objects, and, therefore, Board may seek injunctive relief in cases involving all types of unfair labor practices).

[63]*Compare* Sec. 10(l) *with* Sec. 10(j).

[64]NLRB Casehandling Manual ¶10310.2.

- Whether the continuation of the alleged unfair labor practices will result in exceptional hardship to the charging party;
- Whether the current unfair labor practice is of a continuing or repetitious pattern;
- Whether, if violence is involved, it is out of control of local authorities or otherwise widespread and susceptible to control by 10(j) relief.

While these factors indicate a concern for both public and private interests, courts have stated that Section 10(j) injunctions should issue to protect the public interest and not in vindication of purely private rights.[65] Charging parties should keep these factors in mind in drafting requests for injunctive relief under Section 10(j).

§21.9 Categories of Section 10(j) Cases

In 1979, the Board outlined 14 general categories of Section 10(j) cases. A fifteenth category contains miscellaneous cases that do not fall within the other categories. This section summarizes briefly the Board's description of these categories.[66]

(a) Interference With Union Organizational Campaign (No Majority). These cases concern employer unfair labor practices, such as threats, interrogations, and discharges, designed to undermine the union's organizational campaign before the union obtains majority support. Orders enjoining further violations and reinstating any employees discharged because of union activities usually are sought.[67] Even when the employer allegedly commits only a few illegal actions, Section 10(j) injunctions are issued when it can be shown that the conduct has a significant impact on the organizational campaign in a small unit.[68]

(b) Interference With Union Organizational Campaign (Majority). In these cases, the union obtains majority support, but the employer's unfair labor practices destroy the union's majority and preclude a free and fair election. The Section 10(j) relief sought

---

[65]*Seeler v. Trading Port, Inc.*, 517 F.2d 33, 89 LRRM 2513 (2d Cir. 1975).

[66]*See* Lubbers, *Discretionary Injunction Authority Under Section 10(j)*, 35 LAB. L.J. 259 (1984), and General Counsel Memorandum No. 79-77 (October 15, 1979) for further discussion of these categories. Copies of the General Counsel Memorandum may be acquired from the Board's Information Division.

[67]*See, e.g., Angle v. Sacks*, 382 F.2d 655, 66 LRRM 2111 (10th Cir. 1967) (employer who "interviewed" employees to discern their views on campaigning union and warned employees that union "agitators" would be discharged enjoined from interfering with employees' exercise of their Sec. 7 rights and ordered to reinstate employees who had been discharged for their union activities).

[68]*See, e.g., Zipp v. Shenanigans*, 106 LRRM 2989 (C.D. Ill. 1980) (Sec. (10(j) injunction warranted, even though employer discharged only one employee, because employee discharged was sole union organizer).

is typically an order to bargain pending final Board adjudication, an order to desist from any further violations of the employees' right to organize, and an order to reinstate any alleged discriminatorily discharged employees. The courts of appeals are split on the appropriateness of interim bargaining orders in such cases. The Fifth Circuit has held that such bargaining orders are not appropriate because the union has never enjoyed a bargaining relationship with the employer and therefore a bargaining order would alter rather than maintain the status quo.[69] The Second and Sixth Circuits have issued interim bargaining orders to restore the status quo as it existed prior to the employer's unfair labor practices[70] and to prevent irrevocable harm to the union.[71] The Seventh Circuit has awarded interim bargaining orders.[72]

(c) Subcontracting or Other Change to Avoid Bargaining Obligation.

These cases concern an employer's changes in business operations which adversely affect the working conditions of employees represented by a union. Subcontracting and relocation of plants are typical examples of this activity. These changes may be motivated by a desire to avoid bargaining or to interfere with an organizational campaign, or they may be illegally undertaken without bargaining where the change is a mandatory subject of bargaining. Usually relief sought in these cases is aimed at preserving or restoring the status quo before the violation occurred.[73]

(d) Withdrawal of Recognition From Incumbent Union.

In these cases an employer, without objective considerations upon which to base a good faith doubt of the union's majority status, either withdraws recognition from or refuses to bargain for a new agreement with an incumbent union. Typically, affirmative interim bargaining orders are sought in these cases.[74]

---

[69]*Boire v. Pilot Freight Carriers, Inc.,* 515 F.2d 1185, 89 LRRM 2908 (5th Cir. 1975).

[70]*Levine v. C & W Mining Co.,* 610 F.2d 432, 102 LRRM 3093 (6th Cir. 1979).

[71]*Seeler v. Trading Port, Inc.,* 517 F.2d 33, 89 LRRM 2513 (2d Cir. 1975).

[72]*Wilson v. Liberty Homes, Inc.,* 108 LRRM 2699 (7th Cir. 1981), *vacated as moot,* 664 F.2d 620, 109 LRRM 2492 (7th Cir. 1982) (court of appeals approved bargaining order but later held that Board order had rendered it moot).

[73]*Maram v. Universidad Interamericana de Puerto Rico, Inc.,* 722 F.2d 953, 115 LRRM 2118 (1st Cir. 1983) (restoration of subcontracted maintenance unit ordered because subcontracting designed to thwart union organizing effort). *But see Milwaukee Spring Div. of Ill. Coil Spring Co.,* 268 NLRB 601, 115 LRRM 1065 (1984), *enf'd,* 765 F.2d 175, 119 LRRM 2801 (D.C. Cir. 1985) (midcontract transfer of work outside of bargaining unit for economic reasons not violation); *Otis Elevator Co.,* 269 NLRB 891, 115 LRRM 1281 (1984) (employer's refusal to bargain with union concerning its decision to transfer and consolidate certain unit work not violation of Sec. 8(a)(5)).

[74]*See generally Sachs v. Davis & Hemphill, Inc.,* 71 LRRM 2126 (4th Cir.), *vacated as moot and opinions withdrawn,* 72 LRRM 2879 (4th Cir. 1969) (in original case bargaining order issued because reasonable cause existed to believe that employer did not have a good faith doubt concerning the union's majority status when it withdrew recognition).

(e) Undermining of Bargaining Representative. In these cases the employer allegedly commits unfair labor practices with the intent of undermining the incumbent union, but does not withdraw recognition. In such cases, the Board usually seeks an order to compel the employer to cease its unfair labor practices and return to the status quo as it existed before the unfair labor practices began.[75]

(f) Minority Union Recognition. This category includes cases involving an employer's grant of recognition to a union which does not represent an uncoerced majority of employees in the unit and cases involving an employer's illegal assistance to or domination of a labor organization. An injunction is sought to prevent the minority union from becoming so entrenched that the employees cannot exercise their Section 7 rights.[76]

(g) Successor Refusal to Recognize and Bargain. In these cases an employer who acquires a business and thereby becomes the legal successor to an existing bargaining relationship refuses to recognize and bargain with the incumbent union. Here the harm is in denying to the employees the benefits of union representation while the Board is considering the charge, and in the potential decline of support for the union.[77]

(h) Conduct During Bargaining Negotiations. These cases involve the refusal to bargain in good faith by one of the parties to a collective bargaining relationship. A Section 10(j) injunction may be appropriate when the conduct creates a threat to industrial peace or threatens to undermine employee support for the union.[78]

(i) Mass Picketing and Violence. In these cases a labor organization or its agents restrain or coerce employees, usually when the employees refrain from engaging in Section 7 activities, such as a strike. Because such injury cannot be remedied adequately by a Board order issued much later, Section 10(j) relief often is warranted.[79]

---

[75]*See, e.g., Advertisers Mfg. Co. v. NLRB*, 677 F.2d 544, 110 LRRM 2355 (7th Cir. 1982) (injunction issued when employer made series of unilateral changes while challenging union's certification).

[76]*See, e.g., Fuchs v. Jet Spray Corp.*, 560 F. Supp. 1147, 114 LRRM 3493 (D. Mass. 1983) (when employer aided one employee committee and denied similar benefits to UAW, employer ordered to withdraw recognition from and set aside contract negotiated with employee committee).

[77]*See generally Davis v. Huttig Sash & Door Co.*, 288 F. Supp. 82, 68 LRRM 2936 (W.D. Okla. 1968).

[78]*See generally Douds v. ILA*, 241 F.2d 278, 39 LRRM 2388 (2d Cir. 1957).

[79]*See, e.g., Grupp v. Steelworkers*, 532 F. Supp. 102, 109 LRRM 3257 (W.D. Pa. 1982) (picket line misconduct enjoined).

(j) Notice Requirements for Strike or Picketing. In these cases the union fails to comply with the notice and waiting period provisions in Sections 8(d) (federal and state mediation) and 8(g) (notices to health care institutions) before striking or picketing. Section 10(j) relief often is sought if the union's activity threatens to have a substantial adverse impact on the employer's operations. The Board usually seeks an order to cease the striking or picketing unless and until the union complies with the notice and waiting requirements of Sections 8(d) and 8(g).[80]

(k) Refusal to Permit Protected Activity on Private Property. In these cases the employer allegedly interferes with the employees' right to engage in protected Section 7 activity, or to receive information from nonemployees in nonworking areas of the private property of the employer. Injunctive relief may be warranted when the employer's conduct has a substantial adverse effect on the protected activity.[81]

(l) Union Coercion to Achieve Unlawful Object. These cases involve unlawful coercion on the part of a union to achieve unlawful objectives. For example, the union may bargain to the point of impasse on a permissive or illegal subject of bargaining. If the union's conduct inspires industrial unrest or has a substantial adverse effect on the employer's operations, a Section 10(j) injunction may be sought.[82]

(m) Interference With Access to Board Processes. In these cases an employee resorts to the processes of the Board, typically filing charges or giving testimony, and the union or employer retaliates against the employee for this action. Because such conduct can have a great affect on other employees, a Section 10(j) injunction often is warranted.[83]

(n) Segregating Assets. In these cases employers take actions to segregate their assets, for example by closing down operations and liquidating assets, with the foreseeable consequence that an anticipated backpay order in an unfair labor practice case will not be satisfied. In such cases the employer must make provisions to satisfy the Board order.[84]

---

[80]*See generally McLeod v. Compressed Air Workers Local 147*, 292 F.2d 358, 48 LRRM 2655 (2d Cir. 1961).

[81]*See generally Eisenberg v. Holland Rantos Co.*, 583 F.2d 100, 99 LRRM 2543 (3d Cir. 1978).

[82]*See generally Boire v. Teamsters*, 479 F.2d 778, 83 LRRM 2128 (5th Cir. 1973).

[83]*See, e.g., Hirsch v. Pilgrim Life Ins. Co.*, 112 LRRM 3147 (E.D. Pa. 1982) (employer enjoined from prosecuting groundless lawsuit meant to retaliate against employee for having filed charges with the Board).

[84]*Norton v. New Hope Ind., Inc.*, 119 LRRM 3086 (D. La. 1985).

(o) **Miscellaneous.**   This category includes cases in which the Board believes that injunctive relief is appropriate, but where the issues do not fit within any of the above categories. In general, these cases involve situations in which the Board's final order will be unable to restore fully the status quo.[85]

§21.10   Responsibility of Regional Director to Seek Injunctive Relief

The charging party lacks standing to seek an injunction in federal district court under Section 10(j).[86] Only the Board may seek such an injunction. Therefore, when requesting the issuance of an unfair labor practice complaint, the charging party also should request that the Board seek injunctive relief.[87]

While under Section 10(l) the regional director usually seeks the injunction directly, under Section 10(j) the regional director must seek and obtain the Board's approval before petitioning for injunctive relief. Thus, the director prepares for submission to the General Counsel an analysis of the case setting forth the facts, applicable law, and reasons why an injunction is appropriate. During the General Counsel's review of the director's recommendation, the parties may request an opportunity to present their views.[88] If the General Counsel agrees that Section 10(j) relief is appropriate, a request for authority to proceed will be filed with the Board.

§21.11   Section 10(j) Injunction Proceedings in Federal District Court

(a) **Notice.**   When a petition for a Section 10(j) injunction is filed in district court, the court must serve notice on the party against whom the injunction is sought.[89] Telephonic notice has been held sufficient.[90]

(b) Parties Participating in Proceedings.   As in Section 10(l) proceedings, the regional director is the plaintiff in a Section 10(j) action, and the charging party may not intervene as a matter of

---

[85]*Arlook v. Southwire Co.*, Case No. C-83-114 N (N.D. Ga. 1983) (Board unsuccessfully sought injunctive relief when individual employee who was discriminatorily discharged experienced great financial hardship pending Board's decision on backpay).

[86]*Brown & Sharpe Mfg. Co. v. District 64, Int'l Ass'n of Machinists & Aerospace Workers*, 535 F. Supp. 167, 169 n.2 (D.R.I. 1982).

[87]*See* NLRB Casehandling Manual ¶10310.

[88]The procedure is similar to that discussed in §12.12 regarding the presentation of views to the General Counsel during an appeal of the dismissal of a charge.

[89]Sec. 10(j).

[90]*Squillacote v. Meat & Allied Food Workers Local 248*, 534 F.2d 735, 92 LRRM 2089 (7th Cir. 1976).

right.[91] The district court may, however, in its discretion grant or deny a request for intervention.[92] Even if the court does not allow intervention, it may permit a party to appear as *amicus curiae*.[93]

(c) Evidentiary Hearing. Evidentiary hearings may be held but are not required before issuance of a Section 10(j) injunction. The parties may waive the evidentiary hearing[94] or the court may decide to proceed without a hearing.[95] The failure to hold a hearing is not a basis for reversal absent evidence showing that the court abused its discretion.[96]

(d) Standards Applied by District Court. In determining whether an injunction should issue under Section 10(j), the district court must first decide whether there is "reasonable cause" to believe that the alleged violations have occurred.[97] The court may not decline making this determination on the ground that the matter should be determined by the Board.[98] Under the "reasonable cause" standard the Board does not need to show that the alleged violations actually occurred.[99] Likewise, when anti-union animus must be shown to establish the unfair labor practice charge, such motivation need not be proved in Section 10(j) proceedings. Only reasonable cause to believe that there was such motivation must be shown.[100] In determining whether the "reasonable cause" standard has been satisfied, the court should give the Board the benefit of the doubt on issues of fact.[101] Where more than one inference is possible, inferences favorable to the Board may be drawn.[102] Deference should be accorded to the

---

[91]*Squillacote v. UAW Local 578*, 383 F. Supp. 491, 87 LRRM 2811 (E.D. Wis. 1974).

[92]See note 5 *supra* and accompanying text. *See, e.g., Wilson v. Liberty Homes, Inc.*, 500 F. Supp. 1120, 108 LRRM 2688 (W.D. Wis. 1980) (union's motion to intervene in Sec. 10(j) proceeding denied where no possibility that outcome would adversely affect union's ability to protect its interests); *Youngblood v. Scottex Corp.*, 80 LRRM 2619 (N.D. Tex. 1972) (union was allowed to intervene in Section 10(j) proceeding when its contract with the respondent employer was challenged).

[93]*NLRB v. Committee of Interns & Residents*, 94 LRRM 2605 (S.D.N.Y. 1976).

[94]*See, e.g., Fuchs v. Jet Spray Corp.*, 560 F. Supp. 1147, 114 LRRM 3493 (D. Mass. 1983) (parties waived evidentiary hearing and instead submitted affidavits to court).

[95]*Squillacote v. Meat & Allied Food Workers Local 248*, 534 F.2d 735, 92 LRRM 2089 (7th Cir. 1976).

[96]*Id.*

[97]Although Sec. 10(j) does not explicitly establish the "reasonable cause" standard, courts consistently have applied it in such proceedings. THE DEVELOPING LABOR LAW at 1639 and n.34 *supra. See, e.g., Levine v. C & W Mining Co.*, 610 F.2d 432, 102 LRRM 3093 (6th Cir. 1979); *Solien v. Merchants Home Delivery Serv., Inc.*, 557 F.2d 622, 95 LRRM 2596 (8th Cir. 1977); *Eisenberg v. Hartz Mountain Corp.*, 519 F.2d 138, 89 LRRM 2705 (3d Cir. 1975).

[98]*Solien v. Merchants Home Delivery Serv. Inc.*, 557 F.2d 622, 95 LRRM 2596 (8th Cir. 1977).

[99]*See Davis v. R.G. LeTourneau, Inc.*, 340 F. Supp. 882, 78 LRRM 2616 (E.D. Tex. 1971).

[100]*Wilson v. Liberty Homes, Inc.*, 108 LRRM 2699 (7th Cir. 1981), *vacated as moot*, 664 F.2d 620, 109 LRRM 2492 (7th Cir. 1982).

[101]*See Hirsch v. Trim Lean Meat Prods., Inc.*, 479 F. Supp. 1351, 102 LRRM 2950 (D. Del. 1979).

[102]*Id.*

Board's legal theories as long as they are not frivolous.[103] Furthermore, the court should not make credibility determinations.[104]

If the "reasonable cause" test has been satisfied, the court may grant injunctive relief "as it deems just and proper."[105] The courts of appeals are divided upon the standard to be applied in determining what is "just and proper." Most circuits consider relief just and proper when it is necessary to prevent the frustration of the remedial purposes of the Act.[106] Other circuits have required that the Board show injunctive relief is necessary to preserve the status quo, prevent irreparable harm,[107] or to protect the public interest.[108]

(e) Effect of Delay in Seeking Injunction. Since an injunction is an extraordinary remedy, a delay between the commission of the alleged unfair labor practice and the submission of a petition for an injunction may substantially weaken the argument that an injunction is necessary.[109] In particular, an injunction may not be deemed necessary if the Board's final decision on the underlying case will be issued in the near future.[110] If, however, the delay is caused in part by the respondent, an injunction usually will not be denied.[111] Still other courts have held that the Board's administrative delays should not preclude relief because the injured parties have no control over Board procedure.[112]

§21.12 Effect and Duration of Section 10(j) Injunctions

Just as in Section 10(l) proceedings, the district court's findings in a Section 10(j) proceeding are not binding on the Board when it adjudicates the underlying claim.[113] A Section 10(j) injunction automatically terminates when the Board issues its final order in the

---

[103]*See, e.g., Boire v. Teamsters,* 479 F.2d 778, 83 LRRM 2128 (5th Cir. 1973) (rejecting contention that Sec. 10(j) relief unwarranted because Board's theories were novel); *Mack v. United Mine Workers,* 466 F. Supp. 474, 100 LRRM 3229 (E.D. Tenn. 1979) (stating that Board's legal theory must only be substantial and not frivolous).

[104]*Mack v. United Mine Workers,* 466 F. Supp. 474, 100 LRRM 3229 (E.D. Tenn. 1979).

[105]Sec. 10(j).

[106]*See, e.g., Fuchs v. Hood Indus., Inc.,* 590 F.2d 395, 100 LRRM 2547 (1st Cir. 1979); *Boire v. Teamsters,* 479 F.2d 778, 83 LRRM 2128 (5th Cir. 1973); *see* THE DEVELOPING LABOR LAW at 1639 for a more extensive listing of cases.

[107]*See Seeler v. Trading Port, Inc.,* 517 F.2d 33, 89 LRRM 2513 (2d Cir. 1975).

[108]*See Eisenberg v. Hartz Mountain Corp.,* 519 F.2d 138, 89 LRRM 2705 (3d Cir. 1975).

[109]*Siegel v. Marina City Co.,* 428 F. Supp. 1090, 95 LRRM 2061 (C.D. Cal. 1977).

[110]*Id.* (injunction not warranted where Board waited three months after unfair labor practices allegedly occurred before filing petition for injunction and Board proceedings were scheduled to begin shortly).

[111]*Morio v. North Am. Soccer League,* 501 F. Supp. 633, 106 LRRM 2761 (S.D.N.Y. 1980).

[112]*Fuchs v. Jet Spray Corp.,* 560 F. Supp. 1147, 114 LRRM 3493 (D. Mass. 1983) (employees should not be penalized for actions beyond their control); *DeProspero v. House of the Good Samaritan,* 474 F. Supp. 552, 102 LRRM 2154 (N.D.N.Y. 1978) (neither employees nor public should be penalized for Board's administrative delays beyond their control).

[113]*NLRB v. Acker Indus., Inc.,* 460 F.2d 649, 80 LRRM 2364 (10th Cir. 1972).

underlying unfair labor practice case.[114] A dismissal of the complaint is considered the Board's final order for these purposes.[115]

Some courts, however, have put an express time limit on the duration of Section 10(j) injunctions.[116] The Third Circuit has held that a Section 10(j) injunction should have an explicit time limit no longer than six months with a possible extension of not more than six additional months.[117] Other courts have declined to adopt a strict requirement, but nevertheless place time limits on Section 10(j) injunctions to encourage expeditious handling of the underlying unfair labor practice case.[118]

§21.13 Temporary Restraining Orders Under Section 10(j)

Section 10(j) also provides for the issuance of temporary restraining orders.[119] Where circumstances warrant, the Board requests a temporary restraining order when it petitions for injunctive relief. District courts apply similar standards to judge whether a temporary restraining order should issue as when they consider petitions for injunctive relief.[120]

The Federal Rules of Civil Procedure govern any temporary restraining orders issued under Section 10(j). Rule 65(b) limits such orders to a 10-day period plus an additional 10 days "for good cause shown."[121]

§21.14 Appeal of District Court's Decision in Section 10(j) Injunction Proceedings

At the appellate level, findings of fact[122] and determinations of reasonable cause[123] are reviewed under a clearly erroneous standard. Legal conclusions, however, are more fully analyzed.[124] A district

---

[114]*Levine v. Fry Foods, Inc.*, 596 F.2d 719, 101 LRRM 2417 (6th Cir. 1979).

[115]*See Kennedy v. Warehouse & Distrib. Workers, Local 688*, 43 LRRM 2645 (E.D. Mo. 1959).

[116]See notes 49–55 *supra* and accompanying text for a discussion of duration of Sec. 10(l) injunctions.

[117]*Eisenberg v. Hartz Mountain Corp.*, 519 F.2d 138, 89 LRRM 2705 (3d Cir. 1975).

[118]*See, e.g., Kaynard v. Mego Corp.*, 633 F.2d 1026, 105 LRRM 2723 (2d Cir. 1980) (injunction limited to approximately two months because simplicity of facts of underlying case would allow quick Board adjudication).

[119]Sec. 10(l) specifically authorizes temporary restraining orders while Sec. 10(j) authorizes a court to grant "temporary relief or restraining order as it deems just and proper." Courts have held that the language of Section 10(j) is broad enough to authorize temporary restraining orders. *Squillacote v. Meat & Allied Food Workers Local 248*, 534 F.2d 735, 92 LRRM 2089 (7th Cir. 1976).

[120]*Id.*

[121]FED. R. CIV. P. 65(b).

[122]*Boire v. Teamsters*, 479 F.2d 778, 83 LRRM 2128 (5th Cir. 1973).

[123]*Levine v. C & W Mining Co.*, 610 F.2d 432, 102 LRRM 3093 (6th Cir. 1979).

[124]*Boire v. Teamsters*, 479 F.2d 778, 83 LRRM 2128 (5th Cir. 1973).

court's grant of equitable relief is reversed only when there has been an abuse of discretion.[125]

Subpoena Enforcement

The Act provides for the issuance and enforcement of subpoenas at the request of parties in Board hearings.[126] The discussion at §7.6(c) outlines the procedures to acquire subpoenas in representation proceedings, and the discussion at §15.13 outlines the procedures to obtain subpoenas in unfair labor practice proceedings. This section focuses on procedures to enforce subpoenas.

§21.15   Enforcement of Subpoenas by the Board

The Board, not a private party, may seek enforcement of a subpoena in an appropriate federal district court.[127] If a subpoena is ignored, the party seeking the testimony or evidence may request the General Counsel to institute judicial proceedings to have the subpoena enforced. The General Counsel must comply with this request unless the Board believes that enforcement of the subpoena would be inconsistent with law and with the policies of the Act.[128]

§21.16   Standard of Review in District Court

The scope of the district court's inquiry in subpoena enforcement proceedings is very limited. The Board must show only some reasonable basis for believing that the information sought will prove relevant. The Board does not need to establish probable cause to believe that the Act has been violated.[129]

---

[125]*Id.*

[126]Sec. 11.

[127]Sec. 11(2); *NLRB v. Dutch Boy, Inc.*, 606 F.2d 929, 102 LRRM 2528 (10th Cir. 1979). The Board is precluded from enforcing its own subpoenas through the imposition of sanctions against parties who fail to comply. Authority to enforce subpoenas rests exclusively with the federal district courts. *NLRB v. International Medication Sys., Ltd.*, 640 F.2d 1110, 107 LRRM 2214 (9th Cir. 1981).

[128]NLRB Rules and Regulations §102.31(d); NLRB Casehandling Manual ¶11790.1.

[129]*NLRB v. Frederick Cowan & Co.*, 522 F.2d 26, 89 LRRM 2999 (2d Cir. 1975); *see NLRB v. G.H.R. Energy Corp.*, 707 F.2d 110, 113 LRRM 3415 (5th Cir. 1982) (district court must enforce subpoena as long as evidence called for relates to matter under investigation or in question and evidence is described with sufficient particularity).

§21.17 Standing to Object to Subpoena Enforcement Proceedings

In order to object to subpoena enforcement proceedings, a party against whom a subpoena has been issued must exhaust all available administrative remedies. Specifically, the party must file a motion to revoke, or show that he or she would be irreparably harmed if required to exhaust the administrative process.[130] Parties not named in a subpoena do not have standing to challenge subpoena enforcement.[131]

§21.18 Defenses to Subpoena Enforcement

Among the most common defenses against subpoena enforcement is the claim that the subpoena is designed as a "fishing expedition" to get information for a charge.[132] The success of this defense will hinge on how specifically the subpoena is drafted.[133] District courts generally will deny enforcement only if items requested are not "particularly described."[134] At least one court has held that it is frivolous to contend that the Board is attempting to use a subpoena as a discovery device since Section 11 of the Act grants the Board access to any person's records at all reasonable times, whether records belong to one merely being investigated or to one against whom an action already has been instituted.[135]

Burdensomeness as a defense to subpoena enforcement also may be difficult to establish. Even the production of thousands of documents has been held not to be too burdensome.[136]

Other defenses have had varying degrees of success. The attorney-client privilege has been successfully invoked as a defense.[137] A claim that there was a danger of misuse of information sought by a subpoena has resulted in modification of the subpoena.[138] Defective

---

[130]*Maurice v. NLRB*, 691 F.2d 182, 113 LRRM 3224 (4th Cir. 1982).

[131]*See Fugazy Continental Corp. v. NLRB*, 514 F. Supp. 718, 108 LRRM 3074 (E.D.N.Y. 1981) (alleged alter ego employer not named in subpoena and not served lacks standing to challenge relevancy of documents requested by subpoena).

[132]NLRB Casehandling Manual ¶11798.

[133]*Id.*

[134]*See Oklahoma Press Pub. Co. v. Walling*, 327 U.S. 186, 5 WH Cases 864 (1946).

[135]*NLRB v. G.H.R. Energy Corp.*, 707 F.2d 110, 113 LRRM 3415 (5th Cir. 1982).

[136]*Id.*

[137]*See generally Upjohn Co. v. United States*, 449 U.S. 383 (1981) (questionnaires, memoranda, notes of interviews conducted by employer's attorney among employees protected by attorney-client privilege and constitute work product of attorney prepared in anticipation of litigation).

[138]*See NLRB v. Martins Ferry Hosp. Ass'n*, 649 F.2d 445, 107 LRRM 2569 (6th Cir. 1981) (employer required to provide W-4 forms bearing employees' signatures to ascertain authenticity of union authorization cards, but order modified to protect employees by allowing employer to provide copies of W-4 forms with all irrelevant information excluded); *NLRB v. William Filene's Sons Co.*, 110 LRRM 2423 (D. Mass. 1982) (employer required to provide names and employment information relating to employees, but Board required not to disclose this information to the union).

service of process also has been used successfully as a defense.[139] The First Amendment has been held to bar enforcement of a subpoena against a non-party newspaper editor.[140] Finally, it has been held that a corporation enjoys no Fifth Amendment privilege against self-incrimination.[141]

§21.19　Stay of Injunction Pending Appeal

The unsuccessful party in a subpoena enforcement proceeding may request a stay pending appeal. In general, to determine whether a stay should be granted, the court will balance the likelihood of success on the merits on appeal, the potential harm to the various parties if the stay is granted or denied, and the effect of the grant or denial of the stay upon public interests.[142]

§21.20　Standard of Review in Court of Appeals

The district court's decision in a subpoena enforcement proceeding may be appealed to the appropriate court of appeals. The appellate court may reverse the district court's order only if it finds an abuse of discretion.[143]

---

[139]*See Maurice v. NLRB*, 108 LRRM 2882 (S.D. W.Va. 1981) (temporary restraining order issued against enforcement of Board's subpoena requiring party to appear as witness because subpoena not served in compliance with 28 C.F.R. §50.10).

[140]*Id.*

[141]*Oklahoma Press Pub. Co. v. Walling*, 327 U.S. 186, 5 WH Cases 864 (1946).

[142]*See, e.g., NLRB v. General Motors*, 510 F. Supp. 341, 106 LRRM 2810 (S.D. Ohio 1980) (employer entitled to stay pending appeal where it is likely that employer will prevail on appeal, employer will suffer irreparable harm if stay denied while no potential harm to opposing parties, and public interest best served by granting stay).

[143]*NLRB v. G.H.R. Energy Corp.*, 707 F.2d 110, 113 LRRM 3415 (5th Cir. 1982).

22

Dispute Settlement Procedures

§22.1 In General

Sections 8(a)(5) and 8(b)(3) of the Act make it an unfair labor practice for employers and unions to refuse to bargain collectively. The extent of the duty to bargain is defined in Section 8(d) which requires that the parties confer "in good faith with respect to wages, hours, and other terms and conditions of employment. . . ." The Act does not attempt to establish procedures to evaluate bargaining proposals or, with limited exceptions, to provide a final method for the settlement of disputes between the parties. Most important of these exceptions are the statutory system for resolving questions of representation (see chapters 4-11) and the Board's authority under Section 10(k) to determine the assignment of work in jurisdictional disputes (see chapter 19). Dispute settlement procedures involving the Board also are found in the Postal Reorganization Act (see discussion at §22.6 *infra*).

The Act does contain, however, limited general provisions to aid in the settlement of contract disputes. There are additional procedures to be used when the dispute involves national emergency strikes, Postal Service bargaining, or employees of health care institutions. This chapter outlines these provisions.

§22.2 Notice Requirements

When a party desires to terminate or modify an existing collective bargaining agreement, Section 8(d)(1) requires that a written notice to this effect be served upon the other party 60 days prior to either the expiration date stated in the contract or the time it is proposed that the termination or modification take place. In addition, the party desiring to terminate or modify the agreement must notify the Federal Mediation and Conciliation Service (FMCS) within 30 days after notice is served on the other party, provided no agreement

511

has been reached at that time.[1] Any state or territorial mediation agency for the state or territory where the dispute occurs must be notified at the same time.[2] Failure to notify the mediation services renders a strike unlawful and thereby makes any striking employees vulnerable to lawful discharge.[3]

For the convenience of the parties, the Federal Mediation and Conciliation Service makes available a form which may be used to serve notice of a dispute. (See Exhibit 110.) Copies may be obtained from either a regional office or the Washington, D.C., office of the FMCS. The notice of dispute may be filed with either the Washington headquarters of the FMCS or with the FMCS office having jurisdiction over the region in which the dispute exists. Locations of these offices appear in Appendix H.

Section 8(d)(4) prohibits a strike or lockout during the 60-day period after notice is served on the other party, or until the expiration date of the contract, whichever is longer. The Supreme Court has held that the term "expiration date" means either (1) the expiration date contained in the contract, (2) a mid-term reopening date contained in the contract, or (3) the date proposed for modification or termination to take effect.[4] A violation of Section 8(d)(4) constitutes a refusal to bargain unfair labor practice. Section 8(d) further provides that an employee who strikes within any notice period specified in that section loses his or her status as an employee of the employer, unless rehired.

Section 8(d) has been construed literally to apply only to situations where a party seeks to modify or terminate a contract. The Supreme Court has held that Section 8(d) does not apply to strikes in protest of employer unfair labor practices because such strikes are not called for the purpose of terminating or modifying a contract.[5]

§22.3 Notice Requirements—Health Care Institutions

Whenever the collective bargaining agreement involves employees of a health care institution, a party seeking to terminate or modify the agreement must comply with longer notice periods. Section 2(14) of the Act defines "health care institution" to include "any hospital, convalescent hospital, health maintenance organization, health clinic,

---

[1] Sec. 8(d)(3).

[2] *Id.* The burden of notifying the mediation services of a dispute rests exclusively with the initiating party, and the initiating party's failure to file such a notice cannot preclude the noninitiating party from undertaking otherwise lawful economic action, such as unilateral implementation of new conditions of employment. *United Artist Communications, Inc.*, 274 NLRB No. 17, 118 LRRM 1353 (1985).

[3] *United Furniture Workers, Local 270 v. NLRB*, 336 F.2d 738, 55 LRRM 2990 (D.C. Cir. 1964); *Retail Store Employees, Local 322 (Wilhow Corp.)*, 240 NLRB 1109, 100 LRRM 1384 (1979).

[4] *NLRB v. Lion Oil Co.*, 352 U.S. 282, 39 LRRM 2296 (1957).

[5] *Mastro Plastics Corp. v. NLRB*, 350 U.S. 270, 37 LRRM 2587 (1956).

U.S GPO 1984-0 454 683 1454

FMCS FORM F-7 REVISED 8/84	NOTICE TO MEDIATION AGENCIES	FORM APPROVED OMB NO. 3-076-0004

MAIL TO:
NOTICE PROCESSING UNIT
FEDERAL MEDIATION AND CONCILIATION SERVICE
2100 K STREET, N.W.   AND
WASHINGTON, D.C. 20427

THE STATE OR TERRITORIAL MEDIATION AGENCY

You are hereby notified that written notice of proposed termination or modification of the existing collective bargaining contract was served upon the other party to this contract and that no agreement has been reached.

IF THIS IS A HEALTH CARE INDUSTRY NOTICE PLEASE INDICATE (MARK "X")

(MARK ONE "X") AND GIVE APPROPRIATE: MO. DAY YR.

① CONTRACT EXPIRATION DATE _____ / /

(1) ☐ INITIAL CONTRACT   ☐ EXISTING CONTRACT

② CONTRACT REOPENER DATE _____ / /

NAME OF EMPLOYER OR EMPLOYER ASSOCIATION/ORGANIZATION (IF MORE THAN ONE, SUBMIT NAMES AND ADDRESSES ON AN ATTACHED LIST)

③

ADDRESS OF EMPLOYER/ASSOCIATION

④ NO.   STREET   CITY   STATE   ZIP

EMPLOYER OFFICIAL TO CONTACT

⑤

(AREA CODE) PHONE NUMBER

⑥

NAME OF INTERNATIONAL UNION OR PARENT BODY

⑦

NAME AND NO. OF LOCAL (IF NOT A LOCAL, GIVE NAME AND NUMBER, IF ANY, OF THE UNION ORGANIZATION INVOLVED IN THE NEGOTIATIONS)

⑧

ADDRESS OF LOCAL UNION

⑨ NO.   STREET   CITY   STATE   ZIP

UNION OFFICIAL TO CONTACT

⑩

(AREA CODE) PHONE NUMBER

⑪

A. LOCATION OF AFFECTED ESTABLISHMENT   CITY   STATE   ZIP

B. LOCATION OF NEGOTIATIONS (COMPLETE ONLY IF DIFFERENT FROM 12.A)

⑫   CITY   STATE   ZIP

TOTAL NUMBER EMPLOYED AT AFFECTED LOCATION(S)

⑬

NUMBER OF EMPLOYEES COVERED BY CONTRACT

⑭

INDUSTRY AND TYPE OF ESTABLISHMENT (E.G., STEEL INDUSTRY — FACTORY; FOOD INDUSTRY — RETAIL CHAIN STORE; EDUCATION — PRIVATE COLLEGE; ELECTRICAL INDUSTRY — PUBLIC UTILITY)

⑮

PRINCIPAL PRODUCT OR SERVICE

⑯

THIS NOTICE IS FILED ON BEHALF OF (MARK "X")

⑰ ☐ UNION   ☐ EMPLOYER

TYPE OF NEGOTIATIONS (MARK "X")

☐ SINGLE ESTABLISHMENT
☐ MULTI-PLANT
☐ AREA OR INDUSTRY WIDE
⑱ ☐ OTHER (SPECIFY) _____

TYPE OF EMPLOYEES COVERED BY CONTRACT (MARK "X" ALL THAT APPLY)

☐ PROFESSIONAL/TECHNICAL
☐ PRODUCTION/MAINTENANCE
☐ CLERICAL
⑲ ☐ OTHER (SPECIFY) _____

NAME AND TITLE OF OFFICIAL FILING NOTICE

⑳

SIGNATURE   DATE

㉑

Receipt of this form does not constitute a request for mediation nor does it commit FMCS to offer its facilities. Receipt of this notice will not be acknowledged in writing by FMCS. FMCS does not forward copies of this notice to state or territorial mediation agencies. While the use of this form is voluntary, it will facilitate our service to respondents.

Exhibit 110.   Notice to Mediation Agencies   (FMCS Form F-7)

nursing home, extended care facility or other institution devoted to the care of sick, infirm or aged person." Notice must be given to the health care institution 90 days before the expiration of the agreement or proposed modification date, and to the FMCS and state mediation agencies within 60 days thereof.[6] Strikes and lockouts are barred for 90 days after notice is given or until the expiration date of the agreement, whichever is longer.[7] Where a union has just been certified or recognized and the bargaining is for the initial agreement, the labor organization must give the FMCS and state mediation agencies at least 30 days' notice of the dispute.[8] Section 8(d) further requires the parties to participate fully in meetings held by the FMCS.

Section 8(g) imposes a further requirement on labor organizations to give notice before engaging in any strike, picketing, or other concerted refusal to work at any health care institution. The labor organization must notify in writing both the institution and the FMCS not less than 10 days prior to the action. The notice must state the date and time of the commencement of the intended work stoppage.[9] If the labor organization does not strike at the specified time but intends to strike at some point within the following 72 hours, it should give at least 12 hours' notice of the revised time. The labor organization may not strike or picket more than 72 hours after the previously specified time without affording a new 10-day notice.[10]

The 10-day notice requirement does not apply to an unfair labor practice strike,[11] a threat to strike,[12] or a short, nondisruptive interruption of work.[13] Furthermore, when a labor organization is not involved in the work stoppage, a 10-day notice is not required.[14] It does apply, however, to activities of union organizers.[15]

When a strike or picketing is directed at a health care institution, the notice requirement applies even though there is no contractual relationship between the union and the institution.[16] In addition, the

---

[6]Sec. 8(d)(4)(A).

[7]*Id.*

[8]Sec. 8(d)(4)(B).

[9]Sec. 8(g).

[10]S. REP. NO. 766, 93d Cong., 2d Sess. 4 (1974).

[11]*See, e.g., District 1199-E, Nat'l Union of Hosp. & Health Care Employees (CHC Corp.),* 229 NLRB 1010, 95 LRRM 1214 (1977) (employees need not give 10-day notice when work stoppage is in protest of employer's repeated cancellation of scheduled grievance meetings).

[12]*See District 1199-E, Nat'l Union of Hosp. & Health Care Employees (Greater Penn. Ave. Nursing Center, Inc.),* 227 NLRB 132, 94 LRRM 1083 (1976).

[13]*District 1199-E, Nat'l Union of Hosp. & Health Care Employees (CHC Corp.),* 229 NLRB 1010, 95 LRRM 1214 (1977).

[14]*See, e.g., Montefiore Hosp. & Medical Center v. NLRB,* 621 F.2d 510, 104 LRRM 2160 (2d Cir. 1980) (notice provision not applicable to nonunionized doctors who walked out in sympathy with lawful economic strikers); *NLRB v. Long Beach Youth Center, Inc.,* 591 F.2d 1276, 101 LRRM 2501 (9th Cir. 1979) (notice provision not applicable to unrepresented employees who instituted work stoppage to protest their working conditions).

[15]*See District 1199, Nat'l Union of Hosp. & Health Care Employees (S. Nassau Communities Hosp.),* 256 NLRB 74, 107 LRRM 1190 (1981) (notice provision applied to activities of union organizers who displayed placards, patrolled hospital entrances, and passed out leaflets).

[16]*See, e.g., Bricklayers & Allied Craftsmen, Local 40,* 252 NLRB 252, 105 LRRM 1317 (1980); *Orange Belt Dist. Council No. 48,* 243 NLRB 609, 101 LRRM 1456 (1979).

fulfillment of the requirement by one union does not excuse another union's failure to comply.[17] When picketing is not directed at the health care institution, but rather at another employer, unions need not comply with the notice provision even though picketing occurs on the property of the health care institution.[18]

§22.4 Boards of Inquiry in Health Care Disputes

If the Director of the FMCS believes that a threatened or actual strike or lockout affecting a health care institution will substantially interrupt the delivery of health care services in the locality concerned, the Director may establish an impartial board of inquiry to investigate the issues and make a written report to the parties.[19] The Director's decision to establish a board is not subject to judicial review if he or she acts within 30 days after receiving notice.[20] Any appointment of a board after this 30-day period does not have legal force or effect.[21] Parties involved in the controversy may jointly submit to the Director a list of arbitrators or other impartial individuals as suggested board members. The Director, however, is not obligated to choose the board of inquiry from this list.[22]

Within 15 days after its establishment, the board must issue a written report containing its findings of fact and recommendations for settling the dispute.[23] After the Director has established the board, and for the 15 days following issuance of the board's report, the parties involved in the controversy may not make any change in the status quo as it existed prior to the expiration date of the contract.[24] Nevertheless, the board's recommendations are not binding on the parties.[25]

As an alternative to an FMCS-appointed board, the parties themselves may agree on a private factfinding process. The FMCS will defer to this process and not appoint a board of inquiry as long as the private process satisfies the FMCS' legal responsibilities.[26] The parties must submit to the FMCS a written copy of the agreed-upon factfinding process.[27] The procedure must:

- Be invoked automatically at a specific time;

---

[17]*See, e.g., General Serv. Employees' Union Local 200*, 263 NLRB 400, 111 LRRM 1613 (1982) (union engaged in sympathy strike not excused from notice requirement).

[18]*Painters, Local 452 (Beck Co.)*, 246 NLRB 970, 103 LRRM 1002 (1979).

[19]29 U.S.C. §183(a) (1982); 29 C.F.R. §1420.1(b).

[20]*Sinai Hosp. v. Horvitz*, 621 F.2d 1267, 104 LRRM 2171 (4th Cir. 1980).

[21]*Sinai Hosp. v. Scearce*, 561 F.2d 547, 96 LRRM 2355 (4th Cir. 1977).

[22]*See* 29 C.F.R. §1420.5 and 29 U.S.C. §183(a) (1982) for specific requirements in submission of lists.

[23]29 U.S.C. §183(a) (1982).

[24]29 U.S.C. §183(c) (1982).

[25]29 C.F.R. §1420.1(b).

[26]29 C.F.R. §1420.8(a).

[27]29 C.F.R. §1420.8(a)(4).

- Provide for a fixed and determinate method for selecting impartial factfinders;
- Prohibit strikes or lockouts or changes in conditions of employment except by mutual agreement prior to or during the factfinding procedure and for at least seven days afterward; and
- Provide that the factfinders will make a written report to the parties containing their findings and recommendations for settling the dispute, a copy of which is to be sent to the FMCS.[28]

The FMCS also may defer to a private arbitration procedure agreed to by the parties so long as the FMCS' legal responsibilities are fulfilled by that procedure.[29] The parties must jointly submit a procedure which:

- Provides that there can be no strike or lockout and no changes in conditions of employment except by mutual agreement during contract negotiations covered by the procedure and the period of any subsequent interest arbitration proceedings;[30]
- Provides that the award of the arbitrators is final and binding on both parties;
- Provides a fixed and determinate method for selecting the arbitrators; and
- Provides for a written award by the arbitrators.[31]

§22.5 Notice Requirements—United States Postal Service Employees

When the U.S. Postal Service was established in 1970 and the Board given jurisdiction over its employees, a number of special provisions governing both notice of disputes and contract-settlement procedures were included.[32] (See Appendix I.) Under these provisions:

- No party to an existing collective bargaining agreement is permitted to terminate or modify the agreement without serving a written notice of its intent on the other party not less than 90 days prior to either the expiration date of the agreement or the proposed date of termination or modification.
- A party desiring to terminate or modify an agreement must notify the Federal Mediation and Conciliation Service of the

---

[28] 29 C.F.R. §1420.8(a).

[29] 29 C.F.R. §1420.9(a).

[30] 29 C.F.R. §1420.9(b).

[31] 29 C.F.R. §1420.9(a).

[32] 39 U.S.C. §§1201–1209 (1982). NLRB Rules and Regulations §102.135 provides that to the extent applicable regular Board procedures shall apply to cases arising under the Postal Reorganization Act.

existence of a dispute within 45 days after giving the 90-day notice if no agreement has been reached by that time.[33]

There are no notice requirements in initial contract situations.

§22.6 Settlement Procedures—United States Postal Service Employees

The Postal Reorganization Act also includes provisions to assure settlement of all contract disputes without resort to strikes or lockouts. The following procedures are used:

- If the parties fail to reach agreement or to voluntarily agree upon a method to provide a binding resolution of a dispute by the date of either the contract expiration or the proposed termination or modification, the Director of the Federal Mediation and Conciliation Service establishes a factfinding panel of three persons. This is done by submitting a list of 15 names to the parties. Each party, within 10 days, selects one person, and the two chosen select from the list of 15 a third member who serves as chairman. The panel makes an investigation of the dispute and, not later than 45 days from the date the list of names was submitted to the parties, it must issue a report of its findings. The report may contain recommendations but it is not mandatory that it do so.[34]
- If the foregoing procedures fail to result in an agreement within 90 days after the contract expiration or termination, or the date on which the agreement became subject to modification, an arbitration board is established. The board consists of one person chosen by the Postal Service, one by the union, and the third by the two selected. Arbitration board members may not have served on the factfinding panel.[35]
- After a hearing at which the parties may present evidence in support of their claims, the arbitration board issues a decision which is "conclusive and binding upon the parties." The decision must be rendered within 45 days after the board's appointment.[36]

Costs of the factfinding panel and arbitration board are shared equally by the Postal Service and the bargaining representative.[37]

---

[33] 39 U.S.C. §1207(a) (1982).

[34] 39 U.S.C. §1207(b) (1982). To a considerable extent, matters arising under the Postal Reorganization Act are governed by the Board's Rules and Regulations applicable to other types of cases. *See* NLRB Rules and Regulations §102.135.

[35] 39 U.S.C. §1207(c)(1) (1982).

[36] 39 U.S.C. §1207(c)(2) (1982).

[37] 39 U.S.C. §1207(c)(3) (1982).

§22.7   Settlement Procedures—National Emergency Disputes

Since 1947 the Act has contained provisions for dealing with threatened or actual strikes or lockouts affecting all or a substantial part of an industry. The procedures are invoked when the President believes that the strike, if permitted to occur or to continue, will "imperil the national health or safety."[38] The President has the discretion to appoint a board of inquiry to investigate the issues involved in the dispute and to prepare a written report within whatever time is prescribed. The report must contain a statement of the facts with respect to the dispute and each party's statement of its position but it may not contain any recommendations. The report is made public.[39]

After receiving the report the President may direct the Attorney General to seek an injunction from an appropriate federal district court to prevent or end the strike. If an injunction issues, the parties are directed by the statute "to make every effort to adjust and settle their differences," but they are not required to accept any proposed settlement. Concurrently, the President reconvenes the board of inquiry and, at the end of 60 days, if the dispute has not been settled, the board again reports to the President. This report must include the current positions of the parties and a statement of the employer's last offer of settlement. This report also is made public.[40]

Within 15 days thereafter the Board is required to conduct a secret ballot election to determine whether the employees affected wish to accept or reject the employer's last offer. The results must be certified to the Attorney General within five days and the injunction is then dissolved.[41] Thus, injunctions may last a maximum of 80 days.

Although the Board has conducted such elections, it has never adopted regulations or formalized the procedures to be used. The Board's Casehandling Manual merely states that "last-offer" elections "should be undertaken pursuant to advice procured from the Division of Operations on a case-by-case basis."[42] Generally, preparation for and conduct of such elections closely resemble procedures followed in representation elections.

---

[38]Sec. 206.
[39]*Id.*
[40]Secs. 208, 209.
[41]Secs. 209, 210.
[42]NLRB Casehandling Manual ¶11520.

23

Proceedings for Reimbursement of Attorneys' Fees and Litigation Expenses

Equal Access to Justice Act

§23.1 Purpose

The Equal Access to Justice Act (EAJA)[1] provides that small businesses, public interest groups, and individuals may, in certain circumstances, recover attorneys' fees and other litigation expenses when they prevail in administrative or judicial proceedings in which the federal government is an opposing party. EAJA and Board rules state that a party (other than the United States) prevailing in a "significant and discrete substantive portion" of a proceeding will be reimbursed unless the agency's position in the proceeding was "substantially justified" or "special circumstances make an award unjust."[2] By offering reimbursement of attorneys' fees and other costs, Congress intended that litigants of modest resources would be encouraged to defend themselves against government action.

With regard to the NLRB in particular, EAJA applies only to unfair labor practice and backpay proceedings; it does not cover representation cases.[3] The original EAJA, which was enacted on a three-year trial basis, expired on October 1, 1984. A bill passed by Congress which would have extended EAJA with modifications was vetoed by President Reagan in November 1984. In August 1985, Congress re-

---

[1] 5 U.S.C. §504 (1982).
[2] 5 U.S.C. §504(a)(1) (1982); NLRB Rules and Regulations §102.143(b).
[3] NLRB Rules and Regulations §102.143(a).

519

enacted EAJA on a permanent basis and made the new legislation retroactive to October 1, 1984.

§23.2   Who May Seek Reimbursement

Persons eligible to receive EAJA awards are:[4]

- An individual whose net worth does not exceed $2 million;
- The sole owner of an unincorporated business who has a net worth of not more than $7 million, including both business and personal interests, and not more than 500 employees;
- A charitable or other tax-exempt organization described in §501(c)(3) of the Internal Revenue Code[5] with not more than 500 employees;
- A cooperative association as defined in §15(a) of the Agricultural Marketing Act[6] with not more than 500 employees; and
- Any other partnership, corporation, association, unit of local government, or public or private organization whose net worth does not exceed $7 million and 500 employees.

The applicant has the burden of proving eligibility for receipt of an award.[7] In *W.C. McQuaide, Inc.*,[8] the Board indicated that it is not enough for an applicant to satisfy only one of the eligibility requirements; both the net worth and employee standards must be met in order to be eligible for an award.

Eligibility under both the net worth and number of employee standards is determined as of the date of the notice of hearing (in a backpay proceeding) or the date of the complaint (in an unfair labor practice proceeding).[9]

(a) Calculating Net Worth. EAJA does not permit an applicant to value its assets at a depreciated cost. Net worth is determined by subtracting total liabilities from total assets, with assets valued at their acquisition cost rather than at their fair market value.[10]

The Board also requires that in determining eligibility the net worth of the applicant and all of its affiliates shall be aggregated.[11] The intent of Congress in enacting EAJA was to aid "truly small entities rather than those that are part of larger groups of affiliated

---

[4]NLRB Rules and Regulations §102.143(c).

[5]26 U.S.C. §501(c)(3) (1982).

[6]12 U.S.C. §1141j(a) (1982).

[7]*See Roofers, Local 135*, 269 NLRB 1067, 116 LRRM 1023 (1984).

[8]270 NLRB 1197, 116 LRRM 1265 (1984).

[9]NLRB Rules and Regulations §102.143(d).

[10]Some courts do not agree with the Board's interpretation and permit accumulated depreciation to be deducted in calculating net worth. *American Pacific Concrete Pipe Co. v. NLRB*, __ F.2d __, 122 LRRM 2205 (9th Cir. 1986); *Continental Web Press Inc. v. NLRB*, 767 F.2d 321, 119 LRRM 3125 (7th Cir. 1985).

[11]NLRB Rules and Regulations §102.143(g).

firms."[12] Aggregation is required in all situations where the applicant is directly or indirectly controlled by, or is directly or indirectly in control of, the affiliated organizations.[13] The Board recognizes, however, that certain unspecified financial arrangements may not, standing alone, create a sufficient nexus between two or more organizations to justify aggregation.[14]

(b) Determining Number of Employees.

The term "employees" for purposes of determining EAJA eligibility includes "all persons who regularly perform services for remuneration for the applicant under the applicant's direction and control."[15] Since this definition appears to include management personnel and supervisors it is broader than the definition of employee in Section 2(3) of the National Labor Relations Act.

Several issues remain unresolved concerning the employee complement standard. The General Counsel has interpreted "employees" to include members of an applicant's board of directors. An administrative law judge has disagreed with this interpretation on the basis that corporate directors cannot be considered employees because they do not work under the applicant's "direction and control."[16]

Part-time workers are included in counting the number of employees "on a proportional basis."[17] The precise method of calculating the number of part-time employees, however, has not yet been determined.[18] Suggested methods include the number of hours worked by the part-time employees on the date the complaint issued, during the week in which the complaint issued, during the payroll period in which the complaint issued, or during that year.[19]

Finally, the status of strikers as employees under EAJA is unresolved. In one case an administrative law judge held that they are not to be counted as employees for purposes of EAJA jurisdiction

---

[12]Administrative Conference of the United States, Equal Access to Justice Act: Agency Implementation, 46 Fed. Reg. 32,900, 32,902–32,903 (June 25, 1981).

[13]*Kut-Kwik Corp.*, 273 NLRB No. 112, 118 LRRM 1200 (1984) (net worth statement of applicant must include net worth of sole stockholder of parent corporation); *Noel Produce, Inc.*, 273 NLRB No. 104, 118 LRRM 1303 (1984) (aggregate net worth of applicant and its parent company exceeded $5 million); *Pacific Coast Metal Trades Dist. Council (Foss Launch & Tug Co.)*, 271 NLRB 1165, 117 LRRM 1179 (1984) (aggregation required where trades council derives a majority of its financial support directly or indirectly from monthly affiliation fee of member local councils); *see also Carpenters Local 1361 (Atchinson Foundation Co.)*, 272 NLRB No. 176, 117 LRRM 1462 (1984) (aggregation of local union's assets with those of its international may be appropriate if direct or indirect control exists). *But see Miller v. Hotel and Restaurant Employees and Bartenders, Local 2*, 605 F. Supp. 753, 199 LRRM 2560 (N.D. Cal. 1985) (local union's eligibility should be determined without reference to its affiliation with international union).

[14]NLRB Rules and Regulations §102.143(g).

[15]*Id.* at §102.143(f).

[16]*Lion Uniform*, JD-(ATL)-76-83 (10-CA-12938(E), *et al.*).

[17]NLRB Rules and Regulations §102.143(f).

[18]General Counsel Memorandum No. 83-11 (April 7, 1983), *The Equal Access to Justice Act—The First Year, reprinted in* 1983 Lab. Rel. Yrbk. 222 (BNA). Copies may be acquired from the Board's Information Division.

[19]*Id.*

because they are not regularly performing services for the applicant under the applicant's direction and control.[20]

As with calculating an applicant's net worth, the number of employees an applicant has shall be calculated by aggregating the applicant's own workers with those of its affiliates.[21]

§23.3   Prevailing Parties

For the purpose of EAJA, a prevailing party in an adversary adjudication is one who has "prevailed" in an entire proceeding or in a "significant and discrete substantive portion" of a proceeding.[22] Only a respondent who satifies this standard and who meets the other EAJA eligibility requirements can apply for an award of fees and expenses. Applications from parties who have not prevailed entirely or in a "significant and discrete substantive portion" of a proceeding will be denied.[23]

In *Westerman, Inc.*,[24] an administrative law judge sustained complaint allegations that the company unlawfully had threatened to close its plant, but dismissed allegations that 13 employees had been unlawfully discharged and that one supervisor unlawfully had created an impression of surveillance of employee union activities. In a subsequent EAJA action maintained by the company to recover fees and expenses for the dismissed portions of the complaint, the Board found that the discharge allegations did constitute a significant and discrete portion of the case, but that the impression of surveillance claim, while perhaps discrete, was not "significant."

§23.4   Defenses to Reimbursement Requests

After the applicant has demonstrated eligibility to apply for an EAJA award, the burden of proof then shifts to the General Counsel to demonstrate that an award should not be made.[25]

(a) Substantial Justification. The General Counsel has the burden of proving that its position in the proceeding was substantially

---

[20]*Lion Uniform*, JD-(ATL)-76-83 (10-CA-12938(E), *et al.*).

[21]NLRB Rules and Regulations §102.143(g); see §23.2(a) *supra*.

[22]*Id.* at §102.143(b).

[23]Dismissal of a complaint pursuant to the terms of a negotiated settlement agreement does not make the respondent a "prevailing party." *Carthage Heating & Sheet Metal Co.*, 273 NLRB No. 22, 118 LRRM 1023 (1984); *Duncan Crane Serv., Inc.*, JD-(SF)-270-82 (19-CA-13802(E)) (respondent not deemed "prevailing" where complaint was dismissed before hearing only because parties deferred to arbitration).

[24]266 NLRB 799, 113 LRRM 1054 (1983).

[25]NLRB Rules and Regulations §102.144(a).

justified.[26] If the General Counsel established a *prima facie* case in the underlying administrative proceeding, the Board will find that the General Counsel's position is substantially justified and will dismiss the fee application.[27] The fact that the respondent subsequently rebutted the General Counsel's *prima facie* case is not sufficient to justify a fee award.[28]

The absence of a *prima facie* case, however, does not necessarily mean that a fee award is appropriate.[29] The fact that the Board lost its case does not give rise to a presumption that its position was unreasonable, and the substantially justified standard does not "require the Government to establish that its decision to litigate was based on a substantial probability of prevailing."[30] In cases where a complaint is issued in light of conflicting evidence requiring credi-

---

[26]*Id.* Prior to the permanent enactment of EAJA in 1985, the courts were not in agreement as to precisely what government position had to be substantially justified. Some courts held that EAJA referred to the government's position taken in litigation. *See, e.g. United States v. 2,116 Boxes of Boned Beef,* 726 F.2d 1481 (10th Cir. 1984); *Spencer v. NLRB,* 712 F.2d 539, 113 LRRM 3178 (D.C. Cir. 1983); *Electronic Modules Corp. v. United States,* 702 F.2d 218 (D.C. Cir. 1983). Other courts determined that EAJA referred to the substantial justification of the underlying governmental action that gave rise to the litigation in the first place. *See, e.g., Natural Resources Defense Council v. EPA,* 703 F.2d 700 (3d Cir. 1983); *Moholland v. Schweiker,* 546 F. Supp. 383 (D.N.H. 1982); *Photo Data v. Sawyer,* 533 F. Supp. 348 (D.D.C. 1982); *see also Tyler Business Servs., Inc. v. NLRB,* 695 F.2d 73, 111 LRRM 3001 (4th Cir. 1982) (both underlying action and litigation theories mentioned). Still other courts examined the totality of the circumstances including both the government's prelitigation and litigation conduct in determining whether its position was substantially justified. *Iowa Express Distribution v. NLRB,* 739 F.2d 1305, 116 LRRM 3224 (8th Cir. 1984); *Rawlings v. Heckler,* 725 F.2d 1192 (9th Cir. 1984).

In 1985 EAJA was amended to provide that the "position of the agency" which must be substantially justified means "in addition to the position taken by the agency in the adversary adjudication, *the action or failure to act by the agency upon which the adversary adjudication is based.*" (Emphasis added). Pub. L. No. 99-80, §1(c)(3)(B), 99 Stat. 183, 184, (1985). In commenting upon the meaning of this clarification Senator Grassley observed that

"when deciding whether a prevailing party shall be awarded fees, a court or adjudicative officer shall evaluate both the Government's agreements made in the litigation and the agency action that made it necessary for the private party to seek relief. Thus, if the agency action that led to the litigation is not substantially justified, a prevailing party could be eligible for an Equal Access to Justice Act award, irrespective of the merits of the Government's arguments once they get to court."

131 Cong. Rec. S9992 (daily ed. July 24, 1985) (statement of Sen. Grassley). In determining eligibility, the Board and the courts must confine their review to the administrative record as a whole developed in the underlying adjudicatory proceeding and may not engage in independent discovery. Pub. L. No. 99-80, §1(a)(1), 99 Stat. 183 (1985); 131 Cong. Rec. S9994 (daily ed. July 24, 1985) (statement of Sen. Heflin).

In cases decided since the 1985 amendments, the Board has held that the amendments were not intended to alter, but merely to clarify, the definition of "substantially justified" which means more than "mere reasonableness." *R. and K. Caterers, Inc.,* 277 NLRB No. 2, 120 LRRM 1227 (1985); *Forest Grove Lumber Co.,* 277 NLRB No. 167, 121 LRRM 1272 (1985).

[27]*See Contemporary & Scandinavian Interiors, Inc.,* 272 NLRB No. 82, 117 LRRM 1343 (1984) ("where the General Counsel presents evidence which, if credited by the fact finder, would constitute a *prima facie* case of unlawful conduct, the General Counsel's case has been deemed to be substantially justified . . .").

[28]*Bosk Paint & Sandblast Co.,* 270 NLRB 514, 116 LRRM 1103 (1984).

[29]*Wolf Street Supermarkets (Jim's Big M),* 266 NLRB 665, 113 LRRM 1019 (1983) ("presence or absence of a *prima facie* case is not determinative"; standard to be employed is one of "reasonableness"); *Enerhaul, Inc.,* 263 NLRB 890, 111 LRRM 1085 (1982) (establishment of a *prima facie* case is not a *sine qua non* for the establishment of substantial justification).

[30]S. REP. No. 253, 96th Cong., 1st Sess. 6–7, 14–15 (1979); H.R. REP. No. 1418, 96th Cong., 2d Sess. 10–11 (1980) *quoted in Spencer v. NLRB,* 712 F.2d 539, 557, 113 LRRM 3178, 3192 (D.C. Cir. 1983).

bility resolutions on the part of the administrative law judge, the fact that the resolutions eventually are made against the General Counsel's witnesses does not mean that the General Counsel was unreasonable in issuing the complaint.[31]

EAJA recognizes that in some instances agencies may lose cases which are brought to define the outer limits of the law. Congress thus noted that fee awards would be inappropriate when the government is "advancing in good faith a novel but credible extension and interpretation of the law."[32] Whether this standard is met is an issue which must be decided on a case-by-case basis in light of all of the surrounding circumstances.[33]

A similar issue exists when the General Counsel issues a complaint which reflects or represents a reasonable extension of existing Board precedent, but which is inconsistent with the law of the circuit in which the alleged unfair labor practice occurred. In *Enerhaul, Inc. v. NLRB*,[34] the General Counsel issued a complaint on the theory that individual employee gripes regarding safety issues constituted protected concerted activity. At the time the complaint issued, the General Counsel's theory represented prevailing Board law,[35] but was inconsistent with precedent in the Eleventh Circuit. The Court of Appeals granted the employer's request for fees and expenses "because the NLRB's position in this case was unreasonable under the law of this Circuit."[36] In contrast, the Court of Appeals for the Sixth Circuit in *Wyandotte Savings Bank v. NLRB*[37] reflected a more lenient position stating that "the fact that the NLRB's position was contrary to prior Sixth Circuit precedent does not mean that the Board was not substantially justified in seeking enforcement of its order."[38] The court observed that the Board has broad discretion in the prosecution of unfair labor practice cases and that several other circuits, as well as certain individual judges on the Sixth Circuit,

---

[31]*Wolf Street Supermarkets (Jim's Big M)*, 266 NLRB 665, 113 LRRM 1019 (1983); *see also Contemporary & Scandinavian Interiors, Inc.*, 272 NLRB No. 82, 117 LRRM 1343 (1984); *Charter Mgt. Inc.*, 271 NLRB 169, 116 LRRM 1351 (1984); *Wright-Bernet, Inc.*, 270 NLRB 55, 116 LRRM 1160 (1984).

[32]H.R. REP. No. 1418, 96th Cong., 2d Sess. 10 (1980); *Enerhaul, Inc. v. NLRB*, 710 F.2d 748, 113 LRRM 3636 (11th Cir. 1983); *see also* General Counsel Memorandum No. 81-55 (November 19, 1981), *Casehandling Guidelines Relating to the Equal Access to Justice Act* at 12. Copies may be acquired from the Board's Information Division.

[33]*Compare Iowa Parcel Serv., Inc.*, 266 NLRB 392, 112 LRRM 1415 (1983) (General Counsel argued a novel but credible extension and interpretation of the law relating to alter ego relationships) *with Debolt Transfer, Inc.*, 271 NLRB 299, 117 LRRM 1306 (1984) (General Counsel's theory for a Sec. 8(a)(1), (3) and (5) violation not a "reasonable" novel extension of the law).

[34]710 F.2d 748, 113 LRRM 3636 (11th Cir. 1983).

[35]*Alleluia Cushion Co.*, 221 NLRB 999, 91 LRRM 1131 (1975). In *Meyers Indus.*, 268 NLRB 493, 115 LRRM 1025 (1984), the Board reversed *Alleluia Cushion* and held that an employee's activity must be engaged in with or on the authority of other employees, and not solely by and on behalf of the employee alone, in order to constitute protected concerted activity.

[36]710 F.2d at 751, 113 LRRM at 3639.

[37]682 F.2d 119, 110 LRRM 2929 (6th Cir. 1982).

[38]682 F.2d at 120, 110 LRRM at 2930.

agreed with the Board's position. Accordingly, the fee request was denied.

(b) Lack of Cooperation or Special Circumstances. In addition to cases in which the Board's position is substantially justified, an award will be reduced or denied if the applicant has unduly or unreasonably prolonged the proceeding or if special circumstances make the award sought unjust.[39]

§23.5 Allowable Fees and Expenses

(a) In General. EAJA awards include attorneys' fees and other expenses incurred in unfair labor practice and backpay proceedings but do not include costs incurred in representation proceedings.[40] Fees incurred during the General Counsel's investigation prior to the issuance of an unfair labor practice complaint or prior to the issuance of a notice of hearing in a backpay proceeding are not recoverable under EAJA.[41] Expenses incurred in seeking EAJA awards following issuance of a Board decision, however, are recoverable.[42]

(b) Computing Attorneys' Fees. The following rules are used to compute recoverable fees and expenses:[43]

- Awards shall be based on "rates customarily charged by persons engaged in the business of acting as attorneys, agents, and expert witnesses," even where the applicant has received a reduced rate on services;
- No award shall exceed $75 per hour.

In determining the reasonableness of the fees sought, the Board considers:[44]

- The attorney's, agent's, or expert witness' customary fee for similar services, or if an employee of the applicant, the fully allocated cost of the services;

---

[39]NLRB Rules and Regulations §102.144(b); *International Maintenance Sys. Group, Inc.*, 267 NLRB 1136, 114 LRRM 1138 (1983) (fees denied where applicant uncooperative during investigation); *Duncan Crane Serv., Inc.*, JD-(SF)-270-82 (19-CA-13802(E)) ("special circumstances" existed where EAJA proceedings would entail a trial and litigation as costly as award sought).

[40]NLRB Rules and Regulations §102.143(a).

[41]*Id.*; *see Evergreen Lumber Co.*, JD-(SF)-108-83 (28-CA-64598(E)).

[42]*Debolt Transfer, Inc.*, 271 NLRB 299, 117 LRRM 1306 (1984); *see also Tyler Business Servs., Inc. v. NLRB*, 695 F.2d 73, 111 LRRM 3001 (4th Cir. 1982); *accord Ocasio v. Schweiker*, 540 F. Supp. 1320 (S.D.N.Y. 1982); *Photo Data v. Sawyer*, 533 F. Supp. 348 (D.D.C. 1982).

[43]NLRB Rules and Regulations §102.145(a), (b).

[44]*Id.* at §102.145(c).

- The prevailing rate for similar services within the community in which the attorney, agent, or expert witness usually performs services;
- The time actually spent representing the applicant, and the reasonableness of that amount of time considering the complexity of issues involved.

Any person may file with the Board a petition to increase the maximum rate for recoverable attorney or agent fees.[45] The petition should include the desired rate of reimbursement and should explain fully why the higher rate is warranted (i.e., an increase in the cost of living or some other special factor such as the limited availability of attorneys).

The Board has been extremely reluctant to grant a request to pay more than the maximum statutory rate of $75 per hour.[46] Accordingly, the emphasis generally is placed on the "reasonableness" of hours charged and not on the hourly rate. "Reasonableness" of hours charged customarily is determined by the number of hours spent on a case and whether those hours constituted productive work time.[47]

An award may include in addition to fees the reasonable expenses of the attorney, agent, or witness as a separate item if the person rendering the service customarily charges clients separately for such expenses.[48]

An applicant may be reimbursed for the "reasonable cost" of any study, engineering report, test, project, analysis, or similar matter necessary for preparation of the applicant's case so long as the charge for the service is not greater than the prevailing rate for similar services.[49]

---

[45]*Id.* at §102.146.

[46]The Board has denied requests for rulemaking to raise the statutory $75 per hour ceiling on the basis that higher fees often were requested at the time Congress passed EAJA and there has been no change in the circumstances since then. *See Best Bread Co.*, 272 NLRB 470, 117 LRRM 1445 (1984) ($94 to $128 per hour); *International Maintenance Sys. Group, Inc.*, 262 NLRB 1, 110 LRRM 1196 (1982) (seeking $140 per hour); *see also Abbott House, Inc.*, 272 NLRB No. 173, 117 LRRM 1471 (1984) (Board denied request to raise rate to $83.87 per hour on basis of inflation); *Adams & Westlake, Ltd.*, 271 NLRB 470, 117 LRRM 1007 (1984) (Board denied request to raise hourly rate from $75 to $81.54 in accordance with increase in Consumer Price Index since enactment of EAJA); *Stephens College*, 268 NLRB 1035, 115 LRRM 1149 (1984) (seeking $130 per hour); *Columbia Mfg. Corp.*, 262 NLRB 3, 110 LRRM 1196 (1982) (seeking $145 per hour); *Allied Lettercraft Co.*, 262 NLRB 2, 110 LRRM 1195 (1982) (seeking $140 per hour). *But see Miller v. Hotel and Restaurant Employees and Bartenders Local 2*, 605 F. Supp. 753, 119 LRRM 2560 (N.D. Cal. 1985) (calculation of fees at $85 per hour approved in light of the high caliber of the presentations on behalf of the union, the novel and important issue presented, and the valuable precedent set by the case).

[47]*See Photo Data v. Sawyer*, 533 F. Supp. 348 (D.D.C. 1982) (court found 40 percent of time expended to be nonproductive and accordingly reduced requested attorneys' fees and expenses).

[48]NLRB Rules and Regulations §102.145(b).

[49]*Id.* at 102.145(d); *see also Photo Data v. Sawyer*, 533 F. Supp. 348 (D.D.C. 1982) (clerk, marshal fees, copying and printing costs, and docket fees recoverable, but overtime meals, car, local transportation, and miscellaneous costs not recoverable); Administrative Conference of United States Draft Model Rules, 46 Fed. Reg. 15,895, 15,898 (March 10, 1981).

Filing a Claim for Attorneys' Fees and Expenses

§23.6 Application

An EAJA proceeding is commenced with the filing of an application with the Board in Washington, D.C.[50]

(a) Contents. The application shall include the following:[51]

- Identification of the applicant and the adversary adjudication for which the award is sought, along with a statement of the particulars in which the applicant prevailed, and an identification of the portion of the proceeding in which the applicant alleges the General Counsel's position was not substantially justified;
- A statement of the number, category and work location of employees of the applicant (unless the applicant is an individual) and a description of the type and purpose of its business or organization;
- A statement that the applicant's net worth is not greater than $2 million (if an individual), or $7 million (for all other applicants, including their affiliates);[52]
- A statement of the amount of fees and expenses for which an award is sought;
- Any other matters the applicant wishes the agency to consider when deciding whether and in what amount an award should be made; and
- Full documentation of fees and expenses sought, including, when available, receipts, vouchers, or other substantiation of awards claimed.

The application must be signed by the applicant, an authorized officer, or the applicant's attorney, and must be accompanied by written verification under oath that the information provided is true.[53] An EAJA application must be filed by or on behalf of the applicant and not on behalf of the applicant's attorney.[54]

(b) Timeliness. The application must be filed within 30 days after entry of the Board's final order and shall establish that the applicant has prevailed entirely or in a "significant and discrete sub-

---

[50]NLRB Rules and Regulations §102.148.

[51]*Id.* at §§102.147(a), (b), (c), (d), (h).

[52]Organizations which are tax exempt under Sec. 501(c)(3) of the Internal Revenue Code and agricultural cooperative associations are exempt from this requirement. NLRB Rules and Regulations §§102.147(b)(1), (2).

[53]*Id.* at §102.147(e).

[54]*Power Contractors, Ltd.*, JD-(SF)-268-82 (27-CA-6969(E)).

stantive portion" of that proceeding.[55] The application should be filed in triplicate with the Board in Washington, D.C., along with a certificate of service, and copies should be served on the regional director and all parties.[56]

Where in the absence of exceptions the Board adopts the administrative law judge's decision *pro forma*, the 30-day filing period for an EAJA application begins on the date the Board issues its order.[57] If exceptions to the administrative law judge's decision are filed and the Board issues a decision on the merits, the 30-day filing period begins with the date of the Board's decision and order.[58]

If the end of the 30-day filing period falls on a Saturday, Sunday, or holiday, the application is timely if it is filed on the next regular business day.[59] The Board has determined that the 30-day time limit for filing an application is jurisdictional in nature and therefore cannot be waived or extended.[60] An application will be considered filed when the Board receives it, not when it is placed in the mail.[61] Service must be made on the Board in Washington, D.C.,[62] and service on the regional director is not considered a substitute for service on the Board.[63]

An application must be filed within the 30-day limit even when the applicant intends to file a motion for reconsideration of the Board's order or seek court review. In such instances the EAJA proceeding is held in abeyance pending reconsideration or review.[64]

The withdrawal of a complaint by a regional director shall be treated as a final order, and an appeal of the withdrawal to the General Counsel shall be treated as a motion for reconsideration.[65]

(c) Request for Confidentiality. Except for qualified tax-exempt organizations and agricultural cooperative associations, each applicant must provide along with the fee application a detailed exhibit showing its net worth and that of any of its affiliates.[66]

Any applicant who objects to public disclosure of any portion of the net worth exhibit may submit that portion of the exhibit in a sealed envelope labeled "Confidential Financial Information," accompanied by a motion to withhold that information from disclosure. The

---

[55]NLRB Rules and Regulations §102.148(a).

[56]*Id.*

[57]*T.E. Elevator Corp.*, 268 NLRB 1461, 115 LRRM 1235 (1984).

[58]*Id.*

[59]*B.J. Heating & Air Conditioning, Inc.*, 268 NLRB 643 98, 115 LRRM 1081 (1984).

[60]*Id.*; *Monark Boat Co.*, 262 NLRB 994, 110 LRRM 1431 (1982).

[61]NLRB Rules and Regulations §102.111(b)(2); *Haynes-Trane Serv. Agency Inc.*, 265 NLRB 958, 112 LRRM 1053 (1982).

[62]NLRB Rules and Regulations §102.148(a).

[63]*Lord Jim's*, 264 NLRB 1098, 111 LRRM 1319 (1982).

[64]NLRB Rules and Regulations §102.148(c).

[65]*Id.* at §102.148(d).

[66]NLRB Rules and Regulations §102.147(f).

motion shall describe which information should be withheld, why disclosure would have an adverse affect on the applicant, and why the public does not need access to that information.[67] The exhibit is filed with the administrative law judge and a copy need only be served on the General Counsel.[68]

The fact that a motion to withhold information is granted is not determinative of its availability under the Freedom of Information Act.[69] Moreover, even in the event that information is withheld from the general public, the General Counsel has the authority to disclose the information to others if necessary to verify an eligibility claim.[70]

§23.7 Answer to Application

The General Counsel may file an answer within 35 days following service of the application.[71] Included in the answer is an explanation of any objections to the award and the facts on which the decision of the General Counsel to issue a complaint were based.[72]

Failure to file a timely answer may be treated as consent to the requested award[73] unless:[74]

- An extension of time to answer has been requested;
- A statement of intent to negotiate a settlement has been filed; or
- A motion to dismiss the application has been filed.

An applicant has 21 days to respond to an answer[75] or to a motion to dismiss filed in lieu of an answer.[76] If the motion to dismiss is granted in its entirety, Board review may be requested.[77] Any party to a proceeding other than the applicant and the General Counsel may file comments on an award application within 35 days of its service, and may comment on an answer within 21 days of its service.[78]

---

[67]*Id.* at §102.147(g)(1).

[68]*Id.*

[69]*Id.* at §102.147(g)(2).

[70]*Id.*

[71]*Id.* at §102.150(a).

[72]*Id.* at §102.150(c). If the answer is based on alleged facts not already in the record, supporting affidavits may be provided or a request made for further proceedings under §102.152 of the Board's Rules and Regulations.

[73]*Id.* at §102.150(a).

[74]*Id.*

[75]*Id.* at §102.150(d).

[76]*Id.* at §102.150(a).

[77]*Id.*

[78]*Id.* at §102.150(e).

Proceedings Before the Administrative Law Judge

Upon filing, the application is referred by the Board to the administrative law judge who heard the underlying proceeding.[79] All motions and pleadings from the time the case is referred to the administrative law judge until a decision is issued should be filed in triplicate with the judge along with proof of service. Copies of all documents should be served on the other parties.[80] Rulings made by the administrative law judge are reviewable by the Board in the same manner as rulings made during regular unfair labor practice hearings.[81]

Requests for extensions of time to file motions, documents, or pleadings should be filed with the chief administrative law judge in Washington, D.C., the deputy chief administrative law judge in San Francisco, or the associate chief in New York or Atlanta, as appropriate.[82] Such requests must be filed not later than three days before the document is due. Notice of extension requests must be served on all parties along with proof of service.[83]

§23.8   Settlement of Fee Awards

Under certain circumstances the General Counsel and the applicant may feel that the award application can be settled without formal proceedings. In such cases they jointly shall file a statement of "their intent to negotiate towards a settlement" which has the effect of extending by 35 days the permissible time for filing an answer.[84]

A settlement of an award can be reached at any time before final action on an application. In the event that the applicant and General Counsel agree on a proposed settlement of an award before the application has been filed, the proposal should be filed with the application[85] and is subject to Board approval.

§23.9   Evidentiary Hearings

The Board's rules contemplate that most EAJA awards will be made on the basis of documents in the record without need for an

---

[79]*Id.* at §102.148(b).

[80]*Id.* at §102.149(a).

[81]*Id.* at §§102.152(e), 102.26. Appeals of administrative law judges' rulings are discussed at §16.14.

[82]*Id.* at §102.149(b).

[83]*Id.*

[84]*Id.* at §102.150(b).

[85]*Id.* at §102.151.

evidentiary hearing.[86] The administrative law judge may, however, upon the request of one of the parties or upon his or her own motion, order further proceedings such as an informal conference or additional written submissions.[87] Evidentiary hearings are held only as a last resort.[88]

Any party requesting a hearing should specify the disputed issues, the evidence sought to be introduced at the hearing, and explain why an additional hearing is necessary.[89] An administrative law judge's order for a hearing will specify which issues are to be considered.[90] The hearing is held in accordance with the Board's rules for unfair labor practice hearings[91] described in chapter 16.[92]

§23.10 Administrative Law Judge's Decision

Upon conclusion of the proceedings discussed above, the administrative law judge prepares a decision including written findings and conclusions which dispose of the award application.[93] Each party receives a copy of the decision and a copy of the order transferring the case to the Board.[94]

Proceedings Before the Board

Procedures for filing exceptions to administrative law judges' decisions, and procedures for Board consideration of the decisions, are the same as those for unfair labor practice cases.[95]

The record before the Board includes the application and any amendments or attachments, the answer with any amendments or attachments, replies to the answer, the net worth exhibit, comments by other parties, motions, rulings, stipulations, orders, written submissions, the stenographic transcript of any oral argument or hearing, exhibits, and depositions.[96] The record also contains the

---

[86]*Id.* at §102.152(a).

[87]*Id.*

[88]*Id.*

[89]*Id.* at §102.152(b).

[90]*Id.* at §102.152(c).

[91]*Id.* at §102.152(d).

[92]Evidentiary hearings under EAJA follow the Board's rules for unfair labor practice hearings except that the following sections shall not apply: §102.33 (relating to the consolidation, severance, and transfer of unfair labor practice charges), §102.34 (relating to the initial designation of administrative law judges), and §102.38 (relating to the rights of parties to participate in hearings). NLRB Rules and Regulations §102.152(d).

[93]NLRB Rules and Regulations §102.153(a).

[94]*Id.*

[95]*Id.* at §102.154. Exceptions to administrative law judges' decisions are discussed at §§17.4–17.9.

[96]*Id.* at §102.153(b).

administrative law judge's decision and exceptions, cross-exceptions, answering briefs, and the record of the unfair labor practice or back-pay proceeding upon which the application is based.[97]

To receive payment of an award the applicant must give to the Director of the Board's Division of Administration a copy of the Board's decision granting the award, and a statement that the party will not seek court review. If such a statement is filed, the Board will pay the award within 60 days.[98] If the applicant chooses to seek court review of the fee award or the underlying decision, however, the Board's obligation to pay the fee is stayed.[99]

---

[97]*Id.*
[98]*Id.* at §102.155.
[99]*Id.*

V

Records and Filing Requirements

24

Records and Information

§24.1 In General

The Board makes available to the public bound volumes of its case decisions, copies of its rules and regulations, and its annual reports. During the Board's early days it generally refused to supply most other records and information. During this period the majority of the Board's representation case decisions were issued as "short forms" and were unpublished. Since the delegation of authority over these matters to the regional directors in 1961, however, all Board decisions in representation matters have been included in the bound volumes, but regional directors' decisions continue to be unpublished.

Other materials now are available as a result of decisions under the Freedom of Information Act (discussed at §§24.3–24.4 *infra*) which generally requires greater disclosure by government agencies.

§24.2 Materials Currently Published on a Regular Basis

The Board and the General Counsel regularly publish the materials listed below. Unless otherwise noted, all documents may be purchased from the Superintendent of Documents, U.S. Government Printing Office, Washington, D.C. 20402.

1. *Decisions and Orders of the National Labor Relations Board.* These are bound volumes containing complete decisions of the Board. Only relatively current volumes are available and there are serious delays in publication, frequently more than a year. Copies of individual decisions may be obtained immediately after issuance from the Information Division, National Labor Relations Board, Washington, D.C. 20570. They also are available to the public through commercial services such as the *Labor Relations Reporter* (published by The Bureau of National Affairs, Inc., Washington, D.C. 20037).

2. *Guide for Hearing Officers in National Labor Relations Board Proceedings.* This guide, compiled in the Office of the General Counsel, provides procedures, checklists, and reference materials for NLRB professional personnel in representation case hearings.

3. *Classification Outline With Topical Classified Index for Decisions of the National Labor Relations Board and Related Court Decisions, and Classified Indices of NLRB and Related Court Decisions.* The outline provides a subject matter classification system for procedural and legal issues contained in NLRB and related court decisions. It also contains a topical index to the classification outline headings which provides an alphabetized word or term entry to all outline headings containing that word or term. The classified indices are cumulative volumes that cover NLRB and related court decisions within a prescribed period of time. Given the extraordinary level of detail contained in the Classification Outline and indices, these books are an invaluable reference source for persons researching Board and related court decisions.

4. *Classified Indices of Decisions of Regional Directors of the National Labor Relations Board in Representation Proceedings.* These indices, similar in format to the classified outline described immediately above, are compiled by the Office of the General Counsel and reference the final decisions and orders issued by regional directors in representation proceedings.

5. *NLRB Election Report.* This monthly report lists the outcome of NLRB-conducted representation elections. The report is compiled from results following resolution of postelection objections and/or challenges, and is arranged in two parts—single- and multi-union elections. The election tallies are listed by unions involved along with employer name and location. The subscription service for the NLRB Election Report can be ordered from the Superintendent of Documents.

6. *The Annual Report of the National Labor Relations Board.* After the close of each fiscal year the Board issues an annual report containing statistical material and a review of significant case decisions. These rarely appear until the following calendar year.

7. *Rules and Regulations and Statements of Procedure, Series 8, as Amended.* Formerly a paperback pamphlet, the Board's rules and regulations now are issued in looseleaf form in order that amendments may be added. Copies of the current rules and a subscription to any changes are available through the Superintendent of Documents. Frequently there are long delays before changes are distributed.

8. *Weekly Summary of NLRB Cases.* This service contains a summary of each published Board decision in representation election, unfair labor practice, and Equal Access to Justice Act cases; lists decisions of administrative law judges and directions of elections by

regional directors; reproduces guideline memoranda issued by the General Counsel to field offices on important casehandling subjects; carries notices of publication of bound volumes of Board decisions and orders, NLRB annual reports, and other agency informational literature. The subscription service for the Weekly Summary can be ordered from the Superintendent of Documents. BNA publishes the Weekly Summary in its *Daily Labor Report* service, generally in the Monday editions.

9. *General Counsel's Report of Casehandling Developments.* Each quarter the General Counsel issues a report discussing rulings on whether or not to issue unfair labor practice complaints in cases involving important or unusual issues. The reports are valuable sources of policy changes and developments at their earliest stages. Copies may be obtained from the Information Division, National Labor Relations Board, Washington, D.C. 20570, and also are published by BNA on a current basis as a part of its weekly *Labor Relations Reporter* service and as a permanent reference in its *Labor Relations Yearbooks.*

10. *National Labor Relations Board Casehandling Manual.* This three-part manual provides complete, updated General Counsel procedural and operational guidelines to the Board's regional offices in processing cases. Part One is entitled "Unfair Labor Practice Proceedings"; Part Two, "Representation Proceedings"; and Part Three, "Compliance Proceedings and Settlement Agreements." It is available as a subscription service from the Superintendent of Documents.

11. *NLRB Guide.* This nontechnical guide to basic law and procedures under the National Labor Relations Act can be purchased from the Superintendent of Documents.

12. *Miscellaneous Materials.* The Board issues, through the Information Division, general explanatory pamphlets on its function and the law it enforces. These are not in sufficient detail to be useful as research sources or procedural manuals. Statistical information, news releases, and other miscellaneous materials are also issued by the Information Division from time to time.

§24.3 Records and Information Available for Inspection and Copying Under the Freedom of Information Act

The Freedom of Information Act (FOIA),[1] enacted in 1966 and amended in 1974, was passed to increase public access to government

---

[1] 5 U.S.C. §552.

records. Under FOIA, the NLRB makes available a variety of materials for public inspection and copying.

(a) Information Disclosable Upon Oral Request. The following materials are available to the public upon oral request during normal business hours:[2]

- Final opinions and orders of the Board, available from the Board in Washington, D.C.;
- Administrative staff manuals (with the exception of those described later in this chapter) and instructions that affect any member of the public, available from the Board's Washington office and from each regional, subregional, and resident office;
- A current index of final Board opinions and orders, available from the Board's Washington office and from each regional, subregional, and resident office;
- A record of the final vote of each member of the Board in each agency proceeding, available from the Board's Washington office; and
- Formal documents constituting the record in a case or proceeding, available from the Board's Washington office and from each regional, subregional, and resident office.

(b) Information Disclosable Upon Written Request. The public may use the written request procedure to obtain the following materials:[3]

In Open Case Files[4]

- Formal documents;
- Pleadings;
- Other nonconfidential information in the case file such as collective bargaining agreements, newspaper clippings, arbitrators' decisions, and transcripts from other proceedings;
- After the close of a hearing, all affidavits or portions of affidavits which have been produced during the hearing pursuant to the Board's Rules and Regulations §102.118;
- Documents which are or were in the possession of a party, such as letters to or from that party, will be disclosed to that party; and

---

[2]NLRB Rules and Regulations §§102.117(a), (b).

[3]NLRB General Counsel Memorandum No. 79-6, *FOIA Guidelines in Closed Cases* (January 24, 1979), *reprinted in* 1979 LAB. REL. YRBK. 338, 339 (BNA). This memorandum is reproduced as Appendix J.

[4]An unfair labor practice case is considered open "until there is an approved withdrawal of the charge, final dismissal, or compliance has been effected." *Id.* at 339. A representation case is considered open, "until there is a withdrawal, final dismissal, certification of a representative, certification of results, or until a related unfair labor practice case is closed." *Id.*

- "Advice" and "appeals" memoranda authorizing dismissal of charges.[5]

In Closed Case Files[6]

- Documents in closed case files factually related to another pending proceeding;[7]
- Affidavits after expiration of the buffer period (see note 6 *supra*), except those of current employees of an employer involved in the case, or in a unit represented by any union involved and/or members of those unions;[8]
- Union authorization cards which will be disclosed only in instances where they already have been disclosed at a hearing;
- Nonpublic evidentiary material other than affidavits and authorization cards (deletions may have been made to protect personal privacy); and
- All advice memoranda to regional directors.

These records may be acquired by complying with the written request procedure; the requestor should:[9]

- In writing, "reasonably"[10] describe the requested records;
- Include with the request a statement assuming financial liability in full, or to a specified maximum amount, to cover the cost of the search for the records and for their duplication;[11]
- Submit requests for records in regional or subregional offices to those offices; for records in the General Counsel's office to the FOIA officer, Office of the General Counsel, Washington, D.C.; and for records in the offices of the Board to the Executive Secretary of the Board in Washington, D.C.;

---

[5]*NLRB v. Sears, Roebuck & Co.*, 421 U.S. 132, 89 LRRM 2001 (1975). *But cf. Kent Corp. v. NLRB*, 530 F.2d 612, 92 LRRM 2152 (5th Cir. 1976) (Final Investigative Reports are not disclosable).

[6]NLRB General Counsel Memorandum No. 79-6 at 339–341. In order to assure that a closed case will not reopen after the evidence is disclosed, the Board recognizes "buffer" periods during which no documents will be disclosed that would not be disclosed if the case were still open. In cases closed after settlement or adjusted withdrawal, the buffer period usually lasts one year after settlement. In cases closed by withdrawal or dismissal of a charge, the buffer period is six months. There is no buffer period in cases closed after litigation. *Id.*

[7]*See Polynesian Cultural Center v. NLRB*, 600 F.2d 1327, 102 LRRM 2036 (9th Cir. 1979); *New England Med. Center Hosp. v. NLRB*, 548 F.2d 377, 94 LRRM 2322 (1st Cir. 1976).

[8]NLRB General Counsel Memorandum No. 79-6 at 341. Affidavits of current employees may be disclosed when the employee consents or waives any interest in confidentiality.

[9]NLRB Rules and Regulations at §102.117(c). On July 8, 1975, the General Counsel issued a set of guidelines entitled "NLRB: Guidelines for Processing Requests Under the FOIA." The guidelines have been reproduced in the LABOR RELATIONS EXPEDITER (BNA) 4325–4351.

[10]A description is reasonable "if it [enables] a professional employee familiar with the subject area of the request to locate the records with a reasonable amount of effort." H.R. REP. NO. 876, 93 Cong., 2d Sess. 5–6 (1974).

[11]The charges are: $2.50 for each 15 minutes of clerical time, $6.60 for each 15 minutes of professional time, and 10 cents for each sheet of duplication. NLRB Rules and Regulations §102.117(c)(2)(iv)(a).

- Submit request record form NLRB-4933 with the written request. This form is used to calculate all charges due for processing the request.[12] (See Exhibit 111.)

Decisions concerning whether to provide the requested information will be made within 10 working days of when the appropriate office receives the request, and the requesting party will receive a written notice of the decision.[13]

If the request is granted, the records are made available upon payment of any charges due. In the event the request is denied, the requesting party is notified of the right to appeal.[14] Any party who wishes to appeal a denied request must file the appeal within 20 working days of receipt of the adverse determination.[15] If the request was denied by the Executive Secretary of the Board, the appeal should be filed with the Chairman of the Board in Washington, D.C.; if the request was denied in a regional or subregional office, or by the FOIA officer in the office of the General Counsel, the appeal should be filed with the General Counsel in Washington.

The appeal generally is decided within 20 days of receipt. If the appeal is granted, the records are made available upon payment of any charges due. If the appeal is denied, the requestor is notified of the right to seek judicial review.[16]

§24.4 Nondisclosable Information

The Board has tried to be liberal in its interpretation of disclosure under FOIA and lean toward disclosure even in situations where exemptions could be invoked.[17] Both Congress and the courts have recognized that unlimited access would impair the government's ability to fulfill its mandate. FOIA balances these opposing interests by providing nine exemptions from disclosure. As applied to the Board, the exemptions authorize witholding the following information:

- Administrative staff manuals including instructions for internal personnel practices and rules;
- Individual memoranda issued to instruct the staff on the above matters.[18]

---

[12]NLRB: Guidelines for Processing Requests Under the FOIA at 4342.
[13]*Id.* at 4327; NLRB Rules and Regulations §102.117(c)(2)(i).
[14]NLRB Rules and Regulations §102.117(c)(2)(i).
[15]*Id.* at §102.117(c)(2)(ii).
[16]*Id.*
[17]NLRB General Counsel Memorandum No. 79-6 at 338–339.
[18]NLRB: Guidelines for Processing Requests Under the FOIA at 4333.

In Open Case Files[19]

- All affidavits (except those previously discussed at §24.3(b) *supra*);[20]
- Other nonpublic evidentiary material;
- Deliberative memoranda (except "advice" and "appeals" memoranda previously described at §24.3(b) *supra*).[21]

In Closed Case Files

- Affidavits obtained from individuals who, at the time of the disclosure request, are current employees of the employer involved and/or members of or represented by the union involved and whose affidavits have not been revealed after they testified at the hearing;[22]
- Union authorization cards;[23] and
- Deliberative memoranda such as Final Investigation Reports, agenda minutes, and so forth.

---

[19]NLRB General Counsel Memorandum No. 79-6, *supra* note 4.

[20]*NLRB v. Robbins Tire & Rubber Co.*, 437 U.S. 214, 98 LRRM 2617 (1978).

[21]*See NLRB v. Sears, Roebuck & Co.*, 421 U.S. 132, 89 LRRM 2001 (1975).

[22]NLRB General Counsel Memorandum 79-6 at 340. Most courts which have considered the matter, however, have concluded that witness affidavits in closed case files are disclosable. *See Poss v. NLRB*, 565 F.2d 654, 96 LRRM 2984 (10th Cir. 1977); *Stroock & Stroock & Lavan v. NLRB*, 106 LRRM 2553 (S.D.N.Y. 1981); *Joseph Horne Co. v. NLRB*, 455 F. Supp. 1383, 99 LRRM 2787 (W.D. Pa. 1978). *But see Alirez v. NLRB*, 676 F.2d 423, 110 LRRM 2267 (10th Cir. 1982) (documents protected from disclosure because in view of personal contents of documents release would constitute unwarranted invasion of privacy).

[23]*NLRB v. Martins Ferry Hosp. Ass'n*, 649 F.2d 445, 107 LRRM 2569 (6th Cir. 1981); *Howard Johnson Co. v. NLRB*, 618 F.2d 1, 103 LRRM 2888 (6th Cir. 1980); *Irving v. Dilapi*, 600 F.2d 1027, 101 LRRM 2093 (2d Cir. 1979); *Pacific Molasses Co. v. NLRB*, 577 F.2d 1172, 99 LRRM 2048 (5th Cir. 1978); *Committee on Masonic Homes v. NLRB*, 556 F.2d 214, 95 LRRM 2457 (3d Cir. 1977).

Form NLRB-4933
   (3-75)

NATIONAL LABOR RELATIONS BOARD
PUBLIC INFORMATION REQUEST

Request No.	Date of Request	Date of Receipt	Suspense Date for Determination

Nature of Request

Name and Address of Requester (City, State, Zip Code)	Telephone No.

1. PROCESSING TIME

	Initials	Hours	Minutes
a. Professional Time:			
Total			
b. Clerical Time:			
Total			

2. PROCESSING CHARGES
   (Search and Copying Costs Only)

a. Professional Search Time:			
Total				X $6.60 = $ _____ per quarter hour
b. Clerical Search Time:			
Total				X $2.50 = $ _____ per quarter hour

Estimated Charges $ _____

Deposit Requested _____
(See Guidelines)   (Date)

All checks or money orders should be payable to the National Labor Relations Board. If payment is required, send a completed copy of this form to Finance, Rm. 1300, with payment when received.

Copying _____ Sheets @ .10 = .. $ _____

Other Service Charges .... _____

Total Billable Amount ... _____

Deposit .... _____

Balance Payable .... $ _____

Received Payment _____
                          (Date)

_____
(Region or Office)

Exhibit 111. Public Information Request (Form NLRB-4933)

3. INITIAL ACTION ON REQUEST

    ☐ Denied   Date of Notification _____

    ☐ Provided

    ☐ Denied in part, Provided in part   Date Records Provided _____

4. REMARKS

5. FOIA ANNUAL REPORT SUMMARY
   (Check appropriate box or boxes only if request denied)

RECORDS DENIED:

    ☐ Affidavits or statements of witnesses or parties

    ☐ Advice memoranda

    ☐ Appeals memoranda

    ☐ Intra-agency and file case memoranda

    ☐ Deliberative documents in R cases

    ☐ Other (Specify)

Exhibit 111—*page 2*

25

Filing and Service of Papers

§25.1 In General

NLRB proceedings often entail the filing and service of papers on the Board or on other parties, as well as on their attorneys or representatives of record.[1] Depending upon the document, filing and service requirements vary. Therefore, to avoid procedural errors or complications and the possibility of prejudicing their cases, parties are advised to comply carefully with the Board's filing and service requirements.

At the end of this chapter there are three tables—one for representation cases, one for unfair labor practice cases, and one for miscellaneous cases such as petitions for deauthorization elections, advisory opinions, declaratory orders, and for the recovery of attorneys' fees. The tables give the filing and service requirements for all papers involved in Board proceedings along with a citation to the appropriate Board regulation or other authority. The general procedures for filing and service are discussed below.

§25.2 Service of Papers

Charges, complaints and accompanying notices of hearing, final orders, administrative law judges' decisions, and subpoenas issued by the Board or its agents must be served:

- Personally;
- By registered or certified mail;

---

[1] NLRB Rules and Regulations §102.113(b).

- By telegraph; or
- By leaving a copy at the principal office or place of business of the person to be served.[2]

A party serving other parties to a proceeding may use:

- Registered or certified mail;
- Any manner provided for the service of papers in a civil action by the law of the state in which the hearing is pending;
- The same manner as that used in filing papers with the Board (except for charges, petitions, exceptions, briefs, and other papers for which a time for both filing and response has been otherwise established); however, when filing with the Board is accomplished through personal service, the other parties should be notified promptly of the action by telephone, followed by service of a copy by mail or telegraph.[3]

In addition to serving the parties, the Board's rules also require that a copy be served on any attorney or representative of the party who has entered a written appearance. If a party is represented by more than one attorney or representative, service upon any one of such persons will sufficient.[4] The Board's normal practice is to serve all papers (other than subpoenas), after the initial communication to the parties, upon the attorney or representative of record with copies to the party. It has been held that:

- Service of a charge by ordinary mail, although a technical defect, does not invalidate an unfair labor practice proceeding;[5]
- Service need not be made upon each member of a partnership; it is sufficient to serve the partnership in its usual business name;[6]
- Service is effective where the registered matter is tendered to the addressee by the postal service, the addressee refuses to accept it, and it is not delivered for that reason.[7]

The date of service will be the day the document is deposited in the mail or delivered in person.[8] Proof of service will be the return post office or telegraph receipt when service is made by registered or

---

[2]*Id.* at §102.113(a); NLRB Casehandling Manual ¶11840.1.

[3]NLRB Rules and Regulations §102.114(a); NLRB Casehandling Manual ¶11840.2.

[4]NLRB Rules and Regulations §102.113(b).

[5]*Olin Indus., Inc. v. NLRB*, 192 F.2d 799, 29 LRRM 2117 (5th Cir. 1951).

[6]*NLRB v. McGahey*, 233 F.2d 406, 38 LRRM 2142 (5th Cir. 1956).

[7]*Pasco Packing Co.*, 115 NLRB 437, 37 LRRM 1323 (1956).

[8]NLRB Rules and Regulations §102.112; NLRB Casehandling Manual ¶11840.3.

certified mail or by telegraph.[9] When service is made in a manner provided by state law, the proof of service is made according to that law. [10]

Proof of service is desirable in all cases, even though failure to show such proof does not affect the validity of the service.[11] The Board requires a person or party who serves papers on other parties to submit a written statement to the Board setting forth the names of those served and the date and manner of service. The Board will require proof of service only if, subsequent to the receipt of the statement of service, a question is raised with respect to proper service.[12]

If it is determined that the service requirements have not been complied with, the Board may either reject the document, or withhold or reconsider any ruling on the subject matter raised by the document until such time as proper service has been made and the party served has had a reasonable time to respond.[13]

§25.3   How Time Is Computed

In September 1986, the Board implemented revised rules governing the time periods in which parties must respond to Board action. The new rules simplified the calculation of filing periods. They eliminated the former practice of adding three days to the filing period when service of the Board document initiating the filing period was by mail, and formalized the Board's practice of accepting as timely filed papers deposited in the mails the day before the filing date. With the exception of certain statutory time periods, the changes affected virtually all filing periods for responding to Board action. They expanded the time periods to provide for additional time because of the elimination of the three-day "mailing period." The revised filing periods are seven days from the date of Board action, or some multiple thereof, thereby avoiding the occurrence of any filing date falling on a Saturday or Sunday.

In computing the period of time required by the Board in the submission of any document:[14]

- Start counting with the day following the day on which the particular event occurs.[15] For example, in computing the seven-day period allowed in §102.69(a) of the Board's Rules and Regulations for the filing of objections to an election after the tally

---

[9]NLRB Rules and Regulations §102.113(a).

[10]*Id.* at §102.114(a).

[11]*Id.* at §102.114(b); NLRB Casehandling Manual ¶11840.3.

[12]NLRB Rules and Regulations §102.114(b).

[13]NLRB Rules and Regulations §102.114(a).

[14]*Id.* at §102.111(a); NLRB Casehandling Manual §11840.4.

[15]*Plymouth Locomotive Works, Inc.*, 261 NLRB 595, 110 LRRM 1155 (1982); *Baltimore Transfer Co.*, 94 NLRB 1680, 28 LRRM 1241 (1951).

of ballots has been prepared, do not count the day on which the tally was prepared and made available; begin the count with the following day. Likewise, do not count the day a paper (for example, a letter of dismissal under §102.19(a)) is postmarked; begin the count with the following date.

- Count the last day of the period unless the last day falls on a legal holiday.[16] (The term "holiday," as used by the Board, refers only to federal holidays declared as such by congressional enactment or by presidential proclamation.[17]) If the last day of the period should fall on a legal holiday, the period runs until the end of the next agency business day. Because the Board serves documents only on working days, the seven-day multiples for the filing periods eliminate the possibility of a filing period ending on a Saturday or Sunday, and only those holidays falling on weekdays would serve to extend the filing period to the next agency business day.[18]

- Where the allowed period of time is less than seven days, do not count Saturdays, Sundays, or legal holidays that fall within the period.[19]

- If the allowed period of time is seven days or more, count Saturdays, Sundays, and legal holidays falling within the allowed time.

The requirement for a timely filing means that the document must be *received* by the Board or the officer designated to receive such matter before the close of business on the last day of the allowed period.[20] With the exceptions noted below, materials postmarked the day *before* the due date will be considered timely; any materials postmarked *on* or *after* the due date will be rejected as untimely. Because of statutory time limits and the need for prompt resolution of representation issues, the following documents will *not* be considered timely if postmarked the day before the filing date, but must be actually received on or before the close of business of the last day for filing:[21]

- Unfair labor practice charges filed pursuant to Section 10 of the Act;
- Applications for awards, fees, and other expenses under the Equal Access to Justice Act;

---

[16]NLRB Rules and Regulations §102.111(a).

[17]*Fisher Prods. Co.*, 114 NLRB 161, 36 LRRM 1528 (1955).

[18]Because of statutory requirements, it is possible that Equal Access to Justice Act applications and petitions to revoke subpoenas may fall due during a weekend. *See* NLRB Rules and Regulations §§102.148(a), 102.31(b), and 102.66(c). In such instances, the period runs until the next agency business day. *See* NLRB Rules and Regulations §102.111(a).

[19]NLRB Rules and Regulations §102.111(a). With the change in filing periods, this provision is of relevance primarily to petitions to revoke subpoenas.

[20]NLRB Rules and Regulations §§102.111(b), 102.112.

[21]NLRB Rules and Regulations §102.111(b).

- Election objections and revised tallies;
- Petitions to revoke subpoenas; and
- Election petitions filed pursuant to Section 9(c) of the Act.

§25.4   Extensions of Time

Extensions of time in which to file particular documents will be granted by the Board, the General Counsel, or other appropriate official where good cause is shown. The deadline for filing an unfair labor practice charge or for filing an application for awards, fees, or other expenses under the Equal Access to Justice Act cannot be extended, however, because the time limitations are jurisdictional requirements of the statutes.

In most cases the Board is willing to grant one reasonable extension of time in which to file appeals, exceptions and briefs. Further extensions rarely are granted. The General Counsel follows a similar approach on requests for extending the time to appeal from dismissals of unfair labor practice charges by regional directors.

In requesting any extension of time, the three-day limit uniformly used must be carefully observed. Such requests must be received by the close of business three working days prior to the due date.

TABLE 1

REPRESENTATION CASES

I. Petitions

Document	File With/Serve Upon	When[1]	Number of Copies	Authority[2]
Petitions for elections, amendment of certification, or unit clarification	Regional director[3]	—	Original and 4	RR §§102.60(a),(b), .111(b)(5)
Showing of interest in support of election petition	Regional director	Within 48 hours of filing petition	1	SP §101.17
Appeal from regional director's dismissal or postponement of petition prior to close of hearing[4]	(a) Board (b) Regional director (c) All parties	Within 14 days of service of dismissal or postponement	(a) 8 (b) 1 (c) 1	RR §102.71

[1] On June 20, 1986, the Board issued revised rules regarding the time periods in which parties must respond to Board action. The new rules eliminate the provision of adding 3 additional days when service is by mail and include the Board's practice of accepting as timely filed papers deposited in the mails on the day before the filing date. With exception of statutory time periods, most periods for filing papers with the Board have been expanded because the 3-day service-by-mail period has been eliminated. The new period for responding to Board action is 7 days or some multiple thereof, from the date of Board action, thereby eliminating the occurrence of any filing date on a Saturday or Sunday.

[2] "RR" refers to the NLRB Rules and Regulations Series 8, as amended; "SP" to the Statements of Procedure; and "CHM" to the Casehandling Manual.

[3] RR §102.72 provides that a petition may be filed with the General Counsel in Washington, D.C., whenever it appears necessary in order to effectuate the purposes of the Act.

[4] In the case of petitions for amendment of certification or unit clarification, if the petition is dismissed without a hearing review must be obtained under RR §102.67. Where the unit or certification involved in such a petition arose out of a consent election agreement, no appeal is available.

TABLE 1 (Cont'd)

Document	File With/ Serve Upon	When	Number of Copies	Authority
II. Motions in General				
Request for postponement of hearing[5]	(a) Regional director (b) All parties	At least 3 working days before hearing date	(a) Original and 2 (b) 1	CHM ¶11142.1
Other motions	(a) If made prior to hearing, file with regional director; or (b) If made at hearing, file with hearing officer, or state orally on record; or (c) If filed after hearing but before transfer of case to Board, file with regional director; or (d) If made after transfer of case to Board, file with Board; and (e) All parties	—	(a–c) Original and 2 (d) 8 (e) 1	RR §102.65(a)
III. Subpoenas				
Application for subpoena	(a) Regional director prior to hearing; or	—	(a) 1 (b) 1	RR §102.66(c)

[5]The regional director generally gives each party a notice of hearing at least 5 working days before the hearing.

Paper	Where to file	When to file	No. copies	Rule reference
Petition to revoke subpoena	(b) Hearing officer during hearing (a) Regional director; or (b) Hearing officer if evidence is to be produced at opened hearing	Within 5 working days of service of subpoena	(a) 1 (b) 1	RR §§102.66(c), .111(b)(4)

IV. Request for Interlocutory Appeal[6]

Paper	Where to file	When to file	No. copies	Rule reference
Request for special permission to appeal from ruling of hearing officer	(a) Regional director prior to transfer of case to Board; or (b) Board after transfer of case (must serve copy on regional director after filing with Board); and (c) All parties	Promptly	(a) 1 (b) 8 (c) 1	RR §§102.65(a),(c)
Request for special permission to appeal from ruling of regional director	(a) Board (b) All parties	Promptly	(a) 8 (b) 1	RR §§102.65(a),(c)

V. Briefs and Requests Filed After Close of Hearing

Paper	Where to file	When to file	No. copies	Rule reference
Posthearing briefs before transfer of case to Board	(a) Regional director (b) All parties	Within 7 days after close of hearing	(a) Original and 1 (b) 1	RR §102.67(a)
—request for extension of time in which to file brief	(a) Regional director (b) All parties	At least 3 working days before due date	(a) 1 (b) 1	RR §§102.67(k)(1), (k)(3)

[6]Requests for special permission to appeal and the appeal itself must be filed simultaneously. RR §102.65(c).

TABLE 1 (Cont'd)

Document	File With/Serve Upon	When	Number of Copies		Authority
Posthearing briefs after transfer of case to Board with no decision by regional director[7]	(a) Board (b) Regional director (c) All parties	Within time fixed by regional director after service of order transferring case to Board	(a) 8 (b) 1 (c) 1		RR §§102.67(i), (k)(1), (k)(2)
—request for extension of time in which to file brief[8]	(a) Board (b) Regional director (c) All parties	At least 3 working days before due date	(a) 8 (b) 1 (c) 1		RR §§102.67(k)(1), (k)(3)

VI. Motions for Reconsideration, Rehearing, and Reopening Record

Document	File With/Serve Upon	When	Number of Copies		Authority
Motion to reopen record	(a) Regional director if prior to transfer of case to Board; or (b) Hearing officer if during hearing; or (c) Board if after transfer; and (d) All parties	Promptly upon discovery of evidence sought to be adduced	(a–b) Original and 2 (c) 8 (d) 1		RR §§102.65(a),(e)
Motion for reconsideration or rehearing	(a) Regional director if prior to transfer of case to Board; or (b) Hearing officer if during hearing; or (c) Board if after transfer; and (d) All parties	Within 14 days after service of decision or report	(a–b) Original and 2 (c) 8 (d) 1		RR §§102.65(a),(e)

[7] Briefs originally filed with the regional director may be refiled with the Board. Special permission of the Board must be obtained to file any other briefs. RR §102.67(i).

[8] If the transfer order is served during the hearing, the hearing officer may grant an extension not to exceed an additional 14 days. RR §102.67(i).

—request for extension of time to file motions for reconsideration or rehearing	(a) Regional director if prior to transfer of case to Board; or (b) Hearing officer if during hearing; or (c) Board if after transfer; and (d) All parties	At least 3 working days prior to due date of motion	(a–b) Original and 2 (c) 8 (d) 1	RR §§102.65(a),(e)

VII. Request for Review of Regional Director's Preelection Decision[9]

Request for review of regional director's decision	(a) Board (b) Regional director (c) All parties	Within 14 days after service of decision	(a) 8 (b) 1 (c) 1	RR §§102.67(b),(k)(1), (k)(2)
—request for extension of time to file request for review	(a) Board (b) Regional director (c) All parties	At least 3 days before request due	(a) 8 (b) 1 (c) 1	RR §§102.67(k)(1), (k)(3)
Statement in opposition to request for review of regional director's decision	(a) Board (b) Regional director (c) All parties	Within 7 days after last day on which the request for review must be filed	(a) 8 (b) 1 (c) 1	RR §§102.67(e),(k)(1), (k)(2)
—request for extension of time to file statement in opposition	(a) Board (b) Regional director (c) All parties	At least 3 days before statement due	(a) 8 (b) 1 (c) 1	RR §§102.67(k)(1), (k)(3)
Briefs on review of regional director's decision	(a) Board (b) Regional director (c) All parties	Within 14 days after issuance of order granting review	(a) 8 (b) 1 (c) 1	RR §§102.67(g),(k)(1), (k)(2)
—request for extension of time to file brief on review	(a) Board (b) Regional director (c) All parties	At least 3 working days before brief due	(a) 8 (b) 1 (c) 1	RR §§102.67(k)(1), (k)(3)

[9] Requests for review also may be used for appealing regional directors' postelection decisions in cases where there has been a directed election. RR §102.69(c)(4).

TABLE 1 (Cont'd)

VIII. Elections, Objections, and Challenged Ballots

Document	File With/Serve Upon	When	Number of Copies	Authority
Request for withdrawal of name from ballot	(a) Regional director if two or more labor organizations are included as choices; or (b) Regional director and all other parties if employer-filed petition or petition for decertification	(a) Promptly (b) Timely	(a) 1 (b) 1	RR §102.69(a)
Regional director's issuance of tally of ballots	Each designated representative of the parties	Upon conclusion of the election	1	RR §102.69(a)
Challenged ballots	Board agent conducting election	Before ballot dropped in ballot box	1	CHM ¶11338.1
Objections to election	Regional director	Within 7 days after tally of ballots prepared	Original and 5	RR §§102.69(a), .111(b)(3)
—evidence in support of objections	Regional director	Within 7 days after filing of objections, or such additional time as regional director allows	1	RR §102.69(a)
Notice of hearing ordered by regional director	All parties	Following initial investigation of challenges and/or objections	1	CHM ¶11426.2

Document	Parties	Time limit	Copies	Rule
Report of hearing officer on objections and challenged ballots if requested by regional director	All parties	—	1	RR §102.69(e)
—exceptions to hearing officer's report (with supporting briefs if desired)	(a) Regional director (b) All parties	Within 14 days of date of issuance of report	(a) Original and 1 (b) 1	RR §102.69(e)
—answering brief to exceptions	(a) Regional director (b) All parties	Within 7 days from due date of exceptions	(a) Original and 1 (b) 1	RR §102.69(e)
Regional director's report or decision on objections and/or challenged ballots in stipulated and directed elections	All parties	—	1	RR §§102.69(c)(2)–(c)(4)
—exceptions to regional director's report[10]	(a) Board (b) Regional director (c) All parties	Within 14 days of issuance of report	(a) 8 (b) 1 (c) 1	RR §§102.69(c)(2), (c)(4), (j)(1),(j)(2)
—answering brief to exceptions	(a) Board (b) Regional director (c) All parties	Within 7 days from due date of exceptions	(a) 8 (b) 1 (c) 1	RR §§102.69(c)(2), (j)(1), (j)(2)
Notice of hearing ordered by Board	All parties	—	1	RR §102.69(f)
Report of hearing officer on objections and/or challenged ballots if requested by Board	All parties	—	1	RR §102.69(f)

[10] As stated in note 9, appeals from regional directors' *decisions* (rather than *reports*) in directed election cases are through requests for review rather than exceptions. RR §§102.69(c)(3), (c)(4).

TABLE 1 (Cont'd)

Document	File With/ Serve Upon	When	Number of Copies	Authority
—exceptions to hearing officer's report (with supporting briefs if desired)	(a) Board (b) Regional director (c) All parties	Within 14 days from date of issuance of report	(a) 8 (b) 1 (c) 1	RR §§102.69(f), (j)(1),(j)(2)
—answering brief to exceptions	(a) Board (b) Regional director (c) All parties	Within 7 days from due date of exceptions	(a) 8 (b) 1 (c) 1	RR §§102.69(f), (j)(1),(j)(2)
Revised tally of ballots	Each designated representative of the parties	Upon completion of revised tally	1	RR §102.69(h)
Objections to revised tally of ballots	(a) Regional director (b) All parties	Within 7 working days after revised tally furnished	(a) 1 (b) 1	RR §102.69(h)

IX. Procedures in Expedited Elections

Document	File With/ Serve Upon	When	Number of Copies	Authority
Request for special permission to appeal from regional director's decision that a hearing is not needed	(a) Board (b) All parties	Promptly	(a) 8 (b) 1	RR §102.80(c)
Request for special permission to appeal from regional director's dismissal of petition during hearing	(a) Board (b) Regional director (c) All parties	Within 14 days after service of notice of dismissal	(a) 8 (b) 1	RR §§102.80(a), .71(c)
Request for special permission to file briefs after hearing on petition	(a) Regional director if prior to transfer to Board; or (b) Board after transfer	See Part V, *supra*	See Part V, *supra*	RR §§102.67, .77(b)

TABLE 2

UNFAIR LABOR PRACTICE CASES[1]

Document	File With/ Serve Upon	When	Number of Copies	Authority
I. Charge				
Charge	(a) Regional director (b) Party against whom charge is made	(a) Within 6 months after alleged unfair labor practice (b) Approximately same time	(a) Original and 4, plus 1 for each additional charged party	Sec. 10(b) of the Act, RR §§102.9–.11, .14, .111(b)(1)
Withdrawal of charge	(a) Regional director prior to hearing; or (b) Administrative law judge at hearing and until case transferred to Board; or (c) Board after transfer	—	(b) 1 (a–c) 1	RR §102.9
II. Complaint				
Regional director's complaint and notice of hearing	All parties	At least 14 days before date of hearing	1	RR §§102.15, .90
Appeal from regional director's refusal to issue complaint	(a) General Counsel (b) Regional director	Within 14 days after service of refusal to issue complaint[2]	(a) 1 (b) 1	RR §102.19(a)

[1] See notes 1 and 2 in Table 1 for an explanation of abbreviations and a description of methods used by the Board for computing filing periods.
[2] If the unfair labor practice charge was filed in connection with Section 8(b)(7) proceedings, appeals must be filed within 7 days after service of refusal to issue complaint. §102.81(c)

TABLE 2 (Cont'd)

Document	File With/ Serve Upon	When	Number of Copies	Authority
—request for extension of time to file appeal	(a) General Counsel (b) Regional director	Prior to expiration of filing period	(a) 1 (b) 1	RR §102.19(a)
—request for oral argument of appeal issues	General Counsel	Within 4 days after service of acknowledgment of filing of an appeal	1	RR §102.19(b)
—motion for reconsideration of General Counsel's decision sustaining or reversing Regional director	General Counsel	Within 14 days of service of decision; if based on discovery of new information, promptly after such discovery	1	RR §102.19(c)

III. Answer to Complaint

Document	File With/ Serve Upon	When	Number of Copies	Authority
Answer to complaint	(a) Regional director (b) All parties	(a) Within 14 days from service of complaint[3] (b) Same time	(a) Original and 4 (b) 1	RR §§102.20, .21
Request for review of regional director's decision after hearing	See Table 1, Part VII, *supra*	Promptly after issuance of regional director's decision	See Table 1, Part VII, *supra*	RR §§102.67, .77(b)
Request for special permission to appeal from regional director's rulings on election objections or challenged ballots	(a) Board (b) All parties	Promptly	(a) 8 (b) 1	RR §102.78

[3]A party may file with the regional director a request for an extension of time to file an answer. RR §§102.22, 102.24.

Appeal from regional director's decision to direct election and refusal to issue complaint on charge[4]	Within 7 days of notice of refusal	(a) General Counsel (b) Regional director (c) All parties	(a–c) 1	RR §§102.19(a), .81(a)
Appeal from regional director's refusal to issue complaint on other unfair labor practice filed in conjunction with 8(b)(7) proceedings[4]	Within 7 days of notice of refusal	(a) General Counsel (b) Regional director (c) All parties	(a–c) 1	RR §§102.19(a), .81(c)
Amendment of answer	(a) Any time prior to hearing; or (b) When complaint amended or upon special permission from administrative law judge or Board	See next section at "Other motions"	See next section at "Other motions"	RR §§102.23, .24

IV. Motions in General

Request for hearing postponement or change of location	Within 3 working days prior to hearing date	(a) Regional director (b) All parties	(a) Original and 2 (b) 1	RR §§102.16, .24; CHM ¶10294.2
Motion to intervene	—	(a) Regional director prior to hearing; or (b) Administrative law judge during hearing; and (c) All parties	(a) Original and 4 (b) Original and 4 or orally upon the record (c) 1	RR §§102.24, .29

[4]RR §§102.81(a) and (c) provide that RR §102.19 shall be applicable where not inconsistent. See Part II, Complaint, *supra*.

TABLE 2 (Cont'd)

Document	File With/Serve Upon	When	Number of Copies	Authority
Other motions (including motions to consolidate or sever proceedings under RR §102.33(d))	(a) If made prior to hearing, file with chief administrative law judge in Washington, D.C.,[5] or (b) If made at the hearing, file in writing with administrative law judge or state orally on record; or (c) If filed after hearing but before transfer of case to Board, file with administrative law judge, care of chief administrative law judge in Washington, D.C.,[5] or (d) If made after transfer to Board (while case pending there), file with Executive Secretary of Board in Washington, D.C., and (e) All parties	Promptly	(a–c) Original and 4 (d) 8 (e) 1	RR §§102.24, .47

[5]Prehearing motions also may be filed with the deputy chief judge in San Francisco or the associate chief judge in New York or Atlanta, as appropriate. RR §102.24.

V. Depositions and Subpoenas

Paper	Filed by	Time of filing	Original and 4	Reference
Application to take deposition	(a) Regional director prior to hearing; or (b) Administrative law judge during or after hearing but before transfer of case to Board; and (c) All parties	At least 7 days prior to proposed date of deposition[6]	(a–b) 1 (c) 1	RR §§102.24, .30(a)
Application for subpoena	(a) Regional director prior to hearing; or (b) Administrative law judge during hearing	—	1	RR §102.31(a)
—petition to revoke subpoena	(a) Regional director prior to hearing; or (b) Administrative law judge during hearing; and (c) Party who requested subpoena	Within 5 days after receipt of subpoena	(a–c) 1	RR §§102.31(b), .111(b)(4)
—request for order to compel testimony or give information	(a) Board prior to hearing and after transfer of case to Board; or (b) Administrative law judge prior to issuance of decision	—	(a–b) 1	RR §102.31(c)

[6] Application must be filed 15 days prior to proposed date if the deposition is to be taken outside the continental United States.

TABLE 2 (Cont'd)

VI. Request for Interlocutory Appeal and Appeal From Dismissal of Complaint During Hearing

Document	File With/Serve Upon	When	Number of Copies	Authority
Request for special permission to appeal from regional director's and administrative law judge's rulings on motions and objections	(a) Board (b) Administrative law judge if request involves ruling by judge (c) All parties	Promptly[7]	(a–b) Original and 4 (c) 1	RR §§102.24, .26
Statement in opposition or other response to request	(a) Board (b) Administrative law judge if request involves ruling by judge (c) All parties	Promptly	(a–b) Original and 4 (c) 1	RR §§102.24, .26
Request for review of administrative law judge's dismissal of complaint before issuance of decision	(a) Board (b) Regional director (c) All parties	Within 28 days after order of dismissal	(a) Original and 4 (b) 1 (c) 1	RR §§102.24, .27

VII. Briefs Filed After Close of Hearing

Document	File With/Serve Upon	When	Number of Copies	Authority
Briefs filed after close of hearing with administrative law judge (except jurisdictional dispute cases)	(a) Administrative law judge (b) All parties	(a) Within a period set by administrative law judge not to exceed 35 days after close of hearing (b) Promptly	(a) 3 (b) 1	RR §102.42

[7] An appeal from a denial of a request to compel testimony must be filed within 24 hours of the administrative law judge's ruling. RR §102.31(c).

—request for extension of time to file brief	(a) Chief administrative law judge in Washington, D.C.[8] (b) All parties	(a) At least 3 working days before due date (b) Promptly	(a) 1 (b) 1	RR §102.42
Briefs in jurisdictional dispute proceedings (Sec. 10(k)) not involving national defense	(a) Board (b) All parties	(a) Within 7 days of close of hearing (b) Promptly	(a) 8 (b) 1	RR §102.90
—request for extension of time to file brief	(a) Board (b) All parties	(a) At least 3 working days before due date (b) Promptly	(a) 8 (b) 1	RR §102.90
—request for special permission to file reply brief	(a) Board (b) All parties	(a) Promptly (b) Promptly	(a) 8 (b) 1	RR §102.90
Request for special permission to file briefs in jurisdictional dispute proceedings (Sec. 10(k)) involving national defense[9]	(a) Board (b) All parties	(a) Expeditiously (b) Same time	(a) 8 (b) 1	RR §102.90

VIII. Exceptions to, and Briefs in Support of, Administrative Law Judge's Decision

Exceptions to administrative law judge's decision and brief in support of exceptions	(a) Board (b) All parties	(a) Within 28 days from service of order transferring case to Board (b) Promptly	(a) 8 (b) 1	RR §§102.46(a),(j)

[8]Briefs also may be filed with the deputy chief judge in San Francisco or associate chief judge in New York or Atlanta, as appropriate. RR §102.42.

[9]Provisions regarding extension of time and reply briefs described above also apply to briefs in jurisdictional dispute proceedings involving national defense.

TABLE 2 (Cont'd)

Document	File With/ Serve Upon	When	Number of Copies	Authority
—request for extension of time to file exceptions and brief	(a) Board (b) All parties	(a) At least 3 working days before due date (b) Promptly	(a) 8 (b) 1	RR §102.46(a)
Brief in support of administrative law judge's decision	(a) Board (b) All parties	(a) Within 28 days from service of order transferring case to Board (b) Promptly	(a) 8 (b) 1	RR §§102.46(a),(j)
—request for extension of time to file brief in support	(a) Board (b) All parties	(a) At least 3 working days before due date (b) Promptly	(a) 8 (b) 1	RR §102.46(a)
Answering brief to exceptions	(a) Board (b) All parties	(a) Within 14 days from due date of exceptions and supporting brief (b) Promptly	(a) 8 (b) 1	RR §§102.46(d),(j)
—request for extension of time to file answering brief	(a) Board (b) All parties	(a) At least 3 working days before due date (b) Promptly	(a) 8 (b) 1	RR §102.46(d)(3)
Cross-exceptions to administrative law judge's decision and supporting brief	(a) Board (b) All parties	(a) Within 14 days from due date of exceptions (b) Promptly	(a) 8 (b) 1	RR §§102.46(e),(j)
—request for extension of time to file cross-exceptions	(a) Board (b) All parties	(a) At least 3 working days before due date (b) Promptly	(a) 8 (b) 1	RR §102.46(f)(2)

Answering brief to cross-exceptions	(a) Board (b) All parties	(a) Within 14 days from due date of cross-exceptions (b) Promptly	(a) 8 (b) 1	RR §102.46(f)(1)
—request for extension of time to file answering brief to cross-exceptions	(a) Board (b) All parties	(a) At least 3 working days before due date (b) Promptly	(a) 8 (b) 1	PR §102.46(f)(2)
Request for special permission to file further briefs	(a) Board (b) All parties	(a) Promptly (b) Promptly	(a) 8 (b) 1	RR §102.46(g)
Request for oral argument before Board	(a) Board (b) All parties	(a) Time of filing exceptions or cross-exceptions (b) Promptly	(a) 8 (b) 1	RR §102.46(i)

IX. Motions for Reconsideration

Motion for reconsideration, rehearing or reopening of record	(a) Board (b) All parties	(a) Within 28 days after service of Board's decision (b) Promptly	(a) 8 (b) 1	RR §§102.48(d)(1),(2)
—request for extension of time to file motion for reconsideration	(a) Board (b) All parties	(a) At least 3 working days before due date (b) Promptly	(a) 8 (b) 1	RR §102.48(d)(2)
Motion for leave to adduce additional evidence	(a) Board (b) All parties	(a) Promptly upon discovery of evidence (b) Promptly	(a) 8 (b) 1	RR §§102.48(d)(1),(2)

X. Backpay Specifications

Regional director's issuance of backpay specification and/or notice of hearing	All parties	At least 21 days before hearing	1	RR §102.52

TABLE 2 (Cont'd)

Document	File With/Serve Upon	When	Number of Copies	Authority
Mandatory answer to backpay specification[10]	(a) Regional director (b) Any other respondent jointly liable	(a) Within 21 days of service of specification (b) Immediately	(a) Original and 4 (b) 1	RR §102.54(a)
—request for extension of time for filing answer to backpay specification	Regional director	—	1	RR §102.55
—amendment to answer	(a) Regional director if specification amended prior to opening of hearing; (b) Permission of Board or administrative law judge, as the case may be, must be acquired if specification or answer amended after opening of hearing.	—	(a) 1 (b) 1	RR §102.57
Request for postponement of backpay hearing	(a) Regional director (b) All parties	(a) Within 3 working days prior to hearing date (b) Promptly	(a) 1 (b) 1	RR §102.56

[10]No answer is necessary if the regional director issues a notice of hearing without a backpay specification. RR §102.54(d).

TABLE 3

MISCELLANEOUS[1]

Document	File With/ Serve Upon	When	Number of Copies	Authority
I. Petition to Rescind Union Shop Agreement				
Petition to rescind union shop agreement (hearing on petition and conduct of election same as in Table 1, representation cases)	Regional director	—	Original and 4	RR §102.83
Request for review of regional director's refusal to conduct referendum	(a) Board (b) Regional director (c) All parties	Within 14 days of service of notice of dismissal	(a) 8 (b) 1 (c) 1	RR §102.88
II. Petition for Advisory Opinion				
Petition for advisory opinion regarding Board jurisdiction	(a) Board (b) Regional director (c) All parties	While proceeding is before any agency or court of any state or territory	(a) 8 (b) 1 (c) 1	RR §§102.98–.100
Response to petition for advisory opinion	(a) Board (b) All parties	Within 14 working days after service of petition	(a) 8 (b) 1	RR §102.101
Motion to intervene on petition for advisory opinion	Board	Promptly	8	RR §102.102

[1]See notes 1 and 2 in Table 1 for an explanation of abbreviations and a description of methods used by the Board for computing filing periods.

TABLE 3 (Cont'd)

III. Petition for Declaratory Order

Document	File With/Serve Upon	When	Number of Copies	Authority
Response to petition for declaratory order (petition filed by General Counsel)	(a) Board (b) General Counsel (c) All parties	Within 14 working days after service of petition	(a) 8 (b) 1 (c) 1	RR §102.108
Motion to intervene on petition for declaratory order	Board	—	8	RR §102.109
Briefs in declaratory order cases	(a) Board (b) All parties	—	(a) 8 (b) 1	RR §102.110

IV. Procedures to Recover Attorneys' Fees Under the Equal Access to Justice Act

Document	File With/Serve Upon	When	Number of Copies	Authority
Application for recovery of attorneys' fees	(a) Board (b) Regional director (c) All parties	Within 30 days after entry of Board's final order	(a) 3 (b) 1 (c) 1	RR §§102.148(a), .111(b)(2)
Request for confidentiality of net worth exhibit	(a) Administrative law judge (b) General Counsel	With application	(a) 1 (b) 1	RR §102.147(g)(1)
Motions and pleadings while case before administrative law judge	(a) Administrative law judge (b) All parties	—	(a) 3 (b) 1	RR §102.149(a)
—request for extension of time to file motions, documents and pleadings	(a) Chief administrative law judge in Washington, D.C.[2] (b) All parties	Within 3 working days of due date	(a) 3 (b) 1	RR §102.149(b)

[2]Such requests also may be filed with the deputy chief judge in San Francisco or associate chief judge in New York or Atlanta, as appropriate. RR §102.149(b).

Statement of intent to negotiate toward settlement	(a) Administrative law judge (b) All parties	Within 35 days after service of application	(a) 3 (b) 1	RR §§102.149(a), .150(b)
General Counsel's answer to application	(a) Administrative law judge (b) All parties	Within 35 days after service of application; or if General Counsel files a motion to dismiss, within 35 days after order denying motion. If parties file a statement of intent to negotiate toward settlement, General Counsel has 30 additional days to answer	(a) 3 (b) 1	RR §§102.149(a), .150(a)
Reply to General Counsel's answer or motion to dismiss filed in lieu of answer	(a) Administrative law judge (b) All parties	Within 21 days after service of answer or motion to dismiss	(a) 3 (b) 1	RR §§102.149(a), .150(a),(d)
Request for review of grant of motion to dismiss	(a) Board (b) Regional director (c) All parties	Within 28 days of order of dismissal	(a) 8 (b) 1 (c) 1	RR §§102.27, .150(a)
Comments on application by any party other than General Counsel and applicant	(a) Administrative law judge (b) All parties	Within 35 days after service of application	(a) 3 (b) 1	RR §§102.149(a), .150(e)
Comments on answer by any party other than General Counsel and applicant	(a) Administrative law judge (b) All parties	Within 21 days after service of answer	(a) 3 (b) 1	RR §§102.149(a), .150(e)
Appeal of administrative law judge's rulings		Same as appeal of administrative law judge's ruling in unfair labor practice case. See Table 2, Part VI		RR §102.152(e)

TABLE 3 (Cont'd)

Document	File With/ Serve Upon	When	Number of Copies	Authority
Request for evidentiary hearing or other further proceedings	(a) Administrative law judge (b) All parties	—	(a) 3 (b) 1	RR §§102.149(a), .152(a)
Exceptions to administrative law judge's decision and procedures for Board consideration	Same as with unfair labor practice cases. See Table 2, Part VIII			RR §102.154

APPENDIX A

National Labor Relations Act

As amended by the Labor Management Relations (Taft-Hartley) Act and the Labor-Management Reporting and Disclosure (Landrum-Griffin) Act

§ 141.   Short title; Congressional declaration of purpose and policy

[Sec. 1] (a) This Act may be cited as the "Labor Management Relations Act, 1947."

(b) Industrial strife which interferes with the normal flow of commerce and with the full production of articles and commodities for commerce, can be avoided or substantially minimized if employers, employees, and labor organizations each recognize under law one another's legitimate rights in their relations with each other, and above all recognize under law that neither party has any right in its relations with any other to engage in acts or practices which jeopardize the public health, safety, or interest.

It is the purpose and policy of this Act, in order to promote the full flow of commerce, to prescribe the legitimate rights of both employees and employers in their relations affecting commerce, to provide orderly and peaceful procedures for preventing the interference by either with the legitimate rights of the other, to protect the rights of individual employees in their relations with labor organizations whose activities affect commerce, to define and proscribe practices on the part of labor and management which affect commerce and are inimical to the general welfare, and to protect the rights of the public in connection with labor disputes affecting commerce.

Title V.

§ 142.   Definitions

[Sec. 501] When used in this Act—

(1) The term "industry affecting commerce" means any industry or activity in commerce or in which a labor dispute would burden or obstruct

571

commerce or tend to burden or obstruct commerce or the free flow of
commerce.

(2) The term "strike" includes any strike or other concerted stoppage of
work by employees (including a stoppage by reason of the expiration of
a collective-bargaining agreement) and any concerted slow-down or
other concerted interruption of operations by employees.

(3) The terms "commerce," "labor disputes," "employer," "employee,"
"labor organization," "representative," "person," and "supervisor"
shall have the same meaning as when used in the National Labor
Relations Act as amended by this Act.

§ 143. Saving provision

[Sec. 502] Nothing in this Act shall be construed to require an individual
employee to render labor or service without his consent, nor shall anything
in this Act be construed to make the quitting of his labor by an individual
employee an illegal act; nor shall any court issue any process to compel the
performance by an individual employee of such labor or service, without his
consent; nor shall the quitting of labor by an employee or employees in good
faith because of abnormally dangerous conditions for work at the place of
employment of such employee or employees be deemed a strike under this
Act.

§ 144. Separability of provisions

[Sec. 503] If any provision of this Act, or the application of such provision
to any person or circumstance, shall be held invalid, the remainder of this
Act, or the application of such provision to persons or circumstances other
than those as to which it is held invalid, shall not be affected thereby.

Title I. Amendment of National Labor Relations Act

[Sec. 101] The National Labor Relations Act is hereby amended to read as
follows:

§ 151. Findings and declaration of policy

"[Sec. 1] The denial by some employers of the right of employees to
organize and the refusal by some employers to accept the procedure of
collective bargaining lead to strikes and other forms of industrial strife or
unrest, which have the intent or the necessary effect of burdening or
obstructing commerce by (a) impairing the efficiency, safety, or operation of
the instrumentalities of commerce; (b) occurring in the current of commerce;
(c) materially affecting, restraining, or controlling the flow of raw materials
or manufactured or processed goods from or into the channels of commerce,
or the prices of such materials or goods in commerce; or (d) causing
diminution of employment and wages in such volume as substantially to
impair or disrupt the market for goods flowing from or into the channels of
commerce.

"The inequality of bargaining power between employees who do not
possess full freedom of association or actual liberty of contract, and employ-

ers who are organized in the corporate or other forms of ownership association substantially burdens and affects the flow of commerce, and tends to aggravate recurrent business depressions, by depressing wage rates and the purchasing power of wage earners in industry and by preventing the stabilization of competitive wage rates and working conditions within and between industries.

"Experience has proved that protection by law of the right of employees to organize and bargain collectively safeguards commerce from injury, impairment, or interruption, and promotes the flow of commerce by removing certain recognized sources of industrial strife and unrest, by encouraging practices fundamental to the friendly adjustment of industrial disputes arising out of differences as to wages, hours, or other working conditions, and by restoring equality of bargaining power between employers and employees.

"Experience has further demonstrated that certain practices by some labor organizations, their officers, and members have the intent or the necessary effect of burdening or obstructing commerce by preventing the free flow of goods in such commerce through strikes and other forms of industrial unrest or through concerted activities which impair the interest of the public in the free flow of such commerce. The elimination of such practices is a necessary condition to the assurance of the rights herein guaranteed.

"It is hereby declared to be the policy of the United States to eliminate the causes of certain substantial obstructions to the free flow of commerce and to mitigate and eliminate these obstructions when they have occurred by encouraging the practice and procedure of collective bargaining and by protecting the exercise by workers of full freedom of association, self-organization, and designation of representatives of their own choosing, for the purpose of negotiating the terms and conditions of their employment or other mutual aid or protection."

§ 152. Definitions

"[Sec. 2] When used in this Act—
  "(1) The term 'person' includes one or more individuals, labor organizations, partnerships, associations, corporations, legal representatives, trustees, trustees in cases under Title II of the United States Code, or receivers.
  "(2) The term 'employer' includes any person acting as an agent of an employer, directly or indirectly, but shall not include the United States or any wholly owned Government corporation, or any Federal Reserve Bank, or any State or political subdivision thereof, or any person subject to the Railway Labor Act, as amended from time to time, or any labor organization (other than when acting as an employer), or anyone acting in the capacity of officer or agent of such labor organization.
  "(3) The term 'employee' shall include any employee, and shall not be limited to the employees of a particular employer, unless the Act explicitly states otherwise, and shall include any individual whose work has ceased as a consequence of, or in connection with, any current labor dispute or because of any unfair labor practice, and who has not obtained any other regular and substantially equivalent

employment, but shall not include any individual employed as an agricultural laborer, or in the domestic service of any family or person at his home, or any individual employed by his parent or spouse, or any individual having the status of an independent contractor, or any individual employed as a supervisor, or any individual employed by an employer subject to the Railway Labor Act, as amended from time to time, or by any other person who is not an employer as herein defined.

"(4) The term 'representatives' includes any individual or labor organization.

"(5) The term 'labor organization' means any organization of any kind, or any agency or employee representation committee or plan, in which employees participate and which exists for the purpose, in whole or in part, of dealing with employers concerning grievances, labor disputes, wages, rates of pay, hours of employment, or conditions of work.

"(6) The term 'commerce' means trade, traffic, commerce, transportation, or communication among the several States, or between the District of Columbia or any Territory of the United States and any State or other Territory, or between any foreign country and any State, Territory, or the District of Columbia, or within the District of Columbia or any Territory, or between points in the same State but through any other State or any Territory or the District of Columbia or any foreign country.

"(7) The term 'affecting commerce' means in commerce, or burdening or obstructing commerce or the free flow of commerce, or having led or tending to lead to a labor dispute burdening or obstructing commerce or the free flow of commerce.

"(8) The term 'unfair labor practice' means any unfair labor practice listed in section 8.

"(9) The term 'labor dispute' includes any controversy concerning terms, tenure or conditions of employment, or concerning the association or representation of persons in negotiating, fixing, maintaining, changing, or seeking to arrange terms or conditions of employment, regardless of whether the disputants stand in the proximate relation of employer and employees.

"(10) The term 'National Labor Relations Board' means the National Labor Relations Board provided for in section 3 of this Act.

"(11) The term 'supervisor' means any individual having authority, in the interest of the employer, to hire, transfer, suspend, lay off, recall, promote, discharge, assign, reward, or discipline other employees, or responsibly to direct them or to adjust their grievances, or effectively to recommend such action, if in connection with the foregoing the exercise of such authority is not of a merely routine or clerical nature, but requires the use of independent judgment.

"(12) The term 'professional employee' means—

"(a) any employee engaged in work (i) predominantly intellectual and varied in character as opposed to routine mental, manual, mechanical, or physical work; (ii) involving the consistent exercise of discretion and judgment in its performance; (iii) of such a character that the output produced or the result accomplished cannot be standardized in relation to a given period of time; (iv) requiring knowledge of an advanced type in a field of science or learning customarily acquired by a prolonged course of specialized intellectual instruction and study in an institution of higher learning or a hospital, as distinguished from a general academic education or from an apprenticeship or from training in the performance of routine mental, manual, or physical processes; or

"(b) any employee, who (i) has completed the courses of specialized intellectual instruction and study described in clause (iv) of paragraph (a), and (ii) is performing related work under the supervision of a professional person to qualify himself to become a professional employee as defined in paragraph (a).

"(13) In determining whether any person is acting as an 'agent' of another person so as to make such other person responsible for his acts, the question of whether the specific acts performed were actually authorized or subsequently ratified shall not be controlling.

"(14) The term 'health care institution' shall include any hospital, convalescent hospital, health maintenance organization, health clinic, nursing home, extended care facility, or other institution devoted to the care of sick, infirm, or aged person."

§ 153. National Labor Relations Board

"[Sec. 3] (a) The National Labor Relations Board (hereinafter called the 'Board') created by this Act prior to its amendment by the Labor Management Relations Act, 1947, is hereby continued as an agency of the United States, except that the Board shall consist of five instead of three members, appointed by the President by and with the advice and consent of the Senate. Of the two additional members so provided for, one shall be appointed for a term of five years and the other for a term of two years. Their successors, and the successors of the other members, shall be appointed for terms of five years each, excepting that any individual chosen to fill a vacancy shall be appointed only for the unexpired term of the member whom he shall succeed. The President shall designate one member to serve as Chairman of the Board. Any member of the Board may be removed by the President, upon notice and hearing, for neglect of duty or malfeasance in office, but for no other cause:

"(b) The Board is authorized to delegate to any group of three or more members any or all of the powers which it may itself exercise. The Board is also authorized to delegate to its regional directors its powers under section 9 to determine the unit appropriate for the purpose of collective bargaining, to investigate and provide for hearings, and determine whether a question of representation exists, and to direct an election or take a secret ballot under subsection (c) or (e) of section 9 and certify the results thereof, except that upon the filing of a request therefor with the Board by any interested person, the Board may review any action of a regional director delegated to him under this paragraph, but such a review shall not, unless specifically ordered by the Board, operate as a stay of any action taken by the regional director. A vacancy in the Board shall not impair the right of the remaining members to exercise all of the powers of the Board, and three members of the Board shall, at all times constitute a quorum of the Board, except that two members shall constitute a quorum of any group designated pursuant to the first sentence hereof. The Board shall have an official seal which shall be judicially noticed.

"(c) The Board shall at the close of each fiscal year make a report in writing to Congress and to the President summarizing significant case activities and operations for that fiscal year.

"(d) There shall be a General Counsel of the Board who shall be appointed by the President by and with the advice and consent of the Senate, for a term of four years. The General Counsel of the Board shall exercise general supervision over all attorneys employed by the Board (other than trial examiners and legal assistants to Board members) and over the officers and employees in the regional offices. He shall have final authority, on behalf of the Board, in respect of the investigation of charges and issuance of complaints under section 10, and in respect of the prosecution of such complaints before the Board, and shall have such other duties as the Board may prescribe or as may be provided by law. In case of a vacancy in the office of the General Counsel the President is authorized to designate the officer or employee who shall act as General Counsel during such vacancy, but no person or persons so designated shall so act (1) for more than forty days when the Congress is in session unless a nomination to fill such vacancy shall have been submitted to the Senate, or (2) after the adjournment sine die of the session of the Senate in which such nomination was submitted."

§ 154. National Labor Relations Board; eligibility for reappointment; officers and employees; payment of expenses

"[Sec. 4] (a) Each member of the Board and the General Counsel of the Board shall be eligible for reappointment, and shall not engage in any other business, vocation, or employment. The Board shall appoint an executive secretary, and such attorneys, examiners, and regional directors, and such other employees as it may from time to time find necessary for the proper performance of its duties. The Board may not employ any attorneys for the purpose of reviewing transcripts of hearings or preparing drafts of opinions except that any attorney employed for assignment as a legal assistant to any Board member may for such Board member review such transcripts and prepare such drafts. No trial examiner's report shall be reviewed, either before or after its publication, by any person other than a member of the Board or his legal assistant, and no trial examiner shall advise or consult with the Board with respect to exceptions taken to his findings, rulings, or recommendations. The Board may establish or utilize such regional, local, or other agencies, and utilize such voluntary and uncompensated services, as may from time to time be needed. Attorneys appointed under this section may, at the direction of the Board, appear for and represent the Board in any case in court. Nothing in this subchapter shall be construed to authorize the Board to appoint individuals for the purpose of conciliation or mediation, or for economic analysis.

"(b) All of the expenses of the Board, including all necessary traveling and subsistence expenses outside the District of Columbia incurred by the members or employees of the Board under its orders, shall be allowed and paid on the presentation of itemized vouchers therefor approved by the Board or by any individual it designates for that purpose."

§ 155. National Labor Relations Board; principal office; conducting inquiries throughout country; participation in decisions or inquiries conducted by member

"[Sec. 5] The principal office of the Board shall be in the District of Columbia, but it may meet and exercise any or all of its powers at any other place. The Board may, by one or more of its members or by such agents or agencies as it may designate, prosecute any inquiry necessary to its functions in any part of the United States. A member who participates in such an inquiry shall not be disqualified from subsequently participating in a decision of the Board in the same case."

§ 156. Rules and regulations

"[Sec. 6] The Board shall have authority from time to time to make, amend, and rescind, in the manner prescribed by the Administrative Procedure Act, such rules and regulations as may be necessary to carry out the provisions of this Act."

§ 157. Rights of employees as to organization, collective bargaining, etc.

"[Sec. 7] Employees shall have the right to self-organization, to form, join or assist labor organizations, to bargain collectively through representatives of their own choosing, and to engage in other concerted activities for the purpose of collective bargaining or other mutual aid or protection, and shall also have the right to refrain from any or all of such activities except to the extent that such right may be affected by an agreement requiring membership in a labor organization as a condition of employment as authorized in section 159(a)(3)."

§ 158. Unfair labor practices

"[Sec. 8] (a) It shall be an unfair labor practice for an employer—
"(1) to interfere with, restrain, or coerce employees in the exercise of the rights guaranteed in section 7;
"(2) to dominate or interfere with the formation or administration of any labor organization or contribute financial or other support to it: *Provided,* That subject to rules and regulations made and published by the Board pursuant to section G, an employer shall not be prohibited from permitting employees to confer with him during working hours without loss of time or pay;
"(3) by discrimination in regard to hire or tenure of employment or any term or condition of employment to encourage or discourage membership in any labor organization; *Provided,* That nothing in this Act, or any other statute of the United States, shall preclude an employer from making an agreement with a labor organization (not established, maintained, or assisted by any action defined in section 8(a) of this Act as an unfair labor practice) to require as a condition of employment membership therein on or after the thirtieth day following the beginning of such employment or the effective date of such agreement, whichever is the later, (i) if such labor organization

is the representative of the employees as provided in section 9(a), in the appropriate collective-bargaining unit covered by such agreement when made; and (ii) unless following an election held as provided in section 9(e) within one year preceding the effective date of such agreement the Board shall have certified that at least a majority of the employees eligible to vote in such election have voted to rescind the authority of such labor organization to make such an agreement: *Provided further,* That no employer shall justify any discrimination against an employee for non-membership in a labor organization (A) if he has reasonable grounds for believing that such membership was not available to the employee on the same terms and conditions generally applicable to other members, or (B) if he has reasonable grounds for believing that membership was denied or terminated for reasons other than the failure of the employee to tender the periodic dues and the initiation fees uniformly required as a condition of acquiring or retaining membership;

"(4) to discharge or otherwise discriminate against an employee because he has filed charges or given testimony under this Act;

"(5) to refuse to bargain collectively with the representatives of his employees, subject to the provisions of section 9(a).

"(b) It shall be an unfair labor practice for a labor organization or its agents—

"(1) to restrain or coerce (A) employees in the exercise of the rights guaranteed in section 7: *Provided,* That this paragraph shall not impair the right of a labor organization to prescribe its own rules with respect to the acquisition or retention of membership therein; or (B) an employer in the selection of his representatives for the purposes of collective bargaining or the adjustment of grievances;

"(2) to cause or attempt to cause an employer to discriminate against an employee in violation of subsection (a)(3) or to discriminate against an employee with respect to whom membership in such organization has been denied or terminated on some ground other than his failure to tender the periodic dues and the initiation fees uniformly required as a condition of acquiring or retaining membership;

"(3) to refuse to bargain collectively with an employer, provided it is the representative of his employees subject to the provisions of section 9(a);

"(4)(i) to engage in, or to induce or encourage any individual employed by any person engaged in commerce or in an industry affecting commerce to engage in, a strike or a refusal in the course of his employment to use, manufacture, process, transport, or otherwise handle or work on any goods, articles, materials or commodities or to perform any services; or (ii) to threaten, coerce, or restrain any person engaged in commerce or in an industry affecting commerce, where in either case an object thereof is:

"(A) forcing or requiring any employer or self-employed person to join any labor or employer organization or to enter into any agreement which is prohibited by section 8(e);

"(B) forcing or requiring any person to cease using, selling, handling, transporting, or otherwise dealing in the products of any other producer, processor, or manufacturer, or to cease doing business with any other person, or forcing or requiring any other employer to recognize or bargain with a labor organization as the representative of his employees unless such labor organization has been certified as the representative of such employees under the provisions of section 9: *Provided,* That nothing contained in this clause (B) shall be construed to make unlawful, where not otherwise unlawful, any primary strike or primary picketing;

"(C) forcing or requiring any employer to recognize or bargain with a particular labor organization as the representative of his employees if another labor organization has been certified as the representative of such employees under the provisions of section 9;

"(D) forcing or requiring any employer to assign particular work to employees in a particular labor organization or in a particular trade, craft, or class rather than to employees in another labor organization or in another trade, craft, or class, unless such employer is failing to conform to an order or certification of the Board determining the bargaining representative for employees performing such work:

"*Provided,* That nothing contained in this subsection (b) shall be construed to make unlawful a refusal by any person to enter upon the premises of any employer (other than his own employer), if the employees of such employer are engaged in a strike ratified or approved by a representative of such employees whom such employer is required to recognize under this Act: *Provided further,* That for the purposes of this paragraph (4) only, nothing contained in such paragraph shall be construed to prohibit publicity, other than picketing, for the purpose of truthfully advising the public, including consumers and members of a labor organization, that a product or products are produced by an employer with whom the labor organization has a primary dispute and are distributed by another employer, as long as such publicity does not have an effect of inducing any individual employed by any person other than the primary employer in the course of his employment to refuse to pick up, deliver, or transport any goods, or not to perform any services, at the establishment of the employer engaged in such distribution.

"(5) to require of employees covered by an agreement authorized under subsection (a)(3) the payment, as a condition precedent to becoming a member of such organization, of a fee in an amount which the Board finds excessive or discriminatory under all the circumstances. In making such a finding, the Board shall consider, among other relevant factors, the practices and customs of labor organizations in the particular industry, and the wages currently paid to the employees affected;

"(6) to cause or attempt to cause an employer to pay or deliver or agree to pay or deliver any money or other thing of value, in the nature of an exaction, for services which are not performed or not to be performed; and

"(7) to picket or cause to be picketed, or threaten to picket or cause to be picketed, any employer where an object thereof is forcing or requiring an employer to recognize or bargain with a labor organization as the representative of his employees, or forcing or requiring the employees of an employer to accept or select such labor organization as their collective bargaining representative unless such labor organization is currently certified as the representative of such employees:

"(A) where the employer has lawfully recognized in accordance with this Act any other labor organization and a question concerning representation may not appropriately be raised under section 9(c) of this Act,

"(B) where within the preceding twelve months a valid election under section 9(c) of this Act has been conducted, or

"(C) where such picketing has been conducted without a petition under section 9(c) being filed within a reasonable period of time not to exceed thirty days from the commencement of such picketing: *Provided,* That when such a petition has been filed the Board shall forthwith, without regard to the provisions of section 9(c)(1) or the absence of a showing of a substantial interest on the part of the labor organization, direct an election in such unit as the Board finds to be appropriate and shall certify the results thereof: *Provided further,* That nothing in this subparagraph (C) shall be construed to prohibit any picketing or other publicity for the purpose of truthfully advising the public (including consumers) that an employer does not employ members of, or have a contract with, a labor organization, unless an effect of such picketing is to induce any individual employed by any other person in the course of his employment, not to pick up, deliver or transport any goods or not to perform any services.

"Nothing in this paragraph (7) shall be construed to permit any act which would otherwise be an unfair labor practice under this section (8)(b).

"(c) The expressing of any views, argument, or opinion, or the dissemination thereof, whether in written, printed, graphic, or visual form, shall not constitute or be evidence of an unfair labor practice under any of the provisions of this Act, if such expression contains no threat of reprisal or force or promise of benefit.

"(d) For the purposes of this section, to bargain collectively is the performance of the mutual obligation of the employer and the representative of the employees to meet at reasonable times and confer in good faith with respect to wages, hours, and other terms and conditions of employment, or the negotiation of an agreement, or any question arising thereunder, and the execution of a written contract incorporating any agreement reached if requested by either party, but such obligation does not compel either party to agree to a proposal or require the making of a concession: *Provided,* That where there is in effect a collective-bargaining contract covering employees in an industry affecting commerce, the duty to bargain collectively shall also mean that no party to such contract shall terminate or modify such contract, unless the party desiring such termination or modification—

"(1) serves a written notice upon the other party to the contract of the proposed termination or modification sixty days prior to the expiration date thereof, or in the event such contract contains no expiration date, sixty days prior to the time it is proposed to make such termination or modification;

"(2) offers to meet and confer with the other party for the purpose of negotiating a new contract or a contract containing the proposed modifications;

"(3) notifies the Federal Mediation and Conciliation Service within thirty days after such notice of the existence of a dispute, and simultaneously therewith notifies any State or Territorial agency established to mediate and conciliate disputes within the State or Territory where the dispute occurred, provided no agreement has been reached by that time; and

"(4) continues in full force and effect, without resorting to strike or lockout, all the terms and conditions of the existing contract for a period of sixty days after such notice is given or until the expiration date of such contract, whichever occurs later.

"The duties imposed upon employers, employees, and labor organizations by paragraphs (2), (3), and (4) shall become inapplicable upon an intervening certification of the Board, under which the labor organization or individual, which is a party to the contract, has been superseded as or ceased to be the representative of the employees subject to the provisions of section 9(a), and the duties so imposed shall not be construed as requiring either party to discuss or agree to any modification of the terms and conditions contained in a contract for a fixed period, if such modification is to become effective before such terms and conditions can be reopened under the provisions of the contract. Any employee who engages in a strike within any notice period specified in this subsection, or who engages in any strike within the appropriate period specified in subsection (g) of this section, shall lose his status as an employee of the employer engaged in the particular labor dispute, for the purposes of sections 8, 9, and 10 of this Act, as amended, but such loss of status for such employee shall terminate if and when he is re-employed by such employer. Whenever the collective bargaining involves employees of a health care institution, the provisions of this section 8(d) shall be modified as follows:

"(A) The notice of section 8(d)(1) shall be ninety days; the notice of section 8(d)(3) shall be sixty days; and the contract period of section 8(d)(4) shall be ninety days.

"(B) Where the bargaining is for an initial agreement following certification or recognition, at least thirty days' notice of the existence of a dispute shall be given by the labor organization to the agencies set forth in section 8(d)(3).

"(C) After notice is given to the Federal Mediation and Conciliation Service under either clause (A) or (B) of this sentence, the Service shall promptly communicate with the parties and use its best efforts by mediation and conciliation to bring them to agreement. The parties shall participate fully and promptly in such meetings as may be undertaken by the Service for the purpose of aiding in a settlement of the dispute.

"(e) It shall be an unfair labor practice for any labor organization and any employer to enter into any contract or agreement, express or implied, whereby such employer ceases or refrains or agrees to cease or refrain from handling, using, selling, transporting or otherwise dealing in any of the products of any other employer, or to cease doing business with any other person, and any contract or agreement entered into heretofore or hereafter containing such an agreement shall be to such extent unenforceable and void: *Provided,* That nothing in this subsection (e) shall apply to an agreement between a labor organization and an employer in the construction industry relating to the contracting or subcontracting of work to be done at the site of the construction, alteration, painting, or repair of a building, structure, or other work: *Provided further*, That for the purposes of this subsection (e) and section 8(b)(4)(B) the terms "any employer," "any person engaged in commerce or any industry affecting commerce," and "any person" when used in relation to the terms "any other producer, processor, or manufacturer," "any other employer" or "any other person" shall not include persons in the relation of a jobber, manufacturer, contractor, or subcontractor working on the goods or premises of the jobber or manufacturer or performing parts of an integrated process of production in the apparel and clothing industry: *Provided further*, That nothing in this Act shall prohibit the enforcement of any agreement which is within the foregoing exception.

"(f) It shall not be an unfair labor practice under subsections (a) and (b) of this section for an a employer engaged primarily in the building and construction industry to make an agreement covering employees engaged (or who, upon their employment, will be engaged) in the building and construction industry with a labor organization of which building and construction employees are members (not established, maintained, or assisted by any action defined in section 8(a) of this Act as an unfair labor practice) because (1) the majority status of such labor organization has not been established under the provisions of section 9 of this Act prior to the making of such agreement, or (2) such agreement requires as a condition of employment, membership in such labor organization after the seventh day following the beginning of such employment or the effective date of the agreement, whichever is later, or (3) such agreement requires the employer to notify such labor organization of opportunities for employment with such employer, or gives such labor organization an opportunity to refer qualified applicants for such employment, or (4) such agreement specifies minimum training or experience qualifications for employment or provides for priority in opportunities for employment based upon length of service with such employer, in the industry or in the particular geographical area: *Provided*, That nothing in this subsection shall set aside the final proviso to section 8(a)(3) of this Act: *Provided further*, That any agreement which would be invalid but for clause (1) of this subsection, shall not be a bar to a petition filed pursuant to section 9(c) or 9(e).

"(g) A labor organization before engaging in any strike, picketing, or other concerted refusal to work at any health care institution shall, not less than ten days prior to such action, notify the institution in writing and the Federal Mediation and Conciliation Service of that intention, except that in the case of bargaining for an initial agreement following certification or recognition the notice required by this subsection shall not be given until the expiration of the period specified in clause (B) of the last sentence of section 8(d) of this Act. The notice shall state the date and time that such action will commence. The notice, once given, may be extended by the written agreement of both parties."

§ 158a.   [Omitted.]

§ 159.   Representatives and elections

"[Sec. 9] (a) Representatives designated or selected for the purposes of collective bargaining by the majority of the employees in a unit appropriate for such purposes, shall be the exclusive representatives of all the employees in such unit for the purposes of collective bargaining in respect to rates of pay, wages, hours of employment, or other conditions of employment: *Provided,* That any individual employee or a group of employees shall have the right at any time to present grievances to their employer and to have such grievances adjusted, without the intervention of the bargaining representative, as long as the adjustment is not inconsistent with the terms of a collective-bargaining contract or agreement then in effect: *Provided further,* That the bargaining representative has been given opportunity to be present at such adjustment.

"(b) The Board shall decide in each case whether, in order to assure to employees the fullest freedom in exercising the rights guaranteed by this Act, the unit appropriate for the purposes of collective bargaining shall be the employer unit, craft unit, plant unit, or subdivision thereof: *Provided,* That the Board shall not (1) decide that any unit is appropriate for such purposes if such unit includes both professional employees and employees who are not professional employees unless a majority of such professional employees vote for inclusion in such unit; or (2) decide that any craft unit is inappropriate for such purposes on the ground that a different unit has been established by a prior Board determination, unless a majority of the employees in the proposed craft unit vote against separate representation or (3) decide that any unit is appropriate for such purposes if it includes, together with other employees, any individual employed as a guard to enforce against employees and other persons rules to protect property of the employer or to protect the safety of persons on the employer's premises; but no labor organization shall be certified as the representative of employees in a bargaining unit of guards if such organization admits to membership, or is affiliated directly or indirectly with an organization which admits to membership, employees other than guards.

"(c)(1) Whenever a petition shall have been filed, in accordance with such regulations as may be prescribed by the Board—

"(A) by an employee or group of employees or any individual or labor organization acting in their behalf alleging that a substantial number of employees (i) wish to be represented for collective bargaining and that their employer declines to recognize their representative as the representative defined in section 9(a), or (ii) assert that the individual or labor organization, which has been certified or is being currently recognized by their employer as the bargaining representative, is no longer a representative as defined in section 9(a); or

"(B) by an employer, alleging that one or more individuals or labor organizations have presented to him a claim to be recognized as the representative defined in section 9(a):

the Board shall investigate such petition and if it has reasonable cause to believe that a question of representation affecting commerce exists shall provide for an appropriate hearing upon due notice. Such hearing may be conducted by an officer or employee of the regional office, who shall not make any recommendations with respect thereto. If the Board finds upon the record of such hearing that such a question of representation exists, it shall direct an election by secret ballot and shall certify the results thereof.

"(2) In determining whether or not a question of representation affecting commerce exists, the same regulations and rules of decision shall apply irrespective of the identity of the persons filing the petition or the kind of relief sought and in no case shall the Board deny a labor organization a place on the ballot by reason of an order with respect to such labor organization or its predecessor not issued in conformity with section 10(e).

"(3) No election shall be directed in any bargaining unit or any subdivision within which, in the preceding twelve-month period, a valid election shall have been held. Employees engaged in an economic strike who are not entitled to reinstatement shall be eligible to vote under such regulations as the Board shall find are consistent with the purposes and provisions of this Act in any election conducted within twelve months after the commencement of the strike. In any election where none of the choices on the ballot receives a majority, a runoff shall be conducted, the ballot providing for a selection between the two choices receiving the largest and second largest number of valid votes cast in the election.

"(4) Nothing in this section shall be construed to prohibit the waiving of hearings by stipulation for the purpose of a consent election in conformity with regulations and rules of decision of the Board.

"(5) In determining whether a unit is appropriate for the purposes specified in subsection (b) the extent to which the employees have organized shall not be controlling.

"(d) Whenever an order of the Board made pursuant to section 10(e) is based in whole or in part upon facts certified following an investigation pursuant to subsection (c) of this section and there is a petition for the enforcement or review of such order, such certification and the record of such investigation shall be included in the transcript of the entire record required to be filed under section 10(e) or 10(f), and thereupon the decree of the court enforcing, modifying, or setting aside in whole or in part the order of the Board shall be made and entered upon the pleadings, testimony, and proceedings set forth in such transcript.

"(e)(1) Upon the filing with the Board, by 30 per centum or more of the employees in a bargaining unit covered by an agreement between their employer and a labor organization made pursuant to section 8(a)(3), of a petition alleging the desire that such authority be rescinded, the Board shall take a secret ballot of the employees in such unit and certify the results thereof to such labor organization and to the employer.

"(2) No election shall be conducted pursuant to this subsection in any bargaining unit or any subdivision within which, in the preceding twelve-month period, a valid election shall have been held."

§ 160. Prevention of unfair labor practices

"[Sec. 10] (a) The Board is empowered, as hereinafter provided, to prevent any person from engaging in any unfair labor practice (listed in section 8) affecting commerce. This power shall not be affected by any other means of adjustment or prevention that has been or may be established by agreement, law, or otherwise: *Provided,* That the Board is empowered by agreement with any agency of any State or Territory to cede to such agency jurisdiction over any cases in any industry (other than mining, manufacturing, communications, and transportation except where predominantly local in character) even though such cases may involve labor disputes affecting commerce, unless the provisions of the State or Territorial statute applicable to the determination of such cases by such agency is inconsistent with the corresponding provision of this Act or has received a construction inconsistent therewith.

"(b) Whenever it is charged that any person has engaged in or is engaging in any such unfair labor practice, the Board, or any agent or agency designated by the Board for such purposes, shall have power to issue and cause to be served upon such person a complaint stating the charges in that respect, and containing a notice of hearing before the Board or a member thereof, or before a designated agent or agency, at a place therein fixed, not less than five days after the serving of said complaint: *Provided*, That no complaint shall issue based upon any unfair labor practice occurring more than six months prior to the filing of the charge with the Board and the service of a copy thereof upon the person against whom such charge is made, unless the person aggrieved thereby was prevented from filing such charge by reason of service in the armed forces, in which event the six-month period shall be computed from the day of his discharge. Any such complaint may be amended by the member, agent, or agency conducting the hearing or the Board in its discretion at any time prior to the issuance of an order based thereon. The person so complained of shall have the right to file an answer to the original or amended complaint and to appear in person or otherwise and give testimony at the place and time fixed in the complaint. In the discretion of the member, agent, or agency conducting the hearing or the Board, any other person may be allowed to intervene in the said proceeding and to present testimony. Any such proceeding shall, so far as practicable, be conducted in accordance with the rules of evidence applicable in the district courts of the United States under the rules of civil procedure for the district courts of the United States, adopted by the Supreme Court of the United States pursuant to the Act of June 19, 1934 (U.S.C., title 28, secs. 723-B, 723-C).

"(c) The testimony taken by such member, agent, or agency or the Board shall be reduced to writing and filed with the Board. Thereafter, in its discretion, the Board upon notice may take further testimony or hear argument. If upon the preponderance of the testimony taken the Board shall be of the opinion that any person named in the complaint has engaged in or is engaging in any such unfair labor practice, then the Board shall state its findings of fact and shall issue and cause to be served on such person an order requiring such person to cease and desist from such unfair labor practice, and to take such affirmative action including reinstatement of employees with or without back pay, as will effectuate the policies of this Act: *Provided*, That where an order directs reinstatement of an employee, back pay may be required of the employer or labor organization, as the case may be, responsible for the discrimination suffered by him: *And provided further*, That in determining whether a complaint shall issue alleging a violation of section 8(a)(1) or section 8(a)(2), and in deciding such cases, the same regulations and rules of decision shall apply irrespective of whether or not the labor organization affected is affiliated with a labor organization national or international in scope. Such order may further require such person to make reports from time to time showing the extent to which it has complied with the order. If upon the preponderance of the testimony taken the Board shall not be of the opinion that the person named in the complaint has engaged in or is engaging in any such unfair labor practice, then the Board shall state its findings of fact and shall issue an order dismissing the said complaint. No order of the Board shall require the reinstatement of any individual as an employee who has been suspended or discharged, or the payment to him of any back pay, if such individual was suspended or discharged for cause. In case the evidence is presented before a member of the Board, or before an examiner or examiners thereof, such member, or such examiner or examiners, as the case may be, shall issue and cause to be served on the parties to the proceedings a proposed report, together with a recommended order, which shall be filed with the Board, and if no exceptions are filed within twenty days after service thereof upon such parties, or within such further period as the Board may authorize, such recommended order shall become the order of the Board and become effective as therein prescribed.

"(d) Until the record in a case shall have been filed in a court, as hereinafter provided, the Board may at any time upon reasonable notice and in such manner as it shall deem proper modify or set aside, in whole or in part, any finding or order made or issued by it.

"(e) The Board shall have power to petition any court of appeals of the United States, or if all the courts of appeals to which application may be made are in vacation, any district court of the United States, within any circuit or district, respectively, wherein the unfair labor practice in question occurred or wherein such person resides or transacts business, for the enforcement of such order and for appropriate temporary relief or restraining order, and shall file in the court the record in the proceedings, as provided in section 2112 of title 28, United States Code. Upon the filing of such petition, the court shall cause notice thereof to be served upon such person, and thereupon shall have jurisdiction of the proceeding and of the question determined therein, and shall have power to grant such temporary relief or restraining order as it deems just and proper, and to make and enter a decree enforcing, modifying, and enforcing as so modified, or setting aside in whole or in part the order of the Board. No objection that has not been urged before the Board, its member, agent, or agency, shall be considered by the court, unless the failure or neglect to urge such objection shall be excused because of extraordinary circumstances. The findings of the Board with respect to questions of fact if supported by substantial evidence on the record considered as a whole shall be conclusive. If either party shall apply to the court for leave to adduce additional evidence and shall show to the satisfaction of the court that such additional evidence is material and that there were reasonable grounds for the failure to adduce such evidence in the hearing before the Board, its member, agent, or agency, the court may order such additional evidence to be taken before the Board, its member, agent, or agency, and to be made a part of the record. The Board may modify its findings as to the facts, or make new findings, by reason of additional evidence so taken and filed, and it shall file such modified or new findings, which findings with respect to questions of fact if supported by substantial evidence on the record considered as a whole shall be conclusive, and shall file its recommendations, if any, for the modification or setting aside of its original order. Upon the filing of the record with it the jurisdiction of the court shall be exclusive and its judgment and decree shall be final, except that the same shall be subject to review by the appropriate United States court of appeals if application was made to the district court as herein above provided, and by the Supreme Court of the United States upon writ of certiorari or certification as provided in section 1254 of title 28.

"(f) Any person aggrieved by a final order of the Board granting or denying in whole or in part the relief sought may obtain a review of such order in any circuit court of appeals of the United States in the circuit wherein the unfair labor practice in question was alleged to have been engaged in or wherein such person resides or transacts business, or in the United States Court of Appeals for the District of Columbia, by filing in such court a written petition praying that the order of the Board be modified or set aside. A copy of such petition shall be forthwith transmitted by the clerk of the court to the Board, and thereupon the aggrieved party shall file in the court the record in the proceeding, certified by the Board, as provided in section 2112 of the title 28, United States Code. Upon the filing of such petition, the court shall proceed in the same manner as in the case of an application by the Board under subsection (e) of this section, and shall have the same jurisdiction to grant to the Board such temporary relief or restraining order as it deems just and proper, and in like manner to make and enter a decree enforcing, modifying, and enforcing as so modified, or setting aside in whole or in part the order of the Board; the findings of the Board with respect to questions of fact if supported by substantial evidence on the record considered as a whole shall in like manner be conclusive.

"(g) The commencement of proceedings under subsection (e) or (f) of this section shall not, unless specifically ordered by the court, operate as a stay of the Board's order.

"(h) When granting appropriate temporary relief or a restraining order, or making and entering a decree enforcing, modifying, or enforcing as so modified, or setting aside in whole or in part an order of the Board, as provided in this section, the jurisdiction of courts sitting in equity shall not be limited by the Act entitled 'An Act to amend the Judicial Code and to define and limit the jurisdiction of courts sitting in equity, and for other purposes,' approved March 23, 1932 (U.S.C., Supp. VII, title 29, secs. 101-115).

"(i) Petitions filed under this Act shall be heard expeditiously, and if possible within ten days after they have been docketed.

"(j) The Board shall have power, upon issuance of a complaint as provided in subsection (b) charging that any person has engaged in or is engaging in an unfair labor practice, to petition any district court of the United States (including the District Court of the United States for the District of Columbia), within any district wherein the unfair labor practice in question is alleged to have occurred or wherein such person resides or transacts business, for appropriate temporary relief or restraining order. Upon the filing of any such petition the court shall cause notice thereof to be served upon such person, and thereupon shall have jurisdiction to grant to the Board such temporary relief or restraining order as it deems just and proper.

"(k) Whenever it is charged that any person has engaged in an unfair labor practice with the meaning of paragraph (4)(D) of section 8(b), the Board is empowered and directed to hear and determine the dispute out of which such unfair labor practice shall have arisen, unless, within ten days after notice that such charge has been filed, the parties to such dispute submit to the Board satisfactory evidence that they have adjusted, or agreed upon methods for the voluntary adjustment of, the dispute. Upon compliance by the parties to the dispute with the decision of the Board or upon such voluntary adjustment of the dispute, such charge shall be dismissed.

"(l) Whenever it is charged that any person has engaged in an unfair labor practice within the meaning of paragraph (4)(A), (B), or (C) of section 8(b) or section 8(e) or section 8(b)(7), the preliminary investigation of such charge shall be made forthwith and given priority over all other cases except cases of like character in the office where it is filed or to which it is referred. If, after such investigation, the officer or regional attorney to whom the matter may be referred has reasonable cause to believe such charge is true and that a complaint should issue, he shall, on behalf of the Board, petition any district court of the United States (including the District Court of the United States for the District of Columbia) within any district where the unfair labor practice in question has occurred, is alleged to have occurred, or wherein such person resides or transacts business, for appropriate injunctive relief pending the final adjudication of the Board with respect to such matter. Upon the filing of any such petition the district court shall have jurisdiction to grant such injunctive relief or temporary restraining order as it deems just and proper, notwithstanding any other provision of law: *Provided further*, That no temporary restraining order shall be issued without notice unless a petition alleges that substantial and irreparable injury to the charging party will be unavoidable and such temporary restraining order shall be effective for no longer than five days and will become void at the expiration of such period: *Provided further*, That such officer or regional attorney shall not apply for any restraining order under section 8(b)(7) if a charge against the employer under 8(a)(2) has been filed and after the preliminary investigation, he has reasonable cause to believe that such charge is true and that a complaint should issue. Upon filing of any such petition, the courts shall cause notice thereof to be served upon any person involved in the charge and such person, including the charging party, shall be given an opportunity to appear by counsel and present any relevant testimony: *Provided further*, That for the purposes of this subsection district courts shall be deemed to have jurisdiction of a labor organization (1) in the district in which such organization maintains its principal office, or (2) in any district in which its duly authorized officers or agents are engaged in promoting or protecting the interests of employee members. The service of legal process upon such officer or agent shall constitute service upon the labor organization and make such organization a party to the suit. In situations where such relief is appropriate the procedure specified herein shall apply to charges with respect to section 8(b)(4)(D).

"(m) Whenever it is charged that any person has engaged in an unfair labor practice within the meaning of subsection (a)(3) or (b)(2) of section 8, such charge shall be given priority over all other cases except cases of like character in the office where it is filed or to which it is referred and cases given priority under subsection (l)."

§ 161. Investigatory powers

"[Sec. 11] For the purpose of all hearings and investigations, which, in the opinion of the Board, are necessary and proper for the exercise of the powers vested in it by section 9 and section 10—

   "(1) The Board, or its duly authorized agents or agencies, shall at all reasonable times have access to, for the purpose of examination, and the right to copy any evidence of any person being investigated or proceeded against that relates to any matter under investigation or in question. The Board, or any member thereof, shall upon application of any party to such proceedings, forthwith issue to such party subpoenas requiring the attendance and testimony of witnesses or the production of any evidence in such proceeding or investigation requested in such application. Within five days after the service of a subpoena on any person requiring the production of any evidence in his possession or under his control, such person may petition the Board to revoke, and the Board shall revoke, such subpoena if in its opinion the evidence whose production is required does not relate to any matter under investigation, or any matter in question in such proceedings, or if in its opinion such subpoena does not describe with sufficient particularity the evidence whose production is required. Any member of the Board, or any agent or agency designated by the Board for such purposes, may administer oaths and affirmations, examine witnesses, and receive evidence. Such attendance of witnesses and the production of such evidence may be required from any place in the United States, or any Territory or possession thereof, at any designated place of hearing.

"(2) In case of contumacy or refusal to obey a subpoena issued to any person, any district court of the United States or the United States courts of any Territory or possession, or the District Court of the United States for the District of Columbia, within the jurisdiction of which the inquiry is carried on or within the jurisdiction of which said person guilty of contumacy or refusal to obey is found or resides or transacts business, upon application by the Board shall have jurisdiction to issue to such person an order requiring such person to appear before the Board, its member, agent, or agency, there to produce evidence if so ordered, or there to give testimony touching the matter under investigation or in question; and any failure to obey such order of the court may be punished by said court as a contempt thereof.

"(3) [Repealed.]

"(4) Complaints, orders and other process and papers of the Board, its member, agent, or agency, may be served either personally or by registered or certified mail or by telegraph or by leaving a copy thereof at the principal office or place of business of the person required to be served. The verified return by the individual so serving the same setting forth the manner of such service shall be proof of the same, and the return post office receipt or telegraph receipt thereof when registered or certified and mailed or when telegraphed as aforesaid shall be proof of service of the same. Witnesses summoned before the Board, its member, agent, or agency, shall be paid the same fees and mileage that are paid witnesses in the courts of the United States, and witnesses whose depositions are taken and the persons taking the same shall severally be entitled to the same fees as are paid for like services in the courts of the United States.

"(5) All process of any court to which application may be made under this Act may be served in the judicial district wherein the defendant or other person required to be served resides or may be found.

"(6) The several departments and agencies of the Government, when directed by the President, shall furnish the Board, upon its request, all records, papers, and information in their possession relating to any matter before the Board."

§ 162.   Offenses and penalties

"[Sec. 12] Any person who shall willfully resist, prevent, impede, or interfere with any member of the Board or any of its agents or agencies in the performance of duties pursuant to this Act shall be punished by a fine of not more than $5,000 or by imprisonment for not more than one year, or both."

§ 163.   Right to strike preserved

"[Sec. 13] Nothing in this Act, except as specifically provided for herein, shall be construed so as either to interfere with or impede or diminish in any way the right to strike, or to affect the limitations or qualifications on that right."

§ 164.   Construction of provisions

"[Sec. 14] (a) Nothing herein shall prohibit any individual employed as a supervisor from becoming or remaining a member of a labor organization, but no employer subject to this Act shall be compelled to deem individuals defined herein as supervisors as employees for the purpose of any law, either national or local, relating to collective bargaining.

"(b) Nothing in this Act shall be construed as authorizing the execution or application of agreements requiring membership in a labor organization as a condition of employment in any State or Territory in which such execution or application is prohibited by State or Territorial law.

"(c)(1) The Board, in its discretion, may, by rule of decision or by published rules adopted pursuant to the Administrative Procedure Act, decline to assert jurisdiction over any labor dispute involving any class or category of employers, where, in the opinion of the Board, the effect of such labor dispute on commerce is not sufficiently substantial to warrant the exercise of its jurisdiction: *Provided,* That the Board shall not decline to assert jurisdiction over any labor dispute over which it would assert jurisdiction under the standards prevailing upon August 1, 1959.

"(2) Nothing in this Act shall be deemed to prevent or bar any agency or the courts of any State or Territory (including the Commonwealth of Puerto Rico, Guam, and the Virgin Islands), from assuming and asserting jurisdiction over labor disputes over which the Board declines, pursuant to paragraph (1) of this subsection, to assert jurisdiction."

§ 165.   Conflict of laws

"[Sec. 15] Wherever the application of the provisions of section 272 of chapter 10 of the Act entitled 'An Act to establish a uniform system of bankruptcy throughout the United States,' approved July 1, 1898, and Act amendatory thereof and supplementary thereto (U.S.C., title 11, sec. 672), conflicts with the application of the provisions of this Act, this Act shall prevail: *Provided,* That in any situation where the provisions of this Act cannot be validly enforced, the provisions of such other Acts shall remain in full force and effect."

§ 166. Separability of provisions

"[Sec. 16] If any provision of this Act, or the application of such provision to any person or circumstances, shall be held invalid, the remainder of this Act, or the application of such provision to persons or circumstances other than those as to which it is held invalid, shall not be affected thereby."

§ 167. Short title

"[Sec. 17] This Act may be cited as the 'National Labor Relations Act'."

§ 168. Validation of certificates and other Board actions

"[Sec. 18] No petition entertained, no investigation made, no election held, and no certification issued by the National Labor Relations Board, under any of the provisions of section 9 of the National Labor Relations Act, as amended, shall be invalid by reason of the failure of the Congress of Industrial Organizations to have complied with the requirements of section 9(f), (g), or (h) of the aforesaid Act prior to December 22, 1949, or by reason of the failure of the American Federation of Labor to have complied with the provisions of section 9(f), (g), or (h) of the aforesaid Act prior to November 7, 1947: *Provided*, That no liability shall be imposed under any provision of this Act upon any person for failure to honor any election or certificate referred to above, prior to the effective date of this amendment: *Provided, however*, That this proviso shall not have the effect of setting aside or in any way affecting judgments or decrees heretofore entered under section 10(e) or (f) and which have become final."

§ 169. Employees with religious convictions; payment of dues and fees

"[Sec. 19] Any employee who is a member of and adheres to established and traditional tenets or teachings of a bona fide religion, body, or sect which has historically held conscientious objections to joining or financially supporting labor organizations shall not be required to join or financially support any labor organization as a condition of employment; except that such employee may be required in a contract between such employees' employer and a labor organization in lieu of periodic dues and initiation fees, to pay sums equal to such dues and initiation fees to a non-religious, non-labor organization charitable fund exempt from taxation under section 501 (c)(a) of title 26 of the Internal Revenue Code, chosen by such employee from a list of at least three such funds, designated in such contract or if the contract fails to designate such funds, then to any such fund chosen by the employee. If such employee who holds conscientious objections pursuant to this section requests the labor organization to pursue the grievance-arbitration procedure on the employee's behalf, the labor organization is authorized to charge the employee for the reasonable cost of using such procedure."

Title II. Conciliation of Labor Disputes in Industries Affecting Commerce; National Emergencies

§ 171. Declaration of purpose and policy

[Sec. 201] That it is the policy of the United States that—

(a) sound and stable industrial peace and the advancement of the general welfare, health, and safety of the Nation and of the best interests of employers and employees can most satisfactorily be secured by the settlement of issues between employers and employees through the processes of conference and collective bargaining between employers and the representatives of their employees;

(b) the settlement of issues between employers and employees through collective bargaining may be advanced by making available full and adequate governmental facilities for conciliation, mediation, and voluntary arbitration to aid and encourage employers and the representatives of their employees to reach and maintain agreements concerning rates of pay, hours, and working conditions, and to make all reasonable efforts to settle their differences by mutual agreement reached through conferences and collective bargaining or by such methods as may be provided for in any applicable agreement for the settlement of disputes; and

(c) certain controversies which arise between parties to collective bargaining agreements may be avoided or minimized by making available full and adequate governmental facilities for furnishing assistance to employers and the representatives of their employees in formulating for inclusion within such agreements provision for adequate notice of any proposed changes in the terms of such agreements, for the final adjustment of grievances or questions regarding the application or interpretation of such agreements, and other provisions designed to prevent the subsequent arising of such controversies.

§ 172. Federal Mediation and Conciliation Service

[Sec. 202] (a) There is hereby created an independent agency to be known as the Federal Mediation and Conciliation Service (herein referred to as the "Service," except that for sixty days after the date of the enactment of this Act such term shall refer to the Conciliation Service of the Department of Labor). The Service shall be under the direction of a Federal Mediation and Conciliation Director (hereinafter referred to as the "Director"), who shall be appointed by the President by and with the advice and consent of the Senate. The Director shall not engage in any other business, vocation, or employment.

(b) The Director is authorized, subject to the civil-service laws, to appoint such clerical and other personnel as may be necessary for the execution of the functions of the Service, and shall fix their compensation in accordance with the Classification Act of 1923, as amended, and may, without regard to the provisions of the civil-service laws and the Classification Act of 1923 as amended, appoint and fix the compensation of such conciliators and mediators as may be necessary to carry out the functions of the Service. The Director is authorized to make such expenditures for supplies, facilities, and services as he deems necessary. Such expenditures shall be allowed and paid upon presentation of itemized vouchers therefor approved by the Director or by any employee designated by him for that purpose.

(c) The principal office of the Service shall be in the District of Columbia, but the Director may establish regional offices convenient to localities in which labor controversies are likely to arise. The Director may by order, subject to revocation at any time, delegate any authority and discretion conferred upon him by this Act to any regional director, or other officer or employee of the Service. The Director may establish suitable procedures for cooperation with State and local mediation agencies. The Director shall make an annual report in writing to Congress at the end of the fiscal year.

(d) All mediation and conciliation functions of the Secretary of Labor or the United States Conciliation Service under section 8 of the Act entitled "An Act to create a Department of Labor," approved March 4, 1913 (U.S.C., title 29, sec. 51), and all functions of the United States Conciliation Service under any other law are hereby transferred to the Federal Mediation and Conciliation Service, together with the personnel and records of the United States Conciliation Service. Such transfer shall take effect the sixtieth day after the date of enactment of this Act. Such transfer shall not affect any proceedings pending before the United States Conciliation Service or any certification, order, rule, or regulation theretofore made by it or by the Secretary of Labor. The Director and the Service shall not be subject in any way to the jurisdiction or authority of the Secretary of Labor or any official or division of the Department of Labor.

§ 173. Functions of Service

[Sec. 203] (a) It shall be the duty of the Service, in order to prevent or minimize interruptions of the free flow of commerce growing out of labor disputes, to assist parties to labor disputes in industries affecting commerce to settle such disputes through conciliation and mediation.

(b) The Service may proffer its services in any labor dispute in any industry affecting commerce, either upon its own motion or upon the request of one or more of the parties to the dispute, whenever in its judgment such dispute threatens to cause a substantial interruption of commerce. The Director and the Service are directed to avoid attempting to mediate disputes which would have only a minor effect on interstate commerce if State or other conciliation services are available to the parties. Whenever the Service does proffer its services in any dispute, it shall be the duty of the Service promptly to put itself in communication with the parties and to use its best efforts, by mediation and conciliation, to bring them to agreement.

(c) If the Director is not able to bring the parties to agreement by conciliation within a reasonable time, he shall seek to induce the parties voluntarily to seek other means of settling the dispute without resort to strike, lock-out, or other coercion, including submission to the employees in the bargaining unit of the employer's last offer of settlement for approval or rejection in a secret ballot. The failure or refusal of either party to agree to any procedure suggested by the Director shall not be deemed a violation of any duty or obligation imposed by this Act.

(d) Final adjustment by a method agreed upon by the parties is hereby declared to be the desirable method for settlement of grievance disputes arising over the application or interpretation of an existing collective-bargaining agreement. The Service is directed to make its conciliation and mediation services available in the settlement of such grievance disputes only as a last resort and in exceptional cases.

(e) The Service is authorized and directed to encourage and support the establishment and operation of joint labor management activities conducted by plant, area, and industrywide committees designed to improve labor management relationships, job security and organizational effectiveness, in accordance with the provisions of section 205A.

§ 174. Co-equal obligations of employees, their representatives, and management to minimize disputes

[Sec. 204] (a) In order to prevent or minimize interruptions of the free flow of commerce growing out of labor disputes, employers and employees and their representatives, in any industry affecting commerce, shall—

(1) exert every reasonable effort to make and maintain agreements concerning rates of pay, hours, and working conditions, including provision for adequate notice of any proposed change in the terms of such agreements;

(2) whenever a dispute arises over the terms or application of a collective-bargaining agreement and a conference is requested by a party or prospective party thereto, arrange promptly for such a conference to be held and endeavor in such conference to settle such dispute expeditiously; and

(3) in case such dispute is not settled by conference, participate fully and promptly in such meetings as may be undertaken by the Service under this Act for the purpose of aiding in a settlement of the dispute.

§ 175. National Labor-Management Panel; creation and composition; appointment, tenure, and compensation; duties

[Sec. 205] (a) There is hereby created a National Labor-Management Panel which shall be composed of twelve members appointed by the President, six of whom shall be selected from among persons outstanding in the field of management and six of whom shall be selected from among persons outstanding in the field of labor. Each member shall hold office for a term of three years, except that any member appointed to fill a vacancy occurring prior to the expiration of the term for which his predecessor was appointed shall be appointed for the remainder of such term, and the terms of office of the members first taking office shall expire, as designated by the President at the time of appointment, four at the end of the first year, four at the end of the second year, and four at the end of the third year after the date of appointment. Members of the panel, when serving on business of the panel, shall be paid compensation at the rate of $25 per day, and shall also be entitled to receive an allowance for actual and necessary travel and subsistence expenses while so serving away from their places of residence.

(b) It shall be the duty of the panel, at the request of the Director, to advise in the avoidance of industrial controversies and the manner in which mediation and voluntary adjustment shall be administered, particularly with reference to controversies affecting the general welfare of the country.

§ 175a. Assistance to plant, area, and industrywide labor management committees

[Sec. 205A] (a)(1) The Service is authorized and directed to provide assistance in the establishment and operation of plant, area and industrywide labor management committees which—

> (A) have been organized jointly by employers and labor organizations representing employees in that plant, area, or industry; and
>
> (B) are established for the purpose of improving labor management relationships, job security, organizational effectiveness, enhancing economic development or involving workers in decisions affecting their jobs including improving communication with respect to subjects of mutual interest and concern.

(2) The Service is authorized and directed to enter into contracts and to make grants, where necessary or appropriate, to fulfill its responsibilities under this section.

(b)(1) No grant may be made, no contract may be entered into and no other assistance may be provided under the provisions of this section to a plant labor management committee unless the employees in that plant are represented by a labor organization and there is in effect at that plant a collective bargaining agreement.

(2) No grant may be made, no contract may be entered into and no other assistance may be provided under the provisions of this section to an area or industrywide labor management committee unless its participants include any labor organizations certified or recognized as the representative of the employees of an employer participating in such committee. Nothing in this clause shall prohibit participation in an area or industrywide committee by an employer whose employees are not represented by a labor organization.

(3) No grant may be made under the provisions of this section to any labor management committee which the Service finds to have as one of its purposes the discouragement of the exercise of rights contained in section 7 of the National Labor Relations Act (29 U.S.C. 157), or the interference with collective bargaining in any plant, or industry.

(c) The Service shall carry out the provisions of this section through an office established for that purpose.

(d) There are authorized to be appropriated to carry out the provisions of this section $10,000,000 for the fiscal year 1979, and such sums as may be necessary thereafter.

§ 176. National emergencies; appointment of board of inquiry by President; report; contents; filing with Service

[Sec. 206] Whenever in the opinion of the President of the United States, a threatened or actual strike or lockout affecting an entire industry or a substantial part thereof engaged in trade, commerce, transportation, transmission, or communication among the several States or with foreign nations, or engaged in the production of goods for commerce, will, if permitted to occur or to continue, imperil the national health or safety, he may appoint a board of inquiry to inquire into the issues involved in the dispute and to make a written report to him within such time as he shall prescribe. Such report shall include a statement of the facts with respect to the dispute, including each party's statement of its position but shall not contain any recommendations. The President shall file a copy of such report with the Service and shall make its contents available to the public.

§ 177. Board of inquiry

[Sec. 207] (a) A board of inquiry shall be composed of a chairman and such other members as the President shall determine, and shall have power to sit and act in any place within the United States and to conduct such hearings either in public or in private, as it may deem necessary or proper, to ascertain the facts with respect to the causes and circumstances of the dispute.

(b) Members of a board of inquiry shall receive compensation at the rate of $50 for each day actually spent by them in the work of the board, together with necessary travel and subsistence expenses.

(c) For the purpose of any hearing or inquiry conducted by any board appointed under this title, the provisions of sections 9 and 10 (relating to the attendance of witnesses and the production of books, papers, and documents) of the Federal Trade Commission Act of September 16, 1914, as amended (U.S.C., title 15, secs. 49 and 50, as amended), are hereby made applicable to the powers and duties of such board.

§ 178. Injunctions during national emergency

[Sec. 208] (a) Upon receiving a report from a board of inquiry the President may direct the Attorney General to petition any district court of the United States having jurisdiction of the parties to enjoin such strike or lockout or the continuing thereof, and if the court finds that such threatened or actual strike or lock-out—

  (i) affects an entire industry or a substantial part thereof engaged in trade, commerce, transportation, transmission, or communication among the several States or with foreign nations, or engaged in the production of goods for commerce; and

  (ii) if permitted to occur or to continue, will imperil the national health or safety, it shall have jurisdiction to enjoin any such strike or lock-out, or the continuing thereof, and to make such other orders as may be appropriate.

(b) In any case, the provisions of the Act of March 23, 1932, entitled "An Act to amend the Judicial Code and to define and limit the jurisdiction of courts sitting in equity, and for other purposes," shall not be applicable.

(c) The order or orders of the court shall be subject to review by the appropriate circuit court of appeals and by the Supreme Court upon writ of certiorari or certification as provided in sections 239 and 240 of the Judicial Code, as amended (U.S.C., title 29, secs. 346 and 347).

§ 179. Injunctions during national emergency; adjustment efforts by parties during injunction period

[Sec. 209] (a) Whenever a district court has issued an order under section 208 enjoining acts or practices which imperil or threaten to imperil the national health or safety, it shall be the duty of the parties to the labor dispute giving rise to such order to make every effort to adjust and settle their differences, with the assistance of the Service created by this Act. Neither party shall be under any duty to accept, in whole or in part, any proposal of settlement made by the Service.

(b) Upon the issuance of such order, the President shall reconvene the board of inquiry which has previously reported with respect to the dispute. At the end of a sixty-day period (unless the dispute has been settled by that time), the board of inquiry shall report to the President the current position of the parties and the efforts which have been made for settlement, and shall include a statement by each party of its position and a statement of the employer's last offer of settlement. The President shall make such report available to the public. The National Labor Relations Board, within the succeeding fifteen days, shall take a secret ballot of the employees of each employer involved in the dispute on the question of whether they wish to accept the final offer of settlement made by their employer as stated by him and shall certify the results thereof to the Attorney General within five days thereafter.

§ 180. Discharge of injunction upon certification of results of election or settlement; report to Congress

[Sec. 210] Upon the certification of the results of such ballot or upon a settlement being reached, whichever happens sooner, the Attorney General shall move the court to discharge the injunction, which motion shall then be granted and the injunction discharged. When such motion is granted, the President shall submit to the Congress a full and comprehensive report of the proceedings, including the findings of the board of inquiry and the ballot taken by the National Labor Relations Board, together with such recommendations as he may see fit to make for consideration and appropriate action.

§181. Compilation of collective bargaining agreements, etc.; use of data

[Sec. 211] (a) For the guidance and information of interested representatives of employers, employees, and the general public, the Bureau of Labor Statistics of the Department of Labor shall maintain a file of copies of all available collective bargaining agreements and other available agreements and actions thereunder settling or adjusting labor disputes. Such file shall be open to inspection under appropriate conditions prescribed by the Secretary of Labor, except that no specific information submitted in confidence shall be disclosed.

(b) The Bureau of Labor Statistics in the Department of Labor is authorized to furnish upon request of the Service, or employers, employees, or their representatives, all available data and factual information which may aid in the settlement of any labor dispute, except that no specific information submitted in confidence shall be disclosed.

§ 182. Exemption of Railway Labor Act

[Sec. 212] The provisions of this title shall not be applicable with respect to any matter which is subject to the provisions of the Railway Labor Act, as amended from time to time.

§ 183.   **Conciliation of labor disputes in the health care industry**

[Sec. 213] (a) If, in the opinion of the Director of the Federal Mediation and Conciliation Service a threatened or actual strike or lockout affecting a health care institution will, if permitted to occur or to continue, substantially interrupt the delivery of health care in the locality concerned, the Director may further assist in the resolution of the impasse by establishing within 30 days after the notice to the Federal Mediation and Conciliation Service under clause (A) of the last sentence of section 8(d) (which is required by clause (3) of such section 8(d)), or within 10 days after the notice under clause (B), an impartial board of inquiry to investigate the issues involved in the dispute and to make a written report thereon to the parties within fifteen (15) days after the establishment of such a board. The written report shall contain the findings of fact together with the board's recommendations for settling the dispute, with the objective of achieving a prompt, peaceful and just settlement of the dispute. Each such board shall be composed of such number of individuals as the Director may deem desirable. No member appointed under this section shall have any interest or involvement in the health care institutions or the employee organizations involved in the dispute.

(b)(1) Members of any board established under this section who are otherwise employed by the Federal Government shall serve without compensation but shall be reimbursed for travel, subsistence, and other necessary expenses incurred by them in carrying out its duties under this section.

(2) Members of any board established under this section who are not subject to paragraph (1) shall receive compensation at a rate prescribed by the Director but not to exceed the daily rate prescribed for GS-18 of the General Schedule under section 5332 of title 5, United States Code, including travel for each day they are engaged in the performance of their duties under this section and shall be entitled to reimbursement for travel, subsistence, and other necessary expenses incurred by them in carrying out their duties under this section.

(c) After the establishment of a board under subsection (a) of this section and for 15 days after any such board has issued its report, no change in the status quo in effect prior to the expiration of the contract in the case of negotiations for a contract renewal, or in effect prior to the time of the impasse in the case of an initial bargaining negotiation, except by agreement, shall be made by the parties to the controversy.

(d) There are authorized to be appropriated such sums as may be necessary to carry out the provisions of this section.

Title III.   **Liabilities of and Restrictions on Labor and Management**

§ 185.   **Suits by and against labor organizations**

[Sec. 301] (a) Suits for violation of contracts between an employer and a labor organization representing employees in an industry affecting commerce as defined in this Act, or between any such labor organizations, may be brought in any district court of the United States having jurisdiction of the parties, without respect to the amount in controversy or without regard to the citizenship of the parties.

(b) Any labor organization which represents employees in an industry affecting commerce as defined in this Act and any employer whose activities affect commerce as defined in this Act shall be bound by the acts of its agents.

Any such labor organization may sue or be sued as an entity and in behalf of the employees whom it represents in the courts of the United States. Any money judgment against a labor organization in a district court of the United States shall be enforceable only against the organization as an entity and against its assets, and shall not be enforceable against any individual member or his assets.

(c) For the purposes of actions and proceedings by or against labor organizations in the district courts of the United States, district courts shall be deemed to have jurisdiction of a labor organization (1) in the district in which such organization maintains its principal office, or (2) in any district in which its duly authorized officers or agents are engaged in representing or acting for employee members.

(d) The service of summons, subpoena, or other legal process of any court of the United States upon an officer or agent of a labor organization, in his capacity as such, shall constitute service upon the labor organization.

(e) For the purposes of this section, in determining whether any person is acting as an "agent" of another person so as to make such other person responsible for his acts, the question of whether the specific acts performed were actually authorized or subsequently ratified shall not be controlling.

§ 186. Restrictions on financial transactions

[Sec. 302] (a) It shall be unlawful for any employer or association of employers or any person who acts as a labor relations expert, adviser, or consultant to an employer or who acts in the interest of an employer to pay, lend, or deliver, or agree to pay, lend, or deliver, any money or other thing of value—

(1) to any representative of any of his employees who are employed in an industry affecting commerce; or

(2) to any labor organization or any officer or employee thereof, which represents, seeks to represent, or would admit to membership, any of the employees of such employer who are employed in an industry affecting commerce; or

(3) to any employee or group or committee of employees of such employer employed in an industry affecting commerce in excess of their normal compensation for the purpose of causing such employee or group or committee directly or indirectly to influence any other employees in the exercise of the right to organize and bargain collectively through representatives of their own choosing; or

(4) to any officer or employee of a labor organization engaged in an industry affecting commerce with intent to influence him in respect to any of his actions, decisions, or duties as a representative of employees or as such officer or employee of such labor organization.

(b)(1) It shall be unlawful for any person to request, demand, receive, or accept, or agree to receive or accept, any payment, loan, or delivery of any money or other thing of value prohibited by subsection (a).

(2) It shall be unlawful for any labor organization, or for any person acting as an officer, agent, representative, or employee of such labor organization, to demand or accept from the operator of any motor vehicle (as defined in part II of the Interstate Commerce Act) employed in the transportation of property in commerce, or the employer of any such operator, any money or other thing of value payable to such organization or to an officer, agent, representative or employee thereof as a fee or charge for the unloading, or in connection with the unloading, of the cargo of such vehicle: *Provided,* That nothing in this paragraph shall be construed to make unlawful any payment by an employer to any of his employees as compensation for their services as employees.

(c) The provisions of this section shall not be applicable (1) in respect to any money or other thing of value payable by an employer to any of his employees whose established duties include acting openly for such employer in matters of labor relations or personnel administration or to any representative of his employees, or to any officer or employee of a labor organization, who is also an employee or former employee of such employer, as compensation for, or by reason of, his service as an employee of such employer; (2) with respect to the payment or delivery of any money or other thing of value in satisfaction of a judgment of any court or a decision or award of an arbitrator or impartial chairman or in compromise, adjustment, settlement, or release of any claim, complaint, grievance, or dispute in the absence of fraud or duress; (3) with respect to the sale or purchase of an article or commodity at the prevailing market price in the regular course of business; (4) with respect to money deducted from the wages of employees in payment of membership dues in a labor organization: *Provided,* That the employer has received from each employee, on whose account such deductions are made, a written assignment which shall not be irrevocable for a period of more than one year, or beyond the termination date of the applicable collective agreement, whichever occurs sooner; (5) with respect to money or other thing of value paid to a trust fund established by such representative, for the sole and exclusive benefit of the employees of such employer, and their families and dependents (or of such employees, families, and dependents jointly with the employees of other employers making similar payments, and their families and dependents): *Provided,* That (A) such payments are held in trust for the purpose of paying, either from principal or income or both, for the benefit of employees, their families and dependents, for medical or hospital care, pensions on retirement or death of employees, compensation for injuries or illness resulting from occupational activity or insurance to provide any of the foregoing, or unemployment benefits or life insurance, disability and sickness insurance, or accident insurance; (B) the detailed basis on which such payments are to be made is specified in a written agreement with the employer, and employees and employers are equally represented in the administration of such fund, together with such neutral persons as the representatives of the employers and the representatives of employees may agree upon and in the event the employer and employee groups deadlock on the administration of such fund and there are no neutral persons empowered to break such deadlock, such agreement provides that the two groups shall agree on a impartial umpire to decide such dispute, or in event of failure to agree within a reasonable length of time, an impartial umpire to decide such dispute shall, on petition of either group, be appointed by the district court of the United States for the district where the trust fund has its principal office, and shall also contain provisions for an annual audit of the trust fund, a statement of the results of which shall be available for inspection by interested persons at the principal office of the trust fund and at such other places as may be designated in such written agreement; and (C) such payments as are intended to be used for the purpose of providing pensions or annuities for employees are made to a separate trust which provides that the funds held therein cannot be used for any purpose other than paying such pensions or annuities; (6) with respect to money or other thing of value paid by any employer to a trust fund established by such representative for the purpose of pooled vacation, holiday, severance or similar benefits, or defraying costs of apprenticeship or other training programs: *Provided,* That the requirements of clause (B) of the proviso to clause (5) of this subsection shall apply to such trust funds; or (7) with respect to money or other thing of value paid by any employer to a pooled or individual trust fund established by such representative for the purpose of (A) scholarships for the benefit of employees, their families, and dependents for study at educational institutions, or (B) child care centers for preschool and school age dependents of employees: *Provided,* That no labor organization or employer shall be required to bargain on the establishment of any such trust fund, and refusal to do so shall not constitute an unfair labor practice: *Provided further,* That the requirements of clause (B) of the proviso to clause (5) of this subsection shall apply to such trust funds; or (8) with respect to money or any other thing of value paid by any employer to a trust fund established by such representative for the purpose of defraying the costs of legal services for employees, their families, and dependents for counsel or plan of their choice: *Provided,* That the requirements of clause (B) of the proviso to clause (5) of this subsection shall apply to such trust funds: *Provided further,* That no such legal services shall be furnished: (A) to initiate any proceeding directed (i) against any such employer or its officers or agents except in workman's compensation cases, or (ii) against such labor organization, or its parent or subordinate bodies, or their officers or agents, or (iii) against any other employer or labor organization, or their officers or agents, in any matter arising under the National Labor Relations Act, as amended, or this Act; and (B) in any proceeding where a labor organization would be prohibited from defraying the costs of legal services by the provisions of the Labor-Management Reporting and Disclosure Act of 1959; or (9) with respect to money or other things of value paid by an employer to a plant, area or industrywide labor management committee established for one or more of the purposes set forth in section 5(b) of the Labor Management Cooperation Act of 1978.

(d) Any person who willfully violates any of the provisions of this section shall, upon conviction thereof, be guilty of a misdemeanor and be subject to a fine of not more than $10,000 or to imprisonment for not more than one year, or both.

(e) The district courts of the United States and the United States courts of the Territories and possessions shall have jurisdiction, for cause shown, and subject to the provisions of section 17 (relating to notice to opposite party) of the Act entitled "An Act to supplement existing laws against unlawful restraints and monopolies, and for other purposes," approved October 15, 1914, as amended (U.S.C., title 28, sec. 381), to restrain violations of this section, without regard to the provisions of sections 6 and 20 of such Act of October 15, 1914, as amended (U.S.C., title 15, sec. 17, and title 29, sec. 52), and the provisions of the Act entitled "An Act to amend the Judicial Code and to define and limit the jurisdiction of courts sitting in equity, and for other purposes," approved March 23, 1932 (U.S.C., title 29, secs. 101-115).

(f) This section shall not apply to any contract in force on the date of enactment of this Act, until the expiration of such contract, or until July 1, 1948, whichever first occurs.

(g) Compliance with the restrictions contained in subsection (c)(5)(B) upon contributions to trust funds, otherwise lawful, shall not be applicable to contributions to such trust funds established by collective agreement prior to January 1, 1946, nor shall subsection (c)(5)(A) be construed as prohibiting contributions to such trust funds if prior to January 1, 1947, such funds contained provisions for pooled vacation benefits.

§ 187. Unlawful activities or conduct; right to sue; jurisdiction; limitations; damages

[Sec. 303] (a) It shall be unlawful, for the purpose of this section only, in an industry or activity affecting commerce, for any labor organization to engage in any activity or conduct defined as an unfair labor practice in section 8(b)(4) of the National Labor Relations Act, as amended.

(b) Whoever shall be injured in his business or property by reason of any violation of subsection (a) may sue therefor in any district court of the United States subject to the limitations and provisions of section 301 hereof without respect to the amount in controversy, or in any other court having jurisdiction of the parties, and shall recover the damages by him sustained and the cost of the suit.

NLRB Rules and Regulations, Series 8, as Amended*

PART 102—RULES AND REGULATIONS

Subpart A—Definitions

§102.1 Terms defined in section 2 of the act.

The terms "person," "employer," "employee," "representative," "labor organization," "commerce," "affecting commerce," and "unfair labor practice," as used herein, shall have the meanings set forth in section 2 of the National Labor Relations Act, as amended by title I of the Labor Management Relations Act, 1947.

§102.2 Act; Board; Board agent.

The term "act" as used herein shall mean the National Labor Relations Act, as amended. The term "Board" shall mean the National Labor Relations Board and shall include any group of three or more members designated pursuant to section 3(b) of the act. The term "Board agent" shall mean any member, agent, or agency of the Board, including its general counsel.

§102.3 General counsel.

The term "general counsel" as used herein shall mean the general counsel under section 3(d) of the act.

§102.4 Region; subregion.

The term "region" as used herein shall mean that part of the United States or any Territory thereof fixed by the Board as a particular region.

---

*Authors' note: The Board's Rules and Regulations appear as last amended September 29, 1986.

The term "subregion" shall mean that area within a region fixed by the Board as a particular subregion.

§102.5 Regional director; officer-in-charge; regional attorney.

The term "regional director" as used herein shall mean the agent designated by the Board as the regional director for a particular region, and shall also include any agent designated by the Board as officer-in-charge of a subregional office, but the officer-in-charge shall have only such powers, duties, and functions appertaining to regional directors as shall have been duly delegated to such officer-in-charge. The term "regional attorney" as used herein shall mean the attorney designated as regional attorney for a particular region.

§102.6 Administrative law judge; hearing officer.

The term "administrative law judge" as used herein shall mean the agent of the Board conducting the hearing in an unfair labor practice or Telegraph Merger Act proceeding. The term "hearing officer" as used herein shall mean the agent of the Board conducting the hearing in a proceeding under section 9 or in a dispute proceeding under section 10(k) of the act.

§102.7 State.

The term "State" as used herein shall include the District of Columbia and all States, Territories, and possessions of the United States.

§102.8 Party.

The term "party" as used herein shall mean the regional director in whose region the proceeding is pending and any person named or admitted as a party, or properly seeking and entitled as of right to be admitted as a party, in any Board proceeding, including, without limitation, any person filing a charge or petition under the act, any person named as respondent, as employer, or as party to a contract in any proceeding under the act, and any labor organization alleged to be dominated, assisted, or supported in violation of section 8(a)(1) or 8(a)(2) of the act; but nothing herein shall be construed to prevent the Board or its designated agent from limiting any party to participate in the proceedings to the extent of his interest only.

Subpart B—Procedure Under Section 10(a) to (i) of the Act for the Prevention of Unfair Labor Practices[1]

CHARGE

§102.9 Who may file; withdrawal and dismissal.

A charge that any person has engaged in or is engaging in any unfair labor practice affecting commerce may be made by any person. Any such

---

[1]Procedure under sec. 10(j) to (l) of the act is governed by subparts F and G of this part. Procedure for unfair labor practice cases and representation cases under sec. 8(b)(7) of the act is governed by subpart D of this part.

charge may be withdrawn, prior to the hearing, only with the consent of the regional director with whom such charge was filed; at the hearing and until the case has been transferred to the Board pursuant to §102.45, upon motion, with the consent of the administrative law judge designated to conduct the hearing; and after the case has been transferred to the Board pursuant to §102.45, upon motion, with the consent of the Board. Upon withdrawal of any charge, any complaint based thereon shall be dismissed by the regional director issuing the complaint, the administrative law judge designated to conduct the hearing, or the Board.

§102.10 Where to file.

Except as provided in §102.33 such charge shall be filed with the regional director for the region in which the alleged unfair labor practice has occurred or is occurring. A charge alleging that an unfair labor practice has occurred or is occurring in two or more regions may be filed with the regional director for any of such regions.

§102.11 Forms; jurat; or declaration.

Such charge shall be in writing and signed, and either shall be sworn to before a notary public, Board agent, or other person duly authorized by law to administer oaths and take acknowledgments or shall contain a declaration by the person signing it, under the penalties of the Criminal Code, that its contents are true and correct to the best of his knowledge and belief. Three additional copies of such charge shall be filed together with one additional copy for each named party respondent.[2]

§102.12 Contents.

Such charge shall contain the following:
(a) The full name and address of the person making the charge.
(b) If the charge is filed by a labor organization, the full name and address of any national or international labor organization of which it is an affiliate or constituent unit.
(c) The full name and address of the person against whom the charge is made (hereinafter referred to as the "respondent").
(d) A clear and concise statement of the facts constituting the alleged unfair labor practices affecting commerce.

§102.13 [Reserved]

§102.14 Service of charge.

Upon the filing of a charge, the charging party shall be responsible for the timely and proper service of a copy thereof upon the person against whom such charge is made. The regional director will, as a matter of course, cause a copy of such charge to be served upon the person against whom the

---

[2]A blank form for making a charge will be supplied by the regional director upon request.

charge is made, but he shall not be deemed to assume responsibility for such service.

COMPLAINT

§102.15 When and by whom issued; contents; service.

After a charge has been filed, if it appears to the regional director that formal proceedings in respect thereto should be instituted, he shall issue and cause to be served upon all the other parties a formal complaint in the name of the Board stating the unfair labor practices and containing a notice of hearing before an administrative law judge at a place therein fixed and at a time not less than 14 days after the service of the complaint. The complaint shall contain (1) a clear and concise statement of the facts upon which assertion of jurisdiction by the Board is predicated, and (2) a clear and concise description of the acts which are claimed to constitute unfair labor practices, including, where known, the approximate dates and places of such acts and the names of respondent's agents or other representatives by whom committed.

§102.16 Hearing; change of date or place.

Upon his own motion or upon proper cause shown by any other party, the regional director issuing the complaint may extend the date of such hearing or may change the place at which it is to be held.

§102.17 Amendment.

Any such complaint may be amended upon such terms as may be deemed just, prior to the hearing, by the regional director issuing the complaint; at the hearing and until the case has been transferred to the Board pursuant to §102.45, upon motion, by the administrative law judge designated to conduct the hearing; and after the case has been transferred to the Board pursuant to §102.45, at any time prior to the issuance of an order based thereon, upon motion, by the Board.

§102.18 Withdrawal.

Any such complaint may be withdrawn before the hearing by the regional director on his own motion.

§102.19 Appeal to the general counsel from refusal to issue or reissue.

(a) If, after the charge has been filed, the regional director declines to issue a complaint, or having withdrawn a complaint pursuant to §102.18, refuses to reissue it, he shall so advise the parties in writing, accompanied by a simple statement of the procedural or other grounds for his action. The person making the charge may obtain a review of such action by filing an appeal with the general counsel in Washington, D.C., and filing a copy of the appeal with the regional director, within 14 days from the service of the notice of such refusal to issue or reissue by the regional director, except as a shorter period is provided by §102.81. If an appeal is taken the person doing so should notify all other parties of his action, but any failure to give such notice shall not affect the validity of the appeal. The appeal shall contain a complete statement setting forth the facts and reasons upon which it is based. A request for extension of time to file an appeal shall be in writing and be received by the general counsel, and a copy of such request filed with the regional director, prior to the expiration of the filing period. Copies of the acknowledgement of the filing of an appeal and of any ruling on a request for an extension of time for the filing of an appeal shall be served on all parties. Consideration of an appeal untimely filed is within the discretion of the general counsel upon good cause shown.

(b) Oral presentation in Washington, D.C., of the appeal issues may be permitted a party on written request made within 4 days after service of acknowledgment of the filing of an appeal. In the event such request is granted, the other parties shall be notified and afforded, without additional request, a like opportunity at another appropriate time.

(c) The general counsel may sustain the regional director's refusal to issue or reissue a complaint, stating the grounds of his affirmance, or may direct the regional director to take further action; the general counsel's decision shall be served on all the parties. A motion for reconsideration of the decision must be filed within 14 days of service of the decision, except as hereinafter provided, and shall state with particularity the error requiring reconsideration. A motion for reconsideration based upon newly discovered evidence which has become available only since the decision on appeal shall be filed promptly on discovery of such evidence. Motions for reconsideration of a decision previously reconsidered will not be entertained, except in unusual situations where the moving party can establish that new evidence has been discovered which could not have been discovered by diligent inquiry prior to the first reconsideration.

Answer

§102.20 Answer to complaint; time for filing; contents; allegations not denied deemed admitted.

The respondent shall, within 14 days from the service of the complaint, file an answer thereto. The respondent shall specifically admit, deny, or explain each of the facts alleged in the complaint, unless the respondent is without knowledge, in which case the respondent shall so state, such statement operating as a denial. All allegations in the complaint, if no answer is filed, or any allegation in the complaint not specifically denied or explained in an answer filed, unless the respondent shall state in the answer that he is without knowledge, shall be deemed to be admitted to be true and shall be so found by the Board, unless good cause to the contrary is shown.

§102.21 Where to file; service upon the parties; form.

An original and four copies of the answer shall be filed with the regional director issuing the complaint. Immediately upon the filing of his answer, respondent shall serve a copy thereof on each of the other parties. An answer of a party represented by counsel shall be signed by at least one attorney of record in his individual name, whose address shall be stated. A party who is not represented by an attorney shall sign his answer and state his address. Except when otherwise specifically provided by rule or statute, an answer need not be verified or accompanied by affidavit. The signature of an attorney constitutes a certificate by him that he has read the answer; that to the best of his knowledge, information, and belief there is good ground to support it; and that it is not interposed for delay. If an answer is not signed or is signed with intent to defeat the purpose of this rule, it may be stricken as sham and false and the action may proceed as though the answer had not been served. For a willful violation of this rule an attorney may be subjected to appropriate disciplinary action. Similar action may be taken if scandalous or indecent matter is inserted.

§102.22 Extension of time for filing.

Upon his own motion or upon proper cause shown by any other party the regional director issuing the complaint may by written order extend the time within which the answer shall be filed.

§102.23 Amendment.

The respondent may amend his answer at any time prior to the hearing. During the hearing or subsequent thereto, he may amend his answer in any case where the complaint has been amended, within such period as may be fixed by the administrative law judge or the Board. Whether or not the complaint has been amended, the answer may, in the discretion of the administrative law judge or the Board, upon motion, be amended upon such terms and within such periods as may be fixed by the administrative law judge or the Board.

MOTIONS

§102.24 Motions; where to file; contents; service on other parties; promptness in filing and response.

All motions under §§102.16, 102.22, and 102.29 made prior to hearing shall be filed in writing with the regional director issuing the complaint. All motions for summary judgment made prior to hearing shall be filed in writing with the Board pursuant to the provisions of §102.50. All other motions prior to hearing shall be filed in writing with the chief administrative law judge in Washington, D.C., with the deputy chief judge in San Francisco, California, with the associate chief judge in New York, New York, or with the associate chief judge in Atlanta, Georgia, as the case may be. All motions made at the hearing shall be made in writing to the administrative law judge or stated orally on the record. All motions filed subsequent to the hearing, but before the transfer of the case to the Board pursuant to §102.45, shall be filed with the administrative law judge, care of the chief administrative law judge in Washington, D.C., the deputy chief judge, San Francisco, California, the associate chief judge in New York, New York, or the associate chief judge in Atlanta, Georgia, as the case may be. All motions made subsequent to transfer of the case to, and while it is pending before, the Board shall be filed with the executive secretary of the Board in Washington, D.C., as provided in §102.47. Motions shall briefly state the order or relief applied for and the grounds therefor. All motions prior to transfer of the case to the Board shall be filed by the moving party in an original and four copies and a copy thereof shall be immediately served on the other parties. Unless otherwise provided in these rules, motions and responses thereto shall be filed promptly and within such time as not to delay the proceeding.

§102.25 Ruling on motions.

An administrative law judge designated by the chief administrative law judge, by the deputy chief judge in San Francisco, California, by the associate chief judge in New York, New York, or by the associate chief judge in Atlanta, Georgia, as the case may be, shall rule on all prehearing motions (except as provided in §§102.16, 102.22, 102.29, and 102.50), and all such rulings and orders shall be issued in writing and a copy served on each of the parties. The administrative law judge designated to conduct the hearing shall rule on all motions after opening of the hearing (except as provided in §102.47), and any orders in connection therewith, if announced at the hearing, shall be stated orally on the record; in all other cases the administrative law judge shall issue such rulings and orders in writing and shall cause a copy of the same to be served on each of the parties, or shall make his ruling in his decision. Whenever the administrative law judge has reserved his ruling on any motion, and the proceeding is thereafter transferred to and continued before the Board pursuant to §102.50, the Board shall rule on such motion.

§102.26 Motions; rulings and orders part of the record; rulings not to be appealed directly to Board without special permission; requests for special permission to appeal.

All motions, rulings, and orders shall become part of the record, except that rulings on motions to revoke subpoenas shall become a part of the record only upon the request of the party aggrieved thereby, as provided in §102.31. Unless expressly authorized by the Rules and Regulations, rulings by the regional director or by the administrative law judge on motions and/ or by the administrative law judge on objections, and orders in connection therewith, shall not be appealed directly to the Board except by special permission of the Board, but shall be considered by the Board in reviewing the record, if exception to the ruling or order is included in the statement of exceptions filed with the Board, pursuant to §102.46. Requests to the Board for special permission to appeal from a ruling of the regional director or of the administrative law judge, together with the appeal from such ruling, shall be filed promptly, in writing, and shall briefly state the reasons special permission should be granted and the grounds relied on for the appeal. The moving party shall immediately serve a copy of the request for special permission and of the appeal on the other parties and, if the request involves a ruling by an administrative law judge, on the administrative law judge. Any statement in opposition or other response to the request and/or to the appeal shall be filed promptly, in writing, and shall be served immediately on the other parties and on the administrative law judge, if any. If the Board grants the request for special permission to appeal, it may proceed forthwith to rule on the appeal.

§102.27 Review of granting of motion to dismiss entire complaint; reopening of record.

If any motion in the nature of a motion to dismiss the complaint in its entirety is granted by the administrative law judge before filing his decision, any party may obtain a review of such action by filing a request therefor with the Board in Washington, D.C., stating the grounds for review, and immediately on such filing shall serve a copy thereof on the regional director and the other parties. Unless such request for review is filed within 28 days from the date of the order of dismissal, the case shall be closed.

§102.28 Filing of answer or other participation in proceedings not a waiver of rights.

The right to make motions or to make objections to rulings upon motions shall not be deemed waived by the filing of an answer or by other participation in the proceedings before the administrative law judge or the Board.

INTERVENTION

§102.29 Intervention; requisites; rulings on motions to intervene.

Any person desiring to intervene in any proceeding shall file a motion in writing or, if made at the hearing, may move orally on the record, stating the grounds upon which such person claims an interest. Prior to the hearing, such a motion shall be filed with the regional director issuing the complaint; during the hearing such motion shall be made to the administrative law judge. An original and four copies of written motions shall be filed. Immediately upon filing such motion, the moving party shall serve a copy thereof upon each of the other parties. The regional director shall rule upon all such motions filed prior to the hearing, and shall cause a copy of said rulings to be served upon each of the other parties, or may refer the motion to the administrative law judge for ruling. The administrative law judge shall rule upon all such motions made at the hearing or referred to him by the regional director, in the manner set forth in §102.25. The regional director or the administrative law judge, as the case may be, may by order permit intervention in person or by counsel or other representative to such extent and upon such terms as he may deem proper.

WITNESSES, DEPOSITIONS AND SUBPOENAS

§102.30 Examination of witnesses; deposition.

Witnesses shall be examined orally under oath, except that for good cause shown after the issuance of a complaint, testimony may be taken by deposition.

(a) Applications to take depositions shall be in writing setting forth the reasons why such depositions should be taken, the name and post office address of the witness, the matters concerning which it is expected the witness will testify, and the time and place proposed for the taking of the deposition, together with the name and address of the person before whom it is desired that the deposition be taken (for the purposes of this section hereinafter referred to as the "officer"). Such application shall be made to the regional director prior to the hearing, and to the administrative law judge during and subsequent to the hearing but before transfer of the case to the Board pursuant to §102.45 or §102.50. Such application shall be served upon the regional director or the administrative law judge, as the case may be, and upon all other parties, not less than 7 days (when the deposition is to be taken within the continental United States) and 15 days (if the deposition is to be taken elsewhere) prior to the time when it is desired that the deposition be taken. The regional director or administrative law judge, as the case may be, shall upon receipt of the application, if in his discretion good cause has been shown, make and serve upon the parties an order which will specify the name of the witness whose deposition is to be taken and the time, the place, and the designation of the officer before whom the witness is to testify, who may or may not be the same officer as that specified in the application. Such order shall be served upon all the other parties by the regional director or upon all parties by the administrative law judge.

(b) Such deposition may be taken before any officer authorized to administer oaths by the laws of the United States or of the place where the examination is held, including any agent of the Board authorized to administer oaths. If the examination is held in a foreign country, it may be taken before any secretary of embassy or legation, consul general, consul, vice consul, or consular agent of the United States.

(c) At the time and place specified in said order the officer designated to take such deposition shall permit the witness to be examined and cross-examined under oath by all the parties appearing, and his testimony shall be reduced to typewriting by the officer or under his direction. All objections to questions or evidence shall be deemed waived unless made at the examination. The officer shall not have power to rule upon any objections but he shall note them upon the deposition. The testimony shall be subscribed by the witness in the presence of the officer who shall attach his certificate stating that the witness was duly sworn by him, that the deposition is a true record of the testimony and exhibits given by the witness, and that said officer is not of counsel or attorney to any of the parties nor interested in the event of the proceeding or investigation. If the deposition is not signed by the witness because he is ill, dead, cannot be found, or refuses to sign it, such fact shall be included in the certificate of the officer and the deposition may then be used as fully as though signed. The officer shall immediately deliver an original and two copies of said transcript, together with his certificate, in person or by registered or certified mail to the regional director or the administrative law judge, care of the chief administrative law judge in Washington, D.C., the deputy chief judge, in San Francisco, California, the associate chief judge in New York, New York, or the associate chief judge in Atlanta, Georgia, as the case may be.

(d) The administrative law judge shall rule upon the admissibility of the deposition or any part thereof.

(e) All errors or irregularities in compliance with the provisions of this section shall be deemed waived unless a motion to suppress the deposition or some part thereof is made with reasonable promptness after such defect is or, with due diligence, might have been ascertained.

(f) If the parties so stipulate in writing, depositions may be taken before any person at any time or place, upon any notice and in any manner, and when so taken may be used like other depositions.

§102.31 Issuance of subpoenas; petitions to revoke subpoenas; rulings on claim of privilege against self-incrimination; subpoena enforcement proceedings; right to inspect and copy data.

(a) Any member of the Board shall, on the written application of any party, forthwith issue subpoenas requiring the attendance and testimony of witnesses and the production of any evidence, including books, records, correspondence, or documents, in their possession or under their control. Applications for subpoenas, if filed prior to the hearing, shall be filed with the regional director. Applications for subpoenas filed during the hearing shall be filed with the administrative law judge. Either the regional director or the administrative law judge, as the case may be, shall grant the application, on behalf of any member of the Board. Applications for subpoenas may be made *ex parte*. The subpoena shall show on its face the name and address of the party at whose request the subpoena was issued.

(b) Any person, served with a subpoena, whether ad testificandum or duces tecum, if he does not intend to comply with the subpoena, shall, within 5 days after the date of service of the subpoena upon him, petition in writing to revoke the subpoena. All petitions to revoke subpoenas shall be served upon the party at whose request the subpoena was issued. Such petition to revoke, if made prior to the hearing, shall be filed with the regional director and the regional director shall refer the petition to the administrative law judge or the Board for ruling. Petitions to revoke subpoenas filed during the hearing shall be filed with the administrative law judge. Notice of the filing of petitions to revoke shall be promptly given by the regional director or the administrative law judge, as the case may be, to the party at whose request the subpoena was issued. The administrative law judge or the Board, as the case may be, shall revoke the subpoena if in its opinion the evidence whose production is required does not relate to any matter under investigation or in question in the proceedings or the subpoena does not describe with sufficient particularity the evidence whose production is required, or if for any other reason sufficient in law the subpoena is otherwise invalid. The administrative law judge or the Board, as the case may be, shall make a simple statement of procedural or other grounds for the ruling on the petition to revoke. The petition to revoke, any answer filed thereto, and any ruling thereon shall not become part of the official record except upon the request of the party aggrieved by the ruling.

(c) With the approval of the Attorney General of the United States, the Board may issue an order requiring any individual to give testimony or provide other information at any proceeding before the Board if, in the judgment of the Board, (1) the testimony or other information from such individual may be necessary to the public interest, and (2) such individual has refused or is likely to refuse to testify or provide other information on the basis of his privilege against self-incrimination. Requests for the issuance of such an order by the Board may be made by any party. Prior to hearing, and after transfer of the proceeding to the Board, such requests shall be made to the Board in Washington, D.C., and the Board shall take such action thereon as it deems appropriate. During the hearing, and thereafter while the proceeding is pending before the administrative law judge, such requests shall be made to the administrative law judge. If the administrative law judge denies the request, his ruling shall be subject to appeal to the Board in Washington, D.C., in the manner and to the extent provided in §102.26 with respect to rulings and orders by an administrative law judge, except that requests for permission to appeal in this instance shall be filed within 24 hours of the administrative law judge's ruling. If no appeal is sought within such time, or the appeal is denied, the ruling of the administrative law judge shall become final and his denial shall become the ruling of the Board. If the administrative law judge deems the request appropriate, he shall recommend that the Board seek the approval of the Attorney General for the issuance of the order, and the Board shall take such action on the administrative law judge's recommendation as it deems appropriate. Until the Board has issued the requested order no individual who claims the privilege against self-incrimination shall be required, or permitted, to testify or to give other information respecting the subject matter of the claim.

(d) Upon the failure of any person to comply with a subpoena issued upon the request of a private party, the general counsel shall, in the name of the Board but on relation of such private party, institute proceedings in the appropriate district court for the enforcement thereof, unless in the judgment of the Board the enforcement of such subpoena would be inconsistent with law and with the policies of the act. Neither the general counsel nor the Board shall be deemed thereby to have assumed responsibility for the effective prosecution of the same before the court.

(e) Persons compelled to submit data or evidence at a public proceeding are entitled to retain or, on payment of lawfully prescribed costs, to procure copies or transcripts of the data or evidence submitted by them. Persons compelled to submit data or evidence in the non-public investigative stages of proceedings may, for good cause, be limited by the regional director to inspection of the official transcript of their testimony, but shall be entitled to make copies of documentary evidence or exhibits which they have produced.

§102.32 Payment of witness fees and mileage; fees of persons taking depositions.

Witnesses summoned before the administrative law judge shall be paid the same fees and mileage that are paid witnesses in the courts of the United States, and witnesses whose depositions are taken and the persons taking the same shall severally be entitled to the same fees as are paid for like services in the courts of the United States. Witness fees and mileage shall be paid by the party at whose instance the witnesses appear and the person taking the deposition shall be paid by the party at whose instance the deposition is taken.

TRANSFER, CONSOLIDATION, AND SEVERANCE

§102.33 Transfer of charge and proceeding from region to region; consolidation of proceedings in same region; severance.

(a) Whenever the general counsel deems it necessary in order to effectuate the purposes of the act or to avoid unnecessary costs or delay, he may permit a charge to be filed with him in Washington, D.C., or may, at any time after a charge has been filed with a regional director pursuant to §102.10, order that such charge and any proceeding which may have been initiated with respect thereto:

(1) Be transferred to and continued before him for the purpose of investigation or consolidation with any other proceeding which may have been instituted in a regional office or with him; or

(2) Be consolidated with any other proceeding which may have been instituted in the same region; or

(3) Be transferred to and continued in any other region for the purpose of investigation or consolidation with any proceeding which may have been instituted in or transferred to such other region; or

(4) Be severed from any other proceeding with which it may have been consolidated pursuant to this section.

(b) The provisions of §§102.9 to 102.32, inclusive, shall, insofar as applicable, govern proceedings before the general counsel pursuant to this section, and the powers granted to regional directors in such provisions shall, for the purpose of this section, be reserved to and exercised by the general counsel. After the transfer of any charge and any proceeding which may have been instituted with respect thereto from one region to another pursuant to this section, the provisions of this subpart shall, insofar as applicable, govern such charge and such proceeding as if the charge had originally been filed in the region to which the transfer is made.

(c) The regional director may, prior to hearing, exercise the powers in paragraph (a)(2) and (4) of this section with respect to proceedings pending in his region.

(d) Motions to consolidate or sever proceedings after issuance of complaint shall be filed as provided in §102.24 and ruled upon as provided in §102.25, except that the regional director may consolidate or sever proceedings prior to hearing upon his own motion. Rulings by the administrative law judge upon motions to consolidate or sever may be appealed to the Board as provided in §102.26.

HEARINGS

§102.34 Who shall conduct; to be public unless otherwise ordered.

The hearing for the purpose of taking evidence upon a complaint shall be conducted by an administrative law judge designated by the chief administrative law judge in Washington, D.C., or by the deputy chief judge, San Francisco, California, by the associate chief judge in New York, New York, or by the associate chief judge in Atlanta, Georgia, as the case may be, unless the Board or any member thereof presides. At any time an administrative law judge may be designated to take the place of the administrative law judge previously designated to conduct the hearing. Such hearing shall be public unless otherwise ordered by the Board or the administrative law judge.

§102.35 Duties and powers of administrative law judge.

It shall be the duty of the administrative law judge to inquire fully into the facts as to whether the respondent has engaged in or is engaging in an unfair labor practice affecting commerce as set forth in the complaint or amended complaint. The administrative law judge shall have authority, with respect to cases assigned to him, between the time he is designated and transfer of the case to the Board, subject to the rules and regulations of the Board and within its powers:

(a) To administer oaths and affirmations;

(b) To grant applications for subpoenas;

(c) To rule upon petitions to revoke subpoenas;

(d) To rule upon offers of proof and receive relevant evidence;

(e) To take or cause depositions to be taken whenever the ends of justice would be served thereby;

(f) To regulate the course of the hearing and, if appropriate or necessary, to exclude persons or counsel from the hearing for contemptuous conduct and to strike all related testimony of witnesses refusing to answer any proper question;

(g) To hold conferences for the settlement or simplification of the issues by consent of the parties, but not to adjust cases;

(h) To dispose of procedural requests, motions or similar matters, including motions referred to the administrative law judge by the regional director and motions for summary judgment or to amend pleadings; also to dismiss complaints or portions thereof; to order hearings reopened; and upon motion order proceedings consolidated or severed prior to issuance of administrative law judge decisions;

(i) To approve a stipulation voluntarily entered into by all parties to the case which will dispense with a verbatim written transcript of record of the oral testimony adduced at the hearing, and which will also provide for the waiver by the respective parties of their right to file with the Board exceptions to the findings of fact (but not to conclusions of law or recommended orders) which the administrative law judge shall make in his decision;

(j) To make and file decisions in conformity with Public Law 89-554, 5 U.S.C. section 557;

(k) To call, examine, and cross-examine witnesses and to introduce into the record documentary or other evidence;

(l) To request the parties at any time during the hearing to state their respective positions concerning any issue in the case or theory in support thereof;

(m) To take any other action necessary under the foregoing and authorized by the published Rules and Regulations of the Board.

§102.36 Unavailability of administrative law judges.

In the event the administrative law judge designated to conduct the hearing becomes unavailable to the Board after the hearing has been opened, the chief administrative law judge in Washington, D.C., the deputy chief judge in San Francisco, California, the associate chief judge in New York, New York, or the associate chief judge in Atlanta, Georgia, as the case may be, may designate another administrative law judge for the purpose of further hearing or other appropriate action.

§102.37 Disqualification of administrative law judges.

An administrative law judge may withdraw from a proceeding whenever he deems himself disqualified. Any party may request the administrative law judge, at any time following his designation and before filing of his decision, to withdraw on grounds of personal bias or disqualification, by filing with him promptly upon the discovery of the alleged facts a timely affidavit setting forth in detail the matters alleged to constitute grounds for disqualification. If, in the opinion of the administrative law judge, such affidavit is filed with due diligence and is sufficient on its face, he shall forthwith disqualify himself and withdraw from the proceeding. If the administrative law judge does not disqualify himself and withdraw from the proceeding, he shall so rule upon the record, stating the grounds for his ruling and proceed with the hearing, or, if the hearing has closed, he shall proceed with issuance of his decision, and the provisions of §102.26, with respect to review of rulings of administrative law judges, shall thereupon apply.

§102.38 Rights of parties.

Any party shall have the right to appear at such hearing in person, by counsel, or by other representative, to call, examine, and cross-examine witnesses, and to introduce into the record documentary or other evidence, except that the participation of any party shall be limited to the extent permitted by the administrative law judge: *And provided further*, That documentary evidence shall be submitted in duplicate.

§102.39 Rules of evidence controlling so far as practicable.

Any such proceeding shall, so far as practicable, be conducted in accordance with the rules of evidence applicable in the district courts of the United States under the rules of civil procedure for the district courts of the United States, adopted by the Supreme Court of the United States pursuant to the Act of June 19, 1934, (title 28 U.S.C., secs. 723-B, 723-C).

§102.40 Stipulations of fact admissible.

In any such proceeding stipulations of fact may be introduced in evidence with respect to any issue.

§102.41 Objection to conduct of hearing; how made; objections not waived by further participation.

Any objection with respect to the conduct of the hearing, including any objection to the introduction of evidence, may be stated orally or in writing, accompanied by a short statement of the grounds of such objection, and included in the record. No such objection shall be deemed waived by further participation in the hearing.

§102.42 Filing of briefs and proposed findings with the administrative law judge and oral argument at the hearing.

Any party shall be entitled, upon request, to a reasonable period at the close of the hearing for oral argument, which shall be included in the stenographic report of the hearing. Any party shall be entitled, upon request made before the close of the hearing, to file a brief or proposed findings and conclusions, or both, with the administrative law judge who may fix a reasonable time for such filing, but not in excess of 35 days from the close of the hearing. Requests for further extensions of time shall be made to the chief administrative law judge in Washington, D.C., to the deputy chief judge in San Francisco, California, to the associate chief judge in New York, New York, or to the associate chief judge in Atlanta, Georgia, as the case may be. No request will be considered unless received at least 3 days prior to the expiration of the time fixed for the filing of briefs or proposed findings and conclusions. Notice of the request for any extension shall be immediately served upon all other parties, and proof of service shall be furnished. Three copies of the brief or proposed findings and conclusions shall be filed with the administrative law judge, and copies shall be served on the other parties, and a statement of such service shall be furnished.

§102.43 Continuance and adjournment.

In the discretion of the administrative law judge, the hearing may be continued from day to day, or adjourned to a later date or to a different place, by announcement thereof at the hearings by the administrative law judge, or by other appropriate notice.

§102.44 Misconduct at hearing before an administrative law judge or the Board; refusal of witness to answer questions.

(a) Misconduct at any hearing before an administrative law judge or before the Board shall be ground for summary exclusion from the hearing.

(b) Such misconduct of an aggravated character, when engaged in by an attorney or other representative of a party, shall be ground for suspension or disbarment by the Board from further practice before it after due notice and hearing.

(c) The refusal of a witness at any such hearing to answer any question which has been ruled to be proper shall, in the discretion of the administrative law judge, be ground for striking all testimony previously given by such witness on related matters.

ADMINISTRATIVE LAW JUDGE'S DECISION AND
TRANSFER OF CASE TO THE BOARD

§102.45 Administrative law judge's decision; contents; service; transfer of the case to the Board; contents of record in case.

(a) After hearing for the purpose of taking evidence upon a complaint, the administrative law judge shall prepare a decision. Such decision shall contain findings of fact, conclusions, and the reasons or basis therefor, upon all material issues of fact, law, or discretion presented on the record, and shall contain recommendations as to what disposition of the case should be made, which may include if it be found that the respondent has engaged in or is engaging in the alleged unfair labor practices, a recommendation for such affirmative action by the respondent as will effectuate the policies of the act. The administrative law judge shall file the original of his decision with the Board and cause a copy thereof to be served upon each of the parties. Upon the filing of the decision, the Board shall enter an order transferring the case to the Board and shall serve copies of the order, setting forth the date of such transfer, upon all the parties. Service of the administrative law judge's decision and of the order transferring the case to the Board shall be complete upon mailing.

(b) The charge upon which the complaint was issued and any amendments thereto, the complaint and any amendments thereto, notice of hearing, answer and any amendments thereto, motions, rulings, orders, the stenographic report of the hearing, stipulations, exhibits, documentary evidence, and depositions, together with the administrative law judge's decision and exceptions, and any cross-exceptions or answering briefs as provided in §102.46, shall constitute the record in the case.

EXCEPTIONS TO THE RECORD AND PROCEEDINGS

§102.46 Exceptions, cross-exceptions, briefs, answering briefs; time for filing; where to file; service on parties; extension of time; effect of failure to include matter in exceptions; oral arguments.

(a) Within 28 days, or within such further period as the Board may allow, from the date of the service of the order transferring the case to the Board, pursuant to §102.45, any party may (in accordance with section 10(c) of the act and §§102.111 and 102.112 of these rules) file with the Board in Washington, D.C., exceptions to the administrative law judge's decision or to any other part of the record or proceedings (including rulings upon all motions or objections), together with a brief in support of said exceptions. Any party may, within the same period, file a brief in support of the administrative law judge's decision. The filing of such exceptions and briefs is subject to the provisions of subsection (j) of this section. Requests for extension of time to file exceptions or briefs shall be in writing and copies thereof shall be served promptly on the other parties. Such requests must be received by the Board 3 days prior to the due date.

(b)(1) Each exception (i) shall set forth specifically the questions of procedure, fact, law, or policy to which exceptions are taken; (ii) shall identify that part of the administrative law judge's decision to which objection is made; (iii) shall designate by precise citation of page the portions of the record relied upon; and (iv) shall concisely state the grounds for the exception. If a supporting brief is filed the exceptions document shall not contain any argument or citation of authority in support of the exceptions, but such matters shall be set forth only in the brief. If no supporting brief is filed the exceptions document shall also include the citation of authorities and argument in support of the exceptions, in which event the exceptions document shall be subject to the 50-page limit as for briefs set forth in §102.46(j).

(2) Any exception to a ruling, finding, conclusion, or recommendation which is not specifically urged shall be deemed to have been waived. Any exception which fails to comply with the foregoing requirements may be disregarded.

(c) Any brief in support of exceptions shall contain no matter not included within the scope of the exceptions and shall contain, in the order indicated, the following:

(1) A clear and concise statement of the case containing all that is material to the consideration of the questions presented.

(2) A specification of the questions involved and to be argued, together with a reference to the specific exceptions to which they relate.

(3) The argument, presenting clearly the points of fact and law relied upon in support of the position taken on each question, with specific page reference to the record and the legal or other material relied upon.

(d)(1) Within 14 days, or such further period as the Board may allow, from the last date on which exceptions and any supporting brief may be filed, a party opposing the exceptions may file an answering brief to the exceptions, in accordance with the provisions of subsection (j) of this section.

(2) The answering brief to the exceptions shall be limited to the questions raised in the exceptions and in the brief in support thereof. It shall present clearly the points of fact and law relied upon in support of the position taken on each question. Where exception has been taken to a factual finding of the administrative law judge and it is proposed to support that finding, the answering brief should specify those pages of the record which, in the view of the party filing the brief, support the administrative law judge's finding.

(3) Requests for extension of time to file an answering brief to the exceptions shall be in writing and copies thereof shall be served promptly on the other parties. Such requests must be received by the Board 3 days prior to the due date.

(e) Any party who has not previously filed exceptions may, within 14 days, or such further period as the Board may allow, from the last date on which exceptions and any supporting brief may be filed, file cross-exceptions to any portion of the administrative law judge's decision, together with a supporting brief, in accordance with the provisions subsections (b) and (j) of this section.

(f)(1) Within 14 days, or such further period as the Board may allow, from the last date on which cross-exceptions and any supporting brief may be filed, any other party may file an answering brief to such cross-exceptions in accordance with the provisions subsections (c) and (j) of this section. Such answering brief shall be limited to the questions raised in the cross-exceptions.

(2) Requests for extension of time to file cross-exceptions, or answering brief to cross-exceptions, shall be in writing and copies thereof shall be served promptly on each of the other parties. Such requests must be received by the Board 3 days prior to the due date.

(g) No further briefs shall be filed except by special leave of the Board. Requests for such leave shall be in writing and copies thereof shall be served promptly on the other parties.

(h) No matter not included in exceptions or cross-exceptions may thereafter be argued before the Board, or in any further proceeding.

(i) Should any party desire permission to argue orally before the Board, request therefor must be made in writing to the Board simultaneously with the statement of any exceptions or cross-exceptions filed pursuant to the provisions of this section with a statement of service on the other parties. The Board shall notify the parties of the time and place of oral argument, if such permission is granted. Oral arguments are limited to 30 minutes for each party entitled to participate. No request for additional time will be granted unless timely application is made in advance of oral argument.

(j) Exceptions to the administrative law judge's decision, or to the record, and briefs shall be printed or otherwise legibly duplicated. Carbon copies of typewritten matter will not be accepted. Eight copies of such documents shall be filed with the Board in Washington, D.C., and copies shall also be served promptly on the other parties. All documents filed pursuant to this section shall be double spaced on 8½- by 11-inch paper. A brief filed pursuant to this section shall not be combined with any other brief, and shall not exceed 50 pages in length, exclusive of subject index and table of cases and other authorities cited, unless permission to exceed that limit is obtained from the Board by motion, setting forth the reasons therefor, filed not less than 10 days prior to the date the brief is due. Where any brief filed pursuant to this section exceeds 20 pages, it shall contain a subject index with page references and an alphabetical table of cases and other authorities cited.

§102.47 Filing of motion after transfer of case to Board.

All motions filed after the case has been transferred to the Board pursuant to §102.45 shall be filed with the Board in Washington, D.C., by transmitting eight copies thereof, together with an affidavit of service on the parties. Such motions shall be printed or otherwise legibly duplicated: *Provided, however,* That carbon copies of typewritten matter shall not be filed and if submitted will not be accepted.

PROCEDURE BEFORE THE BOARD

§102.48 Action of Board upon expiration of time to file exceptions to administrative law judge's decision; decisions by the Board; extraordinary postdecisional motions.

(a) In the event no timely or proper exceptions are filed as herein provided, the findings, conclusions, and recommendations of the administrative law judge as contained in his decision shall, pursuant to section 10(c) of the act, automatically become the decision and order of the Board and become its findings, conclusions, and order, and all objections and exceptions thereto shall be deemed waived for all purposes.

(b) Upon the filing of timely and proper exceptions, and any cross-exceptions, or answering briefs, as provided in §102.46, the Board may decide the matter forthwith upon the record, or after oral argument, or may reopen the record and receive further evidence before a member of the Board or other Board agent or agency, or may make other disposition of the case.

(c) Where exception is taken to a factual finding of the administrative law judge, the Board, in determining whether the finding is contrary to a preponderance of the evidence, may limit its consideration to such portions of the record as are specified in the exceptions, the supporting brief, and the answering brief.

(d)(1) A party to a proceeding before the Board may, because of extraordinary circumstances, move for reconsideration, rehearing, or reopening of the record after the Board decision or order. A motion for reconsideration shall state with particularity the material error claimed and with respect to any finding of material fact shall specify the page of the record relied on. A motion for rehearing shall specify the error alleged to require a hearing *de novo* and the prejudice to the movant alleged to result from such error. A motion to reopen the record shall state briefly the additional evidence sought to be adduced, why it was not presented previously, and that, if adduced and credited, it would require a different result. Only newly discovered evidence, evidence which has become available only since the close of the hearing, or evidence which the Board believes should have been taken at the hearing will be taken at any further hearing.

(2) Any motion pursuant to this subsection shall be filed within 28 days, or such further period as the Board may allow, after the service of the Board's decision or order, except that a motion for leave to adduce additional evidence shall be filed promptly upon discovery of such evidence. Any request for an extension of time must be received by the Board 3 days prior to the due date and copies thereof shall be served promptly on the other parties.

(3) The filing and pendency of a motion under this provision shall not operate to stay the effectiveness of the action of the Board unless so ordered. A motion for reconsideration or rehearing need not be filed to exhaust administrative remedies.

§102.49 Modification or setting aside of order of Board before record filed in court; action thereafter.

Within the limitations of the provisions of section 10(c) of the act, and §102.48, until a transcript of the record in a case shall have been filed in a court, within the meaning of section 10 of the act, the Board may at any time upon reasonable notice modify or set aside, in whole or in part, any findings of fact, conclusions of law, or order made or issued by it. Thereafter, the Board may proceed pursuant to §102.50, insofar as applicable.

§102.50 Hearings before Board or member thereof.

Whenever the Board deems it necessary in order to effectuate the purpose of the act or to avoid unnecessary costs or delay, it may, at any time after a complaint has issued pursuant to §102.15 or §102.33, order that such complaint and any proceeding which may have been instituted with respect thereto be transferred to and continued before it or any member of the Board. The provisions of this subpart shall, insofar as applicable, govern proceedings before the Board or any member pursuant to this section, and the powers granted to administrative law judges in such provisions shall, for the purpose of this section, be reserved to and exercised by the Board or the member thereof who shall preside.

§102.51 Settlement or adjustment of issues.

At any stage of a proceeding prior to hearing, where time, the nature of the proceeding, and the public interest permit, all interested parties shall have opportunity to submit to the regional director, with whom the charge was filed, for consideration facts, arguments, offers of settlement, or proposals of adjustment.

BACKPAY PROCEEDINGS

§102.52 Initiation of proceedings; issuance of backpay specification; issuance of notice of hearing without backpay specification.

After the entry of a Board order directing the payment of backpay or the entry of a court decree enforcing such a Board order, if it appears to the regional director that a controversy exists between the Board and a respondent concerning the amount of backpay due which cannot be resolved without a formal proceeding, the regional director may issue and serve upon all parties a backpay specification in the name of the Board. The specification shall contain or be accompanied by a notice of hearing before an administrative law judge at a place therein fixed and at a time not less than 21 days after the service of the specification. In the alternative and at his discretion, the regional director, may under the circumstances specified above, issue and serve upon the parties a notice of hearing only, without the backpay specification, the hearing to be held before an administrative law judge, at a place therein fixed and at a time not less than 21 days after the service of the notice of hearing.

§102.53 Contents of backpay specifications and of notice of hearing without specification.

(a) *Contents of backpay specification.* Where the specification procedure is used, the specification shall specifically and in detail show, for each employee, the backpay periods broken down by calendar quarters, and specific figures and basis of computation as to gross backpay and interim earnings, the expenses for each quarter, the net backpay due, and any other pertinent information.

(b) *Contents of notice of hearing without specification.* The notice of hearing without specification shall contain, in addition to the time and place of hearing before an administrative law judge, a brief statement of the matters in controversy.

§102.54 Answer to specification; no requirement for answer to notice of hearing issued without backpay specification.

(a) *Filing and service of answer to specification.* The respondent shall, within 21 days from the service of the specification, if any, file an answer thereto; an original and four copies shall be filed with the regional director issuing the specification, and a copy thereof shall immediately be served on any other respondent jointly liable.

(b) *Contents of the answer to specification.* The answer to the specification shall be in writing, the original being signed and sworn to by the respondent or by a fully authorized agent with appropriate power of attorney affixed, and shall contain the post office address of the respondent. The respondent shall specifically admit, deny, or explain each and every allegation of the specification, unless the respondent is without knowledge, in which case the respondent shall so state, such statement operating as a denial. Denials shall fairly meet the substance of the allegations of the specification denied. When a respondent intends to deny only a part of an allegation, the respondent shall specify so much of it as is true and shall deny only the remainder. As to all matters within the knowledge of the respondent, including but not limited to the various factors entering into the computation of gross backpay, a general denial shall not suffice. As to such matters, if the respondent disputes either the accuracy of the figures in the specification or the premises on which they are based, he shall specifically state the basis for his disagreement, setting forth in detail his position as to the applicable premises and furnishing the appropriate supporting figures.

(c) *Effect of failure to answer or to plead specifically and in detail to the specification.* If the respondent fails to file any answer to the specification within the time prescribed by this section, the Board may, either with or without taking evidence in support of the allegations of the specification and without notice to the respondent, find the specification to be true and enter such order as may be appropriate. If the respondent files an answer to the specification but fails to deny any allegation of the specification in the manner required by paragraph (b) of this section, and the failure so to deny is not adequately explained, such allegation shall be deemed to be admitted to be true, and may be so found by the Board without the taking of evidence supporting such allegation, and the respondent shall be precluded from introducing any evidence controverting said allegation.

(d) *Answer to the notice of hearing issued without backpay specification.* No answer need be filed by respondent to notice of hearing issued without a specification.

§102.55 Extension of time for filing answer to specification.

Upon his motion or upon proper cause shown by any respondent, the regional director issuing the specification may by written order extend the time within which the answer to the specification shall be filed.

§102.56 Extension of date of hearing.

Upon his own motion or upon proper cause shown, the regional director issuing the specification or notice of hearing without specification may extend the date of hearing.

§102.57 Amendment to backpay specification.

After the issuance of the notice of hearing, but prior to the opening thereof, the regional director may amend the backpay specification and the respondent affected thereby may amend his answer thereto. After the opening of the hearing, the specification and the answer thereto may be amended upon leave of the administrative law judge or of the Board, as the case may be, good cause therefor appearing.

§102.58 Withdrawal.

Any such specification or notice of hearing without specification may be withdrawn before the hearing by the regional director on his own motion.

§102.59 Hearing; posthearing procedure.

After the issuance of a notice of hearing with or without backpay specification, the procedures provided in §§102.24 to 102.51, shall be followed insofar as applicable.

Subpart C—Procedure Under Section 9(c) of the Act for the Determination of Questions Concerning Representation of Employees[3] and for Clarification of Bargaining Units and for Amendment of Certifications Under Section 9(b) of the Act

§102.60 Petitions.

(a) *Petition for certification or decertification; who may file; where to file; withdrawal.* A petition for investigation of a question concerning representation of employees under paragraphs (1)(A)(i) and (1)(B) of section 9(c) of the Act (hereinafter called a petition for certification) may be filed by an employee or group of employees or any individual or labor organization acting in their behalf or by an employer. A petition under paragraph (1)(A)(ii) of section 9(c) of the Act, alleging that the individual or labor organization which has been certified or is being currently recognized as the bargaining representative is no longer such representative (hereinafter called a petition for decertification), may be filed by any employee or group of employees or any individual or labor organization acting in their behalf. Petitions under this section shall be in writing and signed[4] and either shall be sworn to before a notary public, Board agent, or other person duly authorized by law to administer oaths and take acknowledgments or shall contain a declaration by the person signing it, under the penalties of the Criminal Code, that its contents are true and correct to the best of his knowledge and belief. Four copies of the petition shall be filed. Except as provided in §102.72, such petitions shall be filed with the regional director for the region wherein the bargaining unit exists, or, if the bargaining unit exists in two or more regions, with the regional director for any such regions. Prior to the transfer of the case to the Board, pursuant to §102.67, the petition may be withdrawn only with the consent of the regional director with whom such petition was filed. After the transfer of the case to the Board, the petition may be withdrawn only with the consent of the Board. Whenever the regional director

---

[3]Procedure under the first proviso to sec. 8(b)(7)(C) of the Act is governed by subpart D.
[4]Blank forms for filing such petitions will be supplied by the regional office upon request.

or the Board, as the case may be, approves the withdrawal of any petition, the case shall be closed.

(b) *Petition for clarification of bargaining unit or petition for amendment of certification under section 9(b) of the Act; who may file; where to file; withdrawal.* A petition for clarification of an existing bargaining unit or a petition for amendment of certification, in the absence of a question concerning representation, may be filed by a labor organization or by an employer. Where applicable the same procedures set forth in paragraph (a) of this section shall be followed.

§102.61 Contents of petition for certification; contents of petition for decertification; contents of petition for clarification of bargaining unit; contents of petition for amendment of certification.

(a) A petition for certification, when filed by an employee or group of employees or an individual or labor organization acting in their behalf, shall contain the following:

(1) The name of the employer.

(2) The address of the establishment involved.

(3) The general nature of the employer's business.

(4) A description of the bargaining unit which the petitioner claims to be appropriate.

(5) The names and addresses of any other persons or labor organizations who claim to represent any employees in the alleged appropriate unit, and brief descriptions of the contracts, if any, covering the employees in such unit.

(6) The number of employees in the alleged appropriate unit.

(7) A statement that the employer declines to recognize the petitioner as the representative within the meaning of section 9(a) of the act or that the labor organization is currently recognized but desires certification under the act.

(8) The name affiliation, if any, and address of the petitioner.

(9) Whether a strike or picketing is in progress at the establishment involved and, if so, the approximate number of employees participating, and the date such strike or picketing commenced.

(10) Any other relevant facts.

(b) A petition for certification, when filed by an employer, shall contain the following:

(1) The name and address of the petitioner.

(2) The general nature of the petitioner's business.

(3) A brief statement setting forth that one or more individuals or labor organizations have presented to the petitioner a claim to be recognized as the exclusive representative of all employees in the unit claimed to be appropriate; a description of such unit; and the number of employees in the unit.

(4) The name or names, affiliation, if any, and addresses of the individuals or labor organizations making such claim for recognition.

(5) A statement whether the petitioner has contracts with any labor organization or other representatives of employees and, if so, their expiration date.

(6) Whether a strike or picketing is in progress at the establishment involved and, if so, the approximate number of employees participating, and the date such strike or picketing commenced.

(7) Any other relevant facts.

(c) Petitions for decertification shall contain the following:

(1) The name of the employer.

(2) The address of the establishment and a description of the bargaining unit involved.

(3) The general nature of the employer's business.

(4) Name and address of the petitioner and affiliation, if any.

(5) Name or names of the individuals or labor organizations who have been certified or are being currently recognized by the employer and who claim to represent any employees in the unit involved, and the expiration date of any contracts covering such employees.

(6) An allegation that the individuals or labor organizations who have been certified or are currently recognized by the employer are no longer the representative in the appropriate unit as defined in section 9(a) of the act.

(7) The number of employees in the unit.

(8) Whether a strike or picketing is in progress at the establishment involved and, if so, the approximate number of employees participating, and the date such strike or picketing commenced.

(9) Any other relevant facts.

(d) A petition for clarification shall contain the following:

(1) The name of the employer and the name of the recognized or certified bargaining representative.

(2) The address of the establishment involved.

(3) The general nature of the employer's business.

(4) A description of the present bargaining unit, and, if the bargaining unit is certified, an identification of the existing certification.

(5) A description of the proposed clarification.

(6) The names and addresses of any other persons or labor organizations who claim to represent any employees affected by the proposed clarifications, and brief descriptions of the contracts, if any, covering any such employees.

(7) The number of employees in the present bargaining unit and in the unit as proposed under the clarification.

(8) The job classifications of employees as to whom the issue is raised, and the number of employees in each classification.

(9) A statement by petitioner setting forth reasons why petitioner desires clarification of unit.

(10) The name, the affiliation, if any, and the address of the petitioner.

(11) Any other relevant facts.

(e) A petition for amendment of certification shall contain the following:

(1) The name of the employer and the name of the certified union involved.

(2) The address of the establishment involved.

(3) The general nature of the employer's business.

(4) Identification and description of the existing certification.

(5) A statement by petitioner setting forth the details of the desired amendment and reasons therefor.

(6) The names and addresses of any other persons or labor organizations who claim to represent any employees in the unit covered by the certification

and brief descriptions of the contracts, if any, covering the employees in such unit.

(7) The name, the affiliation, if any, and the address of the petitioner.

(8) Any other relevant facts.

§102.62 Consent election agreements.

(a) Where a petition has been duly filed, the employer and any individuals or labor organizations representing a substantial number of employees involved may, with the approval of the regional director, enter into a consent-election agreement leading to a determination by the regional director of the facts ascertained after such consent election. Such agreement shall include a description of the appropriate unit, the time and place of holding the election, and the payroll period to be used in determining what employees within the appropriate unit shall be eligible to vote. Such consent election shall be conducted under the direction and supervision of the regional director. The method of conducting such consent election shall be consistent with the method followed by the regional director in conducting elections pursuant to §§102.69 and 102.70 except that the rulings and determinations by the regional director of the results thereof shall be final, and the regional director shall issue to the parties a certification of the results of the election, including certification of representatives where appropriate, with the same force and effect as if issued by the Board, provided further that rulings or determinations by the regional director in respect to any amendment of such certification shall also be final.

(b) Where a petition has been duly filed, the employer and any individuals or labor organizations representing a substantial number of the employees involved may, with the approval of the regional director, enter into an agreement providing for a waiver of hearing and a consent election leading to a determination by the Board of the facts ascertained after such consent election, if such a determination is necessary. Such agreement shall also include a description of the appropriate bargaining unit, the time and place of holding the election, and the payroll period to be used in determining which employees within the appropriate unit shall be eligible to vote. Such consent election shall be conducted under the direction and submission of the regional director. The method of conducting such election and the post-election procedure shall be consistent with that followed by the regional director in conducting elections pursuant to §§102.69 and 102.70.

§102.63 Investigation of petition by regional director; notice of hearing; service of notice; withdrawal of notice.

(a) After a petition has been filed under §102.61 (a), (b), or (c), if no agreement such as that provided in §102.62 is entered into and if it appears to the regional director that there is reasonable cause to believe that a question of representation affecting commerce exists, that the policies of the act will be effectuated, and that an election will reflect the free choice of employees in the appropriate unit, the regional director shall prepare and cause to be served upon the parties and upon any known individuals or labor organizations purporting to act as representatives of any employees directly affected by such investigation, a notice of hearing before a hearing officer at a time and place fixed therein. A copy of the petition shall be served with such notice of hearing. Any such notice of hearing may be amended or withdrawn before the close of the hearing by the regional director on his own motion.

(b) After a petition has been filed under §102.61(d) or (e), the regional director shall conduct an investigation and, as appropriate, he may issue a decision without a hearing; or prepare and cause to be served upon the parties and upon any known individuals or labor organizations purporting to act as representatives of any employees directly affected by such investigation, a notice of hearing before a hearing officer at a time and place fixed therein; or take other appropriate action. If a notice of hearing is served, it shall be accompanied by a copy of the petition. Any such notice of hearing may be amended or withdrawn before the close of the hearing by the regional director on his own motion. All hearing and posthearing procedure under this paragraph (b) shall be in conformance with §§102.64 through 102.68 whenever applicable, except where the unit or certification involved arises out of an agreement as provided in §102.62(a), the regional director's action shall be final, and the provisions for review of regional director's decisions by the Board shall not apply. Dismissals of petitions without a hearing shall not be governed by §102.71. The regional director's dismissal shall be by decision, and a request for review therefrom may be obtained under §102.67, except where an agreement under §102.62(a) is involved.

§102.64 Conduct of hearing.

(a) Hearings shall be conducted by a hearing officer and shall be open to the public unless otherwise ordered by the hearing officer. At any time, a hearing officer may be substituted for the hearing officer previously presiding. It shall be the duty of the hearing officer to inquire fully into all matters and issues necessary to obtain a full and complete record upon which the Board or the regional director may discharge their duties under section 9(c) of the act.

(b) The hearing officer may, in his discretion, continue the hearing from day to day, or adjourn it to a later date or to a different place, by announcement thereof at the hearing or by other appropriate notice.

§102.65 Motions; interventions.

(a) All motions, including motions for intervention pursuant to paragraphs (b) and (e) of this section, shall be in writing or, if made at the hearing, may be stated orally on the record and shall briefly state the order or relief sought and the grounds for such motion. An original and two copies of written motions shall be filed and a copy thereof immediately shall be served on the other parties to the proceeding. Motions made prior to the transfer of the case to the Board shall be filed with the regional director, except that motions made during the hearing shall be filed with the hearing officer. After the transfer of the case to the Board, all motions shall be filed with the Board. Such motions shall be printed or otherwise legibly duplicated: *Provided, however*, That carbon copies of typewritten matter shall not be filed and if submitted will not be accepted. Eight copies of such motions shall be filed with the Board. The regional director may rule upon all motions filed with him, causing a copy of said ruling to be served on the parties, or he may refer the motion to the hearing officer: *Provided,* That if the regional director prior to the close of the hearing grants a motion to dismiss the petition, the petitioner may obtain a review of such ruling in the manner prescribed in §102.71. The hearing officer shall rule, either orally on the record or in writing, upon all motions filed at the hearing or referred to him as herein above provided, except that all motions to dismiss petitions shall be referred for appropriate action at such time as the entire record is considered by the regional director or the Board, as the case may be.

(b) Any person desiring to intervene in any proceeding shall make a motion for intervention, stating the grounds upon which such person claims to have an interest in the proceeding. The regional director or the hearing officer, as the case may be, may by order permit intervention in person or by counsel or other representative to such extent and upon such terms as he may deem proper, and such intervenor shall thereupon become a party to the proceeding.

(c) All motions, rulings, and orders shall become a part of the record, except that rulings on motions to revoke subpoenas shall become a part of the record only upon the request of the party aggrieved, as provided in §102.66(c). Unless expressly authorized by the Rules and Regulations, rulings by the regional director or by the hearing officer shall not be appealed directly to the Board, but shall be considered by the Board on appropriate appeal pursuant to §102.67 (b), (c), and (d) or whenever the case is transferred to it for decision: *Provided, however,* That if the regional director has issued an order transferring the case to the Board for decision, such rulings may be appealed directly to the Board by special permission of the Board. Nor shall rulings by the hearing officer be appealed directly to the regional director, unless expressly authorized by the Rules and Regulations, except by special permission of the regional director, but shall be considered by the regional director when he reviews the entire record. Requests to the regional director, or to the Board in appropriate cases, for special permission to appeal from such rulings of the hearing officer shall be filed promptly, in writing, and shall briefly state (1) the reasons special permission should be granted and (2) the grounds relied on for the appeal. The moving party shall immediately serve a copy of the request for special permission and of the appeal on the other parties and on the regional director. Any statement in opposition or other response to the request and/or to the appeal shall be filed promptly, in writing, and shall be served immediately on the other parties and on the regional director. If the Board or the regional director, as the case may be, grants the request for special permission to appeal, the Board or the regional director may proceed forthwith to rule on the appeal.

(d) The right to make motions or to make objections to rulings on motions shall not be deemed waived by participation in the proceeding.

(e)(1) A party to a proceeding may, because of extraordinary circumstances, move after the close of the hearing for reopening of the record, or move after the decision or report for reconsideration, for rehearing, or to reopen the record, but no such motion shall stay the time for filing a request for review of a decision or exceptions to a report. No motion for reconsideration, for rehearing, or to reopen the record will be entertained by the Board or by any regional director with respect to any matter which could have been but was not raised pursuant to any other section of these rules: *Provided, however*, That the regional director may treat a request for review of a decision or exceptions to a report as a motion for reconsideration. A motion for reconsideration shall state with particularity the material error claimed and with respect to any finding of material fact shall specify the page of the record relied on for the motion. A motion for rehearing or to reopen the record shall specify briefly the error alleged to require a rehearing or hearing de novo, the prejudice to the movant alleged to result from such error, the additional evidence sought to be adduced, why it was not presented previously, and what result it would require, if adduced and credited. Only newly discovered evidence—evidence which has become available only since the close of the hearing—or evidence which the regional director or the Board believes should have been taken at the hearing will be taken at any further hearing.

(2) Any motion for reconsideration or for rehearing pursuant to this subsection shall be filed within 14 days, or such further period as may be allowed, after the service of the decision or report. Any request for an extension of time to file such a motion must be received 3 days prior to the due date and copies thereof shall be served promptly on the other parties. A motion to reopen the record shall be filed promptly on discovery of the evidence sought to be adduced.

(3) The filing and pendency of a motion under this provision shall not unless so ordered operate to stay the effectiveness of any action taken or directed to be taken, except that if the motion states with particularity that the granting thereof will affect the eligibility to vote of specific employees, the ballots of such employees shall be challenged and impounded in any election conducted while such motion is pending. A motion for reconsideration or rehearing need not be filed to exhaust administrative remedies.

§102.66 Introduction of evidence; rights of parties at hearing; subpoenas.

(a) Any party shall have the right to appear at any hearing in person, by counsel, or by other representative, and any party and the hearing officer shall have power to call, examine, and cross-examine witnesses and to introduce into the record documentary and other evidence. Witnesses shall be examined orally under oath. The rules of evidence prevailing in courts of law or equity shall not be controlling. Stipulations of fact may be introduced in evidence with respect to any issue.

(b) Any objection with respect to the conduct of the hearing, including any objection to the introduction of evidence, may be stated orally or in writing, accompanied by a short statement of the grounds of such objection, and included in the record. No such objection shall be deemed waived by further participation in the hearing.

(c) Any party may file applications for subpoenas in writing with the regional director if made prior to hearing, or with the hearing officer if made at the hearing. Applications for subpoenas may be made ex parte. The regional director or the hearing officer, as the case may be, shall forthwith grant the subpoenas requested. Any person served with a subpoena, whether ad testificandum or duces tecum, if he does not intend to comply with the subpoena, shall, within 5 days after the date of service of the subpoena, petition in writing to revoke the subpoena. Such petition shall be filed with the regional director who may either rule upon it or refer it for ruling to the hearing officer: *Provided however*, That if the evidence called for is to be produced at a hearing and the hearing has opened, the petition to revoke shall be filed with the hearing officer. Notice of the filing of petitions to revoke shall be promptly given by the regional director or hearing officer, as the case may be, to the party at whose request the subpoena was issued. The regional director or the hearing officer, as the case may be, shall revoke the subpoena if, in his opinion, the evidence whose production is required does not relate to any matter under investigation or in question in the proceedings or the subpoena does not describe with sufficient particularity the evidence whose production is required, or if for any other reason sufficient in law the subpoena is otherwise invalid. The regional director or the hearing officer, as the case may be, shall make a simple statement of procedural or other grounds for his ruling. The petition to revoke, any answer filed thereto, and any ruling thereon shall not become part of the record except upon the request of the party aggrieved by the ruling. Persons compelled to submit data or evidence are entitled to retain or, on payment of lawfully prescribed costs, to procure copies or transcripts of the data or evidence submitted by them.

(d)(1) Misconduct at any hearing before a hearing officer or before the regional director or the Board shall be ground for summary exclusion from the hearing.

(2) Such misconduct of an aggravated character, when engaged in by an attorney or other representative of a party, shall be ground for suspension or disbarment by the Board from further practice before it after due notice and hearing.

(3) The refusal of a witness at any such hearing to answer any question which has been ruled to be proper shall, in the discretion of the hearing officer, be ground for striking all testimony previously given by such witness on related matters.

(e) Any party shall be entitled, upon request, to a reasonable period at the close of the hearing for oral argument, which shall be included in the stenographic report of the hearing.

(f) The hearing officer may submit an analysis of the record to the regional director or the Board but he shall make no recommendations.

(g) Witness fees and mileage shall be paid by the party at whose instance the witness appears.

§102.67 Proceedings before the regional director; further hearing; briefs; action by the regional director; appeals from action by the regional director; statement in opposition to appeal; transfer of case to the Board; proceedings before the Board; Board action.

(a) The regional director may proceed, either forthwith upon the record, or after oral argument or the submission of briefs, or further hearing, as he may deem proper, to determine the unit appropriate for the purpose of collective bargaining, to determine whether a question concerning representation exists, and to direct an election, dismiss the petition, or make other disposition of the matter. Any party desiring to submit a brief to the regional director shall file the original and one copy thereof, which may be a typed carbon copy, within 7 days after the close of the hearing: *Provided, however,* That prior to the close of the hearing and for good cause, the hearing officer may grant an extension of time not to exceed an additional 14 days. Copies of the brief shall be served on all other parties to the proceeding and a statement of such service shall be filed with the regional director together with the brief. No reply brief may be filed except upon special leave of the regional director.

(b) A decision by the regional director upon the record shall set forth his findings, conclusions, and order or direction. The decision of the regional director shall be final: *Provided, however,* That within 14 days after service thereof any party may file a request for review with the Board in Washington, D.C. The regional director shall schedule and conduct any election directed by the decision notwithstanding that a request for review has been filed with or granted by the Board. The filing of such a request shall not, unless otherwise ordered by the Board, operate as a stay of the election or any other action taken or directed by the regional director: *Provided, however,* That if a pending request for review has not been ruled upon or has been granted, ballots whose validity might be affected by the final Board decision shall be segregated in an appropriate manner; and all ballots shall be impounded and remain unopened pending such decision.

(c) The Board will grant a request for review only where compelling reasons exist therefor. Accordingly, a request for review may be granted only upon one or more of the following grounds:

(1) That a substantial question of law or policy is raised because of (i) the absence of, or (ii) a departure from, officially reported Board precedent.

(2) That the regional director's decision on a substantial factual issue is clearly erroneous on the record and such error prejudicially affects the rights of a party.

(3) That the conduct of the hearing or any ruling made in connection with the proceeding has resulted in prejudicial error.

(4) That there are compelling reasons for reconsideration of an important Board rule or policy.

(d) Any request for review must be a self-contained document enabling the Board to rule on the basis of its contents without the necessity of recourse to the record; however, the Board may, in its discretion, examine the record in evaluating the request. With respect to ground (2), and other grounds where appropriate, said request must contain a summary of all evidence or rulings bearing on the issues together with page citations from the transcript and a summary of argument. But such request may not raise any issue or allege any facts not timely presented to the regional director.

(e) Any party may, within 7 days after the last day on which the request for review must be filed, file with the Board a statement in opposition thereto, which shall be served in accordance with the requirements of paragraph (k) of this section. A statement of such service of opposition shall be filed simultaneously with the Board. The Board may deny the request for review without awaiting a statement in opposition thereto.

(f) The parties may, at any time, waive their right to request review. Failure to request review shall preclude such parties from relitigating, in any related subsequent unfair labor practice proceeding, any issue which was, or could have been, raised in the representation proceeding. Denial of a request for review shall constitute an affirmance of the regional director's action which shall also preclude relitigating any such issues in any related subsequent unfair labor practice proceeding.

(g) The granting of a request for review shall not stay the regional director's decision unless otherwise ordered by the Board. Except where the Board rules upon the issues on review in the order granting review, the appellants and other parties may, within 14 days after the issuance of an order granting review, file briefs with the Board. Such briefs may be reproductions of those previously filed with the regional director and/or other briefs which shall be limited to the issues raised in the request for review. Where review has been granted, the Board will consider the entire record in the light of the grounds relied on for review. Any request for review may be withdrawn with the permission of the Board at any time prior to the issuance of the decision of the Board thereon.

(h) In any case in which it appears to the regional director that the proceeding raises questions which should be decided by the Board, he may, at any time, issue an order, to be effective after the close of the hearing and before decision, transferring the case to the Board for decision. Such an order may be served on the parties upon the record of the hearing.

(i) If any case is transferred to the Board for decision after the parties have filed briefs with the regional director, the parties may, within such time after service of the order transferring the case as is fixed by the regional director, file with the Board the brief previously filed with the regional director. No further briefs shall be permitted except by special permission of the Board. If the case is transferred to the Board before the time expires for the filing of briefs with the regional director and before the parties have filed briefs, such briefs shall be filed as set forth above and served in accordance with the requirements of paragraph (k) of this section within the time set by the regional director. If the order transferring the case is served upon the parties during the hearing, the hearing officer may, prior to the close of the hearing and for good cause, grant an extension of time within which to file a brief with the Board for a period not to exceed an additional 14 days. No reply brief may be filed except upon special leave of the Board.

(j) Upon transfer of the case to the Board, the Board shall proceed, either forthwith upon the record, or after oral argument or the submission of briefs, or further hearing, as it may determine, to decide the issues referred to it or to review the decision of the regional director and shall direct a secret ballot of the employees or the appropriate action to be taken on impounded ballots of an election already conducted, dismiss the petition, affirm or reverse the regional director's order in whole or in part, or make such other disposition of the matter as it deems appropriate.

(k)(1) All documents filed with the Board under the provisions of this section shall be filed in eight copies, double spaced, on 8½- by 11-inch paper, and shall be printed or otherwise legibly duplicated. Carbon copies of typewritten materials will not be accepted. Requests for review, including briefs in support thereof; statements in opposition thereto; and briefs on review shall not exceed 50 pages in length, exclusive of subject index and table of cases and other authorities cited, unless permission to exceed that limit is obtained from the Board by motion, setting forth the reasons therefor, filed not less than 5 days, including Saturdays, Sundays, and holidays, prior to the date the document is due. Where any brief filed pursuant to this section exceeds 20 pages, it shall contain a subject index with page authorities cited.

(2) The party filing with the Board a request for review, a statement in opposition to a request for review, or a brief on review shall serve a copy thereof on the other parties and shall file a copy with the regional director. A statement of such service shall be filed with the Board together with the document.

(3) Requests for extensions of time to file requests for review, statements in opposition to a request for review, or briefs, as permitted by this section, shall be filed with the Board or the regional director, as the case may be, not less than 3 days before the date the brief or other document is due. The party filing the request for an extension of time shall serve a copy thereof on the other parties and, if filed with the Board, on the regional director. A statement of such service shall be filed with the document.

§102.68 Record; what constitutes; transmission to Board.

The record in a proceeding conducted pursuant to the foregoing section shall consist of: the petition, notice of hearing with affidavit of service thereof, motions, rulings, orders, the stenographic report of the hearing and of any oral argument before the regional director, stipulations, exhibits, affidavits of service, and any briefs or other legal memoranda submitted by the parties to the regional director or to the Board, and the decision of the regional director, if any. Immediately upon issuance by the regional director of an order transferring the case to the Board, or upon issuance of an order granting a request for review by the Board the regional director shall transmit the record to the Board.

§102.69 Election procedure; tally of ballots; objections; certification by regional director; report on challenged ballots; report on objections; exceptions; action of the Board; hearing.

(a) Unless otherwise directed by the Board, all elections shall be conducted under the supervision of the regional director in whose region the proceeding is pending. All elections shall be by secret ballot. Whenever two or more labor organizations are included as choices in an election, either participant may, upon its prompt request to and approval thereof by the regional director, whose decision shall be final, have its name removed from the ballot: *Provided, however,* That in a proceeding involving an employer-filed petition or a petition for decertification the labor organization certified, currently recognized, or found to be seeking recognition may not have its name removed from the ballot without giving timely notice in writing to all parties and the regional director, disclaiming any representation interest among the employees in the unit. Any party may be represented by observers of his own selection, subject to limitations as the regional director may prescribe. Any party and Board agents may challenge, for good cause, the eligibility of any person to participate in the election. The ballots of such challenged persons shall be impounded. Upon the conclusion of the election the ballots will be counted and a tally of ballots prepared and immediately made available to the parties. Within 7 days after the tally of ballots has been prepared, any party may file with the regional director an original and five copies of objections to the conduct of the election or conduct affecting the results of the election which shall contain a short statement of the reasons therefor. Such filing must be timely whether or not the challenged ballots are sufficient in number to affect the results of the election. The regional director will cause a copy of such objections to be served on each of the other parties to the proceeding. Within 7 days after the filing of objections, or such additional time as the regional director may allow, the party filing objections shall furnish to the regional director the evidence available to it to support the objections.

(b) If no objections are filed within the time set forth above, if the challenged ballots are insufficient in number to affect the results of the election, and if no runoff election is to be held pursuant to §102.70, the regional director shall forthwith issue to the parties a certification of the results of the election, including certification of representative where appropriate, with the same force and effect as if issued by the Board, and the proceeding will thereupon be closed.

(c)(1) If timely objections are filed to the conduct of the election or conduct affecting the result of the election, or if the challenged ballots are sufficient in number to affect the result of the election, the regional director shall, consistent with the provisions of §102.69(d), initiate an investigation, as required, of such objections or challenges.

(2) If a consent election has been held pursuant to §102.62(b), the regional director shall prepare and cause to be served on the parties a report on challenged ballots or objections, or both, including his recommendations, which report, together with the tally of ballots, he shall forward to the Board in Washington, D.C. Within 14 days from the date of issuance of the report on challenged ballots or objections, or both, any party may file with the Board in Washington, D.C., exceptions to such report, with supporting documents as permitted by §102.69(g)(3) and/or a supporting brief if desired. Within 7 days from the last date on which exceptions and any supporting documents and/or supporting brief may be filed, or such further period as the Board may allow, a party opposing the exceptions may file an answering brief, with supporting documents as permitted by §102.69(g)(3), if desired, with the Board in Washington, D.C. If no exceptions are filed to such report, the Board, upon expiration of the period for filing such exceptions, may decide the matter forthwith upon the record or may make other disposition of the case. The report on challenged ballots may be consolidated with the report on objections in appropriate cases.

(3) If the election has been conducted pursuant to a direction of election issued following any proceeding under §102.67, the regional director may (i) issue a report on objections or challenged ballots, or both, as in the case of a consent election pursuant to paragraph (b) of §102.62, or (ii) exercise his authority to decide the case and issue a decision disposing of the issues, and directing appropriate action or certifying the results of the election.

(4) If the regional director issues a report on objections and challenges, the parties shall have the rights set forth in paragraph (c)(2) of this section, and in §102.69(f); if the regional director issues a decision, the parties shall have the rights set forth in §102.67 to the extent consistent herewith, including the right to submit documents supporting the request for review or opposition thereto as permitted by §102.69(g)(3).

(d) In issuing a report on objections or challenged ballots, or both, following proceedings under §§102.62(b) or 102.67, or in issuing a decision on objections or challenged ballots, or both, following proceedings under §102.67, the regional director may act on the basis of an administrative investigation or upon the record of a hearing before a hearing officer. Such hearing shall be conducted with respect to those objections or challenges which the regional director concludes raise substantial and material factual issues.

(e) Any hearing pursuant to this section shall be conducted in accordance with the provisions of §§102.64, 102.65, and 102.66, insofar as applicable, except that upon the close of such hearing, the hearing officer shall, if directed by the regional director, prepare and cause to be served on the parties a report resolving questions of credibility and containing findings of fact and recommendations as to the disposition of the issues. In any case in which the regional director has directed that a report be prepared and served, any party may, within 14 days from the date of issuance of such report, file with the regional director the original and one copy, which may be a carbon copy, of exceptions to such report, with supporting brief, if desired. A copy of such exceptions, together with a copy of any brief filed, shall immediately be served on the other parties and a statement of service filed with the regional director. Within 7 days from the last date on which exceptions and any supporting brief may be filed, or such further time as the regional director may allow, a party opposing the exceptions may file an answering brief with the regional director. An original and one copy, which may be a carbon copy, shall be submitted. A copy of such answering brief shall immediately be served on the other parties and a statement of service filed with the regional director. If no exceptions are filed to such report, the regional director, upon the expiration of the period for filing such exceptions, may decide the matter forthwith upon the record or may make other disposition of the case.

(f) In a case involving a consent election held pursuant to §102.62(b), if exceptions are filed, either to the report on challenged ballots or objections, or both if it be a consolidated report, and it appears to the Board that such exceptions do not raise substantial and material issues with respect to the conduct or results of the election, the Board may decide the matter forthwith upon the record, or may make other disposition of the case. If it appears to the Board that such exceptions raise substantial and material factual issues, the Board may direct the regional director or other agent of the Board to issue and cause to be served on the parties a notice of hearing on said exceptions before a hearing officer. The hearing shall be conducted in accordance with the provisions of §§102.64, 102.65, and 102.66, insofar as applicable. Upon the close of the hearing the agent conducting the hearing, if directed by the Board, shall prepare and cause to be served on the parties a report resolving questions of credibility and containing findings of fact and recommendations to the Board as to the disposition of the challenges or objections, or both if it be a consolidated report. In any case in which the Board has directed that a report be prepared and served, any party may within 14 days from the date of issuance of the report on challenged ballots or objections, or both, file with the Board in Washington, D.C., exceptions to such report, with supporting brief if desired. Within 7 days from the last date on which exceptions and any supporting brief may be filed, or such further period as the Board may allow, a party opposing the exceptions may file an answering brief with the Board in Washington, D.C. If no exceptions are filed to such report, the Board, upon the expiration of the period for filing such exceptions, may decide the matter forthwith upon the record or may make other disposition of the case. The Board shall thereupon proceed pursuant to §102.67: *Provided, however,* That in any proceeding wherein a representation case has been consolidated with an unfair labor practice case for purposes of hearing, the provisions of §102.46 of these rules shall govern with respect to the filing of exceptions or an answering brief to the exceptions to the administrative law judge's decision.

(g)(1)(i) In a proceeding pursuant to this section in which a hearing is held, the record in the case shall consist of the notice of hearing, motions, rulings, orders, stenographic report of the hearing, stipulations, exhibits, together with the objections to the conduct of the election or to conduct affecting the results of the election, any report on such objections, any report on challenged ballots, exceptions to any such report, any briefs or other legal memoranda submitted by the parties, the decision of the regional director, if any, and the record previously made as defined in §102.68. Materials other than those set out above shall not be a part of the record.

(ii) In a proceeding pursuant to this section in which no hearing is held, the record shall consist of the objections to the conduct of the election or to conduct affecting the results of the election, any report on objections or on challenged ballots and any exceptions to such a report, any regional director's decision on objections or challenged ballots and any request for review of such a decision, any documentary evidence, excluding statements of witnesses, relied upon by the regional director in his decision or report, any briefs or other legal memoranda submitted by the parties, and any other motions, rulings or orders of the regional director. Materials other than those set out above shall not be a part of the record, except as provided in paragraph (g)(3) of this section.

(2) Immediately upon issuance of a report on objections or challenges, or both, upon issuance by the regional director of an order transferring the case to the Board, or upon issuance of an order granting a request for review by the Board, the regional director shall transmit to the Board the record of the proceeding as defined in paragraph (g)(1) of this section.

(3) In a proceeding pursuant to this section in which no hearing is held, a party filing exceptions to a regional director's report on objections or challenges, a request for review of a regional director's decision on objections or challenges, or any opposition thereto, may support its submission to the Board by appending thereto copies of documentary evidence, including copies of any affidavits, it has timely submitted to the regional director and which were not included in the report or decision. Documentary evidence so appended shall thereupon become part of the record in the proceeding. Failure to timely submit such documentary evidence to the regional director, or to append that evidence to its submission to the Board in the representation proceeding as provided above, shall preclude a party from relying on such evidence in any subsequent related unfair labor practice proceeding.

(h) In any such case in which the regional director or the Board, upon a ruling on challenged ballots, has directed that such ballots be opened and counted and a revised tally of ballots issued, and no objection to such revised tally is filed by any party within 7 days after the revised tally of ballots has been made available, the regional director shall forthwith issue to the parties certification of the results of the election, including certification of representative where appropriate, with the same force and effect as if issued by the Board. The proceeding shall thereupon be closed.

(i)(1) The action of the regional director in issuing a notice of hearing on objections or challenged ballots, or both, following proceedings under §102.62(b) shall constitute a transfer of the case to the Board, and the provisions of §102.65(c) shall apply with respect to special permission to appeal to the Board from any such direction of hearing.

(2) Exceptions, if any, to the hearing officer's report or to the administrative law judge's decision, and any answering brief to such exceptions, shall be filed with the Board in Washington, D.C., in accordance with paragraph (f) of this section.

(j)(1) All documents filed with the Board under the provisions of this section shall be filed in eight copies, double spaced, on 8½- by 11-inch paper, and shall be printed or otherwise legibly duplicated. Carbon copies of typewritten materials will not be accepted. Briefs in support of exceptions or answering briefs shall not exceed 50 pages in length, exclusive of subject index and table of cases and other authorities cited, unless permission to exceed that limit is obtained from the Board by motion, setting forth the reasons therefor, filed not less than 5 days, including Saturdays, Sundays, and holidays, prior to the date the brief is due. Where any brief filed pursuant to this section exceeds 20 pages, it shall contain a subject index with page references and an alphabetical table of cases and other authorities cited.

(2) The party filing with the Board exceptions to a report, a supporting brief, or an answering brief shall serve a copy thereof on the other parties and shall file a copy with the regional director. A statement of such service shall be filed with the Board together with the document.

(3) Requests for extensions of time to file exceptions to a report, supporting briefs, or answering briefs, as permitted by this section, shall be filed with the Board or the regional director, as the case may be, not less than 3 days before the date the brief or other document is due. The party filing the request for an extension of time shall serve a copy thereof on the other parties and, if filed with the Board, on the regional director. A statement of such service shall be filed with the document.

§102.70 Runoff election.

(a) The regional director shall conduct a runoff election, without further order of the Board, when an election in which the ballot provided for not less than three choices (i.e., at least two representatives and "neither") results in no choice receiving a majority of the valid ballots cast and no objections are filed as provided in §102.69. Only one runoff shall be held pursuant to this section.

(b) Employees who were eligible to vote in the election and who are in an eligible category on the date of the runoff election shall be eligible to vote in the runoff election.

(c) The ballot in the runoff election shall provide for a selection between the two choices receiving the largest and second largest number of votes.

(d) In the event the number of votes cast in an inconclusive election in which the ballot provided for a choice among two or more representatives and "neither" or "none" is equally divided among the several choices; or in the event the number of ballots cast for one choice in such election is equal to the number cast for another of the choices but less than the number cast for the third choice, the regional director shall declare the first election a nullity and shall conduct another election, providing for a selection from among the three choices afforded in the original ballot; and he shall thereafter proceed in accordance with paragraphs (a), (b), and (c) of this section. In the event two or more choices receive the same number of ballots and another choice receives no ballots and there are no challenged ballots that would affect the results of the election, and if all eligible voters have cast valid ballots, there shall be no runoff election and a certification of results of election shall be issued. Only one such further election pursuant to this paragraph may be held.

(e) Upon the conclusion of the runoff election, the provisions of §102.69 shall govern, insofar as applicable.

§102.71 Dismissal of petition; refusal to proceed with petition; requests for review by Board of action of the regional director.

(a) If, after a petition has been filed and at any time prior to the close of hearing, it shall appear to the regional director that no further proceedings are warranted, the regional director may dismiss the petition by administrative action and shall so advise the petitioner in writing, setting forth a simple statement of the procedural or other grounds for the dismissal, with copies to the other parties to the proceeding. Any party may obtain a review of such action by filing a request therefor with the Board in Washington, D.C., in accordance with the provisions of paragraph (c) of this section. A request for review from an action of a regional director pursuant to this subsection may be granted only upon one or more of the following grounds:

(1) That a substantial question of law or policy is raised because of (i) the absence of, or (ii) a departure from, officially reported Board precedent.

(2) There are compelling reasons for reconsideration of an important Board rule or policy.

(3) The request for review is accompanied by documentary evidence previously submitted to the regional director raising serious doubts as to the regional director's factual findings, thus indicating that there are factual issues which can best be resolved upon the basis of a record developed at a hearing.

(4) The regional director's action is, on its face, arbitrary or capricious.

(5) The petition raises issues which can best be resolved upon the basis of a record developed at a hearing.

(b) Where the regional director dismisses a petition or directs that the proceeding on the petition be held in abeyance, and such action is taken because of the pendency of concurrent unresolved charges of unfair labor practices, and the regional director, upon request, has so notified the parties in writing, any party may obtain a review of the regional director's action by filing a request therefor with the Board in Washington, D.C., in accordance with the provisions of paragraph (c) of this section. A review of an action of a regional director pursuant to this subsection may be granted only upon one or more of the following grounds:

(1) That a substantial question of law or policy is raised because of (i) the absence of, or (ii) a departure from, officially reported Board precedent.

(2) There are compelling reasons for reconsideration of an important Board rule or policy.

(3) The regional director's action is, on its face, arbitrary or capricious.

(c) A request for review must be filed with the Board in Washington, D.C., and a copy filed with the regional director and copies served upon all the other parties within 14 days of service of the notice of dismissal or notification that the petition is to be held in abeyance. The request shall be submitted in eight copies and shall contain a complete statement setting forth facts and reasons upon which the request is based. Such request shall be printed or otherwise legibly duplicated: *Provided, however,* That carbon copies of typewritten materials will not be accepted. Requests for an extension of time within which to file the request for review shall be filed with the Board in Washington, D.C., and a statement of service shall accompany such request.

§102.72 Filing petition with general counsel; investigation upon motion of general counsel; transfer of petition and proceeding from region to general counsel or to another region; consolidation of proceedings in same region; severance; procedure before general counsel in cases over which he has assumed jurisdiction.

(a) Whenever it appears necessary in order to effectuate the purposes of the act, or to avoid unnecessary costs or delay, the general counsel may permit a petition to be filed with him in Washington, D.C., or may, at any time after a petition has been filed with a regional director pursuant to §102.60, order that such petition and any proceeding that may have been instituted with respect thereto:

(1) Be transferred to and continued before him, for the purpose of investigation or consolidation with any other proceeding which may have been instituted in a regional office or with him; or

(2) Be consolidated with any other proceeding which may have been instituted in the same region; or

(3) Be transferred to and continued in any other region, for the purpose of investigation or consolidation with any proceeding which may have been instituted in or transferred to such region; or

(4) Be severed from any other proceeding with which it may have been consolidated pursuant to this section.

(b) The provisions of §§102.60 to 102.71, inclusive, shall, insofar as applicable, apply to proceedings before the general counsel pursuant to this section, and the powers granted to regional directors in such provisions shall, for the purpose of this section, be reserved to and exercised by the general counsel. After the transfer of any petition and any proceeding which may have been instituted in respect thereto from one region to another pursuant to this section, the provisions of this subpart shall, insofar as applicable, govern such petition and such proceedings as if the petition had originally been filed in the region to which the transfer was made.

(c) The regional director may exercise the powers in paragraph (a)(2) and (4) of this section with respect to proceedings pending in his region.

Subpart D—Procedure for Unfair Labor Practice and Representation Cases Under Sections 8(b)(7) and 9(c) of the Act

§102.73 Initiation of proceedings.

Whenever it is charged that any person has engaged in an unfair labor practice within the meaning of section 8(b)(7) of the act, the regional director shall investigate such charge, giving it the priority specified in subpart G of this part.

§102.74 Complaint and formal proceedings.

If it appears to the regional director that the charge has merit, formal proceedings in respect thereto shall be instituted in accordance with the procedures described in §§102.15 to 102.51, inclusive, insofar as they are applicable, and insofar as they are not inconsistent with the provisions of this subpart. If it appears to the regional director that issuance of a complaint is not warranted, he shall decline to issue a complaint, and the provisions of §102.19, including the provisions for appeal to the general counsel, shall be applicable unless an election has been directed under §§102.77 and 102.78, in which event the provisions of §102.81 shall be applicable.

§102.75 Suspension of proceedings on the charge where timely petition is filed.

If it appears to the regional director that issuance of a complaint may be warranted but for the pendency of a petition under section 9(c) of the act, which has been filed by any proper party within a reasonable time not to exceed 30 days from the commencement of picketing, the regional director shall suspend proceedings on the charge and shall proceed to investigate the petition under the expedited procedure provided below, pursuant to the first proviso to subparagraph (C) of section 8(b)(7) of the act.

§102.76 Petition; who may file; where to file; contents.

When picketing of an employer has been conducted for an object proscribed by section 8(b)(7) of the act, a petition for the determination of a question concerning representation of the employees of such employer may be filed in accordance with the provisions of §§102.60 and 102.61, insofar as applicable: *Provided, however,* That if a charge under §102.73 has been filed against the labor organization on whose behalf picketing has been conducted, the petition shall not be required to contain a statement that the employer declines to recognize the petitioner as the representative within the meaning of section 9(a) of the act; or that the labor organization is currently recognized but desires certification under the act; or that the individuals or labor organizations who have been certified or are currently recognized by the employer are no longer the representative; or, if the petitioner is an employer that one or more individuals or labor organizations have presented to the petitioner a claim to be recognized as the exclusive representative of the employees in the unit claimed to be appropriate.

§102.77 Investigation of petition by regional director; directed election.

(a) Where a petition has been filed pursuant to §102.76 the regional director shall make an investigation of the matters and allegations set forth therein. Any party, and any individual or labor organization purporting to act as representative of the employees involved and any labor organization on whose behalf picketing has been conducted as described in section 8(b)(7)(C) of the act may present documentary and other evidence relating to the matters and allegations set forth in the petition.

(b) If after the investigation of such petition or any petition filed under subpart C of these rules, and after the investigation of the charge filed pursuant to §102.73, it appears to the regional director that an expedited election under section 8(b)(7)(C) is warranted, and that the policies of the act would be effectuated thereby, he shall forthwith proceed to conduct an election by secret ballot of the employees in an appropriate unit, or make other disposition of the matter: *Provided, however,* That in any case in which it appears to the regional director that the proceeding raises questions which cannot be decided without a hearing, he may issue and cause to be served on the parties, individuals, and labor organizations involved a notice of hearing before a hearing officer at a time and place fixed therein. In this event, the method of conducting the hearing and the procedure following, including transfer of the case to the Board shall be governed insofar as applicable by §§102.63 to 102.68, inclusive, except that the parties shall not file briefs without special permission of the regional director or the Board, as the case may be, but shall, however, state their respective legal positions upon the record at the close of the hearing, and except that any request for review of a decision of the regional director shall be filed promptly after the issuance of such decision.

§102.78 Election procedure; method of conducting balloting; postballoting procedure.

If no agreement such as that provided in §102.79 has been made, the regional director shall fix the time and place of the election, eligibility requirements for voting, and other arrangements for the balloting. The method of conducting the balloting and the postballoting procedure shall be governed, insofar as applicable, by the provisions of §§102.69 and 102.70 except that the labor organization on whose behalf picketing has been conducted may not have its name removed from the ballot without the consent of the regional director and except that the regional director's rulings on any objections or challenged ballots shall be final unless the Board grants special permission to appeal from the regional director's rulings. Any request for such permission shall be filed promptly, in writing, and shall briefly state the grounds relied upon. The party requesting review shall immediately serve a copy thereof on each other party. A request for review shall not operate as a stay of the regional director's rulings unless so ordered by the Board.

§102.79 Consent-election agreements.

Where a petition has been duly filed, the parties involved may, subject to the approval of the regional director, enter into an agreement governing the method of conducting the election as provided for in §102.62(a), insofar as applicable.

§102.80 Dismissal of petition; refusal to process petition under expedited procedure.

(a) If, after a petition has been filed pursuant to the provisions of §102.76, and prior to the close of the hearing, it shall appear to the regional director that further proceedings in respect thereto in accordance with the provisions of §102.77 are not warranted, he may dismiss the petition by administrative action, and the action of the regional director shall be final, subject to a prompt appeal to the Board on special permission which may be granted by the Board. Upon such appeal the provisions of §102.71 shall govern insofar as applicable. Such appeal shall not operate as a stay unless specifically ordered by the Board.

(b) If it shall appear to the regional director that an expedited election is not warranted but that proceedings under subpart C of this part are warranted, he shall so notify the parties in writing with a simple statement of the grounds for his decision.

(c) Where the regional director, pursuant to §§102.77 and 102.78, has determined that a hearing prior to election is not required to resolve the issues raised by the petition and has directed an expedited election, any party aggrieved may file a request with the Board for special permission to appeal from such determination. Such request shall be filed promptly, in writing, and shall briefly state the grounds relied upon. The party requesting such appeal shall immediately serve a copy thereof on each other party. Should the Board grant the requested permission to appeal, such action shall not, unless specifically ordered by the Board, operate as a stay of any action by the regional director.

§102.81 Review by the general counsel of refusal to proceed on charge; resumption of proceedings upon charge held during pendency of petition; review by general counsel of refusal to proceed on related charge.

(a) Where an election has been directed by the regional director or the Board in accordance with the provisions of §§102.77 and 102.78, the regional director shall decline to issue a complaint on the charge, and he shall so advise the parties in writing, accompanied by a simple statement of the procedural or other grounds for his action. The person making the charge may obtain a review of such action by filing an appeal with the general counsel in Washington, D.C., and filing a copy of the appeal with the regional director, within 7 days from the service of the notice of such refusal by the regional director. In all other respects the appeal shall be subject to the provisions of §102.19. Such appeal shall not operate as a stay of any action by the regional director.

(b) Where an election has not been directed and the petition has been dismissed in accordance with the provisions of §102.80, the regional director shall resume investigation of the charge and shall proceed in accordance with §102.74.

(c) If in connection with a section 8(b)(7) proceeding, unfair labor practice charges under other sections of the act have been filed and the regional director upon investigation has declined to issue a complaint upon such charges, he shall so advise the parties in writing, accompanied by a simple statement of the procedural or other grounds for his action. The person making such charges may obtain a review of such action by filing an appeal with the general counsel in Washington, D.C., and filing a copy of the appeal with the regional director, within 7 days from the service of the notice of such refusal by the regional director. In all other respects the appeal shall be subject to the provisions of §102.19.

§102.82 Transfer, consolidation, and severance.

The provisions of §§102.33 and 102.72, respecting the filing of a charge or petition with the general counsel and the transfer, consolidation, and severance of proceedings, shall apply to proceedings under this subpart, except that the provisions of §§102.73 to 102.81, inclusive, shall govern proceedings before the general counsel.

Subpart E—Procedure for Referendum Under Section 9(e) of the Act

§102.83 Petition for referendum under section 9(e)(1) of the act; who may file; where to file; withdrawal.

A petition to rescind the authority of a labor organization to make an agreement requiring as a condition of employment membership in such labor organization may be filed by an employee or group of employees on behalf of 30 percent or more of the employees in a bargaining unit covered by such an agreement. The petition shall be in writing and signed, and either shall be sworn to before a notary public, Board agent, or other person duly authorized by law to administer oaths and take acknowledgments or shall contain a declaration by the person signing it, under the penalties of the Criminal Code, that its contents are true and correct to the best of his knowledge and belief.[5] Four copies of the petition shall be filed with the regional director wherein the bargaining unit exists or, if the unit exists in two or more regions with the regional director for any of such regions. The petition may be withdrawn only with the approval of the regional director with whom such petition was filed, except that if the proceeding has been transferred to the Board, pursuant to §102.67, the petition may be withdrawn only with the consent of the Board. Upon approval of the withdrawal of any petition the case shall be closed.

§102.84 Contents of petition to rescind authority.

(a) The name of the employer.
(b) The address of the establishment involved.
(c) The general nature of the employer's business.

---

[5]Forms for filing such petitions will be supplied by the regional office upon request.

(d) A description of the bargaining unit involved.

(e) The name and address of the labor organization whose authority it is desired to rescind.

(f) The number of employees in the unit.

(g) Whether there is a strike or picketing in progress at the establishment involved and, if so, the approximate number of employees participating, and the date such strike or picketing commenced.

(h) The date of execution and of expiration of any contract in effect covering the unit involved.

(i) The name and address of the person designated to accept service of documents for petitioners.

(j) Any other relevant facts.

§102.85 Investigation of petition by regional director; consent referendum; directed referendum.

Where a petition has been filed pursuant to §102.83 and it appears to the regional director that the petitioner has made an appropriate showing, in such form as the regional director may determine that 30 percent or more of the employees within a unit covered by an agreement between their employer and a labor organization requiring membership in such labor organization desire to rescind the authority of such labor organization to make such an agreement, he shall proceed to conduct a secret ballot of the employees involved on the question whether they desire to rescind the authority of the labor organization to make such an agreement with their employer: *Provided, however*, That in any case in which it appears to the regional director that the proceeding raises questions which cannot be decided without a hearing, he may issue and cause to be served on the parties a notice of hearing before a hearing officer at a time and place fixed therein. The regional director shall fix the time and place of the election, eligibility requirements for voting, and other arrangements of the balloting, but the parties may enter into an agreement, subject to the approval of the regional director, fixing such arrangements. In any such consent agreements, provision may be made for final determination of all questions arising with respect to the balloting by the regional director or by the Board.

§102.86 Hearing; posthearing procedure.

The method of conducting the hearing and the procedure following the hearing, including transfer of the case to the Board, shall be governed, insofar as applicable, by sections 102.63 to 102.68, inclusive.

§102.87 Method of conducting balloting; postballoting procedure.

The method of conducting the balloting and the postballoting procedure shall be governed by the provisions of §102.69, insofar as applicable.

§102.88 Refusal to conduct referendum; appeal to Board.

If, after a petition has been filed, and prior to the close of the hearing, it shall appear to the regional director that no referendum should be conducted, he shall dismiss the petition by administrative action. Such dismissal shall be in writing and accompanied by a simple statement of the procedural or other grounds. The petitioner may obtain a review of such action by filing a request therefor with the Board in Washington, D.C., and filing a copy of such request with the regional director and each of the other parties within 14 days from the service of notice of such dismissal. The request shall contain a complete statement setting forth the facts and reasons upon which the request is based.

Subpart F—Procedure To Hear and Determine Disputes Under Section 10(k) of the Act

§102.89 Initiation of proceedings.

Whenever it is charged that any person has engaged in an unfair labor practice within the meaning of paragraph (4)(D) of section 8(b) of the Act, the regional director of the office in which such charge is filed or to which it is referred shall, as soon as possible after the charge has been filed, serve upon the parties a copy of the charge together with a notice of the filing of the charge and shall investigate such charge and if it is deemed appropriate to seek injunctive relief of a district court pursuant to section 10(l) of the act, he shall give it priority over all other cases in the office except other cases under section 10(l) and cases of like character.

§102.90 Notice of filing of charge; notice of hearing; hearing; proceedings before the Board; briefs; determination of dispute.

If it appears to the regional director that the charge has merit and the parties to the dispute have not submitted satisfactory evidence to the regional director that they have adjusted, or have agreed upon methods for the voluntary adjustment of, the dispute out of which such unfair labor practice shall have arisen, he shall cause to be served on all parties to such dispute a notice of hearing under section 10(k) of the act before a hearing officer at a time and place fixed therein which shall be not less than 10 days after service of the notice of the filing of said charge. The notice of hearing shall contain a simple statement of the issues involved in such dispute. Such notice shall be issued promptly, and, in cases in which it is deemed appropriate to seek injunctive relief pursuant to section 10(l) of the act, shall normally be issued within 5 days of the date upon which injunctive relief is first sought. Hearings shall be conducted by a hearing officer, and the procedure shall conform, insofar as applicable, to the procedure set forth in §§102.64 to 102.68, inclusive. Upon the close of the hearing, the proceeding shall be transferred to the Board and the Board shall proceed either forthwith upon the record, or after oral argument, or the submission of briefs, or further hearing, to determine the dispute or make other disposition of the matter. Should any party desire to file a brief with the Board, eight copies thereof shall be filed with the Board at Washington, D.C., within 7 days after the close of the hearing: *Provided, however,* That, in cases involving the national defense and so designated in the notice of hearing no briefs shall be filed, and the parties, after the close of the evidence, may argue orally upon the record their respective contentions and positions: *Provided further,* That, in cases involving the national defense, upon application for leave to file briefs expeditiously made to the Board in Washington, D.C., after the close of the hearing, the Board may for good cause shown grant such leave and thereupon specify the time for filing. Immediately upon such filing, a copy shall be served on the other parties. Such brief shall be printed or otherwise legibly duplicated: *Provided, however,* That carbon copies of typewritten matter shall not be filed and if submitted will not be accepted. Requests for extension of time in which to file a brief under authority of this section shall be in writing and received by the Board in Washington, D.C., 3 days prior to the due date with copies thereof served on the other parties. No reply brief may be filed except upon special leave of the Board.

§102.91 Compliance with determination; further proceedings.

If, after issuance of the determination by the Board, the parties submit to the regional director satisfactory evidence that they have complied with the determination, the regional director shall dismiss the charge. If no satisfactory evidence of compliance is submitted, the regional director shall proceed with the charge under paragraph (4)(D) of section 8(b) and section 10 of the act and the procedure prescribed in §§102.9 to 102.51, inclusive, shall, insofar as applicable, govern: *Provided, however,* That if the Board determination is that employees represented by a charged union are entitled to perform the work in dispute, the regional director shall dismiss the charge as to that union irrespective of whether the employer has complied with that determination.

§102.92 Review of determination.

The record of the proceeding under section 10(k) and the determination of the Board thereon shall become a part of the record in such unfair labor practice proceeding and shall be subject to judicial review, insofar as it is in issue, in proceedings to enforce or review the final order of the Board under section 10 (e) and (f) of the act.

§102.93 Alternative procedure.

If, either before or after service of the notice of hearing, the parties submit to the regional director satisfactory evidence that they have adjusted the dispute, the regional director shall dismiss the charge and shall withdraw the notice of hearing if notice has issued. If, either before or after issuance of notice of hearing, the parties submit to the regional director satisfactory evidence that they have agreed upon methods for the voluntary adjustment of the dispute, the regional director shall defer action upon the charge and shall withdraw the notice of hearing if notice has issued. If it appears to the regional director that the dispute has not been adjusted in accordance with such agreed-upon methods and that an unfair labor practice within the meaning of section 8(b)(4)(D) of the act is occurring or has occurred, he may issue a complaint under §102.15, and the procedure prescribed in §§102.9 to 102.51, inclusive, shall, insofar as applicable, govern; and §§102.90 to 102.92, inclusive, are inapplicable: *Provided, however,* That if an agreed-upon method for voluntary adjustment results in a determination that employees represented by a charged union are entitled to perform the work in dispute, the regional director shall dismiss the charge as to that union irrespective of whether the employer has complied with that determination.

Subpart G—Procedure in Cases Under Section 10 (j), (l), and (m) of the Act

§102.94 Expeditious processing of section 10(j) cases.

(a) Whenever temporary relief or a restraining order pursuant to section 10(j) of the act has been procured by the Board, the complaint which has been the basis for such temporary relief or restraining order shall be heard expeditiously and the case shall be given priority by the Board in its successive steps following the issuance of the complaint (until ultimate enforcement or dismissal by the appropriate circuit court of appeals) over all other cases except cases of like character and cases under section 10 (l) and (m) of the act.

(b) In the event the administrative law judge hearing a complaint, concerning which the Board has procured temporary relief or a restraining order pursuant to section 10(j), recommends a dismissal in whole or in part of such complaint, the chief law officer shall forthwith suggest to the district court which issued such temporary relief or restraining order the possible change in circumstances arising out of the findings and recommendations of the administrative law judge.

§102.95 Priority of cases pursuant to section 10(l) and (m) of the Act.

(a) Whenever a charge is filed alleging the commission of an unfair labor practice within the meaning of paragraph (4)(A), (B), (C), or (7) of section 8(b) of the act, or section 8(e) of the act, the regional office in which such charge is filed or to which it is referred shall give it priority over all other cases in the office except cases of like character and cases under paragraph (4)(D) of section 8(b) of the act in which it is deemed appropriate to seek injunctive relief of a district court pursuant to section 10(l) of the act.

(b) Whenever a charge is filed alleging the commission of an unfair labor practice within the meaning of subsection (a)(3) or (b)(2) of section 8 of the act, the regional office in which such charge is filed or to which it is referred shall give it priority over all other cases in the office except cases of like character and cases under section 10(l) of the act.

§102.96 Issuance of complaint promptly.

Whenever the regional attorney or other Board officer to whom the matter may be referred seeks injunctive relief of a district court pursuant to section 10(l) of the act, a complaint against the party or parties sought to be enjoined, covering the same subject matter as such application for injunctive relief, shall be issued promptly, normally within 5 days of the date upon which such injunctive relief is first sought, except in those cases under section 10(l) of the act in which the procedure set forth in §§102.90 to 102.92, inclusive, is deemed applicable.

§102.97 Expeditious processing of section 10(l) and (m) cases in successive stages.

(a) Any complaint issued pursuant to §102.95(a) or, in a case in which it is deemed appropriate to seek injunctive relief of a district court pursuant to section 10(l) of the act, any complaint issued pursuant to §102.93 or notice of hearing issued pursuant to §102.90 shall be heard expeditiously and the case shall be given priority in such successive steps following its issuance (until ultimate enforcement or dismissal by the appropriate circuit court of appeals) over all cases except cases of like character.

(b) Any complaint issued pursuant to §102.95(b) shall be heard expeditiously and the case shall be given priority in its successive steps following its issuance (until ultimate enforcement or dismissal by the appropriate circuit court of appeals) over all cases except cases of like character and cases under section 10(l) of the act.

Subpart H—Declaratory Orders and Advisory Opinions Regarding Board Jurisdiction

§102.98 Petition for advisory opinion; who may file; where to file.

(a) Whenever a party to a proceeding before any agency or court of any State or Territory is in doubt whether the Board would assert jurisdiction on the basis of its current jurisdictional standards, he may file a petition with the Board for an advisory opinion on whether it would assert jurisdiction on the basis of its current standards.

(b) Whenever an agency or court of any State or Territory is in doubt whether the Board would assert jurisdiction over the parties in a proceeding pending before such agency or court, the agency or court may file a petition with the Board for an advisory opinion on whether the Board would decline to assert jurisdiction over the parties before the agency or the court (1) on the basis of its current standards, or (2) because the employing enterprise is not within the jurisdiction of the National Labor Relations Act.

§102.99 Contents of petition for an advisory opinion; contents of request for administrative advice.

(a) A petition for an advisory opinion, when filed by a party to a proceeding before an agency or court of a State or Territory, shall allege the following:

(1) The name of the petitioner.

(2) The names of all other parties to the proceeding.

(3) The name of the agency or court.

(4) The docket number and nature of the proceeding.

(5) The general nature of the business involved in the proceeding.

(6) The commerce data relating to the operations of such business.

(7) Whether the commerce data described in this section are admitted or denied by other parties to the proceeding.

(8) The findings, if any, of the agency or court respecting the commerce data described in this section.

(9) Whether a representation or unfair labor practice proceeding involving the same labor dispute is pending before the Board and, if so, the case number thereof. Petitions under this subsection shall be in writing and signed, and either shall be sworn to before a notary public, Board agent, or other person duly authorized by law to administer oaths and take acknowledgments or shall contain a declaration by the person signing it, under the penalties of the Criminal Code, that its contents are true and correct to the best of his knowledge and belief.

(b) A petition for an advisory opinion, when filed by an agency or court of a State or Territory, shall allege the following:

(1) The name of the agency or court.

(2) The names of the parties to the proceeding and the docket number.

(3) The nature of the proceeding and the need for the Board's opinion on the jurisdictional issue to the proceeding.

(4) The general nature of the business involved in the proceeding and, where appropriate, the nature of and details concerning the employing enterprise.

(5) The findings of the agency or court or, in the absence of findings, a statement of the evidence relating to the commerce operations of such business and, where appropriate, to the nature of the employing enterprise.

(c) Eight copies of such petition or request shall be submitted to the Board in Washington, D.C. Such petition shall be printed or otherwise legibly duplicated. Carbon copies of typewritten matter will not be accepted.

§102.100 Notice of petition; service of petition.

Upon the filing of a petition, the petitioner shall immediately serve in the manner provided by §102.114(a) of these rules a copy of the petition upon all parties to the proceeding and upon the director of the Board's regional office having jurisdiction over the territorial area in which such agency or court is located. A statement of service shall be filed with the petition as provided by §102.114(b) of these rules.

§102.101 Response to petition; service of response.

Any party served with such petition may, within 14 days after service thereof, respond to the petition, admitting or denying its allegations. Eight copies of such response shall be filed with the Board in Washington, D.C. Such response shall be printed or otherwise legibly duplicated: *Provided, however,* That carbon copies of typewritten materials will not be accepted. Such response shall immediately be served on all other parties to the proceeding, and a statement of service shall be filed in accordance with the provisions of §102.114(b) of these rules.

§102.102 Intervention.

Any person desiring to intervene shall make a motion for intervention, stating the grounds upon which such person claims to have an interest in the petition. Eight copies of such motion shall be filed with the Board in Washington, D.C. Such motion shall be printed or otherwise legibly duplicated: *Provided, however*, That carbon copies of typewritten matter shall not be filed and if submitted will not be accepted.

§102.103 Proceedings before the Board; briefs; advisory opinions.

The Board shall thereupon proceed, upon the petition, responses, and submission of briefs, to determine whether, on the facts before it, the commerce operations of the employer involved are such that it would or would not assert jurisdiction. Such determination shall be in the form of an advisory opinion and shall be served upon the parties. No briefs shall be filed except upon special permission of the Board.

§102.104 Withdrawal of petition.

The petitioner may withdraw his petition at any time prior to issuance of the Board's advisory opinion.

§102.105 Petitions for declaratory orders; who may file; where to file; withdrawal.

Whenever both an unfair labor practice charge and a representation case relating to the same employer are contemporaneously on file in a regional office of the Board, and the general counsel entertains doubt whether the Board would assert jurisdiction over the employer involved, he may file a petition with the Board for a declaratory order disposing of the jurisdictional issue in the cases. Such petition may be withdrawn at any time prior to the issuance of the Board's order.

§102.106 Contents of petition for declaratory order.

A petition for a declaratory order shall allege the following:
(a) The name of the employer.
(b) The general nature of the employer's business.
(c) The case numbers of the unfair labor practice and representation cases.
(d) The commerce data relating to the operations of such business.
(e) Whether any proceeding involving the same subject matter is pending before an agency or court of a State or Territory. Eight copies of the petition shall be filed with the Board in Washington, D.C. Such petition

shall be printed or otherwise legibly duplicated: *Provided, however,* That carbon copies of typewritten matter shall not be filed and if submitted will not be accepted.

Eight copies of the petition shall be filed with the Board in Washington, D.C. Such petition shall be printed or otherwise legibly duplicated: *Provided, however,* That carbon copies of typewritten matter shall not be filed and if submitted will not be accepted.

§102.107 Notice of petition; service of petition.

Upon filing a petition, the general counsel shall immediately serve a copy thereof upon all parties and shall file a statement of service as provided by §102.114(b) of these rules.

§102.108 Response to petition; service of response.

Any party to the representation or unfair labor practice case may, within 14 days after service thereof, respond to the petition, admitting or denying its allegations. Eight copies of such response shall be filed with the Board in Washington, D.C. Such response shall be printed or otherwise legibly duplicated: *Provided, however,* That carbon copies of typewritten materials will not be accepted. Such response shall be served on the general counsel and all other parties, and a statement of service shall be filed as provided by §102.114(b) of these rules.

§102.109 Intervention.

Any person desiring to intervene shall make a motion for intervention, stating the grounds upon which such person claims to have an interest in the petition. Eight copies of such motion shall be filed with the Board in Washington, D.C. Such motion shall be printed or otherwise legibly duplicated: *Provided, however,* That carbon copies of typewritten matter shall not be filed and if submitted will not be accepted.

§102.110 Proceedings before the Board; briefs; declaratory orders.

The Board shall thereupon proceed, upon the petition, responses, and submission of briefs, to determine whether, on the facts before it, the commerce operations of the employer involved are such that it would or would not assert jurisdiction over them. Such determination shall be made by a declaratory order, with like effect as in the case of other orders of the Board, and shall be served upon the parties. Any party desiring to file a brief shall file eight copies with the Board in Washington, D.C., with a statement that copies thereof are being served simultaneously on the other parties.

Subpart I—Service and Filing of Papers

§102.111 Time computation.

(a) In computing any period of time prescribed or allowed by these rules, the day of the act, event, or default after which the designated period of time begins to run, is not to be included. The last day of the period so computed is to be included, unless it is a Sunday or a legal holiday, in which event the period runs until the end of the next agency business day. When the period of time prescribed or allowed is less than 7 days, intermediate Sundays and holidays shall be excluded in the computation.

(b) When the act or any of these rules require the filing of a motion, brief, exception, or other paper in any proceeding, such document must be received by the Board or the officer or agent designated to receive such matter before the close of business of the last day of the time limit, if any, for such filing or extension of time that may have been granted. In construing this section of the rules, the Board will accept as timely filed any document which is hand delivered to the Board on or before the due date or postmarked on the day before (or earlier than) the due date; documents which are postmarked on or after the due date are untimely: *Provided, however,* the following documents must be received on or before the close of business of the last day for filing:

(1) Charges filed pursuant to section 10(b) of the act (see also §102.14).

(2) Applications for awards and fees and other expenses under the Equal Access to Justice Act.

(3) Objections to elections and revised tallies.

(4) Petitions to revoke subpoenas.

(5) Petitions filed pursuant to section 9(c) of the act.

§102.112 Date of service; filing of proof of service.

The date of service shall be the day when the matter served is deposited in the United States mail or is delivered in person, as the case may be. The date of filing shall be the day when the matter is required to be received by the Board as provided by §102.111.

§102.113 Methods of service of process and papers by the Board; proof of service.

(a) Charges, complaints and accompanying notices of hearing, final orders, administrative law judges' decisions, subpoenas, and other process and papers of the Board, its member, agent, or agency, may be served personally or by registered or certified mail or by telegraph or by leaving a copy thereof at the principal office or place of business of the person required to be served. The verified return by the individual so serving the same, setting forth the manner of such service, shall be proof of the same, and the return post office receipt or telegraph receipt therefor when registered or certified and mailed or when telegraphed as aforesaid shall be proof of service of the same.

(b) Whenever these rules require or permit the service of pleadings or other papers upon a party, a copy shall also be served on any attorney or other representative of the party who has entered a written appearance in the proceeding on behalf of the party. If a party is represented by more than one attorney or representative, service upon any one of such persons in addition to the party shall satisfy this requirement.

§102.114 Service of papers by parties; proof of service.

(a) Service of papers by a party on other parties shall be made by registered mail, or by certified mail, or in any manner provided for the service of papers in a civil action by the law of the State in which the hearing is pending. Except for charges, petitions, exceptions, briefs, and other papers for which a time for both filing and response has been otherwise established, service on all parties shall be made in the same manner as that utilized in filing the paper with the Board, or in a more expeditious manner; however, when filing with the Board is accomplished by personal service the other parties shall be promptly notified of such action by telephone, followed by service of a copy by mail or telegraph. When service is made by registered mail, or by certified mail, the return post office receipt shall be proof of service. When service is made in any manner provided by the law of a State, proof of service shall be made in accordance with such law. Failure to comply with the requirements of this section relating to timeliness of service on other parties shall be a basis for either (a) a rejection of the document or (b) withholding or reconsidering any ruling on the subject matter raised by the document until after service has been made and the served party has had reasonable opportunity to respond.

(b) The person or party serving the papers or process on other parties in conformance with §§102.113 and 102.114(a) shall submit a written statement of service thereof to the Board stating the names of the parties served and the date and manner of service. Proof of service as defined in §102.114(a) shall be required by the Board only if subsequent to the receipt of the statement of service a question is raised with respect to proper service. Failure to make proof of service does not affect the validity of the service.

Subpart J—Certification and Signature of Documents

§102.115 Certification of papers and documents.

The executive secretary of the Board or, in the event of his absence or disability, whosoever may be designated by the Board in his place and stead shall certify copies of all papers and documents which are a part of any of the files or records of the Board as may be necessary or desirable from time to time.

§102.116 Signature of orders.

The executive secretary or the associate executive secretary or, in the event of their absence or disability, whosoever may be designated by the Board in their place and stead is hereby authorized to sign all orders of the Board.

Subpart K—Records and Information

§102.117 Board materials and formal documents available for public inspection and copying; requests for described records; time limit for response; appeal from denial of request; fees for document search and duplication; files and records not subject to inspection.

(a)(1) The following materials are available to the public for inspection and copying during normal business hours: (i) All final opinions and orders made in the adjudication of cases; (ii) administrative staff manuals and instructions that affect any member of the public (excepting those establishing internal operating rules, guidelines, and procedures for the investigation, trial, and settlement of cases); (iii) a record of the final votes of each member of the Board in every agency proceeding; and (iv) a current index of final opinions and orders made in the adjudication of cases. Paragraphs (a)(1)(i) through (iv) of this section are available for inspection and copying during normal business hours at the Board's offices in Washington, D.C. Paragraphs (a)(1)(ii) and (iv) of this section are also available for inspection and copying during normal business hours at each regional, subregional, and resident office of the Board. Final opinions and orders made by regional directors in the adjudication of representation cases pursuant to the delegation of authority from the Board under section 3(b) of the act are available to the public for inspection and copying in the original office where issued.

(2) Copies of forms prescribed by the Board for the filing of charges under section 10 or petitions under section 9 may be obtained without charge from any regional, subregional, or resident office of the Board.

(b)(1) The formal documents constituting the record in a case or proceeding are matters of official record and, until destroyed pursuant to applicable statutory authority, are available to the public for inspection and copying during normal business hours, at the appropriate regional office of the Board or at the Board's office in Washington, D.C., as the case may be.

(2) The executive secretary shall certify copies of the formal documents upon request made a reasonable time in advance of need and payment of lawfully prescribed costs.

(c)(1) Requests for the inspection and copying of records other than those specified in paragraphs (a) and (b) of this section must be in writing and must reasonably describe the record in a manner to permit its identification and location. The envelope and the letter should be clearly marked to indicate that it contains a request for records under the Freedom of Information Act (FOIA). The request must contain a specific statement assuming financial liability in accordance with paragraph (c)(2)(iv) of this section, for the direct costs of the search for the requested records and their duplication. If the request is for records in a regional or subregional office of the agency, it should be made to that regional or subregional office; if for records in the office of the general counsel and located in Washington, D.C., it should be made to the Freedom of Information officer, office of the general counsel, Washington, D.C.; and if for records in the offices of the Board in Washington, D.C., to the executive secretary of the Board, Washington, D.C.

Requests made to other than the appropriate office will be forwarded to that office by the receiving office, but in that event the applicable time limit for response set forth in paragraph (c)(2) of this section shall be calculated from the date of receipt by the appropriate office.

(2)(i) Within 10 working days after receipt of a request by the appropriate office of the agency a determination shall be made whether to comply with such request, and the person making the request shall be notified in writing of that determination. If the determination is to comply with the request, the records shall be made promptly available to the person making the request, upon payment of any charges due in accordance with the provisions of paragraph (c)(2)(iv) of this section. If the determination is to deny the request, the notification shall set forth the reasons therefor and the name and title or position of each person responsible for the denial, and shall notify the person making the request of the right to appeal the adverse determination under the provisions of paragraph (c)(2)(ii) of this section.

(ii) An appeal from an adverse determination made pursuant to paragraph (c)(2)(i) of this section must be filed within 20 working days of the receipt by the person of the notification of the adverse determination where the request is denied in its entirety; or, in the case of a partial denial, within 20 working days of the receipt of any records being made available pursuant to the request. If the adverse determination was made in a regional office, a subregional office, or by the Freedom of Information officer, office of the general counsel, the appeal shall be filed with the general counsel in Washington, D.C. If the adverse determination was made by the executive secretary of the Board, the appeal shall be filed with the chairman of the Board in Washington, D.C. Within 20 working days after the receipt of an appeal the chairman of the Board or the general counsel, as the case may be, shall make a determination with respect to such appeal and shall notify the person in writing. If the determination is to comply with the request, the records shall be made promptly available to the person making the request, upon receipt of payment of any charges due in accordance with the provisions of paragraph (c)(2)(iv) of this section. If on appeal the denial of the request for records is upheld in whole or in part, the person making the request shall be notified of the reasons for the determination, the name and title or position of each person responsible for the denial, and the provisions for judicial review of that determination under the provisions of 5 U.S.C. section 552(4)(B). Even though no appeal is filed from a denial in whole or in part of a request for records by the person making the request, the chairman of the Board or the general counsel may, without regard to the time limit for filing of an appeal, sua sponte initiate consideration of an adverse determination under this appeal procedure by written notification to the person making the request. In such event the time limit for making the determination shall commence with the issuance of such notification.

(iii) In unusual circumstances as specified in this subparagraph, the time limits prescribed in either paragraph (c)(2)(i) or (ii) of this section may be extended by written notice to the person requesting the record setting forth the reasons for such extension and the date on which a determination is expected to be dispatched. No such notice or notices shall specify a date or dates that would result in an extension or extensions totaling more than 10 working days with respect to a particular request. As used in this subparagraph, "unusual circumstances" means, but only to the extent reasonably necessary to the proper processing of the particular request:

(a) The need to search for and collect the requested records from field facilities or other establishments that are separate from the office processing the request;

(b) The need to search for, collect, and appropriately examine a voluminous amount of separate and distinct records which are demanded in a single request;

(c) The need for consultation, which shall be conducted with all practicable speed, with another agency having a substantial interest in the determination of the request or among two or more components of the agency having substantial subject-matter interest therein.

(iv) Persons requesting records from this agency shall be subject to a charge of fees for the direct cost of document search and duplication in accordance with the following schedules, procedures, and conditions:

(a) Schedule of charges:

(1) For each one-quarter hour or portion thereof of clerical time $2.50

(2) For each one-quarter hour or portion thereof of professional time..   6.60

(3) For each sheet of duplication (not to exceed 8½ × 14 inches) of requested records 0.10

(4) All other direct costs of search or duplication shall be charged to the requester in the same amount as incurred by the agency.

(b) Each request for records shall contain a specific statement assuming financial liability, in full or to a specified maximum amount, for charges, in accordance with subparagraph (a) which may be incurred by the agency in responding to the request. If the anticipated charges exceed the maximum limit stated by the person making the request or if the request contains no assumption of financial liability for charges, the person shall be notified and afforded an opportunity to assume financial liability. The request for records shall not be deemed received for purposes of the applicable time limit for response until a written assumption of financial liability is received. When the anticipated charges exceed $50, the person making the request, upon notification, shall deposit 50 percent of the anticipated charges with the agency. The request shall not be deemed received for purposes of the applicable time limit for response until such deposit has been made.

(c) Charges may be imposed even though the search discloses no records responsive to the request, or none not exempt from disclosure. The imposition of charges may be waived for the convenience of the agency, and will be reduced or waived when the agency determines that furnishing the information can be considered as primarily benefiting the general public. The agency may, by agreement with the person making the request, make arrangements with commercial firms for required services to be charged directly to the requester.

(v) "Working days," as used in this subsection, means calendar days excepting Saturdays, Sundays, and legal holidays.

(d) Subject to the provisions of §§102.31(c) and 102.66(c), all files, documents, reports, memoranda, and records of the agency, falling within the exemptions specified in 5 U.S.C. section 552(b), shall not be made available for inspection or copying, unless specifically permitted by the Board, its chairman, or its general counsel.

(e) An individual will be informed whether a system of records maintained by this agency contains a record pertaining to such individual. An inquiry should be made in writing or in person during normal business hours to the official of this agency designated for that purpose and at the address set forth in a notice of a system of records published by this agency, in a Notice of Systems of Government-wide Personnel Records published by the Civil Service Commission, or in a Notice of Government-wide System of Records published by the Department of Labor. Copies of such notices, and assistance in preparing an inquiry, may be obtained from any regional office of the Board or at the Board offices at 1717 Pennsylvania Avenue, N.W., Washington, D.C. 20570. The inquiry should contain sufficient information, as defined in the notice, to identify the record. Reasonable verification of identity of the inquirer, as described in paragraph (i) of this section, will be required to assure that information is disclosed to the proper person. The agency shall acknowledge the inquiry in writing within 10 days (excluding Saturdays, Sundays, and legal public holidays) and, wherever practicable, the acknowledgment shall supply the information requested. If, for good cause shown, the agency cannot supply the information within 10 days, the inquirer shall within that time period be notified in writing of the reasons therefor and when it is anticipated the information will be supplied. An acknowledgment will not be provided where the information is supplied within the 10 day period. If the agency refuses to inform an individual whether a system of records contains a record pertaining to an individual, the inquirer shall be notified in writing of that determination and the reasons therefor, and of the right to obtain review of that determination under the provisions of paragraph (i) of this section.

(f) An individual will be permitted access to records pertaining to such individual contained in any system of records described in the notices of systems of records published by this agency, or access to the accounting of disclosures from such records. The request for access must be made in writing or in person during normal business hours, to the person designated for that purpose and at the address set forth in the published notice of systems of records. Copies of such notices, and assistance in preparing a request for access, may be obtained from any regional office of the Board or at the Board offices at 1717 Pennsylvania Avenue N.W., Washington, D.C. 20570. Reasonable verification of the identity of the requester, as described in subsection (i) of this section, shall be required to assure that records are disclosed to the proper person. A request for access to records or the accounting of disclosures from such records shall be acknowledged in writing by the agency within 10 days of receipt (excluding Saturdays, Sundays, and legal public holidays) and, wherever practicable, the acknowledgment shall inform the requester whether or not access will be granted and, if so, the time and location at which the records or accounting will be made available. If access to the record or accounting is to be granted, the record or accounting will normally be provided within 30 days (excluding Saturdays, Sundays, and legal public holidays) of the request, unless for good cause shown the agency is unable to do so, in which case the individual will be informed in writing within that 30-day period of the reasons therefor and when it is anticipated that access will be granted. An acknowledgment of a request will not be provided if the record is made available within the 10-day period. If an individual's request for access to a record or an accounting of disclosures from such a record under the provisions of this subsection is denied, the notice informing the individual of the denial shall set forth the reasons therefor and advise the individual of the right to obtain a review of that determination under the provisions of paragraph (j) of this section.

(g) An individual granted access to records pertaining to such individual contained in a system of records may review all such records. For that purpose the individual may be accompanied by a person of the individual's choosing, or the record may be released to the individual's representative who has the written consent of the individual, as described in paragraph (i) of this section. A first copy of any such record or information will ordinarily be provided without charge to the individual or representative in a form comprehensible to the individual. Fees for any other copies of requested records shall be assessed at the rate of $0.10 for each sheet of duplication.

(h) An individual may request amendment of a record pertaining to such individual in a system of records maintained by this agency. A request for amendment of a record must be in writing and submitted during normal business hours to the person designated for that purpose and at the address set forth in the published notice for the system of records containing the record of which amendment is sought. Copies of such notices, and assistance in preparing a request for amendment, may be obtained from any regional office of the Board or at the Board offices at 1717 Pennsylvania Avenue, N.W., Washington, D.C. 20570. The requester must provide verification of identity as described in paragraph (i) of this section, and the request should set forth the specific amendment requested and the reason for the requested amendment. The agency shall acknowledge in writing receipt of the request within 10 days of its receipt (excluding Saturdays, Sundays, and legal public holidays) and, wherever practicable, the acknowledgment shall advise the individual of the determination of the request. If the review of the request for amendment cannot be completed and a determination made within 10 days, the review shall be completed as soon as possible, normally within 30 days (Saturdays, Sundays, and legal public holidays excluded) of receipt of the request unless unusual circumstances preclude completing the review within that time, in which event the requester will be notified in writing within that 30 day period of the reasons for the delay and when the determination of the request may be expected. If the determination is to amend the record, the requester shall be so notified in writing and the record shall be amended in accordance with that determination. If any disclosures accountable under the provisions of 5 U.S.C. section 552a(c) have been made, all previous recipients of the record which was amended shall be advised of the amendment and its substance. If it is determined that the request should not be granted, the requester shall be notified in writing of that determination and of the reasons therefor, and advised of the right to obtain review of the adverse determination under the provisions of paragraph (j) of this section.

(i) Verification of the identification of individuals required under paragraphs (e), (f), (g), and (h) of this section to assure that records are disclosed to the proper persons shall be required by the agency to an extent consistent with the nature, location, and sensitivity of the records being disclosed. Disclosure of a record to an individual in person will normally be made upon the presentation of acceptable identification. Disclosure of records by mail may be made upon the basis of the identifying information set forth in the request. Depending upon the nature, location, and sensitivity of the requested record, a signed notarized statement verifying identity may be required by the agency. Proof of authorization as representative to have access to a record of an individual shall be in writing, and a signed notarized statement of such authorization may be required by the agency if the record requested is of a sensitive nature.

(j)(1) Review may be obtained with respect to (i) a refusal, under subsection (e) or (k) of this section, to inform an individual if a system of records contains a record concerning that individual, (ii) a refusal, under subsection (f) or (k) of this section, to grant access to a record or an accounting of disclosures from such a record, or (iii) a refusal, under subsection (h) of this section, to amend a record. The request for review should be made to the chairman of the Board if the system of records is maintained in the offices of a member of the Board, the office of the executive secretary, the office of the solicitor, the division of information, or the division of administrative law judges. Consonant with the provisions of section 3(d) of the National Labor Relations Act, as amended, and the delegation of authority from the Board to the general counsel, the request should be made to the general counsel if the system of records is maintained by any office of the agency other than those enumerated above. Either the chairman of the Board or the general counsel may designate in writing another officer of the agency to review the refusal of the request. Such review shall be completed within 30 days (excluding Saturdays, Sundays, and legal public holidays) from the receipt of the request for review unless the chairman of the Board or the general counsel, as the case may be, for good cause shown, shall extend such 30 day period.

(2) If, upon review of a refusal under subsection (e) or (k) of this section, the reviewing officer determines that the individual should be informed of whether a system of records contains a record pertaining to that individual, such information shall be promptly provided. If the reviewing officer determines that the information was properly denied, the individual shall be so informed in writing with a brief statement of the reasons therefor.

(3) If, upon review of a refusal under subsection (f) or (k) of this section, the reviewing officer determines that access to a record or to an accounting of disclosures should be granted, the requester shall be so notified and the record or accounting shall be promptly made available to the requester. If the reviewing officer determines that the request for access was properly denied, the individual shall be so informed in writing with a brief statement of the reasons therefor, and of the right to judicial review of that determination under the provisions of 5 U.S.C. section 552a(g)(1)(B).

(4) If, upon review of a refusal under subsection (h), the reviewing official grants a request to amend, the requester shall be so notified, the record shall be amended in accordance with the determination, and, if any disclosures accountable under the provisions of 5 U.S.C. section 552a(c) have been made, all previous recipients of the record which was amended shall be advised of the amendment and its substance. If the reviewing officer determines that the denial of a request for amendment should be sustained, the agency shall advise the requester of the determination and the reasons therefor, and that the individual may file with the agency a concise statement of the reasons for disagreeing with the determination, and may seek judicial review of the agency's denial of the request to amend the record. In the event a statement of disagreement is filed, that statement (i) will be made available to anyone to whom the record is subsequently disclosed together with, at the discretion of the agency, a brief statement summarizing

the agency's reasons for declining to amend the record, and (ii) will be supplied, together with any agency statements, to any prior recipients of the disputed record to the extent that an accounting of disclosures was made.

(k) To the extent that portions of systems of records described in notices of government-wide systems of records published by the Civil Service Commission are identified by those notices as being subject to the management of an officer of this agency, or an officer of this agency is designated as the official to contact for information, access or contest of those records, individual requests for access to those records, requests for their amendment, and review of denials of requests for amendment shall be in accordance with the provisions of 5 CFR Part 297, Subpart A, §297.101, *et seq.*, as promulgated by the Civil Service Commission. To the extent that portions of systems of records described in notices of government-wide systems of records published by the Department of Labor are identified by those notices as being subject to the management of an officer of this agency, or an officer of this agency is designated as the official to contact for information, access or contest of those records, individual requests for access to those records, requests for their amendment, and review of denials of requests for amendment shall be in accordance with the provisions of 29 CFR Part 70a as promulgated by the Department of Labor. Review of a refusal to inform an individual whether such a system of records contains a record pertaining to that individual, and review of a refusal to grant an individual's request for access to a record in such a system may be obtained in accordance with the provisions of subsection (j) of this section.

§102.118 Board employees prohibited from producing files, records, etc., pursuant to subpoena ad testificandum or subpoena duces tecum; prohibited from testifying in regard thereto; production of witnesses' statements after direct testimony.

(a)(1) Except as provided in §102.117 respecting requests cognizable under the Freedom of Information Act, no regional director, field examiner, administrative law judge, attorney, specially designated agent, general counsel, member of the Board, or other officer or employee of the Board shall produce or present any files, documents, reports, memoranda, or records of the Board or of the general counsel, whether in response to a subpoena duces tecum or otherwise, without the written consent of the Board or the chairman of the Board if the document is in Washington, D.C., and in control of the Board; or of the general counsel if the document is in a regional office of the agency or is in Washington, D.C., and in the control of the general counsel. Nor shall any such person testify in behalf of any party to any cause pending in any court or before the Board, or any other board, commission, or other administrative agency of the United States, or of any State, Territory, or the District of Columbia, or any subdivisions thereof, with respect to any information, facts, or other matter coming to his knowledge in his official capacity or with respect to the contents of any files, documents, reports, memoranda, or records of the Board or the general counsel, whether in answer to a subpoena or otherwise, without the written consent of the Board or the chairman of the Board if the person is in Washington, D.C., and subject to the supervision or control of the Board; or of the general counsel if the person is in a regional office of the agency or is in Washington, D.C., and subject to the supervision or control of the general counsel.

(2) No regional director, field examiner, administrative law judge, attorney, specially designated agent, general counsel, member of the Board, or other officer or employee of the Board shall, by any means of communication to any person or to another agency, disclose personal information about an individual from a record in a system of records maintained by this agency, as more fully described in the notices of systems of records published by this agency in accordance with the provisions of section (e)(4) of the Privacy Act of 1974, 5 U.S.C., section 552a(e)(4), or by the Notices of Government-wide Systems of Personnel Records published by the Civil Service Commission in accordance with those statutory provisions, except pursuant to a written request by, or with the prior written consent of, the individual to whom the record pertains, unless disclosure of the record would be in accordance with the provisions of section (b)(1) through (11), both inclusive, of the Privacy Act of 1974, 5 U.S.C. section 552a(b)(1) through (11).

(b)(1) Notwithstanding the prohibitions of paragraph (a) of this section, after a witness called by the general counsel or by the charging party has testified in a hearing upon a complaint under section 10(c) of the act, the administrative law judge shall, upon motion of the respondent, order the production of any statement (as hereinafter defined) of such witness in the possession of the general counsel which relates to the subject matter as to which the witness has testified. If the entire contents of any such statement relate to the subject matter of the testimony of the witness, the administrative law judge shall order it to be delivered directly to the respondent for his examination and use for the purpose of cross-examination.

(2) If the general counsel claims that any statement ordered to be produced under this section contains matter which does not relate to the subject matter of the testimony of the witness, the administrative law judge shall order the general counsel to deliver such statement for the inspection of the administrative law judge *in camera*. Upon such delivery the administrative law judge shall excise the portions of such statement which do not relate to the subject matter of the testimony of the witness except that he may, in his discretion, decline to excise portions which, although not relating to the subject matter of the testimony of the witness, do relate to other matters raised by the pleadings. With such material excised the administrative law judge shall then direct delivery of such statement to the respondent for his use on cross-examination. If, pursuant to such procedure, any portion of such statement is withheld from the respondent and the respondent objects to such withholdings, the entire text of such statement shall be preserved by the general counsel, and, in the event the respondent files exceptions with the Board based upon such withholding, shall be made available to the Board for the purpose of determining the correctness of the ruling of the administrative law judge. If the general counsel elects not to comply with an order of the administrative law judge directing delivery to the respondent of any such statement, or such portion thereof as the administrative law judge may direct, the administrative law judge shall strike from the record the testimony of the witness.

(c) The provisions of subsection (b) of this section shall also apply after any witness has testified in any postelection hearing pursuant to §102.69(d) and any party has moved for the production of any statement (as hereinafter defined) of such witness in possession of any agent of the Board which relates to the subject matter as to which the witness has testified. The authority exercised by the administrative law judge under subsection (b) of this section shall be exercised by the hearing officer presiding.

(d) The term "statement" as used in subsections (b) and (c) of this section means: (1) A written statement made by said witness and signed or otherwise adopted or approved by him; or (2) a stenographic, mechanical, electrical, or other recording, or a transcription thereof, which is a substantially verbatim recital of an oral statement made by said witness to an agent of the party obligated to produce the statement and recorded contemporaneously with the making of such oral statement.

Subpart L—Practice Before the Board of Former Employees[1]

§102.119 Prohibition of practice before Board of its former regional employees in cases pending in region during employment.

No person who has been an employee of the Board and attached to any of its regional offices shall engage in practice before the Board or its agents in any respect or in any capacity in connection with any case or proceeding which was pending in any regional office to which he was attached during the time of his employment with the Board.

§102.120 Same; application to former employees of Washington staff.

No person who has been an employee of the Board and attached to the Washington staff shall engage in practice before the Board or its agents in any respect or in any capacity in connection with any case or proceeding pending before the Board or any regional offices during the time of his employment with the Board.

Subpart M—Construction of Rules

§102.121 Rules to be liberally construed.

The rules and regulations in this part shall be liberally construed to effectuate the purposes and provisions of the act.

Subpart N—Enforcement of Rights, Privileges, and Immunities Granted or Guaranteed Under Section 222(f), Communications Act of 1934, as Amended, to Employees of Merged Telegraph Carriers

§102.122 Enforcement.

All matters relating to the enforcement of rights, privileges, or immunities granted or guaranteed under section 222(f) of the Communications

---

[1]Attention is directed to Public Law 87-849 (76 Stat. 1119) which amends Chapter 11 of Title 18, United States Code, entitled "Bribery, Graft and Conflicts of Interest" and which provides for the imposition of criminal sanctions under certain circumstances.

Act of 1934, as amended, shall be governed by the provisions of subparts A, B, I, J, K, and M of the Rules and Regulations, insofar as applicable, except that reference in subpart B to "unfair labor practices" or "unfair labor practices affecting commerce" shall for the purposes of this article mean the denial of any rights, privileges, or immunities granted or guaranteed under section 222(f) of the Communications Act of 1934, as amended.

§102.123 Amendment or rescission of rules.

Any rule or regulation may be amended or rescinded by the Board at any time.

Subpart O—Amendments

§102.124 Petitions for issuance, amendment, or repeal of rules.

Any interested person may petition the Board, in writing, for the issuance, amendment, or repeal of a rule or regulation. An original and seven copies of such petition shall be filed with the Board in Washington, D.C., and shall state the rule or regulation proposed to be issued, amended, or repealed, together with a statement of grounds in support of such petition.

§102.125 Action on petition.

Upon the filing of such petition, the Board shall consider the same and may thereupon either grant or deny the petition in whole or in part, conduct an appropriate hearing thereon, or make other disposition of the petition. Should the petition be denied in whole or in part, prompt notice shall be given of the denial, accompanied by a simple statement of the grounds unless the denial is self-explanatory.

Subpart P—*Ex parte* Communications

§102.126 Unauthorized communications.

(a) No interested person outside this agency shall, in an on-the-record proceeding of the types defined in §102.128, make or knowingly cause to be made any prohibited *ex parte* communication to Board agents of the categories designated in that section relevant to the merits of the proceeding.

(b) No Board agent of the categories defined in §102.128, participating in a particular proceeding as defined in that section, shall (i) request any prohibited *ex parte* communications; or (ii) make or knowingly cause to be made any prohibited *ex parte* communications about the proceeding to any interested person outside this agency relevant to the merits of the proceeding.

§102.127 Definitions.

When used in this subpart:

(a) The term "person outside this agency," to whom the prohibitions apply, shall include any individual outside this agency, partnership, corporation, association, or other entity, or an agent thereof, and the general counsel or his representative when prosecuting an unfair labor practice proceeding before the Board pursuant to section 10(b) of the act.

(b) The term "*ex parte* communication" means an oral or written communication not on the public record with respect to which reasonable prior notice to all parties is not given, subject however, to the provisions of §§102.129 and 102.130.

§102.128 Types of on-the-record proceedings; categories of Board agents; and duration of prohibition.

Unless otherwise provided by specific order of the Board entered in the proceeding, the prohibition of §102.126 shall be applicable in the following types of on-the-record proceedings to unauthorized *ex parte* communications made to the designated categories of Board agents who participate in the decision, from the stage of the proceeding specified until the issues are finally resolved by the Board for the purposes of that proceeding under prevailing rules and practices:

(a) In a preelection proceeding pursuant to section 9(c)(1) or 9(e), or in a unit clarification or certification amendment proceeding pursuant to section 9(b) of the act, in which a formal hearing is held, communications to the regional director and members of his staff who review the record and prepare a draft of his decision, and members of the Board and their legal assistants, from the time the hearing is opened.

(b) In a postelection proceeding pursuant to section 9(c)(1) or 9(e) of the act, in which a formal hearing is held, communications to the hearing officer, the regional director and members of his staff who review the record and prepare a draft of his report or decision, and members of the Board and their legal assistants, from the time the hearing is opened.

(c) In a postelection proceeding pursuant to section (c)(1) or 9(e), or in a unit clarification or certification amendment proceeding pursuant to section 9(b), of the act, in which no formal hearing is held, communications to members of the Board and their legal assistants, from the time the regional director's report or decision is issued.

(d) In a proceeding pursuant to section 10(k) of the act, communications to members of the Board and their legal assistants, from the time the hearing is opened.

(e) In an unfair labor practice proceeding pursuant to section 10(b) of the act, communications to the administrative law judge assigned to hear the case or to make rulings upon any motions or issues therein and members of the Board and their legal assistants, from the time the complaint and/or notice of hearing is issued, or the time the communicator has knowledge that a complaint or notice of hearing will be issued, whichever occurs first.

(f) In any other proceeding to which the Board by specific order makes the prohibition applicable, to the categories of personnel and from the stage of the proceeding specified in the order.

§102.129 Communications prohibited.

Except as provided in §102.130, *ex parte* communications prohibited by section 102.126 shall include:

(a) Such communications, when written, if copies thereof are not contemporaneously served by the communicator on all parties to the proceeding in accordance with the provisions of §102.114(a).

(b) Such communications, when oral, unless advance notice thereof is given by the communicator to all parties in the proceeding and adequate opportunity afforded to them to be present.

§102.130 Communications not prohibited.

Ex parte communications prohibited by §102.126 shall not include:

(a) Oral or written communications which relate soley to matters which the hearing officer, regional director, administrative law judge, or member of the Board is authorized by law or Board rules to entertain or dispose of on an *ex parte* basis.

(b) Oral or written requests for information solely with respect to the status of a proceeding.

(c) Oral or written communications which all the parties to the proceeding agree, or which the responsible official formally rules, may be made on an *ex parte* basis.

(d) Oral or written communications proposing settlement or an agreement for disposition of any or all issues in the proceeding.

(e) Oral or written communications which concern matters of general significance to the field of labor-management relations or administrative practice and which are not specifically related to pending on-the-record proceedings.

(f) Oral or written communications from the general counsel to the Board when the general counsel is acting as counsel for the Board.

§102.131 Solicitation of prohibited communications.

No person shall knowingly and willfully solicit the making of an unauthorized *ex parte* communication by any other person.

§102.132 Reporting of prohibited communications; penalties.

(a) Any Board agent of the categories defined in §102.128 to whom a prohibited oral *ex parte* communication is attempted to be made shall refuse to listen to the communication, inform the communicator of this rule, and advise him that if he has anything to say it should be said in writing with copies to all parties. Any such board agent who receives, or who makes or knowingly causes to be made, an unauthorized *ex parte* communication shall place or cause to be placed on public record of the proceeding (1) the communication, if it was written, (2) a memorandum stating the substance of the communication, if it was oral, (3) all written responses to the prohibited communication, and (4) memoranda stating the substance of all oral responses to the prohibited communication.

(b) The executive secretary, if the proceeding is then pending before the Board, the administrative law judge, if the proceeding is then pending before any such judge, or the regional director, if the proceeding is then pending before a hearing officer or the regional director, shall serve copies of all such materials placed on the public record of the proceeding on all other parties to the proceeding and on the attorneys of record for the parties. Within 14 days after the mailing of such copies, any party may file with the executive secretary, administrative law judge, or regional director serving the communication, and serve on all other parties, a statement setting forth facts or contentions to rebut those contained in the prohibited communication. All such responses shall be placed in the public record of the proceeding, and provision may be made for any further action, including reopening of the record, which may be required under the circumstances. No action taken pursuant to this provision shall constitute a waiver of the power of the Board to impose an appropriate penalty under §102.133.

§102.133 Penalties and enforcement

(a) Where the nature and circumstances of a prohibited communication made by or caused to be made by a party to the proceeding are such that the interests of justice and statutory policy may require remedial action, the Board, administrative law judge, or regional director, as the case may be, may issue to the party making the communication a notice to show cause, returnable before the Board within a stated period not less than 7 days from the date thereof, why the Board should not determine that the interests of justice and statutory policy require that the claim or interest in the proceeding of a party who knowingly makes a prohibited communication or knowingly causes a prohibited communication to be made, should be dismissed, denied, disregarded or otherwise adversely affected on account of such violation.

(b) Upon notice and hearing, the Board may censure, suspend, or revoke the privilege of practice before the agency of any person who knowingly and willfully makes or solicits the making of a prohibited *ex parte* communication. However, before the Board institutes formal proceedings under this subsection, it shall first advise the person or persons concerned in writing that it proposes to take such action and that they may show cause, within a period to be stated in such written advice, but not less than 7 days from the date thereof, why it should be take such action.

(c) The Board may censure, or, to the extent permitted by law, suspend, dismiss, or institute proceedings for the dismissal of, any Board agent who knowingly and willfully violates the prohibitions and requirements of this rule.

Subpart Q—Procedure Governing Matters Affecting Employment-Management Agreements Under the Postal Reorganization Act

§102.135 Employment-management agreements.

(a) *Employment-management agreements.* All matters within the jurisdiction of the National Labor Relations Board pursuant to the Postal Reorganization Act (chapter 12 of title 39, United States Code, as revised) shall be governed by the provisions of subparts A, B, C, D, F, G, I, J, K, L, M, O, and P of the rules and regulations insofar as applicable.

(b) *Inconsistencies.* To the extent that any provision of this subpart Q is inconsistent with any provision of title 39, United States Code, the provision of said title 39 shall govern.

(c) *Exceptions.* For the purposes of this subpart, references in the subparts of the Rules and Regulations cited above to (1) "employer" shall be deemed to include the Postal Service, (2) "act" shall in the appropriate context mean "Postal Reorganization Act," (3) "section 9(c) of the act" and cited paragraphs thereof shall mean "39 U.S.C. §§1203(c) and 1204," and (4) "section 9(b) of the act" shall mean "39 U.S.C. §1202."

Subpart R—Advisory Committees

§102.136 Establishment and utilization of advisory committees.

Advisory committees may from time to time be established or utilized by the agency in the interest of obtaining advice or recommendations on issues of concern to the agency. The establishment, utilization, and functioning of such committees shall be in accordance with the provisions of the Federal Advisory Committee Act, 5 U.S.C. app. 1, sections 1–15, and Office of Management and Budget Circular A-63 (rev. March 27, 1975), Advisory Committee Management Guidance, 39 F.R. 12389–12391, to the extent applicable.

Subpart S—Open Meetings

§102.137 Public observation of Board meetings.

Every portion of every meeting of the Board shall be open to public observation, except as provided in §102.139 of these rules, and Board members shall not jointly conduct or dispose of agency business other than in accordance with the provisions of this subpart.

§102.138 Definition of meeting.

For purposes of this subpart, "meeting" shall mean the deliberations of at least three members of the full Board, or the deliberations of at least two members of any group of three Board members to whom the Board has delegated powers which it may itself exercise, where such deliberations determine or result in the joint conduct or disposition of official agency business, but does not include deliberations to determine whether a meeting should be closed to public observation in accordance with the provisions of this subpart.

§102.139 Closing of meetings; reasons therefor.

(a) Except where the Board determines that the public interest requires otherwise, meetings, or portions thereof, shall not be open to public observation where the deliberations concern the issuance of a subpoena, the Board's participation in a civil action or proceeding or an arbitration, or the initiation, conduct or disposition by the Board of particular representation or unfair labor practice proceedings under sections 8, 9, or 10 of the act, or any court proceedings collateral or ancillary thereto.

(b) Meetings, or portions thereof, may also be closed by the Board, except where it determines that the public interest requires otherwise, when the deliberations concern matters or information falling within the reasons for closing meetings specified in 5 U.S.C. section 552b(c)(1) (secret matters concerning national defense or foreign policy); (c)(2) (internal personnel rules and practices); (c)(3) (matters specifically exempted from disclosure by statute); (c)(4) (privileged or confidential trade secrets and commercial or financial information); (c)(5) (matters of alleged criminal conduct or formal censure); (c)(6) (personal information where disclosure would cause a clearly unwarranted invasion of personal privacy); (c)(7) (certain materials or information from investigatory files compiled for law enforcement purposes); or (c)(9)(B) (disclosure would significantly frustrate implementation of a proposed agency action).

§102.140 Action necessary to close meetings; record of votes.

A meeting shall be closed to public observation under §102.139, only when a majority of the members of the Board who will participate in the meeting vote to take such action.

(a) When the meeting deliberations concern matters specified in §102.139(a), the Board members shall vote at the beginning of the meeting, or portion thereof, on whether to close such meeting, or portion thereof, to public observation, and on whether the public interest requires that a meeting which may properly be closed should nevertheless be open to public observation. A record of such vote, reflecting the vote of each member of the Board, shall be kept and made available to the public at the earliest practicable time.

(b) When the meeting deliberations concern matters specified in §102.139(b), the Board shall vote on whether to close such meeting, or portion thereof, to public observation, and on whether there is a public interest which requires that a meeting which may properly be closed should nevertheless be open to public observation. The vote shall be taken at a time sufficient to permit inclusion of information concerning the open or closed status of the meeting in the public announcement thereof. A single vote may be taken with respect to a series of meetings at which the deliberations will concern the same particular matters where such subsequent meetings are scheduled to be held within thirty days after the initial meeting. A record of such vote, reflecting the vote of each member of the Board, shall be kept and made available to the public within one day after the vote is taken.

(c) Whenever any person whose interests may be directly affected by deliberations during a meeting, or a portion thereof, requests that the Board close that meeting, or portion thereof, to public observation for any of the reasons specified in 5 U.S.C. section 552b(c)(5) (matters of alleged criminal conduct or formal censure), (c)(6) (personal information where disclosure would cause a clearly unwarranted invasion of personal privacy), or (c)(7) (certain materials or information from investigatory files compiled for law enforcement purposes), the Board members participating in the meeting, upon request of any one of its members, shall vote on whether to close such meeting, or a portion thereof, for that reason. A record of such vote, reflecting the vote of each member of the Board participating in the meeting shall be kept and made available to the public within one day after the vote is taken.

(d) After public announcement of a meeting as provided in §102.141 of this part, a meeting, or portion thereof, announced as closed may be opened, or a meeting, or portion thereof, announced as open may be closed, only if a majority of the members of the Board who will participate in the meeting determine by a recorded vote that Board business so requires and that an earlier announcement of the change was not possible. The change made and the vote of each member on the change shall be announced publicly at the earliest practicable time.

(e) Before a meeting may be closed pursuant to §102.139, the solicitor of the Board shall certify that in his or her opinion the meeting may properly be closed to public observation. The certification shall set forth each applicable exemptive provision for such closing. Such certification shall be retained by the agency and made publicly available as soon as practicable.

§102.141 Notice of meetings; public announcement and publication.

(a) A public announcement setting forth the time, place and subject matter of meetings or portions thereof closed to public observation pursuant to the provisions of §102.139(a) of this part, shall be made at the earliest practicable time.

(b) Except for meetings closed to public observation pursuant to the provisions of §102.139(a) of this part, the agency shall make public announcement of each meeting to be held at least 7 days before the scheduled date of the meeting. The announcement shall specify the time, place and subject matter of the meeting, whether it is to be open to public observation or closed, and the name, address, and phone number of an agency official designated to respond to requests for information about the meeting. The 7 day period for advance notice may be shortened only upon a determination by a majority of the members of the Board who will participate in the meeting that agency business requires that such meeting be called at an earlier date, in which event the public announcements shall be made at the earliest practicable time. A record of the vote to schedule a meeting at an earlier date shall be kept and made available to the public.

(c) Within one day after a vote to close a meeting, or any portion thereof, pursuant to the provisions of §102.139(b) of this part, the agency shall make publicly available a full written explanation of its action closing the meeting, or portion thereof, together with a list of all persons expected to attend the meeting and their affiliation.

(d) If after public announcement required by paragraph (b) of this section has been made, the time and place of the meeting are changed, a public announcement shall be made at the earliest practicable time. The subject matter of the meeting may be changed after the public announcement only if a majority of the members of the Board who will participate in the meeting determine that agency business so requires and that no earlier announcement of the change was possible. When such a change in subject matter is approved a public announcement of the change shall be made at the earliest practicable time. A record of the vote to change the subject matter of the meeting shall be kept and made available to the public.

(e) All announcements or changes thereto issued pursuant to the provisions of paragraphs (b) and (d) of this section, or pursuant to the provisions of §102.140(d), shall be submitted for publication in the Federal Register immediately following their release to the public.

(f) Announcements of meetings made pursuant to the provisions of this section shall be made publicly available by the executive secretary.

§102.142 Transcripts, recordings or minutes of closed meetings; public availability; retention.

(a) For every meeting or portion thereof closed under the provisions of §102.139 of this part, the presiding officer shall prepare a statement setting forth the time and place of the meeting and the persons present, which statement shall be retained by the agency. For each such meeting or portion thereof there shall also be maintained a complete transcript or electronic recording of the proceedings, except that for meetings closed pursuant to §102.139(a) the Board may, in lieu of a transcript or electronic recording, maintain a set of minutes fully and accurately summarizing any action taken, the reasons thereof and views thereon, documents considered, and the members' vote on each roll call vote.

(b) The agency shall make promptly available to the public copies of transcripts, recordings or minutes maintained as provided in accordance with paragraph (a) of this section, except to the extent the items therein contain information which the agency determines may be withheld pursuant to the provisions of 5 U.S.C. section 552(c). Copies of transcripts or minutes, or transcriptions of electronic recordings including the identification of speakers, shall to the extent determined to be publicly available, be furnished to any person, subject to the payment of duplication costs in accordance with the schedule of fees set forth in §102.117(c)(2)(iv), and the actual cost of transcription.

(c) The agency shall maintain a complete verbatim copy of the transcript, a complete electronic recording, or a complete set of the minutes for each meeting or portion thereof closed to the public, for a period of at least one year after the close of the agency proceeding of which the meeting was a part, but in no event for a period of less than two years after such meeting.

Subpart T—Awards of Fees and Other Expenses

§102.143. "Adversary adjudication" defined; entitlement to award; eligibility for award.

(a) The term "adversary adjudication," as used in this subpart, means unfair labor practice proceedings pending before the Board on complaint, and backpay proceedings under §§102.52 to 102.59 of these rules pending before the Board on notice of hearing, at any time after October 1, 1984.

(b) A respondent in an adversary adjudication who prevails in that proceeding, or in a significant and discrete substantive portion of that proceeding, and who otherwise meets the eligibility requirements of this section, is eligible to apply for an award of fees and other expenses allowable under the provisions of §102.145 of these rules.

(c) Applicants eligible to receive an award are as follows:

(1) An individual with a net worth of not more than $2 million;

(2) The sole owner of an unincorporated business who has a net worth of not more than $7 million, including both personal and business interests, and not more than 500 employees;

(3) A charitable or other tax-exempt organization described in section 501(c)(3) of the Internal Revenue Code (26 U.S.C. §501(c)(3)) with not more than 500 employees;

(4) A cooperative association as defined in section 15(a) of the Agricultural Marketing Act (12 U.S.C. §1141j(a)) with not more than 500 employees; and

(5) Any other partnership, corporation, association, unit of local government, or public or private organization with a net worth of not more than $7 million and not more than 500 employees.

(d) For the purpose of eligibility, the net worth and number of employees of an applicant shall be determined as of the date of the complaint in an unfair labor practice proceeding or the date of the notice of hearing in a backpay proceeding.

(e) An applicant who owns an unincorporated business will be considered as an "individual" rather than a "sole owner of unincorporated business" if the issues on which the applicant prevails are related primarily to personal interests rather than to business interests.

(f) The employees of an applicant include all persons who regularly perform services for remuneration for the applicant, under the applicant's direction and control. Part-time employees shall be included on a proportional basis.

(g) The net worth and number of employees of the applicant and all of its affiliates shall be aggregated to determine eligibility. Any individual, corporation or other entity that directly or indirectly controls or owns a majority of the voting shares or other interest of the applicant, or any corporation or other entity of which the applicant directly or indirectly owns or controls a majority of the voting shares or other interest, will be considered an affiliate for purposes of this part, unless such treatment would be unjust and contrary to the purposes of the Equal Access to Justice Act (94 Stat. 2325) in light of the actual relationship between the affiliated entities. In addition financial relationships of the applicant other than those described in this paragraph may constitute special circumstances that would make an award unjust.

(h) An applicant that participates in an adversary adjudication primarily on behalf of one or more other persons or entities that would be ineligible is not itself eligible for an award.

§102.144 Standards for awards.

(a) An eligible applicant may receive an award for fees and expenses incurred in connection with an adversary adjudication or in connection with a significant and discrete substantive portion of that proceeding, unless the position of the General Counsel over which the applicant has prevailed was substantially justified. The burden of proof that an award should not be made to an eligible applicant is on the General Counsel, who may avoid an award by showing that the General Counsel's position in the proceeding was substantially justified.

(b) An award will be reduced or denied if the applicant has unduly or unreasonably protracted the adversary adjudication or if special circumstances make the award sought unjust.

§102.145 Allowable fees and expenses.

(a) Awards will be based on rates customarily charged by persons engaged in the business of acting as attorneys, agents and expert witnesses, even if the services were made available without charge or at a reduced rate to the applicant.

(b) No award for the attorney or agent fees under these rules may exceed $75.00 per hour. However, an award may also include the reasonable expenses of the attorney, agent, or witness as a separate item, if the attorney, agent or expert witness ordinarily charges clients separately for such expenses.

(c) In determining the reasonableness of the fee sought for an attorney, agent or expert witness, the following matters shall be considered:

(1) If the attorney, agent or expert witness is in practice, his or her customary fee for similar services, or, if an employee of the applicant, the fully allocated cost of the services;

(2) The prevailing rate for similar services in the community in which the attorney, agent or expert witness ordinarily performs services;

(3) The time actually spent in the representation of the applicant;

(4) The time reasonably spent in light of the difficulty or complexity of the issues in the adversary adjudicative proceeding; and

(d) The reasonable cost of any study, analysis, engineering report, test project or similar matter prepared on behalf of an applicant may be awarded, to the extent that the charge for the service does not exceed the prevailing rate for similar services, and the study or other matter was necessary for preparation of the applicant's case.

§102.146 Rulemaking on maximum rates for attorney or agent fees.

Any person may file with the Board a petition under §102.124 of these rules for rulemaking to increase the maximum rate for attorney or agent fees. The petition should specify the rate the petitioner believes should be established and explain fully why the higher rate is warranted by an increase in the cost of living or a special factor (such as the limited availability of qualified attorneys or agents for the proceedings involved).

§102.147 Contents of application; net worth exhibit; documentation of fees and expenses.

(a) An application for an award of fees and expenses under the Act shall identify the applicant and the adversary adjudication for which an award is sought. The application shall state the particulars in which the applicant has prevailed and identify the positions of the General Counsel in that proceeding that the applicant alleges were not substantially justified. Unless the applicant is an individual, the application shall also state the number, category and work location of employees of the applicant and its affiliates and describe briefly the type and purpose of its organization or business.

(b) The application shall include a statement that the applicant's net worth does not exceed $2 million (if an individual) or $7 million (for all other applicants, including their affiliates). However, an applicant may omit this statement if:

(1) It attaches a copy of a ruling by the Internal Revenue Service that it qualifies as an organization described in section 501(c)(3) of the Internal Revenue Code (26 U.S.C. §501(c)(3)) or, in the case of a tax-exempt organization not required to obtain a ruling from the Internal Revenue Service on its exempt status, a statement that describes the basis for the applicant's belief that it qualifies under such section; or

(2) It states that it is a cooperative association as defined in section 15(a) of the Agricultural Marketing Act (12 U.S.C. §1141j(a)).

(c) The application shall state the amount of fees and expenses for which an award is sought.

(d) The application may also include any other matters that the applicant wishes this Agency to consider in determining whether and in what amount an award should be made.

(e) The application shall be signed by the applicant or an authorized officer or attorney of the applicant. It shall also contain or be accompanied by a written verification under oath or under penalty of perjury that the information provided in the application is true.

(f) Each applicant, except a qualified tax-exempt organization or cooperative association, must provide with its application a detailed exhibit showing the net worth of the applicant and any affiliates (as defined in §102.143(g)) when the adversary adjudicative proceeding was initiated. The exhibit may be in any form convenient to the applicant that provides full disclosure of the applicant's and its affiliates' assets and liabilities and is sufficient to determine whether the applicant qualifies under the standards in this part. The administrative law judge may require an applicant to file such additional information as may be required to determine its eligibility for an award.

(g)(1) Unless otherwise directed by the administrative law judge, the net worth exhibit will be included in the public record of the fee application proceeding. An applicant that objects to public disclosure of information in any portion of the exhibit may submit that portion of the exhibit in a sealed envelope labeled "Confidential Financial Information," accompanied by a motion to withhold the information from public disclosure. The motion shall describe the information sought to be withheld and explain, in detail, why public disclosure of the information would adversely affect the applicant and why disclosure is not required in the public interest. The exhibit shall be served on the General Counsel but need not be served on any other party to the proceeding. If the administrative law judge finds that the information should not be withheld from disclosure, it shall be placed in the public record of the proceeding.

(2) If the administrative law judge grants the motion to withhold from public disclosure, the exhibit shall remain sealed, except to the extent that its contents are required to be disclosed at a hearing. The granting of the motion to withhold from public disclosure shall not be determinative of the availability of the document under the Freedom of Information Act in response to a request made under the provisions of §102.117. Notwithstanding that the exhibit may be withheld from public disclosure, the General Counsel

may disclose information from the exhibit to others if required in the course of an investigation to verify the claim of eligibility.

(h) The application shall be accompanied by full documentation of the fees and expenses for which an award is sought. A separate itemized statement shall be submitted for each professional firm or individual whose services are covered by the application, showing the dates and the hours spent in connection with the proceeding by each individual, a description of the specific services performed, the rate at which each fee has been computed, any expenses for which reimbursement is sought, the total amount claimed, and the total amount paid or payable by the applicant or by any other person or entity for the services provided. The administrative law judge may require the applicant to provide vouchers, receipts, or other substantiation for any expenses claimed.

§102.148 When an application may be filed; place of filing; service; referral to administrative law judge; stay of proceeding.

(a) An application may be filed after entry of the final order establishing that the applicant has prevailed in an adversary adjudication proceeding or in a significant and discrete substantive portion of that proceeding, but in no case later than 30 days after the entry of the Board's final order in that proceeding. The application for an award shall be filed in triplicate with the Board in Washington, D.C., together with a certificate of service. The application shall be served on the regional director and all parties to the adversary adjudication in the same manner as other pleadings in that proceeding, except as provided in §102.147(g)(1) for financial information alleged to be confidential.

(b) Upon filing, the application shall be referred by the Board to the administrative law judge who heard the adversary adjudication upon which the application is based, or, in the event that proceeding had not previously been heard by an administrative law judge, it shall be referred to the chief administrative law judge for designation of an administrative law judge, in accordance with §102.34, to consider the application. When the administrative law judge to whom the application has been referred is or becomes unavailable the provisions of §§102.34 and 102.36 shall be applicable.

(c) Proceedings for the award of fees, but not the time limit of this section for filing an application for an award, shall be stayed pending final disposition of the adversary adjudication in the event any person seeks reconsideration or review of the decision in that proceeding.

(d) For purposes of this section the withdrawal of a complaint by a regional director under §102.18 of these rules shall be treated as a final order, and an appeal under §102.19 of these rules shall be treated as a request for reconsideration of that final order.

§102.149 Filing of documents; service of documents; motions for extension of time.

(a) All motions and pleadings after the time the case is referred by the Board to the administrative law judge until the issuance of the judge's decision shall be filed with the administrative law judge in triplicate together with proof of service. Copies of all documents filed shall be served on all parties to the adversary adjudication.

(b) Motions for extensions of time to file motions, documents or pleading permitted by §102.150 or §102.152 shall be filed with the chief administrative law judge in Washington, D.C., the deputy chief administrative law judge in San Francisco, California, or the associate chief administrative law judge in New York, New York, or Atlanta, Georgia, as the case may be, not later than three days before the due date of the document. Notice of the request shall be immediately served on all other parties and proof of service furnished.

§102.150 Answer to application; reply to answer; comments by other parties.

(a) Within 35 days after service of an application the general counsel may file an answer to the application. Unless the general counsel requests an extension of time for filing or files a statement of intent to negotiate under paragraph (b) of this section, failure to file a timely answer may be treated as a consent to the award requested. The filing of a motion to dismiss the application shall stay the time for filing an answer to a date 35 days after issuance of any order denying the motion. Within 21 days after service of any motion to dismiss, the applicant shall file a response thereto. Review of an order granting a motion to dismiss an application in its entirety may be obtained by filing a request therefore with the Board in Washington, D.C., pursuant to §102.27 of these rules.

(b) If the General Counsel and the applicant believe that the issues in the fee application can be settled, they may jointly file a statement of their intent to negotiate toward a settlement. The filing of such a statement shall extend the time for filing an answer for an additional 35 days.

(c) The answer shall explain in detail any objections to the award requested and identify the facts relied on in support of the General Counsel's position. If the answer is based on alleged facts not already in the record of the adversary adjudication supporting affidavits shall be provided or a request made for further proceedings under §102.152.

(d) Within 21 days after service of an answer, the applicant may file a reply. If the reply is based on alleged facts not already in the record of the adversary adjudication, supporting affidavits shall be provided or a request made for further proceedings under §102.152.

(e) Any party to an adversary adjudication other than the applicant and the General Counsel may file comments on a fee application within 35 days after it is served and on an answer within 21 days after it is served. A commenting party may not participate further in the fee application proceeding unless the administrative law judge determines that such participation is required in order to permit full exploration of matters raised in the comments.

§102.151 Settlement.

The applicant and the General Counsel may agree on a proposed settlement of the award before final action on the application. If a prevailing party and the General Counsel agree on a proposed settlement of an award before an application has been filed, the proposed settlement shall be filed with the application. All such settlements shall be subject to approval by the Board.

§102.152 Further proceedings.

(a) Ordinarily the determination of an award will be made on the basis of the documents in the record. The administrative law judge, however, upon request of either the applicant or the General Counsel, or on his or her own initiative, may order further proceedings, including an informal conference, oral argument, additional written submissions or an evidentiary hearing. An evidentiary hearing shall be held only when necessary for resolution of material issues of fact.

(b) A request that the administrative law judge order further proceedings under this section shall specifically identify the disputed issues and the evidence sought to be adduced, and shall explain why the additional proceedings are necessary to resolve the issues.

(c) An order of the administrative law judge scheduling further proceedings shall specify the issues to be considered.

(d) Any evidentiary hearing held pursuant to this section shall be open to the public and shall be conducted in accordance with §§102.30 to 102.44 of these rules, except §§102.33, 102.34 and 102.38.

(e) Rulings of the administrative law judge shall be reviewable by the Board only in accordance with the provisions of §102.26.

§102.153 Administrative law judge's decision; contents; service; transfer of case to the Board; contents of record in case.

(a) Upon conclusion of proceedings under §§102.147 to 102.152, the administrative law judge shall prepare a decision. The decision shall include written findings and conclusions as necessary to dispose of the application. The administrative law judge shall file the original of his decision with the Board and cause a copy thereof to be served on each of the parties. Upon the filing of the decision, the Board shall enter an order transferring the case to the Board and shall serve copies of the order, setting forth the date of such transfer, on all the parties. Service of the administrative law judge's decision and of the order transferring the case to the Board shall be complete upon mailing.

(b) The record in a proceeding on an application for an award of fees and expenses shall include the application and any amendments or attachments thereto, the net worth exhibit, the answer and any amendments or attachments thereto, any reply to the answer, any comments by other parties, motions, rulings, orders, stipulations, written submissions, the stenographic transcript of any oral argument, the stenographic transcript of any hearing, exhibits and depositions, together with the administrative law judge's decision and exceptions, any cross-exceptions or answering briefs as provided in §102.46, and the record of the adversary adjudication upon which the application is based.

§102.154 Exceptions to administrative law judge's decision; briefs; action of Board.

Procedures before the Board, including the filing of exceptions to the administrative law judge's decision and briefs, and action by the Board, shall be in accordance with §§102.46, 102.47, 102.48 and 102.50 of these rules. The Board will issue a decision on the application or remand the proceeding to the administrative law judge for further proceedings.

§102.155 Payment of award.

To obtain payment of an award made by the Board the applicant shall submit to the Director, Division of Administration, a copy of the Board's final decision granting the award, accompanied by a statement that the applicant will not seek court review of the decision. If such statement is filed the Agency will pay the amount of the award within 60 days, unless judicial review of the award or of the underlying decision has been sought.

PART 101—STATEMENTS OF PROCEDURE*

Subpart A—General Statement

§101.1 General statement.

By virtue of the authority vested in it by section 6 of the National Labor Relations Act, 49 Stat. 449, as amended, the National Labor Relations Board has issued and published simultaneously herewith its Rules and Regulations, Series 8, as amended. The following statements of the general course and method by which the Board's functions are channeled and determined are issued and published pursuant to 5 U.S.C. section 552(a)(1)(B).

Subpart B—Unfair Labor Practice Cases Under Section 10(a) to (i) of the Act and Telegraph Merger Act Cases

§101.2 Initiation of unfair labor practice cases.

The investigation of an alleged violation of the National Labor Relations Act is initiated by the filing of a charge, which must be in writing and signed, and must either be notarized or must contain a declaration by the person signing it, under the penalties of the Criminal Code, that its contents are true and correct to the best of his knowledge and belief. The charge is filed with the regional director for the region in which the alleged violations have occurred or are occurring. A blank form for filing such charge is supplied by the regional office upon request. The charge contains the name and address of the person against whom the charge is made and a statement of the facts constituting the alleged unfair labor practices.

---

*Just prior to publication of this volume, the NLRB implemented several changes in its Rules and Regulations but had not yet made conforming changes to its Statements of Procedure. These intended changes have been added in brackets.

§101.3 [Reserved]

§101.4 Investigation of charges.

When the charge is received in the regional office it is filed, docketed, and assigned a case number. The regional director may cause a copy of the charge to be served upon the person against whom the charge is made, but timely service of a copy of the charge within the meaning of the proviso to section 10(b) of the act is the exclusive responsibility of the charging party and not of the general counsel or his agents. The regional director requests the person filing the charge to submit promptly evidence in its support. As part of the investigation hereinafter mentioned, the person against whom the charge is filed, hereinafter called the respondent, is asked to submit a statement of his position in respect to the allegations. The case is assigned to a member of the field staff for investigation, who interviews representatives of the parties and other persons who have knowledge as to the charges, as is deemed necessary. In the investigation and in all other stages of the proceedings, charges alleging violation of section 8(b)(4)(A), (B), and (C), charges alleging violation of section 8(b)(4)(D) in which it is deemed appropriate to seek injunctive relief under section (10)(l) of the act, and charges alleging violations of section 8(b)(7) or 8(e) are given priority over all other cases in the office in which they are pending except cases of like character; and charges alleging violation of section 8(a)(3) or 8(b)(2) are given priority over all other cases except cases of like character and cases under section 10(l) of the act. The regional director may in his discretion dispense with any portion of the investigation described in this section as appears necessary to him in consideration of such factors as the amount of time necessary to complete a full investigation, the nature of the proceeding, and the public interest. After investigation, the case may be disposed of through informal methods such as withdrawal, dismissal, and settlement; or, the case may necessitate formal methods of disposition. Some of the informal methods of handling unfair labor practice cases will be stated first.

§101.5 Withdrawal of charges.

If investigation reveals that there has been no violation of the National Labor Relations Act or the evidence is insufficient to substantiate the charge, the regional director recommends withdrawal of the charge by the person who filed. The complainant may also, on its own initiative, request withdrawal. If the complainant accepts the recommendation of the director or requests withdrawal on its own initiative, the respondent is immediately notified of the withdrawal of the charge.

§101.6 Dismissal of charges and appeals to general counsel.

If the complainant refuses to withdraw the charge as recommended, the regional director dismisses the charge. The regional director thereupon informs the parties of his action, together with a simple statement of the grounds therefor, and the complainant of his right of appeal to the general counsel in Washington, D.C., within 10 [14] days. If the complainant appeals to the general counsel, the entire file in the case is sent to Washington, D.C., where the case is fully reviewed by the general counsel with the assistance of his staff. Oral presentation of the appeal issues may be permitted a party on timely written request, in which event the other parties are notified and afforded a like opportunity at another appropriate time. Following such review, the general counsel may sustain the regional director's dismissal, stating the grounds of his affirmance, or may direct the regional director to take further action.

§101.7 Settlements.

Before any complaint is issued or other formal action taken, the regional director affords an opportunity to all parties for the submission and consideration of facts, argument, offers of settlement, or proposals of adjustment, except where time, the nature of the proceeding, and the public interest do not permit. Normally prehearing conferences are held, the principal purpose of which is to discuss and explore such submissions and proposals of adjustment. The regional office provides Board-prepared forms for such settlement agreements, as well as printed notices for posting by the respondent. These agreements, which are subject to the approval of the regional director, provide for an appeal to the general counsel, as described in §101.6, by a complainant who will not join in a settlement or adjustment deemed adequate by the regional director. Proof of compliance is obtained by the regional director before the case is closed. If the respondent fails to perform his obligations under the informal agreement, the regional director may determine to institute formal proceedings.

§101.8 Complaints.

If the charge appears to have merit and efforts to dispose of it by informal adjustment are unsuccessful, the regional director institutes formal action by issuance of a complaint and notice of hearing. In certain types of cases, involving novel and complex issues, the regional director, at the discretion of the general counsel, must submit the case for advice from the general counsel before issuing a complaint. The complaint, which is served on all parties, sets forth the facts upon which the Board bases its jurisdiction and the facts relating to the alleged violations of law by the respondent. The respondent must file an answer to the complaint within 10 [14] days of its receipt, setting forth a statement of its defense.

§101.9 Settlement after issuance of complaint.

(a) Even though formal proceedings have begun, the parties again have full opportunity at every stage to dispose of the case by amicable adjustment and in compliance with the law. Thus, after the complaint has been issued and a hearing scheduled or even begun, the attorney in charge of the case and the regional director afford all parties every opportunity for the submission and consideration of facts, argument, offers of settlement, or proposals of adjustment, except where time, the nature of the proceeding, and the public interest do not permit.

(b)(1) After the issuance of a complaint, the agency favors a formal settlement agreement, which is subject to the approval of the Board in Washington, D.C. In such an agreement, the parties agree to waive their right to hearing and agree further that the Board may issue an order requiring the respondent to take action appropriate to the terms of the settlement. Ordinarily the formal settlement agreement also contains the respondent's consent to the Board's application for the entry of a decree by the appropriate circuit court of appeals enforcing the Board's order.

(2) In some cases, however, the regional director, pursuant to his authority to withdraw the complaint before the hearing (§102.18 of this chapter), may conclude that an informal settlement agreement of the type described in §101.7 is appropriate. Such an agreement is not subject to approval by the Board and does not provide for a Board order. It provides for the withdrawal of the complaint.

(c)(1) If after issuance of a complaint but before opening of the hearing, the charging party will not join in a settlement tentatively agreed upon by the regional director, the respondent, and any other parties whose consent may be required, the regional director serves a copy of the proposed settlement agreement on the charging party with a brief written statement of the reasons for proposing its approval. Within 5* days after service of these documents, the charging party may file with the regional director a written statement of any objections to the proposed settlement. Such objections will be considered by the regional director in determining whether to approve the proposed settlement. If the settlement is approved by the regional director notwithstanding the objections, the charging party is so informed and provided a brief written statement of the reasons for the approval.

(2) If the settlement agreement approved by the regional director is a formal one, providing for the entry of a Board order, the settlement agreement together with the charging party's objections and the regional director's written statements, are submitted to Washington, D.C., where they are reviewed by the general counsel. If the general counsel decides to approve the settlement agreement, he shall so inform the charging party and submit the agreement and accompanying documents to the Board, upon whose approval the settlement is contingent. Within 7* days after service of notice of submission of the settlement agreement to the Board, the charging party may file with the Board in Washington, D.C., a further statement in support of his objections to the settlement agreement.

(3) If the settlement agreement approved by the regional director is an informal one, providing for the withdrawal of the complaint, the charging party may appeal the regional director's action to the general counsel, as provided in §102.19 of this chapter.

(d)(1) If the settlement occurs after the opening of the hearing and before issuance of the administrative law judge's decision and there is an all-party informal settlement, the request for withdrawal of the complaint must be submitted to the administrative law judge for his approval. If the all-party settlement is a formal one, final approval must come from the Board. If any party will not join in the settlement agreed to by the other parties, the administrative law judge will give such party an opportunity to state on the record or in writing its reasons for opposing the settlement.

(2) If the administrative law judge decides to accept or reject the proposed settlement, any party aggrieved by such ruling may ask for leave to appeal to the Board as provided in §102.26 of this chapter.

(e)(1) In the event the respondent fails to comply with the terms of a settlement stipulation, upon which a Board order and court decree are based,

---

*These time periods were unaffected by the Board's September 29, 1986, rules change.

the Board may petition the court to adjudge the respondent in contempt. If the respondent refuses to comply with the terms of a stipulation settlement providing solely for the entry of a Board Order, the Board may petition the court for enforcement of its order, pursuant to section 10 of the National Labor Relations Act.

(2) In the event the respondent fails to comply with the terms of an informal settlement agreement, the regional director may set the agreement aside and institute further proceedings.

§101.10 Hearings.

(a) Except in extraordinary situations the hearing is open to the public and usually conducted in the region where the charge originated. A duly designated administrative law judge presides over the hearing. The Government's case is conducted by an attorney attached to the Board's regional office, who has the responsibility of presenting the evidence in support of the complaint. The rules of evidence applicable in the district courts of the United States under the Rules of Civil Procedure adopted by the Supreme Court are, so far as practicable, controlling. Counsel for the general counsel, all parties to the proceeding, and the administrative law judge have the power to call, examine, and cross-examine witnesses and to introduce evidence into the record. They may also submit briefs, engage in oral argument, and submit proposed findings and conclusions to the administrative law judge. The attendance and testimony of witnesses and the production of evidence material to any matter under investigation may be compelled by subpoena.

(b) The functions of all administrative law judges and other Board agents or employees participating in decisions in conformity with section 8 of the Administrative Procedure Act are conducted in an impartial manner and any such administrative law judge, agent, or employee may at any time withdraw if he deems himself disqualified because of bias or prejudice. The Board's attorney has the burden of proof of violations of section 8 of the National Labor Relations Act and section 222(f) of the Telegraph Merger Act. In connection with the hearings subject to the provisions of section 7 of the Administrative Procedure Act:

(1) No sanction is imposed or rule or order issued except upon consideration of the whole record or such portions thereof as may be cited by any party and as supported by and in accordance with the preponderance of the reliable probative, and substantial evidence;

(2) Every party has the right to present his case or defense by oral or documentary evidence, to submit rebuttal evidence, and to conduct such cross-examination as may be required for a full and true disclosure of the facts; and

(3) Where any decision rests on official notice of a material fact not appearing in the evidence in the record, any party is on timely request afforded a reasonable opportunity to show the contrary.

(4) Subject to the approval of the administrative law judge, all parties to the proceeding voluntarily may enter into a stipulation dispensing with a verbatim written transcript of record of the oral testimony adduced at the hearing and providing for the waiver by the respective parties of their right to file with the Board exceptions to the findings of fact (but not to conclusions

of law or recommended orders) which the administrative law judge shall make in his decision.

§101.11 Administrative law judge's decision.

(a) At the conclusion of the hearing the administrative law judge prepares a decision stating findings of fact and conclusions, as well as the reasons for his determination on all material issues, and making the recommendations as to action which should be taken in the case. The administrative law judge may recommend dismissal or sustain the complaint, in whole or in part and recommend that the respondent cease and desist from the unlawful acts found and take action to remedy their effects.

(b) The administrative law judge's decision is filed with the Board in Washington, D.C., and copies are simultaneously served on each of the parties. At the same time the Board, through its executive secretary, issues and serves on each of the parties an order transferring the case to the Board. The parties may accept and comply with the administrative law judge's recommended order, which, in the absence of exceptions, shall become the order of the Board. Or the parties or counsel for the Board may file exceptions to the administrative law judge's decision with the Board. Whenever any party files exceptions, any other party may file an answering brief limited to questions raised in the exceptions and/or may file cross-exceptions relating to any portion of the administrative law judge's decision. Cross-exceptions may be filed only by a party who has not previously filed exceptions. Whenever any party files cross-exceptions, any other party may file an answering brief to the cross-exceptions. The parties may request permission to appear and argue orally before the Board in Washington, D.C. They may also submit proposed findings and conclusions to the Board.

§101.12 Board decision and order.

(a) If any party files exceptions to the administrative law judge's decision, the Board, with the assistance of the legal assistants to each Board member who function in much the same manner as law clerks do for judges, reviews the entire record, including the administrative law judge's decision and recommendations, the exceptions thereto, the complete transcript of evidence, and the exhibits, briefs, and arguments. The Board does not consult with members of the trial examining staff or with any agent of the general counsel in its deliberations. It then issues its decision and order in which it may adopt, modify, or reject the findings and recommendations of the administrative law judge. The decision and order contains detailed findings of fact, conclusions of law, and basic reasons for decision on all material issues raised, and an order either dismissing the complaint in whole or in part or requiring the respondent to cease and desist from its unlawful practices and to take appropriate affirmative action.

(b) If no exceptions are filed to the administrative law judge's decision, his decision and recommended order automatically become the decision and order of the Board, pursuant to section 10(c) of the act. All objections and exceptions, whether or not previously made during or after the hearing, are deemed waived for all purposes.

§101.13 Compliance with Board decision and order.

(a) Shortly after the Board's decision and order is issued the director of the regional office in which the charge was filed communicates with the respondent for the purpose of obtaining compliance. Conferences may be held to arrange the details necessary for compliance with the terms of the order.

(b) If the respondent effects full compliance with the terms of the order, the regional director submits a report to that effect to Washington, D.C., after which the case may be closed. Despite compliance, however, the Board's order is a continuing one; therefore, the closing of a case on compliance is necessarily conditioned upon the continued observance of that order; and in some cases it is deemed desirable, notwithstanding compliance, to implement the order with an enforcing decree. Subsequent violations of the order may become the basis of further proceedings.

§101.14 Judicial review of Board decision and order.

If the respondent does not comply with the Board's order, or the Board deems it desirable to implement the order with a court decree, the Board may petition the appropriate Federal court for enforcement. Or, the respondent may petition the circuit court of appeals to review and set aside the Board's order. Upon such review or enforcement proceedings, the court reviews the record and the Board's findings and order and sustains them if they are in accordance with the requirements of law. The court may enforce, modify, or set aside in whole or in part the Board's findings and order, or it may remand the case to the Board for further proceedings as directed by the court. Following the court's decree, either the Government or the private party may petition the Supreme Court for review upon writ of certiorari. Such applications for review to the Supreme Court are handled by the Board through the Solicitor General of the United States.

§101.15 Compliance with court decree.

After a Board order has been enforced by a court decree, the Board has the responsibility of obtaining compliance with that decree. Investigation is made by the regional office of the respondent's efforts to comply. If it finds that the respondent has failed to live up to the terms of the court's decree, the general counsel may, on behalf of the Board, petition the court to hold him in contempt of court. The court may order immediate remedial action and impose sanctions and penalties.

§101.16 Backpay proceedings.

(a) After a Board order directing the payment of backpay has been issued or after enforcement of such order by a court decree, if informal efforts to dispose of the matter prove unsuccessful, the regional director is then authorized at his discretion to issue a "backpay specification" in the name of the Board and a notice of hearing before an administrative law judge, both of which are served on the parties involved. The specification sets forth computations showing gross and net backpay due and any other pertinent information. The respondent must file an answer within 15 [21] days of the receipt of the specification, setting forth a particularized statement of its defense.

(b) In the alternative and at his discretion, the regional director, under the circumstances specified above, may issue and serve upon the parties a notice of hearing only, without a specification. Such notice contains, in addition to the time and place of hearing before an administrative law judge, a brief statement of the matters in controversy.

(c) The procedure before the administrative law judge or the Board, whether initiated by the "backpay specification" or by notice of hearing without a backpay specification, is substantially the same as that described in §§101.10 to 101.14, inclusive.

Subpart C—Representation Cases Under Section 9(c) of the Act and Petitions for Clarification of Bargaining Units and for Amendment of Certifications Under Section 9(b) of the Act

§101.17 Initiation of representation cases and petitions for clarification and amendment.

The investigation of the question as to whether a union represents a majority of an appropriate grouping of employees is initiated by the filing of a petition by any person or labor organization acting on behalf of a substantial number of employees or by an employer when one or more individuals or labor organizations present to him a claim to be recognized as the exclusive bargaining representative. If there is a certified or currently recognized representative, any employee, or group of employees, or any individual or labor organization acting in their behalf may also file decertification proceedings to test the question of whether the certified or recognized agent is still the representative of the employees. If there is a certified or currently recognized representative of a bargaining unit and there is no question concerning representation, a party may file a petition for clarification of the bargaining unit. If there is a unit covered by a certification and there is no question concerning representation, any party may file a petition for amendment to reflect changed circumstances, such as changes in the name or affiliation of the labor organization involved or in the name or location of the employer involved. The petition must be in writing and signed, and either must be notarized or must contain a declaration by the person signing it, under the penalties of the Criminal Code, that its contents are true and correct to the best of his knowledge and belief. It is filed with the regional director for the region in which the proposed or actual bargaining unit exists. Petition forms, which are supplied by the regional office upon request, provide, among other things, for a description of the contemplated or existing appropriate bargaining unit, the approximate number of employees involved, and the names of all labor organizations which claim to represent the employees. If a petition is filed by a labor organization seeking certification, or in the case of a petition to decertify a certified or recognized bargaining agent, the petitioner must supply, within 48 hours after filing but in no event later than the last day on which the petition might timely be filed, evidence of representation. Such evidence is usually in the form of cards, which must be dated, authorizing the labor organization to represent the employees or authorizing the petitioner to file a decertification proceeding. If a petition is filed by an employer, the petitioner must supply, within 48 hours after filing, proof of demand for recognition by the labor organization named in the petition and, in the event the labor organization named is the incumbent representative of the unit involved, a statement of the objective considerations demonstrating reasonable grounds for believing that the labor organization has lost its majority status.

§101.18 Investigation of petition.

(a) Upon receipt of the petition in the regional office, it is docketed and assigned to a member of the staff, usually a field examiner, for investigation. He conducts an investigation to ascertain (1) whether the employer's operations affect commerce within the meaning of the act, (2) the appropriateness of the unit of employees for the purposes of collective bargaining and the existence of a bona fide question concerning representation within the meaning of the act, (3) whether the election would effectuate the policies of the act and reflect the free choice of employees in the appropriate unit, and (4) whether, if the petitioner is a labor organization seeking recognition, there is a sufficient probability, based on the evidence of representation of the petitioner, that the employees have selected it to represent them. The evidence of representation submitted by the petitioning labor organization or by the person seeking decertification is ordinarily checked to determine the number or proportion of employees who have designated the petitioner, it being the Board's administrative experience that in the absence of special factors the conduct of an election serves no purpose under the statute unless the petitioner has been designated by at least 30 percent of the employees. However, in the case of a petition by an employer, no proof of representation on the part of the labor organization claiming a majority is required and the regional director proceeds with the case if other factors require it unless the labor organization withdraws its claim to majority representation. The field examiner, or other member of the staff attempts to ascertain from all interested parties whether or not the grouping or unit of employees described in the petition constitutes an appropriate bargaining unit. The petition may be amended at any time prior to hearing and may be amended during the hearing in the discretion of the hearing officer upon such terms as he deems just.

(b) The petitioner may on its own initiative request the withdrawal of the petition if the investigation discloses that no question of representation exists within the meaning of the statute, because, among other possible reasons, the unit is not appropriate, or a written contract precludes further investigation at that time, or where the petitioner is a labor organization or a person seeking decertification and the showing of representation among the employees is insufficient to warrant an election under the 30-percent principle stated in paragraph (a) of this section.

(c) For the same or similar reasons the regional director may request the petitioner to withdraw its petition. If the petitioner, despite the regional director's recommendations, refuses to withdraw the petition, the regional director then dismisses the petition, stating the grounds for his dismissal and informing the petitioner of his right of appeal to the Board in Washington, D.C. The petition may also be dismissed in the discretion of the regional director if the petitioner fails to make available necessary facts which are in its possession. The petitioner may within 10 [14] days appeal from the regional director's dismissal by filing such request with the Board in Washington, D.C.; after a full review of the file with the assistance of its staff, the Board may sustain the dismissal, stating the grounds of its affirmance, or may direct the regional director to take further action.

§101.19 Consent adjustments before formal hearing.

The Board has devised and makes available to the parties two types of informal consent procedures through which representation issues can be resolved without recourse to formal procedures. These informal arrangements are commonly referred to as (a) consent-election agreement followed by regional director's determination, and (b) consent-election agreement followed by Board certification. Forms for use in these informal procedures are available in the regional offices.

(a)(1) The consent-election agreement followed by the regional director's determination of representatives is the most frequently used method of informal adjustment of representation cases. The terms of the agreement providing for this form of adjustment are set forth in printed forms, which are available upon request at the Board's regional offices. Under these terms the parties agree with respect to the appropriate unit, the payroll period to be used as the basis of eligibility to vote in an election, and the place, date, and hours of balloting. A Board agent arranges the details incident to the mechanics and conduct of the election. For example, he usually arranges pre-election conferences in which the parties check the list of voters and attempt to resolve any questions of eligibility. Also, prior to the date of election, the holding of such election shall be adequately publicized by the posting of official notices in the establishment whenever possible or in other places, or by the use of other means considered appropriate and effective. These notices reproduce a sample ballot and outline such election details as location of polls, time of voting, and eligibility rules.

(2) The actual polling is always conducted and supervised by Board agents. Appropriate representatives of each party may assist them and observe the election. As to the mechanics of the election, a ballot is given to each eligible voter by the Board's agents. The ballots are marked in the secrecy of a voting booth. The Board agents and authorized observers have the privilege of challenging for reasonable cause employees who apply for ballots.

(3) Customarily the Board agents, in the presence and with the assistance of the authorized observers, count and tabulate the ballots immediately after the closing of the polls. A complete tally of the ballots is served upon [made available to] the parties upon the conclusion of the count [election].

(4) If challenged ballots are sufficient in number to affect the results of the count, the regional director conducts an investigation and rules on the challenges. Similarly, if objections to the conduct of the election are filed within 5 [7] days of the issuance of the tally of ballots [after the tally of ballots has been prepared], the regional director likewise conducts an in-

vestigation and rules upon the objections. If, after investigation, the objections are found to have merit, the regional director may void the election results and conduct a new election.

(5) This form of agreement provides that the ruling of the regional director on all questions relating to the election (for example, eligibility to vote and the validity of challenges and objections) are final and binding. Also, the agreement provides for the conduct of a runoff election, in accordance with the provisions of the Board's Rules and Regulations, if two or more labor organizations appear on the ballot and no one choice receives the majority of the valid votes cast.

(6) The regional director issues to the parties a certification of the results of the election, including certification of representatives where appropriate, with the same force and effect as if issued by the Board.

(b) The consent-election agreement followed by a Board determination provides that disputed matters following the agreed-upon election, if determinative of the results, shall be the basis of a formal decision by the Board instead of an informal determination by the regional director, except that if the regional director decides that a hearing on objections or challenged ballots is necessary he may direct such a hearing before a hearing officer, or, if the case is consolidated with an unfair labor practice proceeding, before an administrative law judge. If a hearing is directed such action on the part of the regional director constitutes a transfer of the case to the Board. Thus, except for directing a hearing, it is provided that the Board, rather than the regional director, makes the final determination of questions raised concerning eligibility, challenged votes, and objections to the conduct of the election. Thus, if challenged ballots are sufficient in number to affect the results of the count, the regional director conducts an investigation and issues a report on the challenges instead of ruling thereon, unless he elects to hold a hearing. Similarly, if objections to the conduct of the election are filed within 5 [7] days after issuance of the tally of ballots [the tally of ballots has been prepared], the regional director likewise conducts an investigation and issues a report instead of ruling on the validity of the objections, unless he elects to hold a hearing. The regional director's report is served on the parties, who may file exceptions thereto within 10 [14] days with the Board in Washington, D.C. The Board then reviews the entire record made and may, if a substantial issue is raised, direct a hearing on the challenged ballots or the objections to the conduct of the election. Or, the Board may, if no substantial issues are raised, affirm the regional director's report and take appropriate action in termination of the proceedings. If a hearing is ordered by the regional director or the Board on the challenged ballots or objections, all parties are heard and a report containing findings of fact and recommendations as to the disposition of the challenges or objections, or both, and resolving issues of credibility is issued by the hearing officer and served on the parties, who may file exceptions thereto within 10 [14] days with the Board in Washington, D.C. The record made on the hearing is reviewed by the Board with the assistance of its legal assistants and a final determination made thereon. If the objections are found to have merit, the election results may be voided and a new election conducted under the supervision of the regional director. If the union has been selected as the representative, the Board or the regional director, as the case may be, issues its certification, and the proceeding is terminated. If upon a decertification or employer petition the union loses the election, the Board or the regional director, as the case may be, certifies that the union is not the chosen representative.

§101.20 Formal hearing.

(a) If no informal adjustment of the question concerning representation has been effected and it appears to the regional director that formal action is necessary, the regional director will institute formal proceedings by issuance of a notice of hearing on the issues, which is followed by a decision and direction of election or dismissal of the case. In certain types of cases, involving novel or complex issues, the regional director may submit the case for advice to the Board before issuing notice of hearing.

(b) The notice of hearing, together with a copy of the petition, is served upon the unions and employer filing or named in the petition and upon other known persons or labor organizations claiming to have been designated by employees involved in the proceeding.

(c) The hearing, usually open to the public, is held before a hearing officer who normally is an attorney or field examiner attached to the regional office but may be another qualified official. The hearing, which is non-adversary in character, is part of the investigation in which the primary interest of the Board's agents is to insure that the record contains as full a statement of the pertinent facts as may be necessary for determination of the case. The parties are afforded full opportunity to present their respective positions and to produce the significant facts in support of their contentions. In most cases a substantial number of the relevant facts are undisputed and stipulated. The parties are permitted to argue orally on the record before the hearing officer.

§101.21 Procedure after hearing.

(a) Pursuant to section 3(b) of the act, the Board has delegated to its regional directors its powers under section 9 of the act, to determine the unit appropriate for the purpose of collective bargaining, to investigate and provide for hearings, and determine whether a question of representation exists, and to direct an election or take a secret ballot under subsection (c) or (e) of section 9 and certify the results thereof. These powers include the issuance of such decisions, orders, rulings, directions, and certifications as are necessary to process any representation or deauthorization petition. Thus, by way of illustration and not of limitation, the regional director may dispose of petitions by administrative dismissal or by decision after formal hearing; pass upon rulings made at hearings and requests for extensions of time for filing of briefs; rule on objections to elections and challenged ballots in connection with elections directed by the regional director or the Board, after administrative investigation or formal hearing; rule on motions to amend or rescind any certification issued after the effective date of the delegation; and entertain motions for oral argument. The regional director may at any time transfer the case to the Board for decision, but until such action is taken, it will be presumed that the regional director will decide the case. In the event the regional director decides the issues in a case, his decision is final subject to the review procedure set forth in the Board's Rules and Regulations.

(b) Upon the close of the hearing, the entire record in the case is forwarded to the regional director or, upon issuance by the regional director or of an order transferring the case, to the Board in Washington, D.C. The hearing officer also transmits an analysis of the issues and the evidence, but makes no recommendations in regard to resolution of the issues. All parties may file briefs with the regional director or, if the case is transferred to the Board at the close of the hearing, with the Board, within 7 days after the close of the hearing. If the case is transferred to the Board after the close of the hearing, briefs may be filed with the Board within the time prescribed by the regional director. The parties may also request to be heard orally. Because of the nature of the proceedings, however, permission to argue orally is rarely granted. After review of the entire case, the regional director or the Board, issues a decision either dismissing the petition or directing that an election be held. In the latter event, the election is conducted under the supervision of the regional director in the manner already described in §101.19.

(c) With respect to objections to the conduct of the election and challenged ballots, the regional director may, in his discretion, (1) issue a report on such objections and/or challenged ballots and transmit the issues to the Board for resolution, as in cases involving consent elections to be followed by Board certifications, or (2) decide the issues on the basis of the administrative investigation or after a hearing, with the right to transfer the case to the Board for decision at any time prior to his disposition of the issues on the merits. In the event the regional director adopts the first procedure, the parties have the same rights, and the same procedure is followed, as has already been described in connection with the postelection procedures in cases involving consent election to be followed by Board certification. In the event the regional director adopts the second procedure, the parties have the same rights, and the same procedure is followed, as has already been described in connection with hearings before elections.

(d) The parties have the right to request review of any final decision of the regional director, within the times set forth in the Board's Rules and Regulations, on one or more of the grounds specified therein. Any such request for review must be a self-contained document permitting the Board to rule on the basis of its contents without the necessity of recourse to the record, and must meet the other requirements of the Board's Rules and Regulations as to its contents. The regional director's action is not stayed by the filing of such a request or the granting of review, unless otherwise ordered by the Board. Thus, the regional director may proceed immediately to make any necessary arrangements for an election, including the issuance of a notice of election. However, unless a waiver is filed, he will normally not schedule an election until a date between the 20th and 30th days after the date of his decision, to permit the Board to rule on any request for review which may be filed. As to administrative dismissals prior to the close of hearing, see §101.18(c).

(e) If the election involves two or more labor organizations and if the election results are inconclusive because no choice on the ballot received the majority of valid votes cast, a runoff election is held as provided in the Board's Rules and Regulations.

Subpart D—Unfair Labor Practice and Representation Cases Under Sections 8(b)(7) and 9(c) of the Act

§101.22 Initiation and investigation of a case under section 8(b)(7).

(a) The investigation of an alleged violation of section 8(b)(7) of the act is initiated by the filing of a charge. The manner of filing such charge and the contents thereof are the same as described in §101.2. In some cases, at the time of the investigation of the charge, there may be pending a representation petition involving the employees of the employer named in the charge. In those cases, the results of the investigation of the charge will determine the course of the petition.

(b) The investigation of the charge is conducted in accordance with the provisions of §101.4, insofar as they are applicable. If the investigation reveals that there is merit in the charge, a complaint is issued as described in §101.8, and an application is made for an injunction under section 10(l) of the act, as described in §101.37. If the investigation reveals that there is no merit in the charge, the regional director, absent a withdrawal of the charge, dismisses it, subject to appeal to the general counsel. However, if the investigation reveals that issuance of a complaint may be warranted but for the pendency of a representation petition involving the employees of the employer named in the charge, action on the charge is suspended pending the investigation of the petition as provided in §101.23.

§101.23 Initiation and investigation of a petition in connection with a case under section 8(b)(7).

(a) A representation petition[1] involving the employees of the employer named in the charge is handled under an expedited procedure when the investigation of the charge has revealed that: (1) The employer's operations affect commerce within the meaning of the act; (2) picketing of the employer is being conducted for an object proscribed by section 8(b)(7) of the act; (3) subparagraph (C) of that section is applicable to the picketing; and (4) the petition has been filed within a reasonable period of time not to exceed 30 days from the commencement of the picketing. In these circumstances, the member of the regional director's staff, to whom the matter has been assigned, investigates the petition to ascertain further: (1) The unit appropriate for collective bargaining; and (2) whether an election in that unit would effectuate the policies of the act.

(b) If, based, on such investigation, the regional director determines that an election is warranted, he may, without a prior hearing, direct that an election be held in an appropriate unit of employees. Any party aggrieved may file a request with the Board for special permission to appeal that action to the Board, but such review, if granted, will not, unless otherwise ordered by the Board, stay the proceeding. If the regional director determines that an election is not warranted, he dismisses the petition or makes other disposition of the matter. Should he conclude that an election is warranted, he fixes the basis of eligibility of voters and the place, date, and hours of balloting. The mechanics of arranging the balloting, the other procedures for the conduct of the election, and the postelection proceedings are the same, insofar as appropriate, as those described in §101.19, except that the regional director's rulings on any objections to the conduct of the election or challenged ballots are final and binding, unless the Board, on an application by one of the parties, grants such party special permission to appeal from the regional director's rulings. The party requesting such review by

---

[1]The manner of filing of such petition and the contents thereof are the same as described in §101.17, except that the petitioner is not required to allege that a claim was made upon the employer for recognition or that the union represents a substantial number of employees.

the Board must do so promptly, in writing, and state briefly the grounds relied upon. Such party must also immediately serve a copy on each of the other parties, including the regional director. Neither the request for review by the Board nor the Board's grant of such review operates as a stay of any action taken by the regional director, unless specifically so ordered by the Board. If the Board grants permission to appeal, and it appears to the Board that substantial and material factual issues have been presented with respect to the objections to the conduct of the election or challenged ballots, it may order that a hearing be held on such issues or take other appropriate action.

(c) If the regional director believes, after preliminary investigation of the petition, that there are substantial issues which require determination before an election may be held, he may order a hearing on the issues. This hearing is followed by regional director or Board decision and direction of election, or other disposition. The procedures to be used in connection with such hearing and posthearing proceedings are the same, insofar as they are applicable, as those described in §§101.20 and 101.21, except that the parties may not file briefs with the regional director or the Board, unless special permission therefor is granted, but may state their respective legal positions fully on the record at the hearing, and except that any request for review must be filed promptly after issuance of the regional director's decision.

(d) Should the parties so desire, they may, with the approval of the regional director, resolve the issues as to the unit, the conduct of the balloting, and related matters pursuant to informal consent procedures, as described in §101.19(a).

(e) If a petition has been filed which does not meet the requirements for processing under the expedited procedure, the regional director may process it under the procedures set forth in subpart C.

§101.24 Final disposition of a charge which has been held pending investigation of the petition.

(a) Upon the determination that the issuance of a direction of election is warranted on the petition, the regional director, absent withdrawal of the charge dismisses it subject to an appeal to the general counsel in Washington, D.C.

(b) If, however, the petition is dismissed or withdrawn, the investigation of the charge is resumed, and the appropriate steps described in §101.22 are taken with respect to it.

§101.25 Appeal from the dismissal of a petition, or from the refusal to process it under the expedited procedure.

If the regional director determines after his investigation of the representation petition that further proceedings based thereon are not warranted, he, absent withdrawal of the petition, dismisses it, stating the grounds therefor. If the regional director determines that the petition does not meet the requirements for processing under the expedited procedure, he advises the petitioner of his determination to process the petition under the procedures described in subpart C. In either event, the regional director informs all the parties of his action, and such action is final, although the Board may grant an aggrieved party permission to appeal from the regional director's action. Such party must request such review promptly, in writing, and state briefly the grounds relied upon. Such party must also immediately serve a copy on each of the other parties, including the regional director. Neither the request for review by the Board, not the Board's grant of such review, operates as a stay of the action taken by the regional director, unless specifically so ordered by the Board.

Subpart E—Referendum Cases Under Section 9(e)(1) and (2) of the Act

§101.26 Initiation of rescission of authority cases.

The investigation of the question as to whether the authority of a labor organization to make an agreement requiring membership in a labor organization as a condition of employment is to be rescinded is initiated by the filing of a petition by an employee or group of employee's on behalf of 30 percent or more of the employees in a bargaining unit covered by an agreement between their employer and a labor organization requiring membership in such labor organization. The petition must be in writing and signed, and either must be notarized or must contain a declaration by the person signing it, under the penalties of the Criminal Code, that its contents are true and correct to the best of his knowledge and belief. It is filed with the regional director for the region in which the alleged appropriate bargaining unit exists or, if the bargaining unit exists in two or more regions, with the regional director for any such regions. The blank form, which is supplied by the regional office upon request, provides, among other things, for a description of the bargaining unit covered by the agreement, the approximate number of employees involved, and the names of any other labor organizations which claim to represent the employees. Petitioner must supply with the petition, or within 48 hours after filing, its evidence of authorization from the employees.

§101.27 Investigation of petition; withdrawals and dismissals.

(a) Upon receipt of the petition in the regional office, it is filed, docketed, and assigned to a member of the staff, usually a field examiner, for investigation. He conducts an investigation to ascertain (1) whether the employer's operations affect commerce within the meaning of the act, (2) whether there is in effect an agreement requiring as a condition of employment membership in a labor organization, (3) whether petitioner has been authorized by at least 30 percent of the employees to file such a petition, and (4) whether an election would effectuate the policies of the act by providing for a free expression of choice by the employees. The evidence of designation submitted by petitioner, usually in the form of cards signed by individual employees authorizing the filing of such a petition, is checked to determine the proportion of employees who desire rescission.

(b) Petitioner may on its own initiative request the withdrawal of the petition if the investigation discloses that an election is inappropriate, because, among other possible reasons, petitioner's card showing is insufficient to meet the 30-percent statutory requirement referred to in paragraph (a) of this section.

(c) For the same or similar reasons the regional director may request the petitioner to withdraw its petition. If petitioner, despite the regional director's recommendation, refuses to withdraw the petition, the regional director then dismisses the petition, stating the grounds for his dismissal and informing petitioner of his right of appeal to the Board in Washington, D.C. The petitioner may within 10 [14] days appeal from the regional director's dismissal by filing such request with the Board in Washington, D.C. The request shall contain a complete statement setting forth the facts and reasons upon which the request is made. After a full review of the file, the Board, with the assistance of its staff, may sustain the dismissal, stating the grounds for its affirmance, or may direct the regional director to take further action.

§101.28 Consent agreements providing for election.

The Board makes available to the parties two types of informal consent procedures through which authorization issues can be resolved without resort to formal procedures. These informal agreements are commonly referred to as (a) consent-election agreement, followed by regional director's determination, and (b) consent-election agreement, followed by Board certification. Forms for use in these informal procedures are available in regional offices. The procedures to be used in connection with a consent-election agreement providing for regional director's determination and a consent-election agreement providing for Board certification are the same as those already described in subpart C of the Statements of Procedure in connection with similar agreements in representation cases under section 9(c) of the act, except that no provision is made for runoff elections.

§101.29 Procedure respecting election conducted without hearing.

If the regional director determines that the case is an appropriate one for election without formal hearing, an election is conducted as quickly as possible among the employees and upon the conclusion of the election the regional director furnishes [makes available] to the parties a tally of the ballots. The parties, however, have an opportunity to make appropriate challenges and objections to the conduct of the election and they have the same rights, and the same procedure is followed, with respect to objections to the conduct of the election and challenged ballots, as has already been described in subpart C of the Statements of Procedure in connection with the post-election procedures in representation cases under section 9(c) of the act, except that no provision is made for a runoff election. If no such objections are filed within 5 [7] days and if the challenged ballots are insufficient in number to affect the results of the election, the regional director issues to the parties a certification of the results of the election, with the same force and effect as if issued by the Board.

§101.30 Formal hearing and procedure respecting election conducted after hearing.

(a) The procedures are the same as those described in subpart C of the Statements of Procedure respecting representation cases arising under section 9(c) of the act. If the preliminary investigation indicates that there are substantial issues which require determination before an appropriate election may be held, the regional director will institute formal proceedings by issuance of a notice of hearing on the issues which, after hearing, is followed by regional director or Board decision and direction of election or dismissal. The notice of hearing together with a copy of the petition is served upon petitioner, the employer, and upon any other known persons or labor organizations claiming to have been designated by employees involved in the proceeding.

(b) The hearing, usually open to the public, is held before a hearing officer who normally is an attorney or field examiner attached to the regional office but may be another qualified official. The hearing, which is non-adversary in character, is part of the investigation in which the primary interest of the Board's agents is to insure that the record contains as full a statement of the pertinent facts as may be necessary for determination of the case. The parties are afforded full opportunity to present their respective positions and to produce the significant facts in support of their contentions. In most cases a substantial number of the relevant facts are undisputed and stipulated. The parties are permitted to argue orally on the record before the hearing officer.

(c) Upon the close of the hearing, the entire record in the case is then forwarded to the regional director or the Board, together with an informal analysis by the hearing officer of the issues and the evidence but without recommendations. All parties may file briefs with the regional director or the Board within 7 days after the close of the hearing. If the case is transferred to the Board after the close of the hearing, briefs may be filed with the Board within the time prescribed by the regional director. The parties may also request to be heard orally. Because of the nature of the proceeding, however, permission to argue orally is rarely granted. After review of the entire case, the regional director or the Board issues a decision either dismissing the petition or directing that an election be held. In the latter event, the election is conducted under the supervision of the regional director in the manner already described in §101.19.

(d) The parties have the same rights, and the same procedure is followed, with respect to objections to the conduct of the election and challenged ballots as has already been described in connection with the postelection procedures in representation cases under section 9(c) of the act.

Subpart F—Jurisdictional Dispute Cases Under Section 10(k) of the Act

§101.31 Initiation of proceedings to hear and determine jurisdictional disputes under section 10(k).

The investigation of a jurisdictional dispute under section 10(k) is initiated by the filing of a charge, as described in §101.2, by any person alleging a violation of paragraph (4)(D) of section 8(b). As soon as possible after a charge has been filed, the regional director serves upon the parties a copy of the charge together with a notice of the filing of such charge.

§101.32 Investigation of charges; withdrawal of charges; dismissal of charges and appeals to Board.

These matters are handled as described in §§101.4 to 101.7, inclusive. Cases involving violation of paragraph (4)(D) of section 8(b) in which it is deemed appropriate to seek injunctive relief of a district court pursuant to section 10(l) of the act, are given priority over all other cases in the office except other cases under section 10(l) of the act and cases of like character.

§101.33 Initiation of formal action; settlement.

If, after investigation, it appears to the regional director that the Board should determine the dispute under section 10(k) of the act, he issues a notice of hearing which includes a simple statement of issues involved in the jurisdictional dispute and which is served on all parties to the dispute out of which the unfair labor practice is alleged to have arisen. The hearing is scheduled for not less than 10 days after service of the notice of the filing of the charge, except that in cases involving the national defense, agreement will be sought for scheduling of hearing on less notice. If the parties present to the regional director satisfactory evidence that they have adjusted the dispute, the regional director withdraws the notice of hearing and either permits the withdrawal of the charge or dismisses the charge. If the parties submit to the regional director satisfactory evidence that they have agreed upon methods for the voluntary adjustment of the dispute, the regional director shall defer action upon the charge and shall withdraw the notice of hearing if issued. The parties may agree on an arbitrator, a proceeding under section 9(c) of the act, or any other satisfactory method to resolve the dispute. If the agreed-upon method for voluntary adjustment results in a determination that employees represented by a charged union are entitled to perform the work in dispute, the regional director dismisses the charge against that union irrespective of whether the employer complies with that determination.

§101.34 Hearing.

If the parties have not adjusted the dispute or agreed upon methods of voluntary adjustment, a hearing, usually open to the public, is held before a hearing officer. The hearing is non-adversary in character, and the primary interest of the hearing officer is to insure that the record contains as full a statement of the pertinent facts as may be necessary for a determination of the issues by the Board. All parties are afforded full opportunity to present their respective positions and to produce evidence in support of their contentions. The parties are permitted to argue orally on the record before the hearing officer. At the close of the hearing, the case is transmitted to the Board for decision. The hearing officer prepares an analysis of the issues and the evidence, but makes no recommendations in regard to resolution of the dispute.

§101.35 Procedure before the Board.

The parties have 7 days after the close of the hearing, subject to any extension that may have been granted, to file briefs with the Board and to request oral argument which the Board may or may not grant. However, in cases involving the national defense and so designated in the notice of hearing, the parties may not file briefs but after the close of the evidence may argue orally upon the record their respective contentions and positions, except that for good cause shown in an application expeditiously made to the Board in Washington, D.C., after the close of the hearing, the Board may grant leave to file briefs in such time as it shall specify. The Board then considers the evidence taken at the hearing and the hearing officer's analysis together with any briefs that may be filed and the oral argument, if any, and issues its determination or makes other disposition of the matter.

§101.36 Compliance with determination; further proceedings.

After the issuance of determination by the Board, the regional director in the region in which the proceeding arose communicates with the parties for the purpose of ascertaining their intentions in regard to compliance. Conferences may be held for the purpose of working out details. If the regional director is satisfied that the parties are complying with the determination, he dismisses the charge. If the regional director is not satisfied that the parties are complying, he issues a complaint and notice of hearing, charging violation of section 8(b)(4)(D) of the act, and the proceeding follows the procedure outlined in §§101.8 to 101.15, inclusive. However, if the Board determines that employees represented by a charged union are entitled to perform the work in dispute, the regional director dismisses the charge against that union irrespective of whether the employer complies with the determination.

Subpart G—Procedure Under Section 10(j) and (l) of the Act

§101.37 Application for temporary relief or restraining orders.

Whenever it is deemed advisable to seek temporary injunctive relief under section 10(j) or whenever it is determined that a complaint should issue alleging violation of section 8(b)(4)(A), (B), or (C), or section 8(e), or section 8(b)(7), or whenever it is appropriate to seek temporary injunctive relief for a violation of section 8(b)(4)(D), the officer or regional attorney to whom the matter has been referred will make application for appropriate temporary relief or restraining order in the district court of the United States within which the unfair labor practice is alleged to have occurred or within which the party sought to be enjoined resides or transacts business, except that such officer or regional attorney will not apply for injunctive relief under section 10(l) with respect to an alleged violation of section 8(b)(7) if a charge under section 8(a)(2) has been filed and after preliminary investigation, he has reasonable cause to believe that such charge is true and that a complaint should issue.

§101.38 Change of circumstances.

Whenever a temporary injunction has been obtained pursuant to section 10(j) and thereafter the administrative law judge hearing the complaint, upon which the determination to seek such injunction was predicated, recommends dismissal of such complaint, in whole or in part, the officer or regional attorney handling the case for the Board suggests to the district court which issued the temporary injunction the possible change in circumstances arising out of the findings and recommendations of the administrative law judge.

Subpart H—Declaratory Orders and Advisory Opinions Regarding Board Jurisdiction

§101.39 Initiation of advisory opinion case.

The question of whether the Board will assert jurisdiction over a labor dispute which is the subject of a proceeding in an agency or court of a State or Territory is initiated by the filing of a petition with the Board. This petition may be filed only if (a) a proceeding is currently pending before such agency or court, and (b) the petitioner is a party to such proceedings before such agency or court or is the agency or court itself. The petition must be in writing and signed. When a petition is filed by a private party, it shall either be sworn to or shall contain a declaration under the penalties of the Criminal Code that its contents are true and correct. It is filed with the executive secretary of the Board in Washington, D.C. No particular form is required, but the petition must be properly captioned and must contain the allegations required by §102.99 of this chapter. None of the information sought relates to the merits of the dispute. The petition may be withdrawn at any time before the Board issues its advisory opinion determining whether it would or would not assert jurisdiction on the basis of the facts before it.

§101.40 Proceedings following the filing of the petition.

(a) A copy of the petition is served upon all other parties and the appropriate regional director by the petitioner.

(b) Interested persons may request intervention by a written motion to the Board. Such intervention may be granted in the discretion of the Board.

(c) Parties other than the petitioner may reply to the petition in writing, admitting or denying any or all of the matters asserted therein.

(d) No briefs shall be filed except upon special permission of the Board.

(e) After review of the entire record, the Board issues an advisory opinion as to whether the facts presented would or would not cause it to assert jurisdiction over the case if the case had been originally filed before it. The Board will limit its advisory opinion to the jurisdictional issue confronting it, and will not presume to render an opinion on the merits of the case or on the question of whether the subject matter of the dispute is governed by the Labor Management Relations Act of 1947, as amended.

§101.41 Informal procedures for obtaining opinions on jurisdictional questions.

Although a formal petition is necessary to obtain an advisory opinion from the Board, other avenues are available to persons seeking informal and, in most cases, speedy opinions on jurisdictional issues. In discussion of jurisdiction questions informally with regional office personnel, information and advice concerning the Board's jurisdictional standards may be obtained. Such practices are not intended to be discouraged by the rules providing for formal advisory opinions by the Board, although the opinions expressed by such personnel are not to be regarded as binding upon the Board or the general counsel.

§101.42 Procedures for obtaining declaratory orders of the Board.

(a) When both an unfair labor practice charge and a representation petition are pending concurrently in a regional office, appeals from a regional director's dismissals thereof do not follow the same course. Appeal from the dismissal of a charge must be made to the general counsel, while appeal from dismissal of a representation petition may be made to the Board. To obtain uniformity in disposing of such cases on jurisdictional grounds at the same stage of each proceeding, the general counsel may file a petition for a declaratory order of the Board. Such order is intended only to remove uncertainty with respect to the question of whether the Board would assert jurisdiction over the labor dispute.

(b) A petition to obtain a declaratory Board order may be filed only by the general counsel. It must be in writing and signed. It is filed with the executive secretary of the Board in Washington, D.C. No particular form is required, but the petition must be properly captioned and must contain the allegations required by §102.106 of this chapter. None of the information sought relates to the merits of the dispute. The petition may be withdrawn any time before the Board issues its declaratory order deciding whether it would or would not assert jurisdiction over the cases.

§101.43 Proceedings following the filing of the petition.

(a) A copy of the petition is served upon all other parties.

(b) Interested persons may request intervention by a written motion to the Board. Such intervention may be granted in the discretion of the Board.

(c) All other parties may reply to the petition in writing.

(d) Briefs may be filed.

(e) After review of the record, the Board issues a declaratory order as to whether it will assert jurisdiction over the cases, but it will not render a decision on the merits at this stage of the cases.

(f) The declaratory Board order will be binding on the parties in both cases.

PART 103—OTHER RULES

Subpart A—Jurisdictional Standards

§103.1 Colleges and universities.

The Board will assert its jurisdiction in any proceeding arising under sections 8, 9, and 10 of the Act involving any private nonprofit college or university which has a gross annual revenue from all sources (excluding only contributions which, because of limitation by the grantor, are not available for use for operating expenses) of not less than $1 million.

§103.2 Symphony Orchestras.

The Board will assert its jurisdiction in any proceeding arising under sections 8, 9, and 10 of the Act involving any symphony orchestra which has a gross annual revenue from all sources (excluding only contributions which are because of limitation by the grantor not available for use for operating expenses) of not less than $1 million.

§103.3 Horseracing and dogracing industries.

The Board will not assert its jurisdiction in any proceeding under sections 8, 9, and 10 of the act involving the horseracing and dogracing industries.

Subparts B-E [Reserved]

Subpart F—Remedial Orders

§103.100 Offers of reinstatement to employees in armed forces.

When an employer is required by a Board remedial order to offer an employee employment, reemployment, or reinstatement, or to notify an employee of his or her entitlement to reinstatement upon application, the employer shall, if the employee is serving in the armed forces of the United States at the time such offer or notification is made, also notify the employee of his or her right to reinstatement upon application in accordance with the Military Selective Service Act after discharge from the armed forces.

NLRB Delegation of Powers to General Counsel

Text of Memorandum Describing the Authority and Assigned Responsibilities of the General Counsel of the NLRB effective April 1, 1955, and as last amended effective May 15, 1961

The statutory authority and responsibility of the General Counsel of the Board are defined in Section 3(d) of the National Labor Relations Act as follows:

"There shall be a General Counsel of the Board who shall be appointed by the President, by and with the advice and consent of the Senate, for a term of four years. The General Counsel of the Board shall exercise general supervision over all attorneys employed by the Board (other than trial examiners and legal assistants to Board members) and over the officers and employees in the regional offices. He shall have final authority, on behalf of the Board, in respect of the investigation of charges and issuance of complaints under Section 20, and in respect of the prosecution of such complaints before the Board, and shall have such other duties as the Board may prescribe or as may be provided by law."

This memorandum is intended to describe the statutory authority and to set forth the prescribed duties and authority of the General Counsel of the Board, effective April 1, 1955:

I. Case Handling

A. *Complaint Cases.* The General Counsel of the Board has full and final authority and responsibility, on behalf of the Board, to accept and investigate charges filed, to enter into and approve informal settlement of charges, to dismiss charges, to determine matters concerning consolidation and severance of cases before complaint issues, to issue complaints and notices of hearing, to appear before trial examiners (administrative law judges) in hearings on complaints and prosecute as provided in the Board's

701

rules and regulations, and to initiate and prosecute injunction proceedings as provided for in Section 10(l) of the Act. After issuance of Intermediate Report by the trial examiner (administrative law judge), the General Counsel may file exceptions and briefs and appear before the Board in oral argument, subject to the Board's rules and regulations.

B. *Court Litigation.* The General Counsel of the Board is authorized and has responsibility, on behalf of the Board, to seek and effect compliance with the Board's orders and make such compliance reports to the Board as it may from time to time require.

On behalf of the Board the General Counsel will, in full accordance with the directions of the Board, petition for enforcement and resist petitions for review of Board orders as provided in Sections 10(e) and (f) of the Act, initiate and prosecute injunction proceedings as provided in Section 10(j), seek temporary restraining orders as provided in Sections 10(e) and (f), and take appeals either by writ of error or on petition for certiorari to the Supreme Court, provided, however, that the General Counsel will initiate and conduct injunction proceedings under Section 10(j) or under Sections 10(e) and (f) of the Act and contempt proceedings pertaining to the enforcement of or compliance with any order of the Board only upon approval of the Board, and will initiate and conduct appeals to the Supreme Court by writ of error or on petition for certiorari when authorized by the Board.[1]

C. *Representation and Other Election Cases.* Pursuant to Section 3(b) of the Act, and subject to such instructions and rules and regulations as may be issued by the Board from time to time, the Board has delegated to its regional directors its powers under Section 9 to determine the unit appropriate for the purpose of collective bargaining, to investigate and provide for hearings and determine whether a question of representation exists, and to direct an election or take a secret ballot under Subsection (c) or (e) of Section 9 and certify the results thereof. Such delegation shall be effective

---

[1]On May 27, 1983, the Board clarified its supervisory role over the General Counsel's conduct of court litigation as reflected in the following minute entry:

"The Board has considered how best to carry out its statutory powers to petition courts for enforcement of its orders; resist petitions for review; support its legal positions before the United States Supreme Court; seek compliance with its orders and, where necessary, institute contempt proceedings; and participate in miscellaneous court litigation. In this connection, the Board has reviewed the General Counsel's delegated assignments with respect to these statutory powers as such assignments are set forth in the Board Memorandum Describing the Authority and Assigned Responsibilities of the General Counsel of the National Labor Relations Board effective April 1, 1955.

"In order to exercise its statutory powers more responsibly and effectively, the Board (Member Zimmerman abstaining, Member Dennis not present) today has decided to amend the Minutes of May 4, 1983, to read as follows:

"1. Effective immediately, all pleadings and briefs in proceedings involving enforcement, review, Supreme Court litigation, contempt, and miscellaneous litigation shall be submitted to the Board's Solicitor at least one week before they are due to be filed.

"2. The aforementioned pleadings and briefs shall thereafter be filed by the General Counsel on the Board's behalf only after the Board's approval. This authority may be delegated by the Board to the Solicitor, Deputy, Associate, and Assistant Solicitors.

"3. Briefs and pleadings filed by the General Counsel on the Board's behalf shall list as counsel only:
   (a) the Board's Solicitor or Deputy Solicitor, Associate Solicitor, or Assistant Solicitor if delegated as provided in paragraph 2;
   (b) the attorney immediately responsible for supervising the drafting of the pleading or brief; and
   (c) the attorney or attorneys who actually drafted the pleadings or brief, or who will argue the case.

with respect to any petition filed under Subsection (c) or (e) of Section 9 of the Act on May 15, 1961.

Subject to the foregoing delegation and to the regional director's direct responsibility to perform the delegated functions in accord with the Board's rules and regulations and any other implementing directives of the Board, the General Counsel of the Board is authorized and has responsibility, on behalf of the Board, to facilitate the receipt and processing, in accordance with such instructions and rules and regulations as may be issued by the Board from time to time, all petitions filed pursuant to Section 9 of the Labor Management Relations Act, as amended. The General Counsel is also authorized and has responsibility to conduct secret ballots pursuant to Section 209(b) of the Labor Management Relations Act of 1947, whenever the Board is required to do so by law.

D. *Jurisdictional Dispute Cases*. The General Counsel of the Board is authorized and has responsibility, on behalf of the Board, to perform all functions necessary to the accomplishment of the provisions of Section 10(k) of the Act, but in connection therewith the Board will, at the request of the General Counsel, assign to him for the purpose of conducting the hearing provided for therein one of its staff trial examiners (administrative law judges). This authority and responsibility and the assignment of the trial examiner (administrative law judge) to the General Counsel shall terminate with the close of the hearing. Thereafter the Board will assume full jurisdiction over the matter for the purpose of deciding the issues in such hearing on the record made and subsequent hearings or related proceedings and will also rule upon any appeals.

II. Internal Regulations

Procedural and operational regulations for the conduct of the internal business of the Board within the area that is under the supervision and direction of the General Counsel of the Board may be prepared and promulgated by the General Counsel.

III. State Agreements

When authorized by the Board, the General Counsel may initiate and conduct discussions and negotiations, on behalf of the Board, with appro-

---

"4. Effective immediately, the Board will exercise its statutory authority, set forth in Section 4(a) of the Act, to appoint all attorneys and related employees needed to carry out the functions set forth in the preamble of this minute and in paragraph 1. The Board retains for itself the authority to transfer, promote, discipline, discharge, and take any other necessary and appropriate personnel action with regard to all employees referred to herein. The Board, in turn, delegates this authority to the Chairman, subject to redelegation by him.

"5. The Board desires that the General Counsel exercise general supervisory responsibility over the attorneys and related employees performing the functions listed in the preamble and in paragraph 1. Evaluations and other personnel recommendations shall emanate from the immediate supervisors of the personnel involved and the General Counsel but shall be subject to final approval of the Board.

"6. The Board directs that the Solicitor's office and staff relocate to the area where the attorneys involved in enforcement litigation are located.

"The Executive Secretary is directed to communicate the Board's instructions to the General Counsel forthwith." [Ed.]

priate authorities of any of the States or Territories looking to the consummation of agreements affecting any of the States or Territories as contemplated in Section 10(a) of the Act, provided, however, that in no event shall the Board be committed in any respect with regard to such discussions or negotiations or the entry into of any such agreement unless and until the Board and the General Counsel have joined with the appropriate authorities of the State or Territory affected in the execution of such agreement.

IV.　Liaison With Other Governmental Agencies

The General Counsel is authorized and has responsibility, on behalf of the Board, to maintain appropriate and adequate liaison and arrangements with the office of the Secretary of Labor, with reference to the reports required to be filed pursuant to Sections 9(f) and (g) of the Act and availability to the Board and General Counsel of the contents thereof.[2]

The General Counsel of the Board is authorized and has responsibility, on behalf of the Board, to maintain appropriate and adequate liaison with the Federal Mediation and Conciliation Service and any other appropriate governmental agency with respect to functions which may be performed in connection with the provisions of Section 209(b) of the Act. Any action taken pursuant to the authority and responsibility prescribed in this paragraph will be promptly reported to the Board.

V.　Anti-Communist Affidavits

The General Counsel of the Board is authorized and has responsibility, on behalf of the Board, to receive the affidavits required under Section 9(h) of the Act, to maintain an appropriate and adequate file thereof, and to make available to the public, on such terms as he may prescribe, appropriate information concerning such affidavits, but not to make such files open to unsupervised inspection.[3]

VI.　Miscellaneous Litigation Involving Board and/or Officials

The General Counsel of the Board is authorized and has responsibility, on behalf of the Board, to appear in any court to represent the Board or any of its members or agents, unless directed otherwise by the Board.

VII.　Personnel

1. In order more fully to release the Board to the expeditious performance of its primary function and responsibility of deciding cases, the full authority and responsibility for all administrative functions of the Agency shall be vested in the General Counsel. The authority shall be exercised subject to the limitations contained in paragraph 2 with respect to the

---

[2]Sections 9(f) and (g) were repealed by the Labor Management Reporting and Disclosure Act of 1959 (Landrum-Griffin Act). [Ed.]

[3]Section 9(h) was repealed by the Labor Management Reporting and Disclosure Act of 1959 (Landrum-Griffin Act). [Ed.]

personnel of, or directly related to, Board members, and shall be exercised in conformity with the requirements for joint determination as described in paragraph 4.

2. The General Counsel shall exercise full and final authority on behalf of the Agency over the selection, retention, transfer, promotion, demotion, discipline, discharge, and in all other respects of all personnel engaged in the field, except that personnel action with respect to regional directors and officers-in-charge of subregional offices will be conducted as hereinafter provided, and in the Washington Office (other than personnel in the Board members' offices, the Division of Trial Examiners (administrative law judges), the Division of Information, the Security Office, the Office of the Solicitor, and the Office of the Executive Secretary), provided, however, that the establishment, transfer or elimination of any regional or subregional office shall require the approval of the Board.

The appointment, transfer, demotion, or discharge of any regional director or of any officer-in-charge of a subregional office shall be made by the General Counsel only upon the approval of the Board.

3. The General Counsel will provide such administrative services and housekeeping services as may be requested by the Board in connection with the conduct of its necessary business, and will submit to the Board a quarterly report on the performance of these administrative functions.

4. In connection with and in order to effectuate the foregoing, the General Counsel is authorized to formulate and execute such necessary requests, certifications, and other related documents on behalf of the Agency, as may be needed from time to time to meet the requirements of the Civil Service Commission [Office of Personnel Management], the Bureau of the Budget [Office of Management and Budget], or any other governmental agency, provided, however, that the total amount of any annual budget requests submitted by the Agency, the apportionment and allocation of funds, and/ or the establishment of personnel ceilings within the Agency shall be determined jointly by the Board and the General Counsel.

VIII. Assignment of Authority

To the extent that the above-described duties, powers, and authority rest by statute with the Board, the foregoing statement constitutes a prescription and assignment of such duties, powers, and authority, whether or not so specified.

APPENDIX D

NLRB Delegation of Authority to Regional Directors

Text of Statement Issued by the NLRB May 4, 1961, effective May 15, 1961

Pursuant to section 3(b) of the National Labor Relations Act, as amended, and subject to the amendments to the Board's Statements of Procedure, Series 8, and to its Rules and Regulations, Series 8, effective May 15, 1961 and subject to such further amendments and instructions as may be issued by the Board from time to time, the Board delegates to its Regional Directors "its powers under section 9 to determine the unit appropriate for the purpose of collective bargaining, to investigate and provide for hearings, and determine whether a question of representation exists, and to direct an election or take a secret ballot under subsection (c) or (e) of section 9 and certify the results thereof."

Such delegation shall be effective with respect to any petition filed under subsection (c) or (e) of section 9 of the Act on May 15, 1961.

APPENDIX E

NLRB National, Regional, and Subregional Offices

National Office

National Labor Relations Board
1717 Pennsylvania Avenue, N.W.
Washington, D.C. 20570
202 655-4000

Office of the Board
  Office of the Executive Secretary
  Office of the Solicitor
  Division of Judges
    (1375 K Street, N.W.
    Washington, D.C. 20005)
  Division of Information

Office of the General Counsel
  Division of Operations Management
  Division of Advice
  Division of Enforcement Litigation
  Division of Administration
  Regional Directors

Regional and Subregional Offices

	Region and Subregion Nos.		Region and Subregion Nos.
Alabama	10, 15	Georgia	10
Alaska	19	Hawaii	S-37 (20)
Arizona	28	Idaho	19
Arkansas	26	Illinois	13, 14, 33
California	20, 21, 31, 32	Indiana	9, 13, 25
Colorado	27	Iowa	18, 33
Connecticut	S-39 (1)	Kansas	17
Delaware	4, 5	Kentucky	9, 25
District of		Louisiana	15
Columbia	5	Maine	1
Florida	12, 15	Maryland	5

	Region and		*Region and*
	Subregion Nos.		*Subregion Nos.*
Massachusetts	1	Oregon	S-36 (19)
Michigan	7, 30	Pennsylvania	4, 6
Minnesota	18	Rhode Island	1
Mississippi	15, 26	South Carolina	11
Missouri	14, 17	South Dakota	18
Montana	19	Tennessee	5, 10, 26
Nebraska	17	Texas	16, 23, 28
Nevada	31, 32	Utah	27
New Hampshire	1	Vermont	1
New Jersey	4, 22	Virginia	5
New Mexico	28	Washington	19, S-36 (19)
New York	2, 3, 29	West Virginia	5, 6, 9
North Carolina	11	Wisconsin	18, 30
North Dakota	18	Wyoming	27
Ohio	8, 9	Puerto Rico	24
Oklahoma	16	U.S. Virgin Islands	24

Areas Served by Regional and Subregional Offices

Region 1. Boston, Massachusetts 02116   617 223-3300
Walker Building, 3rd Floor
120 Boylston Street

Serves: Maine, New Hampshire, Vermont, Massachusetts, and Rhode Island.

Subregion 39: Hartford, Connecticut 06103   203 722-2540
750 Main Street, Room 1200

Serves: Connecticut.

Region 2. New York, New York 10278   212 264-0300
Federal Building, Room 3614
26 Federal Plaza

Serves: Bronx, New York; Orange, Putnam, Rockland, and Westchester counties, New York.

Region 3. Buffalo, New York 14202   716 846-4931
Federal Building, Room 901
111 West Huron Street
Resident Office:
    Albany, New York 12207   518 472-2215
    Federal Building
    Clinton Avenue at North Pearl Street

Serves: All New York State counties except the metropolitan area counties served by Regions 2 and 29.

Region 4. Philadelphia, Pennsylvania 19106   215 597-7601
1 Independence Mall, 7th Floor
615 Chestnut Street

Serves: In Pennsylvania, Adams, Berks, Bradford, Bucks, Carbon, Chester, Columbia, Cumberland, Dauphin, Delaware,

Juniata, Lackawanna, Lancaster, Lebanon, Lehigh, Luzern, Lycoming, Monroe, Montgomery, Montour, Northampton, Northumberland, Perry, Philadelphia, Pike, Schuylskill, Snyder, Sullivan, Susquehanna, Tioga, Union, Wayne, Wyoming, and York counties; in New Jersey, Atlantic, Burlington, Camden, Cape May, Cumberland, Gloucester, Ocean, and Salem counties; and in Delaware, New Castle County.

Region 5.   Baltimore, Maryland 21202   301 962-2822
Candler Building, 4th Floor
109 Market Place
Resident Office:
     Washington, D.C. 20037   202 254-7612
     Gelman Building, Suite 100
     2120 L Street, N.W.

Serves: Maryland, Virginia, and the District of Columbia; in Delaware, Kent and Sussex counties; the city of Bristol in Sullivan County, Tennessee; and in West Virginia, Berkley, Grant, Hampshire, Hardy, Jefferson, Mineral, Morgan, and Pendleton counties.

Region 6.   Pittsburgh, Pennsylvania 15222   412 644-2977
1501 Wm. S. Moorhead Federal Building
1000 Liberty Avenue

Serves: In Pennsylvania, Allegheny, Armstrong, Beaver, Bedford, Blair, Butler, Cambria, Cameron, Centre, Clarion, Clearfield, Clinton, Crawford, Elk, Erie, Fayette, Forest, Franklin, Fulton, Greene, Huntingdon, Indiana, Jefferson, Lawrence, McKean, Mercer, Mifflin, Potter, Somerset, Venango, Warren, Washington, and Westmoreland counties; in West Virginia, Barbour, Brooke, Doddridge, Hancock, Harrison, Lewis, Marion, Marshall, Monongalia, Ohio, Pocahontas, Preston, Randolph, Taylor, Tucker, Upshur, Webster, and Wetzel counties.

Region 7.   Detroit, Michigan 48226   313 226-3200
Patrick V. McNamara Federal Building,
     Room 300
477 Michigan Avenue
Resident Office:
     Grand Rapids, Michigan 49503   616 456-2679
     82 Ionia N.W., 3rd Floor

Serves: In Michigan, Alcona, Allegan, Alpena, Antrim, Arenac, Barry, Bay, Benzie, Berrien, Branch, Calhoun, Cass, Charleviox, Cheboygan, Clare, Clinton, Crawford, Eaton, Emmet, Genesee, Gladwin, Grand Traverse, Gratiot, Hillsdale, Huron, Ingham, Ionia, Iosco, Isabella, Jackson, Kalamazoo, Kalkaska, Kent, Lake, Lapeer, Leelanau, Lenawee, Livingston, Macomb, Manistee, Mason, Mecosta, Midland, Missaukee, Monroe, Montcalm, Montmorency, Muskegon, Newaygo, Oakland, Oceana, Ogemaw, Osceola, Oscoda, Otsego, Ottawa, Presque Isle, Roscommon,

Saginaw, St. Clair, St. Joseph, Sanilac, Shiawassee, Tuscola, Van Buren, Washtenaw, Wayne, and Wexford counties.

Region 8.　Cleveland, Ohio 44199　　　　　216 522-3715
Anthony J. Celebrezze Federal Building,
　Room 1695
1240 East Ninth Street

Serves:　In Ohio, Allen, Ashland, Ashtabula, Auglaize, Belmont, Carroll, Champaign, Columbiana, Coshocton, Crawford, Cuyahoga, Darke, Defiance, Delaware, Erie, Fulton, Geauga, Guernsey, Hancock, Hardin, Harrison, Henry, Holmes, Huron, Jefferson, Knox, Lake, Licking, Logan, Lorain, Lucas, Mahoning, Marion, Medina, Mercer, Miami, Morrow, Muskingum, Ottawa, Paulding, Portage, Putnam, Richland, Sandusky, Seneca, Shelby, Stark, Summit, Trumbull, Tuscarawas, Union, Van Wert, Wayne, Williams, Wood, and Wyandot counties.

Region 9.　Cincinnati, Ohio 45202　　　　　513 684-3686
Federal Office Building, Room 3003
550 Main Street

Serves:　In Ohio, Adams, Athens, Brown, Butler, Clark, Clermont, Clinton, Fairfield, Fayette, Franklin, Gallia, Greene, Hamilton, Highland, Hocking, Jackson, Lawrence, Madison, Meigs, Monroe, Montgomery, Morgan, Noble, Perry, Pickaway, Pike, Preble, Ross, Scioto, Vinton, Warren and Washington counties; all counties in Kentucky except Daviess and Henderson; in Indiana, Clark, Dearborn, and Floyd counties; and in West Virginia, Boone, Braxton, Cabell, Calhoun, Clay, Fayette, Gilmer, Greenbrier, Jackson, Kanawha, Lincoln, Logan, McDowell, Mason, Mercer, Mingo, Monroe, Nichols, Pleasants, Putnam, Raleigh, Ritchie, Roane, Summers, Tyler, Wayne, Wirt, Wood, and Wyoming counties.

Region 10.　Atlanta, Georgia 30303　　　　　404 221-2896
Marietta Tower, Suite 2400
101 Marietta Street, N.W.
Resident Office:
　Birmingham, Alabama 35203　　　　205 254-1062
　Bank of Savings Building
　1919 Morris Avenue

Serves:　Georgia; in Tennessee, Anderson, Bledsoe, Blount, Bradley, Campbell, Carter, Clairborne, Clay, Cocke, Cumberland, Fentress, Grainger, Greene, Grundy, Hamblen, Hamilton, Hancock, Hawkins, Jackson, Jefferson, Johnson, Knox, Loudon, McMinn, Marion, Meigs, Monroe, Morgan, Overton, Pickett, Polk, Putnam, Rhea, Roane, Scott, Sequatchie, Sevier, Sullivan, Unicoi, Union, Van Buren, Warren, Washington, and White counties; in Alabama, Autauga, Bibb, Blount, Calhoun, Chambers, Cherokee, Chilton, Clay, Cleburne, Colbert, Coosa, Cullman, DeKalb,

Elmore, Etowah, Fayette, Franklin, Greene, Hale, Jackson, Jefferson, Lamar, Lauderdale, Lawrence, Lee, Limestone, Madison, Marion, Marshall, Morgan, Perry, Pickens, Randolph, St. Clair, Shelby, Sumter, Talladega, Tallapoosa, Tuscaloosa, Walker, and Winston counties.

Region 11.   Winston-Salem, North Carolina 27101   919 761-3201
Federal Building, Room 447
U.S. Courthouse
251 North Main Street

Serves: North Carolina and South Carolina.

Region 12.   Tampa, Florida 33602   813 228-2641
700 Twigg Street, Suite 511
P.O. Box 3322
Resident Offices:
   Miami, Florida 33130   305 350-5391
   Federal Building, Room 916
   51 S.W. 1st Avenue

   Jacksonville, Florida 32202   904 791-3768
   Federal Building, Room 278
   400 West Bay Street

Serves: In Florida, Alachua, Baker, Bradford, Brevard, Broward, Charlotte, Citrus, Clay, Collier, Columbia, Dade, De Soto, Dixie, Duval, Flagler, Gadsden, Gilchrist, Glades, Hamilton, Hardee, Hendry, Hernando, Highlands, Hillsborough, Indian River, Jefferson, Lafayette, Lake, Lee, Leon, Levy, Madison, Manatee, Marion, Martin, Monroe, Nassau, Okeechobee, Orange, Osceola, Palm Beach, Pasco, Pinella, Polk, Putnam, St. Johns, St. Lucie, Sarasota, Seminole, Sumter, Suwannee, Taylor, Union, Volusia, and Wakulla counties.

Region 13.   Chicago, Illinois 60604   312 353-7570
Everett McKinley Dirksen Building
219 South Dearborn Street

Serves: In Illinois, Cook, Du Page, Kane, Lake and Will counties; in Indiana, Lake County.

Region 14.   St. Louis, Missouri 63101   314 425-4167
210 Tucker Boulevard North, Room 448

Serves: In Illinois, Adams, Alexander, Bond, Brown, Calhoun, Christian, Clark, Clinton, Coles, Crawford, Cumberland, Edgar, Edwards, Effingham, Fayette, Franklin, Gallatin, Greene, Hamilton, Hardin, Jackson, Jasper, Jefferson, Jersey, Johnson, Lawrence, Macoupin, Madison, Marion, Massac, Monroe, Montgomery, Perry, Pike, Pope, Pulaski, Randolph, Richland, St. Clair, Saline, Scott, Shelby, Union, Wabash, Washington, Wayne, White, and Williamson counties; in Missouri, Audrian, Bollinger, Butler, Callaway, Cape Girardeau, Carter, Clark, Crawford, Dent, Dunklin, Franklin, Gasconade, Independent City of St. Louis, Iron, Jefferson, Knox, Lewis, Lincoln, Madison, Maries, Marion,

Mississippi, Monroe, Montgomery, New Madrid, Oregon, Osage, Pemiscot, Perry, Phelps, Pike, Ralls, Reynolds, Ripley, St. Charles, St. Francois, St. Louis, St. Genevieve, Scotland, Scott, Shannon, Shelby, Stoddard, Warren, Washington, and Wayne counties.

Region 15. New Orleans, Louisiana 70130   504 589-6361
Federal Building, Room 600
600 South Maestri Place

Serves: Louisiana; in Mississippi, Adams, Amite, Claiborne, Clarke, Copiah, Covington, Forrest, Franklin, George, Greene, Hancock, Harrison, Hinds, Issaquena, Jackson, Jasper, Jefferson, Jefferson Davis, Jones, Kemper, Lamar, Lauderdale, Lawrence, Leake, Lincoln, Madison, Marion, Neshoba, Newton, Pearl River, Perry, Pike, Rankin, Scott, Sharkey, Simpson, Smith, Stone, Walthall, Warren, Wayne, Wilkinson, and Yazoo counties; in Alabama, Baldwin, Barbour, Bullock, Butler, Choctaw, Clarke, Coffee, Conecuh, Covington, Crenshaw, Dale, Dallas, Escambia, Geneva, Henry, Houston, Lowndes, Macon, Marengo, Mobile, Monroe, Montgomery, Pike, Russell, Washington, and Wilcox counties; in Florida, Bay, Calhoun, Escambia, Franklin, Gulf, Holmes, Jackson, Liberty, Okaloosa, Santa Rosa, Walton, and Washington counties.

Region 16. Fort Worth, Texas 76102   817 334-2921
Federal Office Building, Room 8A24
819 Taylor Street
Resident Office:
  Tulsa, Oklahoma 74127   918 581-7951
  Robert S. Kerr Building, Room 210
  440 South Houston Avenue

Serves: Oklahoma; in Texas, Anderson, Andrews, Angelina, Archer, Armstrong, Bailey, Baylor, Bell, Borden, Bosque, Bowie, Brewster, Briscoe, Brown, Burnet, Callahan, Camp, Carson, Cass, Castro, Cherokee, Childress, Clay, Cochran, Coke, Coleman, Collin, Collingsworth, Comanche, Concho, Cooke, Coryell, Cottle, Crane, Crockett, Crosby, Dallam, Dallas, Dawson, Deaf Smith, Delta, Denton, Dickens, Donley, Eastland, Ector, Ellis, Erath, Falls, Fannin, Fisher, Floyd, Foard, Franklin, Freestone, Gaines, Garza, Glasscock, Gray, Grayson, Gregg, Hale, Hall, Hamilton, Hansford, Hardeman, Harrison, Hartley, Haskell, Hemphill, Henderson, Hill, Hockley, Hood, Hopkins, Houston, Howard, Hunt, Hutchison, Irion, Jack, Jeff Davis, Johnson, Jones, Kaufman, Kent, Kimble, King, Knox, Lamar, Lamb, Lampasas, Leon, Limestone, Lipscomb, Llano, Loving, Lubbock, Lynn, Madison, Marion, Martin, Mason, McCulloch, McLennan, Menard, Midland, Milam, Mills, Mitchell, Montague, Moore, Morris, Motley, Nacogdoches, Navarro, Nolan, Ochiltree, Oldham, Palo Pinto, Panola, Parker, Parmer, Pecos, Potter, Presidio, Rains, Randall, Reagan, Red River, Reeves, Roberts,

Robertson, Rockwall, Runnels, Rusk, Sabine, San
Augustine, San Saba, Schleicher, Scurry, Schackelford,
Shelby, Sherman, Smith, Somervell, Stephens, Sterling,
Stonewall, Sutton, Swisher, Tarrant, Taylor, Terrell, Terry,
Throckmorton, Titus, Tom Green, Trinity, Upshur, Upton,
Van Zandt, Ward, Wheeler, Wichita, Wilbarger,
Williamson, Winkler, Wise, Wood, Yoakum, and Young
counties.

Region 17.   Kansas City, Kansas 66101   913 236-3846
           Two Gateway Centre, Room 616
           Fourth at State

Serves: Nebraska and Kansas; in Missouri, Adair, Andrew,
           Atchison, Barry, Barton, Bates, Benton, Boone, Buchanan,
           Caldwell, Camden, Carroll, Cass, Cedar, Chariton,
           Christian, Clay, Clinton, Cole, Cooper, Dade, Dallas,
           Daviess, De Kalb, Douglas, Gentry, Greene, Grundy,
           Harrison, Henry, Hickory, Holt, Howard, Howell, Jackson,
           Jasper, Johnson, Laclede, Lafayette, Lawrence, Linn,
           Livingston, McDonald, Macon, Mercer, Miller, Moniteau,
           Morgan, Newton, Nodaway, Ozark, Pettis, Platte, Polk,
           Pulaski, Putnam, Randolph, Ray, St. Clair, Saline,
           Schuyler, Stone, Sullivan, Taney, Texas, Vernon, Webster,
           Worth, and Wright counties.

Region 18.   Minneapolis, Minnesota 55401   612 349-5357
           Federal Building, Room 316
           110 South Fourth Street
           Resident Office:
           Des Moines, Iowa   515 284-4391
           Federal Building, Room 909
           210 Walnut Street

Serves: North Dakota, South Dakota, and Minnesota; in Iowa,
           Adair, Adams, Allamakee, Appanoose, Audubon, Benton,
           Black Hawk, Boone, Bremer, Buchanan, Buena Vista,
           Butler, Calhoun, Carroll, Cass, Cedar, Cerro Gordo,
           Cherokee, Chickasaw, Clarke, Clay, Clayton, Crawford,
           Dallas, Davis, Decatur, Delaware, Dickinson, Emmet,
           Fayette, Floyd, Franklin, Fremont, Greene, Grundy,
           Guthrie, Hamilton, Hancock, Hardin, Harrison, Henry,
           Howard, Humboldt, Ida, Iowa, Jasper, Jefferson, Johnson,
           Jones, Keokuk, Kossuth, Linn, Lucas, Lyon, Madison,
           Mahaska, Marion, Marshall, Mills, Mitchell, Monona,
           Monroe, Montgomery, O'Brien, Osceola, Page, Palo Alto,
           Plymouth, Pocahontas, Polk, Pottawattmie, Poweshiek,
           Ringgold, Sac, Shelby, Sioux, Story, Tama, Taylor, Union,
           Van Buren, Wapello, Warren, Washington, Wayne,
           Webster, Winnebago, Winneshiek, Woodbury, Worth, and
           Wright counties; in Wisconsin, Ashland, Barron, Bayfield,
           Buffalo, Burnett, Chippewa, Clark, Douglas, Dunn, Eau
           Claire, Iron, Jackson, Pepin, Pierce, Polk, Price, Rusk, St.
           Croix, Sawyer, Taylor, Trempealeau, and Washburn
           counties.

Region 19.   Seattle, Washington 98174   206 442-4532
Federal Building, Room 2948
915 Second Avenue
Resident Office:
   Anchorage, Alaska   907 271-5051
   701 C Street, Room 510

Serves: Alaska, Montana, Idaho, and all counties in Washington
except Clark.

Subregion 36:   Portland, Oregon 97205   503 221-3085
Portland Building, Room 1360
1120 S.W. Fifth Avenue

Serves: Oregon and Clark County, Washington.

Region 20.   San Francisco, California 94102   415 556-3197
Federal Building, Room 13018
450 Golden Gate Avenue, Box 36047

Serves: In California, Butte, Colusa, Del Norte, Glenn, Humboldt,
Lake, Lassen, Marin, Mendocino, Modoc, Napa, Nevada,
Placer, Plumas, Sacramento, San Francisco, San Mateo,
Shasta, Sierra, Siskiyou, Solano, Sonoma, Sutter, Tehama,
Trinity, Yolo, and Yuba counties.

Subregion 37:   Honolulu, Hawaii 96850   808 546-5100
300 Ala Moana Boulevard, Room 7318
P.O. Box 50208

Serves: Hawaii.

Region 21.   Los Angeles, California 90014   213 894-5200
City National Bank Building, 24th Floor
606 South Olive Street
Resident Office:
   San Diego, California 92189   619 293-6184
   U.S. Courthouse, Room 2-N-20
   940 Front Street

Serves: In California, all of Imperial, Orange, Riverside, and San
Diego counties; that portion of Los Angeles County lying
east of Harbor Freeway and south of Pasadena Freeway
(Arroyo Boulevard, U.S. Highway 66).

Region 22.   Newark, New Jersey 07102   201 645-2100
Peter D. Rodino, Jr., Federal Building,
   Room 1600
970 Broad Street

Serves: In New Jersey, Bergen, Essex, Hudson, Hunterdon, Mercer,
Middlesex, Monmouth, Morris, Passaic, Somerset, Sussex,
Union and Warren counties.

Region 23.   Houston, Texas 77002   713 229-3748
Federal Building
Courthouse, Room 4014
515 Rusk Street

Resident Office:
San Antonio, Texas 78206   512 229-6140
Federal Office Building, Room A-509
727 E. Durango Boulevard

Serves: In Texas, Aransas, Atascosa, Austin, Bandera, Bastrop,
Bee, Bexar, Blanco, Brazoria, Brazos, Brooks, Burleson,
Caldwell, Calhoun, Cameron, Chambers, Colorado, Comal,
De Witt, Dimmit, Duval, Edwards, Fayette, Fort Bend,
Frio, Galveston, Gillespie, Goliad, Gonzales, Grimes,
Guadalupe, Hardin, Harris, Hays, Hidalgo, Jackson,
Jasper, Jefferson, Jim Hogg, Jim Wells, Karnes, Kendall,
Kenedy, Kerr, Kinney, Kleberg, La Salle, Lavaca, Lee,
Liberty, Live Oak, McMullen, Matagorda, Maverick,
Medina, Montgomery, Newton, Nueces, Orange, Polk, Real,
Refugio, San Jacinto, San Patricio, Starr, Travis, Tyler,
Uvalde, Val Verde, Victoria, Walker, Waller, Washington,
Webb, Wharton, Willacy, Wilson, Zapata, and Zavala
counties.

Region 24.   Hato Rey, Puerto Rico 00918   809 753-4347
Federico Degatau Federal Building
U.S. Courthouse, Room 591
Carlos E. Chardon Avenue

Serves: Puerto Rico and the U.S. Virgin Islands.

Region 25.   Indianapolis, Indiana 46204   317 269-7430
Federal Office Building, Room 282
575 North Pennsylvania Street

Serves: In Indiana, all counties except Lake, Clark, Dearborn, and
Floyd; in Kentucky, Daviess and Henderson counties.

Region 26.   Memphis, Tennessee 38174   901 521-2725
Mid-Memphis Tower, Eighth Floor
1407 Union Avenue
P.O. Box 41559
Resident Offices:
Little Rock, Arkansas 72201   501 378-6311
1 Union National Plaza, Suite 1120

Nashville, Tennessee 37203   615 251-5922
Estes Kefauver Federal Building
U.S. Courthouse, Room A-702

Serves: Arkansas; in Tennessee, Bedford, Benton, Cannon, Carroll,
Cheatham, Chester, Coffee, Crockett, Davidson, Decatur,
DeKalb, Dickson, Dyer, Fayette, Franklin, Gibson, Giles,
Hardeman, Hardin, Haywood, Henderson, Henry, Hickman,
Houston, Humphreys, Lake, Lauderdale, Lawrence, Lewis,
Lincoln, McNairy, Macon, Madison, Marshall, Maury,
Montgomery, Moore, Obion, Perry, Robertson, Rutherford,
Shelby, Smith, Stewart, Sumner, Tipton, Trousdale, Wayne,
Weakley, Williamson, and Wilson counties; in Mississippi,
Alcorn, Attala, Benton, Bolivar, Calhoun, Carroll,
Chickasaw, Choctaw, Clay, Coahoma, De Soto, Grenada,

Holmes, Humphreys, Itawamba, Lafayette, Lee, Leflore, Lowndes, Marshall, Monroe, Montgomery, Noxubee, Oktibbeha, Panola, Pontotoc, Prentiss, Quitman, Sunflower, Tallahatchie, Tate, Tippah, Tishomingo, Tunica, Union, Washington, Webster, Winton, and Yalobusha counties.

Region 27. Denver, Colorado 80202   303 844-3551
U.S. Custom House, Room 260
721 19th Street

Serves: Colorado, Utah, and Wyoming.

Region 28. Phoenix, Arizona 85004   602 261-3361
234 N. Central Avenue, Suite 440
P.O. Box 33069

Resident Offices:
Albuquerque, New Mexico 87110   617 223-3300
Patio Plaza Building, Upper Level
5000 Marble Avenue, N.E.

El Paso, Texas 79901   915 541-7737
First National Building, Suite 602
109 North Oregon Street

Serves: Arizona and New Mexico; in Texas, Culberson, El Paso, and Hudspeth counties.

Region 29. Brooklyn, New York 11241   212 330-7713
16 Court Street, 4th Floor

Serves: In New York, Kings, Nassau, Queens, Richmond, and Suffolk counties.

Region 30. Milwaukee, Wisconsin 53203   414 291-3861
Henry S. Reuss Federal Plaza, Suite 1240
310 W. Wisconsin Avenue

Serves: In Wisconsin, Adams, Brown, Calumet, Columbia, Crawford, Dane, Dodge, Door, Florence, Fon du Lac, Forest, Grant, Green, Green Lake, Iowa, Jefferson, Juneau, Kenosha, Kewaunee, La Crosse, Lafayette, Langlade, Lincoln, Manitowoc, Marathon, Marinette, Marquette, Menominee, Milwaukee, Monroe, Oconto, Oneida, Outagamie, Ozaukee, Portage, Racine, Richland, Rock, Sauk, Shawano, Sheboygan, Vernon, Vilas, Walworth, Washington, Waukesha, Waupaca, Waushara, Winnebago, and Wood counties; in Michigan, Alger, Baraga, Chippewa, Delta, Dickinson, Gogebic, Houghton, Iron, Keweennaw, Luce, Mackinac, Marquette, Menominee, Ontonagon, and Schoolcraft counties.

Region 31. Los Angeles, California 90024   213 209-7352
Federal Building, Room 12100
11000 Wilshire Boulevard

Resident Office: 702 385-6416
Los Vegas, Nevada 89101
720 South Seventh Street

Serves: In California, Inyo, Kern, San Bernardino, San Luis
Obispo, Santa Barbara, and Ventura counties; that portion
of Los Angeles County lying west of Harbor Freeway and
North of Pasadena Freeway (Arroyo Boulevard, U.S.
Highway 66); in Nevada, Nye, Lincoln, and Clark counties.

Region 32.   Oakland, California 94604   415 273-7200
Breuner Building, 2d Floor
2201 Broadway
P.O. Box 12983

Serves: In California, Alameda, Alpine, Amador, Calavaras, Contra
Costa, El Dorado, Fresno, Kings, Madera, Mariposa,
Merced, Mono, Monterey, San Benito, San Joaquin, Santa
Clara, Santa Cruz, Stanislaus, Tulare, and Tuolumne
counties; in Nevada, Churchill, Douglas, Elko, Esmeralda,
Eureka, Humboldt, Lander, Lyon, Mineral, Ormsby,
Pershing, Storey, Washoe, and White Pine counties.

Region 33.   Peoria, Illinois 61602   309 671-7080
Savings Center Tower, 16th Floor
411 Hamilton Avenue

Serves: In Illinois, Boone, Bureau, Carroll, Cass, Champaign, De
Kalb, De Witt, Douglas, Ford, Fulton, Grundy, Hancock,
Henderson, Henry, Iroquois, Jo Daviess, Kankaee, Kendall,
Knox, La Salle, Lee, Livingston, Logan, Macon, Marshall,
Mason, McDonough, McHenry, McLean, Menard, Mercer,
Morgan, Moultrie, Ogle, Peoria, Piatt, Putnam, Rock
Island, Sangamon, Schuyler, Stark, Stephenson, Tazewall,
Vermillion, Warren, Whiteside, Winnebago, and Woodford
counties; in Iowa, Clinton, Des Moines, Dubuque, Jackson,
Lee, Louisa, Muscatine, and Scott counties.

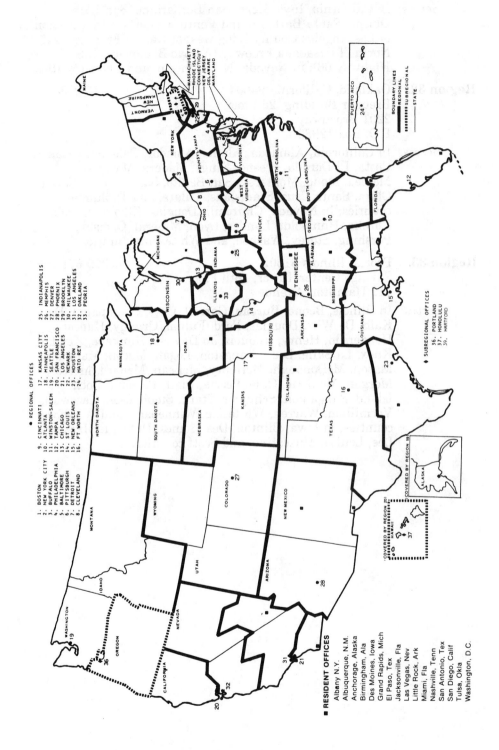

NLRB Decision-Making Process

Text of statement submitted to House Government Operations Subcommittee on Manpower and Housing, November 2, 1983

The organization of the Board, so far as case handling is concerned, consists of the offices of the Chairman and of the four Members, their respective staffs of Counsel, and the Executive Secretary and the Solicitor. Each Board Member has a professional staff consisting of a Chief Counsel, a Deputy Chief Counsel, three Assistant Chief Counsel, a small number of senior Counsel and approximately 10–12 Counsel, for a total of about 21 attorneys on each Board Member's staff.

A Chief Counsel serves in the dual capacity of staff director and legal advisor for his or her respective Board Member. The Executive Secretary is principally concerned with the administrative management of the Board's judicial affairs—in other words, management of the Board's caseload. The Solicitor and his staff are legal advisors and consultants to the Board as a whole.

As permitted by Section 3(b) of the Act, the Board has organized itself into five panels, with three Members comprising a panel; no two panels are composed of the same Members. Each Board Member is the head of one panel, and a member of two others. In general, cases which present novel or unusual issues or require an interpretation for which there is no precedent, or involve questions of policy, are decided by the full five-member Board. The remaining cases are decided by the Board panels. In Fiscal Year 1982, the Board issued 1051 contested unfair labor practice decisions, of which 1017 were issued by Panels, and 34 by four or more Members. In Fiscal 1983, these figures were 602, 591, and 11.

Each case begins by assignment to a Board Member, and is thereby automatically assigned to the panel which he or she heads. Because the handling of unfair labor practice cases before the Board is illustrative of the Board's decisional process generally, the process by which such cases are decided is described below.

In an unfair labor practice proceeding, the Administrative Law Judge issues a decision making findings of fact and conclusions of law, and recommending disposition of the case. Actually, the Executive Secretary's Office issues the Judge's Decision, a purely ministerial act. When the Judge's Decision is received from Reproduction, ready to issue, it is served on the parties with an order transferring the case to the Board, and with an excerpt from the Board's Rules and Regulations which advise how and when to appeal to the Board, if anyone so desires.

The Board's Rules provide 23 days to file exceptions and brief in support of exceptions, or the same period of time to file a brief in support of the Judge's Decision. If exceptions are filed, cross-exceptions and a brief in support of cross-exceptions (not limited in scope) and/or a brief answering exceptions, may be filed within a further period of 13 days. Finally, a brief in opposition to cross-exceptions may be filed within another 13 days. If all of these steps are used by the parties, a minimum period of 49 days is provided by the Board's Rules.

In Fiscal 1983, there were 1106 Judges' decisions received by the Board. Exceptions were filed in 757 cases or 68%.

If no exceptions are filed, the Board issues an Order adopting the Judge's Decision. This occurred in about 32% of the cases in Fiscal 1983. There were 155 summary-judgment decisions issued and 41 10(k) determinations.

Reasonable extensions of time to file exceptions and briefs are granted upon the request of a party. Periodic studies show that such requests are made in approximately 55% of the cases.

In the Board's experience, requests for extensions of time are not usually made for purposes of delay. An effort is made, however, to hold the line, and informal inquiries to other agencies such as FERC, ICC, FCC, and SEC indicate that NLRB is stricter in granting extensions.

If exceptions and briefs are filed with the Board, the Office of the Executive Secretary assigns the case to a Board Member. By and large, cases are assigned to Board Members in rotation, departing only to provide a mix of types of cases, and of length and complexity, or to return a case to the staff from which it originated, if rotation does not accomplish this result. At the beginning of each assignment week, the number of assignable cases is determined; that number is divided into equal "packages" and on a given day for each Board Member, sent to that Member. The result is that, annually, each Board Member is assigned very nearly the same number of cases.

When the Board Member receives the package of cases, a senior attorney, usually the Chief Counsel to that Member, assigns each case to a Counsel who reviews the entire record, including the transcript of the hearing, the exhibits, the ALJ's Decision, and exceptions and briefs.

Decision-making at the Board level is divided into "stages." Stage I is analysis and research; Stage II is drafting of a decision; Stage III is circulation for Board Members' approval or clearance. The final stages, unnumbered, are editorial, reproduction, and issuance.

When the Chief Counsel assigns the case, the Executive Secretary's office is advised of the date when "initial action" will be taken—that is, when a tentative decision will be reached so that the case enters Stage II, the drafting stage. Stage I may be one week or four, but the norm, the objective, is three weeks. There is rarely overdueness in Stage I.

The norm for Stage II is three weeks. Three weeks are allowed for Stage III.

After assignment, the Counsel reads the record and the papers, and researches the issues.

The Counsel reports to his or her supervisor (Assistant Chief Counsel) as to the issues and the facts as reflected in the record. The positions of the parties are thoroughly analyzed and reviewed.

After consultations with the Board Member's Chief Counsel, those cases that appear to be completely routine can be presented to that Member's panel by means of a "draft-in-lieu," to use Board parlance—that is, a proposed draft of Decision and Order ruling on the exceptions and briefs and disposing of the issues raised. In such a case, Stage I ends when the decision is made to prepare a "draft-in-lieu." Before circulating to the other Board Members on the panel, the "draft-in-lieu" has been screened and edited by both the Assistant Chief Counsel and Chief Counsel, or Deputy Chief Counsel, to make sure that it covers fully the issues raised and legal precedent involved, and has been approved by the originating Board Member. The draft-in-lieu procedure is not, however, frequently used.

In those cases that appear to have some substantial issues, the "draft-in-lieu" is not prepared; instead, the case is presented to a subpanel composed of experienced representatives of the Board Members who are the members of the particular panel. This is by far the most frequently used method.

Each subpanel (the originating staff counsel, his/her supervisor, if any, and representatives of the two other Board Members on the panel) holds an agenda one day each week. Thus, there are five Subpanels held each week. At the subpanel agenda, the originating counsel answers questions raised by other subpanel members who, prior to the agenda, have reviewed the Judge's decision and the exceptions and supporting briefs, or the relevant papers in an R case, and, depending on the practice of individual Board Members, will have discussed the case with their Board Members. At the subpanel agenda a tentative decision is reached and the staff counsel is given a due date for circulation of the draft.

After the subpanel's tentative decision, a "flag" (a summary of the case, 3–10 pages in length) and a draft of the proposed Board decision is prepared by staff counsel and cleared through the supervisory hierarchy to the chief counsel. Upon approval by the chief counsel the case is submitted to the originating Board Members, for approval or further discussion or revision. After approval by the Board Member, the "flag" and draft decision are circulated to the other panel members, with courtesy copies going to the non-participating Board Members, for clearance. The proposed draft is "screened" by the subpanel representatives of the two participating Board Members, and forwarded through the supervisory hierarchy of those staffs to the participating Board Members. Separate approvals, concurrences or dissents are circulated to all staffs. The originating staff counsel makes necessary revisions requested by the other two participating Members.

The subpanel may decide that the case should be presented to the panel of Board Members, or to the full Board, either by a draft decision or by means of a memorandum covering certain issues which cannot readily be resolved. In any event, subpanel action marks the dividing line between Stages I and II.

If the case goes to the Board *panel*, the three members of that panel meet, together with their Chief Counsels, the Counsel, and Assistant Chief Counsel, discuss the case, and decide whether it can be disposed of by panel decision or whether it should be referred to the full Board for consideration. In recent years, this procedure has been used only rarely.

If the case is not referred to the full Board, then the draft procedure described above is followed. To repeat, the proposed draft rises through the supervisory hierarchy of the originating Board Member's staff, and is ultimately put into circulation when the draft comports with the tentative decision reached by the subpanel or panel, *and* has the approval of the originating Board Members. The draft then circulates to the other two participating Members for approval. Courtesy copies are sent to the nonparticipating Members, the so-called "clearance" process, so that either of them may request full Board consideration if desired. No decision can issue unless it represents the majority position of the Board.

Cases can also be called up to the full Board by any participating Member. Thus cases reach the full Board directly from the subpanel or panel, or by being called there by any Board Member at any stage.

Cases referred to the full Board are considered at meetings which are scheduled as needed. (The panels or subpanels are regularly scheduled: Panel 1 meeting on Mondays, Panel 2 on Tuesdays, etc.; in addition, other meetings of the full Board or of the panels are held as needed.) Any one Board Member can call a case up to Board Agenda. The Board Members and their Chief Counsels are present at Board agendas, in addition to (as each case is reached) the Counsel to whom that case is assigned, and his or her Assistant Chief Counsel. The Executive Secretary and the Solicitor are also present. These Board adjudicatory meetings are closed to the public under Exemption 10 of the Government in the Sunshine Act and Section 102.139(a) of the Board's Rules. However, such meetings, and the cases being considered, are announced by the Board.

The Board members discuss the questions raised by the legal memorandum or by the draft decision or by the Board Member's request for full Board discussion, and ask other questions based on the briefs, exceptions, and Administrative Law Judge's Decision, which they have read prior to the meeting and have discussed with their respective staffs. The counsel to whom the case has been assigned has the transcript and exhibits on hand, and there is frequent recourse to these documents to check the facts. At the conclusion of this discussion, a decision is usually reached, but sometimes a case is put over to another agenda, or one or more Board Members may reserve their positions until they have seen a draft of the proposed decision.

The assigned counsel, in collaboration with his or her Assistant Chief Counsel, then prepares a proposed Decision and Order, based on the Board's discussion. The draft is then submitted to the Assistant Chief Counsel and, after any necessary revisions, to the Chief Counsel and then to the Board Member for approval, prior to being circulated to the other Board Members.

Each of the Board Members has a number of more experienced counsel who specialize in screening drafts originating from other Members' staffs; circulating drafts are carefully scrutinized by these attorneys. They, in turn, may discuss the draft with their Chief Counsel before submitting it to their Board Members for approval or modification. The Board Member nearly always discusses the draft with both his or her Chief Counsel and "screener" before approving it, or suggesting any changes. If any substantial changes or questions arise as a result of a review of the draft, these are taken up with the originating staff and an attempt is made to resolve such differences. It may be necessary to reschedule the case for further Board or panel discussion. If a majority of the Board or panel has approved the draft, and a Board Member wishes to dissent, that may be done.

All drafts are returned to the Executive Secretary's Office after the review and analysis have been completed by the various Board Members' staffs, and the Board Members have indicated approval, approval with modifications, or disapproval.

At this point all copies of the draft are returned to the assigned Counsel, who is responsible for clearing all changes with all participating Board Members. When final agreement is reached, the Counsel makes a conformed copy, the draft then enters the final edition and reproduction process, and then is issued to the parties by the Executive Secretary's Office. An official, signed copy is placed in the formal, public file.

There is no question but that, under Board procedures, all parties are accorded due process. The basic procedures inherent in Section 4(a) of the Act also assure an opportunity for each Member to participate in or clear every case arising before the Board.

All Board Members, including the Chairman, are present at all full Board meetings and meetings of panels (three) of which they are a member.

Some of the most difficult cases receive exhaustive full Board consideration and oral discussion, before the Board decides that the Judge was right and that nothing more can be added to what has already been written. Thus, the fact that a decision is issued by a Board Panel, simply adopting the decision of the Judge, is not necessarily indicative of the course it has followed through the Board.

Procedures for representation cases are generally along the same lines as those described, except those cases involving requests for a review of a Regional Director's decision. There the Board's Office of Representation Case Appeals provides expedited, specialist attention. These cases, too, each receive personal attention by all three Members on the special panel for that month—and sometimes, in more controversial cases, by all Board Members, to assure that the vote of the panel is representative. Voting on the numerous requests for review that come in each day is a time-consuming job, one that must be given priority attention by Board Members because of the time constraints that are placed by forthcoming election dates. It is also a job that is taken most seriously by all Board Members because of the paramount importance of Board election procedures.

APPENDIX G

NLRB Time Goals for Processing Cases

Unfair Labor Practice Cases Generally

Stage	*Goal*
(1) From filing of charge to beginning of initial investigation	7 days
(2) From filing of charge(s) to completion of investigation and Regional Office determination	30 days
(3) From Regional Office determination to implementation of the decision (issuance of complaint, withdrawal, settlement/adjustment, dismissal, submission to Advice); including former advice cases where such action must be taken within 15 days after return to the Regional Office	15 days
(4) From issuance of complaint to close of hearing	45 days

Priority C Cases

10(l) Cases

Stage	*Goal*
(1) From filing of charge to C.P.'s submission of evidence	24 hours

(2) From filing of charge to completion of investigation and Regional Office determination

72 hours: Regional determination should "immediately" follow the completion of the investigation.

(3) From filing of charge to filing of 10(l) petition in merit cases

After merit determination, if conduct continues or a resumption is threatened, etc., 10(l) petition should be filed "without further delay."

(4) From filing of charge to issuance of complaint in merit cases

5 days after filing of 10(l) petition.

10(j) Cases

Stage	*Goal*
(1) From filing of charge and C.P.'s request or *sua sponte* a Regional Office determination that 10(j) relief is appropriate	Expeditious handling *at all* stages similar to that accorded 10(l) cases. (See G.C. Memo 77–9.)
(2) From authorization to filing 10(j)	48 hours (See G.C. Memo 76–63.)

Summary Judgment Cases

Stage	*Goal*
(1) From filing of charge to complaint	14 days
(2) From issuance of complaint to filing of Motion for Summary Judgment with the Board	20 days

FMCS National, Regional, District, and Field Offices

National Office

Federal Mediation and Conciliation Service
2100 K Street, N.W.
Washington, D.C. 20427
202 653-5300

Office of the Director
Office of the Deputy Director
Division of Operations Support
Office of the Executive Director
Division of Arbitration Services
Division of Automated Information Services
Division of Labor/Management Grant Programs
Division of Administrative Services
Division of Personnel Management

Regional, District, and Field Offices

Eastern Regional Office. New York, New York 10278   212 264-1000
Jacob K. Javits Federal
    Building
26 Federal Plaza, Room 2937

District 1. Boston, Massachusetts 02116   617 223-7345
Park Square Building, Room
    207
31 St. James Avenue

Field Offices: Boston, Massachusetts; Hartford,
Connecticut; Portland, Maine; Providence, Rhode
Island; Albany, New York.

District 2. New York, New York   212 264-1006
Jacob K. Javits Federal
Building
26 Federal Plaza, Room 2937

Field Offices: New York, Hempstead, Buffalo, and
Syracuse, New York; East Orange, New Jersey.

District 3. Philadelphia, Pennsylvania   215 597-7690
19106
William J. Green, Jr., Federal
Building
600 Arch Street, Room 3456

Field Offices: Philadelphia, Allentown, Erie,
Harrisburg, and Pittsburgh, Pennsylvania; Trenton,
New Jersey.

Southern Regional Office. Atlanta, Georgia 30309   404 347-2473
1720 Peachtree Street,
N.W., Suite 318

District 1. Washington, D.C. 20427   202 653-5390
2100 K Street, N.W.

Field Offices: Washington, D.C.; Baltimore,
Maryland; Evansville, Indiana; Louisville, Kentucky;
Charlotte, North Carolina; Cincinnati, Ohio;
Richmond, Virginia; Parkersburg, West Virginia.

District 2. Atlanta, Georgia 30309   404 347-2484
1720 Peachtree Street, N.W.,
Suite 318

Field Offices: Atlanta, Georgia; Birmingham and
Mobile, Alabama; Little Rock, Arkansas; Ft.
Lauderdale, Jacksonville, and Tampa, Florida; New
Orleans, Louisiana; Knoxville, Memphis, and
Nashville, Tennessee.

District 3. St. Louis, Missouri 63141   314 576-3293
Suite 325
12140 Woodcrest Executive
Drive

Field Offices: St. Louis, Springfield, and Kansas City,
Missouri; Wichita, Kansas; Oklahoma City,
Oklahoma; Dallas, Houston, and San Antonio, Texas.

Central Regional Office. Chicago, Illinois 60604   312-353-7350
Insurance Exchange Building,
Room 1659
175 West Jackson Boulevard

District 1. Minneapolis, Minnesota 55414   612 349-3300
Health Association Center
Building
Suite 330
2221 University Avenue, S.E.

Field Offices: Minneapolis, Minnesota; Cedar Rapids and Des Moines, Iowa; Omaha, Nebraska.

District 2. Chicago, Illinois 60604   312 353-7350
     Insurance Exchange Building,
       Room 1659
     175 West Jackson Boulevard

Field Offices: Chicago, Peoria, and Rockford, Illinois; Indianapolis and South Bend, Indiana; Green Bay and Milwaukee, Wisconsin.

District 3. Cleveland, Ohio 44114   216 522-4800
     Room 508 Mall Building
     118 St. Clair Avenue, N.E.

Field Offices: Cleveland, Akron, Columbus, Dayton, and Toledo, Ohio; Detroit, Grand Rapids, Kalamazoo, and Saginaw, Michigan.

Western Regional Office. San Francisco, California   415 974-9850
     94105
     525 Market Street, 29th Floor

District 1. Seattle, Washington 98121   206 442-5800
     Westin Building, Suite 310
     2001 Sixth Avenue

Field Offices: Seattle and Spokane, Washington; Denver, Colorado; Great Falls, Montana; Portland, Oregon; Salt Lake City, Utah.

District 2. San Francisco, California   415 974-9853
     94105
     525 Market Street, 29th Floor

Field Offices: San Francisco and Sacramento, California; Phoenix, Arizona; Honolulu, Hawaii.

District 3. Los Angeles, California 90010   213 468-3114
     4221 Wilshire Boulevard,
       Suite 210

Field Offices: Los Angeles, Santa Ana, and San Diego, California.

APPENDIX I

Excerpts From Postal Reorganization Act*

Sec. 2, Title 39 USC §§ 1201–1209

CHAPTER 12.—EMPLOYEE-MANAGEMENT AGREEMENTS

Sec. 1201. *Definition.* As used in this chapter, "guards" means—

(1) maintenance guards who, on the effective date of this chapter, are in key position KP-5 under the provisions of former section 3514 of title 39; and

(2) security guards, who may be employed in the Postal Service and whose primary duties shall include the exercise of authority to enforce rules to protect the safety of property, mail, or persons on the premises.

Sec. 1202. *Bargaining units.* The National Labor Relations Board shall decide in each case the unit appropriate for collective bargaining in the Postal Service. The National Labor Relations Board shall not include in any bargaining unit—

(1) any management official or supervisor;

(2) any employee engaged in personnel work in other than a purely nonconfidential clerical capacity;

(3) both professional employees and employees who are not professional employees unless a majority of such professional employees vote for inclusion in such unit; or

(4) together with other employees, any individual employed as a security guard to enforce against employees and other persons, rules to protect property of the Postal Service or to protect the safety of property, mail or persons on the premises of the Postal Service; but no labor organization shall be certified as the representative of employees in a bargaining unit of security guards if such organization admits to membership, or is affiliated directly or indirectly with an organization which admits to membership, employees other than guards.

Sec. 1203. *Recognition of labor organizations.* (a) The Postal Service shall accord exclusive recognition to a labor organization when the orga-

---

*Public Law 91–375, 91st Congress, H.R. 17070, August 12, 1970.

nization has been selected by a majority of the employees in an appropriate unit as their representative.

(b) Agreements and supplements in effect on the date of enactment of this section covering employees in the former Post Office Department shall continue to be recognized by the Postal Service until altered or amended pursuant to law.

(c) When a petition has been filed, in accordance with such regulations as may be prescribed by the National Labor Relations Board—

(1) by an employee, a group of employees, or any labor organization acting in their behalf, alleging that (A) a substantial number of employees wish to be represented for collective bargaining by a labor organization and that the Postal Service declines to recognize such labor organization as the representative; or (B) the labor organization which has been certified or is being currently recognized by the Postal Service as the bargaining representative is no longer a representative; or

(2) by the Postal Service, alleging that one or more labor organizations has presented to it a claim to be recognized as the representative;
the National Labor Relations Board shall investigate such petition and, if it has reasonable cause to believe that a question of representation exists, shall provide for an appropriate hearing upon due notice. Such hearing may be conducted by an officer or employee of the National Labor Relations Board, who shall not make any recommendations with respect thereto. If the National Labor Relations Board finds upon the record of such a hearing that such a question of representation exists, it shall direct an election by secret ballot and shall certify the results thereof.

(d) A petition filed under subsection (c)(1) of this section shall be accompanied by a statement signed by a least 30 percent of the employees in the appropriate unit stating that they desire that an election be conducted for either of the purposes set forth in such subsection.

(e) Nothing in this section shall be construed to prohibit the waiving of hearings by stipulation for the purpose of a consent election in conformity with regulations and rules of decision of the National Labor Relations Board.

Sec. 1204. *Elections.* (a) All elections authorized under this chapter shall be conducted under the supervision of the National Labor Relations Board, or persons designated by it, and shall be by secret ballot. Each employee eligible to vote shall be provided the opportunity to choose the labor organization he wishes to represent him, from among those on the ballot, or "no union."

(b) In any election where none of the choices on the ballot receives a majority, a runoff shall be conducted, the ballot providing for a selection between the 2 choices receiving the largest and second largest number of valid votes cast in the election. In the event of a tie vote, additional runoff elections shall be conducted until one of the choices has received a majority of the votes.

(c) No election shall be held in any bargaining unit within which, in the preceding 12-month period, a valid election has been held.

Sec. 1205. *Deductions of dues.* (a) When a labor organization holds exclusive recognition, or when an organization of personnel not subject to collective-bargaining agreements has consultation rights under section 1004 of this title, the Postal Service shall deduct the regular and periodic dues of the organization from the pay of all members of the organization in the unit of recognition if the Post Office Department or the Postal Service has received from each employee, on whose account such deductions are made, a written assignment which shall be irrevocable for a period of not more than one year.

(b) Any agreement in effect immediately prior to the date of enactment of the Postal Reorganization Act between the Post Office Department and any organization of postal employees which provides for deduction by the Department of the regular and periodic dues of the organization from the pay of its members, shall continue in full force and effect and the obligation for such deductions shall be assumed by the Postal Service. No such deduction shall be made from the pay of any employee except on his written assignment, which shall be irrevocable for a period of not more than one year.

Sec. 1206. *Collective-bargaining agreements.* (a) Collective-bargaining agreements between the Postal Service and bargaining representatives recognized under section 1203 of this title shall be effective for not less than 2 years.

(b) Collective-bargaining agreements between the Postal Service and bargaining representatives recognized under section 1203 may include any procedures for resolution by the parties of grievances and adverse actions arising under the agreement, including procedures culminating in binding third-party arbitration, or the parties may adopt any such procedures by mutual agreement in the event of a dispute.

(c) The Postal Service and bargaining representatives recognized under section 1203 may by mutual agreement adopt procedures for the resolution of disputes or impasses arising in the negotiation of a collective-bargaining agreement.

Sec. 1207. *Labor disputes.* (a) If there is a collective-bargaining agreement in effect, no party to such agreement shall terminate or modify such agreement unless the party desiring such termination or modification serves written notice upon the other party to the agreement of the proposed termination or modification not less than 90 days prior to the expiration date thereof, or not less than 90 days prior to the time it is proposed to make such termination or modification. The party serving such notice shall notify the Federal Mediation and Conciliation Service of the existence of a dispute within 45 days of such notice, if no agreement has been reached by that time.

(b) If the parties fail to reach agreement or to adopt a procedure providing for a binding resolution of a dispute by the expiration date of the agreement in effect, or the date of the proposed termination or modification, the Director of the Federal Mediation and Conciliation Service shall direct the establishment of a factfinding panel consisting of 3 persons. For this purpose, he shall submit to parties a list of not less than 15 names, from which list each party, within 10 days, shall select 1 person. The 2 so selected shall then choose from the list a third person who shall serve as chairman of the factfinding panel. If either of the parties fails to select a person or if the 2 members are unable to agree on the third person within 3 days, the selection shall be made by the Director. The factfinding panel shall issue after due investigation a report of its findings, with or without recommendations, to the parties no later than 45 days from the date the list of names is submitted.

(c)(1) If no agreement is reached within 90 days after the expiration or termination of the agreement or the date on which the agreement became subject to modification under subsection (a) of this section, or if the parties decide upon arbitration but do not agree upon the procedures therefor, an arbitration board shall be established consisting of 3 members, not members of the factfinding panel, 1 of whom shall be selected by the Postal Service, 1 by the bargaining representative of the employees, and the third by the 2 thus selected. If either of the parties fails to select a member, or if the members chosen by the parties fail to agree on the third person within 5 days after their first meeting, the selection shall be made by the Director. If the parties do not agree on the framing of the issues to be submitted, the factfinding panel shall frame the issues and submit them to the arbitration board.

(2) The arbitration board shall give the parties a full and fair hearing, including an opportunity to present their case in person, by counsel or by other representative as they may elect. Decisions of the arbitration board shall be conclusive and binding upon the parties. The arbitration board shall render its decision within 45 days after its appointment.

(3) Costs of the arbitration board and factfinding panel shall be shared equally by the Postal Service and the bargaining representative.

(d) In the case of a bargaining unit whose recognized collective-bargaining representative does not have an agreement with the Postal Service, if the parties fail to reach agreement within 90 days of the commencement of collective bargaining, a factfinding panel will be established in accordance with the terms of subsection (b) of this section, unless the parties have previously agreed to another procedure for a binding resolution of their differences. If the parties fail to reach agreement within 180 days of the commencement of collective bargaining, and if they have not agreed to another procedure for binding resolution, an arbitration board shall be established to provide conclusive and binding arbitration in accordance with the terms of subsection (c) of this section.

Sec. 1208. *Suits.* (a) The courts of the United States shall have jurisdiction with respect to actions brought by the National Labor Relations Board under this chapter to the same extent that they have jurisdiction with respect to actions under title 29.

(b) Suits for violation of contracts between the Postal Service and a labor organization representing Postal Service employees, or between any such labor organizations, may be brought in any district court of the United States having jurisdiction of the parties, without respect to the amount in controversy.

(c) A labor organization and the Postal Service shall be bound by the authorized acts of their agents. Any labor organization may sue or be sued as an entity and in behalf of the employees whom it represents in the courts of the United States. Any money judgment against a labor organization in a district court of the United States shall be enforceable only against the organization as an entity and against its assets, and shall not be enforceable against any individual member or his assets.

(d) For the purposes of actions and proceedings by or against labor organizations in the district courts of the United States, district courts shall be deemed to have jurisdiction of a labor organization (1) in the district in which such organization maintains its principal offices, or (2) in any district in which its duly authorized officers or agents are engaged in representing or acting for employee members.

(e) The service of summons, subpena, or other legal process of any court of the United States upon an officer or agent of a labor organization, in his capacity as such, shall constitute service upon the labor organization.

Sec. 1209. *Applicability of Federal labor laws.* (a) Employee-management relations shall, to the extent not inconsistent with provisions of this title, be subject to the provisions of subchapter II of chapter 7 of title 29.

(b) The provisions of Chapter 11 of title 29 shall be applicable to labor organizations that have or are seeking to attain recognition under section 1203 of this title, and to such organizations' officers, agents, shop stewards, other representative, and members to the extent to which such provisions would be applicable if the Postal Service were an employer under section 402 of title 29. In addition to the authority conferred on him under section 438 of title 29, the Secretary of Labor shall have authority, by regulation issued with the written concurrence of the Postal Service, to prescribe simplified reports for any such labor organization. The Secretary of Labor may revoke such provision for simplified forms of any such labor organization if he determines, after such investigation as he deems proper and after due notice and opportunity for a hearing, that the purposes of this chapter and of chapter 11 of title 29 would be served thereby.

(c) Each employee of the Postal Service shall have the right, freely and without fear of penalty or reprisal, to form, join, and assist a labor organization or to refrain from any such activity, and each employee shall be protected in the exercise of this right.

APPENDIX J

Freedom of Information Act Guidelines in Closed Cases

Text of NLRB Memorandum No. 79-6, January 24, 1979, from John S. Irving, General Counsel, to All Regional Directors and Officers-in-Charge

With the Supreme Court's decision in *NLRB v. Robbins Tire and Rubber Co.*, 98 LRRM 2617 (June 15, 1978), it is now clear that affidavits contained in our files in open cases are exempt from disclosure under Exemption 7(A) of the Freedom of Information Act (FOIA). When coupled with the Supreme Court's earlier decision in *NLRB v. Sears, Roebuck & Co.*, 421 U.S. 132 (1975), dealing with intra-agency memoranda, this decision establishes the propriety of our policy of nondisclosure of sensitive material related to our ongoing cases, and virtually assures that our proceedings will not be enjoined under FOIA in the future. We feel that the Agency has been successful in open case litigation largely because we have sought to comply with the spirit of FOIA by strictly limiting nondisclosure to the minimum necessary to protect only those legitimate concerns which are essential to the effective enforcement of the Act. Having obtained judicial approval of that approach, the purpose of this memorandum is to formally establish how that policy is to be applied in closed cases. While, of course, each FOIA request must be given individual consideration taking into account the particular circumstances involved, guidelines will be a most useful tool to insure a uniform application of our commitment to the principles of FOIA.

Both the Courts and the Congress have made it quite clear that the philosophy of FOIA is to encourage as full disclosure of government documents as possible, and that information should not be withheld simply because it comes within the language of one of the exemptions. "Rather, the exemptions 'are only *permissive*' and 'mark the outer limits of information that may be withheld where the agency makes a specific affirmative determination that the public interest and the specific circumstances presented dictate . . . that the information *should* be withheld.'" *Title Guarantee Co. v. NLRB*, 534 F.2d 484, 489 (2d Cir. 1976), *cert. denied*, 429 U.S. 834, quoting from S. REP. NO. 93–854, 93d Cong., 2d Sess. (1974). As Senator Kennedy emphasized in introducing the 1974 FOIA amendments in the Senate:

734

"[A]gencies have a definite obligation to release information—even where withholding may be authorized by the language of the statute—where the public interest lies in disclosure. . . . When in doubt, the department or agency [is] supposed to lean toward disclosure, not withholding."

In this spirit, we have decided to limit the withholding of closed case documents to the minimum which is clearly necessary to safeguard the agency's effectiveness, and have resolved doubts in favor of disclosure even in circumstances where a FOIA exemption could be invoked. The guidelines are the result of analysis and discussion of the problems posed by disclosure in many possible circumstances, and experience with these guidelines may yet demonstrate that the adverse consequences of disclosure of certain types of documents outweigh the public interest in their disclosure. If such substantial adverse consequences materialize, we may have to reevaluate this broad disclosure policy or its application in particular circumstances. If any adverse effects of disclosure are observed, they should be reported to the Division of Operations Management. At this point, however, we are optimistic that the disclosure policy we are instituting will prove successful, and by further opening the agency to public view it will result in a better relationship with the public and the labor bar by increasing public awareness of the high quality of performance by agency personnel.

Guidelines for Public Disclosure of Documents
Obtained in Case Investigations

1. *Documents in Open Case Files.* In open cases, we will continue to disclose formal documents, pleadings, and other nonconfidential material in the case file, such as collective bargaining agreements, newspaper clippings, arbitrators' decisions, transcripts from other proceedings, etc. In addition, following the close of a hearing in the case, we will disclose any affidavits or portions of affidavits which have been produced during the hearing pursuant to the Board's Rules and Regulations, Section 102.118. Finally, we will disclose to a party to the case any documents which are or were in the possession of that party, such as letters to or from that party.

We will continue our policy, approved by the Supreme Court in *Robbins Tire*, of withholding all affidavits (except as provided in the preceding paragraph) and other nonpublic evidentiary material relating to the case so long as the case remains open. As noted by the Court, this policy is essential to encourage co-operation of witnesses during our investigations, and to avoid permitting respondents to use early disclosure of our evidence to undermine our enforcement efforts. In addition, we will continue our policy, approved by the Supreme Court in *Sears, Roebuck & Co., supra,* of withholding deliberative memoranda, except we will provide Advice Memoranda authorizing dismissal of charges. See also, *Kent Corp. v. NLRB*, 530 F.2d 612 (5th Cir. 1976), *cert. denied*, 429 U.S. 920.

For the purpose of these guidelines, an unfair labor practice case is considered "open" until there is an approved withdrawal of the charge, final dismissal, or compliance has been effected. Thus, a case is not considered "closed" merely because an evidentiary hearing is completed. *Abrahamson Chrysler-Plymouth, Inc. v. NLRB*, 561 F.2d 63, 64–65 (7th Cir. 1977); *AMF Head, Inc. v. NLRB*, 564 F.2d 374, 375–376 (10th Cir. 1977). A representation case is considered "open" until there is a withdrawal, final dismissal, certification of a representative, certification of results, or until a related unfair labor practice case is closed. Thus, representation case files are not considered "closed," for the purposes of these guidelines, so long as there is a reasonable expectation that a certification-test 8(a)(5) charge or a *Gissel* bargaining order case may result. See *Trustees of Boston University v. NLRB*, 575 F.2d 301 (1st Cir. 1978); *Wellman Industries v. NLRB*, 490 F.2d 427 (4th Cir. 1974), *cert. denied*, 419 U.S. 834.

2. *Documents in Closed Case Files Which Are Related to Open Cases.* These will be treated the same as documents in open case files. See *New England Medical Center Hospital v. NLRB*, 548 F.2d 377 (1st Cir. 1978).

3. *Documents in Other Closed Case Files.* After the expiration of the appropriate buffer period, as discussed *infra*, we will normally disclose all affidavits obtained from individuals who are not, at the time of the disclosure request, current employees of an employer involved in the case or in a unit represented by any union involved and/or members of those unions.[1]

The only affidavits which we will normally withhold from disclosure after the case is closed are those which were obtained from individuals who, at the time of the disclosure request, are current employees of the Employer involved and/or who are members of, or represented by, the union involved and whose affidavits have not been revealed after they testified at a hearing. This policy is essential to the effectiveness of the agency, for as the courts have consistently recognized, employees are often inhibited from cooperating with investigations of possible wrongdoing by their employers or unions.

"The employee will be understandably reluctant to reveal information prejudicial to his employer when the employer can easily find out that he has done so. No employee will want to risk forfeiting the good will of his superiors thereby lessening his job security and promotion opportunities." *Texas Industries, Inc. v. NLRB*, 336 F.2d 128, 134 (5th Cir. 1964).

"The average employee . . . is keenly aware of his dependence upon his employer's good will, not only to hold his job but also for the necessary job references essential to employment elsewhere. Only by preserving their anonymity can the government obtain the information necessary to implement the law properly." *Brennan v. Engineered Products, Inc.*, 506 F.2d 299, 302 (8th Cir. 1974).

In *Robbins Tire* the Supreme Court recognized that current employees are particularly vulnerable to pressure from their employers, observing (98 LRRM at 2326):

"Not only can the employer fire the employee, but job assignments can be switched, hours can be adjusted, wage and salary increases held up and other more subtle forms of influence exerted. . . . As the lower courts have recognized, due to the 'peculiar character of labor litigation[,] the witnesses are especially likely to be inhibited by fear of the employer's or—in some cases—the union's capacity for reprisal and harassment.' " *Roger J. Au & Son, Inc. v. NLRB*, 538 F.2d 80, 83 (3rd Cir. 1976).

Clearly, the potential for such harassment and reprisal exists regardless of whether the Board's case is open or closed. Thus, if investigative statements of current employees were available in closed cases the potential for disclosure and subsequent reprisals would deter individuals from cooperating with Board investigators and lead them to remain silent in order to

---

[1]If unusual circumstances indicate that the affiant might be subject to retaliation if his or her affidavit is disclosed, then the affidavit will remain confidential. One example would be a situation where there are indications that a former employee might be blacklisted. *Cf. Hodgson v. Charles Martin Inspectors of Petroleum, Inc.*, 456 F.2d 303, 306 (5th Cir. 1972).

protect their economic, physical or social well-being.[2] Disclosure of current employee affidavits may be made, despite these considerations, in special situations, such as when the employee consents to disclosure, or when the employee impliedly waives any interest in confidentiality by suing the employer over the same dispute in another forum (e.g, filing an EEOC or OSHA charge or a contract grievance).

Union authorization cards are not to be disclosed in any circumstances, unless, of course, they have already been introduced into evidence at a hearing (for final disposition of authorization cards, see Case Handling Manual, Part two, Section 11034). Disclosure of authorization cards would not only expose employees to possible retaliation in the same way as disclosure of their affidavits but, as recognized by several courts, in doing so it would undermine the very purpose of a secret ballot election: to permit employees to support or oppose a union anonymously, without fear of exposing themselves to individual retaliation. See *Masonic Homes v. NLRB*, 556 F.2d 214 (3rd Cir. 1977); *Pacific Molasses Corp. v. NLRB*, 577 F.2d 1172 (5th Cir. 1978); *American Airlines, Inc. v. National Mediation Board*, 99 LRRM 3450 (2nd Cir. 1978).

Normally, nonpublic evidentiary material, other than affidavits and authorization cards, will be disclosed upon request. However, deletions will be made in all nonpublic evidentiary materials which are disclosed pursuant to these guidelines, including affidavits, where necessary to protect the personal privacy of an affiant or an individual named in a document (this would include any personal, potentially embarrassing information, such as medical records, personnel records, family problems, etc.), to insure the anonymity of confidential sources of information, and to protect the confidentiality of trade secrets, bargaining positions and strategies, and confidential financial information. If deletions would be inadequate to protect these legitimate interests it will be necessary to withhold disclosure altogether.

With regard to deliberative memoranda in closed cases, we will disclose all Advice memoranda to Regional Directors. However, other deliberative memoranda, such as Final Investigation Reports, Agenda Minutes, etc., will not be disclosed whether the case is open or closed, in order to assure that our internal deliberations are carried on in the candid manner necessary to effective decision making. See *Kent Corp. v. NLRB*, 530 F.2d 612 (5th Cir. 1976), *cert. denied*, 429 U.S. 920.

4. *Closed Case Buffer Periods*. In order to assure that a closed case will not reopen after the evidence is disclosed, we have decided to establish certain buffer periods during which no documents will be disclosed which would not be disclosed if the case were still open. We believe that this policy is necessary both to avoid compromising our enforcement efforts if a case

---

[2]The term "employee" as used in these guidelines does not refer to the definition in the Act, but rather to the broader definition of the term in relation to affidavit disclosure considerations which was used by the Supreme Court in *Robbins* (98 LRRM at 2627):

"The danger of witness intimidation is particularly acute with respect to current employees—whether rank and file, supervisory, or managerial—over whom the employer, by virtue of the employment relationship, may exercise intense leverage. . . . A union can often exercise similar authority over its members and officers."

This principle is inapplicable as to a supervisor/manager or union official who provides an affidavit in the role of a representative of the employer or union which has such "leverage" over him. Accordingly, when acting in that role, their affidavits are not considered to be affidavits of "current employees" as used above and will be provided after the appropriate buffer period.

is reopened, and to avoid unduly encouraging parties to reopen settled cases. We do not believe that this temporary delay in disclosure of documents would significantly impair any legitimate public interest. *Cf. American Airlines v. National Mediation Board, supra,* 99 LRRM at 3456.

a. *Cases Closed After Settlement or Adjusted Withdrawal.* The buffer period will last for a reasonable time after settlement (normally one year), in order to assure that there will be no breach of the agreement and, thus, that the agreement will not be set aside in favor of litigation of the settled charges. Absent such a rule, settlements could be used by respondents as a device to obtain disclosure of the witnesses and evidence against them, with the intention of resuming unlawful conduct leading to litigation after disclosure of the General Counsel's case.

b. *Cases Closed by Withdrawal or Dismissal of the Charge.* There will be a six-month buffer period, in order to avoid compromising enforcement efforts if the same or a related charge is filed within the 10(b) period.

c. *Cases Closed After Litigation.* There will be no buffer period once these cases are finally closed.

We are hopeful that these guidelines will prove to be a workable accommodation between our commitment to the disclosure policies of the FOIA, and our duty to effectively enforce the Act. If you have any questions regarding these guidelines, please contact your Assistant General Counsel.

Table of Cases

Contractors Excavating, Inc., 270 NLRB
1189, 116 LRRM 1248 (1984)   353
Cooper-Hewitt Elec. Co., 215 NLRB 277, 88
LRRM 1475 (1974)   262
Coppus Eng'r Corp., 195 NLRB 595, 79
LRRM 1449 (1972)   312
Corcoran Gallery of Art, Trustees of the,
186 NLRB 565, 75 LRRM 1380
(1970)   39, 42
Cornell Univ., 183 NLRB 329, 74 LRRM
1269 (1970)   42
Cornwell Co., 171 NLRB 342, 68 LRRM
1200 (1968)   453
Coronado Coal Co. v. Mine Workers, 268
U.S. 295 (1925)   17
Coronet Instr. Media, 250 NLRB 940, 104
LRRM 1470 (1965)   229
Cosmetic and Novelties Workers' Union, Lo-
cal 300, 257 NLRB 1335, 108 LRRM 1085
(1981)   225
Coty, J., Messenger Serv.; NLRB v., 763
F.2d 92, 119 LRRM 2779 (2d Cir.
1985)   56
Cowden-Clark Mem. Hosp., 221 NLRB 945,
91 LRRM 1024 (1975)   46
Crompton Co., 260 NLRB 417, 109 LRRM
1161 (1982)   69, 80
Crossett Paper Mills, 98 NLRB 542, 29
LRRM 1396 (1952)   138
Crothall Hosp. Serv. Inc., 270 NLRB 1420,
117 LRRM 1072 (1984)   79
Crown Cork & Seal Co., 203 NLRB 171, 83
LRRM 1088 (1973)   315
—254 NLRB 1340, 106 LRRM 1270
(1981)   226
—v. NLRB, 659 F.2d 127, 108 LRRM 2224
(10th Cir. 1981)   203, 205
Crown Cork de Puerto Rico, Inc., 243 NLRB
569, 101 LRRM 1499 (1979)   418
Cruis Along Boats, Inc., 128 NLRB 1019, 46
LRRM 1419 (1960)   146
Cullen, J.T., Co., 271 NLRB 114, 116 LRRM
1339 (1984)   8
Cumberland Farms Dairy, 266 NLRB 855,
113 LRRM 1048 (1983)   447
Cumberland Nursing & Convalescent Center, 248 NLRB 322, 103 LRRM 1417
(1980)   236
Cuneo v. United Shoe Workers, 181 F. Supp.
324, 45 LRRM 2822 (D.N.J. 1960)   477
Cutter Labs., 116 NLRB 260, 38 LRRM
1241 (1956)   250

D

D & D Health Assoc., Inc., 270 NLRB 181,
116 LRRM 1056 (1984)   8
D & J Gravel Co., 261 NLRB 391, 110
LRRM 1096 (1982)   365
D & L Contracting, Inc., 266 NLRB No. 20,
112 LRRM 1271 (1983)   356
DPM of Kansas, Inc., 261 NLRB 220, 110
LRRM 1022 (1982)   353

D.V. Displays Corp., 134 NLRB 568, 49
LRRM 1199 (1961)   164, 214
Dale's Super Valu, Inc., 181 NLRB 698, 73
LRRM 1427 (1970)   68
Dalewood Rehabilitation Hosp., Inc., 224
NLRB 1618, 92 LRRM 1372 (1976)   269
Dallas Gen. Drivers Local 745 (Macatee,
Inc.), 127 NLRB 683, 46 LRRM 1069
(1960)   476
Daniel Constr. Co., 244 NLRB 704, 102
LRRM 1399 (1979)   295
Danielson
—v. Electrical Workers, Local 501, 509 F.2d
1371, 88 LRRM 2625 (2d Cir. 1975)   496,
497
—v. International Org. of Masters, 521 F.2d
747, 89 LRRM 2564 (2d Cir. 1975)   496
—v. Joint Bd. of Coat Workers' Union, 494
F.2d 1230, 85 LRRM 2902 (2d Cir.
1974)   496
Danzansky-Goldberg Mem. Chapels, Inc.,
264 NLRB 840, 112 LRRM 1108
(1982)   292
Davis
—v. Huttig Sash & Door Co., 288 F. Supp.
82, 68 LRRM 2936 (W.D. Okla.
1968)   502
—v. LeTourneau, R.G., Inc., 340 F. Supp.
882, 78 LRRM 2616 (E.D. Tex. 1971)   505
Davison Chem. Co., 115 NLRB 786, 37
LRRM 1417 (1956)   244
Dawes Labs. Inc., 164 NLRB 935, 65 LRRM
1178 (1967)   251
Dawidoff v. Minneapolis Bldg. & Constr.
Trades Council, 550 F.2d 407, 94 LRRM
2801 (8th Cir. 1977)   498
Dawson, Alexander, Inc. v. NLRB, 586 F.2d
1300, 99 LRRM 3105 (9th Cir. 1978)   394
Day and Zimmerman, Inc., 246 NLRB 1181,
103 LRRM 1076 (1979)   271
Day, J.H., Co., 204 NLRB 863, 83 LRRM
1418 (1973)   259
Daylight Grocery Co. v. NLRB, 678 F.2d
905, 110 LRRM 2915 (11th Cir.
1982)   183, 184, 216
Dayton Motels, Inc.; NLRB v., 474 F.2d 328,
82 LRRM 2651 (6th Cir. 1973)   14
Dayton Power & Light Co., 267 NLRB 202,
114 LRRM 1009 (1983)   418
Dayton Tire & Rubber Co., 234 NLRB 504,
97 LRRM 1308 (1978)   237
Dean Indus., 162 NLRB 1078, 64 LRRM
1193 (1967)   283
Deaton Truck Line, Inc. v. NLRB, 337 F.2d
697, 57 LRRM 2209 (5th Cir. 1964)   422
Debolt Transfer, Inc., 271 NLRB 299, 117
LRRM 1306 (1984)   523, 524
Deena Artware, 112 NLRB 371, 36 LRRM
1028 (1955)   443
De Laval Separator Co., 97 NLRB 544, 29
LRRM 1124 (1951)   137
Delta Hosiery Inc., 259 NLRB 1005, 109
LRRM 1063 (1982)   15
Deluxe Metal Furniture Co., 121 NLRB 995,

G

H

I

L

Q

R

S

U

Y

Z

Index

About the Authors

Kenneth C. McGuiness is a senior partner in the Washington, D.C., law firm of McGuiness & Williams. He has practiced labor law since 1959 representing a wide variety of clients in representation and unfair labor practice proceedings, collective bargaining, arbitration, and equal employment matters. Mr. McGuiness authored the Third and Fourth Editions of *How To Take a Case Before the National Labor Relations Board.*

Prior to entering private practice, Mr. McGuiness served as Associate General Counsel of the NLRB and was a consultant to the Minority of the House Committee on Education and Labor during development of the Landrum-Griffin Act in 1959. A graduate of Iowa State College and the University of California Law School, Mr. McGuiness currently serves as president of the Labor Policy Association, the Equal Employment Advisory Council, and the National Foundation for the Study of Equal Employment Policy.

Jeffrey A. Norris is a partner with McGuiness & Williams. A graduate of Bucknell University and the Cornell University Law School, he has represented clients in NLRB elections and unfair labor practice proceedings, occupational safety and health matters, affirmative action compliance reviews, and a wide variety of race, sex, and age discrimination cases. He is author of *Contract Compliance Under the Reagan Administration: A Practitioner's Guide to Current Use of the OFCCP Compliance Manual.*

Prior to joining the firm in 1977, Mr. Norris spent nearly six years with the NLRB in Washington, D.C. As Chief Counsel to one of the Board members, he participated actively in the Board's substantive decision-making process in both representation and unfair labor practice cases. Mr. Norris currently serves as Secretary and Treasurer to the Equal Employment Advisory Council.